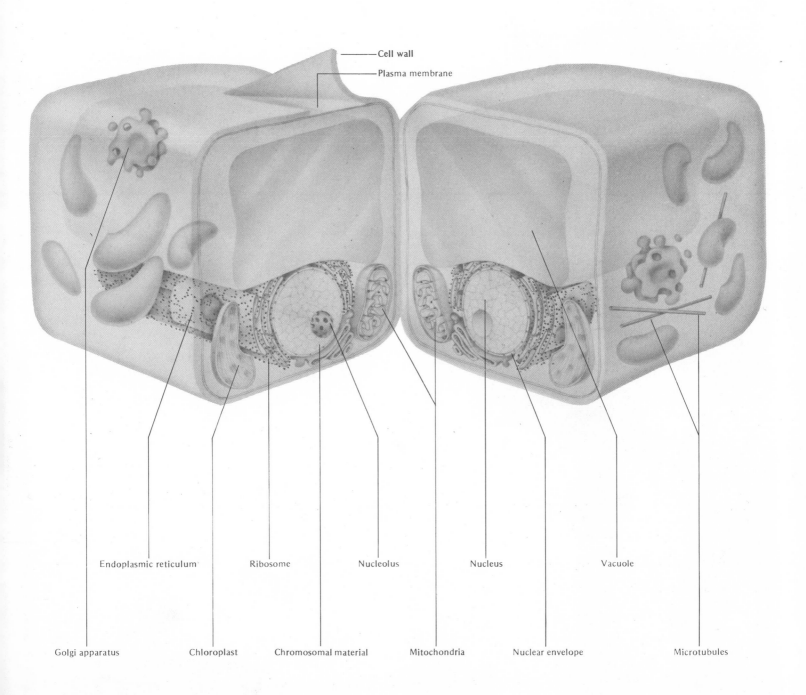

Cell wall

Plasma membrane

Endoplasmic reticulum    Ribosome    Nucleolus    Nucleus    Vacuole

Golgi apparatus    Chloroplast    Chromosomal material    Mitochondria    Nuclear envelope    Microtubules

# BIOLOGY
## A Human Approach

Out of the dreaming past, with its legends of steaming sea and gleaming glaciers, mountains that moved and suns that glared, emerges this creature, man—the latest phase in a continuing process that stretches back to the beginnings of life. His is the heritage of all that has lived; he still carries the vestiges of snout and fangs and claws of species long since vanished; he is the ancestor of all that is yet to come.

Do not regard him lightly—he is you.

DON FABUN, *The Dynamics of Change,*
Englewood Cliffs, New Jersey, Prentice-Hall, 1967.

# BIOLOGY

## A Human Approach

FOURTH EDITION

## IRWIN W. SHERMAN
## VILIA G. SHERMAN

University of California at Riverside

New York   Oxford ♛ OXFORD UNIVERSITY PRESS ♛ 1989

Oxford University Press

Oxford   New York   Toronto   Delhi   Bombay   Calcutta
Madras   Karachi   Petaling Jaya   Singapore   Hong Kong   Tokyo
Nairobi   Dar es Salaam   Cape Town   Melbourne   Auckland

and associated companies in
Berlin   Ibadan

Published by Oxford University Press, Inc.,
200 Madison Avenue, New York, New York 10016

Oxford is a registered trademark of Oxford University Press

Library of Congress Cataloging-in-Publication Data

Sherman, Irwin W.
  Biology : a human approach / Irwin W. Sherman, Vilia G. Sherman.—4th ed.
    p.       cm.        Includes bibliographical references and index.
  ISBN 0-19-505776-7
  1. Biology.   2. Human biology.   I. Sherman, Vilia G.   II. Title.
QH308.2.S5 1989                                              88-23462
574—dc19                                                     CIP

987654321

Printed in the United States of America

For Jonathan and Alexa

# Preface

This book is for you! Students will find this textbook to be somewhat different from others that deal with the subject matter of biology. This text is written so that students like yourself will find biology the dynamic and engrossing subject it really is. We have written it in as interesting a fashion as we know how, and have tried to treat biology in an understandable way for your background. Scattered throughout the text you will find photographs, cartoons, newspaper stories, magazine articles, and boxed materials that we hope will engage your interest and entertain you, but they also have another purpose: to illuminate the remainder of the text. The illustrative materials and the writing style are designed to enlighten and assist in your comprehension. Our aim has been to tell a story that is readable, understandable, and enjoyable—one that has meaning for those of you who are majoring in the arts, humanities, and social sciences.

*Biology: A Human Approach* has been written with both the student and the teacher in mind. Those of us who have spent hours preparing lecture notes and then meeting with students in laboratories and lecture halls have sometimes wondered how we can best convey the vibrance and beauty, as well as the importance, of biology to our students. Frequently we ask ourselves: How can we avoid making the teaching of biology tedious and boring? How can we demonstrate that biology is not a static subject, but one that is dynamic and ever-changing through research? The answers are better lectures and better textbooks. Today's textbooks of biology are lengthier largely because there is an abundance of information that many authors feel compelled to add more and more with each year. These texts, some as bulky as a London or Manhattan telephone directory, have become a kind of "Everything you wanted to know about biology but were afraid to ask" text. Although it is sometimes comforting for teachers using such textbooks to be able to tell the student who has a question to "look it up in your text," the encyclopedic approach frequently loses students in a forest of facts, and provides little guidance toward understanding. Those of us who have used such fact-filled and overwhelming texts have been disappointed that the students frequently do not read the massive amounts placed before them. We have consciously avoided making this text encyclopedic, and have chosen not to write a watered down version of a science majors text. Instead, we have placed the fundamental concepts of biology in a context that hopefully would enable students to better understand themselves and the world in which they live. *Biology: A Human Approach* is a text that students will find not only informative, but a pleasure to read.

Fifteen years have passed since the publication of the first edition of this textbook. Much has happened since then. The restlessness of the 1960s and 1970s, with an almost universal call for an end to an unpopular war, and an overriding concern with ecological balance, have given way to a more settled approach, and a somewhat more materialistic view of the world. The laissez faire curriculum with its emphasis on relevance, has yielded to university and college curricula that are more structured in format, and contain somewhat more emphasis on breadth. During the past decade and a half change has been rapid in the field of biology, and to bring the massive amount of new material within the confines of a single text, with a limited number of pages, has posed a formidable challenge to us. We have had to select, delete, revise, add, and rewrite entire sections of the book. And, in the process not only have we learned a great deal about our subject, but we constantly had to remind ourselves that as teachers our task is not to teach interesting things, but to make interesting that which must be taught.

The primary purpose of this 4th edition is to present the fundamentals of biology to undergraduate students who are likely to pursue careers in fields other than the biological sciences. Because this will be perhaps both an introductory and a final course in the biological sciences we have written the text in such a way that they will be better prepared to understand themselves and the world in which we live. *Biology: A Human Approach* is current, accurate, and appropriate for today's students who will have to make decisions and take stands on biological questions that affect our futures. This text, we hope, will assist in making those decisions well-formed ones.

As implied by the book's title, we have selected the human organism as its central theme. Here we treat biology—the study of life—in its modern and often controversial aspects. Hopefully, biology framed in this way has both meaning and excitement rather than being an abstract stumbling block serving merely to satisfy the breadth requirements of the liberal arts major. By design, we have omitted detailed considerations of the life histories of plants or animals, and plant and animal anatomy. On the other hand, the text goes more deeply into areas relevant to the student's present and future. Basic biological concepts are illustrated by reference to areas of immediate concern, such as cancer, abortion, human genetics, human ecology, transplantation immunity, genetic engineering, and AIDS. When a topic is mentioned, it is given sufficient depth to make exposure meaningful. It is our hope that a human approach to biology will generate sufficient interest in biological phenomena and how these are investigated that, although formal coursework may end here, in depth studies will continue thereafter in an informal way.

The chapters are arranged in a sequential order, the study of advanced areas depending on an understanding of more elementary concepts. Thus, the book progresses from The Cell (Part One) to The Human Organism (Part Two) and ends with a view of us from an ecological perspective, The Human Population (Part Three). Within each section there is also a progression from simple to complex levels so that what goes before is used as a basis for later discussions. The text treatment is flexible enough however, to permit diverse sequences of chapters, so an array of readings can be accommodated to courses of varying length.

To demonstrate the human implications of biological processes, most chapters begin with a photograph, a news article, or a short excerpt from the popular literature. These are designed to pique reader interest and to point up the timeliness of the subject matter. The chapter proper, the academic core of the text, attempts to stress the importance of biological facts to the human condition—where we are and how we might possibly change. At intervals in each chapter, relevant asides are presented in boxes. For example: why cyanide kills; curling of hair and the shape of protein molecules; transplanting a gene; human mammary tumors; smog, smoking, and emphysema. Boxed material serves as motivational cement, holding firm the reader's attention to the text's core material.

Since the book is written for undergraduate college students regardless of their previous scientific background, it seemed important that all students have some of the basic tools of biology at hand. The role of chemistry in biology cannot be minimized. The simple chemistry essential to an understanding of today's biology is presented in an appendix to the text proper so that chapter continuity and student interest are not sidetracked by a "chemistry hurdle" at the book's beginning. Reading the chemistry appendix at appropriate points in the text rather than all at once will serve to reduce the activation–energy barrier of this subject.

At the end of each chapter, there are a summary, a list of key words that are printed in boldface type in the text, and topics for review and discussion. As in previous editions, the index may be used as a glossary; page numbers where definitions of the key terms may be found appear in boldface type in the index, providing a quick and easy reference. We hope that students will find this method of indexing and the list of key words at the end of each chapter to be useful study aids. For example, after reading a given chapter, students may wish to run down the list of key words. If they can successfully define all the key words for themselves, they are well on the way to achieving a good grasp of the chapter's content. Definitions of unknown terms can be checked quickly by looking back through the chapter or by turning to the index.

This book spans its subject from the level of molecules to populations, and no single person can claim excellence in all of these diverse specialties. In the preparation of the text we have been most fortunate in having the able assistance of colleagues who read and gave criticism of these pages so that the text was as error-free as possible. No doubt errors still remain; the fault for these is ours. We continue to hope that the fruits of our labors are enjoyed by the reader with the same delight that we derive from writing about and teaching biology in this way.

*Riverside, California*　　　　　　　　　　　　　　　　I.W.S.
*June 1988*　　　　　　　　　　　　　　　　　　　　V.G.S.

# Contents

PROLOGUE  1

PART I:  THE CELL

1 GENESIS: THE ORIGIN OF LIFE  5

   1-1 What Is Life?  5
Box IA Vitalism Versus Mechanism  6
   1-2 Spontaneous Generation  7
Box 1B The Methods of Science  8
   1-3 History of the Early Earth  9
   1-4 The Primitive Soup  12
   1-5 The Primitive Organism  13
Box 1C Creation: Producing Life in the Laboratory  14
Box 1D The Spiegelman Monster  16
   1-6 Heterotrophs and Autotrophs  17
Box 1E The Earliest Life in the Oldest Rocks  18
Box 1F Does Life Originate Abiotically Today?  20
   Summary  22

2 CELL STRUCTURE: THE ORGANIZATION OF LIFE  25

   2-1 What Is a Cell  25
Box 2A Thereby Hangs a Tail: A Tale of Resolution  32
   2-2 Cell Specialization: Tissues and Organs  49
   2-3 Cells and Organisms  49
   Summary  53
Box 2B Seeing the Unseen: Viruses  54

3 OF MOLECULES AND CELLS  59

   3-1 The Nature of the Living System: The Chemicals of Life  59
   3-2 Carbohydrates: Cellular Fuel  59

Box 3A Through the Looking Glass: Symmetry of Molecules  61
   3-3 Lipids: Fuel, Structure, and Coordination  64
   3-4 Proteins: Fabric of the Cell  68
Box 3B Protein Structure and Making a Meringue  71
   3-5 Enzymes: Proteins That Make Haste  72
Box 3C Curling Hair and the Shape of Protein Molecules  73
   3-6 Vitamins, Coenzymes, and Minerals: Enzyme Helpers  75
Box 3D Beneficial Poison: Sulfanilamide  77
   3-7 Nucleic Acids: Informational Molecules  78
   Summary  78

4 HARVEST OF CHEMICAL ENERGY: CELLULAR RESPIRATION  81

   4-1 What Is Energy?  81
   4-2 Energy Currency: ATP  83
   4-3 Chemical Energy Harvest  84
   4-4 The Energy Cascade  85
   4-5 Getting Along Without Oxygen  86
   4-6 Anaerobic Respiration: Cost Accounting  86
Box 4A Beer, Bread, and Muscle: Molecular Changes in Pyruvic Acid  88
   4-7 Getting Along with Oxygen  89
   4-8 Aerobic Respiration: Cost Accounting  92
Box 4B Why Cyanide Kills  92
   4-9 Where Is ATP Used?  93
   4-10 Chemical Energy Harvest: Evolution and Cellular Location  93
   Summary  94

5 HARVEST OF LIGHT ENERGY: PHOTOSYNTHESIS  97

   5-1 All Flesh Is Grass  97
   5-2 The Energy Cascade Revisited  97

5-3 Light and Chlorophyll: Light Phase  98
5-4 Carbon Dioxide and Sugar Formation: Dark Phase  99
5-5 Cellular Location of Photosynthesis  102
**Box 5A Weed Killers  102**
5-6 Efficiency and Implications of Photosynthesis  102
Summary  104

**6 COMMUNICATION BETWEEN CELL GENERATIONS: NUCLEIC ACIDS  107**

6-1 Inheritance: General Features  107
6-2 Inheritance: Chemical Structure  107
6-3 Genetic Code: Four-Letter Alphabet, Three-Letter Words  111
**Box 6A An Inborn Error: PKU and Idiocy  112**
6-4 Copying and Translating the Genetic Code: RNA and Protein  114
**Box 6B The Library of Heredity  115**
6-5 Implications of the Genetic Code  122
6-6 Genetic Engineering: Recombinant DNA  123
6-7 Prospects for the Refabrication of Human Beings  123
**Box 6C Redesigning Bacteria  124**
Summary  125

**7 CELLS IN ACTION: DUPLICATION AND CONTROL MECHANISMS  129**

7-1 Cell Duplication  129
7-2 Chromosome Structure  134
7-3 Control of Cellular Activity  138
Summary  148

**8 CANCER: CELLS OUT OF CONTROL  151**

8-1 What Is Cancer?  151
8-2 Carcinogens: Cancer-causing Agents  153
**Box 8A The Cancer Screen  156**
**Box 8B Human Mammary Tumors  159**
8-3 The Molecular Basis of Cancer  160
Summary  164

# PART II: THE HUMAN ORGANISM

**9 PERPETUATION OF LIFE I: SEX-CELL FORMATION AND FERTILIZATION  169**

9-1 Sexuality and Meiosis  169
9-2 The Male Reproductive System  171
**Box 9A Sperm Banks  176**
9-3 The Female Reproductive System  177
9-4 Coitus (Copulation)  183
**Box 9B The Month-After Pill  186**
9-5 Fertilization  184
9-6 Contraception  185
**Box 9C Detection of Ovulation  187**
**Box 9D Pregnancy: Signs and Symptoms  189**
9-7 Control of the Female Reproductive Cycle: The Pill  187
Summary  189
**Box 9E AIDS  190**
**Box 9F Sterilization for Both Sexes  192**

**10 PERPETUATION OF LIFE II: HUMAN DEVELOPMENT  195**

10-1 From Egg to Embryo  195
**Box 10A Gene Screen: Early Fetal Checkup  202**
10-2 The Fetus  203
10-3 The Placenta: Lungs, Kidneys, and Digestive Tract for the Human Fetus  206
**Box 10B From Water to Land: A Baby Is Born  208**
10-4 Parturition (Birth)  209
10-5 The Mammary Glands and Lactation  209
10-6 Birth Defects  213
**Box 10C Abortion  214**
Summary  217

**11 THE RESTLESS ENVELOPE: SKIN  221**

11-1 What Is Skin?  221
11-2 The Skin Surface  221
11-3 The Architecture of the Skin  223
11-4 Skin Color  223
**Box 11A Sunburn  225**
11-5 Hair and Nails  226

**Box 11B Gone Today, but Hair Tomorrow  228**
11-6  Glands of the Skin  229
Summary  230

12  PROCESSING FOOD: DIGESTION AND NUTRITION  233

12-1  Why Do We Eat?  233
12-2  Intake Apparatus: Food Processing  233
12-3  Digestion: Food Degradation  235
12-4  Absorption: Food Uptake  235
**Box 12A A Peephole into the Stomach  238**
12-5  Defecation: Waste Expulsion  240
12-6  Nutrition: The Use of Processed Nutrients  240
**Box 12B The Fall and Rise of Nonfood  247**
12-7  Trouble Along the Alimentary Canal  247
**Box 12C Ulcers: The Price of Success  248**
Summary  250

13  INTERNAL TRANSPORT: THE CIRCULATORY SYSTEM  253

13-1  Why Do We Need a Circulatory System?  253
13-2  What Does the Circulatory System Do?  253
13-3  The Heart: A Remarkable Pump  255
**Box 13A Artificial Heart  260**
13-4  Cardiovascular Plumbing at Work  261
**Box 13B Heart Attack  263**
**Box 13C Bypassing the Bypass  266**
**Box 13D Stimulus for Ailing Hearts  270**
Summary  271
**Box 13E The Death of Lenin  272**

14  BLOOD AND IMMUNITY  275

14-1  Blood: A Tissue That Flows  275
**Box 14A Counting the Reds and Whites: Barometer of Disease  280**
14-2  Against the Foreign Peril: Immunity  281
**Box 14B The Bubble Boy's Lost Battle  283**
**Box 14C AIDS, a Failure in Immune Surveillance  290**
**Box 14D Putting Antibodies to Work  290**
**Box 14E The Monospecific Missile: Monoclonal Antibodies  294**
Summary  295

**Box 14F New Organs for Old: Transplantation  297**
**Box 14G Wheezes and Sneezes  298**

15  GASEOUS EXCHANGE: RESPIRATION  301

15-1  Why Do We Need a Respiratory System?  301
15-2  The Respiratory Tree  302
15-3  Alveolus: Rendezvous of Blood and Air  304
**Box 15A Smog, Smoking, and Emphysema  308**
15-4  How Do We Breathe?  309
15-5  Control of Breathing  312
**Box 15B Why Can't We Breathe Under Water?  314**
15-6  Low Pressure, High Pressure  316
Summary  317

16  CHEMICAL BALANCE: THE KIDNEY  321

16-1  What Does the Kidney Do?  321
**Box 16A What Is Urea?  322**
16-2  Structure and Function of the Kidney  323
16-3  Regulation of Fluid and Salt Balance  328
**Box 16B The Artificial Kidney Machine  330**
16-4  Discharge of Urine  332
Summary  333

17  CHEMICAL COORDINATION: HORMONES  337

17-1  The Nature of Hormones  337
17-2  The Human Hormonal Orchestra: Endocrine Glands  337
**Box 17A Giants and Dwarfs  342**
**Box 17B Rickets  348**
**Box 17C The Critical Cortex  353**
**Box 17D The Hypothalamus and History  354**
17-3  Management of the Endocrine Orchestra  357
17-4  The Molecular Activity of Hormones  358
Summary  360

18  ELECTROCHEMICAL COORDINATION: NERVES  365

18-1  What Does the Nervous System Do?  365
**Box 18A 1984 Revisited?  366**
18-2  The Neuron: Signal Cell of the Nervous System  366

18-3 The Nerve Impulse: An Electrochemical
Message 369
18-4 The Nerve Impulse: Production and
Conduction 371
**Box 18B Bugging the Brain 372**
18-5 Signals from Neuron to Neuron: The
Synapse 374
18-6 Integrated Circuits of Neurons: The Nervous
System 377
18-7 Neuronal Circuits in Action: Reflexes 382
**Box 18C An Environmental Cause of Parkinson's
Disease? 383**
18-8 Drugs and the Nervous System 383
Summary 388


19 BUILT-IN SIGNAL CORPS: THE SENSE ORGANS 391

19-1 Sensory Listening Posts 391
19-2 Smell: Detecting Chemical Signals in the Air 391
19-3 Taste: Detecting Chemical Signals in Solution 391
19-4 Sight: Receiving Light Signals 393
19-5 Hearing: Receiving Sound Signals 397
**Box 19A Unwanted Sound: Noise Pollution 400**
19-6 Balance and Equilibrium 401
19-7 Touch, Temperature, and Pressure:
Skin Senses 403
Summary 403


20 ANIMAL AND HUMAN BEHAVIOR 407

20-1 Why Behave? 407
20-2 Toward Understanding Behavior 408
**Box 20A Purpose Is in the Mind of the Beholder 409**
20-3 Simpler Types of Behavior 410
20-4 More Complex Types of Behavior 411
**Box 20B Skinner's Utopia: Panacea or Path to Hell? 412**
**Box 20C Are Human Beings Instinctive Killers? 416**
20-5 Where and How Does Learning Occur? 419
20-6 Memory 420
20-7 Social Behavior 422
**Box 20D The Life of the Honeybee 424**
20-8 Prospects for the Future 427
Summary 427

21 MOVEMENT: SKELETON AND MUSCLE 431

21-1 The Skeleton: Tower of Support and
Protection 431
21-2 Motion: Muscle 435
**Box 21A Myasthenia Gravis 445**
**Box 21B Your Muscles: Use 'em or Lose 'em 447**
Summary 447
**Box 21C Paralytic Poisons 448**


22 STAYING IN PLACE: HOMEOSTATIC CONTROLS 453

22-1 Keeping Things in Order, or, Maintaining the
Steady State 453
22-2 Body-Temperature Control 453
**Box 22A Fever: Resetting the Body's Thermostat 456**
Summary 457


PART III: THE HUMAN POPULATION

23 GENES IN INDIVIDUALS: HUMAN INHERITANCE 461

23-1 Communication Between Parent and
Offspring 461
23-2 Genes, Chromosomes, and Sex-Cell
Formation 461
**Box 23A Preparing Chromosomal Pictures 463**
23-3 Phenotype and Genotype 462
23-4 Transmission of Genes 467
**Box 23B Mendel and His Peas 468**
**Box 23C Hemophilia and History 476**
23-5 Blood Will Tell 478
**Box 23D The Charlie Chaplin Paternity Suit 479**
23-6 Polygenes and Skin Color 481
**Box 23E Of Transplants and Genes 483**
23-7 Chromosomal Abnormalities 482
Summary 489


24 GENES IN POPULATIONS: AN INTRODUCTION TO
EVOLUTION 495

24-1 Sickle Cell: A Molecular Disease 495
24-2 Our Changing Genes: Mutation 496

**Box 24A  Radiation as a Mutagen  498**
   24-3  Genes in Populations  501
   24-4  Natural Selection  503
   24-5  Eugenics: Improving Our Genes by Selection  505
**Box 24B  The Diabolical Disease of Woody Guthrie  506**
   Summary  508


25  HUMAN EVOLUTION  511

   25-1  Our Place in Nature  511
   25-2  What Is a Human Being?  513
   25-3  Darwinism: From Finches to Humans  518
   25-4  The Road to Humans  523
   25-5  The Races of Man  532
   25-6  What Is Our Evolutionary Future?  535
   Summary  536


26  HUMANS AND THE ENVIRONMENT  539

   26-1  What's Ecology?  539
   26-2  Energy Flow  540
   26-3  Food Chains and Ecological Pyramids  541
   26-4  The Danger of Accumulated Chemicals  544
**Box 26A  Hideaways for Nuclear Waste  548**
   26-5  Recycling Matter  549

**Box 26B  Ebbing of the Ogalalla  555**
   26-6  Homeostasis and Succession in the
       Ecosystem  556
   26-7  The Forces That Shape a Community  558
   26-8  Agriculture and Unbalanced Ecosystems  564
   Summary  566


27  ABOARD SPACESHIP EARTH  569

   27-1  The Inhabitants of Spaceship Earth and How They
       Grew  569
   27-2  Implications of Population Growth  578
**Box 27A  Last Chance to Keep Off the Grass?  581**
**Box 27B  Thermal Pollution: We Can't Break Even  583**
**Box 27C  Deep Concern: Groundwater  589**
   27-3  Limits on Population Growth:
       Strategy for Survival  590
       Summary  592


EPILOGUE  595

APPENDIX  597

A: SIMPLE CHEMISTRY FOR BIOLOGY  597

B: WHAT EVER HAPPENED TO METRIC?  603

INDEX  605

# BIOLOGY
## A Human Approach

# Prologue

Man is a threatened species. The twin specters facing him are overpopulation and unbridled technology—both self-induced.

The double threat is aimed most directly at man's environment. As the United States strives to accommodate more human beings than it has ever had to serve before, increased demands are placed on our natural resource bank. Our surroundings become increasingly crowded, noisy, and soiled.

. . . Buffeted by the elements and beset by other life forms, man has always stubbornly insisted on exercising every option open to him. Does he still run his own show today: Or has he finally stumbled upon two forces—population and technology—that he considers two sacred to tamper with: Is he still convinced that the roaring crescendo from babies and bulldozers is the sweet music of progress?

Does he confuse technology with science? Will he continue to accord to the jackhammer the same revered status as the test tube? Or will he recognize in time that the tools he uses to rip up mountains and destroy estuaries must be extensions of his mind as well as his muscle? Will he see that science must remain free, since it is the *search* for truth, but that technology is only a means of *applying* truth—and that these applications need the control and balance of wisdom and a concern for posterity?

Man stands at a fork in his environmental road to the future.

The two arms of the signpost do not state categorically, "Man—Master of Himself" and "Man—An Extinct Species," but it is increasingly apparent that the direction he takes now will move him rapidly along the path toward one or the other designation.

Let us look closely for a moment at this creature who pauses at the crossroads and clamors for attention with our own voice. Who is he? Where has he come from and how has he made the journey this far?

From *Man . . . An Endangered Species?* U.S. Department of the Interior Conservation Yearbook No. 4 (Washington, D.C., U.S. Government Printing Office, 1968).

# THE CELL

Some say that spaceship earth is doomed, that there is only a short time before there will be little oxygen to breathe or food to eat, that the effluents of the inhabitants will soon overcome them, that time has run out, and no matter what we do, nothing can save us. This pessimistic view of our future may eventually become a reality, but let us imagine for the moment that there is ample time to recover the ship and its inhabitants. How can the earth be saved from self-destruction?

Recovery tactics must depend upon a clear understanding of the nature of the earth and its occupants—the substances which make up this self-contained system and how they interact with each other. It would be helpful, indeed desirable, to understand the most fundamental elements that make up this system. In the physical and chemical world the fundamental unit is the atom, and it is impossible to understand physical and chemical events without recognizing what atoms are like and what they do. In the biological world, our world, the cell is the fundamental unit, and similarly we cannot comprehend biological phenomena without an appreciation of the cell and its structure and operation. It is elemental that many of the problems confronting the earth's inhabitants depend upon the nature of the cells which make up earthlings. An understanding of the cell is basic to understanding ourselves and all life.

## Is there life on Mars?

On July 20, 1976, as the sun broke over the Martian horizon, a spindly, three-legged spacecraft sat silently on a dry, barren landscape. Suddenly, a silvery arm stretched out from the Viking Lander and scooped up a heap of reddish soil. The Viking, after an 11-month journey in space, successfully responded to commands from controllers on Earth, 200 million miles away. The robot arm retracted, twisted its wrist, and dropped the soil into an opening on the top of the spacecraft. The search for extraterrestrial life had begun.

How does one look for life that may be very different from our own? How can one be sure that observations reveal living processes rather than nonbiological activity? More than 15 years ago, a Space Study Board agreed that anything organized to draw nourishment from the environment and reproduce itself should be considered "life."

The most obvious way to seek life on Mars is to look for it, and the Lander's cameras were used to see if anything moved or looked suspiciously biological. Another way is to test for the presence of organic molecules. On board Viking, a tiny laboratory was housed in a 1-foot cube weighing only 30 lb. It was crammed with 140,000 electronic components—including 122,000 transistors, 40 thermostats, 3 tiny ovens, bottled radioactive gases, a small xenon lamp to simulate sunshine, and a pocket-sized chromatograph to analyze the chemical components of the soil. Three separate experiments were performed.

One of the experiments sought to learn if anything in the soil assimilates Martian air (mainly carbon dioxide) to form carbon-containing material. The soil sample was exposed to carbon dioxide whose carbon was radioactive, and incubated for up to 5 days under simulated Martian sunlight. The soil was then tested to see if it had become radioactive by incorporating that carbon. This would provide evidence that organisms are growing on Mars. The tests did not find organic molecules; however, small amounts of such carbon-based compounds could go unnoticed.

Living things on Earth use nutrients and release waste products and gases, a process called metabolism. To test for this, a Martian soil sample was moistened with a substance scientists have named "chicken soup," a nutrient broth rich in vitamins and amino acids and containing radioactive carbon. The sample was incubated to see if anything consumed the "soup" and released radioactively labeled products. A rapid release of

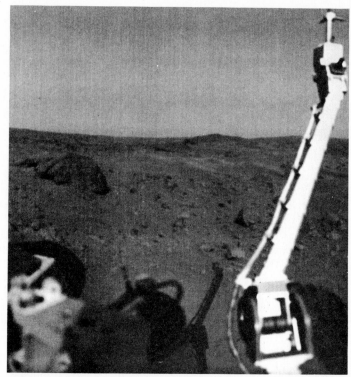

A view of the Martian landscape from the Viking Lander. The outstretched arm of the Lander is used for sampling soil.

carbon dioxide occurred. This could have been the result of microbes metabolizing the soup or simply the chemical activity of soil compounds called peroxides.

In the third test, a soil sample was submerged in a liquid nutrient for 12 days in an atmosphere of helium, krypton, and carbon dioxide. At intervals, the miniaturized laboratory sampled the atmosphere in the chamber for hydrogen, nitrogen, oxygen, methane, and carbon dioxide—gases generally produced by living organisms. The sample released oxygen far more rapidly than plants usually do; such a reaction could be biological or the result of decomposition of soil peroxides.

The results of the three experiments could be explained on the basis of the composition of the Martian soil and atmosphere. No evidence of life was found on Mars.

# 1

# Genesis: The Origin of Life

## 1–1 WHAT IS LIFE?

The business of biology is life. But what is life? What do we really mean when we say that an object is living or nonliving? How do we distinguish between the inanimate and the dead? How shall we recognize living matter on other planets (see facing page), and when can we say that a person is dead and can serve as a donor for organ transplants? It is necessary for us to develop some notion of what life is. We shall find in the process that this is no easy task and no definition of life is completely satisfactory; we can nevertheless make an attempt.

For most of us it is easier to recognize life than to define it. We are aware that we are alive and that someday we shall be dead. Animals and plants are alive; earth, fire, water, and air are not alive. Living things have certain characteristics, no one of which by itself is sufficient to define them as being alive, but which when taken together enable us to distinguish them from the nonliving. The capacity for growth, maintenance, repair, reproduction, movement, responsiveness, change—these are the properties of the living. But how are these characteristics of life different from the growth of crystals, the division of raindrops, the swift movement of a mountain stream, the response and change in a piece of wood as it is consumed by fire? Let us examine the characteristics of living things one by one in greater detail.

### Growth, maintenance, and repair

It is easy for us to recognize living things; however, it is important to recognize that life is not a thing or a substance. **Life** is a property possessed by individuals characterized by the capacity to perform a series of highly organized, interacting processes that occur within a definite structural framework. In order to continue these processes, living systems must obtain materials from the environment, utilizing and altering these substances for the synthesis, maintenance, and repair of their own structures and eliminating those materials that are no longer useful. The flow of materials through the living system is called **metabolism.** The tests for life performed on Martian soil by the Viking Lander attempted to detect metabolism in various ways (see page 4).

The metabolic processes of life involve the performance of work and require an energy supply for their continuance; living systems are capable of converting, transporting, and storing energy. They perform these energy transformations with the aid of organic catalysts called **enzymes.**

One of the end results of all these transformations is an increase in size, or **growth**—from the inside out. Thus, the growth of living systems differs from that of nonliving ones, such as crystals, which grow by the addition of material from the outside and do not transform the added material during the process. Moreover, a crystal is unable to repair or maintain itself except under special conditions.

### Reproduction

Living systems do not only grow and convert, transport, and store energy—they are also capable of self-duplication, or **reproduction.** Many nonliving systems are capable of reproduction, however. Crystals divide, as do streaming raindrops, and fire can be reproduced by incandescent sparks. How does reproduction in living systems differ from this other kind of reproduction? The method of reproduction in living systems is far more complex, exact, and specific than in nonliving ones. Living systems can make identical copies of themselves. Moreover, the process of self-duplication is especially important in living systems because it includes a capacity for **mutation,** or change, and these changes are perpetuated exactly in subsequent generations of the organism involved. The changes in form which may occur during the division of a raindrop or a crystal or the reproduction of fire are not subsequently perpetuated.

A system that cannot change to meet the needs imposed by changes in its environment is at a severe disadvantage, which may eventually prove fatal; in other words, a system incapable of mutation is unable to **evolve** (change with time). Living things exist in endless variety and complexity, and they are able to cope with the demands of the environment because of their ability to mutate, adapt, and evolve.

### Responsiveness and movement

Living systems are not static; they are capable of responding to changes in both the external and the internal environment, not only from generation to generation but within generations. If somebody pricks your finger with a pin, your initial response is probably to withdraw your finger. The capacity for **responsiveness** to stimuli is related to the fact that living systems are self-

5

regulating. A particular stimulus induces an appropriate response, but the response may not always be the same. After withdrawing your finger, you might take the pin from the offending party, you might hit him or her with your fist, or you might simply walk away. Responses are mediated by the living system. A crystal, when it is placed in the right conditions, will always grow; likewise, fire and rain are at the mercy of outside controls. Living systems to a greater or lesser extent can control the end results of stimuli themselves.

The dynamic changes characteristic of the living world are often evidenced as motion. Sometimes the motion is so slow that the change is not immediately apparent (as in plants), and at other times it takes place quite rapidly and is easily recognizable (as in animals). In many living systems the motion takes place over such short distances that it is not perceived by the human eye, but there are conditions where motion covers great distances and is easily observable. Like the capacity for responsiveness, the capacity for movement that living systems have is self-regulating; in nonliving systems it generally is not. A raindrop must fall, and a fire must rage or die.

Thus, life as we have defined it (and the definition is to a large extent arbitrary) involves a series of highly organized, interacting processes that form a system that is potentially capable of perpetual change.

What is the advantage of defining and describing living systems in these mechanistic terms (Box 1A)? First, it avoids mystery, and second, it rules out the concept of the existence of a vitalistic force such as entelechy, or the "soul of life." The reason for avoiding such ideas is that they preclude a scientific examination of the living system; simply stated, such a characterization of life defies testing by scientific methods (Box 1B) and is of little value in biological inquiry.

---

**BOX 1A  Vitalism versus mechanism**

Throughout the history of biological thought, there has raged the controversy of whether or not living phenomena can be described in terms of chemistry and physics. The **vitalists** (adherents to the philosophy of vitalism) take the view that living phenomena cannot be included under the heading of chemistry and/or physics but rather that there is a kind of directing force or spirit resident within the living organism. Vitalists believe that this life force is beyond human comprehension and that a distinct and inviolable barrier exists between the living and the nonliving world. According to the vitalists, the origin of life could be explained only as a result of divine creation.

In contrast, the **mechanists'** view of life states that living phenomena can be described by chemistry and physics; the line of demarcation between the living and the nonliving is not sharply defined, and no vitalistic spirit or soul directs the living organism. The mechanists suggest that living phenomena can be examined and tested by the methods of science (see Box 1B).

Vitalism is an ancient view of living phenomena, but it reappears even in modern times. A distinguished physicist, W. Elasser, in 1958 wrote of "biotonic phenomena," that is, "phenomena in the organism that cannot be explained in terms of mechanistic function." And in 1963 P. Mora suggested, "Living entities, at all levels in almost all their manifestations, have something of a directed, relentless, acquiring and selfish nature, a perseverance to maintain their own being and a continuous *urge* to dominate their surroundings, to take advantage of all possible circumstances and to adjust to new conditions." Perhaps the clearest refutation of vitalism would be the creation of a living organism by completely synthetic means out of simple chemical elements. Disturbing and convincing as such an experiment might be, no doubt a resourceful vitalist would claim that even this system had been taken over by a life force. Vitalistic views, old as well as new, replete with misconceptions and defying examination by objective criteria, are of little value in helping us to understand biology.

As you read this book, you will see that most of the processes having to do with life that we do understand can be explained in terms of chemistry and physics. Those we do not yet understand are potentially explicable in these terms. Superstition and vitalism were early attempts to explain away things that could not be understood at the time because physics and chemistry had not yet advanced far enough.

FIGURE 1–1 (top) Francesco Redi (1626?–1697). (Courtesy of The Bettmann Archive, Inc.)

FIGURE 1–2 (bottom) Anton van Leeuwenhoek (1632–1723). (Courtesy of The Bettmann Archive, Inc.)

FIGURE 1–3 Lazzaro Spallanzani (1729–1799). (Courtesy of The Bettmann Archive, Inc.)

7

GENESIS: THE ORIGIN OF LIFE

## 1–2 SPONTANEOUS GENERATION

If we agree that life can be defined in mechanistic terms, then we can further ask the question, How did life originate? Somewhere in our educational experience, most of us have come across the doctrine of **spontaneous generation,** that is, the sudden appearance of living things from something nonliving. This view held dominion over much of our thinking up until the seventeenth century, and it was supported by some of the greatest and clearest scientific minds of the time. The supporters of this view cited examples and gave recipes for the production of living material from the nonliving: sweaty shirts stored with wheat in a dark place were supposed to give rise to mice, the hairs of a horse's tail when placed in water produced worms, and decaying meat gave rise to maggots (fly larvae). The strangest part about these recipes was that they really appeared to work!

In 1668 an Italian physician and poet named Francesco Redi (Figure 1–1) performed a simple but classic test that shook the foundations of the doctrine of spontaneous generation. Where others were content to observe nature and suggest imaginative explanations for various phenomena, Redi was not content merely to observe natural phenomena as they occurred, but set out to test ideas and to arrange some of the components of nature so that analysis of phenomena could be made; in short, he did an **experiment.** Redi arranged three jars of decaying meat; one of the jars he covered with gauze, another was covered with parchment, and the third was left uncovered. Flies were attracted to the meat samples in the gauze- and parchment-covered jars, but could land only on the meat in the open jar; in this jar maggots developed, but not in either of the others. Decaying meat in itself did not give rise to maggots, he concluded. It was necessary for flies to land on the meat and deposit their eggs, which subsequently hatched and gave rise to maggots.

This simple refutation of the generation of life from substances such as rotting meat held sway for only a short time. In 1675 a Dutch linen merchant with a penchant for grinding magnifying lenses, Anton van Leeuwenhoek (Figure 1–2), found that his lenses showed living microscopic creatures in rainwater. Broth, too, would give rise to all sorts of living creatures if one waited for a while. The resourceful defenders of spontaneous generation argued that although one could not get worms, flies, and rats from the inanimate world, one could get living microorganisms from nonliving broth, rainwater, hay infusions, and other such materials. The first attack on this microlevel doctrine of spontaneous generation came from the Italian scientist Lazzaro Spallanzani (Figure 1–3). In 1767 he discovered that if he boiled meat broth in a flask and then sealed the neck of the flask, no microorganisms developed. If, however, the flask neck was broken, in a short time the broth

BOX 1B The methods of science

Science is the product of people's attempts to understand themselves and the world in which they live; it embodies knowledge about the natural world and ourselves, and it is organized in a systematic fashion derived from experimentation and observation. Scientific knowledge often allows the prediction of specific events and in some cases even permits control of them; scientifically determined facts are repeatable and capable of verification. Science admits "we do not know the answer" and tries to discover it by a variety of repeatable and testable methods rather than by the fabrication of myths which cannot be tested.

There is no one scientific method. Discoveries of a scientific nature are made in a variety of ways, and the methods employed are also quite diverse. The methods of science are not magical or practiced exclusively by scientists working in white coats and surrounded by exotic chemicals and apparatus, but represent a rational approach to understanding the universe. Science assumes that the world about us is knowable.

Scientific method is often described in an idealized fashion; such a formal description bears only a slight resemblance to reality, but it serves to emphasize some of the important elements of scientific inquiry. First, it is important to recognize that a phenomenon exists which demands inquiry. Second, an attempt is made to state the problem in very specific terms. Third, a working **hypothesis** is formulated that attempts to explain the phenomenon. Fourth, the phenomenon is investigated by observation or by experimentation or by both, and evidence is gathered and recorded—the testimony of raw data. Fifth, the data are analyzed and the working hypothesis is reexamined in the light of the evidence provided by the data. Sixth, a conclusion is drawn from the experimental observations about whether the working hypothesis is correct or must be reformulated and reexamined. If it is concluded that the hypothesis is correct, predictions can be made from it. If the hypothesis stands the test of verification and predictability, it becomes a part of the established body of knowledge—a **theory.**

Perhaps no real scientist ever goes through the steps cited above, and obviously such a brief discourse does not take into account the trials, errors, intuitions, and leaps of imagination that are a part of scientific inquiry. Nevertheless, the scientific method represents a powerful tool because of its rigor. Many of the procedures of science are identical to our own daily reasoning, but most of us fail to apply the method stringently in formulating and testing the hypothesis, and when the observations do not satisfy it, we fail to begin anew by reformulating the hypothesis.

Scientific method is a powerful tool for inquiry, but it is not without its limitations. We should not be surprised that sometimes scientific "facts" change or that the practitioners of science harbor decidedly unscientific notions. Since science deals with observable phenomena, its range is limited by our senses or by the machines which sense for us. Refinements in techniques and methods of observation often alter our view of nature and necessitate appropriate modifications in hypotheses and conclusions. Some have therefore characterized science as "the study of errors slowly corrected." The strength of scientific inquiry is that it is self-correcting. Although the scientific method attempts an accurate description of natural phenomena, there is considerable documentation of its mistakes. Scientists are human, with human feelings, failings, and prejudices; on occasion these interfere with their reasoning. This may be particularly true when scientists engage in discussions outside their specialty and neglect the rigorous proof used in their own area of competence. Science can and should be judged apart from the people who practice it; by its very nature science is a productive and important contributor to our knowledge and well-being.

(a)  (1)  (b)  (2)  Sterile broth  (3)

swarmed with microscopic forms of life. Boiling the broth (sterilization) prevented the growth of microorganisms; contamination of it with unheated broth or another substance apparently provided the source of the living creatures. Thus life did not arise spontaneously in the meat broth, but came from an outside source. However, the adherents of the doctrine of spontaneous generation were also imaginative and resourceful. They argued not only that heat destroyed the life in the broth, but also that sealing the flask prevented the vital force of life from entering the flask and bringing forth life. The issue remained in doubt for another century, for it was well known that many organisms required oxygen, a so-called vital principle, and the absence of oxygen in a sealed flask could be expected to inhibit the spontaneous development of living organisms.

In 1862 the French chemist Louis Pasteur (Figure 1–4a) performed an experiment that was both simple and elegant. Pasteur contended that microorganisms (bacteria, yeast, and protozoa) not only cause disease in humans and animals but give rise to decay and change in organic materials, such as broth. In the absence of these microorganisms, he said, no change in the broth should occur. Pasteur placed some meat broth in a flask and boiled it until it was sterile; then he drew out the neck of the flask so that it was formed into the shape of an S (Figure 1–4b). He did not seal the neck, and air could freely communicate with the broth after passing through the twisting neck of the flask. The long, curving neck of the flask trapped the airborne microorganisms and prevented contamination of the broth. In spite of the ease of access of the "vital principle" to the broth, the flasks remained sterile. However, when Pasteur tipped the flask so that some of the broth ran into the bend of the S and then back into the flask, the broth became contaminated with microorganisms. Obviously, something more than broth plus air was necessary to produce life. Kept at the Pasteur Institute in Paris, some of the uncontaminated flasks were sealed to prevent evaporation of the contents, and they remain sterile to this day. The doctrine of spontaneous generation never recovered from the mortal blow provided by this simple experiment of Louis Pasteur.

Such experiments suggest the improbability that life, a complex of organization, can arise in a short time before our eyes, from unorganized organic solutions. We know that today living things perpetuate themselves—roses produce roses, dogs produce dogs, people produce people—but where did it all begin? How did life originate in the first place? Perhaps "spores" came from outer space and upon arrival on this planet flourished and evolved into the creatures that we now recognize as plants and animals. Space exploration convinces us that this is a highly improbable possibility; the kind of spores that could have given rise to life as we know it would be unable to survive the lethal radiations and the low temperatures of outer space. The trip from space to the earth would be disastrous for living substances such as we have on this planet.

Since living things today appear to be produced only by other similar living things and are not generated in a short space of time from nonliving materials, we are drawn almost inescapably to the conclusion that life arose on this planet at some distant period in time. Furthermore, it probably arose in a spontaneous manner from nonliving materials. Thus, the proponents of the doctrine of spontaneous generation may not have been completely wrong after all. They were right about the place, but wrong about the time and the mechanism. Let us go back in time to the period when the earth was being formed and gain some understanding of the conditions that could have fostered the emergence of life as we know it.

## 1–3  HISTORY OF THE EARLY EARTH

If your body was reduced to its constituent elements, we would find that 99% of it consists of carbon, hydrogen, nitrogen, and oxygen (Table 1–1); the remainder is composed of trace quantities of the elements

FIGURE 1–5 The origin of the solar system. (a) Primordial cloud. (b) Condensation of primordial cloud. (c) The primordial cloud forms a flat disc with concentration of matter in the center. (d) Peripheral condensations give rise to the planets, and the matter in the center forms the sun. (e) Planets and sun formed. (f) The present solar system.

**TABLE 1–1 Relative abundance of some of the major elements found in the universe and the human body**

| Element | Relative abundance in atoms (%) | |
|---|---|---|
| | Universe | Human body |
| Hydrogen | 90.79 | 60.3 |
| Carbon | 9.08 | 99.8  10.5 |
| Nitrogen | 0.0415 | 2.42  98.7 |
| Oxygen | 0.0571 | 25.5 |
| Sodium | 0.00012 | 0.73 |
| Magnesium | 0.0023 | 0.01 |
| Aluminum | 0.00023 | — |
| Silicon | 0.026 | 0.00091 |
| Phosphorus | 0.00034 | 0.134 |
| Sulfur | 0.00091 | 0.132 |
| Chlorine | 0.00044 | 0.032 |
| Potassium | 0.000018 | 0.036 |
| Calcium | 0.00017 | 0.226 |
| Iron | 0.0047 | 0.00059 |

sodium, magnesium, phosphorus, chlorine, potassium, iron, and some other metals. The chemical composition of the universe, derived from analyses of the sun, stars, meteorites, and the earth's crust (Table 1–1), demonstrates that the most abundant elements are the very same ones that make up the bulk of living matter. Is this sheer coincidence? Most scientists think not. The relative abundance of elements in the universe and within our own bodies suggests a common origin. To understand the relationship, we must briefly examine the nature of the universe.

If we had a time machine, we could travel backward in time to the remote past and view the beginning of our solar system. Such a machine unfortunately does not exist, and so the solution to the mystery of the origin of our sun and its nine planets must be based on our knowledge of the phenomena that go on in the universe today, most of which are clearly observable through our telescopes.

Where did our solar system come from? How did it arise? The theory that is most popular today and is supported by most **cosmologists** (scientists interested in the origin of stars and planets) is the **primordial cloud** theory. Like other stars, our sun and

(a)

(b)

(c)

(d)

(e)

Planets

(f)

FIGURE 1–6 The history of the earth: formation of the reducing atmosphere.

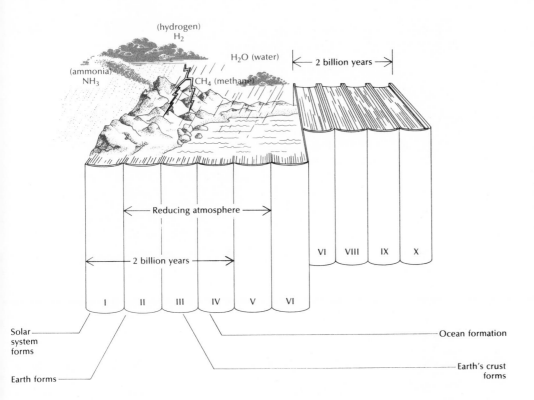

and what remained were virtually naked sunwarmed cores—the planets of today. According to recent estimates, astronomers believe that the formation of the Milky Way took place approximately 10 to 15 billion years ago and our solar system was formed about 5 billion years ago.

Time of the order of billions of years is sometimes a difficult concept to grasp, and so let us use an analogy.[1] Let us assume that the history of the earth can be written in a series of 10 volumes: each volume contains 500 pages, and therefore each page represents 1 million years. The age of the earth and of our solar system is 10 times 500 million, or 5 billion, years. If we could read the history of the earth in these volumes, we would find that the first four volumes (2 billion years) describe the lifeless period (Figure 1–6). What was it like?

According to astronomers, the primeval solar cloud contained principally hydrogen and helium, and present in smaller quantities were carbon, nitrogen, oxygen, and iron. In this interstellar cloud the carbon and nitrogen and some oxygen could combine with the hydrogen to form methane ($CH_4$), ammonia ($NH_3$), and water ($H_2O$). Note that methane is a simple hydrocarbon—an **organic compound**.[2] Thus the atmosphere of the early earth contained organic materials long before there were any organisms. Evidence that tends to confirm these theories comes from present-day spectroscopic analysis of the atmosphere of the planets of our solar system that are farthest from the sun, planets whose residual gases were not completely driven off by the heat of the protosun. Their atmospheres are similar to that suggested for the protoearth: the atmospheres of Jupiter and

all the planets were probably formed from a cloud of primordial gas and dust. There are numerous such clouds in space, some of which are today in the process of forming stars and solar systems. The thinly distributed primordial cloud that ultimately gave rise to our sun and its planets eventually became thicker and more condensed by the gravitational attraction of the molecules composing the cloud; the cloud was in constant motion owing to rotational and gravitational forces and eventually assumed the shape of a flat revolving disc; matter condensed as a series of concentric rings within the cloud. The hub of this spiral cloud had the greatest concentration of matter, and surrounding the center were smaller masses of matter; the center of the condensing cloud formed the sun, and the peripheral condensations that encircled it formed the planets (Figure 1–5). Each planet

became distinctive in character depending on its distance from the central mass and the nature of its raw materials. Over millions of years, the heavier elements composing each planet, mostly nickel and iron, settled to the center and formed the core. Lighter substances, such as granite and basalt, migrated to near the surface. Surrounding this was a surface mantle, or envelope, of lighter gases, mostly hydrogen and helium. The gaseous matter of the sun began to condense further; hydrogen atoms began to undergo fusion into helium, a process that produces a reaction not unlike an H-bomb exploding. With the beginning glow of the sun's thermonuclear furnace, the darkness gave way to light. The radiant heat of the newborn sun drove off the residual gases that surrounded the newly formed planets; after several hundred million years the planets had most of their mass boiled away,

---

[1] Modified from A. I. Oparin.

[2] An organic compound is a substance that is a constituent of organisms. In a broader sense it can be any compound in which the element carbon is combined with hydrogen (hydrogenated). Chemically speaking, the carbon is relatively reduced.

FIGURE 1–7 The history of the earth: formation of the primitive soup.

Saturn contain mostly methane, hydrogen, and ammonia, and the atmospheres of Uranus and Neptune are largely methane. The atmosphere of the early earth was a **reducing atmosphere,** that is, it contained much more hydrogen than today in combination with other elements. In contrast, the atmosphere of the earth today is **oxidizing,** with carbon present as carbon dioxide ($CO_2$, 0.03%), nitrogen as $N_2$ (78%), oxygen as $O_2$ (21%), and hydrogen as $H_2O$. The story of how the reducing atmosphere of the earth became an oxidizing one is bound up with the story of life itself, as we shall see. Radioisotope studies suggest that a reducing atmosphere surrounded the earth for 2 to 3 billion years; in the history of the earth this phase could be read in Volumes II through V (Figure 1–6).

The atmosphere of the early earth contained considerable quantities of water vapor, and as the planet cooled, this vapor condensed and torrents of rain fell. The low places became the ocean basins, the rain that washed down the mountain slopes carved out valleys and river beds. Slowly, salts and minerals, dissolved from the rocks by the rain, accumulated in the newly formed oceans of the early earth, which had a consistency described by some as like that of pea soup. In the history of the earth, this stage could be read in Volumes III and IV (Figure 1–7).

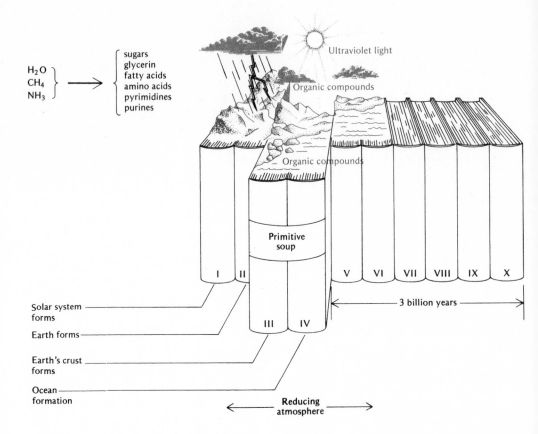

## 1–4 THE PRIMITIVE SOUP

An event of momentous importance took place on the primeval, foul-smelling planet earth some 3.5 billion years ago—the first living organisms appeared. How did this happen? Speculation and science have merged into an imaginative attack on this question and have produced some startling results. In 1924 the Russian biochemist A. I. Oparin published a little book entitled *Origin of Life* (English edition, 1936). Disappointed with the lack of progress in understanding how life originated on the planet earth, he pointed out that scientific inquiry

had reached a no-exit position by limiting studies of possible processes to those that exist on the earth today. Oparin emphasized the differences between the atmosphere of the early earth and that of the earth today and suggested that spontaneous organic synthesis could occur only under the former conditions.

What kinds of compounds can be produced from the gases that made up the atmosphere of the early earth, and what sources of energy are needed for their synthesis? Since we cannot go back in time, some uncertainty exists about the nature of the sources of energy present on the primitive earth; the sources we know of that are available today and that might also have been available then are ultraviolet radiation

(from the sun), electrical discharges (from lightning), cosmic rays (raining down from outer space), radioactivity (from radioactive elements), and heat of volcanic origin. The relative importance of each of these in the prebiological synthesis of organic materials is unknown. Given the nature of the primitive earth's atmosphere and the available sources of energy, can we reproduce the same situation now? By mimicking the conditions present on the early earth in the laboratory today, can we in fact produce organic compounds of the complexity found in living organisms, or even life itself? Just such a challenging problem was given to Stanley L. Miller, then a graduate student at the University of Chicago, by his major professor, Nobel laureate Harold C. Urey.

FIGURE 1–8 Stanley Miller's spark-discharge apparatus. The boiling water provides water vapor that carries the gas mixture upward, and the gases are then subjected to a spark (electrical discharge). Afterward the vapors are condensed by a cool-water jacket and returned to the boiling flask.

**13**

**GENESIS: THE ORIGIN OF LIFE**

In 1953 Miller described an ingenious experiment which sought to simulate the conditions of the early earth. In his experiments, Miller used a sterile, airtight glass apparatus in which he circulated methane, ammonia, hydrogen, and water (Figure 1–8). As the gases passed a set of tungsten electrodes, they were subjected to an electrical discharge; the circulation of gases was maintained by boiling the mixture in one limb of the apparatus and condensing it in the other. After 1 week the condensed liquid was removed and analyzed. What had originally been pure water now contained a number of complex organic compounds including urea, vinegar (acetic acid), and some very simple amino acids. **Amino acids are the building blocks of proteins and basic constituents of living organisms.** The yield of amino acids was surprisingly high. This demonstration created considerable excitement and produced a flurry of experiments along similar lines with similar results.

The amino acids synthesized in the laboratory under primitive-earth conditions are the same amino acids that are most abundant in the proteins of the organisms we see around us. Nevertheless, the early reports of the synthesis of amino acids from gases such as ammonia, methane, and hydrogen were received with skepticism. After all, it was an established fact that "living" molecules such as amino acids are formed only by living organisms, and the doubters suggested that the apparatus used was contaminated with microorganisms. Miller, however, showed not only that his apparatus was sterile but that no living microorganisms could survive the temperature of the boiling water. In adition, amino acids were never formed when oxygen or carbon dioxide was present in the apparatus or in the absence of an electrical discharge; amino-acid synthesis required a reducing atmosphere, not an oxidizing one, and a source of energy.

Living organisms contain many compounds besides amino acids and protein, however. Therefore, it is necessary for us

Electrode

Spark discharge

Gases (methane, hydrogen, ammonia)

Water jacket

Cooling water in

Cooling water out

Trap

Boiling water

Heating mantle

Organic compounds

to account for the formation of other organic compounds. The hereditary material of all organisms consists of nucleic acids. Could these compounds, too, have been formed on the early earth under the conditions that existed at the time? The answer is yes. If a solution of ammonia is heated in the presence of cyanide gas, the purine base adenine (a component of nucleic acids) is produced; variations on this experimental

scheme produce other nucleic-acid precursors. Sugars are important components of living systems, and these can by synthesized in a similar way from a dilute solution of formaldehyde in the presence of hot clay.

We can also envisage and demonstrate in the laboratory the **polymerization** (joining) of these small organic molecules into larger ones—for example, amino acids into proteins and purines into nucleic acids. The experiments of Sidney Fox and his collaborators are of particular interest. These workers took a mixture of dry amino acids and, by heating them to 150° to 180°C, were able to link them to form a small protein chain; when water was added to this mixture, small spherules called **proteinoids** developed (Box 1C).

It is clearly possible that in the ancient seas of the early earth, synthesis and accumulation of organic compounds took place. However, organic molecules are labile entities and are quickly destroyed by oxidation and decay. How did organic materials accumulate, and why weren't they destroyed? Since neither oxygen nor microorganisms that effect decay were present on the primitive earth, the organic molecules were able to persist for very long periods of time. The seas of the earth some 3.5 billion years ago contained a dilute mixture of organic molecules; some scientists estimate that the waters could have been as much as 1% solids. Thus, we can visualize conditions under which a **primitive organic soup** could exist for a long time on the surface of this planet.

## 1–5 THE PRIMITIVE ORGANISM

The warm seas of the primitive earth doubtless contained a rich array of organic molecules, but how did their concentration increase to such a level that chemical reactions could proceed at a reasonable rate? Several mechanisms may have operated. The simplest way may have been by evaporation. In the lakes, lagoons, and pools of the slowly cooling earth we would expect

## CREATION: Producing Life in the Laboratory

### Spheres of living protein made under conditions similar to early earth

In the beginning, there existed on the earth the basic chemicals essential for life—but no life, no living thing capable of reproducing itself. How then did life arise on the early earth?

For a long time, the idea that lifeless molecules could combine into a living substance capable of reproducing itself (spontaneous generation) intrigued both scientists and philosophers, but evidence obtained from carefully controlled experiments always seemed to discredit the idea. Recently, however, there has been renewed interest in a modern theory of spontaneous generation.

Sidney W. Fox and his colleagues at the Institute of Molecular Evolution in Miami have reported a series of exciting experiments: they have been able to synthesize the stuff of life in a laboratory flask. Previously, other workers had shown that if a mixture of gases (methane, ammonia, and water) simulating the atmosphere of the primitive earth is subjected to electric discharge, duplicating on a laboratory scale the lightning bolts that crashed through the atmosphere of the lifeless planet, these simple substances combined into more complex molecules such as amino acids. While not living things themselves, amino acids are the building blocks of proteins, which form the basic structural material of living things. Fox and his colleagues attempted to form assemblages of these amino acids into proteins and thus continue the biological chain reaction toward life itself. By simply heating dry amino acids in the laboratory, chemical blending occurred and proteins were formed. Upon the addition of water these thermally produced proteins gave rise to little spheres which Fox calls "proteinoids." The proteinoids resemble certain bacteria in size and shape, and when viewed under the electron microscope they are so similar to bacteria that their true origins are not recognized. "Expert audiences tend to identify sections of bacteria as sections of proteinoid microspheres and vice versa," Fox said.

To Fox, these proteinoids suggested other similarities to the earliest forms of life. Proteinoids can take up materials from surrounding solutions (their "mother liquor"); they can multiply by a kind of "budding," grow by accretion, and have enzymatic activity. In many of their properties they are very similar to contemporary living cells. The original chain reaction that produced living forms may have been triggered by volcanic eruptions, or perhaps the heat of hot springs. "A well-known region of appropriate geologic character for the formation of proteinoids," Fox said, "is Yellowstone National Park." The laboratory-produced proteinoids demonstrate how primordial life could have arisen in the absence of parental or ancestral systems on a lifeless earth.

The proteinoid (A) shows the spontaneous production of buds (B) as the proteinoid microspheres stand in the mother liquor. When the mother liquor is warmed, buds are released from the parental proteinoid microspheres. (Courtesy of S. Fox.)

FIGURE 1–9 How colloidal droplets become organized. (a) Colloidal droplet with a diffuse orientation of water molecules. (b) Concentration of water molecules around colloidal droplet. (c) Coacervate, a combination of colloidal droplets with a tight boundarty of water molecules.

evaporation to occur and the concentrations of solids to increase. Another mechanism could have been the adsorption of organic substances on the surfaces of claylike materials.

Perhaps the most ingenious mechanism is the one originally suggested by Oparin—the formation of colloidal droplets (**coacervates**). Colloids are produced by the interaction of organic polymers in solution; under the appropriate conditions, drops of the organic compound are formed that become sharply set off from the watery solution that surrounds them. The boundary between the droplet and its surroundings is formed by a shell of rigidly oriented water molecules (Figure 1–9). Such droplets are capable of reacting chemically with their surrounding medium. Coacervate formation is a method of concentrating highly polymerized substances from very dilute solutions. (Gelatin in water at a concentration of 0.001% can form coacervate droplets in which the concentration of gelatin in the droplet is 10%, or a 10,000-fold increase over the concentration in the surrounding medium.) In the laboratory it is possible to produce coacervate droplets containing protein and nucleic acids, and it is possible to produce these at ordinary temperatures.

The fate of these droplets depends on the nature of their internal composition as well as on the array of substances in the surrounding medium. Some droplets are able to concentrate materials better than others and thus interact differently with the environment that produced them. Once favorable combinations of materials are established, coacervates take on a dynamic condition. They persist for a short while in a dynamic state, but when equilibrium is established with the surrounding medium, they become static. The coacervate drops, like the proteinoid spherules, are however, not models of a living system (Box 1C).

We can imagine that in the primitive oceans the surface film of some droplets might have broken down faster than it could be replenished; these droplets must have disintegrated and returned to the primeval soup. Perhaps other droplets were able to maintain their structural integrity; they may have contained bits of iron, copper, or calcium which could have acted as catalysts so that changes in the droplets occurred at a more rapid rate and the droplets were able to persist in a dynamic state. In time some of these metals may have become permanently attached to the protein and functioned as enzymes do today. (See Chapter 3). Rates of processes within the droplet were thus further increased, and some droplets could derive materials from the environment at a greater rate than the other droplets. Droplets now were characterized by individuality. Those that could obtain materials from the environment more efficiently were favored by the selective process. If a particular droplet took up materials faster than its neighbor, the neighbor would not fare as well and perhaps would not survive. These faint beginnings of **natural selection** (survival of the fittest) not only contributed to the preservation of the most efficient droplets, but also influenced their growth in size. Soon the successful droplets incorporated materials that could be laid down as a membrane just below the layer of oriented water molecules; this conferred even greater capacity for differential selection of materials entering the droplet. Soon the growing droplet was so big that the physical forces in the membrane could no longer hold it. It fragmented, and there resulted two or more drops with stable and environmentally interacting components. The division of these droplets was governed by mechanical forces (for example, waves or increased size), and the droplets fragmented in much the same fashion as droplets of oil in water are broken up by shaking. Those droplets that were able to maintain themselves—to grow and to reproduce—were the ones that survived.

---

**BOX 1D  The Spiegelman Monster**

Sol Spiegelman, an American microbiologist, asked a simple evolutionary question: What is the smallest molecule capable of replicating itself? Spiegelman began with a **virus,** called $Q_\beta$, which consisted of a single molecule of ribonucleic acid (RNA) composed of 4,500 nucleotides (roughly equivalent to the information content of a few hundred words). In nature, this virus is normally able to make copies of itself only by invading a living cell, because it requires a cellular enzyme called a replicase. Spiegelman proceeded to strip the virus of its protein coat and to isolate the viral nucleic acid. He placed the viral nucleic acid in a test tube, and added the necessary replicase enzyme so that the virus could replicate itself without going through the trouble of penetrating a living cell. The test tube also contained an ample supply of free nucleotides. The viral nucleic acid continued to replicate for several generations, and then a mutant appeared with fewer than 4,500 nucleotides. Being smaller, the mutant replicated faster than the original virus. Then another mutant appeared to displace the first, and so it went. The virus could survive by getting rid of all the superfluous baggage it might have needed to make its protein coat within the cell. Finally, the virus degenerated into a little piece of nucleic acid with only 220 nucleotides (equivalent to about 10 words)—the smallest bit necessary for recognizing the replicase. This little monster could continue to replicate at high speed, provided it had a source of building blocks. Perhaps this test-tube experiment reveals how, when life arose, protoorganisms were able not only to replicate themselves but also to evolve.

FIGURE 1–10 The development of metabolism in the protoorganism. (a) At first, reactions of organic materials are sporadic. (b) Later, they become linked into a series. (c) Finally, the chain reactions branch and form cycles.

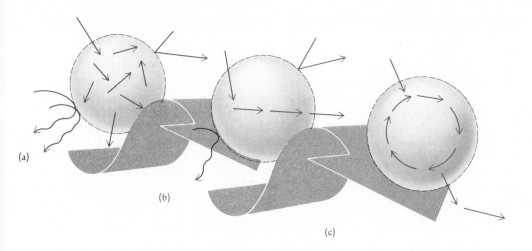

(a)

(b)

(c)

There is not a hard and fast line of demarcation between the structural organization of coacervate droplets, proteinoid spherules, and the earliest organisms; we can recognize in each of them some of the properties that fit our definition of life. Our own origins are in the substance of the successful line of coacervate droplets. The primitive organisms reproduced by mechanical fragmentation, and the daughter droplets initially obtained their constituents by chance. The constitution of the daughter droplets was dependent on the materials they received. Today all organisms have a more precise hereditary mechanism, mediated through the nucleic acids. It would appear that the protoorganisms did not have their composition and inheritance controlled by nucleic acids. The earliest protoorganisms lacked the capacity for exact replication, although they could grow and divide. Persisting for millions of years, diversifying and refining their metabolic pathways, these droplets eventually succeeded in synthesizing ATP, adenosine triphosphate, a molecule that serves as the principal energy-carrying material in modern cells. In time, the protoorganisms accumulated ATP as well as its molecular cousin AMP. ATP is the universal energy carrier,

whereas AMP is one of the nucleotides that makes up nucleic acids; nucleic acids function as carriers of bits of information and also have the capacity to replicate (Box 1D). It has been suggested that by accident one of these protoorganisms became infected with a nucleic acid. At first the infection was lethal, but in time the protein-based droplet adapted to the presence of the nucleic acid. The consequence of the parasitic integration of nucleic acids into a proteinoid was the development of a forerunner of the genetic apparatus of modern cells.

How this complex interaction and control came about remains unknown. Since time is the hero of this story, there was no doubt sufficient opportunity for these interactions to take place.

Living systems are characterized by a high degree of organization. The protoorganism may have been capable of obtaining materials from the environment and by virtue of substances within its body may have been able to alter these materials. The chemical alterations (reactions) occurring in present-day organisms, known as metabolism, are mediated by special proteins with catalytic properties (enzymes). Enzymes do not make impossible reactions occur, but they make

possible reactions proceed at a faster rate. The primitive organisms no doubt had inefficient catalysts, but with time these became more efficient and more specific. Later, the hereditary materials (nucleic acids) specified (encoded) the formation and structure of the catalysts. We know virtually nothing about the details of the metabolism of these early organisms, but we assume that the reactions which were originally sporadic became linked into a series, and as these chains of reactions became longer, some became branched and some became cycles (Figure 1–10). Ability to select materials entering the organism, to trap molecules for synthesis, to control rates of reactions, and to obtain energy was acquired, but we do not know how. It is obvious that improvement in the metabolic machinery of the living system must have involved the development of coordination within the organizational framework; it appears remote that a perfect system developed in a single instant.

We can now consider the self-reproducing and adapting droplet to be a protoorganism, and natural selection acquires its biological meaning—differential reproduction. In our history of the earth, it is in Volume IV that coacervates and protoorganisms make their appearance (Figure 1–13).

## 1–6 HETEROTROPHS AND AUTOTROPHS

It is now commonly believed that the earliest organisms on the planet earth were **heterotrophs** (*hetero*—other, *troph*—feeder; Gk.). Heterotrophic organisms require complex organic nutrients such as proteins, amino acids, and sugars for their survival—you are a heterotroph. The primitive organisms living in their organic soup presumably had adequate supplies of these substances, which were continually being formed by lightning, ultraviolet radiation, and so on, acting on the gases of the reducing atmosphere. As these organisms increased in numbers, they must have depleted the soup at a rate faster

### BOX 1E  The Earliest life in the oldest rocks

Traces of an organic structure, be it the cast of a shell, a footprint, or a part of an organism preserved from prehistoric times, is a **fossil.** The way fossils are formed is that an organism (or its evidence) becomes covered by mud, sand, peat, or some other material destined to become a long-lasting geological formation. Over millions of years the mud may turn to shale, the sand to sandstone, and the peat to coal; and if this occurs, the trace of that organism is preserved for millions or even billions of years in an unaltered form. When such rocks are split open, the fossils are revealed.

Dating of fossils, that is, calculating the age of a fossil, usually can be accomplished by determining the age of the rocks in which the fossil is found. As a general rule, rocks found deeper below the surface are usually the oldest. A more precise way to calculate fossil age, however, is to use a **radioactive clock.** The radioactive clock involves measuring the amount of radioactive element in the rock and is simple and straightforward. A radioactive parent element (such as uranium 238) has its atoms

**FIGURE 1–11 Radioactive decay. Radioactive elements decay at a constant rate. The time it takes for half of the atoms to decay is referred to as the half-life of that element. In the example illustrated note that it takes x amount of time to reduce the amount of the radioactive element by one half, and in twice that time one quarter of the original element is present.**

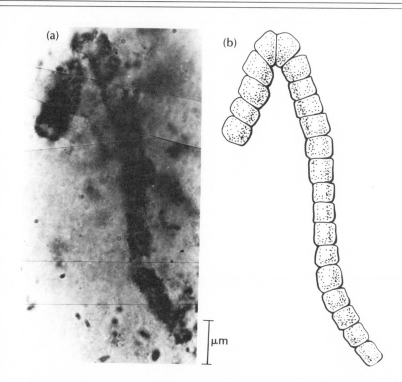

(a) (b)

FIGURE 1–12 The oldest known form of life. On the left is a photograph of a filamentous microfossil, and on the right is a drawing of this organism. Courtesy of J. William Schopf.

decay into one or more daughter elements (such as lead) at a constant rate, the half-life. If one counts the relative number of parent and daughter elements, and knows the time interval of the half-life, it is easy to calculate the time at which the pure parent element was formed (Figure 1–11).

The oldest rocks on the Earth are usually buried under many layers of rock formed in more recent times; however, in some parts of the world these ancient rocks are exposed and accessible. One such spot is western Australia where sedimentary rocks have been dated to be approximately 3.5 billion years old. Digging amongst these oldest deposits, scientists have gathered

such rocks, fractured them, polished their surfaces, and then examined them microscopically. Clearly preserved in these rocks are fossil microorganisms. They look like colonies of spherical cells enclosed by a layered sheath and some are long filaments (Figure 1–12). In their appearance, they resemble modern-day blue-green algae. Because the modern relatives are photosynthetic, it has been hypothesized that these fossil colonies may also have been oxygen-producing. If they were, then as early as 3.5 billion years ago the Earth's surface contained plantlike organisms that were capable of trapping light, fixing carbon dioxide into carbohydrate, and liberating oxygen.

**FIGURE 1-13** The history of the earth: coacervates and protoorganisms.

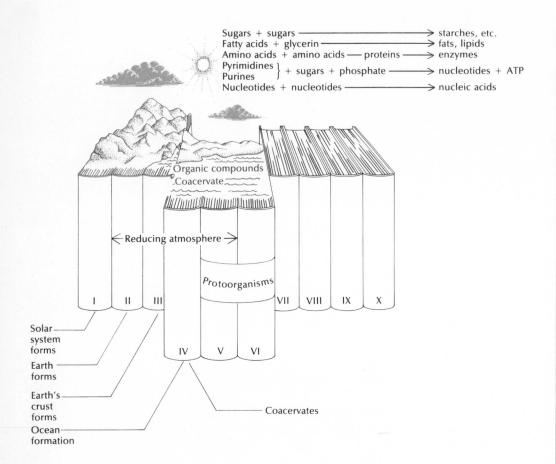

than the organic molecules could be replenished. Eventually the primitive organisms had to compete for materials, and some may even have fed on other droplets. As droplets could not maintain themselves, they returned to the soup and thus provided materials for other growing and reproducing droplets. As the nutrients disappeared from the primitive soup, those organisms that could synthesize needed materials from some other, perhaps simpler and more plentiful, substances present in the soup had an enormous advantage. In such a way we can imagine the stepwise development of metabolic pathways.

Heterotrophy was the primary nutritional mode of life, but life would have ceased long ago if all nutrition had remained heterotrophic. The spontaneous production of organic compounds would have been insufficient to maintain a growing and reproducing population indefinitely, and eventually much of the available organic material would have been tied up in the bodies of the heterotrophic organisms. In order to obtain energy to drive the chemical reactions going on inside them, the heterotrophic organisms degraded (broke down) energy-rich molecules from the soup, such as sugars (carbohydrates). When carbohydrates are degraded, carbon dioxide and water are released, along with energy. In time the reducing atmosphere changed and contained considerable quantities of carbon

**FIGURE 1–14 The history of the earth: one-celled and many-celled organisms.**

dioxide gas just as it does today. Such carbon dioxide in the atmosphere must have screened out some of the high-energy ultraviolet light and reduced the **abiotic synthesis** (a synthesis without organisms) of organic molecules. The decisive step that enabled life to continue on the planet earth was the development of organisms capable of utilizing simple compounds such as carbon dioxide and water for the synthesis of complex organic molecules. This was made possible by the presence in these organisms of pigments that could absorb and make available to them the energy of the sunlight, together with enzymes necessary to catalyze the chemical reactions. Organisms capable of gathering light energy for the production

of organic molecules from simple compounds such as carbon dioxide and water are called **autotrophs** (*auto*—self, *troph*— feeder; Gk.), and the process is called **photosynthesis** (literally "building with light"). All green plants today are photosynthetic autotrophs. An important by-product of their autotrophic activity is molecular oxygen. The appearance of photosynthesis about 3 billion years ago led eventually to the accumulation of oxygen, and this helped transform the reducing atmosphere into an oxidizing one. It is estimated that at present the entire oxygen of our atmosphere is renewed by photosynthetic activity once every 2,000 years. The layer of oxygen that accumulated and surrounded the planet

earth was acted upon by solar radiations and gave rise to a layer of ozone that efficiently screened out most of the lethal effects of the sun's ultraviolet radiation. By this means, the energy source that perhaps played so important a role in the spontaneous generation of life on the primitive earth was effectively reduced so that it could not destroy that life and ultimately permitted living organisms to leave the protective filtering waters of the oceans and colonize the land.

Up to the time that free oxygen first appeared in the atmosphere of the primitive earth, the energy needed to perform all the chemical reactions (metabolism) that went on inside the droplets and first organisms was obtained from the organic molecules of the primitive soup. During the breakdown of these molecules within the organisms, energy was released. If oxygen is utilized during these breakdown reactions, more energy per molecule of fuel material can be released than without oxygen. Thus the development of photosynthesis had important implications in regard to energy yield in metabolism for both heterotrophic and autotrophic organisms. The development of autotrophy was also important because it permitted heterotrophs to maintain themselves by utilizing the autotrophic organisms or their products as nutrients instead of depending on the ever-diminishing supply of organic nutrients in the soup. To this very day we, as heterotrophic organisms, ultimately depend on green-plant photosynthesis for all our food (Chapter 5).

In the history of the earth (Figure 1–14), heterotrophs would appear in Volume IV and autotrophs in Volume V (over 3 billion years ago). What took four volumes (2 billion years) to develop flourishes in abundance and variety on the planet earth in Volumes VI through X (3 billion years). To carry our historical analogy a step further, let us assume that there are 500 words per page in each of the volumes; each word represents 2,000 years. Humans appear 50 words from the end of the last page in Volume X; the birth of Christ is the last

word on the last page, and we are but a speck on the final period!

## SUMMARY

**1.** Characteristics of living things include the capacity for growth, maintenance, repair, reproduction, responsiveness, and change.

**2.** Life can be defined as a property possessed by individuals, characterized by the capacity to perform a series of highly organized interacting processes that take place within a definite structural framework.

**3.** Biologists are usually mechanists, not vitalists. They believe that biology can be understood in terms of physics and chemistry rather than in terms of mystic or spiritual explanations

**4.** To understand and investigate biology, rigorous scientific methods are used. A working hypothesis is repeatedly tested, and if the results of repeated experiments can be predicted accurately, the hypothesis is proved and becomes a theory and part of our knowledge.

**5.** The spontaneous generation of life was a vitalist idea that was refuted by the experiments of Redi, Spallanzani, and Pasteur. Today, living things come only from other living things.

**6.** The first living things probably arose

in the primitive seas of the early earth, which contained a rich array of organic molecules. A variety of theories exists to account for this.

**7.** Our solar system formed 5 billion years ago from a condensing primordial cloud. The early reducing atmosphere of the earth contained no oxygen; it consisted mostly of methane, ammonia, and water. High-energy ultraviolet light from the sun and other energy sources, such as lightning and cosmic rays, permitted the abiotic synthesis of complex organic molecules from these simpler substances.

**8.** Laboratory experiments by Miller and Urey mimicking the conditions of the early atmosphere produced complex organic compounds from an array of simple ones by subjecting them to alternate heat and condensation and an electrical discharge.

**9.** Fox and Oparin have shown how the formation of proteins and coacervates could have occurred in the primitive oceans and perhaps led to the emergence of competing protoorganisms.

**10.** The earliest organisms on the earth were probably heterotrophs. Subsequently, photosynthetic autotrophs appeared.

**11.** The metabolic wastes of autotrophs, specifically oxygen, produced an oxidizing atmosphere. Oxygen destroyed labile organic molecules so quickly that no further abiotic generation of life could occur.

| KEY WORDS | evolve | cosmologists | primitive organic soup | fossil |
| --- | --- | --- | --- | --- |
| | responsiveness | primordial cloud | coacervates | radioactive clock |
| life | spontaneous generation | organic compound | natural selection | |
| metabolism | experiment | reducing atmosphere | heterotrophs | |
| enzymes | vitalists | oxidizing atmosphere | abiotic synthesis | |
| growth | mechanists | amino acids | autotrophs | |
| reproduction | hypothesis | polymerization | photosynthesis | |
| mutation | theory | proteinoids | virus | |

## TOPICS FOR REVIEW AND DISCUSSION

1. What is metabolism? What aspects of metabolism were the Viking Lander experiments designed to detect?

2. What is scientific method? Why is it necessary?

3. Today, all heterotrophs depend ultimately on autotrophs for their food. Explain why heterotophs were probably the first living things and how they survived initially without autotrophs.

4. Why is autotrophy essential for continued life on earth?

5. Why does the spontaneous generation of life not occur today?

6. How was the primitive soup formed? Why are modern oceans not a soup of organic materials?

7. What are the characteristics of living things? Is there one characteristic above all others that distinguishes a living thing from a nonliving thing?

8. How could we recognize life on other planets, or even beyond our solar system?

9. What energy sources were available for the synthesis of organic compounds on the early earth, and of what importance was the earth's reducing atmosphere?

10. Describe some laboratory experiments that illustrate the conditions on the early earth that might have contributed to the origin of life.

11. Contrast the views of vitalists and mechanists.

12. Discuss the pros and cons of the following statement: viruslike particles were the earliest organisms.

13. What was the meaning of "survival of the fittest" to the protoorganism?

## University Days

I passed all the other courses that I took at my University, but I could never pass botany. This was because all botany students had to spend several hours a week in a laboratory looking through a microscope at plant cells, and I could never see through a microscope. I never once saw a cell through a microscope. This used to enrage my instructor. He would wander around the laboratory pleased with the progress all the students were making in drawing the involved and, so I am told, interesting structure of flower cells, until he came to me. I would just be standing there. "I can't see anything," I would say. He would begin patiently enough, explaining how anybody can see through a microscope, but he would always end up in a fury, claiming that I could *too* see through a microscope but just pretended that I couldn't. "It takes away from the beauty of flowers anyway," I used to tell him. "We are not concerned with beauty in this course," he would say. "We are concerned solely with what I may call the *mechanics* of flowers." "Well," I'd say, "I can't see anything." "Try it just once again," he'd say, and I would put my eye to the microscope and see nothing at all, except now and again a nebulous milky substance—a phenomenon of maladjustment. You were supposed to see a vivid, restless clockwork of sharply defined plant cells. "I see what looks like a lot of milk," I would tell him. This, he claimed, was the result of my not having adjusted the microscope properly, so he would readjust it for me, or rather, for himself. And I would look again and see milk.

I finally took a deferred pass, as they called it, and waited a year and tried again. (You had to pass one of the biological sciences or you couldn't graduate.) The professor had come back from vacation brown as a berry, bright-eyed, and eager to explain cell-structure again to his classes. "Well," he said to me, cheerily, when we met in the first laboratory hour of the semester, "we're going to see cells this time, aren't we?" "Yes, sir," I said. Students to right of me and to left of me and in front of me were seeing cells; what's more, they were quietly drawing pictures of them in their notebooks. Of course, I didn't see anything.

"We'll try it," the professor said to me, grimly, "with every adjustment of the microscope known to man. As God is my witness, I'll arrange this glass so that you can see cells through it or I'll give up teaching. In twenty-two years of botany, I—" He cut off abruptly for he was beginning to quiver all over, like Lionel Barrymore, and he genuinely wished to hold onto his temper; his scenes with me had taken a great deal out of him.

So we tried it with every adjustment of the microscope known to man. With only one of them did I see anything but blackness or the familiar lacteal opacity, and that time I saw, to my pleasure and amazement, a variegated constellation of flecks, specks, and dots. These I hastily drew. The instructor, noting my activity, came back from an adjoining desk, a smile on his lips and his eyebrows high in hope. He looked at my cell drawing. "What's that?" he demanded, with a hint of a squeal in his voice. "That's what I saw,' I said. "You didn't, you didn't, you *didn't*!" he screamed, losing control of his temper instantly, and he bent over and squinted into the microscope. His head snapped up. "That's your eye!" he shouted. "You've fixed the lens so that it reflects! You've drawn your eye!"

# 2

# Cell Structure: The Organization of Life

## 2–1  WHAT IS A CELL?

In the living world, the fundamental unit is the cell, and all the processes of life occur within cells. Cells may be broken up by grinding, or they may be extracted to yield particles that perform some of the life processes, but it is only within a unit such as the cell that all the processes of the living system can occur. A **cell** may be defined as the standard unit of biological activity, bounded by a membrane and able to reproduce itself independently of any other living system. All living organisms, large and small, plant and animal, fish and fowl, human and microbe, are made up of cells. All cells are basically similar to each other, having many structural features in common. It is one of the marvels of nature that the endless variety of living organisms should all be constructed of or depend upon such basically similar units.

How can we recognize a cell when we see one? What are universal features of cells? Exactly what do we mean when we say that the cell is the standard unit upon which all living systems are based? Let us take the last question first, and in attempting to answer it we shall find answers to the first two questions. We can more easily understand the concept of the cell by making an analogy and comparing living organisms to buildings; the rooms of buildings are analogous to the cells of organisms.

Both rooms and cells have boundaries with exits and entrances—rooms have walls,

floors, ceilings, doors, and windows, for example, whereas cells have walls or membranes with pores of various sizes. Both rooms and cells come in a variety of sizes and shapes, with various contents; each kind of room or cell has its own particular use, function, or specialty. Buildings may be composed of only one room or of many rooms. In the same way, organisms may be composed of only one cell, in which case we describe them as being **unicellular,** or of many cells, in which case we say they are **multicellular.** By combining rooms of various kinds, we can construct a variety of buildings—homes, apartments, schools, offices, and so on. Similarly, different organisms are constructed of a variety of cell types. Just as there is no building without rooms, so there is no life without cells.

Could you describe a typical room to someone who for some reason had never seen one before? What would you include and what would you leave out? Your final description would probably end up by being somewhat all inclusive, but not applicable to any room that actually exists. It would serve as a kind of map or guide, enabling its users to recognize different features of different rooms as they encountered them, but no one would be likely to find any existing room exactly fitting your description. In the same way, descriptions of the "typical" cell end up by being rather generalized; some features will be universal, some will not. The typical cell is a convenient aid, but no typical cell actually exists.

Like rooms, cells have specialized roles, and correlated with this special function they are specialized in their form. Before examining specialized cells, however, let us construct a typical cell so that we have a guide on our journey through the cells of an organism. Figure 2–1 is a diagrammatic rendition of a typical plant and animal cell.

Cells are separated from their external environment by an interface, or plasma membrane. Everything inside the plasma membrane is sometimes refered to as protoplasm, consisting of the jellylike cytoplasm (*cyto*—cell, *plasma*—thing; Gk.) and various structures collectively known as organelles, including the membrane-bound nucleus with its contained nucleoplasm (*nuci*—nut, *plasma*—thing; Gk.). Each organelle represents a highly specialized compartment or submodule in which particular functions of the cell are localized. Continuing our analogy between cells and rooms, we can think of the organelles as items of furniture or equipment (such as stoves, refrigerators, sinks) that are localized in the room and specialized for specific functions. Just as articles of furniture have a form that is easily recognizable and closely related to their function, cellular organelles also show a form related to their function.

### The plasma membrane: cell boundary

Although the early microscopists conceded that cells were probably bounded by a membrane, they were unable to see such a

**(a) ANIMAL CELL**

Flagellum

Lysosome

Ribosome

Forming pinocytotic vesicle

Mitochondrion

Golgi apparatus

Nucleolus

Endoplasmic reticulum (smooth)

Plasma membrane

Nuclear pore

Centriole

Nuclear envelope

Microtubules

Endoplasmic reticulum (rough)

**(b) PLANT CELL**

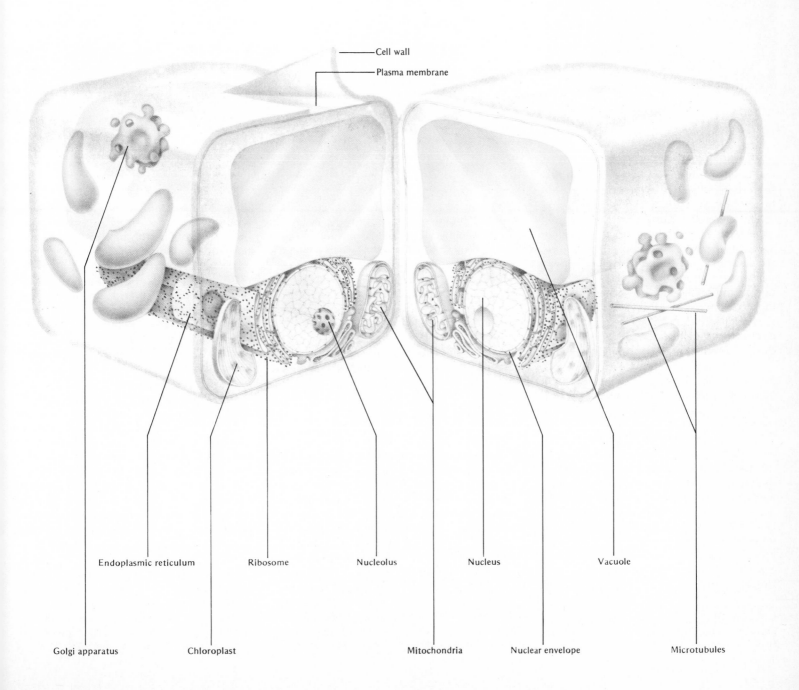

Cell wall

Plasma membrane

Endoplasmic reticulum

Ribosome

Nucleolus

Nucleus

Vacuole

Golgi apparatus

Chloroplast

Mitochondria

Nuclear envelope

Microtubules

FIGURE 2–2 Ghosts of human red blood cells. (Courtesy of Joseph F. Hoffman.)

FIGURE 2–3 The plasma membrane. (a) The fluid mosaic model of the membrane; (b) as revealed by the electron microscope. (Courtesy of J. David Robertson.)

Surface protein

Outer surface

Double layer of lipid

Penetrating protein

Inner surface

(a)

(b)

structure. The reason was that the thickness of the plasma membrane (0.0075 to 0.01 micrometer, μm)[1] is outside the limits of resolution of the light microscope (Box 2A). In spite of the inability of the light microscope to resolve the plasma membrane, considerable information had accumulated about its nature and composition before the development of improved microscopes. Information about the chemical composition of the membrane was obtained from the ghosts of red blood cells; **ghosts** are the membrane remnants of the red cell after it has been placed in water, then washed and extracted with a variety of solutions (Figure 2–2). Chemical analyses of these ghosts indicated that the membrane consists of lipid (fatty material) and protein. How are the lipid and protein molecules arranged in the membrane?

Recent studies suggest that in the plasma membrane, and other membranes as well, the bulk of the protein lies external to a double layer of lipid (fatty) molecules; the water-soluble, or polar, ends of the lipid molecules face outward while the water-insoluble ends face each other. Some proteins are embedded in the lipid layer, and others extend all the way through it. Further, both the lipids and the proteins have considerable freedom of movement, and this

[1] Appendix B contains the conversion of International System (SI) units of measure to the English system and vice versa.

is responsible, in part at least, for some of the membrane's dynamic properties. According to this view, the plasma membrane is like a thick sea of lipid in which protein icebergs float (Figure 2–3a).

Viewed with the electron microscope, the plasma membrane appears as two dark bands separated by a light band (Figure 2–3b); the thickness of the membrane is 75 Angstrom units (Å). Membranes that have this appearance and dimension in electron micrographs have been called **unit membranes,** a term first used by J. D. Robertson.

### Gelatin, protoplasm, and cytoplasm

The internal contents of the cell are sometimes referred to as **protoplasm.** Protoplasm has been considered by some authors to be the substance of life, but as we have already observed, the cell is the unit of life and a constituent part of the cell is not by itself alive. Another serious reservation to the use of the term protoplasm is that it suggests a uniformity of composition, and nothing could be further from the truth. Our own protoplasm differs from the protoplasm of the cells of the dog, the horse, the cat, and the ameba; it is different from the plasms of all other organisms. Your protoplasm is different from that of any

other living creature; it is this which confers a uniqueness upon every organism, large or small. Protoplasm varies in its composition and properties not only between organisms but within organisms; the protoplasm of a red blood cell differs from that of a bone cell, a brain cell, and a liver cell. We shall use the term protoplasm because it is a convenient descriptive word to indicate the material inside a cell; however, do not think of it as a defined chemical entity or as characterized by a life of its own, because this is nonsense.

The protoplasm of the cell bounded by the plasma membrane but lying outside the nucleus of the cell is called the **cytoplasm.** Chemically, cytoplasm consists of proteins and lipids, some carbohydrates, minerals, salts, and a great deal of water (70 to 90%). The proportion of these components varies considerably from cell to cell and from organism to organism. Cytoplasm is a two phase system. The liquid phase is a colloid. What is a **colloid?** A familiar colloidal substance is gelatin, made from the bones, tendons, and ligaments of cattle by treatment with boiling water to solubilize some of the constituents. It is a protein, and when placed in warm water, the protein molecules become finely and uniformly dispersed in the water and remain so because of their

FIGURE 2–4 Molecules in action. Owing to inherent thermal agitation molecules are always moving. This is what we really mean by heat. (a) Colloidal droplets have bound water and are jostled to and fro by bombarding water molecules and repulsive electrical forces on the surface of the colloidal droplets. (b) The path of a single droplet.

Start

Finish

(a)

(b)

FIGURE 2–5 The conversion of a colloid from a solution, or sol, state (a) to a solid, or gel, state (b). In the sol the particles are randomly dispersed, whereas in the gel there is an orderly network.

(a)

(b)

electrostatic charge and because they are being bombarded by the constant activity of the water molecules (Figure 2–4). Because of their charge, the protein (gelatin) molecules bind water molecules; as the particles start to settle out in response to gravitational forces, the gelatin molecules are brought closer together, the like electrical charges on their surfaces cause repulsion, and they move apart once again. Thus, the activity of the water molecules and the electric charge on the molecule of protein maintain the molecules of gelatin in a dispersed phase, and settling does not occur. The size of colloidal particles is on the order of 0.001 μm. Gelatin has another property that is familiar to the household chemist: it can exist as a solid or a liquid. Place some warm dissolved gelatin in the cold and it sets—it gels. The change from the liquid state to the solid state is called a **sol-gel** (solution-solid) **transformation.** In the sol state the gelatin molecules are dispersed randomly in the fluid medium; in the gel state the molecules become more rigidly oriented so that a spongy network results, and the water

is trapped in the interstices of this network (Figure 2–5).

Colloids need not consist of a solid, such as gelatin, in water but can be formed of two liquids. If we place some light oil in water and shake vigorously, it is possible to disperse the oil droplets and obtain a stable suspension of these. In such a case we have produced an **emulsion**—colloidal droplets of a liquid in another liquid. Homogenized milk is a commonplace emulsion in which the fat globules are so small and evenly dispersed that the cream does not rise to the top and separate out. The colloidal material of the cytoplasm of cells is mostly protein molecules and fat globules.

The cytoplasm also contains materials larger than colloidal particles, and such particles do not remain stabilized. If left to gravitational forces, these particles would eventually settle out. Systems that include such materials are referred to as **suspensions.** Sand in water is a common example of a suspension; if kept agitated, the sand particles remain suspended, but if left undis-

turbed, they soon settle to the bottom of the container. Suspensions of crystals and other particulate materials are commonly found dispersed in the colloidal and watery solutions of the cytoplasm.

There also exists within the cell material in **solution,** that is, material dissolved more or less evenly in the water of the cell. The size of such particles may be the dimensions of individual atoms or molecules or small

FIGURE 2–6 The cytoskeleton. (a) Model of the cytoskeleton. The microtrabaculae form the largest part of network and connects the other parts of the cytoskeleton and organelles. (b) Cells stained for cytoskeletal proteins using a fluorescent dye. (Courtesy of Dr. Gopal Murti Science Photo Library, New York).

clusters of these and is usually less than 0.001 μm. Molecules of this dimension cannot be seen with the microscope, do not settle out as a result of gravitational forces, cannot be removed by filtration, and are kept dispersed by the constant agitation of the water molecules. When you add sugar to your coffee or prepare a glass of salt water, you produce a solution of these substances; similar solutions are found in our own cells. In addition, gaseous materials such as carbon dioxide and oxygen are dissolved in the cytoplasm of the cell; these are often the least conspicuous components of the cytoplasm.

Over the years investigators observed that many of the cell's organelles do not flow freely as would be the case if the cytoplasm were a structureless fluid. And, recent studies with the electron microscope have shown that organelles are restrained by an internal scaffolding that not only forms a supporting framework for the cell and its contents, but also provides the machinery whereby cell and organelle movement takes place. This structural framework, by analogy with the bony skeleton of the body, is called the **cytoskeleton.** The cytoskeleton consists of three fiberlike components—microfilaments, microtubules (see p. 41), and the microtrabecular network. Each of these consists of long, unbranched chains of proteins fashioned into cables or interconnecting strands that resemble a spider web. The microtrabecular network (Figure 2–6), which changes its structure in response to changes in cell shape and with environmental changes, such as a drop in temperature, divides the cell into two phases: a protein-rich weblike structure and a fluid, watery phase that fills the spaces. The watery phase contains glucose, amino acids, proteins, and gases such as carbon dioxide and oxygen. With a water content of approximately 50%, the microtrabecular network gives the cytoplasm its gellike consistency.

The cytoskeleton gives the cell a highly organized three-dimensional structure; however, it should not be considered as

**(a)**

**(b)**

rigid or permanent. Just as a group of housepainters, plasterers, and electricians unfold and rearrange ladders and scaffolding to move about a room and get on with their work, so too the scaffolding of the cell is ever changing—being assembled, disassembled, and moved about depending on the activities of the cell.

**Action at the interface: plasma membrane function**

The plasma membrane is a dynamic part of the cell. In addition to performing the obvious function of containing the cell components, it regulates the flow of materials into and out of the cell; all substances entering or leaving the cell must pass across the plasma membrane.

The chemical and physical properties of a particular substance determine its ability to penetrate the plasma membrane. Amino acids (the subunits that make up proteins) penetrate moderately well, but proteins penetrate poorly. Fatty acids (components of fats) penetrate well, but fats penetrate poorly. Table sugar (sucrose) does not penetrate cell membranes, but a simple sugar such as dextrose (glucose) penetrates membranes readily. Salts, which ionize, vary in their ability to penetrate membranes, but usually the negatively charged ions pass across the membrane better than the positively charged ones. In general, molecules that have no electrical charge, that are soluble in lipid, and that are small in size, penetrate the membrane most readily.

If we were to place a small drop of blood on a slide with a drop of water and observe the blood cells under the microscope, we would see that the red blood cells swell and perhaps even burst; conversely, if we placed a drop of blood in a drop of seawater, we would find that the red blood cells shrink and wrinkle. How can we explain such phenomena? In order to understand the properties and the role of the plasma membrane in the swelling and shrinking of cells, it is necessary to examine some of the physical and chemical phenomena that affect the movement of materials from one place to another.

**Diffusion.** In any situation where molecules (or particles) are free to move, they move from a region of greater concentration to a region of lesser concentration. The movement is net movement. That is, any given particle could be moving in any direction at any particular time; an individual particle could be moving toward the center of concentration, but on the average the movement will be away from the center. Given time, the particles eventually distribute themselves randomly within the space available; at this point the system is in equilibrium. The particles are still moving, but there is no net change in the system; that is, the particles remain evenly distributed. The net movement of molecules from a region of high concentration to a region of low concentration is called **diffusion.**

Gas, liquid, and solid are the three common states of matter. Diffusion is fastest in gases and slowest in solids. Diffusion is due to the inherent heat energy of molecules and atoms, as a result of which they are always in constant motion except at absolute zero ($-273°C$). In all cases, the rate of diffusion increases with an increase in temperature. Some familiar examples of the rates of diffusion may be helpful. A woman enters a room, and the fragrance of her perfume penetrates the air very quickly. The air currents carry the volatile perfume oils quickly from the source throughout the room, but even in the absence of these currents distribution of the fragrance is rapid. A crystal of writing ink placed on the bottom of a container of water slowly diffuses through the water if there is little disturbance of the water by agitation or heat; left undisturbed, the coloration of the water by the ink to produce uniform dispersion may take years, but it eventually will occur. A crystal of writing ink placed on an ice cube moves even more slowly, but its movement can be accelerated by melting the ice. It is obvious that the rate of diffusion in the various media depends on the arrangement of the atoms and the molecules in the medium; in a gas the molecules are capable of free movement, in a liquid the molecules are more tightly held together, and in a solid the movement is very restricted. The process of diffusion plays an important role in the entry and distribution of molecules in the living cell.

**Osmosis.** Some molecules can pass through the plasma membrane by diffusion and others cannot. In this sense the membrane is considered to be **semipermeable,** or differentially permeable. Sausage casing is an example of a semipermeable membrane and can be used as a convenient experimental substitute for the plasma membrane. If we placed a watery solution of table salt and gelatin in a sac made of sausage casing and then suspended this sac in a jar containing pure water, we would find that the membrane is permeable to water and salt, but not to gelatin. This means that water molecules and salt molecules can freely pass into and out of the sac, but the gelatin is retained within the sac. More salt molecules pass out of the sac than into it because there are more salt molecules per unit volume inside than outside; conversely, more water molecules pass into the sac than in the other direction because there are more water molecules per unit volume outside the sac. In both instances, there is a net movement of particles from a region of higher concentration to one of lower concentration owing to the purely physical phenomenon of diffusion (Figure 2–7). In time, the fluid content inside the sac will increase owing to the movement of water into it; the amount of water in the jar will decrease by an equal amount. Since the volume of the sac is limited and some of it is obviously occupied by molecules other than water (salt and gelatin), there is a limit to the amount of water that can enter the sac. The increasing amount of fluid within the sac exerts pressure against the sac membrane until, even though the concentration of salt and water is not the same on each side of the membrane, a point of equilibrium is reached and no further change of volume occurs. The diffusion of water through the semipermeable membrane is called **osmosis;** the pressure exerted by the water in the sac at equilibrium is called the **osmotic pressure.** At equilibrium the concentrations of salt and gelatin in the sac will have become somewhat lower than originally, that is, the solution has become more dilute, and salt can be detected outside the sac by simply dipping a finger into the jar and tasting the fluid that once was pure water. Gelatin cannot be detected outside the sac since the membrane is impermeable to it.

The osmotic pressure of a solution is

FIGURE 2–7 Osmosis: the diffusion of water through a semipermeable membrane. (a) Initially, the sac contains a watery solution of gelatin and salt. The sac is permeable to salt and water only. Because the number of water molecules is greater outside the membrane, more water molecules collide with the outer face of the sac and enter it; the converse is true for the salt. (b) Hence, there is a net movement of water into the sac, the sac swells owing to the influx of water, and the volume of fluid in the container remains constant.

Start

Water

(a)

12 hours later

Water

(b)

Salt          • Gelatin

independent of the kinds of particles but proportional to the number of particles per unit volume. Thus, the higher the osmotic pressure of a particular solution, the greater the number of particles per unit volume in it and the greater the tendency for water to flow into it.

In our sample of blood placed in water,

the blood cells became swollen (Figure 2–8) for the same reason the sac did. Our blood cells normally exist in a moderately dilute salt solution (as you know if you have ever placed a cut finger in your mouth), and this solution has the same osmotic pressure as the inside of red blood cells. The cells are in an **isosmotic medium** (osmotic pressure of the external environment is equal to that inside the cell). When a red cell is placed in water, a medium **hypoosmotic** to blood cells (osmotic pressure less on the outside than inside), there are fewer salt particles outside the cell, and water molecules move into the cell, dilute its contents, and stretch the plasma membrane (Figure 2–8). A red blood cell placed in seawater shrinks because the medium is **hyperosmotic** to the blood cell (osmotic pressure greater on the outside than inside), water passes out of the cell, and the membrane collapses (Figure 2–8).

### Against the tide: active transport

Charged molecules do not penetrate the plasma membrane readily. Nevertheless, and in spite of the fact that potassium ions ($K^+$) are higher in concentration inside the cell and sodium ions ($Na^+$) are higher in concentration outside the cell, sodium ions can pass out of the cell and potassium ions can pass into the cell, that is, they can move against their concentration gradients. These passages apparently defy the principles of diffusion we talked about in our previous discussion of concentration gradients; therefore, some mechanism other than diffusion must be operating. The cell has to expend energy or do work in order to transport materials against a concentration gradient. This process is known as **active transport** and involves the movement of materials across the plasma membrane by the expenditure of cellular energy.

Since the plasma membrane is slightly permeable to sodium, sodium moves into the cell by diffusion, but instead of continuing until equilibrium is established, the

sodium which enters is rapidly expelled. In so doing, the cell is working against a concentration gradient and in effect is pumping the sodium out; the system is therefore called the **sodium pump** and may perhaps be crudely likened to a bilge pump bailing water from a leaky ship. The situation for potassium is just the reverse; it is retained at a higher concentration within the cell. The fact that energy is required for the system to work is easily demonstrated, since if we poison the cell with cyanide (a respiratory inhibitor) or remove dextrose (a source of cellular energy), then the cell leaks potassium and sodium enters freely until equilibrium is established. All cells engage in active transport, and they accumulate many kinds of materials. For example, sugars and amino acids are moved into the cell by active transport.

What is the mechanism of active transport? One mechanism involves the transported molecule being bound to a material in the membrane called a carrier (Figure 2–9). The carrier and the molecule move across the membrane, and at the inner surface of the membrane the transported molecule is released and enters the cytoplasm. Now the carrier acquires energy at the inner face of the membrane and returns to the outer surface to pick up another molecule for transport. Conversely, the carrier could also move molecules from the inside to the outside.

### Cell drinking and cell eating: pinocytosis and phagocytosis

The processes of diffusion, osmosis, and active transport are not the only mechanisms whereby the cell can acquire materials from the external environment. In 1931 W. H. Lewis made a remarkable discovery while observing some human cells he had grown in a sterile medium outside the body. He observed that the cells produced fingerlike projections at the surface, and within these projections fine channels developed. Small amounts of fluid from the medium flowed

FIGURE 2–8 (top) The swelling or shrinkage of a red blood cell depends on the osmotic pressure of the solution in which it is suspended.

FIGURE 2–9 (bottom) Active transport as described by a hypothetical model. Carrier substances in the membrane combine with molecules to be transported across the membrane. Material is moved "uphill," against the concentration gradient, by the expenditure of energy.

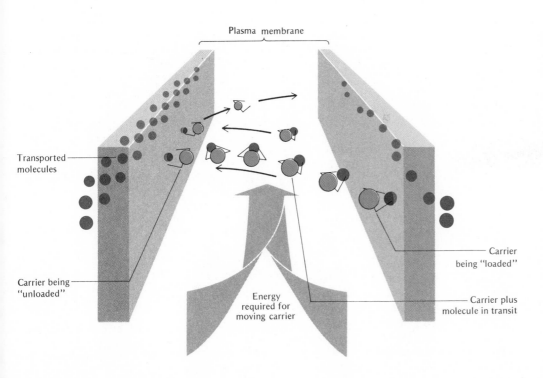

into these channels, and at the base these were pinched off to form tiny droplets, each enclosed by a portion of the plasma membrane (Figure 2–10a, b). In time the fluid was released from the membrane-enclosed vesicle and became mixed with the cytoplasmic materials. Lewis called the phenomenon **pinocytosis,** which in Greek means "cell drinking." In this manner the cell is capable of taking in soluble molecules that ordinarily would have difficulty in penetrating the membrane. The cell can, as one author has said, "take them [the molecules] by the scruff of the neck and pull them pinocytotically into its interior." The phenomenon of pinocytosis is an energy-dependent process, highly selective for certain substances, such as salts, amino acids, and certain proteins, all of which are water soluble. This process, which occurs widely in a variety of cells, could account for some of the phenomena described by some workers as active transport, since both situations show selectivity and energy dependence. The phenomenon of pinocytosis may be of considerable medical importance. For example, suppose it were necessary to treat a group of cells with a drug that ordinarily does not penetrate the plasma membrane owing to its size or its electrical charge. If these cells were treated with the drug made up in a solution containing a pinocytosis-inducing material, such as albumin, then the drug would enter in piggyback fashion along with the albumin and could do its job inside the cell.

**Phagocytosis,** or "cell eating," is in many respects similar to pinocytosis, but whereas in pinocytosis the material engulfed by the plasma membrane is in solution, in phagocytosis the material is in particulate form. Our own white blood cells react to foreign materials such as bacteria, cell debris, or even a damaged cell by engulfing the material and surrounding it in a vesicle lined by an infolding of the plasma membrane (Figure 2–10c). Once inside the phagocytic cell, cytoplasmic enzymes are secreted into the vesicle by the cell, and these effectively

**FIGURE 2–10** Pinocytosis and phagocytosis. (a) Cell drinking (pinocytosis) in a living cell. (b) Pinocytosis in schematic detail. (c) Cell eating (phagocytosis).

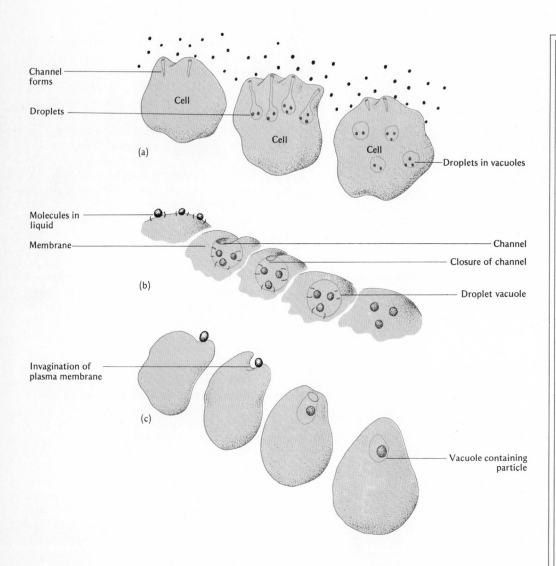

Channel forms

Droplets

Cell

Cell

Cell

Droplets in vacuoles

(a)

Molecules in liquid

Membrane

Channel

Closure of channel

Droplet vacuole

(b)

Invagination of plasma membrane

Vacuole containing particle

(c)

degrade the material into a harmless form; the smaller molecules then pass across the membrane of the vesicle and enter the cytoplasm.

### Microspecialists: cytoplasmic organelles

The word **organelle** means "little organ" and is obviously not to be taken literally. The early microscopists, who used relatively poor microscopes to study the cell, had vivid imaginations, and some of the structures they observed they described as "hearts," "stomachs," and "kidneys." Today it is recognized that the objects these early cell explorers discovered are not true organs, but subcellular structures within the cell. However, since organs (composed of many cells) are the functional units within our bodies and these subcellular structures are

The power to distinguish as separate two objects that lie close together, such as lines, dots, or the letters of words, is known as the power of **resolution.** The quality of any optical system, our own included, depends on its resolving power. For example, as you look at the words in the mouse's tale, you are able to see those at the top more clearly than those at the bottom. If the resolving power of your eye is low, you are unable to read the words at the bottom of the tale unaided—the letters merge and become indistinguishable from one another. If your vision is 20/20, you can see two letters, lines, or dots as being separate if the distance between them is 0.1 mm (4/1000 in.) or greater. If the letters, lines, or dots are closer than this, they are indistinguishable from each other even if you have perfect vision.

Resolution and magnification are two different things. By the combination of their lenses microscopes enlarge (**magnify**) objects for us; however, if the optical system employed does not permit objects to be resolved into separate entities, no matter how many times they are enlarged they will still be blurred. Indeed, the measure of the performance of an optical system such as a microscope is its enhanced power to record fine detail (increased resolution); without this, higher magnification is worthless, since it merely makes a small blur into a big blur. Resolving power is limited by the kind of illumination used. Objects that are closer to each other by less than one half the wavelength of their illuminating light cannot be clearly distinguished as separate entities. Objects or details of objects that are smaller than 2750 Å (or 0.275 $\mu$m) cannot be resolved by white (visible) light as the source of illumination. To increase resolution beyond this level, an illuminating source with a wavelength shorter than that of white light must be used. When electrons (generated by a cathode-ray tube) are energized or propelled by a charge of 50,000 V of electricity, they have a wavelength of 0.05 Å. The electron microscope, using electrons as the "light," never achieves its maximum resolution owing to limitations imposed by materials used in construction, but it does have a resolving power of 2 Å. To gain some idea of the new dimensions revealed by microscopes, let us become quantitative: the human eye can see objects as small as 100 $\mu$m, the light microscope permits us to view objects as small as 0.2 $\mu$m, and the electron microscope reveals objects as small as 0.001

(a)  (b)  (c)

FIGURE 2–11 Cells from a dog's thyroid gland. (a) Unstained. (b) Stained. (c) Unstained but viewed with the phase-contrast microscope. (Courtesy of Carl Zeiss, Inc.)

$\mu$m. Looked at in another way, the light microscope has improved our vision 500 times, and the electron microscope has improved it 10,000 times.

Magnification and resolution are not the only factors involved in the study of cells. Under a conventional light microscope, most living cells appear transparent and almost structureless. It is imperative to be able to distinguish the different parts of the cell from one another and from their surrounding materials. Contrast between the various parts of the cell can be achieved by killing the cell (also called **fixing**) in such a way that minimum damage to its parts occurs and then selectively **staining** (dyeing) certain parts of it (Figure 2–11b). Such techniques are employed in both light and electron microscopy. However, when cells are fixed and stained, there is always the possibility that they may be altered in such a way that the structures seen in a prepared cell are not in fact present in the intact, living cell but are produced by the techniques employed in the preparation of the cell for examination. A special type of light microscope called the **phase-contrast microscope** does permit living cells to be viewed with sharp contrast between their parts without staining and fixing (compare Figures 2–11a and c). With a combination of fixation, staining, phase contrast, and electron microscopy techniques, a rather accurate and more complete view of the cell can be achieved.

Quotation from Lewis Carroll, *Alice's Adventures in Wonderland,* 1865.

FIGURE 2–12 **The endoplasmic reticulum. (a) Reconstruction. (b) As revealed by the electron microscope. (Courtesy of K. R. Porter.)**

functional units within cells, the name organelle has been retained.

**Endoplasmic reticulum and ribosomes: transport, storage, and synthesis.** In 1945 Keith Porter found that cells have a system of internal membranes which form an extensive network in the cytoplasm, and he called this system the **endoplasmic reticulum.** The endoplasmic reticulum is visible in great detail with the electron microscope (Figure 2–12) and consists of an extensive network of membrane-enclosed spaces.

The membranes of the endoplasmic reticulum may appear smooth along their outer surface. However, sometimes the outer surface is studded with small particles called **ribosomes,** and in this case the endoplasmic reticulum has a coarse appearance and is spoken of as rough. The rough endoplasmic reticulum is found with greater frequency and abundance in cells which are actively synthesizing protein. The manufacture of proteins in the cell is associated with the ribosomes, which are dense particles containing protein and ribonucleic acid (RNA). Ribosomes need not always be associated with the endoplasmic reticulum, but may exist free or in clusters in the cytoplasm; these clusters are called **polyribosomes.**

The endoplasmic reticulum, by virtue of its extensive branching, functions in transport; in some cases, the endoplasmic reticulum accumulates large masses of protein and acts in a storage capacity. Of considerable importance is the fact that the endoplasmic reticulum provides a kind of structural framework or a compartmentalization of the cytoplasm. The presence of these sheets and tubules, lined by membrane, provides a tremendous surface area within the cell, and if certain areas of the membrane are specialized for a particular function, the cell shows local patterns of synthesis or breakdown of substances.

**The Golgi apparatus: packaging and distribution center.** In 1898 the Italian scientist Camillo Golgi observed a series of vesicles in the nerve cells of a barn owl. These structures, which could be stained with

certain stains containing silver and which accumulated other dyes, were subsequently found to exist not only in nerve cells but in a number of other cells. The vesicles came to be called the **Golgi apparatus,** after their original discoverer.

Since the structures could be seen at the level of the light microscope only with the help of stains and dyes, some workers contended that they were artifacts produced by the microscopists and their dyes and did not really exist in the living cell. The electron microscope has revealed that Golgi was right and his detractors and critics were

FIGURE 2–13 The Golgi apparatus. (a) Reconstruction. (b) As revealed by the electron microscope. (Courtesy of D. Friend.)

Secretory vesicles leaving Golgi

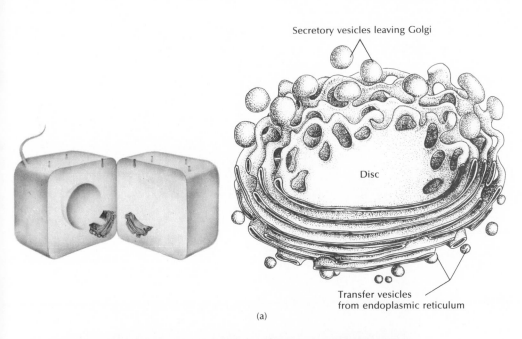

Disc

Transfer vesicles
from endoplasmic reticulum

(a)

(b)

wrong. The Golgi apparatus as disclosed by the electron microscope (Figure 2–13) consists of a group of parallel membranes in flattened saclike configurations (cisternae). The individual sac (cisterna) in the stack of Golgi membranes is usually thin in its center and dilated, or distended, at the edge. At the edge of the Golgi membranes, vesicles of various sizes are seen. Golgi membranes are found in both plant and animal cells.

Some electron microscopists believe the Golgi apparatus is a part of the endoplasmic reticulum and that it may be a site at which new membranes for the endoplasmic reticulum are manufactured. Other workers suggest that its primary function is packaging and sorting of materials. Proteins synthesized in the endoplasmic reticulum, and destined to be secreted from the cell, move from their site of manufacture to the Golgi apparatus by the endoplasmic reticulum budding off bits of membrane enclosing the protein (Figure 2–14). These protein-containing vesicles fuse with the Golgi membranes, and then the Golgi apparatus assumes the role of a traffic officer directing the various proteins to their proper destination in the cell. To accomplish this, the enzymes of the Golgi apparatus react with and modify the proteins that reach them so they are tagged for a specific destination. In some cases, the Golgi enzymes add substances, such as carbohydrates, whereas in other cases they cut the proteins into smaller fragments. Bigger or smaller, the modified protein is given a signal that enables it to be directed to another location. Once a secretory protein, such as a digestive enzyme, is modified in the Golgi apparatus, then the vesicles containing the protein leave the surface of the stack, the vesicles move through the cell, fuse with the plasma membrane, and release their contents into the space outside the cell. Recent evidence indicates that lysosomal enzymes are packaged and secreted by Golgi membranes. Much remains to be learned about the Golgi apparatus and its special cellular roles.

**Mitochondria: the powerhouse.** Mitochon-

**dria** are microscopic bodies that can be stained with certain dyes. They were described in 1890 and called bioplasts ("life germs") because they were thought to be the smallest living things. In 1897 these structures were renamed mitochondria (singular, mitochondrion; *mito*—thread, *chondrion*—granule; Gk.) and recognized as true organelles of the cell. Mitochondria vary in number and shape: some are rods, others are granules, and still others are filaments (Figure 2–15). There may be a single mitochondrion in a cell, or a thousand or more. They are widely distributed in almost all cells and function in cellular metabolism. Carbohydrates, fats, and proteins, which provide the metabolic fuel for the machinery of the cell, are broken down by enzymes of the cytoplasm to smaller molecules that can enter the mitochondrion. Through a series of complex chemical reactions, together called respiration (discussed later), these organic molecules are oxidized to carbon dioxide and water, and the energy released during the reactions is trapped for useful work by the cell. Approximately 90% of the cell's energy is obtained through the chemical reactions that take place in the mitochondrion. It is for this reason that the mitochondrion is sometimes called the powerhouse of the cell.

In living cells viewed under the light microscope, mitochondria appear as lively little organelles that tend to aggregate where energy is required; they move back and forth, change their shape, and fragment to give rise to new mitochondria. The activity is probably due not to inherent movement but to the jostling by other particles and the streaming activity of the cytoplasm. Although it is great fun to watch the active particles under the light microscope, it is with the electron microscope that greater detail of their structure can be observed. A mitochondrion is bounded by two membranes; the outer membrane is smooth and encloses the organelle, and the inner membrane is thrown into a series of folds or pleats (Figure 2–15). These pleats, called

FIGURE 2–14 Pathways of movement in the cell. The path traced here shows the movement of a protein from the point of synthesis in the rough endoplasmic reticulum and into the smooth endoplasmic reticulum. There it receives a specific carbohydrate marker, which makes it a glycoprotein, and becomes part of a vesicle transporting proteins to the Golgi apparatus; it is then incorporated into the membrane of that organelle. Subsequently the same molecule, perhaps with a new or modified carbohydrate marker, moves to the outer layer of the Golgi apparatus, where it becomes part of a secretory vesicle that is carried to the plasma membrane. There, the vesicle fuses with the plasma membrane of the cell.

mitochondrial crests or **cristae,** extend well into the mitochondrion itself and provide either a series of shelflike partitions or a mass of fingerlike projections. Cristae are most abundant in cells with high metabolic activity, and it is here that most of the respiratory activities of the cell take place. The central space or matrix consists of enzymes, small circular threads of deoxyribonucleic acid (DNA) and ribosomes. The mitochondria have their own genetic material, and the capacity, albeit limited, for producing proteins.

**Chloroplast: energy fixation.** The food we eat and the oxygen we breathe are produced by organelles called **chloroplasts.** Chloroplasts ("green bodies") are found in green plants; they are disc-shaped bodies about 5 to 8 μm in diameter and up to 3 μm in width, and they contain a green pigment called **chlorophyll.** From 1 to 300 chloroplasts are found in each green plant cell, and new chloroplasts are produced by division of other chloroplasts. The complex chemical processes of **photosynthesis** take place in the chloroplast, where the energy of sunlight is trapped and utilized for the synthesis of complex organic materials (carbohydrates) from simple inorganic molecules (carbon dioxide and water). Chloroplasts, like mitochondria, contain DNA. This DNA does contain information for the synthesis of some chloroplast proteins, however, most of the proteins of the chloroplast are made on the endoplasmic reticulum.

There is considerable structural organization to a chloroplast, and this is best revealed by the electron microscope (Figure 2–16). Each chloroplast is surrounded by two membranes that enclose its contents

FIGURE 2–15 The mitochondrion. (a) Reconstruction. (b) A longitudinal section as revealed by the electron microscope. (Courtesy of K. R. Porter.)

**39**

CELL STRUCTURE:
THE ORGANIZATION OF LIFE

Matrix

Cristae

Intermembrane space

Outer membrane

Inner membrane

(a)

(b)

and separate it from the cytoplasm. The internal portion of the chloroplast consists mainly of two parts: a fluid matrix (**stroma**) surrounding a complex membrane system. The membrane system of the chloroplast generally consists of a series of multilayered fluid-filled discs (**grana**) resembling a stack of coins or pancakes and a system of closed flat sacs (**lamellae**) extending throughout the chloroplast and connecting the grana. The

grana are so called because they appear as small green grains under the light microscope, and it is here that chlorophyll, carotenoids, lipids, and proteins are associated into units that can convert the radiant energy of the sun into biologically usable forms of chemical energy; the grana are also the site of oxygen production. The chemical energy made in the grana is used in the stroma for the fixation of carbon

dioxide into carbohydrate. It is clear that even within the chloroplast itself there is a division of labor.

Chloroplasts do not develop in the dark, and so plants that have been grown in the dark appear colorless or pale green. However, if one puts such a plant in the light, there is a rapid elaboration of the grana and chlorophyll, and greening occurs. Chloroplasts do not develop in all plant cells, and root tissues even when exposed to the light ordinarily do not green up. (Carrot, pea, and morning glory roots are exceptional cases.)

Higher plants contain a variety of intracellular bodies called **plastids.** Usually we distinguish two types of plastids: **chromoplasts** ("colored bodies") and **leucoplasts** ("white or colorless bodies"). Chloroplasts belong to the chromoplast group. Other kinds of chromoplasts give many flowers and leaves their colors of yellow, orange, or red; these do not show the extensive membrane development seen in the chloroplast, but are membrane-bound vesicles containing pigment. Leucoplasts serve as food-storage depots for the cell and contain oil, starch grains, and protein. The edible part of the potato plant consists of starch-laden leucoplasts.

The color changes in ripening fruit and in leaves during the autumn are due to the decline of chloroplasts and the unmasking of other chromoplasts. In some cases the chloroplasts themselves turn yellow or red because there is a decline in the chlorophyll content and an unmasking and synthesis of the yellow-orange carotenoids present in the grana. When bananas, tomatoes, or sweet peppers ripen, they change from green to yellow or from green to red as the chlorophyll is broken down and the carotenoids originally present become dominant. The reasons that underlie such changes remain obscure.

**Lysosomes: digestive bags. Lysosomes** have been found only in animal cells and are rich in hydrolytic enzymes, which are capable of breaking down and destroying a number

FIGURE 2–16 The chloroplast. (a) Reconstruction. (b) As revealed by the electron microscope. (Courtesy of W. W. Thomson and K. Platt-Aloia.)

of important cellular constituents. Lysosomes are separated from the cytoplasm by a single unit membrane; under normal conditions the enzymes within remain inactive and cannot contact the cellular materials, which they would soon destroy. However, if the lysosomal membrane becomes damaged, the enzymes are released and result in the destruction of the cell. It seems puzzling that the cell manufactures the seeds of its own destruction and then isolates them; however, there may be a sensible explanation for this. In some cases cell death is a natural event in development. For example, when a tadpole changes into a frog, a number of bodily alterations occur. Perhaps the most dramatic of these is the loss of the tadpole's tail. As is evident to every small child who has ever collected pollywogs, the tail does not simply drop off, but is reabsorbed by the developing adult frog. During the resorptive process, the tail cells disintegrate, and part of their demise is due to the activity of the lysosomes. The end result of the digestion and reabsorption of the tadpole's tail is a tailless adult frog.

Lysosomes also play a role in cellular digestion. Bacteria and other foreign bodies are phagocytized by the ameboid white blood cells of our body and contained in membrane-enclosed spaces called vacuoles; lysosomes migrate to the surface of these vacuoles, the membranes of the vacuole and the lysosome fuse, and the lysosomal enzymes enter the vacuole (Figure 2–17). In such a manner, the foreign substances are broken down in the vacuole by the enzymes contributed by lysosomes and, once degraded, are utilized by the cell.

Lysosomes may also play a role in drug action. Vitamin A destroys lysosomal membranes, and when animals receive excess vitamin A, a condition known as vitamin-A intoxication results, which is associated with spontaneous fractures and other lesions in bones and cartilage. Cortisone has the opposite effect; it stabilizes the lysosome, and this property may account for the anti-inflammatory effect of this drug.

Granum

Lamellae

Stroma

Granum

Lamellae

(a)

(b)

FIGURE 2–17 The lysosome. (a) Role of the lyso-some in intracellular digestion. (b) Electron micro-scope view of lysosome. (Courtesy of K. R. Porter.)

(a)

(b)

accumulation of glycolipid in the brain tis-sues of the Tay-Sachs child results in mental derangement, and ultimately early death.

**Vacuoles: inner space.** The cell may contain fluid-filled spaces surrounded by a mem-brane, called **vacuoles.** We have already discussed the formation of vacuoles in an-imal cells during the processes of pinocy-tosis and phagocytosis.

Plant cells have more prominent vacu-oles; in young plant cells the vacuoles are many and they are rather small, but as the plant gets older, these vacuoles fuse to form a large, conspicuous central vacuole (Figure 2–1). The hydrostatic (fluid) pressure of the vacuole forces the cytoplasm to the periph-ery of the cell, and there it remains as a thin layer closely pressed against the plasma membrane. The vacuole of plant cells con-tains primarily water and a variety of other substances together called **cell sap;** because cell sap has a higher osmotic pressure than the external medium, water moves into the cell and the cell becomes turgid. It does not burst because it is surrounded by a rigid cell wall (see Figure 2–25). The turgid nature of the plant cell contributes to the strength of certain plant stems and the crispness of vegetables such as celery and lettuce. Limp celery and wilted lettuce are produced when large amounts of water are lost from the cells of the plant. The cells lose their rigid form and then become limp in much the same way that a tire of your automobile goes flat when it loses air. The plant cell stores a number of important substances in the watery fluids of the vacuole, and these include amino acids, proteins, salts, sugars, and the red pigment anthocyanin. The red color of roses, red onions, and beets is due to the presence of anthocyanins in the vacuolar fluid.

**Microtubules and microfilaments: minimus-cles.** Cellular movements involve two kinds of rodlike structures: microtubules and mi-crofilaments (Figure 2–18). Microtubules are capable of rapid assembly and disassembly and are primarily composed of the protein tubulin. **Microtubules** are the structural

Tay-Sachs disease is an inherited disorder that results in mental retardation, blindness, and death usually before the age of 6 years. Tay-Sachs disease is the result of a failure of lysosome function. In healthy individuals, one of the constituents (a glycolipid) of the plasma membrane of nerve cells is synthe-sized and then degraded, a recycling proc-ess. Individuals who suffer from Tay-Sachs disease lack the lysosomal enzyme, hexos-aminidase, which is involved in the degra-dation of the glycolipid, and as a conse-quence, the membranes of the nerve cell contain a 300-fold excess. This abnormal framework of cilia and flagella; in the mitotic spindle, microtubules act to move the chromosomes during cell division.

The threadlike **microfilaments** are smaller in diameter than microtubules and do not contain tubulin. They are often associated with the inner surface of the plasma membrane, where they occur in bundles and sheets. The musclelike contractions of microfilaments are involved in cell movement, in changes of cell shape, and in cytoplasmic streaming.

**Centrioles, cilia, and flagella: motion.** As early as 1887, microscopists found that their stains showed a dark central body just outside the nucleus; it was given the name **centriole** ("central body"). This densely staining granule plays an important role in the division of animal cells, a function that will be discussed in Chapter 7. Centrioles are not indispensable during cell division, however; the cells of higher plants contain no centrioles and yet are still capable of dividing properly. Centrioles are found in pairs, oriented perpendicularly to one another. When the centriole is studied with the electron microscope we can see that in cross section it consists of a circlet of nine microtubules, each of which is further subdivided into three smaller tubules (Figure 2–19). If we reconstruct a three-dimensional picture from the two-dimensional thin sections viewed with the electron microscope, we find that the nine triplets of the centriole form a short, hollow cylinder. Centrioles are self-replicating, but their chemical nature and exact function remain obscure.

The surfaces of many cells have short hairlike or long whiplike appendages that move fluid across the surface of the cell. If the cell is free to move on its own, the appendages can propel the cell in a watery medium (Figure 2–20). The hairlike appendages are called **cilia** (*cilium*—eyelash; L.), and the whiplike appendages are called **flagella** (*flagellum*—whip; L.). The cells of the trachea (windpipe, see Chapter 15) are covered with cilia that move mucus across

Centriole         Chromosomes         Microtubules

the delicate surfaces so that foreign materials such as soot and tobacco tars do not lodge directly on the plasma membrane (Figure 2–20a). In the human female, the cells of the Fallopian tubes of the reproductive system (Chapter 10) are lined with cilia that move the egg from the ovary along the tube and toward the uterus (Figure 2–20b). Spermatozoa produced in the testes of the human male are motile because of the activity of their lashing tails, which are really flagella (Figure 2–20c).

What do cilia and flagella have to do with centrioles? In cells that bear cilia and flagella, the centriole replicates itself, and the

copies migrate to the cell surface, where they become basal bodies that in turn give rise to the cilia and flagella (Figure 2–20). Every cilium and every flagellum has the same structure when viewed with the electron microscope. Each cilium and flagellum is covered by the plasma membrane, and internal to this is a ring of nine pairs of microtubules surrounding two central tubules (Figure 2–20). The basic structure of these organelles is often referred to as a nine-plus-two arrangement of tubules. Only the cylinder of nine tubules continues below the cell surface (Figure 2–20), and there it forms the basal body, which appears

FIGURE 2–19 The centriole. (a) Reconstruction. (b) Electron microscope view of centrioles cut in cross and longitudinal section. (Courtesy of K. R. Porter.)

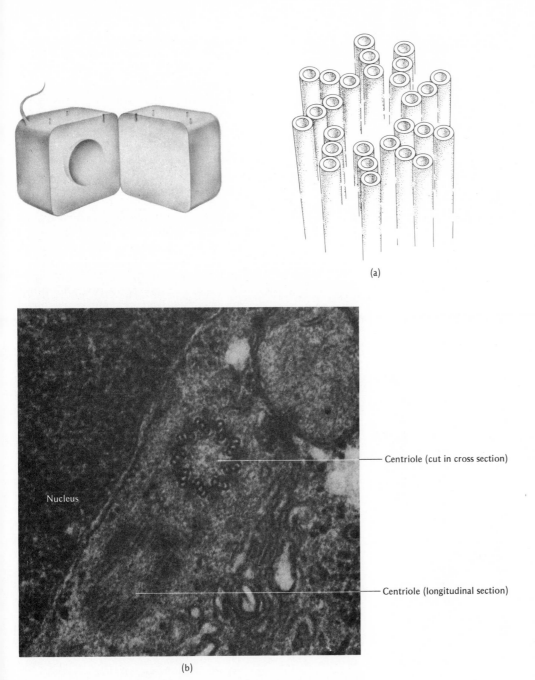

(a)

Nucleus

Centriole (cut in cross section)

Centriole (longitudinal section)

(b)

structurally identical to the centriole. The ability to move rhythmically or to beat is an inherent property of cilia and flagella, and even when detached from the cell, they can be made to move. The mechanism by which the microtubules produce such movements is as follows. Microtubules contain dynein arms, and these arms can split adenosine triphosphate (ATP), cross-bridging the adjacent outer doublet and causing that doublet to slide. This sliding is converted into a bending motion by structures in the cilium or flagellum that act to resist the sliding movements.

**Nucleus: control center.** The most conspicuous feature of a cell viewed with a microscope is the **nucleus.** This organelle was first described from the cells of a flowering plant in 1833 by Robert Brown, but it was soon recognized that both plant and animal cells contain a nucleus. The nucleus, as we shall see, is the control center of the cell, and it contains the genetic material that determines the characteristics of the cell and its offspring. The nucleus is quite obvious in living cells, but it becomes even more recognizable if we add a stain such as iodine, which binds strongly to substances in the nucleus called **d**eoxyribonu**c**leic **a**cid (DNA) and protein. The DNA and protein are organized into structures called **chromosomes** (*chroma*—color, *some*—body; Gk.). In a nondividing cell the chromosomes are in an extended and diffuse state (Figure 2–21), their most active metabolic condition.

The nucleus is a relatively large structure, spherical in shape and separated from the cytoplasm by a nuclear envelope. The electron microscope reveals that the nuclear envelope really consists of two membranes and that the membranes have pores that appear to connect the inside of the nucleus **(nucleoplasm)** with the cytoplasm (Figure 2–21b). In addition to lumps and strands of chromosomes, the nucleoplasm contains a small, dense, roughly spherical body known as the **nucleolus** ("little nucleus"). Under the light microscope, the nucleolus appears

FIGURE 2–20 Cilia and flagella. (a) Cilia line the surface of tracheal cells. (b) Cilia line the cells of the Fallopian tube. (c) Sperm tail (flagellum). (d) Cross section of the flagellum as seen with electron microscope. (Courtesy of D. Friend.) (e) Diagrammatic reconstruction of a cilium (or flagellum).

Plasma membrane

Radial spoke

Central singlet microtubule

Central sheath

Nexin

Inner dynein arm

Outer dynein arm

Outer doublet microtubule

Trachea

(a)

Fallopian tube

(b)

Sperm

Tail

(c)

Central pair of tubules

Nine doublet microtubules

(d)

Cilium (or flagellum)

Plasma membrane

Centriole

(e)

to contain a relatively fluid phase as well as a more solid or dense phase; the dense phase appears dark and consists of clusters of ribosomes, which are rich in RNA; the lighter-appearing, more fluid areas of the nucleolus are made up of tiny granules that are presumably protein. The nucleolus is formed by particular chromosomes that have an active region called the **nucleolar organizer,** and it is here that ribosome precursors are manufactured and accumulated. The dense accumulation of these ribosomal components surrounding the nucleolar organizer forms the major part of the nucleolus as seen under the microscope. The ribosomal components pass out of the nucleolus region, through the nuclear envelope, and into the cytoplasm, where they are assembled and function in the manufacture of proteins. The nucleolus is absolutely fundamental for the growth of the cell. If there is no nucleolus, ribosomes are not synthesized; then there is no protein synthesis, and without protein synthesis the cell cannot grow or maintain itself. The nucleolus may be thought of as the cell's pacemaker, since any change in the activity of the nucleolus will result in a change in the growth rate of the cell.

The nucleus is the control center of the cell, and its role as such can easily be demonstrated. If you cut an ameba in half with a fine glass needle so that one half contained the nucleus and the other half contained only cytoplasm, you would find that the half containing the nucleus could grow and reproduce itself, whereas the portion consisting exclusively of cytoplasm could not maintain itself and would eventually disintegrate (Figure 2–22a and b). Similarly, it is possible to restore normal activity to an ameba that lacks a nucleus by transplanting a nucleus from another ameba (Figure 2–22c to g). Lacking a nucleus, the donor ameba rounds up and dies.

Our own mature red blood cells lack a nucleus and cannot reproduce themselves; their life span is limited to about 120 days, after which they disintegrate and are re-

FIGURE 2–21 The nucleus. (a) Reconstruction. (b) As revealed by the electron microscope. (c) Detail showing nuclear pores. (Electron micrographs courtesy of K. R. Porter.)

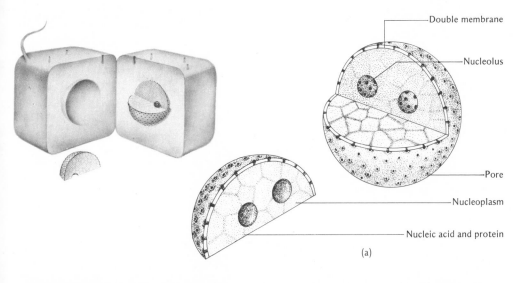

Double membrane

Nucleolus

Pore

Nucleoplasm

Nucleic acid and protein

(a)

(b)

NUCLEUS

PORE

PORE

(c)

placed by new ones developed from nucleated juvenile cells found in the bone marrow and spleen. Although the nucleus directs the activities of the cell and the cell cannot survive for long without it, it is not independent of the cytoplasm, for an isolated nucleus devoid of cytoplasm cannot survive either. It is obvious that there must be dynamic interplay between nucleus and cytoplasm, and for coordinated function a cell must have both.

The nucleus determines the direction of development a cell will take. This can be illustrated by an elegant experiment with an unusual one-celled plant called *Acetabularia*. *Acetabularia* is an umbrella-shaped marine alga that grows to a length of about 1 in., but consists of a single cell with a single nucleus (Figure 2–23). Because of its large size, surgical manipulations are relatively easy. Two kinds (species) of *Acetabularia* differ in their external appearance; in one the umbrella portion (cap) has a smooth edge (*A. mediterranea*), whereas in the other species it is fringed (*A. crenulata*). In both *A. mediterranea* and *A. crenulata*, the cap is supported by a stem and the nucleus is contained in its rootlike base, called the rhizoid. If we removed the caps from some specimens of both kinds, we would find that the caps regenerate; they would look just like the caps that were present in each specimen before surgery. However, if we removed the caps from fresh specimens of both species and then grafted the rhizoid of one species onto the capless stem of the other, we would find that the cap that grew back on any specimen would look like the cap of the cell that donated its nucleus (Figure 2–23c). If these caps were then removed, the caps that regenerated would still be identical to those of the species from which the transplanted nucleus came. It seems that the nucleus exercises its control by secreting messages into the cytoplasm; upon arrival in the cytoplasm, the message is converted into information that details the type of cap to be formed.

FIGURE 2–22 Surgery on the ameba. (a) A fine glass needle is used to cut the ameba in half, one piece with a nucleus and one without. (Courtesy of the Carolina Biological Supply Company.) (b) If left in this condition, only the piece containing the nucleus survives. (c) to (g) If the nucleus from one ameba is transplanted into the cytoplasm of another enucleate ameba, it survives. The donor, without a nucleus, dies.

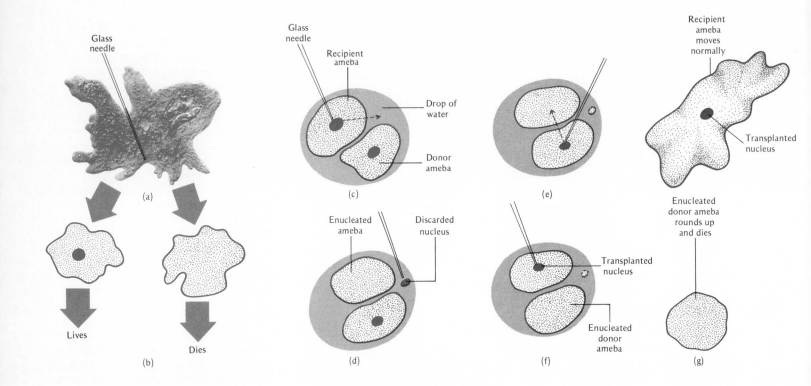

How does the nucleus send out these directive messages? In our description of the nuclear envelope we noted that it is periodically interrupted along its surface by pores. These pores are not empty holes in the same sense as a doughnut hole, but are often filled with a protein-containing plug that probably confers specific properties of selectivity upon the nuclear envelope, enabling it to determine the type of materials that cross into the cytoplasm; chemical messages of a specific nature do in fact pass through these pores. There is another way in which the nucleus can communicate with the cytoplasm. The electron microscope has shown that the outer membrane of the nuclear envelope is continuous in some areas with the membranes of the endoplasmic reticulum. In this way, the materials of the nucleus may be provided with a direct connecting passage to a portion of the cytoplasm (Figure 2–21). The nature of the nuclear message and the manner of its expression in the cytoplasm will be considered in another chapter.

**Extracellular substances: glue, support, and protection.** The cell is a delicate entity. Although the plasma membrane confers a certain amount of protection and support upon the contents of the cell, it is in itself a rather fragile component. Many cells are covered with one or more external substances that give the cell support, protection, and elasticity and provide for adhesiveness and for the retention of water. Most of these coating substances consist of large molecules, such as protein and carbohydrate, fabricated from smaller molecules within the cell.

If the cells of our bodies had no adhesiveness, then no doubt we would exist as loose lumps, constantly coming apart. Obviously, cells must have a type of intercellular glue to hold them together; there are two kinds: **hyaluronic acid** and **chondroitin sulfate.**

Hyaluronic acid is a carbohydrate; when combined with protein, it is a viscous, jellylike material with no definite form. Its viscosity and adhesiveness depend on the amount of calcium present. This material acts as glue and binds cells together. For example, it is possible to convert a live sponge into a mass of separate cells which will not reaggregate by placing it in seawater free of calcium. The human egg is surrounded by numerous small cells glued to each other by hyaluronic acid, making the egg virtually impregnable. However, the hyaluronic acid can be dissolved by an

FIGURE 2–23 The nucleus controls the direction of the development. (a) and (b) If the cap of *Acetabularia* is amputated, the nucleus directs the regeneration of a species-specific cap. (c) Grafting of the nucleate rhizoid of *A. crenulata* onto the stem (with cytoplasm only) of *A. mediterranea* produces a cap with the characteristics of *A. crenulata*.

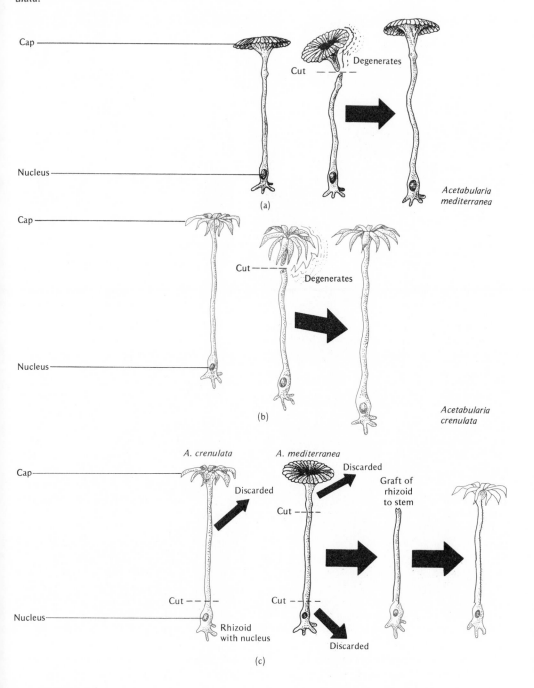

enzyme, hyaluronidase, which is present in the heads of human spermatozoa. This permits penetration of the egg by the sperm. Hyaluronic acid may function in other capacities: in the fluid of our bone joints, it acts as both a lubricant and a shock absorber; in the fluid of our eyes (vitreous and aqueous humors), it helps give the eye a fixed shape.

Chondroitin sulfate is also a carbohydrate, and when combined with protein it forms a rather rigid gel. It is produced and secreted by cartilage cells and forms the intercellular matrix (substance) of cartilage (gristle); it provides for architectural support in the human body. When cartilage contains fibrous materials such as collagen, increased flexibility and rigidity result, a situation not unlike that of steel-reinforced concrete. The cartilage of our ears, nose, and windpipe and much of the skeleton of an infant are good examples of the occurrence of chondroitin sulfate in this capacity.

Fibrous protein elements, such as **collagen** (commercial gelatin), **reticulin,** and **elastin,** are also found in the interstices of cells. Collagen is a long, fibrous protein with a distinct pattern of dark and light bands (Figure 2–24); it confers properties of rigidity and firmness on muscles and tendons. Elastin and reticulin do not show banding in their protein fibers. Elastin, as its name suggests, is elastic in nature and is present in the skin and in the major blood vessels. Reticulin, closely related to collagen, also helps to bind cells together and give organs their shape; it is well developed in the skin.

Finally, it should be mentioned that the mucus secretions of cells help to trap foreign materials. For example, fine particles of dust and the like are trapped in the mucus secretions of the cells of our nasal passageway; by means of cilia which protrude into the mucus layer and beat toward the throat, the mucus and the trapped particles are removed and eventually swallowed. Such a mechanism is extremely efficient in cleansing and filtering the air we breathe and ensures that relatively few particulate materials reach the delicate surfaces of our lungs. Sometimes the copious amounts of mucus produced during a bacterial or viral infection such as the common cold become troublesome and continue as the familiar postnasal drip; here, too, the function of the mucus is to remove the source of irritation.

Plants also have supportive and protective materials outside the plasma membranes of their cells. It is these substances that provide most of our fuel, clothing, building materials, food, and innumerable other conveniences which make our lives more comfortable. The most striking difference between plant and animal cells is that plant cells are surrounded by a nonliving cell wall. The cell wall may consist of three parts: an intercellular cement called the middle lamella, a primary cell wall, and a secondary cell wall (Figure 2–25). The middle lamella is of jellylike consistency and is formed between adjacent cells during division; it is rich in **pectin,** the cement that binds the plant cells together. During ripening, fruit becomes soft (as any shopper poking a ripe tomato or melon knows) owing to the dissolution of the pectin and the loosening of the cells. Pectin is commonly added to jams and jellies to ensure that these materials set, or jell. The **primary cell wall** is found in all plant cells, lies between the plasma membrane and the middle lamella, and is generally formed during early development of the cell. It is thin and quite flexible and forms the outer covering of the cells of fruits, roots, and fleshy stems. When growth of the cell ceases, certain mature cells form a **secondary cell wall** between the primary wall and the plasma membrane. It may be thick or thin, hard or soft, colorless or colored. The secondary cell wall may be as much as 10 μm thick, and it gives the plant cell strength and mechanical support. For us, the secondary cell walls of plants provide lumber, cotton, flax, and hemp. The major component of the cell wall is **cellulose,** a large molecule

Cytoplasm
Nucleus
Vacuole (cell sap)
Plasma membrane
Primary wall

Young

Middle lamella

Secondary wall
Plasma membrane
Primary wall

Vacuole

Mature

Middle lamella

made up of long chains of sugar (glucose) molecules; derivatives of cellulose are used in the manufacture of rayon, cellophane, and plastics. Present in the walls of some plant cells is **lignin,** a complex, nonfibrous molecule unrelated to glucose that forms between the fibrils of cellulose. The arrangement of the cellulose fibers provides for elastic strength, with the harder, resistant material, lignin, acting as a rigid support; in many respects it is like reinforced concrete used in the construction industry—the cellulose acts like the steel rods in providing flexibility, while the cementlike lignin is effective in resisting pressure. Balsa wood is an example of cell walls that lack lignin; it is a soft, brittle wood.

**Membranes: compartmentalization and specialization.** One of the most striking features of cellular organization is the way in

which organelles are constructed of membranes. Plasma membrane, nuclear membrane, Golgi apparatus, endoplasmic reticulum, mitochondria, chloroplasts, and lysosomes are all membranous structures. The membranes of these organelles at first glance appear similar when viewed with the electron microscope, and this structural unity has been emphasized by the application of the descriptive term unit membrane. However, with increasing resolution and newer techniques of electron microscopy, differences in membrane structure are beginning to be shown. These differences are not entirely unexpected, since the various organelles composed of these membranes do differ greatly in function.

Membranes increase the internal surface area and compartmentalize the cell so that considerable specialization can be effected within specific regions of the cell. It is apparent that the cell is not an amorphous blob characterized by randomness and chaos, but a highly structured and well-organized living system. Its structural organization depends intimately upon the use of membranes in the formation of organelles.

## 2–2 CELL SPECIALIZATION: TISSUES AND ORGANS

We cannot see the cells of which we are composed in any detail with the naked eye, yet the most casual glance reveals that these cells are not all the same. For example, each of us recognizes that the cells on the surface of our skin are quite different from those that appear when we cut through the skin and bleed. Just as there are no typical buildings composed of typical rooms, so organisms are not composed of uniformly structured typical cells. According to their function, cells vary in their shape and size and in the degree of development of their constituents. Thus, the cells that make up our muscles are elongate and capable of contraction, whereas the cells that cover

the various surfaces of the body, both external and internal, have a characteristic shape that may be cuboidal, columnar, or platelike so that they fit together and function in lining and protection. Cells that occur together and have a similar structure and function are called **tissues.** Table 2–1 details the structure and function of the major tissues that are found in the human body.

Groups of tissues may be organized to form structural and functional units known as **organs.** The kidney is an organ composed of highly specialized epithelial and connective tissues; our skin is not a simple tissue but a complex organ consisting of epithelial, muscular, nervous, and connective tissues. Organs do not function apart from one another, but form an integrated whole, a smoothly functioning organism, but some groups of organs have particularly integrated functions and are referred to as **organ systems.** Thus, the digestive system includes such organs as the mouth, esophagus, stomach, intestines, liver, and pancreas, and the respiratory system is made up of organs that include the ribs, lungs, diaphragm, and so forth. It should be emphasized that the functional attributes of organ systems reflect the organs and tissues of which they are composed and these in turn are only products of their specialized cells. What makes a cell specialize and become, for example, a red blood cell (with no nucleus and lots of pigment) rather than a skin cell (with nucleus and little or no pigment) during the course of its development from a nonspecialized embryonic cell is another question entirely, and one that lies at the frontiers of modern biology.

## 2–3 CELLS AND ORGANISMS

From the time of Aristotle, people have attempted to categorize the kinds of living creatures around them. The simplest classification of organisms was the system of two kingdoms—plants and animals. Classi-

**TABLE 2–1  A morphological classification of human tissues**

| Type | Function | Form and location | Appearance |
|---|---|---|---|
| I. Epithelial | Cells that form a continuous layer and cover external and internal surfaces; protect, repair, and regulate the passage of substances across themselves; may be absorptive or secretory. | | |
| | A. Covering and lining<br>   May be stratified (layered), ciliated, or keratinized. | i. Squamous<br>   Flattened, thin, irregularly shaped cells. Line the body cavities, blood, and lymphatic vessels. Stratified and keratinized squamous epithelium forms the outer layer of the skin. |  |
| | | ii. Cuboidal<br>   Cube-shaped cells. Line kidney tubules. Cover ovary. | |
| | | iii. Columnar<br>   Elongate pillar-shaped cells with nucleus usually located near the base. Often ciliated at outer surface. Widely distributed as linings of ducts, digestive tract, etc. | Cilia |
| | B. Glandular<br>   Cells specialized to secrete substances such as milk, wax, perspiration, sex cells, or hormones. Cuboidal or columnar in shape. | i. Exocrine<br>   Glands with a duct to the outside surface, e.g., sweat and mammary glands. | Duct<br><br>Secretory cells |

**TABLE 2–1 (Continued)**

| Type | Function | Form and location | Appearance |
|---|---|---|---|
| | | ii. Endocrine<br>Ductless glands that secrete their products directly into the bloodstream, e.g., thyroid, pituitary. | Secretory cells<br><br>Blood vessel |
| II. Connective | Cells whose intercellular secretions (matrix) support and hold together the other cells of the body. | | Fibers<br><br>Connective tissue cell<br>Matrix |
| | A. Fibrous<br>Widely distributed cells with supportive carbohydrate and flexible protein secretions including collagen and elastic fibers. Form tendons and ligaments and wrap many organs, muscles, and nerves. | | |
| | B. Supporting | i. Cartilage<br>Cells secrete a firm, rubbery matrix. Support embryonic skeleton and parts of adult skeleton. | Cartilage cell<br><br>Cartilage (matrix) |
| | | ii. Bone<br>Calcium salts secreted into cartilage, imparting great strength. Supports skeleton and protects nervous system. | Blood vessel<br>Bone (matrix)<br>Bone cells |

**TABLE 2–1** (Continued)

| Type | Function | Form and location | Appearance |
|------|----------|-------------------|------------|
| | C. Blood-forming tissue | Blood, including plasma, red cells, white cells, and platelets, derived from cells resembling connective tissue. | Cells — Plasma (matrix) |
| III. Nervous | Elongate cells or neurons specialized for the expression of irritability and conductivity. | i. Central nervous system: brain and spinal cord<br>ii. Peripheral nervous system: peripheral nerves, ganglia, autonomic nervous system (sympathetic and parasympathetic nerves), and sense-organ nerve endings. | Nerve endings — Nucleus — Cell body |
| IV. Muscle | Elongate, cylindrical, or spindle-shaped cells containing contractile fibers. Perform mechanical work by contraction. | i. Cardiac<br>Branching fibers with many nuclei and striations. Involuntary. Located only in the walls of the heart. | Nuclei — |
| | | ii. Skeletal<br>Elongate cylindrical fibers with many nuclei and striations. Under voluntary control. In general, attached in bundles to bones of skeleton. | Cross striations — Nuclei — |
| | | iii. Smooth<br>Spindle-shaped uninucleate cells with no visible striations. Involuntary. Generally occur in sheets in walls of viscera, digestive tract, etc. | Nuclei — |

fied as **plants** were nonmotile, photosynthetic autotrophs with cellulose cell walls. Classified as **animals** were generally motile, nonphotosynthetic heterotrophs without cellulose cell walls.

However, during the early nineteenth century it was recognized that the two-kingdom system was in difficulty, especially when it came to the classification of one-celled organisms. In the unicellular creature the body is not divided up into tissues and organs, but its organelles are the functional equivalent of organs found in multicellular organisms. Various authors suggested that the single-celled organisms be placed in a kingdom all of their own—neither plant nor animal—and that it be given the name **Protista** (*proto*—first; GK.). For a time the three-kingdom system of plants, animals, and protists was in popular usage; however, as knowledge about the Protista accumulated it became apparent that these one-celled organisms had two very different types of structural organization. One group, the **prokaryotes,** typified by the bacteria, rickettsiae, and blue-green algae, lack a well-defined, membrane-enclosed nucleus and other organelles. The fine filaments of nucleic acid lie free in the cytoplasm, and no nuclear membrane can be seen, nor can one identify an organization of fibrils corresponding to chromosomes. (The term prokaryote comes from the Greek words *pro*—before, and *karyon*—nucleus.) The cytoplasm contains no mitochondria, endoplasmic reticulum, or Golgi apparatus, but is richly endowed with ribosomes. Photosynthesis and respiration are localized in the plasma membrane and its local invaginations. Flagella, when present, do not show microtubules arranged in the nine-plus-two pattern and contain a protein called flagellin. These prokaryotes, it has been proposed, should be placed in a kingdom called **Monera.**

The remaining protists, the **eukaryotes** (*eu*—true; Gk.), include organisms such as the green, yellow-green, and golden algae, protozoans, and diatoms. These have a membrane-bound nucleus and other orga-nelles. Nucleic acid is combined with protein to form chromosomes, which are enclosed by a nuclear membrane. Photosynthesis and respiration are localized in the chloroplast and mitochondrion. Flagella and cilia, when present, have a nine-plus-two arrangement. Currently, such eukaryotic unicellular organisms are classified in the kingdom Protista.

Most plants and animals, including ourselves, are multicellular. They are, like the Protista, eukaryotic in their cell structure, having a membrane-enclosed nucleus and organelles. As multinucleate heterotrophs with cellulose cell walls, the fungi form a kingdom of their own. The major kingdoms for these many-celled eukaryotes are Animalia, Plantae, and Fungi. The diversity of all these living creatures is a reflection of the plasticity of the cell.

## SUMMARY

**1.** The basic unit of life is the cell. Cells are bounded by membranes and capable of self-reproduction.

**2.** The cell or plasma membrane is composed of a double layer of lipid molecules with proteins embedded in or extending through it.

**3.** The cytoplasm of the cell consists of a viscous, colloidal complex of proteins, lipids, carbohydrates, minerals, and salts. Other materials in the cell exist in solution as emulsions and suspensions.

**4.** The plasma membrane regulates the flow of materials into and out of the cell. Regulation is a product of the physical and chemical properties both of the membrane and of the materials that cross it.

**5.** Entrance to and distribution of molecules in the cell are largely governed by the laws of diffusion and osmosis.

**6.** Osmotic pressure is a measure of the concentration of particles in a solvent enclosed by a semipermeable membrane.

**7.** Active transport of materials across the cell membrane against their concentration gradient requires the expenditure of energy. By this means, cells may accumulate or get rid of particular substances.

**8.** Cells may also acquire liquids and solids by pinocytosis ("cell drinking") and phagocytosis ("cell eating").

**9.** The cell is compartmentalized by the endoplasmic reticulum, an intracellular network of membranes which functions in transport and storage. It may be studded with RNA-containing ribosomes, important in protein synthesis.

**10.** The Golgi apparatus consists of a stack of saclike membranes, or cisternae. It plays a role in secretion.

**11.** Mitochondria are membrane-bound structures that are the site of cellular respiration and energy release.

**12.** Chlorophyll-containing chloroplasts, found in green plants, are the site of photosynthesis—the fixation of energy from the sun into complex organic molecules (carbohydrates). Chloroplasts develop in the light; they consist of layers of fluid-filled grana and flat lamellae surrounded by a fluid stroma or matrix. Other plant plastids include chromoplasts, which give plants their color, and leucoplasts, which store oil, starch, and protein.

**13.** Lysosomes contain hydrolytic enzymes and are important in cellular digestion.

**14.** Vacuoles are fluid-filled areas surrounded by a membrane. The prominent central plant cell vacuole keeps the cytoplasm peripheral. The plant contains a watery cell sap with a high osmotic pressure that keeps the cell turgid.

**15.** Microtubules and microfilaments are important in cellular movement: microtubules in the movement of cilia and flagella and chromosome movements in cell division (the mitotic spindle); microfilaments affect changes in cell shape and play a role in cytoplasmic streaming.

**16.** The centriole, just outside the nucleus, is important in cell division. Its microtubular structure is similar to the arrangement in cilia and flagella.

### BOX 2B  Seeing the unseen: viruses

As human beings we sometimes doubt that what we cannot perceive with our senses, and in particular see with our eyes, really does exist. Viruses are a case in point. Although the existence of viruses has been known for a great many years because of the diseases they produce in animals and plants, they are invisible with the light microscope. Indeed, because of their small size they pass through the finest porcelain filters, making it impossible to collect them by filtration. Before the advent of the electron microscope their structure was very poorly characterized.

**Viruses** come in various shapes and sizes and cause a variety of diseases (more than 500 animal viruses have been identified and described so far), but they all have the same basic composition: an outer protein coat and a central core of nucleic acid. Viruses do not have a plasma membrane, and therefore, according to our definition of a cell, viruses are not cells. Some biologists would go a step further and suggest that they are not alive: they have no metabolic machinery of their own, they contain no raw materials for making a new virus, and they can be crystallized, just as a salt can be crystallized, and still remain infective when the crystals are dissolved and come in contact with a suitable host cell.

How do these nonliving noncells exist? Viruses cannot be grown on nonliving substances, but must have a living cell to supply the raw materials and the enzymatic machinery necessary for their reproduction. The virus provides the blueprint for new virus particles (in the form of nucleic acid, the genetic material) and directs the living host cell to perform the actual synthetic operation of viral reproduction. Although it is not exactly clear how all viruses enter cells and take over the host cell's machinery to manufacture new viruses, it is quite clear how the viruses of

FIGURE 2–26  The life cycle of a bacteriophage. (Courtesy of Lee D. Simon.) (a) Bacteriophage. (b) Attachment of bacteriophage to bacterial cell. (c) Injection of DNA into bacterial cell by bacteriophage. (d) Reproduction of bacteriophage heads. (e) Production of bacteriophage heads and tails. (f) Lysis of bacterial cell and release of bacteriophage.

(a)

(b)

(c)

bacteria take over. The viruses of bacteria were discovered in 1917 by the French scientist F. d'Herelle, who noticed them destroying his cultures of dysentery bacteria. He named them **bacteriophages** because they appeared to eat the bacteria (*phago*— eat; Gk.). In actuality the viruses had caused the bacteria to burst, or **lyse.**

The life cycle of a bacteriophage, or phage virus, is illustrated in Figure 2–26. The bacteriophage is tadpole-shaped, and it attaches to the cell wall of the bacterium by its tail. The phage nucleic acid (DNA) is then injected into the host cell, and its protein coat remains outside. Once inside, the phage DNA takes over the metabolic machinery of the cell; for the first 10 to 15 minutes (called the **eclipse period**) nothing is readily apparent inside the phage-infected bacterium, but then virus particles appear in the cytoplasm of the bacterial cell. In time (20 to 30 minutes) the entire host cell is filled with phage particles containing a protein coat and a nucleic-acid core. Eventually the bacterial cell bursts, and the phage viruses (100 or more) are liberated and capable of infecting new bacteria. The entire cycle may take less than half an hour.

Viruses are obviously parasites, but in some cases there is no evidence of injury to the host organism. Most of the viruses we are aware of cause effects that we call disease and therefore are regarded as pathogenic. Viruses are responsible for such human maladies as rabies, smallpox, influenza, polio, the common cold, fever blisters (cold sores), shingles, encephalitis, infectious hepatitis, mumps, measles, yellow fever, viral pneumonia and acquired immunodeficiency disease syndrome (AIDS). Some cancers are caused by viruses, but there is no unanimity among scientists in thinking that all cancers are caused by virus particles. (A discussion of cancer is found in Chapter 8.) Some of the viruses that afflict us are shown in Figure 2–27 as they appear with the electron microscope.

FIGURE 2–27 **Viruses that cause human disease as revealed by the electron microscope. (Courtesy of Robley C. Williams and the Virus Laboratory, University of California, Berkeley.) (a) Poliovirus × 300,000, (b) influenza (spheres) and potato virus (elongate rods) × 150,000, (c) smallpox virus × 100,000 and (d) the virus that causes AIDS, acquired immunodeficiency disease syndrome (p. 56).**

The human immunodeficiency virus (HIV) is the causative agent of AIDS. The scanning electron micrographs on the left side of the figure show budding virus particles (arrows). The transmission electron micrographs on the right side of the figure show the budding virus, the outer envelope of the virus and in some a dark nucleic acid core. (Courtesy of E. Palmer and C. S. Goldsmith)

**17.** The nucleus is the control center of the cell and contains the genetic material. The nucleus contains the chromosomes, composed of deoxyribonucleic acid (DNA). An active region of particular chromosomes organizes the nucleolus, which is important in ribosome synthesis and therefore in cellular growth. The nucleus and cytoplasm communicate across the nuclear membrane and via nuclear pores. The nuclear membrane is also continuous with the endoplasmic reticulum in some areas.

**18.** Cellular adhesiveness and support are provided by hyaluronic acid and chondroitin sulfate, collagen, reticulin, and elastin. Mucus secretions lubricate and protect against dehydration and trap foreign materials. In plant cells, support is provided by the primary and secondary cellulose cell wall, and sometimes by woody lignin and other materials. Plant cells are bound together by a jellylike middle lamella containing pectin.

**19.** Resolution is the power to distinguish between objects, whereas magnification is the enlargement of objects. Both are important in microscopy. Resolution depends on illumination. The electron microscope improves the resolution of objects closer together than one half of the wavelength of white light, using an electron beam as a source of illumination.

**20.** Tissues are composed of groups of cells with similar structure and function. Epithelial tissues may be covering and lining or glandular. Connective tissue may be fibrous, supporting, or blood forming. Nervous tissue forms the nervous system, and muscle tissue provides for movement.

**21.** Organs are structural and functional units composed of groups of tissues. Groups of organs form organ systems.

**22.** Viruses are noncellular, submicroscopic parasites consisting of a nucleic acid core and a protein coat. They invade cells and take over their genetic machinery, redirecting it to make new viruses. They cause many human diseases. Bacteriophages, much used in research, are bacterial viruses.

## KEY WORDS

cell
unicellular
multicellular
ghosts
unit membranes
protoplasm
cytoplasm
colloid
sol-gel transformation
emulsion
suspensions
solution
resolution
magnify
fixing
staining
phase-contrast microscope
diffusion
cytoskeleton
semipermeable membrane
osmosis
osmotic pressure
isosmotic medium
hypoosmotic
hyperosmotic
active transport

sodium pump
pinocytosis
phagocytosis
organelle
endoplasmic reticulum
ribosomes
polyribosomes
Golgi apparatus
mitochondria
cristae
chloroplasts
chlorophyll
photosynthesis
stroma
grana
lamellae
plastids
chromoplasts
leucoplasts
lysosomes
vacuoles
cell sap
microtubules
microfilaments
centriole
cilia
flagella
nucleus

chromosomes
nucleoplasm
nucleolus
nucleolar organizer
hyaluronic acid
chondroitin sulfate
collagen
reticulin
elastin
pectin
primary cell wall
secondary cell wall
cellulose
lignin
tissues
organs
organ systems
plants
animals
Protista
prokaryotes
Monera
eukaryotes
viruses
bacteriophages
lyse
eclipse period

## TOPICS FOR REVIEW AND DISCUSSION

1. Why is the cell considered to be the basic unit of life?

2. Is the statement that viruses are nonliving noncells nonsense? Defend the statement.

3. How are cilia, flagella, and centrioles related to one another?

4. How have developments in optical instrumentation increased our understanding of the cell?

5. How is the structure of the cell (plasma) membrane related to its function?

6. What are the cellular roles of the Golgi apparatus, the endoplasmic reticulum, and lysosomes?

7. Give experimental evidence for the following statement: the nucleus is the control center of the cell.

8. How is the form of cells related to their specific roles in the body?

9. Describe the three-dimensional appearance of the organelles in a typical cell.

10. Contrast the structure of a plant cell with that of an animal cell. Are there similarities? Differences?

# 3

# Of Molecules and Cells

## 3–1 THE NATURE OF THE LIVING SYSTEM: THE CHEMICALS OF LIFE

A living system such as our own body consists of several dollars' worth of shelf chemicals. This low price does not reveal the true value of such a marvelous machine, for we and all living things are much more than a heap of granular materials that can be purchased in the local pharmacy or supermarket. Nevertheless, we *are* composed of chemicals—substances that obey the same physical laws whether they are a part of a living or a nonliving system—and it is virtually impossible to comprehend how life operates without some understanding of these chemicals.

Before becoming unduly discouraged by a chapter devoted to chemistry, remember that chemicals are a part of daily life. We consist of chemicals, and the energy we need to run our bodies is obtained from chemicals. We replenish our supply each day from the food we eat. Most mornings we sit down for breakfast, open a package of breakfast cereal, and eat some of the contents. What we fail to observe is that the "breakfast of champions" or the "snap, crackle, pop" is loaded with chemicals. The side panel of the cereal box tells some of the story. This cereal, it says, contains proteins, fats, carbohydrates, vitamins, minerals, and so on. It also designates what percentage of our minimum daily requirement for certain chemicals the cereal provides. Does everybody really need all these chemicals every day? What are these chemicals, and why do we need them? Where do these materials come from? How are we able to utilize them?

Just as we need not be mechanics to understand the basic operation of automobiles, so we need not be chemists to understand the basic workings of the living cell. The rudiments presented here are designed as a guide to the fundamental components of each and every living entity. This text cannot teach you all the chemistry required for a complete understanding of the workings of the living system, but it can give you some insight into the roles played by chemicals in the living organism—in you and me. We shall confine our discussion to the five major organic molecules of life: (1) carbohydrates, (2) fats, or lipids, (3) proteins, (4) vitamins, and (5) nucleic acids.

Those who have no background in chemistry or who require a brief refresher course should consult Appendix A, which provides a summary of the simple chemistry necessary for understanding this and subsequent chapters.

## 3–2 CARBOHYDRATES: CELLULAR FUEL

**Carbohydrates,** commonly known as sugars and starches, are the primary source of chemical energy needed to run the cells of our bodies; in addition they, or their carbon skeletons, form part of the building materials of a variety of cellular constituents. Carbohydrates are the cheapest foods available, and for this reason they probably represent a large fraction of the average diet. The poorer the economic situation, the higher the proportion of carbohydrate in the diet.

In the economy of the cell, carbohydrates serve as fuel. The carbohydrates used directly by the cell for the production of energy are generally sugars; because of their small molecular size and the process of active transport they can readily pass across the plasma membrane, enter the cellular "engine," and upon combustion yield useful energy. However, if not used at once by the cell, they might pass out and be lost; if retained they would contribute to an increased osmotic pressure within the cell. If our cells had to depend for energy on soluble and easily lost sugars alone, a continuous supply of these molecules would be necessary. How does the cell prevent loss of sugars, how does it avoid being without a ready supply of these fuel molecules, and how does it reduce the osmotic effect?

In order to store fuel and reduce the osmotic effect, the cell converts the fuel into a form that cannot pass across the membrane and therefore cannot exit. The cell stores carbohydrates in the form of large and insoluble molecules such as glycogen or starch. However, the cellular engine cannot use these large molecules as fuel, and so, when needed, they must be converted back into the smaller soluble sugars. In this manner, the cell has conveniently solved the problem of having both the storage and usable forms of carbohydrate within the confines of its plasma membrane.

How is starch converted back into usable sugar? The conversion of available fuel into storage form and vice versa by living cells is based on the fact that all carbohydrates are composed of simple units—building-block compounds of small molecular size. These can be linked together (**polymerized**) to yield large, complex molecules; in turn, the large molecules can be broken apart again to yield their constituent building blocks when required. Very simply, the situation is as follows. We eat carbohydrates such as starch. In the digestive tract (mouth, intestine) these foods are broken down into soluble units of small molecular size which can pass across the plasma membrane and be taken up by the cells of the body. Once inside the cell, the simple molecular units can be polymerized into storage products that are of large molecular size. When the cell needs energy, the storage products can be broken down into metabolically manageable units once again, and these are then metabolized to yield energy or they may be fabricated into other products required by the cell (Figure 3–1).

The mechanisms involved in the synthetic (building up) and degradative (breaking down) processes of carbohydrate metabolism can be understood with the aid of some simple chemistry; this is what follows.

### Single sugars: monosaccharides

Sugars are the simplest of carbohydrates, but in chemical terms what exactly are carbohydrates? As their name implies, they are "hydrates of carbon"; that is, they contain both carbon and water, and for every carbon atom in a carbohydrate there are, with some exceptions, two hydrogen atoms and one oxygen atom. We can therefore write the chemical formula of a carbohydrate as $CH_2O$, but since there are always more than two carbon atoms present, we must modify this formula as $(CH_2O)_n$, where *n* is a number greater than 2.

**Monosaccharides** (*mono*—one, *saccha*—sugar; Gk.), or single sugars, are the simplest kind. The simplest monosaccharides contain at least 3 carbon atoms and may contain as many as 10. Thus, we may write their formulas as follows:

$(CH_2O)_3$ or $C_3H_6O_3$

$(CH_2O)_4$ or $C_4H_8O_4$

$(CH_2O)_5$ or $C_5H_{10}O_5$

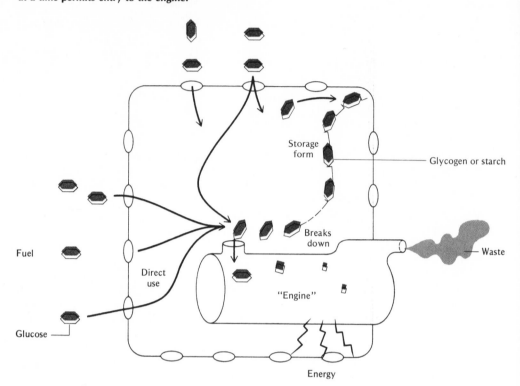

Glycogen or starch

Storage form

Breaks down

Waste

Fuel

Direct use

"Engine"

Glucose

Energy

$(CH_2O)_6$ or $C_6H_{12}O_6$

and so on, up to

$(CH_2O)_{10}$ or $C_{10}H_{20}O_{10}$

These sugars are relatively small molecules and are called **trioses** (*tri*—three), **tetroses** (*tetra*—four), **pentoses** (*penta*—five), and **hexoses** (*hexa*—six).[1] Both trioses and pentoses play important roles in the living cell, and these we shall treat in a later chapter; here we shall confine our discussion to the hexoses, or six-carbon sugars, that act as fuel and building blocks for more complex carbohydrates.

**Glucose** (also known as **dextrose;** see Box 3A), **fructose,** and **galactose** are the most common hexose sugars; they are represented by the chemical formula $(CH_2O)_6$ or

---

[1] The names of sugars usually end in *-ose;* this may help you recognize them as you read on.

$C_6H_{12}O_6$. Although the molecular formulas for these sugars are exactly the same, their three-dimensional configurations are not. Molecules of the same chemical composition but different in their structural organization, and consequently in their chemical properties, are called **structural isomers.** The structural formulas (Figure 3–2) show these different geometries; at first glance the differences appear slight, but they produce significant differences in both chemical and physical properties. For example, fructose is more than twice as sweet as glucose, and glucose is much sweeter than galactose.

Glucose (dextrose) is the most common single sugar (monosaccharide) found in the body; it is the most important fuel sugar for our cells. Normally glucose is present in the blood at a concentration of about 0.15%, and this level is rather rigidly regulated by a complex mechanism involving

FIGURE 3–2 Structural formulas of the common monosaccharides—glucose, fructose, and galactose—shown in the ring form.

Glucose

Galactose

Fructose

the nervous system, liver, pancreas, adrenal glands, and pituitary gland. Brain cells are particularly sensitive to glucose concentrations, and below a certain level their function is impaired; it is for this reason that a severe drop in blood glucose level often results in convulsions and unconsciousness, and perhaps even in death. Foods rich in glucose (Figure 3–3) provide quick energy because the glucose dissolves easily in water and is of a molecular size that can easily pass across the plasma membrane and into the cell, where it is metabolized.

### Double sugars: disaccharides

In nature the single sugars are rare. More commonly the sugars of beets, honey, milk, and other foods consist of two monosaccharide molecules bonded together chemically as a **disaccharide** (*di*—two, *saccha*—sugar; Gk.), or a double sugar molecule (Figure 3–5). Common table sugar (cane sugar or maple sugar or beet sugar) is called **sucrose,** and it is a double sugar consisting of the combination of glucose and fructose; sucrose has the formula $C_{12}H_{22}O_{11}$. Although

**BOX 3A Through the looking glass: symmetry of molecules**

Substances in the universe exist in two optical forms called **stereoisomers,\*** which are mirror images of each other; the two forms are called D and L, because of their spatial configurations: right-handed or left-handed (D for *dextro*—right; L., and L for *laevo*—left; L.). Sugar molecules come in D- and L-forms; when sugars are synthesized in the laboratory, the two kinds are produced in equal amounts, but it is one of nature's curiosities that only the D-form appears in living organisms. The glucose we utilize is the dextro-, or right-handed, form and is therefore sometimes called dextrose (Figure 3–3). If you glance at the illustration of the structure of glucose and

\* Do not confuse stereoisomers with structural isomers, which are molecules with the same chemical composition but a different structure, such as glucose and fructose (Figure 3–2).

FIGURE 3–3 Food into fuel. Dextrose, or D-glucose, is directly absorbed in the intestine and can be directly utilized by the cell. (Courtesy of Peter Paul, Inc.)

dextrose (Figure 3–4), you will see that the D-form (dextrose) is the mirror image of the L-form (glucose), and there is no way of rearranging the atoms so that one form can be converted into the other. Similarly, all amino acids exist in both the right- and left-handed forms (except for the simplest, glycine). Remarkably, all the proteins found in living material contain only the left-handed form of the amino acids. Nobody knows why almost all naturally occurring sugars are right-handed and why we and other organisms contain only left-handed amino acids. Is there something special about the L-form of amino acids or D-sugars? So far as we can tell, none. Molecules that are left-handed or right-handed have exactly the same chemical and physical properties except when they interact with living organisms.

If, like Alice in ''Through the Looking Glass'' you were suddenly to become a mirror image of yourself, there would not be much noticeable change in you; you might part your hair on the opposite side of your head, your heart would be on the right side instead of the left, you would write with your opposite hand, and so on. Except for some of these slight anatomical differences you would look much the same as usual. You would breathe oxygen in and exhale carbon dioxide, and all of your body functions could be carried out except one—you would be unable to eat ordinary food. As soon as you tried to eat natural food, you would find it impossible to digest it; the geometry of the food molecules would be all wrong for you. You could be maintained only on a diet of laboratory-manufactured D-amino acids and L-sugars. You could not even reproduce yourself unless there were other ''mirror humans'' like yourself.

The living system can be compared with a machine composed of interchangeable parts held together by nuts and bolts. If the machine parts were held together with two kinds of bolts having a left- or a right-handed thread, then two separate kinds of bolts and nuts would be required to put the machine together and the nuts and bolts and machine parts would not be interchangeable. Clearly, the construction and operation of a machine requiring two separate kinds of noninterchangeable fasteners would be very inefficient. In the same way, if both left- and right-handed molecules were present in the living cell, two metabolic systems would be required to handle them. Proteins are very specific in their configuration for attachment to right- or left-handed molecules, so that, just as it is impossible to fit a glove for the left hand correctly on the right hand, an improper fit of enzyme and substrate molecules in the cell would result in a malfunctioning metabolism. The design of a machine that is simple, efficient, and effective must involve the selection of right-handed or left-handed threads; which system is adopted does not matter so long as one system is used throughout. In the living machine, the cell, we can assume that once the pattern of left-handed amino acids and right-handed sugars was established in the earliest organisms (probably by chance), the subsequent introduction of the opposite stereoisomer, the mirror image, would have fouled things up structurally. Since the emergence of life, living things have used only one molecular form: right or left, not both.

FIGURE 3–4 Mirror molecules. Note that although these molecules consist of the same atoms, the molecules cannot be superimposed one on top of the other. (a) The amino acid alanine. (b) Glucose and dextrose shown in the straight chain form.

Left (*laevo*) L-alanine      (a)      Right (*dextro*) D-alanine

$$\begin{array}{c} CHO \\ | \\ HO—C—H \\ | \\ H—C—OH \\ | \\ HO—C—H \\ | \\ HO—C—H \\ | \\ CH_2OH \end{array} \qquad \begin{array}{c} CHO \\ | \\ H—C—OH \\ | \\ HO—C—H \\ | \\ H—C—OH \\ | \\ H—C—OH \\ | \\ CH_2OH \end{array}$$

L-glucose (glucose)      (b)      D-glucose (dextrose)

FIGURE 3–5 The formation of disaccharides (double sugars) and polysaccharides (many sugars). Only the reactive OH groups are indicated here. (a) By linking two glucose (monosaccharide) units, the disaccharide maltose is formed. (b) The addition of other glucose units produces an elongated chain, the polysaccharide starch.

droxyl, OH, from one monosaccharide and a hydrogen, H, from the other) is formed in the process, and the monosaccharides are connected by an oxygen atom shared between them (Figure 3–5).

### Many sugars: polysaccharides

In the same way that cells make disaccharides from monosaccharides by condensation reactions, they can make long chains of sugar molecules called **polysaccharides,** or multiple sugars (*poly*—many; *saccha*—sugar; Gk.). **Starch** is formed of long chains of glucose molecules and is an example of a polysaccharide (Figure 3–5b). Starch is poorly soluble, but when it is hydrolyzed (Figure 3–6c), soluble and directly utilizable glucose is released. Starch is the main storage product of many plants (the potato tuber, the carrot, the seeds of wheat and corn) and provides a major source of glucose when we eat these plants. The large molecular size and insolubility of starch admirably suit it to be a storage substance. We are able to store carbohydrate within our bodies, principally in liver and muscle; however, we store it not in the form of starch, but as the polysaccharide glycogen, sometimes called animal starch. **Glycogen** is also a polymer of glucose; it differs from starch in the way in which the glucose molecules are joined together (compare Figures 3–6b and 3–6c). Unlike most starches, glycogen is soluble, but it is of such large molecular size that once fabricated inside the cell it cannot leave; however, when glucose is required by other cells of the body, the stored glycogen in the liver is broken down into glucose and passed into the blood, from where it is carried to the cells requiring it.

Some polysaccharides, such as cellulose, function in a structural capacity rather than as a fuel reserve. **Cellulose** is abundant in the cell walls of plants, where it functions for support and protection. Like starch, it is composed of long chains of glucose molecules. It differs from other polysaccha-

sucrose is soluble in water, its molecular size prevents it from entering the living cell; to be used by the cell, it must first be broken apart in the presence of water **(hydrolysis),** as shown in the following equation:

$$C_{12}H_{22}O_{11} + H_2O \longrightarrow C_6H_{12}O_6 + C_6H_{12}O_6$$
sucrose    water    glucose    fructose

Hydrolysis of sucrose takes place in the small intestine during digestion and yields monosaccharide units—glucose and fructose; these pass across the intestinal wall, enter the blood stream, and then enter the body cells. Another double sugar is **lactose** (milk sugar); lactose is found only in milk, and although it has the same chemical formula as sucrose, it has quite different properties, as it is composed of the monosaccharides glucose and galactose. Maltose, sucrose, and lactose are structural isomers that are made up of different monosaccharide isomers. Milk provides energy because of its lactose content (about 2 to 6%), but lactose, like sucrose, cannot be directly utilized by the body cells because of its molecular size. It, too, must first be digested, and the resultant products of hydrolysis serve as chemical fuel. In the production of beer, the disaccharide malt sugar **(maltose)** is a common starting material; upon hydrolysis of maltose, two molecules of glucose are liberated and then fermented to yield alcohol and carbon dioxide, the active ingredients of beer.

Having considered the breakdown of disaccharides into monosaccharides, let us consider the reverse—the synthesis of disaccharides from monosaccharides. The cell chemically fuses the monosaccharide units to form disaccharides, a process known as **condensation.** A molecule of water (a hyrides, such as starch and glycogen, in the manner by which the glucose units are joined together (Figure 3–6a). If we could digest cellulose, it would provide a rich source of glucose. Perhaps unfortunately, we do not have the proper digestive enzymes to degrade it; cattle, on the other hand, harbor microorganisms in their stomachs capable of digesting cellulose to useful glucose molecules, and this enables them to derive glucose from hay and grass. For us, grass and hay do not provide food; if we were to eat them, they would provide only roughage. Paper is made of plant materials and is largely cellulose; thus, these pages could provide a useful meal for a cow, but for you they provide food only for the mind.

## 3–3 LIPIDS: FUEL, STRUCTURE, AND COORDINATION

**Lipids** include fats and fatlike molecules such as steroids. They are components of membranes, serve as fuel, act as chemical messengers (hormones), and as fat deposits in the skin provide good insulation against loss of body heat. Generally lipids are insoluble in water, but they are soluble in organic solvents such as alcohol, ether, acetone, and chloroform.

### Fats

**Fats,** like carbohydrates, consist of the elements carbon, hydrogen, and oxygen, but the ratio of hydrogen to oxygen is greater than 2:1. The larger hydrogen content of fats allows a greater degree of **oxidation** (removal of hydrogens) and correspondingly more energy per molecule than carbohydrates. Most fats provide twice as many calories per pound as do carbohydrates and thus are a concentrated source of metabolic fuel. Fats may be taken in directly in the diet, or carbohydrate and other nutrients may be converted into fat and stored as fat by the body cells. As we age, we ordinarily become fatter; young men average 13% of

FIGURE 3–6 The polysaccharides cellulose, glycogen, and starch consist of many glucose molecules linked together to form straight and branched chains. (a) The pattern of bonding in cellulose. (b) The branching pattern in glycogen. (c) The hydrolysis of starch yields glucose.

FIGURE 3–7 (top) The formation of a neutral fat involves the bonding of three fatty acids to a molecule of glycerol.

FIGURE 3–8 (bottom) Hydrolysis of fats.

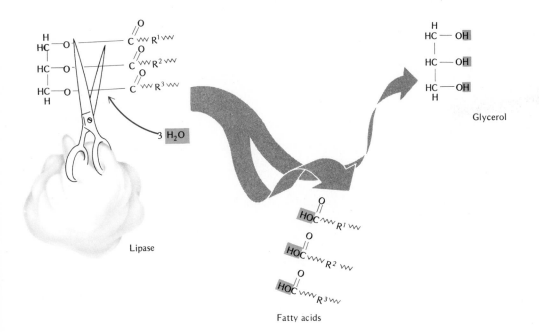

Lipase

Fatty acids

Glycerol

their body weight as fat; the amount of fat in the bodies of older men around age 50 increases to about 20%.

True fats, including animal fats and plant oils, are composed of two kinds of molecules: (1) an alcohol (usually glycerol, sometimes called glycerine) and (2) fatty acids. The **glycerol** molecule has a backbone of three carbon atoms, and attached to each is a hydroxyl group (OH) (Figure 3–7). A **fatty acid** consists of a hydrocarbon chain and like all organic acids contains an acidic group, the carboxyl group (COOH) (Figure 3–7). When glycerol reacts with a fatty acid, an H from the glycerol and an OH from the carboxyl end of the fatty acid combine to form water. This chemical combination of glycerol and fatty acid is another example of a condensation reaction; we have already seen that this kind of reaction is important in the formation of complex carbohydrates. The linkage of the fatty acid and the glycerol (chemically called an **ester linkage**) can occur at three places, since there are three OH groups in the glycerol molecule (Figure 3–7).

Fats differ in their properties because

different kinds of fatty acids may be linked to glycerol to form a fat. The fats we eat may contain fatty acids with backbones of from 4 to 24 carbon atoms, but the most commonly occurring fatty acids are those with 16 and 18 carbon atoms. The hydrolysis of fats, which occurs in the intestine, is accomplished by the enzyme lipase (derived from the term lipid), which breaks the ester linkage, liberating glycerol and fatty acids (Figure 3–8).

The fatty acids that are chemically bound to glycerol vary not only in the length of their carbon chains, but also in the amount of their saturation. Current advertising tells us that polyunsaturated fats are better for our health than saturated ones, but what do these terms actually mean? If the carbon atoms in the hydrocarbon portion of the fatty acids have most or all of their bonds filled with hydrogen atoms, these molecules are described as **saturated fats.** This type of fat is solid at room temperature. If a large proportion of the carbon atoms in the hydrocarbon chain of the fatty acid are not bonded to hydrogens, the **unsaturated** condition is obtained; these fats are liquid at room temperature and are commonly called **oils.** Most vegetable oils are unsaturated; they can be converted by **hydrogenation** (chemically adding hydrogens) to saturated fats such as the familiar vegetable shortening (for example, Crisco) or margarine (from cottonseed oil).

Atherosclerosis, a disease of the arteries, is caused by accumulation and deposition of lipids, chiefly cholesterol (a steroid) in combination with fatty acids and proteins, as plaques in the arterial walls (Figure 3–9). Such deposits are common during and after middle age, when the percentage of body weight that is fat is higher, and the disease is promoted by diets rich in lipids. Polyunsaturates may in fact be better for one's health than saturated fats because they depress the synthesis of cholesterol and are not deposited in the walls of arteries to the same extent as are saturated fats. However, factors other than diet play a role in athero-

(a)

(b)

FIGURE 3–10 (top) Phospholipids. (a) The form of lecithin, a phospholipid. (b) Phospholipid and plasma-membrane structure.

FIGURE 3–11 (bottom) The structure of some common steroids: (a) Basic steroid ring structure. (b) Cholesterol. (c) Estrogen (female hormone) and testosterone (male hormone).

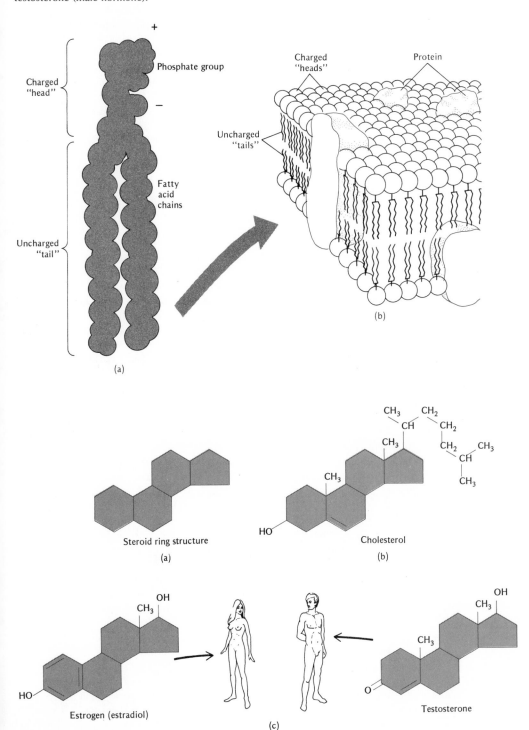

## Phospholipids

**Phospholipids** are important structural components of the plasma membrane and other membrane systems of the cell. As their name indicates, they are lipids that contain the element phosphorus; one of the three fatty acids linked to the glycerol is replaced by a group containing phosphorus and nitrogen (Figure 3–10a). This makes the molecule highly charged, in contrast to the fats previously discussed, which are therefore sometimes called neutral fats. This charged portion of the molecule is soluble in water, but the uncharged portion is not, resulting in a polarity. In the plasma membrane (Figure 3–10b), the water-soluble portion of the phospholipid is external and the water-insoluble ends are internal and face each other.

The best known of the phospholipids are the lecithins and cephalins. Lecithin is found in egg yolk, brain, yeast, liver, and wheat germ; it is used commercially in foods as an emulsifying agent. Brain tissue is rich in cephalin.

## Steroids

**Steroids** are classed as lipids, but they are not fats; they are considered to be lipids because of their solubility in organic solvents. Steroids have a complex structure of four fused rings of carbon atoms (Figure 3–11a). Probably the most familiar steroid is **cholesterol** (Figure 3–11b), which is important in membrane structure, in atherosclerosis, and as the building block for many hormones (Figure 3–11c). Simple addition or deletion of hydrogens, oxygens, and carbons on the basic ring structure creates profound functional change and is indicative of the parsimony of cellular chemistry. For example, the beard and deep voice of a man depend on minor changes in the

sclerosis. For example, blood cholesterol levels are increased as a result of smoking, stress, and lack of exercise.

steroid molecule; a slight molecular alteration is associated with the high-pitched voice, lack of facial hair, and well-developed breasts of a woman (Figure 3–11c).

## 3–4 PROTEINS: FABRIC OF THE CELL

All living cells and all living organisms contain proteins. Although 60 to 70% of the body consists of water, most of our tissues contain between 10% and 20% protein, the exact amount varying with the individual tissue. Proteins are essential to living systems; the word itself comes from Greek roots meaning "first rank of importance." If carbohydrates and lipids are principally the fuels of the living machine, then protein can be considered the structural material of which the machine is made. Furthermore, since all enzymes, without which life could not exist, are proteins, the preeminent position of proteins is well justified. Not all proteins are enzymes; some function in myriad other roles: oxygen and carbon dioxide transport, immune reactions, chemical regulation, and structural support. Common and important proteins found within the body include hemoglobin (the red pigment in red blood cells which carries oxygen), keratin (a fibrous protein that forms nails and hair), fibrin (a fibrous protein involved in clotting), collagen (the most abundant protein of all, the principal fibrous protein of skin, tendons, ligaments, bone, cartilage, etc.), insulin (the hormone regulating blood sugar level), gamma globulin (containing antibodies), oxytocin and vasopressin (hormones that regulate, respectively, uterine contractions during childbirth and the diameter of blood vessels). It has been estimated that a single cell in our body may have at least 10,000 different proteins.

### Protein structure

Proteins are organic molecules that contain nitrogen in addition to carbon, oxygen, and hydrogen; the fundamental building blocks of proteins are the **amino acids.** Amino acids are nitrogenous compounds having an amino ($NH_2$) group, a carboxyl (COOH) group, and another characteristic group of atoms often referred to as an **R group,** since it is variable. We can, therefore, write the generalized formula:

$$NH_2-\overset{\displaystyle R}{\underset{\displaystyle H}{\overset{|}{\underset{|}{C}}}}-COOH$$

Amino acids occur in nature, and they differ from each other in the structure of the R group. Of the 150 naturally occurring amino acids, only 20 are used for the fabrication of proteins. Amino acids combine in various ways to form different proteins in much the same fashion as the letters of the alphabet can be arranged to form a variety of words; amino acids are the alphabet of protein structure, and all the proteins that exist in nature, whether they be of cabbage or of king, are constructed from this universal 20-letter alphabet. Insofar as proteins are concerned, all living things are not equal. The proteins of a person differ from those of a dog, cat, elephant, and baboon. They differ from those of other living creatures because of a different arrangement of amino acids. This is what we mean by **species specificity.**

Since proteins may contain several hundred or a thousand amino acids, it is obvious that the number of possible combinations of the 20 kinds of amino acids is almost infinite; thus, there are endless possible kinds of proteins. The possible number of proteins of average size (containing about 200 amino acids) is so large that it would be expressed as the number 1 followed by 600 zeros! To understand the magnitude of the situation, imagine taking the 26 letters of the alphabet and counting the number of words that can be constructed. Additionally, to make the comparison equivalent to the structure of a protein, you would have to make words that contained 500 letters.

Proteins are long, complex chains of amino acids linked end to end. The connecting link between two amino acids is formed by a chemical bonding of the carboxyl group (COOH) of one amino acid with the amino group ($NH_2$) of another; its formation (a condensation reaction) involves the loss of a water molecule between the two amino acids (an OH from the carboxyl group and an H from the amino group), and the bond thus formed is called a **peptide bond** (—CONH; Figure 3–12). The linking together of amino acids is much like attaching "pop-it" beads together to form a long chain. The joining of up to 50 amino acids results in a **polypeptide chain,** and generally speaking, 50 or more linked amino acids are called a **protein.** Proteins are generally large molecules having molecular weights of thousands to millions. Hemoglobin, for example, has a molecular weight of 64,000; insulin has a molecular weight of 5,000; and the protein of a virus weighs about 40,000,000. By comparison, water has a molecular weight of 18, glucose a molecular weight of 180, and table sugar (sucrose) a molecular weight of 342. Size and function in proteins are not related: vasopressin (the hormone controlling the diameter of blood vessels) contains only nine amino acids, whereas gamma globulin (the antibody molecule) contains hundreds of amino acids; both are indispensable for normal body function.

The variety of proteins existing in nature is due both to the kinds of amino acids composing the peptide chain and to the particular sequence in which they are arranged. On occasion, a single variation in an amino acid out of a chain of hundreds of amino acids makes the molecule behave entirely differently. To illustrate this point, let us once again use our alphabet analogy. If a sequence of letters spells out the word *good,* then a single alteration in one letter could change the entire meaning—for example, *gold* or *food* or *goof.* Sometimes an alteration can produce a word that is meaningless, such as *lood.* For example, the hemoglobin in red blood cells is a protein composed of four individual polypeptide chains, two called alpha and two called beta.

**FIGURE 3–12 (a) The formation of peptide bonds. (b) The formation of proteins.**

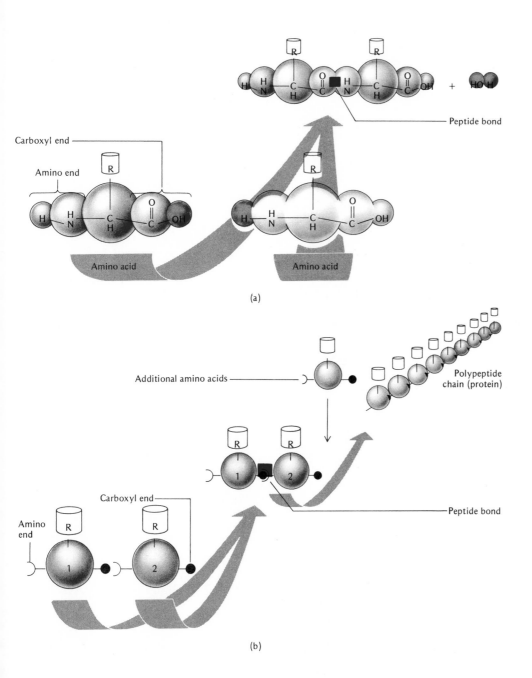

Carboxyl end

Amino end

Amino acid

Amino acid

Peptide bond

(a)

Additional amino acids

Polypeptide chain (protein)

Amino end

Carboxyl end

Peptide bond

(b)

Some persons have a variant kind in their blood cells called sickle-cell hemoglobin. When the red blood cells of persons so affected are deprived of oxygen, the cells assume a sickled shape and can no longer function normally. This striking change in the properties of a red blood cell containing sickle-cell hemoglobin is produced by a change in only 1 of the 146 amino acids in the beta chain!

The protein chain of amino acids formed by peptide bonding makes up the so-called **primary structure** of the protein. Few proteins, however, exist as a straight chain, and most polypeptide chains are coiled or twisted to yield a springlike, or helical, form (Figure 3–13). The most common kind of coiling arrangement is called an **alpha helix;** in its precise geometry there is a turn of the helix every 3.6 amino acids (5 turns involve 18 amino acids). The helix is stabilized by the formation of hydrogen bonds between successive turns of the spiral; the hydrogen bonds are formed between the C=O group of one amino acid and the NH group of another (Figure 3–13). The spiral-staircase arrangement of the polypeptide chain is often called the **secondary structure** of the protein.

Proteins undergo other contortions, for the helical polypeptide chain can be further twisted to yield a globular or an elongated shape (Figure 3–13). This folding of the alpha helix into a variety of shapes produces what is called the **tertiary structure** of the protein.

The secondary and tertiary structures of a protein are easily destroyed by harsh environmental conditions such as heat, excessive acidity, chemical reagents, and radiation. If a protein solution (for example, the white of an egg) is subjected to high temperature (boiling), the helical arrangement is destroyed and the protein becomes **coagulated,** or **denatured** (Figure 3–14). In this condition, although the amino-acid sequence in the protein is unchanged, the spatial orientation of the molecule is severely altered; the helix does not re-form spontaneously, and the molecule loses its original properties. This process of denaturation of proteins may also occur by drying or by exposing the protein solution to acid or alkaline conditions.

Denaturation may be reversible or irreversible. If the diffuse or uncoiled condition can be returned to the coiled configuration, the solubility and other properties of the normal (or native) state are obtained, and this is reversible denaturation, whereas if the native state is not reestablished (as in coagulation) it is irreversible denaturation.

The structure of proteins is important in a practical sense because it tells us something about their properties (Box 3B). The reason for refrigerating blood plasma and other protein solutions becomes apparent; the three-dimensional configuration of proteins is maintained by relatively weak interactions and hydrogen bonds that are easily disrupted by elevated temperatures. Consequently the geometry as well as the function of the protein is destroyed by heat.

## Conjugated proteins

Many proteins consist entirely of amino acids, but some include other components (called **prosthetic groups**) and are called **conjugated proteins.** Conjugated means bound, and in conjugated proteins, the protein portion is bound to a prosthetic group. One of the most familiar of all conjugated proteins is hemoglobin. Hemoglobin consists of four polypeptide chains wound about four ring structures called heme, each of which bears an atom of the metal iron (Figure 3–15). The heme is the prosthetic group. The globular, protein portion of the molecule is called globin, and by its conjugation (binding) with heme it becomes hemoglobin. Other conjugated proteins containing heme are the cytochromes, important in the energy transformations of the cell.

Other examples of conjugated proteins are nucleoproteins (nucleic acid plus protein), found in the nucleus and ribosomes; glycoproteins (carbohydrate plus proteins),

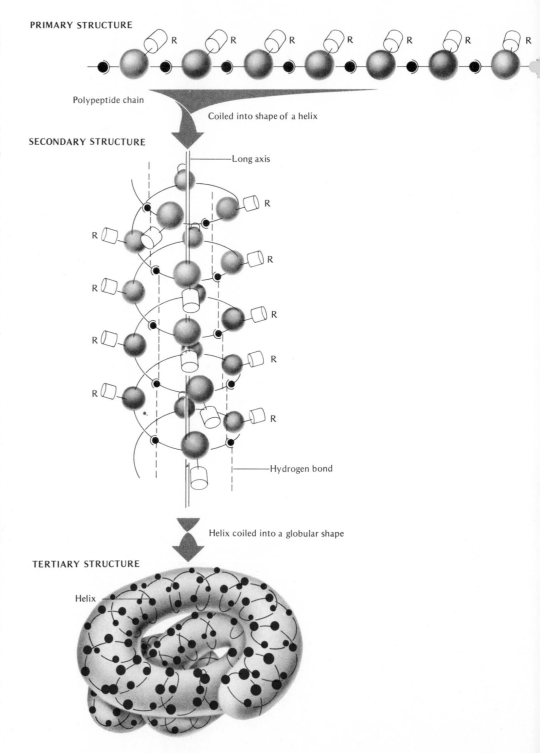

PRIMARY STRUCTURE

Polypeptide chain

Coiled into shape of a helix

SECONDARY STRUCTURE

Long axis

Hydrogen bond

Helix coiled into a globular shape

TERTIARY STRUCTURE

Helix

FIGURE 3–14 Protein and prosthetic-group organization in hemoglobin. The molecule is folded in a complicated way, and the iron-containing heme group (called the prosthetic group) is embedded in one region. Four such protein chains, each with a heme, form a single hemoglobin molecule.

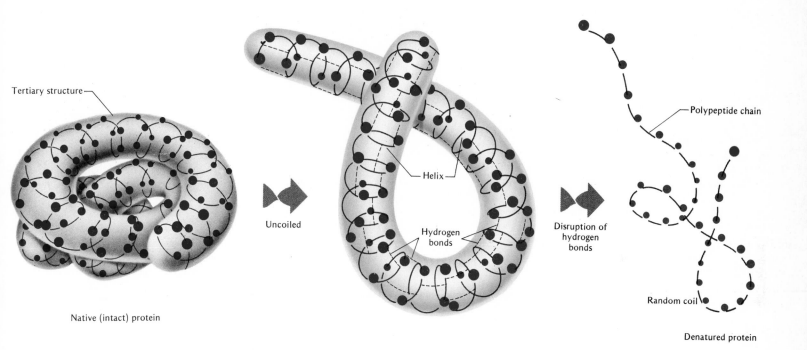

Tertiary structure

Native (intact) protein

Uncoiled

Helix

Hydrogen bonds

Disruption of hydrogen bonds

Polypeptide chain

Random coil

Denatured protein

---

**BOX 3B Protein structure and making a meringue**

Meringue is a fluffy topping that consists of beating and cooking egg whites to which a bit of sugar has been added. Beating the white of an egg, which consists primarily of the proteins ovalbumin and globulin, tends to alter their structure. Ovalbumin and globulin consist of spaghettilike strands of protein rolled up in such a way that they form a sphere. When an egg white is beaten with a whisk, some of the weaker bonds that hold the spaghetti strands together are broken, and there is an unraveling of the sphere. The unraveling of the globular protein to form a tangled mass of strands is called **denaturation,** and a good cook knows when this happens because the transparent egg whites become opaque. Once unraveled, the spaghettilike protein strands form a meshwork or gel, and beaten further this gel traps air bubbles. If this mixture is heated in an oven, the air bubbles expand and a fluffy meringue results. Heating further denatures the proteins, and also coagulates them, producing a stiffening of the meringue.

If yolk is accidentally added to the egg white, the lipids of the yolk attach to the albumin strands, and acting like a grease, the bonding of albumin molecules one to another is prevented. As a consequence, it is harder to form a meshwork and less air is trapped. A poor meringue results. Sugar should be added to the egg white, only after a stable foam results from beating. If sugar is added before the gel forms, it tends to remove water from the protein, and this thickens the whites sufficiently so that getting it to foam is more difficult. Excessive beating can also ruin a meringue, as it unravels the proteins too much. This produces a firm gel, and water separates from the protein; when heated, the white cannot expand properly, the air bubbles burst, and the meringue collapses before coagulation can occur. The result is a flat pancake of baked egg whites.

FIGURE 3–15 Protein and prosthetic group organization in myoglobin. This space-filling model represents each amino acid as a larger blue sphere, whereas the smaller spheres of the prosthetic group atoms are colored green, with the iron atom at its center colored red.

present on the surface of erythrocytes and responsible for blood types; and lipoproteins (lipid plus protein), which are structural elements in all cellular membranes.

## 3–5 ENZYMES: PROTEINS THAT MAKE HASTE

An old adage states, "Haste makes waste." However, in all cells hasty chemical reactions make life possible. Before we see how cells are able to speed up chemical changes, let us briefly consider the conditions under which chemical reactions themselves take place.

Before molecules can react to form new chemical configurations, their atoms must be so oriented that electrons may be lost, gained, or shared. The sharing and rearrangement of electrons form the basis of all chemical change. However, spontaneous electron alterations do not commonly occur in nature: if they did, matter in the universe would be very unstable and constantly undergoing change.

The bringing together of molecules so that atomic collisions can occur and electron sharing can take place requires energy. That is, to effect the molecular collisions which allow chemical reactions to occur, there must be an increase in the amount of energy in the reacting substances. This is called **activation energy.** Once molecules have acquired the necessary activation energy, the chemical reaction can begin. In other words, each chemical reaction has an energy barrier; the higher the barrier, the more stable are the substances involved and the less likely they are to react. We can compare the situation to a skier who must get to the top of a hill in order to ski down the other side. She or he starts at the bottom of the hill and to get to the top must expend energy; a strong push of the arms on ski poles, and the skier moves up the slope. The energy expended to get the skier to the top of the hill corresponds to the activation energy necessary to overcome the energy barrier in a chemical reaction (Figure

3–17a and b). The skier at the top of the hill can be considered to be in an activated state and can easily go down the opposite side of the hill; the barrier has been hurdled. In just the same way, chemical reactions can proceed only when the reacting molecules have acquired the energy of activation. Thus, a molecule may never react or change unless activation energy is supplied to it. If this happens, the molecule is lifted over the top of the energy hill and rolls down the other side. In rolling down, it is chemically altered.

How can we influence the activation energy of molecules so that rates of chemical reactions can be increased? We can visualize a number of ways of making molecules more reactive. For example, we can increase the concentrations of the reactants so that the frequency of molecular collision is increased, or we can increase the energy of the reactants by heating the materials, or we can add an accelerating substance called a **catalyst.** Catalysts are substances that affect the rate of a reaction without themselves being changed in the process. Catalysts are not magic substances. They do not make impossible reactions possible, but they do

accelerate the rates of reactions that would occur spontaneously (but very slowly) in their absence. Thus, catalysts have similar effects upon reactants as do temperature and increased concentration. Catalysts are widely used in industry to reduce the energy of activation of reactants. They lower the energy barrier, and chemical reactions proceed rapidly at ordinary temperatures with reduced concentrations of reactants. Iron filings and finely divided platinum are common industrial catalysts. We can demonstrate the catalytic effects of iron filings quite easily. For example, hydrogen peroxide (used in bleaching hair or as an antiseptic) is a naturally unstable material which breaks down slowly at room temperature to yield oxygen and water. Its decomposition can be accelerated by warming the solution or by adding a pinch of a catalyst such as iron filings. As the iron filings are added the hydrogen peroxide froths; the liquid turns almost white as oxygen is rapidly liberated. The iron filings, however, remain unchanged.

How do catalysts produce their effects? One mechanism is by providing a site of adsorption for the reactants—a sort of meeting place or rendezvous so that the reactants can find each other more easily and are more likely to meet. Molecular contacts are thus more frequent and assured, facilitating molecular rearrangements (Figure 3–18). Other factors, still obscure, probably also play a role in catalytic activities. Catalysts are economical materials for producing chemical change; they are usually effective in very small quantities, and since they are unchanged by the chemical reactions they effect, they can be used over and over again.

Now let us consider how the cell makes chemical reactions occur at a quickened pace. Clearly heat cannot be used, since it would coagulate (irreversibly denature) the cellular proteins; the concentrations of reactants cannot be increased beyond a certain level because many of these key materials are unavailable in large quantities; and the addition of substances such as

### BOX 3C Curling hair and the shape of protein molecules

The major protein of hair and wool is keratin. Long protein molecules are lined up alongside each other to form a fibrous arrangement and bound together by numerous cross linkages that give the hair its elasticity and strength (Figure 3–16a). About 10% of all the amino acids forming keratin are cysteine, which contains sulfur. These amino acids form sulfur-sulfur linkages called **disulfide bridges,** which link the protein chains. The position of a disulfide bridge contributes to the straightness or curl of hair (Figure 3–16). To change the arrangement of the bonds, one must break the bridges and re-form them in another configuration. This is what is done in a permanent-wave treatment. If the keratin fibers in hair are forcibly coiled and subjected to heat of over 200°F, the strained sulfur-sulfur linkages snap, and new ones re-form on cooling; the hair remains permanently curled. Such treatment often damages the hair itself, and so the cold-wave or home-permanent-wave treatment, which does not involve high temperatures and is less harmful, has largely replaced the hot-wave permanent. Permanent-wave kits for home use contain a strong, odoriferous chemical, which is applied to the hair; the chemical contains a so-called reducing substance, which breaks the disulfide bridge. The hair is then curled or straightened with rollers, and a neutralizer is applied. The neutralizer reestablishes the disulfide bridges in the configuration of the rollers, and the protein chains are reoriented. The normal configuration of hair proteins and the position of the disulfide bridges are determined by hereditary constitution, so when new hair grows it must, in turn, be treated.

Disulfide bridges also help to stabilize other proteins or polypeptides. For example, insulin is composed of two chains held together by disulfide bridges (Figure 3–16b); even small molecules such as vasopressin and oxytocin, with only nine amino acids, are formed into a ring by the disulfide bridge (Figure 3–16c). A contorted protein chain achieves additional stability by the strong binding produced by the sulfur-sulfur linkage.

FIGURE 3–16 Disulfide bridges. (a) Hair curling. (b) Insulin, a hormone, contains two polypeptide chains held together by disulfide bridges. (c) Oxytocin and vasopressin, hormones, each consists of nine amino acids; six of these are linked via disulfide bridges. Note that the two hormones differ in only two amino acids (shaded).

FIGURE 3–17 Skiing and activation energy. (a) Skiing requires energy input to reach the hilltop (energy barrier). Once this is reached, the skier is activated and can easily ski downhill without additional energy. (b) Ordinary chemical reaction. The energy of the reactants is insufficient to carry them over the energy barrier, and so they do not react until additional energy is supplied (activation energy) to allow movement across the energy barrier. (c) Enzyme-catalyzed reaction. Required energy of activation is lowered, permitting more molecules to cross the energy barrier and the reaction to proceed at a faster rate.

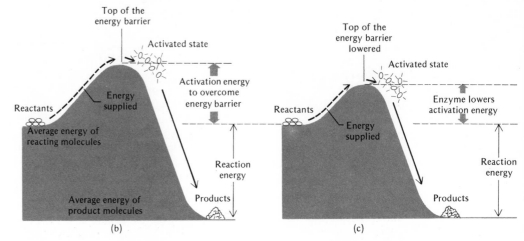

platinum or iron filings is quite out of order. Living cells hasten chemical reactions by employing certain kinds of proteins as catalysts—**enzymes.** All enzymes are proteins, and they are involved as catalysts in almost all the chemical reactions that take place in the living organism. Without enzymes, life would not be possible.

How do enzymes work? Enzymes operate in much the same fashion as other catalysts, that is, they lower the amount of energy necessary to start the reaction and thus assist molecules in jumping over the activation-energy barrrier (Figure 3–17c). To do this an enzyme must initially combine with its **substrate** (the substance[s] acted upon by the enzyme) and form a chemical complex (Figure 3–19a and b); in forming the complex, the enzyme steers the electrons of the substrate into deformed orbits, orienting them so they can be shared between reactants, and then the chemical reaction occurs. Once the reaction has been completed, the product is released and the enzyme is free to participate once again with new substrate (Figure 3–19c).

Unlike inorganic catalysts, enzymes are specific in their action and often catalyze only a single reaction. The degree of their specificity is probably dependent upon the structure of the protein. The substrate, which is usually a smaller molecule, fits into a specific area on the surface of the large-protein enzyme. The region of attachment is called the **active site** of the enzyme. Since an enzyme must have a specific geometry for its active site to fit the substrate properly, it becomes clear why enzymes are easily inactivated by heat, acid, and alkali. Such treatments denature the protein and destroy the three-dimensional structure of the enzyme; the active site and the substrate cannot fit properly, and because of the misalignment no chemical reaction takes place.

The specificity of enzyme and substrate suggests mechanisms whereby enzymes may be inhibited or **poisoned.** Poisoning occurs when the enzyme is prevented from affecting the substrate even though they are in proximity. If molecules resembling the substrate are introduced into a living cell (or to an isolated enzyme), but these molecules cannot be acted upon by the enzyme, binding of the mimic compound (called an **antimetabolite** or **competitive inhibitor**) to the enzyme may occur, and then the enzyme is prevented from carrying out its function with its normal substrate (Figure 3–20). If the binding process is irreversible, the enzyme is permanently poisoned. Fluoride acts as an irreversible inhibitor for the enzymes involved in glucose breakdown. The nerve gases, agents of chemical warfare, operate by blocking the enzymes involved in the transmission of the nerve impulse and thus produce their paralyzing and lethal effects.

Over a thousand different enzymes are known, and undoubtedly many more exist that have not yet been identified. Each enzyme is involved in a rather specific chemical reaction. The names given to enzymes generally end in *-ase* and are derived either from the substrate on which they act or from the kind of reaction in which they are involved. For example, lipase acts on lipids, amylase attacks starch (*amylum*— starch; L.), and sucrase attacks sucrose (table sugar). This uniformity of enzyme nomenclature is convenient, logical, and of recent vintage. Some of the first enzymes discovered escaped this systematic approach and were given names that end in *-in;* these have been so commonly used that they are retained to this day. Trypsin and pepsin, which digest proteins, and ptyalin (present in saliva), which digests starch, are examples of these oldtime enzymes.

Enzymes are organic catalysts; like indus-

**FIGURE 3–18** How a catalyst works. (a) Molecules react chemically if they collide; however, such collisions are rare. (b) If an adsorption site for the molecules is present, collisions occur more easily. Catalysts provide adsorption sites, thus facilitating chemical reactions and increasing their rates.

**FIGURE 3–19** (top) The interaction of enzyme and substrate. (a) Enzyme and substrate have geometries that allow them to fit together. (b) Enzyme and substrate form a complex. (c) Product is liberated, and enzyme is free to participate with a new molecule of substrate.

**FIGURE 3–20** (bottom) Competitive enzyme inhibition. (a) Inhibitor molecule is mixed with the enzyme. (b) Enzyme–inhibitor complex forms and prevents the natural substrate from attaching to the enzyme; no reaction occurs as the enzyme is blocked, or poisoned.

(a)  (b)

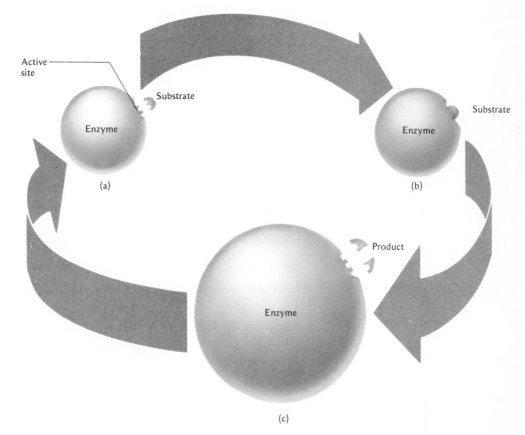

trial catalysts, they are effective in very small amounts, they are relatively unchanged by the chemical reactions they effect, and they can be used over and over again; this is highly advantageous to the cellular economy, since only a minute amount of each required enzyme need be synthesized by the cell, and the organism need not expend energy and materials for the synthesis of enzymes at a rate proportional to the reactions they effect. Life depends on enzyme function, and when enzymes are inactivated, death may eventually be the outcome.

## 3–6 VITAMINS, COENZYMES, AND MINERALS: ENZYME HELPERS

### Vitamins

Sailors on extended voyages used to be prone to the disease scurvy, characterized by skin hemorrhage, bleeding gums, extremely tender joints, and great pain upon movement. An English surgeon named Lind demonstrated that food alone would cure scurvy and that the disease could easily be prevented by drinking lemon and lime juices. Since British sailors were required to drink lime or lemon juice daily as a preventive measure, they were nicknamed "limeys." In 1870 sailors of the newly created Japanese navy fell ill with a painful and crippling disease that paralyzed the legs, affected the

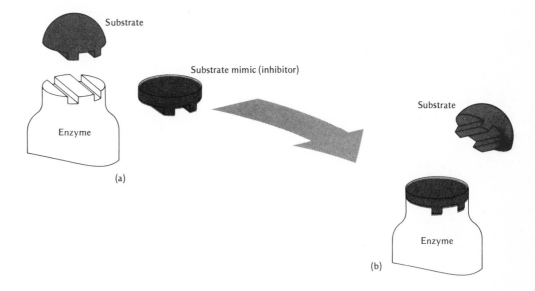

heart, and produced loss of appetite and severe constipation. The disease, called beriberi, was cured by having the sailors eat less polished rice and more wheat, meat, and vegetables. In 1914 a debilitating disease, pellagra, was widespread in the southern United States. Persons affected showed a roughening of the skin, diarrhea, and dementia. Dr. Joseph Goldberger claimed that the disease was not spread by infection, and to prove the point he and his wife and 22 volunteers swallowed capsules containing the blood, feces, and urine of pellagra patients. None of them developed pellagra. A diet of whole-grain cereals quickly cured the afflicted.

Miracle cures for scurvy, beriberi, and pellagra? No, the diseases were obviously related to diet; today it is well known that these diseases are the result of deficiencies in specific dietary materials called **vitamins.**

Vitamins, the miracle workers in deficiency diseases, are molecules that must be acquired from food because they cannot be manufactured by the body. A glance at the side panel of a cereal package (page 58) indicates that we require these materials in very small quantities, what we might call catalytic amounts. Do vitamins play a role as catalysts? Yes, but in a special way. Vitamins are misnamed because they are not "vital amines" as was once thought, but represent a diverse group of chemical compounds. However, most vitamins have a similar function: within the body they are converted into substances known as **coenzymes,** which are esential participants in a number of enzyme-catalyzed reactions. Not all enzyme reactions involve coenzymes, but in those that do, the characteristics of vitamin deficiency are produced by the absence of required coenzymes.

How do enzymes and coenzymes differ? Coenzymes are not proteins, they are of much smaller molecular size, and they do not ordinarily lose their normal properties and activity when subjected to treatments which inactivate (denature) most proteins. How do coenzymes work? They may act as

FIGURE 3–21 The role of coenzymes. (a) Coenzyme acts as an adapter, permitting substrate to attach to the enzyme. (b) Coenzyme binds to enzyme. (c) Enzyme-substrate complex is formed. (d) Release of product. Enzyme and coenzyme are now free to begin the cycle anew with additional substrate.

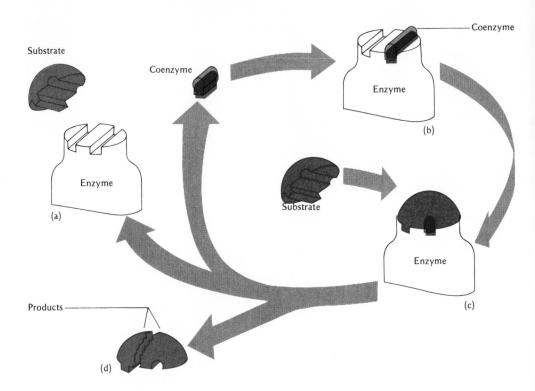

adapter molecules, facilitating binding of enzyme and substrate or removing one of the products of the chemical reaction, thus making the reaction tend to proceed in one direction only.[2] Like enzymes, coenzymes are not consumed in the reaction and are effective in small quantities. However, unlike enzymes, they are generally not as specific with respect to substrate. The relationship of coenzyme and enzyme to catalytic function is illustrated in Figure 3–21.

In the treatment of disease considerable gains have been made from the simple recognition that coenzymes function in a wide variety of enzyme-catalyzed reactions (Box 3D). As we have observed, enzyme function can be inhibited or enzymes can be poisoned by substances that resemble the natural substrate (Figure 3–20); this type

of inhibition is quite specific, since enzymes themselves ordinarily act in restricted catalytic capacities. On the other hand, a coenzyme inhibitor causes a more generalized inhibition or poisioning because it affects all enzymes requiring that coenzyme. For example, folic acid is a vitamin and coenzyme required by all our cells for the synthesis of nuclear materials. A deficiency of folic acid prevents the operation of enzymes involved in nuclear synthetic reactions, and eventually cell growth and division are inhibited. Certain drugs (such as aminopterin) structurally resemble folic acid, but cannot serve as the coenzyme; they are called folic acid analogs. When cancer patients, particularly those with leukemia, are treated with such drugs, there is remission of the disease. The remission is due to the nature of the greedy cancer cell, which avidly takes up the drug; the drug inhibits synthesis of nuclear materials and causes destruction of

---

[2] Refer to Appendix A for reasons for this.

---

### BOX 3D  Beneficial poison: sulfanilamide

The vitamin *p*-aminobenzoic acid (PABA) is required by many bacteria for the synthesis of the coenzyme folic acid. Folic acid is a coenzyme that is required by all organisms, including ourselves. Unlike bacteria we cannot take PABA and make folic acid; we require a supply of preformed folic acid and obtain it from our diet. It may be a matter of semantics, but for bacteria PABA is a vitamin, and for us folic acid is a vitamin.

Since bacteria require PABA, anything that will interfere with its utilization will ultimately prevent the manufacture of the critical coenzyme folic acid. Sulfanilamide, a sulfa drug discovered in the 1930s, was found to be effective in controlling bacterial growth; it was especially valuable in the treatment of pneumonia. Why does sulfanilamide kill bacteria but not humans? The answer lies in the similarity of structure of PABA and sulfanilamide (Figure 3–22). When bacteria are presented with the sulfa drug, they are "fooled" into incorporating this material into their folic acid, but this sulfa-bearing folic acid molecule is completely functionless. Enzyme reactions in the bacterial cell requiring folic acid cannot be carried out, and so the bacteria die. Since we do not manufacture folic acid from PABA there is little chance that the cells of our body will utilize the sulfa drug.

FIGURE 3–22  The structure of PABA and sulfanilamide.

---

the cancer cells. Aminopterin also affects the requirements of normal cells for folic acid, but to a much lower degree, since normal cells divide at a much slower rate. Hence, adequate precautions must be taken not to overdose the patient; the effectiveness of drug treatment depends on the delicate balance between the administered dose and the requirement of the cancer cells for folic acid.

Vitamins (especially the water soluble ones such as B– vitamins and vitamin C) must be supplied regularly in the diet because the body cells cannot manufacture these key materials, and they are broken down and excreted during cell metabolism. This means that although vitamins are required in very small amounts, any deficiency in the diet can cause a disruption in cellular function and the symptoms of disease. If the diet is well balanced, there is no need for vitamin supplements, but if the diet is poorly balanced, then vitamin supplements may be helpful. Vitamin pills are relatively expensive, and the paradox is that "those who need vitamin pills can't afford them, and those who can afford them don't need them."[3] The best advice on vitamin pills is, buy them if you can afford them, but if your diet is balanced and varied you can save your money.

### Minerals

We are conscious that **minerals** in the soil are necessary for good plant growth, and we assure healthy plants by supplementing garden soil with iron, phosphorus, and magnesium. We may not yellow like the leaves of a plant when suffering from a lack of iron or magnesium, but we certainly do show some ill effects from deficiencies of mineral elements. The cereal packet (page 58) indicates that the cereal supplies certain amounts of trace elements—magnesium, cobalt, iron, manganese, zinc, and copper.

The minerals we obtain in our food are not degraded by digestive juices, but are simply freed from their complex associations with food components and absorbed across the intestinal wall to enter the bloodstream. Unlike carbohydrates, fats, and proteins, minerals supply no energy, but they play important roles in the structure of the body, and in trace quantities they perform essential metabolic functions. For example, calcium and phosphorus are major structural components of bones and teeth, and iodine is necessary for the synthesis of thyroid hormone. Some minerals function as part of the prosthetic group of conjugated proteins. For example, iron is a part of the prosthetic group (heme) of both blood hemoglobin and the cytochrome enzymes. Minerals may also function much like coenzymes in assisting the enzyme to bind its substrate.

---

[3] Quoted in Garrett Hardin, *Biology: Its Principles and Implications*, 2nd ed., San Francisco, Freeman, 1966, p. 494.

## 3–7 NUCLEIC ACIDS: INFORMATIONAL MOLECULES

Like proteins, **nucleic acids** are generally large molecules. They have two principal functions in the cell. First, they are the materials that record the hereditary information that every living thing carries with it; second, they translate this information so that they can direct the cell's activities. The latter function is mediated through their direction of the synthesis of proteins, particularly proteins with an enzymatic function. We shall discuss the structure and function of these very important molecules at greater length in Chapters 6 and 7.

## SUMMARY

**1.** The organic molecules that make up living things fall into five major categories: carbohydrates, fats or lipids, proteins, vitamins, and nucleic acids.

**2.** *Carbohydrates* (sugars and starches) have the basic composition $(CH_2O)_n$. They are the primary source of cellular energy.

**3.** Polymerization of carbohydrate units into larger storage molecules prevents them from leaving the cell, where they can later be degraded and used as needed. Monosaccharides contain from 3 to 10 carbon atoms. The commonest are six-carbon, hexose sugars, with the formula $(CH_2O)_6$ or $C_6H_{12}O_6$. Structural hexose isomers include glucose (dextrose), fructose, and galactose. Of these, glucose is the most common in cells, and its level in the blood is rigidly controlled.

**4.** Glucose occurs only in the right-handed or D-form (stereoisomer) in living things and is known as dextrose. (Proteins in living things contain only the left-handed or L-isomer of amino acids.)

**5.** Two monosaccharide units bonded together form a double sugar, or disaccharide. Disaccharides are formed by condensation reactions with the loss of a water molecule. Conversely, they can be broken apart during digestion with the addition of a water molecule, a process called hydrolysis. Common disaccharides are table sugar, or sucrose (glucose + fructose), milk sugar, or lactose (glucose + galactose), and malt sugar, or maltose (glucose + glucose).

**6.** Long chains of sugar molecules linked by condensation reactions are called polysaccharides or multiple sugars. Starch, glycogen, and cellulose are formed from long chains of glucose molecules. Polysaccharides are usually insoluble in water and are important storage and structural components of cells.

**7.** *Lipids* include fats and steroids; insoluble in water but soluble in organic solvents, they are important fuels, storage materials, and components of membranes and of hormones.

**8.** Like carbohydrates, fats contain CHO, but the ratio of hydrogen to oxygen is greater than 2:1. Thus fats contain more hydrogen than carbohydrates, which permits a greater degree of oxidation by removal of hydrogen; therefore fats provide about twice as much energy as the same amount of carbohydrate.

**9.** True fats are composed of an alcohol (usually glycerol) and fatty acids:

Alcohol    +    Fatty acid
(usually glycerol)    (hydrocarbon chain + acidic carboxyl group)

condensation

$\longrightarrow H_2O$

$$H-\overset{|}{\underset{|}{C}}-O-\overset{O}{\overset{||}{C}}-\text{hydrocarbon chain}$$

ester linkage

The link between the alcohol and fatty acid is called an ester linkage.

**10.** The ester linkage of glycerol to fatty acid, each with its long hydrocarbon chain and carboxyl group, can occur at three places because there are three hydroxyl groups in glycerol.

**11.** Digestion of fats is by hydrolysis with the help of the enzyme lipase.

**12.** Saturated fats are solid at room temperature; all the carbons in their hydrocarbon chains are filled with hydrogens. Unsaturated fats contain less hydrogen and are not solid at room temperature.

**13.** Phospholipids contain a phosphorus and nitrogen group in place of one hydrocarbon chain, which polarizes the molecule. Phospholipids are important constituents of membranes.

**14.** Steroids consist of four fused carbon rings and are important constituents of hormones, membranes, and cholesterol. Cholesterol causes atherosclerosis when deposited on arterial walls in combination with fatty acids from fats. A diet high in saturated fats appears to speed this process.

**15.** *Proteins* contain C, H, and O plus nitrogen. They are built of amino acids, whose formula is:

$$NH_2-\overset{R}{\underset{H}{\overset{|}{\underset{|}{C}}}}-COOH$$

The R group is variable. Only 20 kinds of amino acids in nature form polypeptide chains and proteins by condensation reactions:

$$H_2N-\overset{R}{\underset{H}{\overset{|}{\underset{|}{C}}}}-COOH \quad + \quad H_2N-\overset{R}{\underset{H}{\overset{|}{\underset{|}{C}}}}-COOH$$

$$\searrow H_2O$$

$$N_2H-\overset{R}{\underset{H}{\overset{|}{\underset{|}{C}}}}- CONH -\overset{R}{\underset{H}{\overset{|}{\underset{|}{C}}}}-COOH$$

peptide bond

**16.** Peptides consist of up to 50 amino acids joined together, and more than 50 amino acids joined together make a protein.

**17.** Primary structure of a protein is the polypeptide chain.

Secondary structure is the helical coiling

(alpha helix) because of H-bond formation.

Tertiary structure is the twisting of the helically coiled chain into globular form by means of various interactions and bondings.

**18.** Denaturation (coagulation) is the uncoiling of the tertiary or secondary structure and breaking of various bonds. It may be caused by heat, excess acidity, chemical reagents, radiation, etc, and it may be reversible.

**19.** Subsidiary bonds such as sulfur-sulfur links between molecules of the R group stabilize proteins and can produce changes in protein geometry.

**20.** Some molecules exist in two geometric forms, called stereoisomers, which are mirror images of each other. In living things, carbohydrates are all right-handed (D-form) and amino acids are all left-handed (L-form).

**21.** Conjugated proteins have a nonprotein prosthetic group attached and include nucleoproteins, glycoproteins, lipoproteins, and metal-containing proteins.

**22.** All enzymes are proteins and are cellular organic catalysts. Enzymes combine with their substrates, making it possible for substrate and reactant to share electrons. Following the reaction, the enzyme is released. Enzymes are reaction-specific, unchanged by the reactions they catalyze, and effective in minute quantitites. Enzymes can be poisoned by mimics called analogs or antimetabolites.

**23.** *Vitamins,* components of coenzymes, are needed for many enzyme-catalyzed reactions. The body cells cannot manufacture vitamins, and so they must be supplied in the diet. Deficiency of particular vitamins causes various diseases related to the lack of the vitamin coenzyme.

**24.** Some minerals obtained in the diet are important in structural components of the body; others function as part of the prosthetic group of conjugated proteins or assist in binding a substrate to its enzyme.

**25.** *Nucleic acids* record hereditary information and translate it to direct the cell's functions.

## KEY WORDS

| | | | |
|---|---|---|---|
| carbohydrates | lactose | oils | denatured |
| polymerized | maltose | hydrogenation | prosthetic groups |
| monosaccharides | condensation | phospholipids | conjugated proteins |
| trioses | stereoisomers | steroids | disulfide bridges |
| tetroses | polysaccharides | cholesterol | activation energy |
| pentoses | starch | amino acids | catalyst |
| hexoses | glycogen | R group | enzymes |
| glucose | cellulose | species specificity | substrate |
| dextrose | lipids | peptide bond | active site |
| fructose | fats | polypeptide chain | poisoned |
| galactose | oxidation | protein | analog |
| structural isomers | glycerol | primary structure | antimetabolite |
| disaccharide | fatty acid | alpha helix | vitamins |
| sucrose | ester linkage | secondary structure | coenzymes |
| hydrolysis | saturated fats | tertiary structure | minerals |
| | unsaturated fats | coagulated | nucleic acids |

## TOPICS FOR REVIEW AND DISCUSSION

1. How is the structure of a protein related to its function?

2. What is denaturation?

3. Compare and contrast the structure of carbohydrates with that of fats.

4. Explain the role of condensation reactions in the formation of a polysaccharide.

5. What is the functional significance of hydrolysis reactions to living organisms?

6. What is activation energy and how does it relate to enzyme function?

7. Which amino acid stereoisomer is commonly found in living systems? Why don't both stereoisomers occur in living organisms?

8. Why is it that carbohydrates tend not to be species-specific whereas proteins generally are?

9. What is the relationship of vitamins to coenzymes?

10. By what mechanism(s) do enzymes work?

11. What is the difference between saturated and unsaturated fats? Of what importance is this to human health?

12. Discuss the use of molecular building blocks in living systems.

## YOUR USE OF ENERGY FOR ONE DAY*

| Activity | Hours spent in activity | Energy used (Calories per pound per hour) | Total Calories used per pound (Calories × hours) |
|---|---|---|---|
| Asleep | 8 | 0.4 | 3.2 |
| Lying still, awake | 1 | 0.5 | 0.5 |
| Dressing and undressing | 1 | 0.9 | 0.9 |
| Sitting in class, eating, studying, talking | 8 | 0.7 | 5.6 |
| Walking | 1 | 1.5 | 1.5 |
| Standing | 1 | 0.8 | 0.8 |
| Driving a car | 1 | 1.0 | 1.0 |
| Running | ½ | 4.0 | 2.0 |
| Playing ping-pong | ½ | 2.7 | 1.3 |
| Writing | 2 | 0.7 | 1.4 |
| TOTAL | 24 | — | 18.2 |

**Total Calories used per pound**      18.2
**Weight in pounds**      × 115.0
**Total Calories expended for the day**      2,093.0

* Adapted from Helen S. Mitchell *et al.*, *Cooper's Nutrition in Health and Disease*, 15th ed., Philadelphia, J. P. Lippincott, 1968. Used by permission of the publisher.

# Harvest of Chemical Energy: Cellular Respiration

## 4–1 WHAT IS ENERGY?

The human heart is about the size of a clenched fist. In a life span of 70 years it beats 2.5 billion times and pumps 40 million gallons of blood. The heart is indispensable to one's very being, for in the pumping of blood, oxygen and food are carried to every cell of the body, and by the return circuit of the bloodstream, cellular wastes and carbon dioxide are removed. The heart, we humans, and indeed all our cells are composed of matter and, as such, occupy space and have both weight and density. **Matter** is something we can perceive through our senses—we can feel it and see it. However, it takes more than matter to constitute a living cell, an organ such as the beating heart, or an entire organism like one's self. What makes matter in the living system go, or maintain itself, is energy. The human heart has an energy demand, and this varies with its work load. For example, no mathematics, chemistry, or physics is required to recognize that the heart of an obese individual requires more energy to operate effectively than that of a person of more normal girth. The same size heart has to pump blood a greater distance in the overweight individual; it has been estimated that for every pound of fat there are three miles of blood vessels, and to pump blood over these distances, the heart needs more energy in a person with more pounds of fat. It is not profitable to be overweight. Similarly, the energy requirements of all our cells depend directly on their work load. Energy is quite different from matter: en-

ergy has no mass, occupies no space, has no density; yet we know it exists. We refer to energy frequently when we say, "I wish I had his energy," or, "Atomic energy has changed the course of modern history." What is this thing called energy?

**Energy** can be measured by the effects it produces on matter and is defined as the capacity to do work. **Work** can be thought of as any process requiring energy. You can see that this kind of circular reasoning does not get us very far, but it does indicate that there is a close relationship between work and energy. The greater the amount of energy available, the greater the amount of work that can be performed; the more matter to be moved, for example, the greater the energy required to move it.

Energy is considered to exist in two states: potential and kinetic. **Potential energy** is stored or inactive energy; the stored energy confers the capacity for work, but no work is actually being done. **Kinetic energy,** on the other hand, is energy in action—the energy used during the performance of work. Let us consider an example. If your automobile can go 15 miles per gallon of gasoline, we can say that the potential energy of 1 gallon of gasoline for your car is 15 miles of travel, and when the car is actually moving, the energy contained in the fuel is being released and is in a kinetic state.

Energy can take a variety of forms: potential energy may be chemical, electrical, or atomic; kinetic energy may be in the form of motion, light, or heat. The forms of energy are interchangeable; for example,

electrical energy can be converted into light and heat (as when electricity flows through the tungsten filament in a light bulb), and light can be changed into electrical energy (as occurs in an exposure meter). Just as there are different forms of energy, so, too, there are different kinds of work: mechanical, chemical, osmotic, and electrical. The forms of energy and their uses are everyday occurrences. Let us briefly examine one of these: the starting of the automobile engine. When you activate the starter, the stored chemical energy in the battery is converted into electrical energy, which produces a spark at the spark plugs; this ignites the gasoline vapors, and by the process of combustion (burning) the gasoline's potential chemical energy is released as kinetic energy in the form of heat, light, and an expanding gas. (Heat, you may recall, is simply the random motion of molecules.) The kinetic energy of the expanding gas moves the pistons, producing mechanical work, and the car moves.

What has energy to do with life processes? As you sit and read these words, your cells are in ceaseless activity. All living cells depend on the release and use of energy for the maintenance of the living state. Living systems are highly organized, and to maintain this order, energy must be fed into the system. When a living cell can no longer obtain, release, and use energy, it is dead. However, no machine or living system can produce energy out of nothing; it can only change energy from one form to another. Automobile engines obtain energy and produce work from fuels such as gasoline or diesel oil. Living machines—cells—obtain, release, and use energy for growth, maintenance, and repair from the energy-rich molecules that constitute their food. Like the automobile engine, cells are transducers of chemical energy and perform work, but as we shall see, there are significant differences between cells and gasoline engines as energy-exchange systems.

In both living and nonliving things, transformations of energy are governed by a number of constant factors, which we formalize by stating them as laws. The principal laws dealing with energy conversions are called the **laws of thermodynamics** ("heat-energetic" laws). The First Law, often called the Law of Conservation of Energy, states that when energy goes from one form to another no energy is gained or lost. In other words, the total energy of the universe remains constant: energy does not perish, it is transformed. The Second Law of Thermodynamics states that during an energy transformation the amount of usable energy is reduced and some of the energy is not available to do work. Succintly stated, **entropy**[1] (the tendency toward randomness and disorder in the universe) increases.

Let us consider some examples. If we put a fixed amount of fuel into a gasoline engine, we obtain a certain amount of mechanical work, but a fraction of the fuel energy is lost to the surroundings in the form of heat. Proof of this is easily obtained by holding your hand over a running engine. By saying energy is lost, we do not mean the energy disappears, but only that it is unable to produce work. The total available energy of the gasoline liberated by combustion is the sum of the work of the pistons of the engine plus the heat that is unavailable to that system for work. (This satisfies the First Law of Thermodynamics.) The conversion of one form of energy into another is never 100% efficient, and some of the

---

[1] Entropy is a randomized state of energy that is unavailable to do work.

FIGURE 4–1 Model of an open thermodynamic system. The "organized" level at A can be maintained only if the loss by outflow is matched by the gain through inflow. If the outflow exceeds the inflow, the level drops below the steady state and approaches the "disorganized" level at B; the system has lost its order.

energy is liberated in a useless form. (This satisfies the Second Law of Thermodynamics.)

Now let us consider the living machine. A living cell is an open thermodynamic system, that is, it must continually be supplied with energy in order to maintain itself. When the energy supply ceases, the cell ceases to work; it becomes disorganized, and death ensues. A convenient way of looking at the energy relationships in the living system is illustrated in Figure 4–1. The organized state of the living cell is represented by level A; to maintain this level at a steady state, energy must constantly be

fed in, because the system is open and there is a certain loss that must be compensated. The level will decline and the system will approach level B (entropy will increase) if energy is not brought into the system. The continual energy loss from the living, open thermodynamic system is represented predominantly by heat, which is dissipated and unavailable for work to maintain the organized state. Energy received in the form of food cannot be utilized with 100% efficiency for work, and at every energy transformation there is a reduction in the usable energy of the system—usually in the form of heat.

We have said that carbohydrate in the form of glucose is one of the fuels of the living cell. How does the cell convert glucose into energy? When the fuel of an automobile engine is burned, energy is liberated in a single, quick burst. If we took 0.5 lb of glucose, burned it, and measured the heat released, we would obtain about 700 Calories. (A **Calorie** is a unit of measure of heat. It is the amount of heat necessary to raise the temperature of 1 kg of water 1 C°—from 14.5° to 15.5°C.)[2] In a living system that burned glucose and liberated 700 Calories in a single burst, there would result a sharp rise in temperature owing to the sudden release of heat. If a person ate 0.5 lb of glucose and all the energy was liberated in a single burst, the body temperature would rise about 10 C°, from 37° to 47°C. From what you already know about proteins and cells, it is obvious that such a temperature rise would coagulate most proteins. In effect, the single-step liberation of heat energy from food in a human would mean self-incineration with every meal.

Unlike heat engines, cells must obtain their energy from the chemicals that are their fuel so that large bursts of heat do not occur. The mechanism of trapping energy and storing it involves breaking the energy-rich chemical bonds of molecules; a portion of the energy obtained from these molecules is trapped in the chemical bonds of other molecules. Energy is thus redistributed among reacting molecules rather than liberated all at once in a free form. The energy obtained in this way is called **bond**

---

[2] A **calorie** (c) is the amount of heat required to raise the temperature of 1 g of water 1 C°; this unit is so small that most nutritionists prefer to use the larger calorie, written **Calorie** (capital C), which is a kilocalorie, or 1,000 times greater than the small calorie. We shall use Calorie, the common way of writing kilocalorie, and drop the *kilo.* A Calorie is roughly equivalent to the work available in 0.10 horsepower; put another way, 100 Calories are needed to keep a 100-W light bulb burning for 1 hour.

**energy,** for obvious reasons, and it is obtained in stepwise fashion, that is, during a sequence of chemical reactions. The remainder, unavailable for cellular work, is dissipated into the environment as almost imperceptible amounts of heat. Heat is liberated in step with the chemical reactions, and in this way the release of large amounts of heat and energy at one time is avoided and waste is minimized.

## 4–2 ENERGY CURRENCY: ATP

The fires of life burn at a low heat. The fuels of the living cell are the chemicals that make up its food, and energy is obtained by breaking the bonds of these various chemicals. The released energy is trapped and stored in other chemicals in the cell and can be released again when needed. What are these chemicals? How does the cell make all these energy conversions?

The oxidation of carbohydrates and other energy-rich compounds (such as lipids and proteins) provides the main source of energy for many cells and organisms. **Oxidation** is a process by which oxygen is added to a molecule or hydrogens and electrons are removed. In spite of the name, therefore, oxygen is not always necessary for an oxidative reaction to take place. Since hydrogens may be removed from molecules during an oxidative reaction, these reactions are sometimes called **dehydrogenations.** When oxygen is added to a substance, it must be obtained from somewhere, and when hydrogens or electrons are removed, they have to go someplace. Thus, for every oxidation reaction there must be a corresponding reduction reaction. **Reduction** in the chemical sense does not mean a diminution in size, but indicates the removal of oxygen or the addition of hydrogens or electrons to a substance. (Remember the reducing atmosphere of the primitive earth and the important role it played in the formation of organic compounds?) The following equation illustrates the general form

of an oxidation-reduction reaction: the substance X is being oxidized and Y is being reduced; X is the reductant (it supplies the hydrogens) and Y is the oxidant (it receives the electrons or hydrogens):

| electron donor | electron acceptor | | oxidized substance | reduced substance | |
|---|---|---|---|---|---|
| $XH_2$ | $+ \quad Y$ | $\rightleftharpoons$ | $X$ | $+ \quad YH_2$ | $+$ energy |
| energy rich | energy poor | | energy lost | energy gained | |

In the human body carbohydrate serves as fuel and is oxidized to carbon dioxide and water; during the process energy is liberated. The simplified formula for this reaction is:

| electron donor | electron acceptor | | | |
|---|---|---|---|---|
| $CH_2O +$ | $O_2$ | $\rightarrow$ | $CO_2 \quad + \quad H_2O$ | $+$ energy |
| carbohydrate | oxygen | | carbon dioxide $\quad$ water | |

The carbohydrate ($CH_2O$) corresponds to the $XH_2$ molecule (plus an O), and the molecular oxygen corresponds to the $Y$; the carbohydrate becomes oxidized, not by a loss or gain of oxygen but by a loss of hydrogens. The hydrogens derived from the carbohydrate are passed to the molecule of oxygen and chemically reduce the latter, and a molecule of water is formed. The carbohydrate without its hydrogens yields the molecule carbon dioxide.

The significant feature of this oxidation-reduction shuttle system is that when an electron (or a hydrogen) flows from a reducing system to an oxidizing system, energy is liberated. As electrons are transferred, they fall from a higher energy state to a lower one. In a storage battery or a dry cell, the electrons flow from one electrode to the other when the electrodes are connected by a wire, and energy is produced in the form of electricity; this energy can be made to produce heat or light or to perform work (Figure 4–2). In much the same manner, the oxidation of foodstuffs liberates energy; such energy is trapped and conserved in the form of a high-energy

FIGURE 4–2  The dry-cell battery. Chemical energy is transformed into heat and light.

FIGURE 4–3  ATP: its role in the cell can be likened to that of a storage battery.

phosphate compound called **adenosine triphosphate (ATP)**[3] and can later be released for work. ATP can be likened to the "charged" form of the storage battery with energy available for cellular work (Figure 4–3). Just as a battery runs down and becomes discharged when the chemicals in the electrodes no longer donate electrons, so, too, there is a "discharged" form of ATP called **adenosine diphosphate (ADP).** The molecule of ATP has three phosphate groups; ADP has only two. The link between the second and third phosphates of ATP releases a great deal of energy when it is broken and is sometimes spoken of as a **high-energy bond** (Figure 4–4). It is of primary importance in conserving the energy that is released by oxidation of foodstuffs. When phosphate and energy are added to ADP, it becomes ATP and is thus "energized." The ATP↔ADP reaction shuttles energy back and forth between energy-requiring and energy-yielding reactions of the cell; ADP is charged to ATP during the oxidation of foodstuffs, and ATP is discharged to ADP during the performance of cellular work (Figure 4–4).

Most energy-dependent reactions within the cell are tied to ATP. What is the advantage of this? A similar question is, What is the advantage of money or currency? Our society could, as do many primitive societies, exist perfectly well on a barter system. The payment for goods and services could easily be made by other goods and services. If, for example, you wanted to purchase a loaf of bread and a pound of meat, you could do a chore as payment. If you didn't have the time to do the work, you could pay off the debt by giving the shopkeeper a gallon of oil or some other item. However, if the shopkeeper had no desire for the oil, you could not pay for the bread and meat.

---

[3] Other energy-rich compounds in the cell also trap energy (for example, $NADPH_2$, $NADH_2$, GTP, and CoA); however, we shall omit detailed consideration of these and focus attention primarily on ATP.

Clearly, if there were some universally exchangeable and therefore universally desirable object, transactions could be carried out more conveniently and efficiently. In commerce, the universally exchangeable material is money; in the cell, the currency is ATP. Energy is liberated from ATP as needed, and in this way the cell can conveniently and efficiently pay for most of its work. By having such a common currency for energy transactions, considerable flexibility of energy supply is attained. For example, the body can satisfy its energy requirements by the oxidation of carbohydrates, proteins, and fats (and on occasion even by peculiar nutrients such as alcohol); all these can provide energy for cellular work. The living machine is thus capable of using a variety of fuels, roughly equivalent to an automobile engine that could run on oil, wood, gasoline, coal, or gas. The automobile engine lacks such versatility, but living organisms have it; this is largely achieved because ATP is the single mediator between the energy suppliers and the energy users. The food or fuel does not directly drive the energy-requiring processes of the cell; this is handled by ATP.

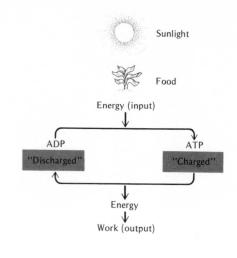

## 4–3  CHEMICAL ENERGY HARVEST

In what manner do the cells of our bodies obtain their energy? How is the harvest of energy accomplished? We have indicated that we are dependent upon a supply of food (carbohydrates, lipids, proteins) as a source of energy. These are our fuels; however, we cannot manufacture these for ourselves and ordinarily require other organisms to make them for us. We consume and then digest (break down) these organisms (plants and animals) or their products; some of the digested materials are then stored within our bodies as food reserves. (The process of digestion is the subject of Chapter 12.) Foodstuffs are rich in potential energy, and our cells release this energy and use it for growth, maintenance, reproduction, and other life functions.

How do living things release the potential energy of digested materials? In human beings, as in most organisms, energy is released from the various digested foodstuffs by oxidation. Although many substances may be oxidized to yield energy, we shall confine our discussion to glucose,

FIGURE 4–4 The ATP molecule. The terminal phosphate bonds are energy-rich. When these bonds are broken, more calories are released than if other bonds in the molecule were broken.

a material that is our prime source of energy.

The breakdown of glucose in the living cells of the body is carried out by a complex series of chemical reactions, each catalyzed by a specific enzyme. The early sequence of steps in the oxidation of glucose is completely independent of oxygen and is called **anaerobic respiration.** Some organisms can carry out the entire sequence without oxygen; such organisms can, therefore, live in the absence of oxygen and are called **anaerobes** (*an*—without; *aero*—air; Gk.). The tetanus bacterium and yeast are examples of anaerobes. However, we and many other organisms cannot complete the extraction of energy from foodstuffs without oxygen; in such organisms the sequence of reactions that constitutes anaerobic respiration is followed by a sequence of reactions which depends on the availability of molecular oxygen. The sequence is called **aerobic respiration,** and organisms like ourselves in whom aerobic respiration is the rule are called **aerobes.** Oxygen is involved only in the final steps of aerobic respiration, but all the preceding steps indirectly depend on it because they could continue for only a short time if oxygen were not available to participate in the terminal reactions of the process. We obtain the oxygen used by our cells in aerobic respiration by breathing, and we can live for only a short time when

breathing stops; without oxygen, too little ATP is generated, the processes in our cells become disorganized, and the cells are damaged beyond repair. In many parts of the body the cells can be restored to normal function if oxygen should become available before total death has occurred, but after only 2 minutes without oxygen, irreparable brain damage occurs. This is because brain cells require a rich supply of ATP, which comes principally from glucose via aerobic respiration.

### 4–4 THE ENERGY CASCADE

Before we examine the sequence of events that occurs within our cells during anaerobic and aerobic respiration, let us first understand what can be called the **energy cascade.** A flowing river has a great deal of kinetic energy that can be useful if some way can be found to harness it. If the river is dammed to prevent it from flowing, a reservoir is created and the river's energy is converted into potential energy. This energy can be harvested by allowing the water to spill over the dam and flow downhill, and by making it do useful work on the way, such as driving waterwheels or electrical generators. To get the energy out of the reservoir, the sluice gate of the dam must be opened; this requires energy (a kind of pump priming,

to get things going), and then during the water's fall, energy and work are obtained. The amount of energy obtained from this system depends on the initial volume of the reservoir, the quantity of water permitted to flow out of the dam, and the vertical distance traveled by the water. Energy for work can no longer be obtained when the water has completed its downhill run and reached the lowest level. Allowing the water to flow downhill in a single sharply declining slope supplies a large, but unmanageable, spurt of energy. Greater control is achieved if a series of sluice gates or dams is included, creating a number of cataracts. At each cataract, a waterwheel or electrical generator is positioned. The opening and closing of the sluice gates releases energy in manageable steps rather than in a single big rush (Figure 4–5).

This cascade of water, producing energy in stepwise fashion, provides us with a simple model somewhat analogous to the release of energy in the cell. The cellular regulators (gatekeepers) of energy are specific proteins called enzymes. In the living cell, molecules that are rich in potential energy are activated by means of enzymes to get them over the barrier of chemical reactivity and then degraded in stepwise fashion to release small, discrete amounts of energy. Just as it is impossible to convert

FIGURE 4–5 The energy cascade. Water in the reservoir is allowed to leave and flow downhill. At certain places there are sluice gates and waterwheels. The flowing water can move the wheels to produce mechanical work, and the rate of flow is controlled by opening or closing the sluice gates.

all the kinetic energy of the flowing water into mechanical work, since some is lost through friction, so there is some wasted energy in the conversions that take place in the cell. The process of energy conversion is always less than 100% efficient (the Second Law of Thermodynamics).

## 4–5 GETTING ALONG WITHOUT OXYGEN

When your cells are working, glucose, serving as the fuel for this work, is rapidly consumed. The degradation of energy-rich glucose yields energy, and the process may or may not involve oxygen. The breakdown of glucose and the removal of hydrogens occur in stepwise fashion, and the energy released is trapped in the form of ATP. If oxygen is not present, the partial oxidation of glucose is by anaerobic respiration, as follows.

Glucose, a 6-carbon compound, is broken down to 2 molecules of **pyruvic acid,** a 3-carbon compound, by 11 enzymatic steps (Figure 4–6). Glucose is prepared initially for its molecular dismemberment by the attachment of phosphate groups, donated by ATP. This is significant, because the adding of phosphate (**phosphorylation**) to glucose converts it from a substance that can leave the cell to one that cannot pass across the plasma membrane. Now the glucose molecule is trapped inside the cell, where cytoplasmic enzymes can alter its molecular architecture. The phosphorylation of glucose also boosts it to a higher energy level (activates it), and this renders it more reactive chemically: the sluice gates have been opened. Two molecules of ATP are used to activate the glucose initially, and during the following steps, there is the synthesis of 4 molecules of ATP; the net yield to the cell is 2 ATP molecules (Figure 4–6).[4]

During the degradation of glucose, hy-

[4] This value pertains only if pyruvic acid is subsequently converted to lactic acid or alcohol.

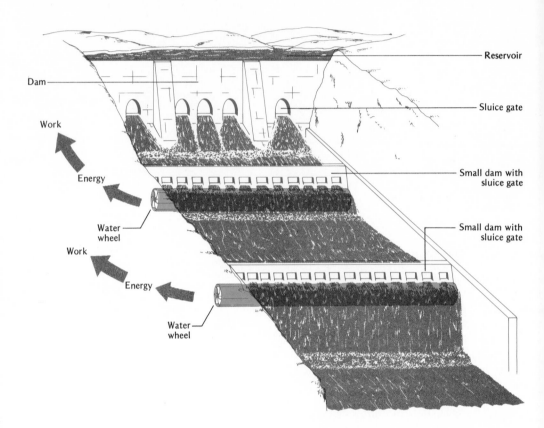

FIGURE 4–5 The energy cascade. Water in the reservoir is allowed to leave and flow downhill. At certain places there are sluice gates and waterwheels. The flowing water can move the wheels to produce mechanical work, and the rate of flow is controlled by opening or closing the sluice gates.

drogens and electrons are removed and transferred to an acceptor molecule, the coenzyme **NAD** (**n**icotinamide **a**denine **d**inucleotide).[5] Two molecules of $NADH_2$ are produced.

The end product of anaerobic respiration, the 3-carbon fragment known as pyruvic acid, is subsequently converted into lactic acid or ethyl alcohol and carbon dioxide, which can leave the cell (Box 4A).

[5] The coenzyme NAD is formed from the vitamin niacin; a deficiency of niacin results in a decrease in the amount of NAD, a slowing of anaerobic degradation of glucose, and production of the disease known as pellagra. The situation is analogous to the gatekeeper of the energy cascade not allowing water to exit and flow downhill; energy release is thus prevented.

## 4–6 ANAEROBIC RESPIRATION: COST ACCOUNTING

The efficiency of any machine is measured not by the rate at which the fuel is degraded, but by the amount of energy that is made available for work. A cell is not simply a machine for burning sugar, any more than an automobile is just a machine for burning gasoline. If breaking down fuel molecules into small size for disposal were the only object of combustion, it would be simpler and cheaper for cells to burn fuel by some other means. The object of breaking down a fuel is to get energy for work—in an automobile, to get the car moving; in the cell, to produce ATP for storage of energy and ultimately cellular work. The more efficient the automobile engine, the less fuel

FIGURE 4–6 A schematic representation of the anaerobic respiration of glucose.

**87**

**HARVEST OF CHEMICAL ENERGY:
CELLULAR RESPIRATION**

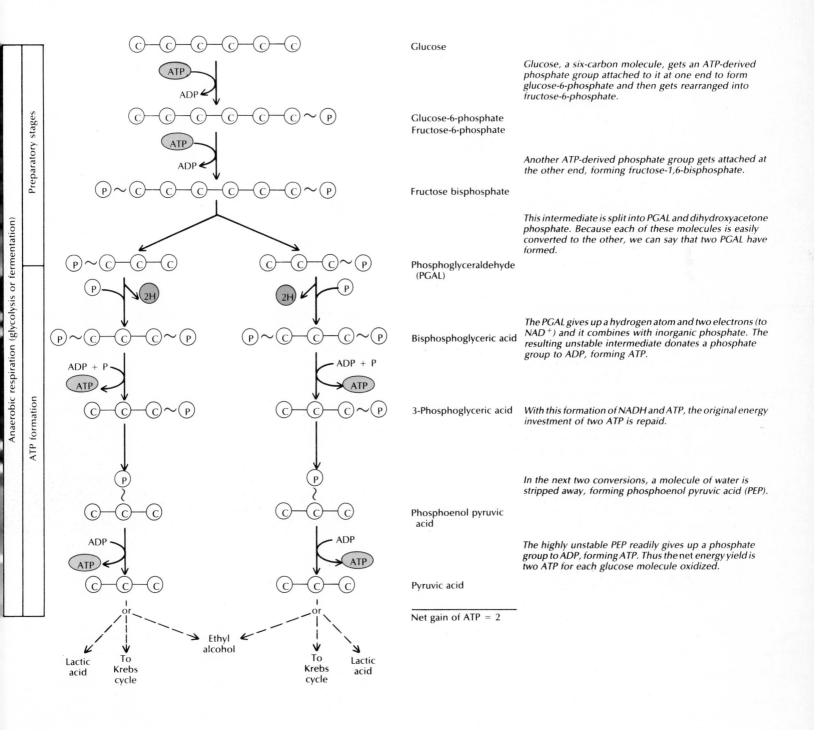

Glucose

*Glucose, a six-carbon molecule, gets an ATP-derived phosphate group attached to it at one end to form glucose-6-phosphate and then gets rearranged into fructose-6-phosphate.*

Glucose-6-phosphate
Fructose-6-phosphate

*Another ATP-derived phosphate group gets attached at the other end, forming fructose-1,6-bisphosphate.*

Fructose bisphosphate

*This intermediate is split into PGAL and dihydroxyacetone phosphate. Because each of these molecules is easily converted to the other, we can say that two PGAL have formed.*

Phosphoglyceraldehyde
(PGAL)

*The PGAL gives up a hydrogen atom and two electrons (to NAD⁺) and it combines with inorganic phosphate. The resulting unstable intermediate donates a phosphate group to ADP, forming ATP.*

Bisphosphoglyceric acid

*With this formation of NADH and ATP, the original energy investment of two ATP is repaid.*

3-Phosphoglyceric acid

*In the next two conversions, a molecule of water is stripped away, forming phosphoenol pyruvic acid (PEP).*

Phosphoenol pyruvic
acid

*The highly unstable PEP readily gives up a phosphate group to ADP, forming ATP. Thus the net energy yield is two ATP for each glucose molecule oxidized.*

Pyruvic acid

Net gain of ATP = 2

BOX 4A Beer, bread, and muscle:
molecular changes in pyruvic acid

Pyruvic acid plays a pivotal role in reactions that take place in such diverse occurences as muscular work, the manufacture of alcohol, and the baking of bread. The fact that the fermentation of sugars produces alcohol and carbon dioxide has been known for thousands of years, but the cause of the phenomenon was discovered only about a century ago. Under anaerobic conditions, the yeast cell utilizes glucose and performs enzymatic conversions similar to those we have discussed. The pyruvic acid is then further degraded to a 2-carbon compound, acetaldehyde, and eventually this forms ethyl alcohol plus carbon dioxide (Figure 4–7). The enzyme that carries out this split of pyruvic acid is called **carboxylase,** and it requires the coenzyme thiamine pyrophosphate, (or **TPP**), a derivative of vitamin $B_1$ (thiamine).

When our muscle cells are heavily exercised, they run out of oxygen and glycogen is utilized anaerobically. First, glycogen is converted into phosphorylated glucose molecules, and up to a point, the molecular dismemberment of glucose takes place in the same way as in yeast cells. The principal difference between the process in fatigued muscle and in yeast is the product formed: yeast produces alcohol and carbon dioxide, and muscle produces lactic acid. In both cases there is a reduction (acetaldehyde → ethyl alcohol; pyruvic acid → lactic acid) and the donor of hydrogens is reduced NAD ($NADH_2$) formed earlier during anaerobic respiration (Figure 4–8). This step makes the product of glucose degradation its own hydrogen acceptor, and at the same time NAD is regenerated for continued participation earlier in the sequence. In yeast, the process is called **fermentation,** and it is responsible for the production of alcoholic beverages such as beer; the carbon dioxide is used in the baking of bread (it causes the rising of the dough). In muscle the process is called **glycolysis,** because glycogen is the original fuel molecule. The products of glycolysis (lactic acid) and of fermentation (carbon dioxide and ethyl alcohol) leave the cell easily and become a part of the external cellular environment. A twist of enzymatic fate has determined that lactic acid rather than alcohol be poured into the blood when our muscles are exercised. Were our muscle enzymes slightly different, heavy physical effort might be both popular and intoxicating!

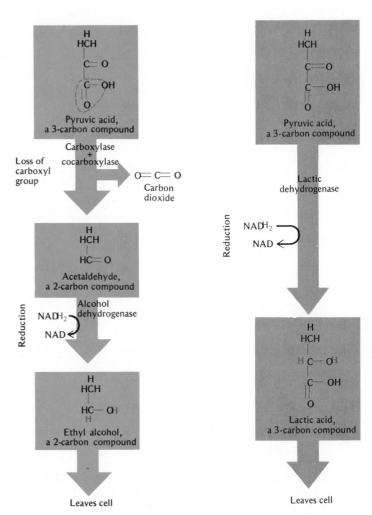

FIGURE 4–7 (left) The fermentation of sugar by yeast.

FIGURE 4–8 (right) Anaerobic respiration of pyruvic acid by muscle.

it consumes in moving the car from place to place; the more miles per gallon, the happier the automobile owner. Similarly, the more efficient the cell, the less fuel consumption required for its work load.

How efficient is the anaerobic degradation of glucose in providing a cell with energy in the form of ATP? To evaluate efficiency, it is necessary to do some simple arithmetic. The amount of energy potentially available to the cell from glucose can be estimated by completely burning the glucose in a device called a **bomb calorimeter** and measuring the caloric output. The calorie tables that you use to determine how much you should or should not eat have been worked out by using a bomb calorimeter or a similar device. If glucose is burned in this device, it is found that 1 **mole**[6] of glucose (180 g) yields approximately 700 Calories of energy. The burned glucose in the calorimeter ends up as carbon dioxide and water. When 1 mole of ATP is hydrolyzed to ADP, about 10 Calories is released. By anaerobic respiration of 1 mole of glucose, the cell obtains a net yield of 2 ATP, or approximately 20 Calories; the total available was 700 Calories, and so the cell obtains about 3% of the total energy available (20/700 × 100 = 3%). Looked at another way, the breakdown of 1 mole of glucose in anaerobic respiration yields 2 moles of lactic acid. A mole of lactic acid burned in a calorimeter yields approximately 325 Calories and produces carbon dioxide and water. The cell has potentially available to it 700 Calories per mole of glucose, and it produces lactic acid which has a caloric value of 650 Calories. Thus, when glucose is broken down to lactic acid, the amount of energy available (as determined by calorimetry) is 50 Calories (700 − 650). The cell has trapped 20 Calories in ATP and lost 30 Calories; it is about 40% efficient as an energy-trapping machine (20/50 × 100). By comparison, the modern steam-generating

---

[6] A mole is the molecular weight in grams.

plant and the automobile engine are only 25 to 30% efficient.

Let us now do a cost accounting of the degradation of glucose under anaerobic conditions. The energy-rich glucose may be thought of as a large denomination of currency, let us say a five-dollar bill. In order for the cell to pay for goods and services, that large bill must be exchanged for smaller change, of the order of 10 cents. The 10-cent pieces are used by the cell to pay all outstanding debts. The 10-cent piece is the only currency used; dollar bills or other amounts must be made up out of multiples of 10 cents. The commission for converting the large bill into small change is about 60 cents on the dollar. By financial standards it appears exorbitant, but for the cell it is the only means of operation. If 1 mole of glucose represents a 5-dollar bill, the cell only gets 20 cents' worth of usable currency from each 5 dollars' worth of glucose; it loses about 30 cents as a result of the exchange rate (as heat, which cannot be used for paying debts), and about 4 dollars and 50 cents is not converted into small change. It would appear that the cell using anaerobic respiration has let a great deal of money slip through its fingers by producing pyruvic acid, lactic acid, or ethyl alcohol.

The efficiency expert might say that this system of generating small change from larger currency is a highly inefficient way to run an economy. Why does the cell not dispense with all the enzyme reactions that make ATP from glucose and form ATP directly? As simple as this scheme sounds, it would mean that the cell would have to handle a lot more material in the form of ATP in order to gain an amount of energy equal to that contained in a molecule of glucose. It would be equivalent to the cell's obtaining all its fuel energy in the form of dimes instead of dollars. (Just imagine receiving your paycheck in dimes!) Glucose does not provide energy in an immediately available form, but it is compact, easy to transport, and quite convenient to handle. The ATP-generating system using energy-

rich molecules is, after all, quite economical and efficient for the cell.

## 4–7 GETTING ALONG WITH OXYGEN

During anaerobic respiration, pyruvic acid forms either alcohol (as in yeast cells) or lactic acid (as in fatigued muscle) (Box 4A), but when oxygen is plentiful, these products are not formed and pyruvic acid has another fate. As we have seen, this 3-carbon compound is still quite energy-rich, and it is apparent that a cell which loses such a molecule also loses a potential source of ATP. If a cell were to exist only on anaerobic respiration, then another molecule of glucose must be consumed for the cell to derive another 2 molecules of ATP. In discarding pyruvic acid or other related molecules (lactic acid, alcohol), the anaerobic cell is throwing away chemical potential energy; if the pyruvic acid could be further degraded, the cell could obtain additional amounts of energy without taking in any more glucose. This is what happens during aerobic respiration, and the pyruvic acid is broken down to carbon dioxide and water. The principal yield of energy to the cell occurs during this phase. Clearly, as the name aerobic implies the degradation of pyruvic acid involves oxygen.

During aerobic respiration, pyruvic acid is split to produce a 2-carbon fragment (called an **acetyl group**) and carbon dioxide (Figure 4–9). Simultaneously, the carbon dioxide passes out of the cell and the 2-carbon fragment is linked to a coenzyme called **coenzyme A,** producing a molecule called **acetyl coenzyme A** (Figure 4–9).

It is apparent that one third of the carbon atoms of the glucose have become carbon dioxide; the remaining two thirds are now in the form of the acetyl group of acetyl coenzyme A. The carbons of the acteyl group are oxidized to carbon dioxide, by a cyclic series of enzyme-catalyzed reactions called the **Krebs,** or **citric acid, cycle** (Figure 4–9).

When acetyl coenzyme A enters the Krebs

FIGURE 4–9 A schematic representation of the Krebs (citric acid) cycle. Each reaction is catalyzed by a separate enzyme.

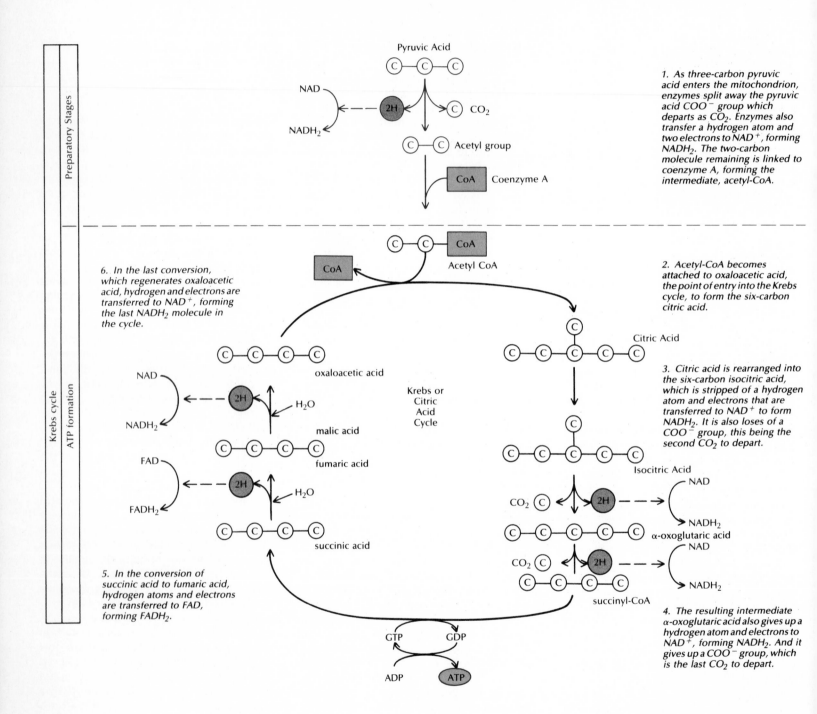

1. As three-carbon pyruvic acid enters the mitochondrion, enzymes split away the pyruvic acid $COO^-$ group which departs as $CO_2$. Enzymes also transfer a hydrogen atom and two electrons to $NAD^+$, forming $NADH_2$. The two-carbon molecule remaining is linked to coenzyme A, forming the intermediate, acetyl-CoA.

6. In the last conversion, which regenerates oxaloacetic acid, hydrogen and electrons are transferred to $NAD^+$, forming the last $NADH_2$ molecule in the cycle.

2. Acetyl-CoA becomes attached to oxaloacetic acid, the point of entry into the Krebs cycle, to form the six-carbon citric acid.

3. Citric acid is rearranged into the six-carbon isocitric acid, which is stripped of a hydrogen atom and electrons that are transferred to $NAD^+$ to form $NADH_2$. It is also loses of a $COO^-$ group, this being the second $CO_2$ to depart.

4. The resulting intermediate α-oxoglutaric acid also gives up a hydrogen atom and electrons to $NAD^+$, forming $NADH_2$. And it gives up a $COO^-$ group, which is the last $CO_2$ to depart.

5. In the conversion of succinic acid to fumaric acid, hydrogen atoms and electrons are transferred to FAD, forming $FADH_2$.

cycle, the acetyl group is joined by a 4-carbon compound (oxaloacetic acid) to form a 6-carbon compound (citric acid), and the coenzyme A molecule is released in the process. The coenzyme A liberated by the acetyl group entering the cycle is available for ferrying more acetyl groups to the enzymes of the Krebs cycle. By a series of enzyme-catalyzed reactions, the citric acid is broken down to oxaloacetic acid, the starting material, which can then pick up another acetyl group; in the process, the original acetyl group has been broken down to yield 2 molecules of carbon dioxide. The Krebs cycle provides a continuous mechanism for breaking down acetyl groups. During the operation of the cycle, the acetyl group also loses its hydrogens; they are linked to molecular oxygen and turned into water through the operation of a series of reactions called the **respiratory chain** (Figure 4–10).

The respiratory chain consists of an energy cascade involving a series of enzyme-coenzyme reactions that pass hydrogens and electrons down the line eventually to reduce oxygen and form water (Figure 4–10). For each turn of the Krebs cycle, there are four dehydrogenation steps, each involving a pair of electrons and hydrogens. Thus, at each turn of the Krebs cycle, four pairs of electrons and hydrogens are produced. Each pair of electrons and hydrogens moving down the respiratory chain generates 3 molecules of ATP; thus for every turn of the cycle 12 ATP molecules are generated (Figure 4-10). In addition to the release of hydrogens for the production of energy via the respiratory chain, the cell derives another benefit from the Krebs cycle, and that is the production of building blocks. Some of the compounds formed during the cycle can be used to manufacture amino acids and other essential cellular components; these intermediate products can be siphoned off at different points in the cycle. In the same way, molecules not needed for biosynthesis can be fed into the cycle at different places, allowing the cell a greater

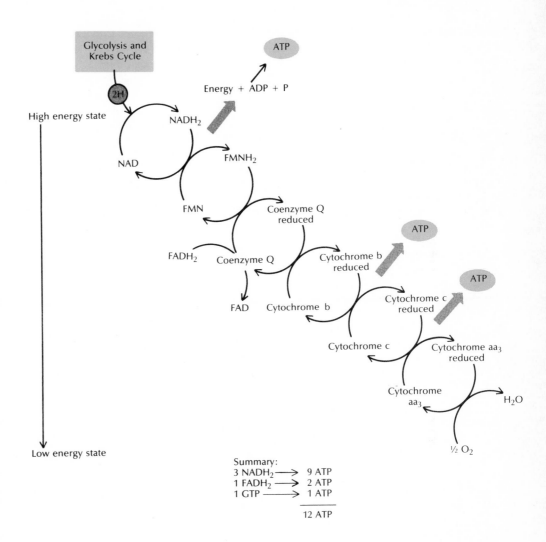

Summary:
$$3\ NADH_2 \longrightarrow 9\ ATP$$
$$1\ FADH_2 \longrightarrow 2\ ATP$$
$$1\ GTP \longrightarrow 1\ ATP$$
$$\overline{\qquad\qquad 12\ ATP}$$

diversity of usable foodstuffs. The Krebs cycle can be thought of as the metabolic hub of the cell.

Now let us examine some of the details of the flow of energy through the respiratory chain that enable the cell to obtain energy currency, ATP. When pyruvic acid is split to yield acetyl coenzyme A and carbon dioxide, it also loses a pair of electrons in the form of hydrogens; these hydrogens, as well as those from the Krebs cycle acids, are passed to the coenzyme NAD, which becomes reduced ($NADH_2$ (Figure 4–10).

The $NADH_2$ passes its hydrogens to another acceptor, the coenzyme **FMN** (flavin mononucleotide, a derivative of the vitamin riboflavin); the transfer of hydrogens again is an oxidation-reduction reaction. The FMN bearing hydrogens ($FMNH_2$) can pass the hydrogens via the coenzyme called Q or ubiquinone, to a series of enzymes called the **cytochromes.** The cytochromes are conjugated proteins containing iron in a ring structure (heme) and resemble hemoglobin. There are three types of cytochromes, and the last one donates its hydrogens to

BOX 4B  Why cyanide kills

Cytochromes are capable of reacting with cyanide. The lethal effect of the gas chamber (cyanide gas is generated by the addition of sodium cyanide pellets to an acid such as hydrochloric acid) results from the fact that the iron of the cytochrome binds these materials irreversibly. In this way the cytochrome enzymes are poisoned and incapable of acting in the capacity of transferring electrons. Aerobic cells unable to obtain energy from glucose become disorganized and die. It is for this reason that cyanide kills.

molecular oxygen (Figure 4–10). The respiratory chain consists of NAD, FMN, coenzyme Q, and the cytochromes.

At this point you may wonder why the cell goes through such a series of complicated reactions. The answer is that with each respiratory-chain transfer (an oxidation-reduction reaction) the electrons are lowered from a higher energy state to a lower energy state; at some of these transfers, ATP is formed. We might analogize the transfer of electrons down the respiratory chain to the movement of water down the energy cascade, releasing discrete amounts of energy along the way.

In summary, let us write our general equation for oxidation-reduction:

$$XH_2 + Y \longrightarrow X + YH_2$$

In the respiratory chain, pyruvic acid or the acids of the Krebs cycle are $XH_2$, and $Y$ is NAD; the next reaction would be:

$$\underset{YH_2}{\overset{NADH_2}{}} + \underset{Z}{\overset{FMN}{}} \longrightarrow \underset{Y}{\overset{NAD}{}} + \underset{ZH_2}{\overset{FMNH_2}{}}$$
$$\downarrow$$
$$ATP$$

in the next series of steps:

$$\underset{ZH_2}{\overset{FMNH_2}{}} + \underset{CoQ}{\overset{coenzyme\ Q}{}} \longrightarrow \underset{Z}{\overset{FMN}{}} + \underset{CoQH_2}{\overset{reduced\ coenzyme\ Q}{}}$$

$$\underset{CoQH_2}{} + \underset{Cy}{\overset{cytochrome}{}} \longrightarrow CoQ + \underset{CyH_2}{\overset{reduced\ cytochrome}{}}$$
$$\downarrow$$
$$2ATP$$

and finally:

$$\underset{CyH_2}{\overset{reduced\ cytochrome}{}} + \underset{O_2}{\overset{oxygen}{}} \longrightarrow \underset{H_2O}{\overset{water}{}} + \underset{Cy}{\overset{cytochrome}{}}$$

The overall equation for the aerobic degradation of glucose is:

$$\underset{XH_2}{\overset{}{C_6H_{12}O_6}} + \underset{Y}{\overset{}{6O_2}} \longrightarrow \underset{X}{\overset{}{6CO_2}} + \underset{H_2Y}{\overset{}{6H_2O}}$$

## 4–8 AEROBIC RESPIRATION: COST ACCOUNTING

The degradation of pyruvic acid by the enzymes of the Krebs cycle and the transfer of hydrogens along the respiratory chain yield energy that is available for cellular work; in the process the pyruvic acid becomes carbon dioxide and the hydrogens removed from it become water. Just how efficient is aerobic respiration? Each molecule of pyruvic acid going to acetyl coenzyme A produces 1 molecule of $NADH_2$, and by passing the hydrogens and electrons through the cytochromes 3 ATP molecules are formed. Since 2 pyruvic acid molecules are formed per molecule of glucose, the net yield to the cell is 6 ATP molecules. In each revolution of the Krebs cycle there are generated 12 ATP molecules; since there are two turns of the cycle for the 2 molecules of acetyl coenzyme A formed from the original molecule of glucose, the net yield is 24 molecules of ATP. Now recall that during anaerobic respiration 2 molecules of $NADH_2$ were produced. If these hydrogens are passed down the respiratory chain, 3 ATP molecules are generated per pair of hydrogens for a total of 6 ATP molecules. Now for the grand total: 6 ATP from pyruvic acid going to acetyl coenzyme A, 24 ATP from the Krebs cycle–respiratory chain sequence, and 6 ATP from the glycolysis–respiratory chain sequence. The total yield from aerobic respiration is 36 ATP molecules; to this must be added the 2 ATP from anaerobic respiration, and thus the cell gains 38 ATP molecules from the complete oxidation of glucose.

Now for some simple arithmetic to calculate efficiency. We noticed previously that the total energy available in 1 mole of glucose was about 700 Calories. By both anaerobic and aerobic respiration, the cell traps 38 ATP molecules, which is equivalent to 380 Calories. The efficiency of the combined anaerobic and aerobic respiratory scheme is, therefore, 54% ($380/700 \times 100 = 54\%$). This efficiency is considerably better than any heat engine yet invented (the efficiency of the average heat engine is about 30%). If we could manufacture an engine employing principles similar to those incorporated in the design of the cell, shortages of electricity and heat and problems of transportation would be alleviated; there would be plenty of energy for all.

## 4-9 WHERE IS ATP USED?

ATP provides the driving force for most cellular activities, including muscular and nervous activity, the movement of cilia and flagella, active transport, and a wide variety of energy-dependent metabolic processes. We shall describe some of these events more fully later (Chapters 18 and 21).

When materials have to be moved into or out of cells against a concentration gradient, energy is required. In some cases, this is called uphill transport. The pumping of sodium out of the interior of a cell is an ATP-requiring process; if ATP is withdrawn from participation (by a poison, for example) the process stops. The work of bailing out the water that enters the cell by osmosis requires ATP. In this manner, ATP is a participant in the work of the cells of our kidneys, which maintain our water balance.

Nerve cells perform electrical work, and here again ATP functions in the movement of charged molecules (called ions) across the plasma membrane, thus generating an electrical potential; the movement of this electrical charge is the basis of transmission of nerve messages. If the ATP system is poisoned by a substance such as nerve gas, paralysis results because electrical messages cannot be generated.

The fabrication of molecules, that is, the formation of new chemical bonds, is dependent upon ATP. In green plants, ATP is formed during the so-called light phase of photosynthesis, and subsequently this is used for the synthesis of carbohydrate (sugar) from $CO_2$. It is this carbohydrate we all depend on for energy.

Thus, in the economy of life, the coin of

FIGURE 4–11 ATP, the currency of the cell. Debts for mechanical, chemical, osmotic, and electrical work are paid for with ATP. (From *Biological Science* by William T. Keeton. By permission of W. W. Norton & Company, Inc. Copyright © 1967 by W. W. Norton & Company, Inc.)

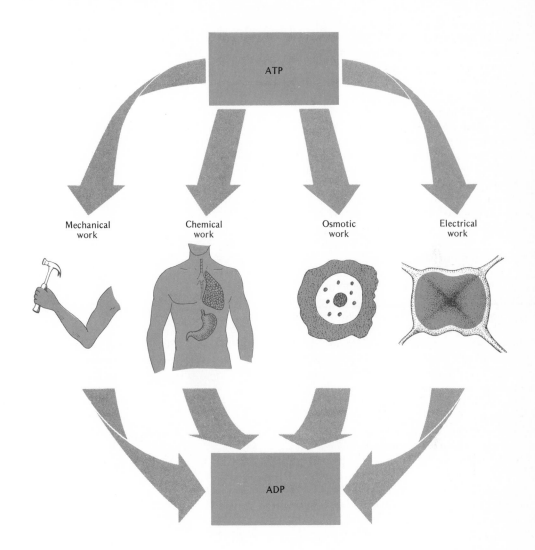

the realm is ATP (Figure 4–11). ATP is the common intermediate of exchange in reactions that require energy and those that yield energy.

## 4-10 CHEMICAL ENERGY HARVEST: EVOLUTION AND CELLULAR LOCATION

All cells, whether they be anaerobic or aerobic, have the anaerobic scheme for extracting energy from glucose. It would

appear, therefore, that during the evolution (development) of cellular life, anaerobic organisms arose first and the aerobic respiratory system was later added on to the anaerobic system. This line of reasoning fits well with our thoughts about the origin of life, since the atmosphere of the early earth was a reducing one and aerobic organisms could not function in it; later, once oxygen became available, anaerobic organisms must have acquired the ability to use oxygen in

FIGURE 4–12 The fractionation of liver.

cellular respiration. Because of this, their metabolism became more efficient, and they were able to conserve greater quantities of energy (in the form of ATP) for every molecule of energy-rich material they fed upon.

Cells are specialized transducers of chemical energy, but where in the cell is the energy factory located? How does the machinery for energy production fit inside the cell? We have seen that there is considerable division of labor within cells, that some cellular functions are restricted to specific structures or compartments of the cell known as organelles. The energy-yielding processes that occur inside every cell are also compartmentalized.

If you put some liver in a blender and whirled it at high speed so that it became homogenized, and then spun it in a centrifuge, you would obtain two fractions—a watery solution and a solid pellet (Figure 4–12). The enzyme-catalyzed sequences of anaerobic respiration occur in the soluble portion of the cytoplasm, in the liver fraction that you separated into a solution and a pellet. Although the enzymes are probably organized, they do not occur in a fixed, observable geometric configuration. The enzymatic events that take place during aerobic respiration do not occur in the soluble cytoplasmic portion of the cell, but are arranged in a fixed spatial orientation in a special organelle, the mitochondrion. These mitochondria would be found in the pellet portion of your fractionated liver sample. The mitochondrion has been called the powerhouse of the cell because it is here that the major harvest of energy from glucose is obtained.

You have seen pictures of the mitochondrion as it is revealed by the electron microscope (page 39). The matrix contains the Krebs-cycle enzymes, whereas the enzymes of the respiratory chain are located on the inner mitochondrial membranes, the mitochondrial crests or cristae. Imagine the systematic degradation of a molecule of pyruvic acid; the 15 enzymes of the sequence are located in sequence in the mitochondrion, and the electrons and hy-

Liver

Sugar or salt solution

Homogenize in blender

Filter through cheesecloth to remove unbroken cells

Suspension of broken cells

Solution (liquid) with cytoplasmic enzymes

Pellet with mitochondria nuclei

Spin in centrifuge

drogens are removed in a stepwise fashion. The enzymatic sequence fits the geometric structure of the mitochondrion beautifully. We can compare the situation to the assembly line of a factory; the enzymes and coenzymes are lined up and, in bucket-brigade fashion, they remove electrons and hydrogens and pass them along to where they eventually reach molecular oxygen; in

the process ATP is produced and made available to the entire cell.

## SUMMARY

**1.** Energy is the capacity to do work. Potential energy is stored energy; kinetic energy is energy in action. All living cells depend on the release and use of energy from food for maintenance of the living state.

**2.** The laws of thermodynamics state that I. When energy goes from one form to another, no energy is gained or lost. II. During energy transformations, the amount of *usable* energy is reduced.

**3.** Living cells are open thermodynamic systems: to maintain an organized, steady state, energy must be supplied. Living cells obtain energy for growth, maintenance, and repair by the stepwise release of energy from organic molecules. During this process, heat is dissipated into the environment.

**4.** Oxidation (= dehydrogenation) of energy-rich compounds such as carbohydrates liberates energy. For every oxidation reaction (addition to oxygen) there is a corresponding reduction reaction (removal of hydrogen). When an electron (hydrogen) flows from a reducing system, energy is released.

**5.** In living systems, energy is stored primarily in the high-energy bonds of ATP, which can be discharged to ADP when energy is needed.

**6.** The oxidation of glucose to provide energy in living cells is called respiration. It occurs into two stages: anaerobic and aerobic.

**7.** During the anaerobic respiration of glucose, it is broken down from a 6-carbon compound to 2 molecules of pyruvic acid, a 3-carbon compound, by 11 enzymatic steps. During this process, hydrogens are removed and there is a net yield of 2 molecules of energy-rich ATP to the cell.

**8.** Pyruvic acid may form alcohol (fermentation of yeast) or lactic acid (glycolysis of muscle), or it may be further metabolized in the presence of oxygen (aerobic respiration) to produce more energy-rich ATP, carbon dioxide, and water. Carbon dioxide and water are energy-poor molecules and freely leave the cell.

**9.** During aerobic respiration, pyruvic acid is first broken down to carbon dioxide and an acetyl group. The acetyl group is itself metabolized via the Krebs cycle to carbon dioxide. During both sets of reactions, hydrogens and electrons are removed; the hydrogens and electrons are transported by a series of reactions called the respiratory chain and ultimately combine with molecular oxygen to form water. During the transport of electrons down the respiratory chain, energy is released and stored as ATP.

**10.** For every mole of glucose metabolized in respiration, the cell obtains 38 energy-rich molecules of ATP from ADP, a 54% efficiency rate. (The average heat engine is only 30% efficient.)

**11.** The reactions of anaerobic respiration occur in the soluble cytoplasm. Aerobic respiration occurs in the mitochondrion.

## KEY WORDS

| | | | |
|---|---|---|---|
| | Calorie | aerobic respiration | bomb calorimeter |
| | bond energy | aerobes | mole |
| matter | oxidation | energy cascade | acetyl group |
| energy | dehydrogenation | pyruvic acid | coenzyme A |
| work | reduction | phosphorylation | acetyl coenzyme A |
| potential energy | adenosine triphosphate (ATP) | nicotinamide adenine dinucleotide (NAD) | Krebs or citric acid cycle |
| kinetic energy | adenosine diphosphate (ADP) | carboxylase | respiratory chain |
| laws of thermodynamics | high-energy bond | thiamine pyrophosphate (TPP) | flavin adenine dinucleotide (FAD) |
| entropy | anaerobic respiration | fermentation | cytochromes |
| calorie | anaerobes | glycolysis | |

## TOPICS FOR REVIEW AND DISCUSSION

1. Explain how potential and kinetic energy differ from each other.

2. How do the laws of thermodynamics govern the operations of living cells?

3. Why is ATP called the "energy currency" of the cell?

4. Compare anaerobic and aerobic respiration.

5. Why can yeast cells survive anaerobically?

6. What is the significance of enzymes in the release of energy by cells?

7. Explain the similarities and differences between glycolysis and fermentation.

8. What is energy and how is it measured?

9. Describe the cellular compartmentalization of aerobic and anaerobic respiration.

10. How are oxidation-reduction reactions involved in the release of energy from cells?

Reprinted by permission Sawyer Press, Los Angeles, California.

# 5

# Harvest of Light Energy: Photosynthesis

## 5–1 ALL FLESH IS GRASS

Humans can change the course of rivers, build mountains out of rubble, create machines that think, split the atom, and travel through outer space. Surely nothing on this planet is more impressive than our capacity to think creatively and alter the environment to suit our needs. However, in spite of our apparent dominion over much of the planet, we are totally dependent upon other organisms for all our food.

For example, in an average day's meals you might consume the following:

Breakfast: Eggs, orange juice, toast, coffee, butter, milk

Lunch: Hamburger, salad, french fries, milk

Dinner: Roast beef, potatoes, carrots, peas, ice cream, coffee

We can divide these foods into two categories: those that came from plants and those that were derived from animal materials, the latter being eggs, milk, and meat products. The chickens, cows, and beef-on-the-hoof from which the latter products came obtained their nourishment, in turn, from plant materials. When we sit down to a juicy steak or drink a glass of creamy milk, we are consuming nothing more than converted plants. All animals that feed on other animals are in the same situation. A chain or pyramid of food organisms exists, linked by producers and consumers and headed by flesh eaters; all food pyramids are based on plant material of one kind or another (**Figure 5–1**). Many food pyramids, such as

the one we have described for ourselves, exist in nature, and some of them are so complex that they form webs rather than pyramids. This is the subject of Chapter 26. The point to be made here is that we and all other animal life depend on plants to produce our food or the food of organisms upon which we feed. Everything we eat is thus either plant material or derived from plant material. The author of Isaiah recognized this when he wrote: "All flesh is grass" (Isa. 40:6). But what do plants depend on for their food?

Plant cells, green-plant cells to be more exact, combine the simple inorganic substances carbon dioxide ($CO_2$) and water ($H_2O$) to form complex organic carbohydrates such as sugar or starch ("$CH_2O$"). They obtain the energy needed for this process from sunlight. This process, upon which all life on this planet depends, is called **photosynthesis** (literally, "putting together with light"). As a by-product of such activity, the photosynthetic plant liberates molecular oxygen.

If all flesh is grass, then the amount of flesh that the earth can support is dependent on the amount of energy trapped by the grass (green plants) through photosynthesis. The photosynthetic process is enormous in magnitude. Each year 690 billion tons of carbon dioxide and 280 billion tons of water are combined by photosynthesis to produce 500 billion tons of carbohydrate. About 80% of this production occurs in the sea. Some 90% of the total carbohydrate goes into materials that cannot be used as food, such as wood, and some is used by

the plants themselves as their energy source. Even so, the total sugar yield available for use by other organisms is about 4 billion tons each year; this amounts to about 0.8 tons of sugar per person per year, or 7 lb of sugar per person per day. As an additional bonus there is the liberation of about 500 billion tons of oxygen into the atmosphere. Every 2,000 years the atmospheric oxygen of our planet is completely renewed by the activities of green plants.

The population of the earth continues to grow. Calculation of the number of people the planet can support must involve some recognition of the photosynthetic process. Can the energy-trapping efficiency of photosynthesis be increased? Can we increase photosynthetic food production? Will the capacity of green plants to carry out photosynthesis finally determine the number of persons who can live on the planet earth? Before we can attempt to answer these questions, we must have some appreciation of the mechanisms of photosynthesis itself.

## 5–2 THE ENERGY CASCADE REVISITED

By the oxidation of complex foodstuffs such as sugar, living things obtain chemical energy (in the form of ATP), lose energy (in the form of heat), and in the process form carbon dioxide and water, energy-poor molecules. We have seen that the energy is released in gradual steps rather like water flowing from a reservoir down through a series of controllable sluice gates. (See Chapter 4, Figure 4–5.) Consequently, the reservoir is slowly and continually being

FIGURE 5–1 A simple food pyramid. This food pyramid involves several transformations of chemical energy. The cow eats the grass, and the chemical fuel of the plant is used to form the chemicals of the cow's flesh and milk. Humans drink the milk and eat the flesh (meat), thus obtaining chemical fuel. Because at each transformation there is a loss of energy, it takes a greater amount of the supplier to support an equal amount of consumers (i.e., 100 lb of grass to support 10 lb of cow to produce 1 lb of human).

depleted. In order to maintain a store of potential energy, it must have its water supply replenished. There must be uphill transport of water, and this requires a massive input of energy from the outside. In nature, water is cycled continually from reservoir to ocean or sea and back to the reservoir; the heat energy of the sun evaporates water from the oceans and seas, and via precipitation (rain, snow, etc.) the reservoir can be refilled (Figure 5–2a). The reservoir can also be refilled by mechanical means, such as a pump (Figure 5–2b). As long as it is replenished, water from the reservoir can continue to flow downhill and create a cascade of energy. In the same way, cells and organisms require an energy reservoir for their work. The energy reservoir of life would run dry if only the oxidation of food took place, and life could no longer continue. How is life's energy reservoir replenished?

The energy of sunlight in photosynthesis acts in a way analogous to the sunlight that evaporates water from oceans and seas or the electric pump that lifts water to a reservoir. The input of solar energy via photosynthesis enables $CO_2$ and $H_2O$ to be chemically fused into an energy-rich molecule ("$CH_2O$") which acts as a reservoir or energy source for life (Figure 5–3). In this way, photosynthesis makes the energy cascade operate on a continuing basis and permits the continuity of life.

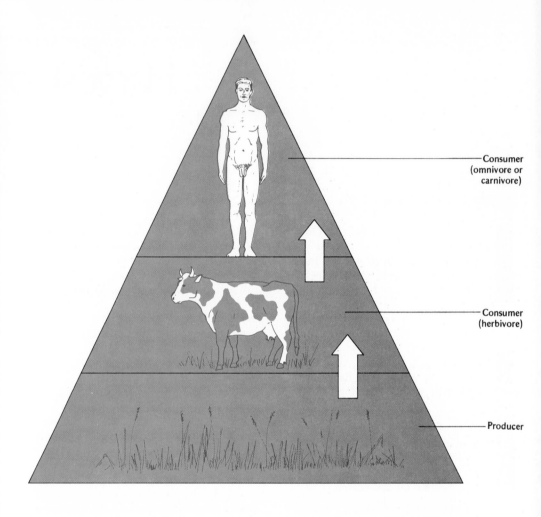

Consumer (omnivore or carnivore)

Consumer (herbivore)

Producer

## 5–3 LIGHT AND CHLOROPHYLL: LIGHT PHASE

The sun, that thermonuclear furnace which warms us and lights our way, is the ultimate energy source for every living creature on the earth. Our sun is like a gigantic hydrogen bomb in which hydrogen is converted into helium; in the process, radiant energy is released as light and heat.

Light is made up of particles or radiant energy packets, called **photons** or **quanta.** Light energy is converted into chemical energy by photosynthesis, but first it must be absorbed by plant pigments, principally the green pigment **chlorophyll** located in the chloroplast. (This phase of photosynthesis is thus called the **light phase.**) There are two kinds of chlorophyll: chlorophyll *a* and chlorophyll *b*, which differ slightly in their molecular structure (Figure 5–4) and in the way in which they absorb visible light. Only chlorophyll *a* is active in photosynthesis. Other pigments present in a leaf (carotenoids, phycobilins, and chlorophyll *b*) help to gather light energy and pass it on to chlorophyll *a*.

The ability of a pigment to absorb light depends on its molecular architecture and in particular on the arrangement of the electrons within its atoms. Certain pigments, by virtue of their structure, possess particularly mobile electrons that are associated not with individual atoms but with the molecular system as a whole, and chlorophyll is one of these. When light strikes chlorophyll *a* in the chloroplast, a particle of light energy (a photon) is absorbed, and an electron is raised to a higher energy level; this electron is then passed on to neighboring molecules, and thus energy is transferred from chlorophyll molecule to

FIGURE 5–2 The energy cascade. (a) The natural water cycle involving sunlight and precipitation. (b) Water cycle in which an electric pump is used to refill the reservoir.

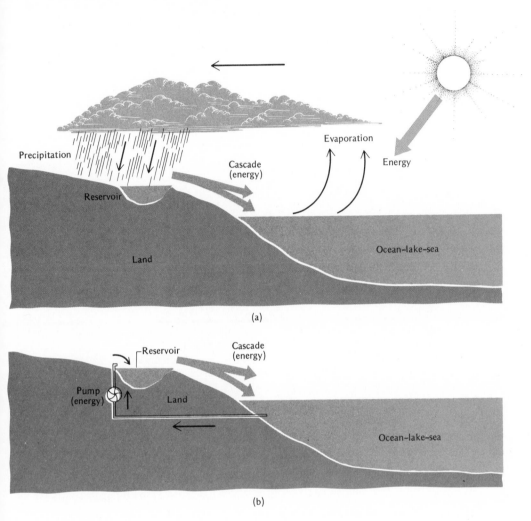

The chlorophyll $a_1$ of system I, excited by light energy, has generated $NADPH_2$, but in the process it has lost its electrons; now electron-deficient, this "hole" must be filled with another ground-state electron. That replacement comes from another chlorophyll molecule, $a_2$; this is called **system II**. In this system the absorption of light energy by the chlorophyll produces an "excited" state, and in some manner (as yet unknown) water is split into hydrogen ($H^+$) ions, electrons, and molecular oxygen:

$$2H_2O \longrightarrow 4H^+ + 4e^- + O_2$$
water      hydrogen    electrons    oxygen
            ions

The chlorophyll $a_2$ electrons are carried downhill through a series of electron acceptors (plastoquinone, plastocyanin, and cytochrome), eventually reaching the ground state and filling the "hole" in the chlorophyll $a_1$ of system I. This downhill transit of electrons is more than a "digging of an electron hole" to "fill an electron hole," for during the process ATP is generated from ADP and inorganic phosphate. The electrons to replace those lost from the chlorophyll $a_2$ of system II are derived from the splitting of water. Now the chlorophyll of system II has recovered ground-state electrons and is no longer "excited." The hydrogen ions, also produced by the splitting of water, are used for the formation of $NADPH_2$ in system II. The reactions of system II are shown schematically in Figure 5–6.

So far, we have seen how the energy of light is trapped and conserved in the high-energy bonds of ATP. However, we said that one of the main results of photosynthesis was the production of carbohydrate. How does this occur? We shall now examine this process.

## 5–4 CARBON DIOXIDE AND SUGAR FORMATION: DARK PHASE

The chemicals ATP and $NADPH_2$, generated rapidly during the light-driven phase of

chlorophyll molecule. The freely migrating electrons react with molecules called **electron acceptors.** Upon receiving an electron, an electron acceptor becomes reduced and in turn donates its electrons to a series of other electron acceptors. In bucket-brigade fashion, the electrons flow from one compound to another, as electricity flows in a wire. Eventually, light energy is traded for chemical energy, by a process called **noncyclic photophosphorylation.** Noncyclic photophosphorylation occurs in two phases or systems, and both involve chlorophyll a. In **system I**, chlorophyll $a_1$ is "excited" by pho-

tons of light, and electrons are boosted to a high energy level; the electrons are passed to an iron–sulfur center, then to the electron acceptor ferredoxin. The ferredoxin in turn passes the electrons on to the coenzyme NADP, which combines with hydrogen ions ($H^+$) in the medium to become reduced ($NADPH_2$). (**NADP** stands for **n**icotinamide **a**denine **d**inucleotide **p**hosphate and is a derivative of niacin; it is not identical to, or exchangeable in function with, its coenzyme cousin, NAD, but they play similar roles in cellular metabolism.) The situation is shown schematically in Figure 5–5.

FIGURE 5–3 A highly schematic view of the energy cascade in the biological world.

FIGURE 5–4 The molecular structure of chlorophyll. In chlorophyll *a*, $X$ = —$CH_3$, whereas in chlorophyll *b*, $X$ = —CHO.

photosynthesis, are used to produce carbohydrate in a more leisurely fashion, by a process that does not require light and is called the **dark phase** of photosynthesis. (It can go on in the light or the dark.)

In the dark phase a 5-carbon phosphorylated sugar (called **ri**bu**l**ose **p**hosphate or **RuP**), already present in the chloroplast, receives another phosphate group from ATP to form a molecule with two phosphates, one on each end of the molecule (called **RuBP** for **ri**bu**l**ose **b**is**p**hosphate). Now carbon dioxide (from the air and in solution in

the cell sap) is joined to this diphosphorylated 5-carbon sugar, and the resulting 6-carbon molecule is split immediately to produce 2 molecules of a 3-carbon compound (**PGA** or **p**hospho**g**lyceric **a**cid) (Figure 5–7). By the energy supplied from ATP and the reducing power of $NADPH_2$ (derived from the light reactions), the PGA becomes modified into a 3-carbon sugar (**PGAL** or **p**hospho**g**lycer**al**dehyde). These two 3-carbon molecules are then combined to give a 6-carbon sugar with two phosphates (hexose diphosphate). The 6-carbon sugar (hex-

FIGURE 5–5 (top) Photosystem I in photosynthesis.

FIGURE 5–6 (bottom) Photosystem II in photosynthesis.

FIGURE 5–7 Simplified reactions of the dark phase of photosynthesis.

ose) with its two phosphates is then altered and added on to a starch molecule,[1] and in this manner can serve as a reserve energy fuel (Figure 5–7).

It should be noted that for every 3 molecules of carbon dioxide used, 6 molecules of PGAL are produced, but only 1 of these will be converted into starch. The remaining 5 molecules of PGAL are converted into 3 molecules of the starting material, the 5-carbon phosphorylated sugar (RuP). The 5-carbon sugars can then react with more carbon dioxide to initiate another cycle of dark reactions; if the regeneration of the 5-

[1] Glucose in a free state is not directly produced in photosynthesis.

**101**

FIGURE 5–8 The photosynthetic process visualized as a series of mechanically driven gears. Light energy turns the NADPH₂-synthesis and ATP-synthesis gears. Both these gears cause the carbon-dioxide-fixation gear to turn, yielding PGAL. (From *Biological Science* by William T. Keeton. By permission of W. W. Norton & Company, Inc. Copyright © 1967 by W. W. Norton & Company, Inc.)

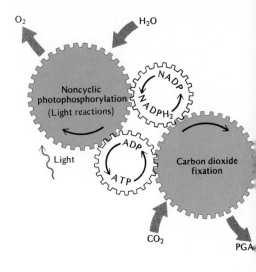

carbon sugar does not occur, the sequence of reaction stops.

Thus, in the dark phase of photosynthesis, carbon dioxide, is chemically reduced to form "CH₂O," carbohydrate, at the expense of the energy of ATP and the reducing power of NADPH₂. Note that in the production of carbohydrate within the chloroplast the intermediates are all phosphorylated and, therefore, do not leak out of their place of manufacture; by being directly converted to starch, the carbohydrate is conveniently stored within the chloroplast. When energy is needed for cellular work, the starch is enzymatically converted to glucose or fructose, and via oxidation energy is made available to the plant cell. (Thus, plants respire, too!)

The process of photosynthesis can be seen as a mechanical model (Figure 5–8).

## 5–5 CELLULAR LOCATION OF PHOTOSYNTHESIS

The processes of photosynthesis take place in the chloroplast. The chloroplast is compartmentalized, and the light and dark reactions take place in different parts of it (Figure 2–14). Chlorophyll is incorporated in the grana in a series of membranes stacked one on top of the other, resembling a pile of coins. The chlorophyll molecules are arranged in layers in these stacks of membranes, presumably sandwiched between layers of protein and lipid. The chlorophyll is thus rigidly oriented, and it behaves much like a crystal. When light (photons) strikes the chlorophyll in the grana, the electrons are free to move in the crystal and in their cyclic path generate ATP, NADPH₂, and oxygen. Thus the grana are solar power plants. The dark reactions take place in the stroma of the chloroplast, the region devoid of membrane stacks. In the stroma are the enzymes necessary for the fixation of carbon dioxide into carbohydrate. The reducing agent, NADPH₂, and the energy source, ATP, which are generated in the grana, move into the stroma and

there participate in the synthesis of carbohydrate. Then the NADP and ADP return to the grana to repeat the cycle.

## 5–6 EFFICIENCY AND IMPLICATIONS OF PHOTOSYNTHESIS

Let us examine the efficiency of the photosynthetic process as it relates to us. The surface of the earth receives annually about $500 \times 10^{18}$ Calories of solar energy. About one third of the total annual solar radiation reaching the earth is expended in the evaporation of water (from the surfaces of oceans, lakes, ponds, etc.), which leaves about $150 \times 10^{18}$ Calories available for photosynthesis. Plants convert less than 1% (actually closer to 0.34%) of this available energy into the chemical energy of carbohydrate. Even so, this amounts to $1.5 \times 10^{18}$ Calories stored by land plants alone, and if we calculate only the fertile areas (about 20% of the land area of the earth), the stored energy equals $0.3 \times 10^{18}$ Calories. Of this, humans use only about 1%, or $0.003 \times 10^{18}$ Calories, annually—about $2 \times 10^3$ (2,000) Calories per day for each of the approximately 5 billion persons presently on the earth. Based on these values, it should in theory be possible

FIGURE 5–9 A summary of the light and dark reactions of photosynthesis (reactants in circles and products in diamonds).

to support a population of 400 billion persons.

This argument has obvious fallacies. First, many of the photosynthetically produced Calories in the previous statistics are useless to us as food. For example, an acre of pine trees is useful to people in many ways, but not directly as food. Second, to be of any use, the enormous annual production of photosynthetic energy must be harvested. Our means of harvesting are not good. Optimistic assumptions indicate that, under present farming conditions, about one acre of land is required to support one person. The total potentially arable (meaning harvestable) land of the earth is about 7 billion acres. The term "potentially arable" is misleading, as much of this land cannot really be farmed because of problems of irrigation, clearing, low yields, and the exorbitant costs of making it produce. Hence, even supposing all this acreage could be farmed efficiently in the next few years, the absolute maximum number of persons the earth can support is finite.

The population of the earth continues to increase (see Chapter 27). Of course, the more people there are, the less food there will be to go around, and the greater the probability of malnutrition or starvation. Since there is an unequal distribution of populations and food resources, starvation is already occurring in many countries of the world, especially in lesser developed countries, and the United States is not immune to the problem. (See Chapter 27.)

What can be done about it? One way is to increase food production so that less than one acre of arable land is needed to feed one person adequately. Much has been done already, with the use of fertilizers, insecticides, etc. However, the effects of these chemicals have not been totally beneficial, because they are not easily degraded and they accumulate in the environment to dangerous levels (Chapter 27).

Another way to increase food production is to produce more efficient photosynthetic plants; again, something along these lines

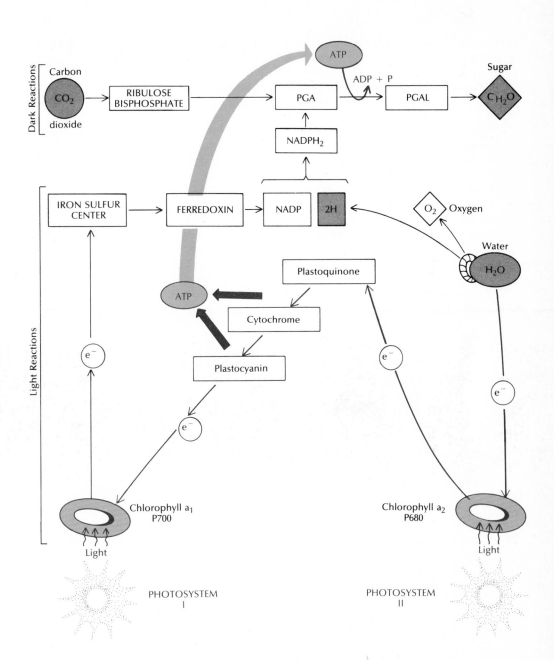

has already been done. The Nobel Peace Prize for 1970 was presented to Norman E. Borlaug, whose efforts in producing higher-yield wheat and rice plants have greatly contributed to feeding the world. When we understand the genetic mechanism of photosynthesis in detail, we may be able to breed superefficient plants and perhaps even create a synthetic chloroplast to substitute for the living green-plant cell.

Even if we could feed more people, it is questionable how pleasant life would be under such crowded conditions (Chapters 26 and 27). There is one other way out of our dilemma: to decide what number of persons can comfortably live on the earth and then find a way to restrict the population to that number (Chapter 27). For now, suffice it to say that it is clearly not the energy-conversion system of the photosynthetic plant, the amount of carbon dioxide, or the availability of sunlight that will limit the earth's population. Rather, the number of persons the earth can support will be restricted by the amount of space people need for living. No conceivable increase in food supply can long keep pace with the current growth rate of world populations; what happens depends on the political, religious, social, and economic considerations that affect measures which must be taken now.

## SUMMARY

**1.** All life depends on the sun.

**2.** Plants trap solar energy by using it to convert $CO_2$ and $H_2O$ into carbohydrate; oxygen is liberated into the atmosphere as a by product. This process is called photosynthesis.

**3.** Animals obtain their energy in turn from plants or animals that feed on plants.

**4.** Photosynthesis is essentially the opposite of respiration:

**Photosynthesis:**

$6CO_2$ + $6H_2O$ + solar energy
carbon    water
dioxide

$$\longrightarrow C_6H_{12}O_6 + 6O_2$$
carbohydrate    oxygen

**Respiration:**

$C_6H_{12}O_6$ + $6O_2$
carbohydrate    oxygen

$$\longrightarrow 6CO_2 + 6H_2O + energy$$
carbon    water
dioxide

**5.** Solar energy is trapped as ATP in the light phase of photosynthesis (Figure 5–9). The green pigment chlorophyll, present in the chloroplast, is excited by a photon; in the process an electron is raised to a higher energy level and is passed along a chain of electron acceptors, including ferredoxin and NADP. This series of reactions is called system I.

**6.** At the same time, chlorophyll $a_2$ in a second system (system II) is excited by light energy (photons); this energy is used to split water into $H^+$ ions, electrons, and oxygen, which is released. The hydrogen ions go to system I to reduce NADP to $NADPH_2$. The electrons are passed along a series of acceptors (plastoquinone plastocyanin, and cytochrome) and replace the original electrons in systems I and II.

**7.** During the passage of electrons from system II to system I, ATP is formed from ADP and inorganic phosphate.

**8.** The reduced $NADPH_2$ and ATP formed in the light phase of photosynthesis are subsequently used during the dark phase to form carbohydrate (sugar) from $CO_2$.

**9.** In the dark phase, the energy of ATP is used to phosphorylate ribulose phosphate (RuP) and convert it to a 6-carbon sugar (ribulose bisphosphate, RuBP) using $CO_2$ as the carbon source ($5C \rightarrow 6C$). The 6-carbon sugar is then split to 2 molecules of PGA (phosphoglyceric acid). More ATP energy and the reducing power of $NADPH_2$ (from the light reactions) convert the PGA into PGAL (phosphoglyceraldehyde). Two such 3-carbon molecules are then combined into a diphosphorylated 6-carbon sugar (hexose bisphosphate), which is altered and added onto a starch molecule.

**10.** The light reactions occur in the grana of the chloroplast. The dark reactions occur in the stroma.

**11.** The earth receives $500 \times 10^{18}$ Calories of solar energy annually. Land plants trap $1.5 \times 10^{18}$ Calories of this.

## KEY WORDS

photosynthesis
photons
quanta
chlorophyll
light phase
electron acceptors
noncyclic photophosphorylation
system I
nicotinamide adenine dinucleotide
   phosphate (NADP)
system II
dark phase
ribulose phosphate (RuP)
ribulose bisphosphate (RuBP)
phosphoglyceric acic (PGA)
phosphoglyceraldehyde (PGAL)

## TOPICS FOR REVIEW
## AND DISCUSSION

1. What is the role of light in the process of photosynthesis?

2. How can a knowledge of photosynthesis be used for the improvement of crop yields?

3. What is the biological meaning of the statement, "All flesh is grass"?

4. What functional roles are served by plant pigments?

5. Describe in some detail the light and dark reactions of photosynthesis.

6. Does the oxygen produced during photosynthesis come from water or from carbon dioxide?

7. Contrast cellular respiration with photosynthesis.

8. How does the Second Law of Thermodynamics relate to photosynthesis?

9. How does photosynthesis keep the energy cascade operating?

10. Why are green plants green? Of what significance is this?

# MIGHTY MICE

## Gene transfer creates giants

It was the sort of biological alchemy that abounds in science fiction. Take a trait from one species, genetically transfer it to another species, and voila! a hybrid emerges that nature could never have produced.

This remarkable feat has been accomplished several times, but even today it is considered one of the extraordinary successes of genetic engineering. The experiment involved taking the gene for growth hormone from a rat and incorporating it into mouse embryos. The result: mice that grew to nearly twice the normal size. The super mice not only produced large quantities of rat growth hormone, but in some cases even passed on this trait to a second generation.

The size achieved by each mouse was dependent on how many copies of the rat gene the mouse embryos received. One mouse with 20 copies had 800 times the normal level of growth hormone in its blood. It grew to almost twice the size of litter mates that had no copies of the rat gene.

The implications of this experiment for medicine, agriculture, and biological research are enormous. The most obvious application would be creation of giant domesticated cattle capable of yielding vast quantities of meat and milk. The extraordinary levels of hormones produced by the giant mice also suggest the possibility of genetic farming, that is, using animals to produce large quantities of medically useful substances, as *Escherichia coli* is used today. The study also may help unravel the mysteries of how gene regulation goes awry in cancer.

The rapid advance of genetic engineering as illustrated here raises a fundamental question as to the evolution of our species: Should engineered, heritable, alterations to the human gene set be permitted?

Courtesy of Ralph Brinster.

# 6

# Communication Between Cell Generations: Nucleic Acids

## 6-1 INHERITANCE: GENERAL FEATURES

"Chip off the old block" is an expression that indicates the relationship between parent and offspring. It simply suggests that offspring generally resemble their parents, that like begets like. Humans give birth to humans, cats give birth to cats, and dogs give birth to dogs; this is the way of nature, and the phenomenon occurs (at least to date) without exception. The phenomenon is more complicated than this: not only do cats always produce other cats and dogs other dogs, but black cats tend to produce black kittens and brown dogs brown puppies. Tall humans tend to have tall children. Not only this, but when liver and skin cells reach a certain size and stage of development, they divide and produce more liver and skin cells, respectively. Nowhere does it occur within our bodies that on occasion one of our cells makes a mistake and slips in a dog cell or a cat cell, or even a human skin cell among the cells of the liver. Cells pass on their specific and characteristic messages from one generation to the next with great fidelity; otherwise chaos would reign within us.

Although these phenomena may not surprise you because they are everyday occurrences, they are remarkable because they imply the existence of a system capable of accurately retaining information and passing it on with equal accuracy from generation to generation. In our culture, information is recorded in books, on records, or on tapes and is stored and available to

anyone who has access to it. During the building of a house, a builder works from a plan—a blueprint prepared by an architect for the client. In much the same way, the cells of the body record and store information about the kinds of cells they are, and when new cells arise, this information can be translated and is available to those cells in a form much like a blueprint. A new cell can be constructed using the directions of the blueprint.

**Genetics,** the study of inheritance, deals with the transfer of information (or passing on of traits) from parent to offspring, whether this be at the level of the cell or of the organism. In the present context we shall explore the chemical nature of the genetic blueprint (so-called genes) and show how that material performs its function in making us what we are. In the next chapter we shall deal with the mechanisms whereby cells are able to duplicate themselves, and much later (Chapters 23 and 24) we shall see how human traits are inherited.

Considerable fear and excitement surround discussions of the nature of the inherited message, for once we understand how the genetic blueprint is constituted and how it can be read and translated, we should be able to manipulate it (see page 106). The implications of this are far-reaching. Will this knowledge be used to change defective traits into beneficial ones? It is not difficult to see that a child born with an inherited defect, such as cystic fibrosis, muscular dystrophy, or diabetes, would be better off if this defect could have been

prevented by the manipulation of the parents' genetic material prior to conception. If taken further, the subject of genetic manipulation raises interesting questions. Could we and shall we create an entire race of superhumans with predictable and "desirable" characteristics? Who is qualified to decide what is desirable and what undesirable in a human being? Understanding the chemical nature of inheritance may provide a "second genesis," but it is fraught with the same kinds of social and political questions that surrounded the suggested programs of eugenics that were popular not too long ago (breeding for beneficial traits in human populations, just as cows are bred to produce more milk, poodles for more interesting hair patterns, and so on). This chapter will detail the mechanism of inheritance; the use to which this information is put rests with all of us as individuals and as citizens.

## 6-2 INHERITANCE: CHEMICAL STRUCTURE

The disease pneumonia is caused by a bacterium called *Streptococcus pneumoniae*. When grown in the laboratory on a plate of nutrient jelly or agar, the bacteria multiply rapidly and form colonies that appear smooth and shiny to the naked eye. The smooth kind of *S. pneumoniae* is the normal, virulent disease-producer. The smooth appearance is the result of the presence of mucilaginous capsules, which probably prevent the bacteria from being engulfed (phagocytized) by the white blood cells of the body and enable them to multiply and cause the symptoms of the disease. Some strains of *S. pneumoniae* have lost the ability to produce the mucilaginous capsule; when grown on agar, the colonies appear rough. The cells that form rough colonies are not virulent and do not cause pneumonia because they are easily ingested and destroyed by the white blood cells. Each strain of bacterium breeds true: rough strains give rise to rough strains and smooth strains to smooth strains. In 1928 F. Griffith studied these strains of *S. pneumoniae* and obtained some puzzling results. If he injected living cells of the rough strain into a mouse, the mouse lived; if he injected living cells of the smooth strain into another mouse, the mouse died (Figure 6–1). When he killed the bacteria (he heated the broth in which they were growing to 60°C) and then injected each strain into mice, the mice did not become infected (Figure 6–1). So far, there are no puzzles. However, for the sake of completeness Griffith injected into a mouse a mixture of living rough cells and some killed smooth cells; unexpectedly, the mouse died (Figure 6–1). The cause of death was pneumonia, and bacteria recovered from the body multiplied on agar and formed smooth colonies. Obviously, there had been a conversion of rough cells into smooth cells, and Griffith postulated that an agent had been given off by the dead smooth cells which was taken up by the living rough cells; this agent was transmissible and conferred heritable properties upon the recipient. The agent was called **transforming principle.** What was this mysterious material?

In 1944 O. T. Avery, C. M. Macleod, and M. McCarty carefully collected and purified transforming principle; they found that it was a chemical compound called **d**eoxyribo**n**ucleic **a**cid **(DNA).** It has since been found that this chemical is the material universally responsible for inheritance—recording and transmitting the characteristics

FIGURE 6–1 The transformation experiments of Griffith.

Live rough pneumococcus

Lives

Live smooth pneumococcus

Dies

Killed

Lives

Killed

Lives

BUT:

Killed smooth + Live rough

Dies

FIGURE 6–2 Structure of a nucleotide (deoxyribonucleotide), with detailed structure of the sugar deoxyribose.

FIGURE 6–3 The nitrogenous bases found in DNA.

**109**

**COMMUNICATION BETWEEN CELL GENERATIONS: NUCLEIC ACIDS**

of a cell or an organism from generation to generation.[1]

What is the structure of DNA, and how does it work? What properties must DNA have in order to qualify as the chemical substance of hereditary material? It must have two fundamental properties: first, it must have the ability to duplicate itself, otherwise it could not be passed undiluted from generation to generation; and second, it must be able to contain all the information necessary for directing cellular activities that must be carried from one generation to the next.

Chemical analysis of DNA shows it to belong to a class of molecules known as the nucleic acids. Each DNA molecule is made up of a series of building blocks called **nucleotides** (more specifically, **deoxyribonucleotides**), each of which contains three major constituents: (1) phosphate, (2) a 5-carbon sugar called **deoxyribose,** and (3) a nitrogenous base (Figure 6–2). The phosphate and sugar portions of the nucleotide are a constant feature, but the nitrogenous bases come in four varieties: **adenine, guanine, thymine,** and **cytosine** (Figure 6–3). Adenine and guanine are structurally similar, consisting of two fused rings (Figure 6–3), and are called **purines.** Thymine and cytosine, having a single ring, are structurally alike but differ from the purines and are called **pyrimidines** (Figure 6–3).

In 1950 Erwin Chargaff purified DNA from a variety of sources and measured the amounts and kinds of nitrogenous bases present in each type of DNA. The data from some of his analyses are shown in Table 6–1. Three facts become apparent from examination of Chargaff's data. First, within the limits of experimental error, the proportion of the bases from the tissues of any particular species is the same; for example, human tissues all have about 28% adenine, 19% guanine, 28% thymine, and 19% cytosine. Second, the composition of DNA varies from species to species; the DNA of the ox is different from the DNA of yeast. Third, the percentage of purines (adenine plus guanine) equals, within the limits of experimental error, the percentage of pyrimidines (thymine plus cytosine); moreover, the amount of adenine equals the amount of thymine and the amount of guanine equals the amount of cytosine. Let us now substitute the letters A, T, G, and C for the nitrogenous bases that begin with those letters and abbreviate the discovery of Chargaff as A = T and G = C, and A + G = T + C.

How are the nucleotides arranged to form a molecule of DNA? As we have already mentioned in our discussion of proteins, the spatial, or three-dimensional, appear-

---

[1] Some viruses, which are not cells, have ribonucleic acid (RNA) as their genetic material.

**TABLE 6–1 The percentage of nitrogenous bases present in DNA**

| Source of DNA | Adenine | Guanine | Cytosine | Thymine |
|---|---|---|---|---|
| *Human* | | | | |
| Sperm | 29% | 18% | 18% | 30% |
| Thymus | 28 | 19 | 16 | 28 |
| Liver | 27 | 19 | * | * |
| *Ox* | | | | |
| Thymus | 26 | 21 | 18 | 25 |
| Liver | 26 | 21 | 17 | 14 |
| Spleen | 26 | 20 | * | * |
| *Yeast* | 31 | 17 | 18 | 33 |

* These determinations were not made by Chargaff. What do you think the values should be?

ance of a molecule is often related to the functions of the molecule. Thus, in order to comprehend the functional properties of DNA, it is necessary to understand the spatial arrangement of nucleotides in the molecule. As we shall see, it is the three-dimensional nature of the DNA that is the key to how it really works. As with proteins, which you recall are composed of long chains of amino acids, DNA consists of nucleotides linked in a long strand. Are the nucleotides of the DNA molecule arranged to form a single strand, two strands, three strands, or four strands? Are the strands twisted, and how are the nitrogenous bases oriented? The problem of the structure of DNA was solved in 1953 by the efforts of M. H. F. Wilkins, James D. Watson, and Francis Crick. Wilkins was an x-ray crystallographer, that is, he studied the arrangement of atoms in crystals by bombarding the crystal with x rays. The way in which the x rays are scattered by the atoms in the crystal (**diffraction pattern**) gives information on the spatial arrangement of atoms forming the crystal. (Similarly, the manner in which x rays are scattered by your bones, muscles, and skin gives information on the density of these tissues and on the arrangement of atoms within them.) Wilkins examined purified crystalline DNA by this method and found that there were three spacing arrangements (**periodicities**) in the crystalline DNA; these were 3.4 Å, 20 Å, and 34 Å. Why did the diffraction pattern always indicate this repetitive spacing? It became a jigsaw puzzle to arrange these pieces of information into a meaningful picture. The puzzle was solved elegantly by Watson and Crick. Aware of the molecular structure of the nitrogenous bases and of their organization in the nucleotide, Watson and Crick built scale models of DNA, using the structure and size of the purines and pyrimidines and the dimensions of the DNA crystal. They arranged the nucleotides in a linear sequence, the backbone of the chain being formed of repetitive sequences of sugar-phosphate-sugar-phosphate; furthermore,

FIGURE 6–4 Organization of the DNA double helix as proposed by Watson and Crick. The uprights of the helix consist of alternating sugar-phosphate groups, and the rungs are formed by pairs of nitrogenous bases held together by hydrogen bonding.

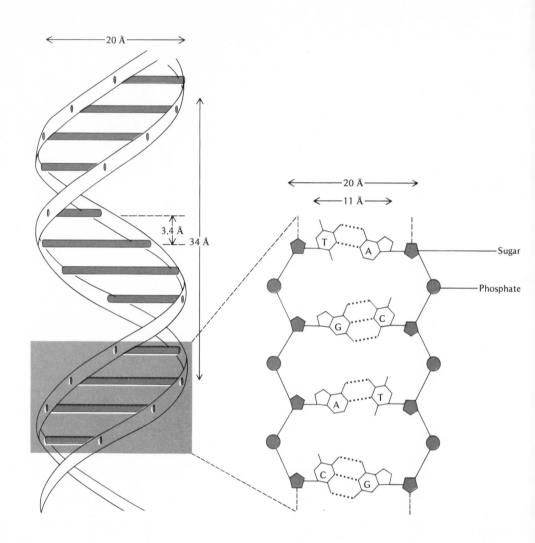

FIGURE 6–4 Organization of the DNA double helix as proposed by Watson and Crick. The uprights of the helix consist of alternating sugar-phosphate groups, and the rungs are formed by pairs of nitrogenous bases held together by hydrogen bonding.

they proposed that the DNA molecule consisted of two long chains, each with a sugar-phosphate backbone. The position of the bases proved somewhat troublesome, but soon it became apparent that adenine could bond only with thymine (by two hydrogen bonds) and guanine could bond only with cytosine (by three hydrogen bonds). Such a specific pairing of a purine with a pyrimidine would account for the identical amounts of adenine-thymine and cytosine-guanine. Furthermore, when the two nitrogenous

bases were joined as A-T or G-C they were 20 Å in width. Watson and Crick proposed that the nucleotides were arranged lengthwise forming two long chains; the backbone of each chain consisted of sugar and phosphate groups, and the two chains were linked by the inward-pointing bases (Figure 6–4). It then became obvious that the bases formed the rungs of a ladder and the uprights consisted of sugar and phsophate arranged in an alternating sequence; the distance between successive bases (rungs)

FIGURE 6–5 A diagrammatic representation of the manner in which DNA is replicated. (a) Intact double helix of DNA. (b) Complementary strands separate. (c) Free nucleotides are lined up in a specific order (complementary to the nucleotides in the DNA strand); by means of the enzyme DNA polymerase, phosphate bonds between adjacent nucleotides are formed. (d) Two new complementary DNA strands result.

was 3.4 Å. The 34-Å periodicity that Wilkins had found in crystalline DNA is 10 times 3.4 Å, and Watson and Crick proposed that the ladder was twisted in the form of a helix (similar to a spiral staircase), with a full twist (360°) at every tenth base. The Watson-Crick model for DNA was complete. They called it the double helix, since it was made of two strands of nucleotides wound around one another (Figure 6–4).

One of the properties that DNA must have in order to function in inheritance is the ability to duplicate itself. The Watson-Crick model provides for this. One strand of the DNA is complementary to the other, since when adenine occurs in one strand, thymine occurs in the opposite strand, and guanine in one strand is matched by cytosine in the other strand. The helical strands separate by the paired bases moving apart; this "unzipping" of the strands, resulting

from reduced hydrogen bonding between the bases, allows a new complementary strand to be formed from nucleotides and other materials present in the cell, under the direction of a specific enzyme called **DNA polymerase** (Figure 6–5). All the information necessary for arranging these bases in a linear sequence to complement the original strands of DNA is provided for by this mechanism of **complementary base pairing.** For example, if the strand of DNA contains adenine, a nucleotide containing thymine will pair with it; and if the next base in the DNA strand is guanine, the nucleotide which will pair must contain cytosine; and so on. In this manner, the old strands of DNA direct the **sequence,** or order, of nucleotides that form the new sister strands; the new strand is a complementary copy of the original strand. The formation of two new chains identical to

the original two chains is thus effected, but in addition and most important, the exact sequence of base pairs in the original strands will have been faithfully reproduced (Figure 6–5d). This process of DNA duplication is called **replication.**

### 6–3 GENETIC CODE: FOUR-LETTER ALPHABET, THREE-LETTER WORDS

As we have seen, the double helical strands of DNA have built into them all the information necessary for their own duplication; by means of base pairing, the old strand builds onto itself a new and complementary DNA strand. Thus, DNA satisfies one of our criteria for being the genetic material. How does the DNA carry information from one generation to the next? How can the bases of the DNA provide all the necessary information to build an entirely new cell? It

### BOX 6A An inborn error: PKU and idiocy

Phenylketonuria (PKU) is a rare hereditary disease of human beings. About 1 in 15,000 infants have this disease, which is characterized by severe mental retardation, the daily excretion in the urine of large amounts of phenylpyruvic acid, and high concentrations of the amino acid phenylalanine in the blood plasma. Normal individuals metabolize phenylalanine to tyrosine, but individuals with PKU lack the enzyme that catalyzes this reaction, and instead the blood plasma contains high levels of phenylalanine (Figure 6–6). In other words, in a child with the symptoms of PKU, the gene that codes for the enzyme that catalyzes the conversion of phenylalanine to tyrosine is faulty or missing altogether. Because of this, phenylalanine and several derivatives of phenylalanine, such as phenylpyruvic acid and phenylacetic acid, accumulate. A specific incriminating factor involved in brain cell damage has not been identified, however it has been hypothesized that high levels of phenylalanine itself as well as the toxic metabolites of phenylalanine result in mental retardation or idiocy.

Knowledge of PKU, its genetic basis, and the nature of the enzymatic deficiency provides a means for the prevention of mental retardation due to this disease. At birth each child is tested for the PKU trait; urine is examined for phenylpyruvic acid, or a drop of blood is placed on a card saturated with chemicals to ascertain the level of phenylalanine. If urine and blood are high in phenylpyruvic acid and phenylalanine, the child bears the defective genes for PKU. Idiocy in the bearer of PKU trait is easily prevented by a controlled diet.

Human beings are unable to synthesize eight amino acids (so-called **essential amino acids**)\* which are necessary for protein synthesis, and these must be obtained from our dietary proteins. Phenylalanine is one of these. In a child with the PKU trait it is necessary to prevent the production of phenylpyruvic acid, derived from phenylalanine in the diet and responsible for damage to the brain. The treatment of PKU is to maintain the dietary level of phenylalanine just sufficient for protein synthesis, but low enough to prevent a buildup of phenylpyruvic acid. Once brain development has proceeded beyond the sensitive stages and there is no longer any chance that phenylpyruvic acid and excess phenylalanine will influence mental capacity, a normal diet can be instituted.

The simple recognition of the relationship of genes to enzymes in PKU has virtually eliminated idiocy produced by this disease in the United States.

FIGURE 6–6 The metabolic basis of phenylketonuria (PKU). (a) Normal metabolism of phenylalanine. (b) Abnormal metabolism of phenylalanine in a person with PKU.

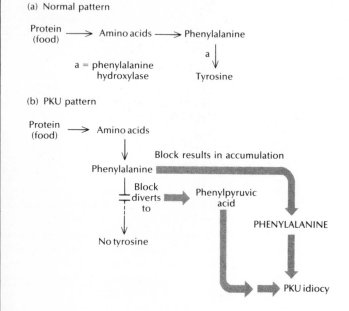

(a) Normal pattern

Protein (food) ⟶ Amino acids ⟶ Phenylalanine

a = phenylalanine hydroxylase

a ↓

Tyrosine

(b) PKU pattern

Protein (food) ⟶ Amino acids

Block results in accumulation

Phenylalanine

Block diverts to ⟹ Phenylpyruvic acid

No tyrosine

PHENYLALANINE

PKU idiocy

\* Because valine, leucine, isoleucine, lysine, methionine, threonine, phenylalanine, and tryptophan cannot be synthesized from other diet-derived molecules or the various intermediates of metabolism, they are called essential amino acids. The nonessential amino acids (glycine, alanine, serine, glutamic acid, glutamine, tyrosine, aspartic acid, asparagine, cysteine, histidine, proline, and arginine) can be made in the body using metabolic intermediates and the essential amino acids as amino donors. "Essential" is an unfortunate term, since all amino acids must be present in the cell for protein synthesis to take place. (Only plants are capable of synthesizing all the amino acids from substances simpler than the amino acids themselves).

FIGURE 6–7 Coding genetic information in the DNA molecule using nucleotide sequences of one, two, or three.

**113**

COMMUNICATION BETWEEN CELL GENERATIONS: NUCLEIC ACIDS

becomes obvious that somehow the DNA must contain a **code,** a symbolic message that directs the cell to manufacture what the code specifies.

Before we explore the nature of the code itself, let us briefly look at inheritance. Studies with a variety of organisms amply demonstrate that enzyme synthesis depends upon specific entities within the nucleus known as **genes.** In 1940 G. W. Beadle and E. L. Tatum proposed that for every enzyme there is a specific gene; the concept became known as the **one gene–one enzyme hypothesis.** This hypothesis states that genes exert their control over cellular metabolism by controlling the synthesis of enzymes; since enzymes control all the reactions that take place in the cell, the form and function of the cell depend directly upon enzyme function and therefore upon gene action (Box 6A). To illustrate this very simply, let us consider an example. In order to have brown pigment in your hair there must occur a series of chemical reactions in the cells that produce a pigmented hair. The reaction sequence can be represented by $A \rightarrow B \rightarrow C \rightarrow D \rightarrow$ brown pigment. The enzymes that catalyze this sequence of reactions can be represented as $a$, $b$, $c$, $d$. Thus, the reaction can be represented:

$$A \rightarrow B \rightarrow C \rightarrow D \rightarrow \text{brown pigment}$$
$$\uparrow \quad \uparrow \quad \uparrow \quad \uparrow$$
$$a \quad b \quad c \quad d$$

When all the enzymes are present, brown pigment is produced, as long as substance $A$ is present in the body. If substance $A$ is lacking, then we get no brown pigment and the hair is colorless; and if enzyme $a$, $b$, $c$, or $d$ is lacking, we get no brown pigment.

Genes direct the production of enzymes. What do genes have to do with DNA? Let us say for the time being that specific regions of the DNA helix present in the cell are the stuff of which genes are made; in a simplistic way, a portion of the DNA molecule equals a gene. (How much DNA makes up one gene is a complex question that we shall allow to rest for the time being.) The

question that remains is, How does the DNA direct the synthesis of enzymes? Enzymes, as we have seen, are proteins, and so the question can be rephrased: how do we get from DNA to a protein?

This brings us once again to our problem of coding. The DNA of most organisms exists as a long, unbranched, double helical strand localized within the nucleus. In each strand of the double helix there are four different kinds of nitrogenous bases. It must be that the sequence of bases determines the nature of the information available to the cell. But what do we need to code for, and what is the product of the sequence of nitrogenous bases? If the DNA that composes a gene or genes makes a protein, the sequence of bases must code for the subunits of a protein—the amino acids. There are 20 different kinds of amino acids present in most proteins; therefore, the base sequence must be able to code for at least 20 different amino acids. How many bases, of which only four kinds exist, are needed to code for 20 amino acids? To put it another way, let us think of the nitrogenous bases as the letters A, G, T, and C. How many words can we construct using these four letters? If we use one letter for each word,

we can make only four words (A, G, T, and C); if each word is composed of two letters, and four letters are available, we can make 16 words (AA, AG, AT, AC, GT, GG, GC, and so on); and if we make three-letter words and have four letters available, we can compose 64 words (Figure 6–7). Clearly, if the genetic code were to use only one- or two-letter "words" it could not code for 20 amino acids, but three-letter "words" (or "words" composed of three bases) can code for more than is required. The genetic code, it has been established, is a **triplet code;** that is, it consists of sequences of three nitrogenous bases. The nature of the triplet code words has been completely deciphered. This is shown in Figure 6–8. As you can see, there is some redundancy in the code, since some combinations signify the same amino acid; for example, the DNA code words which specify alanine are CGA, CGG, CGT, and CGC. We have a similar situation in the English language, where several different words can be used to specify the same object: house, home, dwelling, residence. Codes in which several different code words describe the same thing are called **degenerate codes;** the genetic code is a degenerate code.

| Singlet code (4 words) | Doublet code (16 words) | | | | Triplet code (64 words) | | | |
|---|---|---|---|---|---|---|---|---|
| | | | | | AAA | AAG | AAC | AAT |
| | | | | | AGA | AGG | AGC | AGT |
| | | | | | ACA | ACG | ACC | ACT |
| | | | | | ATA | ATG | ATC | ATT |
| | | | | | GAA | GAG | GAC | GAT |
| | | | | | GGA | GGG | GGC | GGT |
| A | AA | AG | AC | AT | GCA | GCG | GCC | GCT |
| G | GA | GG | GC | GT | GTA | GTG | GTC | GTT |
| C | CA | CG | CC | CT | CAA | CAG | CAC | CAT |
| T | TA | TG | TC | TT | CGA | CGG | CGC | CGT |
| | | | | | CCA | CCG | CCC | CCT |
| | | | | | CTA | CTG | CTC | CTT |
| | | | | | TAA | TAG | TAC | TAT |
| | | | | | TGA | TGG | TGC | TGT |
| | | | | | TCA | TCG | TCC | TCT |
| | | | | | TTA | TTG | TTC | TTT |

**(a)**

Second base in DNA triplet

First base in DNA triplet / Third base in DNA triplet

| First base | Second base A | Second base G | Second base T | Second base C | Third base |
|---|---|---|---|---|---|
| **A** | AAA AAG } phenylalanine; AAT AAC leucine | AGA AGG AGT AGC } serine | ATA ATG } tyrosine; ATT ATC } "terminator" | ACA ACG } cysteine; ACT "terminator"; ACC tryptophan | A G T C |
| **G** | GAA GAG GAT GAC } leucine | GGA GGG GGT GGC } proline | GTA GTG } histidine; GTT GTC } glutamine | GCA GCG GCT GCC } arginine | A G T C |
| **T** | TAA TAG TAT } isoleucine; TAC methionine | TGA TGG TGT TGC } threonine | TTA TTG } asparagine; TTT TTC } lysine | TCA TCG } serine; TCT TCC } arginine | A G T C |
| **C** | CAA CAG CAT CAC } valine | CGA CGG CGT CGC } alanine | CTA CTG } aspartic acid; CTT CTC } glutamic acid | CCA CCG CCT CCC } glycine | A G T C |

**(b)**

Second letter in mRNA triplet

First letter in mRNA triplet / Third letter in mRNA triplet

| First letter | Second letter U | Second letter C | Second letter A | Second letter G | Third letter |
|---|---|---|---|---|---|
| **U** | UUU UUC } phenylalanine; UUA UUG } leucine | UCU UCC UCA UCG } serine | UAU UAC } tyrosine; UAA UAG } "terminator" | UGU UGC } cysteine; UGA "terminator"; UGG tryptophan | U C A G |
| **C** | CUU CUC CUA CUG } leucine | CCU CCC CCA CCG } proline | CAU CAC } histidine; CAA CAG } glutamine | CGU CGC CGA CGG } arginine | U C A G |
| **A** | AUU AUC } isoleucine; AUA; AUG methionine | ACU ACC ACA ACG } threonine | AAU AAC } asparagine; AAA AAG } lysine | AGU AGC } serine; AGA AGG } arginine | U C A G |
| **G** | GUU GUC GUA GUG } valine | GCU GCC GCA GCG } alanine | GAU GAC } aspartic acid; GAA GAG } glutamic acid | GGU GGC GGA GGG } glycine | U C A G |

It has been found that the genetic code is universal, that is, the same triplet stands for the same amino acid in all organisms from viruses to humans. This suggests that the genetic code probably evolved only once. The differences among viruses, bacteria, human beings, and all other living organisms are due not to differences in the kinds of nitrogenous bases found in their DNA, but to variations in the sequential order of these bases. It is much like using the letters of the alphabet to construct different words. The letters used are always the same; however, the words formed and their meaning (message) may differ depending on the manner in which the letters have been arranged. Similarly, different arrangements of triplets (letters) along the length of the DNA strand will result in a varying amino-acid sequence (words) in a protein (sentence); it is possible to produce an almost infinite number of triplet arrangements in DNA, and thus it is possible to have an endless variety of amino-acid sequences in proteins. Species-specificity has as its basis the different amino-acid sequences in a protein (that is, dog hemoglobin differs from human hemoglobin in a number of amino acids), but it must be emphasized that this is ultimately a reflection of the specific arrangement of the three-letter words in the hereditary blueprint, DNA (Box 6B).

## 6–4 COPYING AND TRANSLATING THE GENETIC CODE: RNA AND PROTEIN

The genetic code of the DNA is localized within the nucleus of the cell; the nucleus is in a sense a library of blueprints, but the blueprints cannot be taken out of the library. How then does the information encoded in the DNA reach the rest of the cell? The manufactured product specified by the code is a protein, and the apparatus for protein synthesis is in the cytoplasm. Thus, a number of problems must be solved by

FIGURE 6–9 The general structure of a ribonucleotide. For comparative purposes, the structural
differences between the sugars of a ribonucleotide
(ribose) and a deoxyribonucleotide (deoxyribose) as
well as between the unique nitrogenous bases
(uracil and thymine) are shown.

Nucleotide

the cell before it can utilize the information
contained in the DNA.

First, a means must be available for copying or transcribing the genetic code and
transporting this copy of the code to the
cytoplasm, where the information can be
put to use. Second, the coded message
must be deciphered; if the code is in a

cryptic or symbolic language, a key to the
code will be needed in order to translate
its contained information. Let us now introduce the transcriber and the translator of
the genetic code: ribonucleic acid, or **RNA.**

RNA, like DNA consists of three molecular
constituents: (1) phosphate, (2) a 5-carbon
sugar called **ribose,** and (3) a nitrogenous
base. As with DNA, these constituent groups
together form a nucleotide, or, more specifically, a **ribonucleotide** (Figure 6–9). Although RNA, like DNA, contains four different nitrogenous bases, only three of
these are the same as those of DNA. RNA
contains the bases adenine, guanine, cytosine, and uracil. **Uracil** is a pyrimidine
almost identical to thymine, and in RNA the
uracil replaces the thymine of DNA.

There are three important distinctions
between DNA and RNA: (1) RNA contains
ribose, a sugar slightly different from that
found in DNA (Figure 6–9); (2) RNA is usually
single-stranded in contrast to double-
stranded DNA; and (3) RNA is distributed
throughout the cell, whereas DNA is found
(almost) exclusively within the nucleus.[2]

A look at the nucleotides of RNA suggests
that the base sequences are similar to those
of DNA and could in themselves represent
a language or code written in four letters.
This RNA alphabet of nitrogenous bases is
exactly like that of DNA, except for the
substitution of uracil for thymine. Even with
this one-letter substitution, the bases of
DNA can be copied or transcribed into RNA
bases, and in so doing the genetic message
is unchanged. In the cell the transcription
or copying of code words of the DNA into
RNA results in a specific kind of RNA called
messenger **RNA (mRNA),** and is achieved by
a specific enzyme called **RNA polymerase.**

In order for the sequence of nucleotides
in the DNA to be read and copied, the DNA
strands must separate; a region of the DNA

---

[2] Mitochondria and chloroplasts contain small
amounts of DNA, which may code for specific
mitochondrial and chloroplast proteins.

FIGURE 6–10 A schematic representation of transcription. (a) DNA strands separate, exposing a sequence of bases. This serves as a guide for the synthesis of a complementary strand of mRNA. The nucleotides of the incipient RNA are bonded together by means of RNA polymerase. (b) DNA strands zip closed, and the strand of mRNA leaves the nucleus.

double helix "unzips" and a sequence of bases is exposed (Figure 6–10); only one of the exposed strands of the DNA serves as a guide for the synthesis of a complementary strand of mRNA. Using the mechanism of specific complementary base pairing, the nucleotides of the incipient mRNA, which are free in the nucleus, line up and match the DNA nucleotides: mRNA-uracil with DNA-adenine, mRNA-guanine with DNA-cytosine, mRNA-cytosine with DNA-guanine, and mRNA-adenine with DNA-thymine. The base-pairing mechanism assures that the sequence of nucleotides in the DNA strand is followed exactly by the sequence in which the nucleotides of the incipient mRNA are lined up. The mRNA molecule detaches from the strand of DNA and leaves the place of synthesis in the nucleus: the DNA strands now "zip" closed (Figure 6–10). In this manner the nucleotide sequences of DNA, corresponding to genes, are copied in the nucleotide sequences of mRNA; the genetic code has been rewritten, or copied, without any change in the wording; the process is called **transcription.**

As we have already seen, the language of the genetic code, contained in the DNA molecule, is written in three-letter words using an alphabet of four letters. The mRNA, using an alphabet of four letters, only one of which is different from the alphabet of DNA, faithfully represents these three-letter code words. The four letters of the DNA alphabet are capable of making 64 different three-letter code words, or triplets, and it is easy to see that in the mRNA the four-letter code can also make 64 three-letter words; the 64 code words of the mRNA are called **codons** (Figure 6–8).

The problem of getting the genetic information out of the nucleus without the release of DNA has been solved by the formation of a strand of mRNA. Messenger RNA is appropriately named, for it not only is a complementary copy of the genetic code, but it also moves out of the nucleus, where it was synthesized, and enters the

(a)

DNA

RNA polymerase
Enzyme

Ribonucleotides

= U
Uracil

= C
Cytosine

= G
Guanine

= A
Adenine

(b)

DNA

mRNA

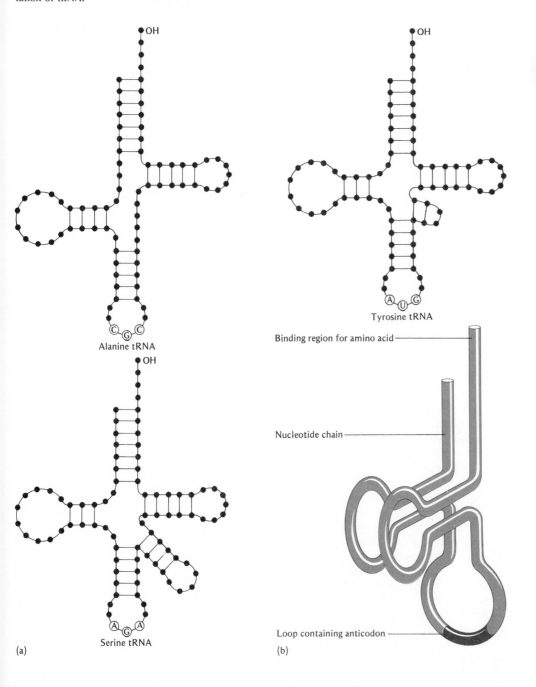

FIGURE 6–11 (below and right) Transfer RNA, a single-stranded molecule that exists in the cytoplasm. (a) Cloverleaf pattern of three tRNAs from yeast showing the free end for binding to an amino acid and the bend with a region for binding to mRNA (anticodon). (b) Three-dimensional representation of tRNA.

Alanine tRNA

Tyrosine tRNA

Serine tRNA

Binding region for amino acid

Nucleotide chain

Loop containing anticodon

(a)

(b)

cytoplasm. In the cytoplasm the mRNA attaches to an organelle, the **ribosome.** The ribosome contains protein and a special kind of RNA called ribosomal **RNA (rRNA).** (The rRNA also arises as a result of transcription.) The ribosome is the site within the cell where proteins are synthesized.

How is the coded message of the mRNA translated into a protein? It is clear that before a protein can be synthesized it is necessary to move the constituent amino acids into position, arrange them in the proper sequence, and forge the peptide bonds between adjacent amino acids so that a protein is produced. This cannot be accomplished by the amino acids themselves, since they will not bond directly to the mRNA; the process depends upon an adapter-type molecule that will pick up an individual amino acid and together they are transferred to the mRNA–ribosome complex. This adapter is called **transfer RNA (tRNA).** Each transfer RNA is a molecule of RNA that is twisted in such a manner that it forms a cloverleaf pattern (Figure 6–11). There are more than 20 kinds of tRNAs present in the cytoplasm, and each one binds to a specific amino acid at its free end (Figure 6–11). At the bend of the middle loop in the cloverleaf-shaped molecule of tRNA, there is a specific triplet region of nucleotides which is complementary to a particular triplet (codon) of the mRNA; the specific triplet of the tRNA is called an **anticodon.**

We have introduced all the participants in the assembly of proteins; now let us see how they function. Each amino acid, free in the cytoplasm, is activated by ATP and an enzyme, and then this activated amino acid is transferred to one of the prongs of the cloverleaf-shaped tRNA, which is specific for that particular amino acid. The tRNA carries the activated amino acid to the ribosome, which is composed of two globular regions, one larger than the other (Figure 6–12). Protein synthesis actually begins when a single strand of mRNA attaches to the

FIGURE 6–12 The ribonucleic acids (RNAs) of the cell.

smaller region of the ribosome. By means of specific base pairing, the triplet region of the tRNA (anticodon) becomes attached to the complementary triplet region of the mRNA (codon) (Figure 6–13a). The tRNA, carrying its amino acid, is held in position on the larger portion of the ribosome; in this manner the ribosome acts like a jig or a vise, holding the mRNA in position and guiding the tRNA anticodon into proper alignment for coupling to the codon of the mRNA. The next step involves the movement of a second tRNA with its amino acid to the ribosome and the specific coupling of its anticodon region with the next mRNA codon. Thus, when the two adjacent codons of the mRNA are read, two tRNAs are present on the ribosome, properly aligned and attached to the mRNA and each bearing an activated amino acid. With the aid of two enzymes and an energy-rich molecule of GTP (similar to ATP but containing guanosine instead of adenosine), a peptide bond is formed between the adjacent amino acids and the bonding of the first tRNA to the mRNA and the amino acid is weakened (Figure 6–13b). The ribosome then moves along the strand of mRNA as the third codon is read, and the first tRNA, now minus its amino acid, becomes discharged from the mRNA (Figure 6–13c). A new tRNA carrying its activated amino acid can now attach to the third codon of the mRNA. The movement of the ribosome along the strand of mRNA produces a sequential reading of codon after codon. With each reading, the following takes place: (1) an amino acid is brought into position, (2) a peptide bond is formed between adjacent amino acids, (3) the tRNA in the first position is released, and, (4) as the next codon is read, there is room for another tRNA with its amino acid to be bound to another mRNA codon further down the line. The free tRNAs move away from the ribosome and can be used over and over again to pick up other activated amino acids. By this one-by-one addition of amino acids, a long, free polypeptide chain is formed (Figure 6–13d); its sequence of

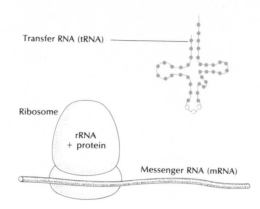

Transfer RNA (tRNA)

Ribosome

rRNA + protein

Messenger RNA (mRNA)

amino acids is determined by the codon sequence of the mRNA and the proper alignment of the complementary anticodons of the tRNA. In this manner, a nucleotide sequence of mRNA becomes the amino-acid sequence of a protein. The assembly of a protein or polypeptide chain using the information in mRNA is called **translation.**

There are three codons that are not recognized by any tRNA; these are called **chain terminator** codons and signal the end of the message (Figure 6–8); the final amino acid in the polypeptide chain is released from the last tRNA, the tRNA is released from the mRNA, and a complete free polypeptide chain results. Since molecules of mRNA are often very long (thousands of nucleotides in length), only a small portion of the molecule is in contact with the ribosome at any one time. Frequently other ribosomes attach at the beginning of the mRNA, so that the message is being read by several ribosomes in succession; this creates a chain of ribosomes held together by a strand of mRNA, and such a group is called a **polyribosome** or **polysome** (Figure 6–14).

How is the genetic code read? The reading of the DNA strand of nucleotides apparently begins at the beginning, just the way you begin reading a paragraph. The triplets are

read in a nonoverlapping sequence in groups of three. For example, if the DNA nucleotide sequence is TGAGCACAACTT and if TGA is at the beginning of the DNA message, the sequence would be read TGA, GCA, CAA, and CTT. To support this notion, Crick suggested that if he treated DNA (in this case the DNA of a virus) with a dye that deleted certain nucleotides, this would produce an altered sequence and therefore a different protein. In the case of the sequence just cited, suppose that the deleted base was A in the second triplet— GCA; the sequence would become TGA GCC AAC TT. Obviously the first amino acid in the polypeptide chain would be identical to the synthesized product coded by the untreated DNA, but the remainder would be incorrect. This is exactly the type of result that Crick obtained.

Not all base deletions or alterations cause the same functional change in a polypeptide chain. The deletion or insertion of one or more nucleotides generally leads to completely nonfunctional genes. By contrast, simple exchanges of one nucleotide for another may lead to "leaky" genes, those in which the protein product often shows partial enzymatic activity. To visualize the difference between these situations, consider the following sentence: seethecatatetherat. If such a sentence is read in triplets, the meaning becomes clear: see the cat ate the rat. If there was a deletion or insertion of one letter, and again the sequence of letters is read as triplets, the reading frame is completely upset and a meaningless sentence is produced:

insertion: seethecatbatetherat ⟶ see the cat bat eth era t

deletion: seethectatetherat ⟶ see the cta tet her at

However, a single-letter substitution may produce a meaningful result:

seethecatatatethebat ⟶ see the cat ate the bat.

As we have already mentioned, the ge-

FIGURE 6–13 Diagrammatic view of peptide-bond formation and the role of the ribosome in translation. (a) A strand of messenger RNA (mRNA) attaches to the small subunit of the ribosome, and by means of specific base pairing the triplet region (anticodon) of the transfer RNA (tRNA) becomes attached to the complementary region of the mRNA (codon). The tRNA carrying an amino acid is held in position on the large subunit of the ribosome. A second tRNA bearing an amino acid then moves to the ribosome, and its anticodon region binds to the second codon of the mRNA. (b) A peptide bond is formed between the adjacent amino acids, and the bonding of the first tRNA to the mRNA is weakened. (c) The first tRNA minus its amino acid leaves the ribosome as the ribosome moves along the strand of mRNA. (d) Another tRNA carrying an activated amino acid can now attach to the third codon of the mRNA. Thus, a sequential reading of codon after codon is produced by the movement of the ribosome along the mRNA; with each reading an amino acid is brought into position by the tRNA, a peptide bond is formed between adjacent amino acids, the tRNA in the first position is released, and as the next codon is read, there is room for another tRNA bearing an amino acid.

FIGURE 6–14 The ribosome: assembly site of polypeptide chains. (a) Electron microscope view of isolated ribosomes, with inset showing ribosome at higher magnification. (Courtesy of Masamichi Aikawa.) (b) Ribosomes move (in direction of the small arrows) along a strand of mRNA, reading and translating the message into a polypeptide chain. A chain of ribosomes held by a strand of RNA is called a polysome (polyribosome). (c) Electron micrograph of genes being transcribed. The growing polypeptide chain is not visible in the micrograph. (Courtesy of Oscar L. Miller).

(a)

Free ribosome about to attach to mRNA

Growing polypeptide chains

Complete polypeptide chain

tRNA

Messenger RNA

Polysome

Free ribosome

(b)

RNA polymerase

Inactive chromosome segment

Active chromosome segment

Direction of RNA synthesis

Polyribosome

DNA

Ribosome

Messenger RNA

RNA polymerase

RNA polymerase

DNA

0.25 μm

Ribosome    mRNA

(c)

netic code is degenerate, that is, more than one triplet may code for a particular amino acid. Degeneracy most often occurs in the third letter of the triplet; thus AAG and AAA both code for lysine. If a base substitution occurred that converted AAA into AAG, there would be no amino acid alteration and a normal protein would be produced. One of the speculations on the reason for degeneracy in the genetic code is that it provides a buffer against alterations that could lead to unfavorable effects.

James Joyce in *Ulysses* wrote without any punctuation, and in such a narrative the meaning sometimes becomes ambiguous because the sentences run together. How does the machinery of the cell know when to begin reading a sequence of nucleotides and when to stop? Since DNA is a long strand of nucleotides, it is difficult to see why the cell does not manufacture one gigantic polypeptide chain: a molecular run-on sentence. What are the punctuation marks that determine sentence length and tell the cell where the beginning and end of a gene are?

The necessary punctuation marks (equivalent to a period or a space) between linear sequences of nucleotides in the DNA have been found. Transcription of a stretch of DNA involves the enzyme RNA polymerase, which catalyzes the formation of a strand of mRNA. First there must be a mechanism to ensure that the proper gene is transcribed. This is accomplished by the RNA polymerase having an affinity for a particular region of the DNA, a site approximately 10 bases before the site at which transcription itself is to begin. This site generally contains the sequences TATAATG. The RNA polymerase not only recognizes the proper place on the DNA to bind, but it also selects only one of the two strands of the DNA that will be transcribed. During the binding of the polymerase to the DNA, the double helix unwinds. The RNA polymerase moves along the DNA separating the strands of the helix and at the same time fabricating a complementary molecule of mRNA from one of the two strands. Once the polymerase is past a particular site, the double helix is reformed.

Just as there are start signals for transcription, there are also stop signals that act to terminate mRNA synthesis at specific locations along the length of the DNA. The reading of these stop signs or periods is achieved when the polymerase reaches a specific region often identified by a stretch of GC pairs; at this point transcription terminates, the RNA polymerase leaves the DNA, and then another gene may be transcribed.

Once a strand of mRNA has been transcribed from the DNA, it attaches to the ribosome, where protein synthesis takes place. To ensure that the ribosome becomes attached to the mRNA in the correct alignment, there is a recognition site on the mRNA called the **ribosome binding site,** positioned approximately seven nucleotides ahead of an AUG triplet, the start site for protein synthesis. Once the ribosome attaches to this codon it moves along the RNA in blocks of three nucleotides. AUG is more than just an attachment site, it is also the codon that specifies the amino acid methionine. In nature, however, not all proteins have this amino acid at their starting end, so how can AUG be the universal initiation codon? In the cell there are two kinds of tRNA molecules for methionine. One tRNA picks up the normal methionine, but another tRNA attaches to a methionine that subsequently receives a formyl (O=C—H) group. The methionine having a formyl group is a blocked amino acid, that is, it can only begin a polypeptide chain, it cannot be inserted in the middle of a polypeptide. Later, once the polypeptide chain is complete, enzymes in the cell remove the blocked methionine so that a protein chain can begin with almost any of the amino acids.

The termination of a protein chain requires a stop signal, a special termination codon, and a release factor capable of recognizing this stop sign. In mRNA there are 61 triplets, codons, which code for amino acids, but three triplets (UAA, UAG, and UGA) do not, and these are called chain terminators or nonsense triplets. If in the DNA strand a nonsense triplet is inserted between a series of meaningful triplets, the mRNA would faithfully contain this codon (UAA). When such a codon is read, the terminal tRNA drops off the mRNA, no amino acid is inserted at this codon, and a single polypeptide chain of definite length is produced.

In summary, let us once again look at the genetic code and the synthesis of proteins. The hereditary information of all living cells is contained in molecules of DNA; a sequence of nucleotides in the DNA (a gene) carries all the necessary information for the fabrication of the gene product, a protein. A sequence of three nucleotides on the DNA strand codes for an amino acid—this triplet genetic code is specific and universal. In addition, the DNA molecule is self-duplicating and contains all the information necessary for making additional copies of itself. DNA is ordinarily restricted to the nucleus of the cell, and we can consider that the coded hereditary blueprint resides in a library of heredity, but the blueprint does not circulate. It is as if the master blueprint were so precious that it is kept confined so that it cannot be lost. In order for the coded message of the DNA to be put into operation, it is necessary to get the message to the cytoplasm of the cell, where the site of protein synthesis is located. Since the DNA is locked in the nucleus, the coded blueprint is copied, and only the copy of the blueprint leaves the nucleus to enter the cytoplasm. Messenger RNA, a copy of a single strand of the DNA, is a faithful transcript of the triplets that make up the genetic message. In the cytoplasm the mRNA attaches to a ribosome; another kind of RNA (tRNA) binds to a specific amino acid and carries it to the ribosome. At the ribosome the copied blueprint of the mRNA is read and the message is translated into an amino-acid sequence. In this manner the

DNA of the genetic code becomes transcribed into a molecule of mRNA and this in turn is translated into a polypeptide or protein.

In 1977 it was discovered that in eukaryotes, (as opposed to prokaryotes), the genetic messages do not occur in long, linear, uninterrupted sequences. Instead, in birds, amphibians, reptiles and mammals there exist long stretches of DNA that do not correspond to the primary sequence of the protein being coded. These intervening sequences (**introns**) are present in nearly all eukaryotic genes, but it remains a mystery as to why such genes occur in pieces. What is known, however, is that an RNA copy (pre-mRNA) is made in the nucleus from the entire length of the DNA containing the fragmented gene, the intervening sequences in the pre-mRNA are then snipped out enzymatically, and the cut ends of the RNA are spliced together to give a shortened, mature mRNA. This mRNA is itself now a copy of the gene, and it moves from the nucleus to the cytoplasm, where the genetic message is read and made into a protein.

## 6–5 IMPLICATIONS OF THE GENETIC CODE

So far we have suggested that the nucleotide sequences of DNA code for amino acids; via mRNA and tRNA, amino acids are assembled in specific, ordered arrangements dictated by the DNA and enzymatically linked to form proteins. Originally we restricted our discussion of genes and the genetic code to a specific group of proteins, enzymes, because it is in enzyme activity that gene function is most clearly observed. The one gene–one enzyme hypothesis of Beadle and Tatum is true, but as you will already have surmised, it should be modified and broadened in its scope to include more than proteins with enzymatic activity. Recent evidence indicates that a better statement of the genetic code would be "one

gene–one polypeptide chain." (Remember that a polypeptide chain is a subunit of a protein; Chapter 3.) Let us return to an example of a protein which is not an enzyme but which illustrates the nature of the genetic code and its importance in the function of the body.

There exists in human populations a variant of normal hemoglobin called sickle-cell hemoglobin. **Sickle-cell hemoglobin** differs from normal hemoglobin in only 1 amino acid among those that compose the protein chain of hemoglobin. If we look at five amino acids in the normal hemoglobin sequence, we find the following:

-threonine-proline-glutamic acid-
glutamic acid-lysine-

Looking at the same region in a person with sickle-cell hemoglobin, we find:

-threonine-proline-valine-
glutamic acid-lysine-

The difference between the two hemoglobins is the substitution of valine for glutamic acid in sickle-cell hemoglobin. To see how such a small change produces such a profound effect, let us look at the nucleotide sequence in the DNA that codes for both these amino-acid sequences. The DNA code words for valine are CAT and CAC; those for glutamic acid are CTT and CTC. Essentially, the difference between valine and glutamic acid (as far as the nucleotide sequence in DNA is concerned) is a change in the middle nucleotide; when A is substituted for T in the triplet, glutamic acid is transcribed and translated as valine. It is apparent that one way of producing a genetic change (**mutation**) in a cell or an organism is by the simple exchange of one nucleotide for another. In Chapter 24 we shall discuss in some detail changes in our genetic constitution (mutations) and their effect on our body functions.

How do nucleotide substitutions occur? One type of error might be a "typographical" error. It is conceivable that during the replication of the nucleotide strands of DNA,

when the strands separate, a rearrangement of the hydrogen atoms of the nucleotide might occur, resulting in faulty hydrogen bonds; this would permit binding of the wrong nucleotide in the new chain being synthesized. For example, instead of A binding T, perhaps because of defective hydrogen bonding, it would bind C. When the next round of replication occurred, the chain with the C would pair with a G; the original parent strand would pair with a T. Thus, there would arise a DNA molecule in the next generation which had AT substituted by GC. Other errors might occur as the result of unnatural effects. For example, there is evidence that mutations can arise in double-stranded DNA as a result of exposure to x rays, ultraviolet rays, cosmic rays, and certain chemical agents such as nitrous acid; such agents alter either the base sequence (by cutting out a base) or the base itself.[3] Thus, mutational changes can be considered to result, at least in some cases, from changes in the nucleotide sequence of DNA. A major hazard of radiation (to be discussed in Chapter 24) is the hazard to the genetic code itself. As typographical errors rarely improve a sensible printed message, so, too, random changes in the base sequence are rarely favorable. Many mutations are lethal, and so we never see them and they are not perpetuated. If the mutations are not lethal, their favorable or unfavorable nature often depends on the environment and the genetic constitution in which the gene functions, so that a hard-and-fast rule is impossible.

An important implication of the Watson-Crick model for DNA and the mechanism of protein synthesis is that it tells us why

---

[3] Nitrous acid works as a mutagen by converting the pyrimidine cytosine to uracil. This means that in the DNA strands GC, for example, is converted to GU; when replication occurs one of the daughter strands will contain GC, but the other will contain UA. In a second round of replication this mutant strand will give rise to a daughter molecule with AT and UA. The error or alteration in bases is perpetuated.

humans differ from mice, cats, dogs, and elephants. We manufacture human proteins and not any other kind because of the specific order of the nucleotides in our DNA. We may eat a variety of proteins in our diet, but after digestion and absorption, the building blocks of amino acids are fabricated within our cells into our very own proteins because each cell of our body contains very specific coded directions in the DNA. It can be said that the more similar the order of the bases, the more closely related are the organisms; in identical twins the DNA base sequences are all identical.

## 6–6 GENETIC ENGINEERING: RECOMBINANT DNA

We said earlier that a cat is a cat and a dog is a dog because they respectively have cat DNA and dog DNA. What if one could combine dog and cat DNA? How would it be expressed? Would we create a new organism?

**Recombinant DNA** research techniques have made it possible to splice the DNA sequences of organisms such as dogs and cats and to insert them into the DNA sequences of the bacterium *Escherichia coli.* The foreign DNA is then replicated along with the bacterial DNA (Box 6C). What is the promise of recombinant DNA research?

First, by carving up the genetic material of particular species and inserting the genes, one at a time, into *E. coli,* it is possible to study the organization and expression of genes as well as the function of different genes, something that up to now has required long and costly breeding programs, most often with limited results. With understanding comes control, possibly of genetic diseases such as hemophilia and diabetes. We could construct, say, bacterial strains that produce massive amounts of antibodies, antibiotics, or hormones, or we could develop bacteria that enable all plants to draw their nitrogen from the air rather

than from costly fertilizers. Already, bacteria have been manufactured that can produce the human brain hormone somatostatin. Somatostatin inhibits the secretion of pituitary growth hormone. The researchers who first isolated somatostatin needed almost half a million sheep brains to produce 5 mg of the substance, an amount that can be produced rapidly by only 2 gallons of altered bacterial culture.

## 6–7 PROSPECTS FOR THE REFABRICATION OF HUMAN BEINGS

We have deciphered messages written in the DNA strands and can isolate single genes; now we are on the road toward learning to spell new words, words of our own creation—in effect, writing new genetic messages. Can we change the pattern of the machinery that predestines our being?

The idea of correcting a human genetic defect by introducing a new piece of DNA into a cell has been obvious on theoretical grounds and has been much discussed in recent years. The transfer of foreign genes into cells which then incorporate and express them has now been successfully carried out. For example, a bacterial plasmid (see p. 124) containing the genes from a herpes simplex virus (the cold sore virus) has been injected into fertilized mouse eggs, which were then implanted into female mice. At the end of the gestation period the fetuses were removed and analyzed for the presence of the foreign genes. Quite remarkably, 15% of the developing mice had donor DNA containing the foreign genes, and the genes were intact. Such experiments provide a beginning toward genetic manipulation, for if gene control is to be exercised, the foreign DNA must be incorporated into the host-cell chromosomes and then transmitted to future generations via sperm and egg. Recent studies with injected mouse eggs that were permitted to develop to maturity showed that the adult tissues contained foreign DNA.

Only a few mice successfully integrated these new genes, and why such transfers succeed in some cases and fail in others is still unclear. However, despite such limitations, all of the necessary preliminary steps for studying foreign gene expression in a living cell have been successfully accomplished, and mice which carry genes that are both foreign and functional have been bred.

At the same time, things are not as simple as they seem. Responsible scientists warn that the possibilities of genetic intervention (genetic engineering) in humans are not without limitations. The number of diseases (for example, hemophilia and PKU) and normal traits (for example, eye color) that are controlled by a single gene (relatively short lengths of DNA) is small and forms a special class of the genetic spectrum. Most human characteristics are **polygenic,** that is, they depend on the interaction of many genes (long stretches of DNA), and they vary continuously rather than producing an all-or-none effect. For example, instead of a trait such as skin color being represented as white or brown, there exists a continuum of shades of tan between these extremes. Especially important is the fact that characteristics, such as intelligence and temperament, as well as physique, are highly polygenic. Human beings probably have hundreds of thousands of genes for polygenic characteristics compared with the few hundred recognizable monogenically (single gene) controlled ones. Polygenic inheritance is difficult to study and control because so many combinations are possible and gene interactions are extremely frequent. Also it should be emphasized that, singly or in clusters, genes can determine the range of potential for a given trait in an individual, but the environment may determine the nature of its expression within that range. In other words, having a certain set of genes does not assure its expression; the conditions for its manifestation must be appropriate.

There is another fly in the ointment when

BOX 6C  Redesigning bacteria

The development of the recombinant DNA technique ushered in a new era of genetic engineering—with all of its promise and possible peril. The lowly organism that currently plays the largest role in the process is the *E. coli* bacterium. This microbe—a laboratory derivative of a common inhabitant of the human intestine—lends itself to being engineered because its genetic structure has been so well studied. In the first step of the process, scientists place the bacterium in a test tube with a detergent-like liquid. This dissolves the microbe's outer membrane, causing its DNA strands to spill out in a disorderly tangle. Most of the DNA is included in the bacterium's chromosome, in the form of a long strand containing thousands of genes. The remainder is found in several tiny, closed loops called plasmids, which have only a few genes each and are the most popular vehicles for the recombinant technique.

After the plasmids are separated from the chromosomal DNA in a centrifuge, they are placed in a solution with a chemical catalyst called a restriction enzyme. This enzyme cuts through the plasmids' DNA strips at specific points. It leaves overlapping, mortise-type breaks with "sticky" ends. The opened plasmid loops are then mixed in a solution with genes—also removed by the use of restriction enzymes—from the DNA of a plant, animal, bacterium, or virus. In the solution is another enzyme,

called a DNA ligase, which cements the foreign gene into place in the opening of the plasmids. The result of these unions is new loops of DNA called **plasmid chimeras** because, like the Chimera—the mythical lion-goat-serpent after which they are named—they contain the components of more than one organism.

Finally, the chimeras are placed in a solution of cold calcium chloride containing normal *E. coli* bacteria. When the solution is suddenly heated, the membranes of the *E. coli* become permeable, allowing the plasmid chimeras to pass through and become part of the microbes' new genetic structure. When the *E. coli* reproduce, they create carbon copies of themselves, new plasmids—and DNA sequences—and all. Thus they become forms of life potentially different from what they had been before—imbued with characteristics dictated not only by their own *E. coli* genes but also by genes from an entirely different species.

Reprinted by permission from TIME, The Weekly Newsmagazine; copyright Time Inc. 1977.

FIGURE 6–15 Gene transplantation in *E. coli* bacteria. (a) Plasmid is isolated from *E. coli* bacterium. (b) Plasmid undergoes enzymatic cleavage. (c) Foreign DNA segment is prepared. (d) Foreign DNA is inserted into plasmid. (e) The plasmid chimera is introduced into a fresh *E. coli* bacterium. (f) The "engineered" *E. coli* bacterium reproduces itself.

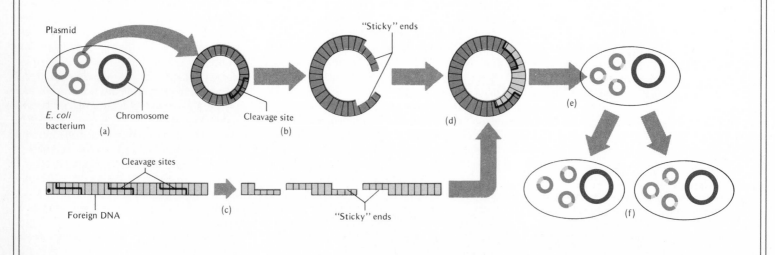

it comes to genetic manipulation of the human being, namely, that redirection often cannot be accomplished. For example, although genes direct the development of the brain and its billions of constituent nerve cells, the insertion of a new piece of DNA following the establishment of the brain could not alter that organization; neither could learning processes be altered by means of a shot of DNA, because they depend so much on previous occurrences, such as experience and conditioning (Chapter 20). The transfer of genetic defects to produce debilitation for political or military purposes also seems more in the realm of science fiction than science. Most monogenic diseases produce behavioral aberrations whose usefulness to a tyrant is hard to conceive; even if such a malevolent end result is desired, it would seem that a genetic bomb could not easily and secretly be introduced to mass populations and affect already developed individuals.[4]

Sensational pronouncements about the dangers of genetic manipulation and the Promethean predictions of unlimited control are without scientific evidence; blueprinting a human personality is not on the horizon. Genetic intervention could be used in a limited way for improvement of the human condition, and while dangers may exist, it is necessary to evaluate and regulate them in a rational way.

## SUMMARY

**1.** Genetics, the study of inheritance, deals with the transfer of information from parent to offspring.

---

[4] It should be noted that any society wishing to direct the evolution of its genetic composition has an alternate solution to genetic engineering, and that is selective breeding. This method has been used for thousands of years to produce better stocks of animals and plants. It was the basis of the eugenics movement, which faltered because humans could not be induced to mate and breed by directive. Inbreeding, selection, and eugenics are discussed in Chapter 24.

**2.** Griffith found in 1928 that rough *S. pneumoniae* can be altered into a lethal strain by transforming principle from a killed smooth strain. Avery, McCleod, and McCarty purified transforming principle in 1944 and found it to be DNA (deoxyribonucleic acid).

**3.** In all cells DNA is responsible for recording and transmitting the genetic blueprint.

**4.** DNA is composed of deoxyribonucleotides, composed of a sugar (deoxyribose) linked to a phosphate and to one of four nitrogenous bases: adenine, guanine (purines), thymine or cytosine (pyrimidines).

**5.** In 1950, Chargaff found that in any DNA (a) the proportion of bases from any given species is always the same; (b) the composition varies between species; and (c) the amounts of A = T and G = C, and A + G = T + C.

**6.** In 1953, Watson and Crick proposed that the nucleotides of DNA are arranged in a linear sequence. Each DNA molecule consists of two such sequences, and the bases of each strand bond with each other in a complementary way so that A always bonds with T and G with C. The bonded bases form the rungs of a ladder, with sugar-phosphate uprights. The entire DNA molecule is twisted helically at every tenth base.

**7.** DNA replicates itself by unzipping and matching complementary base pairs, which are bonded together by DNA polymerase.

**8.** Specific regions of the DNA helix code for, and direct, the synthesis of proteins. These regions are the genes.

**9.** A specific sequence of three bases codes for a specific amino acid. Each triplet is called a codon. The triplet code is degenerate because more than one triplet may code for the same amino acid. (There are 64 possible triplet combinations to code for the 20 amino acids in most proteins.)

**10.** The code is universal—the same triplet codes for the same amino acid in all organisms.

**11.** Many diseases are genetic. Phenylketonuria (PKU), for example, is caused by a fault in the genetic code for an essential enzyme that metabolizes phenylalanine in the diet. Build up of phenylpyruvic acid, derived from phenylalanine, and excess phenylalanine, cause mental retardation in the young. It can be prevented by controlling the diet.

**12.** The genetic message is contained in the DNA of the nucleus; proteins are synthesized in the cytoplasm. The genetic instructions in DNA are copied, or rather transcribed, into a ribonucleic acid, which resembles DNA except that the sugar is ribose and uracil replace thymine. The transcribed RNA, called messenger RNA, then travels to the cytoplasm.

**13.** Messenger RNA is transcribed from one strand of DNA by specific complementary base pairing, with the aid of RNA polymerase. The mRNA moves from nucleus to cytoplasm and attaches to a ribosome.

**14.** Transfer RNA is a cloverleaf-shaped molecule in the cytoplasm. Each of the 20 amino acids is carried by a specific kind of tRNA molecule. At the bend of the cloverleaf of tRNA is a triplet region of nucleotides (anticodon) which is specifically complementary to a triplet region (codon) of the mRNA.

**15.** Activated by ATP, cytoplasmic amino acids are picked up by the prongs of their specific cloverleaf tRNA and carried to the mRNA on the ribosome, where the anticodons match and bond with their complementary codons. Peptide bonds are forged enzymatically between adjacent amino acids on the ribosome, which moves along the strand of mRNA "reading" the codons. This process is called translation. Following translation of the genetic message into a polypeptide chain, the tRNAs are discharged and can be reused.

**16.** Codons in the mRNA, called chain terminators, signal the end of the message and of the polypeptide chain.

**17.** Long strands of mRNA may be read by more than one ribosome at once. Such associations are called polyribosomes, or polysomes.

**18.** One gene codes for one polypeptide chain.

**19.** The sequence of triplets (codons) in the DNA determines the sequence of codons in the RNA and hence the kind of protein made. Species specificity and individuality are determined by codon sequence.

**20.** Changes in the genetic message, or mutations, occur when nucleotide base substitutions or deletions occur.

**21.** Recombinant DNA research, or gene splicing, has given us the capacity to add a small number of genes from any organism to bacterial cells (*E. coli*) and hence to reproduce them in large quantities. The potential for solving biological and medical problems is offset by the novel risks presented by this research and has led to the development of government guidelines.

**22.** Prospects for changing the genetic code of organisms other than bacteria are remote since most characteristics of an organism are polygenic and it is difficult to change an organism once it is fully developed. Correction of some genetic diseases may be accomplished in the future by using viruses as delivery vehicles for the insertion of genetic messages into the nuclei of human cells, however.

## KEY WORDS

genetics
transforming principle
deoxyribonucleic acid (DNA)
nucleotides
deoxyribonucleotides
deoxyribose
adenine
guanine
thymine
cytosine
purines
pyrimidines
diffraction pattern
periodicities
DNA polymerase
complementary base pairing
sequence
replication
code
genes
one-gene–one-enzyme hypothesis
triplet code

degenerate code
essential amino acids
ribonucleic acid (RNA)
ribose
ribonucleotide
uracil
messenger RNA (mRNA)
RNA polymerase
transcription
codons
ribosome
ribosomal RNA (rRNA)
transfer RNA (tRNA)
anticodon
translation
chain terminator
polyribosome or polysome
introns
sickle-cell hemoglobin
mutation
recombinant DNA
polygenic
plasmid chimeras

## TOPICS FOR REVIEW AND DISCUSSION

1. How is DNA able both to duplicate itself and to carry information?

2. How did transformation in bacteria lead to the discovery that DNA is the hereditary material?

3. What is the hereditary basis of sickle-cell hemoglobin?

4. Discuss the validity of the one gene–one enzyme hypothesis.

5. What is the relationship of codon to anticodon?

6. Explain the significance of the universality of the genetic code.

7. Describe the cause of phenylketonuria (PKU) and how it may be "cured."

8. During gene expression, the genetic code is transcribed and translated. Describe these molecular events.

9. What is genetic engineering?

10. What is the Watson-Crick model for the structure of DNA? How can it be confirmed experimentally?

11. Name three different kinds of RNA and list their functions.

12. Describe the role of polyribosomes in the manufacture of protein.

## Closing In on Cloning

**In 363 tries, three rare mice and hints of things to come**

In the book and movie *The Boys from Brazil,* a demented Nazi doctor uses blood and tissue cells from Adolf Hitler to clone dozens of copies of the German dictator in the hope that at least one of them will seize power and conquer the world. Though the cloning of human beings is likely to be confined to fantasy for decades—perhaps forever—other kinds of cloning have long been possible. The Greek word *klon* means twig, and the simplest kind of vegetable cloning consists of cultivating cuttings from a plant. By the mid-1950s scientists had succeeded in cloning amphibians, producing frogs that were genetically identical to each other and carried the inherited characteristics of only a single parent. Most animal cloning has been done by transplanting nuclei into egg cells to produce an entire organism from a single cell. But the cloning of higher forms of life, like mammals, is hard to achieve. Mammal eggs are microscopic, 10 to 20 times smaller in diameter than frogs' eggs, and vastly more difficult to manipulate. Consequently, the barriers to cloning laboratory mice had, until recently, proved insurmountable. But now biologists have successfully done just that.

First a mass of embryonic cells from the womb of a pregnant gray mouse was removed. Using microscopes and a micropipette much finer than a human hair, the cells' nuclei were sucked out and, one by one, each was transplanted into a recently fertilized egg extracted from another mouse. That mouse was black and functioned as a kind of genetic control. Then the egg and sperm nuclei that were already in the black mouse's egg were removed so that their genetic information could not influence the resulting clone. Next the cell was cultured in a solution of nutrients until it divided and grew into an early embryo, which was then inserted into the womb of a third mouse, this one white. The white mouse gave birth to a gray mouse, genetically identical to the original embryo.

In 363 tries, several mice were produced from a single embryo, all genetically identical to each other and thus true clones.

Almost every cell in an organism contains all the genetic information needed for reproducing the entire organism. But getting that information to turn on or, as biologists put it, to "express" itself, is

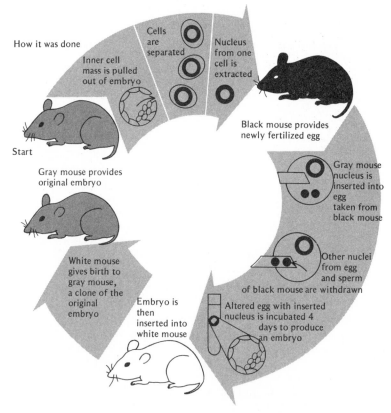

How it was done

Inner cell mass is pulled out of embryo

Cells are separated

Nucleus from one cell is extracted

Black mouse provides newly fertilized egg

Gray mouse nucleus is inserted into egg taken from black mouse

Other nuclei from egg and sperm of black mouse are withdrawn

Altered egg with inserted nucleus is incubated 4 days to produce an embryo

Embryo is then inserted into white mouse

White mouse gives birth to gray mouse, a clone of the original embryo

Gray mouse provides original embryo

Start

TIME Chart by Karen Karlsson

# 7

# Cells in Action: Duplication and Control Mechanisms

the main problem in animal cloning. It has been done now with immature cells. But as cells become differentiated, they seem to lose the ability to release genetic instructions for anything other than what they have become. A red blood cell can become only another red blood cell, for example. For that reason, researchers have been able to clone mice only from embryonic cells that had not yet differentiated into cells for skin, bones, brains, eyes, and other parts of the body. So far, there have been no undisputed reports of cloning from mature animal cells.

Nonetheless, such mice, if they are produceable in large numbers, open many new avenues for research. The mice are, in fact, less important as clones than as vehicles for experiments in embryology, cell differentiation, and immunology as well as in the study of birth defects and cancer. They enable medical researchers to introduce variables into otherwise genetically identical subjects and then observe the results.

Some variation of the technique may one day be used to clone prize bulls or even human beings. But other scientists question the ethics, as well as the scientific use, of trying to clone humans from undifferentiated cell masses. Whatever the original genetic imprint, the results would not be predictable, and mistakes would be stamped indelibly not on mice but on men.

## 7–1  CELL DUPLICATION

In the last chapter, we saw how a molecule of DNA is able to reproduce itself and how it contains within it information for directing the synthesis of proteins. Now we shall see how the DNA is packaged within the cell and how synthesis of DNA and of protein is involved in cellular reproduction—one of the fundamental properties of life.

### Mechanics of cell division

It is a paradox of nature that living things change, yet stay the same. Viewed over a life-span, we can recognize that we grow old and die, but on a shorter time scale, say minutes or hours, we notice hardly any difference in our appearance—we are the same. Or are we? Critical examination shows that we are in fact not the same as we were an instant ago. Our bodies are in constant activity, and change is unending. The cells of which we are composed are restless: they reproduce, they grow, they specialize, and they die. Our cells must work hard to maintain the status quo, for they must replace those that are lost from wear and tear. No cell lives forever, and every second that passes sees the death of some 50 million body cells; during that same period 50 million new cells are produced to take their place. Cells, like people, vary in the duration of their life-span; an intestinal cell lives for 36 hours, then it dies and passes out of the body; a white blood cell lives for about 2 weeks, a red blood cell for about 4 months, and a nerve cell for 60 years or more.

What kind of delicate balance operates within our bodies to preserve our integrity? How is it that the body's active cells, which may number in the millions of millions, are capable of regulating themselves? And how is it that every so often some cells lose their regulatory controls and, no longer subject to ordinary restrictions, become lawless cancer cells?

Let us consider our cellular origins and see how we became what we are today—an organized population of diverse cells. We began life as a single cell, and through a series of dramatic events, that cell became divided into many smaller cells. Later, by utilizing externally supplied raw materials, the cells grew in size, again they multiplied, and soon there were thousands of cells; as the process continued cells propagated their kind, and eventually there were millions of cells: the cells became organized into distinctive nerve cells, skin cells, liver cells, and so on. How did the original cells recognize that multiplication was their role? When did the cells receive the signal to stop dividing continuously, and instead to just keep pace with cellular death? Why and how did our cells specialize? Before we can answer questions such as these, we must understand a basic activity of the living cell—its reproduction. Cells reproduce themselves by dividing. **Cell division** is a commonplace occurrence, in that it happens with great frequency; however, the process is intricate and beautiful to observe. As we shall see, the division of a cell is a remarkable event.

As the living cell prepares to divide, the

**129**

FIGURE 7–1 (top) Mitosis in the living cell. Shown here are stages in the reproduction of cells from the African blood lily. (Courtesy of Andrew S. Bajer.)

FIGURE 7–2 (bottom) The interphase cell. (Whitefish blastula photograph courtesy of Carolina Biological Supply Company.)

nucleus, which is ordinarily translucent, begins to cloud up, and within it distinct threadlike bodies called **chromosomes** appear (Figure 7–1). The nuclear membrane disintegrates. The chromosomes, which are now free, split lengthwise, and one set migrates to one pole of the cell while the other moves to the opposite pole. Each set then is reestablished within a nucleus, and the cytoplasm divides, producing two new daughter cells, each with a full set of chromosomes.

Thus, the division of the cell involves a complex pattern of events and is not merely a mechanical fragmentation of the parent cell to form daughter cells. The process can be looked upon as a cycle of events or steps, each of which depends or is conditional upon what precedes it. The entire process is, for the sake of convenience, divided into stages, but it must be remembered that these stage designations are somewhat arbitrary, and during division one stage merges into another to form a continuum. We can compare the cycle of cell division to a dramatic play that is divided into a series of scenes or acts to focus attention on a particular situation. A detailed view of cell division, like a view of a continuously running play, can begin at any time, but for simplicity let us begin with an undividing (**resting**) cell. This cell, like most cells, is in fact doing all sorts of things, for in the living state cells are never at rest; the only thing the cell has not begun to do is divide. Such a cell is described as containing an **interphase nucleus,** that is, the nucleus is between the phases of activity that make up cell division. At this stage, the nucleus is large and nucleoli are evident. The internal contents of the nucleus show a fine network of stainable material, called **chromatin** (*chrom*—color; Gk.), but there is little discernible structure to it (Figure 7–2). Near the nucleus are two pairs of small, deep-staining bodies called **centrioles.** The centrioles are often not visible in the living cell. The interphase nucleus of the resting cell is not inactive, but quite the opposite; it is

Metaphase

Anaphase

Cell plate

Prophase

Interphase

Telophase

during this stage that nucleic-acid synthesis occurs. Interphase may be looked upon as a preparation stage for the process of nuclear division, and it occupies the major portion of the cycle of cellular reproduction.

When the cell enters the initial stage of nuclear division, called **prophase** (*pro*—first; L.), the dynamic processes within the nucleus become visible (Figure 7–3). The chromatin material undergoes a striking change in organization. The diffuse network of chromatin forms dense threads, and the nucleus begins to resemble a carelessly rolled ball of yarn; the chromatin is not a single continuous thread, but consists of discrete and separate threads that are easily stained with a variety of dyes. These are the chromosomes ("colored bodies"; *chroma*—color, *soma*—body; Gk.). The increasing visibility of the chromatin and its distinct longitudinally double appearance in the chromosome are due to the coiling and consequent shortening of the chromatin threads. You can visualize the process that is occurring in the nucleus by thinking of

the chromatin as a wire coiled into the shape of a bedspring (Figure 7–4); as it goes from an elongated, barely visible entity to one that is short and thick, it becomes clearly visible. The larger the diameter of the coil, the more infrequent the number of turns and the more apparent the chromosome becomes. Why does the chromosome coil and shorten during nuclear division? One suggested reason is that in the shorter, more compact form the chromosome can be moved about more easily without becoming hopelessly tangled and snarled. Now we might turn the question around and ask, Why does the chromosome not remain coiled even during interphase? Again the answer is speculative: it could be that the synthetic activity of the chromosome is directly related to the amount of exposed surface, and since during interphase synthetic activity is maximal the uncoiled form, presenting the greatest exposed surface, is its functional condition. Careful inspection of the chromosome shows that each actually consists of two spiral

filaments, called **chromatids,** closely associated along their length but not actually fused (Figure 7–5); the chromatids are held together at a specific region, the **centromere.** During prophase the originally distinct nucleoli of interphase disappear and the nuclear membrane also breaks down and disappears.

Now there is the appearance of activity within the cytoplasm. The centrioles separate. Radiating outward from each centriole are protein fibrils, called **asters** or **astral rays,** and between the centrioles there is another group of fibrils, the **spindle,** arranged in the shape of two cones lying base to base. The centrioles, along with their asters, migrate in opposite directions describing a semicircle, until they reach the poles of the cell. With the dissolution of the nuclear membrane, the chromosomes lie free in the center (**equator**) of the cell and orient themselves in a characteristic manner in this location. The appearance of the spindle and the positioning of the chromosomes on the equator of the cell[1] begin the stage called **metaphase** (*meta*—middle; Gk.) (Figure 7–6). The metaphase chromosomes are clear and distinct, and at this point it is quite easy to count the number of individual chromosomes. Ordinarily, to make certain that the chromosomes remain arrested at this stage so that they can be counted easily, the dividing cell is treated with the drug colchicine. This prevents the aggregation of

---

[1] Actually it is the centromeres that are precisely positioned on the equator, while the chromosomal arms may extend in any direction (Figures 7–1 and 7–6).

FIGURE 7–5 Chromosome structure as it appears just before division. The two chromatids of the chromsosome remain attached at the centromere until separation. The sketch at the left illustrates the complex coiling of the chromatin in the chromosome shown in the electron micrograph on the right (after E. J. DuPraw).

the spindle proteins, and without a spindle the chromosomes are incapable of moving away from their position on the cell equator. Such a colchicine-arrested condition of the metaphase chromosomes from the cells of a human female is shown in Figure 7–7. Notice how each centromere differs in its location along the chromosome, conferring a distinctive appearance upon each chromosome; thus, each chromosome can be recognized by the length of its chromatid arms on either side of its centromere.

The metaphase chromosomes, lying on the equatorial plate of the cell, become connected to the spindle fibers at the centromere. Each centromere separates, and as it does so the fibers of the spindle contract and the chromatids separate and move toward opposite poles of the cell. The separate chromatids, each with its own centromere, are now called **daughter chromosomes,**[2] and their separation signals the start of the stage called **anaphase** (*ana*—further or later; Gk.).

Anaphase chromosomes, which appear to be pulled by the contracting spindle fibers, often resemble rods or are V- or J-shaped. The shape each chromosome takes is related to the position of the centromere along its length and is produced as a passive response to the contractile force of the spindle. The situation is much like the arm movement of a string-manipulated puppet. As the puppeteer pulls on the string attached to the puppet's elbow, the arm moves and is bent into the shape of a V, whereas a tug on the string attached to the wrist of the puppet moves the arm as a stiff rod; the shape assumed by the arm is a passive response to the pull of the string. At the end of this chromosomal dance, two dense groups of chromosomes are located at opposite ends of the cell (Figure 7–8); this concludes anaphase.

---

[2] In determining the number of chromosomes, we count the number of centromeres present in the nucleus, not the number of strands.

Chromosome

Centromere region

Chromatid

The next phase, **telophase** (*telo*—final; Gk.), begins when the movement of the chromosomes ends. During this phase (Figure 7–9), the nuclear membrane is reconstructed from endoplasmic reticulum remnants, the chromosomes uncoil to become slender chromatin threads, the spindle disintegrates, and the nucleoli appear at specific regions along the length of certain chromosomes (**nucleolar organizer** regions). The events of telophase are essentially the reverse of those that took place during prophase, but there is an added dimension; segmentation and separation of the cyto-

plasm (**cytokinesis**) occur. The cytoplasm constricts along a plane perpendicular to the spindle, and a process known as **furrowing** (or **cleavage**) divides the cytoplasm into two as if the cell were being constricted by a tightly drawn string around its equator.

This process of cell division, or, strictly speaking, nuclear division, is called **mitosis;** it comes from the Greek word for thread (the prefix *mito* is already familiar to you from the name of the threadlike body of the cytoplasm, the mitochrondrion, or powerhouse of the cell). The precise mitotic ballet of the chromosomal threads assures

FIGURE 7–6 (top) The cell in metaphase. (White-fish blastula photograph courtesy of Carolina Biological Supply Company.)

FIGURE 7–7 (bottom) Chromosomes of the human female. (Courtesy of W. R. Centerwall.)

**133**

**CELLS IN ACTION: DUPLICATION
AND CONTROL MECHANISMS**

equal distribution of nuclear materials between the daughter cells, and the chromosome number is reproduced with great fidelity. The cycle of division begins in a parent cell with a certain number of chromosomes, and the cycle ends with two daughter cells having exactly the same number of chromosomes as the parent cell did (Figure 7–10).

We have been describing mitosis as it occurs in animal cells. The process in higher plant cells is basically the same; the differences are related to the fact that plant cells differ from animal cells in certain aspects of their anatomy. For example, higher plant cells lack centrioles but do form a spindle. Obviously a centriole as a visible entity is not an absolute requirement for the organization of the spindle fibers. Plant cells are surrounded by a rigid, nonliving cellulose cell wall, and therefore furrowing is impossible. Instead, in telophase of plant cells, the division of cytoplasm occurs by the laying down of a cell plate between the daughter nuclei (Figure 7–1).

### Timing of cell division

The division of a cell during mitosis is like a continuously running play. How long does it take for the cell to perform a complete cycle of division? The answer to this question is, Quite variable, depending on the particular cell type. Some cells, such as nerve cells and muscle cells, never divide again once they are formed. Other cells of the human body may divide at different rates at different times. For example, if a portion of your skin is removed by accident or surgery, the remaining cells begin to divide rapidly to replace the lost tissue; at other, more normal times, the division rate of skin cells is much slower. A human connective-tissue cell takes about 20 hours to undergo mitosis. It is evident from Figure 7–11 that most of a cell's time is spent in interphase (90%), and it may take as little as 45 to 90 minutes for the cell to go from prophase to telophase of one division. In-

FIGURE 7–8 (top) The cell in anaphase. (Whitefish blastula photograph courtesy of Carolina Biological Supply Company.)

FIGURE 7–9 (bottom) (a) The cell in telophase and (b) daughter cells. (Whitefish blastula photograph courtesy of Carolina Biological Supply Company.)

(a)

(b)

terphase, the longest phase of a cell's life, can be subdivided into three periods: a gap (G₁) after telophase, a time of DNA synthesis (S), and then another gap (G₂) just before prophase commences. Exactly what goes on in the nucleus during the gap phases is obscure; however, it is presumed that those metabolic events which must precede prophase occur during these times.

### Implications of cell division

Cells, like humans, progress through a series of transitions from birth until death. Cells divide, grow, fabricate new materials from the raw stuff of their environment, and divide again; in this way they obtain a freshness and vitality—their substance is constantly renewed. As soon as a cell reaches a certain age, it divides and begins again; the aging process is thus avoided or dimin-

CELLS IN ACTION: DUPLICATION
AND CONTROL MECHANISMS

FIGURE 7–10 Diagrammatic representation of mitosis in an animal cell.

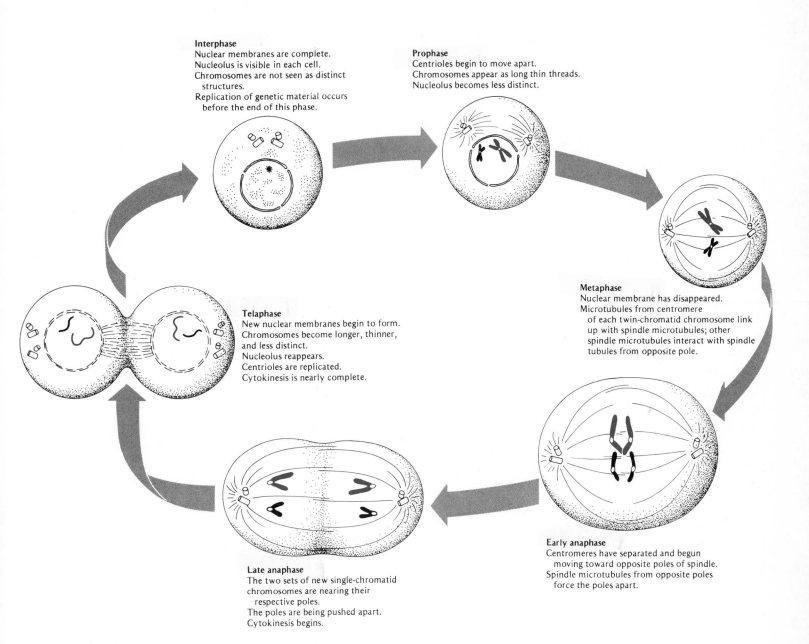

**Interphase**
Nuclear membranes are complete.
Nucleolus is visible in each cell.
Chromosomes are not seen as distinct
   structures.
Replication of genetic material occurs
   before the end of this phase.

**Prophase**
Centrioles begin to move apart.
Chromosomes appear as long thin threads.
Nucleolus becomes less distinct.

**Metaphase**
Nuclear membrane has disappeared.
Microtubules from centromere
   of each twin-chromatid chromosome link
   up with spindle microtubules; other
   spindle microtubules interact with spindle
   tubules from opposite pole.

**Telaphase**
New nuclear membranes begin to form.
Chromosomes become longer, thinner,
   and less distinct.
Nucleolus reappears.
Centrioles are replicated.
Cytokinesis is nearly complete.

**Early anaphase**
Centromeres have separated and begun
   moving toward opposite poles of spindle.
Spindle microtubules from opposite poles
   force the poles apart.

**Late anaphase**
The two sets of new single-chromatid
chromosomes are nearing their
   respective poles.
The poles are being pushed apart.
Cytokinesis begins.

ished. A cell that retains the ability to divide is always young; through this mechanism, life to a degree thwarts time. In contrast, cells that do not divide eventually become senescent and die.

The division of cells and their increase in numbers and size by growth provide the raw material for differentiation and division of labor within the organism of which they are a part. The cells of our bodies are grouped into units called tissues and organs, which perform varied but specialized functions. The differentiation of a cell toward a specific role is the beginning of its eventual death, since the most highly differentiated cells do not divide; a return to youth and cell division may come about only by a loss of the differentiated state (called dedifferentiation). The paradox of cellular life is that youth belongs to the generalized cell, but the specialized cell, which is probably much more efficient for its job, is destined to die.

Mitosis is the mechanism whereby continued genetic similarity of cells is assured. Although mitotic mistakes do occur, they are rare. For example, if one or more chromosomes did not attach to the spindle for some reason, such as loss of the centromere, they might lag behind during division and end up in the wrong daughter cell. As a result of such a mitotic mistake, the daughter cells would contain unequal numbers of chromosomes, which could lead to death or to abnormal patterns of cellular behavior. Some human disorders, such as Down syndrome, are produced by the unequal distribution of particular chromosomes during the cell divisions that are preliminary to formation of the egg cell. If mistakes were a part of the natural process of cell division and the products of division all varied in their constitution, our bodies would consist of a random assortment of cells. By assuring the similarity of inherited characteristics in each and every cell derived from the original fertilized egg, it is possible to construct organisms like ourselves, which have both uniformity and specialty in function. The mechanism by which cells of uniform genetic character become differentiated is poorly understood and remains one of the most intriguing of all biological problems. We shall speculate on some aspects of the situation later in this chapter.

## 7–2 CHROMOSOME STRUCTURE

### Packaging the DNA

Chromosomes of eukaryotes contain DNA, but they also contain proteins called **histones** and **nonhistone proteins.**[3] The proteins play a role in the organization of chromosome structure and function, but do not carry

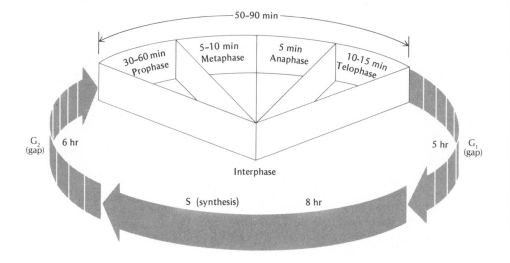

FIGURE 7–11 The cell cycle in a human connective tissue cell.

hereditary information; that function is restricted to the DNA. As we saw in Chapter 6, the Watson-Crick model for DNA shows that it is a double helix, and the genetic code is embodied in the nucleotide sequence of the DNA. The problem that now confronts us is, How are the DNA and protein organized in the chromosome?

It has been shown that the chromatid consists of two complementary strands, suggesting that a chromatid is in fact a chain of DNA. However, the matter is not as simple as this. Some indication of the packaging problem is evident from Figure 7–12, and the statistics in Table 7–1. The nucleus of a human cell contains about 3 billion nucleotide pairs distributed among 46 chromosomes. Thus each chromosome, composed of two chromatids, contains an average of 60 million nucleotide pairs, and the double helix twists once for every 10 nucleotide pairs—6 million times! If a chromatid consisted of a single linear chain of DNA, then the DNA chain of a virus would be 60 µm long, that of a bacterium would be 1 mm in length, and that of a person

---

[3] In prokaryotic cells, such as bacteria, the chromosome contains only DNA.

would be almost 1 in. long. The total length of the DNA chains in each cell of a human being would be about 1 yd! When we consider that all this DNA must be packaged into cells with diameters many times smaller than the length of the DNA chains, we can begin to appreciate the nature of the problem (Figure 7–12). It seems unthinkable that DNA strands inches long could ever uncoil, as they must each time transcription or replication occurs. Furthermore, when fully extended, each chromatid is 100 times thicker and only 1/10,000 as long as it ought to be if it consisted of a linear DNA chain. How then are DNA chains packaged into chromosomes?

Staining methods and light microscopy have revealed that each chromosome at mitosis consists of transverse alternating dark and light bands. (Figure 7–13). It can also be seen that the strand of material forming a chromatid is very tightly wound in a helical coil, which may wind upon itself like a coiled telephone cord twisted into a series of secondary coils (Figure 7–5). This would in some measure account for the amount of DNA that can be accommodated in such a small space as that afforded by the nucleus of a cell.

**FIGURE 7–12** Extracted DNA from a variety of organisms compared to scale with the structure into which the DNA is organized. (a) A virus (60-μm DNA). (b) A bacterium (1-mm DNA). (c) A fruit fly (16-mm DNA.)

**FIGURE 7–13** The appearance of chromosomes from the salivary-gland cells of the fruit fly *Drosophila*. (Courtesy of Carolina Biological Supply Company.)

Virus

60-μm length

0.5 μm

(a)

Bacterium

1-mm length

5 μm

(b)

Fruit fly chromosomes

16-mm length

5 μm

(c)

It is impossible by light or electron microscopy to see how the DNA and protein molecules are arranged in an intact chromatid; therefore, its structure has been studied by isolating its constituents. When chromatin is extracted using mild enzymatic digestion and an appropriate salt solution the individual chromatin threads can be seen with the electron microscope. The fragments of chromatin prepared in this way resemble beads on a string (Figure 7–14). Each bead consists of a protein (histone) core and approximately 150 base pairs of DNA, and the string connecting the beads consists of approximately 50 base pairs of DNA. The repeating, beadlike units of chromatin are called **nucleosomes**. In a nucleosome the DNA is arranged in such a way that the 150 base pairs are tightly wound around the outside of the histone core, and then the strand of DNA continues as the linker "string" until it reaches another histone core where again it is wrapped around the outside of the "bead." In forming the chromatid the "beads on a string" are further wound into a helix, and this in turn coils upon itself into a series of super coiled loops (Figure 7–14). There is enough flexibility in this arrangement so that a 20,000-μm strand of DNA and its associated histone can be packed into a space equal to only a few microns. And, by the tight association of the DNA with the histone, the DNA itself is protected from enzyme attack by nucleases, which are known to be present in the nucleus.

### Implications of chromosome structure

As we have seen, the hereditary material or DNA of which the genes are composed, is organized into structures known as chromosomes. What exactly is a gene, and what is the significance of the organization of genes into chromosomal structures? Let us say that a gene is a nucleotide sequence of the DNA which codes for a specific protein

**TABLE 7–1 The genes in different organisms**

| Organism | DNA nucleotide pairs per cell | Number of genes (estimated) |
|---|---|---|
| φ 174 (virus) | 5,500 | 12 |
| T4 (virus) | $2 \times 10^5$ | 450 |
| *Escherichia coli* (bacterium) | $3 \times 10^6$ | 13,300 |
| *Drosophila* (fruit fly) | $6 \times 10^6$ | 25,000 |
| Frog | $7 \times 10^{10}$ | 120,000,000(?) |
| Human | $3 \times 10^9$ | 3,000,000* |

* Although 3,000,000 are possible, only 1,487 genetic traits have been catalogued. From E. Carlson, *The Gene: A Critical History*, Philadelphia, Saunders, 1966, table 1, p. 268.

**137**

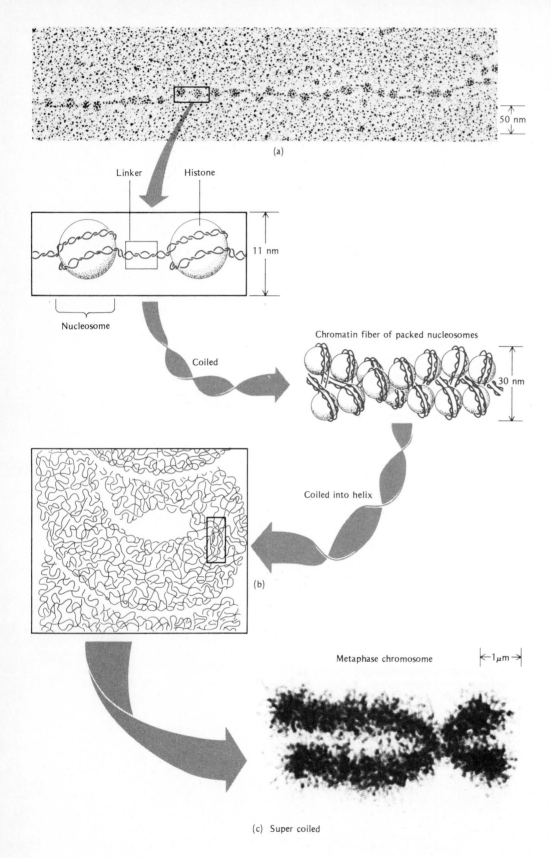

**FIGURE 7–14** Levels of chromosome organization. Nucleosomes are regions of DNA wound around an histone core. The electron micrograph (a) shows the "beads" of histone on a "string" of DNA. The nucleosomes are further coiled (b) to form an helix. By coiling coils upon coils a supercoiled DNA forms a chromosome (c). (Part *a* courtesy of Barbara A. Hamkalo.)

50 nm

Linker   Histone

11 nm

Nucleosome

Chromatin fiber of packed nucleosomes

Coiled

30 nm

Coiled into helix

(b)

Metaphase chromosome   ←1μm→

(c)  Super coiled

product. The number of genes an organism has is to some extent related to the complexity of the organism. The number of genes of a variety of organisms is represented in Table 7–1. It is obvious that a small virus has fewer proteins, less DNA, fewer nucleotides, and fewer genes than a larger and more complex virus. Similarly, the intestinal bacterium *Escherichia coli* has about 20 times as many genes as a complex virus, and when we come to our own DNA we see that we have enough DNA in each of our cells to provide for 3 million genes. Are we really a thousand times more complex than a bacterium? Probably we are, but notice also that DNA content and degree of complexity do not always go hand in hand; for example, the cells of the fruit fly *Drosophila* have twice the number of nucleotides as those of *E. coli*, and the cells of some frogs have 20 times the DNA content of human cells.

How many genes do each of our cells contain? To approach the solution to this question, we could catalog all the human traits that have been shown to be controlled by a single gene; a recent catalog of such traits indicates the number to be 1,487. Of course, this value is the lower limit for the number of human genes, since there are a great many genetic traits that are undescribed; estimates for the total number range from 5,000 to 15,000 (with little good evidence for either). Thus, there is a sharp discrepancy between the potential number of genes a human cell could have (3 million) and the number it may actually have (thousands); such a discrepancy indicates that we have a great deal of extra DNA in every cell, and to some biologists this suggests that a considerable fraction of our DNA is redundant, consisting of duplicated genes. The functions of all of these duplicated messages have as yet been worked out in only a few instances.[4] The whole mechanism

---

[4] For example, in the fruit fly there are 130 copies of the genes involved in making the ribosomes, in the chick there are 100 copies, in a salamander

is highly complex, and manipulation of hereditary material involving the insertion of linear stretches of DNA into cells may be further away than the headlines in newspapers would have us believe. We must not only work out the mechanism by which genetic insertions can be made, but determine how to eliminate specific portions of the message already in the cell. These and many other problems will have to be solved before a special-to-order human can be manufactured.

The calculation that there are 3 million genes in every human cell, or even the conservative estimate of thousands of genes, makes it plain that if each gene were localized in a discrete particle, and each had to segregate at cell division, a haphazard and chaotic state would be produed every time a cell divided. The organization of genes into a linear array on the chromosome (Figure 7–13) minimizes the number of segregating units, increases the efficiency of segregation by diminishing the possible loss or gain of individual genes, and permits gene-gene interaction. This is not to say that the process would be impossible with thousands of individually separate gene bodies, but it would probably be much less efficient. A cell obtains many advantages from its structural organization, including the organization of genetic material into chromosomes; a more independent and less organized condition of the genetic material would be less advantageous for the cell and the organism.

## 7–3 CONTROL OF CELLULAR ACTIVITY

### Seeing gene activity

It has been said that we are what our enzymes make us. Each of us is a product of the subtle activities of the many enzymes

that control our cellular processes. Ultimately these cellular activities depend on the nature of the genetic material and its manner of expression. As we have seen, the genetic material is composed of nucleotide units of DNA—genes—which are organized into discrete nuclear structures called chromosomes. Therefore, it seems logical to look for evidence of the activities of genes in or on the chromosomes. Can we with our own eyes directly observe the activities of submicroscopic entities such as genes? The answer, quite surprisingly, is yes.

We are fortunate that there exist in nature certain organisms with cells that have giant chromosomes, for without such structures it would be impossible to see gene activity directly. Our own chromosomes are much too small for studies of chromosome function, and even the electron microscope with its increased powers of resolution is of no help. However, in the cells of the salivary glands of certain flies, **giant chromosomes** are formed by the repeated division of chromatids without nuclear division. After 9 or 10 multiplication cycles, there may be up to 2,000 chromatids. These do not separate, but remain in parallel association so that there results a giant chromosome resembling a multistranded cable (Figure 7–15). At full size they are 100 times thicker and 10 times longer than ordinary chromosomes like our own. These large chromosomes provide us with a better view of chromosome organization and behavior than do the normal-sized chromosomes of ordinary cells, because not only their size but their activities are magnified. Studied under the light microscope, the giant salivary-gland chromosome appears to have transverse bands; the dark bands can be shown to contain DNA and histone (the main chromosomal protein) in high concentration, whereas in the light bands these substances are present in lower concentrations. Investigators studying these giant chromosomes found that particular regions of certain chromosomes at various times in the life of a fly

(not the same fly, of course) showed a reversible change in their circumference. These inflated regions were called **chromosomal puffs.** The puff pattern of chromosomes changed during the life cycle of the fly, and this was interpreted to mean that different regions of the chromosome were active. In addition, puffing could be induced by applying certain hormones to the fly. What sort of activity was taking place at the chromosomal puff? Studies using special stains and radioactive materials have shown that the puffs are regions of uncoiling, and in the vicinity of the puff significant amounts of RNA can be detected (Figure 7–15). By the use of radioactive uridine, which is a specific precursor molecule for RNA but not for DNA, it is possible by special techniques to find radioactivity in the region of the puff but not in the giant chromosome itself. It appears that RNA is manufactured on the DNA template, and this is interpreted to be messenger RNA (mRNA). The mRNA leaves the region of the puff, migrates out of the nucleus, enters the cytoplasm, and interacts with the ribosomes to make new protein. Puffing can be inhibited by preventing nucleic-acid synthesis, but not by blocking protein synthesis. There seems to be little question that puffing represents the activity of certain genes at the level of the chromosome; gene activity thus represents the DNA-directed synthesis of mRNA.

### Control mechanisms

Now that we have morphological evidence for gene activity, we can ask the question, Are gene activities one-way avenues of communication out of the nucleus with the rest of the cell playing a passive role, or is it possible to influence gene activity? If the latter is the case, what turns the genes on and how can synthesis of protein, the gene product, be controlled? There are thousands of genes in every cell of the body, and theoretically each is capable of provid-

---

1,000 copies, and in *E. coli* 5 copies. Similar redundancy has been found for transfer RNA, where there are 13 copies in the chromosomes of the fruit fly.

ing the information necessary for the synthesis of a protein. Yet it is quite apparent that not all genes are active at the same time, and in the case of certain cells some genes are never active. For example, every cell in the body has the gene for making hemoglobin, and yet only certain cells (juvenile red blood cells) make this particular protein; similarly, all our cells have the gene for producing the protein of hair, keratin, but only specific cells produce this protein. Furthermore, a gene may be active for a period of time, then inactive, and perhaps reactivated again after this. Such on-off genetic switching may continue for the entire lifetime of the cell. Thus, the genes of every cell are regulated in their pattern of activity; behind their regulation lies a complex system of controls.

By the regulation of gene or enzyme activity, it should be possible to control the destiny of a cell and ultimately the entire organism. By turning protein and especially enzyme production on or off, or by controlling the action of genes responsible for enzyme synthesis, it should be possible to regulate cell growth and specialization. Some of the most intriguing problems in biology center on understanding the mechanisms that control cellular activities. At present, the state of our knowledge concerning this is quite incomplete. Nevertheless, let us now examine what is known about some of these control mechanisms.

**Mechanical systems.** Frequently in this text we have compared cells to machines, and although such an analogy is often useful in helping us to understand the activities of cells, it is well to recognize its limitations. Living things, cells included, are machines with some remarkable properties, such as the ability to duplicate themselves, to change, and to perpetuate such changes. However, when we come to the regulatory mechanisms that operate within a living organism, the similarity between cells and machines is striking. Cells, like many machines, consist of an array of structures that work in a coordinated fashion; processes are inte-

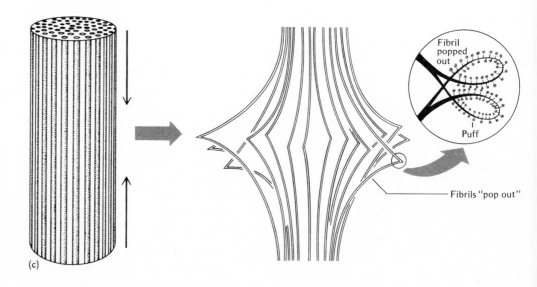

grated and the metabolic maelstrom is organized so as to produce a smoothly running living system. For a cell to regulate its pattern of activity, there must be a systematic organization of the control systems.

What is that organization? Two types of control systems are found in cells, and in principle these greatly resemble those of machines: (1) a rigid or **fixed control system,** that is, a system with a preset, unchanging pattern, and (2) a **feedback control system,** that is, a self-correcting and oscillating system.

The first kind of control is seen in a machine such as the automobile engine. The combustion of fuel in the cylinder moves the pistons, the piston rod moves the crankshaft, and the latter moves the drive shaft. The organization is rigid in such a machine, in that movement of the piston always produces a similar response in the drive shaft. The duplication of the genetic material resembles a rigid control system. DNA is duplicated in a fixed manner according to the rules of complementary base pairing. The precise replication of DNA is necessary to ensure the inherited characteristics of each daughter cell, and in addition, the information content of the DNA must be such that the cell can function in a normal manner. Special mechanisms have evolved for making certain that the replication of DNA is as error-free as possible. This is accomplished in the same way that you might ensure that there are no errors in this sentence or in something that you have written: proofreading for spelling, punctuation, and meaning. In the cell there are a variety of enzymes that act to proofread the DNA sequences, and if an error is encountered, the mistake is selectively removed and a proper substitution inserted.

Despite elaborate repair mechanisms, mistakes and changes in the genetic messages do occur, albeit rarely. Typically, a particular gene is altered only once in a million replications of the DNA. A permanent heritable change in the genetic message, that is a mutation, may result from exposure to chemicals, ionizing radiation, ultraviolet radiation, or heat. Ultraviolet radiation when absorbed by the DNA may produce the covalent bonding of two adjacent thymines in the same DNA strand. If such thymine dimers are left unrepaired DNA replication could be hampered, and this could lead either to cell death or to abnormal cellular growth. Generally when

such a thymine dimer occurs an enzyme recognizes the dimer, it and an adjacent stretch of bases are excised, and then using complementary base pairing the damage is repaired. In the very rare human disease, xeroderma pigmentosum, the enzymes involved in repair of thymine dimers are deficient. As a result such individuals are extremely sensitive to sunlight and run a high risk of skin cancer.

Although there may be more than 50 enzymes involved in locating and correcting errors, changes in the DNA do occur. These uncorrected changes lead to altered messages, and from then on, the new sequence is itself duplicated in succeeding rounds of replication.

In contrast to a fixed control system, a feedback control system is self-correcting. The response to a given command or stimulus is quantitative, specific, and automatic. Such systems operate within the living cell, but before we study these, let us briefly examine a mechanical one, the thermostat. When we set the thermostat in a room to a specific temperature (set point), we are initiating a regulatory mechanism (Figure 7–16a). When the temperature drops below the set point, a metallic strip in the thermostat moves and makes a complete electrical circuit and the heating system is turned on. When the room warms to the temperature set on the thermostat, the circuit is broken, and the heating system is turned off. The essential feature of this system is that it is represented by a closed loop (or circle); such a closed loop is called a feedback system (Figure 7–16b). Information about this system (in this case, temperature) is fed back to change the response. This is called a **negative feedback** because it compensates for, or negates, any change in the system (the temperature remains constant); negative feedback systems are error-actuated (that is, an error in the temperature of the room sets in operation the corrective process) and tend to stabilize the system. (Note that the set point can be moved to produce another system for stability.) A

system that is controlled by such feedback controls, which tends automatically to correct for errors, is far more flexible and less vulnerable to damage than a rigid one. Moreover, it is economical to operate because it is self-correcting and does not require the intervention of a separate control.

There is, as you might imagine, an opposite kind of feedback which would result in a lack of correction by changes in the system. This is a **positive feedback.** It produces an unstable situation and is sometimes called a **runaway feedback.** As an example, let us suppose that in the thermostat, when the circuit was broken, the heating system was turned on; the temperature in the room rises, but this causes no change in the thermostat, and the temperature rise continues indefinitely. Another mechanical representation of negative and positive feedback controls is illustrated in Figure 7-17.

The mechanical control systems just discussed are quite simple compared with the controls found in the living cell. The brief survey of metabolic pathways (Chapters 4 and 5) and of the synthesis of proteins and nucleic acids (Chapter 6) convinces us that in order for cells to maintain their status quo, the traffic in chemicals must move in an orderly fashion and there must be certain priorities established that channel energy into certain activities and not others. A metabolically regulated cell can function without interruption during periods of nutritional feast or famine and can adjust to adverse or injurious situations—the cell maintains what may be called its set point or **steady state.** It is important to recognize that both change in the performance of a pattern of metabolic activity (alteration of the set point) and maintenance of the steady state (fixed set point) operate in the same way: effects act back upon the cause. Signals are received by cellular receptors, and these signals are translated into biological activity; typically it is found that small, mobile molecules are the signals and large

FIGURE 7–16 A mechanical feedback circuit: the thermostat. (a) When the bimetallic strip is cooled, it moves the plate downward; this completes the electrical circuit, and the heating system goes on. When contact is broken by an elevation in temperature, the circuit is broken and the heating system is shut off. (b) The room temperature oscillation in a thermostatically regulated heating system. (c) The negative feedback loops in temperature control of room temperature. (From Garrett Hardin, *Biology: Its Principles and Implications,* 2nd ed., San Francisco, W. H. Freeman and Company. Copyright © 1966.)

molecules are the receptors. The on-off feedback system of the cell (or the thermostat) usually shows a delay in response and then a slight overshoot, and there results an oscillation around the set point. Let us now look at these feedback controls of the living cell.

**Enzyme induction.** Much of the detailed information we have about enzyme regulation in cells comes from studies of microorganisms, but many biologists feel that what goes on in such creatures may be similar to what occurs in the cells of higher organisms. However, at present we have little direct evidence that this optimistic notion is true. In the bacterium *E. coli,* it is possible to stimulate the synthesis of certain enzymes by environmental factors. If *E. coli* is grown in a medium containing glucose, it has only traces of the enzyme β-galactosidase (an enzyme that catalyzes the breakdown of lactose into glucose and galactose); however, if the bacteria are grown with lactose alone in the medium, then the enzyme activity may be increased over a thousand times. It is a "clever" bacterium that makes the right kind of enzyme when the right nutrient substance (food) is available. How does the bacterium "know" what kind of and how much enzyme to produce? Is it due to an activation of the enzyme, that is, does the lactose make the enzyme itself more active, or does it affect the amount of the enzyme produced? It has been shown that lactose acts as an inducer for the synthesis of the enzyme in a process called **enzyme induction.** The lactose affects the rate of manufacture of the enzymatic protein, and new protein can be detected within the cell only 3 minutes after the inducer has been added to the medium. When the inducer is removed, the synthesis of the enzyme ceases. Here we have an example of an environmental substance that turns specific genes on, and when the substance is lacking these genes are switched off; it is a negative feedback system. Not all enzymes exhibit these properties; many are produced and are active regardless of

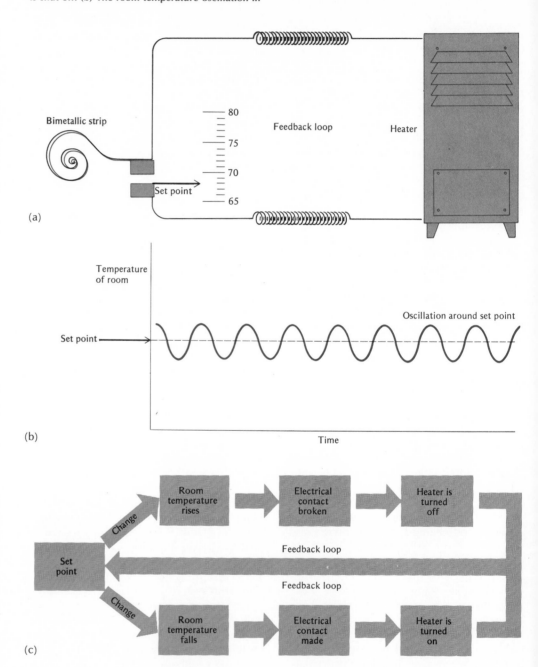

FIGURE 7–17 A mechanical model of feedback control systems. (a) Negative feedback. As water enters the flask, the valve automatically compensates for the inflow and maintains a constant level. (b) Positive feedback. As water enters the flask, the float is raised; this closes the valve and the water rises above the set point. Similarly, if water evaporates, this lowers the float; the valve opens and water runs out of the flask. Instability results.

Set point

Float

Valve

(a)

(b)

the presence or absence of substrates (inducers). Such enzymes are called **constitutive** because they are always present in the cell at a fixed level—the genes that code for them are always turned on and, therefore, the enzymes are a permanent part of the cell's normal constitution. They are part of a rigid control system.

How is the induced enzyme genetically controlled? The production of β-galactosidase is actually controlled by two genes: one (A) codes for the amino-acid sequence of the enzyme itself, and another (B) codes for a permease that moves lactose into the cell. An alteration (mutation) in the nucleotides of any of these genes (so-called **structural genes** because they code for a functional product such as a protein) changes the structure of the enzyme but does not affect the rate of enzyme synthesis. The rate

of synthesis is controlled by a third gene, called the **regulator** (R); if this gene mutates, then enzyme synthesis may become continuous and the inducer, lactose, need not be present; in other words the loss of gene activity in the regulator gene (R) causes enzyme synthesis to be switched to the on position (alternatively, it can be thought of as not switched off; the reason for this will become apparent momentarily). How does the regulator work? In 1961 F. Jacob and J. Monod proposed that the regulator gene (R) produces a substance called **repressor,** and that this material diffuses through the cell and shuts off the genes (A and B) responsible for the synthesis of β-galactosidase and the permease. They hypothesized that the repressor substance does not act on the structural genes (A and B) directly, but binds to a special region of the chro-

mosome located next to the A and B genes. This special region of the DNA they called the **operator** (designated as O), and it can be thought of as a switch that turns on genes A and B. The genes O, A, and B are called the **operon.** According to the Jacob-Monod model, this region of the bacterial chromosome can be represented as follows:

$$\cdots - \boxed{R} - \boxed{O} - \boxed{A} - \boxed{B} - \cdots \text{ chromosome}$$

operon

Let us see what the operon model predicts. When repressor is produced by the R gene, it binds to the DNA at the operator gene (O), and this switches off the activity of the adjacent genes, A and B—the operon is repressed. However, when lactose is present, repressor binds to it, and by virtue of a change in the shape of the repressor molecule, it falls off the operator gene (Figure 7–18). Now the operator is switched on, the gene (A + B) is transcribed, mRNA is made, β-galactosidase and permease are formed, and lactose is utilized by the cell.

The Jacob-Monod model of the operon has been experimentally substantiated. RNA polymerase recognizes a specific region of the DNA called the **promoter region**. It is at this site that mRNA synthesis begins. The promoter region is adjacent to the operator (Figure 7–19). Repressor substance is a protein that consists of 360 amino acids, and it binds to a base sequence of the DNA that corresponds to the operator, but it also overlaps a portion of the promoter region. As a consequence of this overlap the binding of the repressor to the operator blocks the attachment of the RNA polymerase to the promoter, and no mRNA can be transcribed. However, when repressor protein is not bound to the operator (i.e., when lactose is present in the environment) then the RNA polymerase is able to attach to the promoter region, and transcription of the structural genes can occur. Repressor substance is very specific in its binding to a specific region of the bacterial chromosome; it turns off only the lactose operon.

FIGURE 7–18 The operon and enzyme induction. (a) **Operator off.** Repressor protein attached to operator gene blocks the beginning of transcription by RNA polymerase; no synthesis of mRNA occurs at the operon. (b) **Operator on.** Inducer attaches to repressor, changes its shape, and releases it from the operator gene. RNA polymerase attaches to DNA, and mRNA synthesis begins. The translation of mRNA at the ribosome gives rise to enzymes.

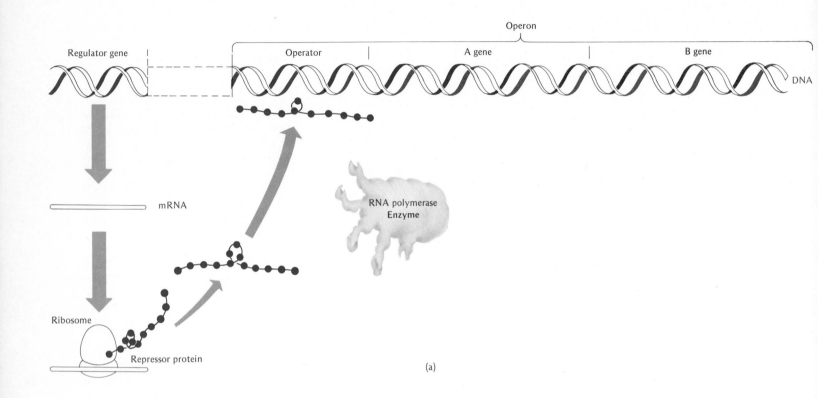

(a)

The operon model provides us with a situation whereby switching on of genes can alter the functional properties of cells; if the product of a gene were a division protein, it could even initiate cell division. The possibilities for future understanding of differentiation and division of cells through promoters, repressors, and the like are quite encouraging.

Through repressor substances and enzyme induction, as well as another mechanism to be discussed shortly, the chemical machinery of the cell is self-regulating and the amount of energy used in the manufacture of enzymes (a major cellular expenditure because a different enzyme is required for every reaction) is effectively and economically controlled; in a frugal and systematic way the cell produces only the kinds and amounts of enzyme molecules neces-sary to metabolize the amount of available nutrients (in this case, lactose).

**Feedback inhibition.** In the previous discussion we saw how chemical reactions within the cell can be genetically regulated by controlling the kinds and amounts of enzymes produced. There is another mechanism of cellular control that involves regulation of enzymatic activity in direct response to environmental situations; this mechanism, called **feedback inhibition,** is not directly controlled by the genes.

Several years ago it was found that when *E. coli* was grown in the presence of an excess of the amino acid isoleucine the cells stopped producing this amino acid. It was known that the synthesis of this amino acid required several intermediate materials and that the conversion of these into the final product (isoleucine) was controlled by spe-cific enzymes. This situation is illustrated in Figure 7–20.

It was also shown that when excess isoleucine is present, it directly affects only the first enzyme in the series; all the other enzymes are unaffected. Moreover, no other amino acid can turn off the system, and the inhibition does not even require an intact cell, for inhibition can be produced by an extract of the cells containing only the enzymes and totally lacking any nucleic acids.

Here we have another example of a negative feedback control system. When the supply of isoleucine is adequate, the cell no longer continues its manufacturing processes; the control mechanism is simply to turn off the first enzyme in the sequence, and since this prevents the formation of subsequent materials in the pathway, the

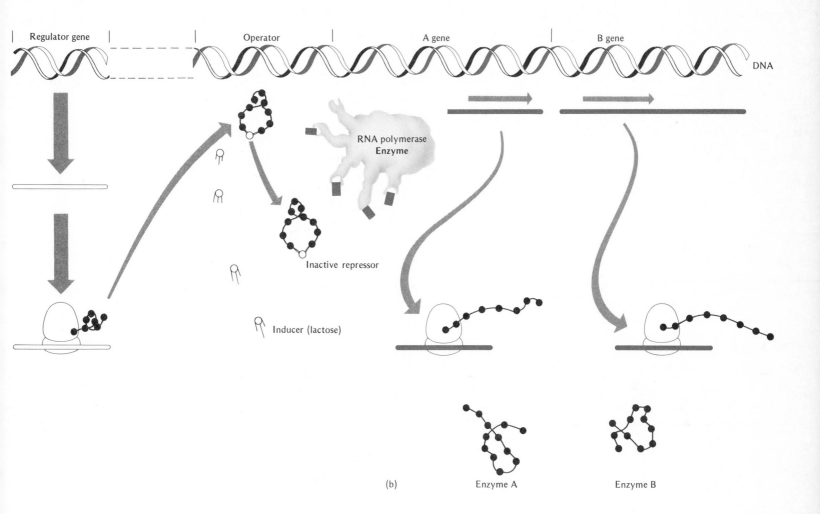

(b)

whole production line is brought to a standstill. The mechanism is as follows: isoleucine combines with the first enzyme to produce an enzyme-isoleucine complex, and this prevents the enzyme from binding to its natural substrate (a in Figure 7–20); as a result the enzyme is inhibited in its activity. The binding of isoleucine is not at the active site of the enzyme (that is, the site at which the enzyme would bind to its natural substrate), but nevertheless it does interfere with the usual binding of this enzyme with the natural substrate. The reason for this can be visualized as shown in Figure 7–20b. If the level of isoleucine diminishes, isoleucine is no longer bound to the enzyme, and then the natural substrate can once again bind to the active site of the enzyme and set in motion the reaction sequence to produce more isoleucine.

Such a control mechanism adjusts itself quickly and automatically to the changing needs of the cell and requires no additional expenditure of cellular energy once the first enzyme is made. This control system is perhaps the ultimate in efficiency, since it requires no energy for its operation. (Consider what the effects of this would be in an industrial process!)

**Regulation of gene action in higher organisms.** The differences between cells depends on the particular proteins that are being made or have been made. This being

FIGURE 7–19 The arrangement of the promoter and operator sequences that regulate the *lac* operon. The promoter and operator sequences overlap (a) so that when the repressor occupies the region of the operator the RNA polymerase cannot bind to the operator (b). When the repressor is not present or the cell is de-repressed RNA polymerase binds to the operator and transcription may begin (c).

so then a key question for understanding gene regulation is: At what level is the synthesis of a protein controlled? Does it involve transcription, does it involve translation, or does it involve the transport of RNA molecules to the ribosome? At the time of this writing the answers to these questions remain incomplete, but if we did have a fuller understanding of the molecular mechanisms that underlie gene activation then perhaps problems of differentiation, cancer, and the like, could not only be understood, they might even be controlled.

The chromosome of a bacterium consists of a circular DNA molecule that contains about 3 million base pairs and contains enough information to code for about 2,500 proteins. As already discussed in this chapter a bacterial cell interacts with its environment in a precise way. Fluctuations in the environment in which a bacterium lives are likely to occur quite suddenly, and the bacterium must be able to cope with such changes or suffer the consequences. A bacterium is confronted with feast or famine, and its control switches must be turned on or off rapidly. Nearly all gene regulation in bacteria is known to occur at the level of transcription. The lactose operon (p. 143) is one of the best described examples of this kind of regulation.

The cells of a eukaryotic organism, such as you and I, also have genes that are responsive to environmental signals (e.g., hormones), and in this way we resemble prokaryotes. It is rare, however, that such genes are turned on or off with such rapidity. More frequently when a particular set of genes does become active in a eukaryotic cell it is in a gradual manner, and once the direction of differentiation (specialization) has been established it may be unaffected by other changes in the environment. That is, in eukaryotes reversibility of gene activation is the exception rather than the rule. During the development of a eukaryotic organism the presence of an activator molecule (such as steroid hormone) may activate a few regulatory gene proteins (so-

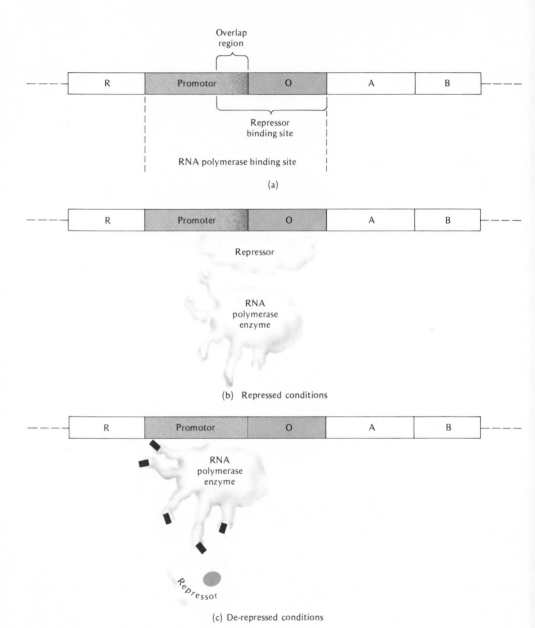

(a)

(b) Repressed conditions

(c) De-repressed conditions

FIGURE 7–20 Feedback inhibition. (a) The biosynthesis of isoleucine requires five enzymes, and the end products of the pathway act as a regulatory signal to inhibit the first enzyme in the pathway. (b) The mechanism by which isoleucine inhibits or restores activity to the first enzyme. The first enzyme in the pathway has two sites for binding to its natural substrate (a) and to the end product, isoleucine (b). When the end product (b) is bound, it changes the configuration of the enzyme so that it cannot bind to the substrate, and this effectively stops enzyme activity in the pathway. Activity can be restored by release of the end product.

(a)

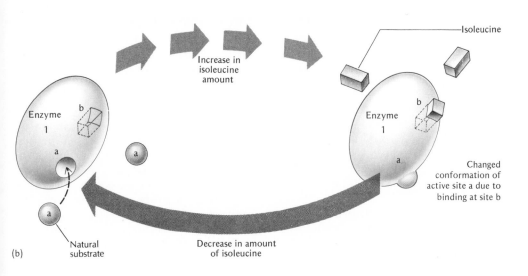

(b)

called master genes) that in turn switch on or off large numbers of other genes. The molecular mechanisms involved in such master gene effects are, at present, not understood.

The regulatory mechanisms of eukaryotes differs from those of prokaryotes because of two unique features: (1) the DNA is tightly associated with histones and (2) the genes are interrupted with noncoding sequences (introns). It has been observed that in those eukaryotic genes that are being transcribed the regions of the chromatin are uncoiled. This suggests that it is the state of the chromatin itself rather than the process of transcription that is important in the regulation of eukaryotic genes. The uncoiling of chromatin may involve nonhistone proteins or highly acetylated histones, but exactly how these act to produce uncoiling is not completely understood.

In the DNA of eukaryotic cells there are long stretches of noncoding DNA called **introns**. These introns are initially transcribed into RNA (so-called primary transcripts) that may be 10 times longer than the active mRNA. Before leaving the nucleus the noncoding portions of the primary transcript are cut out, and the coding ends are spliced together to form an active mRNA that then leaves the nucleus. It has been observed that a substantial fraction of the primary transcript is completely degraded within the nucleus. And, although the discarded portions of the primary transcript represent portions of the mRNA that cannot be read, it is also possible that these represent a store of potential mRNA molecules that can only be transcribed in certain cells at certain times. Thus, it may be that introns serve in a regulatory capacity in the eukaryotic cell.

Much of what we know about gene regulation in prokaryotes was determined in a period of intense research covering the years since Jacob and Monod proposed the operon model. Unraveling the specific mechanisms involved in eukaryotic gene activation remains one of the most exciting and challenging research frontiers of the next decade.

## SUMMARY

1. Mitotic cell division involves the replication and separation of the chromosomes and the production of two cells with sets of genetic information identical to that of the parent cell. It occurs in several definable stages.

2. The undividing, or resting, cell contains an interphase nucleus with a diffuse network of stainable chromatin and an obvious nucleolus. Nucleic acid synthesis occurs during this stage.

3. During prophase, the chromatin threads coil and shorten and are increasingly stainable and visible as chromosomes. Each chromosome consists of two closely associated chromatids, held together at the centromere. The nuclear membrane and nucleoli break down.

4. During metaphase, the centrioles separate. The spindle and astral rays form. The chromosomes orient themselves at the equator of the cell, and individual chromosomes can be recognized according to the location of their centromeres, by which they attach to the spindle.

5. At anaphase, the centromeres separate and the sister chromatids are pulled by contracting spindle fibers. The chromatids move to opposite poles of the cell, and are now called chromosomes.

6. During telophase, the nuclear membrane is reconstituted, the chromosomes uncoil, and nucleoli appear at the nucleolar organizer regions of certain chromosomes. In animal cells, cytokinesis divides the cytoplasm by cleavage.

7. Higher plant cells lack centrioles and have a rigid cellulose cell wall. Cytokinesis occurs by the laying down of a cell plate rather than by cleavage.

8. Cells spend most of their time in interphase, which can be divided into three phases: $G_1$, S, and $G_2$. DNA synthesis occurs during the S phase, and the chromosomes are double by the time of the next prophase.

9. Chromosomes consist of DNA and structural proteins (histones and nonhistones). A chromatid consists of a tightly coiled DNA strand which coils on itself and is packed in protein.

10. Structural genes are nucleotide sequences of DNA that code for specific products such as a protein. The number of genes an organism has is related to its complexity. Most eukaryotic cells seem to have many duplicated, redundant genes. The linear organization of genes on chromosomes increases the efficiency of replication and segregation and permits gene-gene interaction.

11. Fly salivary glands have cells with giant chromosomes formed by the repeated divison of chromatids without nuclear division. Their banded structure reflects functional differences, possibly at the level of the gene. Chromosomal puffing reflects uncoiling and RNA synthesis.

12. DNA replication is not error-free.

13. Maintenance of the steady state in a cell involves negative feedback systems comparable to the thermostat.

14. The regulation of gene activity and the switching on and off of genes often involve negative feedback systems. In E. coli, lactose induces synthesis of the enzyme β-galactosidase, which digests it. The enzyme is not produced unless lactose is present. (Enzymes that are produced all the time, regardless of the presence or absence of the substrate, are constitutive enzymes.)

15. Induced enzyme synthesis is controlled by more than one gene. In β-galactosidase synthesis in E. coli, gene A codes for the amino-acid sequence of the enzyme, gene B for a permease that moves lactose into the cell, and gene R (regulator) for the rate of synthesis. R produces minute amounts of a repressor substance that binds to an operator gene (O) next to A and B. This binding switches off the activity of genes A and B. Genes O, A, and B are called the operon.

16. When repressor binds to O it prevents RNA polymerase from initiating transcriptioh. When lactose is present, repressor binds to it rather than to O so that the operator is switched on and A and B are transcribed. Hence, β-galactosidase and permease are made and lactose is used by the cell.

17. The production of a substance by a cell may be inhibited by the presence of adequate amounts of that substance in the cellular environment, with no genetic control. Feedback inhibition of the production of the amino acid isoleucine by E. coli occurs when isoleucine combines and thus interferes with the first enzyme of a sequence that normally produces isoleucine. This prevents it from binding to its substrate and stops the production sequence. Production does not resume until isoleucine levels drop.

18. Control of genetic switching on and off in higher organisms is under intense investigation.

## KEY WORDS

| | | |
|---|---|---|
| | metaphase | negative feedback |
| | daughter chromosomes | positive (or runaway) feedback |
| cell division | anaphase | steady state |
| chromosomes | telophase | enzyme induction |
| resting cell | nucleolar organizer | constitutive enzymes |
| interphase nucleus | cytokinesis | structural genes |
| chromatin | furrowing or cleavage | regulator gene |
| centriole | mitosis | repressor |
| prophase | histones | operator |
| chromatids | genes | operon |
| centromere | giant chromosomes | promoters |
| asters or astral rays | chromosomal puffs | feedback inhibition |
| spindle | fixed control system | introns |
| equator | feedback control system | |

## TOPICS FOR REVIEW AND DISCUSSION

1. Describe the stages of mitosis. What is the significance of mitotic cell division?

2. Can gene activity be seen? How?

3. What is the meaning of negative feedback? How does it operate in cellular metabolism?

4. Describe the operon theory.

5. Why may mitosis be thought of as cellular immortality?

6. Explain the relationship of genes to chromosomes.

7. Illustrate the chromosomal movements during mitotic division of a cell containing four chromosomes.

8. What is the relationship of chromatid to chromosome?

9. Describe the packaging of DNA into chromosomes.

10. What would happen to a cell's chromosomes during mitosis if a centromere were lost? If a centriole were lost?

11. What is the difference between plant and animal cell mitosis?

## Did Roosevelt Have Cancer?

Little strokes, a heart attack, cancer. Rumors of these illnesses—and worries about how they would affect his fitness for office—hovered around Franklin Delano Roosevelt as early as 1936. By 1944, when he was 62 and running for an unprecedented fourth term as President, the rumors had become persistent. Vice Admiral Ross McIntire, Roosevelt's personal physician, insisted during the campaign that the President was in "excellent condition for a man of his age." But on April 12, 1945, less than three months after his fourth inauguration, F.D.R. died.

Though no autopsy was performed (at Eleanor Roosevelt's request), there is little doubt that his death was caused by a massive cerebral hemorrhage. But speculation has continued about Roosevelt's health in the last years of his life; any serious illness could have affected his performance in office and led to what many believe were unwise concessions to Stalin at the momentous Yalta Conference. Now a doctor has raised anew the suggestion that Roosevelt had terminal cancer, knew it, but chose to run for re-election in 1944 anyway so that the country, engaged in the war effort, would not be disrupted by a change in leadership.

Spot above left eye is evident in 1939 photograph (left) but missing in 1944 photograph. A suggestion that F.D.R. had terminal cancer, knew it, but ran for re-election in 1944.

# Cancer: Cells Out of Control

## 8–1 WHAT IS CANCER?

Cancer is a killer that will touch most of us directly or indirectly. One in three Americans will get cancer at some time in his or her lifetime. And one person dies of cancer every 65 seconds. Worldwide, over 3 million people each year die of cancer, and in the United States more than 500,000 deaths are annually attributed to this disease. In morbidity statistics for the United States, cancer ranks second as the principal disease causing death, surpassed in importance only by the cardiovascular diseases. It has been estimated that about 70,000 person-years are lost annually because of disabilities caused by cancer and $20 billion are lost yearly in goods and services. Cancer is indiscriminate; it affects young and old, male and female, rich and poor. What is cancer and how can it be recognized?

One of the inherited tendencies of living matter is to multiply. Cellular growth and multiplication are dynamic processes, but in our bodies such events are under some sort of restraining influence; unchecked or unlimited cell division ordinarily does not occur. For example, if a wound is made in the skin, let us say a cut, some striking changes in the pattern of cell growth take place (Figure 8–1a). The cells that surround the gaping wound detach themselves, become ameboid, and move into the wound area; on the way, these cells begin to divide. The cells continue the process of division until the entire wound is filled. Now cell touches neighboring cell, the proliferation

of cells ceases, and the wound is healed. Similarly, when a tissue or an organ is in the process of growing, the cells multiply, but once a certain size is reached the multiplication process ceases.

Suppose a few of our skin cells, especially those that divide to replace the cells continually being lost at the surface, escape from controlling factors and the daughter cells continue to multiply; eventually a cluster of cells is produced (Figure 8–1b). Similar uncontrolled cell division in any part of the body could result in an abnormal, functionless lump or mass of cells—a **cancer** or **tumor** (the terms are synonymous). The cancer cell is often described as being **neoplastic** (*neos*—new; *plasma*—a thing formed; Gk.), since it has been transformed from a cellular condition of rest with the synthetic machinery turned off to a condition of continuous growth and multiplication.[1] Cancer cells contribute nothing to the tissue from which they arose; they often interfere with and damage neighboring normal cells and monopolize the food supply.

To most people, cancers are "rampant, predatory, savage, ungovernable, greedy cells—flesh destroying itself." To a biologist, the cancer cell is one with an inherited capacity for autonomous growth, that is, it determines its own activities irrespective of the laws that precisely regulate the growth

[1] The time spent in mitosis by a cancer cell is the same as that of normal cells, but the frequency of cell division is greater for the cancer cell.

of all normal cells. The clinical physician distinguishes tumors by their appearance and their manner of distribution, designating them as **benign** (harmless) or **malignant** (deadly). Malignant tumors are usually classified according to the cells or tissues involved. Cancers of the epithelial tissues or the skin are called carcinomas, and those of the muscles, bone, and connective tissue are called sarcomas. Tumors of the nervous system are called gliomas. When classified according to the type of cell, cancers are basal cell carcinomas if they involve basal skin cells, or squamous cell carcinomas if they involve the squamous cells of the lung or the skin, and melanomas if they involve the pigment cells. Most tumors are solid masses, but the leukemias, which are a type of sarcoma, grow as individual white cells in the blood.

The property of autonomy is expressed in both benign and malignant tumors; how then do they differ from one another? Normal cells of the body tend to respond to the presence of abnormal objects such as tumors by attempting to surround them in an envelope of tissue, thus isolating them and cutting them off from the rest of the body. If a tumor is surrounded by a connective-tissue capsule and is thus restricted in its growth, it is called a benign, or harmless, tumor (Figure 8–2a). Of themselves, benign tumors do not kill, but they can interfere with normal function; for example, they can obstruct the bowel. Benign tumors can be cured because they can be removed by surgical means; warts are ex-

FIGURE 8–1 Patterns of skin growth. (a) Wound healing. (b) Cancer.

amples of benign tumors, caused by a virus.

Sometimes benign tumors give rise to another kind, called an **invasive tumor.** In such a condition the normal tissue cannot keep pace with the rapidly dividing cancer cells, and the capsule breaks down. The cancer cells break out of the connective-tissue capsule, grow outside the capsule, and infiltrate the surrounding tissues (Figure 8–2b). Such a condition is more difficult to handle and may cause a diseased condition; this is a malignant tumor. The malignant invasive tumor may eventually become surrounded by blood vessels and lymphatics; the tumor, or cancer, cells may then enter these vessels and be transported to other parts of the body (Figure 8–2c). This is a malignant **metastatic tumor** and is extremely difficult to treat by surgical procedures. The cancer cells may eventually lodge in the lungs, liver, or kidney or be held in the lymph nodes; there they may proliferate and cause further damage and destruction to the vital organs of the body. Whole-body treatment with drugs or irradiation must be instituted to control such a malignant metastatic cancer.

It is apparent from this discussion that the cancer cell differs from ordinary normal cells in its relationship with neighboring body cells. Ordinarily, normal cells are confined within specific tissues and maintain themselves in a precise and orderly architectural pattern; the cancer cell does not remain confined to the tissue from which it originated, but moves into the surrounding tissues and there continues its proliferative ways. Many cancers show this invasive tendency, and in this way they "claw" their way through the body, injuring and killing other cells. To the early physicians who first observed these cellular tendencies, the hardened body of tumor tissue resembled the body of a crab and the rapidly dividing cancer cells projecting out of this mass and invading surrounding tissues appeared like the crab's claws; it was imaginative, if perhaps not quite logical, to call

Epidermis

Basal cell layer

Blood vessel

(a)

Normal skin

Wound. Gap fills with blood; epidermal cells begin to divide and migrate into wounded area

(b)

Cancerous growth

Scab

Scab. Epidermal cells meet under scab

"Lump"

Cluster of cells

FIGURE 8–2 Clinical diagnosis of cancer. (a) Benign. (b) Invasive. (c) Metastatic.

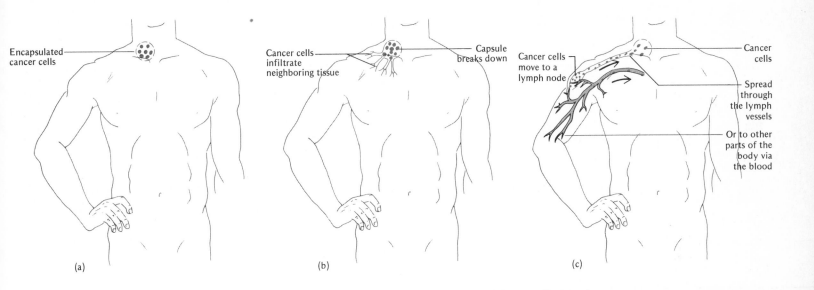

FIGURE 8–2 Clinical diagnosis of cancer. (a) Benign. (b) Invasive. (c) Metastatic.

the disease "cancer" after the Greek word *karkinos*, meaning "crab."

## 8–2 CARCINOGENS: CANCER-CAUSING AGENTS

Agents capable of causing cancer are called **carcinogens;** they come from a variety of sources and can be classified into three basic groups: chemical, physical, and viral.

### Chemical agents

**Occupational.** The first occupational cancer caused by a chemical was described in 1775 by the English physician Percival Pott as "a scrotal cancer of chimney sweeps." The frequency of skin cancer, particularly in the area of the scrotum, was greater in sweeps who had started as climbing boys early in childhood, yet the symptoms appeared only in sweeps who had been in the profession for 20 years or more. Pott surmised that the tumors had originated from soot which accumulated and persisted longer in the scrotal region because of poor hygiene. The clinical observation of the relationship be-

tween soot and scrotal cancer resulted in a set of safety regulations, in the form of bathing requirements. As a result, the incidence of scrotal cancer among sweeps showed a sharp decrease. It was not until 150 years later that Pott's clinical observations were confirmed experimentally. In 1932, Kennaway and his colleagues isolated a specific chemical from coal tar, 3:4-benzpyrene, and this alone induced cancerous lesions.

Workers in the dye industry show a high incidence of bladder cancer, and the carcinogen involved is β-naphthylamine, which is used as the starting material for the synthesis of many dyestuffs. Petroleum workers, too, show a higher incidence of cancers than the general populace, but the agents involved have not yet been identified. Asbestos, nickel, uranium, chromates, and arsenic have all been shown to be involved in cancerous lesions.

**Dietary.** Recent evidence indicates that we are surrounded by numerous dietary agents that may be carcinogenic. A potent carcinogen popularly known as "butter yellow" (*N*-dimethylaminobenzene) used to be

routinely added to butter to make it more yellow and presumably more attractive to the consumer; fortunately, the quantity used for coloring was quite low and the practice has now been prohibited. Certain other food additives, such as cyclamates and saccharin, have been implicated in bladder cancer in mice, and older case studies showed that the hormone diethylstilbestrol, used for caponizing fowl, could also produce animal cancers. Dietary factors in some countries are associated with or implicated in cancer of the esophagus and the stomach. In Sri Lanka and India, cancers of the mouth and throat are common and are related to the habit of chewing mixtures of tobacco, betel nut, and lime. The evidence at present, as with most cancer research on humans, is strictly statistical, but diet itself does represent a potential source of carcinogens.

**Hormonal.** Within our own bodies there may be agents potentially capable of inducing cancer. Particularly suspect is the female hormone estrogen. Long-term application of estrogen to the skin has caused cancers in experimental animals, and the continued application of estrogen in guinea pigs causes

FIGURE 8–3 Relation between smoking and the subsequent rise in the death rate from lung cancer, for men and women in England. (After Royal College of Physicians, *Smoking and Health Now*.)

uterine tumors; mice can be induced to produce pituitary tumors by estrogen administration. For humans, the effects of hormones on cancer development are not as clear-cut. In men under treatment with estrogen it is not unusual to find an enlargement of the breasts, and some of these show precancerous lesions. It is suspected, but by no means proved, that estrogen may play a significant role in the development of certain forms of cancer.

**Atmospheric pollution.** Whenever hydrocarbons such as gasoline, coal, oil, gas, or other fuels are incompletely burned, a variety of compounds are produced that have been identified as carcinogenic. In the atmosphere over most large cities, a dense blanket of air pollutants causes eye irritation, difficulty in breathing, and a range of other discomforts. In every month in every square mile of Manhattan more than 1,520 lb of tar settle down, a small fraction of the 176 tons of solids that rain down on the inhabitants each month. The soot of the air contains the powerful carcinogen 3:4-benzpyrene, and the amount of that chemical increases during the winter with increased burning of fossil fuels. The frequency of lung cancer is directly related to the density of the population, indicating that atmospheric pollution may play a significant role. With continued increase in population and an increased utilization of fossil fuels, there seems little doubt that the larger amounts of carinogens produced will enhance the incidence of cancer.

**Smoking and lung cancer.** At the present time, the side panel of every package of cigarettes manufactured in the United States carries the statement "Surgeon General's Warning: Smoking Causes Lung Cancer, Heart Disease, Emphysema, And May Complicate Pregnancy."

The American Cancer Society estimates that cigarette smoking is responsible for about 83% of the lung cancers. The death rate due to cancer for male smokers is twice that of nonsmokers. Yet despite these grim statistics and the warning of the Surgeon General 30% of the U.S. population continues to smoke, and the output of cigarettes is 659 billion (in 1986).

Much experimental evidence for a variety of laboratory animals indicates that inhaled cigarette smoke can be carcinogenic. Cigarette smoke contains 6,800 different chemicals, several of which (dimethylnitrosamine, hydrazine, and vinyl chloride) have been shown in animal tests to be powerful carcinogens. For example, in experiments where dogs smoked cigarettes and extracts

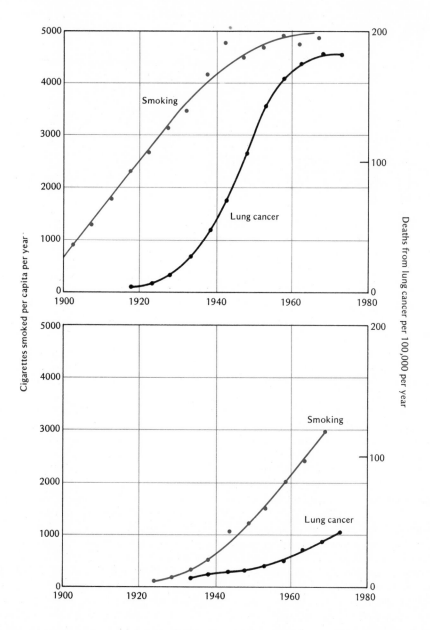

FIGURE 8–4 Smoking and cancer. (a) Mean death rate from lung cancer for cigarette smokers and their cigarette consumption. (b) Mean death rate from lung cancer for cigarette smokers who have stopped smoking for varying periods of time. (Courtesy of *Journal of the American Medical Association* and American Cancer Society, Inc.)

(a)

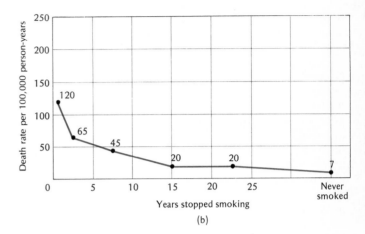

(b)

from cigarette smoke were painted on the backs of mice, tumors developed. Critics of these tests maintain that the results cannot be extrapolated to humans. They may be correct, but continually accumulating evidence indicates that the critics are probably wrong. No direct experiments using cigarette-smoke carcinogens can be performed on humans, and so the evidence is primarily statistical. Be that as it may, the statistics show that smoking is hazardous to one's health.

If the incidence of lung cancer in England is plotted against the increased cigarette consumption, then it is clearly seen that the rise in deaths due to cancer follows that nation's cigarette consumption (Figure 8–3). Also, because of social habits, the rise in lung cancer increased in men long before it did in women. Notice also that there is about a 20-year interval between the time people begin to smoke and the measurable increase in lung cancer.

If every smoker in America stopped smoking today, hundreds of thousands of premature deaths from cancer could be prevented, and an estimated 30% of all cancer incidence could be eliminated. Since such warnings are likely to go unheeded, we can expect 140,000 persons to die annually from

lung cancer alone; more persons will die from lung cancer than from automobile accidents!

The data in Figure 8–4 show that the longer an individual smokes, the greater the possibility of developing lung cancer. The most important factor in the development of lung cancer is that the risk increases with the amount of smoke inhaled and the duration of the smoking habit. Cigarette smoking also bears a causal relationship to other disorders, such as Buerger's disease (an inflammation of the arteries), emphysema, chronic bronchitis, and heart disease. These correlations do not prove a cause-and-effect relationship, but they do suggest a strong link between the smoking of cigarettes, cancer, and related diseases.

Over the last 40 years, overwhelming evidence has accumulated that Americans, and others elsewhere around the world, are increasingly filling their environment with carcinogenic chemicals. The World Health Organization currently estimates that environmental agents are responsible for more than 75% of human cancers. A National Cancer Institute map shows the areas of the United States with the highest death rates from lung, liver, and bladder cancer (Figure 8–5); these are the same regions that have

the greatest amount of chemical pollution. Yet there is hope: if the main causes of cancer are indeed environmental, then potentially this disease could be prevented (Box 8A).

**Physical carcinogens**

**Ultraviolet light and skin cancer.** One of the diversions considered fashionable in modern society is to lie in the radiant sunshine for hours at a time, covered with some kind of greasy substance; at the end of this time the sunbather hopes to have acquired a deep brown suntan. The effect of the sun's ultraviolet light upon the skin of most humans is to produce first a redness that may be accompanied by a soreness; then if the dose is not severe enough to cause blistering and peeling, the red fades and is replaced by a brown coloration—the much-desired tan. The redness is produced by the dilation of blood vessels creating increased blood flow in the area, and the skin becomes red and warm. In the tanning process, ultraviolet light causes the deeper layers to produce the pigment melanin, which migrates to the more superficial layers (Figure 8–6). If the skin is not reexposed, the tan fades. In many respects the effect

FIGURE 8–5 (top) Mortality among white males suffering from lung, liver, and bladder cancer (1950–1969). The national average is 174 per 100,000 yearly. (Reprinted by permission from TIME, The Weekly Newsmagazine; copyright Time Inc. 1975.

FIGURE 8–6 (bottom) Changes in the skin induced by sunburn. (a) Before sunburn. (b) After sunburn, there is increased blood flow in the capillary bed (arrows), greater deposition of melanin, death of epidermal cells, increased cell division, and a thickening of the keratin layer.

of ultraviolet light represents a type of inflammation, and commonly there is some damage to the skin cells. Such injury results not only in the elaboration of melanin but in the thickening of the skin itself by a proliferation of cells and a greater deposition of keratin.[2] Does this ultraviolet-light-induced aging and cellular proliferation eventually lead to cancer? There is some uncertainty and doubt regarding this question, but certain factors suggest that this may indeed be the case. It is estimated that 10% of human cancers are related to exposure to ultraviolet rays; most of these are cancers of the skin, and 95% of such cancers are curable if treated in time—while they are still benign and before they metastasize. Skin cancers occur more frequently on the parts of the body that are habitually exposed to sunlight, skin cancer is more prevalent among populations dwelling in the sunnier regions of the globe, and skin cancer appears more frequently in light-skinned than in dark-skinned persons and more frequently among outdoor than indoor workers. Mice can be induced to produce skin cancers by treatment with low doses of ultraviolet light for 5 days a week over 161 days; human beings have 70 years or so for exposure and therefore a greater likelihood of developing skin cancer (the life-span of a mouse is about 2 years). If the effects of sunlight are cumulative, as experiments with mice suggest, the risk of skin cancer in humans due to the effects of sunlight increases with age and is very great indeed.

**X radiation.** X rays are much more energetic than ultraviolet rays and, as one would expect, are much more effective in producing skin cancer. The early radiologists, unaware of the carcinogenic effects of x rays,

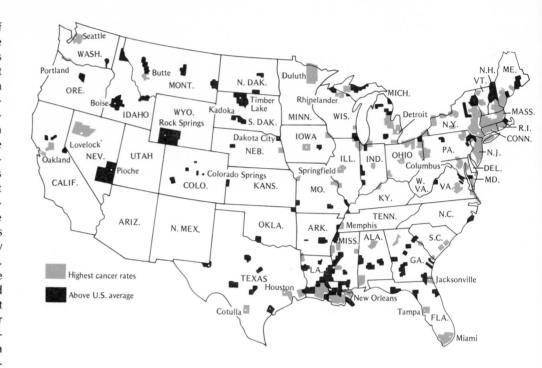

Highest cancer rates

Above U.S. average

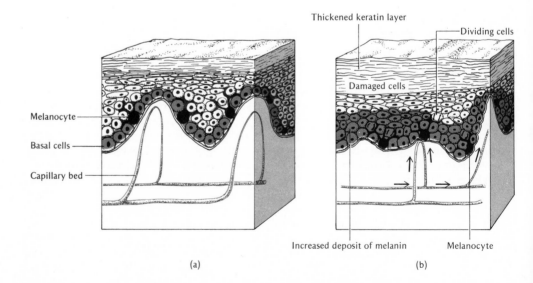

Thickened keratin layer

Dividing cells

Damaged cells

Melanocyte

Basal cells

Capillary bed

Increased deposit of melanin    Melanocyte

(a)    (b)

---

[2] Microscopic examination of skin from the face and arms of fair-skinned but overtanned individuals shows that the cells resemble those taken from the skin of very old men and women (cells from unexposed areas such as the buttocks retained a youthful appearance). Sunburning and suntanning tend to age the skin prematurely.

---

## BOX 8A  The cancer screen

Medical scientists have been trying for decades to identify those chemicals that are carcinogenic. That task is not easily accomplished. During a lifetime we are exposed to literally millions of chemical compounds, both natural and synthetic. To screen each of these compounds for their carcinogenic properties would require extensive animal testing, involving many years and costing millions. However, there may be a way to speed up the process. A simple and inexpensive cancer screening test was developed by Bruce Ames, a biochemist at the University of California. The **Ames test** is based on the theory that carcinogens damage nucleic acids, causing mutations and thereby inducing cancer. Bacteria do not get cancer but are vulnerable to mutations. Ames used a mixture of four mutants of the bacterium *Salmonella typhimurium* that were unable to make the amino acid histidine; such mutants do not grow unless histidine is added to the agar on which they are placed. When exposed to agents causing mutations (**mutagens**), these strains may mutate further; some of these mutations, by chance, will repair the original genetic defect, making their possessor normal. If this occurs, the bacteria will grow on agar containing no histidine and colonies will form on the agar surface. The colonies show up as white dots and can easily be counted. The more powerful the mutagen, the more colonies there are that will grow in the absence of histidine. Thus, colony numbers give some measure of the potency of the mutagenic agent. Of 174 known carcinogens tested, 157 (90%) were mutagenic in the Ames test. Out of a group of 180 so-called noncarcinogens, 14 were mutagenic. Some of these mutagens may well cause cancer. For example, a food additive called furylfuramide that was used in Japan for 8 years had been shown to be noncarcinogenic in animal tests; however, recent studies show it to be both mutagenic and carcinogenic. Furylfuramide is positive in the Ames test.

All evidence indicates that certain chemicals and radiation in the environment damage DNA; over a lifetime this cumulative damage is probably the cause of most human cancers. The Ames mutagenicity test is a cheap way of determining whether a chemical compound is likely to be dangerous to humans. It may also enable us to tell whether an individual who has been exposed to a suspected carcinogen is carrying a lethal time bomb within her or him. A physician suspicious of such a condition could take a sample of the patient's urine, add it to a culture of *Salmonella*, and see if it is mutagenic. If detected early, treatment could be initiated. Mutagenic screening could make it possible to protect the public against hazardous substances before and not after they have been in widespread use.

---

developed severe carcinomas of the hands after repeated brief exposures to low doses of x rays. The frequency of leukemia among radiologists is 10 times greater than among other physicians. The leukemia incidence among the survivors of Nagasaki and Hiroshima is five times that of the rest of the Japanese population; the incidence of breast cancer among the female survivors is also increased (approximately three times).

X rays, by virtue of their energy, break molecules down into charged particles called ions. These highly reactive ions stimulate mitosis or destroy cells, depending on the dose and the tissue involved. How these effects are produced, and what factors trigger normal cells to divide and retain these proliferative properties, remain speculative, but mutations may be involved. We shall return to this later in the chapter.

### Viruses and cancer

As early as 1910 Peyton Rous found evidence that a fibrous connective-tissue tumor (sarcoma) in the breast muscle of chickens was due to the presence of a virus (Rous sarcoma virus, or RSV), but this was lightly dismissed as a peculiarity of chickens. Later, the evidence made such criticisms less valid. In 1932 Rous, Beard, and Shope found that a nonmalignant skin cancer in wild rabbits was caused by a virus (Shope papilloma virus);[3] when the purified virus was transferred to other rabbits, it metastasized and eventually killed the animal. Today it is well recognized that viruses are responsible for a great many cancers. (In fact, Rous was awarded the 1966 Nobel Prize in medicine for his 1910 work on RSV.)

---

[3] Perhaps the best known of all human cancers that is viral in origin is the nonmalignant skin tumor known as the common wart. Electron microscopy reveals the presence of viruses in wart tissues; isolation of these viral particles and introduction into a susceptible host produce warts. (Handling toads has nothing to do with the transmission of warts.)

Finding virus particles in the cells of a human tumor does not prove that viruses are the causative agents of a human cancer. For example, it is conceivable that the viruses are harmless cellular occupants, and it is quite by chance that they occur within these cells, or it could be that viruses invade cells after the cells have been transformed into cancer cells and so have not contributed to the transformation process itself. A convincing demonstration that a virus does induce cancer is required, and certain criteria (called **Koch's postulates**) must be satisfied before we can say that proof positive has been obtained:

1. The virus must be isolated from the cancer.
2. The virus must be inoculated into a healthy animal and produce the disease.
3. The same virus must be reisolated from this experimentally induced cancer.

It is obvious that to apply such methods to the direct study of human cancers is almost impossible, and therefore other techniques have been employed. The transmission of human cancers to animals (other than humans) and to human cells grown outside the body in tissue-culture systems has provided a great deal of information on the nature of the relationship between viruses and human cancers, but the results are still far from conclusive. Presently, it is suspected that viruses may be involved in human cancers such as breast cancer (Box 8B), leukemia, and Hodgkin's disease (a cancer of the spleen and lymph nodes). However, the assumption held by some that all cancers are caused by viruses, and that carcinogens such as chemicals and irradiations are effective because they activate the virus, is presently without foundation.

One of the problems involved in investigating virally induced cancers is that the behavior of viruses may depend on the host or the particular tissue that is invaded; in one tissue a virus may have no ill effects (it is simply a passenger virus), in another it may cause lethal effects, and in still others

it may induce malignancy. To illustrate this let us look at a particular case.

In the early 1950s, Sarah E. Stewart and Bernice E. Eddy isolated a virus that caused salivary-gland tumors in mice. When reisolated and grown in tissue culture, the viruses multiplied, and upon reinjection into newborn mice, the viruses produced 20 different kinds of cancers in addition to the one found originally only in the salivary gland. This broad-spectrum virus was named **polyoma virus.** Other experiments using tissue cultures showed that, on occasion, polyoma virus not only induced cells to become cancerous but resulted in cell death. What is responsible for these many faces of the polyoma virus?

The explanation may in part relate to the protein coat that surrounds the virus. The viral protein coat readily provokes an **immune response** by the host (that is, specific proteins called **antibodies** develop in the blood of the host upon contact with foreign proteins and the antibodies neutralize or inactivate the virus); when viruses are contracted in small quantities, the animal builds an immunity to the virus. In nature, polyoma virus is spread among mice in the saliva and in the feces, and the young gradually build an immunity to it.[4] Antibodies are also passed to the offspring via the mother's milk. This acquired immunity probably accounts for the low incidence of spontaneous tumors in mice. Experimentally, massive quantities of virus can be produced in tissue cultures, and then these can be injected into highly susceptible animals. In young animals death often results because the defense system is unable to cope with the virus, but in older, more resistant animals the same virus may allow the host cells to live and cause them to proliferate; in this latter case, malignant cancers are produced.

How does the polyoma virus cause cancer? Electron microscopy shows the po-

lyoma virus to be a round particle with a diameter of 2.7 Å, made up of a protein coat surrounding a core of DNA. When polyoma viruses enter a susceptible cell, the cell has two possible fates: (1) death, as a consequence of virus production, or (2) transformation into a cancer cell without the formation of new viruses. In both cases, viral particles are taken up by the host cell into small sacs, these sacs accumulate around the host-cell nucleus, some of the viruses lose their protein coats, and the naked viral DNA enters the nucleus. In the lethal infection, within 48 hours the host-cell nucleus becomes filled with viral particles; the progeny of the infecting viruses eventually fill the host cell and cause it to burst, and the released viral particles can begin a new round of infection. However, on rare occasions the polyoma virus can create a cancerous condition in the host cell. Viral particles are not seen in the transformed cell; rather, the naked viral DNA is inserted into the DNA of the host-cell chromosomes. These viral genes usurp and corrupt the host cell, making it act in a malignant way.

Polyoma viral DNA carries about six to eight genes (it has 5,000 nucleotide base pairs); these genes are actively responsible for the production of a cancer cell. One of the viral genes probably codes for a protein that is a regulator (a promoter or repressor substance), and this turns on or off specific genes of the host cell or virus. (Genetic regulators are discussed in Chapter 7.) For example, the viral genes that code for viral coat protein are silent, or off, since once a cell is transformed, viruses with protein coats are never formed. On the other hand, the virus does turn on the cellular enzymes involved in DNA synthesis, presumably at the transcription level, thus causing both host-cell and viral genes to be duplicated and the cell to divide. In addition, viral genes direct the production of a specific coat on the host cell; this change in the host-cell surface may be responsible for the altered relations of the cancer cell with its neighbors.

---

[4] Laboratory experimenters working with polyoma virus also build antibodies to it.

## BOX 8B Human mammary tumors

Breast cancer is the most common type of cancer in women in the United States: there are 130,000 new cases each year and 40,000 deaths annually. In human breast cancer the earliest symptom is a lump in the breast; most commonly these are nonmalignant, or benign, tumors. Breast cancer risk increases with age, and the tumor seldom occurs in young women. As the cancer develops, it tends to spread to the lymphatics and then to other parts of the body; it is at this stage that the cancer is dangerous. Detection of cancer in the early stages is simple and effective. By mammography and self-examination of the breast more than 90% of breast cancers are discovered.

There is a tendency for breast cancer to occur more frequently in certain females, and this makes it likely that a genetic predisposition for it may exist (the genetic factor, if it exists, does not appear to be strong). Human breast cancers show a hormone dependency. As early as 1896 G. Beatson, a British physician, found that surgical removal of the ovaries in patients with breast cancer caused a remission of the tumor. However, since breast cancer occurs more frequently among women who have never married and those who have not had children, the mechanism of hormonal action in human breast cancer remains an enigma. In mice, tumors of the mammary gland are also influenced by hormonal factors, but it has been conclusively shown that mammary tumors in mice are caused by a virus that is passed on in their mothers' milk. Although it seems to be different from the situation in the mouse, it may be that some human breast cancers are also viral in origin.

Treatment for breast cancer is variable depending on the woman's preference and the medical situation—surgery, radiation therapy, chemotherapy and hormone therapy are employed. Cancer of the breast also occurs in men (the frequency is 1 case of male breast cancer for 100 cases of female breast cancer). The most common treatment for male breast cancer is surgical removal.

In summary, we can say that we know little about the events

Xeroradiographs of normal breast (left) and of breast with tumor (right). *Dr. John E. Martin/Time Magazine.*

that initiate human breast cancer, but we do know that hormones play an important role in the development and growth of mammary tumors. It is conceivable that the effect of hormones on the breast tissue produces an environment conducive to tumor formation; it is also possible that a combination of genetic and hormonal factors alone can induce tumor formation. Which, if any, of these is the causal mechanism remains uncertain at present.

FIGURE 8–7 Patterns of growth of normal and cancerous cells.

Why do viruses induce cancer? The induction of cancer by some viruses may be a by-product of viral functions that have developed for their own multiplication. Because the virus is small, it cannot contain much genetic information and must therefore exploit the synthetic machinery of the cell to achieve its own replication. The viral activities induce cancer because they are similar to the activities and mechanisms by which cells regulate their own replication. In other words, viruses enter cells in order to reproduce their kind. To do this, they must turn on the DNA-replicating machinery of the host cell and redirect it to make viral materials. A side effect of continued DNA replication is likely to be continued cell division and proliferation—cancer.

## 8–3 THE MOLECULAR BASIS OF CANCER

What is the difference in
these lethal shapes
that makes them deathful deviates
from quiet harmony
with those around?
CHAUNCEY D. LEAKE

Cancer, as we have seen, is a descriptive term for a galaxy of diseases having a common biological pattern: the breakdown of the regulatory controls that precisely govern the growth of cells within the body. Cancers also show another property: an escape from normal cell-cell contact relations. Let us examine this loss of "stick-togetherness" of cancer cells and see how it contributes to their ability to infiltrate normal tissues, detach, migrate, and metastasize to distant sites.

If a small piece of your skin was removed and placed in a glass dish containing a nutrient solution, the cells would settle down and attach to the glass surface. For a time, if there were very few cells, there would be rapid cell division, and the skin cells would spread out to form a uniform sheet of cells one cell thick (Figure 8–7). Having reached the edge of the dish, and now with each cell touching another, cell

Contact-inhibited monolayer of normal cells

Multilayer of uninhibited cancer cells

Growth medium     Plastic tissue—
culture dish

division would slow down. The sheet of cells would continue to live if supplied with nutrients, and when cells died they would be replaced by limited divisions in certain cells of the sheet. In this manner the continuity of the single layer of cells would be maintained. It appears that cell contact inhibits cell division; we have already seen this type of growth pattern in wound healing. A similar type of experiment can be performed with a cancer of the skin, but here the results would be quite different. Once the cancer cells were placed in the glass dish containing nutrient solution, they would divide and spread out in a single layer in the same way as normal cells, but division would not cease at this point. Rather, growth and division would continue without limit, and the cells would pile one upon the other producing a lump of cells several layers deep. There appears to be no boundary limiting the growth of the cancer cell. Division of cancer cells can occur in the living organism (in vivo) or in a glass dish (in vitro) over and over again; it occurs not only with skin cancer but with cancers derived from liver, nerve, kidney, bone, and so on. All cancers show the same sort of phenomenon: uncontrolled growth and loss of normal contact relations.

This phenomenon, where cells cease to divide when they touch one another, is

called **contact inhibition.** It is not clear what factors are responsible for contact inhibition, but it may be related to a greater stickiness of normal cells so that their contacts are firm; the cancer cells, in contrast, are less adhesive and can separate and pile upon one another. This local regulation of growth makes good sense, for inside our own bodies or the body of any other multicellular organism there is a limited amount of space; thus it would be a great disadvantage if cells continued to divide once the space was filled—there would be no room for them. At the same time, if for some reason a space appears, as, for example, in a wound, then division can begin and the space is filled up. Stickiness of cells is also rather specific: liver cells adhere to liver cells, and kidney cells to kidney cells, but cancer cells show no preferences. Thus, we can begin to see why cancer cells are able to invade and maintain themselves in a variety of tissues irrespective of their tissue of origin.

One of the puzzling things about cancer concerns the diversity of physical, chemical, and biological agents that are capable of producing what appears to be the same end result: an inherited pattern of cell growth that is abnormal, unregulated, permanent, and autonomous, accompanied by a loss of cellular contact inhibition. When we begin to ask, "How is cancer caused?" rather than, "What is cancer?" we move from an area of descriptive science to the realm of speculative science. A plethora of hypotheses concerning the mechanisms of cancer formation is available: each hypothesis has its merits and each has its limitations. We shall discuss three of them here.

### Hypothesis: mutations cause cancer

Since cancer is usually a permanent (irreversible) change, it has been suggested that cancers develop as a result of mutations. It is well known that physical agents such as ultraviolet light and x rays as well as certain chemical agents are both carcinogenic and

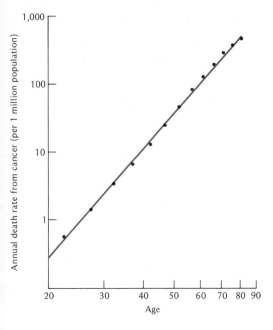

mutagenic (capable of producing mutations). Hermann Muller, a Nobel laureate in genetics, suggested that the carcinogenic properties of these agents are due to the accumulation of changes in individual genes (mutations) in certain cells of the body and that these reduce the cell's susceptibility to inhibition of cell division. This hypothesis also states that several mutations are necessary for inducing the cancerous state, and as such fits well with what we know about the slow rate of development of most cancers and their increased incidence with advancing age. The older a person gets, the mutation hypothesis holds, the greater the chance that some of the body cells could accumulate these mutations, thereby becoming transformed into cancer cells. The essential mutations are those directly involved in cell division and could have as their basis the removal of an essential protein, such as the repressor substance that regulates the expression of genes involved in mitosis. Thus, the mutational hypothesis attempts to correlate chemical and physical

agents with the capacity for tumor induction. Some investigators suggest that these agents could also activate a latent virus gene and thus could play a role in virally induced cancers. Once the carcinogen induces such a change, it no longer has to be present to perpetuate the tumorous condition; since the change affects the genetic material, it is permanent, and autonomous growth results.

What evidence is there to support the view that mutations are involved in cancer? The death rate from cancer of the large intestine increases about 1,000 times between ages 20 and 80, but significantly most of this increase occurs after age 40 (Figure 8–8). The relationship between age and death rate shown in the graph (Figure 8–8) is logarithmic and can be explained by the hypothesis that it takes both time and a series of mutations to produce a cancer. The slope of the line suggests about five mutations are required to produce a cancer, and the incubation period for a cancer may encompass a lifetime. Thus, the incidence of lung cancer may be related not to the number of cigarettes an individual smokes today, but the number he or she smoked 20 years ago. Similarly the scrotal cancer of chimney sweeps described by Pott was initiated during childhood and took many years for its full development.

If mutations cause cancer, is it due to normal errors in DNA replication or are environmental mutagens responsible? Current evidence implicates the environment. Cancer of the stomach is more common in Japan than in the United States, whereas for cancers of the breast, prostate, and bladder the reverse is true. When Japanese leave Japan and come to live in the United States, these differences are lost within two generations despite the fact that such immigrants tend to marry within the group. The time factor, the changed environment, and the rather constant genetic background tend to implicate environmental mutagens.

What is the mechanism involved in mutagenicity? The basic mechanism of muta-

tion is either by base-pair substitutions or frameshift mutations. In the base-pair substitution the mutagen resembles the normal nucleotide base so that it is mistakenly inserted in the DNA during replication. This substitution alters base pairing; the coding for an amino acid would then be incorrect, producing an abnormal protein (or a shortened polypeptide if the new triplet coded for termination). Frameshift mutations occur when the mutagen slips between the base-pair "rungs" of the DNA, and by distortion of the molecule—a stretching or shortening—the precise reading of the triplets is upset. As a consequence, bases are read in an entirely new sequence of triplets and the protein produced may be either novel or functionless. No matter what the mechanism, if mutations are responsible for many human cancers, then prevention and eradication should be possible.

### Hypothesis: genetic transpositions cause cancer

The two most common cancers are those of the skin and the lungs, and both are strongly dependent on a single factor: sunlight in the former and smoking in the latter. Skin cancers are undoubtedly caused by ultraviolet light, which causes localized lesions in the DNA of skin cells, and the mutagens in cigarette smoke are believed to be the responsible agents for carcinogenicity of lung cells. However, there are other common cancers whose origins are more difficult to identify and which develop rather slowly, occupying a significant portion of the animal's life-span. Recently, some scientists have claimed that x rays, ultraviolet light, and some other conventional mutagens are probably responsible for less than 10% of the deaths attributable to cancer. If this is true, then we must search elsewhere for the causes of these cancers. One possibility is that cancers are the result not of a small lesion in the DNA, a point mutation, but of a shuffling of short DNA sequences from one position of the chromosome to another. Such reshuffled DNA sequences, called **transposons**, or "jumping genes," may in their new location alter the expression of the genes that flank them. For example, a transposon could act as a new start and stop signal for neighboring genes, or it could make a particular region of the chromosome highly unstable and thus contribute to its alterability.

What is the evidence that transposons are involved in cancer? A case in point may be Bloom's syndrome, an inherited disease associated with a high frequency of chromosomal rearrangements. In persons suffering from the disease, the death rate from cancer (especially lymphomas and leukemias) is increased 100-fold over that of the normal population. Also, people suffering from two other inherited diseases, Fanconis anemia and ataxia telangiectasia, which are also associated with chromosomal rearrangements, show a high incidence of leukemia. Thus, large-scale changes in the arrangement of genes could be involved in some cancers.

If transposons are indeed the basis for some cancers, and the idea is highly speculative, then it will be important to determine what kinds of external agents increase the frequency of the process and in what manner transposons exert control over gene expression so that a normal cell becomes one with abnormal properties. It will not be simple to devise experiments to measure the factors that provoke carcinogenic transpositions, but it is certainly an exciting area for future research.

### Hypothesis: oncogenes cause cancer

The hypothesis that cancer is caused by viruses is not really a hypothesis, since there already is considerable evidence for the viral origin of certain kinds of cancer. However, questions persist: Are all cancers induced by viruses? How do viruses contribute to the transformation of a normal cell into a neoplastic one?

FIGURE 8–9 The developmental cycle of the Rous sarcoma virus.

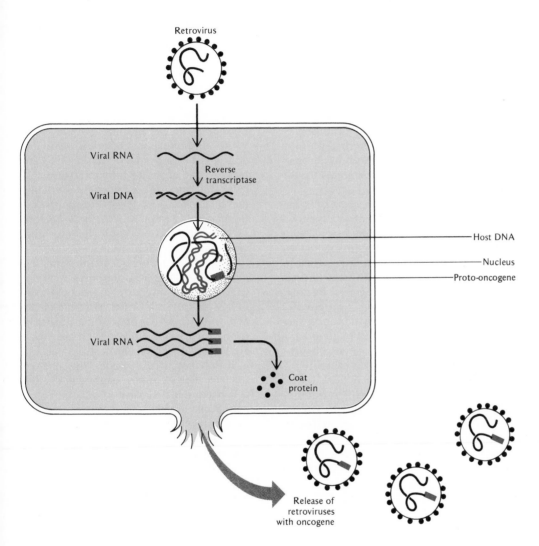

Retrovirus

Viral RNA

Reverse transcriptase

Viral DNA

Host DNA

Nucleus

Proto-oncogene

Viral RNA

Coat protein

Release of retroviruses with oncogene

cell. Through integration the viral genes become a part of the chromosomes of the host cell. A sarcoma virus has only four genes, and one of these, designated src, encodes a protein that causes the conversion of a normal chicken cell into a cancerous one; the remainder of the virus' genes are involved in viral multiplication (Figure 8–9).

In 1968, it was theorized that viruses caused cancers by inserting a portion of their genome into a normal cell thereby causing its transformation. The viral cancer-causing gene was called an oncogene, and the src gene described previously is an example of how theory has been verified by fact. At first it was assumed that the src gene and the other 20 oncogenes that have now been identified were peculiar to the retroviruses that cause cancer, but recent studies have shown that oncogenes have their counterparts in normal animal cells. It appears that the viral oncogenes are copies of the normal cellular genes (or protoon-cogenes) that were plucked out of the vast array of genes in the infected animal cell by virtue of the way the retrovirus replicates itself (Figure 8–10). The presence of oncogenes in the virus appears to be an accident that allows the host cell to be in a condition most suitable for virus multiplication. Simply put, oncogenes are normal genes in another cellular guise.

Retroviruses are not the only source of oncogenes. Oncogenes have been discovered in DNA tumor viruses, such as the Epstein-Barr virus and the polyoma virus, and they have been found to occur in cancer cells that have arisen without any known viral infection, that is through exposure to chemical carcinogens. (Of course, it is always difficult to state with absolute certainty for any cancer cell that at some point in the distant past it did not acquire a bit of DNA from a viral invader.)

Protooncogenes can be found in the cells of all animals including humans, and because they have been retained by cells for many millions of years, it has been assumed

We have considered two cancer hypotheses: one in which there was change in or deletion of genetic information (mutations) and another in which there was no change in the genetic constitution (genetic transpositions). Now let us consider a third hypothesis: oncogenes cause cancer.

**Oncogenes** are, as their name implies, cancer-causing genes. Much of what we know about them has been discovered in the past 10 years although the oncogene

story actually begins in 1910 when Peyton Rous discovered the sarcoma virus of chickens. Later work showed that the genetic material of the sarcoma virus is not DNA, but RNA. It is, therefore, a retrovirus, so-called because it replicates *backwards* by means of an RNA-directed synthesis of DNA. The RNA genes of the invading virus are first copied into DNA by the enzyme reverse transcriptase, and then the DNA is inserted (or integrated) into the DNA of the host that they must be important for the normal activities of the cell. But, you might wonder, why would a cell carry in it the potential for aberrant growth? The answer seems to lie in the similarity of the proteins encoded by oncogenes and protooncogenes. One of the proteins encoded by oncogenes is an enzyme, protein kinase. Protein kinases catalyze the phosphorylation of specific proteins that are involved in maintaining cell shape and also control the growth of cells. The src oncogene encodes a protein kinase that is specifically bound to the region of the cell membrane where actin filaments are anchored. When this enzyme phosphorylates the cytoskeletal proteins, it disorganizes them, cell surface adhesiveness is lost, and the propensity for that cell to become metastatic is substantially increased. Another oncogene codes for a protein closely resembling the amino acid sequence of the receptor for epidermal growth factor (EGF). The oncogenic protein is a truncated form of the receptor: it lacks the binding region for EGF, but retains the portion that is embedded in the membrane, and it also contains the catalytic site in the cytoplasm. It may be that this modified EGF receptor leads to uncontrolled growth because it can function without the presence of an external growth factor signal. And, finally, some oncogenic proteins are localized in the nucleus where they may alter the rates of transcription of other genes involved in cell growth.

How does a protooncogene become an oncogene? One means is to increase the transcription rate. This may result from the insertion of a protooncogene into a high transcription region. That is, near a promoter. A second kind of conversion involves the loss of some portion of the protooncogene that results in unregulated activity, and a third way is a single point mutation. Such alterations in protooncogenes give rise to increased levels of the protein product, and structural and functional changes of the protein. Oncogenes may also be activated by the movement of the gene to

another place on the chromosome, a translocation. Tumor cells from human patients with Burkitt's lymphoma, a cancer of the antibody-producing B cells, consistently show chromosomal abnormalities especially an exchange of segments between chromosomes 8 and 14. One consequence of this is the translocation of a protooncogene (called myc) from its normal position on chromosome 8 to a region on chromosome 14 near the region that codes for the antibody molecule.

The discovery of oncogenes and the characterization of their protein products allows us to understand some of the mechanisms involved in the transformation of healthy cells into cancer cells, but the questions that still remain are: How many human cancers are caused by oncogenes? Because most human tumors develop in progressive stages, resulting in a metastatic cancer, are multiple oncogenes involved in generating the initial event? How do nongenetic changes influence the development of cancer?

The hypotheses presented here by no means exhaust all the possibilities, but they do offer attractive suggestions for future work. Perhaps by the time you read this we may have a better view of how viruses, mutations, transposons, carcinogens, and oncogenes act to produce the cancerous state.

## SUMMARY

**1.** Cancer is one of the principal diseases causing death in the United States.

**2.** A cancer, or tumor, is composed of neoplastic cells in a state of autonomous growth and multiplication.

**3.** Clinically, cancers may be benign or malignant. Malignant tumors arise from benign tumors which become invasive. If invasive cancer cells are transported to other parts of the body by blood or lymph, they are metastatic.

**4.** Carcinogens are agents capable of causing cancer; they may be chemical, physical, or viral.

**5.** Chemical carcinogens include many environmental substances, thought to be responsible for more than 75% of human cancers; example are soot (3:4-benzpyrene), dyes (β-napthylamine), asbestos, nickel, chromates, and arsenic; dietary additives such as cyclamates and saccharin; hormones, including some synthetic estrogens; air pollutants, including fossil fuel and coal tar derivatives such as 3:4-benzpyrene; and cigarette smoke (DMBA).

**6.** The Ames test is a screen for environmental carcinogens. It depends on the mutation rate of a strain of *Salmonella* bacteria.

**7.** Physical carcinogens include the ultraviolet rays of the sun and x rays.

**8.** Some viruses are carcinogenic. The effect of a cancer-causing virus may vary with the tissue invaded. For example, polyoma virus causes a broad spectrum of cancers in newborn laboratory mice, possibly owing to lack of antibodies and absence of an immune response in these animals.

**9.** Polyoma virus invades the host-cell nucleus. The virus may cause cell death as a consequence of virus production, or it may transform the cell into a cancer cell; then viral DNA is replicated along with host-cell DNA, and the host-cell surface is changed, altering cell-cell interactions.

**10.** Cancer cells show a loss of contact inhibition.

**11.** There may be a genetic factor in human breast cancer, although it seems to be hormone dependent. Mammary tumors in mice are caused by a virus that is passed on in their mothers' milk.

**12.** Cancer may be caused by cumulative mutations. Mutagens may have their effect by altering the DNA itself (base-pair substitutions or frameshift mutations) or by activating a latent virus.

**13.** Carcinogens may selectively and permanently activate the genes that switch cell division on, or repress those that keep it switched off.

**14.** Oncogenes cause cancer by activating cell division or altering adhesiveness.

KEY WORDS

cancer
tumor
neoplastic
benign
malignant
invasive tumor
metastatic tumor
carcinogens
Ames test
mutagens
Koch's postulates
polyoma virus
immune response
antibodies
contact inhibition
mutations
transposons
oncogenes

TOPICS FOR REVIEW
AND DISCUSSION

1. How may viruses cause cancer?

2. Why is it difficult to determine the role of viruses in the establishment of human cancers?

3. Describe the varied behavior of the polyoma virus and its significance to cancer.

4. Describe how environmental carcinogens are related to the incidence of cancer.

5. What are some of the ways that scientists use to screen potential carcinogens?

6. What is loss of contact inhibition?

7. How may somatic mutations be related to the development of cancer?

8. How is cancer defined biologically? Clinically?

9. How can an understanding of normal cell division aid in an understanding of cancer?

10. The cancerous condition is usually a permanent, heritable change in a cell. What does this tell us about the mechanism of induction?

## WHAT IS A HUMAN BEING?

A self-balancing, 28-jointed adapter-base biped; an electrochemical reduction plant, integral with segregated stowages of special energy extracts in storage batteries for subsequent actuation of thousands of hydraulic and pneumatic pumps with motors attached; 62,000 miles of capillaries. . . .

The whole, extraordinary complex mechanism guided with exquisite precision from a turret in which are located telescopic and microscopic self-registering and recording range finders, a spectroscope, etc.; the turret control being closely allied with an air-conditioning intake-and-exhaust, and a main fuel intake. . . .

R. BUCKMINSTER FULLER, *Nine Chains to the Moon*, Philadelphia, J. B. Lippincott Co., 1938

Illustration by Masami Miyamoto, from "Telemobility," *Kaiser Aluminium News*, III, 1966. Reprinted by permission of Kaiser Aluminum Chemical Corporation.

# THE HUMAN ORGANISM

What is a human being? Anthropologists regard humans as the tool-making descendants of an apelike stock and the makers of culture. Psychologists view us as behavioral systems capable of learning, memory, and reason. To sociologists we are of interest because of the institutions and societies we form. Poets see the human organism as the abode of the soul, and for artists humans are forms of transcendent beauty. To a biologist human organisms are anatomically complex, highly adaptable, self-reproducing animals who can accumulate experience and use it to alter their environment and their fate.

The machinery of the human body can be most conveniently studied by taking it apart piece by piece, examining each part in detail, and then putting the parts together again and determining the way in which they function to make a smoothly operating whole. The parts of the body are known as organs, and organs that function together constitute systems. The chapters that follow describe the various systems of the human body. The classification is merely a didactic convenience, and there is nothing fixed in any arrangement; one may split or lump organs into systems in a variety of ways. It is important to remember that all the body's systems interact and that the simplest of bodily functions requires more than one system. A malfunction in one system can lead to breakdown or dysfunction of others.

Study of the human organism has intrinsic interest for us, because we are the subject of our own study. Moreover, it is of considerable importance for all of us to know what we are and how we came to be, for in understanding these we hold the key to our future. As far as we know, human beings are the only creatures to have developed on earth who are able to stand apart, as it were, and to examine themselves in their own setting. No other animal has altered its environment to the degree that civilized human beings have. To a large extent, all other creatures are at the mercy of their particular environment and adapt themselves to it. Humans adapt the environment to themselves. The implications of this are, of course, enormous, and the more all of us understand about ourselves and our relationship to the world in which we find ourselves, the better equipped we will be to adjust ourselves to that world and that world to us. The admonition "know thyself" is the prime reason for studying the human organism. As a consequence we may be more reasonable in our relations with other human beings, other forms of life, and our total environment.

## The Age of the Test-tube Baby Is Here

Recently, a professor of law at Georgetown University stood in front of a blackboard and began writing formulas. One formula read: $X_D$ and $Y_M$ by IVF with gestation M. He explained to his audience that the formula represented that the beginnings of life could be created through the uniting in a laboratory dish (in vitro fertilization or IVF) of a woman's donated egg and a man's sperm. One reason for the law professor's resorting to formulas is that biology is creating concepts of birth and parenthood faster than the English dictionary can define them. He said, "Many of the new reproductive possibilities remain so novel that terms are lacking to describe the human relationships they create."

In vitro fertilization, heralded in by the birth of the world's first test-tube baby in 1978, now accounts for several hundred babies in the United States, but there are virtually no laws dealing with this method. And, there are many legal and moral considerations. For example, if a married couple can use a donor to create a baby, should a single woman who wants a child be allowed the same right? What about a lesbian, a transsexual, or a homosexual couple? Does a surrogate mother have a right to an abortion?

Before we are able to take a position on these complex issues, we must understand the science of conception.

(Left) Conception in a glass. (1) The woman is treated with a hormone to stimulate maturation of eggs in the ovary. (2) Through an incision in the abdomen a needle is inserted and eggs are removed. (3) The egg is placed in a dish with nutrients, serum and sperm. (4) After fertilization, the fertilized egg is transferred to another dish where development to a multicellular blastocyst takes place. (5) The blastocyst is placed in the uterus where it implants, and development of the embryo proceeds as it would from a natural conception. (Right) Droplets containing sperm are added to eggs in nutrient solution. (*Time, Sept. 10, 1984*)

# 9

# Perpetuation of Life I:
# Sex-Cell Formation and Fertilization

## 9–1 SEXUALITY AND MEOISIS

"And this," said the Director opening the door, "is the Fertilizing Room." . . . "These," he waved his hand, "are the incubators." And opening an insulated door he showed them racks upon racks of numbered test-tubes. "The week's supply of ova. Kept," he explained, "at blood heat; whereas the male gametes," and he opened another door, "they have to be kept at thirty-five instead of thirty-seven. Full blood heat sterilizes."

Still leaning against the incubators he gave . . . a brief description of the modern fertilizing process; spoke first, of course, of its surgical introduction—"the operation undergone voluntarily for the good of Society, not to mention the fact that it carries a bonus amounting to six months' salary"; continued with some account of the technique for preserving the excised ovary alive and actively developing; . . . referred to the liquor in which the detached and ripened eggs were kept; and . . . showed them how this liquor was drawn off from the test-tubes; . . . how the eggs which it contained were inspected for abnormalities, counted and transferred to a porous receptacle; how (and he now took them to watch the operation) this receptacle was immersed in a warm bouillon containing free-swimming spermatozoa—at a minimum concentration of one hundred thousand per cubic centimetre, he insisted; and how, after ten minutes, the container was lifted out of the liquor and its contents reexamined; how, if any of the eggs remained unfertilized, it was again immersed . . .; how the fertilized ova went back to the incubators; where the Alphas and Betas remained until definitely bottled; while the Gammas, Deltas and Epsilons were brought out again after only thirty-six hours, to undergo Bokanovsky's Process.

"Bokanovsky's Process," repeated the Director. . . . "One egg, one embryo, one adult—normality. But a bokanovskified egg will bud, will proliferate, will divide . . . and every bud will grow into a perfectly formed embryo, and every embryo into a full-sized adult. Making ninety-six human beings grow where only one grew before."

From *Brave New World* by Aldous Huxley, pp. 2 and 3. Copyright 1932 by Aldous Huxley; renewed 1960 by Aldous Huxley. Reprinted by permission of Harper & Row Publishers, Inc., Mrs. Laura Huxley, and Chatto and Windus Ltd.

So it went in the Central London Hatchery and Conditioning Centre as described in Aldous Huxley's 1932 novel, *Brave New World.* Even in such a soulless, streamlined Eden, human reproduction could be mechanized but the human donors could not be completely abandoned. Bokanovsky's Process produced 96 carbon-copy adults from one fertilized egg, but to get the fertilized egg required sperm and eggs from adult individuals.

Bokanovsky's Process—that is, the mitotic division of a fertilized egg—provides for the continuity of life. All our cells, numbering in the million of millions, are derived from such mitotic divisions. Thus, each of us is essentially a complex organization of carbon-copied cells, for mitosis ensures that genetic information remains more or less constant from cell generation to cell generation (Chapter 7). Identical human twins or triplets are the result of the separation of cells that are mitotic products of a single fertilized egg—to use Huxley's term, identical twins are derived by Bokanovsky's Process.

We replace lost cells in our body by mitosis, and we grow from a single cell to 100 million million ($10^{14}$) cells by the same process, but we do not reproduce ourselves by this method. Even in *Brave New World,* Bokanovsky's Process could not make an Alpha from an Epsilon or vice versa; that required the combination of a sperm with an egg. Why? The answer lies in our sexuality. Bacteria and one-celled plants and animals are asexual; that is, they usually do not produce sex cells, and all the offspring come from a single parent. Most other living creatures on this planet, ourselves included, reproduce by sexual means. Sexually reproducing organisms produce sex cells that fuse in pairs to form a new cell, the **zygote,** and from this the many-celled organism eventually develops. The fusion of sex cells (**gametes**) is called **syngamy,** or **fertilization;** thus, sexually produced progeny have not one but two parent cells. It is of critical importance to recognize that when fusion of gametes takes place there is an intermingling of two separate sets of genetic messages. (More about this in Chapter 23.)

Recall that the messengers of inheritance in our cells are called **genes** and that these are localized in discrete nuclear bodies called **chromosomes** (Chapter 7). Chromosomes move from one cell generation to the next during cell division and are the vehicles of inheritance. Let us consider our own chromosomal condition for a moment. Each cell of the body contains 46 chromosomes, and if we assume that our gametes (sperm and egg) arise by mitosis, then the chromosome number of our gametes would

FIGURE 9–1 A diagrammatic rendition of mitosis and meiosis in a cell having a single pair of homologous chromosomes.

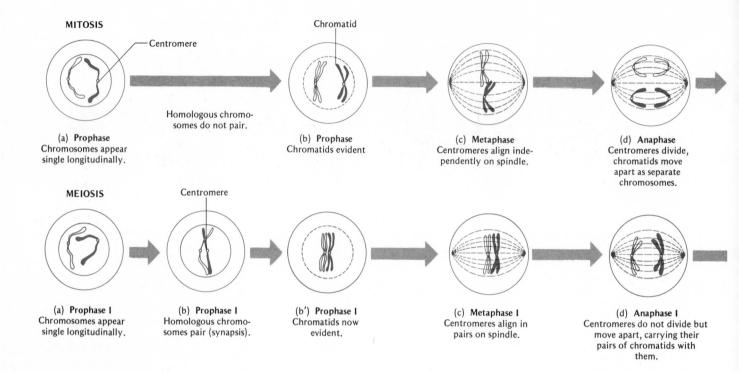

**MITOSIS**

(a) **Prophase**
Chromosomes appear single longitudinally.

Homologous chromosomes do not pair.

(b) **Prophase**
Chromatids evident

(c) **Metaphase**
Centromeres align independently on spindle.

(d) **Anaphase**
Centromeres divide, chromatids move apart as separate chromosomes.

**MEIOSIS**

(a) **Prophase I**
Chromosomes appear single longitudinally.

(b) **Prophase I**
Homologous chromosomes pair (synapsis).

(b′) **Prophase I**
Chromatids now evident.

(c) **Metaphase I**
Centromeres align in pairs on spindle.

(d) **Anaphase I**
Centromeres do not divide but move apart, carrying their pairs of chromatids with them.

also be 46, since mitosis maintains a constant chromosome number. When fertilization occurred, the zygote would contain double the number of chromosomes—92. Such individuals would also produce eggs and sperm containing 92 chromosomes, and the resulting zygote would contain 184 chromosomes. In each succeeding generation the chromosome number would double if mitosis were the only type of cell division. In 10 generations, about the time since the United States declared its independence, the number of chromosomes would increase from 46 in the cells of first-generation individuals to 23,332 in the cells of members of the tenth generation. Clearly, this is not what occurs.

It is obvious that in a sexually reproducing population of organisms, the gametes cannot be formed by simple mitotic division.

Sexually reproducing organisms like ourselves produce gametes by a process that includes a special type of cell division through which the number of chromosomes in the daughter cells is reduced. This process is called **meiosis.** Meoisis encompasses two nuclear divisions but involves only one replication of the chromosomes; in this way the number of chromosomes in each daughter cell is halved. Let us examine the process of meoisis and compare it with the process of mitosis by looking at the dance of a single pair of chromosomes in each type of nuclear division (Figure 9–1).

A number of important differences between mitosis and meoisis are apparent. At the outset of both types of cell division the number of chromosomes is the same, and the chromosomes occur in pairs. Members of each pair of chromosomes are identical

in size and shape and are called **homologous chromosomes.** Cells having two of each type of chromosome are said to be **diploid** and have the $2n$ number of chromosomes ($n$ stands for the number of different types of chromosomes). At the start of both meiosis and mitosis, the cells are diploid, and in the example illustrated the $2n$ number is 2 ($n = 1$). First, in meiosis homologous chromosomes pair (this is called **synapsis**); in mitosis this does not occur. Second, in meoisis there are two cell divisions without replication of the genetic material between divisions; in mitosis there is one division. Third, mitosis reproduces the chromosome number exactly in each daughter cell; in meoisis the number in each is halved. At the end of mitosis the chromosome number is $2n$ (diploid); in meiosis the products have only a single member of each chromosome

(e) **Telophase**
Chromosomes group
into nuclear region.

Cells formed have the
same number of chromo-
somes as were present
in the parental cell.

Chromatid replication
would occur during
interphase before
another division took
place.

(e) **Telophase I**
Chromosomes group into nuclear region. (Each nuclear
region contains a chromosome
with two chromatids.) The
cells formed contain half the
number of chromosomes present
in the parental cell.

(f) **Prophase II**
No replication of genetic
material prior to this, hence
no new chromatids are formed.
Therefore, each cell is haploid,
containing half the number of
parental chromosomes.

(g) **Metaphase II**
Centromeres arranged on a
new spindle.

(h) **Anaphase II**
Centromeres divide for the first
time; sister chromatids (now
separate chromosomes)
separate and move to
opposite poles.

(i)
Four cells, each with
a single chromosome
or half the number
present in the
parental cell.

pair present, and the chromosome number
is n (**haploid**). In the illustrated example, the
cells derived from the two divisions of
meiosis have a single chromosome, whereas
each of the cells derived from the mitotic
division have two chromosomes.

A human body cell, such as a skin or liver
cell, contains 46 chromosomes, and whenever it divides mitotically the daughter cells
also have 46 chromosomes—the diploid (2n)
number. If a body cell containing 46 chromosomes divides meiotically, the products
of such a nuclear division will have 23
chromosomes, the haploid (n) number.

Where in the human body does meiosis
take place? In sexually reproducing organisms such as ourselves, the body consists
of two basic kinds of cells, which are called
**somatic cells** and **germ cells.** The germ cells
divide meiotically to give rise to sex cells,

or gametes, the sperm and eggs. The germ
cells are usually located in organs called
**gonads.** Indeed, the only place in the body
where meiosis occurs is in the gonads.
Somatic, or body, cells do not contribute
to the germ line, and although they may
assist in the act of reproduction in higher
organisms, they never contribute directly
to the cells of a new individual. Somatic
cells reproduce themselves solely by mitosis, and in this manner they provide for
growth in bulk or increase in body-cell
number.

Meiosis enables us and all other sexually
reproducing creatures to reproduce our
kind without multiplying the number of
chromosomes in the cells of succeeding
generations. More important, it provides a
mechanism whereby the genetic heritage
of two individuals may be reassorted and

recombined in new ways in a new individual. The result is that every generation
produced by sexual means has new genetic
possibilities. Meoisis provides a bridge between succeeding generations—parents
passing on to offspring a minute fraction of
their own matter. Somatic cells are mortal;
they die with the individual, but through
the germ cells, eggs and sperm, we gain a
kind of physical immortality.

## 9–2 THE MALE REPRODUCTIVE SYSTEM

### Producing sperm and semen

The human male reproductive system is
designed for the production of gametes
(**spermatogenesis**) and their transfer to the
female, where fertilization will take place.
It is also concerned with the production of
the chemical messages (hormones) that

FIGURE 9–2 The male reproductive system. (a) External anatomy. (b) Detailed view of male pelvic organs shown in cross section.

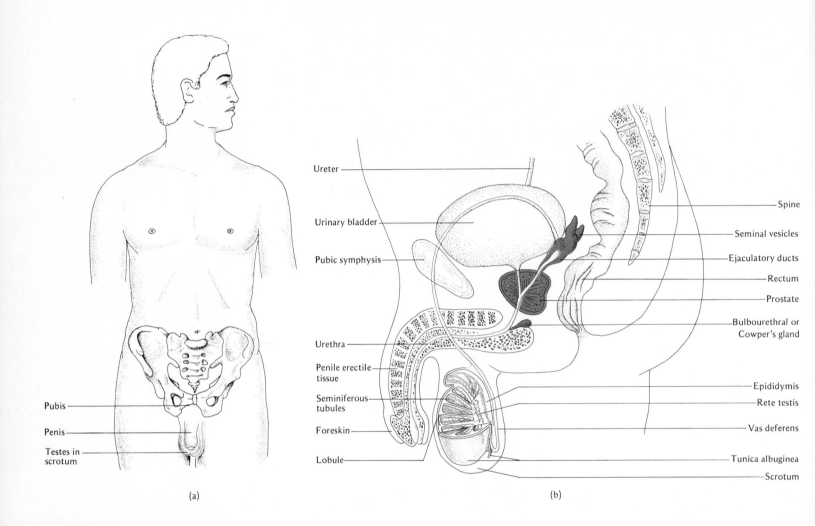

(a)

(b)

control development of the male secondary sexual characteristics—for example, hair on the face and body, deepening voice, body size and shape. Figure 9–2 illustrates the male reproductive system, which consists of the following: (1) the testes, paired male gonads (*gonos*—seed; Gk.) contained within the scrotum, (2) a duct system leading from the testes to the penis, including the seminiferous tubules and vas deferens, (3) accessory glands, and (4) a copulatory organ, the penis.

Each **testis**[1] consists of two functional parts: one produces endocrine secretions (*endo*—within, inside; Gk.), the male sex hormones (**androgens**) which circulate in the blood, and the other produces an exocrine secretion (*exo*—out; *krinein*—to separate; Gk.)

---

[1] The singular of testes is testis. The diminutive form of testis is testicle; the two words are synonymous. For some reason the popular literature commonly uses testicle, where the scientific literature uses testis.

which leaves the body, the **spermatozoa,** or **sperm.** At maturity the testis is a solid, egg-shaped structure (Figure 9–2b) that contains highly coiled tubules, the **seminiferous tubules,** enmeshed in connective tissue and blood vessels. In each testis there are approximately 800 tubules, whose combined length is about 0.5 mile. In the fetus and up to the time of puberty, the seminiferous tubules are represented by solid cords of cells. These cords contain primordial germ cells (**spermatogonia**) and nurse cells (**Sertoli**

FIGURE 9–3 Meiotic events in spermatogenesis. Spermatogonia are diploid germ cells that divide by mitosis to produce a large number of cells. Some of these cells continue to function as spermatogonia; others enlarge and become primary spermatocytes. The primary spermatocytes undergo the two divisions of meiosis followed by a series of morphological changes (spermiogenesis) that culminate in the formation of mature sperm.

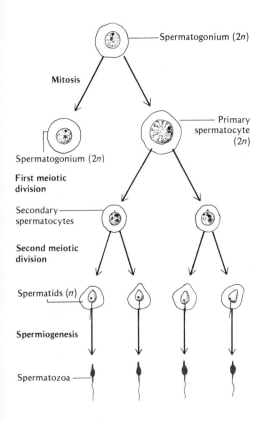

Spermatogonium ($2n$)

Mitosis

Spermatogonium ($2n$)

Primary spermatocyte ($2n$)

First meiotic division

Secondary spermatocytes

Second meiotic division

Spermatids ($n$)

Spermiogenesis

Spermatozoa

cells) that will eventually nourish the developing spermatozoa. Some cord cells also secrete male hormones that markedly affect the maleness of the developing child.

At puberty the young male child becomes an adolescent, and these are times of turbulent change until the boy becomes a man. The changes depend upon a small, pea-sized gland, the pituitary gland, suspended by a short stalk from the base of the brain. The pituitary gland receives signals from the brain and secretes hormones that travel throughout the body via the blood. (The pituitary gland and hormones are discussed in Chapter 17.)

The maturation of male reproductive function is controlled by a series of hormones. A gonadotropin-releasing hormone from the hypothalamus stimulates the se-cretion of two gonadotropins from the anterior lobe of the pituitary gland: **follicle-stimulating hormone** (FSH) and **luteinizing hormone** (LH). FSH acts on the Sertoli cells of the seminiferous tubule to trigger growth and maturation of sperm, and LH stimulates the interstitial cells to secrete the male androgenic hormone **testosterone**. In the adolescent, it is testosterone that initiates development of those characteristics we recognize as male, such as a deepening voice, development of a beard, and muscular body shape.

Testosterone is transported from the interstitial cells to the Sertoli cells, and via the Sertoli cells, testosterone acts to facilitate spermatogenesis, that is, the formation of sperm. Spermatogenesis involves meiosis, maturation, and differentiation. Details of the process are shown in Figures 9–3, 9–4, and 9–5. In the human male it requires about 74 days for a spermatogonium to become a spermatozoan, and each day several million sperm are manufactured.

Spermatids are released into the seminiferous tubules and pass through a half-mile of highly convoluted tubing (Figure 9–2). The still-immature sperm move from the tubule to straight collecting ducts, and then they enter a network of smaller tubules (**rete testis**); eventually, those unite to form about 20 collecting tubules that join to form a single duct within the **epididymis**. Sperm removed directly from the seminiferous tubules cannot fertilize the ovum. During passage through the epididymis, which takes about 12 days, fluid and debris that accompany the sperm are removed, and the sperm undergo maturation that enables them to swim and fertilize the ovum after a period of time in the female tract. Maturation is dependent on testosterone stimulating the epididymis.

Sperm are routinely stored (up to a month) in the epididymis. The tubules of the epididymis are continuous with the long, thick-walled, relatively straight **vas deferens.** The muscular vas deferens passes upward from the scrotum and enters the abdominal cavity through the **inguinal canal.** (The inguinal canal, located in the groin, is the opening through which the testis descended from the abdomen at birth, and this is routinely checked by a physician for an inguinal hernia.) The vas deferens continues upward and across the surface of the bladder, then turns downward and crosses under the bladder. Eventually the two vasa deferentia join the tube leaving the bladder and enter the penis as a common duct called the **urethra.** Shortly before ejaculation the part of the urethra that lies between the points of entry of the vasa deferentia and Cowper's glands receives, in addition to sperm cells, fluid secretions from three sets of accessory glands—the two **seminal vesicles,** the **prostate gland,** and the two Cowper's (**bulbourethral) glands.** These secretions, together with the sperm cells, constitute the **semen** (seed; L). The climax of sexual excitation in the male occurs when the accumulated semen is forcibly ejaculated by spasms or contractions of the muscle layers that surround and are adjacent to the urethra. By a remarkable system of engineering, urine and semen never pass through the urethra at the same time.

In older men it is not uncommon for the prostate to enlarge sufficiently to obstruct the urethra and to make passage of urine difficult; this calls for surgical removal of the gland. In elderly males the prostate is also a common site of cancer.

**Seminal fluid,** a complex liquid material, contains fructose, citric acid, amino acids, choline, enzymes, prostaglandins, and mucus and is slightly alkaline. The tiny sperm cells can store very little food themselves and are entirely dependent upon extrinsic nutrients for use in respiration to provide the ATP necessary to keep the flagella lashing to and fro. Most of the energy for sperm motility is derived from the metabolism of fructose, a unique property of sperm, since most cells use glucose as their metabolic fuel. Seminal fluid also plays other roles; it lubricates the passageways through which the sperm pass during ejaculation, it helps

FIGURE 9–4 Spermatogenesis in the human male. (a) The seminiferous tubules are the factory for sperm production. Below the connective-tissue sheath are the spermatogonia. In layers approaching the lumen of the tubule, consecutive stages of developing sperm can be seen. Mature sperm are nearest the lumen. (b) Spermiogenesis (spermatid maturation). The spermatid loses most of its cytoplasm. The nucleus shrinks and becomes the sperm head. The Golgi aggregates to form a cap, the acrosome, which helps the sperm to penetrate the egg. The centrioles migrate behind the nucleus, where one gives rise to the axial filaments of the sperm tail (flagellum). The mitochrondria move to the middle piece providing power for the lashing tail.

(a)

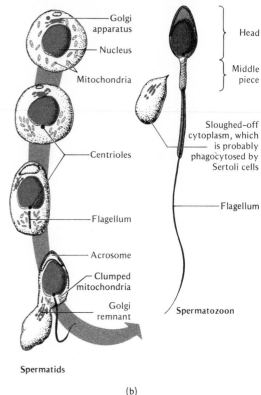

(b)

protect the sperm from the acidity of the female vagina, and it serves as a medium for carrying sperm to the vagina. Immediately after ejaculation, the sperm are motionless, as they were before ejaculation, because the seminal fluid is thick and mucuslike in consistency, but within 30 minutes the fluid thins (owing to proteolytic enzymes contained in the fluid) and the sperm become highly motile—swimming as fast as 3 in. per hour. Sperm deposited in the vagina can remain motile for as long as 2 hours; the entire trip along the female canal from the cervix to the Fallopian tube (a distance of 5 to 7 in.), where fertilization takes place, may take less than 70 minutes. Figure 9–6 illustrates the route taken by the sperm.

Human ejaculate (semen) may be about a teaspoonful in amount (3 to 4 ml), although the quantity varies from 1 to 11 ml. Each milliliter contains about 100 million sperm, so that there are about 300 to 400 million per ejaculate. There is, however, considerable variation in the actual number. Some 3 or 4 males out of every 100 are sterile, or infertile. Infertile males have fewer than 150 million sperm per ejaculate, and more than 25% of these sperm are abnormal in appearance (all ejaculates contain some abnormal-looking sperm). The causes of male sterility are variable and include infections (such as mumps, typhus, or gonorrhea), ionizing radiation, and congenital defects. It may be difficult to realize why sterility should result when so many sperm are present, since it takes only a single sperm to fertilize the egg, but it is believed that the others are necessary to assist that sperm in reaching the egg.

If the male is continuously producing sperm, what happens if there is no ejaculation? That is, what happens to sperm that are not utilized? There are indications that unused sperm are resorbed by the tubules so that ejaculation after a period of rest usually produces a more or less constant volume of semen.

**External genitalia: scrotum and penis**

The most obvious parts of the male reproductive system are the penis and scrotum. Shortly before birth the testes descend from

FIGURE 9–5 Diagrammatic reconstruction of the human sperm as revealed by the electron microscope (side view).

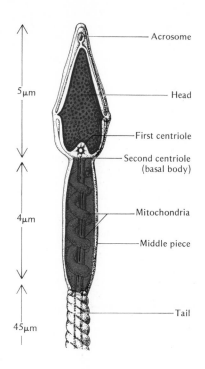

- Acrosome
- Head
- First centriole
- Second centriole (basal body)
- Mitochondria
- Middle piece
- Tail

5 μm
4 μm
45 μm

FIGURE 9–6 Coitus: the route taken by a sperm from its origin (testis) to the place where it fertilizes the egg (Fallopian tube).

- Site of fertilization
- Egg
- Fallopian tube
- Ovary
- Uterus
- Cervix
- Site of deposition of semen
- Vagina
- Erect penis
- Urethra
- Vas deferens
- Epididymis (sperm storage)
- Testis (site of manufacture)
- Release of seminal fluid

the abdomen and enter the scrotal sac by way of the inguinal canals. The **scrotum** is a wrinkled sac of skin with a midline seam that indicates its double origin in the embryo. In the small child, the inguinal canal may remain open and the testes may be withdrawn into the abdomen on occasion (for example, when it gets cold). Normally the canal is closed by the growth of connective tissue, and testicular retraction becomes impossible; however, if it fails to close properly, a loop of the intestine may drop into the scrotum via the enlarged ring of the inguinal canal and cause obstruction and pain in the groin. This is called an **inguinal hernia**. Even when the inguinal canal is properly closed, it is a point of weakness and easily ruptures. The weight of the abdominal organs rests on the lower abdomen, and thus when this area is subjected to excessive strain—as by lifting a heavy object, for example—the probability for de-

velopment of an inguinal hernia is increased. Such hernias are uncommon in four-legged mammals, in which the weight of the organs is more evenly distributed.

A major function of the scrotal sac is to keep the testes cool, or cooler by 0.5 to 4.5 °C than the rest of the body. Spermatogenesis will not proceed at normal body temperatures; the scrotum acts as a thermoregulator: when the temperature surround-

ing the testes is too cold the scrotal muscles contract, bringing the testes closer to the body; another set of scrotal muscles causes the scrotal skin to shrink and pucker. Increased environmental temperatures cause these scrotal muscles to relax. It is crucial for the testes to descend prior to adolescence; if they do not, they atrophy, and sterility results. The condition of undescended testes is called **cryptorchidism**

BOX 9A Sperm banks

## From the Day of Deposit—
## A Lien on The Future

Ever since 1776, when Lazzaro Spallanzani found that human sperm could be frozen and then thawed out and revived, biologists have predicted a day when a man might have his semen put into cold storage and, perhaps after his death, used to beget a child.

That day is here now, not just as a laboratory curiosity but as a commercially available sperm banking service that brings much closer the prospect of controlled breeding programs to produce superior members of the human species.

Some experts predict that enlightened couples may come to prefer having a child by the frozen semen of a modern-day Einstein or Lincoln rather than by the husband. Others, equally expert, say that, on a large scale, such a program could actually redound to the disadvantage of the species by diminishing genetic variability and, therefore, adaptability to changing environments.

Whatever the consequences, it appears that we are soon to learn them, for two private corporations announced that they plan to open frozen sperm banks in New York City within the next few weeks.

Both companies will offer their services to anyone who wishes to have quantities of his semen specially treated, frozen and kept at 321 degrees below zero until wanted for use. At that time, which may be many years later, the sperm bank will thaw out the semen and hand it over to a physician, who will place it in the uterus of the woman intended to be the mother of the child.

At this point, the procedures of artificial insemination are similar to those currently used with freshly collected semen. Since the 1960s about 250,000 children were born following insemination of the mother with fresh semen from an anonymous donor.

Frozen semen, on the other hand, has been used by researchers over the years to initiate thousands of successful pregnancies. The rate of miscarriages and birth defects has been somewhat lower than normal.

With sperm banks, the use of frozen semen can be expanded to offer the woman not just the semen of a donor the doctor chooses, usually on the basis of superficial physical characteristics, but the semen of a broad range of outstanding men, living and dead, who have contributed, or sold, their semen to the bank.

For their part, the men who are setting up the commercial sperm banks wish to avoid the question of whose semen shall be used for what purposes. They intend to exercise no control over the use of the semen, except to say that it shall remain the property of the client and his to use as he sees fit.

Some 85 per cent of the clients in the two existing sperm banks are men who stored quantities of semen before undergoing vasectomies. Proprietors of the new sperm banks believe that the current boom in such male sterilizations will increase as men learn there is a method by which they may still have children.

Beyond the medical and scientific questions are many legal and moral issues to be resolved. If a man undergoes a vasectomy in the belief that he may have children by his frozen semen, and then the sperm bank folds, what recourse has he? If artificial insemination programs are to use sperm banks for eugenics purposes, who shall determine which men exemplify worthwhile characteristics—and, indeed, just what these characteristics are?

Many such questions have already come up with respect to artificial insemination with fresh semen. There the questions have been dealt with by avoiding them. That procedure is usually carried out in the utmost privacy, with no records or legal sanction. Now that sperm banks are going commercial, the questions again ask for answers.

BOYCE RENSBERGER, *The New York Times*, Aug. 22, 1971. © 1971 by The New York Times Company. Reprinted by permission.

FIGURE 9–7 (a) Reflex pathway for ejaculation. Reflex can be initiated from higher centers, or these centers can inhibit arousal; mechanoreceptors in the penis can also initiate the reflex. (b) Cross section through the penis.

(a)

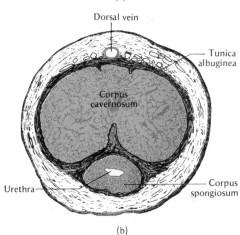

(b)

(*cryptos*—hidden, *orchis*—testis; Gk.). (The name of the familiar orchid plant is derived from the same Greek word, because in some species the bulbous roots resemble human testes). Cryptorchidism often can be treated by surgery or administration of hormones.

The **penis** hangs in front of the scrotum and is the copulatory organ used for transferring sperm to the vagina of the female reproductive tract. At its tip is the slitlike opening of the urethra. The head of the penis, the **glans** (acorn; L.), is covered with a fold of thin skin attached at the neck region; this is the **foreskin,** or **prepuce,** and it is this portion that is surgically removed at circumcision. Under normal circumstances, the penis is limp, or flaccid, but in order to function as a copulatory organ it must become rigid and erect. Penile erection depends upon a spinal reflex (Figure 9–7a) and can be induced by physical and/ or psychic stimuli. Most carnivorous mammals, such as cats, dogs, and seals, have a stiffening bone, the os penis, but primates like ourselves have no such supporting element. The tissues of the human penis are so organized that there are two large cavernous beds of blood vessels above the urethra, the **corpora cavernosa,** and a smaller bed surrounding the urethra, the **corpus spongiosum** (Figure 9–7b). Under appropriate reflex stimulation, the cavernous blood spaces fill rapidly with blood. This increases the fluid pressure, compresses the veins, and prevents blood from leaving the penis. As a result of this engorgement the penis enlarges, stiffens, and becomes erect; it can then be introduced into the vagina. (There is no relation between penis size and virility or sterility, although a considerable mythology has developed about this.)

Ejaculation occurs when the penis is erect. Wavelike (peristaltic) contractions of the smooth muscles of the testes spread to the epididymis, vasa deferentia, seminal vesicles, and prostate gland, and at the same time the entrance from the bladder to the urethra is closed by a sphincter. Muscles in the penis itself contract, and sperm and

seminal fluid are discharged. The entire process can take as little as a few seconds.

## 9–3 THE FEMALE REPRODUCTIVE SYSTEM

### Producing eggs

The human female reproductive system is organized (1) to produce eggs (**oogenesis**), (2) to receive sperm and provide a milieu where fertilization of the egg by the sperm can take place, (3) to provide for the development of the embryo, and (4) to produce hormones to control the development of the secondary sex characteristics, such as pubic hair, the breasts, and the feminine form. These are much more complex tasks than mere sperm production and ejaculation, and this is reflected by the greater complexity of the reproductive organs of the human female. The essential organs of the female system are (1) a pair of gonads (the ovaries); (2) a duct system including uterine tubes called the Fallopian tubes, the uterus (womb), and a copulatory organ (the vagina); and (3) the external genitalia (vulva) (Figure 9–8). The mammary glands (breasts) are also part of the female reproductive system.

The **ovaries** are almond-shaped glands about 1.5 in. long, lying completely within the body and located on each side of the pelvic cavity (Figures 9–8 and 9–9). Just as the testes are designed for sperm and hormone production, so the ovaries are designed for the production of eggs (ova) and hormones. Like the testes, the ovaries contain germs cells, but these are not arranged in tubules as in the testes; instead they are distributed in a cortical layer of varying thickness (Figure 9–10a). The ovaries are attached to the back wall of the pelvis by a fold of connective tissue called the **broad ligament** (Figure 9–9). Along the top edge of the broad ligament and close to the ovary lie the **Fallopian (uterine) tubes,** which connect to the uterus. They are called Fallopian tubes after the sixteenth-century anatomist Gabriel Fallopius (1523–1563), who de-

FIGURE 9–8 The female reproductive system. (a) External anatomy. (b) Internal anatomy.

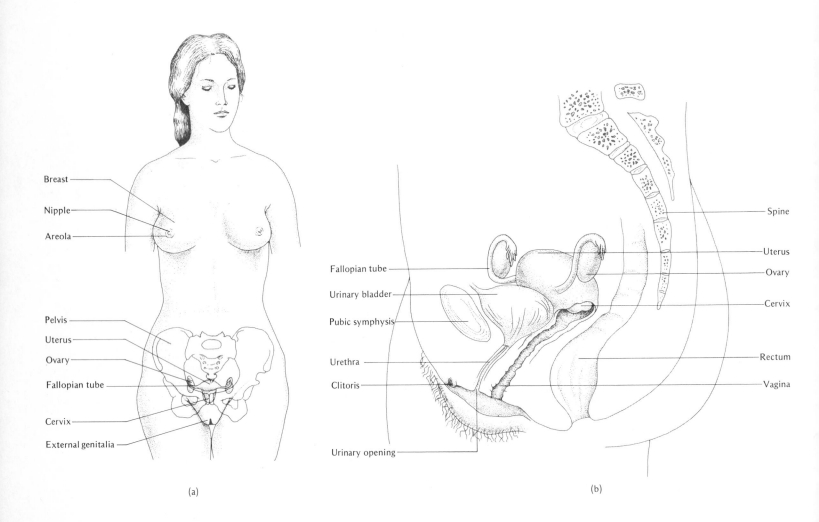

Breast

Nipple

Areola

Pelvis

Uterus

Ovary

Fallopian tube

Cervix

External genitalia

Fallopian tube

Urinary bladder

Pubic symphysis

Urethra

Clitoris

Urinary opening

Spine

Uterus

Ovary

Cervix

Rectum

Vagina

(a)

(b)

scribed them. Curiously, he did not recognize their true function, but thought they were chimneys for the escape of "sooty humors" from the uterus. The end of the Fallopian tubes closest to the ovary is fringed with projections that appear to caress the surface of the ovary. The Fallopian tubes provide a passageway to the uterus for the secondary oocyte after it has been liberated from the ovary.

During infancy and childhood the immature egg cells exist as primary **oocytes** numbering 2 million at birth, but reduced

by age 21 to 300,000. The ripening of the primary oocytes begins at puberty, usually between ages 9 and 17 (the average is 12.5 years). Like the male, at puberty the female child becomes an adolescent, and many physical and psychological changes take place. The most obvious signal of the onset of puberty is the first menstrual discharge of blood (**menarche**) from the vagina. The first menstrual flow, or period, marks the beginning of a female's reproductive life.

Menarche signals the beginning of cyclic changes in the ovary. Oocytes that were

quiescent are now roused to activity. Each month (on the average, every 28 days) an **ovarian cycle** takes place: an oocyte matures in the ovary and is released and carried down the Fallopian tubes. The uterus undergoes changes in its lining to prepare for pregnancy; if the oocyte is not fertilized, the uterine lining breaks down and is shed as a bloody discharge (**menstruation**).

During the reproductive years the monthly liberation of oocytes from the ovary results in a continued decline in oocyte numbers, and at **menopause** (about age 50), when

FIGURE 9–9 View of the female reproductive system with the organs of the right side cut away to show their internal structure.

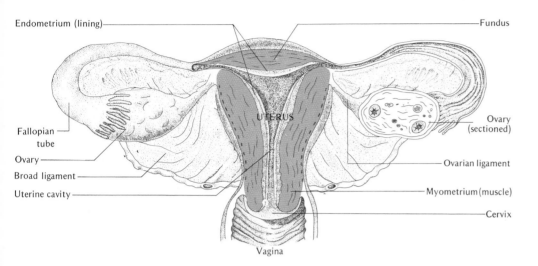

Endometrium (lining)
Fundus
Fallopian tube
Ovary
Broad ligament
Uterine cavity
UTERUS
Ovary (sectioned)
Ovarian ligament
Myometrium (muscle)
Cervix
Vagina

menstruation ceases, oocyte development ceases, the remaining oocytes degenerate, and a woman's reproductive life ends. Although ovalation ceases, sexual life continues and frequently improves. The psychological and physiological changes that characterize menopause do not end abruptly, but may last years. Primitive human females probably never lived long enough to experience menopause. Improved health care and civilization have made menopause the obvious sign of the termination of a woman's reproductive activity.

### The ovarian cycle

The events of an ovarian cycle are shown in Figures 9–10 and 9–11. The hormonal factors controlling ovarian function are similar to those described for the testis, that is, there is a series of hormones: Gonadotropin-releasing hormone (from the hypothalamus), and FSH and LH (from the pituitary), and sex hormones (estrogen and progesterone). In men there is a pulselike secretion of gonadotropin-releasing hormone that is due to an oscillating pattern either in secretory cells or in neurons of

the hypothalamus, and in women, too, such a rhythmic pattern occurs. During childhood estrogens are secreted in small quantities, but at puberty, under the influence of releasing hormone, the amount of FSH and LH increases substantially. Estrogen levels rise. The female sexual organs—Fallopian tubes, uterus, vagina—increase in size, and there is deposition of fat in the breasts, buttocks, thighs, mons pubis, and labia. And, the lining of the uterus, the endometrium, comes to be influenced by the estrogens leading to its thickening and glandular development.

Oocytes begin to ripen in one or both ovaries under the influence of FSH, LH, and estrogen. Each oocyte is surrounded by a nest of epithelial cells constituting a follicle. Different follicles mature at different rates; some are slower and others faster. A few of the follicles show a greatly expanded fluid-filled cavity and resemble inflated balloons. The enlargement is rapid, and the follicle becomes many times its original size, almost 0.5 in. in diameter. At this inflated stage the follicle protrudes slightly and appears as a swollen blister on the surface of the ovary; it is called a **Graafian follicle**

(Figure 9–10b and c) after the seventeenth-century Dutch embryologist Regnier de Graaf (1641–1673), who first described it.

By the time the follicle develops its cavity, the primary oocyte has undergone its first meiotic division, producing a large secondary oocyte and a tiny polar body. This secondary oocyte contains a haploid number of chromosomes. The other set of chromosomes is extruded into the polar body. The unequal division of cytoplasm in the first meiotic division assures that the secondary oocyte will have a large amount of cytoplasm, needed for subsequent development (Figure 9–13).

Final follicular growth and ovulation requires luteinizing hormone (Figure 9–11). Without this hormone, even if large quantities of FSH are present, the follicle will not mature to the stage of ovulation. In concert, FSH and LH cause an accelerated growth of the follicle, and the cells of the follicle produce estrogen.

The mature Graafian follicle contains the oocyte embedded in a small mound of cells called the **cumulus oophorus** (literally "heap holding the egg"). The mature follicle is now prepared for ovulation, that is, expulsion of the secondary oocyte from the follicle. Ovulation is triggered by a brief but substantial increase in LH; this causes the oocyte to complete meiosis, enzymes break down the follicle membrane enclosing the oocyte, and prostaglandins (PGF$_2$) cause contractions, and the oocyte is squeezed out the way a seed is pushed out of a ripe grape. The shed secondary oocyte is surrounded by a thick jellylike layer (the **zona pellucida**) and a loose covering of cells (the **corona radiata**).

As a rule only one follicle ripens sufficiently and releases its oocyte each month. On occasion, however, two mature, and if both liberate their oocytes the possibility of multiple fertilizations and multiple births exists. Those follicles that do not shed their oocytes regress, die, and are replaced by scar tissue; no other trace of them remains.

The secondary oocyte is liberated into

FIGURE 9–10 (a) Cross section of the mature ovary showing the events of the ovarian cycle. (b) Schematic representation of the ovarian cycle (oogenesis). (Modified from M. B. V. Roberts, *Biology: A Functional Approach.* Copyright © 1971 by M. B. V. Roberts. Published by The Ronald Press Company, New York, 1972. Used with permission of The Ronald Press Company and Thomas Nelson & Sons Limited.) (c) Scanning electron micrograph of the human Graafian follicle. (From P. Bagavadoss.*The Reproductive Endocrinology Program*, Department of Anatomy, The University of Michigan.)

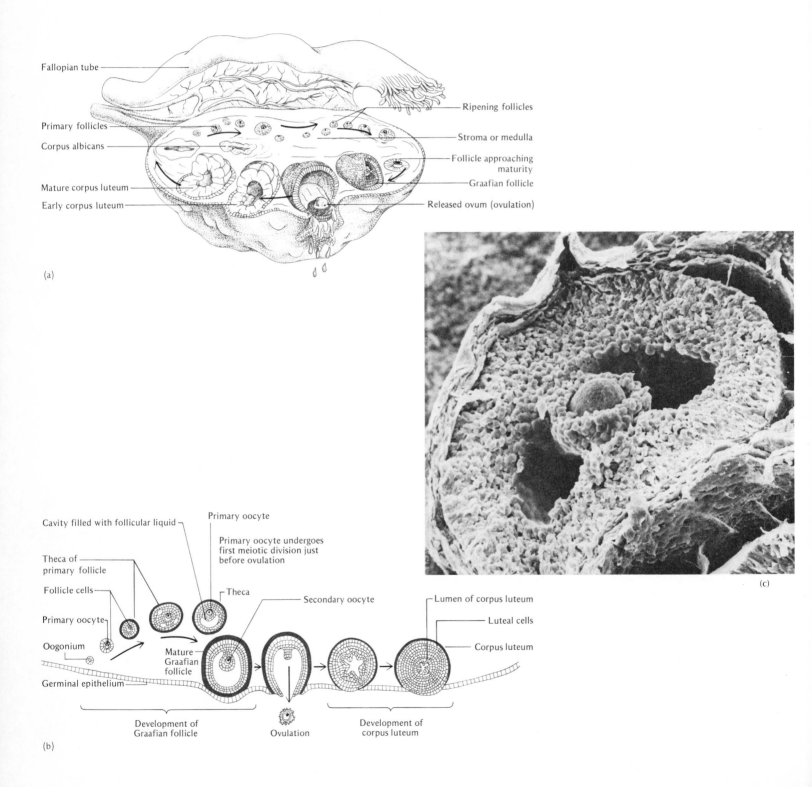

(a)

Fallopian tube

Primary follicles

Corpus albicans

Mature corpus luteum

Early corpus luteum

Ripening follicles

Stroma or medulla

Follicle approaching maturity

Graafian follicle

Released ovum (ovulation)

(b)

Cavity filled with follicular liquid

Primary oocyte

Primary oocyte undergoes first meiotic division just before ovulation

Theca of primary follicle

Follicle cells

Primary oocyte

Oogonium

Germinal epithelium

Theca

Secondary oocyte

Mature Graafian follicle

Development of Graafian follicle

Ovulation

Development of corpus luteum

Lumen of corpus luteum

Luteal cells

Corpus luteum

(c)

FIGURE 9–11 A summary of the events taking place in the pituitary gland, ovary, uterine lining (endometrium), and vagina during the ovarian cycle and the uterine cycle.

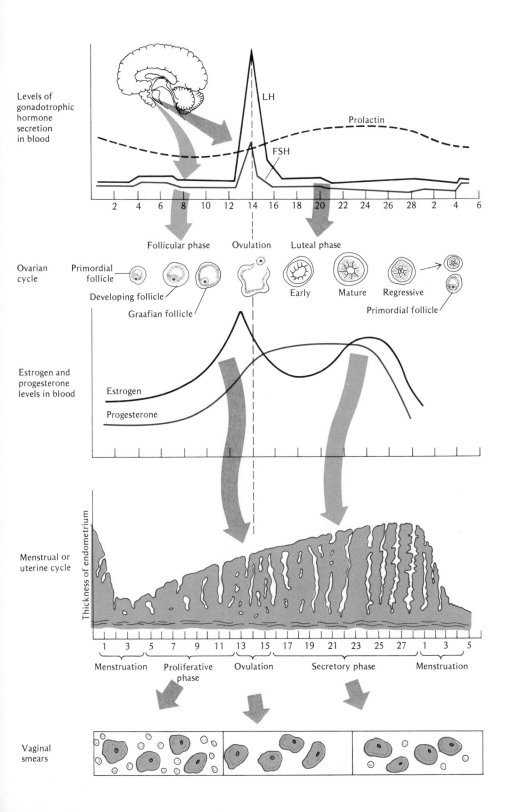

Levels of gonadotrophic hormone secretion in blood

LH

Prolactin

FSH

Follicular phase    Ovulation    Luteal phase

Ovarian cycle

Primordial follicle

Developing follicle

Graafian follicle

Early    Mature    Regressive

Primordial follicle

Estrogen and progesterone levels in blood

Estrogen

Progesterone

Menstrual or uterine cycle

Thickness of endometrium

Menstruation    Proliferative phase    Ovulation    Secretory phase    Menstruation

Vaginal smears

the abdominal cavity, but its time there is quite brief. Only a few millimeters away lie the finger-like processes of the Fallopian tube, covered with cilia. The cilia beat in waves toward the interior of the tube, and this current sweeps the egg into it. In less than a few hours the oocyte enters the Fallopian tube and starts to move toward the uterus. The viability of the oocyte is probably about 24 hours, and if not fertilized during this time, it dies.

After ovulation the follicular cavity collapses and becomes filled with cells. The remains of the follicle, now called the **corpus luteum** ("yellow body" because de Graaf noted that color in the cow ovary; in the human ovary it is cream-colored), develops rapidly during the next 4 days (Figure 9–10). By 9 days it is solid and almost 1 in. across. Under the influence of LH, the corpus luteum begins to secrete the hormones estrogen and progesterone. The progesterone and estrogen circulate in the blood, arrive at the pituitary, and act on it to suppress production of LH (Figure 9–11). In addition, the follicular cells produce a hormone called inhibin that suppresses the production of FSH. Thus no new follicles are stimulated at this point, and egg production is arrested. In the event that fertilization does not occur, the corpus luteum becomes inactive in 13 or 14 days and is transformed into a fibrous mass of scar tissue, the **corpus albicans** (Figure 9–10). In about 2 months there is hardly a trace of the scar tissue left.

About 7 females out of 100 are infertile. The causes of infertility may be infection (most commonly gonorrhea), which blocks the Fallopian tubes, or failure to ovulate because of either insufficient hormone or an excessively thick capsule on the ovary. Sometimes these conditions can be remedied by hormone treatment or surgery. Hormone treatment involves the use of FSH or some synthetic steroid to stimulate follicular growth; occasionally, more than one follicle is stimulated, several oocytes are released at the same time, and multiple fertilizations and births may result.

### The uterus and the uterine cycle

The ovarian cycle of egg maturation and release is intimately related to the events taking place in the uterus, collectively described as the **uterine** or **menstrual cycle.** Menstruation and ovulation are different events occurring in different organs at different times, but are linked to each other by hormonal action.

The **uterus** is a hollow muscular organ about the size and shape of a pear (Figures 9–8 and 9–9). It is loosely anchored to the bony pelvis by ligaments and is suspended in the pelvic cavity between the bladder in front and the rectum in the rear. The upper part of the uterus, the body, is mostly muscle, and it is this portion that enlarges greatly during pregnancy. The smaller, lower end of the uterus, the **cervix,** points downward toward the vagina. It can readily be felt by inserting a finger into the vagina; it feels like the tip of the nose. The uterus is where the developing child, first as an embryo and then as a fetus, is nourished and sheltered. The lining of the uterus (**endometrium**) is elaborately prepared for implantation of the fertilized egg.

Menstruation is a time of uterine bleeding, accompanied by a regression and shedding of the endometrium. It usually indicates that the egg has not been fertilized, the preparations of the uterus for implantation are in vain, and the entire lining is torn down and discarded. (For obvious reasons, menstruation has been described as the "weeping of a disappointed uterus.") The building up and tearing down of the endometrium constitute the menstrual cycle. It is a continuum that runs for about a lunar month, or 28 days (*menses*—lunar, Gk.) before repeating itself (Figure 9–11). Cycles have no beginning or end, but for convenience we can designate four stages in the menstrual cycle. We begin with a landmark in the cycle: the start of bleeding.

Stage 1. Menstruation. The beginning of menstruation or bleeding is designated as day 1 of the cycle. The bleeding (often referred to as a period) lasts on the average for 4 days (range 3 to 7 days); at the end of this time the endometrium is only 1 to 2 mm thick and is rather smooth (Figure 9–11).

Stage 2. Proliferation. Under the influence of LH and FSH, ovarian follicles begin to develop and to produce estrogen. As the estrogen level increases, endometrial repair begins and the thickened uterine lining acquires blood vessels (Figure 9–11). The proliferative stage lasts 8 to 10 days.

Stage 3. Ovulation. On or about day 14 of a standard cycle a rise in LH causes the ovarian follicle to rupture, releasing the oocyte. This is called ovulation.

Stage 4. Secretion. Estrogen and progesterone (produced by the corpus luteum) act upon the endometrium to prepare it for the embryo. Blood vessels in the uterine wall become more abundant, and glycogen accumulates in the glands of the endometrium. The secretory phase lasts about 13 to 14 days.

On about the twentieth or twenty-first day of the uterine cycle, the corpus luteum receives a message, in the form of a hormone, indicating whether the embryo has been implanted in the endometrium. If implantation has not occurred, the corpus luteum starts to degenerate on day 22 or 23, and the progesterone and estrogen levels drop. The endometrium begins to break down, fragments are shed along with mucus from the uterine glands, blood oozes from the denuded endometrium, and on the average 1 to 8 oz of blood are lost. (Menstrual blood is distinctive in that it does not clot, probably because it contains large amounts of fibrinolysin that dissolves the fibrin.) The decreased production of progesterone and estrogen causes removal of the block on FSH production by the pituitary. New FSH production initiates new ovarian and menstrual cycles.

### The vagina

The **vagina** is a tubular canal about 4 to 6 in. in length, directed upward and backward to connect the uterus with the vestibule of the vulva (Figures 9–8b and 9–9). Like the uterus, it is situated between the rectum and the bladder. The vagina has muscular walls and is ordinarily folded to form a collapsed tube. It serves as a copulatory organ, receiving the shaft of the penis, and during childbirth it functions as a part of the birth canal. The vaginal walls contain no glands and normally are kept moist by a slightly acidic secretion of the cervix; a bacterium aids in maintaining this state. If acidity is not maintained, the vagina becomes prone to infection. Cells from the vaginal fluid are useful in determining the time of ovulation (Figure 9–11) and as a diagnosis of cervical (uterine) cancer.

The opening of the vagina into the vestibule may be partially covered by a mucous membrane, the **hymen.** The absence of a hymen is no more proof of sexual promiscuity than its presence is proof of virginity. Frequently it is absent in women who have never had sexual intercourse, and it may persist in women who have.

In the vaginal vestibule, mucus glands, called **Bartholin's glands** (homologous to the bulbourethral glands of the male), secrete a viscous fluid and are stimulated to activity during sexual play.

### External genitalia

The external genitalia of the female (Figure 9–12), collectively called the **vulva,** consist of the **mons veneris** (pubis), the **labia majora and minora,** the **clitoris,** and the **vestibule.** These organs play a minor role in the reproductive process per se, but do function in foreplay and the sexual act (coitus). The labia majora are fatty skin folds which pass

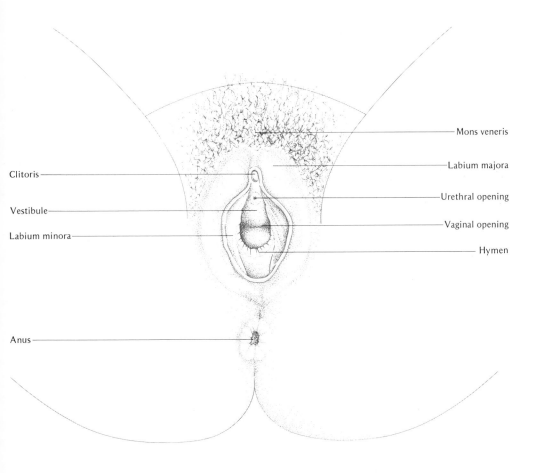

occurs because blood is forced through the arteries faster than it can be drained by capillaries and veins. In the female, the cervix begins to secrete a fluid that lubricates the vagina. At first, individual droplets line the vaginal wall, and these then coalesce to form a uniform surface coating. The production of lubricating fluid, the first physiological evidence of the female's response to sexual stimulation, is involuntary and results from the marked dilation of blood vessels and massive localized vasocongestion in the region of the vagina. Occasionally, vaginal muscles contract and cause this vaginal fluid to squirt out (this is not ejaculation, for which it is sometimes mistaken). The inner two thirds of the vagina dilates, and the uterus contracts rapidly and irregularly. The labia minora swell and Bartholin's glands in the vaginal vestibule secrete a small amount of fluid. In both male and female, the heart beats faster and the blood pressure rises.

Erection of the penis facilitates insertion into the vagina.

The clitoris serves both as a receptor and a transformer of sensual stimuli, and in some women stimulation of the clitoris is the major cause of female **orgasm.** During sexual stimulation, the clitoris becomes enlarged and erect and then the entire clitoral body withdraws beneath a sheath of skin, the clitoral sheath. This retraction is reversible, and if there is a reduction in sexual activity it will return to its unstimulated overhanging position. Because of clitoral retraction the penis rarely comes in direct contact with it during sexual intercourse. However, secondary stimulation may occur via the sensitive labia minora and the vagina. The onset of female orgasm is indicated by contractions in certain organs: at first the labia minora and outer third of the vagina show long spasmodic contractions lasting 2 to 4 seconds, and then contractions about 1 second apart occur; this phase is followed by less regular contractions of the uterus and the muscles of the pelvic floor. The strength and number of orgasmic contrac-

backward from the mons veneris and in postpubertal females are covered with hair. The labia minora are two fleshy folds of skin which enclose the vestibule. The vestibule of the vagina is a cleft between the labia minora, and situated within are the hymen and the openings of the vagina and the urethra (leading from the bladder).

The clitoris is a pea-shaped projection of erectile tissue well supplied with nerves and blood vessels; located at the upper end of the labia minora, it is partially covered by them. The clitoris is the homolog of the male penis, is highly sensitive, and is important in sexual stimulation and satisfaction. (It does not contain the urethra.)

## 9–4 COITUS (COPULATION)

Courtship is the prelude to **coitus** (also called **copulation** or **sexual intercourse**). In humans the courtship process varies and may run the gamut of sensory experiences including touch, taste, smell, and sight—all usually pleasurable. The sexual foreplay of courtship serves one primary biological function: arousal and preparation for coition.

The result of sensory stimulation is tumescence—swelling of the breasts and genitals as they become engorged with blood. The nipples become erect, as do the clitoris and penis. The erection of these organs tions vary with the individual. No particular orgasmic reaction in the breasts or clitoris has been observed. During orgasm, the muscular contractions are accompanied by a diffuse feeling of pleasure. Hearing, vision, taste—all the senses are diminished or lost during orgasm, and it seems to pervade the entire body.

It has long been believed by many women and their physicians that clitoral and vaginal orgasms were distinctly different from each other. Indeed, in the Freudian view the human female progressed during sexual maturation from a maximal response to clitoral stimulation to a maximal response to vaginal stimulation. Recent anatomical evidence shows that vaginal and clitoral orgasms are not physiologically distinguishable; the organs involved in orgasm respond exactly the same way to effective sexual stimulation of any kind.

The orgasmic phase is explosive and brief, usually lasting 3 to 10 seconds. Female orgasm corresponds to ejaculation in the male, but there is no fluid expelled in the female. Whether orgasm in the female facilitates conception is unknown, but it is not essential for conception to occur. In many women orgasm must be learned, and some women never experience it in spite of frequent intercourse. Emotional and psychological factors have profound effects. Aside from ejaculation, the female differs from the male in two respects with regard to orgasm: (1) the female is capable of several orgasms, one immediately after the other, and (2) the orgasmic experience can be maintained for a relatively long period of time.

In the male, orgasm and ejaculation occur at the same time. Ejaculation consists of two distinct activities: (1) semen is delivered from the sperm ducts to the urethra by contraction of smooth muscles in the vasa deferentia, seminal vesicles, and prostate gland (this is often called **emission**) and (2) seminal fluid is forcibly expelled by contraction of muscles surrounding the urethra. The process is controlled by a spinal reflex located in the lower back (Figure 9–7), although higher centers can alter the response, and ejaculation can occur without tactile stimulation of the penis (influenced by erotic thoughts, petting, and so on). Higher centers may also inhibit erection or ejaculation under certain conditions.

Following orgasm there is a return to the unstimulated condition. In the male, detumescence of the penis occurs rapidly, and the organ becomes flaccid. After orgasm the male experiences a refractory period, that is, a resistance to sexual stimulation. Those events that elicited excitement no longer do so; in fact, they may even be irritating and distasteful. The relaxation of the penis after ejaculation-orgasm precludes a second intromission for a varying period of time.

## 9–5 FERTILIZATION

Ovulation takes place between the tenth and the sixteenth day of the average menstrual cycle. The oocyte is quickly caught on the fringed edges of the Fallopian tube, and through muscular and ciliary activity the oocyte is whisked into the tube's upper portion (ampulla). In order for fertilization to occur, sperm must be introduced at about this time. Ejaculation during copulation sends almost 0.5 billion sperm into the vagina. The alkaline seminal fluid is mixed with acidic cervical secretions that lubricate the vagina; sperm first must survive this acid bath and then must swim upstream to the farthest reaches of the Fallopian tube, almost 6 in. away, to contact the oocyte (Figure 9–6). By means of the lashing motion of the whiplike tail, the sperm move against the ciliary currents in the Fallopian tubes, which are directed downward toward the uterus. Within seconds after ejaculation, sperm are in the cervical canal, and they continue to swim upstream against the prevailing current. The Fallopian tubes have many folds, constricted regions, and blind passages, and the number of swimming sperm is reduced all along the way. (Although sperm from the epididymis are mature, they are not able to fertilize the oocyte until they have resided in the female genital tract, and undergone capacitation and activation.) Probably only 1 million sperm ever reach the uterine lumen, and by the time they enter the Fallopian tubes only thousands remain. Perhaps less than a few hundred actually arrive at the vicinity of the oocyte in the upper part of the Fallopian tube.

Sperm are fragile and can survive for about 48 to 72 hours inside the female reproductive tract. Indeed, if they have not found and fertilized the oocyte by then, they perish. The oocyte is even more sensitive and cannot survive for more than about 24 hours. For fertilization to take place, coitus must occur less than 72 hours before the oocyte reaches the Fallopian tube or else the sperm will not be viable; if coitus occurs more than 24 hours after the oocyte reaches the uterine tubes, the oocyte may undergo deterioration with the increased risk of the production of an abnormal embryo or fetus. Thus, there is a critical maximum period of 72 to 96 hours during a monthly ovarian cycle during which coitus must occur if an oocyte is to be fertilized.

The sperm, numbering about 100, arrive in the vicinity of the oocyte about 1 to 2 hours after coitus. The sperm, which are relatively small (they are 54 μm long, but only 5 μm of this length encompasses the head), quickly surround the enormous (150 μm) oocyte. The oocyte itself is enclosed by a layer of cells, the corona radiata, and prior to entry the sperm must first disperse these (Figure 9–10). Each sperm contains in its caplike acrosome the enzyme hyaluronidase; upon release of this enzyme, the hyaluronic acid cement which holds the cells of the corona radiata together is broken down and the cells of the corona become dispersed. Now the remaining sperm confront another barrier, the jellylike zona pellucida. A single sperm moves through the zona pellucida and reaches the plasma membrane of the oocyte. The plasma mem-

FIGURE 9–13 Meiotic events in oogenesis. A primary oocyte that undergoes oogenesis produces one functional ovum and three (or two) minute, functionless polar bodies. The unequal cytoplasmic division during the two meiotic divisions ensures that the ovum is well endowed with the cytoplasmic components essential for development of the fertilized egg. In this way, chromosome reduction occurs without loss of cytoplasm from the egg cell.

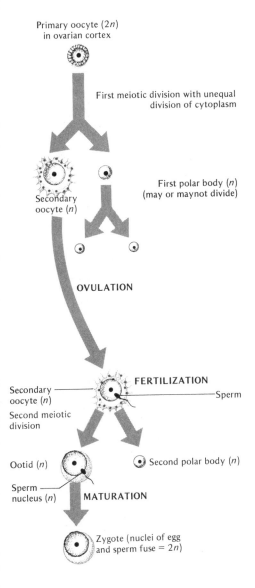

Primary oocyte (2n) in ovarian cortex

First meiotic division with unequal division of cytoplasm

First polar body (n) (may or maynot divide)

Secondary oocyte (n)

**OVULATION**

Secondary oocyte (n)

Second meiotic division

**FERTILIZATION**

Sperm

Ootid (n)

Sperm nucleus (n)

Second polar body (n)

**MATURATION**

Zygote (nuclei of egg and sperm fuse = 2n)

branes of the sperm and the oocyte fuse, and the contents of the sperm enter the oocyte. As soon as this occurs, the oocyte becomes impermeable to all other sperm; they are barred from entry.

As the sperm nucleus enters, the cytoplasmic activity of the secondary oocyte becomes violent. The oocyte completes its second meiotic division and expels the second polar body (Figure 9–13). The remaining egg nucleus and the sperm nucleus, lose their enclosing nuclear membranes, and merge. The merging of chromosomes from sperm and egg is called syngamy, or fertilization, and this occurs within 12 hours after sperm penetration. The fertilized egg is now called a zygote, and it contains the diploid number of 46 (23 pairs) chromosomes. Now the cytoplasm of the zygote becomes less agitated, and the period of embryo development (**embryogenesis**) begins.

## 9–6 CONTRACEPTION

Anything that interferes with fertilization of the egg can be termed **contraception**, and anyone who deliberately avoids conception during sexual intercourse is employing a contraceptive measure. There are about half a dozen ways that conception can be avoided:

1. Limiting time of intercourse to a period during the female reproductive cycle when the oocyte is not available for fertilization
2. Preventing sperm from being deposited in the vagina
3. Preventing sperm from entering the cervix
4. Preventing the release of sperm in the seminal fluid
5. Preventing ovulation or entry of the oocyte into the Fallopian tube
6. Interfering with oocyte transport in the Fallopian tube or preventing implantation of the blastocyst

Let us consider the effectiveness of each of the six methods.

1. The **rhythm method** is quite simple: couples do not engage in sexual intercourse when a fertilizable oocyte is present in the Fallopian tubes. In theory, the oocyte is fertilizable for only a brief time (72 to 96 hours), and, therefore, by avoiding intercourse during an unsafe period—2.5 days before and after ovluation—conception can be avoided. This is the ideal situation, but for many women there is no regularity of ovulation. Detection of the timing of ovulation presents the most difficult aspect of using the rhythm method. Analysis of the cervical mucus and measurement of body temperature are often used to determine the dangerous, or unsafe, period (Figure 9–14 and Box 9B). How effective is the rhythm method? It is estimated to be 74% effective, that is, of 100 women using this method for 1 year, 26 will become pregnant.[2]

2. Sperm may be prevented from deposition in the vagina by a variety of natural and artificial methods. The oldest is **coitus interruptus,** or withdrawal of the penis prior to ejaculation; this is mentioned in the Old Testament (*Gen.* 38:9), was practiced by the ancient Hebrews, and is still widely practiced. The method requires self-control by the male and has a high failure rate. It is generally unacceptable to Americans, who believe it limits full sexual expression by both partners. Even the smallest amount of semen deposited in the vagina can cause pregnancy, and many couples employing coitus interruptus do not realize that it is so failure-prone.

The **condom** is an effective artificial male contraceptive (83 to 88% effective). Invented in the 1700s in the court of Charles II, it is a rubber sheath 7 to 8 in. in length worn over the erect penis during intercourse. The sheath captures the sperm in the sealed end and prevents their deposition in the vagina. The condom is effective if it does not rip or slip off during intercourse. Condoms are made of latex rubber, can be purchased without prescription, and are frequently used to prevent the contraction of sexually transmitted diseases such as AIDS, gonorrhea, and syphilis. (Premature ejaculation in the male, which is not uncommon during the early months of marriage, may be alleviated by wearing two condoms. This substantially reduces the sensitivity of the glans penis and makes

---

[2] In the absence of any birth-control procedures, the pregnancy rate is about 40%.

BOX 9B The Month-After Pill

It is being heralded as the long-sought, safe, morning-after pill. But there is a difference: it is really a month-after pill. A team of doctors from the Hôpital de Bicêtre near Paris reported in last week's *New England Journal of Medicine* that a substance known as RU 486, taken within ten days after a missed period, effectively terminates pregnancies without causing any major side effects.

In tests supervised by Dr. Béatrice Couzinet and Dr. Gilbert Schaison, 100 women volunteers who were less than a month pregnant were given RU 486. Of these, 85 aborted within four days, largely without the discomfort and psychological problems that can accompany other forms of abortion. Because of these remarkable results, the drug is expected to be approved for use in France and Sweden as early as next spring. In the U.S., where abortion is hotly debated, the drug's future is less certain. John Willke, the president of the National Right to Life Committee, has already referred to the drug as "chemical warfare against the unborn."

RU 486 works by adhering to certain hormone receptors in the uterus that under normal circumstances accept progesterone, the substance that prepares the uterine lining to receive a fertilized egg. Because the presence of RU 486 blocks the action of progesterone, the uterine lining sloughs off, and the embryo is expelled, as an unfertilized egg is during a normal period. Although bleeding is usually heavier than during menstruation, only a pregnancy test prior to receiving the drug will tell a woman for certain whether she has actually conceived.

The psychological consequences of this uncertainty can be significant. "We call it contragestation, not abortion," says Couzinet. "Many women think of it as an induction of a menstrual period. Compared with classical abortion, the procedure is so much better tolerated emotionally by women." RU 486 is expected to be a boon to victims of rape and incest, and to women who cannot, or do not, take the pill—"especially," says Couzinet, "young women and teenagers whose sexual activity is very irregular and infrequent."

Part of the reason RU 486 appears to cause so few side effects is that it remains in the body for less than 48 hours. In addition, it apparently does not impair fertility. One woman in the test group took RU 486 one month, aborted, then became pregnant again and came back for another dose the next month. No information is yet available on what effect RU 486 might have on the fetus if the drug fails to induce abortion; all of the 15 women who sustained their pregnancies after receiving the drug had clinical abortions.

Dr. Couzinet hopes to improve the success rate of RU 486 even further by mixing it with small amounts of prostaglandins, biological compounds that cause the uterus to contract and help expel the embryo. That combination, the French researchers say, should provide a 100% effective form of after-the-fact birth control. "There are between 40 million and 50 million abortions performed annually around the world," Couzinet says. "If we have found a safe, convenient medical method of terminating pregnancy, I think it will turn out to be very important."

By Jamie Murphy. Reported by B. J. Phillips/Paris. © Time Dec. 29, 1986

ejaculation occur later in sexual intercourse.)

3. Sperm may be blocked from entering the cervical canal by a variety of artificial methods: douche, spermicidal solutions or foams, and the diaphragm.

The **vaginal douche** is perhaps the oldest of contraceptives; however, it is also the least effective (40 to 66%). Shortly after ejaculation, the vagina is flushed with a spermicidal solution to kill spermatozoa. Since sperm enter the cervix 90 seconds after deposition in the vagina, it is difficult to prevent sperm from moving out of the vaginal region. The method is judged unacceptable from the point of view of sexual expression.

**Spermicidal solutions,** foams, suppositories, jellies, or creams contain chemicals that kill sperm and make them incapable of penetrating the cervical mucus. The jellies and creams are inserted in the vagina with a special applicator, the foams and suppositories are inserted without an applicator. The chemical methods are about 80% effective. Their prime disadvantage is that they must remain in place for 1 to 6 hours after intercourse; oozing of the spermicide from the vagina may be objectionable.

The **diaphragm** is a mechanical device that fits over the cervix and prevents sperm entry (86 to 88% effective). It must be used in conjunction with a spermicide; it must be kept in place for 6 hours after intercourse and can be worn for 24 hours. The diaphragm must be fitted by a physician and refitted after each pregnancy. If inserted improperly, it will not perform satisfactorily.

4. Prevention of sperm release into the semen involves **vasectomy** (sterilization; Box 9F).

5. Prevention of oocyte release or transport to the uterus involves the oral **contraceptive pill** (Section 9–7) or **tubal ligation** (sterilization; Box 9E).

6. Conception can be prevented by use of the **intrauterine device,** or IUD. These are 98% effective. The IUD is a small object (loop, ring, spiral, or bow) made of steel or

plastic, which is inserted by a physician into the uterus (Figure 9–15). The physician inserts the IUD by straightening it in a tubelike instrument, pushing this through the cervix, and then pushing the IUD out the end of the tube. Free in the uterus, the IUD assumes its original shape. Usually the IUD is provided with nylon threads that protrude through the cervix so that the woman can check whether the device is still in place. Since the IUD does not alter the hormonal balance, it may offer advantages over the pill. However, there may be discomfort, bleeding, cramps, and spontaneous expulsion. And, there are instances of uterine perforation, pelvic inflammation, and a higher incidence of tubal pregnancies. Usually the IUD cannot be used until after the first pregnancy. The mechanism by which the IUD prevents conception is via prostaglandin release, production of an inflammatory response, and stimulation of uterine contractions all of which interfere with implantation of the embryo into the uterine wall.

## 9–7 CONTROL OF THE FEMALE REPRODUCTIVE CYCLE: THE PILL

The complete understanding of how hormones influence the ovarian cycle provided the necessary background for developing a method of suppressing ovulation, the oral contraceptive, commonly called the pill. The contraceptive pill is 97 to 99% effective, that is, out of 100 women taking the pill for 1 year, less than 2 will become pregnant. According to the best estimates there are millions of women in the world today using oral contraceptives by their own choice. Some 8 million women in the United States not only choose the oral contraceptive, but find its use pleasant and easy.

How does the oral contraceptive pill work? Recall from our discussion of the normal ovarian cycle that ovulation is triggered by a change in the relative levels of FSH and LH and that the secretion of these hormones is inhibited by estrogen and progesterone

BOX 9C  Detection of ovulation

Along with the liberation of oocyte and follicular fluid during ovulation, there may be some hemorrhage. The hemorrhage, if excessive, may cause a local inflammation, which may in turn cause low abdominal pain, called **mittelschmerz** (middle pain; Ger.) because it occurs in the middle of the month between menstrual bleedings.*
If it does occur it may be an indication that ovulation has taken place.

Changes in the cervical mucus occur during the ovarian cycle, and two tests indicate the time of ovulation. In the **fern test** a drop of cervical mucus is placed on a microscope slide and allowed to dry. If the donor is in the middle of her cycle, the mucus dries in a fernlike pattern. In the **spinnbarkheit** test, mucus from the cervix is placed between the thumb and the forefinger and is drawn out to form a thread. Midcycle mucus usually stretches to 4 in.: mucus obtained at other times stretches less.

Some women find that ovulation can be detected by changes in body temperature. The body temperature is recorded daily, and ovulation is indicated by a drop in temperature (Figure 9–14). After ovulation a rise in temperature may be observed, and this is maintained during the rest of the menstrual cycle. It is important to note that this method tells the safe period *after* ovulation, not before.

None of these tests are foolproof, there is considerable variation from woman to woman, and from cycle to cycle in a woman.

* Some physicians believe mittelschmerz is not caused by an irritation from blood, but is a result of spasmodic contractions of the Fallopian tubes.

FIGURE 9–14 Body temperature and the ovarian cycle.

FIGURE 9–15 Insertion and position of the IUD. (a) Insertion of IUD into syringelike device. (b) Insertion of IUD into uterus. (c) IUD in place. (Modified from Robert Demarest and John Sciarra, *Conception, Birth and Contraception: A Visual Presentation,* New York, McGraw-Hill, 1969.)

(Figure 9–11). If the levels of estrogen and progesterone could be adjusted sufficiently to interfere with the normal change in relative levels of the two pituitary hormones, ovluation could be inhibited artificially. Estrogens such as estradiol and progesterone are ineffective when taken by mouth (they are degraded during digestion), and so they must be injected to produce an effect. Synthetic estrogens and progesterones (progestins) have been developed that are not so degraded and act like the natural hormones, that is, they inhibit LH accumulation, and therefore LH surges. Theoretically, estrogen alone could suppress FSH secretion, and indeed it does, but estrogen alone will not suppress midcycle production of LH; in fact it stimulates LH secretion. Therefore, if there were developing follicles, an oral contraceptive that possessed only estrogenic activity would allow the possibility of an escape ovulation. Thus, the contraceptive effect of a pill employing the estrogenic method alone would be uncertain. The oral steroid contraceptive procedures most commonly used are the combination method and the sequential method. In the combination method a pill containing estrogen and progestin is taken for 20 to 21 days after menstruation (day 5). The period usually starts 1 to 3 days after the last pill is taken. (The progestin plus estrogen maintains the endometrial lining, and when its production is diminished menstrual bleeding results.) This establishes an artificial 28-day menstrual cycle.

Side effects from taking the pill are not uncommon. Indeed, it would be unfair to say that all the questions about its long-term effects are settled. For example, estrogens have widespread effects on body tissues aside from those involved in reproduction. They affect protein and carbohydrate metabolism, they play a role in calcium balance, they affect blood pressure, water and salt retention, and they act on the adrenal and thyroid glands as well as the pituitary. Some women taking the pill experience water retention and weight gain.

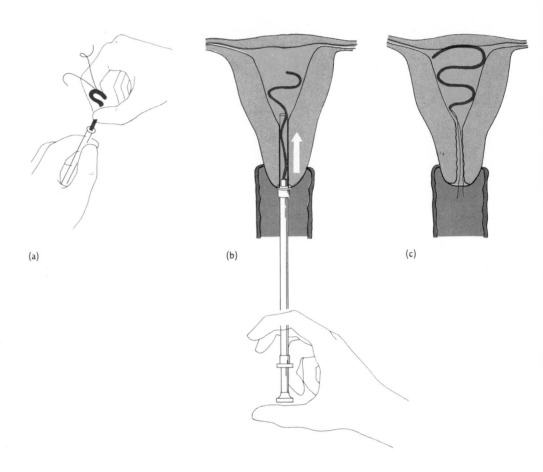

(a)          (b)          (c)

In large doses, progestins have effects similar to those produced by male hormones. The contraceptive pills usually balance these steroids and reduce the amount of synthetic hormone to a minimum. Still there are women taking the pill who experience acne, headaches, nausea, and tenderness of the breasts. There are indications of enhanced clot formation in women taking the pill. In some women the pill causes the veins to dilate abnormally, causing slow blood flow, and this may in turn produce a sludging of blood and clot formation. Moreover, the pill may change the chemistry of the clotting reaction itself. A clot that develops in the veins (**thrombophlebitis**) may break loose from its point of origin, travel through the

body (as an **embolus**), and lodge in the blood vessels of the lungs or the brain. Many such pulmonary (lung) and cerebral (brain) embolisms are fatal. The use of oral contraceptives increases the risk of being admitted to a hospital for a thromboembolism. This statistic must be balanced against the dangers of pregnancy itself. Today, in a developed country, a woman's chances of dying during pregnancy are 1 in 3,000. Although death is a tragic event and the risk of it is not to be dismissed lightly, the risk of complications from the pill is in fact as low as or lower than that from other drugs and is equivalent to the risk of death that a woman runs in her own kitchen in the same period of time. Clearly, the decision to use

BOX 9D  Pregnancy: signs and symptoms

**Pregnancy** lasts 9.5 lunar months (38 weeks, or 266 days) after conception. Physicians usually calculate the date of birth by adding 14 and 266 and tell the mother that the baby will be born 280 days after the first day of the last menstrual period (the figure 14 signifies that fertilization occurred on the fourteenth day of the menstrual cycle). Another frequently used method for calculating the date of confinement (birth) is to add 7 days to the first day of the menstrual cycle, substract 3 months, and add 1 year. If the last menstrual period began on June 17, the delivery date would be March 24 of the following year (June 17 + 7 = June 24 − 3 months = March 24 + 1 year). It should be noted that the calculation of date of confinement is a rough approximation; less than 10% of normal pregnancies run 280 days exactly. There is less than a 50-50 chance that the child will be born within a week of the due date, and the odds are 1 out of 10 that labor will occur 2 weeks later.

Although conception and implantation take place about 7 days after ovulation, the prospective mother is not aware of her condition until 2 weeks later. During the third week after fertilization, the telltale sign of pregnancy becomes apparent: **amenorrhea,** a cessation of menstruation. Her awareness is heightened by a tingling sensation in her breasts, more frequent urination, and constipation. Nausea and vomiting—**morning sickness**—appear in about two thirds of pregnant women. The cause of morning sickness is uncertain, but may be due to stretching of uterine tissues. A hormone appears in her urine, called **chorionic gonadotropin,** which is produced by the cells of the trophoblast.* Secretion of this hormone causes the corpus luteum to continue to secrete estrogen and progesterone; thus the endometrium is maintained in its thickened, highly vascularized state. Detection of chorionic gonadotropin in a urine sample is the basis of most pregnancy tests.

The pregnancy tests most commonly employed today are immunological ones. The urine from the possibly pregnant female is placed in contact with a reagent, consisting of an antiserum to human chorionic gonadotropin. If the urine contains gonadotropin, it reacts with the antiserum and the combination precipitates or produces a colored reaction product. The test results may be read within 2 hours and because of the test's sensitivity and high degree of specificity, pregnancy can be detected as early as 6 days after the missed period.

Later in pregnancy the effects of hormonal changes and the developing fetus become more obvious; the breasts enlarge, veins are more prominent, the nipples and areolae become more deeply pigmented. The oil glands around the areolae enlarge and look like tiny bumps. The pressure of the enlarging uterus may be distressing; the shifting of the center of gravity by an extra 20 lb forward can cause unpleasant sensations of falling forward. Cravings for foods may develop, and there may be a change in attitude. The so-called mask of pregnancy (**chloasma**), a deep coloration of the face, may develop, as well as dark lines (**striae**) on the abdomen. Most of this will disappear after childbirth. The pituitary gland doubles in size, the thyroid, parathyroids, and adrenals grow larger. Engorged and dilated blood vessels are visible in the skin. Varicose veins and hemorrhoids often accompany or follow pregnancy. Edema and swelling are common, and there is a sluggish return of blood from the extremities to the heart.

* The outermost covering of the developing embryo (Chapter 10).

oral contraceptives should be based on individual choice after consultation with a physician.

## SUMMARY

**1.** Meiosis is the method of cell division by which germ cells (gametes) are produced in the gonads. Following meiosis, the gametes are haploid. The diploid number of chromosomes is restored at fertilization.

**2.** Meiosis involves two cell divisions. During the first reduction division, synapsis of homologous chromosomes is followed by a halving of the chromosome number. This first division is followed by a mitotic division. Four haploid cells are thus produced from one diploid cell.

**3.** Male gametes, or spermatozoa, are produced from spermatogonia in the seminiferous tubules of the paired testes by spermatogenesis: this involves meiosis, differentiation and maturation. At puberty, the pituitary gland produces FSH and LH, which stimulate both spermatogenesis and testosterone production in the testes. Testosterone and other male hormones produced in the testes control the development of secondary sex characteristics.

**4.** Mature sperm pass via a series of collecting ducts and tubules and the coiled epididymis to the vas deferens. The two vasa deferentia join with the tube leaving the bladder and enter the penis as the urethra.

**5.** The seminal vesicles, prostate, and Cowper's (bulbourethral) glands add secretions to the sperm cells, constituting semen or seminal fluid.

**6.** The testes normally hang in the scrotal sac. In prepubertal males, they may be retracted via the inguinal canal, which closes after puberty. An inguinal hernia is caused by the dropping of an intestinal loop into the scrotum. Cryptorchidism is due to undescended testes.

**7.** The muscular penis is the male copulatory organ. The glans (head) is covered by a prepuce (foreskin). Erection occurs in response to stimulation and depends on the filling of the corpora cavernosa and corpus spongiosum with blood. During ejaculation, the entrance from the bladder to the urethra is closed by a sphincter.

**8.** Female gametes, or ova, are produced from oocytes in the paired ovaries by oogenesis, involving meiosis and maturation.

**9.** FSH produced by the pituitary signals the onset of menarche and the development of secondary sex characteristics. It also signals the onset of oogenesis.

**10.** The oocytes develop in Graafian follicles. Unequal division of the cytoplasm at each meiotic division produces one mature ovum and two (or three) polar bodies from each primary oocyte.

**11.** The secondary oocyte requires LH from the pituitary for maturation. FSH and LH induce the follicle cells to produce estrogens.

**12.** The changing balance of FSH and LH produces ovulation of the oocyte, which is surrounded by the cumulus oophorus. When a secondary oocyte is shed, it is picked up by the Fallopian tubes and moved toward the uterus.

**13.** Influenced by LH, the postovulatory follicle the corpus luteum, secretes estro-

**BOX 9E  AIDS\***

Viruses have plagued humans through the ages, but none has been more formidable than the one that causes acquired immunodeficiency syndrome (AIDS). In 1987 about 130 of the world's 160 countries had reported a total of 56,000 cases, and of these 40,000 were in the United States. At present, the death toll in the United States due to AIDS is 15,000, but in 5 years time it is expected that the number dying will reach 200,000. Although we understand the cause of the disease (p. 56 and p. 290), no vaccine or cure is in sight.

One of the most worrisome features of AIDS is that between 5 and 10 million people worldwide are asymptomatic carriers of the virus. In the United States there may be a million carriers who have no symptoms at all or very minimal symptoms, yet they have persistent infections and are probably infectious to others. The vast majority of people who will contract AIDS will be through sexual contact with infected individuals. Hundreds of thousands of persons worldwide may be exposed through virus-contaminated blood, and some newborns will become infected from their AIDS-carrying pregnant mothers.

What advice can be given about AIDS that can save lives and reduce the spread of the disease?

Although the AIDS virus is found in several body fluids, a person acquires the virus during sexual contact with an infected person's blood or semen, and possibly vaginal secretions. Small (unseen by the naked eye) tears in the surface lining of the vagina or rectum may occur during insertion of the penis, fingers, or other objects, thus opening an avenue for entrance of the virus directly into the bloodstream; therefore, the AIDS virus can be passed from penis to rectum and vagina and vice versa without a visible tear in the tissue or the presence of blood.

Although the initial discovery was in the homosexual community, AIDS is found in heterosexual people as well. AIDS is not a black or white disease. AIDS is not just a male disease. AIDS is found in women; it is found in children. In the future AIDS will probably increase and spread among people who are not homosexual or intravenous drug abusers.

Unless it is possible to know with *absolute certainty* that neither you nor your sexual partner is carrying the virus of AIDS, you must use protective behavior. *Absolute certainty* means not only that you and your partner have [had] a mutually faithful monogamous sexual relationship [for at least 5 years], but . . . that neither you nor your partner has used illegal intravenous drugs.

If you suspect that [your partner] has been exposed by previous heterosexual or homosexual behavior or use of intravenous drugs with shared needles and syringes, a rubber (condom) should always be used during (start to finish) sexual intercourse (vagina or rectum).

Do not have sex with prostitutes. Infected male and female prostitutes are frequently also intravenous drug abusers; therefore, they may infect clients by sexual intercourse and other intravenous drug abusers by sharing their intravenous drug equipment. Female prostitutes also can infect their unborn babies.

The risk of infection increases according to the number of sexual partners one has, *male or female*. The more partners you have, the greater the risk of becoming infected with the AIDS virus.

No one should shoot up drugs . . . However, many drug users are addicted to drugs and for one reason or another have not changed their behavior. For these people, the only way not to get AIDS is *to use a clean, previously unused* needle, syringe, or any other implement [for injection].

Almost all babies with AIDS have been born to women who were intravenous drug users or the sexual partners of intravenous drug users who were infected with the AIDS virus. More such babies can be expected.

*You cannot get AIDS by donating blood.*

Every blood donation is now tested for the presence of antibodies to the AIDS virus. Blood that shows exposure to the AIDS virus by the presence of antibodies is not used. [But] because antibodies do not form immediately after exposure to the virus, a newly infected person may unknowingly donate blood after becoming infected but before his/her antibody test becomes positive. It is estimated that this might occur less than once in 100,000 transfusions.

Shaking hands, hugging, social kissing, crying, coughing, or sneezing will not transmit the AIDS virus. Nor has AIDS been contracted from swimming pools or hot tubs or from eating in restaurants (even if a restaurant worker has AIDS or carries the AIDS virus). AIDS is not contracted from sharing bed linens, towels, cups, straws, dishes, or any other eating utensils. You cannot get AIDS from toilets, doorknobs, telephones, office machinery, or household furniture. You cannot get AIDS from body massages, masturbation, or any nonsexual body contact.

None of the identified cases of AIDS in the United States are known or are suspected to have been transmitted from one child to another in school, day care, or foster care settings.

Quarantine has no role in the management of AIDS because AIDS is not spread by casual contact. The only time that some form of quarantine might be indicated is in a situation where an individual carrying the AIDS virus knowingly and willingly continues to expose others through sexual contact or sharing drug equipment.

* Based on the U.S. Surgeon General's report, AIDS, and reported in Time November 3, 1986.

gen and progesterone. In turn, the latter suppress FSH production and hence further egg production. Estrogen and progesterone also act on the uterine lining to prepare it for implantation. In the absence of fertilization, the corpus luteum is transformed to a corpus albicans and eventually is resorbed.

**14.** The uterus consists of the uterine body and cervix. A uterine cycle begins with menstruation, that is, with breakdown of the endometrium; this is followed by endometrial proliferation under the influence of estrogen and progesterone produced by the ovarian follicles and the corpus luteum. If fertilization does not occur following ovulation on about day 14, the corpus luteum degenerates on about day 22 or 23. Progesterone and estrogen levels drop, and menstruation recommences about day 28.

**15.** The muscular vagina is the female copulatory organ. Its entrance may be partly covered by the hymen. Vestibular Bartholin's glands secrete a lubricant during sexual intercourse. Externally, the female vulva consists of the mons veneris (pubis), labia majora and minora, clitoris, and vestibule.

**16.** During coitus, sexual arousal causes vasocongestion that results in the erection of nipples, clitoris, and penis and produces secretions from the various glands. Sexual orgasm and emission coincide in the male. Vaginal and clitoral orgasm are physically indistinguishable in females. Males experience a postorgasmic refractory period.

**17.** Fertilization occurs high in the Fallopian tube. The fertilizing sperm penetrates the corona radiata and zona pellucida, and the oocyte becomes impenetrable to other sperm. The oocyte and sperm plasma membranes fuse, the oocyte completes its second meiotic division, the oocyte and sperm nuclei fuse, and fertilization is complete. The zygote is now diploid.

**18.** Conception can be avoided by preventing the sperm from reaching the egg. Methods include use of rhythm, coitus interruptus, condoms, vaginal douche, spermicides, diaphragm, vasectomy, tubal liga-

BOX 9F Sterilization for both sexes

One drastic way to practice birth control is by means of sterilization. The surgeon's knife is now being sought by increasing numbers of Americans, both men and women, who want to be sure that they will have no more babies. Sterilization operations for men and women are based on the same strategy: cutting the tubes that carry the sex cells on their paths toward junction and conception.

Because of anatomical differences, the male operation is the simpler. After a local anesthetic, the surgeon makes an incision about half an inch long on one side of the scrotum, draws out one vas, and cuts out a section up to an inch long. He usually cauterizes the remaining stumps of the vas and ties them shut with nonabsorbable thread. The surgeon then sutures the small wound and repeats the procedure on the other side.

Because patients have some discomfort for two or three days after a vasectomy, the Margaret Sanger Research Bureau in Manhattan schedules all such operations on Fridays: thus the patient will be able to return to work on Monday. The vasectomy patient undergoes no hormonal changes, and if he has fully understood the operation beforehand he should have no emotional problems. His capacity for sexual relations may even be increased, because he no longer fears conception. His sperm, trapped in the testicles, are reabsorbed, and eventually his body manufactures fewer of them. However, some sperm are left "in the pipeline" at the time of operation, so for the next six to twelve acts of coitus a contraceptive must be used. Most surgeons require that their patients return after four to twelve months and leave a semen sample for analysis to make sure

that neither vas deferens has joined itself up again.

For women there are a variety of surgical procedures. The most obvious is used on the woman who is having a baby by Caesarean section, and has decided that this will be her last. Since her abdomen is already open, the obstetrician simply reaches in for the Fallopian tubes, ties them off and severs them—much as the urologist does in a vasectomy. Most surgeons also remove part of the tube. This procedure is called tubal ligation.

Equally common is the operation on a woman who has just given birth to a baby normally. Within 36 hours after the delivery, the surgeon makes a three- or four-inch incision in her lower abdomen to reach the tubes. The surgical wound is almost healed by the time the woman goes home with her baby.

In recent years, especially in Britain and Europe, gynecological surgeons have been seeking means of reaching and severing the Fallopian tubes without a long pelvic incision. They have succeeded with the aid of the laparoscope, a tube containing a "light pipe," less than half an inch in diameter. The techniques vary in detail. At Johns Hopkins Hospital in Baltimore, Dr. Clifford R. Wheeless makes two incisions less than half an inch long just below the navel. Through one, after blowing in carbon dioxide to separate the organs, he inserts the laparoscope to locate a tube. Through the second he inserts the electric cautery and a tiny surgical knife. The operation, under general anesthesia, takes about 30 minutes and allows the patient to leave the hospital the same day.

In a modified version of the operation, Dr. Alvin Siegler of New York's Downstate Medical Center makes his first incision for the laparoscope so close to

the navel that no separate scar will be visible, then inserts the cautery and knife through two punctures not much bigger than those made by a heavy-gauge hypodermic needle.

The simplest development in sterilization of women, requiring only local anesthesia, is reported by Dr. Martin Clyman at Manhattan's Mount Sinai School of Medicine. He has designed special instruments that enable him to operate through an incision little more than an inch long in the vaginal wall, reaching and tying off both tubes in about ten minutes. This vaginal approach leaves the patient with no visible scars, and she can go home in 24 to 48 hours after the operation.

Why do couples prefer sterilization to the long-term use of contraceptives? "Because they know that failure rates from most forms of contraception are too high," one doctor says. "Or they are afraid of side effects from the Pill, or they have aesthetic objections to having to remember to insert something at what is emotionally the wrong time."

**Rates of Reversal.** One nagging question that still deters many men from seeking sterilization: is the operation reversible? The answer is that in some cases, after either male or female sterilization, fertility can be restored by a reverse operation to rejoin the severed tubes. The success rate of these operations is disputed. Some physicians put it as high as 80%; most think 30% is more realistic. But the question seldom arises. Most urologists' records show that not more than 1% or 2% of their male patients have ever asked for a reverse operation.

tion, intrauterine devices, and oral contraceptive pills.

**19.** Ovulation is normally triggered by changes in LH level. Secretion of FSH and LH is inhibited by estrogen and progester-one. Contraceptive pills depend on oral administration of synthetic estrogen and progesterones; they are not without side effects.

**20.** Ovulation can be detected by a va-riety of methods, including the fern and spinnbarkheit tests, or by monitoring changes in body temperature. Mittelschmerz indi-cates ovulation in some women.

## KEY WORDS

| | | | | |
|---|---|---|---|---|
| zygote | spermatogonia | corpora cavernosa | cervix | vaginal douche |
| gametes | Sertoli cells | corpus spongiosum | endometrium | spermicidal solutions |
| syngamy | follicle-stimulating | oogenesis | vagina | diaphragm |
| fertilization | hormone (FSH) | ovaries | hymen | vasectomy |
| genes | testosterone | broad ligament | Bartholin's glands | contraceptive pill |
| chromosomes | rete testis | Fallopian (uterine) tubes | vulva | tubal ligation |
| meiosis | epididymis | oocytes | mons veneris | intrauterine device (IUD) |
| homologous chromosomes | vas deferens | menarche | labia majora | mittelschmerz |
| diploid | inguinal canal | ovarian cycle | labia minora | fern test |
| synapsis | urethra | menstruation | clitoris | spinnbarkheit |
| haploid | seminal vesicles | menopause | vestibule | pregnancy |
| somatic cells | prostate gland | Graafian follicle | coitus | amenorrhea |
| germ cells | bulbourethral glands | luteinizing hormone (LH) | copulation | morning sickness |
| gonads | semen | estrogens | (sexual intercourse) | chorionic gonadotrophin |
| spermatogenesis | seminal fluid | cumulus oophorus | orgasm | chloasma |
| testis | scrotum | zona pellucida | emission | striae |
| androgens | inguinal hernia | corona radiata | embryogenesis | thrombophlebitis |
| spermatozoa (sperm) | cryptorchidism | corpus luteum | contraception | embolus |
| seminiferous tubules | penis | corpus albicans | rhythm method | AIDS |
| | glans | uterine or menstrual cycle | coitus interruptus | |
| | foreskin (prepuce) | uterus | condom | |

## TOPICS FOR REVIEW AND DISCUSSION

1. What is the relationship of meiosis to sexual reproduction?

2. What are the biological advantages of sexual reproduction (meiosis) as contrasted with asexual reproduction?

3. Describe spermatogenesis. Compare and contrast the process with oogenesis.

4. How are the structural attributes of the sperm and egg related to their functional roles in reproduction?

5. Discuss the hormonal basis of the contraceptive pill.

6. What are some of the methods used for detecting ovulation and pregnancy?

7. Describe the functional roles of the external genitalia.

8. Contrast vasectomy with castration.

9. Describe the ovarian and uterine cycles.

10. Describe the nature and possible causes of infertility in humans.

11. Discuss the exocrine and endocrine functions of the testes or the ovaries.

A 12-week-old human fetus still within its amniotic sac held in an obstetrician's hand.
(Courtesy of Roberts Rugh and Landrum B. Shettles.)

# 10

# Perpetuation of Life II: Human Development

## 10–1 FROM EGG TO EMBRYO

The fertilized egg cell, or zygote, is one of the largest cells in the body, with a high ratio of cytoplasm to nuclear material. Following fertilization, the zygote divides mitotically into a number of smaller cells, a process known as **cleavage** (Figures 10–1 and 10–2). The main function of cleavage is to produce new cells for specialized tasks. This is accomplished by reduction in cell size through subdivision and the formation of new nuclear material. Although the total mass of the zygote is not substantially reduced during cleavage, the arrangement of its components is radically altered. Cleavage lasts until developmental processes other than mere subdivision begin to assume importance (Figures 10–3 and 10–4). These processes involve the movement of the cells of the subdivided zygote relative to one another; the cells in the different regions interact and affect each other's fate. From this time onward, the developing organism is referred to as an **embryo.** After implantation in the wall of the mother's uterus the embryo begins to obtain nourishment (Figure 10–5). Only then does an increase in total size of the developing organism begin to occur.

Let is now trace these events in more detail by looking at a series of remarkable photographs that show human development from the moment of fertilization until the seventh week, when the embryo begins to assume a clearly recognizable human form (Figures 10–6 to 10–11).

FIGURE 10–2 Cleavage: one cell into two. Cleavage of the zygote into two cells takes place in about 36 hours. Surrounding the cells is the transparent zona pellucida, which helps to hold the cells together and also protects against precocious implantation. (Courtesy of Carnegie Institution of Washington.)

FIGURE 10–1 The moment of fertilization. The oocyte, barely visible to the naked eye, is about the size of the period at the end of this sentence and is 2,000 times larger than the sperm that fertilizes it. At the moment of fertilization shown here, sperm and oocyte fuse, producing a zygote weighing one twenty-millionth of an ounce. In 30 days this zygote will increase its size 40 times and its weight 3,000 times. (Courtesy of Landrum B. Shettles.)

FIGURE 10–3 Cleavage and morula formation. By the third day there is a clump of 16 to 32 cells—the morula (literally, "mulberry")—enclosed by the zona pellucia. The total mass of the morula is not greater than that of the egg, since cleavage has simply divided the egg into smaller and smaller cells. (Courtesy of Carnegie Insitution of Washington.)

FIGURE 10–4 The blastocyst. At 4 days fluid enters through the zona pellucida, and the solid morula becomes the hollow blastocyst (blastula). The cells at one pole form a thickened mass, the internal inner cell mass, and this will ultimately contribute cells to the embryo as well as to the extraembryonic membranes. The exterior blastocyst cells form the trophoblast, which functions in implantation and contributes to the chorion. (Courtesy of Carnegie Institution of Washington.)

FIGURE 10–5 Implantation of the blastocyst. After 7 to 9 days the blastocyst, free of its zona pellucida, becomes implanted in the endometrial lining. (Courtesy of Carnegie Institution of Washington.)

197

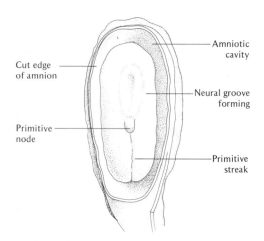

FIGURE 10–6 A two-layered embryo: the second week. The 2.5-week embryo with its two layers of cells, the ectoderm and the endoderm. The ectoderm will form the skin and nervous system and the endoderm the digestive tract and its derivatives. The bulge in the ectoderm, called the primitive streak, marks the long axis of the embryo, and it is along this line that the spinal column will form.

 Actual size

FIGURE 10–7 A three-layered embryo: the third week. The 3-week embryo contains three layers: ectoderm, endoderm, and a middle layer—mesoderm. The ectoderm thickens, has a groove, and begins to fold its edges in such a way that it forms the neural tube, which will ultimately give rise to the brain and the spinal cord. (Courtesy of Carnegie Institution of Washington.)

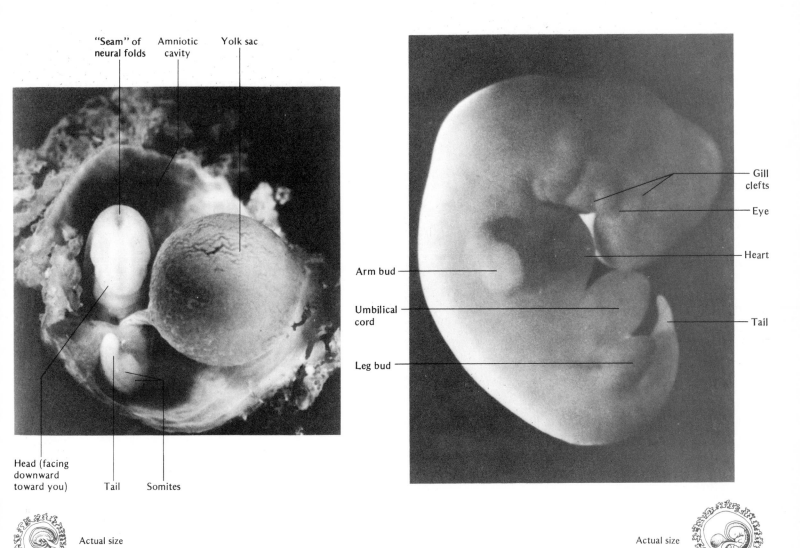

FIGURE 10–8 Organ systems develop: the fourth week. A 4-week embryo is about the size of a small fingernail. The neural tube has closed, the brain begins to develop, and the heart appears. Segmentation shows up in the 30 pairs of mesodermal blocks (somites) that will form muscle and the vertebrae of the spinal column. (Courtesy of Carnegie Institution of Washington.)

FIGURE 10–9 At 5 weeks of development the embryo is almost complete, although its size and weight are about the same as those of an aspirin tablet. About one third of the embryo is head, and this is bent forward (cranial flexure) in such a way that it almost touches the rudimentary tail. The heart bulges outward from the body and pulsates, forcing blood through the circulatory channels. At this time the heart is a simple tube, and only later will chambers develop. The arm and leg buds are formed. It is at this stage that the tranquilizer thalidomide had its tragic effects, producing flipper limbs. Gill clefts and the outline of the eyes appear. (Courtesy of Robert Rugh.)

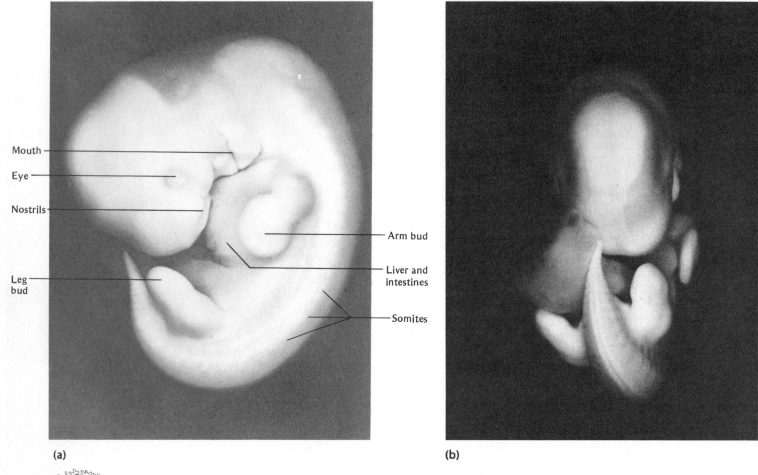

Mouth

Eye

Nostrils

Leg
bud

Arm bud

Liver and
intestines

Somites

(a)

(b)

Actual size

FIGURE 10–10 At 6 weeks the eyes become pigmented, the jaw is well formed, and the gill clefts have almost disappeared. The head still curls downward, almost touching the tail. Muscle blocks (somites) are clearly seen. The embryo is now about 0.5 in. long, and the earliest reflexes appear. The heart is partitioned into chambers, the liver begins to manufacture red blood cells, the diaphragm is formed, and the intestines and liver are so enlarged that they bulge outward. The germ cells have completed their migration from the yolk sac and are settled into the gonad region. (a) Side view. (b) Front view. (Courtesy of H. Nishimura and Roberts Rugh.)

**(a)**　　　　　　　　　　　　　　　　　　　　　　　　**(b)**

FIGURE 10–11 By the seventh week the embryo begins to assume a more human form. The rudimentary tail has diminished in size; the ears and eyes are developing rapidly. The fingers and toes are present, and the development of the face is evident. One of the temporary gill pouches becomes part of the ear (Eustachian tube). The embryo is about 1 in. long, and because of the large head appears top-heavy. (a) Side view. (b) Front view. (Courtesy of E. Ludwig and Roberts Rugh.)

### BOX 10A Gene screen: Early fetal checkup

For Donna and Steven Roehl and Debbie and Maury Fisher, having a baby is a risky business. The Roehls both carry the gene for Niemann-Pick disease, a metabolic disorder that has already taken the life of their first child. The Fishers are carriers of Tay-Sachs disease, a fatal ailment that afflicts their two-year-old son. For both couples, the odds are one in four that any child they bear will be defective. When the two wives became pregnant earlier this year, they intended to undergo amniocentesis, a test to determine if the fetuses were normal. Each planned to abort if it was not.

But amniocentesis usually cannot be done until the 16th or 17th week of pregnancy, when there is enough amniotic fluid to obtain a sample safely via a needle through the abdomen. Results are not available for another four weeks. Eager to avoid five months of anxious waiting, the two women volunteered for a new, early test of fetal health, under study at Michael Reese Hospital in Chicago. Fisher had the procedure in her

ninth week "and found out the next day that my baby did not have Tay-Sachs." Roehl also got good news, fast.

The test, called chorionic villi sampling (CVS), is a painless procedure and can be done in a physician's office as early as the fifth week of pregnancy. To perform it, the obstetrician inserts a long thin tube through the vagina into the uterus. A second doctor, following the procedure on an ultrasound monitor, helps the obstetrician position the catheter between the lining of the uterus and the chorion, a layer of tissue that surrounds the embryo during the first two months and later develops into the placenta. The goal is to suction up a sample of the chorionic villi, finger-like projections of tissue that transfer oxygen, nutrients and waste between mother and embryo. "It's like vacuuming a shag rug; you get about half a dozen villi," explains Dr. Laird Jackson of Philadelphia's Jefferson Medical College, which has helped pioneer the technique in the U.S. Since the tiny chorion sample is composed of the same cells as the fetus, genetic defects present in the child should show up in laboratory analysis.

Dr. Eugene Pergament of Michael Reese is convinced that CVS "will eventually replace amniocentesis as the first line of genetic diagnosis." Earlier detection not only means less anxiety for the mother, it also means that should she choose to terminate the pregnancy, she can have a simple outpatient abortion after six to eight weeks rather than a far more complex one at five months, requiring hospitalization. "And no matter how you feel about abortion," says Jackson, "there is a difference in our perception of pregnancy at eight weeks and at 20."

The cost of CVS, is about the same as amniocentesis. The risks, though not fully known, are probably also the same: one in 200 women who have undergone amniocentesis suffers complications (infection, for example) that may lead to miscarriage. For this reason the new test will be recommended only for women known to have a high risk of delivering an abnormal baby, including the growing number who wait until age 35 or later to have their first child. CVS may some day prove to be valuable for another reason: Early detection of genetic defects may make it possible for doctors to intervene and correct problems while the child is in the womb.

© Time Aug. 23, 1983

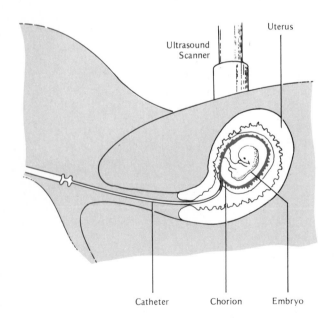

Ultrasound
Scanner

Uterus

Catheter    Chorion    Embryo

FIGURE 10–12 The fetus at eight weeks. (Courtesy of E. Ludwig and Roberts Rugh.)

**203**

**PERPETUATION OF LIFE II:
HUMAN DEVELOPMENT**

Actual size

## 10–2 THE FETUS

By the eighth week of development, the ground plan of differentiation has been established and all the human features are evident (Figure 10–12). No longer called an embryo, the developing child has become a **fetus.** One and a quarter inches in length from the top of its enlarged head to its buttocks, it appears top-heavy because of the large head; indeed, the head composes almost one half of the fetus. The eyes, slitlike in appearance, have moved from the sides of the head and are directed forward, and the jaws are almost fully developed, as is the nose; there are small earlobes, and the face is now unmistakably human. The mouth region forms, and the alimentary canal runs downward from this. The arms and legs are gracefully proportioned, the hands well formed, the fingers and toes distinctly human, and simple reflexes occur. The skeleton, which was once cartilage, now begins to harden with the deposition of bone. The abdomen bulges outward like a potbellied stove, and the external sexual organs can clearly be seen.

Now the fetus grows (Figures 10–13 to 10–15). Growth depends on nutrition from the mother via the placenta, the umbilical cord, and the fetal blood vessels (Section 10–3).

### The sixth month

The fetus averages 12 in. in length and weighs 1.5 lb. It appears to be a miniature

FIGURE 10–13 The third month. Between weeks 9 and 12 the fetus grows from 1.5 to 3 inches in length. The head no longer bends forward, and the fetal posture becomes upright. Weight goes from 1/7 to 1/2 ounces. Fingernails, toenails, and hair appear. The face becomes more human in appearance because the eyes (which are closed) are moved forward; tooth buds and bones form. Blood is now manufactured in the bone marrow instead of in the spleen and the liver. A fetal pulse can be heard; the skeleton and muscles take on human contours. The male fetus is recognizable by its external penis, and the female forms a uterus and vagina. The kidneys begin to function. The fetus is sensitive to touch, and the motions of breathing and swallowing become coordinated and purposeful. Individuality in fetal facial expressions appears. Now the mother can feel her enlarging uterus just below her navel. (Courtesy of Roberts Rugh and Landrum B. Shettles.)

human. The internal organs occupy their normal positions, and the abdomen no longer bulges outward so much. Sucking of the thumb and swallowing of amniotic fluid occur. The eyelids separate, and eyebrows and lashes form. The oil glands in the skin produce a protective cheeselike covering called the **vernix caseosa.** The intestine becomes filled with a green pastelike material **(meconium),** which is derived from the breakdown of red blood cells and debris from the liver, gallbladder, and pancreas; it remains there until birth. The hands develop a strong grip. Scalp hair becomes abundant. The first bones develop (breastbone), and cartilage in the limbs is slowly replaced. Survival is usually not possible for the baby delivered after only 6 months of fetal life, since body temperature cannot be regulated and the lungs and digestive system cannot function on their own.

### The seventh month

By the seventh month the child has at least a chance of independent survival. (Premature births are the cause of 50% of infant mortality in the United states.) If born at this time, there would be a 10% chance that the premature infant (preemie), given proper care in an incubator, could live. Essentially

FIGURE 10–14 The fourth month. During the fourth month there is a rapid burst in fetal growth: now the fetus grows to 6 in. and weighs 4 oz. Posture becomes more erect, fingerprints appear, and the fetus shows a startle reflex. It moves, stretching its arms and legs, but ordinarily these movements are not felt by the mother. If prematurely delivered, it would curl its fingers and toes when tickled on the palms or soles. The heart beats 120 to 160 times a minute, twice the rate of the mother's heart. The lungs are collapsed and functionless. The fetal membranes surrounding the fetus are shown. (Courtesy of Carnegie Institution of Washington.)

FIGURE 10–15 The fifth month. The fetus, 8 in. long and weighing 0.5 lb, is shown attached to the placenta by the umbilical cord. Gripping reflexes develop now. Fetal movements, such as kicking and turning, can easily be felt by the mother. The fetus may hiccup and sleep. Suspended in a quart of amniotic fluid, the fetus is in a state of weightlessness. The body is covered by a fine down called lanugo. Although the baby appears capable of a great deal if delivered prematurely at this time, it cannot survive more than a few minutes, since its lungs, skin, and digestive tract are unprepared for independent existence. The heart beats rapidly, and the sounds are easily recognized by a physician listening in with a stethoscope on the mother's abdomen. (Courtesy of Roberts Rugh.)

an incubator is an artificial womb: warm, moist, sterile air aids in protection and survival. The baby's nervous system has developed sufficiently so that breathing is under control, swallowing is regular, and body temperature is regulated. The fetus is about 1 ft in length and weighs 2 to 3 lb. The downy fur coat, **lanugo,** which was more plentiful in the sixth month, is now found only on the back and the shoulders. Movements continue to be random, and there is thumb-sucking. The brain enlarges greatly, its surface becomes furrowed, and functional localization in the brain becomes evident. Sexual differences also manifest themselves: in the male, the testes descend into the scrotum.

### The eighth month

During the eighth month the rate of weight gain slows down, the fetus weighs 4 to 5 lb and is 13 in. long. Fat tends to accumulate under the skin, and the fetus appears chubby—a change from its wrinkled condition in previous months. The fetus can perceive light and taste sweet substances, but remains deaf. If born at this time, the probability of survival rises to 70%. Fat deposits help to regulate the body temperature of the eight-month preemie, but it still has difficulty in breathing because the air sacs of the lungs are not prepared for gas exchange. In addition, the digestive tract is immature. For this reason premature ba-

bies are given supplemental oxygen, but they live on stored nutirents for a while.

### The ninth month

Fetal activity diminishes during this month because all the available space within the uterus is occupied. The fetus is 19 or 20 in. long and weighs between 6 and 8 lb. Boys may weigh more than girls. Shortly before delivery the fetus turns so that its head rests in the pelvic basin—a comfortable position for the fetus and a safe position for delivery. The movements of the fetus in this position are even more restricted than before. The cheesy coating, the vernix caseosa, becomes dislodged and muddies the amniotic

FIGURE 10–16 The uterus and embryo at 7 weeks.

waters; the intestines are filled with green meconium. Fingernails and toenails grow so long that they require trimming shortly after birth; the gums are ridged; the eyes are almost always blue. The baby acquires disease-resisting antibodies from the maternal blood supply, which will give it temporary immunity against certain diseases that could adversely affect the newborn child. Immunities acquired in this way usually persist for the first 6 months or so of life and then gradually wear off as the baby begins to develop its own immune reactions. The hormones of the mother that cause her breasts to enlarge in preparation for lactation also cause the unborn child's breast to become firm and protrude. The newborn child may even secrete a few drops of milk (witches' milk). A few days after birth, when the effects of maternal hormones wear off, breast enlargement in the infant subsides and further secretion of milk ceases.

A week or two before delivery, the growth of the fetus slows down as the placenta regresses and becomes fibrous. Blood clots appear, indicating that placenta blood vessels have degenerated. The placenta begins to fail, and the fetus must prepare to take care of itself.

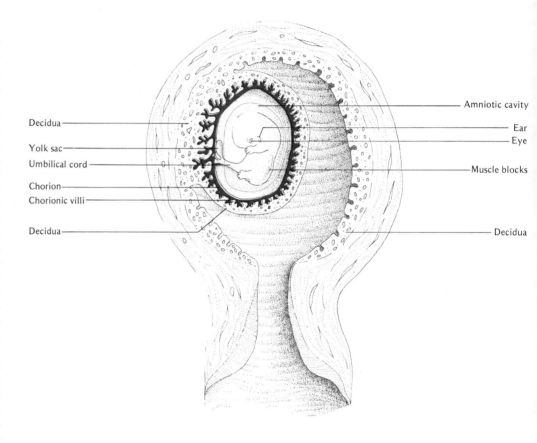

## 10–3 THE PLACENTA: LUNGS, KIDNEYS, AND DIGESTIVE TRACT FOR THE HUMAN FETUS

A chick, a frog, or a fish embryo survives apart from the mother because its egg contains a rich food suply—yolk. A human embryo has no such abundant resource and, therefore, requires considerable maternal care.

The first source of maternal nourishment is the glycogen-rich secretion of the endometrium (uterine milk). The egg implants by burrowing into the endometrium, where it derives its nourishment from then until birth. Since this elaborately prepared layer is shed at birth, it is given the name **decidua**

(*deciduus*—falling off; L.). As early as the first week of development, the embryo begins to form an enclosing membrane, the **amnion,** within which it secretes amniotic fluid. This bag of water cushions and protects the early embryo. The trophoblast cells also burrow deeper into the endometrial lining. About 5 to 6 days after attachment to the uterus the trophoblast has eroded spaces (**lacunae**) in the endometrium, giving it a spongy appearance (Figure 10–5). Blood from the mother fills these spaces and bathes the growing trophoblast. The outermost membrane of the embryo (the **chorion**) begins to form fingerlike projections called **chorionic villi,** which project into the

lacunae. By the third week the chorionic villi contain blood vessels that absorb nourishment from the mother's blood and carry it into the blood vessels of the developing embryo. These blood vessels are called the **allantoic arteries** and **veins,** and they run from the body of the developing child via a stalk, the **umbilical cord,** and connect up with the chorionic blood vessels (Figures 10–16 and 10–17).

The **placenta** then develops. It is a disc-shaped mass of tissue that has a double origin. The fetal portion consists of the branched chorionic villi (called the **chorion frondosum**), and the maternal portion consists of a part of the decidua. It is principally

**FIGURE 10–17** (a) Section through the uterus showing fetal membranes, umbilical cord, and placenta. (b) Detail of circulation of maternal and fetal blood through placenta.

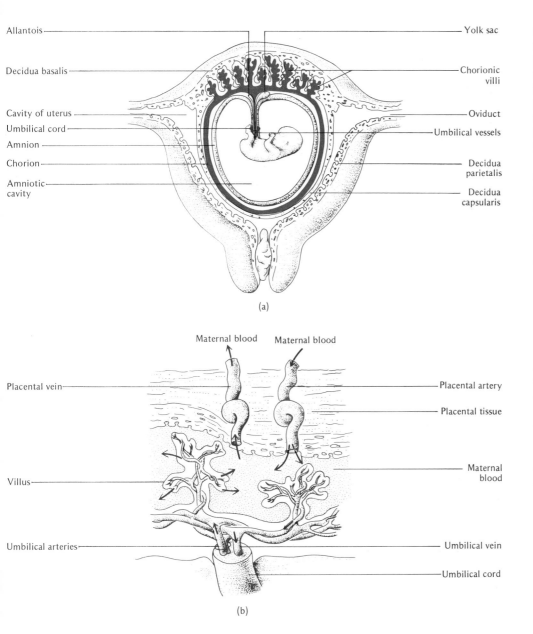

Allantois

Decidua basalis

Cavity of uterus

Umbilical cord

Amnion

Chorion

Amniotic cavity

Yolk sac

Chorionic villi

Oviduct

Umbilical vessels

Decidua parietalis

Decidua capsularis

(a)

Maternal blood          Maternal blood

Placental vein

Villus

Umbilical arteries

Placental artery

Placental tissue

Maternal blood

Umbilical vein

Umbilical cord

(b)

via the chronic villi that most of the exchanges between mother and fetus take place. The placenta provides for gaseous transfer, for elimination of wastes, and for the fetus's supply of predigested nutrients. In a sense, it is lungs, kidneys, and digestive tract for the fetus during life in the womb. How does the placenta perform these functions?

The fetus floats in an almost weightless state in a fluid-filled sac (the amnion), but it is connected to the placenta from the very beginning by the umbilical cord (Figure 10–17), a conduit carrying two fetal arteries and one fetal vein. The umbilical cord provides a connection to life-support systems provided by the mother. In the fetus, the umbilical cord grows from a few inches to a length of up to 4 ft. Its blood vessels are cushioned in a substance known as **Wharton's jelly,** which prevents them from kinking. Just prior to birth about 300 qt of blood are moved across the placenta each day, each round trip between fetus and mother taking only 30 seconds. The waste products of the fetus are carried away by the umbilical arteries and delivered to the chorionic villi, from which they diffuse into the mother's blood. The cleansed blood returns to the fetus via the single umbilical vein, laden with nutrients and oxygen picked up from the mother's blood. Maternal blood enters the placenta via the uterine arteries, and these open into an **intervillous space.** The spaces in turn are drained by uterine veins.

Thus, in the placenta, blood of the fetus and the mother circulate in distinct and separate channels; normally the two are never in direct contact. Materials are exchanged across the placenta by diffusion across capillary membranes. To facilitate exchange, the surface area of the placenta is quite large, amounting to many square yards. The placenta functions for nutrition, respiration, and excretion; acts as a barrier against disease organisms; and secretes hormones to maintain the endometrium. All these functions (except hormone) are

### BOX 10B  From water to land: a baby is born

We emerge from water to the land at birth and announce the event by screaming. The change from fetus to newborn is dramatically seen in the circulatory system. If changes in the circulatory system did not occur, our chances for survival would be poor indeed. As we live warm and protected within the womb, our lungs are collapsed and idle. The fetal heart contains a bypass for the lungs: blood entering the right side of the heart from the body can pass directly to the left side through an opening called the **foramen ovale,** the oval window (Figure 10–18a). Together with another short circuit in the fetal circulation, the heart-lung bypass ensures that only 10% of the fetus's blood is sent to the lungs, 55% goes to the placenta for oxygenation, and 35% is circulated through the blood vessels. The blood that enters the fetus via the umbilical vein is sent on a bypass around the liver.

At birth the circulatory routing must be changed and the short circuits removed. The newborn infant can no longer depend on the placenta for food and oxygen; now lungs and liver assume important functional roles, and blood must be routed through these organs. Ordinarily, the shock of birth triggers the first breath of life. If not, the traditional slap on the baby's bottom provides a sensory stimulus that triggers the respiratory center of the brain to initiate breathing (Chapter 14). Failing this, the umbilical blood vessels close following delivery of the placenta, and there is a sharp rise of carbon dioxide in the blood; this triggers the respiratory center into activity. As a result blood flow between the heart and the lungs is increased, this equalizes the pressure on the heart, and the foramen ovale in the heart closes. Closure of the umbilical blood vessels results in increased flow from the body organs through the liver, the other heart-lung short-circuit vessel closes, and the land-type pattern of circulation takes over (Figure 10–18b).

If by chance there is some slipup and the heart-lung bypasses do not close, arterial and venous blood mix and a "blue baby" results. Surgery can be used to seal the foramen ovale and tie off the short-circuit vessel, restoring normal land type circulation.

FIGURE 10–18 (a) Human fetal circulation (diagrammatic). (b) Circulatory system following birth (diagrammatic).

FIGURE 10–19 First stage of labor: dilation of the cervix. This stage takes the longest time: 8 to 20 hours for the first baby and 3 to 8 hours for the second or later babies. During pregnancy the cervix has remained closed; now it must be opened to a diameter of 4 in. to permit the baby to pass through.

The cervix also becomes softer during pregnancy, and the uterine muscles rearrange themselves to produce maximum expulsive force. As the body of the uterus contracts, considerable pressure is placed on the cervix, and it dilates and effaces itself. The uterus, cervix, and vagina become a single canal,

the birth canal. **The baby's head itself acts as a wedge, widening the birth canal and slowly moving downward. If there is difficulty at this stage of labor, the child may be delivered by** Cesarean section, an incision into the abdomen and uterus.

tremendous forces created by the muscular contractions of the uterine wall and the fluid pressure of the amniotic fluid, the cervix begins to be forced open. The dilation, or opening, of the cervix is the first stage in labor and permits the baby to enter the birth canal. A pink vaginal discharge (show) is also indicative of cervical dilation. The amnion, placed under 25 or 30 lb of pressure by the uterine muscles, may rupture, and the breaking of the waters occurs. Once the uterine contractions are occurring at 10-minute intervals, it is time to set off for the hospital (Figures 10–19 to 10–21).

## 10–5 THE MAMMARY GLANDS AND LACTATION

The **mammary glands** (breasts) are accessory reproductive organs in females (Figure 10–22). Prior to puberty the breasts in the male and female are similar. At about 10 years of age a girl's breasts begin to enlarge owing to the influence of estrogen and progesterone.

Estrogen causes duct development and increase in the supporting connective tissue, whereas progesterone is responsible for growth of 15 to 20 glandular lobes of tissue embedded in fat and connective tissue (Figure 10–22). The absence of significant quantities of these hormones in the male makes his breasts remain rudimentary. Growth continues until late adolescence, when the breasts assume a firm and rotund condition. After puberty the breasts fluctuate in size in cyclic fashion during each menstrual cycle because of the slight rise in progesterone and estrogen (Figure 10–23). At puberty the nipples become more sensitive, as does the pigmented area around each nipple (the **areola**). Each breast lobule is drained by a **lactiferous duct** that runs to the nipple.

Just prior to their termination beneath the aerola, the ducts dilate into **lactiferous sinuses,** which serve as reservoirs for milk. The actual size of the breasts bears little relation to the amount of mammary tissue

accomplished by purely physical means and require no special mechanisms other than semipermeable capillary walls. The growth of the placenta is phenomenal: by 1 month it lines 20% of the uterus, and by 5 months 50%. When the baby is delivered, the placenta is shed as the afterbirth and weighs 1.5 lb.

## 10–4 PARTURITION (BIRTH)

After 37 weeks in the womb, the baby is ready for birth **(parturition).** The fetus in the amniotic sac has been surrounded by amniotic fluid for 9 months. The fluid capsule acts as a shock absorber and enables the fetus to grow without restriction. The uterus

in turn has increased to 16 times its normal size, and its elastic walls have been stretched to capacity. Now, approximately 280 days after the last menstrual period, labor begins. **Labor** brings about the expulsion of the fetus from the uterus; it will mean departure from the watery world and the beginning of a new life on land (Box 10B).

It begins as a series of rhythmic movements in the uterine muscles and those in the abdomen. Oxytocin a hormone secreted by the posterior lobe of the pituitary specifically causes the uterine muscles to contract. The muscular contractions, called **labor pains,** produce discomfort beginning in the lower abdomen and spreading to the back and thighs. As a consequence of the

FIGURE 10–20 Second stage of labor: delivery of the baby. The uterus, cervix, and vagina have become a single canal, the birth canal, and the child moves outward through it. Now the mother bears down with each contraction. (This is involuntary and is stimulated by distension of the vagina and vulva by the fetus's head.) Usually the duration of this stage is shorter in women who have given birth previously and in those with strong uterine musculature. It usually lasts between 20 minutes and 2 hours. Moving downward through the birth canal, the newborn is rotated by the bones of the mother's pelvis. The obstetrician often guides the child at the delivery stage. Abnormal positions of the baby's limbs and the umbilical cord can complicate labor, but most physicians are well versed in handling these nonroutine births. As the child passes down the birth canal, its head may be pressed out of shape, but this produces no damage to the underlying brain, since the bones of the skull are pliable and separated by sutures which allow some degree of overlap. A few days after birth, the head resumes its normal shape. With expulsion of the baby, the uterus now shrinks in size, and by shearing forces at its base the placenta is separated. (Courtesy of Roberts Rugh.)

FIGURE 10–21 Third stage of labor: delivery of the placenta. About 15 minutes after the baby is delivered, the placenta and its associated membranes, together called the afterbirth, are expelled. Usually this is effected by the mother. The blood loss during this stage is about 200 ml and is minimal because the firm contractions of uterine muscles serve to constrict blood vessels. Blood loss can be further lessened by intramuscular administration of Pitocin (an oxytocic drug), which helps the uterine muscles regain their tone. The umbilical vein collapses and the cord is tied. Life on land begins. (See Box 10B.)

FIGURE 10–22 (a) External and internal anatomy of the mature female breast as seen in front view. (b) Side view of the internal anatomy of the breast.

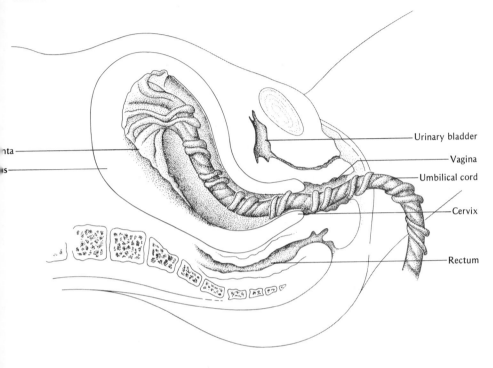

Urinary bladder
Vagina
Umbilical cord
Cervix
Rectum

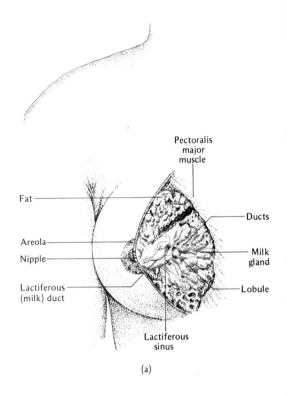

Pectoralis major muscle
Fat
Areola
Nipple
Lactiferous (milk) duct
Lactiferous sinus
Ducts
Milk gland
Lobule

(a)

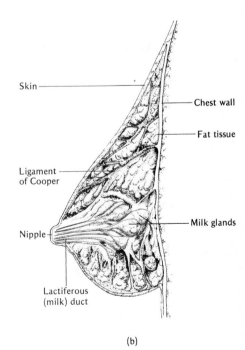

Skin
Ligament of Cooper
Nipple
Lactiferous (milk) duct
Chest wall
Fat tissue
Milk glands

(b)

present. In a mature nonlactating woman there may be no more than a spoonful of mammary tissue; the rest of the breast is occupied mostly by fat and connective tissue. These contribute to the ornamental features of the female body, not the primary function of the breast. At menopause, there is contraction and shrinkage of the connective tissue and the lobes, and as a result a woman's breasts sag and lie closer to her chest.

Early in pregnancy there is an alteration in the breasts that is more marked than during menstruation—the glandular tissue becomes more complex and larger and the areolae darken. Sebaceous (oil) glands in the areolae enlarge, and their oily secretion keeps the nipples supple and prevents the skin from cracking. Growth is brought about by ovarian and placental hormones (estrogen and progesterone). However, **lactation** (milk secretion and release from the mammary gland) is suppressed by progesterone. At parturition, the levels of estrogen and progesterone decline with the expulsion of the placenta. This decline removes the inhibitory influence and permits the mammary gland to be stimulated. Stimulation for lactation comes from the action of the pituitary hormones prolactin and oxytocin (Figure 10–24). In addition, the placenta secretes large quantities of human chorionic somatomammotropin that has a lactogenic effect. True milk is not produced until a day or two after partuition, and the first secretion is a watery, yellowish-white fluid called **colostrum.** Colostrum has the same concentrations of proteins and lactose as milk but contains little or no fat; it serves as the baby's first food.

Although milk secretion begins about 2 days after the child is born, the milk remains stored within the gland until the breast is suckled. Suckling on the nipples of the

**211**

FIGURE 10–23 Hormonal changes during a human female's lifetime and their relation to breast development.

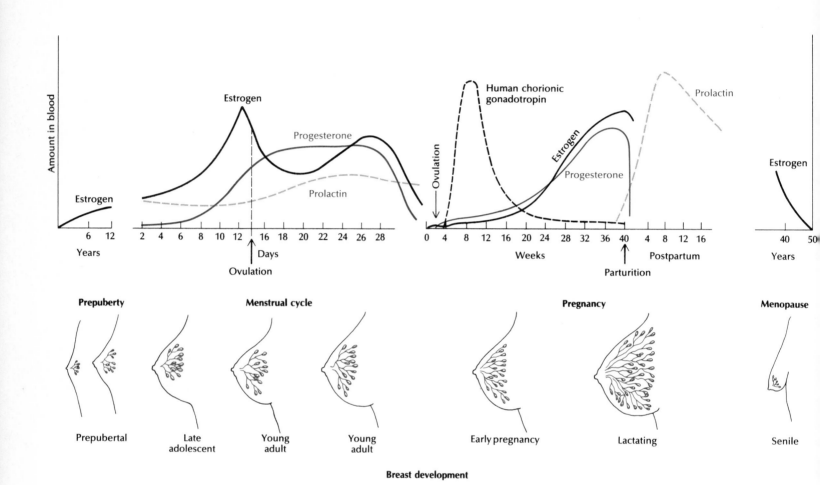

breast triggers a **letdown reflex** and the flow of milk. The letdown reflex is a complex affair (Figure 10–24). As the baby suckles the nipple, the nerves in the nipple are excited and impulses are transmitted to the hypothalamus of the brain, which releases the hormone oxytocin. The actual release of the hormone occurs via the posterior lobe of the pituitary gland, and when the hormone arrives at the breasts, it triggers the contraction of the small muscles that surround the milk-engorged lobules of the mammary glands. As a result, the glands are squeezed and milk is moved into the main ducts and out of the holes in the surface tip of the nipple. The more milk is removed, the more hormone is released. Thus, the suckling infant regulates its own supply. Once established, milk production can continue for many months, and once suckling is instituted, the letdown process may take less than a minute.

If the mother does not suckle her young, the mammary glands do not receive local stimulation, milk formation stops within 1 or 2 weeks, and the milk stored in the gland, if not expressed manually, is resorbed. Lactation is a delicately balanced process, and psychogenic stimuli can prevent letdown. Because of this possibility, nursing mothers are advised to remain calm during lactation.

At the peak of lactation milk production by the mother may amount to 1.5 qt each day. Lactation in humans may continue for as long as the infant is suckled. The production of prolactin during this time usually inhibits the menstrual cycle. It is important to know that a nursing mother can become pregnant, and nursing does not constitute a reliable contraceptive method.

The composition of milk in cows and humans is shown in Table 10–1. Cow's milk

FIGURE 10–24 (top) Suckling reflex control of the milk letdown in the mammary gland.

FIGURE 10–25 (bottom) A thalidomide victim. (Courtesy of W. Lenz.)

**213**

**PERPETUATION OF LIFE II: HUMAN DEVELOPMENT**

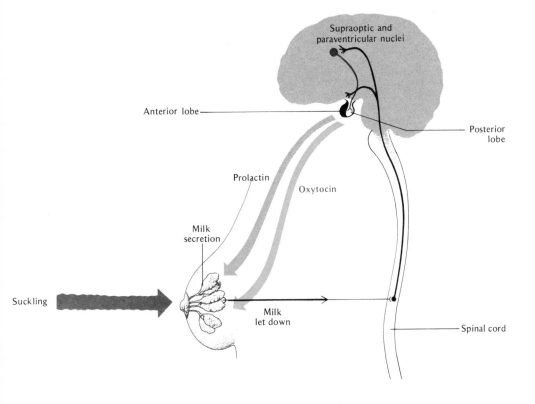

**TABLE 10–1 The composition of milk**

| Component | Approximate concentration (gm/100 ml) | |
| --- | --- | --- |
| | Human milk | Cow's milk |
| Water | 88.5 | 87.0 |
| Lactose (milk sugar) | 7.0 | 4.8 |
| Lipid | 3.3 | 3.5 |
| Protein | | |
|   Casein | 0.9 | 2.7 |
|   Lactalbumin and other proteins | 0.4 | 0.7 |
| Minerals | | |
|   Potassium | 0.041 | 0.150 |
|   Calcium | 0.030 | 0.120 |
|   Phosphorus | 0.013 | 0.095 |
|   Sodium | 0.011 | 0.050 |

is richer in protein than human milk and curdles in a human infant's stomach.

## 10–6 BIRTH DEFECTS

The boy shown in Figure 10–25 is a victim of thalidomide, a "harmless" sedative taken by his mother during her second month of pregnancy. His plight tragically illustrates the intricate complexities of human development and shows how interference at some crucial stage can produce defective offspring.

Development and growth can go awry to produce Siamese twins, hydrocephalics with balloon-shaped heads, children with six fingers or harelip or clubfoot, fetuses without brains or with split spines. How does this happen?

The processes of development are not always perfect, but usually the final product of embryonic development fits a statistical description that we call normal. ("Normal" simply means that the variable in question most frequently fits within a certain range—for example, normal height for a human adult male is between 5 ft 2 in. and 6 ft 4 in.; outside this range, the individual is considered to be abnormal.) When tissue interactions go awry, as indeed they often

BOX 10C Abortion

Abortion refers to the interruption of pregnancy before the embryo or fetus can live on its own outside the uterus. (To have a minimum chance of survival, the fetus must be 7 months old.) Premature expulsion of an embryo or nonviable fetus constitutes abortion, and 96% of all such are spontaneous. Spontaneous abortions (**miscarriages**) are probably due to abnormalities of fetus or placenta, and about 10% of pregnancies end in spontaneous abortion, the majority occurring in the first 3 months.

Prior to 1967, millions of American women underwent illegal abortions, and hundreds of these died as a result of incompetent bunglers performing the operations under unsanitary conditions. Recently, however, the status of abortion in the United States has changed dramatically. At first only a dozen states provided for legal abortion, but by 1973 the Supreme Court ruled that abortion could not be denied to any women in her first 3 months of pregnancy; after 3 months, regulation by states was permissible if it related to maternal health. Although the availability of safe, legal abortions has significantly reduced the number of deaths due to illegal operations, the practice is not without controversy. Some opponents say abortion destroys a potential and sacred life, penalizes the poor and the unmarried, induces psychiatric problems, and promotes irresponsibility and sexual promiscuity. The proponents say it is necessary to curb overpopulation, protect against the delivery of an abnormal child, and precludes adverse effects for the mother who desires no more children and the pregnant young adolescents. At present a vast gulf exists between science and religion, and between law and morality, and the abortion laws yet to be drafted must satisfactorily bridge that gap.

How is a therapeutic abortion performed, and how safe is it? This depends on the length of the pregnancy. During the first 3 months, either **suction** or **dilation and curettage** (D and C) is most frequently used. Suction, or vacuum aspiration, is performed under local anesthesia; the cervix is distended or dilated sufficiently to permit introduction of a suction tube, and the uterus is emptied by gentle suction. The dilation process may produce some cramps, but the suction is quick and usually quite painless. The entire procedure, including preparation, takes less than 20 minutes, and the patient can return home after several hours' rest. In over 54,000 patients aborted by suction, there was not a single fatality due to the method.

Performance of a D and C involves dilation of the cervix and the insertion of a curette (a wide loop of steel attached to a special handle) to scrape the inside of the uterus to remove the implanted embryo and the surrounding endometrial tissue. General anesthesia is often used because somewhat greater discomfort is produced by the dilation. The procedure takes 20 minutes, and the patient may be admitted to the hospital for an overnight stay. When properly done, there is less than a pint of blood lost.

Beyond 12 weeks of pregnancy the risk and difficulty of abortion increase. Most physicians find that the risk of hemorrhage during the thirteenth to sixteenth weeks precludes abortions by suction or D and C, but by the seventeenth week a **saline abortion** can be employed. The procedure takes from 1 to 3 days. Under local anesthesia, a long, hollow needle is inserted through the abdominal wall into the amniotic sac, and a small amount of amniotic fluid is withdrawn and replaced with a concentrated solution of salt water. The salt injection ends fetal life within hours, labor contractions are induced, and the fetus plus placenta are expelled within 24 to 72 hours after the injection. There is little discomfort during the saline injection, and the labor is quite similar to a normal delivery, though not as intense. The risk of complications by saline abortion is three times greater than with the procedures used for early abortions. Beyond 20 weeks most physicians will not attempt a saline abortion.

Two other methods for later abortion are a small **Cesarean section** (cutting through the walls of the abdomen and uterus to remove the fetus) and **hysterectomy** (total removal of the uterus). Both are considered major surgery, may cause complications, and are ordinarily performed only when the mother's health demands (for example, diseased uterus).

The death rate for legal abortions averages less than 8.2 fatalities per 100,000 cases. This means that early abortion is far safer than childbirth and saline abortions are somewhat safer than full-term delivery. Cesarean section and hysterectomy incur greater risks than normal childbirth. Notwithstanding the safety of legal abortion, it remains the least desirable method of birth control.

do, a functional or a structural abnormality may result. These developmental aberrations are probably more common than many people believe. In 1964 Columbia-Presbyterian Medical Center studied 6,000 infants from the fourth month of fetal life through the first year after birth and tabulated all the malformations. Of the babies born alive (by far the majority of abnormal embryos never reach full term), 4% had severe disorders such as heart defects, mental retardation, and imperfect closure of the neural folds resulting in a neural canal open to the exterior of the body **(spina bifida).** Extrapolated to the country at large, this means that over 250,000 seriously abnormal children are born in the United States each year, 700 each day, or 1 every 2 minutes.

Most of the abnormalities occur prior to birth, for the embryo is the most vulnerable stage of development. The embryo passes through a series of developmental stages at any of which it can be changed from normal to abnormal. Birth defects are generally caused by three conditions: (1) defective genes, (2) abnormal arrangements of chromosomes, and (3) teratogens. **Teratogens** are environmental agents that act on the embryo, directly or indirectly, during its intrauterine existence to produce malformations. We shall discuss the first two causative elements in Chapter 23. Here we shall concern ourselves with the teratogens that are responsible for 80% of the distortions (so-called **congenital aberrations**) in the architectural plan of development.

**Thalidomide and other drugs**

The thalidomide tragedy of the 1960s points up how birth defects can be induced by subjecting the pregnant mother to an environmental hazard. During 1960–1962 in West Germany numerous reports of deformed infants appeared in newspapers

**TABLE 10–2 Drugs and pregnancy**

| Drugs taken by mother | Possible effects on fetus or newborn |
| --- | --- |
| Androgens (male hormones) | Masculinization of fetus |
| Anesthetics | Depression of fetus, asphyxia |
| Antimetabolites | Hydrocephalus, cleft palate, eventual infertility |
| Antihistamines | Abortion, malformations |
| Aspirin | Persistent truncus arteriosus, abnormal heart |
| Barbiturates | Depressed breathing, drowsiness for 6 days after birth |
| Chloramphenicol (an antibiotic) | Gray spinal syndrome, death, leukemia, damage to chromosomes |
| Cortisone acetate | Anomalies, cleft palate (?), withdrawal syndrome |
| Demerol | Brain damage(?) |
| Diuretics and potassium-depleting agents | Polycystic kidney disease |
| Erythromycin | Liver damage(?) |
| Estrogens (female hormones) | Malformations, hyperactivity of fetal adrenals |
| Gantrisin | Hyperbilirubinemia (a blood disorder) |
| Heroin and morphine | Convulsions, tremor, neonatal death |
| Insulin shock | Fetal death |
| Lead | Anemia, hemorrhage, abortion, lead line on gums |
| LSD (d-lysergic acid diethylamide) | Chromosomal anomalies, deformity |
| Nicotine (from smoking) | Stunting, accelerated heartbeat, premature birth, organ congestion, fits and convulsions |
| Norethisterone or Enovid | Androgenesis, masculinization |
| Oral progestogens | Secondary sex anomalies(?) |
| Phenacetin | Anemia, death |
| Phenobarbital in excess | Asphyxiation, brain damage(?), neonatal bleeding, death |
| Sodium seconal | Electrical depression of brain waves |
| Stilbesterol | Virilization of females |
| Streptomycin | Damage to auditory nerve |
| Sulfonamides | Jaundice, kernicterus |
| Thalidomide | Hearing loss, abnormal appendages, death |
| Tranquilizers | Retarded development(?) |
| Thiazine (a diuretic) | Thrombocytopenia, polycystic kidney disease |
| Vaccination against influenza | Anemia |
| Vaccination against smallpox | Fetal vaccinia |
| Vitamin K analogs in excess | Hyperbilirubinemia, jaundice in premature infants |

From R. Rugh and L. B. Shettles, *From Conception to Birth*, New York, Harper & Row, 1971.

around the country. The arms of these babies had failed to grow, and their heads extended almost directly from their shoulders, producing a seallike flipper (Figure 10–25). Careful sleuthing revealed that the condition was not genetic, but that the mothers of the flipper-limbed infants (and there were hundreds of cases in 1961, and as many as 6,000 by 1962) had taken a sedative preparation containing thalidomide. The drug was used in cough syrups and was recommended for patients with morning sickness. Little is known about the metabolism of thalidomide and how it produces its effects, but it seems to act on the embryo between the twenty-eighth and forty-second days of development, a time when the future limbs of the embryo are forming. The limbs first appear as microscopic buds

at 10 days, and by 42 days they can easily be identified by eye in the 1-in. embryo (Figure 10–9). The arms develop first and then the legs; this may be the reason that the arms are malformed more frequently than are the legs. Thalidomide does not produce limb abnormalities in mice, rats, or rabbits. In November 1961 the German manufacturer stopped production of the drug, but the thalidomide victims continue to suffer to this day. Americans were spared a thalidomide disaster because the drug was not approved by the U.S. Food and Drug Administration. (The few American babies deformed by thalidomide were damaged by pills brought in from Europe.)

Other drugs that can cause malformations when taken during pregnancy are listed in Table 10–2.

### Disease and birth defects

The uterus, which harbors the developing embryo, is a protected place indeed, but it is not entirely safe. As we have seen, drugs such as thalidomide do penetrate the placental barrier and can produce malformations. The pregnant mother can also transmit diseases and toxins to her unborn offspring, and such agents can be teratogenic. The agents that cause smallpox, chickenpox, measles, mumps, scarlet fever, tuberculosis, syphilis, influenza, and rubella (German measles) are all capable of crossing the placenta. During the first month of development rubella often produces eye cataracts; in the second month heart malformations are likely; and in the third month fever may result in deafness of the fetus.

**TABLE 10–3 Maternal diseases and the fetus**

| Maternal infection | Possible effects on fetus or newborn |
| --- | --- |
| Chickenpox or shingles | Chickenpox or shingles, abortion, stillbirth |
| Congenital syphilis (*Treponema pallidum*) | Miscarriage |
| Coxsackie B virus | Inflammation of heart muscles |
| Cytomegalovirus (salivary-gland virus) | Small head, inflammation and hardening of brain and retina, deafness, mental retardation, enlargement of spleen and liver, anemia, giant cells in urine from kidneys |
| Hepatitis | Hepatitis |
| *Herpes simplex* | Generalized herpes, inflammation of brain, cyanosis, jaundice, fever, respiratory and circulatory collapse, death |
| Influenza A | Malformations |
| Mumps | Fetal death, endocardial fibroelastosis, anomalies |
| Pneumonia | Abortion in early pregnancy |
| Poliomyelitis | Spinal or bulbar poliomyelitis, acute poliomyelitis of newborn |
| Rubella (German measles) | Anomalies; hemorrhage; enlargement of spleen and liver, inflammation of brain, liver, and lungs; cataracts; small brain; deafness; various mental defects; death |
| Rubeola | Stillbirth, abortion |
| Scarlet fever | Abortion in early pregnancy |
| Smallpox | Abortion, stillbirth, smallpox |
| Syphilis | Stillbirth, premature birth, syphilis |
| Toxoplasmosis (protozoan parasite infection) | Small eyes and head, mental retardation, water on the brain (encephalitis), heart damage, fetal death |
| Tuberculosis | Fetal death, lowered resistance to tuberculosis |
| Typhoid fever | Abortion in early pregnancy |
| Western equine, encephalitis | Encephalitis, idiocy |

From R. Rugh and L. B. Shettles, *From Conception to Birth*, New York, Harper & Row, 1971.

The nervous system begins its formation about the third week, but continues its development long after birth. Thus, for a considerable period of time the structure and function of the embryonic and fetal nervous system can easily be affected by disease agents, toxins, and viruses. Table 10–3 lists some dangerous maternal diseases and possible effects on the embryo and fetus.

### X rays and birth defects

Hereditary defects from ionizing radiations such as x rays occur because sperm and oocyte genes are altered (more about this in Chapter 20). Congenital defects can develop in the embryo as a result of direct exposure of the pregnant mother to x rays. Dividing cells are more sensitive to ionizing radiation than are nondividing cells. Since the major part of development involves cell division and specialization, it is no wonder that it takes less x-ray exposure to damage a fetus than an adult. The embryo is most sensitive during the second to the sixth week, because this is the period of fastest embryonic growth when cell division of the germ layers is most active. Based on the experiences of the victims of Hiroshima and Nagasaki, we know that ionizing radiation causes leukemia, cataracts, microcephaly, and other malformations. Seven out of 11 Hiroshima children were born retarded if their mothers were less than 20 weeks pregnant and were less than 0.5 mile from ground zero. Those whose mothers were farther away showed deformed hips, eyes, and hearts.

Laboratory experiments have shown that a minimum exposure of 10 roentgens will affect the fetus. Usually a single x-ray exposure involves 0.1 roentgen, but fluoroscopy may involve greater doses. When exposure to 10 roentgens or more during the first 6 weeks of pregnancy is necessary (for example, when radiation therapy must be used to treat a pelvic tumor), a therapeutic abortion may be recommended by the physician.

### SUMMARY

**1.** After fertilization the zygote divides mitotically into a number of smaller cells; this process constitutes cleavage. Cleavage lasts until developmental processes other than mere subdivision begin to occur.

**2.** By the morula stage (16 to 32 cells), the fate of each cell is committed.

**3.** The morula hollows out to a blastocyst at 4 days. The blastoderm cells will form the embryo; the remaining trophoblast cells will form embryonic membranes.

**4.** Following implantation of the blastocyst, the embryo increases in size and cell-cell relationships change. Embryonic development begins.

**5. Embryonic development**

| Weeks | Stage of embryonic development |
|-------|-------------------------------|
| 2–5 | Ectoderm, endoderm, and primitive streak appear. |
| 3 | Mesoderm and neural plate appear. |
| 4 | Neural tube; organ systems begin to develop; brain, heart, and somites appear. |
| 5 | Tubular heart pumps blood; cranial flexure becomes acute; limb buds form; gill clefts and outline of eyes appear. |
| 6 | Jaws form; gill clefts disappear; eye pigment, diaphragm, gonads, and reflexes appear; heart is partitioned; liver and intestine enlarge; cranial flexure is apparent. |
| 7 | Tail diminishes; eyes and ears, fingers and toes, and inner ear are well formed. Male reproductive system begins to develop. |

**6. Fetal development.** At 2 months, the embryo is well developed and is now called a fetus.

| Months | Size | Stage of fetal development |
|--------|------|---------------------------|
| 2 | 1.5 in., 1/7 oz | Eyes directed forward; jaws, nose, earlobes, limbs, external genitalia, mouth, and alimentary canal well formed. Skeleton hardens; simple reflexes occur. Blood made in fetal liver and spleen. Growth ensues. |
| 3 | 3 in., 1/2 oz | Cranial flexure disappears. Fingernails, toenails, hair, tooth buds, and bones appear. Blood manufactured in bone marrow. Fetal pulse apparent; kidneys function; coordinated motion improves. |
| 4 | 6 in., 4 oz | Posture erect; startle and other reflexes appear; fingerprints appear, refinements in development continue. |
| 5 | 8 in., 0.5 lb | Gripping reflexes appear; fetal movements and rapid heartbeat apparent. Lanugo covers fetus. Lungs, skin, and digestive tract well developed, but fetus incapable of independent existence. |
| 6 | 12 in., 1.5 lb | Thumb-sucking, swallowing, and vernix caseosa appear; meconium fills intestine; hair and bones well developed. |
| 7 | 12 in., 2–3 lb | Chance of survival following birth is 10%. Breathing, temperature regulation, and swallowing possible, though systems immature. Lanugo reduced. Brain enlarges and differentiates; testes begin to descend. |
| 8 | 13 in., 4–5 lb | Growth slows. Fat accumulates; temperature regulation capacity improves; light and taste perception develop. Lungs and digestive tract immature; no sound perception. |

| Months | Size | Stage of fetal development |
|--------|------|---------------------------|
| 9 | 19–20 in., 6–8 lb | Activity diminishes; fetus turns and acquires immunities; development to prenatal state completed. Placenta and umbilical cord regress. |

**7.** The embryo implants into the endometrium (decidua), and the protective amnion forms. The trophoblast erodes lacunae; the chorion (outermost membrane) forms villi and blood vessels. Chorion and amnion form the allantoic sac; the embryo is suspended in amniotic fluid. Two allantoic arteries and one vein run along the umbilical cord to and from the embryo, protected by Wharton's jelly.

**8.** The chorionic villi (chorionic frondosum) + decidua = placenta. The placenta has a large surface area and functions in fetal respiration, excretion, and nutrition. It also secretes hormones and bars many maternal disease organisms. Placental exchange occurs by diffusion, with no mixing of maternal and fetal blood.

**9.** At 40 weeks, cervical softening, dilation, and effacement and muscular uterine contractions (labor pains) signal imminent parturition. The amnion ruptures; the baby moves into the birth canal and is born. Placenta and membranes (afterbirth) follow.

**10.** At birth, the fetal umbilical vessels, foramen ovale, and heart-lung bypass close. Rising $CO_2$ levels trigger the respiratory center and breathing ensures. Postnatal circulatory patterns take over.

**11.** Female mammary glands develop in response to progesterone and estrogen, which also suppress lactation. Levels of these hormones drop with placental expulsion. Prolactin and oxytocin stimulate lactation. True milk flow is preceded by colostrum flow. A letdown reflex is triggered by suckling on the nipples. Prolactin may also inhibit menstruation during lactation.

**12.** Miscarriages and/or birth defects may be caused by defective genes, by chromosome abnormalities, or by teratogens such as drugs, viruses, and x rays.

**13.** Pregnancy termination (abortion) may be performed by suction, D and C, saline abortion, Cesarian section, or hysterectomy.

## KEY WORDS

cleavage
embryo
zona pellucida
morula
blastocyst
trophoblast
ectoderm
endoderm
primitive streak
mesoderm
neural tube
somites
cranial flexure
fetus
vernix caseosa
meconium
lanugo
decidua
amnion
lacunae
chorion
chorionic villi
allantoic arteries and veins
umbilical cord

placenta
chorion frondosum
Wharton's jelly
intervillous space
parturition
labor
labor pains
birth canal
Cesarean section
afterbirth
foramen ovale
mammary glands
areola
lactiferous duct
lactiferous sinuses
lactation
colostrum
letdown reflex
spina bifida
teratogens
congenital aberrations
miscarriages
suction
dilatation and curettage (D and C)
saline abortion
hysterectomy

## TOPICS FOR REVIEW AND DISCUSSION

1. Discuss the role of cleavage in development.
2. What are the differences between the embryo and the fetus?
3. List the functions of the placenta.
4. Discuss methods of therapeutic abortion.
5. How may birth defects arise?
6. What structural changes take place in the circulatory system at birth?
7. Describe the events taking place during the first eight weeks of embryonic life.
8. What are the feedback controls involved in lactation?
9. Describe the various stages of labor.
10. To what organs do the embryonic ectoderm, endoderm, and mesoderm give rise?

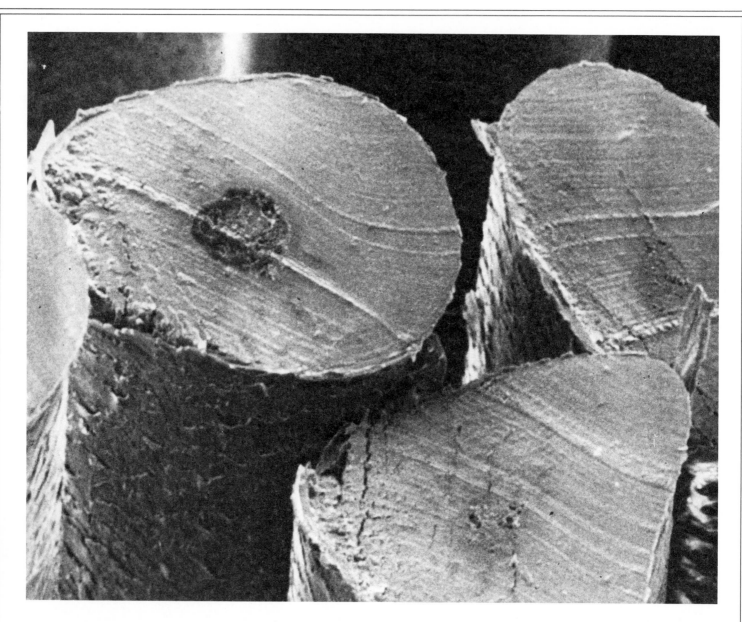

The photograph you are looking at is not a picture of the cut stumps of a cluster of trees but of human hairs magnified 5,000 times, viewed with the scanning electron microscope. You can clearly see the shingled appearance of the hair's external surface and the cut edge shows two distinct regions: an outer barklike cortex and a central core of medulla. Hair is just one of the many products of our skin (nails, oil, and sweat are some others). Why does hair grow or not grow? What does our skin do for us? What happens when we get sunburned? What causes our skin color? What is this cellular wrapper called skin?

# 11

# The Restless Envelope: Skin

## 11–1 WHAT IS SKIN?

This is an age of wonder drugs, miracle fibers, and a thousand other man-made products that contribute to our health and comfort; one of the body's largest organs can be described as a kind of miracle wrap, and that organ is our skin.

Skin covers the entire surface of the body and it marks us as individuals, each distinct in appearance from the other. Nowhere on the earth are there two individuals identical in face or form. This unique outward appearance confers upon each of us a badge of identity that we show in our body as a whole and especially in our faces and fingerprints. Our individuality is in large part due to the manner in which our skin is molded over the underlying tissues, and the organization of the skin itself. Skin shows a striking lability, and is capable of undergoing profound alterations in response to changes in both the internal and external environments. It is restless, constantly being worn away at the surface, and continually being renewed from layers deep within it. However, skin is quite durable and sturdy; it is able to withstand and adjust itself to an infinite number of insults and abuses. Think of how we nick and scratch it, cream it, bake it in the sun, expose parts of it to icy winds, scrub and clean its surface with harsh detergents, and in general expect it to perform in a variety of ways that stretch its capacities to their limits. Americans spend more for cosmetics each year than the entire budget for the National Institutes of Health. Baked, beaten, chilled, washed, creamed, and painted for decades, we finish up with the dry, furrowed, flabby skin of old age—a shabby and worn result of such continual abuses.

Our skin acts as a mirror of our general health. Warning signals of body malfunctions are read by trained physicians when they examine our nails and hair, note the presence of a rash, the texture of the skin, and the abundance of fat. Skin is a "jack of all trades" organ. It acts as a shield against environmental hazards, it maintains the integrity of the body by not allowing foreign invaders (physical, chemical, and microbial agents) to penetrate its surface, it retains the body fluids, helps to regulate our body temperature, and contains the senses of touch, pain, and temperature. In addition, it is one of the principal organs of sexual attraction.

## 11–2 THE SKIN SURFACE

Our **skin** is an organ composed of many tissues. It varies in its characteristics in different parts of the body. For example, the outer covering (cornea) of our eyes is modified skin, which forms a perfectly transparent windshield permitting free entry of light to the retina. The skin at our joints, such as the knuckles, elbows, and knees, is pliable and loosely attached to the fat and muscle below so that the joints can move freely and flexibly. If you look at the skin on your forearm, you will see that it is more taut; a gentle tug and it snaps back into place demonstrating the elastic properties of skin. During pregnancy (or when one gains weight), the skin must stretch considerably; after delivery and the associated weight loss when there is a return to the normal condition, the skin springs back to its original configuration. Sometimes the skin is stretched beyond its elastic limits, and more or less permanent scars are left when the skin shrinks again, producing so-called *stretch marks*. These are particularly common in the abdomen and breasts after pregnancies.

The skin surface has a waterproof quality conferred on it by the products of oil (**sebaceous**) **glands** in the skin. The oily film that covers most of the body also acts to prevent the loss of excessive amounts of moisture. On the face, the forehead, cheeks, and nose are normally more oily than the chin and the neck, and this is related to the distribution of oil glands in the skin.

The skin may bear nails and hair in certain parts of the body. The kind of hair varies with location: coarse and thick on the head and eyebrows, velvety on the forehead, absent on the lips, soles of the feet, and palms of the hands. If you look at the palm of your hand, you will find that the skin is rather taut, and its surface contains ridges and furrows; it is also moist. These tiny ridges (Figure 11–1a), similar to the treads on an automobile tire, aid in gripping. If the fingertips were smooth, gripping would be less effective. (Recall how difficult it is to grasp a pin while wearing a pair of rubber gloves.) The design of the ridges and furrows in the skin give each area of the body a characteristic topography and such a map is well established even before birth. Be-

FIGURE 11–1 (a) and (c) Surface structure of the skin and its relation to the epidermis and dermis (diagrammatic). (b) Structure of the skin as seen with the scanning electron microscope.

cause of the fine detail of these individual markings, they can be used as a means of identification. Almost any part of the body could be used as an identity key, but fingerprints are most often used because they have a high relief, and they can easily be obtained time and time again. The fingerprint pattern is inherited and appears during the third or fourth month of fetal life. The fingerprints of every individual are different from those of every other individual except those of identical twins, and even here a fingerprint expert can detect slight differences.

Some other lines, such as the furrows in the palm and sole, are inherited and it is these lines that supposedly tell of our past and our future. There is no scientific evidence for the predictions of the palm readers. Other furrows and lines are not inherited, but are acquired after birth. The lines in our brow and the crow's feet around the corners of our eyes are produced by the repeated wrinkling of the skin, the orientation of the muscles and fat that underlie the skin, and the pull of the muscles themselves. These lines give our faces character and attempts to modify them provide a rich source of raw material for the cosmetic industry.

Under continued pressure or friction, the skin surface becomes thickened and a callus is produced. The pattern of calluses on the hands can often be used to identify a person's occupation; for example, the "pencil pusher" shows calluses on the index and middle fingers, the guitarist at the fingertips, and the laborer on the surfaces of the palms and the fingers.

The skin contains a number of sense receptors so that we are able to detect pressure, pain, and temperature. (These are discussed in more detail in Chapter 19.) The fingertips are particularly rich in the nerve endings of these receptors so that we can distinguish slight differences in texture, weight, and temperature with our fingertips. The nerve endings on the back of the hand are sparsely scattered when the area is compared with the fingertips, and thus this location is not as sensitive as our fingers, and sensory discrimination is not as fine.

An outstanding property of the skin is its ability to repair itself; in this respect it is very much like a self-renewing, self-sealing puncture-proof tire. Considering the number of cuts and bruises that our skin surface suffers during the course of a few weeks or months, it becomes evident that if our skin did not have the capacity for repair it would be an extremely shabby and worn cloak, virtually useless in a very short time.

The blood supply to the human skin is very rich and assists in sealing a wound and protecting against foreign invaders, but it also acts in conjunction with other tissues of the skin to thermostatically control the temperature of the body.

## 11–3 THE ARCHITECTURE OF THE SKIN

The average adult has about 3,000 square inches of skin, and this amount of skin weighs about 6 pounds (nearly twice the weight of our liver or our brain). Our skin is at no point thicker than three-sixteenths of an inch, testimony to the truthfulness of the term *skin deep!* In spite of its thinness, skin is an intricate organ and is composed of two principal parts: a thin outer cellular layer, which contains no blood vessels, called the epidermis, and a thick, inner layer, fibrous in nature, containing blood vessels, nerve endings, and glands, called the dermis.

The thin **epidermis** is composed of four or five sheets of cells layered one on top of another (Figure 11–1a). The top layer consists of a compact veneer of flattened, dead cells (Figure 11–1b), called the horny layer (**stratum corneum).** It is this layer that serves as the principal shield of the body. The epidermis is self-renewing. The deeper layers of the epidermis steadily replenish the horny layer by cell division; a layer called the basal layer or **stratum germinativum,** which lies just above the dermis, produces new cells and these push upward and replace the dead cells at the surface; in their transit from the basal layer to the surface, they form keratin (*keras*—horny; Gk.) a horny, waterproof material. You can easily demonstrate this horny layer for yourself by scratching your skin with your fingernail, and see that you obtain thin flakes of the dead epidermal cells. Dandruff is another example of the flaky, dead epidermal cells of the scalp. The basal cells of the epidermis divide in a rhythmic and cyclical fashion. It is estimated that the movement of a cell from the lowest layer where it was formed to the topside where it is dead and sloughed off takes about 4 weeks; the time may be shortened in injured areas. The horny layer of the epidermis is quite an effective barrier against foreign materials, but it falls short of perfection. Among the materials that do penetrate are the metals mercury and nickel, as well as the oleoresins of poison ivy, and these produce violent reactions in the living tissues below the surface.

Beneath the epidermis is the **dermis,** a soft, thick cushion with rolling hills and valleys at its surface into which the overlying epidermis fits exactly. If we were to separate the epidermis from the dermis, we would see that the lower surface of the epidermis is the exact negative mold of the upper surface of the dermis; they fit into one another like a hand in a glove. The arrangement and distribution of the hills and valleys of the epidermis–dermis contribute in part to the texture of the skin. The dermis consists of connective tissue containing collagen and elastin, fat, nerves, hair follicles, sweat and oil glands, and a rich supply of blood vessels (Figure 11–1b). The interlacing connective tissues account for the toughness and elasticity of the skin. Leather is nothing more than the tanned dermis with the epidermis removed; the thicker the dermis, the more bulky the leather. Human skin has a relatively thick dermis and can be fashioned into leather. One of the most shocking cases of the use of human skin for leather was by the sadistic World War II criminal, Ilse Koch, who fashioned the tattoed skin of concentration camp victims into lampshades.

Fat tends to accumulate in the deeper regions of the skin (dermis), acting as insulation against heat loss and as a cushion against mechanical injury. The distribution of fat is characteristic of the sex. For example, in women the fat layer is on the average thicker than it is in men, giving the skin of a woman a velvety quality. Because the fat is deposited in localized regions (buttocks, hips, and breasts) the body contours of women are smoother, rounder, and less pronounced than in men.

## 11–4 SKIN COLOR

The human races are white, black, brown, yellow, and red. The coloration is literally only skin deep, and depends on the amount of pigmentation present in the epidermis. There are a number of pigments that contribute to our skin coloration: **melanin,** a

FIGURE 11–2 The melanocyte and its location in the basal region of the epidermis. The arrows indicate the manner of injection of melanin granules into the surrounding cells.

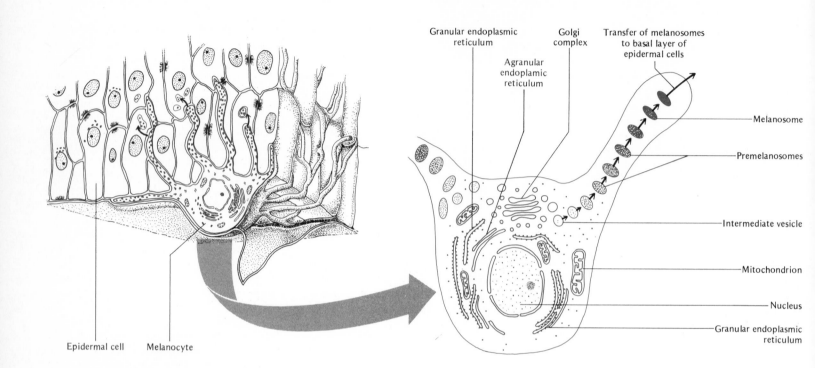

Epidermal cell    Melanocyte

Granular endoplasmic reticulum

Agranular endoplamic reticulum

Golgi complex

Transfer of melanosomes to basal layer of epidermal cells

Melanosome

Premelanosomes

Intermediate vesicle

Mitochondrion

Nucleus

Granular endoplasmic reticulum

yellow to black pigment; carotene, a yellow to orange substance, and hemoglobin, the red pigment of the blood. Melanin is the most important of all the skin pigments, and it functions primarily as a shield against the injurious rays of the sun (Box 11A).[1] The yellowish-black melanin is formed by irregularly-shaped cells, melanocytes, located between the cells in the basal layer of the epidermis (Figure 11–2). The melanocytes have long fingerlike processes that extend some distance from the cell body and worm their way between the epidermal cells. The melanocyte produces melanin granules, and these are injected in hypodermic syringe fashion into the neighboring epidermal cells. Within the epidermal cell the melanin is arranged as a protective sheath around the nucleus, thus screening out the ultraviolet rays and protecting the nucleic acid inside.

---

[1] Melanin is also responsible for eye color and hair color.

Differences in human skin color depend on the distribution of pigments, primarily melanin, and the thickness of the skin itself. No matter what race of human beings we study, we find that skin coloration is not due to the number of melanocytes present but is a result of the amount of pigment manufactured and its distribution in the epidermal layers. The number of melanocytes is roughly the same in all races, and the color of a person's skin depends on the activity of melanocytes and their capacity for melanin production. These factors are genetically determined, and so the color of a person's skin is a product of genetic constitution. The darkest and the lightest individuals have exactly the same number of melanocytes—the blackest black has a great deal of pigment, and the whitest albino, almost none.

Melanocytes react to ultraviolet light by producing increased amounts of pigment and a suntan (Box 11A). Light rays activate

the pigment-synthesizing machinery of the melanocytes so that more melanin is produced, and the skin darkens or tans. In heavily pigmented skin the melanin is distributed evenly and abundantly in all the epidermal layers. Groups of active melanocytes surrounded by groups of less active ones produce islands of pigment called freckles. Fair-skinned people have pinkish-colored skin because their melanocytes produce less melanin and the visibility of the red blood cells in their blood vessels beneath the skin surface is greater than in darker-skinned people. Variations in skin thickness (the range is 0.5 mm in the eyelids to 6 mm on the palms and the soles) also influence skin coloration, and persons with a thin epidermal layer have a ruddier complexion than those with a thicker layer, which is less transparent and gives the skin a yellowish color. Calluses are usually paler in color than the surrounding skin, for this reason. Light-scattering qualities of the skin

## BOX 11A  Sunburn

The main defense of the skin against the lethal rays of the sun is a shield of the pigment melanin, produced by special cells called melanocytes located in the basal layer of the epidermis. The sun's rays stimulate the activity of these cells and there results a darkening of the skin producing the much desired tan, a demonstration of one's health, affluence, and time for leisure activities. It should be recognized, however, that the ultraviolet rays of the sun do more than stimulate tanning; they cause considerable damage to the skin, and in some cases induce cancer (see p. 155).

When skin is exposed to ultraviolet light, the blood vessels near the skin surface dilate, producing a warm sensation and the skin reddens. It is thought that this inflammation (redness and warmth) is due to the action of the ultraviolet light on the lysosomes of the epidermal cells. When these cells are irradiated with ultraviolet light, the lysosomes are ruptured and release their hydrolytic enzymes. It is possible that these enzymes cause the dilation of blood vessels and, in severe sunburn, the elevation of body temperature (fever). If the epidermis alone is burned by the sun (or some other agent), the injury is called a first-degree burn. Sunburn also causes increased frequency of cell division in the epidermis, and the skin becomes thickened within 48 hours (Figure 11–3); this abnormal thickening of the epidermis may last up to 6 weeks. Concomitant with the increased frequency of epidermal cell division is activation of the enzyme tyrosinase in the melanocytes. How the ultraviolet light induces this activation is not clear, but it may inactivate an inhibitor of tyrosinase that is ordinarily present in such cells. The activation of the tyrosinase leads to increased production of melanin and injection of increased amounts of this pigment into the neighboring cells. The process takes 4 or 5 days to develop, and the tan reaches its

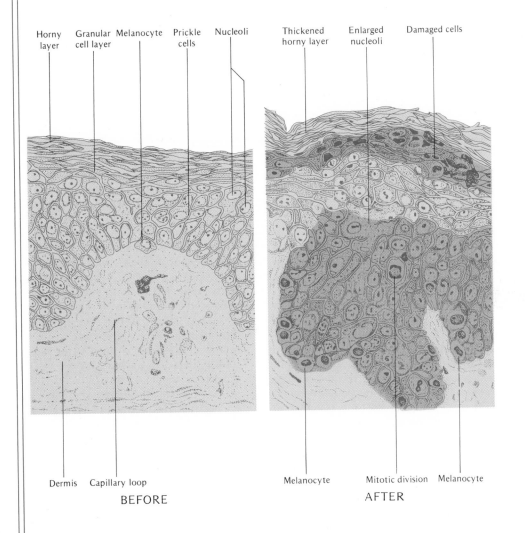

BEFORE — Horny layer, Granular cell layer, Melanocyte, Prickle cells, Nucleoli, Dermis, Capillary loop

AFTER — Thickened horny layer, Enlarged nucleoli, Damaged cells, Melanocyte, Mitotic division, Melanocyte

FIGURE 11–3  Sunburn.

peak in about 1½ weeks; if the skin is not re-exposed, the tan fades, gradually disappearing in a matter of months.

Overexposure to the sun may produce blistering of the skin (a second degree burn), fever, chills, nausea, and occasionally fainting. The hazards of sunburn are increased at high altitudes where the ultraviolet light has to pass through a thinner layer of atmosphere, and on the ski slopes or beach where radiation is intensified by reflection from snow and sand. The safest period of exposure is when the sun is low, that is early morning or late afternoon; at this time, the ultraviolet rays are filtered out because the sunlight has to pass through a greater thickness of the atmosphere. (Long wavelengths penetrate thicker layers of air better than the short wavelengths, and thus the red-orange color of sunrise and sunset.) To protect against sunburn, limit exposure to the sun (1 hour is quite a long exposure), sunbathe in early morning or late afternoon when the sun is low and use sun block lotions or ointments (which contain substances to absorb ultraviolet light or are themselves opaque).

also modify skin color; the deeper layers of melanin-containing cells appear blue because of the scattering effect of light in the overlying coarser layers. Blue light is more readily scattered than red light by tiny particles such as melanin granules. Thus, people with heavily pigmented skin sometimes appear to be blue-black.

Extreme lack of skin pigmentation is called **albinism.** Albinos characteristically have white hair, pink eyes, and pinkish-white skin because of the red blood in their blood vessels that shows through their unpigmented eyes and skin very easily. Albinism is not due to a deficiency in the numbers of melanocytes but to a lack of the enzyme tyrosinase, which converts the amino acid tyrosine to melanin. This is a genetic defect. The greatest (in size) example of an albino may have been Moby Dick, the white whale!

## 11–5 HAIR AND NAILS

### Hair

Humans have been called *naked apes* because they lack the heavy coat of hair possessed by most other related species such as gorilla, orangutang, and chimpanzee. To be quite accurate, the human body is not really devoid of hair, but the hairs on many parts of it are small, colorless, and difficult to see, giving the appearance of hairlessness. This is particularly true of the forehead, the inner surfaces of the thighs, and parts of the abdomen. Considerable controversy exists concerning the reasons for human nakedness and the hairy character of our ape-like relatives; one speculation suggests that early humans were more hairy than we are today, and the reduced amount of hair may have been an adaptation to hunting in the tropical savannahs. In hairy animals the coat of hair prevents the loss of heat from the body, and thus enables the animal to live more comfortably in a cold environment; in warmer climates it acts as a protective shield against the sun. It is obvious that without a furry covering

humans would not be able to survive in colder climates without clothing; for this reason it has been suggested that humans first arose in a tropical clime.

What hair we do have on our bodies serves primarily a protective function. This is particularly true on the scalp where hair acts as a cushion against mechanical damage and protects against extremes of temperature and the harmful rays of the sun. The hairs of the eyebrows and eyelashes protect the eyes by trapping particles of dirt and dust. Hairs in the nostrils and in the ears act as filters for trapping and removing foreign substance and dust particles. Hair may also play a role in sexual activity by promoting the evaporation of sweat and producing a characteristic odor. Ornamental hair, such as in the region of the genitalia, may function as a sexual attractant.

Hairs are produced in follicles, which are tubelike organs attached to and continuous with the epidermis (Figure 11–1b); these penetrate deep into the dermis. The end buried in the dermis is enlarged into an onion-shaped region called the **bulb;** the bulb is invaginated slightly to form a cavity that is filled with connective tissue and a tuft of blood vessels, the dermal papilla. The dermal papilla, nourished by the blood, is the region of hair growth. Hair is not produced continuously, but growth occurs in cycles. When a hair has reached its characteristic length, the cells at the base of the club cease to divide and the hair follicle detaches. When a new cycle of growth is initiated, the old club hair is pushed toward the surface where it is eventually shed, This process of cyclical growth is seasonal in some animals, such as the dog, and there is a periodic shedding of hair; in humans this seasonal shedding of hair does not occur. The lifespan of a hair varies with its location: eyelashes live for 6 months, the scalp hairs of men last 3 to 4 years, those of women about 7 years, and in young girls the hairs may be as old as 15 years.

Hairs may be round, round-oval, or ribbon-shaped in cross section; this makes the hair appear straight, curly, or kinky, respectively. The kind we possess is determined genetically. The color of the hair depends on the amount and distribution of melanin in it, and this too is inherited. Among the cells in the dermal papillae are melanocytes, and these inject their pigment granules into the cells that will eventually form the shaft of the hair. When these hair shaft cells die and become keratinized, the pigment remains and gives the hair its characteristic shades of brown-red to deep black-brown. With little pigment present, the yellow color of the keratin predominates and the hair is white to blonde. Color of hair may be modified by environmental conditions such as diet (a deficiency in tyrosine or protein deficiency) or even emotional crises. Lighter colored hair may be present in infancy and darken with the maturation of the melanin-synthesizing system. Whitening of the hair with age is due to reduced production of melanin. Stories of hair turning white overnight due to shock or fright are mythical.

Hair is composed of keratinized cells cemented together. Hairs are dead, and clipping, shaving, and singeing have no effect on the skin cells that produce them. The observation that hair gets bristly and coarse due to shaving is not true. When elongated and soft hairs are clipped to short stubs, they no longer have the tapering ends that contribute to the soft feel of hair, and thus one gets the impression of coarseness; permitted to grow to full length the soft quality returns. Another myth concerning hair is that it grows after death. The explanation for this phenomenon is that even after a very close shave, a millimeter or two of the hair shaft remains below the skin surface; after a person dies the skin shrivels and shrinks and these hairs are exposed.

Hair grows at an acute angle to the skin surface, and about 2/3 of the way along its length are attached a group of smooth muscle fibers forming the erector muscle (Figure 11–1b). When this muscle contracts,

the hair shaft is pulled perpendicular to the skin surface and the hair "stands up." This action causes the skin surface around the hair to bulge up, and the mound thus formed is called a goose pimple or bump. Gooseflesh is a result of the widespread reflex contraction of the erector muscles upon exposure of the skin to cold. (These same muscles are involved when the hairs stand up on the neck or body of an angry dog or a frightened cat.)

Hair also plays a role in the sense of touch. The base of the hair follicle is surrounded by a collar of nerves that record the movement of the hair. The most sensitive hair follicles are located on the face, around the anus, and the genitalia. The sensitivity of the skin itself is due to an abundance of sense organs (see Chapter 19), and those involving the hair may play an important role in the development and security of the infant as he or she is bathed, stroked, and cuddled; in addition, such nerves and hairs contribute to the erogenous (eros—love; Gk.) zones of the body.

The presence of body hair is a relatively vestigial trait in humans, and humans of the future may be even more naked in appearance than we are today. The progressive loss of scalp hair is characteristic of most people's lifespan. Wigs, hair weaving, and surgical techniques can all be applied to conceal the development of hairlessness. Baldness in many men and women produces anxiety (Box 11B); it is of psychological as well as cosmetic and biological interest.

As human beings we begin life in a bald condition. The hairs that develop on our face and head are rather uniformly distributed and there is no clear line of demarcation for the scalp. By the fifth fetal month, the hair follicles on the forehead undergo involution, and by birth they are so small as to give the forehead a naked look. With passage of time the hairs in the region of the forehead become even smaller so that they are barely visible, and during early youth the hairline becomes established.

The male (androgenic) hormones are re-

sponsible for stimulating the growth of all body hairs in both men and women.[2] There is a tendency in later life, in the early twenties and thirties, for hair loss or baldness to occur. This baldness shows itself in a characteristic manner (called pattern baldness) and is apparently inherited; however, it does not manifest itself unless there is a certain critical concentration of the androgenic hormone in the blood. As a result, the scalp hair follicles respond to the hormonal signals and, in the same way as the forehead follicles of a fetus, they involute and cause the scalp to appear naked. The number of scalp hair follicles remains the same, but the hairs produced are small and almost invisible. Once involution of hair follicles has occurred, a new crop of hairs will not develop.

The tendency to pattern baldness is genetically determined, explaining why baldness runs in families. The fact that pattern baldness is induced by a high level of male sex hormones explains why eunuchs and young women deficient in androgenic hormones, are rarely bald on their heads. Baldness in women sometimes occurs after menopause. The adrenal glands, situated above the kidneys, produce a small amount of male sex hormone throughout a woman's life. They have various functions in women, including the control of hair development; not enough is produced to masculinize women, and any tendency this way is counteracted by the female hormones (estrogen and progesterone) produced by the ovaries, and responsible for femaleness (see Chapter 9). At menopause, however, the ovaries atrophy and the level of female hormones goes down. The androgenic hormones then contribute to more or less masculinization of the postmenopausal women, including the development of pattern baldness, depending, of course, on her inherited tendency toward it. Today, these effects can

---

[2] Women have small amounts of male hormones, just as men have small amounts of female hormones.

### BOX 11B Gone today, but hair tomorrow

Vanity, thy name is woman? A bald lie if you ask doctors. For one of the most common cosmetic procedures in the world is usually requested by men: hair transplants. In recent years, medical efforts to reforest bare scalps have become increasingly sophisticated. A combination of new surgical procedures can now mask baldness so faithfully that "only the patient and his doctor will know for sure" according to Dermatologist Theodore Tromovitch of San Francisco. At the same time, research on a new drug treatment suggests the hair-raising possibility that baldness can be prevented in the first place, even for those fated by heredity to lose their hair.

Many of the new methods of treating sparsely covered scalps are based on a transplant technique developed in the 1950s: about 50 "plugs," each consisting of twelve to 15 hairs with follicles intact, are removed from the back of the head and implanted in the bald spots. But the process is tedious and expensive. Transplanting each plug costs $25, and three to four sessions may be necessary. Moreover, not everyone has enough hair to provide sufficient plugs.

A solution is scalp-reduction surgery, which can shrink a bald spot the size of a palm to the width of a finger. The procedure, developed about eight years ago in Canada, is performed in a doctor's office under local anesthesia. The plastic surgeon or dermatologist makes an incision in the crown and then tugs firmly on the scalp, pulling hair-covered areas from the sides of the head toward the bare area on top *(see diagram)*. A section of the bald scalp is cut away, and the incision is closed with stitches. The 60-min. procedure may be repeated to reduce further the size of the bald spot, which is eventually filled in with transplanted plugs. The approximate cost of surgery each time: $1,200. However, says Alan Gaynor, in one out of four cases the patient's scalp is too tight to be stretched.

Another new procedure has made it possible to avoid the artificial-looking hairline left by transplants. Using a Danish technique, doctors can now insert plugs of just one or two hairs in front of an implanted area to simulate a natural hairline.

The latest hope in treating baldness is a drug originally designed to combat hypertension: minoxidil, made by Upjohn. It proved to have the bizarre side effect of promoting hair growth everywhere on the body, probably because it increases blood supply to the hair follicles. Trying to make a virtue of necessity, Upjohn began a number of studies in which minoxidil ointment was rubbed onto the scalp. In Washington, D.C., early this month, Dr. Hideo Uno, of the University of Wisconsin, reported that "minoxidil stopped the natural process of balding" in monkeys that normally lose their hair. So far, results in humans have been less clear-cut. "There is no question that minoxidil can stimulate growth in some patients," says San Francisco Dermatologist Vera Price, but the yield is often nothing more than a fine peach fuzz. It may be that minoxidil will be most effective as a preventive measure, applied at the earliest signs of balding. Researchers are also investigating a dozen other chemicals, including hormones, all of which require further testing. One thing is certain: there will be no shortage of volunteers.

By Claudia Wallis. Reported by Robert Buderi/San Francisco and Mary Carpenter/ New York. © Time, May 28, 1984.

Cosmetic surgery for baldness. 1. An incision is made, and scalp is pulled toward the bald area on top. 2. Excess skin is cut away, and scalp is sewn together. 3. Remaining bald spot is implanted with plugs of hair taken from the sides and back.

(1)

(2)

(3)

be simply prevented by the administration of hormone therapy to menopausal and postmenopausal women.

### Nails

Nails on the fingers and toes develop from inpocketings of the epidermis, similar to those described for hair (Figure 11–4). Nails are first formed during early embryonic life, and growth continues thereafter.[3] They are composed of keratinized cells that are densely packed together. The dead cells are translucent, and the pink color of the nail comes from the underlying blood vessels that show through it. The nail grows by the continuous addition of material at its base, marked by the white half-moon of the nail. Nails grow at a rate of about an inch in 6 months, but this varies with the state of one's health. The toenails and fingernails function to protect the sensitive tips of the toes and fingers. Fingernails, the counterpart of claws, are useful in picking up tiny objects, as any frustrated nail biter is aware.

### 11–6 GLANDS OF THE SKIN

The skin of humans has two principal kinds of glands: oil (sebaceous) glands and sweat glands (Figure 11–1).

### Oil Glands

The waterproof properties and the softness and pliability of the skin surface are due, in part, to the secretions of oil (sebaceous) glands, which are usually attached to the hair follicle. When a hair emerges from the skin, it is coated with a fine film of oil (sebum) that gives it some of the luster. It also contributes to a greasy look if not washed off regularly. **Sebum** is a complex, semi-liquid material containing a mixture of

FIGURE 11–4 Nail structure (section through the fingertip).

Labels: Lunule (half moon); Nail; Corneal layer; Growth region; Bone; Stratum germinatium; Horny layer; Dermal papilla; Nail root; Nail bed

fats, fatty acids, waxes, cholesterol, and cellular debris. Very little is known about the specific functions of this complex material except that it prevents the hair from drying out and becoming brittle. (Lanolin, highly touted in advertising for hair preparations, is sheep sebum.) The secretions of the sebaceous glands are under the control of hormones and sebum production increases during puberty and pregnancy and decreases with advancing age. The relative dryness of the skin in later life is due to the diminished activity of these glands; excessive washing and soaping of the skin also contribute to the loss of sebum.

The sebaceous glands are most numerous on the face and especially on the nose, producing the "shiny nose" that women must constantly attack with powder. Sebum formed in the ears collects as earwax. Sebaceous glands are particularly abundant around the anus and the genitalia; these latter locations suggest that they must have a special function in addition to a simple lubrication of hairs, but their role remains obsure. Sebaceous glands are better known for their abnormal than for their normal function. Nearly every teenager or adult has at one time or another developed sebaceous glands that have become plugged with se-

bum; the plugged opening is often darkened due to an oxidation of the fatty materials by the air, producing blackheads or acne. Acne seems to be a human condition, for none of our close primate relatives develop such plugged glands. Acne is probably influenced by androgenic (male) hormones, diet, and genetic constitution. It has been suggested that in the human female, the hormone progesterone may influence the activity of the sebaceous glands. Nervous stimulation may also influence the secretion of sebum, and could play a role in acne formation. Since puberty is a time of great hormonal changes, it is not surprising that acne occurs most commonly at this time in our lives. The secretions of the sebaceous glands provide a medium for the growth of certain bacteria, and may result in the formation of pus. The bacteria and the pus together produce pimples or boils that either heal spontaneously or must be treated with antibiotics or minor surgery.

### Sweat glands

Sweat is produced by simple tubular glands with the coiled, glandular portion deep in the dermis (Figure 11–1). The straight, duct-like portion passes up from the coil and

---

[3] If the growing zone of a nail does not develop or is destroyed, a nail will not be produced.

terminates in an opening at the skin surface. There are two kinds of **sweat glands;** those associated with hair follicles (apocrine) and those that are not (eccrine).

The apocrine sweat glands are not randomly distributed over the body, but are localized in the region of the armpits, around the nipples of the breasts,[4] around the anus, genitalia, and umbilicus. The apocrine secretion is a milky, viscous, pale gray-white fluid, which is decomposed rapidly by bacteria living on the skin surface producing the typical unclean underarm odor. The breakdown product may aid in protecting the skin from invasion by potential disease-producing organisms. Apocrine glands produce so little in the way of fluid that they play no role in regulating the temperature of the body. Speculation has it that their original function was to produce an odor that was retained by the pubic and axillary hairs and served as a sexual attractant; however, the use of deodorants and perfumes has largely supplanted this function, and now we have artifically created odors that are said to perform this role.

Eccrine sweat glands are the principal source of human sweat, a weak salt solution (Table 11–1); the sweat glands are widely distributed over the body, and there may be as many as 2½ million tubules in the skin of one person. Placed end-to-end, they would form a tube 6 miles long! The glands are not uniformly distributed over the body surface, and are more numerous on the palms of the hand, soles of the feet, and in the armpits. Some individuals have more sweat glands than others, but there does not seem to be much difference between men and women. The amount of sweating by an individual is not strictly related to the number of sweat glands, as many glands that are normal in appearance are apparently functionless. As we all know from experience, the amount of sweat produced

---

[4] The mammary gland itself is a modified apocrine gland that produces milk for the newborn infant.

**TABLE 11–1 Average compositions of sweat and plasma**

| Substance | Conc. in sweat, mg/100 ml | Conc. in plasma, mg/100 ml |
|---|---|---|
| Sodium | 185 | 325 |
| Potassium | 15 | 15 |
| Calcium | 4 | 10 |
| Magnesium | 1 | 3 |
| Chloride | 310 | 370 |
| Lactate | 35 | 15 |
| Urea nitrogen | 20 | 15 |
| Glucose | 2 | 100 |
| Protein | 0 | 7400 |

Adapted from Y. Kuno, *Human Perspiration*, Thomas, Springfield, Ill., 1956.

varies with the temperature. Under extremely hot conditions, as much as 3 gallons of sweat may be produced in 24 hours. The basal rate of sweat production, that is in an air-conditioned environment at 25°C, is about a pint a day.

The advertising campaigns against perspiration and body odor by toilet goods industries are misleading, for sweating is both normal and essential. The primary function of the eccrine sweat glands is to secrete water on the skin surface, which cools the body as it evaporates. They are indispensable for the maintenance of a constant body temperature. Sweat plays a secondary role on the palms and soles; it keeps these areas soft and pliable and thus assists in the fine sense of touch and aids in the gripping of objects.

Eccrine glands in different parts of the body show different responses to stimuli and appear at different stages of embryonic development. The eccrine glands of the body are responsive to heat stimuli, and develop relatively late in fetal life (fifth month), whereas the eccrine glands of the palms and soles produce sweat in response to psychogenic (*psyche*—mind; Gk.) stimuli and develop early in fetal life (3½ months). The sweating response of the palms of the hands to psychogenic stimuli is the basis of the lie detector test.

Sweating can, of course cause problems if considerable quantities of fluid are lost without replacement. In addition, because sweat is 99% water and 1% solid (mainly sodium chloride, or common salt), it is possible to produce not only severe dehydration but salt imbalance as well. Usually the excessive loss of water by sweating is compensated by decreased output of urine from the kidneys, and the development of an insatiable thirst sensation. As a result, fluid intake increases, which restores the internal fluid balance. As a result of drinking water, however, the concentration of salt within the body fluids is diluted. Salt loss in the sweat, together with dilution of body fluids by increased intake, make it advisable to increase the intake of salt with food as well as to drink water in hot weather. This is especially true if considerable physical labor or exercise is to be performed.

## SUMMARY

**1.** Skin in an organ composed of many tissues.

**2.** The outermost layer of skin is the epidermis, and the innermost is the dermis. The deeper layers of the epidermis replenish the horny layer (stratum corneum).

**3.** Blood vessels, nerves, and fat are located in the dermis.

**4.** Melanin, produced by melanocytes, is the most important of the skin pigments. It aids in screening out the harmful effects of ultraviolet light.

**5.** Overexposure to the sun (or ultraviolet light) may produce reddening, blistering, and tanning.

**6.** Hair and nails are products of epidermal cells. Hair, composed of keratinized cells, functions primarily for protection; it also plays a role in the sense of touch.

**7.** Oil (sebaceous) glands contribute to the waterproof and pliability characteristics of the skin and the hair.

**8.** Sweat glands occur in two forms, apocrine and eccrine. Apocrine glands are localized to certain body regions, whereas eccrine glands are widely distributed. Eccrine glands are the principal source of sweat. The primary function of eccrine sweat glands is to assist in the maintenance of a constant body temperature.

## KEY WORDS

skin
sebaceous glands
epidermis
stratum corneum
stratum germinativum
dermis
melanin
albinism
sunburn
hair
bulb
nails
sebum
sweat glands

## TOPICS FOR REVIEW
## AND DISCUSSION

1. Why is skin sometimes called a "jack of all trades" organ?

2. Why is skin considered an organ rather than a tissue?

3. What glands are associated with the skin and what are their functions?

4. Why might one claim that fingerprints and lie detector tests are legal extensions of the skin?

5. How is skin color produced?

6. What are the processes that take place in tanning? in a sunburn?

7. Of what importance to the body is melanin?

"Why should I eat it? I got my daily essential Vitamin A and all the thiamine and riboflavin I need in the fortified Dynaflakes and irradiated milk I had for breakfast."

# 12

# Processing Food: Digestion and Nutrition

## 12–1 WHY DO WE EAT?

We all recognize what food is. Just the thought of food may make the mouth water. But why is it necessary for us to eat? Most of us would respond by saying, "We eat to live." Intuitively, each of us recognizes that life depends upon a supply of food, and we all know that we have a continuing and constant demand for matter and energy (Chapters 3 and 4). From our food we obtain the materials we need for growth, repair, and energy. As Walter de la Mare put it:

It's a very odd thing—
As odd as can be—
That whatever Miss T. eats
Turns into Miss T.[1]

Our own cells as well as those of Miss T. require that the nutrients or regulatory substances contained in food be available in the tissue fluids in a soluble form. However, the food we eat is a complex material that is often insoluble. Therefore, the problem presented to the body with breakfast, lunch, or dinner is to break down these complex foodstuffs into small, soluble molecules that can pass across the plasma membranes of the cells of the digestive system. The process by which our food is broken down from complex, insoluble substances into simple, soluble ones is called **digestion.** This is a special function of the organ system known

as the **digestive tract** (also called the **gut, alimentary canal,** or **gastrointestinal [GI] tract**). Once the food is digested, the digestive tract functions in another capacity: it permits absorption of the soluble substances and makes them available to the cells of the body via body fluids. Finally, the digestive tract eliminates the food residues that cannot be digested or absorbed.

## 12–2 INTAKE APPARATUS: FOOD PROCESSING

The digestive tract is a continuous tube running from the mouth to the anus (Figure 12–1a); if stretched out, it would measure nearly 30 ft in length. In life, however, **muscle tonus** (a sustained state of partial contraction) shortens the length of the digestive tube to between 12 and 15 ft. The walls of the tube have four layers: the innermost lining (the **mucosa**) consists of epithelial cells; the layer beneath this (the **submucosa**) is connective tissue with fibers, blood vessels, and nerve endings; and the outermost layers are muscle, with the inside layer having a circular orientation of the fibers and the outer one a lengthwise arrangement (Figure 12–1b). The mucosal lining of the digestive tract secretes a slimy, mucous material, and in some regions it also produces digestive juices. This mucus lubricates the tube, facilitates the movement of food along its length, protects the delicate epithelial cells against the abrasive substances in the food, and provides a coating that resists the action of enzymes in the digestive juices.

Although the digestive tract is often called one's "innards," in a very real sense any substance present within it is not in the body at all. The digestive tube goes through the body and is surrounded by the body, but substances in the tube are as much outside the body as a finger placed in a doughnut hole is outside the substance of the doughnut.

The processing of food by the digestive tract occurs in the following way. Three times a day, more or less, a bulk cargo of foreign goods—food—enters the alimentary canal through its gateway, the mouth. In the mouth the cargo is mechanically degraded by the ripping, grinding, and cutting action of the teeth; the rolling action of the tongue and the secretion of saliva form the food into a pliable ball, or a **bolus.** Food then moves on to the throat (pharynx) and is swallowed. From the throat it is transported to the stomach by way of the esophagus and then on through the intestine; passage of food along the canal is accomplished by rhythmic muscular movements called **peristalsis** (Figure 12–2). Pushed and shoved along by muscles, the bulk cargo is mechanically and chemically changed: the stomach churns the food and mixes it with mucus so that it assumes a pastelike consistency, and here digestion begins. Later, food is moved into the small intestine, where "tributaries" carrying digestive enzymes empty; most digestion takes place in the small intestine, and what was bulk cargo becomes a mixture of soluble, fluid materials. The soluble materials are transported across the intestinal wall

[1] From "Miss T" by Walter de la Mare. Reprinted by permission of The Literary Trustees of Walter de la Mare and The Society of Authors as their representatives.

**TABLE 12–1 Functional organization of the digestive system**

| Structure | Description | Activity | Time spent by food |
|---|---|---|---|
| Mouth | Countains teeth and tongue, openings of salivary glands | Teeth grind and break down food, exposing large surface area for action of enzymes. Tongue assists teeth and rolls food into bolus preparatory to swallowing. Saliva dilutes and moistens food. Mucus sticks food together and lubricates bolus for swallowing. From 1 pt to 0.5 gal of saliva is produced each day. | Minutes |
| Pharynx | Crossroads of digestive and respiratory pathways | Bolus of food is pushed into pharynx voluntarily by tongue. From there, involuntary (reflex) action continues swallowing action. | Seconds |
| Esophagus | A 10-in. tube connecting pharynx and stomach | Folded walls distend, and peristaltic waves of muscle contraction propel food to stomach. Liquids pass more rapidly along, assisted by gravity. | 5–10 sec for solids |
| Cardiac constrictor | A muscle band closing the stomach entrance | Peristaltic wave pushes against constrictor and causes it to open. Fluids are held until peristaltic wave arrives. | Seconds |
| Stomach | A J-shaped muscular bag of about 1-qt capacity below ribs, acts as food reservoir; gastric and mucous glands secrete about 2 qt of gastric juice each day | Muscular walls churn and subdivide food further. Fine particles are mixed with gastric juice and mucus, producing soupy chyme. Gastric secretion and stomach motility are regulated by nervous and hormonal factors. Storage function eliminates need for many small meals. | 2–6 hr |
| Pyloric sphincter | Muscle closing the exit of the stomach to the small intestine | Gastric chyme is periodically squirted into small intestine. (Emptying of stomach is controlled by various factors acting on sphincter.) | Seconds |
| Small intestine | A 21-ft coiled muscular tube, 1 in. in diameter, lined by glands and absorptive villi Consists of three regions: Duodenum Jejunum Ileum | Keeps chyme in motion by churning movements. Glands secrete 1.5 gal of mucus and water each day. Disintegrating epithelial cells sloughed off from walls release digestive enzymes. Hydrolytic digestion continues. Absorption of digested materials take place. Absorption of digested materials takes place. | 5–6 hr |
| Pancreas | Large gland opening into the duodenum, producing pancreatic juice* | Pancreatic enzymes continue hydrolytic digestion of nutrients. Pancreatic secretion is regulated by nervous and hormonal factors. | |
| Liver† and gallbladder | Liver produces dark-green, watery bile, which is concentrated and stored in the gallbladder; bile duct connects gallbladder and duodenum | Bile is poured into duodenum, and its secretion is regulated by nerves and hormones. Helps to emulsify fats (break them into small droplets), providing greater surface area for action of the enzyme lipase. | |
| Ileocolonic sphincter | Valve guarding opening between small and large intestines | Prevents backflow from large to small intestine. | Seconds |
| Cecum and appendix | Blind sacs at junction of small and large intestines | Nonfunctional (vestigial) in humans. In herbivores, contain bacteria that are important for the digestion of cellulose. | |
| Colon and large intestine | Thick walled, U-shaped tube 2.5 in. in diameter about 5 ft long; secretes mucus; contains large numbers of bacteria | Absorbs water from chyme. Peristalis compacts residue as feces. Stores feces prior to discharge. Mucus lubricates feces and protects against digestive juices from small intestine. Bacteria act on any undigested food and synthesize useful substances, e.g., vitamins and gases such as methane and hydrogen sulfide, which give feces their odor. | 12–24 hr |
| Rectum | Continuation of large intestine guarded by ileocecal valve proximally and anal sphincters distally; storage depot for feces | Some 0.5 lb of compacted, undigestible material plus bile pigments (giving feces color) and bacteria (10%–50% of feces) are eliminated daily as feces. Ileocolonic and anal sphincters regulate emptying of rectum, controlled by defecation reflex. | |

* The pancreas also produces the hormones insulin and glucagon, but these are secreted directly into the blood (Chapter 17).
† The liver is an important regulator of dietary substances following digestion and absorption of nutrients.

**FIGURE 12–1** (a) The digestive tract. (b) Detail of the wall of the digestive tract. (c) Scanning electron microscope view of the digestive tract (intestine).

**FIGURE 12–2** Peristalsis. (a) The movement of food along the length of the digestive tract can be visualized as a squeezing action, forcing the food along. (b) This mechanism is shown diagrammatically in a section through the intestine. Although in peristalsis the muscular waves of contraction can move food in both directions, one-way movement is usual. Food distending the tract causes contraction on the headward side and relaxation on the anal side of the distention, producing an easy forward movement.

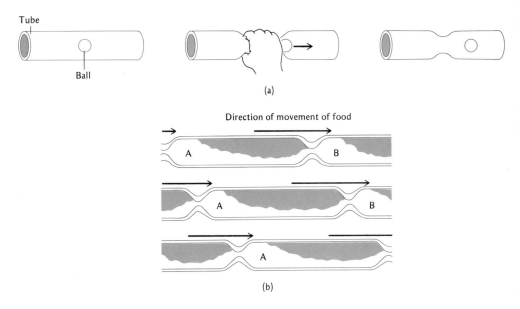

Tube

Ball

(a)

Direction of movement of food

A    B

A    B

A

(b)

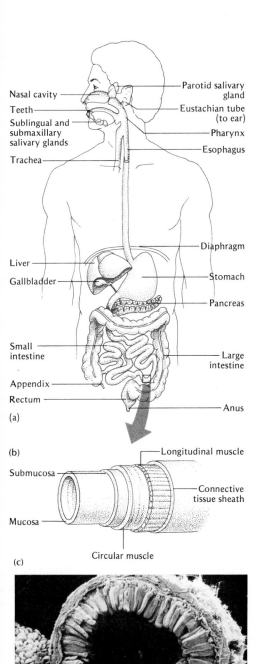

Nasal cavity

Teeth

Sublingual and submaxillary salivary glands

Trachea

Liver

Gallbladder

Small intestine

Appendix

Rectum

Parotid salivary gland

Eustachian tube (to ear)

Pharynx

Esophagus

Diaphragm

Stomach

Pancreas

Large intestine

Anus

(a)

(b)

Longitudinal muscle

Submucosa

Connective tissue sheath

Mucosa

Circular muscle

(c)

into the riverways of the circulatory system.

Absorbed and circulated, the molecular constituents of the food enter the body cells, where they are utilized for energy, repair, and building of new cells. The remaining undigested materials (**feces**) pass into the large intestine and leave the digestive tube via the anus.

Now that we have surveyed the general organization of the digestive tube, let us take a more detailed tour and observe its functional specializations. The details of the journey taken by the food we eat are shown in Table 12–1.

## 12–3 DIGESTION: FOOD DEGRADATION

The digestive tract is relatively indiscriminate. Almost anything and everything digestible that we eat is absorbed without any kind of selectivity. (Other organs, such as the liver and pancreas, actually set the levels of nutrients carried in the blood.) Enzymatic breakdown of food within the digestive tract involves one kind of mechanism: **hydrolysis.** Hydrolysis splits molecules by the addition of water. (See Chapter 3 for a discussion of hydrolytic reactions.) In this kind of reaction, the energy change in the molecules themselves is insignificant, that is, little chemical energy of the food is lost. Furthermore, hydrolytic reactions do not require energy (no ATP is consumed). In the stomach and intestine, proteins are digested to polypeptides and ultimately to amino acids, fats are broken down into glycerol and fatty acids, sugars and starches are hydrolyzed to monosaccharides, and nucleic acids are degraded to nucleotides.

Table 12–2 lists the enzymes and other substances secreted by the alimentary canal and its associated organs and indicates their action on the components of our food.

## 12–4 ABSORPTION: FOOD UPTAKE

Chemical digestion reduces what was once a tasty morsel of food to a solution of fatty acids, glycerol, glucose, fructose, nucleotides, and amino acids. If these small, soluble molecules are to be of any use to the cells of the body, they must be moved out

**TABLE 12–2  Digestive enzymes and associated products of the digestive tract and its related organs**

| Organ | Enzyme | Action | Other comments |
|---|---|---|---|
| Mouth | Salivary amylase (ptyalin) | Starch → maltose | 5%–10% is hydrolyzed in mouth; up to 50% is continued in stomach. Neutral pH of saliva is ideal for action of ptyalin. |
| Stomach | 0.5% hydrochloric acid (ph 1–3)* | Pepsinogen → pepsin | Acidity inactivates ptyalin when bolus is subdivided, sterilizes food, and destroys bacteria. |
| | Pepsin | Proteins → polypeptides | Stomach secretes inactive pepsinogen, which is activated by low pH. This prevents self-digestion, since the cells lining the stomach are not exposed to pepsin intracelluarly. |
| | Mucus* | Protects lining of stomach from pepsin | |
| | Gastric lipase | Fats → fatty acids | |
| | Rennin | Aids digestion of milk Casein → milk curd | High in infants and children. Curdles milk, causing it to remain in stomach longer for digestion of proteins by gastric juice. Optimum pH is 5–6, found only in young. |
| Small intestine | PSodium carbonate (pH8–9)* | Neutralizes acid chyme | Provides proper pH for the action of pancreatic and intestinal enzymes. |
| | IMucus* | | Coats intestinal walls with protective effect. |
| | IEnterokinase | Trypsinogen → trypsin | |
| | PTrypsin | Proteins → polypeptides | |
| | PChymotrypsin | Proteins → polypeptides | Chymotrypsin is activated by trypsin. |
| | PCarboxypeptidase | Proteins → polypeptides | |
| | IAminopeptidase | Polypeptides → amino acids | ⎫ Protein digestion |
| | IPAmylase | Starch → maltose | |
| | IPMaltase | Maltose → glucose | |
| | ILactase | Lactose → galactose and glucose | |
| | IPSucrase | Sucrose → fructose and glucose | ⎫ Carbohydrate digestion |
| | IPLipase | Fatty acids and glycerol | |
| | Bile* | Emulsifies fats | Contains bilirubin (a breakdown product of hemoglobin), various salts, and cholesterol. ⎫ Fat digestion |
| | IPRibonuclease | Nucleic acids → mononucleotides | |
| | IPDeoxyribonuclease | | ⎫ Nucleic-acid digestion |

I  Released by the disintegrating epithelial cells of the intestine.
P  Secreted by the pancreas.
*  These products are not enzymes, but assist the digestive process as indicated.

FIGURE 12–3 The small intestine. (a) Structure of the small intestine (duodenal region) and associated glands. (b) Detail of duodenal wall. (c) Structure of the villus.

**237**

**PROCESSING FOOD: DIGESTION AND NUTRITION**

of the intestine into the bloodstream. The process of moving nutrients and water from the intestine to the blood constitutes **absorption**.

### The stomach

By the time it reaches the stomach, what was a bolus of finely divided food has been broken down to an acid solution of polypeptides, finely suspended globules of fat, and partially degraded starches.

Only a few substances are absorbed directly across the walls of the stomach. Aspirin, a weak acid, is one of these, and so is ethyl alcohol. Ethyl alcohol is lipid- as well as water-soluble, and it quickly diffuses across the epithelial surface of the stomach to enter the blood. This is why its effects show up so rapidly. Although it is absorbed by the stomach, alcohol is more quickly absorbed across the intestinal walls because of the latter's greater surface area. It is possible to reduce the immediate effects of alcohol, that is, dulling of the higher centers of the brain and the associated euphoria, by diminishing intestinal absorption. Drinking milk before imbibing alcohol or snacking on cheese dips or high-fat hors d'oeuvres delays the emptying of the stomach and consequently slows down alcohol absorption, but it does not prevent it altogether.

### The intestine

Approximately 90% of the digested food is absorbed in the 20 to 25 ft of the small intestine (the duodenum is about 1 ft in length, the jejunum 7 to 8 ft, and the ileum about 12 ft; Figure 12–1). Additionally, about 10% of the body's total water and salt enters the small intestine each day as secretions from the various digestive glands, and approximately 90% of this is resorbed into the bloodstream. Were all the water secreted into the gut lost with the feces, we would have a severe dehydration problem.

Since the small intestine is the place where nutrient and most water absorption

takes place, we should expect it to have a large exposed surface area. This is exactly the case. The small intestine is quite long and is packed into the abdominal cavity as a series of coils (Figure 12–1) so that by its length alone a large surface for absorption is provided. However, this is not all, for the

surface of the small intestine also contains folds and enormous numbers of fingerlike processes called **villi** (sing. **villus**—shaggy hair; L.) that project into its cavity (Figure 12–3). Both the folds and the villi vastly increase the absorptive surface of the intestinal wall over what it would be if it were

### BOX 12A  A peephole into the stomach

On June 6, 1812, in a small community at the Canada-Michigan border, Alexis St. Martin accidentally discharged his musket and tore a large, gaping hole in the left side of his abdomen. William Beaumont, an army surgeon stationed at nearby Fort Mackinac, examined the young man within 30 minutes of the accident and treated St. Martin for his wound, but held out little hope that the 18-year-old boy would recover. St. Martin was young and vigorous, and he not only survived but recuperated remarkably well. However, his wound healed peculiarly: a tunnel 2.5 in. wide remained open in his side, and this led through the skin and muscle of the abdominal wall directly into the stomach. Food and drink constantly exuded from the perforation unless prevented by a compress and a bandage.

St. Martin's **fistula** (abnormal opening) provided Beaumont with a remarkable opportunity to peep into the digestive system, and he retained the young man as a servant in his home. St. Martin performed a variety of household duties; he fathered children and enjoyed good health and vigor as do men in general.

Periodically, Beaumont used the boy for experiments on the digestive processes by introducing materials into the stomach via the hole, sealing the opening with a bandage to prevent leakage, and later removing the materials from the stomach to evaluate the changes. Here is his first recorded experiment:

August 1, 1825. At 12 o'clock, M., I introduced through the perforation, into the stomach, the following articles of diet, suspended by a silk string, and fastened at proper distances, so as to pass in without pain—viz.:—a piece of high-seasoned à la mode beef; a piece of raw, salted, fat pork; a piece of raw, salted, lean beef; a piece of boiled, salted beef; a piece of stale bread; and a bunch of raw, sliced cabbage; each piece weighing about two drachms; the lad continuing his usual employment about the house.

At 1 o'clock, P.M., withdrew and examined them—found the cabbage and bread about half digested: the piece of meat unchanged. Returned them to the stomach.

At 2 o'clock, P.M., withdrew and examined them again—found the cabbage, bread, pork, and boiled beef all cleanly digested, and gone from the string; the other pieces of meat but very little affected. Returned them into the stomach again.

At 3 o'clock, P.M., examined again—found the à la mode beef partly digested: the raw beef was slightly macerated on the surface, but its general texture was firm and entire. The smell and taste of the fluids of the stomach were slightly rancid; and the boy complained of some pain and uneasiness at the breast. Returned them again.

W. BEAUMONT, *Experiments and Observations on the Gastric Juice and the Physiology of Digestion*, Pittsburgh, Allen, 1833.

St. Martin and Beaumont collaborated off and on for 8 years; St. Martin remained healthy and outlived Beaumont by 27 years, dying at the age of 76. Today we know much about the function of the digestive tract, but it was a remarkable set of circumstances that permitted Beaumont a glimpse into the stomach for the first time 155 years ago.

entirely smooth. It has been estimated that the total surface area of the small intestine is 2,000 ft$^2$, or about 100 times the surface area of the skin. Additionally, each villus is covered with epithelial cells, and the plasma membrane of each cell is thrown into many minute fingerlike projections called **microvilli**, which further enhance the absorptive surface area (Figures 12–1c, and 12–4). Thus, the surface of the small intestine is much like a thirsty Turkish towel, with its many fine projections that facilitate the absorption of water; a worn bathtowel, without its nap, absorbs less well.

The villi move back and forth independently of each other, much as a field of wheat sways in the breeze, and these movements are muscular in origin. Motion is greater following a meal, so the absorption proceeds at an even greater rate. The cells at the top surface of the villi are continuously sloughed off and replaced as a result of the mitotic activity of cells at the base, and the entire intestinal epithelium is replaced every 36 hours. The continuous discharge of cells into the intestinal space amounts to about 0.5 lb of cells every day!

The passage of nutrient materials across the cellular border of the small intestine is not passive, and the speed with which it takes place cannot be explained by diffusion alone. Rather, it depends on the ceaseless side-to-side bending and shortening of the villi as well as on the active and selective accumulation of materials requiring the expenditure of a considerable amount of metabolic energy. Why is energy required for this selective absorption of nutrients? To move molecules from a region of lower concentration (in the intestine) to one that has a higher concentration (the bloodstream) requires active transport of the molecules "uphill," so to speak, and the energy for such driving movements is provided by ATP. As you may have anticipated, the cells that line the villi of the small intestine are well endowed with mitochondria to generate this "moving power."

Where do the absorbed nutrients go? As

FIGURE 12–4 Electron micrograph of the fine, hairlike microvilli lining the duodenum. (Courtesy of K. R. Porter).

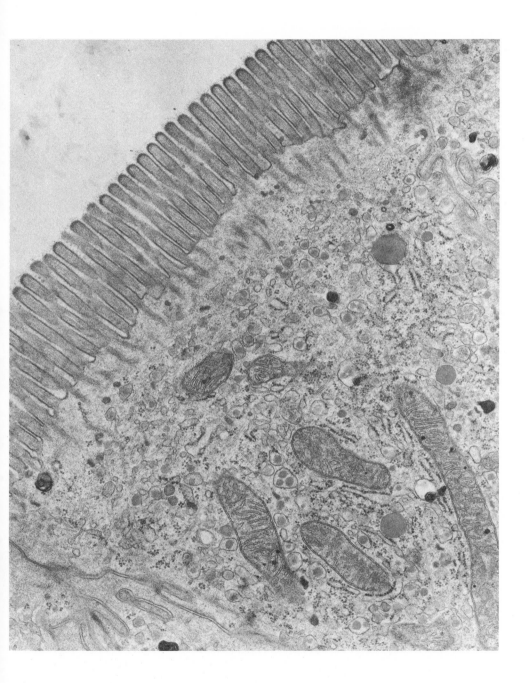

FIGURE 12–5 The hepatic portal system. Blood is carried directly from the stomach and intestines to the liver via the mesenteric, gastric, and hepatic portal veins. Hepatic veins then convey it to the heart by way of the inferior vena cava.

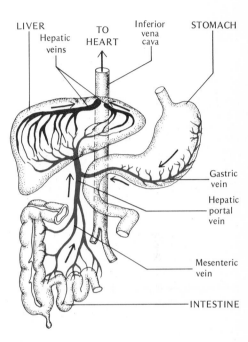

the nutrients cross the epithelial lining of the villus, they enter the core region, which contains a capillary bed of blood vessels (Figure 12–3), an arteriole, a venule, and a lymph vessel, the **lacteal.** The amino acids and sugars are pumped across the surface of the villus, enter the bloodstream, and then are carried directly to the liver via mesenteric, gastric, and hepatic portal veins (Figure 12–5). In this way, the liver gets first choice of the nutrients for processing and storage, before they are distributed to the rest of the body. Amino acids will be used for growth, repair, and energy. The liver regulates the level of amino acids and sugar in the blood and acts as a buffer zone between the digestive tract's indiscriminate absorption of nutrients and the rigid requirements of the body's cells. Vitamins, minerals, and water also enter the blood and are transported to the various cells.

Although fatty acids and glycerol do enter the epithelial cells, they recombine to form neutral fats (called **triglycerides**). More than 60% of the fat enters the lacteals in the form

**239**

of tiny droplets, giving them a milky appearance (*lacteus*—milky; L.). The lacteals drain into the lymphatic vessels that ultimately empty into the blood circulation at the junction of the jugular and subclavian veins in the neck (Chapter 13). A portion of the absorbed fat will be stored in connective-tissue cells called **adipose tissue,** some will be used for the synthesis of membranes, and the rest will be used for energy.

## 12–5 DEFECATION: WASTE EXPULSION

The residues of food that cannot be digested or absorbed leave the small intestine and pass through the ileocolonic valve into the large intestine. There, water and vitamins (produced by intestinal bacteria) are absorbed and waste materials are compacted into feces.

Peristaltic movements in the colon are slow, and 99% of the time there are no contractions, but when the colon becomes overfilled, strong peristaltic waves occur and the fecal material is propelled long distances along the length of the colon. The lower part of the colon (**rectum**) is surrounded by two circular bands of muscle called the **anal sphincters** (literally "that which binds tight"; Gk.). When the sphincters are relaxed, the passageway is opened and material can pass out; when they are contracted the passageway is closed.

When fecal material accumulates in the rectum, it initiates a special defecation reflex by exciting nerve endings that send their impulses to the spinal cord. Return impulses are transmitted to the colon, rectum, and internal anal sphincter, causing contraction of the muscles in the walls of the colon and rectum and relaxation of the sphincter, which in turn causes emptying of the **bowels** (colon and rectum), provided the external anal sphincter is also relaxed. The external anal sphincter is a voluntary skeletal muscle that guards the outer opening of the anus, and it can be controlled consciously. If the time is not convenient for emptying the bowels, the external anal sphincter prevents defecation in spite of the defecation reflex. Any parent who has lived through bowel training an infant recognizes how long it takes for such conscious control of the external anal sphincter to develop.

Almost all of us are familiar with the natural desire to defecate after a heavy meal or after the first meal of the day. This is caused by the **gastrocolic** and **duodenocolic reflexes.** The filling of the stomach and duodenum results in the stimulation of receptor nerves in the walls of these organs. Impulses travel to the spinal cord and back to the colon, stimulating the muscles in its walls and increasing peristalsis. As a result, fecal material is rapidly moved along the length of the colon, and the defecation reflex is brought into play. The emptying of the rectum after each meal is most evident in infants and the elderly, in whom control of the external anal sphincter is poor.

## 12–6 NUTRITION: THE USE OF PROCESSED NUTRIENTS

### A balanced diet

Antoine Laurent Lavoisier (1743–1794) was an elegant aristocrat and a brilliant scientist who met his end beneath the guillotine during the French Revolution. He was executed not because of his scientific pursuits, but because he was a tax collector for Louis XVI. When the judge was asked at his trial to spare Lavoisier's life, he replied, "The Republic has no need of scientists." After the execution, an old friend of Lavoisier remarked, "It took but a second to cut off his head; a hundred years will not suffice to produce one like it."

Before his untimely demise, Lavoisier clearly stated that food was burned (oxidized) in the body's chemical factories and it was in this way that living organisms derived their energy. Lavoisier also demonstrated that the energy content of any fuel—a lump of coal as well as a cube of sugar or a pound of meat—could be simply determined by burning and then measuring the heat liberated as calories.

Since the days of Lavoisier, we have been calorie-counters. Indeed, we all know that different foods as well as differing amounts of the same food have different caloric values. Generally it can be said that a given amount of fat contains over twice the number of calories as an equal amount of protein or carbohydrate.

All the energy in the food oxidized by the body appears ultimately as heat, which is dissipated into the environment. The rate at which heat is produced is equal to the energy demands of the body, and this is called the **metabolic rate.** The metabolic rate is a measure of energy demands over a certain period of time. It can be measured and expressed in terms of calories. For an average person weighing 150 lb, the bare minimum, that is, the amount of energy required to lie in bed and do absolutely nothing, is 1,500 to 1,800 Calories. This is called the **basal metabolic rate** (BMR), and the energy is used for keeping the heart going and the breathing movements operational and in general for keeping the body's cells alive. The basal rate varies with sex and other factors (including age, hormones, and nutritional state of the body). An average woman has a somewhat lower metabolic rate (15 to 20% lower) than an average man and thus requires fewer calories. Over and above the basal rate, an individual requires calories for work. Caloric requirements vary with different kinds of activities. For example, women require more calories when pregnant or nursing, and a growing child requires more calories per pound of body weight than does an adult; an infant requires 50 Calories per pound of body weight, whereas an adult requires only 18 Calories when sedentary and 35 when active.

Carbohydrates and fats provide energy, and carbohydrates are readily converted into fat in the body. The simple exchange of carbohydrate for fat explains why fat is deposited when a person eats a carbohy-

**TABLE 12–3 Chemical composition and recommended daily allowance of a 70-kg (150-lb) human male**

| Component | Content (g) | Daily requirement | |
|---|---|---|---|
| Water | 41,400 | | |
| Fat | 12,600 | Approximately 100 g | |
| Protein | 12,600 | 70–100 g | Approximately 2,500 Calories* |
| Carbohydrate | 300 | Approximately 400 g | |
| Na (sodium) | 63 | 2.5 g | |
| K (potassium) | 150 | 5.0 g | |
| Ca (calcium) | 1,160 | 800 mg | |
| Mg (magnesium) | 21 | 350 mg | |
| Cl (chlorine) | 85 | 270 g | |
| $PO_4$ (phosphate) | 670 | 800 mg | |
| S (sulfur) | 112 | | |
| Fe (iron) | 3 | 10 mg | |
| I (iodine) | 0.014 | 140 μg | |
| Vitamin A | | 1 mg | |
| Thiamin | | 1.5 mg | |
| Riboflavin | | 1.8 mg | |
| Niacin | | 20 mg | |
| Ascorbic acid | | 45 mg | |
| Vitamin D | | .01 mg | |

* On the average, organic foods (that is, organic in the chemical sense and as defined on p. 11) contain about 5 Calories per gram; therefore for an adequate caloric supply, the body requires about 500 g of organic food (1–2 lb) each day. About 15% of the food intake should be protein.

drate-rich diet. Protein, too, may contribute to the energy supply, but the energy demands of the cells are satisfied by carbohydrates and fats as long as these materials are available. This is called **protein sparing**. During starvation the stores of carbohydrate and fat are depleted first, then amino acids serve as fuel. The amount of energy available from amino acids under these conditions can suffice for only a few days, since they must be derived from the structural tissues of the body. Beyond this short time the body begins to consume itself; cells are unable to grow and repair themselves, and ultimately this may lead to death.

Unlike carbohydrates and fats, proteins contain nitrogen. Although proteins, fats, and carbohydrates can all serve as a source of energy, fats and carbohydrates cannot serve as a source of amino-acid building blocks because they lack atoms of nitrogen. Amino acids and proteins cannot be stored (except in eggs and nuts), and excessive amounts of protein are quickly transformed into glycogen and fat and their nitrogen excreted as urea. Thus, although we can exist for some time without fat or carbohydrate, we must have a continuing supply of protein in our diet.

Carbohydrates and lipids from the various species of plants and animals differ only slightly in their composition and in their nutritional value to us. Proteins, however, are unique, and not all proteins contain all 20 different kinds of amino acids. Indeed, certain kinds of proteins are deficient in some amino acids. In general, complete proteins, which are capable of supporting growth when used as the sole dietary supply, are derived from animal sources. Consequently, adequate nutrition solely from plant proteins usually requires a mixed diet of plant foods. Most vegetable matter is low in protein; this means that a vegetable diet ordinarily is suppplemented with meat or other protein-rich foods to meet the daily dietary requirements for protein. Roughly, it can be said that a human being requires about 1 g of protein per kilogram of body weight per day. Lack of adequate amounts of protein in the daily diet, or deficiency of amino acids due to imbalance in protein foods, is probably the severest problem facing the impoverished of this world. (See Chapter 27.)

The well-balanced daily diet should consist of protein (15%), carbohydrate (65%), and fats (15 to 20%) to supply the energy and structural needs of the body, together with vitamins, minerals, trace elements, and water. These last four substances are important constituents of coenzymes and other metabolic regulators, as well as structural components of the body (Chapter 3). The amounts of the various classes of nutrients included in the diet depend on their role in metabolism. Table 12–3 gives the amounts of food substances required each day and compares them with the amounts found in the body.

**Obesity**

Obesity[2] may be the most serious health problem in the United States. Ten to 15% of our children are overweight and 80% of all overweight children become overweight adults. Obesity kills indirectly through its complications. Obese people have an increased risk of heart disease, high blood pressure, and adult-onset diabetes. Obesity is more common among women than men. There are also psychological problems associated with obesity, as thin is the image that Americans aspire to and the person who is overweight is made the butt of jokes and shunned.

What causes obesity? Because our eating

---

[2] Obesity and overweight are often used synonymously but they are in fact distinct. **Obesity** is excess fat deposition, whereas overweight is determined by norms on height–weight tables. An individual who is muscular can be overweight without being obese.

**TABLE 12–4  Caloric values for common snacks**

| Food | Amount or average serving | Calories | Food | Amount or average serving | Calories | Food | Amount or average serving | Calories |
|------|---------------------------|----------|------|---------------------------|----------|------|---------------------------|----------|
| "Just a little Sandwich" | | | Fruits | | | Desserts | | |
| Hamburger on bun | 3-in patty | 330 | Apple | 1 medium | 70 | Mince | ⅙ pie | 400 |
| | | | Banana | 1 small | 85 | Pumpkin with whipped | | |
| Peanut butter | 1 tbsp. p. b | 330 | Grapes | 30 medium | 75 | cream | ⅙ pie | 460 |
| Cheese | 1-oz. cheese | 280 | Orange | 1 medium | 70 | Cake: | | |
| Ham | 1-oz. ham | 320 | Pear | 1 | 65 | Chocolate | | |
| Pizza, cheese | ⅛ pie | 180 | | | | layer | 3-in. section | 350 |
| | | | Salted nuts and potato chips | | | Doughnut, sugared | 1 average | 150 |
| Beverages | | | Almonds, fiberts, | | | | | |
| Carbonated drinks, soda, | | | hazelnuts | 12–15 | 95 | Sweets | | |
| root beer, etc. | 6-oz. glass | 80 | Cashews | 6–8 | 90 | Ice cream: | | |
| Pepsi-Cola | 12-oz. glass | 150 | Peanuts | 15–17 | 85 | Plain vanilla | ⅙ qt. | 200 |
| Club soda | 8-oz. glass | 5 | Peanuts, walnuts | 10–15 halves | 100 | Cocolate and | | |
| Chocolate | | | Potato chips | 1 serving | 108 | other flavors | ⅙ qt. | 260 |
| malted milk | 10-oz. glass | 500 | | | | Orange sherbet | ½ cup | 120 |
| Ginger ale | 6-oz. glass | 60 | Candies | | | Sundaes, small | | |
| Tea or coffee, | | | Chocolate bars: | | | chocolate nut | | |
| straight | 1 cup | 0 | Plain, sweet | | | with whipped | | |
| Tea or coffee, | | | milk | 1 bar (1 oz.) | 155 | cream | average | 400 |
| with 2 tbsp. | | | With almonds | 1 bar (1 oz.) | 140 | Ice-cream sodas, | | |
| cream and | | | Chocolate- | | | chocolate | 10-oz. glass | 270 |
| 2 t. sugar | 1 cup | 90 | covered bar | 1 bar | 270 | | | |
| | | | Chocolate | | | Midnight snacks | | |
| Alcoholic drinks | | | cream, | | | for icebox | | |
| Ale | 8-oz. glass | 155 | bonbon, | | | raiders | | |
| Beer | 8-oz. glass | 110 | fudge | 1 piece 1-in. sq. | 90–120 | Cold potato | ½ medium | 65 |
| Highball (with | | | Caramels, plain | 2 medium | 85 | Chicken leg | 1 average | 88 |
| ginger ale) | 8-oz. glass | 185 | Hard candies, | | | Milk | 7-oz. glass | 140 |
| Manhattan | average | 165 | Lifesaver type | 1 roll | 95 | Roast beef | ½ in. × 2 in. × | |
| Martini | average | 140 | Peanut brittle | 1 piece 2½ × | | | 3 in. piece | 130 |
| Wine, muscatel | | | | 2½ × ⅜ in. | 110 | Cheese | ¼ in. × 2 in. × | |
| or port | 2-oz. glass | 95 | | | | | 3 in. piece | 120 |
| Sherry | 2-oz. glass | 75 | Desserts | | | Leftover beans | ½ cup | 105 |
| Scotch, | | | Pie: | | | Brownie | ¾ in. × 1¼ in. | |
| bourbon, rye | 1½-oz. jigger | 130 | Fruit | ⅙ pie | 375 | | × 2¼ in. | 140 |
| | | | Custard | ⅙ pie | 265 | Cream puff | 4-in. diam. | 450 |

Source: Helen S. Mitchell *et al. Cooper's Nutrition in Health and Disease*, 15th ed. (Philadelphia, 1968), pp. 282–83. Data provided by Smith, Kline, and French Laboratories.

habits and appetite patterns are established when we are young, and our caloric demand declines with decreasing activity and age, there is a strong tendency to put on weight. Only a small percentage of the population is obese because of hormonal or inherited tendencies, and these should be diagnosed and treated by a physician. Most obesity is due to overeating and lack of exercise. An excess caloric intake of only 10 Calories per day can lead to an increase of 1 to 2 pounds in weight per year! The "snack" of a chocolate bar, the highball, the chocolate eclair, have more calories than we tend to realize (these three alone are equal to the Calories in a serving of roast beef, two potatoes, and six eggs! (Table 12–4).

What controls our eating habits? The appetite center or appestat in the hypothalamus of the brain regulates how much we eat in much the same way that the thermostat regulates room temperature. The stimuli that activate the appestat are not known, but it could be a drop in the glucose concentration of the blood, a temperature drop in the body, a change in the metabolism of the fat cells, or a decrease in the concentration of amino acids in the blood plasma. Consciously or unconsciously, due to emotional stress the appestat may be

**TABLE 12–5 Desirable weights in pounds for people 21 or over***

| Men | | | | Women | | | |
|---|---|---|---|---|---|---|---|
| Height† Ft. In. | Small frame | Medium frame | Large frame | Height† Ft. In. | Small frame | Medium frame | Large frame |
| 5 2 | 112–120 | 118–129 | 126–141 | 4 10 | 92– 98 | 96–107 | 104–119 |
| 5 3 | 115–123 | 121–133 | 129–144 | 4 11 | 94–101 | 98–110 | 106–122 |
| 5 4 | 118–126 | 124–136 | 132–148 | 5 0 | 96–104 | 101–113 | 109–125 |
| 5 5 | 121–129 | 127–139 | 135–152 | 5 1 | 99–107 | 104–116 | 112–128 |
| 5 6 | 124–133 | 130–143 | 138–156 | 5 2 | 102–110 | 107–119 | 115–131 |
| 5 7 | 128–137 | 134–147 | 142–161 | 5 3 | 105–113 | 110–122 | 118–134 |
| 5 8 | 132–141 | 138–152 | 147–166 | 5 4 | 108–116 | 113–126 | 121–138 |
| 5 9 | 136–145 | 142–156 | 151–170 | 5 5 | 111–119 | 116–130 | 125–142 |
| 5 10 | 140–150 | 146–160 | 155–174 | 5 6 | 114–123 | 120–135 | 129–146 |
| 5 11 | 144–154 | 150–165 | 159–179 | 5 7 | 118–127 | 124–139 | 133–150 |
| 6 0 | 148–158 | 154–170 | 164–184 | 5 8 | 122–131 | 128–143 | 137–154 |
| 6 1 | 152–162 | 158–175 | 168–189 | 5 9 | 126–135 | 132–147 | 141–158 |
| 6 2 | 156–167 | 162–180 | 173–194 | 5 10 | 130–140 | 136–151 | 145–163 |
| 6 3 | 160–171 | 167–185 | 178–199 | 5 11 | 134–144 | 140–155 | 149–168 |
| 6 4 | 164–175 | 172–190 | 182–204 | 6 0 | 138–148 | 144–159 | 153–173 |

* These figures are based on the person's wearing indoor clothing. For nude weight, women should subtract 2 to 4 pounds; men 5 to 7 pounds. Women between the ages of 18 and 25 should subtract 1 pound for each year under 25.
† Height is measured with shoes on: 1-inch heels for men, 2-inch heels for women.
Source: Metropolitan Life Insurance Company. Derived primarily from data of the Build and Blood Pressure Study, Society of Actuaries, 1959.

turned on or off. Many people overeat because they are bored, frustrated, or unhappy with their family, job, social contacts, and a whole array of other factors. When the caloric intake is less than the daily energy requirement, the body draws on its chemical energy reserves. Carbohydrates (in the form of a glycogen) are used first, then fats (from fat deposits), and finally proteins. The calories from glycogen (of which there is only about one-fourth of a pound in an individual) are used up in a day or two, but stored fat will supply energy for 5 or 6 weeks of life. Because fat donates more energy than does a comparable amount of carbohydrate and protein, even under conditions of prolonged starvation the body's weight loss is gradual (much to the disappointment of those people on crash diets!).

How can we control our weight? There are as you might imagine no magic formulas. Weight control requires intelligence and

will power, and it takes time to reduce weight. First, know what your desirable weight should be (Table 12–5). Second, calculate the calories required to maintain a desirable body weight by using the following formula:

Calories allowed for men: (814 + 36.6W) 0.95
Calories allowed for women: (580 + 31.1W) 0.95
W + desirable weight in kilograms
(A kilogram equals about 2.2 pounds).

Now regulate your caloric intake. A pound of body fat equals 3,500 Calories and on a 1,200-Calorie-a-day diet, the average person will lose a little more than a pound a week—so do not expect miraculous slimming. In addition to calorie counting, make certain your diet is tasteful, varied, and includes milk, meat, vegetable–fruit, and bread–cereal. Do not cut out food you like, just cut down, but remember that high protein content diets aid in weight loss, whereas high carbohydrate ones do not. Cut out snacks!

## Excess vitamins and minerals

In the past 25 years there has been a tendency for people to consume larger and larger quantities of vitamins to prevent or cure diseases. Advocates of the megavitamin approach have claimed to have used vitamins to cure the common cold, as well as schizophrenia. There is little scientific documentation to support such claims. It is difficult to set a normal vitamin requirement; however, it is critical to recognize that vitamins and minerals are used in the body in trace quantities. When the dose is increased, the efficacy and toxicity of these pharmacologic substances must be assessed. Because fat-soluble vitamins, such as vitamins A and D, can be stored in the body, the effects of excessive amounts in the diet are cumulative.

In adults, chronic toxicity of vitamin A results in headache, nausea, vomiting, weakness, and profound psychiatric disturbances. Skin changes occur, such as loss of hair, skin dryness, and there is also liver malfunction.

Large doses of vitamin D are also toxic. Ingestion of 10,000 IU/day (10 times the RDA) produced weakness, anorexia, vomiting, diarrhea, hypercalcemia, and impaired renal function. Table 12–6 gives information regarding the role of vitamins in metabolism, the deficiency diseases that result from their absence or insufficiency in our diet, the sources of vitamins, and the estimated safe and adequate daily dietary requirement.

Megadoses of minerals, although not so common a practice as megavitamin "therapy," can be potentially dangerous. At least two minerals are consumed in excess by most Americans: sodium and phosphorus. Other minerals recommended in current advertising as a supplement to prevent against nonspecific diseases, such as iron for fatigue, and zinc, copper, and magnesium for deficiency states, must be regarded with suspicion as such states do not exist.

Sodium chloride is required on average

**TABLE 12–6  Vitamins necessary for normal cell functioning**

| Vitamin | RDA* (milligrams) | Dietary sources | Major body functions | Possible outcomes of deficiency | Possible outcomes of excess |
|---|---|---|---|---|---|
| **Water-Soluble** | | | | | |
| Vitamin B₁ (thiamine) | 1.5 | Pork, organ meats, whole grains, legumes | Coenzyme (thiamine pyrophosphate) in the removal of carbon dioxide | Beriberi (peripheral nerve changes, edema, heart failure) | None reported |
| Vitamin B₂ (riboflavin) | 1.8 | Widely distributed in foods | Constituent of two flavin nucleotide coenzymes involved in energy metabolism (FAD and FMN) | Reddened lips, cracks at corner of mouth (cheilosis), lesions of eye | None reported |
| Niacin | 20 | Liver, lean meats, grains, legumes (can be formed from tryptophan | Constituent of two coenzymes involved in oxidation-reduction reactions (NAD⁺ and NADP⁺) | Pellagra (skin and gastriointestinal lesions, nervous, mental disorders) | Flushing, burning and tingling around the neck, face, and hands |
| Vitamin B₆ (pyridoxine) | 2 | Meats, vegetables, whole grain cereals | Coenzyme (pyridoxal phosphate) involved in amino acid metabolism | Irritability, convulsions, muscular twitching, kidney stones | None reported |
| Pantothenic acid | 5–10 | Widely distributed in foods | Constituent of coenzyme A, which plays a central role in energy metabolism | Fatigue, sleep disturbances, impaired coordination, nausea (rare in humans) | None reported |
| Folic acid | 0.4 | Legumes, green vegetables, whole wheat products | Coenzyme (reduced form) in carbon transfer in nucleic acid and amino acid metabolism | Anemia, gastrointestinal disturbances, diarrhea, red tongue | None reported |
| Vitamin B₁₂ | 0.003 | Muscle meats, eggs, dairy products | Coenzyme in carbon transfer in nuclei acid metabolism | Pernicious anemia, neurological disorders | None reported |
| Biotin | Not established. Usual diet provides 0.15–0.3 | Legumes, vegetables, meats | Coenzymes in fat synthesis, amino acid metabolism, glycogen formation | Fatigue, depression, nausea, dermatitis, muscular pains | None reported |

at 500 mg/day, but most of us receive much larger doses due to the hidden amounts of sodium in processed foods. Supplementation of our diet is not only unnecessary, it is dangerous. For most of us reducing sodium intake is needed. Sodium chloride increases blood pressure in hypertensive individuals and may contribute to high blood pressure in individuals who have a genetic predisposition to this disease. Excess phosphorus obtained largely through carbonated drinks, milk, and meats can also cause problems especially in bone resorption and

possibly contributes to osteoporosis in the elderly. The evidence, although suggestive, would indicate that phosphorus intake should be reduced. Table 12–7 summarizes the important roles played by minerals in the structure of the body and its metabolic performance.

### Alcohol excess

Since prehistoric times, alcohol has been used by human societies. In moderate amounts, imbibing of alcohol is a socially

accepted custom in many parts of the world. In the United States (and elsewhere), the consumption of alcoholic beverages is probably the most unrecognized nutritional excess. Alcoholic beverages are produced by yeast fermentation of carbohydrates such as sugar in fruit juices or other plant extracts. Barley, corn, rye, potatoes, and rice cannot be fermented directly by yeast, and therefore, they first must be germinated, a process known as malting. Fermentation can continue until the alcohol content is approximately 14%, at which point the yeast

**TABLE 12–6 Vitamins necessary for normal cell functioning (cont'd)**

| Vitamin | RDA* (milligrams) | Dietary sources | Major body functions | Possible outcomes of deficiency | Possible outcomes of excess |
|---|---|---|---|---|---|
| Choline | Not established. Usual diet provides 500–900 | All foods containing phospholipids (egg yolk, liver, grains, legumes) | Constituent of phospholipids. Precursor of neurotransmitter acetylcholine | None reported for humans | None reported |
| Vitamin C (ascorbic acid | 45 | Citrus fruits, tomatoes, green peppers, salad greens | Maintains intercellular matrix of cartilage, bone, and dentine. Important in collagen synthesis | Scurvy (degeneration of skin, teeth, blood vessels, epithelial hemorrhages) | Relatively nontoxic. Possibility of kidney stones |
| **Fat-Soluble** | | | | | |
| Vitamin A (retinol) | 1 | Provitamin A in green vegetables. Retinol in milk, butter, cheese, margarine | Constituent of rhodopsin (visual pigment). Maintenance of epithelial tissues | Xerophthalmia (keratinization of ocular tissue), night blindness, permanent blindness | Headache, vomiting peeling of skin, anorexia, swelling 6 long bones, liver damage |
| Vitamin D | 0.01 | Cod liver oil, eggs, dairy products, margarine | Promotes bone growth, mineralization. Increases calcium absorption | Rickets (bone deformities) in children. Osteomalacia in adults | Vomiting, diarrhea, weight loss, kidney damage |
| Vitamin E (tocopherol | 15 | Seeds, green leafy vegetables, margarine | Functions as an antioxidant to prevent cell membrane damage | Possibly anemia; never observed in humans | Relatively nontoxic |
| Vitamin K (phylloquinone) | 0.03 | Green leafy vegetables. Small amount in cereals, fruits, and meats | Important in blood clotting (involved in formation of active prothrombin | Deficiencies associated with severe bleeding, internal hemorrhages | Synthetic forms at high doses may cause jaundice |

* Recommended daily allowance, for an adult male in good health.
From "The Requirements of Human Nutrition," by Nevin S. Scrimshaw and Vernon R. Young. Copyright © 1976 by Scientific American, Inc. All rights reserved.

cells are killed. Stronger alcoholic beverages such as whiskey, gin, and vodka are obtained by distillation.

The major nutrient in alcoholic beverages is ethanol, which represents 5% of the calories in the human diet. The caloric food value of ethanol is less than carbohydrate; consequently, substituting the same number of calories in the form of ethanol for carbohydrate causes less weight gain. As a result, alcoholic beverages provide little nutritive value other than calories. But, before one considers going on a diet by increasing the consumption of ethanol, consider the toxic effects. Chronic drinking of alcohol results in a series of progressive changes in the liver. Initially, fatty deposits accumulate, then there is liver inflammation (**hepatitis**), and finally there is cirrhosis. Cirrhosis of the liver is the seventh leading cause of death in the United States.

Alcohol, when swallowed, is absorbed in the stomach, passing into the bloodstream and carried to the liver. Ninety-five percent of the alcohol is metabolized in the liver, and the remainder is excreted unchanged in urine and breath. This unmetabolized alcohol forms the basis of breathalyzer tests for drunk driving. Upon reaching the liver, the alcohol is metabolized by the enzyme alcohol dehydrogenase yielding acetaldehyde, which can be further metabolized to carbon dioxide and water and eliminated from the body. With alcohol overload, however, there is a shift in the breakdown of fatty acids for energy. As a consequence, some of the fat that would have been metabolized accumulates. When alcohol is metabolized, fatty acid synthesis increases and protein synthesis decreases. Massive fat droplets accumulate in the liver cells, blocking their normal function, and ultimately leading to their demise. This is **fatty liver disease**. Fatty deposits also occur in the walls of the veins; this reduces blood flow and

**TABLE 12–7 Minerals necessary for normal cell functioning**

| Mineral | Amount in adult body (grams) | RDA* (milligrams) | Dietary sources | Major body functions | Possible outcomes of deficiency | Possible outcomes of excess |
|---|---|---|---|---|---|---|
| Calcium | 1,500 | 800 | Milk, cheese, dark-green vegetables, dried legumes | Bone and tooth formation Blood clotting Nerve transmission | Stunted growth Rickets, osteoporosis | Not reported for humans |
| Phosphorus | 860 | 800 | Milk, cheese, meat, poultry, grains | Bone and tooth formation Acid-base balance, ATP formation, etc | Weakness, demineralization of bone, loss of calcium | Erosion of jaw (fossy jaw) |
| Sulfur | 300 | (Provided by sulfur amino acids) | Sulfur amino acids (methionine and cystine) in dietary proteins | Constituent of active tissue compounds, cartilage and tendon | Related to intake and deficiency of sulfur amino acids | Excess sulfur amino acid intake leads to poor growth |
| Potassium | 180 | 2,500 | Meats, milk, many fruits | Acid-base balance Body water balance Nerve function | Muscular weakness Paralysis | Muscular weakness Death |
| Chlorine | 74 | 2,000 | Common salt | Formation of gastric juice Acid-base balance | Muscle cramps Mental apathy Reduced appetite | Vomiting |
| Sodium | 64 | 2,500 | Common salt | Acid-base balance Body water balance Nerve function | Muscle cramps Mental apathy Reduced appetite | High blood pressure |
| Magnesium | 25 | 350 | Whole grains, green leafy vegetables | Activates enzymes Involved in protein synthesis | Growth failure Behavioral disturbances Weakness, spasms | Diarrhea |
| Iron | 4.5 | 10 | Eggs, lean meats, legumes, whole grains, green leafy vegetables | Constituent of hemoglobin and enzymes involved in energy metabolism | Iron-deficiency anemia (weakness, reduced resistance to infection) | Siderosis (iron deposition in tissues) Cirrhosis of liver |
| Fluorine | 2.6 | 2 | Drinking water, tea, seafood | May be important in maintenance of bone structure | Higher frequency of tooth decay | Mottling of teeth, increased bone density. Neurological disturbances |
| Zinc | 2 | 15 | Widely distributed in foods | Constituent of enzymes involved in digestion | Growth failure Small sex glands | Fever, nausea, vomiting, diarrhea |
| Copper | 0.1 | 2 | Meats, drinking water | Constituent of enzymes associated with iron metabolism | Anemia, bone changes (rare in humans) | |
| Iodine | 0.011 | 0.14 | Marine fish and shellfish, dairy products | Constituent of thyroid hormones | Goiter (enlarged thyroid) | Very high intakes, depress thyroid activity |
| Cobalt | 0.0015 | (Required as vitamin $B_{12}$) | Organ and muscle meats, milk | Constituent of vitamin $B_{12}$ | None reported for humans | Industrial exposure : dermatitis and diseases of red blood cells |

* Recommended daily allowance, for an adult male in good health.

contributes to tissue death. The dead and dying cells trigger an inflammatory response that may be accompanied by pain and a yellowing of the skin (jaundice). Inflammation also results in a compression of the portal vein; this obstructs blood flow, and the number of dying cells is increased further. The progressive destruction of liver cells is accompanied by an increase in the amount of nonfunctional fibrous connective tissue (**cirrhosis**), and as a result the detoxifying power of the liver is reduced.

In chronic alcoholics, vitamin intake as a result of poor diet is reduced. Hepatic stores of folate, vitamins B$_6$ and B$_{12}$, and niacin are depleted, and a critical coenzyme, pyridoxal phosphate, is decreased. Folate deficiency leads to anemia, and neurological symptoms result from reduced levels of thiamin.

The most important therapy for alcoholism is to stop drinking. This may be easier said than done as alcoholism is an addiction. Behaviorial modification and other supportive measures are therefore necessary. In human volunteers fed a high protein and low fat diet and given six drinks of 86 proof alcohol (about 10 oz) daily, there was an eightfold increase in fat deposits in only 18 days. Fortunately, fatty liver without other complications may be reversed by abstinence and a balanced diet. Hepatitis should be treated by hospitalization with replacement of fluid and salts, administration of dextrose, vitamins, and protein. In patients with cirrhosis, similar treatment is given; however, greater care is necessary to avoid renal failure, salt-water imbalance, and brain inflammation.

## 12–7 TROUBLE ALONG THE ALIMENTARY CANAL

Under normal circumstances the passage of food along the alimentary canal is regulated by a variety of nervous and hormonal mechanisms, and eating, swallowing, digesting, and defecating all occur without problem. However, the large volume of over-the-

---

**Box 12B  The fall and rise of nonfood**

The only current way in which we can make nutritional use of cellulose, is to feed grass to cows or other ruminants, and then to eat the beefsteak. Direct degradation with the enzyme cellulase, which is made by bacteria in the cow's stomach, is successful in the laboratory but not commercially.

One biochemist, while looking for a better tire cord material at the American Viscose Corporation, did discover how to make a form of cellulose that was at least edible although nutritionally worthless. O. A. Battista sheared cellulose molecules mechanically in a Waring blender and produced a low-molecular-weight cellulose product that could be used in diet foods in place of flour. It was not absorbed in the digestive tract and had no taste, no calories, no vitamins, no nutritional or food value whatever. Cookies and cakes made with the material would stave off hunger pangs for a few hours, fooling the stomach into equating "full" with "fed." It was hailed by *Life* magazine in 1961 as the answer to the average American's tendency to overeat, but sank into rapid oblivion.

More recently, however, "edible" cellulose has found a use in diet foods and as a substitute for milk and ice cream in milk shakes. The inventor received a promotion and a pay raise, but as is often the case in industrial laboratories, had signed his patent rights away in advance for the token sum of one dollar, making him ineligible to share in any financial bonanza from the use of his product in diet foods. As *Life* concluded, it was somehow fitting that the inventor of nonfood be paid in nonmoney.

From: Life, Cells, Organisms, Population, E. O. Wilson et al Sinauer, 1977

---

counter remedies sold every year for everything from indigestion to constipation testifies to the number of things, real or imagined, that can go wrong.

### Tooth decay

Dental **caries,** or cavities, are the most common human ailment. Certain bacteria ferment sugars and secrete acid, and the acid eats away at the teeth and produces cavities. Development of cavities depends on tooth susceptibility, ability of the saliva to neutralize the acids, and the presence of sugar in the mouth. Rinsing or brushing the teeth after meals helps prevent cavities because

food particles and the acid secretions of the bacteria are removed and salivary secretion enhanced. Pain (toothache) results when destruction has reached nerve endings in the tooth. Unchecked caries may eventually cause an abscess. It pays to take care of the teeth, not only for reduced dental bills, but because tooth loss causes a marked change in the appearance, as the lips and cheeks sink inward, and in nutrition, since the ability to chew depends on the condition of the teeth.

An old gag has the punch line, "The teeth are all right, but the gums have got to go." It bears a grain of truth, for more teeth are lost because of gum disease, especially after age 35, than because of dental caries themselves. The gum tissues surrounding the tooth (**periodontal tissues**) often become inflamed, a condition called **pyorrhea;** the teeth loosen and fall out. Pyorrhea can be caused by the deposition of calculi (bacteria-laden plaques that calcify), improper brushing, trauma from toothpicks and gingivitis (redness or swelling of the gums caused by poor hygiene), deficiencies of vitamins B and C, and bacterial infections such as Vincent's angina (trench mouth).

## Heartburn and indigestion

The condition known as **heartburn** actually has nothing to do with the heart except anatomical proximity. It is caused by a backflow into the lower end of the esophagus of highly acidic gastric juice which irritates the lining of the esophagus and causes a burning sensation. In some individuals this condition is chronic, caused by improper closure of the cardiac constrictor muscle at the junction of the stomach and esophagus. Closure of the cardiac constrictor is normally assisted by pressure in the abdominal cavity (the lower part of the esophagus lies below the diaphragm; Figure 12–1a). If the terminal segment of the esophagus is pushed upward through the diaphragm to lie in the thoracic cavity (as occurs in the last 5 months of pregnancy owing to the large size of the fetus), the barrier is not as effective, and there is a tendency for some of the stomach contents to be regurgitated into the esophagus. The stomach acidity leads to the heartburn characteristically present during late pregnancy. It subsides in the last weeks as the fetus moves downward. The tendency for a newborn infant to regurgitate is due to the fact that the lower portion of its esophagus does not lie in its abdominal cavity, so that the constriction between the esophagus and the stomach is weak. Current advertising notwithstanding, an "acid stomach" is both natural and functional. If the stomach were not acid, protein digestion could not begin. However, heartburn

---

### Box 12C Ulcers: the price of success

Peptic ulcers occur at any age, but most often they develop at about the age of 30 to 35. About four times as many men develop ulcers as women. There is a strong relationship between ulcers and personality. Ulcer victims are ordinarily conflict-ridden, hard-driving, fast-eating, superiority-craving individuals; they are more of the action type than the phlegmatic, introspective sort. The highest frequency of ulcers occurs in people under pressure: bus drivers, taxi drivers, executives in the business world.

About fifteen years ago some interesting experiments were initiated to investigate the cause of ulcers. Monkeys were trained to avoid an electric shock by depressing a lever, a learning situation that was an easy task for them to master. Although the monkeys learned well, they often died of severe peptic ulcers. Further tests showed that if a monkey was restrained in a chair and shocked at intervals, it developed no ulcers. To clarify the situation, a pair of monkeys were linked to each other by an electrically wired floor and given shocks simultaneously. Thus the treatment administered was exactly the same for each of them. However, one monkey had a lever which would turn off the shock, but the other monkey had a dummy lever; both monkeys received the same number of shocks, but only one of them, the "executive" monkey, could turn off the shock. The executive monkey alone developed ulcers. (Note that the executive monkey received no warning of the shocks to come.)

These studies suggest that physical stress (shocks in this case) is itself not a major factor in ulcer formation, but that psychological or emotional factors are. Of critical importance is the cyclic character of the emotional stress; with 6 hours on and 6 hours off, ulcer development was maximum. Continuous stress, it would appear, produces a kind of stable adjustment to the situation, consequently ulcers tend not to develop.

More recent investigations have attempted to separate the psychological and physical factors involved in the production of stomach ulcers, using rats. Like the monkeys, two rats received electric shocks simultaneously through electrodes placed on their tails. One of the rats heard a beeping tone a few seconds before the shock so that it could predict when the shock would occur, whereas the other received no warning signal. Rats hearing the warning beep developed severe ulceration, whereas those that received shocks without warning developed no ulcers. Hence the psychological effect of predictability rather than the shock itself determined ulcer severity. If the animal was provided with a lever by which it could avoid and escape, that is, cope with, the shock after the warning beep, ulceration was much less severe.

The latter result was apparently opposed to that obtained with monkeys. This contradiction may be explained by the effects of feedback on coping behavior, that is, if an animal is able to cope with a shock by turning it off, it is obtaining positive reinforcement or so-called relevant feedback from its environment. If the animal attempts to cope with the shock and gets some shock anyway, as did the executive monkeys, it is getting negative reinforcement or poor relevant feedback from its environment; this produces anxiety, the stressor stimulus that ultimately leads to peptic ulcers. If the animal is not offered the opportunity to cope with shock, that is, it gets the shock and can do nothing about it, it is not getting positive or negative feedback. The psychological stress is correspondingly reduced, and although the animal is in a stressful situation, ulcer development is reduced because the total amount of stress is reduced.

In a similar situation, people given inescapable shocks but who think they can avoid them by clenching their fist or pressing a button showed less emotional arousal than those given the same shocks, also asked to press a button or clench a fist, but who understand that the shocks are unavoidable. Those who thought they had control over the shock saw their responses as producing relevant feedback—as positively reinforcing—whereas in contrast people who thought they were helpless saw their responses as producing no relevant feedback.

It has further been found that animals receiving positive feedback, that is, those able to avoid and escape shock, show an increase in the levels of nervous transmitter substances (norepinephrine) in the brain, whereas their helpless counterparts receiving the same shocks show a decrease. Decreased levels of nervous transmitters in the brain are suspected causes of nervous depression and consequent inability to cope. Thus, initial helplessness in a particular situation may induce biochemical changes in the nervous system; these intensify depressed behavior and the inability to cope could be perpetuated in the nervous system in a vicious cycle.

Once ulcers develop, how can they be treated? Treatment of ulcers involves attempts to reduce the secretion of gastric juice by administration of drugs that block the nervous stimuli for acid secretion. If this does not work, the treatment is to surgically cut the vagus nerve, the principal stimulatory nerve to the secretory portion of the stomach. How can ulcers be controlled without resort to surgery? The simplest method is often the most difficult: avoidance of a stressful environment. Change of job and way of life often help, as do frequent feedings of a bland diet containing milk and milk products and complete abstinence from stimulants such as tobacco, alcohol, and coffee.

can usually be relieved by drinking a solution of an alkaline substance such as bicarbonate of soda.

**Indigestion** is common when one is emotionally upset. Secretion of gastric juice by nervous reflex is inhibited by such emotions as anger and fear, so that it is no wonder digestion is impaired when we are under emotional stress.

### Peptic ulcers

Peptic ulcers are small, craterlike holes eroded in the walls of the stomach (where they are called **gastric ulcers**) or the small intestine (**duodenal ulcers**) and are estimated to affect 1 of 10 adults in the United States; most victims are men. There is some correlation between stress and ulcer development (Box 12B). Ulcers result from insufficient secretion of mucus and oversecretion of gastric juice in the stomach; this erodes the mucosal wall and may perforate the stomach or duodenum itself, causing **peritonitis**[3] and bleeding (hemorrhage). Most commonly a peptic ulcer is found in the duodenum, just beyond the stomach. The pain associated with a duodenal ulcer probably results from irritation of exposed nerve fibers and muscle cells in the region of the ulcer; muscle spasms initiated by acid acting on the muscle may be contributing factors. Ingestion of milk, alkali, and food may temporarily relieve the pain, since these substances tend to buffer the acid in gastric juice and also to delay stomach emptying. The burning abdominal pain in ulcer sufferers generally begins 2 to 3 hours after eating, when unbuffered acid begins to enter the duodenal region.

### Gallstones, bile, and jaundice

Bile is a complex fluid: it contains the pigments **bilirubin** (brown-red) and **biliver-**

---

[3] Peritonitis is a bacteria-induced inflammation of the lining of the body cavity; prior to the advent of antibiotics, it was almost always fatal.

din (green), which are breakdown products of hemoglobin; a variety of bile salts; and some cholesterol. If the bile duct is obstructed or if the gallbladder, in which bile is stored, has been removed surgically, absorption and digestion of fat are impaired. The bile pigments give the feces their characteristic brown color; thus, bile-duct obstruction, liver damage, or a blood disorder such as anemia (often caused by a lack of hemoglobin) may be reflected by chalky or grayish feces since the bile pigments cannot be poured into the intestine. Occasionally the bile pigments accumulate in the blood because they cannot be excreted and give the skin a yellowish cast—a condition known as **jaundice** (*jaune*—yellow; Fr.). Jaundice has various origins: obstruction of the bile duct, damage to the liver cells caused by cirrhosis, hepatitis, toxic substances such as poisons or alcohol, and excessive red cell destruction due to pernicious anemia or malaria. Since the causes are so varied, treatment of jaundice must be adjusted to its mode of production.

Perhaps the most common ailment involving bile is the condition known as **gallstones.** It is normal for bile in the gallbladder to be concentrated 5 to 10 times by the resorption of water, and under ordinary circumstances the concentrated bile contains no deposits. On occasion, precipitation of crystals of cholesterol occurs, and these are combined with bile salts and bile pigments to produce gallstones. These pretty, yellow-green-tinted gallstones may produce pain and can block the bile duct, thereby stopping the flow of bile into the intestine and seriously impairing the digestion and absorption of fat. Some gallstones pass out with undigested food, but the obstructive kind must be removed by surgery.

## Appendicitis

The blind-ending sac at the tip of the cecum, the **vermiform appendix** (Figure 12–1), is a lymphoid organ that does not perform any digestive function in human beings. Al-though it protects against infection, it may become infected itself with bacteria from the rest of the gut, producing an inflamed condition called **appendicitis.** The condition can be treated with antibiotics, or the appendix may have to be removed surgically. The danger of appendicitis is that the infected appendix may burst, spewing its bacterial contents into the body cavity and causing peritonitis.

## Terminus: constipation, diarrhea, and colitis

The feces eliminated from the body generally are soft and columnar. If emptying is delayed, there is excessive water absorption, and the fecal matter becomes dry and hard, causing difficulty in evacuation, a condition known as **constipation.** Constipation may also be caused by such emotions as fear, anxiety, or fright, which inhibit the defecation reflex. The headaches and other symptoms that accompany constipation result not from toxins or poisons absorbed from the feces, but from mechanical distension of the rectum. Similar symptoms appear under experimental conditions if the rectum is stuffed with a nontoxic substance such as cotton or an inflated balloon.

The walls of the rectum contain blood vessels. Occasionally, owing to constipation, abdominal pressure (as in pregnancy or severe obesity), or hereditary predisposition, these vessels enlarge, producing **hemorrhoids.** Hemorrhoids may be external or internal and can cause pain and bleeding.

If the contents of the colon are moved too rapidly, there is less time for water absorption, and the fecal materials reaching the rectum are more fluid—a condition known as **diarrhea.** Diarrhea, characterized by loose and frequent evacuations, may result from irritation of the lining of the colon due to the presence of dysentery bacteria, irritants in the food (such as prunes, which stimulate intestinal movements), or toxic substances. Prolonged or severe diarrhea may cause excessive water loss or **ulcerative colitis**, owing to rapid flow of digestive juices from the small intestine into the colon. This may, in turn, lead to ulcers in the colon wall.

## SUMMARY

1. Digestion is the process during which food is broken down from complex, insoluble substances into simple, soluble ones. It takes place in the digestive tract, which also absorbs the soluble materials and eliminates residues.

2. The digestive tract secretes mucus and enzymes.

3. Peristalsis moves food along the tract from mouth and pharynx via the esophagus to the stomach, to the small and large intestines, and to the rectum, from which feces are expelled.

4. Carbohydrate digestion begins in the mouth.

5. In the stomach, food is churned and subdivided to chyme in an acidic medium. Hydrolytic digestion of proteins to polypeptides and fats to fatty acids begins.

6. In the small intestine, protein, carbohydrate, and fat digestion continue in an alkaline medium. Products of the liver and pancreas aid in digestion and empty into the duodenum. The duodenum, ileum, and jejunum have a large surface area for absorption owing to their lining of villi and the microvilli of epithelial cells. Absorption occurs by active transport as well as diffusion.

7. Amino acids and sugars enter the bloodstream via the capillaries of the villus and are carried directly to the liver via the hepatic portal system. Fats, as fatty acids and glycerol, are recombined to neutral triglycerides and enter the lymphatic system via the lacteals of the villi.

8. The gastrocolic and duodenocolic reflexes result in emptying of the bowels (colon and rectum) via the anus.

9. The energy demands of the body are measured in terms of heat (calories) as the

metabolic rate. The metabolic rate and caloric requirements vary with sex and daily activity. Energy is usually supplied by fats and carbohydrates, and proteins supply energy as well as building-block materials for structural growth and repair.

**10.** Unlike carbohydrates and fats, proteins cannot be stored. So-called complete proteins generally come from animal sources, whereas plants are lower in protein and usually incomplete in their amino-acid content.

**11.** We need to eat a well-balanced diet containing fats, carbohydrates, and proteins as well as vitamins, minerals, trace minerals, and water.

**12.** The digestive process is normally regulated by hormones and nerves.

**13.** Disorders of the digestive system can include tooth decay (caries), pyorrhea, heartburn, indigestion, peptic ulcers, peritonitis, jaundice, gallstones, appendicitis, constipation, diarrhea, and hemorrhoids. Some of these, particularly heartburn and ulcers, can be aggravated by psychological factors that produce increased acid secretion by the stomach.

## KEY WORDS

| | | | | |
|---|---|---|---|---|
| digestion | submucosa | adipose tissue | periodontal tissue | gallstones |
| digestive tract | bolus | rectum | pyorrhea | vermiform appendix |
| gut | peristalsis | anal sphincters | heartburn | appendicitis |
| alimentary canal | feces | bowels | indigestion | constipation |
| gastrointestinal (GI) tract | hydrolysis | gastrocolic reflex | gastric ulcers | hemorrhoids |
| fistula | absorption | duodenocolic reflex | duodenal ulcers | diarrhea |
| muscle tonus | villus (villi) | metabolic rate | peritonitis | obesity |
| mucosa | microvilli | basal metabolic rate (BMR) | bilirubin | hepatitis |
| | lacteal | protein sparing | biliverdin | fatty liver disease |
| | triglycerides | caries | jaundice | ulcerative colitis |

## TOPICS FOR REVIEW AND DISCUSSION

1. What is digestion? What is its significance to human nutrition?

2. Discuss the structure of the digestive tract and how the structure of specific regions is related to their functions.

3. What is the significance of Beaumont's experiments?

4. How does defecation differ from excretion?

5. Why does the stomach not digest itself?

6. How is the structure of the mucosa related to its absorptive function?

7. Defend the contention that the gut is outside the body.

8. In what ways are digestive enzymes involved in human nutrition?

9. Describe the role of the liver in digestion.

10. How are proteins digested in the human digestive tract?

## Bad Heart Would Have Killed Lincoln, Doctor Says

"President Abraham Lincoln had a bad heart and probably would have died in office even if he had not been assassinated," a doctor says. Although his diagnosis is based on circumstantial evidence, Dr. Harold Schwartz feels certain that Lincoln suffered from a genetic defect known as the Marfan Syndrome. Indications of the syndrome are abnormally long arms and legs, a sunken chest, crossed eyes and a leaking heart valve.

Lincoln had the long arms and legs, the sunken chest, frequent crossing of the eyes, and most likely also had a leaking heart valve when he went to the Ford Theater. In the last two months of his life, Lincoln became easily fatigued, suffered frequent headaches and was bedridden for a time. Schwartz says this is an indication that Lincoln's heart was failing. During this period Lincoln told a friend, "I am very unwell now. My hands and feet of late seem to be always cold, and I ought perhaps to be in bed." This is a sign of bad blood circulation, as would be expected with a failing heart.

Reprinted by permission from the Associated Press.

Today, more than one million Americans die annually of disturbances involving blood vessels and the heart—the cardiovascular diseases. Indeed, more than 55% of all such deaths in the United States this year will be caused by such disorders. To understand these problems we must know something about the circulatory system and how it operates.

# 13

# Internal Transport: The Circulatory System

## 13–1 WHY DO WE NEED A CIRCULATORY SYSTEM?

Life arose in the sea. The sea not only spawned tiny blobs of living matter, it also nourished them. The early sea, a dilute organic broth, provided the primitive cells with the raw materials necessary to support their metabolism. The cells received food and, if they were aerobes, oxygen from the fluid environment in which they were suspended. Metabolic trash—carbon dioxide and nitrogenous compounds—natural products of cellular activity, were dumped back into the sea. For the earliest creatures, minute in size, exchanges with the environment were a simple affair: across the cell's plasma membrane, the process of diffusion carried in what was needed and carried off what was not. Diffusion worked well because the exchange surface, the loading and unloading platform, was never very far from the innermost recesses of the cell. Even today, all one-celled and some minute many-celled plants and animals rely on similar mechanisms (Figure 13–1a).

As organisms increased in bulk, becoming structurally more complex and consisting of larger and larger communities of cells, problems of transport arose. The "seafront" exchange surface came to be far removed from those cells lying in the interior—the regions of supply and demand came to lie farther and farther apart. How could food and oxygen in the surrounding sea reach the "landlocked" interior cells, and how could their wastes be carried off to be

dumped outside the body's surface? One mechanism for providing a seafront to land-locked cells was to hollow out the body in the form of a tube and move the environmental fluid in and out. This is the situation in saclike organisms, whose modern representatives are sponges, hydras, sea anemones, and jellyfishes (Figure 13–1b). However, as animal size continued to increase, the simple tube of internal seawater (or fresh water) was no longer enough for efficient exchanges between animal and environment. To allow food and oxygen to reach the cells a considerable distance from the body surface, the tube containing environmental fluid became branched, creating a complicated canal system which assured that exchanges with the fluid environment were possible for most, if not all, cells (Figure 13–1c). Internal cells again obtained a place on the seafront.

Now other problems developed. Having a canal system filled with a portion of the sea might suffice for small, moderately active creatures such as flatworms, but it certainly would not do for bulky, highly active organisms. Efficiency of exchange and maintenance of a more or less constant internal environment are of paramount importance to such organisms; diffusion is simply not effective over great distances, and ebb and flow in a tubular network fall short of adequacy. In the course of time the problem was solved: the internal sea became enclosed in a tubular network, ebb and flow were replaced by a swift continuous one-way stream, and regulatory mech-

anisms gradually evolved for maintenance of internal constancy. The fluid was kept moving by a pumping device—a pulsating vessel or heart. As the fluid circulated past the food-and-oxygen-loading platforms at the body's surface, nutrients and oxygen diffused in, and these were then carried to the cells, where they were received; the cells, in turn, gave up their wastes to the circulating fluid, and at the surface unloading platform these were expelled. The circulating fluid became a trade route for effecting rapid exchanges between the outside and the inside of the body.

Thus, in most of the larger active animals, humans included, specialized regions for nutrient procurement, gas exchange, and waste expulsion, restricted more or less to the body surface, were linked to the countless deep-lying cells by a system of fluid-filled tubes—the **circulatory system.** Once this had occurred, the cells of the body were bathed from within, and such creatures were to a certain degree independent of the watery environment from which they had come. These organisms could move onto the land, and so some of them did. We are but one of those many land creatures that emerged ages ago from the primeval watery habitat.

## 13–2 WHAT DOES THE CIRCULATORY SYSTEM DO?

The circulatory system, including the heart, blood vessels, and blood, is in bulk, twice the size of the liver. If the tubular conduits

FIGURE 13–1 Exchange of materials between cells and the environment. (a) The one-celled animal *Amoeba.* (b) The hydra. (c) The flatworm *Dugesia.*

of your circulatory system were laid end to end, they would stretch one fourth of the way from the earth to the moon—60,000 miles.

The muscular **heart** pumps the blood into the arteries, and these branch like a tree to distribute the cargo of the blood to all parts of the body (Figure 13–2). When blood leaves the left side of the heart, it enters the great artery[1] of the body, the **aorta.** The aorta is about 1 in. wide; it curves upward

[1] Note that an **artery** carries blood away from the heart and a **vein** carries blood to the heart or between other organs (**portal veins,** Figure 12–5). Although the majority of arteries carry oxygenated blood and the majority of veins carry deoxygenated blood, oxygen content cannot be relied upon to distinguish an artery from a vein.

in an arch as it leaves the heart and then runs downward along the backbone into the abdomen. Leading from the aorta are other large arteries that supply blood to the head, the internal organs, the arms, and the legs. These branch into smaller and smaller arteries, and the smallest branches of the arterial system are the microscopic **arterioles.** The arteries are tubes with rela-

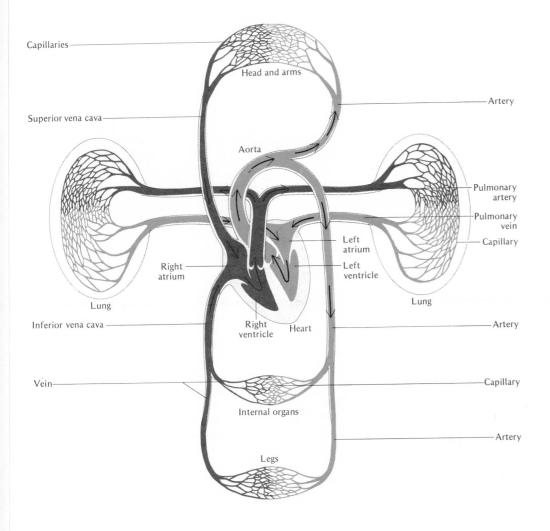

cargo for the cells and the carrying away of the products of cellular metabolism. In a sense, the other components of the circulatory system are secondary plumbing for carrying blood to and from the capillaries. From the capillaries blood enters the smallest veins, the **venules,** and these combine to form larger veins. The veins return the blood to the heart. Veins differ from arteries in that their thin walls are not rich in elastic or muscle tissue, but are composed primarily of connective tissue (Figure 13–3d). As a result these vessels are more extensible and less elastic than the arteries; in addition, the veins are provided with one-way valves, so that backflow of blood into the capillaries is prevented. Heart, artery, capillary, and vein form a closed system of channels through which the internal river of the blood circulates over and over again.

In summary, the circulatory system is a fluid-filled dynamic system that permits the community of cells to perform their individual but interconnected roles and provides a stable environmental medium for the cells of the body.

## 13–3 THE HEART: A REMARKABLE PUMP

### The double pump

An adult human heart is about the size and shape of a clenched fist (Figure 13–4). It is about 5 in. long and 3.5 in. wide and weighs less than 1 lb. (12 to 13 oz). The heart is a muscular pump that keeps blood circulating, and without its continued throbbing, life soon ceases. If blood flow to the brain is cut off for more than 5 seconds, we lose consciousness; after 15 to 20 seconds the muscles twitch convulsively, and after 9 minutes of interrupted circulation the cells of the brain are irreversibly damaged.

The heart lies just behind the breastbone, between the lungs and above the diaphragm. Surrounding the heart is a double-walled sac, the **pericardium.** The fluid in the

tively thick walls containing elastic and muscle tissues (Figure 13–3a–d). The strength and elasticity of the walls prevent them from bursting under pressure, and the muscle permits control of their diameter. The finer branches, the arterioles, have their walls composed almost entirely of smooth muscle and are capable of broadening or narrowing their tubular width. The smallest arterioles branch into tiny **capillaries,** composed of a single layer of flat cells (Figure 13–3b). This

layer not only forms the walls of the capillaries but also lines the other blood vessels and the heart, so that all the blood in the body is contained within a single continuous envelope. There are thousands of miles of capillaries in an adult person, and they permeate every tissue of the body; indeed, no cell is more than a few thousandths of an inch from a capillary. In the capillary the primary function of the circulatory system takes place: the continuous unloading of

FIGURE 13–6 (a) The Starr-Edwards artificial heart valve. (Courtesy of Edwards Laboratories, Santa Ana, California.) (b) X-ray photograph showing two artificial valves implanted in a patient. (Courtesy of World Health Organization.)

(a)

Direction of blood flow

(b)

giving any trouble. However, recent reports indicate that occasionally the valves become infiltrated with fatty materials that cause clot formation; modifications in design are being attempted with a view toward reducing these tendencies.

The wall of the heart consists of three layers: the outer **epicardium,** composed of connective tissue and frequently infiltrated with fat; the inner **endocardium,** lining the cavity of the heart, covering the valves, and continuous with the lining of the blood vessels; and the middle layer, or **myocardium,** consisting of a complex meshwork of muscle. The myocardium is responsible for the ability of the heart to contract.

The arrangement of muscle groups in the wall of the heart is such that when the atrial cells are stimulated both atria contract together, and similarly both ventricles contract together when stimulated. The thick ventricular walls have the muscle arranged in rings, whorls, and loops that are connected to each other. This arrangement is very efficient mechanically: ventricular contraction not only pushes blood out of the ventricles but wrings it out with a twisting motion; the ventricular chambers are the primary elements of the cardiac pump. Before a contraction, the ventricles fill almost completely with blood by elastic recoil from the previous contraction—not, as one might expect, by contraction of the atria themselves. The contraction of the atria completes the transfer of blood, so to speak, by squeezing out the last drops.

### Electrical activity of the heart

A heart completely removed from the body but provided with adequate nutrition will continue to beat rhythmically almost indef-initely. The heartbeat originates in the muscle itself and is therefore said to be **myogenic** (*myo*—muscle, *gennan*—to produce; Gk.). The tempo starts in a region known as the **pacemaker,** or **sinoatrial** (SA), **node,** which is a group of specialized cells located in the posterior wall of the upper part of the right atrium (Figure 13–5a). These cells generate a brief electrical impulse approximately 72 times a minute, and this impulse spreads quickly over the atria, exciting them almost simultaneously, so that both atria contract at the same time. The impulse also reaches another node of specialized muscle cells situated between the atria and ventricles— the **atrioventricular** (AV) **node.** Here the impulse is delayed briefly (0.07 second) and then is conducted across an insulating ring between the atria and ventricles by a special conducting system called the **AV bundle.** The fibers of this bundle are modified car-

FIGURE 13–7 Control of the heartbeat. The parasympathetic (vagus) nerve is inhibitory, and under normal conditions it holds down the beat of the heart by a steady stream of nerve impulses. Excitement, exercise, or emotion triggers impulses from the vasomotor center to accelerate the heartbeat via the sympathetic nerve.

diac muscle cells that transmit impulses six times faster than ordinary cardiac muscle. The AV bundle divides into two main branches, which ramify throughout both the ventricles as myriad fine branches called the **Purkinje fibers.** The cardiac impulse spreads via the Purkinje fibers, and as a result the ventricles contract almost simultaneously, making the heart a very effective pump.

In a normal heart, a second impulse cannot be generated or conducted for at least 0.3 second; during this interval the heart is said to be **refractory.** However, if the conducting pathway is lengthened owing to enlargement of the heart, if there is a decrease in the refractory period owing to disease or drug administration (for example, epinephrine), or if the Purkinje system fails to conduct, then the impulse continues to travel around the heart muscle indefinitely and causes a muscle flutter, or **fibrillation.** Atrial fibrillation is not serious, but if there is ventricular fibrillation, no blood is pumped by the ventricles, and death results. Ventricular fibrillation is easily initiated by an electric shock, especially 60-cycle alternating current, one reason why touching a live household electrical outlet is dangerous.

An isolated heart beats at its own rate without nervous connection. Even when small bits of heart tissue are isolated and placed in a dish containing an artificial nutrient medium, they continue to beat in rhythmic fashion. As we all know, however, within the body the heartbeat is modified according to work load or state of mind. At rest the heart rate slows; during heavy exercise or because of excitement, its pace is stepped up. When we sleep, the heart pumps 1 gal of blood per minute, but if we exercise vigorously, it pumps faster, increasing its output up to 5 gal per minute.

Regulation of the heartbeat occurs via the nervous system. The SA node is supplied by two sets of nerves: **parasympathetic** and **sympathetic** (Figure 13–7). Stimulation of the sympathetic nerve fibers increases the ac

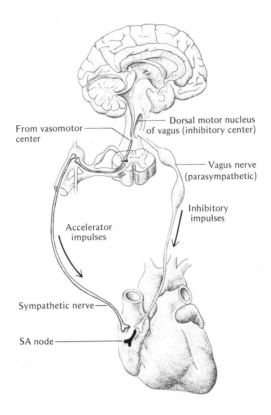

tivity of the heart: the heart rate increases, contractions of the heart muscle are stronger, and more blood flows into the coronary arteries, which supply the heart muscle itself. Increased heartbeat from exercise or excitement is due to discharge of the sympathetic nerves and clearly is a response to the body's demand (real or anticipated) for rapid transit of blood through the circulatory system. The fibers of the parasympathetic system are inhibitory, and they decrease the activity of the heart.

Although the principal regulatory mechanisms of the heart rate are nervous, other factors modify its action. The hormone epinephrine (adrenaline) acts directly on the heart muscle as well as on the nerve fibers to accelerate the heart; carbon dioxide in

creases the pumping rate. Mechanical factors, such as the pressure of blood within the heart, affect the beat.

### Cardiac cycle and the electrocardiogram

Physicians listen to sounds of the cardiac cycle by placing a stethoscope on the left side of the chest about 1 in. below the nipple. The sounds heard can be represented as *lubb, dupp,* pause, *lubb, dupp,* pause. The *lubb* sound is sharp and booming and represents the slamming shut of the atrioventricular valves and the contracting of the ventricles; the *dupp* sound occurs simultaneously with the closing of the semilunar and aortic valves. Peculiar wooshes or swishes heard through the stethoscope are called **murmurs,** and many have no clinical significance. However, some murmurs do represent valve malfunction, such as incomplete closure owing to an enlarged orifice or too great a spread in the valve flaps, and in this case there is backflow of blood. In other cases, the murmur indicates a constricted valvular opening due to a hardening of the valvular flap.

The recording of the electrical activity of the heart during a cardiac cycle is known as an electrocardiogram **(ECG).** Since the heart muscle acts as an electrical conducting system, its activity is detected by placing electrodes on the body (a good conductor of electricity). The electrodes lead to an instrument that records the heart's electrical activity. Such a record of activity can be seen in Figure 13–8. As you can see from Figure 13–8b, the first component of the ECG, the **P wave,** represents electrical activity of the atria preceding contraction (**systole**); following this there is a sharp triangular peak, the **QRS wave,** which represents electrical potentials of the ventricles just prior to contraction; then there is a large, slow wave, the **T wave,** which represents electrical activity just prior to ventricular relaxation (**diastole**).

The most important aspects of an electro-

### BOX 13A  The Artificial Heart

The human heart is a pump that beats 100,000 times a day, and over an average lifetime pumps enough blood through circulatory system tubing to cover 60,000 miles. According to the U.S. Office of Technology Assessment, nearly 75,000 Americans suffer from such significant problems with their heart that they could benefit from either a transplanted heart or an artificial heart. Because there are insufficient numbers of donors of hearts, problems of rejection, and high costs, research on developing mechanical hearts continues.

In December 1982, Dr. William DeVries implanted the Jarvik 7, an artificial heart named for its designer Robert Jarvik, in the first human recipient, Barney Clark. The heart Barney Clark received was made of plastic and aluminum and was powered by electricity. The surgical procedure involved cutting away the heart's lower chambers, the ventricles, leaving the upper chambers, the atria, intact. Dacron fittings were sewn to the aorta, pulmonary artery, and the atria, and then the artificial heart, which is actually two ventricles, was snapped into place "like Tupperware" (see the accompanying figure). Two 6-foot long plastic tubes from each ventricle were arranged so that they emerged from beneath the rib cage to connect the artificial heart to an electrically powered air pump as well as emergency tanks of compressed air and other equipment, all of which were stored on a cart.

The total weight of the awkard external system was 375 lbs. Barney Clark remained alive, supported by the Jarvik 7, for 112 days. In April 1983, however, beset by kidney failure, chronic respiratory problems, inflammation of the colon, and loss of blood pressure, Clark, aged 62, died quietly. The official cause of death was circulatory collapse due to multiorgan failure. The $9,050 artificial heart itself was found to be in good working order, having beat steadfastly nearly 13 million times.

Since that first implant, four other patients have received artificial hearts designed to win a few more months of life, but in each case the recipients developed a serious kidney condition known as tubular necrosis, which generally started within four days of

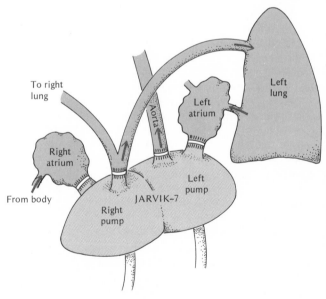

Surgeons cutting away the heart's lower chambers so that the artificial heart (Jarvik 7) can be sewn into place (Left). Diagrammatic representation of the attached artificial heart to the aorta, atria, and pulmonary arteries (Right).

FIGURE 13–8 (a) An electrocardiogram (ECG). (b) The spread of electrical activity across the heart.

**261**

**INTERNAL TRANSPORT: THE CIRCULATORY SYSTEM**

(a)

(b)

surgery and lasted up to two weeks. For reasons that remain obscure, all four experienced impairment of their immune systems in the weeks following surgery, and all suffered from some form of infection, ranging from urinary-tract problems to pneumonia. Experience with the four patients has also shown that the artificial heart batters the red blood cells, causing a form of anemia.

The drawbacks of the artificial heart have led many doctors to conclude that the device should be used only as a temporary measure to sustain a patient until a human donor heart can be found. "I'm not sure that it should be considered a permanent transplant," says famed Houston heart surgeon Michael DeBakey.

Still, few physicians are openly critical of the implants; many point out that pioneering efforts in open-heart surgery and human heart transplants also met with many disappointments and failures. One surgeon has said, "This is a new technical endeavor, and naturally it is going to be fraught with complications"; with a few more cases DeVries and his colleagues will learn to control problems like bleeding.

For his part, DeVries insists that his work is largely experimental and if anything is to be gained from it, more experience is needed. "You must realize that heart transplantation has [been tried on] almost 800 patients, and we're looking at five. We're still in our embryonic beginnings."

Modified from Time, May 6, 1985.

FIGURE 13–9 Abnormal electrocardiograms.

Ventricular fibrillation

Ventricular fibrillation

Complete heart block (atrial rate, 107; ventricular rate, 43)

Atrial fibrillation

Intermittent right bundle branch block

cardiogram are the time relationships between the various waves. Some abnormal examples are shown in Figure 13–9.

## 13–4 CARDIOVASCULAR PLUMBING AT WORK

### Blood pressure

One of the measurements taken during a routine medical examination is arterial blood pressure. The measuring device, a **sphygmomanometer,** consists of an inflatable wrapper (the cuff), a rubber bulb and some tubing, and a glass tube filled with mercury (the manometer) (Figure 13–11). The cuff is wrapped securely around the upper arm and is inflated by means of the rubber bulb. The physician places the bell of the stethoscope on a blood vessel just in front of the elbow and slowly releases the pressure in the cuff. In less than a minute the doctor says, "Quite normal. Your blood pressure is $^{120}/_{80}$." What does this cryptic fraction-style notation indicate? How is blood pressure measured? Why are there two pressures indicated?

With each beat of the heart 2 oz of blood are driven from the ventricles into the elastic arteries. The contraction (systole) of the ventricle acting on the blood causes a rise in pressure. While the ventricle fills with blood, it is relaxed (diastole) and the blood pressure in the ventricle is zero. In the artery receiving blood during systole, there is a rise in pressure, and during diastole the pressure falls (but not to zero). Thus, with each beat of the heart there is a rise and fall in the blood pressure of the artery and a corresponding expansion and contraction of the arterial wall.

When the blood-pressure cuff is inflated, the artery in the upper arm collapses when the pressure applied to the artery externally is greater than the pressure exerted by the blood within the vessel. As the pressure in the cuff is gradually released, the first spurts of blood pass through the artery and cause an intermittent sound that can be heard with the stethoscope. A glance at the manometer at this time shows the maximum pressure in the artery—the **systolic pressure**—and this is recorded as millimeters of mercury. When the cuff pressure is reduced even further, the pressure falls sufficiently low so that blood flows through the artery without any intermittance (the throbbing sounds are no longer heard with the stethoscope). This reading on the manometer corresponds to the **diastolic pressure**—when the heart is resting between contractions and the arteries are contracting by elastic recoil. The diastolic and systolic pressures are recorded fraction-style, with the numerator being the systolic and the denominator being the diastolic pressure. Thus, if the diastolic pressure is 80 and the systolic pressure is 120 mm Hg, the value is written 120/80. There is a wide range of normal pressures: 100 to 140 for systolic, 60 to 90 for diastolic.

BOX 13B  Heart attack

Each year over a million people in the United States succumb
to the nation's number-one killer—heart attack. More than two
thirds of the deaths occur within hours (often minutes) after
the onset of the attack. Many people believe that a heart attack
is an easy way to go—it is quick, simple, painless, and complete;
often forgotten are the many thousands who do not die this
way, but linger on for years, suffering as heart disease cripples
them. What causes heart attack, and why its usual sudden
course?

FIGURE 13–10  The progression of atherosclerosis. (a) Normal artery. (b)
Partial blockage of artery. (c) Severe blockage of artery. (Courtesy of The
American Heart Association.)

(b)

(a)

(c)

In an average lifetime, the heart does enough work to raise a weight of 45 tons to a height of 5 miles. To perform such work its demands for fuel and oxygen are great. Unlike skeletal muscle, the muscle of the heart cannot build up an oxygen debt; it must be continuously supplied with oxygen. Whereas other tissues use only 25% of the oxygen carried to them by the blood, the heart uses 80% of its available supply; there is little margin for safety.

The blood passing through the heart chambers cannot be used to supply oxygen to the heart muscle itself; instead blood is piped directly to the muscle cells by two **coronary arteries,** each about the diameter of a soda straw. The coronary arteries originate from the aorta and wrap themselves around the surface of the heart, ramifying to send small branches to all the muscle cells (Figure 13–4). The networks of each coronary artery do not overlap much. Blood returns to the right atrium by a pocket or trough in the wall of the right atrium, the **coronary sinus,** into which the coronary veins empty.

A heart attack is usually caused by a blockage in the coronary arteries, and the muscle and connective tissue fed by the vessels downstream from the blockage soon become starved of oxygen and die. Such blocking may occur quickly or slowly, but in almost all cases it is associated with atherosclerosis. **Atherosclerosis** is a degenerative condition in which the walls of the arteries are invaded with fatty materials, mainly cholesterol. Eventually these deposits become fibrous and impregnated with calcium, forming plates, or plaques, similar in consistency to bone (Figure 13–10). As the deposits grow, the opening of the blood vessel becomes smaller, until a small blood clot, or thrombus, perhaps no bigger than a BB shot, is able to plug it up. If the blockage is in the coronary artery, the individual suffers a "heart attack" or a "coronary," which often causes death. If damage is not extensive because blockage has affected only a small blood vessel, it is possible that the weakened condition may be only temporary.

It will probably surprise you to learn that if you are over 30 years old you are already carrying a few dead areas in your heart, the scar-tissue remains of such local damage. By the age of 40 you will probably experience a few minor coronary blockages, quite tiny, and often mistaken for indigestion pains. Why does such blockage not always produce a coronary attack? If the blockage is gradual, auxiliary blood vessels usually develop, and mild exercise accelerates the development of these accessory blood vessels. As a consequence new blood-supply routes are made available to cells in the region of the blocked artery, and damage is minimal. Yet the coronary occlusion that kills may not always be large. Most deaths are a result of disturbances in the electrical rhythm of the heart. The dying patch of heart muscle downstream from the occlusion may block normal conduction as if it were a tiny electrical signal. An abnormal rhythm is triggered, and ventricular fibrillation results. A fibrillating ventricle pumps no blood, and if the heart is not defibrillated in minutes, death ensues.

Mercury manometer

Hand bulb

Pressure cuff

Stethoscope

Artery (upper arm)

Artery (lower arm)

(1)   No flow
Pressure in cuff = 120 mmHg

(2)   Flow near end of systole
Pressure in cuff = 115 mmHg

(3)   Flow during most of cycle
Pressure in cuff = 85 mmHg

(4)   Flow is continuous
Pressure in cuff = under 80 mmHg

FIGURE 13–12 Blood pressures and flow rates in various parts of the circulatory system.

**265**

INTERNAL TRANSPORT:
THE CIRCULATORY SYSTEM

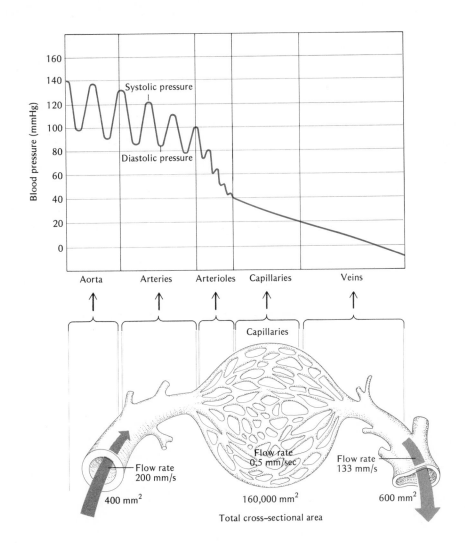

Total cross–sectional area

arteries. The pressure reaches its low point in the veins, especially those near the heart. Why is it that the blood pressure drops as blood is moved farther away from the heart?

The frictional resistance of the walls of the blood vessels slows down blood flow, and the narrower their diameter the greater their frictional resistance. Thus, as blood travels away from the pumping force of the heart and passes through narrower and narrower blood vessels, the frictional forces it encounters cause a decline in the flow rate. This accounts for the drop in blood pressure from artery to capillary. Blood-pressure decline is also related to the larger total cross-sectional area of the capillaries (Figure 13–12).

The diameter of an individual capillary is so narrow, that the blood cells slide sideways in single file. This slow amble of blood through the extensive capillary network allows oxygen, nutrients, and other key materials time to move across the capillary wall into the surrounding fluid-filled tissue spaces. Similarly, wastes move from the cell into the fluid space and into the capillary. (The watery fluid surrounding the cells, which acts as a medium for the loading and unloading, is called **interstitial fluid.**)

Now the blood, laden with cellular wastes, starts its journey back to the heart by moving from the capillaries into the venules. The pressure in the venules and the small veins is quite low because they are even farther away from the pump force of the heart and because of the frictional forces in the capillaries. However, the flow rate in the veins is increased greatly because they have a smaller total cross-sectional area than does the extensive capillary network. It is obvious that the pressure in the veins is not sufficient for return to the heart; also, since we humans are usually in an upright position, a good deal of the blood must be driven uphill. Faced with this pressure deficit, how does blood return to the heart?

The movement of blood toward the heart is effected by what is called the **venous pump.** All the peripheral veins contain valves

If the blood pressure recorded for an individual was 200/120, this would be abnormally high. The cause of this high blood pressure may be decreased elasticity in the walls of the artery, most frequently due to atherosclerosis. The deposition of calcified plaques prevents the artery from stretching during systole and minimizes elastic recoil during diastole. Low blood pressure can be caused by shock, reduced blood volume, or both.

If we look at the blood pressure in the different blood vessels (Figure 13–12), we see a characteristic rise and fall in the arteries, but the average blood pressure decreases continuously as the blood moves farther and farther away from the heart. The pressure is greatest in the aorta, falls off slightly in the arteries, and in the arterioles is about one half that in the arteries. By the time blood reaches the capillaries, the pressure is one fifth that found in the large

Open valve

Direction of blood

Direction of
muscle
contraction

Closed valve

BOX 13C  Bypassing the bypass

Introduced 20 years ago, bypass surgery has become the most commonly performed heart operation in the United States. The purpose of bypass surgery is, quite simply, a way around fat-clogged coronary arteries, thus allowing blood to keep flowing to the heart. The re-routing is done by taking a section of vein from the leg and grafting it into the chest where it provides a detour around the obstruction. In patients with a blockage in the left coronary artery, the principal supplier of blood to the heart, the bypass is the best hope of prolonging life. And, bypass surgery is also the treatment of choice in those individuals who have several coronary arteries clogged. In 10% of the cases, however, the buildup of fatty deposits continues to occur in the newly grafted blood vessel and in 6 months that vessel is completely blocked. In others the process of fatty deposition is slower, but it does occur. The ultimate result is that 5 years after surgery about one half of all bypass patients are no better off than they were before. A second and third bypass may be necessary, but this is risky because the tissues involved are scarred and damaged. To avoid a second bypass, it has been suggested that the first bypass be put off as long as possible by controlling the pain of angina with drugs such as calcium channel blockers or beta blockers.

Alternatives to bypass surgery do exist. In the mid-1970s, an ingenious method of unclogging arteries using an inflated balloon was developed. The procedure called angioplasty is now performed on more than 12,000 patients a year and involves insertion of a narrow tube into the diseased artery until it reaches the clogged area. Then a tiny balloon at the tip of the tube is alternately inflated and deflated so that it flattens the fatty deposits against the walls of the artery and widens the channel. In a Star Wars modification of the balloon technique, a laser is aimed and fired through the tube at the obstruction. The lumps of fat, which literally melt like butter, are then swept up through a vacuum tube.

Techniques, such as bypass surgery and angioplasty, are life-saving treatments but they do pose a significant risk to the patient. The real challenge in combating heart disease is to find a way to prevent or reverse the process of atherosclerosis. Only then can the bypass be bypassed once and for all.

that prevent backflow, allowing the blood to flow only toward the heart (Figure 13–13): In addition, every time a muscle contracts or a limb is moved, the veins are compressed. Since the valves prevent backflow, the muscles are always "milking" the veins and pushing blood in the direction of the heart. Thus, swinging the arms, walking, running, and other body movements all aid in returning blood to the heart. In addition, slight constriction of the muscles in the walls of the veins aids in return flow and prevents pooling of blood in the extremities.

### Exchange of materials across the capillary wall

In a 1-in. cube of muscle, it has been estimated, there are over 1.5 million capillaries. The extensive branching, small diameter, thin walls, and great surface area

FIGURE 13–14 Diagrammatic representation of nutrient and waste movement between the blood and tissue cells. Substances move across the capillary walls primarily by diffusion, and thus depend on the maintenance of a concentration gradient between capillary and interstitial fluid.

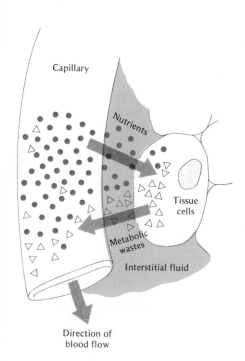

Capillary

Nutrients

Tissue cells

Metabolic wastes

Interstitial fluid

Direction of blood flow

FIGURE 13–15 (a) An electron micrograph showing a cross section of a capillary. The junction of the endothelial cells with an obvious intercellular space is indicated by arrows. In addition, numerous pinocytotic vesicles can be seen in the endothelial cells making up the capillary wall. (Courtesy of K. R. Porter.) (b) Fluid exchange between capillary and tissue space.

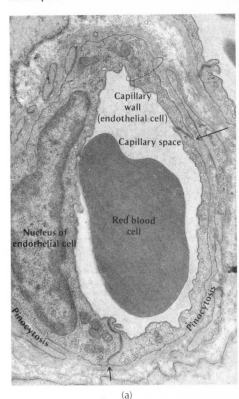

Capillary wall (endothelial cell)

Capillary space

Red blood cell

Nucleus of endothelial cell

Pinocytosis

Pinocytosis

(a)

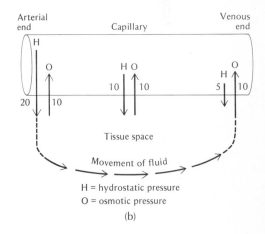

Arterial end

Venous end

Capillary

Tissue space

Movement of fluid

H = hydrostatic pressure
O = osmotic pressure

(b)

of the capillaries ensure that transfers between the cells and the bloodstream occur fairly rapidly.

The walls of the capillary are freely permeable to water and most small molecules; transport of these material across the capillary is primarily by diffusion. Exchanges between the blood (contained in the capillaries) and the tissue cells do not occur directly; the tissue cells are surrounded and bathed by interstitial fluid, which acts as the go-between: substances pass from the blood across the capillary wall into the interstitial fluid and into the cell, or the other way around. Because the movement of materials through the capillary wall involves diffusion, a concentration gradient is required to provide the driving force for the net movement of a substance. The maintenance of this gradient is basically dependent on actively metabolizing tissue cells. Let us see why.

The nutrients dissolved in the blood diffuse out of the capillary and into the tissue

cells via the interstitial fluid. Since nutrients are continuously being utilized by the tissue cells, there is a rather steady removal of these substances from the interstitial fluid, and as a consequence, a gradient is established in which the concentration of nutrients is greater in the blood than in the interstitial fluid or the cells themselves. Conversely, metabolic wastes are continuously produced by the actively metabolizing tissue cells, and as the intracellular concentration increases, these substances move from the cell into the interstitial fluid; this movement, in turn, results in an increased concentration of wastes in the interstitial fluid, and by diffusion these materials enter the capillary. The sequence of events involved in exchanges between capillary and tissue cell is shown in Figure 13–14.

Since fat-soluble materials penetrate the plasma membrane quite easily, these probably pass directly through the capillary wall. Charged molecules (**ions**) and substances that are not fat soluble would have considerable difficulty getting across were it not for the fact that spaces exist between the endothelial cells that form the capillary wall (Figure 13–15). It is believed that these slow-diffuser molecules move through the intercellular spaces by filtration rather than by direct diffusion across the plasma membrane, and thus they exchange more rapidly than would be anticipated from their diffusion characteristics alone. Additionally, the electron microscope reveals that bulk transport of large and small molecules into and out of the capillaries may take place by pinocytosis (Figure 13–15).

In summary, bulk transport (pinocytosis), filtration, and diffusion are the mechanisms whereby dissolved substances move across the capillary walls, and as a result tissue cells exchange useless wastes for essential nutrients.

### Control of fluid movement across the capillary

What determines the direction in which fluids (principally water) move into or out

267

### BOX 13D Stimulus for ailing hearts

A large percentage of heart disease deaths in the U.S. are the direct result of arrhythmias, irregular heart beats. If the potentially dangerous rhythms are detected in time then corrective measures can be taken. Indeed, nearly a million people now rely on artificial pacemakers which can last from six to twelve years.

The artificial pacemaker is a mechanical device that supplies to the heart electrical pulses that give the heart muscle a rhythmic beat. The artificial pacemaker is used when the natural pacemaker, the SA node, fails to deliver an electrical signal that can excite the atria and ventricles to activity. For thousands of individuals it is the gift of life.

In the early 1950s the first artificial pacemakers were introduced. These consisted of an externally worn battery with a connection that ran directly to the heart by wires passed through the skin. Since the heart beats about 40 million times a year, and this would flex the pacemaker wires 80 million times, the problem that most often developed was wire fatigue and breakage. Interruption of the signal by a broken circuit meant heart failure. Recent techniques have gotten around this problem, and at present the wire from the power supply is threaded down the inside of the neck vein, through the vena cava, into the right atrium, through the tricuspid valve, and into contact with the interior wall of the right ventricle (Figure 13–16). The method does not require open-heart surgery and minimizes wire flexion; if the batteries are replaced at regular intervals, a pacemaker can operate for up to 7 years.

The normal heart beats at 70 times each minute; during sleep it drops down to 55 or 60 beats; and during times of stress it may pulsate at 150 beats per minute. Thus for a normal life a person

FIGURE 13–16 The artificial pacemaker. (a) Pacemaker lead passing through a neck vein, vena cava, right atrium, and right ventricle. (b) Two types of pacemakers held in the hand. The one on the right is about the size of a book of matches. In the x-ray film in the background, the larger pacemaker held in the left hand is shown actually implanted. (Courtesy of World Health Organization.)

Subclavian vein

Right atrium

Superior vena cava

Right ventricle

(a)

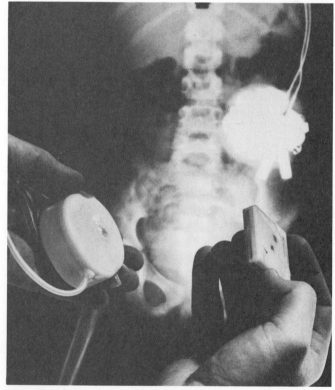

(b)

fitted with an artificial pacemaker should have the capacity for varying the electrical impulses between 55 and 150. Such an elaborate device would be not only costly but more failure-prone than one of a simpler design. In practice, therefore, most pacemakers have three switch positions: slow, normal, and fast. These are controlled by the wearer so that the heart beats approximately in accord with its work load.

The most successful modern artificial pacemaker is a transistorized model that picks up impulses from the patient's own SA node; the signals are amplified, delayed for an appropriate interval, and then sent on to the ventricular muscle. In the event the SA node fails to deliver an electrical signal, the implanted pacemaker switches to its own pulse generator and gives 72 pulses per minute. In cases where the heart is blocked irregularly, the artificial pacemaker works on demand and produces a pulse only when the natural pacemaker fails. Since the electrical pulses from the SA node are best picked up on the outside of the heart, the attachment is relatively simple.

The pacemaker has also been used in a remarkable muscle transplant operation. In this procedure, the latissimus dorsi muscle of the back is stripped from its attachments near the spine, and is slipped into the chest cavity with its nerves and blood supply intact. The muscle is then wrapped around the damaged heart like a towel. After a week of recovery, the transplanted muscle is stimulated with a pacemaker. The procedure itself is remarkable because skeletal muscle, such as that used for the transplant, is very different from cardiac muscle, yet when electrically conditioned by electrical stimulation, it functionally resembles the heart's own muscle. Such a novel approach has several benefits: the borrowed muscle is the individual's own and is not rejected, and the procedure reduces the need for risky open heart surgery.

As one physician put it when discussing pacemakers:

We have had luck. The electrical pulse that stimulates the ventricles happens to be reproducible, using an effect discovered by Luigi Galvani as long ago as 1791. Wrap Galvani's discovery up in some rather commonplace surgical and electrical skill, and you have the present pacemaker. The real achievement would be to match the adaptability of the natural pacemaker with a device linked to the body's own feedback pathways. No one is seriously contemplating that—yet.

of the capillary? The amount of fluid entering or leaving the capillary is determined by the relative differences in magnitude between the hydrostatic (fluid) and osmotic pressures at each end of the capillary. At the arterial end of the capillary, the blood (hydrostatic) pressure is about 30 mmHg and that of the surrounding tissue fluid is 10 mmHg. Thus, the effective hydrostatic pressure tending to drive fluid from the capillary into the tissue spaces is 20 mmHg. Counterbalancing this force is the difference in the colloidal osmotic pressures of the blood and interstitial fluid. Blood contains relatively large amounts of plasma proteins, to which the capillary walls are not readily permeable; consequently, the interstitial fluid is low in the large-molecular-weight proteins. Because of this, the osmotic pressure of the blood at the arteriole end is higher (25 mmHg) than that of the interstitial fluid (15 mmHg). Thus, the effective osmotic pressure, tending to return fluid to the capillary, is 10 mmHg. When both the hydrostatic and the osmotic forces are considered, there is an outward filtration pressure of 10 mmHg (20 − 10 mmHg) at the arteriole end (Figure 13–15b). At the venous end the situation is reversed. The blood pressure at this end of the capillary is 15 mmHg, the tissue fluid pressure is 10 mmHg, and therefore the effective hydrostatic pressure is 5 mmHg. The effective osmotic pressure at the venous end of the capillary is the same as at the arterial end—10 mmHg. Because the osmotic pressure exceeds the hydrostatic pressure at the venous end, tissue fluid is forced back into the capillary. In the middle of the capillary, the hydrostatic and osmotic pressures are about equal, and there is no net movement of fluid (Figure 13–15b).

As long as the osmotic and hydrostatic forces are balanced, there is no net fluid movement (that is, equal quantities of fluid pass into and out of the capillaries); however, any alteration in the balance may allow swelling or shrinking of the tissues. The accumulation of excessive amounts of fluid

FIGURE 13–17 The lymphatic system. (a) Diagram of the relationship between the lymphatic system and the circulatory system. (b) Schematic diagram of the lymphatic system. (c) Detail of blood capillary and lymph vessel.

in the tissue spaces is known as **edema. Shock,** which frequently occurs after surgery, severe burns, injury, or fright, is characterized by increased capillary permeability with escape of blood proteins into the tissue spaces. This reduces the osmotic pressure gradient between the blood and the tissue fluids, return flow is impeded, the blood volume decreases, and, if this continues for an extended time, death can result.

### Lymph and the lymphatic system

The body contains an extensively branched tubular network for carrying off excess amounts of interstitial fluid and returning this to the circulatory system. The tubes of this network are thin-walled, blind-ending vessels called **lymphatics,** and they merge to form larger and larger vessels. Eventually, the largest of these drain into two large ducts, the **right lymphatic duct** and the **thoracic duct,** which empty into the blood system in the region of the neck (Figure 13–17). While it is in the lymphatic system, interstitial fluid is called **lymph.** The essential difference between circulatory fluid (plasma) and lymph is that plasma is much richer in proteins.

The lymphatics play an important role in returning fluid and protein to the circulatory system. As we have noted, the capillary wall is slightly permeable to protein; as a consequence of this, there is a slow but steady loss of protein from the blood into the interstitial fluid surrounding the cells. However, such proteins cannot return to the circulatory system across the capillary wall because there is insufficient tissue fluid pressure to move them in that direction. The lymphatics themselves provide the mechanism for returning proteins to the blood, since they are quite permeable to these materials (Figure 13–17c). In fact, if such a return did not occur, the osmotic pressure of the blood would fall so low that blood volume would continuously be reduced and death would occur in less than

(a)        (b)        (c)

24 hours. Failure to reduce the buildup of proteins in the interstitial fluid interferes with the mechanism that moves water from the regions surrounding the tissue cells into the venous end of the capillary, there is a net movement of fluid into the tissue spaces, and edema results. The grotesque swelling of limbs seen in elephantiasis (Figure 13–18) is caused by the blockage of the draining lymph channels by a parasitic worm called filaria.

What pushes the lymph along the extensive network of lymphatic ducts to the point where it drains into the blood system in the

neck? Lymph flows slowly in the lymph vessels, much more slowly than the blood in its vessels. Two factors determine how fast lymph flows in the lymphatics: (1) tissue pressure and (2) the lymphatic pump. Wherever the tissue fluid pressure rises above normal, the faster is the flow of lymph into the lymphatics. This greater movement of fluid enhances the flow rate of lymph. The **lymphatic pump** is not actually a muscular organ but is the compression exerted during body movement by muscle and other tissues surrounding the lymph vessels. It operates in the following way. Lymph vessels, like

FIGURE 13–18 A normal leg compared with that of a patient with elephantiasis.

FIGURE 13–19 Lymph nodes and drainage of an infected area.

**271**

INTERNAL TRANSPORT:
THE CIRCULATORY SYSTEM

Leg with
elephantiasis

Normal
leg

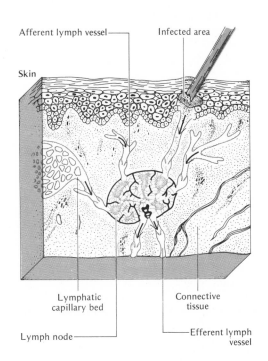

Afferent lymph vessel

Infected area

Skin

Lymphatic
capillary bed

Connective
tissue

Lymph node

Efferent lymph
vessel

veins, have one-way valves that permit flow in only one direction. As each lymph vessel is compressed, fluid is forced toward the neck region and flows into the venous system. Exercise, running, or walking assists in pumping lymph from the tissue spaces back into the bloodstream.

At certain points of juncture of small lymph vessels with large ones (the groin, armpits, and neck, in particular) are located lumpy masses of cells known as **lymph nodes** (Figure 13–19). These play an important role in the body's defense against disease by producing lymphocytes and antibodies and by filtering out bacteria and foreign particles. The **lymphocytes** are specialized ameboid white blood cells that can engulf foreign particles (Chapter 14). All the lymph that drains from the tissue spaces to return to the channels of the circulatory system must pass through the filters of the lymph nodes. In this way lymph is continuously cleansed of foreign debris and bacteria and the blood is scrubbed clean and pure. It is not unusual that during a severe infection the lymph nodes become inflamed, for they are engaged in protective battle. For example, an infection in the finger or hand may cause a lymph node in the armpit to swell and to become tender and painful. Swollen glands are sometimes in reality enlarged lymph nodes.

Since the lymphatic network is such an extensive drainage system (Figure 13–17), you can readily appreciate the reason why it is often involved in metastatic cancer. Once cancer cells have invaded the lymph vessels, they may become lodged and proliferate in the nodes. If diagnosed in time, there is the possibility that removal of the downstream lymph ducts and nodes can prevent further spread of such a cancer.

## SUMMARY

**1.** The evolution of circulatory systems was probably linked with increase in body size.

**2.** Blood flows from heart → aorta → arteries → arterioles → capillaries → venules → veins and back to the heart.

**3.** Arteries conduct blood away from the heart, veins conduct blood toward the heart or between other organs (portal veins).

**4.** In the four-chambered heart, one-way blood flow is directed from right atrium to right ventricle by the tricuspid valve, and from right ventricle to pulmonary artery by the semilunar valve. From the pulmonary artery blood flows to the lungs.

**5.** From the lungs, blood returns to the left atrium via the pulmonary vein. One-way blood flow from left atrium to left ventricle is controlled by the bicuspid valve, while the aortic valve directs flow from left ventricle to aorta.

**6.** The right side of the heart is the pulmonary pump, the left side is the systemic pump.

**7.** The heart valves operate passively to prevent backflow of blood when the heart contracts. Diseased valves can be replaced with artificial materials.

**8.** The heart wall consists of epicardium, endocardium, and the muscular myocardium. Both atria contract together, as do both ventricles.

**9.** The heart beat is myogenic, that is, it is generated electrically by specialized muscle cells: the pacemaker, or sinoatrial, node and the atrioventricular node. Fast-conducting muscle cells, called the AV bundle, radiate from the AV node as Purkinje fibers and help to coordinate ventricular beat. Transistorized artificial pacemakers reproduce or regulate the electrical activity of faulty or failing SA nodes.

**10.** During a normal heartbeat cycle, there is a refractory period; if this period is decreased, fibrillation ensues. Ventricular fibrillation is especially dangerous and can be caused by 60-cycle electric current.

### BOX 13E  The death of Lenin

It was a bitter cold day in Gorki, a suburb of Moscow. The time was January 1924. Early that afternoon the body of Lenin, leader of the Russian Revolution, had been brought into the autopsy room. Ten physicians and Joseph Stalin were in attendance. Scalpels and bone scissors cut through the skull and revealed Lenin's brain. The cause of death was clear: the entire left side of the brain was destroyed. A closer examination of the brain showed the reason. A main artery serving an extensive portion of the brain was blocked, and the tissue on the downstream side of the occlusion had died of starvation. As the scalpel blade cut into the blocked artery the knife struck something hard and gritty, as if it were cutting a piece of stone. What was once a resilient, rubberlike artery was now a solid, bonelike rod.

The death of Lenin was not totally unexpected; this was his third stroke. He succumbed to a degenerative disease of the circulatory system called atherosclerosis (commonly referred to as "hardening of the arteries"). Even today over 28 million people in this country have some form of cardiovascular disease. Among your friends, relatives, the people that live in your home town and your county, one out of every seven is afflicted by cardiovascular disease.

**11.** Nervous control of the heart beat is via parasympathetic (inhibitory) and sympathetic (stimulatory) nerves, which act on the SA node. Hormones (epinephrine, or adrenaline), $CO_2$, and blood pressure may also affect the rate of heart beat.

**12.** Heart murmurs may represent the malfunctioning of valves.

**13.** The electrical activity of the heart can be recorded as an ECG. Electrically, each complete heartbeat cycle shows as a P wave (prior to atrial contraction or systole), a QRS wave (prior to ventricular contraction), and a longer, slower T wave (reflecting ventricular relaxation, or diastole).

**14.** Heart attacks are usually caused by blockage of the coronary arteries owing to atherosclerosis.

**15.** Blood pressure is taken with a sphygmomanometer and reflects pumping efficiency of the heart. Systolic pressure reflects heart contraction; diastolic pressure reflects heart relaxation. High pressures may be caused by atherosclerosis, low pressures by shock and/or reduced blood volume. Pressure is greatest in the arteries and least in the veins. The return of venous blood to the heart is assisted by valves in the peripheral veins and contractions of body muscle; together these constitute the venous pump.

**16.** Exchange of nutrients and wastes between tissue cells and blood occurs by diffusion, filtration, and bulk transport across the capillary and tissue cell walls via the interstitial fluid. Direction of fluid movement across the capillary wall is determined by the relative balance between hydrostatic and osmotic pressures. Alteration of this balance may cause edema.

**17.** Excess interstitial fluid is returned to the blood via the extensive lymphatic system. When in lymphatic vessels, the fluid is called lymph; it is lower in proteins than blood plasma. Tissue pressure and the lymphatic pump (muscular and tissue compression) as well as valves assist the flow of lymph in the lymphatics.

**18.** Lymph nodes contain lymphocytes and are important in fighting infection and disease.

## KEY WORDS

| | | |
|---|---|---|
| | systemic pump | diastole |
| | epicardium | coronary arteries |
| circulatory system | endocardium | coronary sinus |
| heart | myocardium | atherosclerosis |
| aorta | myogenic | sphygmomanometer |
| artery | pacemaker or sinoatrial (SA) node | systolic pressure |
| vein | atrioventricular (AV) node | diastolic pressure |
| portal veins | AV bundle | interstitial fluid |
| arterioles | Purkinje fibers | venous pump |
| capillaries | refractory period | ions |
| venules | fibrillation | edema |
| pericardium | parasympathetic nerve | shock |
| atrium | sympathetic nerve | lymphatics |
| ventricle | murmurs | right lymphatic duct |
| tricuspid valve | ECG | thoracic duct |
| pulmonary or semilunar valve | P wave | lymph |
| pulmonary pump | systole | lymphatic pump |
| bicuspid valve | QRS wave | lymph nodes |
| aortic valve | T wave | lymphocytes |

## TOPICS FOR REVIEW AND DISCUSSION

1. List the major functions of the circulatory system.

2. Why do animals of large dimensions require a more complex circulatory system than smaller ones?

3. What are some of the feedback controls involved in the regulation of heartbeat?

4. Why is the heart called a "double pump"?

5. Discuss the relationship of coronary blood vessels to heart attacks.

6. Compare and contrast artificial pacemakers with the heart's natural pacemaker.

7. Describe the relationship of the electrical activity of the heart to the cardiac cycle.

8. How is blood pressure determined and recorded?

9. How is the structure of blood vessels related to their function?

10. What is the lymphatic system? List its major functions.

The chances of saving Professor Benes were slim; a blood clot in the brain would kill him in a matter of hours. To save Benes' life a rather unorthodox plan was developed: miniaturization of a submarine and its occupants, injection into the dying man's carotid artery, transport to the clot by the bloodstream, and destruction of the clot by the piercing rays of a laser gun. Once miniaturization was complete the entire mission had to be completed within 60 minutes for, if not, the submarine and occupants both would return to normal size and kill Benes whether the surgery was successful or not.

In the control room, the television receiver seemed to spring back to life. . . . "They're out of the ear and heading rapidly for the clot." "Twelve minutes. Can they make it? . . ."

"We've entered the brain itself," announced Owens. . . .

He doused the ship's lights again and all of them looked forward in a moment of wonder that put everything else, even the climax of the mission, out of their minds for a moment.

As they drifted through the interstitial fluid along passageways between the cells, they could see the dendrites tangling overhead and for a moment they were passing under what seemed to be the twisted limbs of a row of ancient forest trees. . . .

The submarine came to a halt. For an instant or two, there was silence, then Owens said quietly, "That's our destination, I think. . . ."

Duval nodded, "Yes, the clot."

No human has yet been miniaturized to journey through the body as did the characters in Isaac Asimov's novel *Fantastic Voyage*, but modern techniques in biology have made it possible to blow up and enlarge microscopic structures in such a way that we can gain a "bacterium's eye view" of our own cells. The photograph shows a red blood cell caught in the tangled web of a fibrin clot, a situation much like that encountered by the voyagers in Asimov's science fiction story. (The horizontal black line in the lower right of the photo is about the size of the miniaturized submarine—1 μm!) This chapter will take you on a fantastic voyage through our blood—described by some as "the river of life."

EMIL BERSTEIN, cover photograph for *Science*, August 27, 1971. Copyright © 1971 by The American Association for the Advancement of Science.

# 14

# Blood and Immunity

## 14–1 BLOOD: A TISSUE THAT FLOWS

Blood has always held a special position in human thought. The ancients recognized that continued loss of blood led to weakness and eventually to death; it was as if a person's life drained out of the body with the outpouring of blood. In days gone by, blood was considered to have many wonderful properties, some of them quite mystical. Even today, we speak metaphorically of the special qualities of blood: virile men are "red-blooded," aristocrats are "blue bloods," undesirable individuals have "bad blood," and close family relations are "blood relatives." Some of these expressions, as we shall see, are biologically unsound, but they emphasize our long-standing preoccupation with this special fluid.

The quantity of blood in the body is substantial, making up about 7% of the total body weight. On the average we have about 5 qt (almost 10 lb) of blood. In a single day about 5,000 qt of blood (5 qt making 1,000 circuits) course through the body. As a result of this continuous flow, food and oxygen are delivered to the hungry cells and potentially lethal wastes are carried away; excess heat derived from the metabolic furnaces of our tissue cells is carried off and dissipated in the skin; regulatory substances (hormones) are moved to every part of the body, so that chemical contact between remote organs is maintained; and by virtue of the presence of specific defense agents, foreign invaders are challenged and repelled.

Blood and its derivative, lymph, form a kind of internal sea that continuously bathes our cells. Blood is a liquid tissue, and it flows readily because its constituent cells are not joined together in a rigid or semirigid network, but are suspended in a watery medium. The cells float singly and separately and are carried along like flotsam and jetsam in the streaming current. As blood flows through the vessels of the circulatory system, it consists of a complex, straw-colored fluid plasma in which float the suspended red blood cells, white blood cells, and platelets. The fluid plasma composes about 55% of the total volume, and the cells (so-called formed elements) make up the remaining 45% of the total volume (Figure 14–1).

### Plasma: our internal sea

Blood **plasma** is basically similar to a dilute solution of seawater, and indeed they share the same salts, but in different concentrations (Table 14–1). For some biologists this confirms the speculation that when life arose in the sea those organisms that developed circulatory systems took along with them the seawater characteristic of that ancient geological period, a time when the seas were less salty. (Blood plasma is roughly 0.85% salt, and today's seawater about 3.5% salt.) You know the salty character of plasma if you have ever tasted blood—and who has never sucked on a cut finger?

Since the prime function of the plasma is to act as a medium of transport, it contains substances other than salts. Most of the nonprotein substances are cargo on their way to or from the tissues. These include nutrients such as sugars (mainly glucose), lipids, and vitamins; hormones; and waste products such as urea (Table 14–2). The concentrations of nutrients and salts, though small, are kept relatively constant; this is in spite of the fact that blood is continuously exchanging materials with the countless numbers of body cells. The constancy of the blood composition (homeostasis) is maintained by a series of negative feedback controls—a decline or elevation in the amount of a substance initiates responses in a variety of organs, especially the liver and kidneys, until equilibrium is reestablished.

Nonprotein substances make up only a small part of the plasma (about 1%). More than 92% of the plasma is water; the rest consists mainly of proteins—more than 70 different kinds! We need not concern ourselves with all of them, but can focus our attention on three main groups of plasma proteins: **albumin, globulin,** and **fibrinogen.** Most of the plasma protein is albumin. The globulin fraction consists of a mixture of proteins: the **alpha globulins** are glycoproteins or mucoproteins (carbohydrate plus protein), the **beta globulins** are lipoproteins (lipid plus protein), and the **gamma globulins** are proteins that include most of the circulating antibody. Fibrinogen is the protein that forms the blood clot.

Plasma proteins serve a variety of functions, but their most important role is in the maintenance of the proper osmotic pressure between the circulatory fluid and the fluid in the tissue spaces, so that ex-

FIGURE 14–1 The separation of whole blood into plasma and solids by means of centrifugation.

Withdraw blood from vein    Place blood in tube          Spin blood in a centrifuge

Fluid fraction = 55%

Solid fraction = 45%

**TABLE 14–1 A comparison of seawater with blood**

| Component | Seawater (g/liter) | Blood (g/liter) |
|---|---|---|
| Na (sodium) | 10.7 | 3.2–3.4 |
| K (potassium) | 0.39 | 0.15–0.21 |
| Ca (calcium) | 0.42 | 0.09–0.11 |
| Mg (magnesium) | 1.34 | 0.012–0.036 |
| Cl (chloride) | 19.3 | 3.5–3.8 |
| $SO_4$ (sulfate) | 2.69 | 0.16–0.34 |
| $CO_3$ (carbonate) | 0.073 | 1.5–1.9 |
| Protein | | 70 |

| Relative composition (sodium taken as 100) | | |
|---|---|---|
| Na (sodium) | 100.00 | 100.00 |
| K (potassium) | 2.70 | 3.99 |
| Ca (calcium) | 2.80 | 1.78 |
| Mg (magnesium) | 13.90 | 0.66 |
| Cl (chloride) | 136.80 | 83.97 |
| $SO_4$ (sulfate) | 7.10 | 1.73 |

change of materials between blood and the cells is facilitated. (See Chapter 13 for details of their function in this capacity.) They contribute to the viscosity of the blood and thus play a role in the maintenance of normal blood pressure. Plasma proteins also act to buffer the blood, so that the pH of the plasma is almost always slightly alkaline (pH 7.4).

Where do the plasma proteins come from? The liver is the sole source of fibrinogen, albumin, and most of the alpha and beta globulins, but the gamma globulins originate in lymphoid tissues—from plasma cells and lymph-node cells. Impairment of liver function, such as occurs in chronic liver disease (cirrhosis), is often reflected by a decline of plasma proteins, particularly albumin.

### Blood cells: the red and the white

Almost all our blood cells are **erythrocytes** (*erythros*—red; Gk.), or **red blood cells,** and these give our blood its characteristic color. The major function of the red blood cells is the transport of oxygen from the lungs to all the cells of the body. They are red because they contain **hemoglobin,** an iron-containing protein that readily combines with oxygen. Oxygen binding to hemoglobin is reversible: in the lungs, where the oxygen concentration is high, hemoglobin loads up and becomes bright red **oxyhemoglobin;** when it arrives at cells where the oxygen concentration is low, it unloads oxygen and becomes maroon hemoglobin once again. (Transport of gases by hemoglobin is discussed in Chapter 15.) About 1 out of every 500 cells in the blood does not

contain hemoglobin, and these colorless cells are called **leukocytes** (*leukos*—white; Gk.), or **white blood cells.** White blood cells have a variety of functions, but the most important of these is to protect the body against foreign invaders. Platelets are quite numerous in the blood; they are fragments of a special kind of bone-marrow cell and play an essential role in the clotting of blood.

**Red cells.** In the time it takes you to scan this page (about 1 minute) you will produce 140 million new red blood cells to replace the old and the dead. In a single drop of blood there are about 200 million such biconcave discs, each resembling a minute inflated rubber raft, 7 to 8 μm in diameter and 1 to 2 μm thick (Figure 14–2). Altogether, the number of red blood cells in the body exceeds 25 million million ($2.5 \times 10^{13}$).

Red cells are unlike any other cells of the body. A mature red cell cannot multiply because it lacks a nucleus. It is in large part a specially designed container for hemoglobin, and its architecture exposes maximum surface area for exchange of oxygen and carbon dioxide. If it were spherical, we should require much greater numbers of cells to do the job of gaseous transport with the same efficiency.

If mature red cells cannot grow or repro-

**TABLE 14–2 Major components of plasma (per100 ml)**

| Electrolytes and metals (mg*) | | Metabolic intermediates (mg*) | |
|---|---|---|---|
| Bicarbonate | 152–190 | Bile acids | 0.2–3.0 |
| Calcium | 8.5–10.5 | Choline | 26–35 |
| Chloride | 355–380 | Citric acid | 2.0–3.0 |
| Cobalt | 0.4–0.7 μg | Lactic acid | 6–16 |
| Copper | 88–124 μg | Lipids | 360–820 |
| Iodine | 5–6 μg | Cholesterol | 150–280 |
| Iodine | 50–150 μg | Fatty acids | 200–450 |
| Magnesium | 1.8–3.6 | Phospholipids | 135–170 |
| Manganese | 4–6 μg | Pyruvic acid | 1.0–2.0 |
| Phosphate | 3.0–4.5 | | |
| Potassium | 15–20 μg | **Waste products (mg*)** | |
| Sodium | 315–330 | Acetone | 0.3–2.0 |
| Sulfate | 0.5–1.5 | Ammonia | 40–70 μg |
| Zinc | 250–350 μg | Bilirubin | 0.5 |
| | | Creatine | 0.8–1.0 |
| **Nutrients (mg*)** | | Creatinine | 0.7–1.5 |
| Amino acids | 30 | Urea | 25–52 |
| Glucose | 70–100 | Uric acid | 3–6 |
| | | | |
| **Vitamins (mg*)** | | **Proteins (g)** | |
| Ascorbic acid | 0.4–1.5 | Albumin | 4.6 |
| Biotin | 1.0–1.7 μg | Antibodies | 1.5 |
| Carotenoids | 100–200 μg | Clotting factors | ? |
| Folic acid | 0.6–2.5 | Enzymes | ? |
| Niacin | 0.2–0.3 μg | Fibrinogen | 0.38 |
| Pantothenic acid | 6–35 μg | Globulins | 2.6 |
| Riboflavin (B₂) | 2.6–3.7 | | |
| Vitamin A | 50–100 | **Hormones (traces)** | |
| Vitamin B₁₂ | 20–50 μg | | |
| Vitamin E | 0.6–1.6 | Dissolved gases (CO₂, O₂, N₂, etc.) | |

\* Unless otherwise noted.

formation of more hemoglobin or it goes to the liver for storage in the form of ferritin. When the marrow requires iron, the ferritin is released from the liver, iron is made available, and hemoglobin is synthesized.

About 95% of the protein in a red blood cell is hemoglobin, a thick molasseslike solution enclosed by the plasma membrane. The remaining red-cell proteins are an array of enzymes that enable the cell to survive for about 120 days, though not to grow or reproduce. Why is hemoglobin contained in such a special cell? Would it not be just as easy to dissolve hemoglobin in the plasma? The answer is no. Hemoglobin in cells rather than in solution is less likely to be lost as the kidneys filter the plasma. Moreover, the hemoglobin in the plasma tends to become oxidized and to be quickly bound to other proteins, both of which occurrences would impair its oxygen-transport capacity. Finally, red cells expedite gaseous transport by causing turbulence in the blood vessels, much as pebbles do in a stream.

**White cells.** Human white cells (leukocytes) are larger than red cells and have large, often irregularly shaped nuclei. At

duce, how are new red blood cells made? Erythrocytes in adults are formed exclusively in the bone marrow (located in the central core of bones of the body such as the ribs and the sternum) from nucleated cells called **erythroblasts.** Erythroblasts (*erythros*—red, *blastos*—sprout; Gk.) are actively dividing cells that give rise through a series of stages to erythrocytes. The mature erythrocyte squeezes its way through the walls of the capillaries in the marrow and in this way enters the bloodstream. There it lives for an average of 4 months before disintegrat-

ing. The cell fragments are engulfed by phagocytic cells in the liver and spleen—the graveyard of the erythrocyte. The hemoglobin released by the rupture of the aged erythrocyte flows freely in the blood, and in less than an hour it leaks into the tissue spaces. Here it is ingested by phagocytic cells and chemically dismembered to form iron, bilirubin, and amino acids. The amino acids return to the amino-acid pool of the body, while the bilirubin is excreted from the liver in the bile. Iron is recycled: either it is transported to the bone marrow for the least five different kinds can be distinguished by their staining properties and the shape of the nucleus. Normally, 65% of the white cells are **granulocytes,** that is, they contain granules that stain readily. About 35% are devoid of such granules and are called **agranulocytes.** The granulocytes are formed in the bone marrow and come in three varieties (Figure 14–3). The agranulocytes come in two varieties, are formed in lymphoid tissue (lymph nodes, spleen, tonsils, and thymus), and are more abundant in the lymphatic system than in the blood. White blood cells are capable of ameboid movement; they wander by squeezing between the cells that form the walls of the lymph and blood vessels and thus reach the tissues of the body. These wandering cells are important in the body's defense reactions against disease and infection, since they can engulf foreign bodies such as bacteria.

### Self-sealing: blood platelets and fibrinogen

If you attach a garden hose to a faucet and turn on the water, it comes out through the nozzle. Puncture the hose and water squirts from the point of puncture—it does not all go where you want it to, and you lose water. Similarly, if one punctures a blood vessel, blood pours out and is wasted. Unimpeded flow of blood (**hemorrhage**) from damaged vessels causes wasting and eventually death. Cuts, scrapes, and tears in the skin with rupture of blood vessels are everyday occurrences; however, in general the flow of blood from a small wound does not continue for long. The blood soon thickens, or clots, a scab forms, and the puncture is sealed. In time the scab drops off, and newly formed skin replaces that which was ripped away. Blood contains a self-sealing material that effectively plugs leaks in the plumbing of the circulatory system.

You can demonstrate blood clotting by collecting some fresh blood in a test tube. If you tip the tube upside down immediately, the blood flows out; it is liquid. Wait

FIGURE 14–3 The various types of white blood cells. Neutrophils contain lavender-colored granules. Eosinophils stain a deep red. The cytoplasm of basophils contains granules that stain deep blue. Lymphocytes have a nucleus that stains a deep purple; their cytoplasm stains pale blue. The nucleus of a monocyte stains a pale blue, its cytoplasm a paler blue.

| | Diameter ($\mu$m) | Number/mm$^3$ | % Among leukocytes |
|---|---|---|---|
| Erythrocyte | 7–8 | 5–6 million | |
| Granulocytes | | | |
| Neutrophil | 9–12 | 3,000–6,750 | 60–65 |
| Eosinophil | 10–14 | 100–360 | 2–4 |
| Basophil | 8–10 | 25–90 | 0.5–1.0 |
| Agranulocytes | | | |
| Lymphocyte | 6–12 | 1,000–2,700 | 20–35 |
| Monocyte | 12–15 | 150–170 | 3–8 |
| Platelets | 2–3 | 200,000–300,000 | |

FIGURE 14–4 Stages in clot formation. Intact blood vessels have a continuous lining of endothelial cells so that during normal blood flow the platelets do not come into direct contact with the blood vessel wall itself; however, when the blood vessel is cut, blood flows out and platelets make contact with the connective tissue substance collagen (a). Platelets adhere to the collagen, and this initiates the secretion of ADP; the platelet changes shape (it spreads out) and disintegrates (b). In addition, the cut blood vessel wall releases tissue factor, and in the presence of calcium ions and other clotting factors prothrombin of the plasma is converted to thrombin (c). The thrombin in turn converts the plasma fibrinogen into fibrin strands, and this causes further platelet aggregation (d). Fibrin strands form a meshwork that reinforces the plug and traps red blood cells (e), producing a blood clot.

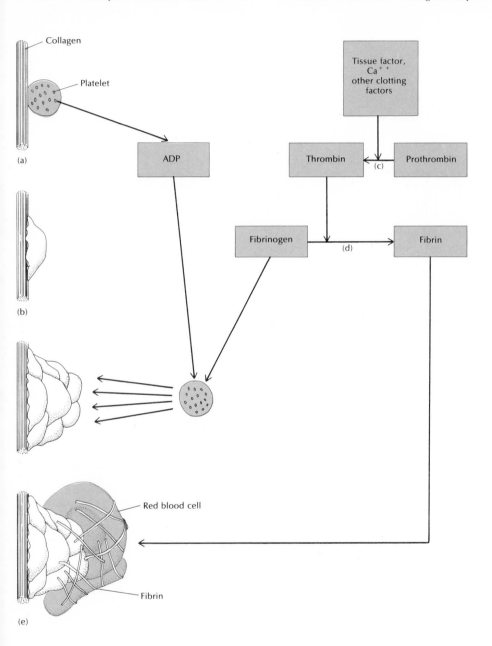

a few minutes (4 to 10 minutes is the normal range) and then tip the tube; the blood does not flow. It has solidified and formed a clot. If the reddish clot is allowed to shrink and then is carefully removed from the tube, a clear yellow fluid remains. This is the same material that oozes out of a wound after a clot is formed. The pale-yellow fluid, **serum,** is much like plasma save for one important difference: it lacks a protein called **fibrin.** Fibrin forms the meshwork that traps red blood cells to form the reddish clot.

The sealant is fibrin, but what is the mechanism that leads to clot formation? The patching material of the blood includes a group of soluble proteins and tiny particles called **platelets,** or **thrombocytes.** Every cubic millimeter of blood contains 5,000,000 red cells and about 7,500 white cells. It also contains about 250,000 exceedingly small platelets. Each platelet is a cytoplasmic fragment of a giant cell known as a **megakaryocyte,** a normal resident of the bone marrow. Platelets are quite stable within the bloodstream, but are fragile outside. When a cut is made in the skin and a blood vessel is torn, the platelets at the wound disintegrate, and the machinery of clot formation begins. Clotting does not occur simply by exposure of blood to air. If blood is carefully drawn from a blood vessel so that no tissue damage results, and this blood is placed in a wax (or other nonwettable) container, it remains liquid. Only when platelets disintegrate, as occurs by contact with a wettable surface such as glass or by contact with damaged tissue, is clot formation initiated.

Clot formation is a complex affair (Figure 14–4). Discoveries since 1947 of the mechanisms involved in clotting have revealed that in addition to the platelets, calcium ions, vitamin K, and at least 10 proteins (called **clotting factors**) found in small amounts in the plasma are required. Deficiency of any one of these can lead to delayed clotting—bleeder's disease, or **hemophilia.** Hemophilic individuals bruise easily, and hemorrhages occur in the nose, gums, intestines, and skin—and sometimes even in the brain.

BOX 14A  Counting the reds and whites: barometer of disease

The slip shown in Figure 14–5 is a request for blood analysis; such an analysis is often ordered by a physician to determine the state of a patient's health. Most of us are directly involved in just the first stage of blood analysis: donation of a drop or a tubeful of blood. What happens next? If the physician has requested a total blood count, a few drops of blood are diluted with a special fluid. This is mixed well, and a drop of the diluted blood is placed on a counting chamber (a **hemocytometer**) and covered with a coverglass. The counting chamber is placed under a microscope, and the cells are counted (Figure 14–6). A simple calculation correcting for the dilution gives the cell count per cubic millimeter of undiluted blood. Some normal cell counts of blood are given in Table 14–3.

A rising white cell count is often an early clue to a dangerous infection. As the body mobilizes its forces to defend against attack, production of white blood cells increases, and these cells appear in great numbers in the blood. For example, in a person with appendicitis the white cell count may reach 50,000 per cubic millimeter of blood—about seven times the average normal value.

Each red cell contains about 265 million molecules of hemoglobin, and 100 ml of blood normally contains about 15 g of hemoglobin. It has been shown that iron, vitamin B$_{12}$, and folic

FIGURE 14–6  Method used in counting blood cells.

FIGURE 14–5  The laboratory slip requesting blood analysis.

Hemoglobin

Leucocyte

Erythrocyte

Eosinophils

Complete blood
count—red
and white

Two types
of neutrophils

BLOOD COUNT - 04

☐ Hb (8318)_____  ☐ Hct.(8317)_____

☐ W.B.C. (8339)_____

☐ R.B.C. (8329)_____

☐ Platelets(8328)_____

☐ Reticulocytes(8332)_____ Corrected_____

☐ Total EOS Count (8311)_____

☐ Leucocyte Alk. P'tase(8321)_____

☐ Sickle Cell Prep.(8334)_____

☐ C.B.C. (8305)_____

☐ Misc._____

_____

☐ Differential(8309)

| Seg. | Band | Lymphs | Monos | Eosins | Baso | | | |
|------|------|--------|-------|--------|------|--|--|--|
| | | | | | | | | |

Aniso_____

Poik_____

Hypochromasia_____

Polychromasia_____

Lab Directors
12-9010(11-70)     BLOOD COUNT - 04

Initiated by | Requesting Doctor | Hosp. Rm | Send report to

Name

Cov.           Med. Rec. No.

Medicare No.            Group No.

Sex       Dep. code     Mo. & Yr. of birth

Date

Comments:_____

Date of specimen | Date reported | By

acid, as well as other substances, are necessary for the manufacture of hemoglobin. Thus, a dietary deficiency of any of these substances may produce the condition we know as "tired blood," or anemia, and it may be necessary to supplement the diet with iron, vitamin pills, or both. Anemia is defined in medical terms as deficiency in the amount of circulating red blood cells or hemoglobin (or both). When for some reason (for example, hemorrhage) the level of red cells declines to one third of normal and hemoglobin concentration falls to one tenth of normal, oxygen is transported with reduced efficiency, and the energy available for cellular work is correspondingly reduced. Consequently, the anemic individual tires easily and often appears pale. The causes of anemia are many, and the disorder should be treated promptly, since a decrease in oxygen-carrying capacity of the blood can result in tissue damage. In addition, decreased viscosity of the blood due to diminished numbers of red cells causes too rapid a flow of blood in the circulatory channels, a condition that promotes excessive strain on the heart and could cause heart failure.

Another aspect of blood analysis involves quality rather than quantity. A drop of blood is smeared out on a glass slide in a thin film. This is dried and stained. The stain shows mature erythrocytes as pink-orange. Abnormalities are indicated if the erythrocytes are too pale or have an abnormal appearance when examined under the microscope. A trained laboratory technician can easily identify the five different kinds of white cells and by simple count can determine their relative proportions, which may indicate a pathological condition. For example, if a person is infected with parasitic worms, such as those that cause trichinosis or hookworm, the eosinophil count rises sharply. In acute appendicitis, neutrophils may rise from 62% to 95%. In infectious mononucleosis, monocytes increase in number and may constitute a major fraction of the white-cell population. Leukemia (literally "white blood": *leukos*—white, *emia*—blood; Gk.) is a cancer of the white-cell-producing tissue, typified by an excessive number of white blood cells in the circulation. The white cells gradually crowd out the red-cell-forming tissue, and there is a corrosive anemia. Ultimately, if the disease is unchecked, death may result.

**TABLE 14–3 Normal cell counts in peripheral blood**

| Cell | Average count (cells/mm³) | Range of count in 95% of normal population (cells/mm³) |
| --- | --- | --- |
| Red cells | 5,400,000 (men)<br>4,800,000 (women)<br>4,500,000 (infants) | 4,500,000–6,500,000 (men)<br>3,900,000–5,600,000 (women)<br>4,000,000–5,600,000 (infants) |
| White cells | 7,500 (adults)<br>12,000 (infants) | 4,500–11,000 (adults)<br>10,000–25,000 (infants) |
| Platelets | 250,000 (all ages) | 140,000–440,000 (all ages) |

The failure to clot causes one kind of problem, but the reverse situation also causes difficulty. If for some reason platelets gather in large numbers in blood vessels when there is no injury, a thrombus, or clot, may plug the vessel. If this occurs in an artery, the vital supply of blood to the organ normally fed by the artery could be cut off, with disastrous consequences. For example, a clogged coronary artery can produce a heart attack, a clogged brain artery causes a stroke or worse, and a clogged pulmonary artery may result in death. A clot may form in a leg because of platelet malfunction in an area of sluggish flow. If such a clot breaks loose, it forms an **embolus**, a traveling clot that moves through the bloodstream, and may come to rest and clog a vital artery. The reasons for the spontaneous development of these wayward clots are unknown.

The body has mechanisms for the prevention of clot formation in uninjured vessels. One of these safety factors involves the intact linings of blood vessels, which, by virtue of their electrical charges, repel the platelets and prevent their aggregation. Another is the presence in the plasma of **anticlotting factors** such as **antithrombin,** which inactivates thrombin, and **heparin,** which enhances the activity of antithrombin, thus preventing platelet breakdown and inhibiting the action of thrombin on fibrinogen. Heparin is often added to samples of blood drawn by syringe to prevent clotting so that plasma and cell samples can be obtained for diagnostic purposes (Box 14A).

### 14–2 AGAINST THE FOREIGN PERIL: IMMUNITY

Alien agents continually attempt to penetrate the borders of the body. When we bruise or cut our skin, they slip past the skin cells and enter the body; foreign materials creep into the body by way of the nose or any of the other passages from outside the body to the interior; some invaders are carried inside when we swallow our food; dust, microbes, and viruses slip through whatever breach can be found. The continued integrity of the body depends upon its ability to repel the foreign intruder. How is this accomplished?

The body has an elaborate array of defensive weapons geared to prevent foreign agents from invading, establishing themselves, and taking over. The foreign material may be living (such as bacteria) or nonliving (protein or toxin); it may be friend (organ transplant) or foe (filth contaminating a wound). No matter how varied the alien material may be, the defense system depends for its function on a simple and straightforward mechanism: the ability to distinguish between the body tissues (self) and those substances that are dissimilar (not-self). Once a substance is recognized as not-self, the stage is set for battle.

## Natural immunity

The close-fitting cells of the skin form a protective wall, providing a natural barrier between the body and the environment. In addition, the body produces watery barriers; for example, mucous secretions in the nose and mouth contain antimicrobial substances to trap and kill bacteria. The salivary glands that open into the mouth produce saliva, which contains bactericidal substances. Coughing repels foreign materials and acts as a watchdog for the lungs. Tears flush the eyes and contain the enzyme lysozyme, which destroys the cell walls of certain bacteria. The ears are protected by waxy secretions, and the acidity of the stomach provides a hazard for bacteria to traverse in their passage from mouth to intestine. The acidity of urine and the regular flushing action of urination contribute to the antimicrobial activity of the urinary system. These systems of defense constitute a part of our **natural immunity** to intruders. We are endowed with them at birth, and they involve anatomical barriers as well as special secretions.

The physical barriers of the body are not impregnable, however. Occasionally invaders sneak past the outer defenses and enter the body itself. (Think of all the small breaks in the skin produced by brushing the teeth, shaving, scratching, and so on.) This could cause problems for the community of cells, especially if the agent penetrates the bloodstream, in which it is likely to be carried to all the internal organs. Moreover, the bloodstream is in many ways a hospitable home for thousands of microscopic organisms, since it provides plenty of oxygen, virtually unlimited food, and usually freedom from competition for the available resources.

Fortunately, there is a second line of natural defenses standing ready to repel those invaders that manage to cross the body's walls and waterways. Maintaining this line of defense are the cells of the **reticuloendothelial system.** The reticuloendothelial system consists of fixed phagocytic cells lining the sinusoids of the spleen, lymph nodes, liver, and bone marrow. (**Sinusoids** are expanded areas in small blood vessels.) The foreign substances that enter these organs are not pursued, but instead are plucked from the bloodstream by phagocytosis as they pass through the tortuous maze of circulatory channels.

Sometimes a breach in the defense system is counteracted by an active search-and-destroy mission, called **inflammation.** Inflammation is an immediate, localized response to the presence of a foreign substance or, more generally, to tissue injury. Whenever tissue is damaged, the cells release materials that attract white blood cells (**neutrophils**) from the bloodstream, capillary permeability is increased, and fluid accumulates in the tissue spaces. As a result, the area becomes red, warm, and puffy—in a word, inflamed. The presence of extra fluid dilutes toxic materials, and because some local clotting occurs the damaged area is walled off, thus preventing the spread of the foreign invader.

Neutrophils not only engulf and destroy foreign particles, especially bacteria, but also clean up the remnants of the damaged cells. When a neutrophil contacts a foreign substance, it quickly surrounds it, and the intruder soon becomes securely enclosed in a membranous sac. Complete engulfment may take less than 0.01 second! The next step is destruction of the alien agent. The lysosomes of the neutrophil move toward the sac, the membranes of the two fuse, and the powerful digestive enzymes of the lysosome are discharged into the sac. The enzymes kill the invader and degrade its molecular constituents into harmless products that are released or are used as a nutrient source by the neutrophil. Some neutrophils die as a result of the phagocytic process, but others continue to ingest, degrade, and inactivate foreign intruders. The mixture of dead cells, bacteria, and neutrophils that accumulates at the site constitutes **pus,** and an extensive accumulation of pus is testimony to the body's battle against invasion.

To summarize: the natural barriers such as the skin, the secretions of cells (tears and mucus), the fixed and mobile phagocytes of the reticuloendothelial and circulatory systems, and the localized inflammatory response are all elements in the natural immune reactions of the body. The system of natural immunity is the first line of defense to clear the body of invaders on initial encounter.

## Acquired immunity

Whenever the body encounters an intruder, it attempts to eliminate it by producing an effective countermeasure, one specifically tailored to match the offender. In addition, the body attempts to render itself permanently resistant to that invader and others of its kind. Those mechanisms developed as a consequence of exposure to the foreigner are called **acquired immune reactions.** Acquired immunity may involve specific cells as well as special products of cells, called **antibodies.** An antibody is a specific protein produced in response to the presence in the bloodstream of some material

## BOX 14B  The bubble boy's lost battle

It had been his simple wish to walk barefoot on the grass and some day to live normally in the world. For this hope David, 12, and his family took the ultimate gamble: they traded the safety of a germ-free plastic bubble at Houston's Texas Children's Hospital for the slim chance that a bone-marrow transplant would allow the immunologically defenseless boy to live freely. Last week they lost their gamble, and his death was felt across the country.

David's case was unprecedented: no other human being had lived so long without a functioning immune system, a defect that can turn even the common cold into a fatal disease. David (the family always insisted on anonymity) owed his survival to doctors who had anticipated the condition before his birth because an older brother had died of immunodeficiency. Inside a series of sterile "bubbles," David progressed from a baby in a crib to an A student who attended school by telephone; his food was sterilized and slipped in through air locks. Only briefly, in 1977, was he able to explore the world outside, thanks to a special suit presented to him by NASA. More than a million dollars in federal research grants helped cover the cost of his care.

The only hope for a cure was a transplant of bone marrow, which could provide the body with a rapidly multiplying source of defender cells to ward off disease. Such transplants were once possible only if a genetically matched donor, generally a sibling, could be found. Sadly, David's older sister's cell type did not match his. In the past few years, however, new technology has made it possible to transplant imperfectly matched marrow, making obsolete the isolation approach to David's illness. "There will be no more bubbles," said Dr. William Shearer, the boy's physician. Last October David received 1⅔ oz. of his sister's treated marrow.

On Feb. 7 David finally emerged from his sterile world, crawling through an air lock into his mother's waiting arms. But that brief reunion was clouded by worry: a persistent fever, diarrhea and vomiting had made it necessary for doctors to treat him outside the bubble. The symptoms, doctors feared, were signs of the often fatal graft *vs.* host disease, which occurs when cells from donated marrow attack the recipient's body. During the next 15 days, David developed severe ulceration of his

digestive tract and a dangerous accumulation of fluid in his lungs and around his heart. The exhausted child finally died of cardiac failure. Shearer recalled that at the end David asked, "Why don't we just pull out all these tubes and let me go home?"

Post-mortem examination disclosed "totally unexpected" complications, according to Shearer. Accumulations of abnormally large white blood cells known as B cells were found in the boy's intestines, lungs and spleen. The fact that the cells were David's and not his sister's suggested that the transplant had not taken hold. For doctors, the more interesting question was whether these cells were malignant. The answer could provide valuable clues to the immune system and how it defends against cancer. "David's life," said an emotional Shearer, "has been important for medicine, but his greatest contribution was his death."

**A wistful David ponders his twelfth birthday from his germ-free cell. (Courtesy of Baylor College of Medicine.)**

FIGURE 14–7 Human thymus in a child is a flat, two-lobed organ lying high in the chest behind the breastbone. The thymus is large in relation to the rest of the body in early childhood; by the age of puberty, it begins to atrophy.

that is foreign to the body. The antibody circulates in the blood, combines with the foreign substance, and destroys it in one way or another.

What enables the body to know that it should produce an antibody and that the invader is a foreigner and not-self? The answer lies in the uniqueness of the molecules of life. Each substance carries its own chemical identification tags, and the molecular configurations of foreign substances that differ from those of the body act as **anti**body **gen**erators, or **antigens.** Thus, antigens are materials (or entire organisms) capable of eliciting an immune response, that is, stimulating antibody production. Antigens can vary: bacteria and viruses that enter the body can be antigens, a skin graft on the body of another person can be an antigen, and proteins, fats, carbohydrates, and nucleic acids can be antigens under the appropriate circumstances. In general, antigens have a common characteristic: they are large molecules, ranging in size from 50,000 to 100,000 molecular weight. For example, water, with a molecular weight of 18, and glucose, with a molecular weight of 180, are not antigens, because of their small molecular size.

On occasion the body makes a mistake and starts producing antibodies against its own tissues. The disease that develops when this occurs may be quite severe and is called an **autoimmune disorder.** To date there is no good way of undoing the body's immunological confusion, and a progressive wasting away results.

**The primary immune response.** The human immune system, weighing about 2 lb, consists of a number of tissues and organs, including the spleen, thymus, tonsils, bone marrow, and lymph nodes. All of these tissues are linked to one another by blood vessels and lymphatics.

Three kinds of cells are involved in the immune response—macrophages, T lymphocytes, and B lymphocytes. **Macrophages,** found in tissue, are derived from the bone marrow white cells (macrophages that cir-

culate freely in the blood are known as monocytes). Macrophages are voracious phagocytes that ingest and degrade foreign substances.

The second and third types of cells of the immune system that respond to foreign invaders are small, round white cells called **lymphocytes.** Lymphocytes respond to antigens either by producing sensitized cells or by forming antibodies, both of which bind to antigen. Numbering about a trillion in the body, lymphocytes are constantly being formed from precursor stem cells in the bone marrow. In the time it has taken you to read the last few paragraphs, your body has produced about 10 million new lymphocytes to replace those that are damaged or destroyed.

About half of the lymphocytes, those called **T cells,** migrate from the bone marrow to the thymus, a gland that lies in the upper chest (Figure 14–7). Here they remain for a time and multiply; then some of the progeny leave the thymus and, by way of the bloodstream, either settle down in the spleen, tonsils, lymph nodes, or appendix or continue to circulate in the blood.

The T cells recognize foreign antigens because they contain receptor molecules on their surface. Once a T cell has recognized an antigen, its function depends on the particular subclass to which it belongs. One type of T cell, the cytotoxic T cell, actively and independently defends the body by destroying infected, foreign, or malignant cells, whereas the remaining T cell types affect the immune response by secreting messenger proteins or by cooperating with other cells. For example, inducer T cells trigger the maturation of T lymphocytes from precursor cells and helper T cells precondition other cells so that when a foreign antigen is recognized the B cells are induced to secrete antibody. Another kind of T cell is called a suppressor cell, it "turns off" the B and T cells, and dampens the immune response several weeks after an infection has activated them. Helper and inducer cells belong to a subset of T lym-

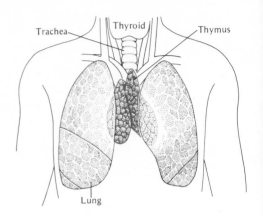

phocytes called $T_4$, whereas the suppressor and cytotoxic cells belong to the subset called $T_8$.

The third kind of lymphocyte, is called the **B cell.** B cells arise in the bone marrow, have antibody on their surface, circulate in the blood, and are also located in the lymph nodes, but they are not thymus-derived. A T cell may activate a B cell causing the B cell to divide a number of times and to differentiate into a clone,[1] or a colony of B cells. Such B cells, in turn, will produce antibody.

Once the T and B lymphocytes have been processed, they either enter the circulation or settle down in the lymphoid tissues; now they are capable of reacting with antigen. As we shall see presently, the T and B lymphocytes have entirely different roles in the immune system; however, both are essential for life, and if either the one or the other is lacking, the animal soon dies of infection.

Resting B lymphocytes, prior to antigen activation, produce a number of specific antibody molecules (approximately 100,000), which are strategically placed on the outer surface of their plasma membranes. These molecules are called **receptors,** and in es-

---

[1] **clone:** a mitotically produced colony of cells of identical genetic constitution.

sence each "waits" for an encounter with its specific antigen. Each lymphocyte displays only one kind of receptor. It is believed that by a more-or-less random replacement of amino acids in a particular region of the molecule, millions of different kinds of lymphocytes can be generated, each with different kinds of receptors, and these receptors will fit practically any kind of antigen. If this is indeed so, then how does one's own immune system distinguish between antigens that are part of one's own body and those that are not? The body's immune system avoids reacting with self-antigens not because it is genetically programmed to avoid the manufacture of such receptors, but because in embryonic life the immune system "learned" that certain antigens are "self" and others are "not-self." This property, called **self-tolerance,** is induced when a lymphocyte in the embryo makes contact with self-antigen; lymphocytes with receptors for self-antigen are eliminated or paralyzed. As a consequence, all lymphocytes that display receptors for self-antigen are purged from the immune system during embryonic or neonatal life. What remains is an army of a million or more lymphocytes, each with receptors capable of combining with antigens that are not-self.

T cells are involved in a process called **cell-mediated immunity.** Some antigens, such as those of the bacterium that causes the disease tuberculosis (TB), when presented to the T cells, bind to receptors on the surface of the T cell, causing the secretion of lymphokines. As a result blood vessels become dilated and more blood flows to the region. Other lymphokines make the vessels leaky so that fluid and blood cells move into the surrounding tissue causing swelling. Some lymphokines activate macrophages causing them to congregate in the area. As a result of lymphokine secretion, the bacteria are ingested and destroyed by the macrophages, and the body is protected. When you are given a tuberculin, or Schick, test to determine whether you

have ever been exposed to TB (and most city dwellers have), the tuberculin antigen is injected under the skin. In 48 to 72 hours, an inflammation develops at the site of injection if the test is positive. This reaction is called a **delayed hypersensitivity reaction** because the reaction takes days to develop. By contrast, someone who reacts to an antigen within minutes of exposure is said to show **immediate hypersensitivity.** Good examples of such a reaction are the hay fever some people experience after breathing ragweed pollen and the severe reaction seen in some hypersensitive people who have been sensitized by previous exposure to penicillin or the venom from a bee sting.

The antigen-activated T cell that produces the delayed hypersensitivity reaction does not secrete antibody; however, it does recognize foreign antigens because specific receptors are present on its surface. Instead, the activated T lymphocyte divides, releases lymphokines, and participates in a localized mobilization of phagocytic cells at the site of antigen—a response that is called cell-mediated immunity. The tuberculin sensitivity test is just one example of cell-mediated immunity. Cell-mediated immunity is involved in contact dermatitis, such as that seen when one touches poison ivy, and it is also involved in the rejection of foreign grafts. If a piece of an organ from one animal is grafted to a genetically dissimilar animal, such a graft is rejected. Usually, a skin graft is successful only if the graft is from another part of the individual's own body or comes from an identical twin. If the graft is foreign, wandering T cells enter the area where the graft has been made, lymphokines are produced, and these ultimately kill the cells of the graft; the graft has been rejected. Under some circumstances, activated T lymphocytes will act as aggressor, cytotoxic cells that serve to eliminate certain kinds of tumor cells. Some biologists believe that the immune system evolved not to protect an animal against disease agents or to prevent grafts from being made between different organisms,

but to police the surfaces of all the body's cells continuously so that if antigenically different and potentially deranged cells appeared, they would promptly be destroyed by the mechanisms of cell-mediated immunity.

Certain antigens, especially those of large molecular size with repeating units, as well as bacteria and viruses, do not activate T cells; instead they directly trigger B lymphocytes to activity in a process known as **humoral,** or **antibody-mediated, immunity.** The surface of the B lymphocyte, like that of the T cell, bears receptors for a specific antigen, and when the antigen reaches the lymph nodes and the spleen, these B lymphocytes (also called **plasmablasts**) divide and then differentiate into plasma cells. The plasma cells in turn divide rapidly producing a clone, or colony of cells (Figure 14–8). This clone of plasma cells includes some that are mature and specialized for the production of antibody and others that will divide at a later time to produce more plasma cells (in the secondary immune response, discussed later). The antigen itself need not enter the plasma cell in order to stimulate division and antibody production. All that is necessary is that antigen be bound to the surface receptor. The plasma cell is a factory for producing antibody molecules (Figure 14–9). By the fifth day after exposure to the antigen, the protein factory is in full production: the antibody genes are transcribed into 20,000 molecules of messenger RNA, which serve 200,000 ribosomes, enabling each plasma cell to produce 2,000 antibody molecules per second. The antibody formed is released from the plasma cells into the circulatory system, where it combines with the antigen and neutralizes it. It may take only a few thousand antibody molecules—each specifically tailored to the molecular architecture of the antigen—to completely inactivate a virus or bacterial cell. The situation has been compared to the state of affairs in which a factory manager (antigen) has only to walk up to the correct building (plasma cell) to set off feverish activity within, and there is produced a steady stream of custom-built merchandise (antibody) that is designed to suit the manager exactly.

When the invader cells or their antigens are neutralized, the primary response to the attack is over. During the ensuing period of 4 to 6 weeks, the antibodies formed during the primary response tend to disappear from the circulation.

The usual sequence of events in response to an infectious agent, let us say by a measles virus, follows a rather characteristics pattern and involves both T and B lymphocytes, a process called **immunological cooperation.** In the first step, macrophages engulf the invader and produce two proteins, gamma interferon and interleukin-1 (IL-1).[2] Macrophages also process the viral antigens so that they can be recognized by the helper and inducer T cells. The IL-1 activates those T cells that have recognized the viral antigen, and triggers them to differentiate and divide. The gamma interferon stimulates macrophages and cytotoxic T cells helping them to amplify the response to the invading virus. It is IL-1 and gamma interferon that cause the fever and malaise that frequently accompanies an infection.

Once T cells are activated, they produce the protein interleukin-2 (IL-2). IL-2 is secreted both by T$_4$ and T$_8$ cells, and when present, those T cells, which had been previously stimulated by antigen and IL-1, proliferate into clones of mature T cells: cytotoxic, suppressor, and helper T cells. This burst of cytotoxic activity usually peaks about a week after the measles virus gained entry to the body, and usually results in the elimination of virus-infected cells. The suppressor cells help to shut down the T cell response after several weeks, but there persists a population of T cells, called memory cells, which remain for life. These memory T cells mediate recall reactions and

---

[2] IL-1 and IL-2 are called **lymphokines**, proteins secreted by lymphocytes that affect the behavior of other cells such as T lymphocytes and macrophages.

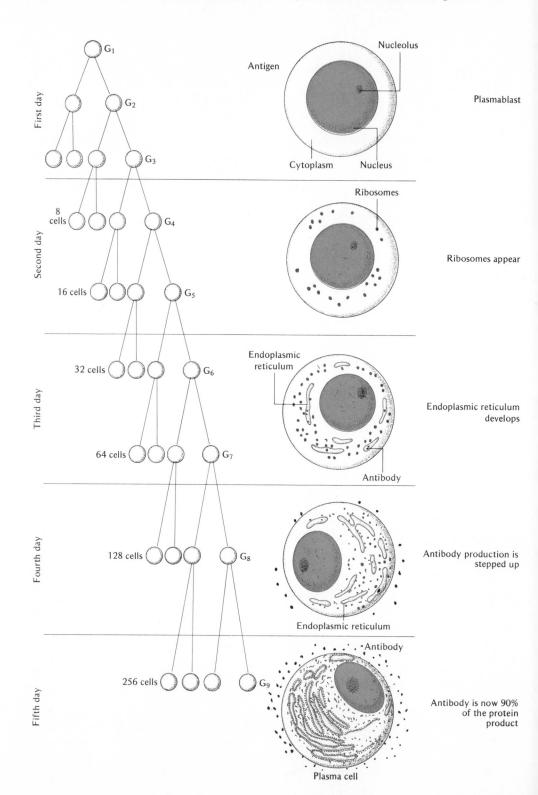

FIGURE 14–9 Plasma cells as revealed by the electron microscope. (Courtesy of K. R. Porter.)

**287**

**BLOOD AND IMMUNITY**

accelerate responses to subsequent encounters with the antigen. It is the $T_4$ helper cell that interacts with the B cell enabling it to produce antibody specific for viral antigens, and neutralizing the virus. The $T_4$ lymphocyte plays a key role in the immune response as it recognizes foreign antigen, causes proliferation of cytotoxic and suppressor functions and also triggers B cell activity. It is not difficult to imagine the devastating consequences that might occur were $T_4$ cells killed or their numbers diminished. Indeed, virtually all of the infectious complications of acquired immunodeficiency disease syndrome (AIDS) are related to specific damage to the $T_4$ cells by the AIDS virus (Box 14C).

**The secondary immune response.** Once the primary response to antigen is ended, all is quiet. However, if antigenic challenge again presents itself, then the T- or B-cell response is highly reactive. How is it that the immune system becomes more highly responsive with each additional challenge from antigen?

Recall that not all members of a particular T- or B-cell clone are involved in the primary response of lymphokine production or antibody secretion. Instead, some revert to the resting state and represent the "memory" of the occurrence. Should a particular antigen reappear—be it a graft or a viral infection—immunological memory will produce both an accelerated and an enhanced response. Thus, when an additional antigenic challenge presents itself in the form of a skin graft, the graft may be rejected in a matter of days instead of weeks; if the challenge is in the form of reinfection with a virus, antibody will be formed quickly, it will persist for a greater length of time, and it will be more abundant (Figure 14–10). This is called the **secondary immune response.** As a consequence, the body's defenses are quickly mobilized and the foreign intruder is quickly overwhelmed. The prompt secondary immune response is of great consequence to someone who has been vaccinated or who has recovered from an

FIGURE 14–10 The formation of antibody with repeated challenges of antigen.

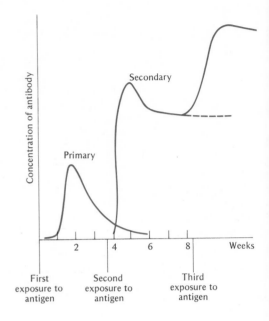

---

**BOX 14C  AIDS, a failure in immune surveillance**

AIDS is a frightening disease that is spreading rapidly. There are more than 30,000 patients in the United States, and there are millions of Americans who are silent carriers of the infection. AIDS does not kill on its own, but rather death results from a range of lethal opportunistic infections and unusual cancers. AIDS is a new infection of humans that began in Africa in the early 1950s, later spreading to the Caribbean and then to the United States and Europe. The first sign of the new disease was the appearance of a rare cancer of blood vessel tissues in the skin and the internal organs called Kaposi's sarcoma. Many of these sarcoma patients turned out to have a history of homosexuality. Later, AIDS was discovered among users of intravenous drugs, recipients of frequent blood transfusions, and heterosexuals with multiple sex partners who had contact with AIDS infected individuals.

Only 3 years after the disease was described its cause was identified: a human retrovirus, called HTLV-III (human T lymphotropic virus III) or HIV (**human immunodeficiency virus**). Recent work has shown that HTLV-III homes on to the $T_4$ cell, indeed, the $T_4$ cell surface acts as a receptor for the virus. Once inside the cell, the virus multiplies. One of the viral genes stimulates translation of viral RNA directly into protein, allowing for increased viral replication and building up the numbers of cells that are infected and killed.

The viral particles released from the dead cells, may then proceed to invade other T cells, and it is the depletion of the $T_4$ helper cells that results in a defective immune surveillance system. As a consequence of viral destruction of cells, lymphocyte numbers decline, delayed hypersensitivity reactions are absent, lymphokine production is reduced, cytotoxic T-cell activity is impaired, macrophages are diminished in their ability to attack foreign substances, and B cell function is virtually lost. "Blinded" to foreign invaders, the body of an AIDS patient is at an increased risk from bacterial infections, and other pathogens, as well as tumors; diseases that would ordinarily cause little or no harm now become a threat to life.

The AIDS virus indergoes rapid antigenic change and in this way possibly is able to evade immune detection even early in the infection. This also hampers the development of an effective vaccine. Nevertheless, the search for a vaccine continues.

The drug azidothymidine (AZT), which inhibits reverse transcription, has some clinical benefit in treating AIDS; however, it is a highly toxic compound, and a course of treatment is quite expensive. Drugs that specifically affect the replication of the virus or inhibit its capacity to invade cells are being developed; these in conjunction with vaccines hold out promise for both protection and cure of AIDS.

---

infection; a second attack by the same antigen stimulates so prompt and massive an outpouring of the correct antibody that the infection is stopped in its tracks. In much the same way that training refines one's physical competence (practice makes perfect), the priming of the immune system through "memory" enhances its capacity to defend the body against alien agents. A summary of the origin of the cells of the immune system is illustrated in Figure 14–11. The operation of the immune system is shown in Figure 14–12.

**Two kinds of acquired immunity: active and passive.** The development of antibodies in response to an alien antigen is called **active immunity.** It can come about in either of two ways: (1) infection, that is, by having the disease—the usual occurrence when we recover from such childhood illnesses as measles, mumps, and chickenpox—or (2) immunization, the deliberate inoculation of the disease agent or a close relative (Box 14B).

How does immunization by inoculation,

FIGURE 14–11 A summary of the origin of the cells of the immune system.

**289**

**BLOOD AND IMMUNITY**

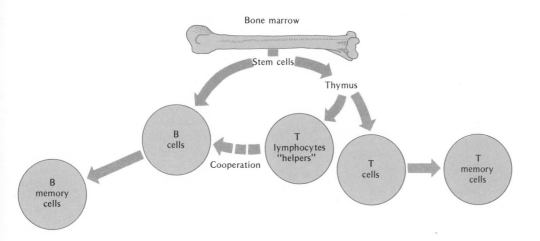

or vaccination, work? The mechanism is that already described in the discussion of the primary and secondary immune responses. When we are vaccinated against a particular disease agent, we receive a series of graded challenging doses of antigen— small at first and larger later on. The antibody response to the first challenge is usually slow, and the antibodies circulate in the bloodstream for only a short time. Periodic booster shots of antigen subsequent to this initial series serve to keep the immune system primed, and thus immunity remains strong and long. Since the immune reaction is highly specific, immunity gained by vaccination against one disease does not ordinarily protect against another. Thus, commonly we must be vaccinated against each kind of disease with a specific material.

**Passive immunity** is borrowed immunity. In passive immunity, the antibodies developed in another individual (by infection or immunization) are injected into the body of a person to be protected against that disease. Thus, recipients of the immune serum containing antibodies do not build their own antibodies against the disease agent (or its product), but simply borrow antibodies that have been made by another. Usually these antibodies on loan circulate in the recipients' bodies for 3 to 5 weeks and then are destroyed by their own reticuloendothelial systems. Passive immunization almost invariably causes recipients to form antibodies against the proteins in the immune serum, and 2 to 3 weeks later the individuals may show signs of serum sickness. Repeated exposure—that is, a second or third dose of immune serum—is often quite dangerous.

Why is passive immunity used when it is such a temporary protective device? Passive immunity is useful because it is immediate, whereas active immunity takes time to develop. Therefore, passive immunity is used in the treatment of virulent diseases such as acute diphtheria, tetanus (this is the shot of antitoxin), measles, and infectious hepatitis—cases where there is insufficient time for the afflicted individual to produce a strong active immunity. In snakebite, borrowed antibody (if available) can prevent death if administered quickly. A baby is born with antibody borrowed from its mother; the antibody crosses the placenta to enter the child's circulation. Some temporary protection is also transferred to the young via the mother's milk (colostrum), which contains antibodies to a variety of disease agents. In this way a newborn child is protected against poliomyelitis, measles, and mumps. The passive immunity of the infant against poliomyelitis lasts 6 weeks, and measles and mumps immunity lasts for less than 1 year after birth. To gain lasting acquired immunity, the child must develop its own active immunity.

## What is an antibody and what does it do?

Antibodies may be thought of as molecular missiles designed to hit and inactivate a specific alien target, formed in response to the presence of the alien substance (antigen) in the bloodstream. How do antibodies recognize the antigen they are to neutralize, and how do they accomplish their task? These highly specific, tailor-made proteins are of large molecular size, consisting of about 1,500 amino acids strung together to form four chains, and are located in the gamma globulin fraction of the blood plasma. Two of the four chains are identical to one another, are longer and therefore heavier, and are called the heavy chains; the other two, again identical to one another, are shorter and lighter and are called the light chains. The antibody molecule can be represented in such a way that the heavy chains form a Y, and the light chains sit on the outside of the V-shaped portion of the Y, producing a thickened region. The binding of the heavy-heavy chains and the heavy-light chains is accomplished by sulfur-sulfur (disulfide) bridges (Figure 14–13).

All antibodies are alike in their amino acid composition except for about 50 positions in the V-shaped portion. This is called the variable region (Figure 14–13). It is the variable region that is the antibody's **recognition site**. The three-dimensional configuration of this region is complementary to a small region of the antigen called the **antigenic determinant**. Substitution of different amino acids in the variable region of the antibody provides different surface configurations in almost infinite array—one to fit almost every conceivable kind of antigen. (A conservative estimate, involving 50 positions of both

FIGURE 14–12 The operation of the immune system.

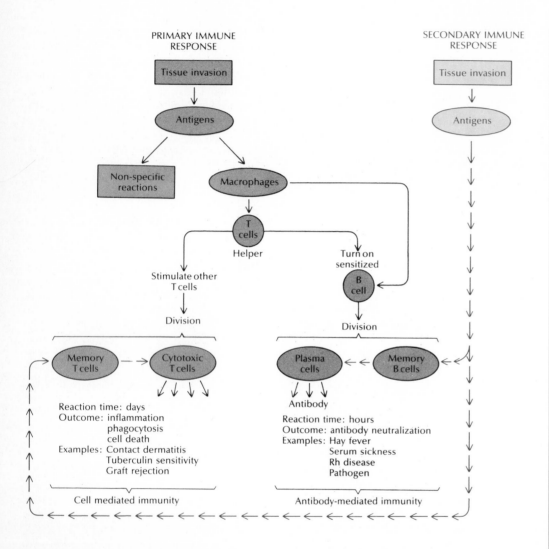

PRIMARY IMMUNE RESPONSE

SECONDARY IMMUNE RESPONSE

Tissue invasion

Antigens

Non-specific reactions

Macrophages

T cells

Helper    Turn on sensitized

Stimulate other T cells    B cell

Division    Division

Memory T cells — Cytotoxic T cells

Plasma cells ← ← Memory B cells

Antibody

Reaction time: days
Outcome: inflammation
phagocytosis
cell death
Examples: Contact dermatitis
Tuberculin sensitivity
Graft rejection

Reaction time: hours
Outcome: antibody neutralization
Examples: Hay fever
Serum sickness
Rh disease
Pathogen

Cell mediated immunity

Antibody-mediated immunity

Tissue invasion

Antigens

---

chains with an independent choice between just two amino acids, would provide $2^{100}$, or $10^{30}$, different kinds of molecules!)

By virtue of their specific geometric configurations, the recognition site of the antibody molecule is complementary to the antigenic determinant region, and one fits into the other just as a key matches its lock (Figure 14–14). The particular form of the recognition site is produced by slight variations in the sequence of amino acids in the terminal ends of the antibody mole-

cules. As a consequence of such variations in amino-acid sequence, slight differences in the folding of the ends of the protein chains are produced, and these contribute to a different geometric configuration of the recognition site. Each configuration is tailor-made to fit on a specific antigen. Thus, an extra bump or depression in the antibody molecule may completely change its fit with a particular antigen, in much the same way that an extra tooth, a burr, or a notch on a key prevents its being used to open a

---

**BOX 14D  Putting antibodies to work**

There was a time when smallpox was the most feared disease in the world. In eighteenth-century England it killed one out of three children before they reached their third birthday. Those that survived were blind or their skin was pitted with deep, angry scars (pockmarks), bitter reminders of their battle with this "most terrible of all the ministers of death." Smallpox played an important role in the colonization of the Americas. The men of Cortez carried smallpox with them, and shortly after their arrival in Mexico (1520) the disease ravaged the Aztec Indians. More than half the Indians were killed by the epidemic, and this was so demoralizing that their defeat was hastened. The early settlers in the American colonies brought their diseases with them, and smallpox was one. Epidemics broke out frequently; in 1721 more than half of the inhabitants of Boston fell ill with smallpox, and the mortality rate was 15%. This highly infectious disease was also an early kind of germ warfare. It was not uncommon that when the English fought the Indians in North America they contaminated blankets with smallpox, spread them among the highly susceptible Indians, and rejoiced when their enemies died.

Today smallpox is virtually unknown outside the laboratory thanks to the development of the first vaccine by Edward Jenner, an English physician, in 1796. Essentially, Jenner took advantage of local folklore and turned it into a reliable and practical device against the ravages of smallpox. The farmers of Gloucestershire believed that people who contracted the mild disease cowpox were assured of immunity to smallpox. Indeed, hardly a milkmaid or a farmer who had contracted cowpox showed any of the disfiguring scars of smallpox. Jenner did an experiment to test this. On May 14, 1796, he took a small drop of fluid from a pustule on the wrist of Sarah Nelms, a milkmaid, who had an active case of cowpox. Jenner smeared the material from the cowpox pustule on the unbroken skin of a small boy, James Phipps. Six weeks later Jenner tested his vaccine (*vacca*—cow; L.) and its ability to protect against smallpox by deliberately inoculating the boy with material from a smallpox pustule. The boy showed no reaction—he was immune to smallpox. In the years that followed, "poor Phipps" (as Jenner called him) was tested for immunity to smallpox about a dozen times, but he never contracted the disease.

To this day the same treatment works, and in most developed countries smallpox is unknown because of vaccination. Indeed, after Jenner's work it became common to call all immunization shots "vaccinations" after the first practical technique developed by Jenner nearly 200 years ago. But why does cowpox protect against smallpox?

Smallpox is caused by a virus—a tiny bit of nucleic acid enclosed in a protein jacket. Each virus has its own kind of protein coat, conferring specificity upon its owner. Thus, the various kinds of pox viruses—smallpox, cowpox, and chickenpox—are all distinguishable by their protein coats and, of course, by their genetic codes). The smallpox virus (called **variola**) enters the body through the mucous membranes of the nose and throat when a contaminated article or a droplet containing the viruses comes in direct contact with the body. The viruses spread rapidly via the bloodstream and then localize in the skin and mucous membranes, where they develop into pus-filled sores. In severe cases death may result. (An old curse was "A pox on you and your house!")

Cowpox is a viral disease of cattle, and it is a close relative of the smallpox virus. Cowpox virus (**vaccinia**) and smallpox virus (variola) are antigenically similar, that is, their protein coats have a similar molecular architecture. As a consequence, an individual vaccinated with live cowpox virus develops a mild, single-pustule infection and builds antibodies that will neutralize cowpox virus; such antibodies will also neutralize smallpox virus. Thus, protection is afforded by this vaccination procedure because of the cross reaction of cowpox antibodies with smallpox virus, a condition called **cross immunity**.*

The recent conquest of poliomyelitis by vaccination provides an excellent example of how effective vaccination can be. In 1950–1954 the annual incidence of polio in the United States was more than 20,000 cases; in 1961, after immunization had been developed and practiced, this country had only 61 cases! Initially, live poliovirus was treated with chemicals that inactivated its disease-producing capabilities but allowed antigens to remain for induction of antibodies upon injection into a recipient. Later, poliovirus was grown in monkey kidney cells, and from these cultures three mutant lines were isolated that had lost their disease-producing capacity but not their antigenic properties. As a result effective vaccination with live polio-viruses became practical.

Similarly, live but nonvirulent viruses and bacteria are used in vaccines to provide protection against such maladies as rabies, yellow fever, measles, influenza, diphtheria, whooping cough, and tetanus. The introduced inactivated microbes (or their products) engender immunity without producing disease, and as a consequence sickness and death are virtually unknown from these diseases in the United States and many other countries where vaccination is practiced.

---

* The vaccine for smallpox is prepared today by scratching smallpox or cowpox virus onto the shaved and disinfected skin of a calf. When the pustules are ripe, fluid is collected from them and placed in sterile tubes ready for use.

FIGURE 14–13 (top) (a) Diagram of the antibody molecule. The four protein chains, heavy and light, are held together by disulfide bridges. Each "V" indicates a variable region and each "C" a constant region. (b) A molecular model. Each amino acid is represented by a small sphere. The heavy chains are colored red, the light chains brown. The four chains wind about one another to form a Y shape, with two identical antigen-binding sites at the arms of the Y.

FIGURE 14–14 (bottom) The combination of antigen and antibody involves complementary sites so that a lock-and-key fit is obtained

Light chain

Heavy chain

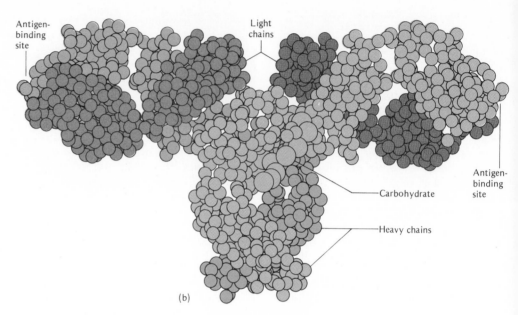

Antigen-binding site

Light chains

Carbohydrate

Antigen-binding site

Heavy chains

(b)

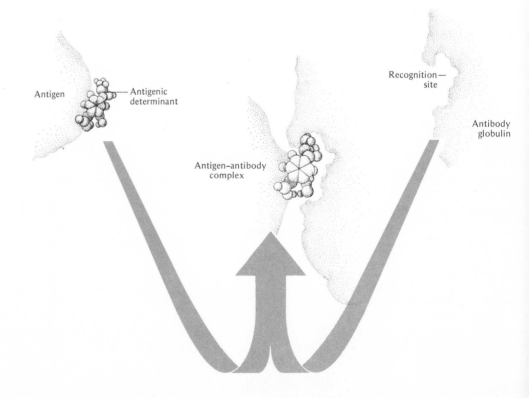

Antigen

Antigenic determinant

Antigen–antibody complex

Recognition—site

Antibody globulin

**TABLE 14–4 The five immunoglobulin classes in humans**

| Class | Structure | Mean adult serum level (mg/ml) | Characteristics | Protective functions |
|-------|-----------|--------------------------------|-----------------|----------------------|
| IgM | (pentamer) | 1.0 | Increases phagocytosis; initiates complement reaction | Assists in engulfing foreign microorganisms; leads to lysis (destruction) of foreign organisms |
| IgG | (monomer) | 12.0 | Crosses placenta; stimulates ingestion by phagocytes; initiates complement reaction | Protects fetus and newborn infant; assists in destroying foreign microorganisms; leads to lysis of foreign organisms |
| IgA | (dimer with secretory piece) | 1.8 | Present in secretions (tears, saliva, intestine, milk) | Protection "outside" the body's tissues |
| IgD | (monomer) | 0.03 | Found on surfaces of B cells | Stimulates B cells to produce specific antibodies |
| IgE | (monomer) | 0.0003 | Causes histamine release from mast cells | Inhibits penetration of parasites (?); leads to lysis of parasites (?) |

particular lock. It has been estimated that the human body can distinguish at least 10,000 different antigens.

Five classes of circulating antibodies are found in the blood plasma. These are designated IgG, IgM, IgA, IgE, and IgD, with Ig standing for immunoglobulin. As Table 14–4 shows, the various immunoglobulins have different structures and functions.

We have thousands of antibody missiles in our immunological defense arsenal, but what exactly does an antibody do, once it recognizes and reacts with its antigen? That depends on the nature of the particular antigen. For example, some disease-producing microorganisms secrete poisons (**toxins**) that destroy host tissue. As a rule these toxins are antigenic, and the antibod-

ies produced against them are called **antitoxins.** Antitoxins can be produced against the toxins of diphtheria and tetanus, thus preventing disease. Active immunity can be engendered by injection of a modified toxin (called **toxoid**), which is nontoxic but antigenic.[3] Some of the snake poisons are enzymes, and neutralization of snakebites can be effected by an **antivenin,** which is an antibody (antitoxin) prepared against the venom toxin.

The antibodies produced against viruses may act in a variety of ways. Some antibodies may prevent the adsorption of the virus onto the host cell; other antibodies may prevent discharge of viral nucleic acid into the host cell by the adsorbed virus (this occurs with poliovirus and influenza virus). In the case of vaccinia virus (cowpox), antibody prevents the escape of the virus from the phagocytic entry vacuole so that viral replication does not occur, and in time the virus is digested within this vacuole. In effect, these varying activities of antibodies neutralize the viral invader.

Certain antibodies react with the lipid layer of the cell walls of bacteria. Antibodies that coat the bacteria in such a way that the bacteria are more easily phagocytized are called **opsonins.** Antibodies that act to clump particles such as bacteria or red blood cells, rendering them more susceptible to removal by phagocytes, are called **agglutinins.** Antibodies that act to dissolve organisms are called **lysins,** and those that react with soluble substances to render them insoluble (and thus much easier to phagocytize) are called **precipitins.**

Although it was once believed that each

---

[3] It is possible to treat toxins with chemicals or heat to destroy their poisonous properties, and then to use these as vaccines. Such an inactivated toxin, called a toxoid, is antigenic and promotes antibody synthesis against the active toxin. The booster shot of tetanus antitoxin is usually a toxoid that results in a buildup of antibody against the toxin.

### BOX 14E  The monospecific missle: monoclonal antibodies

A foreign invader, such as a virus or a bacterium, consists of a vast array of antigens. When they breach the body's outer defenses and contact the cells of the immune system, they trigger a response that consists of the outpouring of a diverse population of antibody molecules with differing specificities. As a consequence of this battery of missles, each with a different target, the body is able to effectively dispose of such a complex threat. In some instances, a show of force from millions of antibody missles is neither necessary nor desirable; indeed, there may be considerable advantage in having a monospecific target-seeking missile, that is, an antibody that will react with only a single antigen. (A likely target might be a specific antigen of a particular kind of cancer cell.) Because the antiserum produced against a virus, a bacterium, or any complex mixture of foreign substances consists of an equally complex array of antibodies that are difficult to separate from one another, the isolation of a single antibody with the specificity of a single antigen remained an elusive goal for decades. The work of Cesar Milstein and Georges Kohler in the mid-1970s changed all that.

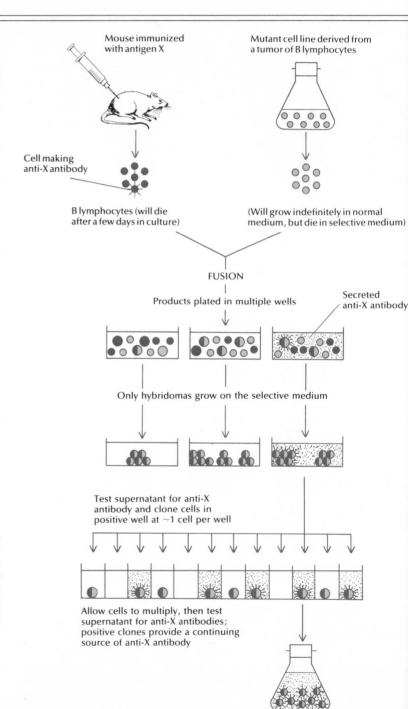

FIGURE 14–15 Schematic diagram showing how hybridomas, which secrete monoclonal antibodies against a particular antigen (X), are prepared. The selective growth medium used contains an inhibitor (aminopterin) that blocks the normal biosynthetic pathways by which nucleotides are made. The cells must, therefore, use a bypass pathway to synthesize their nucleic acids, and this pathway is defective in the mutant cell line to which the normal B lymphocytes are fused. Because neither cell type used for the initial fusion can grow on its own, only the hybridomas survive.

It is known that a single lymphocyte (plasmablast), triggered by antigen, divides into a clone of 256 lymphocytes (plasma cells), each of which secretes one kind of antibody. Unfortunately, such plasma cell clones cannot be grown indefinitely in culture; and, therefore, to recover a large number of antibody producers requires that these antigen-stimulated lymphocytes be transformed into cells capable of continued division in culture—in short, immortalized plasma cells. In contrast, malignant tumor cells, myelomas, rapidly proliferate in culture (as clones) and produce large amounts (10 mg/ml of serum) of immunoglobulin. The myeloma cells are immortal, that is, they continue to grow and divide as long as they are provided with nutrients, and wastes are removed. But, although the myeloma cell can go on dividing and producing immunoglobulin, it is not possible to specify the antigen to which the antibody is directed. The best of both worlds would be to take the ability of one plasma cell to make a specific antibody, and couple that with the myeloma cell's properties of immortality and enhanced antibody production. Milstein and Kohler did just that—they developed a method for fusing a myeloma cell with a lymphocyte that had been triggered by antigen. The result of such a fusion is a cell that consists of a mixture of chromosomes from both cells, and is a hybrid or a **hybridoma,** an immortalized plasma cell. The hybridoma can be grown indefinitely in culture and secretes a large amount of antibody with the specificity for a single antigen, a **monoclonal antibody.** The antibody produced is the one that was being synthesized by the plasma cell before fusion with the myeloma cell. (To ensure that only hybrid cells are recovered, the myeloma cells used are lacking in an enzyme, and will not grow in a medium deficient in the product of the reaction catalyzed by the enzyme; however, a myeloma cell that has successfully fused with a lymphocyte will contain the gene for the enzyme and can grow and reproduce in the deficient medium [Figure 14–15]. The recovery of hybridomas is simple: examine cultures that contain growing clones, which secrete a specific antibody and remove these to fresh medium.)

An important feature of the hybridoma technique is that not only can monoclonal antibodies be made from a complex mixture of antigens, but that monospecific antibodies can be made against an antigen that is a minor component of the mixture. This latter feat is achieved because individual hybridoma clones producing one antibody can be picked out from among the many other hybrid cells producing antibodies of other specificities.

Monoclonal antibodies have been used to determine specific antigens on a complex cell, and have been used for tissue typing before transplantations are undertaken. And, monoclonal antibodies specific for certain cancer cells have been coupled to a toxic chemical so that the poisonous effects are directed specifically to cells bearing the tumor antigen leaving the other normal cells untouched. Countless other medical applications of monoclonal antibodies are now being developed, one of which is the production of highly purified monovalent vaccines. The value of the work of Milstein and Kohler was recognized by their receipt of the Nobel prize in 1984.

of the foregoing phenomena was due to a different kind of antibody, it now is considered that these are merely the many faces of the same antigen-antibody reaction.

Another nonantibody component of the immune system is called complement. **Complement** refers to a complex group of 20 proteins, many of which are enzyme precursors found in normal serum; complement works in conjunction with antibody to destroy foreign cells. The relationship between antibody and complement is similar to that of the ignition key and the engine of an automobile. The antibody is the key with a specific surface configuration that fits into the ignition lock, the antigen. It is the interaction of lock and key in the ignition system, which starts the engine, that does the actual work; similarly, it is the binding of antibody and antigen that triggers complement to be activated. In a complement-dependent reaction, the complement is fixed on the invader's cell surface. Complement has its own recognition sites for antibody and antigen, and its activity is usually of limited duration. The binding of complement to antibody (only IgM and IgG can bind complement) is the basis of the complement fixation test that has long been used for the laboratory diagnosis of syphilis.

One component of complement when bound to a cell surface promotes phagocytosis by macrophages and neutrophils, that is, it is involved in opsonization. Another complement protein attaches to the lipid bilayer of the cell membrane forming a doughnut shape that penetrates the bilayer. The hollow core of the doughnut serves as a pore through which water enters the cell, ultimately causing it to burst. Complement is also involved in the inflammatory response by provoking the release of histamine and attracting white blood cells.

## SUMMARY

**1.** Blood functions in the transport of food, oxygen, waste materials, and hor-

BOX 14F  New organs for old: transplantation

"I am a new Frankenstein," Louis Washkansky told the nurse at his bedside. The macabre humor was appropriate: Washkansky, a sturdy 53-year-old grocer from Capetown, South Africa, had just received the heart of a 25-year-old girl who had died in a traffic accident. Washkansky had literally been brought back to life by a remarkable surgical technique, performed by Dr. Christiaan N. Barnard on December 3, 1967. On that day Barnard made medical history. Other surgeons around the world have performed similar transplants, but of the 6,403 patients who received hearts, only 3,952 are still alive. Now, on the average 81.6% of the recipients are alive after the first year, and 78.7% survive after 5 years. The number of individuals who could benefit from a heart transplant is estimated at 100,000 per year at an average cost of $150,000 per operation.

Between 1936 and 1957, many attempts were made to transplant kidneys, but none survived for more than 7 months. By 1977 thousands of kidneys had been transplanted; 55% of the kidneys from related donors (siblings or parents) and 20% of the kidneys from unrelated donors (mostly cadavers) were functioning 1 year after the transplant operation. There are even reports of kidney transplants functioning for 7 years in related donors and for 4 years in unrelated donors.

The recent success of organ transplants is not due solely to greatly improved surgical skill or to methods of preserving the transplanted organ itself, although these are important. A key factor has been the development of methods to bypass the rejection of the transplant; tissue typing of organs (in much the same way that blood is matched for transfusion purposes) and the use of immunosuppressive agents.

It has been determined that acceptance or rejection of a graft depends on a relatively small number of genes (called **histocompatibility genes**). The closer the genetic constitution of the graft and the host, the better the antigenic match, and the more likely the graft will survive. Before any transplant is attempted, an evaluation of the tissue-transplant antigens is made, using lymphocytes or other white blood cells that carry the histocompatibility antigens. In practice, the genetic constitution of the host is matched as closely as possible with that of the donor. Ideally, grafts should be made between twins or close relatives (brothers and sisters). Once tissue typing is satisfactory the patient who is to receive the donor organ may be surgically drained of some lymphocytes to diminish the immune response.

Administration of immunosuppressive agents helps to blunt the rejection mechanism. Drugs such as azathioprine, a nucleic-acid antagonist, inhibit the division of lymphocytes and diminish antibody formation. Cyclosporin, a fungal product that blocks T cell function, is commonly used to delay the rejection response. Another practice is to bombard the lymphocyte centers with ionizing radiations such as x rays. This disrupts the lymphoid cells and inhibits the rejection of the graft.

Immunosuppression is at best a poor expedient. Upsetting the defense mechanism of the body does more than promote graft acceptance; it promotes the possibility of successful invasion by disease organisms. The graft may be accepted by the host, but the host may die of viral or bacterial pneumonia or of a disease produced by some other infectious agent. Thus, an attempt must be made to keep lymphocyte production at such a level that grafts are accepted while an immune response for disease protection is maintained. The balance is obviously very delicate. One hope for overcoming graft rejection lies in the development of blood-soluble tolerance-inducing antigens. These would swamp the immune centers of the host before rejection could be initiated; they would not permit the host to reject the graft and thus would permit acceptance of the graft. Work on these drugs is progressing, and the hope is that they will be available soon so that "spare-part" surgery will become commonplace.

mones; in the regulation of temperature; and in the control of disease.

2. Blood consists of plasma, red cells (erythrocytes), white cells (leukocytes), and platelets (thrombocytes).

3. The plasma consists of 92% water plus proteins (albumin; alpha, beta, and gamma globulins; and fibrinogen), salts, sugars, lipids, vitamins, hormones, and waste materials. Its composition is controlled by a series of feedback mechanisms. The proteins maintain osmotic pressure, contribute to the maintenance of blood pressure, buffer the blood, and are important in clotting and antibody formation.

4. Erythrocytes are formed in bone marrow. When mature, they are enucleate, biconcave sacs of hemoglobin that can reversibly bind oxygen, forming oxyhemoglobin. Oxygen is picked up at the lungs, where the pressure is high, and released in the tissues, where the pressure is low.

5. Leukocytes are of two basic types: granulocytes (formed in the bone marrow) and agranulocytes (formed in the lymphoid tissue). Both are important in combating disease and infection.

6. A rising white cell count signals disease. Increase in a particular kind of white cell may indicate a specific kind of disease. Anemia may be due to a lowered red cell count or to lack of iron, vitamin $B_{12}$, or folic acid, which interferes with hemoglobin formation.

7. Platelets, fragments of megakaryocytes, disintegrate when in contact with damaged tissue. Along with calcium ions, vitamin K, and protein (clotting factors), a series of reactions produces a fibrin meshwork that traps red cells and forms a clot, sealing the wound. Lack of clotting factors causes bleeder's disease (hemophilia). Anticlotting factors (antithrombin, heparin) in the plasma prevent platelet breakdown and embolus formation in the absence of tissue damage.

8. Natural physical barriers such as the skin, mucous secretions, saliva, tears, ear wax, stomach acid, urine acidity and flushing action, coughing, and sneezing all protect the body against foreign substances and disease organisms. Cells of the reticuloendothelial system (fixed phagocytes) that line the sinusoids of the liver and spleen act as a second line of natural defense.

9. Inflammation is a local response to tissue damage. White cells (neutrophils) and fluid accumulate, and some local clotting occurs. The neutrophils engulf and destroy the foreign material by means of lysosomes; pus may accumulate.

10. The human immune system consists of the spleen, thymus, tonsils, bone marrow, and lymph nodes, all linked by blood vessels and lymphatics.

11. Acquired immunity involves antibody production by lymphocytes in response to antigens. The reaction is highly specific, and each antigen engenders production of a specific antibody. Autoimmune disorders involve production of antibodies against the body's own tissues.

12. T lymphocytes and B lymphocytes are formed in the bone marrow, but T cells spend some time in the thymus. Each T lymphocyte has on its surface about 40,000 molecules, all of one kind: these are receptors specific for one kind of antigen. Receptors specific for the body's own tissues (self-antigens) are normally destroyed early in embryonic life so that the immune system is self-tolerant.

13. During the primary immune response to an antigen, macrophages process antigens so that they can be recognized by helper and inducer T cells. T lymphocytes divide and form cytotoxic T cells that destroy the foreign substance. This reaction, called cell-mediated immunity, is also responsible for graft rejection and any natural destruction of cancer cells. T cells are also involved in hypersensitivity reactions.

14. B lymphocytes are involved in humoral immunity. In response to antigen, a clone of plasma cells is formed from a specific B lymphocyte. Antigen is bound to antibody molecules on the surface of the lymphocyte, and this triggers the B lymphocyte to produce specific antibody in massive amounts.

15. T and B cells may both cooperate in response to a particular antigen.

16. A repeated challenge by the same antigen produces a secondary immune response. Members of previously activated T- and B-cell clones retain immunological "memory" of the first antigen, and so an accelerated and enhanced response is induced.

17. Active immunity is produced in response to infection or immunization. Immunization involves inoculation with graded doses of antigen, attenuated disease agents, or closely related antigens (cross immunity).

18. Passive immunity involves direct injection of antibodies into infected or poisoned individuals who have had insufficient time to develop their own active immunity.

19. Antibodies are gamma-globulin molecules (macroglobulins), whose recognition site is complementary in geometric form to the antigenic determinant region; the form of the recognition site is produced by variations in amino-acid sequences. The matching mechanism allows antibody to specifically bind antigen. Inactivation of antigen may be by combination with antibody, forming a complex.

20. Antitoxins are produced in response to toxins. Active immunity is produced by inoculation with toxoid, such as antivenin against snake venom.

21. Viral antibodies may prevent viral adsorption to cells, discharge of viral nucleic acid, or escape of the virus from a cellular vacuole.

22. Bacterial antibodies dissolve bacteria (lysins), or they may clump them (agglutinins), coat them (opsonins), or precipitate them (precipitins), thus making them more easily phagocytized.

23. Allergens cause B lymphocytes to form IgE antibodies, which are bound to the mast cell's surface. On reexposure to the same

## BOX 14G Wheezes and sneezes

Whatever turns your skin to scum
Or turns your blood to glue,
Why that's the what, the special what
That you're allergic to.

OGDEN NASH, 1938

If your eyes tear from pollen, or if you break out in a rash from penicillin, then you know what Ogden Nash was referring to when he penned these lines. And, if it is of any consolation, you are not alone in your allergies. Some 37 million Americans suffer from one allergy or another, and 2,000 to 4,000 die of asthma, a respiratory disorder often caused by allergy. The offending substances, **allergens,** range from nuts, fruits, milk, chocolate, pollen, dust, feathers, hair dander, and drugs to bee stings. To be allergic to these agents, a susceptible individual must be assaulted twice. With the first assault, the person becomes sensitized, and with the second he or she reacts with the symptoms of allergy: sneezing, running nose, itching, coughing, hives, and swelling.

The basis of the allergic response is this. Allergens trigger B lymphocytes to form IgE. However, these antibody molecules do not circulate freely; the tails of these Y-shaped molecules are embedded in the membranes of mast cells, which resemble the basophils of the blood. The mast cells contain membrane-enclosed granules that are rich in substances called **histamines.** Upon subsequent exposure to an allergen, the allergen combines with the V-shaped ends of two adjacent IgE molecules, forming a bridge. This bridge formation causes the permeability of the mast cell to change, and calcium enters rapidly. The membrane of the granule fuses with the cell membrane and its contents, including histamine, are discharged into the circulation. The entire process of degranulation takes only 2 to 3 minutes. The histamine travels to remote points in the body and sets up the secondary allergic response—hives, burning in the eyes, shock, and shortness of breath. Although allergic responses are quite specific, all have one common property:

they are annoying. The release of histamine causes capillaries to exude fluid at a rapid rate, blood volume is reduced, venous return to the heart is slowed, and cardiac output is diminished; all these symptoms may cause a state of shock to develop, called **anaphylactic shock.** Sometimes histamine causes localized arteriole dilation, there is excessive blood flow in the area, leakage of fluid from the capillary is enhanced, and the skin swells and becomes reddened, causing welts or hives to develop. In hay fever the swelling of tissues due to histamine release occurs in the nose and produces difficulty in breathing; bronchiolar constriction may develop and this may make the individual gasp for breath. Asthma is usually an allergic reaction involving bronchiolar constriction.

There is often a hereditary predisposition toward allergic responses; some individuals seem to produce higher quantities of IgE antibodies than others. The best treatment for allergies is avoidance of the cause. Other tactics include the use of antihistamines or desensitization. In desensitization the individual is repeatedly injected (usually under the skin) with small amounts of allergen so that increased immunity develops slowly; the antibodies formed act to destroy the allergens before they can reach the IgE antibodies bound to tissue cells. **Antihistamines** neutralize histamine and relieve allergy symptoms, such as the sneezy, runny, stuffy nose; the tearing eyes; and the dulled hearing, taste, and smell. They do not prevent tissue destruction, however, and their effects are temporary. Without further treatment the allergy could become dangerous. Total treatment, such as desensitization, should be sought, rather than self-medication with over-the-counter antihistamine remedies.

What is the function of IgE antibody? Some investigators believe that such antibody molecules provide a front-line defense against invaders at the surface of the body—skin, respiratory tract, and gastrointestinal tract. It may be that the simple act of sneezing is effective in repelling an unwanted foreign substance or that the allergic response prevents some animal parasite from establishing itself in the skin, lungs, or gut. It is possible that allergy may represent a hyperactive immune system primed to resist infectious diseases.

allergen, swelling or destruction of the mast cells with release of histamine causes allergic reactions. Severe reactions may cause a state of anaphylactic shock.

**24.** Desensitization to allergens involves the induction of active immunity and formation of antibodies by inoculation with graded doses of allergen.

**25.** Individuals who are allergic to certain substances often take antihistamine drugs to relieve the symptoms of allergic reactions. It is important to realize that such drugs simply relieve the symptoms, but do not eliminate the cause of the allergic response.

---

**KEY WORDS**

| | | | |
|---|---|---|---|
| | platelets | macrophages | recognition site |
| | thrombocytes | monocytes | antigenic determinant |
| plasma | megakarocyte | lymphocytes | toxin |
| albumin | clotting factors | T cells | antitoxin |
| globulin | hemophilia | B cells | toxoid |
| fibrinogen | embolus | clone | antivenin |
| alpha globulins | anticlotting factors | receptors | opsonins |
| beta globulins | antithrombin | self-tolerance | agglutinins |
| gamma globulins | heparin | cell-mediated immunity | lysins |
| erythocytes | hemocytometer | lymphokines | precipitins |
| red blood cells | natural immunity | delayed hypersensitivity reaction | histocompatibility genes |
| hemoglobin | reticuloendothelial system | immediate hypersensitivity | allergens |
| oxyhemoglobin | sinusoids | humoral or antibody-mediated immunity | histamines |
| leukocytes | inflammation | immunological cooperation | anaphylactic shock |
| white blood cells | neutrophils | plasmablasts | antihistamines |
| erythroblasts | pus | secondary immune response | human immunodeficiency virus |
| granulocytes | acquired immune reactions | active immunity | AIDS |
| agranulocytes | antibodies | passive immunity | complement |
| hemorrhage | antigens | variola | hybridoma |
| serum | autoimmune disorder | vaccinia | monoclonal antibody |
| fibrin | primary immune response | cross immunity | |

---

**TOPICS FOR REVIEW AND DISCUSSION**

1. How is the body able to distinguish between self-antigens and foreign antigens?

2. What are antibodies and how do they work?

3. Contrast passive immunity with active immunity.

4. What are the special and distinct roles performed by T and B lymphocytes?

5. Describe the mechanisms involved in the formation of a blood clot.

6. List the components of blood and give a function for each.

7. What is immunization and why does it work?

8. How is antibody specificity related to protein structure?

9. What is a reasonable explanation for the similarity of blood plasma to sea water?

10. Why are transplants from genetically dissimilar animals rejected?

11. List and describe several methods of circumventing graft rejection.

## Tragedy under the sea

It was scheduled to be a routine mission, a dive of about an hour's duration in only a few hundred feet of water off Key West, Fla. The 23-foot-long submersible, designed by famed inventor-oceanographer Edwin A. Link, seemed more than equal to the task. Since it began operating as an oceanographic research vessel for the Smithsonian Institution two years ago, *Sea-Link* had easily plunged to depths of 1,000 feet. But this time, as the minisub maneuvered in swift currents of the Gulf Stream, routine turned abruptly into tragedy.

*Sea-Link* was checking and collecting fish traps near the wreckage of an old destroyer scuttled last year to create a man-made reef that would encourage marine growth. Suddenly, *Sea-Link*'s crew heard the harsh, rasping sound of metal rubbing against metal. Apparently pushed off course by an unexpectedly strong current the sub had become ensnarled in cables and other debris. As rescue ships hurried to the scene *Sea-Link*'s crewmen were told to exert themselves as little as possible in order to conserve oxygen. The crew could do little else. At the pressure that exists at a depth of 360 feet (162 lb per square inch) a free swim to the surface was far too risky.

By the time the sub was freed the men had been under water 31 hours. It was a bittersweet success. Two crewmen emerged unharmed from the forward compartment, where the atmosphere had remained at about sea level pressure. But rescuers had to leave two others (whose motionless bodies could be seen through portholes) inside the aft compartment while it was slowly depressurized; if the men were still alive, suddenly opening the hatch at sea level would have caused a possibly fatal case of bends. When the hatch was opened, the fears were confirmed: both crewmen had died of carbon dioxide poisoning.

# 15

# Gaseous Exchange: Respiration

## 15-1 WHY DO WE NEED A RESPIRATORY SYSTEM?

We live aboard the spaceship earth. Our precarious existence depends on a self-contained life-support system that provides fuel (food), water, and air. Without these we cannot survive for long. Deprived of food, earthlings like ourselves can live for weeks, without water for a few days; in the absence of air, life is snuffed out in a matter of minutes. Why is this so?

The countless millions of cells of the body all require energy for their operation. They must be supplied with energy-rich fuel molecules, but to release the energy locked within the chemical bonds, oxygen is required. The oxidative combustion of fuel (food), taking place within the metabolic furnace of the cell, liberates energy for the performance of work. The fuel molecules contain carbon atoms, and when the fuel is burned a gaseous ash, carbon dioxide, is produced as a by-product. Since carbon dioxide is a cellular poison, it must be eliminated directly. Unlike food and water, neither the carbon dioxide that results from metabolism nor the oxygen of the air can be stored within the body. Consequently, oxygen must be continuously supplied from the air around us and carbon dioxide must be disposed of. How do our cells exchange essential oxygen for useless, poisonous carbon dioxide?

The exchange of gases between the living organism and its environment is called **respiration.** Respiration in human beings involves three related processes (Figure 15–1). The direct exchange of gases between environment and organism is called **breathing** or **ventilation;** it primarily involves physical phenomena and is performed by the external respiratory system. Oxygen is transferred from the respiratory system to the blood, by which it is carried to every cell of the body and exchanged for carbon dioxide. The carbon dioxide is carried in the blood back to the respiratory system, where it, in turn, is given up in exchange for more oxygen. The transfer of gases between the blood and other tissues of the body is called **internal respiration** and strictly speaking is a function not of the external respiratory system but of the circulatory system. It completes the essential second stage of the total exchange process between the air and the body's cells. Finally, there is **cellular respiration**—the chemical reaction of oxygen with organic fuel molecules within the cell to release energy, carbon dioxide, and water. This chapter will concern itself with external and internal respiration; cellular respiration is discussed in Chapter 4.

We and all other inhabitants of the surface of the earth are surrounded by an immense ocean of air, the **atmosphere.** The atmosphere presses down on all that live at the surface of this planet of ours, and we live at the bottom of that ocean of air, moving about in it like deep-sea fish. Air is a mixture of gases consisting of 21% oxygen, 78% nitrogen, 0.04% carbon dioxide, and less than 1% argon, helium, neon, and other rare gases. Probably 80% of all the animals that inhabit the earth breathe free air—mammals, birds, reptiles, amphibians, insects, land snails, and earthworms. The remaining 20% "breathe" air dissolved in water—fishes, amphibians, and aquatic invertebrates (such as lobsters, clams, starfish, and sponges).

Gas exchange between an organism and its environment always takes place by diffusion[1] across a moist plasma membrane. Diffusion is a relatively slow process, and in liquids a gas can traverse only very short distances by this mechanism (a maximum distance of 1 mm); thus animals that rely solely on diffusion to obtain sufficient oxygen for metabolic needs and to eliminate carbon dioxide must be small, have a low metabolic rate, or be constructed in such a way that the cells are nowhere very distant from the surrounding medium. Larger creatures require the maintenance of a respiratory surface of dimensions large enough to allow sufficient oxygen and carbon dioxide to be exchanged to meet the metabolic requirements of the body; the larger and more active the organism, the more oxygen is required and the larger the respiratory exchange surface must be. The respiratory exchange surface is usually thin, delicate, and moist and must be not only exposed to the environment for gas transfer but protected against injury. Here is the dilemma: how can a respiratory surface be thin, delicate, large, exposed, protected, and (especially in air) kept moist all at the same time?

One obvious way to expose a large surface

---

[1] Refer to Chapter 2 for definition of diffusion.

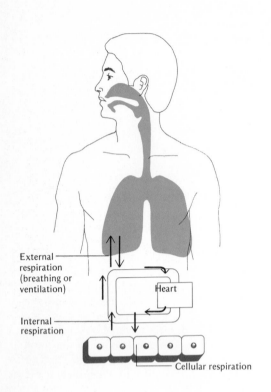

FIGURE 15–1 The three kinds of respiration.

External respiration (breathing or ventilation)

Heart

Internal respiration

Cellular respiration

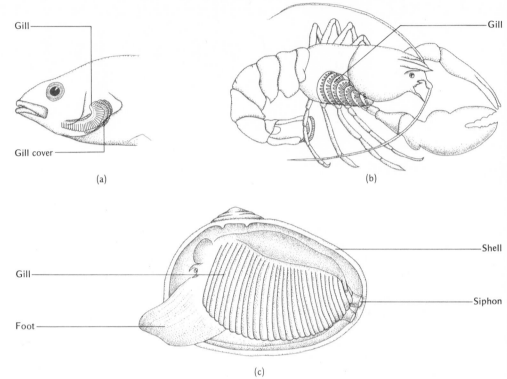

FIGURE 15–2 A variety of gills. (a) Gills of a fish. (b) Gills of a lobster, with a portion of the gill cover removed. (c) Gills of a clam, with one of the shell valves removed.

Gill

Gill cover

(a)

Gill

(b)

Shell

Gill

Siphon

Foot

(c)

area for respiratory exchange would be to utilize the entire body surface; however, such an arrangement would readily suffer mechanical damage and could not be protected easily. Nevertheless, some organisms manage this way—particularly small aquatic animals such as flatworms, sponges, hydras, and frogs. On land, however, the moist and fragile surface would easily dry out and soon be functionless, so that in most organisms the respiratory surface is confined to a specific region of the body where it is protected from damage and desiccation. The respiratory surfaces of water-dwelling animals (such as clams, lobsters, and fishes) are outgrowths of the body called **gills;** these are kept moist by the water in which the animal lives and are enclosed and protected by a gill cover (Figure 15–2). The land-air

dwellers have ingrowths of the body wall called **lungs** (or **tracheal tubes** in insects) that are protected by being tucked inside the body (Figure 15–3); they are kept moist by mucous secretions and communicate with the environment through a chimneylike opening so that water loss and injury are minimized. Since the amount of gas that can be exchanged by diffusion across moist interfaces depends upon the area exposed, the respiratory surface can be increased tremendously by extensive folding. If the environment (air and water) is actively pumped across the respiratory surface (as in ventilation or breathing), efficiency of gas exchange can be further increased. Once the gas has passed across the respiratory surface, efficiency of distribution is increased greatly if the respiratory surface

is amply supplied with blood; therefore larger animals usually have an efficient circulatory system (Chapter 13). By means of the circulatory fluid, oxygen can be swiftly carried to, and carbon dioxide away from, all the tissues, a system much more effective than transport by diffusion alone.

Gills and lungs have several common properties, including moist surfaces, greatly enlarged surface areas, a gas or water pump, protection against mechanical injury, and a circulatory system for transfer of gas between the external environment and the internal body cells.

### 15–2 THE RESPIRATORY TREE

Air passes from the outside of the body to the respiratory exchange surface, the lungs,

FIGURE 15–3 The respiratory system of an insect and a mouse. (a) The insect's tracheal system consists of highly branched tubes that carry oxygen directly to the cells. The entrances-exits for the tracheal tubes are porelike spiracles. (b) In the mouse, air enters via the nose and mouth and gas exchange between the air and the blood takes place across the surface of the lung.

into the windpipe (**trachea**), which is a cylindrical tube, 4 to 5 in. long, supported by regularly spaced rings of cartilage. You can feel these rings by running your finger down the front of your throat (Figure 15–4a). Ciliated and mucus-secreting cells line the trachea and help to trap debris and sweep it upward toward the mouth, where it is either swallowed or spat out (Figure 15–6). The trachea divides into two **bronchi**, which enter the lungs and divide 20 to 22 times, producing smaller and smaller tubes, the **bronchioles** (Figure 15–4b). The smallest have no cilia or cartilage, but an abundance of smooth (involuntary) muscle, and communicate directly with grapelike clusters of thin-walled air sacs (**alveoli**). The bronchioles normally widen and narrow as we alternately inhale and exhale. The alveoli are surrounded by a network of capillaries, and there gas exchange occurs (Figure 15–4b). Oxygen from the incoming air diffuses across the moist alveolar membrane into the blood, and carbon dioxide diffuses in the other direction, from blood to alveolus, from where it can be exhaled.

Our lungs weigh only 2.5 lb. They consist of the millions of tiny alveoli, so numerous that their combined surface area is 70 $yd^2$, more than 40 times the area of our skin and equivalent in surface area to about one fourth of a tennis court. The alveoli and associated bronchioles give the lung a soft, spongy texture. In addition, there are elastic tissue, numerous nerves, and blood vessels. The pair of lungs lies free in the chest (thoracic) cavity, attached to each other by the bronchi. The two lungs are not mirror images of each other. In humans, the right lung is the larger of the two and is partially divided into three lobes; the left lung is divided into two lobes (Figure 15–4a). The space provided by the smaller left lung is occupied by the heart.

A thin sheet of epithelial cells, called the **pleural membrane**, snugly surrounds and encloses each of the lungs and is continuous with the lining of the chest cavity. The pleural membranes secrete a lubricating fluid

via the **respiratory tree,** a complex branching network of passages resembling a tree trunk and its ramifying roots and rootlets (Figure 15–4). As air moves along the respiratory passages, it is both filtered and conditioned.

Air first enters the respiratory tree through the nostrils, where projecting hairs filter out dust and debris (Figure 15–5a). The air then enters the nasal cavity, which is divided by a septum and lined by a ciliated epithelium. The cilia distribute a mucus film that traps debris, and in conveyor-belt fashion this mucus sheet is moved toward the throat, where it is swallowed or spat out. Beneath the nasal epithelium is a rich network of blood vessels that helps to warm the air as it eddies about in the nasal cavity. Scroll-like turbinate bones and air spaces in the skull (**sinuses**) form a complex labyrinth of

passages that further assist in filtering, warming, and moisturizing the incoming air (Figure 15–5b and c). Even our tears help moisturize the air we breathe, since tear ducts drain the continuously operating tear glands and empty directly into the nasal chamber (Figure 15–5b).

Warmed, humidified, and scoured of dust and small particles, the air passes from the nasal cavity to the throat (**pharynx**), where the air and food passages cross. From the pharynx the air enters the **larynx** (voice box, or Adam's apple) through a slitlike opening, the **glottis,** which is guarded by an elastic flap, the **epiglottis.** The glottis remains open at all times except when we swallow. The larynx, made of cartilage, ligaments, membranes, and muscles, includes the **vocal cords,** by which we speak. It leads directly that reduces friction and allows the lungs to expand and contract without becoming irritated. The amount of fluid secreted is quite small, and it is normally absorbed by lymph vessels as rapidly as it is produced.

We take 4 to 10 million breaths a year. During the passage of air from the nose to the lungs, any number of things may go wrong. Table 15–1 catalogs some of the afflictions of the respiratory tree, from coughing to bronchitis.

## 15–3 ALVEOLUS: RENDEZVOUS OF BLOOD AND AIR

The alveoli of the lungs are moist, diaphanous exchange surfaces with three layers: a thin, fragile epithelium lining the sac; an interstitial layer, also very thin; and an overlay of capillaries arranged in a delicate lacework pattern (Figure 15–4b). The capillary network of the lungs is extensive. Consider the following: in each pound or two of our fatty tissue there are about 6 miles of blood vessels, but if the pulmonary capillaries of our lungs (which weigh a little over 2 lb) were laid end to end, their total length would equal some hundreds of miles.

Gas exchange in the lung occurs in the following way. Air entering the lung has been conditioned and filtered, and it now comes to the blind air sacs, 300 million or more, each enmeshed in a capillary network. Blood enters the capillary network of the alveoli via the pulmonary artery, which in turn comes directly from the heart (Figure 15–7). The meshwork of the microscopic capillaries covers the air sacs as a glove covers a hand, and the interface between air and blood is very thin indeed. Each capillary is only wide enough to permit the blood cells to pass through in single file, and so the diffusion path from gas-filled alveolus to blood-filled capillary is extremely short. Oxygen molecules, relatively more abundant on the alveolar side of the interface than in the blood, dissolve in the filmy moisture coating the alveolus, pass across its thin walls, and diffuse into the

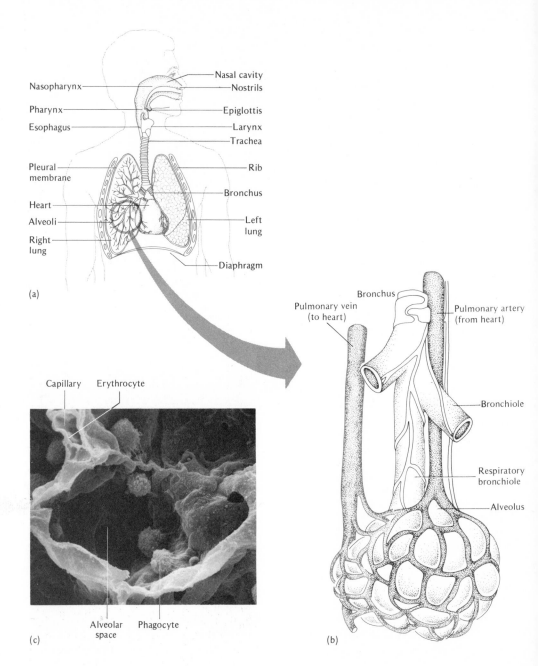

(a)

(c)

(b)

FIGURE 15–5 The nasal cavity, sinuses, and nasal labyrinth. (a) External view of the nose. (b) Frontal view showing the internal arrangement of the sinuses and the turbinate bones. (c) A section through the nasal cavity and two sinuses.

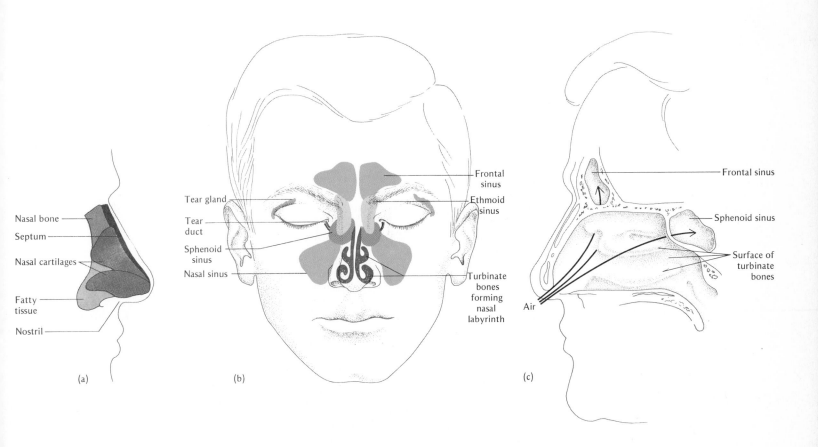

(a)

Nasal bone
Septum
Nasal cartilages
Fatty tissue
Nostril

(b)

Tear gland
Tear duct
Sphenoid sinus
Nasal sinus

Frontal sinus
Ethmoid sinus
Turbinate bones forming nasal labyrinth

(c)

Frontal sinus
Sphenoid sinus
Surface of turbinate bones
Air

bloodstream, where they are bound by the hemoglobin of the red blood cells. Oxygen is swept along in the bloodstream, carried back to the heart via the pulmonary vein, and from there distributed by the systemic circuit to the cells of the body.

The lungs do more than deliver oxygen to the blood. Simultaneously they remove the waste product of cellular oxidation, carbon dioxide. Since carbon dioxide is continuously being formed by the oxidative metabolism of the body's cells, it is more concentrated in the blood than it is in the alveolar air. The net movement of carbon dioxide is from the blood into the lung, and in this way, at exhalation, it leaves the body.

Although oxygen and carbon dioxide both cross the alveolar interface, they move independently of each other. They are like total strangers who simultaneously touch the station platform, one boarding and the other leaving the same train.

The delicate meshwork of capillaries surrounding the alveoli of the lungs contains only 2 oz of blood, a volume exactly equal to the amount of blood pumped out of the right side of the heart with each contraction. Thus, with each heartbeat the oxygenated blood in the lung capillaries is pushed back toward the heart, which it enters at the left side, and a new volume of deoxygenated blood is pumped from the heart to refill the

pulmonary vessels. When we are at rest, each red blood cell remains in the pulmonary capillaries for only 0.75 second, but this is time enough for it to unload its carbon dioxide and take on a fresh cargo of oxygen.

At rest the cells of the body require 250 ml of oxygen each minute, and with exercise this requirement is increased 10 to 20 times— to 5 liters of oxygen each minute (over 1 gal). Any interruption in the delivery of oxygen to the blood or the tissues, which can occur in any number of ways, results in impairment of cellular function and can cause asphyxia. Plasma in equilibrium with air can take up about 0.25 ml of dissolved oxygen per 100 ml. This being so, the heart

**TABLE 15–1 Trouble along the respiratory tree**

| Location | Problem | Possible cause | Cure |
|---|---|---|---|
| Nasal cavity | Bloody nose | Blowing nose too hard | Time |
| | Deviated septum: difficulty in breathing | Punch in the nose | Surgery |
| | Copious secretion from tear glands | Peeling onions or crying | Stop crying, cook onions |
| | Runny nose: inflammation of nasal lining spreading to sinus lining and causing sinusitis and headaches | Severe head cold | Antihistamines relieve symptoms by constricting capillaries and reducing secretion of mucus |
| | Sneezing (a cough in the nose); a reflex action | Irritants in nasal passageway | None, since it is a reflex |
| Pharynx | Tonsillitis: sore throat | Enlarged tonsils | Surgery |
| | Interference with breathing, snoring, restless sleep, dull expression from open mouth, which is necessary for breathing | Enlarged adenoids (lymphoid tissues at rear of pharynx) | Surgery |
| Larynx | Coughing | Talking and eating simultaneously; epiglottis remains open too long and food enters larynx | None, since it is a reflex |
| | Persistent hoarse voice, difficulty in breathing | Cancer of the vocal cords | Surgery |
| Trachea | Asphyxia: choking | Blockage with food, mucus, or blood from an accident | Surgery (cutting an opening and bypassing the trachea, a tracheotomy); Heimlich maneuver* |
| Bronchioles | Asthma: difficulty in exhaling but not inhaling. The resistance in the airways decreases during inhaling because as the lungs expand the bronchioles and alveoli widen, but during exhaling the resistance in the airways increases due to narrowing. | Allergic reaction involving histamine release or nervous stimulation contracts muscles and reduces size of passage | Epinephrine (adrenaline) or other muscle-relaxing drugs directly act on bronchioles to dilate them |
| | Bronchitis: inflammation of bronchiolar tree (excess secretion of mucus blocks bronchioles as phlegm, coughing up phlegm weakens linings, and area is susceptible to infection) | Persistent irritaton, as from colds, infection, cigarette smoke, smog | Wait for cold to get better, stop smoking, reduce air pollution |
| Lungs | Emphysema: impaired lung function, pain (Box 15A) | Chronic expansion and destruction of alveoli | Stop smoking, reduce air pollution |
| | Pleurisy: pressure, painful breathing, impairment of lung function | Inflamed pleural membranes | |
| | Pulmonary edema: impaired breathing, pressure, pain | Oozing of body fluid into lungs | Rest, aspiration |

* The Heimlich maneuver involves placing the rescuer's fist below the choking person's abdomen just slightly above the navel and pushing upward quickly. This rapid elevation of the diaphragm causes a sharp increase in alveolar pressure and the forceful expulsion of air from the lungs expels the foreign object choking the person.

FIGURE 15–6 Scanning electron microscope view of the ciliated epithelial cells of the windpipe. A mucus droplet is supported by the cilia. (C. Port and I. Corvin, "Ciliated and Nonciliated Epithelial Cells from Hamster Trachea." Cover photograph for *Science*, September 22, 1972.)

FIGURE 15–7 Diagrammatic view of the circulatory pathways leading from the heart to the lung and back to the heart.

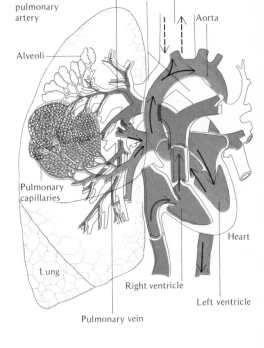

would have to pump 83 liters per minute through the lungs[2] just to meet our needs at rest. This is virtually an impossible task for the heart and is obviously not the way the body's oxygen demands are met. A critical factor in increasing oxygen uptake by the blood is the ability of hemoglobin, present in the red blood cells, to combine with oxygen. In the presence of plentiful oxygen, hemoglobin forms a complex called **oxyhemoglobin** (Figures 15–8); this is unstable, and under conditions where the oxygen is low (as in the tissues) the oxygen

is released from the complex to form hemoglobin again. As a consequence, hemoglobin loads up with oxygen at the lungs and unloads it at the tissue cells. Because of the presence of hemoglobin, the oxygen-carrying capacity of the blood is increased 65 times, to 20 ml per 100 ml, and this means that at rest the heart need pump only 5.5 liters of blood each minute (which it does). Thus, when oxygen diffuses across the alveolus, less than 2% dissolves in the blood plasma and 98% combines with the hemoglobin, the principal oxygen carrier.

Hemoglobin and its association with oxygen are rather remarkable. Hemoglobin is a conjugated protein. The protein portion, **globin,** is combined with the nonprotein prosthetic group, **heme,** a flat, ringlike struc-

ture containing iron in the ferrous state ($Fe^{2+}$). There are four molecules of heme to each molecule of hemoglobin (Figure 15–8). Oxygen combines with the iron of hemoglobin, and for every molecule of hemoglobin four molecules of oxygen are bound: the loose combination converts the hemoglobin to oxyhemoglobin. The reversibility of oxyhemoglobin to reduced hemoglobin depends on the presence of iron in the ferrous state and intact globin. If the globin is denatured or the iron oxidized to the ferric form ($Fe^{3+}$), it can no longer carry oxygen.

Two factors influence the carrying capacity of hemoglobin for oxygen: hydrogen ion or carbon dioxide concentration, and temperature. With increased concentrations of carbon dioxide, the combining capacity of the hemoglobin for oxygen is less, allowing a greater liberation of oxygen from the blood to the tissues (Figure 15–9);

---

[2] This assumes 100% of the oxygen in the blood is delivered to the tissues, which is not the case. Normally the tissues extract only 20 to 25% of the oxygen carried to them.

**307**

BOX 15A Smog, smoking, and emphysema

Each day an average New York City dweller inhales the equivalent of half a pack of cigarettes, even if that individual does not smoke! The dirty air we breathe daily contains about 20 billion foreign particles, and in a lifetime each of us may take in as much as 45 lb of dust. Polluted air, **smog** (*smoke* plus *fog*), blankets most large cities of the world, and our lungs bear scars from breathing this. Smog consists of an aerosol of carbon particles about the size of bacteria, and these settle on the walls of the trachea and bronchioles to be carried out with the mucus sheet. If this were all, we might be in trouble; however, also present in our filthy air are smaller particles—less than 0.3 μm— and these do reach the alveoli. Their cumulative effects are most clearly seen when the lungs of a newborn child are compared with those of an adult city dweller. The infant's lungs are bright and pink, but those of the adult have a dull pink-gray-mottled coloration.

Smog contains not only particles but noxious and toxic gases, such as nitrogen oxides, ozone, sulfur dioxide, and peroxides, and these are not removed by filtration. On a smoggy day in Los Angeles you can smell the ozone and see the brown haze of smog that blankets the basin, choking the inhabitants. With every fire we make, we pollute the air. Coal and low-grade fuel oil send both soot and sulfur dioxide into the air; petroleum refineries, chemical factories, and automobile engines contribute their share of toxic gases. Smog is a by-product of the combustion of hydrocarbons, and the automobile is a prime offender. Every thousand cars that move through a congested city discharge 3.2 tons of carbon monoxide, 400 to 800 lb of hydrocarbon gases, 100 to 300 lb of nitrogen oxides, and other lethal fumes. These poison gases, together with cigarette smoke, cause bronchitis, pulmonary edema, and emphysema (Table 15–1). Bronchitis and emphysema were rare diseases 30 years ago; now they constitute a major respiratory ailment afflicting nearly 20 million Americans. How do smog and smoking produce these respiratory disorders?

The smoke from the burning of tobacco or gasoline contains gases that paralyze the cilia of the trachea and the bronchi. The inactivity of the cilia prevents the mucous blanket from moving, and it accumulates in the bronchioles. (The early morning cough of a smoker is an attempt to clear this mucus from the airways.) Inhaled air easily moves past the mucus and swells the bronchioles, but as the air is exhaled the bronchiole walls collapse, and the air is trapped and held by the mucus plugging the bronchiole. The trapped air stretches the air sacs, they balloon out forming air blisters, and some burst. In the process the alveolar and elastic tissues of the lung are destroyed. Elastic recoil of the lung tissue is lost. The lungs stretch to compensate for the loss of respiratory surface, they press against the walls of the chest and the diaphragm, and the muscles lose efficiency. As a result, the emphysema patient develops a barrel-shaped chest, breathing is difficult, severe oxygen deprivation produces brain damage, and the heart is enlarged and weakened; in severe cases there is a clubbing of the fingers (**pulmonary osteoarthropathy**).

The symptoms begin slowly. Paralysis of the cilia by the toxic fumes, with stagnation of mucus, means that bacterial invaders are no longer swept out, infections develop in the alveoli and spread to the bronchioles—chronic bronchitis develops. Inflammation damages blood vessels, they leak fluid into the lung, and edema results. Respiratory exchange is impaired, and oxygen deprivation ultimately takes its toll. The mortality rate from bronchitis and emphysema due to smog is undetermined, but among cigarette smokers it is 700% higher than among nonsmokers. The Geneva Protocol, which the United States sponsored in 1925 and which all major powers have ratified, bans chemical and biological weapons in war. Gas warfare in our cities, however, is at present not only permitted but prevalent.

FIGURE 15–8 Hemoglobin. (a) Association of hemoglobin with oxygen. Only two of the four protein chains of a hemoglobin molecule are shown. (b) Detail of the chemical nature of the heme in hemoglobin.

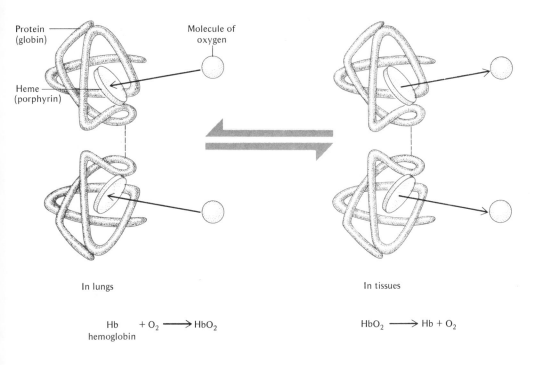

Protein (globin)

Molecule of oxygen

Heme (porphyrin)

In lungs

$$Hb + O_2 \longrightarrow HbO_2$$
hemoglobin

In tissues

$$HbO_2 \longrightarrow Hb + O_2$$

Oxygen molecule attaches here to heme molecule. Since there are 4 hemes per hemoglobin molecule, 4 molecules of oxygen are carried.

(a)

(b)

carbon dioxide levels are especially high where cells are most actively respiring, producing larger amounts of carbon dioxide and requiring more oxygen. A rise in temperature also decreases the oxygen-hemoglobin combination. During increased muscular activity, there occur both an elevation in temperature and an accumulation of acid (due to the production of carbon dioxide and lactic acid), which help to liberate oxygen from the hemoglobin to these tissues.

Oxygen is carried by hemoglobin, but how is the carbon dioxide carried from the cells to the lungs? A small amount (7%) of the carbon dioxide is dissolved in the plasma, and a smaller quantity combines with the water in the plasma to form carbonic acid. An additional 23% is carried in combination with hemoglobin. Most of the $CO_2$ (70%) is carried in the form of bicarbonate in the plasma and red blood cells. Carbon dioxide is 20 times more soluble in water than is

oxygen, and because of this it rapidly diffuses from the blood into the alveolus, is unloaded into the lung, and is subsequently exhaled.

## 15–4 HOW DO WE BREATHE?

We have seen how the respiratory tree is organized and how oxygen and carbon dioxide are exchanged across the alveolar surface. In order to keep a sufficient supply of oxygen in the lungs and to carry away the carbon dioxide, the air in the lungs must constantly be changed. How do we ventilate the respiratory system?

The lungs lie in the chest cavity, bounded on the top and sides by the rib cage with its associated muscles and on the bottom by a strong, dome-shaped sheet of skeletal muscle, the **diaphragm** (Figure 15–4). The pleural membranes surrounding the lungs are continuous with the diaphragm. The

lungs are virtually in a closed chamber. If you watch your chest during a breathing cycle (inhale slowly and exhale slowly), you will see the chest move up and expand as you inhale and move down and shrink in size as you exhale. If you were carefully to open the chest cavity of an anesthetized animal, the breathing movements of the chest would continue; however, the lungs would not inflate, but would remain collapsed. Thus, it appears that the lungs are acting passively in response to changes in the size of the chest cavity. To keep the air moving in and out of the lungs, a bellowslike air pump is at work, operated by the muscles in the rib cage and the diaphragm. How does this air pump work? If we were to take a pair of balloons and place them in a bell jar (Figure 15–10) with the openings into the balloons connected to the outside by a hollow glass tube and the open bottom of the bell jar covered by a rubber sheet, we

FIGURE 15–10 A mechanical model illustrating the filling and collapse of the lungs during inhalation and exhalation.

FIGURE 15–9 The loading and unloading of oxygen by hemoglobin. In the lungs (A) hemoglobin loads up with oxygen and is about 100% saturated, but when such fully loaded hemoglobin reaches the tissues (B), where the oxygen concentration is lower, it begins to release oxygen. This release is further accentuated by the presence of carbon dioxide, acid, or high temperature (arrow). For example, under ordinary conditions, when the oxygen concentration is about 25 mm Hg, the hemoglobin is only 50% saturated, but in the presence of actively metabolizing cells releasing carbon dioxide, acids, and where the temperature is elevated the saturation curve shifts so that the hemoglobin saturation is below 25%. In other words, it has given up 25% of its oxygen to the cells. The shift of the saturation curve favors oxygen release at sites requiring oxygen, and the loading of oxygen at the lungs, where it is more plentiful.

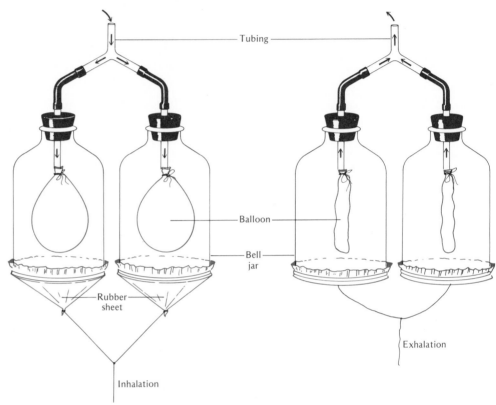

would then have a setup mechanically similar in its operation to that of the lungs. If we pull down on the rubber sheet, the pressure inside the balloons is reduced and, because the air pressure outside is greater, air enters the balloons until the pressure is equalized: the balloons inflate. Anything tending to decrease the gas pressure inside the balloons causes an intake of air. Similarly, a decrease of gas pressure in the lung causes it to fill with air. During inhalation

(also called **inspiration**) the rib muscles contract, drawing the front ends of the ribs upward and outward, an action made possible because the ends of the ribs are attached in a hingelike fashion to the backbone (Figure 15–11). The diaphragm contracts and flattens, and the chest cavity is enlarged. The increased volume of the chest cavity results in a reduced gas pressure in the lungs, and air from the outside rushes in through the windpipe and bronchi to fill the air sacs: the lungs inflate.

Some alveolar cells secrete a protein with detergentlike properties that decreases the surface forces of the fluid film that coats the inner surfaces of the air sacs. This allows for easier expansion of the lung. In some premature babies, however, the secretion of this detergentlike substance is decreased.

Infants who have this condition, called **hyaline membrane disease,** have difficulty with lung expansion, and frequently they die soon after birth because of inadequate ventilation.

The lungs deflate when we exhale (also called **expiration**) by the relaxation of the rib muscles and the diaphragm. The ribs are rotated downward, and the abdominal organs push upward on the diaphragm so that it returns to its original dome shape. This causes the volume of the chest cavity to decrease, and the elasticity of the lungs causes them to recoil, contract, and expel the air to the outside. In contrast to inhalation, exhalation is generally a passive process involving lung elasticity (the lungs themselves are not contractile, having no musculature to speak of).

FIGURE 15–11 Breathing movements. (a) Arrangement of ribs and diaphragm produces an enlarged or reduced chest cavity. (b) A mechanial representation of how the ribs are attached to the backbone. Upward movement of the rib cage increases the size of the chest cavity, and downward movement reduces it.

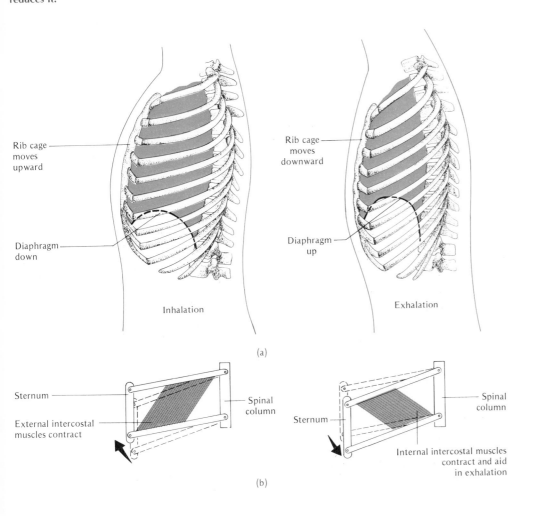

Rib cage
moves
upward

Diaphragm
down

Inhalation

Rib cage
moves
downward

Diaphragm
up

Exhalation

(a)

Sternum

External intercostal
muscles contract

Spinal
column

Sternum

Spinal
column

Internal intercostal muscles
contract and aid
in exhalation

(b)

When we cough or sneeze the abdominal muscles contract and push against the diaphragm, decreasing the thoracic volume suddenly, and there is rapid expulsion of air from the lungs via the nose and mouth. Hiccups are the result of muscular spasms in the diaphragm that cause the chest cavity to enlarge so that air tends to rush inward very quickly. Through a reflex, the epiglottis is quickly closed, the inrushing air sharply strikes the epiglottis, and the characteristic sound of the hiccups is produced. Persistent hiccups can be stopped by inhalation of 5 to 7% carbon dioxide (thus breathing into a paper bag often helps, since one is rebreathing the same air, which consequently has a higher carbon dioxide content). If the condition becomes pathological, the phrenic nerve, which runs to the diaphragm and initiates the spasm, may have to be cut.

With each breath we take in 500 ml of air (Figure 15–12), but only 350 ml of that air actually reaches the alveoli, since the remainder is trapped in the upper respiratory passages (trachea, bronchi, and bronchioles). This 150 ml of trapped air is in dead space, and its oxygen cannot be exchanged across the alveolar surface. The air in the dead space is the first to be expelled with the next expiration. The last 150 ml of air expelled from the alveoli with each breath also remains in this region, and though rich in carbon dioxide, it is the first to be drawn into the alveoli with the next breath. Thus, with each inhalation only 350 ml of new air reaches the lungs to mix with the 2.5 liters already within.

The air in the dead space, as we have seen, plays no role in gaseous exchange and is richer in carbon dioxide than fresh air. If the dead space of the lungs is increased, as, for example, by breathing through a long tube such as a garden hose, the air reaching the alveoli is further enriched in carbon dioxide and depleted in oxygen; this could be fatal. At a concentration of 7% carbon dioxide, we gasp for breath, and at 14% we cannot survive.

The compositions of alveolar and atmospheric air are shown in Table 15–2.

**TABLE 15–2 Gas composition of the air we inspire, the air we expire, and the air in the alveoli**

| Gas | Inspired air | | Expired air | | Alveolar air | |
|---|---|---|---|---|---|---|
| | Partial pressure (mmHg) | % | Partial pressure (mmHg) | % | Partial pressure (mmHg) | % |
| $O_2$ (oxygen) | 157.0 | 20.71 | 110 | 14.6 | 105 | 13.2 |
| $CO_2$ (carbon dioxide) | 0.3 | 0.04 | 30 | 4.0 | 40 | 5.3 |
| $H_2O$ (water) | 9.5 | 1.25 | 45 | 5.9 | 45 | 5.9 |
| $N_2$ (nitrogen) | 593.0 | 78.00 | 574 | 75.5 | 574 | 75.6 |

FIGURE 15–12 Measuring lung function. (a) By the use of a spirometer it is possible to determine lung capacity. Breathing 10 to 14 times a minute, we pass into and out of our lungs about 0.5 liters of air. (b) The working lung capacity is about 4.5 liters as measured by deep breathing in and out, but in actual fact the total lung capacity is 5.5 liters, with 1 liter as residual air.

(a)

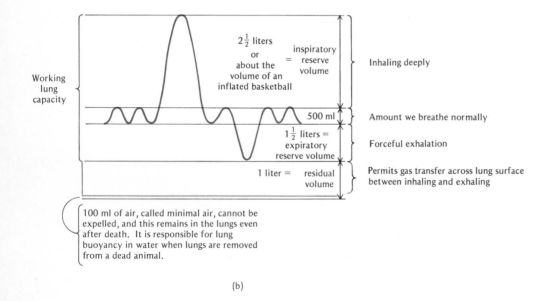

(b)

### 15–5  CONTROL OF BREATHING

Try to hold your breath for as long as you can. In a short time you *must* breathe. This simple exercise clearly demonstrates that gas exchange (ventilation) is so vital to our being that it is not primarily under voluntary control and there exist safeguards to ensure maximum performance under continuous operation.

**Nervous control**

In 1811 the Frenchman César Legallois found that if the cerebrum, cerebellum, and part of the upper brain stem (medulla) (Figure 18–14)[3] were removed from a rabbit, the animal still continued to breathe in a rhythmic pattern. However, if a small region in the lower medulla was damaged or cut out, breathing ceased. Today, it is still generally accepted that the rhythmic pattern of respiration is controlled by a group of interconnected nerves (neurons) in the lower medulla, the **respiratory center** (Figure 15–13). Within the respiratory center there are inspiratory and expiratory neurons, which interact with each other and receive input from other sources to regulate breathing rhythms.

Although the respiratory center of the medulla is the primary region for control of respiration, it is not the only part of the brain that can influence respiration. A reflex is involved in preventing overinflation of the lungs. When the lungs are expanded, nerve endings within the walls are stimulated, and impulses pass from the lungs via the vagus nerve to the medulla, where they inhibit inspiration and excite expiration. This prevents excessive lung distention, so that the lungs are not ripped like an overinflated balloon and do not take up too much blood, depriving the left side of the heart of its supply. Thus, the respiratory center has a built-in safety factor with two feedback loops: one loop is intrinsic in the

---

[3] The nervous system and brain are treated in detail in Chapter 18.

FIGURE 15–13 Location of the respiratory center of a human being.

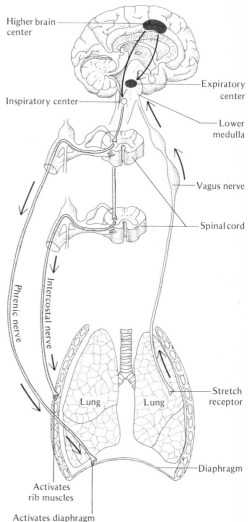

medulla and the other is extrinsic through the reflex system (Figure 15–14). This double control system is characteristic of many important body functions and is essential for a system that must operate without failure for 70 years or more.

The higher centers of the brain (the cerebral cortex) also play a role in respiratory control, and by sending impulses from these centers to the medulla you can voluntarily hold your breath. Such voluntary control of respiration can be maintained for only about 40 seconds, and then you breathe even against your will. The threat of a small child to hold its breath until it dies is just a threat; this cannot be done.

The oscillating mechanism of the respiratory center can, on occasion, fail. Most commonly this is due to a cerebral concussion or an abnormal excessive pressure on the medulla. The pressure causes blood vessels that supply the neurons of the respiratory center to collapse; deprived of oxygen, the neurons cease to function and the respiratory rhythm ceases.

The most common way in which the respiratory center becomes inactivated is by the action of drugs that induce sleep—chloroform, ether, morphine, barbiturates, or other central-nervous-system depressants in excessive and toxic amounts. These substances interfere with oxygen utilization by the cells in the respiratory center, impair nerve impulse transmission and depress

blood flow into this region of the brain. If such damage to the respiratory center is irreversible, death results. Unfortunately, there are few chemical agents that can excite the respiratory center, and so a chemical antidote for an overdose of a sleep preparation is not available; in most cases prolonged artificial respiration is the only means of counteracting severe respiratory depression.

### Chemical control

The nervous signals within the respiratory centers of inspiration and expiration oscillate back and forth to produce a resting rhythm of 10 to 14 breaths per minute, but a short run or sudden fright will convince you that the depth and rate of breathing can be quite variable. During exercise, the breathing rate may be 75 breaths per minute and the volume of air entering and leaving the lungs goes from about 6 liters per minute to between 80 and 120 liters per minute. The maximum possible rate of breathing is about 300 breaths per minute with a flow of 150 to 200 liters of air. We obviously have a great reserve capacity for ventilation. When for some reason (for example, increased exercise) the body needs more oxygen or more carbon dioxide must be expelled, the ventilation rate must be increased. How does the respiratory center "know" what the body's oxygen requirements are?

At first glance it might seem sensible for the amount of oxygen in the blood to influence the respiratory center directly, so that when the blood oxygen level goes down, ventilation increases to compensate; however, this turns out not to be the case. If a person is allowed to breathe and rebreathe air in a closed container, the oxygen in the air gradually decreases, the carbon dioxide content of the air increases, and

**313**

FIGURE 15–15 Chemical receptors acting on the respiratory center.

the respiratory rate increases. If, however, sodium hydroxide or some other chemical is placed in the container to absorb the carbon dioxide so its content does not increase but the oxygen content still decreases, the breathing rate is only slightly increased. Obviously, increased levels of carbon dioxide rather than decreased levels of oxygen stimulate the respiratory center to activity. Convincing proof of this can be obtained by allowing an individual to breathe a gas mixture containing normal amounts of oxygen but increased amounts of carbon dioxide; the respiratory rate is increased even though oxygen levels are normal.

Emotional state, excitement, and exercise increase the metabolic rate, thus increasing carbon dioxide levels in the blood; the rate and depth of breathing are adjusted to meet the body's demand for more oxygen and to prevent accumulation of carbon dioxide. The increased carbon dioxide in the blood travels to the brain and excites the neurons of the inspiratory center; there results an increased volley of impulses to the muscles involved in inspiration, lung expansion becomes greater, and the frequency of the breathing cycle is increased. When the carbon dioxide level returns to normal, the respiratory center returns to its normal oscillatory rhythm.

Carbon dioxide is a poison to most cells, but its complete removal from the blood would be fatal, since it triggers the respiratory center to activity. Rapid, deep breathing (**hyperventilation**), voluntarily undertaken, can so severely deplete the blood of carbon dioxide that the respiratory center may become inactive; dizziness, unconsciousness, and cessation of breathing may result. If the cessation of breathing (**apnea**) lasts long enough, death may ensue.

At birth we take our first breath of fresh air. As the newborn baby is separated from the placenta, its oxygen supply is cut off, the level of carbon dioxide in its blood increases, and this stimulates the respiratory center to send nerve impulses to the muscles of the rib cage and the diaphragm;

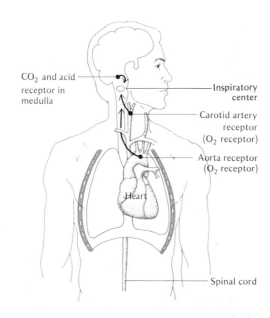

CO$_2$ and acid receptor in medulla

Inspiratory center

Carotid artery receptor (O$_2$ receptor)

Aorta receptor (O$_2$ receptor)

Heart

Spinal cord

these contract, and the first breath is taken. If the newborn baby has difficulty in taking its first breath, air containing 10% carbon dioxide may be administered via the mouth, and this usually triggers the respiratory center to become active. Why does the obstetrician slap a newborn baby, so that all of us enter the world crying? Painful stimuli almost anywhere in the body trigger a reflex reaction of the respiratory center, and a good slap on the infant's bottom starts respiration. Other shocks, such as a cold shower, also trigger receptors to send impulses to the respiratory center and stimulate it; this gives us a breath of fresh air and thus we find it invigorating.

Although the respiratory centers of the brain monitor carbon dioxide levels in the blood and thus regulate ventilation, there is an independent, or backup, system that registers changes in the amount of oxygen in the blood. Receptors chemically sensitive to oxygen are located at the branching of the carotid arteries in the neck and the aortic arch; they are connected to the medulla by nerves (Figure 15–15). If the oxygen

**BOX 15B Why can't we breathe under water?**

The body requires about 300 ml of oxygen per minute. Why can't we swim around in the water and obtain oxygen in much same fashion as we swim in a sea of air? Seawater, or any kind of well-aerated water, contains about 0.3 ml of oxygen per 100 ml of fluid. Each breath of air we take in (about 500 ml) contains about 100 ml of oxygen. Thus in order to process enough water to satisfy our resting need for oxygen for a single minute, we should have to pump 100 liters (about 25 gal) of water into and out of our lungs every minute. This is impossible for a number of reasons. Our lungs operate on a back-and-forth tidal system, and we move a relatively small mass of respiratory medium (air). If water were to enter our lungs laden with oxygen, it would be mixed with oxygen-deficient water. If the flows were not kept separate we would get very little out of the incoming water.

There is another drawback to ventilating our lungs with water as the respiratory medium; water is heavy, and to move it into and out of our lungs (that is, an acceleration-deceleration and reversal of flow of sufficient water) would be very costly in terms of energy expended. To perform such a feat we would require a set of muscles 20 times more effective than the heart (which pumps

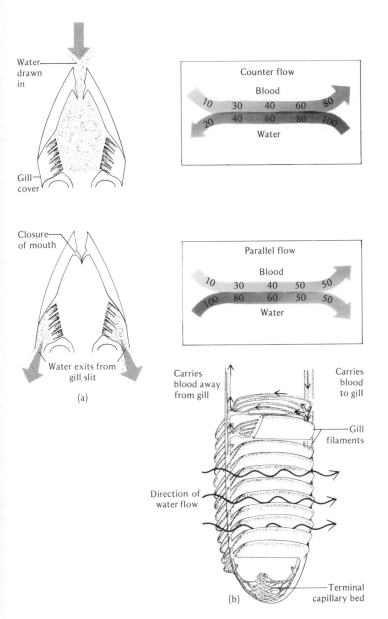

about 5 liters per minute). Another problem posed in using a lung under water is that the diffusion of the gas from the water to alveolar surface would be very slow because of the slow rate of diffusion of oxygen in water. The rate of diffusion of oxygen in air is 300,000 times faster than it is in water. Clearly, for a warm-blooded animal with a high metabolic rate and a high oxygen demand, air breathing is the preferred mode of respiration. It has one major disadvantage: the danger of desiccation. This is combatted by continuous production of mucus by the cells lining the lungs.

Our lungs are designed to breathe air, not water, and attempts to convert the air-breathing lung to a water-breathing lung have disastrous consequences: drowning. How does a fish breathe under water? In a "water-breathing" gill the anatomy of the respiratory system is very different from that found in a lung. Gill-bearing animals do not use a tidal, back-and-forth type of respiration, because to move water in, stop it, and then push it out is energetically uneconomical. Fish and other gill-bearing animals have a one-way flow system. Water enters a fish via the mouth and is drawn into the pharynx with the gill covers (opercula) closed (Figure 15–16a). Then the mouth closes, and the opercula move outward; this enlarges the gill cavity, and water is drawn past the gills and exits via the gill slits. A fish does not "rebreathe" its respiratory medium, but constantly takes in new water as it swims along. The direction of water flow over the gill filaments and across the thin-walled gill lamellae is opposite the flow of blood through the gill, and such a countercurrent flow permits a more efficient and complete oxygenation of the blood than would occur if the currents flowed parallel to one another in the same direction (Figure 15–16b).

If we were to breathe under water, we would need gills and a redesigned ventilation system, but gills would be useless on land, for they would quickly dry out; the soft gill filaments would collapse and stick to one another, and air could not reach most of the gill surface. A fish out of water or a human being under water cannot respire without some kind of accessory equipment.

FIGURE 15–16 Fish gills. (a) Diagram of the movement of water through the gill chamber of a fish. (b) Detail of water movement across the gill, showing how the countercurrent flow enriches the oxygen content of the blood.

FIGURE 15–17 The air (barometric) pressure varies with altitude. There are fewer gas molecules per unit volume at a high altitude than at a lower one. Thus, the air thins out at higher altitudes. A barometer is a long glass tube, open at one end, filled with mercury, and placed with the open end in a dish of mercury. At sea level the height of the mercury (Hg) in the tube is 760 mm, and at higher altitudes the air pressure is less and the column height is shorter.

level in the blood falls, impulses are sent out from these receptors to stimulate the inspiratory center of the medulla, and ventilation is increased. In the disease, **sudden-infant death syndrome,** it has been found that more than half of the infants who outwardly appear healthy have an undeveloped carotid artery receptor.

Just as there are receptors that activate the ventilation system, so there are receptors that produce a temporary inhibition of breathing. When an irritating gas such as ammonia or acid fumes passes down the respiratory tree, we cannot inhale even if we want to. By stimulating receptors in the larynx, these noxious substances produce a volley of impulses to the respiratory center to inhibit breathing, and we catch our breath. This is a valuable protective device, since it prevents many harmful substances from entering the lungs.

## 15–6 LOW PRESSURE, HIGH PRESSURE

### Low pressure: high altitude

The traveler who desires to visit Machu Picchu, the lost city of the Incas, must suffer a little to view the prehistoric site of an Andean civilization. This ancient city of the Incas lies nestled high in the Andes Mountains, and to reach it one must first fly to Cuzco, Peru, 12,700 ft above sea level. Breathing the Cuzco air leaves one exhilarated, talkative, and euphoric. These pleasant feelings, however, do not last; one often feels nauseous, a violent headache develops, shortness of breath occurs with the slightest exertion. Some individuals react even more unfavorably: inability to think clearly, irritability, irrationality, speech difficulty, and coldness in the feet. These are the symptoms of mountain sickness, and their only cure is time: in the course of several days these symptoms diminish and disappear.

Why does mountain sickness occur? The

FIGURE 15–17 The air (barometric) pressure varies with altitude. There are fewer gas molecules per unit volume at a high altitude than at a lower one. Thus, the air thins out at higher altitudes. A barometer is a long glass tube, open at one end, filled

Mt. Everest (29,000 ft)

↓ 237 mmHg

630 mmHg ↓

Denver (5,280 ft)

760 mmHg ↓

Air pressure supporting column

Sea level

basis for such symptoms is a simple fact: gases are compressible. The atmosphere surrounding the earth varies in its air (barometric) pressure with altitude: the higher the altitude, the lower the barometric pressure; in other words the higher the altitude, the fewer molecules of gas there are per unit volume (Figure 15–17). The amount of oxygen in the air is approximately 20%, but at higher altitudes, where there is less air, there is correspondingly less oxygen available and consequently less oxygen is absorbed by the blood. Because of this oxygen deficiency, and since breathing does not occur more quickly, the tissues become starved of oxygen. The brain is particularly susceptible, and symptoms of blurred vision and mental confusion are among the first to appear (up to 15,000 ft). The higher one

goes, the greater the problem: at 18,000 to 24,000 ft the individual gets slaphappy, irrational, and drowsy. The time required at various altitudes for oxygen deficiency to cause collapse or coma in a person unaccustomed to high altitudes is shown in Figure 15–18.

People who live at high altitudes, such as those inhabiting villages high in the Andes, tend to **acclimate,** that is, they develop compensatory mechanisms for coping with the low oxygen content of the air they breathe. Ventilation rates increase, there is an increase in the number of red blood cells, hemoglobin levels are higher, and there is a shift in the hemoglobin–oxygen dissociation curve to the right (Figure 15–9). Acclimatization, however, is a mixed blessing as the increase in numbers of red cells "thickens" the blood, and blood flow resistance is increased.

Fliers and mountain climbers use oxygen masks to ascend to greater and greater heights. In modern aircraft the cabin is pressurized to about 5,000-ft simulated altitude. The big jets fly at 30,000 ft, yet the passengers and crew have no mountain sickness since the air breathed is at the barometric pressure of 5,000 ft. If the cabin were to leak at this altitude, there would be only a minute of consciousness in which to begin breathing pure oxygen from emergency sources. Most aircraft have automatic devices to provide oxygen in the event cabin pressure is lost.

### High pressure: deep-sea diving

There is a beauty beneath the sea that lures one to dive deeper and deeper. There is, however, danger down below, and not only from sharks and other denizens of the deep. As one dives into the ocean, the weight of water pressing down on the body increases with increasing depth, and this causes the barometric pressure of the air in the lungs to increase, too—an effect that can be mimicked in a compression chamber. At in-

FIGURE 15–18 The time required at different altitudes for oxygen deficiency to cause collapse or coma. (From Harry G. Armstrong, *Principles and Practice of Aviation Medicine,* Baltimore, The Williams and Wilkins Company, 1952.)

**317**

GASEOUS EXCHANGE: RESPIRATION

creased depths the amount of gas that can pass from the alveolus into the blood, where it may become dissolved in the body fluids, also increases; this can cause serious disturbances in body function.

A diver can breathe compressed air to 200 ft below the sea without any problem of excess absorption, but deeper than this oxygen intoxication results. At pressures encountered below 200 ft (seven times the atmospheric pressure at sea level), oxygen is transported into the blood and body fluids and there it dissolves. The brain is most sensitive to this oxygen excess; metabolism is deranged and nervous twitching, convulsions, and coma result. The danger of oxygen poisoning can be achieved by supplying less and less oxygen in the breathing mixture as the diver descends to greater depths.

Nitrogen, although inert, also dissolves in the body fluids under high pressures. Nitrogen so dissolved may form bubbles as the diver surfaces. At a depth of 200 ft the pressure is seven times that at sea level, and if an individual is rapidly brought to the surface, the gases come out of solution because the pressure outside the body is now lower than the pressure of the gases dissolved in the fluid. Bubbles of gas form in the cells, blood, and spinal fluid, causing **decompression sickness** (also called the bends, caisson disease, and diver paralysis). The bubbles can plug blood vessels, rupture fiber pathways in the nervous system, and lead to mental disorder or permanent paralysis (see ''Tragedy under the Sea'' on page 300). There may be severe pain from nervous-system damage and bubble formation in the joints. Decompression sickness can be prevented by allowing a diver to come to the surface slowly or by controlling decompression in a decompression chamber so that release of gas is slow.

## SUMMARY

**1.** Respiration is the exchange of gases (carbon dioxide and oxygen) between an organism and its environment. Breathing, or ventilation, is the direct physical exchange of gases at the respiratory surfaces (gills or lungs). Internal respiration involves gas exchange between the blood and tissues, and cellular respiration involves the reaction of oxygen with fuel molecules to produce energy, carbon dioxide, and water.

**2.** Gas exchange between organisms and the environment takes place by diffusion across a large moist surface. In land vertebrates, the exchange surfaces are the extensive lungs.

**3.** Ventilation of the lungs occurs via the respiratory tree; air passes via the nasal passages and sinuses to the pharynx and larynx and via the glottis (guarded by the epiglottis) to the trachea, bronchi, bronchioles, and lungs. During its passage, the air is filtered, conditioned, and cleaned.

**4.** Smoking or breathing polluted air can cause emphysema.

**5.** The lungs consist of thin-walled alveoli. Oxygen from the incoming air diffuses across the alveoli to the blood, where it is lower in concentration. Carbon dioxide diffuses in the opposite direction, from blood, where it is high in concentration, to the lungs, where it is low in concentration.

**6.** In the blood, oxygen combines with the iron in the ring-shaped heme of hemoglobin to form an unstable complex: oxyhemoglobin. Carried from the lungs to the heart and then to the tissues, where the oxygen pressure is low, the oxyhemoglobin gives up its oxygen to the tissues. Higher carbon dioxide concentration in the tissues and rising temperatures in actively respiring cells such as muscle, lower the combining capacity of hemoglobin for oxygen and assist its release.

**7.** Carbon dioxide is carried by the red blood cells as bicarbonate, combined with hemoglobin, and dissolved in the blood.

**8.** During inspiration, the rib muscles and diaphragm contract and enlarge the chest cavity, and the lungs inflate in response to reduced air pressure. During expiration, the rib muscles and diaphragm relax, the volume of the chest cavity decreases, the lungs recoil and contract, and the inhaled air is expelled.

**9.** About 350 ml of air is exchanged with each breath; 150 ml is in dead space.

**10.** Nervous control of breathing is centered in the respiratory center of the lower medulla (brainstem). Overinflation of the lungs is prevented by a reflex mediated by the vagus nerve. Voluntary control of breathing is mediated by the cerebral cortex, thus enabling an individual to hold his or her breath. Nervous-system depressants can inactivate the respiratory center causing possible death.

**11.** Carbon dioxide in the blood stimulates the respiratory center. Breathing rate increases when carbon dioxide blood levels increase. Depletion of carbon dioxide by hyperventilation may inactivate the respiratory center, causing apnea and possible death. Increasing carbon dioxide levels in the newborn trigger the respiratory center to activity. Painful stimuli also trigger the respiratory reflex.

**12.** Depressed blood oxygen levels cause stimulation of the inspiratory center via impulses from carotid receptors that monitor blood oxygen. Laryngeal receptors inhibit breathing when stimulated by irritating gases during inspiration.

**13.** Mountain sickness is caused by low oxygen levels at high altitude.

**14.** Oxygen poisoning can result from breathing compressed air at great ocean depths; less oxygen must be supplied as divers descend deeper and are subjected to increasing pressure. Decompression sickness may occur if a diver surfaces too rapidly: excess nitrogen dissolved in the blood while under increased pressure may form bubbles in the blood and tissues if the pressure is released too quickly.

**15.** We cannot breathe underwater as fish do because we cannot move enough water into and out of our respiratory tree to allow complete oxygenation of the blood and efficient gas exchange. Fish have an efficient one-way flow of water with a countercurrent flow of blood in their gills.

## KEY WORDS

| | | | |
|---|---|---|---|
| | respiratory tree | alveoli | hyaline membrane disease |
| | sinuses | pleural membrane | respiratory center |
| respiration | pharynx | smog | hyperventilation |
| breathing or ventilation | larynx | pulmonary osteoarthropathy | apnea |
| internal respiration | glottis | oxyhemoglobin | sudden infant death syndrome |
| cellular respiration | epiglottis | globin | acclimate |
| atmosphere | vocal cords | heme | decompression sickness |
| gills | trachea | diaphragm | |
| lungs | bronchi | inspiration | |
| tracheal tubes | bronchioles | expiration | |

## TOPICS FOR REVIEW AND DISCUSSION

1. Why can't humans breathe underwater?

2. What are the three types of respiration?

3. How are respiration and breathing related to one another?

4. Give the structure and function of the various components of the respiratory tree.

5. How do smog and smoking affect lung function?

6. What are some of the nervous and chemical controls involved in breathing?

7. How is gas exchange accomplished in small and in large animals?

8. Draw a mechanical model that can show the manner of expansion and contraction of the lungs. Describe its operation.

9. What is the cause of bends, or caisson disease?

10. Discuss the statement, Speech is a by-product of breathing.

## Kidney in a suitcase

For other vacationers, the trip would have been routine. But when Josephine Berman, 43, and her husband toured the Grand Canyon, stopped at Las Vegas and then visited San Francisco last summer, it was something of a medical miracle. For 11 years the pretty Brooklyn housewife has suffered from chronic kidney disease. Like 24,000 other similarly afflicted Americans, she could never go far from the massive dialysis machines that purge her blood of the toxic wastes her kidneys are no longer able to remove. Yet during her 16-day trip, she shunned kidney centers entirely. Her unexpected freedom was the result of a remarkable new device: a portable mechanical kidney so compact it is built into a small metal valise.

"The idea came to me out of simple frustration," says Dr. Eli A. Friedman, inventor of the suitcase kidney. Friedman, director of the renal diseases section at New York's Downstate Medical Center, had planned to take 25 kidney patients on a European holiday, dialyzing them at stopovers en route. But at the last minute, medical authorities in Copenhagen concluded that they did not have enough dialysis machines to handle so many additional patients. Forced to cancel the trip, Friedman resolved to build a dialysis machine that kidney patients could carry on their travels and operate by themselves.

Suitcase kidneys, he feels, will be a boon not only to dialysis patients who want to travel but also to smaller rural hospitals which could use them in emergencies. The little machines could also be used for happier occasions: another of Friedman's patients took a suitcase kidney on his honeymoon.

What is a mechanical kidney?
What is a real kidney, and how does it work?

# 16

# Chemical Balance: The Kidney

## 16–1 WHAT DOES THE KIDNEY DO?

The lungs serve to maintain the composition of the extracellular fluid with respect to oxygen and carbon dioxide, and with this their duty ends. The responsibility for maintaining the composition of this fluid in respect to other constituents devolves on the kidneys. It is no exaggeration to say that the composition of the body fluids is determined not by what the mouth takes in but by what the kidneys keep; they are the master chemists of our internal environment, which, so to speak, they manufacture in reverse by working it over completely some fifteen times a day. . . . Our bones, muscles, glands, even our brains, are called upon to do only one kind of physiological work, but our kidneys are called upon to perform an innumerable variety of operations. Bones can break, muscles can atrophy, glands can loaf, even the brain can go to sleep, and not endanger our survival; but should the kidneys fail in their task neither bone, muscle, gland, nor brain could carry on.

Recognizing that we have the kind of internal environment we have because we have the kidneys that we have, we must acknowledge that our kidneys constitute the major foundation of our physiological freedom. Only because they work the way they do has it become possible for us to have bones, muscles, glands, and brains. Superficially, it might be said that the function of the kidneys is to make urine; but in a more considered view one can say that the kidneys make the stuff of philosophy itself.

HOMER W. SMITH, *From Fish to Philosopher*, Boston, Little, Brown and Company, 1953.

Perhaps Smith exaggerated somewhat in stating that "kidneys make the stuff of philosophy itself," but as we shall soon see, his statement is correct in recognizing the central role of the kidney as a regulator of our internal environment.

As the blood flows through the body, its composition is in a state of flux: cellular "ashes" such as carbon dioxide and urea are dumped into it, and oxygen, regulatory materials, fuels, and building materials are removed. Many organs of the body play a role in this dynamic exchange with blood. The digestive system serves to replenish the supply of raw materials. The respiratory system functions in the removal of carbon dioxide and in the replenishment of the supply of oxygen. The liver aids in the chemical processing of the blood; it breaks down hemoglobin, regulates the availability of sugar, and forms urea. However, most chemical exchanges with the bloodstream take place in the kidneys. The **kidneys** are primarily concerned with the disposal of liquid sewage and constitute the principal organs of excretion.[1] They are vital to our economy, and although these two organs are only about the size of a clenched fist and account for less than 0.5% of the total body weight, every day they process more than 1,700 qt of blood; with every beat of the heart, 20% of the heart's blood volume flows through the kidneys. The kidneys filter

and chemically process this blood and produce urine. The kidney is the body's chemist par excellence, regulating the chemical composition of the body fluids and in effect maintaining the constancy of the internal environment.

What is the internal environment? The human body consists mainly of water; roughly 60% of the body weight is water. Over half is contained in the cells themselves, and the remainder is a dilute salt solution that surrounds and bathes all the cells (Figure 16–1). The liquid portion of the blood (plasma) is part of this bath; as the blood courses through the tiny capillaries that pass close to every cell, some of the salty fluid plasma diffuses out, carrying nutrients into the watery solution that bathes the cells (interstitial fluid). Waste products, on the other hand, leave the cells and pass into the blood plasma. In this way, materials essential for cell maintenance, growth, and reproduction are supplied and poisonous wastes are discarded. The composition of this extracellular solution is quite important, for cells can function properly only if it is chemically balanced; that is, there must be proper proportions of ingredients. Accumulated poisonous wastes such as urea (Box 16A) must be discarded; the ingredients essential to life, such as salts, sugars, amino acids, and other nutrients that are depleted by cell utilization, must be retained; acidity-alkalinity (pH) must be balanced; and the volume of the fluid itself must remain fairly constant.

---

[1] Excretion involves ridding the body of waste metabolities that it has itself produced, as opposed to defecation, which involves ridding the body of undigested food materials it cannot use.

**FIGURE 16–1** (top) The distribution of fluid in the body.

**FIGURE 16–2** (bottom) The kidney and associated structures.

### BOX 16A  What is urea?

Much of the food we eat contains proteins. Proteins are nitrogenous compounds, and when their building blocks, amino acids, are used as fuel by cells, the metabolic ashes are carbon dioxide and water plus nitrogen-containing substances. The waste nitrogen must be eliminated from the body, but it cannot be liberated as gas because too much energy is required to perform such a reaction. Instead, most organisms produce ammonia, urea, or uric acid. Ammonia is a highly toxic gas and is extremely soluble in water. A thousandth of a milligram of ammonia in a liter of blood is sufficient to kill a person. Therefore, ammonia must be eliminated quickly, and aquatic animals flush the gas into the water as quickly as it is formed. Land creatures cannot form ammonia as a waste product because they (and we) must conserve water: instead they convert it to nontoxic urea in the liver.

The actual quantity of urea we excrete each day is quite variable and depends on the quantity of protein in our diet, since it is from protein that urea is derived. If we eat a protein-rich diet, we may eliminate about 1 oz of urea each day.

The nitrogenous portion of the urea is derived by **deamination** (removal of the amino group) of amino acids. Deamination results in the formation of ammonia:

Ammonia formed in the tissues passes to the blood and is carried to the liver. By a series of enzyme-catalyzed reactions (the **urea cycle**), the highly toxic ammonia is combined with carbon dioxide to produce urea, a much less poisonous material.

$$CO_2$$
$$NH_3$$
$$2ATP$$ $$\longrightarrow$$ $$2ADP$$
Carbamyl phosphate — Citrulline
Ornithine — UREA CYCLE — Aspartic acid
urea  C=O — Arginosuccinic acid
NH₂ — Arginine — Fumaric acid

The urea leaves the liver, enters the blood, is carried to the kidney, and is then eliminated.

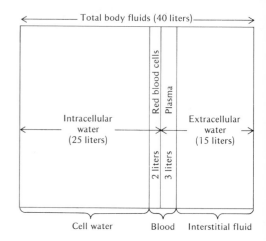

Total body fluids (40 liters)

Intracellular water (25 liters) — Red blood cells — Plasma — Extracellular water (15 liters)

2 liters — 3 liters

Cell water — Blood — Interstitial fluid

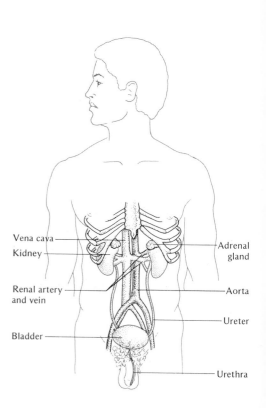

Vena cava
Kidney
Renal artery and vein
Bladder
Adrenal gland
Aorta
Ureter
Urethra

FIGURE 16–3 The entire nephron with Bowman's capsule cut away.

FIGURE 16–4 A scanning electron micrograph of the nephron. (Courtesy of Peter M. Andrews and Keith R. Porter.)

Our kidneys maintain salt balance, excrete nitrogenous wastes such as urea, regulate the acidity of the body fluids, and control the volume of the cellular bathing solution. In short, they critically control the concentrations of most of the substances in the sea within us.

## 16–2 STRUCTURE AND FUNCTION OF THE KIDNEY

What is a kidney? The human kidney is a dark red, bean-shaped organ about 4 in. long, 2.5 in. wide, and 1 in. thick. It weighs about 0.5 lb. Each of us normally has a pair of kidneys attached to either side of the backbone above the small of the back (lower abdominal wall) just behind the stomach and liver (Figure 16–2). Attached to each kidney are three tubes: (1) the **renal artery** (*ren*—kidney; L.), which conducts blood from the aorta to the kidney; (2) the **renal vein,** which carries blood from the kidney to a large vein going to the heart; and (3) a **ureter,** which carries urine from the kidney to the bladder (Figure 16–2). The kidneys receive blood, process it, and excrete urine, and the processed blood passes on its way.

How is the kidney organized to process blood and form urine? Each kidney contains about 1 million miniaturized chemical filtration units called **nephrons.** A nephron consists of a twisted hollow tube, closed at one end and open at the other, and a network of associated blood vessels (Figure 16–3). Let us consider the blood supply first. The renal artery that enters the kidney branches to form a series of arterioles, and these distribute blood to each nephron as a spherical cluster of capillaries, the **glomerulus** (little ball; L.) (Figure 16–4). There filtration of the blood takes place. The blood that leaves the glomerulus then flows through another capillary bed surrounding the tubular portion of the nephron. These blood vessels then converge and form a system of veins that merge to form the large renal vein, by which blood leaves the kidney (Figure 16–3).

Now let us look at the tubules of the nephron. The blind end of the kidney tubule is greatly expanded to form a double-walled funnel or capsule, called **Bowman's capsule** (Figure 16–4). Each of the two walls of Bowman's capsule is separated by a fluid-filled space and consists of a single layer of flattened epithelial cells. The invaginated, or cuplike, portion of the capsule almost completely surrounds the coiled ball of glomerular capillaries.

The glomerulus-capsule relationship can be visualized by thinking of a fist that is pushed into an inflated rubber balloon (Figure 16–5). The layer of rubber directly overlying the fist represents the inner surface of the invagination of Bowman's capsule, and the point where the wrist makes contact with the balloon is the opening into the capsule. The blood supply to Bowman's capsule enters at the position of the wrist, and the clenched fist represents the glomerulus that nestles in the capsule. The outer surface of the balloon represents the outer surface of the capsule, which, in the nephron, is continuous with the tubule leading from it. The tubule leading from the capsule twists in a complicated manner in the vicinity of the glomerulus; then it takes a straight course into the interior of the kidney, where it makes a hairpin turn (the **loop of Henle**); the tubule then runs back to the region of the glomerulus, winds about in a second series of twists, and finally discharges into a **urine-collecting duct** that later connects with the main ureter (*ouron*—urine; Gk.) (Figure 16–3). The meandering of the kidney tubule with its twists and turns serves to compact the length into a small space, microscopic in diameter and only about 1.25 in. long; if the 2 million nephrons

in both kidneys were straightened out and laid end to end, they would produce a tunnel about 50 miles long!

The nephrons of the kidney are not arranged in a haphazard manner. If a kidney is sliced longitudinally, two regions can be distinguished: an outer, reddish-brown region, the **cortex,** and an inner, grayish area, the **medulla** (Figure 16–6). Microscopic examination of the cut surface of the kidney shows that the glomeruli, Bowman's capsules, and convoluted portions of the kidney tubules are located in the cortex (Figure 16–6), whereas the straight portions of the

Cortex ——

Medulla ——

Pelvis ——

Ureter ——

tubules, Henle's loops, and urine-collecting ducts are located in the medulla.

Each kidney tubule and its associated capillaries constitute a nephron, and this is the functional unit of the kidney. Because each nephron operates in almost exactly the same way as all the others, we can describe most of the functions of the entire kidney by explaining the function of a single nephron.

The capillaries of the glomerulus have very thin walls, and the electron microscope reveals that they are permeated with many tiny pores (Figure 16–7). The glomeruli of the kidney are mechanical filters, and they permit a cell-free, protein-free fluid to pass from the blood into the tubule. The pores in the capillary wall are of such a size that blood cells and proteins cannot leave, but water and smaller molecules (both useful substances and dissolved wastes) flow out. Thus, the fluid that passes out of the glomerulus contains water, amino acids, glucose, salts, and urea in exactly the same

FIGURE 16–7 A small portion of the glomerulus, showing the pores (arrows) that act as a filter for the blood. (Courtesy of Marilyn G. Farquhar.)

**325**

CHEMICAL BALANCE: THE KIDNEY

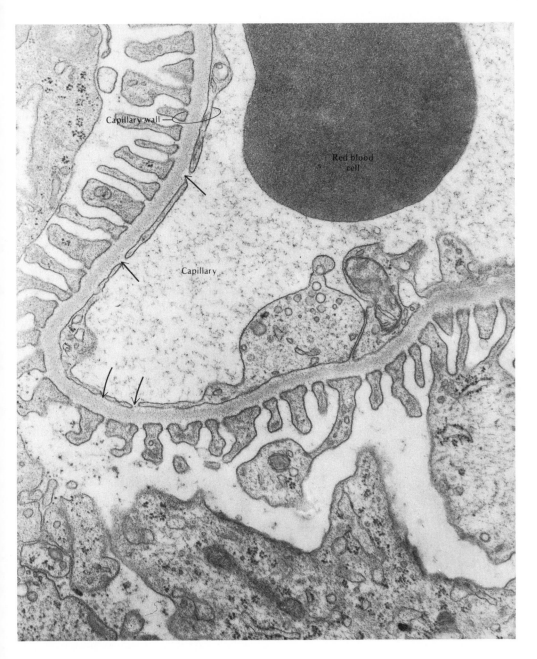

Capillary wall

Red blood cell

Capillary

**TABLE 16–1 Comparison of the composition of blood, glomerular filtrate, and urine**

| Component | Blood plasma (g/liter) | Glomerular filtrate (g/liter) | Urine (g/liter) |
|---|---|---|---|
| Glucose | 1.0 | 1.0 | 0 |
| Sodium | 3.0 | 3.0 | 3.0 |
| Chloride | 3.5 | 3.5 | 6.0 |
| Potassium | 0.15 | 0.15 | 1.5 |
| Uric acid* | 0.03 | 0.03 | 0.3 |
| Urea | 0.25 | 0.25 | 20.0 |
| Sulfate | 1.0 | 1.0 | 1.0 |
| Creatinine† | 0.15 | 0.15 | 0.7 |
| Phosphate | 0.03 | 0.03 | 1.0 |
| Amino acids | 0.3 | 0.3 | 0 |
| Protein | 70.0 | 0.2 | 0 |

Blood passing through kidney: 500 gal/day
Glomerular filtrate formed: 50 gal/day
Glomerular filtrate reabsorbed: 49.5–49.75 gal/day
Urine volume excreted: 0.25–0.50 gal/day

\* End product of purine metabolism.
† By-product of muscle metabolism.

amounts as are found in blood plasma (Table 16–1); this filtrate of the blood is also nearly identical to the dilute salt solution surrounding all the cells of the body. The total blood flow through the kidneys is normally about 750 ml per minute, or about one fifth of the blood volume pumped by the heart in the same amount of time. Approximately 125 ml per minute of protein-free filtrate is pressed out of the glomerular capillaries and passes into the kidney tubules. The remainder of the blood leaves the glomerulus by way of an (efferent) arteriole.

What supplies the energy for the filtration process? The driving force for moving fluid out of the glomerulus and into Bowman's capsule is the blood pressure in the capillaries, which is ultimately a result of the work of the beating heart (Figure 16–8). The pressure in the glomerulus is higher than the pressure in Bowman's capsule. Therefore, fluid moves out of the glomerulus via the microscopic pores in the walls of the capillaries and passes into the capsule. After the glomerular filtrate enters Bowman's capsule, it passes into the tubular system of the nephron. Each day about 45 gal (180 liters) make this journey from the blood to the kidney tubule, but, of course, this is far in excess of what is passed out of the body as urine. Normally we excrete only 1% of the total glomerular filtrate (about 1 to 2 qt). Where does the remainder go? More than 99% of the glomerular filtrate that enters the kidney tubule is reabsorbed into the blood by way of the capillary network surrounding the tubule. In this manner the tubules send back to the blood that which is valuable and reusable and leave the wastes inside to be discharged. Additionally, much of the fluid lost from the circulatory system is recaptured by the blood. Indeed, if reabsorption did not take place, we would simply excrete our body fluids into the urine and the sea within us would soon be depleted.

The cleansing of the blood by the kidney can be analogized to a housekeeper who wants to clean up a dirty room: instead of merely sweeping up the dust and dirt and disposing of them, the cleaner empties the room of all its portable furniture (pictures, tables, chairs, and so on) as well as the disposable materials. The furniture and other useful items are returned to the room leaving only disposable material out in the hall. At first glance this seems an inefficient way for a kidney to handle purification—throwing out almost everything by filtration and retrieving what the body requires by reabsorption. Indeed, there are certain drawbacks, but consider the advantage: every 20 minutes of our lives, our entire blood supply is chemically cleansed in a complete and thorough way, without cutting any corners.

The nondiscriminatory process of filtration is a function of the glomerulus. Selective retrieval of essential materials by reabsorption and secretion takes place in the kidney tubules; let us examine the retrieval processes.

The glomerular filtrate entering the kid-

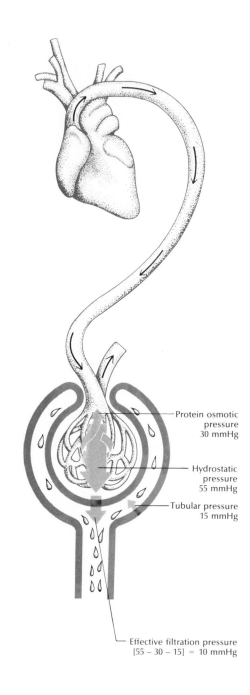

Protein osmotic pressure 30 mmHg

Hydrostatic pressure 55 mmHg

Tubular pressure 15 mmHg

Effective filtration pressure [55 – 30 – 15] = 10 mmHg

ney tubule from Bowman's capsule passes first through the proximal convoluted tubule, then through the loop of Henle, then through the distal convoluted tubule, and finally into a straight collecting duct. Although the initial filtrate is similar in salt composition to the blood plasma (it is **isosmotic**), in its passage through the kidney tubules it will become concentrated, and the urine excreted will be higher in salt concentration (**hyperosmotic**) relative to the blood plasma (Table 16–1). As the glomerular filtrate passes through the proximal convoluted tubule, approximately 85% of the water, sodium ions, and chloride ions; most of the bicarbonate; and all of the glucose, vitamins, and amino acids are reabsorbed into the surrounding network of capillaries. So powerful and efficient is this reabsorption process that virtually no glucose, vitamins, or amino acids are found in the excreted urine. The proximal convoluted tubule is admirably suited for its reabsorptive role. The cells lining the proximal tubule have millions of microscopic, fingerlike microvilli that serve to increase the reabsorptive surface area, thus facilitating rapid transfer of water and other essential materials (Figure 16–9).

Water reabsorption occurs by osmosis because the proximal tubule is permeable to water and most of the solutes (sodium and chloride ions) are reabsorbed across the membrane by active transport. Other essential substances, such as glucose, amino acids, and vitamins, are moved against a concentration gradient, and for such metabolic work energy must be expended. The immediate energy source for this "uphill" (active) transport of materials is ATP. The ATP-generating system of the proximal tubule is found in the large numbers of mitochondria located within the tubule cells themselves. The mitochondria supply the energy for transport, but specificity of active transport is due to the presence of specific **carrier proteins** in the membrane. There are carrier proteins specific for moving certain amino acids across the membrane, other

FIGURE 16–9 The proximal tubule of the kidney as revealed by the electron microscope. Note the many microvilli and the mitochondria in the cells that make up this tubule, aiding in the active transfer of materials from the glomerular filtrate into the blood. (Courtesy of K. R. Porter.)

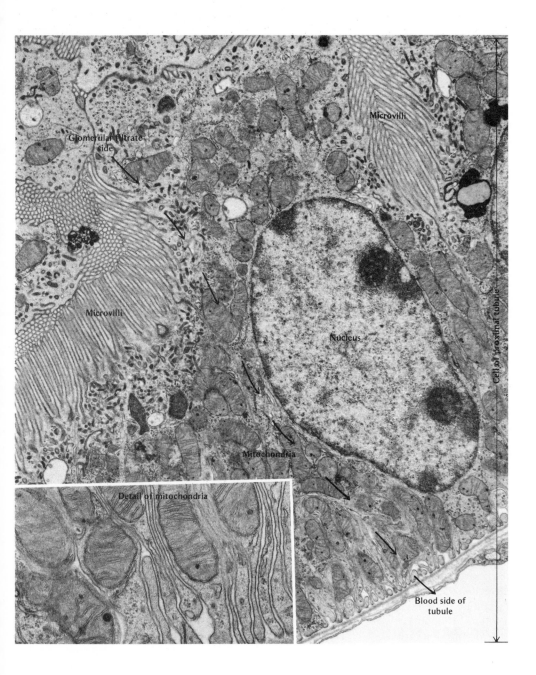

Glomerular filtrate side

Microvilli

Microvilli

Nucleus

Mitochondria

Cell of proximal tubule

Detail of mitochondria

Blood side of tubule

carriers for transporting vitamins, and so on. (The situation is shown diagrammatically in Figure 16–10.)

The tubular fluid, now free of amino acids, sugar, vitamins, and so on, passes from the proximal convoluted tubule to the descending loop of Henle, and from there to the ascending loop. The cells of the ascending limb of the loop of Henle actively pump sodium ions out of the tubule and into the surrounding tissue fluid (chloride ions passively follow to maintain electrical neutrality). Some but not all of this sodium then diffuses from the tissue fluid into the descending limb so that there is a recirculation of sodium from the ascending limb, into the tissue fluid, to the descending limb, and back again to the ascending limb (Figure 16–11). As a result of the cyclic pumping and reabsorption of sodium, and by virtue of the organization of the loops of Henle in the medulla of the kidney, a salt (sodium chloride) concentration gradient is maintained in the tissue fluid surrounding the loops of Henle. The concentration is highest in the medulla (at the hairpin turn in the loop of Henle) and lowest in the cortex (at the region of the convoluted tubules). The walls of the ascending limb are impermeable to water, so that only sodium leaves the tubule. As a result, the filtrate in the loop of Henle loses much of its sodium, but little water. Thus, when the filtrate reaches the distal convoluted tubule, it contains less salt than there was in the original glomerular filtrate. Concentration of the filtrate by osmotic resorption of water occurs in the collecting duct. As the filtrate moves from the distal convoluted tubule into the collecting duct (which progresses downward from cortex to medulla), it encounters a region of ever-increasing salt concentration in the tissue fluid surrounding the duct. The walls of the collecting duct are permeable only to water, so that water moves passively, by osmosis, from the duct into the sodium-rich (hyperosmotic) fluid surrounding it. As a result the fluid in the duct, now called **urine,** eventually becomes isos-

**FIGURE 16–10** Diagram of active transport in the kidney. Specific carriers in the kidney tubule cells pick up molecules and transfer them from the glomerular filtrate to the blood. The energy source for this transport is ATP, generated by the mitochondria of the tubule cells.

**FIGURE 16–11** The mechanism by which urine is concentrated by a nephron in the human kidney.

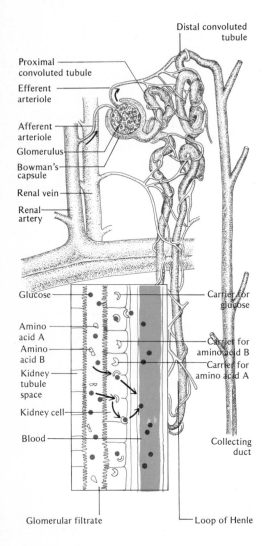

Distal convoluted tubule

Proximal convoluted tubule

Efferent arteriole

Afferent arteriole

Glomerulus

Bowman's capsule

Renal vein

Renal artery

Glucose

Amino acid A

Amino acid B

Kidney tubule space

Kidney cell

Blood

Glomerular filtrate

Carrier for glucose

Carrier for amino acid B

Carrier for amino acid A

Collecting duct

Loop of Henle

Cortex

Medulla

Na ions

Proximal convoluted tubule

Distal convoluted tubule

Na ions

Isosmotic

Osmosis

$H_2O$

Na

Hyposmotic or isotonic

Osmosis

$H_2O$

Isosmotic

Salt gradient

Descending loop of Henle

Na
Na
Na
Na

$H_2O$

Na

$H_2O$

Osmosis

Blood vessel

Collecting duct

High salt concentration (hyperosmotic)

Hyperosmotic

Permeable to water

Henle's loop

Impermeable to water

motic with the fluid around the duct, and at the end of the duct the urine is not only much more concentrated than the original glomerular filtrate but also hyperosmotic to the blood plasma. Thus, of the 180 qt of dilute glomerular filtrate produced in a day, less than 2 qt appear as concentrated urine. (The concentration of the various salts is shown in Table 16–1.)

The composition of urine depends to a large extent on what is left behind in the tubules, that is, on what the nephrons do not remove from the glomerular filtrate by selective reabsorption. However, there is also active secretion of certain substances from the capillaries surrounding the tubule into the tubule itself. In the human kidney the amount of such secretion (called **augmentation**) is small and occurs mainly in the convoluted tubules. *p*-aminohippuric acid, a minor nitrogenous waste product, is secreted into the proximal convoluted tubules, and $K^+$ and $H^+$ ions are secreted by the distal convoluted tubules. Secretion of $H^+$ ions helps to maintain the pH (acidity) of the blood at a relatively constant level. When the antibiotic drug penicillin is taken, it is secreted into the urine by the distal convoluted tubule. Similarly, the antimalar-

ial drug Atabrine is secreted by these tubules. Because these drugs are excreted in the urine, blood levels eventually drop, and for effective therapy administration of the drug must be maintained during the course of the infection.

## 16–3 REGULATION OF FLUID AND SALT BALANCE

As you undoubtedly realize from personal experience, the output of urine by the kidneys is not constant in amount. A few examples will illustrate how the rate of urine formation varies. If you were to drink about a quart of water over a short span of time (let us say in 15 to 30 minutes), you would find that your urine production over the next few hours would be greater than your

FIGURE 16–12 Regulation of urine output. This depends on the secretion of a hormone (ADH) and resorption of water across the walls of the collecting duct.

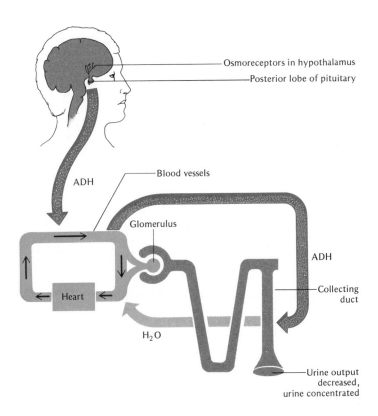

Osmoreceptors in hypothalamus
Posterior lobe of pituitary
ADH
Blood vessels
Glomerulus
ADH
Heart
Collecting duct
H₂O
Urine output decreased, urine concentrated

to the posterior lobe of the pituitary gland, and there ADH is released (Figure 16–12). The ADH passes by way of the blood to the kidney, where it affects reabsorption. The hormone ADH controls the water permeability of the cells of the distal convoluted tubule and the collecting duct. If ADH is present, these tubules become highly permeable to water, so that water leaves the tubules and seeps back into the bloodstream. As a result of this loss of water from the tubules, the urine becomes concentrated. If, on the other hand, the osmoreceptors are not stimulated, as is the case when water in the body fluids is at a normal level, ADH is not released and the tubules remain impermeable to water. The result of an absence of ADH is the formation of a dilute urine, since salt is reabsorbed but water is not.

A disease characterized by the production of abnormal quantities of urine is called **diabetes** (to pass through; Gk.), because water that is drunk seems to siphon from the body at such a rapid rate. There are two kinds of diabetes, called **mellitus** and **insipidus.** In the rare disease diabetes insipidus (*insipidus*—tasteless; L.), the urine output may reach 10 gal a day instead of the more normal quantity of 1 qt. Persons so afflicted have an incessant thirst and suffer from a salt imbalance in the body fluids. The disease is caused by a deficiency in the supply of ADH; reabsorption of water is low, and the urine produced is copious and quite dilute.

The more common type of diabetes is mellitus, or sugar, diabetes, characterized by the presence of sugar in the urine. The primary abnormality in this kind of diabetes is a failure to regulate properly the utilization of glucose because of a deficiency of the hormone insulin (Chapter 17). As a result there is too much glucose in the blood, the glomerular filtrate contains excessive amounts, and only a fraction of this can be reabsorbed. The excess glucose in the tubule increases the osmotic pressure of the contents and thus reduces reabsorption of

normal output. In fact, if you were to collect the urine produced in the period subsequent to the drinking of the fluid, you would find the excess urine volume to be just about a quart. It is as if the kidneys knew exactly how much liquid was ingested, and to maintain the amount of body fluid at a constant level, they eliminated the excess.

Let us imagine that you spent a day in the desert with only a single canteen of water available. What would be the output and appearance of your urine? Probably you would find that the urine produced was more concentrated, dark yellow, and below normal in amount. Exposed to the hot, dry desert air, you would tend to lose body fluids via sweating, but a considerable fraction of the body fluids would be conserved by the kidneys, as their fluid output was

reduced. Again, the kidneys know about the body's fluid balance.

These situations demonstrate that the rate of urine formation is increased or decreased in direct relation to the amount of hydration or dehydration. How do the kidneys know when to excrete water and how do they know when to conserve it?

The control mechanism that regulates the body fluids involves the secretion of a hormone called **antidiuretic hormone** (ADH) or **vasopressin.** The system for controlling water conservation or excretion involves the effect of ADH on the reabsorptive properties of the kidney tubule. When the body fluid supply is low, special sensory receptors located in the hypothalamus of the brain are stimulated. These osmoreceptors send out impulses that are carried by nerve fibers water. The diabetic thus excretes large quantities of water and sugar and may become dehydrated. Today the disease is easily treated by regular injections of insulin.

As we have already noted, water reabsorption in the kidneys is a passive process. The prime factor responsible for water reabsorption is the active transport of sodium from the tubule into the tissue fluid, as described earlier. Sodium pumping here is regulated by the hormone **aldosterone**, secreted by the cortex of the adrenal glands. The mechanism of action of this hormone is not completely understood, but by its action sodium is conserved and so is water. When the body fluid volume is decreased owing to dehydration, the amount of sodium in the body fluids increases, and this leads to the production of aldosterone. Aldosterone promotes resorption of sodium (and water), reduces urine output, and conserves water. If, on the other hand, aldosterone secretion is diminished,[2] resorption of sodium is low and sodium is lost in the urine.

In normal individuals the regulatory mechanisms for retention or excretion of sodium are so precise that the sodium balance in the body does not vary by more than 2% in spite of large variations in salt intake and salt loss (sweating, vomiting, and diarrhea). When the kidneys fail to excrete adequate amounts of sodium, the individual accumulates sodium and water in the body spaces, leading to swelling of the tissues, a condition known as **edema.**

### Diuresis

Substances that increase the flow of urine are called **diuretics;** the flow process itself is called **diuresis.** Glucose, salt, and amino acids present in excess cannot be resorbed, and water is retained in the tubule to keep

[2] This can occur by administration of the diuretic drug spironolactone, or in individuals suffering from Addison's disease, a condition in which the adrenal cortex no longer secretes aldosterone.

**BOX 16B  The artificial kidney machine**

Perhaps up to 5 million people in the United States suffer from undiagnosed disorders of the kidney. Sometimes kidney disease reveals itself clearly, and treatment and recovery are possible, but for others there is no warning, and a slow wasting proceeds. No age group, no group of any kind is spared from disorders of the kidneys.

Uremia (urea in the blood), a progressive toxic condition due to kidney failure and related kidney diseases, kills hundreds of thousands of Americans each year. Uremia can occur by accidental ingestion of a poison, shock, physical injury, and disease. Without kidney function, poisonous wastes accumulate in the blood and destroy the body's cells. What would happen if at this moment your kidneys simply stopped working?

Until recently there was little hope for persons suffering from kidney failure, but recent developments in the manufacture of artificial kidney machines provide a mechanism for ridding the body of its poisons. This device permits Josephine Berman (page 320) and countless others to live. How does the artificial kidney machine work?

The natural kidney regulates the body fluid composition by filtration and selective reabsorption. An artificial kidney does the same things; however, it does not look like a real kidney nor does it operate exactly the same way. The filter of the natural kidney is the glomerulus,

FIGURE 16–13 Diagrammatic representation of the artificial kidney machine. (Modified from John P. Merrill, *The Artificial Kidney*. Copyright 1961 by Scientific American, Inc. All rights reserved.)

and the efficiency per unit surface area of these 2 million microscopic filters cannot be matched by any machine at the present time; the natural kidney is a marvel of compact efficiency. The artificial kidney machine (Figure 16–13) consists of a steel tub 2 ft deep and 2 ft wide. In the center of the tub is the filter, a narrow, tubular coil of cellophane 25 yd long, providing a large surface area for exchange of materials. Cellophane has pores of the same dimensions as the glomerular capillaries so that the same substances pass across its surface (molecules smaller than 50,000 molecular weight). As blood passes through the cellophane tubing, molecules move across the cellophane according to their concentration in the blood and the surrounding solution (Figure 16–14). For example, if the concentration of substance A is higher in the blood than in the external solution, substance A leaves the blood; if the reverse is true, substance A enters the blood from the external solution. The diffusion of small molecules across a semipermeable membrane is called **dialysis,** and it is the mechanism by which the artificial kidney works. By changing the composition of the solution surrounding the cellophane tubing, the artificial kidney can move materials into or out of the blood.

An artificial kidney treatment, or **hemodialysis** (dialysis of the blood), requires that the cellophane tubing of the artificial kidney be primed with an anticoagulant plus blood matched exactly to that of the patient. This assures a continuous flow of unclotted blood from patient to machine and back. The tub surrounding the coils is filled with warm water containing the proper concentration of chemicals (glucose, salt, bicarbonate, amino acids, and other small molecules). The patient is plugged in to the machine by connecting an artery and a vein to the machine (Figure 16–13). Blood, pumped by the patient's heart, flows through the artery into the machine and traverses the long cellophane coil. Purified by dialysis, the blood passes from the cellophane tubing into a clot-and-bubble trap and then back to the body via a tube into the vein. Dialysis takes 6 to 10 hours, but varies with the individual condition and frequency of treatment.

The artificial kidney cannot secrete or reabsorb; it can only filter by dialysis, and therefore balance of ingredients in the wash solution is critical. If such balance is not controlled, the blood could eliminate useful materials and take up worthless ones. Clearly hemodialysis is not a procedure that can easily be adapted for home use (see Chapter opener).

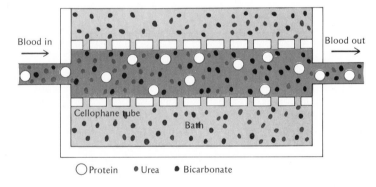

Blood in

Blood out

Cellophane tube

Bath

○ Protein   ● Urea   ● Bicarbonate

FIGURE 16–14  The artificial kidney operates by the principle of dialysis. Note how the urea, high in concentration in the blood, moves into the bath and bicarbonate, high in concentration in the bath, moves into the blood; proteins are retained in the blood because they are larger than the pores of the dialysis (cellophane) tubing. (Modified from John P. Merrill, *The Artificial Kidney.* Copyright 1961 by Scientific American, Inc. All rights reserved.)

these substances in solution. Similarly, meals rich in protein produce diuresis because their by-products, amino acids and urea, remain in the tubules, water is retained in the tubules to keep these in solution, and urine flow is increased. Caffeine (in coffee, tea, and cola drinks) and alcohol act as diuretics by inhibiting the secretion of ADH. One estimate suggests that 100 ml of water are excreted for every 10 g of alcohol ingested. The well-known diuretic effect of beer is due largely to its water content, not its alcohol content; since beer is less than 4% alcohol, it is less dehydrating than whisky (40 to 45% alcohol) and therefore provides a better way of quenching one's thirst.

Emotions may increase or decrease diuresis by affecting epinephrine secretion. Minute quantities of epinephrine cause a constriction of the arterioles leaving the glomerulus, the blood pressure in the glomerulus is elevated, and urine production is increased. Large amounts of epinephrine constrict the arteriole leading to the glomerulus and thus decrease glomerular pressure and diminish the formation of urine.

Diuretic drugs (Diamox, mercurial compounds, thiazides), commonly called water pills, are used to increase the excretion of salt and water in individuals suffering from edema. These diuretic drugs act principally by blocking the specific enzymes involved in tubular reabsorption, especially those promoting sodium uptake; as a consequence of sodium remaining in the tubules, water reabsorption is decreased and urine flow is increased. **Dropsy,** a chronic condition of bloating due to excessive reabsorption of water resulting from heart failure or other causes, may be alleviated by administration of diuretic drugs.

**Thirst**

Water intake is under voluntary control; we can, of course, drink at will. There is, however, an unconscious control mechanism that tells us when we are thirsty. When water loss has reached 1% of the body weight, the sensation of thirst is experienced. In the hypothalamus there is a localized region of nerve cells called the **drinking center;** when this area is stimulated either electrically or by the presence of high salt concentrations in the body fluids, a reflex is initiated that produces the sensation of thirst. This stimulates us to drink and prompts the kidneys to conserve water. Thirst symptoms develop because the mouth and pharynx become dry (parched) as a result of declining saliva production. This produces discomfort in swallowing, and relief is obtained only by drinking (wetting the mouth doesn't work). The thirst reflex is much stronger than that of hunger, and the limit of endurance for thirst is a matter of days whereas hunger can go on for weeks. When water loss reaches 5% of the body weight, a state of collapse ensues; when the water loss is over 10% of an individual's body weight, death is likely to occur.

"Water, water, everywhere/nor any drop to drink."[3] A person adrift in the ocean with only seawater available cannot satiate thirst. Drinking salt water will not quench thirst because the salt content of seawater is three times that of the blood. The excess ingested salt has to be excreted, and this requires more water than was consumed in the seawater. It is a losing battle, and the result is accelerated water loss and a quicker death.

## 16–4 DISCHARGE OF URINE

Once the filtrate has been processed, all that remains is to carry the urinary wastes out of the body. Exclusive of the nephrons of the kidney, the remainder of the urinary system is simply plumbing for conducting urine to the outside.

---

[3] S. T. Coleridge, *The Rime of the Ancient Mariner.*

Urine passes from the collecting ducts into the pelvis of the kidney, where the ducts unite to form a series of funnels drained by a 1-ft-long tube, the **ureter** (Figure 16–15). Urine is carried along the length of the ureters to the bladder by spontaneous, rhythmic, peristaltic contractions of the ureter walls, aided by gravity. Ordinarily the urine takes only a minute to go from the kidney to the bladder. Any abnormality of the ureter may impair its ability to contract, causing urine to collect in the kidney pelvis. This leads to swelling and may promote infection. Urine is stored in the bladder prior to discharge.

Some of the substances contained in the urine are only sparingly soluble in water, and when stagnation of urine occurs, microscopic crystals of calcium phosphate and calcium oxalate may aggregate to form concretions called **kidney stones** or **urinary calculi.** These materials grow in size, and eventually they may fill the kidney pelvis and obstruct the flow of urine in the ureter. These stones cause extreme pain, and passing a stone can be an excruciatingly painful experience. Organic substances such as amino acids (cysteine, for example, is sparingly soluble) and uric acid may also form stones. If it is impossible to redissolve or pass the stones, they must be removed surgically.

The bladder is a muscular bag situated in the pelvic cavity just above the pubic bone. When empty, it resembles a deflated balloon, but as it fills it assumes a pearlike shape and may contain a volume of about 1 qt. Its ability to expand is related to its highly extensible epithelial lining and the stretchability of the layers of smooth muscle on its outer surface. The ureters enter the bladder at an oblique angle to form a flaplike valve (Figure 16–15b). Therefore, any pressure in the bladder tends to close the opening of the ureters, preventing backflow.

Urine leaves the bladder via a single tube, the **urethra** (Figure 16–15), which varies in

FIGURE 16–15 (a) The structure of the bladder and its relation to the kidney. (b) Detail of the bladder wall and the ureter. As the bladder fills, the pressure (arrow) tends to close the opening from the ureter into the bladder.

(a)

(b)

length according to sex: in males it is about 8 in. long and passes through the penis, and in females it is 1.0 to 1.5 in. in length. The part of the urethra closest to the bladder is surrounded by two sphincter muscles controlled by the nervous system; one is under voluntary control and the other is not. Oridinarily both sphincters remain closed, so that urine cannot escape from the bladder except when there is some to pass and the individual wills it.

Urination (**micturition**) in humans is controlled by a combination of voluntary and involuntary nervous activity. When the bladder fills with about a pint of urine, stretch receptors in the bladder wall are stimulated; these transmit impulses to the spinal cord and initiate a conscious desire to urinate and a subconscious micturition reflex. The subconscious reflex involves motor fibers to the bladder wall and to the internal sphincter muscle of the urethra. The bladder contracts, and the internal sphincter relaxes; then for urine to pass out of the body the external sphincter of the urethra must be relaxed. If the time is suitable for urination, by the conscious activity of the brain (or merely by passage of urine into the urethra), there is relaxation of the external sphincter and urination occurs. If a person wishes to urinate before the micturition reflex occurs naturally, the reflex can be started by contracting muscles in the abdominal wall which push the viscera down onto the bladder; this excites the stretch receptors and the reflex of urination begins. Emotional conditions or exictement also tend to produce the urination reflex.

It is possible to override or inhibit the urination reflex and not succumb to the urge; in this case the desire to urinate passes within a few minutes. However, in a matter of minutes to hours, the reflex returns, and once the bladder fills to capacity the reflex becomes so strong that urination can no longer be prevented by conscious action. A baby has no control over the external sphincter of its urethra, and urination oc-

curs whenever the bladder fills and the urination reflex is initiated. Similarly, a person whose spinal cord has been severed has no bladder control. This loss of voluntary control of micturition is called **incontinence.** Such individuals may require a catheter, a tube inserted into the urethra, so that urine can flow into a convenient receptacle.

Inflammation of the bladder (**cystitis**) may be caused by bacterial infection and occasionally is a result of an inflammation in the kidney itself. Inflammation of the bladder is likely to be more apparent than a kidney inflammation, since it usually causes painful urination. Treatment involves antibiotics that attack the bacteria causing the infection.

## SUMMARY

**1.** The kidneys are the principal organs of excretion, ridding the body of waste and maintaining the constancy of the internal environment.

**2.** Blood supply to the kidney is via the renal artery and vein. The functional unit of the kidney is the nephron. The renal artery distributes blood to each nephron as a spherical cluster of capillaries called the glomerulus.

**3.** Owing to the effects of capillary blood pressure, a cell-free, protein-free blood filtrate passes from the glomerulus to Bowman's capsule.

**4.** From each Bowman's capsule, there is a series of convoluted tubules and an extended loop of Henle. The distal convoluted tubule leads via a urine-collecting duct to the ureter.

**5.** Henle's loops and the collecting ducts are found in the renal medulla; the rest of each nephron is in the cortex of the kidney.

**6.** Selective reabsorption and secretion of 99% of the filtrate occurs in the kidney tubules. The proximal convoluted tubule has a large surface area because of its microvilli. Here, 85% of the water, sodium and chloride ions, bicarbonate, glucose, vitamins, and amino acids is reabsorbed into the surrounding capillary network. Water enters by osmosis; the other components are actively transported by carrier proteins.

7. Sodium is actively pumped out by cells of the ascending loop of Henle. Chloride passively follows. Sodium then diffuses to the descending limb. Thus, sodium is recirculated and a sodium concentration gradient surrounds the loops of Henle. The concentration is higher in the medulla than the cortex. Since the ascending loop is impermeable to water, sodium is lost here but not water.

8. The dilute filtrate reaches the collecting duct, which is permeable only to water. As the tubule passes through the hyperosmotic renal medulla, the filtrate is concentrated by osmotic resorption of water. The concentrated filtrate is urine.

9. Augmentation of the urine may occur by selective capillary secretion.

10. Urine output depends on a fluid and salt balance that is regulated by antidiuretic hormone (ADH). ADH increases permeability of the distal convoluted tubule and collecting ducts. Hypothalamic osmoreceptors stimulate ADH secretion from the posterior pituitary as necessary.

11. ADH deficiency causes diabetes insipidus, with copious, dilute urine. Diabetes mellitus is due to insulin deficiency and increased blood sugar, which spills into the urine, causes osmotic imbalance, and may lead to dehydration.

12. The renal sodium pump is regulated by an adrenal hormone, aldosterone. Failure to excrete adequate sodium causes osmotic imbalances, water retention, and edema.

13. Diuretics increase urine flow and include high-protein diets (which increase amino acids and urea in the tubules), caffeine and alcohol (which inhibit ADH secretion), increased epinephrine secretion in response to emotional stimuli (which increases glomerular pressure and filtration), and diuretic drugs (which block tubular reabsorption enzymes).

14. The hypothalamic drinking center is stimulated by water loss and initiates a thirst reflex.

15. The collecting ducts unite in the renal pelvis to form a ureter, which carries the urine to the extensible bladder for storage. Urine stagnation may cause kidney stones to form.

16. Urine leaves the bladder via the urethra. Backflow from bladder to ureter is prevented by valves. Discharge of urine is controlled by two urethral sphincters.

17. A full bladder initiates the micturition reflex, which, within limits, can be consciously overridden. Incontinence involves the loss of voluntary control. Cystitis is inflammation of the bladder, which causes painful urination.

18. Ammonia is the nitrogenous waste material of protein metabolism. Soluble and toxic, it is carried to the liver and combined with $CO_2$ to form urea. Urea passes to the kidneys via the blood and is excreted.

19. Uremia can be treated by hemodialysis using an artificial kidney machine.

---

**KEY WORDS**

| | | | |
|---|---|---|---|
| | urine-collecting duct | antidiuretic hormone (ADH) or vasopressin | ureter |
| | cortex | diabetes | kidney stones or urinary calculi |
| kidneys | medulla | diabetes mellitus | urethra |
| renal artery | deamination | diabetes insipidus | micturition |
| renal vein | urea cycle | aldosterone | incontinence |
| ureter | isosmotic | edema | cystitis |
| nephrons | hyperosmotic | diuretics | dialysis |
| glomerulus | carrier proteins | diuresis | hemodialysis |
| Bowman's capsule | urine | dropsy | |
| loop of Henle | augmentation | drinking center | |

TOPICS FOR REVIEW
AND DISCUSSION

1. Why do animals require kidneys?

2. What is the nephron and how does it work?

3. How is blood pressure involved in kidney function?

4. What are the similarities and differences between the natural and the artificial kidney?

5. How is urea formed? How is urine formed?

6. Why is the drinking of seawater dehydrating?

7. What is the role of ADH in water balance?

8. How does the kidney regulate the fluid volume of the body?

9. What is the function of the bladder?

10. What is the fate of 99% of the glomerular filtrate?

Broom–Hilda by Russell Myers

# 17

# Chemical Coordination: Hormones

## 17-1 THE NATURE OF HORMONES

Look at yourself. Immediately you recognize what sex you are and so does everyone else. It is a fact of life that in the human species males and females look different. Indeed, our male or female appearance is so important to us that a plaque aboard a U.S. spacecraft headed for the far reaches of the Milky Way galaxy shows us naked. If it is found by intelligent life outside the earth, even those beings will know what we look like! Our sex differences are present not only externally but in the organs tucked away inside the body (Chapter 9). What mechanisms bring about such differences?

As we saw in Chapter 9, hormones are produced by ovaries and testes, and the action of these chemicals on a variety of tissues determines the external form we recognize as male or female. Indeed, if a boy is castrated before puberty, he grows into a eunuch. The effects of castration make it abundantly clear that for normal development of masculine characteristics there must be a chemical produced by the testes and transported by the bloodstream to all parts of the body. Such chemicals are called **hormones,** a word meaning "to arouse" or "to excite" in Greek. In essence, this is what a hormone does: it activates processes that, prior to its presence, were inactive or operating at a much lower level. A hormone can be defined as a specific chemical substance elaborated by cells in a particular part of an organism (plant or animal) that controls or helps control cellular processes elsewhere in the organism.

Why is it necessary to have a system of hormonal controls in an organism? The division of labor among cells is one of the primary characteristics of the multicellular condition, and it provides for certain advantages. However, division of labor is advantageous only if the component cells are coordinated and integrated by a communications network. In multicellular organisms the communications systems are both hormonal and nervous. The hormonal system generally provides for coordination on a slow-acting basis. Hormonal messages are distributed throughout the body, influencing specific cells in various parts of the body. By contrast, the nervous system is specialized for rapidly conducting electrochemical messages and mediating short-term responses. The signals that traverse the nervous system move along well-defined cables (nerves) and activate a limited number of cells at their terminal ends. Although the hormonal and nervous systems are usually regarded as separate—and in some organisms, such as plants, only one system (hormonal) exists—the two systems have much in common. Both systems influence processes in organs or tissues located some distance from the control center. To a considerable degree both systems operate on negative feedback principles. That is, a message sent out from the control center causes the target organ to increase or decrease its activity, and this response then acts back on the control center; as a consequence the system is self-correcting. The operation of the hormonal and nervous coordinating systems by negative feedback contributes to an organism's functional stability. Because they are error actuated and the controls are built in, such systems are economical and flexible. This is a point to which we shall return in Chapter 22.

## 17-2 THE HUMAN HORMONAL ORCHESTRA: ENDOCRINE GLANDS

Some glands of the body pour their products into tubes or ducts, and in this way the secretions pass to the outside of the body or to the cavity of one of the internal organs (Figure 17-1a). Among these **exocrine** (*exo*—outside, *krinein*—to separate; Gk.) **glands** are the mammary glands, sweat glands, salivary glands, gastric glands, and the liver. In contrast, hormones are produced by ductless **endocrine glands** (*endo*—within; Gk.), poured directly into the bloodstream, and swiftly carried throughout the body (Figure 17-1b).

Hormones are effective in minute quantities. The endocrine glands are tucked away in various places in the body—head, neck, abdominal cavity, and gonads (Figure 17-2). They provide an excellent example of the old adage that size is no criterion of function (together they weigh less than 5 oz); the endocrines exercise profound control over such functions as growth and development, regulation of tissue activity, and reproduction. Malfunction of an endocrine gland can lead to serious disturbances, usually owing to either underproduction (**hyposecretion**) or overproduction (**hypersecretion**). The causes are manifold: diet, disease, tumors, genetic disorders, and so on.

How is a specific response mediated by the hormonal system? Why does a hormone

FIGURE 17–1 A comparison of (a) exocrine and (b) endocrine glands. (Modified from A. J. Vander, J. H. Sherman, and D. Luciano, *Human Physiology: The Mechanism of Body Function.* Copyright © 1970, McGraw-Hill Book Company. Used with permission of McGraw-Hill Book Comany.)

FIGURE 17–2 Human endocrine glands.

produce activity in organ A and not in organs B, C, and D? As we might expect, the response of a particular organ to a hormonal stimulus is determined by the specific makeup of that organ. Thus, in coordinating body activity, each hormone has its **target organ** or organs—those it can trigger into activity; the other organs carry on normally. The nature and degree of response of the target organ to a hormone may vary from one time to another, from one individual to another, and from one species to another. This variation in response contributes to an organism's individuality.

### Maestro of the orchestra: the pituitary gland

The **pituitary gland,** or **hypophysis,** is a pea-sized organ nestled in a bony cavity below the base of the brain and above the nasal passages (Figure 17–3a). It was first described by the anatomist Vesalius (1514–1564), who mistakenly believed it produced mucus that was discharged into the nose and who therefore called the gland "pituitary" from the Latin word meaning "nasal secretion." The pituitary gland is actually two glands in one, consisting of an anterior lobe and a posterior lobe (Figure 17–3b and 17–3c). Although the anterior and posterior lobes lie side by side, with a portion of the anterior lobe wrapped around the posterior one, the two lobes are quite distinct functionally.

   **The anterior pituitary (adenohypophysis).** The anterior lobe of the pituitary is essential for life. It is the master gland, for many of the hormones it produces control the growth, development, and activity of other endocrine glands (for example, thyroid, adrenals, and gonads). If an animal's pituitary gland is removed or does not function properly, these endocrine organs degenerate or become functionless. In some respects the pituitary functions as the conductor of an orchestra. The maestro calls each orchestral section into activity at the proper time so that a harmony of function is produced.

(a)

(b)

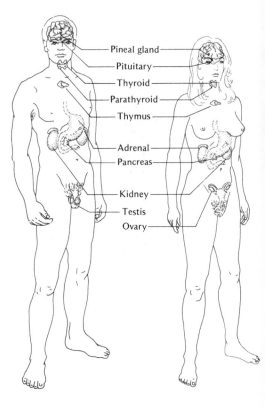

Without a maestro the musicians play when and what they will (as they do while tuning up), and noise instead of music is produced. When the pituitary's stimulatory hormones (called **tropic hormones**) arrive at their particular target organ, they call that gland into activity, and it in turn secretes its own product (usually a hormone). The rate of hormonal secretion by the pituitary and its target glands is controlled by negative feedback mechanisms. They work this way: when the tropic hormone reaches the target organ, the latter produces hormone; when sufficient hormone is produced, it affects the pituitary gland so that output of tropic hormone is diminished. When, on the other hand, the target organ is undersecreting, the pituitary steps up tropic hormone production, and the target organ is triggered

**FIGURE 17–3 The pituitary gland. (a) Location in the head region. (b) Detail of the gland. (c) Structure of the lobes of the pituitary. (d) Feedback control of the pituitary.**

Hypothalamus region of brain

Pituitary stalk

Pituitary gland

Posterior lobe

Anterior lobe

Pituitary vault

(b)

(a)

HYPOTHALAMUS

Nerve cells

Nerve fibers

Artery

Hypothalamic releasing hormone

Artery

Capillary network

Tropins

ANTERIOR LOBE

POSTERIOR LOBE

Vein

Vein

Vasopressin Oxytocin

ACTH
LH
FSH
TSH
PROLACTIN
STH

(c)

Anterior pituitary

Inhibitory action

Tropic hormone stimulation

Thyroid

Hormone

Adrenal cortex

Hormone

Gonads

Hormone

(d)

FIGURE 17–4 The hormones of the anterior pituitary and their sites of action.

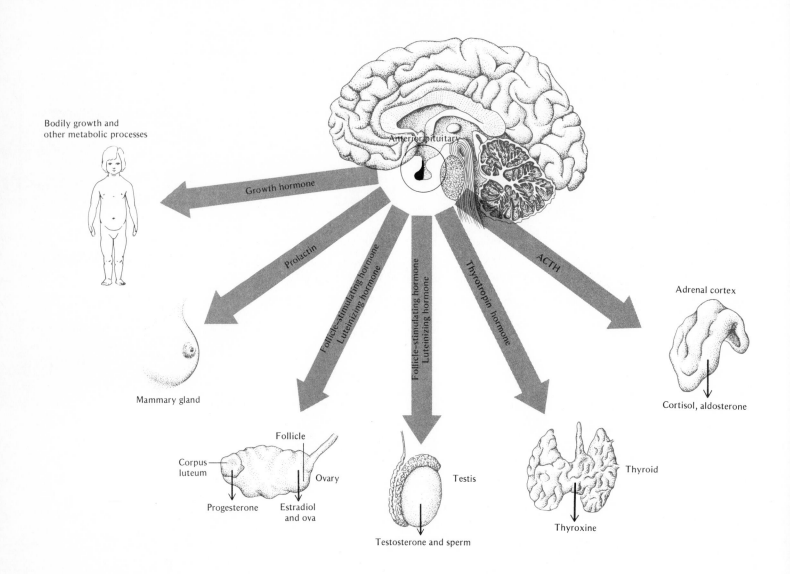

Bodily growth and other metabolic processes

Growth hormone

Prolactin

Mammary gland

Follicle-stimulating hormone
Luteinizing hormone

Anterior pituitary

Follicle-stimulating hormone
Luteinizing hormone

Thyrotropin hormone

ACTH

Adrenal cortex

Cortisol, aldosterone

Corpus luteum

Follicle

Ovary

Progesterone

Estradiol and ova

Testis

Testosterone and sperm

Thyroid

Thyroxine

**TABLE 17-1  Anterior pituitary (adenohypophyseal) hormones**

| Hormone | Target organ(s) | Principal effects | Diseases |
| --- | --- | --- | --- |
| Follicle-stimulating hormone (FSH) | Ovarian follicle and seminiferous tubules of testis | Stimulates growth of follicles and tubules | Hyposecretion: hypogonadism<br>Hypersecretion: hypergonadism |
| Luteinizing hormone (LH) | Corpus luteum and interstitial cells of testis | Stimulates formation of corpus luteum from follicle; stimulates production of progesterone by the ovaries and testosterone by the testes | Hyposecretion: hypogonadism<br>Hypersecretion: hypergonadism |
| Prolactin | Female mammary gland | Stimulates milk production after parturition | |
| Somatotropic growth hormone (STH) | Body tissues | Increases synthesis of protein | Hyposecretion: dwarfism<br>Hypersecretion: gigantism and acromegaly (Box 17A) |
| Adrenocorticotropic hormone (ACTH) | Cortex of adrenal gland, skin, liver, mammary gland | Stimulates production of corticosteroids; increases metabolic rate, glycogen deposition in liver, darkening of skin, milk production | Hyposecretion: Addison's disease (Box 17B) |
| Thyrotropic hormone (TH) | Thyroid gland | Stimulates production of thyroxine | Hyposecretion: cretinism, myxedema<br>Hypersecretion: goiter |

**TABLE 17-2  Posterior pituitary (neurohypophyseal) hormones***

| Hormone | Target organ(s) | Principal effects | Diseases |
| --- | --- | --- | --- |
| Vasopressin, or antidiuretic hormone (ADH) | Smooth muscle, especially of arterioles and kidney tubules | Constricts blood vessels, thus raising blood pressure; stimulates resorption of water by kidney (Chapter 16) | Hyposecretion: diabetes insipidus (Chapter 16) |
| Oxytocin | Uterus and ducts of mammary gland | Stimulates contraction of uterus if primed by ovarian hormones; enables milk-letdown reflex by mammary gland | Hypersecretion: water retention, edema |

* Produced by the hypothalamus.

into greater activity (Figure 17–3d). Thus, by negative feedback the pituitary and its target organs are integrated in their function, and body activities are coordinated.

The anterior pituitary produces six hormones, all of which are polypeptides, peptides, or proteins: two **gonadotropic hormones,** which regulate sexual functions in men and women; **adrenocorticotropic hormone** (ACTH), which controls one function of the adrenals; **thyrotropic hormone,** which controls the thyroid; **somatotropic (growth)** **hormone;** and **prolactin** (Figure 17–4). Table 17–1 shows the roles and functions of the hormones of the anterior pituitary.

**The posterior pituitary (neurohypophysis).** The posterior lobe of the pituitary is both structurally and functionally an extension of the hypothalamic region of the brain (Figure 17–3c). Although at one time it was believed to manufacture the hormones **vasopressin** (also called ADH or antidiuretic hormone) and **oxytocin,** it is now known that these hormones are produced by nerve

cells in the hypothalamus and are transported by the long terminal nerve fibers to the posterior lobe. This again shows how closely related the nervous and endocrine systems are, since oxytocin and vasopressin are produced by nerve cells, flow along the nerves in the stalk connecting the hypothalamus and the pituitary, and are later released from the pituitary gland via a capillary network. A summary of the functions of the posterior pituitary hormones is given in Table 17–2.

### BOX 17A Giants and dwarfs

The mention of giants and dwarfs conjures up memories of the fairy tales we heard when we were young. Yet these people who live in a make-believe world pressed between the covers of a children's book have their counterparts in the real world (Figure 17–5). In engravings, paintings, and stories of the past we find descriptions of dwarfs, court curiosities believed to be endowed with magical talents. Today the dwarf is frequently regarded as a freak, a part of the circus menagerie. The most famous of all modern dwarfs was Charlie Stratton ("Tom Thumb") and his bride, Lavinia Warren, both less than 3 ft tall; they were displayed on many continents by P. T. Barnum, the master showman. Giants, too, occur in the real world. Robert Wadlow (1919–1940) of Alton, Illinois, measured 8 ft 10.75 in., weighed 495 lb, wore size 37 shoes, and towered over his 5-ft 11-in. father. He was appropriately called the "Alton Giant."

These extremes in size, the short and the tall, are a result of too little or too much pituitary hormone. The **pituitary dwarf** does not produce an adequate supply of human growth hormone; as a result, the growth rate during childhood is diminished, and in some cases adult size is only twice that at birth. The body is normally proportioned and intelligence is normal. Treatment of a pituitary dwarf is possible if the condition is diagnosed early and includes the injection of human growth hormone. There are probably about 5,000 pituitary dwarfs in the United States. In the past the only source of human growth hormone was from the pituitary glands of deceased human donors. To treat a single patient with an underactive pituitary required the processing of hormone from 650 pituitary glands. In 1971, C. H. Li, an endocrinologist-biochemist at the University of California, and his colleagues announced that after 15 years of painstaking effort they had determined the order of the 191 amino acids in human growth hormone. This breakthrough, as

FIGURE 17–5 Too little or too much growth hormone. Insufficient quantities of growth hormone produce a pituitary dwarf; excessive amounts of this hormone result in gigantism. (Courtesy of Syndication International Ltd.)

well as genetic engineering advances whereby bacteria are induced to produce the hormone, now enable a production-line synthesis of growth hormone in the laboratory.

Overproduction of growth hormone (usually due to a pituitary tumor) can produce two conditions: if it occurs during pread-olescent years it causes **gigantism,** a condition in which the individual is unusually large. If it occurs in an adult, whose long bones have matured so that the shaft has fused with the ends (Chapter 21), there is enlargement of the cartilaginous regions and the bony joints, producing a condition called **acromegaly.**

Individuals with acromegaly show disproportionate thickening of the face, the feet, and the hands (Figure 17–6). The chin protrudes; the nose, lips, and extremities enlarge. The face of the individual tends to lack an intelligent expression; the individual suffers from lethargy and severe headaches. Treatment of acromegaly and gigantism is difficult because of the inaccessible position of the pituitary. If oversecretion is due to a pituitary tumor, some benefit may be obtained by surgical removal or bombardment with ionizing radiation (x rays), and in some cases treatment with dopamine is effective.

FIGURE 17–6 The progression of acromegaly. (a) At age 20, normal. (b) At age 24, early coarsening of features. (c) At age 40, well-established acromegaly with enlargement of nose and jaw. (Courtesy of Milton G. Crane, Loma Linda University Medical School.)

FIGURE 17–7 Marie de Medici, painted by Peter Paul Rubens in 1625.

FIGURE 17–8 An extreme case of goiter. (Courtesy of J. Nelson.)

### The thyroid gland: controlling the fires of life

The **thyroid gland** is a butterfly-shaped mass of tissue lying in the front of the neck, just below the voice box (Adam's apple). If you place your finger into the notch at the uppermost border of the breast bone, the tip of your finger will touch the lower edge of the gland. The thyroid produces three hormones: **thyroxine, triiodothyronine,** and **calcitonin.**

**Thyroxine and triiodothyronine.** Maria de Medici, wife of Henry IV of France, sat for the painter Peter Paul Rubens in 1625, and the portrait (now hanging in Spain's Prado Museum) is today considered a masterpiece. The painting not only attests to Rubens' skill as an artist and his fine eye for detail, but shows quite clearly that Henry's wife suffered from a mild **goiter** (Figure 17–7), an enlarged thyroid gland (*gutter*—throat; L.). Many portraits and paintings from this period show the regular and rounded neck, an obvious sign of goiter but considered a mark of beauty in the late Renaissance. Goiter is characteristic of people living in those parts of the world where there is an insufficient iodine supply in the food and water, such as the Alps of Europe and the Great Lakes region of the United States. Although mild goiter might be considered beautiful, extreme enlargement of the gland creates a far from pleasing appearance (Figure 17–8). Goiter is often associated with other symptoms, including dry and puffy skin, loss of hair, lethargy, mental dullness, and a slower-than-normal heartbeat. How is goiter related to thyroid function?

The formation of the thyroid hormones takes place in the thyroid gland. Ingested iodine is transported as iodide via the blood to the thyroid where it is pumped into the gland cells, concentrated and trapped. The iodide, is then converted to iodine, combined with the amino acid tyrosine, and linked to the protein thyroglobulin. The tyrosine first receives one iodide, then two to form thyroxine. And when a tyrosine bearing one iodide is linked to another bearing two, a molecule of triiodothyronine is produced. Thyroxine and triiodothyronine attached to thyroglobulin can be stored in the gland for several months; therefore, even when thyroid hormone synthesis has ceased entirely, the effects may not be observed for several months. Thyroglobulin is not released into the bloodstream; instead, thyroxine and triiodothyronine are first cleaved from the protein, and only the free hormones enter the blood.

Thyroid hormone secretion is controlled by the anterior pituitary hormone, thyrotro-

FIGURE 17–9 Goiter, the result of impaired negative feedback control in the formation of thyroid hormone.

pin (also called TSH, thyroid-stimulating hormone). Thyrotropin increases the liberation of thyroid hormones from thyroglobulin, increases iodide trapping and tyrosine iodination by the gland cells, and also increases the size of the cells. Increased thyroid hormone in the body fluids decreases the secretion of thyrotropin either by a direct effect on the anterior pituitary itself or by acting indirectly via the hypothalamus. Decreased levels of thyroid hormone result in an increased release of thyrotropin. It is this feedback mechanism that maintains an almost constant level of thyroid hormone in the body.

The development of the goiterous condition results from malfunction of the feedback mechanism that operates between the pituitary and its target organ, the thyroid. Tyrosine can be produced from a wide variety of substances that occur in the body and therefore offers no problems of supply, but iodine must be obtained in the food or water. If the diet is deficient in iodine, synthesis of thyroid hormones is diminished; this releases the brakes on the pituitary, and production of thyrotropin is increased. As a consequence of its oversecretion, the thyroid gland enlarges and the goiter forms. Increased size of the thyroid may or may not compensate for the hormonal insufficiency.

Disease and abnormal development may cause a goiter, but a dietary lack of iodine can also cause a goiter. Minute quantities of iodine in the diet (as little as 50 mg per year) prevent development of the iodine-deficiency goiter. The introduction of iodized salt has markedly reduced the incidence of goiter in many parts of the world, although it has been estimated that even today 200 million people are afflicted with the condition. Unfortunately, dietary iodine has little effect on an already established goiter.

What do thyroid hormones do? They increase the metabolic rate of almost all tissues of the body. Glucose metabolism and protein synthesis increase; mitochondria increase in size and number, and translation and transcription rates are stimulated. Mental processes are excited, growth may be accelerated, and fat stores, blood flow, and respiration rates increase. In some respects the thyroid hormones act like the gas pedal in an automobile, regulating the amount of gasoline fed into the engine, and thus controlling the rate of engine activity.

The symptoms of thyroid deficiency, as seen in individuals with severe goiter, reflect a lowered hormone activity; the manifestation of other thyroid disorders depends on when the deficiency of hormone sets in. If severe thyroid deficiency starts in

early infancy or prior to birth, the result is a mentally defective dwarf, a **cretin** (Figure 17–10a). A cretin never matures sexually, and growth never proceeds beyond that achieved by a 7 or 8 year old. If thyroid hormone administration is begun early enough, there may be some restoration of normal development, but in most cases of arrested development normal growth patterns cannot be initiated again. If thyroid deficiency develops in childhood or adult life, the disease is called **myxedema** (Figure 17–10b). Juvenile myxedema produces a short, squat child with an enlarged head, a short and heavy neck, dry skin, and a face with a dull and stupid expression. In an adult myxedema produces lethargy, obesity, edema, slowed heartbeat, decreased intelligence, and a coarseness of the hair and skin; the individual feels cold—the metabolic fires have been damped. Thyroid hormones administered orally often dramatically reverse these hypothyroid conditions, and the person can lead a normal life by taking daily medication.

Excessive thyroid activity produces an acceleration of bodily functions. The hyperthyroid individual suffering from **Graves' disease** (Figure 17–11) is nervous and excitable, the appetite is increased enormously but the person loses weight, movements are quick and restless, the heart rate is accelerated, the skin is hot and flushed, and sweating is increased; the eyes stare and sometimes they protrude (**exophthalmos**). Patients with Graves' disease show normal levels of thyrotropin, but the blood contains antibodies with properties similar to thyrotropin. These antibodies bind to the gland cells of the thyroid and result in continual activation of the gland. These antibodies are almost certainly the result of autoimmunity, that is, antibodies formed against the thyroid gland itself. Treatment involves administration of propylthiouracil or methimazole (drugs that block the synthesis of thyroid hormone), surgical removal of a major portion of the gland (thyroidectomy), or the injection of radioactive iodine

FIGURE 17–10 Too little thyroid hormone: childhood and adult effects. (a) Cretinism in a 2.5-year-old child. (b) Myxedema. (Courtesy of Sanford Schneider.)

FIGURE 17–11 Hyperthyroidism (Graves' disease), with exophthalmos (protruding eyes). Courtesy of J. Nelson.)

FIGURE 17–12 Scan of the thyroid area after administration of radioactive iodine ($^{131}$I).

FIGURE 17–10 Too little thyroid hormone: childhood and adult effects. (a) Cretinism in a 2.5-year-old child. (b) Myxedema. (Courtesy of Sanford Schneider.)

(a)

(b)

FIGURE 17–11 Hyperthyroidism (Graves' disease), with exophthalmos (protruding eyes). Courtesy of J. Nelson.)

FIGURE 17–12 Scan of the thyroid area after administration of radioactive iodine ($^{131}$I).

Radioactivity

(a)

($^{131}$I). In the last case, advantage is taken of the fact that an overactive thyroid concentrates massive amounts of iodine; 80 to 90% of the injected radioactive iodine is localized in the thyroid (Figure 17–12), enough radioactivity to destroy the hyperactive gland cells.

**Calcitonin.** Bones function as structural supports, but they also play a role in the metabolism of calcium. About 99% of the calcium in the body is deposited in the bones (Chapter 21); the remainder is found in cells and tissue fluids, where it is important in blood clotting, in neuromuscular function, and in cementing cells together. The levels of calcium in the body fluids are controlled and regulated by the hormones **calcitonin** (produced by the thyroid gland) and parathyroid hormone.

In young animals calcitonin rapidly decreases the level of calcium in the body fluids by reducing the amount of calcium released from bone. It does this by inhibiting specialized bone cells called osteoclasts (Chapter 21) so that there is decreased reabsorption of calcium salts in the bones (Figure 17–13). Calcitonin secretion is increased when the blood calcium level is raised above normal. Calcitonin increases the deposition of calcium into bone, how-

ever, in the adult human this does not substantially alter blood calcium levels because the daily rate of bone deposition is so small.

**The parathyroid glands**

The parathyroids are four small, egg-shaped glands about the size of a raisin, embedded in the back surface of the thyroid. They produce parathyroid hormone, which plays a vital role in the metabolism of calcium and phosphorus. Parathyroid hormone regulates the level of calcium in the body fluids by causing an increase in the movement of calcium from bone into the extracellular fluid, increasing calcium reabsorption by the kidney, and increasing intestinal absorption of calcium. As a consequence, the calcium level in the blood rises (Figure 17–13).

The secretion of parathyroid hormone is regulated by environmental factors. For example, when the blood level of calcium is low, owing to an insufficiency of calcium in the diet or a lack of calciferol (or vitamin D, which controls uptake of dietary calcium from the intestine; see Box 17B), the parathyroid glands increase their output of parathyroid hormone and the calcium level of

**FIGURE 17–13 A summary of the control of calcium metabolism by parathyroid hormone, calcitonin, and DHC (vitamin D).**

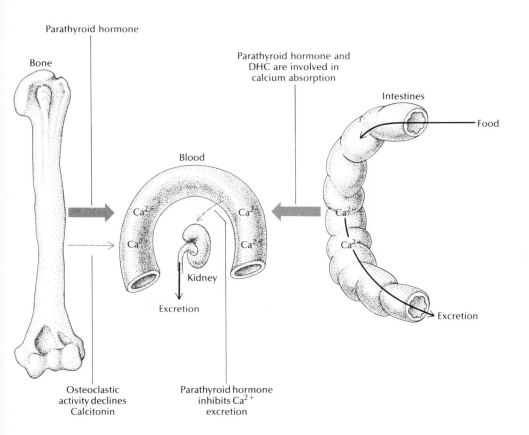

the extracellular fluids increases (derived from the release from the bone). Ordinarily it takes very little bone to maintain an adequate level of calcium in the body fluids, and since the bones contain a thousand times the content of the fluids, the structure of the bone itself is not impaired.

Overactivity of the parathyroids can cause the removal of so much calcium from the bones that they become honeycombed with cavities and so fragile that even walking can induce fractures. Since the parathyroids are embedded in the thyroid and are difficult to distinguish, the most common cause of parathyroid hormone deficiency is the inadvertent removal of the parathyroid glands during surgical removal of a portion of the thyroid (for example, in the treatment of

Graves' disease). If the calcium level falls to half that required for normal nerve function, the person develops tetany and dies of spasms in the respiratory muscles (Chapter 15). If parathyroid hormone is administered in time, the increased level of extracellular calcium restores normal function.

Parathyroid hormone thus produces an effect opposite that of calcitonin, but it differs from calcitonin in another way: it acts slowly, whereas calcitonin acts quickly. It may take hours for the effects of parathyroid hormone to become apparent. Calcitonin action is weak and functions mainly, as a short-term regulator, whereas parathyroid hormone is long-term and is the major regulator of the levels of calcium in the extracellular fluids (Figures 17–13 and 17–14).

**The pancreas: control of fuel supply**

**Diabetes mellitus,** meaning "sugar siphon," was described by Hippocrates over 2,000 years ago as a condition in which the urine contains excessive amounts of sugar. In seventeenth-century England, the disease was called the pissing evil because there was a marked loss of weight in spite of huge food intake, and it was believed that the substance of the body was being dissolved and poured out through the urinary tract. Before 1913, a child suffering from diabetes would die within 2 years, and if the disease developed at maturity, the afflicted individual could expect to live only 3 to 4 years. Today a diabetic individual can expect to live for 60 years or more. The miracle therapy for this disease is administration of the hormone **insulin.**

Insulin is produced in the **pancreas,** a gland that lies just beneath the stomach (Figure 17–15). The pancreas is a double gland: it produces digestive enzymes and hormones. In 1869 a German anatomist, Paul Langerhans, observed that the pancreas contains tiny clumps of cells that are sharply separated from the surrounding glandular tissue; these clumps make up only 1 to 2% of the total mass of the pancreas and appear as tiny cellular islands or, as Langerhans called them, islets. The **islets of Langerhans** are endocrine glands that produce insulin. Insulin facilitates the transport of glucose into the cell across the plasma membrane. In the presence of insulin the entry of glucose is 25 times faster than in its absence. The exact mechanism by which insulin affects the plasma membrane remains uncertain.

How is insulin related to diabetes mellitus? When we eat starch or sugar, enzymes in the digestive juices convert them to glucose; this simple sugar is transferred across the intestinal wall and passes into the blood. When the blood glucose level begins to rise, the islets of Langerhans in the pancreas are triggered to secrete insulin. Part of the absorbed glucose remains in

### BOX 17B  Rickets

Rickets is due primarily to insufficient deposition of calcium in growing bones. Although rickets is generally considered to result from a dietary lack of vitamin D, it is in fact caused not by a poor diet but by a deficiency of the sun's ultraviolet radiation. How is ultraviolet light related to vitamin D, and what do both of these have to do with rickets?

Normally, ultraviolet radiation from the sun acts on a prehormone (7-dehydrocholesterol) that occurs naturally in the skin and converts it to a substance called vitamin $D_3$ (or calciferol). Vitamin $D_3$ is released from the skin into the bloodstream and reaches the liver, where it undergoes chemical conversion (into 25-hydroxycalciferol) and then travels to the kidney via the blood to become the active material 1,25-dihydroxycalciferol **(DHC).** DHC promotes the uptake of calcium

from the intestine and aids in the deposition of calcium salts in the bones. Thus, any factor that reduces the amount of sunlight (and, therefore, of ultraviolet light) reaching the skin reduces the formation of vitamin $D_3$ and DHC. When DHC is not manufactured, not enough calcium can be absorbed from the intestine, and if such a condition persists for many months, the blood calcium level drops and calcium in the bone is automatically removed (under the control of parathyroid hormone) to reestablish the normal concentration. The depletion of calcium salts from the bones causes a severe weakening and bowing of the bones: rickets. (Lack of calcium in the diet per se rarely is a cause of rickets.)

FIGURE 17-14 The feedback loops involved in the regulation of the blood level of calcium. Compare the regulatory process shown here with the feedback circuit in the thermostat (Figure 7-16).

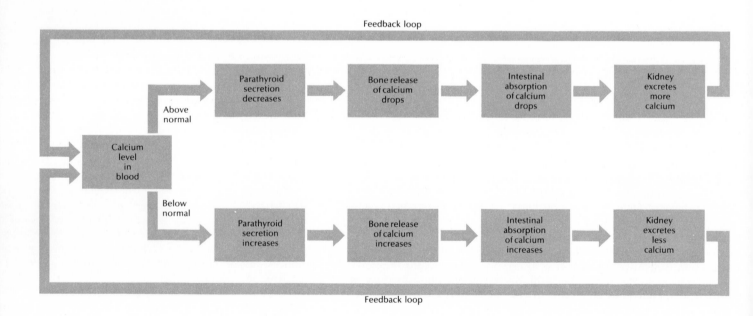

The history of rickets is quite interesting in itself. As early as 1650 the disease was described in England; its appearance coincided with the Industrial Revolution, which produced widespread use of coal and smoke and increased population densities in the cities with their narrow, dingy, and sunless streets. Rickets was probably the first recognized disease associated with air pollution. Many European physicians noted not only that rickets was a disease of industrialized and urbanized populations, but that it had a seasonal variation. The long, dark winters of Europe and the prolonged confinement of infants during these months predisposed these children toward rickets. Indeed, it was noted in 1906 that nearly all German children who were born in the fall and died in the spring had rickets, whereas those who were born in the spring and died in the fall were free of rickets. Thus, by the early 1900s sufficient evidence had accumulated to show that rickets was caused by a lack of sunlight. The problem that confronted the physicians was, How can sunlight be provided during the European or North American seasons when the amount of solar radiation is low? In the 1920s it was discovered that ultraviolet irradiation of linseed oil, cottonseed oil, or the plant sterol ergosterol made such materials capable of curing rickets. In fact, the irradiation of ergosterol is now a routine procedure, and the resultant material, ergocalciferol, or vitamin $D_2$, is added to almost all milk sold in the United States and Europe (0.01 mg per quart); since vitamin $D_2$ is a metabolic precursor of DHC, it prevents rickets. If you look at a carton or a bottle of milk you will find the words "400 USP units of Vitamin D added per quart." The demonstration that dietary materials could cure rickets was further strengthened by the finding that cod-liver oil has a preventive therapeutic effect against rickets. Soon the belief that diet influenced rickets became widespread, and when laboratory animals were fed diets deficient in vitamin D and developed rickets it was "established as fact" that rickets was a vitamin-deficiency disease. Over the years the evidence that rickets is a climate-related disorder was forgotten and the vitamin basis became widely accepted.

Is DHC a vitamin or a hormone? The answer lies in its chemical structure and metabolic role. Calling DHC a hormone links it to the other hormones (parathyroid hormone and calcitonin) that function in the control of calcium and phosphate metabolism in the body (Figure 17–14). Moreover, DHC is a steroid, synthesized in the body as are all other hormones. Thus vitamin D is actually best described as a hormone precursor.

the circulation, but most of it is carried to the liver, where it is transported rapidly across the cell membrane and stored as glycogen.

Diabetes may be due to insufficient activity of the cells in the islets of Langerhans. Insulin deficiency causes glucose to accumulate in the blood instead of being transported into the cells, and the unused glucose spills over into the urine. The excess amount of glucose in the glomerular filtrate of the kidney osmotically draws water into the urine and there is excessive output of dilute urine. To compensate for the lack of available fuel (glucose) and energy for cellular activities, fat is mobilized, and fatty acids are released; protein is also used as a source of energy. Repair of injured tissue is slowed, and resistance to infection is low. Impaired lipid metabolism results in the formation of ketone bodies as well as keto acids. Both increase in amount in the blood, and acidosis develops; the urine and breath may smell of acetone. Glucose-deprived cells degenerate; the individual eats voraciously, but remains hungry and loses weight. Acidosis may become severe, resulting in coma and death. Prolonged diabetes causes heart disease, kidney damage, and atherosclerosis. Diabetes is treated simply: daily injections of insulin and a restricted intake of carbohydrate. Most diabetics live active, normal lives when properly treated.

Too little insulin causes cells to be deprived of glucose because the cells are impermeable to the fuel. Too much insulin (because of a pancreatic tumor or injection of too large a dose of insulin) produces the same effect, but for a different reason. Excessive quantities of insulin promote too rapid an uptake of blood glucose; low blood glucose results, and this causes brain cells to be deprived of a constant supply of fuel energy. The brain cells are extremely sensitive to blood glucose concentration and become highly excitable, convulsions occur, then the nerve cells of the brain become depressed, and the individual falls into a coma. Treatment for this may be simply a

FIGURE 17–15 The pancreas produces both hormones and digestive enzymes. The islets of Langerhans are endocrine organs; they secrete the hormone insulin into the bloodstream.

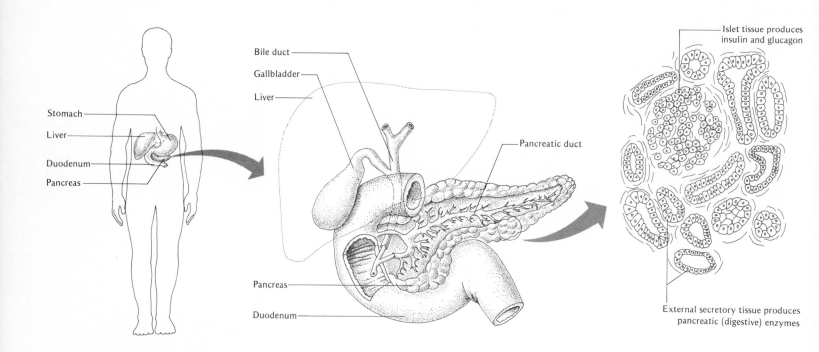

glucose-restricted diet to decrease insulin secretion.

If insulin turns up the set point of the metabolic thermostat, what turns it down? The hormone **glucagon.** Glucagon is an antagonist of insulin, and its secretion by the pancreas[1] results in the breakdown of liver glycogen and release of glucose into the blood. Secretion of glucagon is elicited by a fall in blood glucose level (below 60 to 80 mg per 100 ml of blood), and an immediate release of glucose from the liver restores the normal level (90 to 100 mg per 100 ml).

### The adrenal glands

The adrenal glands (*ad*—on, *ren*—kidney; L.) sit perched like a three-cornered hat on the upper surface of each kidney (Figure 17–16). Each gland is really a gland within a gland, consisting of a pea-sized central core, the **medulla,** and a thicker outer bark, the **cortex.**

**The adrenal medulla.** In the developing embryo the medulla arises from nervous tissue; it is really an overgrown sympathetic ganglion whose cell bodies do not send out nerve fibers, but instead release their chemical products directly into the bloodstream, again illustrating the close relationship between the nervous and endocrine systems. The hormone released by the medulla is for the most part **epinephrine** (*epi*—on, *nephros*—kidney; Gk.), with smaller quantities of a closely related substance, **norepinephrine.**[2]

What does epinephrine do? If epinephrine is injected into the body, a complex series of physiological changes occurs: arterioles constrict, and the blood pressure is elevated; liver glycogen is mobilized, and the blood sugar level rises; the pacemaker of the heart is activated, and the cardiac output is increased; blood vessels in the skeletal muscles dilate, as do the coronary arteries; the bronchioles dilate, permitting maximal gas flow to the lungs; the spleen contracts, ejecting the stored blood cells into the bloodstream; smooth muscles in the intestine are relaxed, and the sphincters of the anus, urethra, and stomach are constricted. In short, the body is mobilized for unusual exertion. In times of stress, anxiety, or fear the adrenal medulla is activated, and this series of responses is collectively called the **emergency response** or the **fight-or-flight reaction.** These emergency-response activities of the adrenal medulla are like those produced by the sympathetic nervous system (Chapter 18). The similarity is easily explained by the fact that sympathetic nerves

---

[1] The islets of Langerhans contain two kinds of cells, alpha and beta: alpha cells produce glucagon and beta cells produce insulin.

[2] Epinephrine is equivalent to the substance known by the trade name Adrenalin; likewise norepinephrine is the same as Noradrenalin.

FIGURE 17–16 Adrenal gland sliced to show internal organization.

FIGURE 17–17 The steroid hormones of the adrenal cortex. The steroid ring structure common to all these molecules is outlined in color.

secrete norepinephrine at their terminal ends. Because of this, loss of the adrenal medulla is not fatal; it is backed up by compensatory activity of the nerve fibers of the sympathetic system. However, response to stress and the ability to sustain muscular activity are severely impaired.

**The adrenal cortex.** For more than a century it has been known that the adrenal cortex (unlike the medulla) is absolutely essential for life. In 1855 Thomas Addison, an English physician, described a rare condition in a patient who had suffered from tuberculosis. The afflicted individual showed a bronzing of the skin, muscle weakness, impairment of kidney function, water retention in the tissue spaces, loss of weight, decreased levels of blood glucose, apathy, and a severe decline of sodium in the blood and tissue fluids. Shortly thereafter the patient died, and upon autopsy it was found that his adrenal cortex was almost completely functionless. The disease syndrome came to be called Addison's disease; President Kennedy had a mild form of this disease (Box 17C).

Addison's disease involves the failure of the adrenal cortex to secrete its hormones. The cortex of the adrenal gland is literally an endocrine factory secreting many hormonelike materials (about 50 have been identified so far), of which 10 are very active. All the hormones produced by the cortex have the same basic chemical ring structure (Figure 17–17), referred to as the **steroid ring** (Figure 3–11), and they are called **adreno-**

FIGURE 17-18 An abbreviated scheme of the synthesis of the adrenal cortical hormones from cholesterol.

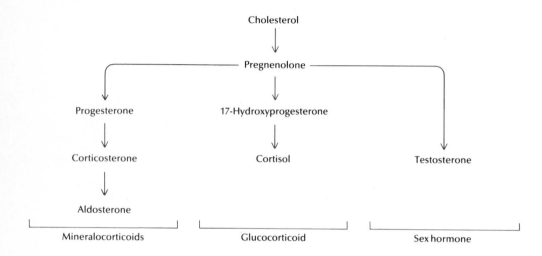

TABLE 17-3 Adrenal cortical hormones

| Hormone | Chemical nature | Target organ(s) | Principal effects | Diseases |
|---------|-----------------|-----------------|-------------------|----------|
| Testosterone | Steroid (mineralocorticoid) | Kidney | Controls absorption of sodium and potassium by kidney tubules | Hypersecretion: retention of water in tissues (edema) and high blood pressure |
| Cortisol | Steroid (glucocorticoid) | Body tissues | Regulates storage of glycogen by liver and conversion of protein into glucose; reduces action of insulin on peripheral tissues | Hyposecretion: Addison's disease (Box 17C) Hypersecretion: Cushing's syndrome |
| Androgens | Steroid | Body tissues | Secondary sex characteristics | Hypersecretion: precocious sexual development |

**corticosteroids** or **corticosteroids.** Although the steroid hormones of the adrenal cortex appear to have only minor chemical differences, they do have strikingly different functional properties. The parsimony of chemical synthesis coupled with target-organ specificity produces the economy and variety of control exercised by these molecules. The starting material for the adrenal hormones is cholesterol, and by a complex branching pathway involving addition and deletion of oxygen or hydrogen atoms or of small molecules, a group of steroids is produced (Figure 17-18). The steroid hormones fall into three types: (1) **glucocorticoids,** which act primarily in regulating sugar and protein metabolism; (2) **mineralocorticoids** (aldosterone, corticosterone, and deoxycorticosterone), which regulate the amount of sodium and other minerals in the extracellular fluids; and (3) the **sex hormone** testosterone. The synthesis of these hormones is affected by the pituitary gland and by enzymes. ACTH, secreted by the pituitary, affects only the first step (that is, the conversion of cholesterol to pregnenolone); subsequent reactions and conversions are enzyme-catalyzed. If the pituitary gland does not secrete ACTH, the adrenal glands remain inactive; if the cortex is underactive, owing to disease or some other cause, the individual shows the signs of Addison's disease (Box 17C). Table 17-3 summarizes the functions of the most important hormones secreted by the adrenal cortex.

### Sex hormones

Development from youth to maturity in humans is marked by dramatic changes in both mind and body, and these changes require coordination. The regulatory processes need not be rapid in action, but they must be continuous, often extending over months and years. The mechanisms for effecting such controls are hormones, especially the sex hormones.

**Male hormones (androgens).** Removal of the testes (**castration**) clearly reveals that maleness is related to this organ. The male hormones (**androgens**) are secreted by the testicular interstitial cells situated between the sperm-producing seminiferous tubules. Two androgens are produced, **testosterone** and **androstenedione,** of which testosterone is the predominant one. At puberty the pituitary gland begins to secrete large amounts of LH, and this triggers the testis to produce testosterone. Aided by FSH, the testis increases in size, and early spermatogenic activity is induced. Acting in concert, these hormones ensure maturation of sperm, and ejaculation becomes possible. The androgens of the testis are the dominant influence in the production of masculine characteristics (Chapter 9).

**Hypogonadism** (deficient gonadal function) is present in 0.13% of all males. If it occurs before puberty and involves only pituitary gonadotropins, testicular activity is impaired, spermatozoa and male hormones are not manufactured, and a eunuchoid individual results. The physique remains adolescent, the pubes and the face remain hairless, the features are delicate, the voice

## BOX 17C  The critical cortex

The early 1960s were years of optimism and youthful vigor—or so it appeared to some in the United States at the time. John F. Kennedy, 44 years of age, was the president, and his face and mannerisms contributed to the country's feeling of optimism (Figure 17–19). The Peace Corps was formed; the country survived the Cuban missile crisis, but got deeper into war in Vietnam. Although war always loomed on the horizon, the nation seemed to be in good hands. The president had charisma: a flashing smile, sparkling eyes, an easy air, and a deeply tanned skin. However, all in fact was not as it should have been: the smile and relaxed manner covered pain and illness. During the presidential campaign of 1960, the nature of Kennedy's illness came to light. Once or twice a year he required examinations to check on his adrenal insufficiency (Addison's disease). Kennedy had to take regular doses of cortisone from 1947 to 1951 and again from 1955 to 1958 to combat the disease. He said he took oral doses of corticosteroids "frequently when I have worked hard." Full disclosure of Kennedy's adrenal disorder and the effects of the administered hormones on his physical condition has never been made. Yet, it could be said that for a time the health of the chief executive and the fate of the United States depended upon replacement therapy for a pair of adrenal glands.

A patient with Addison's disease cannot cope with stress or resist infection, largely because insufficient amounts of cortisol are produced. Cortisol not only regulates the storage of glycogen in the liver and the amount of glucose formed from protein, but also reduces the action of insulin on peripheral tissues. Thus, in a person suffering from adrenal insufficiency, the blood sugar level may fall dangerously low. As a consequence the individual suffers from lethargy and muscle weakness.

Cortisol* is an especially effective anti-inflammatory agent, and acts by inhibiting the effects of mediators of inflammation such as histamines and prostaglandins.

Cortisol also affects other endocrine glands: it suppresses thyroid function by inhibiting TSH secretion. In Addison's disease the skin bronzes because more melanocyte-stimulating hor-

mone is secreted, and this causes melanocytes in the epidermis to form more of the pigment melanin. The activity of cellular respiration is diminished (owing to underproduction of TSH with consequent decline in the amount of thyroxine circulating in the blood).

The actions of cortisol are so important to the functioning of the body that there exists a special feedback control to ensure that adequate levels are always present in the blood and that these amounts will be increased when necessary. Stress, shock, pain, or any physical damage to the body triggers the hypothalamus to secrete a releasing factor that passes to the pituitary by way of the blood. This, in turn, causes the release of ACTH, which stimulates the adrenal cortex to synthesize and release cortisol into the bloodstream. As the level of cortisol rises, it inhibits further release of ACTH.

FIGURE 17–19 John F. Kennedy. (Courtesy of Wide World Photos, Inc.)

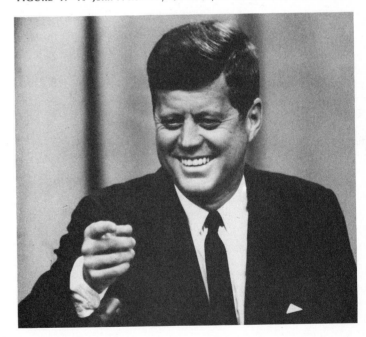

---

* The common name for cortisol is hydrocortisone.

FIGURE 17–20 Sex hormone and gonadotropic hormone levels (a) in the human male and (b) in the human female.

remains high-pitched, there is little sexual desire, and fat tends to accumulate in the hips, breasts, and below the umbilicus. Similar consequences arise from prepubertal castration and **cryptorchidism** (failure of the testes to descend from the pelvic cavity into the scrotum).

Hypogonadism may also occur after puberty, owing to disease (mumps virus causes inflammation of the testes in 20 to 30% of affected adult males, but rarely leads to male sterility if the disease is properly treated by a physician), radiation, castration, or chromosomal abnormalities such as Klinefelter's syndrome (Chapter 23). The form of the body remains approximately normal, but there is some enlargement of the breasts and excessive deposition of fat, owing to a lack of testosterone production; such individuals are sterile.

The opposite side of the coin, **hypergonadism** in the male (caused by hereditary factors or by tumor of the adrenal, pituitary, or testis), leads to excessive development of the genitalia and of the secondary sex characteristics: broad shoulders, hairy and muscular body, etc. Prepubertal hypergonadism in males causes precocious sexual development and shortness of stature because fusion of the ends of the long bones with the shaft occurs prematurely.

In their late forties and early fifties many men experience **male climacteric** (male menopause), with a diminution of sexual drive. This is due partly to psychological factors and partly to a decline in secretion of androgens (Figure 17–20) coupled with a rise in secretion of FSH; occasionally there is atrophy of the seminiferous tubules. In some cases of male climacteric the individual benefits from administration of testosterone.

**Female hormones.** The feminine characteristics of body form, menstruation, ovulation, pregnancy, and menopause are all dependent on the female hormones **estrogen** and **progesterone**. The estrogens are produced from cholesterol by the follicle cells of the ovary under the stimulus of the

pituitary gonadotropins (FSH and LH) (Figure 17–18). The pituitary does not secrete these tropic hormones in significant quantities until a child is about 7 or 8 years old. Then production increases to age 11 to 13, after which time the level remains as in the adult (Figure 17–20). Once the gonadotropin levels are high enough, the ovaries begin to produce estrogen and progesterone, and body changes become evident. The breasts enlarge, the pelvis broadens, the uterus increases in size, pubic hair develops and menstruation and ovulation begin. (The hormonal interactions during the ovarian and uterine cycles, menstruation, menopause, and pregnancy are discussed in Chapter 9).

Estrogen concentrations in females rise

nine characteristics. The body was heavily covered with fat. There was scarcely a hair on the body, and that on the head was thin, fine, and silky. Penis and testes were small, the pubis resembled the mons veneris in a woman, and the shoulders were narrow and the hips wide. The emperor had changed his secondary sex characteristics. It seems that he suffered from adiposogenital dystrophy, a disease of the hypothalamus that causes deranged pituitary function and abnormal adrenals, thyroid, and reproductive organs.

With this speculative look at Napoleon,

**FIGURE 17–21** (a) Napoleon, first consul. (b) Napoleon, emperor. (Courtesy of the Mansell Collection.)

(a)

(b)

can we explain why the great military genius failed to destroy the Russia army at Borodino and then was left with nothing to support his army in Moscow? In 1812 the French grand army retreated from Russia in defeat. Was it because Napoleon was unable to make a decision to attack? Had he delayed too long? A year later at Dresden his indecision converted victory into defeat once more, when instead of pursuing the enemy he stopped and turned back. At the battle of Leipzig he did not oversee the battle at all, but slept. Waterloo was the final battle: he delayed the attack for 6 hours, and by that time Wellington had received additional support. Much of the time he was fast asleep in a chair! He was physically and mentally worn out at age 45. The fall of the French Empire may well have been caused by the impaired hypothalamic function of Napoleon's brain. What course would European history have taken had the emperor been able to receive treatment for the hypothalamic changes he endured? We can only speculate.

at puberty, and this level tends to inhibit pituitary secretion of growth hormone. Thus at puberty or shortly thereafter in the female, long bones cease to grow and the ends of the bones fuse with the shaft. Male hormone produces no such inhibition of growth hormone, and consequently men tend to be larger in stature than women. Estrogen causes fat to accumulate in the hips and breasts and promotes the retention of body water. Female hormones, particularly estrogen, tend to reduce the level of cholesterol in the blood, a fact which may have some bearing on the lower incidence of atherosclerosis in women.

If the ovaries of a female are removed prior to puberty, a childlike physique is retained; if they are removed after puberty, sex drive diminishes, and menstruation ceases. Treatment of a normal female with male hormone produces masculinization. Overactive adrenal glands and diseased ovaries have been shown to produce excessive amounts of androgens, and this can lead to baldness and excessive facial hair in women.

### Other endocrine organs

It has recently been discovered that the **thymus gland,** situated in the neck region (Figure 17–2), secretes several hormones essential for functional maturation of lymphocytes involved in the immune response. The **pineal gland,** a small pea-shaped organ lying on the upper surface of the brain (Figures 17–2 and 18–14e), produces a hormone called **melatonin,** which has been implicated in the control of reproduction. The synthesis of melatonin from serotonin is suppressed by light and stimulated by darkness; as a consequence, there is a daily rhythm of pineal gland secretion: melatonin levels are higher at night and lower during the daytime. Melatonin suppresses the onset of puberty, and it is the marked decrease in the synthesis of this hormone that affects sexual development in the human. In children with pineal tumors, and with increased levels of melatonin, sexual development is

delayed. When melatonin is administered to human volunteers, it induces sleep, and therefore, it may be the increased levels of melatonin in children that contributes to their requiring more sleep than do adults.

The plasma membranes of the cells of a variety of tissues have recently been found to synthesize a family of 20-carbon fatty acids in small amounts. Called **prostaglandins,** these are rapidly degraded, but seem to perform a variety of roles in the body. "Prostaglandins," as one research worker put it, "are hormonelike substances that do anything and everything." He may not be exaggerating. The name prostaglandin is a misnomer based on the erroneous belief that the active substances are derived from the prostate gland alone. Seminal fluid contains 100 times the amount found in any other tissue, and it is probably for this reason alone that prostaglandins were discovered.

One prostaglandin ($PGE_2$) lowers blood pressure; a closely related one ($PGF_2\alpha$) raises blood pressure. An intravenous injection of a low dose of either of these stimulates contractions of the uterine muscles. Since prostaglandins are found in the amniotic fluid of women during labor, these substances are probably the major factor in delivery. If a woman in labor is experiencing difficulty, the injection of a small amount of $PGE_2$ induces delivery in a matter of hours. Some have suggested that $PGE_2$ could be a useful agent for inducing abortions. In trials with female monkeys, an injection of $PGE_2$ shortly after mating produces a sharp reduction in the secretion of progesterone by the corpus luteum, thus preventing implantation of the fertilized egg. This means that $PGE_2$ could potentially be used as a morning-after, or after-the-fact, contraceptive agent.

$PGE_2$ inhibits gastric secretions in dogs and may be a promising new tool in the prevention of human peptic ulcers. Administered as an aerosol, it constricts the bronchial passages and aids asthmatic patients in their breathing. Applied topically to the

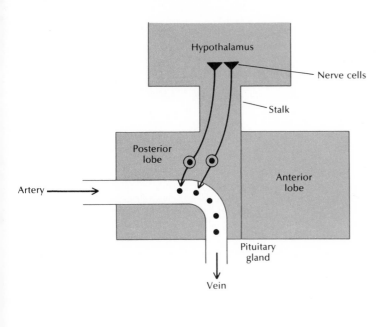

FIGURE 17–22 The relation of the hypothalamus to the posterior lobe of the pituitary. The nerve cells in the hypothalamus have long axons that terminate in the posterior lobe. The hormones synthesized by the neurons are released at the terminal ends and enter the capillary beds.

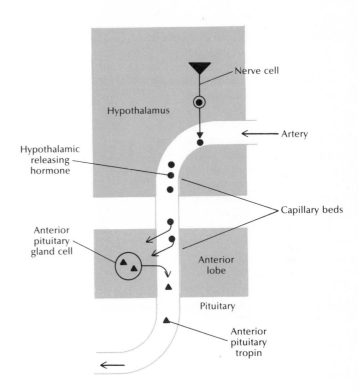

FIGURE 17–23 The relation of the anterior pituitary to the hypothalamus. Releasing factors from the hypothalamus pass to the pituitary via the blood, and these trigger secretion of the anterior pituitary tropin hormones.

nose, $PGE_2$ clears nasal passages by constricting blood vessels. The prostaglandins may regulate the function of the plasma membrane itself, and in so doing may influence the movement of materials into and out of cells, the formation of cellular metabolites responsible for cell-cell communication, and consequently the transmission of signals from nerve cell to nerve cell.

The future holds great promise for investigation of these substances, and no doubt by the time you read these words we shall know a great deal more about how they act at the molecular level.

## 17–3 MANAGEMENT OF THE ENDOCRINE ORCHESTRA

The orchestra of endocrine organs is conducted by the maestro, the pituitary gland. The interaction between the pituitary and the other endocrine glands is delicately balanced by negative feedback controls mediated by the hypothalamic region of the brain. (See Box 17D) The **hypothalamus** is a small mass of brain tissue lying just above the pituitary (Figure 17–3c). The pituitary is physically connected to the hypothalamus by a stalk that contains nerves and small blood vessels. The posterior lobe of the pituitary is actually an extension of the hypothalamus. Nerve cells in the hypothalamus have long extensions called axons that pass down the stalk and their terminal branches end in the posterior lobe in close proximity to a capillary bed. The hormones oxytocin and vasopressin, each synthesized by different nerve cells, move downward from their place of synthesis in the hypothalamus, are released at the terminal branch, and enter the capillaries (Figure 17–22). Stimulation of these nerve cells occurs in much the same way as in other nerve cells (see Chapter 18).

In contrast to the posterior lobe, there are no direct nerve cell connections between the anterior lobe and the hypothalamus, but there is an unusual capillary-to-capillary connection. The axons that originate in the hypothalamus have their terminal endings in close proximity to the uppermost capillary bed, and when these nerve cells are triggered to activity, they release one or more of the hypothalamic releasing hormones (Figure 17–23). Each releasing hormone is named after the anterior pituitary hormone whose secretion it controls. The hypothalamic releasing hormones enter the capillary bed and move to the anterior lobe where they act on the gland cells causing them to inhibit or provoke secretion of one or more of the peptide hormones. These anterior pituitary hor-

FIGURE 17–24 The second messenger of hormone activity, cyclic AMP.

mones enter the second capillary network and are carried throughout the body.

In this way, gonadotropin releasing hormone triggers secretion of FSH and LH, thyrotropin releasing hormone stimulates secretion of TSH, corticotropin releasing hormone causes ACTH to be secreted, prolactin releasing hormone causes secretion of prolactin, and growth hormone releasing hormone provokes secretion of growth hormone. Two of the hypothalamic hormones inhibit secretion: somatostatin and prolactin release inhibiting hormone.

The hypothalamic releasing factors control the activity of the anterior pituitary, but what controls the secretion of releasing factors? The answer: nerve impulses and hormones. The hypothalamus, a small area of nervous tissue, is a crossroad of nerve-cell connections, and it receives nerve inputs from almost all parts of the body. In addition, it is well supplied with blood vessels, so that it comes in contact with the hormones circulating in the bloodstream. Each specific input to the hypothalamus is monitored, and the hypothalamus responds by secreting the appropriate releasing factor. The nerve cells of the hypothalamus are transducers, that is, they convert one kind of signal into another—neural messages become hormonal messages, and sensory information is transferred from the nervous system to the pituitary. Thus, neural activity may promote endocrine change, and hormonal secretions may influence neural activity. Again, the endocrine and nervous systems act as an integrated unit; the anterior lobe of the pituitary is maestro of the endocrine orchestra, but the hypothalamus manages the maestro.

## 17–4 THE MOLECULAR ACTIVITY OF HORMONES

Hormones provide integrative function between groups of cells, but how do hormones act at the cellular level? What is the effect of a hormone on its target cell? In recent years it has become apparent that

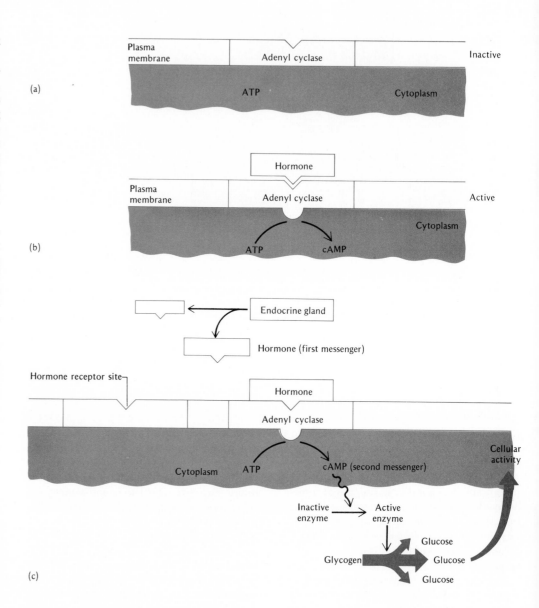

FIGURE 17–24 The second messenger of hormone activity, cyclic AMP.

hormones exert their effects by alteration of enzyme activity, alteration of membrane transport, and gene activation.

### Enzyme activity and cyclic AMP

During the 1960s laboratory experiments demonstrated that certain polypeptide hor-

mones (vasopressin, epinephrine, glucagon, tropic hormones) interact with their target cells in such a way that the target cells respond by the formation of **cyclic adenosine monophosphate** (**cyclic AMP** or **cAMP**). Cyclic AMP is made from ATP by the enzyme adenyl cyclase, which is present in the plasma membrane. Hormones acti-

FIGURE 17–25 A model for the mode of action of steroid hormones.

**359**

CHEMICAL COORDINATION: HORMONES

vate adenyl cyclase by changing its shape, and the active adenyl cyclase then converts ATP into cAMP. Cells that have cAMP immediately break down glycogen to glucose and thus receive an additional spurt of energy for the performance of metabolic work (Figure 17–24). It is presumed that the specific response of target cells to different hormones is a consequence of different cell types having different hormone-specific receptor sites. Thus, the thyroid gland cells have receptors that react only with the hormone TSH and will not react with other tropic hormones. On the other hand, cells that respond to a variety of hormones presumably have many receptor sites on their plasma membranes. Liver cells have receptors for glucagon, epinephrine, thyroxine, and so on.

In some cases cAMP formation activates enzymes that catalyze reactions important to the function of the cell involved. For example, the cAMP elicited in kidney tubule cells by the hormone vasopressin activates the enzymes that bring about water resorption by these cells. Similarly, cAMP induced in thyroid cells by TSH activates the enzymes in these cells that promote iodine uptake, and the cAMP in liver cells, induced by glucagon, activates the enzymes necessary for fat mobilization. Hormone action in these cases may be viewed as a two-messenger system: the first is an extracellular messenger, the hormone itself, which travels from the endocrine gland via the bloodstream to the target cell; the second messenger is an intracellular one, cyclic AMP, which receives the hormonal message in the target cell and initiates molecular (enzymatic) activity.

### Membrane transport

Two types of diabetes can be distinguished clinically: juvenile-onset (also called Type I diabetes) and maturity-onset (also called Type 2 diabetes). Maturity-onset diabetes is the much more common form of diabetes, representing 90% of the cases, and generally

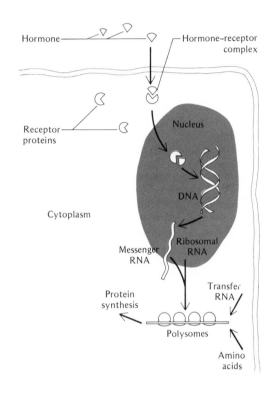

occurs in people who are over 40 and overweight. Diabetes of the mature type results not from a deficiency of insulin but from a defect in the molecular machinery that affects the action of insulin on its target cells, muscle and adipose tissues.

Insulin acts by binding to receptor molecules on the surface of target cells. Once bound to the cell surface, the cell's metabolism is so altered that glucose uptake by membrane transport from the blood plasma is increased and the glucose is either metabolized or stored in the form of glycogen or fat. Whereas in juvenile diabetes there is a defect in the synthesis of insulin, in the mature type there is a decrease in the number of insulin receptors. This decrease in insulin receptors makes the membranes of the target cells less responsive to insulin, and the increased amounts of insulin in circulation produce a further reduction in

the number of insulin receptors. The maturity-onset type of diabetes tends to run in families, and the likelihood of an individual developing the disease is increased if one parent is diabetic and further increased if both are diabetic. Thus there may be a genetic basis for this kind of diabetes. Juvenile diabetes, too, may be influenced by genetic factors, but there is also evidence that autoimmunity, viruses, and/or toxic chemicals may be responsible. However, the way in which each factor influences the onset of the disease is still not clear.

### Gene activation

Many actions of steroid hormones are exerted at the level of the gene. In pregnancy and throughout the menstrual cycle, women produce abundant quantities of estrogens and progesterone. One effect of these hormones is the development of secondary sex characteristics, but in addition there is a rapid mobilization of metabolic activities in target cells: the linings of the uterus, cervix, and vagina thicken and become vascularized; their liquid content increases; and new proteins are formed. Evidently under hormonal influence these target organs express bits of their genetic information.

Recent investigations have shown that steroid hormones, such as estrogen and progesterone, easily diffuse into the target cells, as well as into many other kinds of cells. In nontarget cells the hormone concentration remains low because the hormone diffuses out as easily as it diffuses in, but in target cells the hormone molecules continue to diffuse in, causing their concentration to increase within the cell. The reason for this increase is that, within the target cell cytoplasm, the hormone quickly associates with specific receptor proteins (Figure 17–25). The binding of hormone to the receptor alters the latter in such a way that it becomes activated, and the hormone-activated receptor complex moves from the cytoplasm to the nucleus. In the nucleus the hormone-receptor complex binds to the

Photograph by Eliot Elisofon, Time/Life Picture Agency, © Time, Inc.

# 18

# Electrochemical Coordination: Nerves

## 18-1 WHAT DOES THE NERVOUS SYSTEM DO?

The animal is anesthetized, and a metal halo is clamped on its head to prevent movement. By means of a high-speed drill, a small shaft is bored through the bony skull and into the coverings of the brain. The shiny, wrinkled surface of the brain is exposed. Using a micromanipulator, the operator carefully guides a tiny electrode—fine wires insulated with Teflon and scraped bare at the tips—into the soft, jellylike tissue of the brain itself. There is no pain, since the brain has no sensory receptors or free nerve endings in its own tissue. Deeper and deeper within the brain the operator moves the bare stainless-steel wires of the electrode, until the right position has been reached. Once the electrode has been implanted, the wires at the scalp end of the electrode are soldered to a small electrical socket, and this is permanently cemented to the skull. The operation is quick, and the instrument implant is so small that in time it will be completely covered by the scalp hairs. After the anesthesia has worn off, plugging into the brain is as simple as putting a lamp plug into a wall socket. When the electrode wires are connected to a power supply, a small pulse of electricity can be sent into the brain and the animal made to perform certain specific movements like an electrical toy. When electrodes are connected to the correct region of the brain, the animal gives involuntary but coordinated movements.

The experimental animal we have been describing is not a rat, a cat, or a monkey, but a human—under treatment for psychomotor epilepsy. By delivering electric shocks to the patient's brain, the operator can produce a slow clenching of the patient's hands into a fist. When one such patient was asked to keep his fingers extended through the next stimulation, he replied that he could not do so. He commented, "I guess your electricity is stronger than my will."

The wired and electrically manipulated brain represents our latest method of control over our own behavior. By means of electrodes placed in precisely located spots (more than 400 have been implanted in an experimental monkey for 4 years), the subject can be made to act in a specific way (Box 18A). For example, electrode implantation has been used in the diagnosis and treatment of involuntary movements, intractable pain, and severe epilepsy. When patients with an implanted electrode feel an epileptic seizure coming on, they can, by using a self-stimulator, induce electrical excitation in a competing area of the brain; this stops the discharge from spreading, and the fit does not develop. Before we can understand how such techniques are possible, it is appropriate to ask two questions: Why do we need a nervous system, and how does the nervous system work?

The body receives messages from its own organs and from the external world. We perceive light, sound, odors, pressure, temperature, chemicals, and the like; we think, we move, we have unconscious thoughts and conscious ones. The normal functioning of the body depends both on receipt of stimuli and on production of integrated responses. For the body to perform its activities in coordinated fashion, there must exist a connecting link between stimulus and response, between receptor organ and effector organ; that link must be a system capable of channeling information from one to the other.

Two systems in our bodies act as coordinating links between stimulus and response: the endocrine system and the nervous system. The endocrine system, as we saw in Chapter 17, regulates the activities of cells in other parts of the body by means of hormones. When a hormone is released directly into the blood, some time elapses before the response is evident. The lag may be seconds, minutes, or hours. Moreover, since the hormone circulates in the blood for a time with little decay in activity, the period during which it can affect the target organ may last for hours or days. Thus, the hormonal system provides for slow communication on a long-term basis. The nervous system, on the other hand, provides for rapid communication between the various tissues and organs of the body. In large organisms, many of the organs involved in the reception of stimuli are on the surface and usually are far removed from those involved in reacting to the stimuli (glands and muscles). To link the peripheral "listeners" with the more internal responders and to effect rapid reactions to stimuli, quick and direct pathways for conducting messages are required, and that function involves nerve cells. The nervous system em-

---

**BOX 18A  1984 Revisited?**

If the late George Orwell were writing a sequel to *1984* today, he would probably reject as archaic the propaganda techniques for controlling people's minds described in his famous anti-Utopian classic. Today, for example, he might envisage a society in which a newborn baby's first experience would be neurosurgery, an operation in which the child's brain was fitted with miniaturized radio devices connected to every major center controlling reason and emotion. Children in such a society might be raised as flesh-and-blood electrical toys, whose ideas and behavior were directed by computer signals. Any aberrant or heretical ideas would be transmitted to the computer, which would be programmed to take appropriate action to restore control.

This may not be as fantastic as it sounds. Some years ago it was discovered that if rats had a stimulating electrode implanted into a particular region of the brain, they could be trained to press a lever that would turn on a stimulating current. Such a rat, when given a choice between feeding and pressing, would prefer to stimulate its median forebrain bundle rather than eat. Indeed, some animals press the lever as many as 8,000 times in 1 hour. The area came to be known as the reward or pleasure center of the brain. Similar techniques and experiments have been performed on cats, dogs, monkeys, and even man. In one human case where the individual had an electrode implanted in the septal region, the patient declared after electrode stimulation that he felt "good," as if he were building up to a sexual orgasm, although the end point was not achieved. Similarly, unpleasant emotions can be produced in man: stimulation of the amygdala region of the temporal lobe induces fear reactions, and stimulation of particular regions of the hypothalamus incites a variety of emotional responses including rage and terror.

Fortunately, human ignorance about the brain remains so vast that there is no imminent prospect that the techniques being worked on could have Orwellian significance. Nevertheless, the horrifying prospect rises that in the twenty-first century the lexicographers may have to drop the verb "to brainwash" and replace it with "to brainwave."

---

ploys electrochemical messages, **nerve impulses,** that run along specialized nerve pathways receiving and transmitting information to and from various organs. Nerve cells, or **neurons,** are specialized to conduct electrochemical messages at high speed and, when bundled together in cablelike form as **nerves,** are able to regulate the direction in which information flows. Groups of nerve cells form control centers, such as in the brain and spinal cord, which act as central clearinghouses of information, loci of coordination. Some scientists have contended that without nervous control, active multicellular animals could never have developed.

## 18–2 THE NEURON: SIGNAL CELL OF THE NERVOUS SYSTEM

The human nervous system is often likened to a switchboard or a computer, since all three receive signals and send out messages. Electrochemical signals cause the nervous system to "flash," "blink," and "hum." It is a complex array of "wiring" made up of over 100 billion neurons, interspersed with supportive elements, the **glial cells** (Figure 18–1). In order to arrive at an understanding of how the nervous system works, it is necessary to consider the nature and mode of operation of the structural components themselves, the neurons.

The neuron is the basic unit of the nervous system, and although neurons vary in size and shape (Figure 18–2a), they do show a common functional organization that makes it possible to describe the "typical" neuron (Figure 18–2b). Like other cells, the neuron has a plasma membrane, a nucleus, and various organelles within its cytoplasm. It is a single cell and not structurally continuous with any other cell. The neuron cell body, like that of most other cells, contains the nucleus, Golgi apparatus, mitochondria, ribosomes, endoplasmic reticulum (Nissl bodies), and a granular cytoplasm. Projecting from this region are many fine rootlike processes called **dendrites;** these receive

FIGURE 18–1 The "wiring" of the nervous system, as drawn by the Flemish anatomist Vesalius in 1543. (Courtesy of The New York Academy of Medicine.)

FIGURE 18–2 (a) A variety of neurons from different parts of the human nervous system. Dendrites receive excitation from other cells and conduct impulses toward the cell body, whereas axons conduct nerve impulses away from the cell body. (b) The "typical" neuron shows many short dendrites and a single, elongate axon.

BIPOLAR CELL FROM RETINA

MITRAL CELL FROM OLFACTORY BULB

PYRAMIDAL CELL FROM CORTEX

Dendrites

Cell bodies

Axon

Dendrite

Cell body

Axons

MOTOR NEURON FROM SPINAL CORD

Dendrite

Cell body

Axon

(a)

Dendrites

Cell body

Nucleus

Axon

Myelin sheath

Node

Synaptic knob

(b)

messages from adjacent cells or directly from the environment. Also extending from the cell body is a single, long, fiberlike extension, the **axon,** which ramifies near its end into fine branches, each terminating in a tiny bulb **(synaptic knob).** The axon passes signals to other neurons or effectors.

Some axons are covered by a sheath, formed by special **glial cells.** The glial cell completely encircles the axon (Figure 18–3a) and may play a role in the nutrition of neurons and in their regeneration following damage. The glial cells of some axons, called Schwann cells, wind their plasma membranes tightly around the surface of the axon, forming a spiral envelope containing many turns (Figure 18–3b). These tightly wrapped membranes, rich in fatty materials, form an effective insulating layer called the **myelin sheath.** The myelin sheath helps to increase the speed of transmission of signals along the axon it surrounds. At intervals along the axon's length the myelin sheath is interrupted; the interruptions (called **nodes of Ranvier**) represent points where one encircling cell ends and another begins.

**Multiple sclerosis** (MS), a disease characterized by jerky body and limb movement, double vision, slurred speech, and paralysis, is caused by a patchy destruction of the myelin sheath. Since the myelin sheath is like living electrical tape, similar to the insulation around a telephone wire, the destruction of myelin reduces the neuron's ability to conduct impulses. Either the impulses travel slowly, or else the axons cannot conduct at all. The victim of multiple sclerosis suffers from a decrease in the function of neurons in the spinal column and brain.

FIGURE 18–3 The relationship of the glial Schwann cell to the myelin sheath. (a) Diagrammatic reconstruction of the myelin sheath wrapped around an axon. (b) Formation of the myelin sheath, a tightly packed coil of the plasma membrane of the Schwann cell. (1) The Schwann cell partially wraps itself around the axon, and in successive stages (2) and (3) the number of coils is increased until a packed spiral of membranes lying between most of the Schwann cell cytoplasm and the axon is formed (4). (c) Electron micrograph showing the myelin sheath, axon, and nucleus of the Schwann cell. (Courtesy of Mary and Richard Bunge.)

The plasma membrane of the neuron is highly specialized for the transmission of electrochemical impulses. Since the functioning of the entire nervous system depends upon the electrical events occurring in the neurons of which it is composed, understanding that function requires comprehension of some basic principles of electricity.

There are two types of electrical charges in the universe—positive and negative. Like charges repel each other, and opposite charges attract each other. When positive and negative charges are separated, an electrical force tends to draw these charges

FIGURE 18–4 The neuron and its associated ions. (a) The resting nerve is polarized, with the inside negative to the outside. (b) Intracellular recording from a neuron. The tip of a microelectrode has to be inserted into a nerve cell. In a neuron that is at rest there is a potential difference of about 70mV; the inside is negative with respect to the outside.

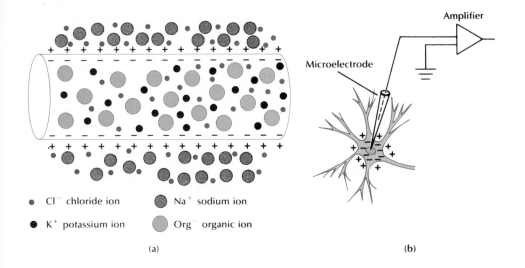

Cl⁻ chloride ion

K⁺ potassium ion

Na⁺ sodium ion

Org⁻ organic ion

(a)

Amplifier

Microelectrode

(b)

together. The force that draws these unlike charges together can be measured, and its strength increases when the charges are moved closer together as well as when there is an increasing quantity of charge. The separated electrical charges of opposite sign have the potential of doing work if they are allowed to come together. This potential of separated electric charges to do work is called an electrical potential, and it is measured in units called volts. The movement of electric charge is called **current.**

These principles of electricity apply directly to the neuron. Consider for the moment that the axon of the neuron is a long, thin tube, the walls of which are the plasma membrane. The key to the electrical activity of the neuron lies in the chemical contents of that tube and of the tissue fluid surrounding it. Organic molecules and salts dissolved in the intracellular and extracellular water dissociate to yield electrically charged particles, **ions.** There are important differences between the ionic composition of the tissue fluid and the neuronal fluid. The tissue fluid bathing the neuron contains a high concentration of sodium chloride so that more than 90% of its charged particles are the positive sodium ions (Na⁺) and the negative

chloride ions (Cl⁻). Inside the cell these ions are very low in concentration (less than 10%); the principal positive ion is potassium (K⁺), and the negative ions are a variety of organic substances (Org⁻) made by the cell itself, such as proteins, amino acids, and citric acid (Figure 18–4a).

At rest, the concentration of sodium is 10 times higher outside the neuron than within, and that of potassium is 30 times higher within the neuron than without. The membrane of the neuron is highly permeable to potassium and chloride ions, and only slightly to sodium ions; hence there is a tendency for the potassium ions (K⁺) to leak out of the cell at a high rate. As a result of this, as well as the inability of the large, negative organic substances to diffuse across the plasma membrane, the inside of the cell tends to become electrically negative. This tends to attract the positive sodium ions from the cell's exterior to reestablish electrical neutrality. The attraction is counteracted by the cell's lack of permeability to sodium as well as its active extrusion of sodium ions against their own concentration gradient by the so-called **sodium-potassium pump** (Figure 18–5). The pump is energy-dependent, but the work expended

amounts to only a small fraction of the energy made available by the cell's own metabolism. The pump moves three sodium ions out of the cell for every two potassium that it brings in, and because of the outward leakage of potassium and the presence of negatively charged organic ions within, the cell maintains a separation of charges; the inside of the neuron is made negative relative to the outside and is thus polarized. The resulting membrane voltage can be measured by inserting into a cell minute electrodes that are connected to a sensitive voltmeter or oscilloscope (Figure 18–4b). Measured in this way, the voltage amounts to about 70 millivolts (mV), or approximately 0.1 V. This is called the **membrane resting potential,** and although it may seem small (it is about ¹⁄₅₀ the voltage of a flashlight battery), in biological terms it is quite substantial.

## 18–3 THE NERVE IMPULSE: AN ELECTROCHEMICAL MESSAGE

The language of the neuron is an electrochemical one. Sometimes it is difficult to comprehend that thoughts, emotions, learning, and the myriad functions that are a property of the human mind are carried by neurons via electrochemical changes known as nerve impulses, but this is indeed the case. How is a nerve impulse produced?

When active neurons (and muscle cells) are stimulated, the membrane resting potential changes; hence, these are often called **excitable cells** and the cause of the change is called the **stimulus.** The membrane potential of a stimulated neuron drops from a negative value toward zero; that is, the membrane becomes **depolarized.** This is followed by a temporary reversal of polarity so that the outside of the membrane is negative relative to the inside, and then almost as quickly as this occurs the membrane is restored to its original condition (**repolarization**) (Figure 18–6). The rapid depolarization-repolarization of the membrane is called the **action potential** and in-

FIGURE 18–5 Diagram of the membrane of a resting nerve cell, and changes with an action potential. (a) Resting state with almost all sodium channels closed. (b) Action potential. Sodium channel opened.

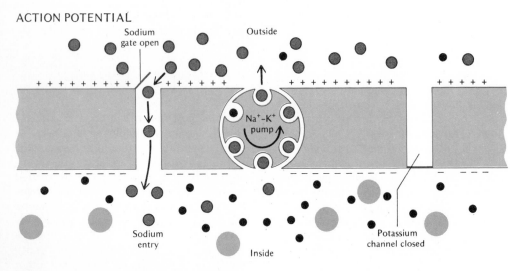

volves a change in the membrane voltage lasting only about 0.001 second. The action potential moves along the length of the neuron, and it is this pulse of electricity that constitutes the neuronal message. How does the membrane become depolarized and then repolarized, and how can a wave of depolarization (the action potential) be propagated along the length of the nerve

without any decrease in strength so that a message gets from one point to another without distortion?

The resting potential of the membrane of the neuron is about $-70$ mV (the voltage is measured relative to the outside, and since the inside of the cell is more negative than is the outside, the voltage is written as a minus value). When the membrane is

excited at some point by an appropriate stimulus (such as pressure, electricity, or a chemical agent), the region so affected becomes much more permeable to sodium ions (Na$^+$) than to potassium ions (K$^+$), and the sodium ions rush into the cell via specific gated channels faster than potassium ions can leave (Figure 18–6b). As a result of this, the voltage drops toward zero and then there is a slight overshoot so that the inside of the membrane becomes positively charged in this particular region (Figure 18–6c). The resultant action potential spreads to adjacent areas and is self-reinforcing. How does this occur? The flow of sodium ions through the membrane makes it easier for others to follow, and as the voltage changes, there is a change in membrane permeability immediately adjacent to the region of excitation; this localized current causes the sodium channels to open favoring sodium flow in this region as well. This process continues, producing an electrical current that flows in wavelike fashion from the original region of stimulation along the entire length of the membrane. The moving action potential is the nerve impulse.

Immediately after the peak of the action potential, the process of membrane repolarization begins. The membrane once again becomes impermeable to sodium ions (the sodium gates that were opened are now closed), and the potassium ions, which are more numerous in the cell, are moved outward (the potassium gates are opened wider than during the resting condition). This once again creates a negative charge on the inside of the membrane (repolarization). Repolarization begins at the point of excitation, spreading out as a wave immediately behind the region of depolarization and following a few ten-thousandths of a second after depolarization has occurred. The entire process of depolarization and repolarization takes only a millisecond or two.

For a few milliseconds after a particular region has been depolarized, a second action potential cannot be produced, for the

FIGURE 18–6 The nerve impulse. (a) At rest the voltage is −70mV and the membrane is polarized; the concentration of potassium and organic ions is higher inside, and sodium is abundant outside. (b) At the start of depolarization, sodium ions enter the axon and the voltage drops to zero. An action potential has begun. (c) As the action potential develops, the membrane is depolarized; as a consequence of the rapid influx of sodium ions, the interior becomes slightly positive. (d) With outward movement of potassium ions and prevention of sodium entry, the membrane becomes repolarized.

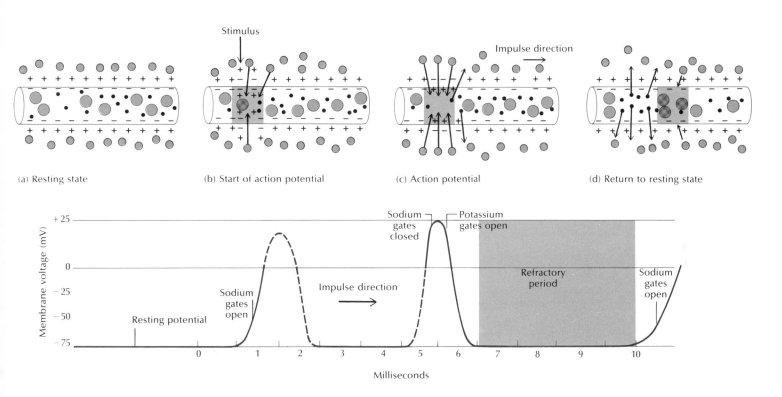

(a) Resting state     (b) Start of action potential     (c) Action potential     (d) Return to resting state

membrane must be repolarized, and the membrane is said to be in an inexcitable, or **refractory, state** (Figure 18–6d). No matter how strong the stimulus, a depolarized nerve will not conduct an impulse. Because of the refractory period, the action potential is unable to reexcite that region of the membrane that it has just passed, and so travels away from its point of origin.

The movement of the action potential along the length of the neuron is often compared to a burning fuse of gunpowder. Once ignited, the heat of the gunpowder burning in one section causes the next section to ignite, and so it burns in a self-propagating manner. Although this analogy has merit, it also has limitations. The gunpowder fuse works but a single time and carries only one impulse, whereas the neuron can carry impulse after impulse over the same pathway. Furthermore, heat tra-

verses the length of a gunpowder fuse, but an electrochemical event produces self-propagating change along a neuron.

In order for the membrane of the neuron to become repolarized to its resting potential, sodium ions that moved inside and potassium ions that leaked outside must be returned to their original positions. The restoration is accomplished by the sodium–potassium pump (Figure 18–5), an activity that requires energy (ATP is used). However, even when the pump is not operating (as when it is turned off by a metabolic poison such as cyanide; Chapter 4), thousands of action potentials can still be generated in a neuron before it quits functioning altogether. The reason for this is that only a minute amount of sodium passes into the neuron with each impulse, and it takes a considerable amount of sodium in the cell to prevent depolarization completely.

## 18–4 THE NERVE IMPULSE: PRODUCTION AND CONDUCTION

A nerve impulse can be triggered by a variety of stimuli: chemicals, electricity, and mechanical forces. What determines whether a stimulus will produce a nerve impulse (action potentials) in a neuron?

If a neuron were set up in the laboratory so that the axon could be electrically stimulated under controlled conditions (Figure 18–7a), we would find that, depending on the particular axon, there would be a minimum voltage necessary to produce an action potential. This minimal strength is called a **threshold stimulus,** and stimuli weaker than this (subthreshold) would normally produce no action potential (Figure 18–7b). Stimuli greater than threshold (suprathreshold) would elicit an action potential, but this action potential would be no different from

(a)

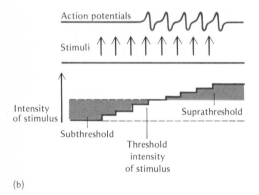

(b)

one produced by a threshold stimulus. One of the most important characteristics of the excitation process in a neuron is that it either leads to an action potential or it does not. If an action potential is produced, its magnitude, character, and duration are independent of the strength or the nature of the stimulus. This relationship is called the **all-or-none law,** and it applies to a single neuron. It means that once the threshold level of stimulation is reached, the response initiated in the neuron does not depend on the kind of initiator or on its strength. It is like setting a mousetrap or cocking the

### BOX 18B  Bugging the brain: EEG

There are about 100 billion nerve cells in the body, and most of these are always in some state of activity. Even when we are asleep, electrical activity occurs in the network of nerves. These electrical events can be measured with instruments that monitor fluctuations in voltage. We can "eavesdrop" on these electrical activities by placing a number of electrodes on the various regions of the scalp and recording neuronal signals. To be sure, the signals are weak and not all neurons are active, but a single electrode taped to the scalp can record as little as 0.00001 V. Electrical activity arising in the brain was first reported in 1875 by Richard Caton, an English physician, but it was not until the 1920s that Hans Berger, a German neurologist, devised a system for recording electrical activity on a moving sheet of paper on a polygraph or a physiograph apparatus (Figure 18–8). Berger found that there were rhythmic cycles in the brain, and since

FIGURE 18–8 Recording an electroencephalogram.

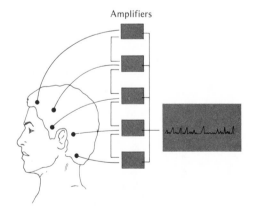

they appeared as waves on the paper, he called them **brain waves.** The record of such brain waves, that is, the pattern of electrical activity of the brain, is called an electroencephalogram (*encephalos*—brain; Gk.) or **EEG.** By placing electrodes on various sites on the scalp, we can "bug" different groups of neurons, and although the patterns are extremely complex it is possible to correlate brain waves with various behavioral states.

When we are awake, but at rest with our eyes closed, the EEG shows a regular pattern of activity, **alpha waves** (Figure 18–9a), and this changes markedly when the eyes are opened (Figure 18–9b). When we open our eyes or when there is muscular activity, different waves, **beta waves,** replace the alpha waves. When we are asleep the electrical activity shows a slow, rolling pattern (Figure 18–9c), and when the sleep becomes deeper the waves become greater in amplitude (Figure 18–9d). If the brain is damaged by hemorrhage, tumor, infection, epilepsy (Figure 18–9e), or injury the EEG can sometimes monitor the brain waves and record the location and extent of damage. (Emotional disorders are usually not detected by the EEG.)

**Epilepsy** is a disorder in the brain's electrical activity. About 1 person out of 200 in the United States suffers from some form of epilepsy. Some famous epileptics were Julius Caesar, Peter the Great, Mohammed, and Dostoevski. It is believed that epileptic seizures are a result of spontaneous, uncontrolled reverberating cycles of electrical activity in the brain's neurons. One portion stimulates another, this activates another, and this in turn stimulates the first, so that a cycle of activity begins and runs its course until the neurons fatigue. While such reverberations are taking place, the individual may have hallucinations and a seizure; the confused circuitry causes a loss of consciousness, and neuronal fatigue promotes sleep. The grand mal, or severe seizure, is uncommon, but milder attacks (petit mal) may occur frequently: the afflicted person "sees" flashes of light, and there may be sensations of sound and odor and a blackout of consciousness. The majority of epileptics lead near-normal lives owing to treatment with the drug Dilatin (diphenylhydantoin), which suppresses seizures.

**Cats and Pets**

In the realm of neurons, CATS and PETS are not animals; instead, these are acronyms that stand for the latest series of machines being used to "bug" the brain and diagnose disorders of the nervous system. PET stands for positron emission tomography, and it is a cousin of the CAT scanner, which couples x-ray techniques with computer technology to give a series of cross-sectional views of the internal structures of the body—soft tissues as well as bones. The CAT scanner reveals the form and shape of the internal structures of the body, and provides the physician with valuable information about organ structure but reveals almost nothing about its function. The PET scanner, on the other hand, tells something about the metabolic activity of the body's tissues and organs. In the PET scanning method, an individual inhales or is injected with a radioactively tagged substance, a substance that emits positively charged particles (positrons) as it decays. These positrons when they combine with the negatively charged electrons normally present in the body's cells give off gamma rays that can be detected by a scanning gamma-ray detector, the PET scanner. Collected and translated into color-coded images, the resulting patterns indicate the intensity of metabolic activity. PET scanning is a noninvasive method for studying the workings of the internal organs of the body, and it is now being used to explore the brain activities of individuals suffering from schizophrenia, manic–depression, dementia, multiple sclerosis, and Huntington's disease with the hope that a metabolic basis for these disorders can be detected. Because the radioactive substances used in PET scanning are so short-lived, anyone undergoing this technique is exposed to very little radiation.

**FIGURE 18–9** Typical EEG recordings from the scalp. **(a)** Normal rhythms characteristic of the relaxed state with eyes closed are called alpha waves. **(b)** Beta waves appear during wakefulness, at rest with eyes open. **(c)** Brain waves recorded during rapid-eye-movement (REM) sleep. When subjects are awakened during REM sleep 80–90% of the individuals reported that they were dreaming. **(d)** Brain waves during moderate deep sleep. **(e)** Petit mal epileptic seizure.

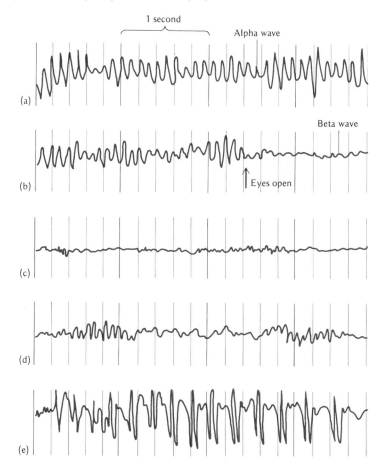

trigger of a gun. Once triggered to activity, the force generated is built in and cannot be increased by stronger stimulation.

Now there develops an important question: if neurons exhibit an all-or-none property with regard to stimulus intensity, how do we detect differing intensities of stimulation—for example, the difference between a sheet of paper and a rock held in the hand or between a light tap and a hard slap on the back? The intensity of stimuli can be determined because different neurons have different thresholds, and a more intense stimulation involves greater numbers of neurons, each of which exhibits the all-or-none phenomenon. Furthermore, although the speed of travel of the action potential along the length of the axon is constant, a more intense stimulus will produce a greater number of action potentials moving down the axon per unit time (greater frequency). We can visualize the situation as follows: the code of the neuron can be thought of as a dot that moves across the page at a fixed rate; if the stimulus intensity is low, the dots are less frequent and few neurons send out dots:

Neuron 1 •      •      •      •
Neuron 2 •  •  •  •  •  •

However, if the stimulus is of high intensity, the dot frequency is high, and many neurons send out signals:

Neuron 1 •  •  •  •  •  •  •
Neuron 2 •  •  •  •  •  •  •
Neuron 3 •  •  •  •  •  •
Neuron 4 •  •  •  •  •
Neuron 5 •  •  •  •  •  •
Neuron 6 •  •  •  •  •  •

Thus, to make up for limitations in the coding system, the nervous system employs a large number of channels (or neurons), each capable of transmitting signals of variable frequency. From the eye alone a million channels run to the brain!

The velocity of transmission varies with the diameter of the axon and whether it is myelinated or not. The myelinated regions along the length of the axon are not continuous, and about every millimeter there is a constriction devoid of myelin (the **node**). Action potentials do not occur along sections of the membrane protected by myelin, but can occur where the myelin is interrupted, that is, at the nodes, and impulses in this type of nerve skip along from node to node, producing a jumping (saltatory) conduction of impulses via relay stations. This is a valuable mechanism for transmission of nerve impulses, since it diminishes cross talk between neurons, increases conduction velocity, and minimizes sodium leakage. As a result there is a considerable saving of metabolic energy, and nerve transmission is highly efficient. Next time you pull your hand away from a hot stove, remember that such a reaction is possible because a nerve impulse travels at a rate of about 300 ft—the length of a football field—in 1 second!

## 18–5 SIGNALS FROM NEURON TO NEURON: THE SYNAPSE

If the neuron is to function as a signal transmitter and as a part of a communications network, it must be able to send the signal it receives to another neuron or to an effector organ, such as a muscle or gland. The junction between one neuron and the next or between neuron and effector is called a **synapse,** and the intervening space is called the **synaptic cleft.** The synapse has the capacity to transmit some signals and not others, and thus it acts as a gate for neuronal transmission. A neuron stimulated artificially in the middle of its axon can conduct impulses spreading out in both directions, but normally it transmits its impulses in only one direction. Dendrites usually receive signals and pass them on to the cell body, and the axon carries them from there and transmits them to the next cell. This unidirectional function is imposed

upon the neurons by the nature of the synapse.

### Synaptic transmission

The dendrites and/or cell body of a typical neuron receive hundreds of small fibers from the ends of the axons of adjacent neurons. These axonal fiber ends terminate in small bulblike swellings called **presynaptic knobs** (Figure 18–10). The electron microscope has shown that a presynaptic knob has many small sacs, or vesicles, containing molecules of a transmitter substance (Figure 18–11a). When an impulse moves along the axon and reaches the presynaptic knob, it causes a temporary change in the knob's permeability to calcium ions, and the vesicles discharge their transmitter substance. The transmitter molecules released into the synaptic cleft (about 200 Å in distance) diffuse across it and alter the membrane potential of the adjacent (postsynaptic) neuron (Figure 18–11b). The electrical change in the postsynaptic cell membrane induced by the transmitter substance is very brief, but if depolarization occurs, an action potential is triggered in the postsynaptic cell.

Let us consider, for example, the case of a particular transmitter chemical, acetylcholine (ACh). When an action potential arrives at the synaptic terminal, transmitter molecules of ACh are released into the synaptic cleft. The ACh diffuses across the space and attaches to receptor sites on the postsynaptic membrane (Figure 18–11b). The receptor site functions in two capacities: (1) it inactivates ACh because it has enzymatic properties (acetylcholinesterase, which degrades ACh) and (2) it activates the postsynaptic membrane. During activation, there is a rapid influx of sodium ions (the sodium gates are opened), and as a result of the net movement of these positively charged ions into the postsynaptic cell, there is a slight depolarization. When this depolarization, called the **excitatory postsynaptic potential (EPSP),** reaches a threshold level, it initiates an action potential in the postsyn-

FIGURE 18–10 (a) Scanning electron micrograph of the synaptic knobs lying on the cell body of an adjacent neuron. (b) Detail of the synaptic knobs as shown by the scanning electron microscope. (From E. R. Lewis, T. E. Everhart, and Y. Y. Zeevi, *Science*, September 1969. Copyright 1969 by the American Association for the Advancement of Science.)

(a)

(b)

aptic cell (Figure 18–12). The EPSP is a local, passively propagated current, and its only function is to help trigger the action potential; it is not all-or-none, but can vary in amplitude. The fact that the EPSP is graded is of critical importance, for it means that a neuron bombarded by signals across many synapses is capable of integrating this information; when the level of chemical transmitter reaches threshold, a distinct action potential is triggered.

The ACh released from the presynaptic knobs does not persist for long, since it is quickly destroyed by acetylcholinesterase. Indeed, such destruction is of considerable functional significance, for if ACh were not rapidly degraded, the stimulatory action would continue indefinitely. Many of the organophosphate insecticides (malathion and parathion) as well as some of the nerve gases are inhibitors of cholinesterase and block the destruction of ACh; as a result the affected animal's nervous system is overstimulated, uncontrolled tremor and spasms result, and death ultimately ensues.

**Catecholamines** (derived from the amino acid tyrosine) include the neurotransmitter substances L-dopa, dopamine, epinephrine, and norepinephrine. These transmitters, like acetylcholine, are released from presynaptic neurons; however, when catecholamines interact with the membrane of the postsynaptic cell, they do not directly open up ion channels. Instead, they first activate the membrane enzyme adenyl cyclase. This enzyme catalyzes the conversion of ATP into cyclic AMP, and it is the latter that activates enzymes within the cell to open the ion gates leading to membrane depolarization of the postsynaptic neuron. Thus, catecholamines control ion channels indirectly by means of a secondary messenger.

The brain and other neuronal centers do not contain solely excitatory synapses; if they did, neural activity would cause a buildup of excitation, and action potentials would continually be generated, such as occurs during an epileptic seizure (Box 18B).

In addition, there are times when inhibition is required for normal action; for example, when you withdraw your hand from a hot stove some of the muscles must be inhibited while others are excited. Obviously there must be some kind of inhibitory transmitter substance to inhibit neurons, the opposite number of excitatory substances. The simplest way of inhibiting synaptic transmission would be to increase the negativity of the resting potential, thus making depolarization more difficult. In a sense, this lessens the likelihood that threshold will be reached. How can such an effect be produced? One of the known inhibitory transmitters is the amino acid gamma aminobutyric acid (**GABA**). It is believed that this material increases the permeability of the postsynaptic membrane mainly to chloride ions but not to sodium ions. Thus, chloride leaks into the cell at an accelerated rate, the membrane potential is shifted from $-70$ mV to $-75$ mV or $-80$ mV, and an EPSP of 10 mV, which previously would have caused depolarization, now shifts the potential to $-65$ mV or $-70$ mV, a value that is below threshold. Thus, inhibition is attained by a brief increase in negativity of the membrane potential. The shift (from $-70$ mV to $-80$ mV) is called the **inhibitory postsynaptic potential** (IPSP). The IPSP can grow in graded fashion, as can the EPSP, but with opposite effects on nerve excitation.

Transmission across a synapse depends on diffusion, a relatively slow process; as a consequence, crossing the synaptic cleft is slower than transmission along the length of the neuron. In addition, since synaptic transmission involves release of molecules, which must be resynthesized after depletion, fatigue occurs more quickly at the synapse than in the neuron itself when repetitive stimuli of similar intensity are delivered. At first, neurons may discharge rapidly, but then, owing to synaptic fatigue, there is a decreased response; such a mechanism permits nervous reactions to fade away with time.

The human nervous system is a blend of

FIGURE 18–11 Structure of the synapse. (a) Diagram of synaptic knobs and synaptic cleft. Transmission electron micrograph of the synapses at low magnification (b) and higher magnification (c). (d) Schematic representation of the release of transmitter substance from the synaptic vesicles into the synaptic cleft. After discharge, the vesicle must be recharged with transmitter substance.

FIGURE 18–12 Initiation of an action potential (nerve impulse) by transmitter substance. Transmitter substance reaches the postsynaptic neuron, reducing its potential and creating an EPSP (excitatory postsynaptic potential). If the EPSP reaches a threshold level, an action potential is triggered.

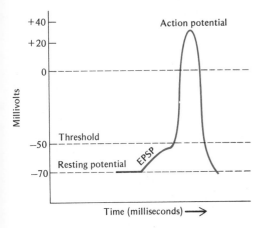

excitation (EPSP) and inhibition (IPSP) between neurons. Every neuron is covered with literally thousands of synaptic knobs (Figure 18–10a) and is subject to a number of excitatory and inhibitory influences. The dynamic balance between these opposing influences produces the events that occur in the nervous system and that we see recorded in EEG wave patterns.

### Summation and facilitation

Stimulation of a single presynaptic knob may not cause a postsynaptic neuron to generate an action potential. Oftentimes, for an excitatory postsynaptic cell to generate an impulse, many synaptic knobs must release their transmitter substances simultaneously. As each knob is recruited toward vesicle discharge, the potential generated on the postsynaptic neuron comes closer and closer to threshold. This progressive recruitment of synaptic knobs is called **summation.** Summation can occur in two ways: time (temporal) and space (spatial). In temporal summation the same presynaptic knob fires several times in rapid succession, so that the transmitter substance is added in amount. For this to be effective, successive firings must occur within less than 0.01 second of each other or else the transmitter

substance is destroyed. (Recall that acetylcholinesterase is present on the ACh receptor.) In spatial summation, two or more synaptic knobs fire simultaneously and their individual effects are additive.

Let us imagine that a number of synaptic knobs secrete their chemical substances into the synaptic cleft, but this is insufficient to produce a potential big enough to generate an action potential; in other words, it is subthreshold. This subthreshold discharge of synaptic knobs may not be completely without effect because it can produce a condition known as **facilitation.** That is, even though no action potential is generated in the postsynaptic neuron, the neuron is primed for excitation and can subsequently be triggered to activity by a subthreshold stimulus. For example, let us say that it takes the discharge of 50 presynaptic knobs to generate an action potential in an adjacent neuron. If only 40 discharge simultaneously, the postsynaptic neuron does not generate an action potential; however, the presence of the chemical transmitter substance in the synaptic cleft facilitates transmission, so that when 10 or more synaptic knobs fire shortly thereafter, an action potential is generated and a nerve impulse begins.

### 18–6 INTEGRATED CIRCUITS OF NEURONS: THE NERVOUS SYSTEM

#### Basic design

Pry open the back of a television set or a radio and you will see a maze of wires and printed circuits. Look inside a computer or a telephone switchboard and you will find a tangle of interconnecting wires and other electronic gadgetry. The wires and circuits of these communication devices are the fundamental units of operation, but the sequence and arrangement of the components determine how the machine operates. The fundamental unit of structure in the nervous system is the neuron, and similarly the way neurons are hooked together de-

termines the manner in which the nervous system functions (Figure 18–13).

There are three different functional classes of neurons: **sensory neurons,** which receive stimuli from the environment and transmit information to the central nervous system (brain and spinal cord); **motor neurons,** which conduct messages from the brain and spinal cord to the glands and muscles; and **interneurons,** which act in an integrative capacity and shuttle signals back and forth between the neurons of various parts of the brain and spinal cord. Over 99% of the neurons of the body and brain are interneurons.

In a simplified way Figure 18–13 illustrates a schematic wiring diagram of the nervous system. Note that an impulse entering the spinal cord via a sensory neuron has many possible pathways. Rarely does the signal that traverses a sensory neuron directly activate a motor neuron leading to an effector (for example, muscle); typically the signal travels upward via the spinal cord interneurons and through a number of relay centers in the brain before reaching the higher centers. From there the command signals travel down the spinal cord, again via relay centers, and via a motor neuron the effector is triggered to activity. Note that the more neuronal cells in the circuitry, the more flexible can be the response.

The nervous system's circuitry is composed of two basic subdivisions: the central nervous system **(CNS),** comprising the structures encased within the skull and the vertebral column, and the peripheral nervous system **(PNS),** which lies outside the skull and vertebral column but connects up with the CNS via spinal and cranial nerves.

#### The central nervous system

The central nervous system consists of the brain and spinal cord (Figure 18–14). It serves as a clearing-house for all nerve impulses, controlling, directing, and integrating all messages within the body. The brain and spinal cord embrace a series of hollow spaces (ventricles in the brain and

FIGURE 18–13 Simplified circuitry of the nervous system. Neurons are arranged into cables consisting of many axons and dendrites. Axons, bundled together to form a multistranded cable, form the nerve fiber or nerves we commonly see in a dissected specimen. The collection of axons and dendrites in the brain and spinal cord—the information centers—are called tracts.

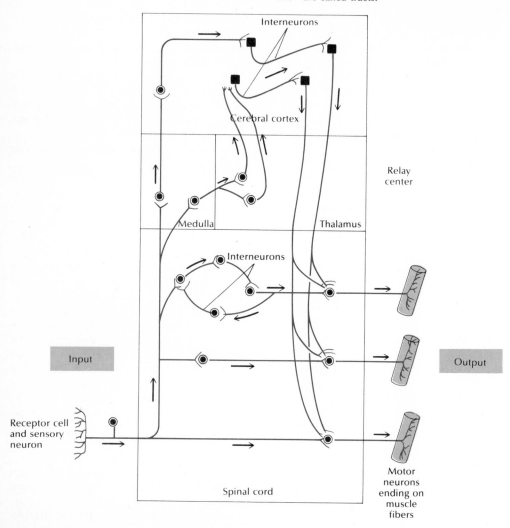

The brain is commonly divided into three main geographical areas: the **forebrain,** the **midbrain,** and the **hindbrain.** The forebrain consists of the **cerebrum,** divided into two lobes, or **cerebral hemispheres,** together with internal structures such as the **thalamus** and **hypothalamus** (Figure 18–14e) and the **limbic system** (Figure 18–14c). The surface layer of the cerebrum is deeply infolded into creases and furrows and constitutes the **cerebral cortex.** The midbrain is an intermediate zone connecting the forebrain to the hindbrain. The hindbrain consists of the **medulla (brain stem), pons,** and **cerebellum.** The brain gives rise to 12 pairs of cranial nerves, running to various regions of the body (Figure 18–14d). Some are sensory, some are motor, and some contain both motor and sensory neurons. Table 18–1 describes the structure and function of the various regions of the brain.

**The spinal cord.** The brain communicates with the spinal cord through an opening in the base of the skull and is continuous with the spinal cord (Figure 18–14a). The spinal cord is nearly 18 in. long and about as wide as your thumb. It is a hollow tube encased in an elongated, bony tunnel formed by the rings of the vertebrae (the backbone) and consists of millions of neurons arranged for the most part in cablelike fashion. Like the brain, the spinal cord contains gray and white matter, but the arrangement in the cord has the gray matter on the inside and the white matter on the outside (Figure 18–14b). The spinal cord controls many of the involuntary actions (**reflexes**) of the body. From the spinal cord arise 31 pairs of nerves, which pass out through openings between the vertebrae, and these branch and rebranch to innervate the limbs and torso. The spinal nerves and their branches form the PNS, discussed in the next section.

Most sensory neurons have their cell bodies outside the cord (in a spinal ganglion)[1] and enter the cord via the dorsal

central canal in the spinal cord) that are filled with fluid. This fluid, called **cerebrospinal fluid,** also communicates with and fills spaces between three investing membranes, called **meninges,** that cover and protect the brain and spinal cord.

**The brain.** The brain—soft, gray, and furrowed—lies protected from harm within a bony vault, the **cranium** (skull). It is about the size and shape of a head of cauliflower and has been described as a "great raveled

knot," a "modest bowl of pinkish jelly," and "a rather messy substance of the consistency of porridge." The exterior of the brain is gray, and its inner portions are white. The gray matter consists of the cell bodies of neurons; the white matter is made up of axons. The white appearance is due to the fatty myelin sheaths that surround these axons and act as intercommunicating cables (tracts) between various regions of the brain.

---

[1] Ganglia are made up of concentrations of neuronal cell bodies. The singular is ganglion.

FIGURE 18–14 The organization of the central nervous system. (a) Anatomic subdivisions. (b) The spinal cord and the vertebral column. (c) Section through the brain to show the limbic system. (d) The brain viewed from the right side, showing regions of structure and function. (e) Section through the brain, showing the left half.

**TABLE 18–1  The structures of the human brain**

| Structure | Description | Function |
|---|---|---|
| Cerebrum | | |
|   Cortex (outer surface) | Thin (3–6 mm), highly folded sheet with large surface area; most recent evolutionary development; high degree of development | Center of the mind; seat of conscious thought, memory, speech, intelligence, personality, and judgment; center of sensory-motor coordination |
|   White matter (inner cerebrum) | Composed of nerve tracts connecting parts of cortex to each other and to rest of brain and spinal cord | Center of sensation, including sight, hearing, taste, etc. |
| Corpus callosum | Consists of 300 million separate neuronal lines | Connects the halves (hemispheres) of the cortex |
| Thalamus | Groups of cell bodies arranged in shape of a football | Relays sensory information to cortex (vision, hearing, touch, taste); regulates sleep and wakefulness in conjunction with limbic system |
| Limbic system<br>  Hippocampus<br>  Fornix<br>  Cingulate gyrus<br>  Amygdala | Internal region of forebrain, divided into several regions | Involved in emotion, motivation, and reinforcement |
| Hypothalamus | Linked to sympathetic nervous system and pituitary | Controls basic drives (eating, drinking, sleeping, sexual behavior); regulates temperature, blood pressure, heart rate |
| Cerebellum ("little brain") | Baseball-sized lump of gray-white tissue lying on either side of the brain stem | Involved in sensory-motor coordination; if damaged, loss of equilibrium and motor coordination results |
| Brain stem (medulla) | Extension of spinal cord within the skull | Involved in control of respiration, heart rate, and gastrointestinal function |
| Reticular formation | Consists of fibers and cell bodies running from spinal cord to cerebral hemispheres | Involved in control of arousal and alertness |
| Pons | Consists mainly of white matter lying anterior to cerebellum and between midbrain and medulla | Acts as bridge linking the various parts of the brain and as relay station from medulla to higher centers |

(back side) root; all motor neurons have their cell bodies within the cord, and their axons leave the cord via the ventral (front side) root. Shortly after leaving the spinal cord, the dorsal and ventral roots, at the same level of the cord combine to form a pair of spinal nerves one on each side of the cord. Thus, all the spinal nerves are mixed, that is, they contain the axons of both sensory and motor neurons (Figure 18–14b).

If the motor root is damaged, there is muscle paralysis, but sensation is not lost. In poliomyelitis, there is damage to the cell bodies of the motor neurons within the cord itself, and there results a flaccid paralysis of muscles without sensory impairment. If the dorsal root is damaged, there is a loss of sensation in that part of the body which sends neurons to the cord via that root, but muscle paralysis does not occur. Some forms of syphilis cause dorsal-root degeneration, producing uncoordinated movements and muscle weakness. A complete cut across the cord results in spastic paralysis, loss of all sensation, and loss of urinary and rectal sphincter control. However, spinal reflexes still persist in such paraplegics.

### The peripheral nervous system

The CNS is concerned with integrating and coordinating all nervous functions, both voluntary and involuntary. All sensory input arises from the environment (external and internal), and the effector organs (muscles and glands) are the ultimate destination of nerve impulses. Lying between the CNS and the environment and the CNS and the effector organs is a vast network of nerves and ganglia that constitute the peripheral nervous system. Most of the nerves are mixed and so include both sensory and motor components. Hardly any tissue or organ is missed by the complex array of nerves, and thus, through them, the CNS is in continuous contact with nearly every part of the body. We are aware of some of the nervous associations: these are the ones that ultimately connect with conscious centers in the cerebral cortex, and we interpret their activities as either sensations (via sensory nerves) or voluntary actions (via motor nerves). But there are other nerve components whose functions ordinarily lie outside our consciousness or volition. These components connect with our visceral organs (heart, lungs, kidneys, blood vessels, intestines), and we neither are aware of what these organs are doing nor have voluntary control over them. This is because the nervous impulses go mainly to the medulla

FIGURE 18–15 **The peripheral nervous system (PNS) comprises all of the neurons and nerve fibers outside the central nervous system (CNS) and has two subdivisions: (1) the somatic nervous system, with nerves running directly from spinal cord to effector organs, and (2) the autonomic nervous system (ANS),** with nerves leading from spinal cord to effector synapse, first with neurons (ganglia) outside the CNS, and then these send nerve fibers to the effector organs. The ANS, shown below, is composed of two anatomical subdivisions: (1) the sympathetic, where ganglia lie on either side of the spinal cord some distance from the effectors, and (2) the parasympathetic, where the ganglia are in or near the effectors. The sympathetic system mobilizes the body's resources for work or an emergency, whereas the parasympathetic is an energy-conserving system.

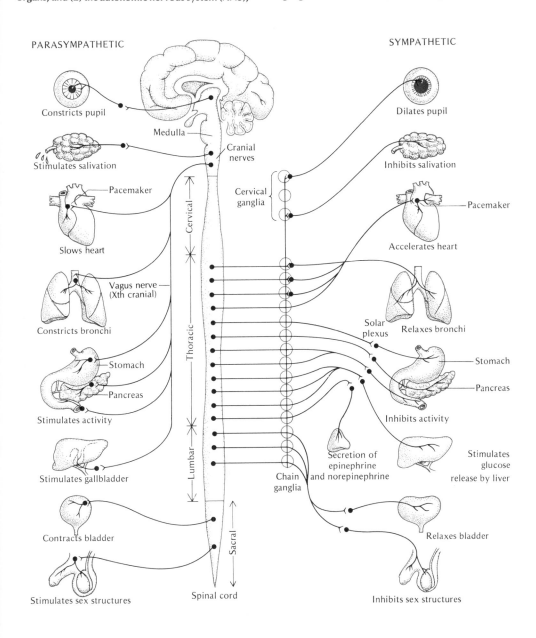

PARASYMPATHETIC

SYMPATHETIC

Constricts pupil

Medulla

Stimulates salivation

Cranial nerves

Pacemaker

Cervical

Slows heart

Vagus nerve (Xth cranial)

Constricts bronchi

Thoracic

Stomach

Pancreas

Stimulates activity

Lumbar

Stimulates gallbladder

Contracts bladder

Sacral

Stimulates sex structures

Spinal cord

Dilates pupil

Inhibits salivation

Cervical ganglia

Pacemaker

Accelerates heart

Solar plexus

Relaxes bronchi

Stomach

Pancreas

Inhibits activity

Secretion of epinephrine and norepinephrine

Stimulates glucose release by liver

Chain ganglia

Relaxes bladder

Inhibits sex structures

parallel to and on each side of the middle region of the spinal cord (Figures 18–14b and 18–15). The sympathetic nerves exit ventrally from the spinal cord and run to sympathetic ganglia near the cord, where they synapse with motor neurons whose cell bodies are located in the ganglia. The axons of the motor neurons arising from the ganglia innervate the heart, lungs, and sweat glands, and the smooth muscles in the digestive tract, excretory system, reproductive system, and blood vessels. Activation of the sympathetic system causes constriction of certain arteries, acceleration of heartbeat, elevation of blood sugar level, inhibition of gastrointestinal contractions and secretions, dilation of pupils, and many other effects. The sympathetic system mobilizes resources of the body for emergency, effects that are sometimes called flight-or-fight responses. Thus, in stressful situations (fear, anger, and the like) the heart beats faster, the stomach muscles relax, the pupils widen, and energy is made available. As you may recall, these same responses are produced by the adrenal hormone epinephrine. The reason for the similarity is related to the nature of the transmitter substance in sympathetic neurons: norepinephrine. In actual fact the adrenal medulla is derived from presumptive nervous tissue during development and can be considered a glandular part of the sympathetic nervous system that hormonally augments that system. Thus, sympathetic neuron and endocrine function are related both chemically and developmentally.

**Parasympathetic nervous system.** The parasympathetic division is an energy-conserving system; it slows the heart rate, enhances digestive action, promotes muscle relaxation, and causes many arteries to dilate, pupils to constrict, and blood sugar levels to drop. Nerves of the parasympathetic system innervate most of the same organs as those of the sympathetic system, but originate mainly in the cranial nerves (principally the Xth cranial nerve, the vagus) and in the posterior (sacral) region of the spinal

and hypothalamus rather than the thalamus and the cerebral cortex. The motor components of these visceral nerves are extremely interesting and important, and they differ in several respects from all other parts of the PNS. They constitute what is known as the **autonomic nervous system** (ANS). There are two divisions within the ANS—the **sympathetic** and the **parasympathetic.**

**Sympathetic nervous system.** The sympathetic division is composed of motor nerves and of ganglia that appear as a pair of chains

FIGURE 18–16 The reflex. (a) Simple reflex arc. (b) Complex reflex arc involving higher centers (brain).

cord (Figure 18–15). The nerves of the parasympathetic system run from their point of origin in the spinal cord directly to their target organs. There they synapse with a motor neuron whose cell body is located in a ganglion close to the organ or even inside it. The parasympathetic neurons have ACh as their transmitter substance, and the nerves are therefore sometimes said to be **cholinergic** (as opposed to sympathetic neurons, which are **noradrenergic**). The sympathetic and parasympathetic systems are usually antagonistic: sympathetic nerves are involved in excitation and emotional stress, whereas parasympathetic nerves are involved in relaxation and maintenance activites. The condition of a particular organ receiving neurons from the autonomic system is determined by the relative amount of stimulation from the parasympathetic and sympathetic nerves. As a consequence, in the heart, many glands, and smooth muscle, which are innervated by both sympathetic and parasympathetic nerves, a dynamic seesaw balance in organ function is attained.

## 18–7 NEURONAL CIRCUITS IN ACTION: REFLEXES

Perhaps the most familiar of all the neuronal circuits is that involved in the knee-jerk reflex. This is an involuntary stretch reflex—a motor response following sensory stimulation controlled primarily by the spinal cord and not by the conscious thinking portion (higher centers) of the brain.

If you sit on the edge of a table and your knee tendon is gently tapped, your leg jerks forward in an involuntary kick. The tapping stretches the extensor muscle, and a sensory neuron relays the electrical signal to the spinal cord. There the signal is transmitted via an interneuron to a motor neuron, which transmits the signal from the cord to a muscle. This causes the extensor muscle to contract, and the lower leg raises upward. This is one of the simplest of responses; it involves a neuronal arc (called a **reflex arc**) (Figure 18–16a).

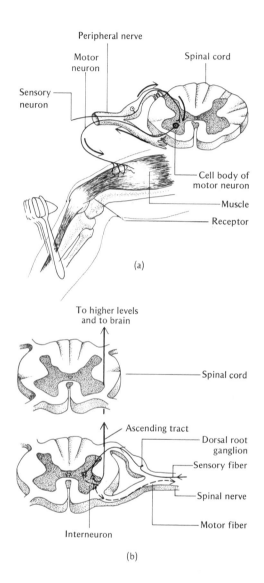

(a)

(b)

Now let us consider a more complicated situation: pricking one's finger. You are about to pick a rose when your finger hits a thorn. Sensory endings (receptors) are stimulated, an impulse travels to the spinal cord, the motor nerves are triggered to action, and almost instantaneously the entire hand is withdrawn. The stimulus that sent action potentials along sensory neurons not only set off a series of impulses in

the motor neurons but also triggered some interneurons within the spinal cord to fire. These signals were transmitted via ascending nerve tracts to the higher centers of the brain (Figure 18–16b). In the brain, the speech center neurons were activated and you exclaimed, "Ouch!" At the same time the cerebral cortex became aware of pain, and there was initiated a complex series of thoughts: "What happened? Is it bleeding? Let's look at it. You are a fool not to be more careful!" Then there was initiated a series of motor responses carried by a descending nerve tract from the brain to the effectors: "Move the hand in front of the eyes and check on the damage." Again a volley of sensory inputs to the brain: "Looks all right, forget about it." Finally, there was the storage of the event (memory): "Next time you pick a rose be careful to avoid the thorns." During this simple occurrence, thousands of neurons were brought into play: sensation, reflex action, motor response, awareness, speech, observation, evaluation, and storage of information in a memory bank all occurred. With remarkable speed, information was received, sorted, and acted upon.

The reflex involved in withdrawal from injury is quite simple; yet it is purposeful and coordinated. The movement of the body is away from the stimulus, and thus further damage to the body is prevented. Thus, the reflex response has purpose, even without the conscious sensation of pain, and most often the sensation of pain occurs after the response has been elicited. Indeed, this withdrawal reflex can be performed even after the spinal cord has been severed from connection with the brain!

Biologists-psychologists say that reflexes are the instantaneous, automatic responses to sensory stimuli and that the more complex patterns of the nervous system are not reflexes but activities of the higher centers. These higher centers process information and produce an integrated response; they also store information and play an important role in memory so that appropriate actions will be taken when a similar situation arises. (See Chapter 20.)

## 18-8 DRUGS AND THE NERVOUS SYSTEM

A chemical agent other than a nutrient that can effect a functional and/or structural change in living tissues is a **drug.** Illegal neurological drugs are called **dope.** Drugs used as a shortcut to happiness, for kicks, are often the same substances employed in medicine for treating disease and alleviating pain; the behavioral difference induced by a drug is often related to the frequency of use, the amount used, and psychic dependence.

How and at what sites do drugs affect the nervous system? While some drugs exert their influence on behavior by affecting the physiology of the nerves themselves, one of the most likely sites of action is at the neural gateway, the synapse. A gate is a control point; locked, it keeps a pathway from being traversed; open, it permits free access. Since the synapse is the neural gate, modifications in neural transmission depend on the status of the gatekeeper, the transmitter substances. Increasing or decreasing the amount of transmitted chemicals, or substitution of molecules with similar action, will profoundly alter the nervous system's activity. Selective action of drugs at the synapse can variously alter thinking, learning, memory, and complex patterns of behavior.

So far, scientists have found more than 100 peptides and amines that act on neurons. Each of these molecules has a unique chemical configuration, such that it fits only into specific receptor sites on the neuron. If a drug has a molecular configuration similar to that of the natural neurotransmitter, it may be able to bind to the membrane receptor and mimic the action of the neurotransmitter. Drugs of this type are called **receptor agonists.** One example of this is the drug L-dopa. Parkinson's disease, or shaking palsy, results from the degeneration of a group of neurons which secrete the

neurotransmitter dopamine (See Box 18C). This causes the receptors of the neurons in the base of the brain, which ordinarily are the receivers of the neurotransmitter, to have less dopamine available. As a result, the neurons function abnormally and cause tremor, rigidity, and delay in movement. Although the brain of a person with Parkinson's disease has been depleted of dopamine, the neurons of the base of the brain still have undamaged receptors; consequently the administration of L-dopa makes up for the dopamine deficiency and the disease symptoms are reduced.

If a drug has a similar, but not identical, configuration to that of the natural neurotransmitter, it may bind to a receptor without activating it. Indeed, in this instance the drug will act as a block to neuron activation, and such drugs are called **receptor antagonists.** A drug such as chlorpromazine is an antagonist of the dopamine receptor, and thus acts as a tranquilizer. **Endorphins** (literally "the morphine within") or **enkephalins** (head; Gk.) are brain peptides whose effects are similar to those of opiates, such as morphine. These endogenous opiates probably act as neurotransmitters in the brain and spinal cord, suppress pain under some conditions, and may

---

**BOX 18C  An environmental cause of Parkinson's disease?**

When the heroin addict arrived at the Medical Center, he had the classical symptoms of a person suffering from Parkinson's disease: drooling, immobilized muscles, and tremors in the extremities. Yet, because the victim was quite young, the examining physician doubted that he had parkinsonism, a disease that characteristically occurs in individuals 50 years or older. Further investigation showed that the addict developed the symptoms of parkinsonism after he tried a new synthetic heroin. That drug contained a toxic contaminant known as MPTP. MPTP on its own was not the cause of the addict's symptoms; however, once the chemical had entered the body it was rapidly converted to another compound called MPP. MPP acts like a guided missile, homing in and attacking the substantia nigra, the part of the brain that is affected in all Parkinson's victims. MPTP-induced parkinsonism has now been confirmed in other studies with heroin addicts in various parts of the United States, and this has led some scientists to speculate that Parkinson's disease may be due to exposure to toxic substances similar to MPTP. Even with this tantalizing evidence of an environmental cause of a brain disorder, there are still unanswered questions. Why is the substantia nigra the target? What is the cause of naturally occurring parkinsonism? Why is the progress of Parkinson's disease usually so slow, and symptoms do not develop until later in life? Is it possible to prevent the disease by reducing exposure to some toxic materials in the environment? Can function be restored to damaged cells in the substantia? In time many of these questions will surely be answered, but for the present the toxin hypothesis of parkinsonism provides a basis for better understanding a disease that in the United States alone afflicts 50,000 people each year.

**TABLE 18–2 Drugs that affect behavior through neurotransmitter substances**

| Neurotransmitter | Receptor type | Receptor agonist | Receptor antagonist | Drugs that alter level of neurotransmitter | |
|---|---|---|---|---|---|
| | | | | Increase | Decrease |
| Dopamine | Dopamine | Apomorphine | Thorazine | L-dopa, dexedrine, Ritalin | α-Methylparatynsine |
| Norepinephrine | Adrenergic | Epinephrine | Propanolol | Cocaine, Elavil, Tofranil (tricyclic antidepressants) | Reserpine, α-methyldopa |
| Serotonin | Serotonin | 5-Methoxy-NN-dimethyl-tryptamine | LSD | Tricyclic antidepressants (Elavil, Anafranil) | Parachlorophenylalanine |
| Acetylcholine | Cholinergic | Pilocarpine, muscarine | Atropine, belladonna, curare, anectine | Parathion, malathion, nerve gas | Botulinus toxin |
| Enkephalin | — | Morphine, heroin, methadone | Naloxone | — | — |

also affect behavior. It is believed that elaboration of such chemicals may explain why some wounded individuals do not complain of pain and why placebos are effective pain killers. Table 18–2 summarizes the drugs that act to alter neurotransmitter levels and those that block or activate the receptors for neurotransmitters.

Stimulants, tranquilizers, and four other commonly known drugs are discussed here in some detail. Table 18–3 summarizes available information on a number of classes of drugs that affect behavior.

**Stimulants.** A stimulant is a chemical substance that "peps" us up, enhances the amount and duration of excitatory synaptic transmitters, and in effect permits more impulses to be transmitted across the synapse. As a consequence the neurons in the nerve network are overactive and most stimuli (even those which are normally subthreshold) trigger the events of excitation. Stimulants such as caffeine, nicotine, amphetamines or "uppers" (dexedrine, benzedrine and methedrine), and strychnine facilitate synaptic transmission. Strychnine in high doses is lethal because neurons tend to discharge spontaneously even in the absence of stimuli. As a result muscles contract spasmodically, ultimately causing

death by spastic paralysis of the respiratory muscles. Nicotine acts by mimicking ACh. Amphetamines probably act by inducing excessive release of excitatory transmitter substances, such as norepinephrine and serotonin, in the brain, particularly the reticular system. They may also block uptake from the synapse so that the transmitter molecules persist, or increase their synthesis, or increase the sensitivity of receptors. Thus, amphetamines lessen depression and fatigue while increasing alertness, motor activity, and verbal activity. However, these elevations of mood are soon followed by severe depression. Often judgment is impaired so that the heart is overtaxed: when exhaustion sets in it is not felt because of the stimulant cover. Taken orally or intravenously, the results are dangerous. Tolerance and psychic dependence (addiction) develop quickly, within weeks. Continued usage ultimately leads to the development of physical and mental problems, and sometimes death ensues. Caffeine is a popular and widely consumed powerful stimulant. It increases activity, suppresses drowsiness and fatigue, and has few side effects. The earliest behavioral effects are increased mental alertness, wakefulness, and restlessness. Most of these actions are due to

an augmentation of cellular metabolism. One cup of coffee (200 mg of caffeine) stimulates the central nervous system sufficiently. Heavy consumption (12 or more cups of coffee a day) may result in agitation, anxiety, rapid breathing, and cardiac arrhythmia. Physiological dependence does occur with ingestion of large doses, and withdrawal symptoms may occur if there is abrupt cessation of drinking a daily amount of five or more cups of coffee.

**Tranquilizers and sedatives.** The effects of tranquilizers are the opposite of those of stimulants. They antagonize synaptic transmitter substances and turn off neural transmission, especially in the higher centers of the brain, and numb one's awareness of the external and internal world—the nerve network "sleeps." The emotions of rage and aggression are centered in the hypothalamus and limbic regions of the brain. The entire brainstem contains a core of tissue composed of small highly branched neurons called the reticular formation. The reticular formation receives and integrates information from many incoming pathways as well as other regions of the brain. The ascending components affect wakefulness and attention to specific events, hence the reticular formation is called the brain's "stay awake" center. Norepinephrine, dopamine, and serotonin are important neuronal transmitters in these regions of the brain. The tranquilizer reserpine acts by blocking the uptake of norepinephrine into synaptic knobs, and its depressant chemical cousin chlorpromazine blocks the receptors of dopamine.

These potent tranquilizers are usually not a part of the drug culture; for the common user and abuser, the barbiturate sedatives ("downers") provide relief from the everyday stresses of life and aid the insomniac. We must be a nation of insomniacs because we consume hundreds of tons of barbiturates a year, and one out of every two Americans uses barbiturates! Sedatives and barbiturates work in ways similar to tranquilizers, probably through interference with the release of the transmitter substances serotonin and norepinephrine, prevention of their synthesis, decreasing the sensitivity of post-synaptic receptors, or enhancment of the decay of the materials once they are released. Barbiturates first affect the reticular formation and then, directly or indirectly, the cortex of the brain. Barbiturates, taken in excessive amounts, can produce oversedation or drunkeness. They are also strongly addictive, and it is not long before there is physical and psychic dependence on these "goofballs." Chronic barbiturate use leads to tolerance within a short period, and excessive doses must be taken to achieve the same state of calm. Abrupt removal from the drug precipitates withdrawal symptoms: "shakes," convulsions, hallucinations. Unable to eat or retain food, panic sets in, fever is present, and if the individual is not healthy, death may result.

**Marijuana.** Marijuana is derived from the weed *Cannabis sativa*. It contains a sticky, golden, resinous subtance that is rich in a chemical known as tetrahydrocannabinol or THC. The THC is responsible for the euphoric effects of marijuana, which tend to be both individualistic and highly variable. Marijuana smokers report feeling detached and free-floating. Visual and auditory perceptions are enhanced, short-term memory is interfered with, speech patterns become disorganized, and thoughts seem to be more lucid, although the train of thought is often lost entirely. THC tends to accumulate in the neurons of specific areas of the brain, in particular the frontal cortex and the hippocampus. The time distortion frequently reported by marijuana users may be related to this, since the hippocampus is involved in the recall of recent events and the frontal cortex is presumed to play a role in evaluating one's actions (Figure 18–14 and Table 18–1).

**LSD.** The powerful hallucinogen LSD (lysergic acid diethylamide) appears to affect other parts of the brain than does THC. During an LSD "trip" the individual might experience psychoses, disruption of the time sense, strange visions, and behavioral detachment. LSD blocks the effects of serotonin, a neurotransmitter contained in the raphe cells of the medulla, a region that controls slow-wave sleep (Figure 18–14). This increases dreaming or even hallucinations while awake. How does LSD produce its effects? The brain-stem cells function in an analogous fashion to a boss's secretary. The secretary is the barrier that must be passed before the boss, that is, the cortex, can be influenced. Under normal circumstances the brain stem, like a good secretary, acts to filter, block, and scan all the information received from various parts of the body, en route to the brain. When LSD is present the filtering action of the secretary is disrupted; no longer can the secretary discriminate among the information—sensory events are both enhanced and distorted; what was once considered insignificant becomes important; sensory inputs are disturbed, producing strange feelings, confusion, alarm, and the like. Unpleasant consequences may result.

**Cocaine.** Whatever the price and by whatever name, cocaine is becoming the fashionable drug for recreational use. Known on the street as coke, C, snow, blow, toot, leaf, flake, freeze, happy dust, and nose candy, it is chemically an alkaloid derived from the leaves of the coca plant. Devotees of the drug habit (usually in the form of cocaine sniffing) believe it is a relatively risk-free drug that makes one alert and witty, is not carcinogenic, and leaves the user with no hangover. It is an abused drug, however, that has its highs followed by a severe letdown; depression and edginess as well as weight loss frequently result from its use. Increased usage often leads to sleeplessness, loss of appetite, hallucinations, paranoia, devastation of the nasal membrane, and physical collapse. Psychological dependence does occur, and with the most potent and dangerous forms (called freebase), it may be addictive.

Cocaine, similar in chemical structure to synthetic local anesthetics, such as lidocaine or procaine, also produces local anesthesia because it dissolves in the membrane lipid and binds to receptor sites within the sodium channels. This binding interferes with depolarization of the membrane and the nerve impulse is blocked. Cocaine also acts on sympathetic nerves preventing norepinephrine uptake, and this increased persistence of transmitter substance leads to a faster heart rate and elevated blood pressure. Like an overburdened telephone switchboard, the brain of a cocaine user suffers from message overload, there is too much information coming in, and the user becomes hyperaroused.

The specific effects of cocaine depend on the dosage, the form of the drug, the route of administration, as well as the setting and personality of the user. Cocaine is a medically useful drug as a local anesthetic, but when abused it can be a dangerous drug that can lead to self-destructive behavior.

**Alcohol.** Alcohol reduces the ability of the nerve cell to conduct messages by its action on the function of the nerve cell membrane. In general, alcohol is a central nervous system depressant that produces a marked decrease in motor performance and mental abilities. Its initial stimulatory effects are probably caused by suppression of the nerv-

**TABLE 18–3 Some drugs that affect behavior**

| Drug type | Official name | Slang name | Legitimate medical use | Psychological dependence | Potential for physical dependence |
|---|---|---|---|---|---|
| Stimulants | Caffeine<br>NoDoz*<br>Coca Cola*<br>Coffee<br>Tea | <br><br>Coke<br>Java | Lessen fatigue and drowsiness; promote alertness | Slight | No |
| | Nicotine | | None | High | No |
| | Strychnine | | None (used in some rat poisons) | | |
| | Amphetamines<br>Benzedrine*<br>Methedrine*<br>Dexedrine* | Uppers<br>Bennies, beans, cartwheels<br>Crystal, speed, meth, crank<br>Dexies, Christmas trees | Lessen fatigue and depression; treatment of obesity; promote alertness, motor activity, verbal activity | High<br>(in weeks) | High |
| Tranquilizers | Reserpine<br>(Rauwolfia) | | Treatment of moderate depression | Minimal | No |
| | Chlorpromazine<br>Thorazine*<br>Compazine*<br>Stelazine* | | Treatment of schizophrenia, depression, delerium | Minimal | No |
| | Benzodiazepines<br>Librium*<br>Valium* | | Treatment of anxiety | High | Yes |
| | Barbiturates<br>Seconal*<br>Amytal*<br>Nembutal*<br>Tuinal* | Downers, goofballs<br>Red devils<br>Blue angels<br>Yellow jackets<br>Rainbows | Treatment of insomnia and tension | High | Yes |
| Narcotics | Derivatives of opium poppy<br>Opium<br>Morphine<br>Heroin | <br>Op<br><br>Horse, H | Treatment of severe pain, diarrhea, cough | High | Yes |
| | Synthetics<br>Methadone<br>Demerol* | | Treatment of persons addicted to heroin, morphine | | |
| Anesthetics | Ether<br>Chloroform | | General anesthesia | | |
| | Procaine<br>Novocaine* | | Local anesthesia for minor surgery or dental work | No | No |
| | Cocaine | Coke, snow | Topical anesthesia, made systemic by eating (coca leaves), injection or sniffing | Yes | Yes |
| | Ethyl alcohol<br>(whisky, gin, beer, wine) | Booze, hooch, juice | Sedative, although there is a primary excitatory phase | Moderate | Yes |
| Hallucinogens | Psilocybin<br>Mescaline (peyote) | <br>Cactus | Experimental studies on brain function | | |
| | LSD (d-lysergic acid diethylamide) | Acid, sugar | | Yes | No |
| | Marijuana<br>Hashish | Pot, grass, tea, Mary Jane<br>Weed, hash | | Moderate | No |

* Registered trade name.

386

| Tolerance | Physiological effects (short term) | Long-term effects (psychological and physiological) |
|---|---|---|
| Yes | Facilitate synaptic transmission in CNS; therefore, enhance amount and duration of excitatory transmitters. Inhibits phosphodiesterase and allows cAMP accumulation to keep ion channels open for a longer than usual time | Produce insomnia or restlessness; habituation |
| Yes | Mimics ACh; excitatory in low doses from smoking | Causes lung cancer, heart and blood-vessel damage, emphysema |
| . . . . | Facilitates transmission by mimicking ACh and depresses IPSP; lethal in high doses because neurons discharge spontaneously in absence of stimuli, resulting in convulsions | Produces death due to spastic paralysis of respiratory muscles |
| Yes | Stimulate excessive release or synthesis of excitatory transmitters norepinephrine and serotonin in brain; may also block uptake from synapse and increase sensitivity of receptors; structurally resemble epinephrine | Cause malnutrition, paranoid schizophrenia, hallucinations, psychoses; judgment is impaired, heart is overtaxed, exhaustion results from stimulant cover |
| No | Depletes stores of norepinephrine, dopamine, and serotonin from CNS. | Produces drowsiness, drying of mouth, blurring of vision, diarrhea, ulcers |
| No | Monoamine antagonist blocks dopamine receptors in the brain; CNS depressant | Induces hypothermia, acts as antiemetic, depresses stay-awake reticular network, suppresses hallucinations and delusions |
| Yes | Stimulates receptors on GABA neurons, and thereby increases neural inhibition | |
| Yes (quickly) | Interfere with synthesis and release of the transmitters norepinephrine and serotonin, especially in reticular system; decreased sensitivity of postsynaptic receptors; may enhance breakdown of transmitter substances | Induces sleep, euphoria, drowsiness, impaired judgment, irritability, weight loss; highly addictive; abrupt withdrawal is severe and unsafe, producing shakes, convulsions, hallucinations |
| Yes | Act as CNS depressant, inducing muscle relaxation, hypnosis (drowsiness and lethargy), euphoria (well-being), and sleep | Produce constipation, loss of appetite, temporary impotence, addiction with unpleasant symptoms of withdrawal; overdose kills, probably by depressing respiratory center |
| | Mechanism of action unknown | |
| | Inhibit axonal transmission of nerve impulses | |
| No | Prevent synaptic transmission to neurons of CNS | None |
| Yes | Prevents or reduces uptake of transmitters such as norepinephrine into nerve terminals | Produces euphoria, alertness, addiction |
| Yes | Acts as CNS depressant, producing loss of motor coordination (high doses) and alertness (low doses); induces euphoria; exact mechanism of action unknown | Causes cirrhosis of liver, physiological dependence, obesity, brain damage, addiction with severe withdrawal symptoms |
| . . . . | May enhance serotonin and norephinephrine levels in the brain because of their chemical similarity to these transmitters; therefore, sensory input enhanced | Precipitate existing psychoses; psychotic symptoms may recur without drug taking |
| Yes | Rich visual imagery, sensory awareness, "trip," hallucinations Decreases serotonin release and synthesis | |
| Yes | Acts as CNS depressant in high doses, euphoric and stimulant in low doses; exact mode of action unknown | Causes loss of appetite, judgment, and motivation |

ous system's inhibitory controls. Alcohol causes increased aggressiveness in many heavy users and may have adverse effects on the liver, stomach, intestines, and even the brain, producing delerium tremens (DTs) if the supply is withdrawn. Alcohol is addictive, and treatment of alcoholism is extremely difficult.

## SUMMARY

1. The nervous system provides for rapid communication between various tissues and organs, and links the sense organs with effectors.

2. Neurons, or nerve cells, transmit nerve impulses. Glial cells are supportive in function. The brain, spinal cord, and ganglia are concentrated centers of nerve cells and supporting elements.

3. Neurons conduct messages from dendrites via the cell body to the long axon, whose terminal ramifications end in synaptic knobs. The axonal sheath, or neurilemma, is formed by glial cells. Glial cells form a tightly wrapped insulating myelin sheath around many neurons. The sheath is interrupted by nodes. Multiple sclerosis is due to destruction of the myelin sheath.

4. A potential difference is maintained across the neuronal plasma membrane, which is electrically negative inside and positive outside. The concentration of $Na^+$ ions is higher outside, whereas the concentration of $Cl^-$, $Org^-$, and $K^+$ is higher on the inside. The membrane resting potential is $-70$ mV.

5. When a neuron is stimulated, membrane permeability temporarily changes. Sodium enters, and the membrane becomes rapidly depolarized and then just as rapidly repolarized as permeability to sodium is reversed. This is the action potential (impulse), and it passes along the nerve with no decrease in strength.

6. A second action potential cannot be produced until the membrane is completely repolarized and sodium ions are pumped out (the sodium pump). During this period, the neuron is in a refractory state (inexcitable).

7. Stimuli must be stronger than threshold level to produce an action potential. The magnitude, character, and duration of the impulse are independent of the strength or nature of the stimulus (the all-or-none law). Stimulus intensity is determined by variation in neuronal threshold, numbers of neurons stimulated, and frequency of action potentials.

8. Transmission velocity varies with neuronal diameter and myelination. Transmission is saltatory, from node to node.

9. Nerve impulses are transmitted in only one direction because of the synapse. When a neuron is stimulated, presynaptic axonal knobs discharge transmitter substance, which diffuses across the synaptic cleft to the dendrites of the postsynaptic neuron; here, an excitatory postsynaptic potential (EPSP) is triggered, which in turn triggers an action potential when threshold levels are reached.

10. The postsynaptic membrane inactivates the transmitter substance enzymatically. Excitatory transmitters include acetylcholine (ACh).

11. Inhibitory substances such as GABA can lower the resting potential and thus raise the threshold necessary for generation of an impulse (inhibitory postsynaptic potential, IPSP). Nervous activity results from a balance in EPSP and IPSP between neurons.

12. The nerve impulse is subject to accommodation because of synaptic fatigue.

13. Summation involves the progressive recruitment and discharge of presynaptic knobs. It can be temporal and/or spatial. It is subject to facilitation (subthreshold discharge of synaptic knobs).

14. The central nervous system (CNS) comprises the brain and spinal cord. The peripheral nervous system (PNS) comprises all of the neurons and nerve fibers of the CNS.

15. Sensory neurons transmit environmental stimuli to the CNS. Motor neurons transmit messages from the CNS to glands and muscles, and interneurons are integrative.

16. The brain and spinal cord are surrounded and protected by membranes called meninges. Cerebrospinal fluid fills the spaces in the brain, the central canal of the spinal cord, and the spaces between the meninges.

17. The exterior, gray matter of the brain consists of neuronal cell bodies; the internal, white matter is made up of axons and their myelin sheaths.

18. The forebrain consists of the bilobed cerebrum, thalamus, hypothalamus, and limbic system. The exterior cerebral cortex, which is extensively furrowed and highly developed in humans, is the center of consciousness. The hindbrain consists of the brain stem, or medulla, pons, and cerebellum, and the midbrain connects the fore- and hindbrain. Twelve pairs of cranial nerves arise from the brain.

19. The gray matter is interior to the white matter in the spinal cord. It controls many involuntary actions (reflexes) and gives rise to 31 pairs of mixed nerves. The sensory elements have dorsal roots and ganglia; the motor elements have ventral roots and ganglia.

20. The autonomic nervous system consists of the sympathetic and parasympathetic systems and is concerned with involuntary control.

21. The sympathetic nerves exit ventrally from the spinal cord and synapse with motor neurons in the ventral ganglia. Norepinephrine is the transmitter substance, and adrenergic sympathetic nerves innervate heart, lungs, sweat glands, and involuntary smooth muscles. The system is involved in the emergency response.

22. Parasympathetic nerves originate in the Xth cranial neve (vagus) and the spinal sacral region. They are cholinergic (ACh is the transmitter) and generally inhibitory. They innervate the same body organs as the sympathetic nerves, and thus a functional balance is maintained between excitation and relaxation and maintenance.

**23.** Simple reflex arcs involve transmission from a sense organ along a sensory neuron via spinal interneuron and motor neuron to an effector organ. In this way a simple involuntary response is produced. Secondary impulses along the spinal cord to the higher centers of the brain may be generated simultaneously, so that information is processed and a further (perhaps conscious) integrated response may be produced.

**24.** A chemical other than a nutrient that can effect a functional and/or structural change in a living tissue is a drug. Neurological drugs may affect behavior by acting on nervous physiology or on the synapse, by increasing, decreasing, or substituting for transmitter substances.

## KEY WORDS

| | | | |
|---|---|---|---|
| | excitable cells | excitatory postsynaptic potential (EPSP) | thalamus |
| | stimulus | inhibitory postsynaptic potential (IPSP) | hypothalamus |
| nerve impulses | depolarized | summation | limbic system |
| neurons | repolarization | facilitation | cerebral cortex |
| nerves | action potential | GABA | medulla (brain stem) |
| glial cells | refractory state | catecholamine | pons |
| dendrites | threshold stimulus | sensory neurons | cerebellum |
| axon | all-or-none law | motor neurons | reflexes |
| synaptic knob | node | interneurons | autonomic nervous system |
| neurilemma | synapse | central nervous system (CNS) | sympathetic system |
| interstitial cells | synaptic cleft | peripheral nervous system (PNS) | parasympathetic system |
| myelin sheath | presynaptic knobs | cerebrospinal fluid | cholinergic |
| nodes | brain waves | meninges | adrenergic |
| multiple sclerosis | electroencephalogram (EEG) | cranium | reflex arc |
| voltage | alpha waves | forebrain | drug |
| current | beta waves | midbrain | dope |
| ions | endorphin | hindbrain | receptor agonists |
| sodium pump | enkephalin | cerebrum | receptor antagonists |
| membrane resting potential | epilepsy | cerebral hemispheres | cocaine |

## TOPICS FOR REVIEW AND DISCUSSION

1. Draw and label a nerve synapse.
2. What is the function of the synapse? How is drug action related to the synapse?
3. Discuss polarity in the nervous system.
4. What are the differences between the parasympathetic and sympathetic nervous systems?
5. Draw a "typical" neuron and label its parts.
6. Describe a reflex arc.
7. How is the human nervous system organized?
8. In what ways are the nervous and endocrine systems related?
9. Why can't a complete description of the function of a neuron be used to describe the entire operation of the nervous system?
10. Define and describe summation, facilitation, fatigue, and inhibition in the nervous system.

The film *2001: A Space Odyssey* is an adventure concerning deep space exploration. En route to Jupiter the giant antenna system of the spaceship *Discovery* malfunctions, and Mission Commander Bowman must leave the ship to repair it. The antenna system of the spaceship enables the crew to keep in touch with the Earth, almost half a billion miles away, and this receptor system must operate perfectly or else the mission will fail. (Courtesy of Metro-Goldwyn-Mayer, Inc., © 1968.)

# Built-in Signal Corps: The Sense Organs

## 19–1 SENSORY LISTENING POSTS

This morning the alarm clock buzzed, and with eyes closed you pressed the lever that turned it off. With barely opened eyes you checked the weather outside and found the sun shining. Then your eyes opened fully as the lids moved upward. You rolled out of bed, washed your face with cold water to perk yourself up, listened to the early-morning news on the radio, and were completely aroused by the aroma of fresh-brewed coffee. Each day of our lives, mundane or exciting, the world about us is continually being monitored by a battery of listening posts—our sense organs. Our view of the world is imparted by our senses; deprived of all sensation a human being experiences fright, terror, hallucinations, and ultimately madness.

Structurally our communications network consists of signal receivers (receptors), conduction pathways (nerves), and a means for interpreting and/or responding to the signals (brain and muscles or glands). The receptors that monitor the external world are those with which we are most familiar—those of the five senses: sight, hearing, touch, smell, and taste. These are, however, only a few of the many senses with which we are endowed, since, in addition to receiving information from the outside environment, the nervous system receives messages from the internal environment, for example, tension in muscles, tendons, and joints or the feeling of fullness. These sensory receptors are groups of specialized neurons; together they provide us with a wide range of sensory experience and enable us to keep tabs on the workings of the body.

Although sense organs—the eye, nose, tongue, skin, and ear—are responsible for distinct sensations, the sensory receptor itself does not determine what we see, feel, hear, taste, or smell. Indeed, you can prove this to yourself by closing your eyes and lightly tapping on the lids. You see flashes of light that are produced not by light but by touch (pressure). How can pressure signals be received as light? It is clear that what we sense depends not so much on the nature of the stimulus, as on where it is transmitted. Sense organs are essentially **transducers,** designed to collect information of one kind or another and convert it into nerve impulses.

Neurons have a limited code of information: the signals are either off or on, and when they are turned on, only the signal frequency can be altered. Only when the signals are transmitted to the cerebral cortex of the brain, where they are decoded and interpreted, do we sense a stimulus. The brain's cortex puts together the coded messages it receives from a variety of sources and integrates, interprets, stores, and acts on them. There is a systematic organization in the cortex, and different regions seem to be responsible for decoding and interpreting different signals (Figure 18–14). Just as tapping on the closed eye produces a sensation of light, so does pressure on the back of the skull. "Seeing stars" as a result of a blow to the head indicates that the light-interpreting region of the brain has received a signal, in this case as a result of a direct pressure stimulus.

One of the frontiers of modern biology involves the mechanism whereby information in the nervous system is coded and decoded to produce the richness of sensation we all recognize. No doubt the future will see this frontier crossed and much advancement in decoding nerve messages and understanding sensation and behavior.

## 19–2 SMELL: DETECTING CHEMICAL SIGNALS IN THE AIR

The organs responsible for detecting odors, called **olfactory organs,** lie high up in the interior of the nose (Figure 19–1a). The receptor cells of the olfactory organs each bear a cluster of hairlike filaments at its free end (Figure 19–1b). The olfactory cells run toward the brain as the olfactory nerve (cranial nerve I); at the brain they end in the olfactory bulb. From the olfactory bulb signals are sent for interpretation to the higher centers within the cerebral cortex (Figure 18–14).

Because the olfactory organs are recessed deep within the nasal passages, the material to be smelled must have certain properties. First, it must be volatile, that is, so organized chemically that its molecules evaporate rapidly and can diffuse upward to the receptor or be drawn upward by sniffing. Second, it must be capable of being absorbed by and soluble in water and lipids. This enables the molecule to pass through the mucus covering the sensory epithelium. Third, the substance must be one that is not already present on the surface epithelium of the olfactory organ, so that it elicits a change upon arrival; only change will cause the sensation of smell. Once the odor molecule has acted on the receptor cell, it causes depolarization of the membrane and triggers an action potential. Information on the chemistry of the odor, recorded as action potentials in the olfactory nerves, is then decoded in the brain.

How are we able to discriminate among odors, which number in the thousands? Are there different receptors for each odor? A current theory suggests that discrimination among odors depends upon the presence of a number of olfactory receptors in the nose, each of which has at its tip an absorbent site specific for a particular odor or class of odors. Each receptor terminus will accept only its appropriately shaped odor molecule, just as a lock and key fit exactly. Thus molecules have different odors because they cannot fit into the same absorbant site on the olfactory receptor, but if substances of different chemical composition have the same configuration, they can have the same odor because they fit the same site. Differences in orientation of the atoms in a molecule that do not alter surface architecture do not alter odor. Odors may be modified if fatigue has occurred in neighboring receptors. For example, if receptor site A is fatigued, the molecules that would ordinarily fit into A, B, and C can occupy only B and C. This is why, when shopping for perfume, one can smell only a few before they all begin to smell alike—the capacity for discrimination is lost or diminished.

## 19–3 TASTE: DETECTING CHEMICAL SIGNALS IN SOLUTION

You bite into a thick juicy steak smothered in mushroom sauce, and you savor the food. It is really good! Taste is, like smell, a chemical sense. Odorous materials are wafted by air currents into the nose; however, taste chemicals must be put into the mouth in solution, where they excite taste

Olfactory bulb

Olfactory area

Turbinate bones

Tongue

(a)

To olfactory bulb

Axons

Supporting cell

Receptor cell

Mucus

Cilia

(b)

(a)

(b)

(c)

(a)

(b)

receptors, the **taste buds,** found primarily on raised papillae on the surface of the tongue (Figure 19–2a). Taste is a short-distance sense, for chemicals in solution must be placed directly in contact with the receptors. There are approximately 10,000 taste buds, and they are distributed over the tongue in a definite pattern (Figure 19–2a). The tip of the tongue senses sweet tastes, the sides sense salty and sour tastes, and the back of the tongue detects bitter flavors. Although we have four primary tastes, and all other tastes are combinations of these, all the taste receptors look alike.

Within each taste bud the receptor cells, which are modified neurons, are arranged like the segments of an orange, with the upper tips of the receptor cells extending into a small pore at the tip of the taste bud (Figure 19–2c). The tips contain microvilli, and these provide the contact point between taste molecules and receptor cells. The impulses from the taste buds are transmitted by nerves up the brain stem and then to the cortex. The full detection of taste is related to smell, and often the two cannot be separated. For example, during a stuffy head cold, we lose the sense of taste because we cannot smell!

## 19–4 SIGHT: RECEIVING LIGHT SIGNALS

Let there be light: and there was light.
Gen. 1:3

The light of the body is the eye.
Matt. 6:22

We and our closest primate relatives are so extremely visual as animals that eyesight is probably our most important environmental sense. Indeed, so reliant are we upon our eyesight that without it we are virtually incapable of surviving unaided.

### Eye structure

The human eye is a tender ball about 1 in. in diameter, protected by its location in a socket of the skull. The position of the eyes in front of the head allows for superimposition of the images from each eye, and we see stereoscopically in three dimensions (length, width, and depth).

The optical system for detecting light within the eye is much like that of a camera. The eyeball has a three-layered wall, each concentric layer, or coat, functioning in a specific capacity (Figure 19–3). The outer covering is a tough, fibrous capsule called the **sclera,** the white of the eye; it maintains the shape of the eye and protects it. Muscles responsible for moving the eye in the socket are attached to the outside of the sclera. The front of the sclera, facing the outside world, is perfectly transparent and is called the **cornea.** This is truly the window of the eye, and it is composed of five layers of flat cells arranged like sheets of plate glass. The layer just inside the sclera, called the **choroid coat,** contains blood vessels and a nonreflecting pigment that acts as a light shield and prevents the light from scattering. Light penetrates the cornea and enters the interior of the eye through the front portion of the choroid coat, which is interrupted to

**393**

produce a small opening, the **pupil.** The region of the choroid visible through the cornea and surrounding the pupil as a colored band is called the **iris.** The iris gives the eye its color, depending on the presence or absence of pigment. If there is a lot of pigment (melanin), the eye color is brown; if pigment is sparse and localized only in the back layer of the choroid, the light is scattered to a greater extent and the eye appears blue. We are all born with blue eyes because it takes time for melanin production to get under way after birth. In the absence of pigment, as occurs in **albinism,** the eye appears pink because the blood in the blood vessels of the choroid shows through.

To allow for changes in light intensity, most expensive cameras are equipped with a diaphragm (so-called *f* stops). When the light is dim, the diaphragm is wide open; when the light is too bright, it is closed down. The automatic diaphragm of the eye is the iris. The iris can expand and contract, thus enlarging and decreasing the size of the pupil by means of iris muscles that function like the drawstring around a purse. The iris can expand the pupil's diameter sixfold (from $\frac{1}{16}$ to $\frac{1}{3}$ in.), and 40 times as much light can enter the eye when the pupil is expanded as when it is contracted. This dark adaptation takes time, as you know if you have stumbled in a darkened theater after entering from bright daylight.

The elastic **lens** is suspended from the **ciliary body** just below the iris. Composed of concentric layers of fibers and crystal-clear proteins in solution, it serves to focus the light rays onto the receptor cells of the "film" of the eye, the **retina.** The retina is the innermost layer of the eyeball. It is about the size of a postage stamp, not much thicker, and lines the back two thirds of the choroid coat. It contains special nerve cells, called **rods** and **cones** (Figure 19–5), which convert light rays into nerve impulses.

The coats of the eye are rather soft, and to maintain their position the entire eye is filled with fluid kept under pressure; for the eye to work, the eyeball must be turgid. The space in front of the lens (**anterior chamber**) is filled with a lymphlike watery fluid, **aqueous humor** (Figure 19–3). It is provided by filtration from capillaries and is ordinarily drained off into blood vessels supplying the cornea. Behind the lens in the **posterior chamber** is a jellylike but clear fluid, the **vitreous humor.**

The eye is protected in front on its outer surface by a thin transparent layer of epidermal cells, the **conjunctiva.** The conjunctiva is continuous at its periphery with two folds of skin, the **eyelids,** which are aided in their protective function by hairs on their edges, the **eyelashes.** The eyelashes and the **eyebrows** above the eye help to prevent dust, sweat, and so on from reaching the sensitive, moist surface of the eye. The eye is kept moist at all times by the **tears,** a watery secretion of two special lacrimal glands (*lacrima*—tear; L.). Excess tears are drained from the eye into the nasal sinuses by the **lacrimal duct,** opening from the inner corner of the lower eyelid (Figure 19–4).

This then is the eye, a living device for photoreception.

**Filming the world around us: the retina.** The light-sensitive film of the eye, the retina, consists of about 130 million neurons stacked up in three layers. Their function is to convert the electromagnetic radiation of light into electrical signals that can be sent to the brain, where they produce the sensation of seeing.

Light that enters the eye first passes through the curved surface of the cornea, continues on through the aqueous humor, and enters the lens by way of the pupil. In the lens the ultraviolet light is filtered out, and the rays of light pass through the vitreous humor and then impinge on the retina. Light hitting the retina first strikes the axons of the optic neurons, next passes through a layer of bipolar cells, and then, at the very back, hits the light-sensitive neuronal elements, the rods and cones (Figure 19–5). It is a curiosity of development that puts the light-sensitive neurons at the back of the retina,

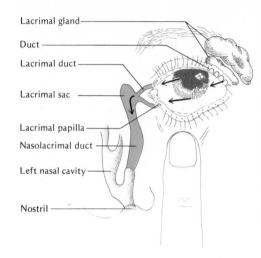

FIGURE 19–4 The lacrimal glands, above and on the outer edge of the eye socket, secrete tears that wash away foreign substances and dilute irritants on the eye's surface. Excess fluid drains through minute openings near the nasal side of each eyelid and enters the nasal cavity through the lacrimal sac and the nasolacrimal duct.

Lacrimal gland

Duct

Lacrimal duct

Lacrimal sac

Lacrimal papilla

Nasolacrimal duct

Left nasal cavity

Nostril

directed away from the light, and requires light to pass through two other layers before it strikes the photoreceptor cells.

The rod cells are very sensitive and are more abundant toward the periphery of the retina. They enable us to see in light too dim to stimulate the cone cells, but they do not give a clear or well-defined image and cannot differentiate color. The cone cells, responsible for detection of color, are more abundant toward the center of the retina and give rise to more detailed and better defined images than the rod cells. They are used for vision in bright light. When light hits the rods and cones, it causes a chemical change in the pigments they contain.

The pigment of the rods consists of a protein called rhodopsin and a derivative of vitamin A called retinaldehyde. Absorption of light energy by the retinaldehyde molecule causes it to change form (technically from the *cis* to the *trans* configuration) and subsequent reactions lead to a split of the rhodopsin into opsin and retinaldehyde. Absorption of light energy by the rhodopsin leads to a change in membrane potential, and this subsequently affects the bipolar cell to produce an electrical potential, the neuron is triggered to fire, and this impulse travels to the visual region of the

FIGURE 19–5 The human retina is composed of several layers of cells. Incoming light strikes the retinal layers in the following order: nerve fibers, ganglion cells, bipolar nerve cells, rod and cone cells, and pigment cells. The pigment layer acts like the black surface inside a camera and prevents light from being reflected backward; the rods and cones are light-sensitive neurons that transmit their signals to the ganglion cells via the bipolar nerve cells; the axons of the ganglion cells run along the surface of the retina, eventually converging to form the optic nerve.

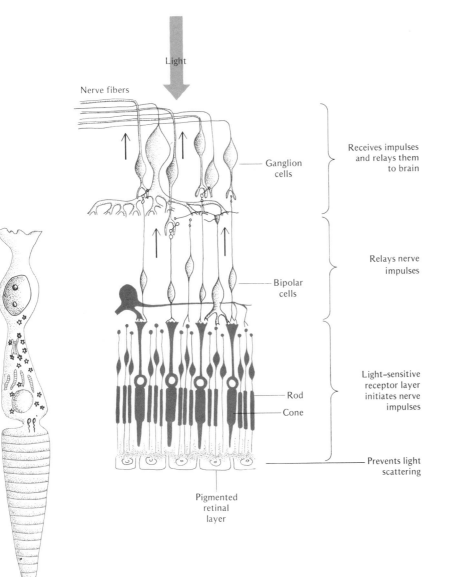

Light

Nerve fibers

Ganglion cells — Receives impulses and relays them to brain

Bipolar cells — Relays nerve impulses

Rod
Cone — Light–sensitive receptor layer initiates nerve impulses

Prevents light scattering

Pigmented retinal layer

Detail of rod cell

Detail of cone cell

brain, where it is decoded and interpreted as light. The split pigments are reduced in the retina to vitamin A and must be resynthesized if we are to continue perceiving light. If the diet is deficient in vitamin A, pigment synthesis is impaired, and the disease known as **night blindness** results. The rods contain only one kind of pigment, rhodopsin, or visual purple, but the protein pigments in the cones come in three different kinds of opsins, and are sensitive to blue, red, and green light, respectively. We can distinguish 160 different colors, and this ability depends on the amount and kinds of cones stimulated—a sort of neuronal pigment mixing to produce a particular hue, just as the artist mixes colors on a palette. White is perceived if all three cone pigments are equally stimulated by light. Color intensity is determined by the number of nerve impulses produced by the light hitting the cones.

The cornea and lens of the eye focus the light to the **fovea,** a region on the retina no bigger than the head of a pin. The cones are abundant in this region, and there are no rods. The nerve layer above the fovea is quite thin, so that light hits the photoreceptor cells directly. The fovea is the region of keenest vision. On this spot the eye focuses the letters and words you see on this page. Light that strikes the retinal cells outside the region of the fovea gives rise to less well-defined images because there are fewer cones; we cannot make out fine details. This constitutes **peripheral vision.** Peripheral vision is in a sense looking out of the corner of your eye; when it is restricted the person is said to have **tunnel vision.**

If we were to look at the retina through an ophthalmoscope, we would see two things: the fovea, as a small depression, and a creamy white disc, the **optic disc,** or **blind spot** (Figure 19–6a). The optic disc contains no rods or cones, but consists only of nerve fibers that are gathered from the retina to form the optic nerve (cranial nerve II). We are unaware of the blind spot be-

FIGURE 19–7 The optic chiasma viewed from below.

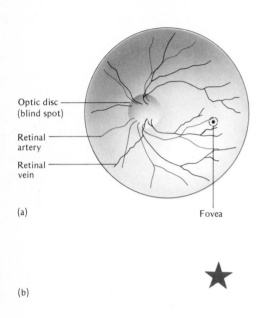

Optic disc (blind spot)

Retinal artery

Retinal vein

(a)

Fovea

(b)

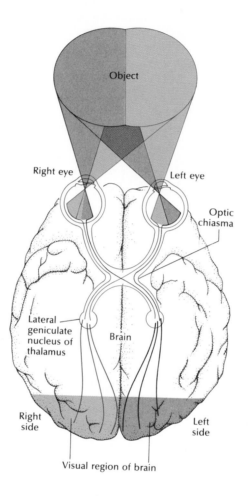

Object

Right eye

Left eye

Optic chiasma

Lateral geniculate nucleus of thalamus

Brain

Right side

Left side

Visual region of brain

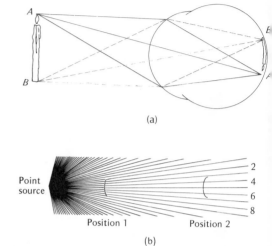

(a)

Point source

2
4
6
8

Position 1

Position 2

(b)

FIGURE 19–8 (a) Image formation on the retina. Incoming light rays from the object being viewed are bent in such a way that the rays from each point come together at a single point on the retina and produce an image. When you look at a candle, all rays reflected from the tip of the flame must be brought together at a point on your retina, all rays from the base must be brought together at another point, and so on for all parts of the candle. The image formed on the retina is inverted. (b) The divergence of light rays from near and far sources. Light rays from a point source travel outward in all directions. The cornea of a viewer standing near the source will be struck by rays traveling at divergent angles (rays 1 to 9), but the cornea of a viewer 20 ft or more away will be struck by fewer rays (rays 4 to 6).

cause the eye ordinarily focuses light rays on the fovea. Your own blind spot can be located by following the directions in the caption to Figure 19–6b.

The **optic nerve** passes backward from the retina to the brain. Just in front of the pituitary gland, the optic nerves from each eye partially cross, forming the **optic chiasma.** The nerve fibers originating from the temple sides of the two retinas remain uncrossed, but those from the nasal sides do cross over (Figure 19–7). Thus, the optic nerves that leave the optic chiasma are composed of outside signals of one retina and inside signals of the other. Each optic nerve synapses with cells in a region below the thalamus of the brain and then spreads out to the visual cortex of the brain. The peculiar anatomic distribution of nerves from the two retinas means that damage (such as is caused by an enlarged pituitary or a pituitary tumor) to a single optic nerve affects both retinal images.

**Image formation.** Just as clear photographs depend upon precise focusing of light on the film of a camera, so clear vision depends

upon precise focusing of light rays on the retina. If focusing is poor, the image is blurred.

What is focus? The lens of the eye bends incoming rays of light from objects we are looking at and brings them together (focuses them) on the retina (Figure 19–8a). If the rays of light are bent incorrectly and come together in front of the retina or behind it, the image is blurred, and we say it is out of focus (Figure 19–9).

As you may know, the image formed on the film of a camera is upside down. The same is true of the image formed on the

retina (Figure 19–8a). The world is perceived as right side up because the coded action potentials received by the brain are inverted. This ability to invert retinal images is partly inherited and partly learned. The visual connections of a newborn kitten without visual experience are much the same as in an adult cat. But a kitten deprived of visual experience for 2 to 3 months loses much of its ability for visual reflexes and is unable to perceive form. A human wearing prism glasses that invert objects so that the retinal image is right side up is at first disoriented, but in time there is reevaluation

**FIGURE 19–9 Focus and the eye. (a) Accommodation. (b) Myopia (nearsightedness). (c) Hyperopia (farsightedness). (d) Astigmatism.**

(a)

Ciliary muscle *contracts* and lens thickens

Close objects

Ciliary muscle *relaxes* and lens thins

Distant objects

(b)

Focus in front of retina

Normal eye

Biconcave lens

Correction

(c)

Focus in back of retina

Normal eye

Biconvex lens

Correction

(d)

Lens

Correction

the distance of objects from the eye. (In the camera, we focus on an object by moving the position of the lens rather than by changing its shape.) Why is it necessary to adjust focus for distance? Light rays reflected from a particular point travel away from that point in all directions (Figure 19–8b). The angle of divergence of rays of light entering the eye or the camera from a near object is much greater than that of rays of light from a distant object, which are almost parallel to one another. Obviously, much less bending is necessary to focus the rays coming from a distant object than is needed to focus the rays coming from a near object. When nearby objects are viewed, the lens thickens; when distant objects are viewed, it flattens out (Figure 19–9a). The change in lens shape to permit focus of close and distant objects is called **accommodation**.

Sometimes the cornea and the lens are so constructed that too much or too little bending of light rays occurs, or the eyeball depth is too shallow or too deep. As a result, light does not focus properly on the retina, and this produces conditions of nearsightedness, farsightedness, or astigmatism (Figures 19–9b–d). In **nearsighted** people, light rays from near objects tend to fall on the retina, but rays from distant objects focus in front of it, producing a blurred image. This is caused either by a lens that bends the incoming light rays too strongly or by an abnormally long distance between cornea and retina. In **farsighted** people, the distance from cornea to retina may be too short or the capacity of the lens to bend incoming light rays may be weak. Light rays focus behind the retina; the lens may accommodate for this by thickening, but near vision is poor. **Astigmatism** is caused by an irregular curvature of the cornea. As a result, light rays focus at different points behind and in front of the retina, and the image is blurred. These conditions, nearsightedness, farsightedness, and astigmatism, can often be helped by glass lenses constructed according to the defect involved—spectacles, or eyeglasses.

of the information on the retina and proper orientation results. Thus, experience as well as neuronal wiring plays a role in our ability to see things as they are.

The cornea of the eye rather than the lens is responsible for most of the bending of incoming light rays. The importance of the lens lies in the fact that it can change its shape by contracting or relaxing the ciliary muscles, thus bending incoming light rays to a greater or lesser degree. This makes it possible to adjust the focus depending on

FIGURE 19–10 The ear. (a) Internal structure. (b) Mechanical model for the working of the ear.

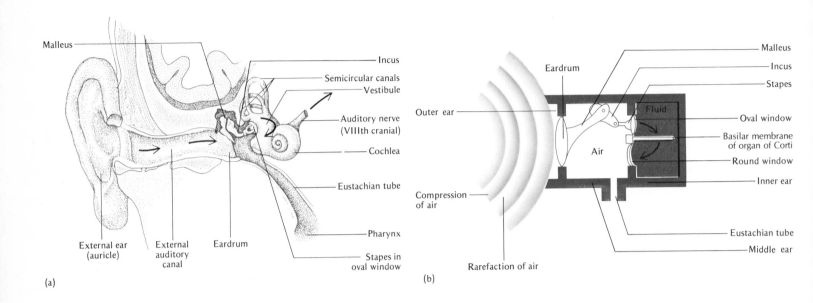

(a)

(b)

## 19–5 HEARING: RECEIVING SOUND SIGNALS

The buzz of a mosquito, the blended tones of a symphony orchestra, the voice of someone you hold dear, the emotion-laden words of an actor are all sound signals. In order for them to mean anything to us, they must be heard. The ear is a sensitive instrument for detecting air vibrations (sound), and it does this with remarkable acuity.

Before we discuss the reception of sound signals (hearing), let us first ask, What is sound? You are sitting quietly reading when a gust of wind blows against the open door and it slams shut. The kinetic energy of moving air has pushed the door; it moves, but once closed it moves no farther. The air rebounds off the door as it slams and sets the adjacent air particles in motion, and causes them to vibrate. The air particles pass the vibrations on to their adjacent neighbors, so that vibrating waves travel from the door to your ear, and you hear the door close with a slam. The variable compression of the air produces regions of

compression and rarefaction, similar to the ripples or waves of water created by a pebble dropped on its surface. Thus, **sound energy** is a disturbance of air molecules transmitted by air.

Our ears can translate air vibrations between extremes of frequency (between 16 and 20,000 cycles per second) into nerve impulses that we interpret as sound. The **frequency** is the number of wave peaks (or cycles) that passes a given point in 1 second. The faster the vibration, the greater the frequency and the higher the **pitch.** Our best range is above 1,000 cycles per second (to 5,000), and it is this insensitivity to low frequency that allows us to avoid the distraction of noises produced by our own muscles contracting and by everyday bodily movements. (You can hear these low frequencies produced by muscle contraction by sticking a finger in each ear, thus shutting out airborne sound; you will hear a low hum.) Think how unpleasant it would be to hear every step you took or every beat of your heart as a loud thud.

The **volume** of the sound we hear is a

function of the amplitude of the vibrations; the higher the **amplitude** (height of the sound waves), the louder the sound. If a piano, a violin, and a flute all play a note at the same pitch and volume, they will still sound different from each other. The differences are produced by secondary air vibrations, and we call such differences **tone quality.**

The pitch, the volume, and the quality of sound we hear depend upon the interpretation put upon the stimulations received by the sound receptor within the ear. How does the ear collect sound and make us aware of it? The human ear consists of three regions: the **external ear (auricle),** the **middle ear,** and the **inner ear (labyrinth)** (Figure 19–10a). The external ear consists of a flesh-covered, cartilaginous funnel for collecting sound waves. At its narrow end there is stretched a delicate membrane like the head of a drum, the **tympanum (eardrum).** When air waves strike the eardrum, they set it vibrating (Figure 19–10b); this membrane forms the outer wall of the middle ear, which contains a connected chain of three

FIGURE 19–11 (a) The cochlea. (b) The cochlea unwound. (Modified from G. Hardin, *Biology: Its Principles and Implications,* 2nd ed., San Francisco, W. H. Freeman, 1966.) (c) Cross section through the unwound cochlea showing position of the organ of Corti. (d) Cochlear hair cell, the receptor for sound.

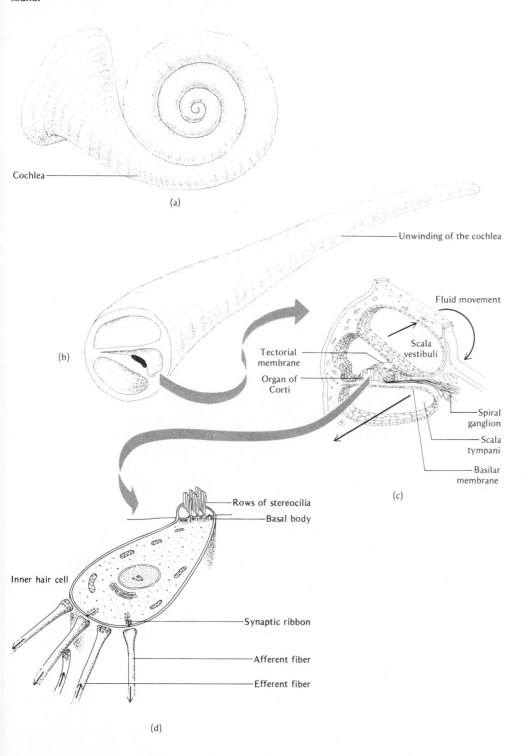

bones, and these tiny bones are set in motion also. The eardrum is in direct contact with the handle of the outermost of the three middle-ear bones—the **hammer (malleus).** The hammer articulates with the **anvil (incus),** which in turn articulates with the innermost bone, the **stirrup (stapes).** The stirrup's base is shaped like a plunger, and this is attached by a ligament to a membrane called the **oval window** on the inner wall of the middle ear. Two muscles operate the bones of the middle ear; one of these is attached to the handle of the hammer, and its contractions serve to keep the eardrum taut and cone-shaped; the other is attached to the stirrup and makes sure that the bones operate smoothly and do not move apart from one another as they transmit the vibrations from the eardrum to the oval window. The bones of the middle ear are not free to move about, but are anchored in place by elastic ligaments and covered over by mucous membrane. If the middle-ear cavity becomes inflamed, infected, or filled with pus, the bones do not function and hearing is impaired. The oval window and another membrane just below it, the **round window,** separate the middle ear from the inner ear. The round window, like the oval window, is stretched tightly across the entrance to the inner ear.

The inner ear consists of a series of fluid-filled chambers and coiled canals lying in the bones of the skull. The upper group is concerned with the senses of balance and equilibrium. The lower portion of the inner ear contains a long, coiled tube, the **cochlea** (*cochlea*—snail shell; L.). The cochlea is divided into three ducts by membranes. The delicate sound receptor, the **organ of Corti,** lies on one of these membranes (Figure 19–11). Specialized hair cells on the organ of Corti are the actual sensory receptors. Vibrations of the oval window are transmitted to the cochlear fluid, the oscillations of the fluid cause the hairs to move, and they rub against an overhanging membrane (the **tectorial membrane**). Their displacement causes the hair cells to release

### BOX 19A Unwanted sound: noise pollution

Sound can convey precious information or be totally useless. Noise is useless and unwanted sound, and it can be disturbing and damaging. Today in the United States alone there are over 90 million automobiles, 16 million trucks, and 3 million motorcycles that pollute the air not only with hydrocarbons but with the roar of their engines as well. The clatter of trash collection, the grinding of dishwashers, disposal units, and blenders all contribute to noise in the home. Even the skies rain down noise from jet planes.

The ear, as we have seen, is a sensitive detector of air pressure. The smallest air disturbance that can be heard under ideal conditions in a normal ear is known as the **threshold of hearing.** This forms the baseline for sound measurement in terms of loudness. The unit for measuring loudness of sound is called a **bel,** after Alexander Graham Bell, the inventor of the telephone. A **decibel** (0.1 bel) is used most frequently to describe audible sounds. The bel scale of loudness is logarithmic, just as is the Richter scale for measuring earthquake intensity. This means that a value difference of 1 unit indicates an intensity difference of 10. Thus, 1 decibel, which is the softest sound a human ear can hear, is one tenth as loud as a sound of 10 decibels (or 1 bel) and is one hundredth as loud as a 20-decibel (2-bel) sound. A whisper is 30 decibels (Table 19–1) and is 1,000 times louder than the threshold of hearing. As decibels increase, the sound energy increases rapidly, and the greater the energy, the higher the amplitude of the sound waves. Very high amplitude sound waves (very loud sounds), especially if they are of high frequency, may damage the hair cells of the ear. Sound can be destructive: a sound of 170 decibels focused on a small animal will kill it. Ordinary conversation is about 60 decibels, but the sound in a discotheque may reach 120 decibels. A guinea pig subjected to rock-and-roll music at 122 decibels for periods similar to those to which teenagers subject themselves had widespread and irreversible damage to the hair cells in the organ of Corti (Figure 19–12).

Since sound travels as waves with areas of compression and

**TABLE 19–1 Sound level readings**

|  | Decibels |
|---|---|
| Threshold of pain | 130 |
| 10 ft away from rock drill | 130 |
| Discotheque | 120 |
| Motorcycle, power mower | 115 |
| 2,000 ft from jet taking off | 105 |
| Subway station with train coming in | 95 |
| 50 ft from a moving heavy truck | 90 |
| Noisy kitchen in city | 85 |
| 50 ft from a highway | 70 |
| Noisy office | 65 |
| Quiet conversation | 60 |
| Quiet office | 45 |
| Quiet rural night | 30 |
| Whisper | 30 |
| Threshold of hearing | 0 |

Prolonged exposure to sound between 85 and 115 decibels will begin to cause hearing loss; limited exposure to sound over 115 decibels will cause hearing loss.

Source: Office of Noise Abatement and Control, U.S. Environmental Protection Agency.

(a)　　　　(b)

FIGURE 19–12 Destruction of hair cells in organ of Corti. Scanning electron micrographs of hair cells from the organ of Corti before (a) and after (b) exposure to 24 hours of loud noise, comparable to that of a loud rock concert. On some of the hair cells, the orderly arrangement of cilia has been disrupted. Other hair cells have degenerated, losing their cilia.

rarefaction (Figure 19–10), higher-amplitude waves have greater compression and can produce great pressure. A loud noise, such as the roar of a jet engine, can cause enough pressure within the external auditory canal to rupture the eardrum. Workers around jetports must wear ear defenders to avoid such damage.

Millions of people are going deaf, although they do not realize it. Since we converse at 60 decibels, losses below that level often go unnoticed. For example, a person who has suffered a 40% hearing loss may not be aware of the loss because such a person still can hear other people conversing. Higher levels of speech comprehension may cover up the actual damage. We all tend to tune out extremes of noise. Unfortunately, the insidious damage goes on, and the ability to turn off sound in the brain by accommodation may result in an irreversible change and inability to turn on hearing.

transmitter substances that activate the neurons with which they synapse. The neurons then produce action potentials that travel along the auditory nerves to the brain for interpretation. The hair cells of the cochlea are arranged in sequence, from those stimulated by low-frequency waves (low-pitched sounds) at the base all the way up to those stimulated by high-frequency sounds at the apex, rather like the keys of a piano. The neurons from each region of the cochlea run to slightly different areas in the brain, and the pitch sensation we experience depends upon the brain area stimulated. High-amplitude vibrations cause similar high-amplitude oscillations of cochlear fluid, which in turn produce more intense stimulation of the hair cells and transmission of more impulses to the brain per unit time, interpreted by the brain as loudness. Very high amplitude waves (very loud sounds) can damage the sensitive hearing apparatus (Box 19A). Variations in the pattern of hair cells stimulated by secondary sound waves are interpreted by the brain as variation in tone quality.

Why is it necessary to have such a complex setup to stimulate the organ of Corti? If sound waves were to strike the cochlear fluid and the organ of Corti directly, they could not exert sufficient pressure to make it vibrate because fluid is more resistant to flow than air. The eardrum is a relatively large surface (70 mm²) and amplifies the sound waves that strike it. The sound waves are transmitted to the oval window, which has a small surface area (3.2 mm²), by the bones of the middle ear. The total force on the oval window is the same as that on the eardrum, but because the oval window is much smaller, the pressure, that is, the force per unit area, is increased about 22 times ($70 = 3.2 \times 22$). Thus, in transit the increased force per unit area (pressure) of the sound waves is sufficient to set up a rhythmic vibration in the cochlear fluid. This vibrates back and forth in the channel of the cochlea between the oval and round windows and is further amplified. The am-

plified vibrations are then sufficient to stimulate the organ of Corti.

If the middle ear were a closed unit between inner and outer ear, there would be great risk of a ruptured eardrum whenever the air pressure on the eardrum changes. For proper function, the air pressure of the middle ear must equal that outside the eardrum. The safety valve of the ear is the **Eustachian tube,** a short passage connecting the middle ear with the pharynx (Figure 19–10). The pharyngeal opening of the Eustachian tube is opened during swallowing, which allows equalization of pressure; normally it is kept closed by pharyngeal muscles. During ascent or descent in an airplane, the pressures on each side of the eardrum are unequal, and you relieve this condition by "popping" your ears; the procedure allows air to enter the Eustachian tube as you swallow and equalizes the pressure on both sides of the ear drum.

## 19–6 BALANCE AND EQUILIBRIUM

Although it is usually described as a single sense organ, the ear is really concerned with the perception of two totally different kinds of stimuli and fulfills two distinct purposes in our lives. The ear is a sound receptor responsible for the sense of hearing, but it also receives stimuli that make us aware of our movements and enable us to orient ourselves and maintain our equilibrium. The function of orientation is associated with the upper group of fluid-filled **semicircular canals** of the inner ear (Figure 19–13). Three semicircular canals are connected to the cochlea by a **vestibule** containing two chambers called the saccule and the utricle. Each chamber is lined with sensory hairs on which rest crystals of calcium carbonate, called **otoliths.** When we move our head, these crystals pull on some of the hair cells more than others, stimulating them more. These differences in stimulation give rise to action potentials in the axons, which are interpreted by the brain and signal the position of the head at any

Utricle

Membranous duct in superior semicircular canal

Membranous duct in posterior semicircular canal

Membranous duct in lateral semicircular canal

Saccule

Cochlea

(a)

(b)

Grelatinous matrix

Otoconia

Otolithic membrane

Filamentous base

Stereocilia

Hair cell

Supportive cells

Efferent nerve

Afferent nerve

(c) Hair cells in the vestibule

given moment. This gives us our sense of balance.

The three semicircular canals give us our sense of movement and equilibrium. Each canal is oriented in a different plane, and each has a tuft of sensory hairs in a small chamber at its base. When the head is moved, the fluid in the canals lags behind because of its inertia (fluid is resistant to flow). This can be easily understood by a simple experiment. If we place a glass of water in the center of a turntable and start the turntable spinning at first the water in the glass remains stationary. In time, the water will also rotate in the glass, but when we stop the turntable the water continues to spin inside the glass because of its inertia. The lagging fluid within the semicircular canals, like the water in the glass, does not move when the head is first rotated and it exerts increased pressure on the hair cells on the lag side and stimulates action potentials. The different stimuli from the three canals are integrated by the brain, and we can determine the direction and movement of our head from these signals.

The semicircular canals are concerned not

FIGURE 19–14 The sense organs of the skin. (a) Section through the fingertip. (b) The hair and its associated nerve ending.

**403**

**BUILT-IN SIGNAL CORPS: THE SENSE ORGANS**

just with motion itself but with changes in motion. If we move at a constant speed, no motion is detected in the semicircular canals, but stopping or starting motions are both equally effective triggers for activity in the auditory nerve. If we spin on a chair and then stop suddenly, the fluid in the canals keeps moving and continues to stimulate the hair cells so that we detect motion; however, we know from the signals of other sense organs (eyes, touch receptors, and others) that we are stopped and not moving, and so the brain signals that the surroundings must be in motion—the room appears to spin and we may lose our balance.

Impulses in the vestibular apparatus excite the centers of the hindbrain involved in the maintenance of posture and equilibrium, but their activity can stimulate closely related centers and produce other effects—vomiting, for example. The rocking motion of a ship or a plane stimulates the semicircular canals, and these initiate feelings of motion sickness, nausea, headache, and eyestrain because of the secondary involvement of other centers.

## 19–7 TOUCH, TEMPERATURE, AND PRESSURE: SKIN SENSES

Perhaps nothing is more important to a small baby or a person in love than a fond caress, a gentle stroking of the skin with the fingers and the palm of the hands. Even the pressure of a handshake feels good—warm and friendly. The body surface is covered with a thin, touch-sensitive wrapper, the **skin.** The skin is composed of two layers: the thin, veneered upper surface, the **epidermis,** and the much thicker and deeper layer, the **dermis** (Figure 19–14a). The dermis forms a mantle containing arrays of nerve endings, and it is these that represent the major sensory receptors of the skin. Touch, pain, heat, and cold are all felt because signals are sent from the skin to the central nervous system. What are these receptors?

Most of our responses to temperature are

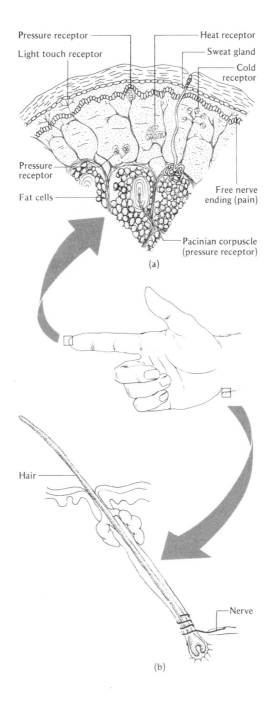

(a)

(b)

probably mediated by superimposed nerve endings (Figure 19–14a); when activated by thermal agitation (heat), these alter membrane permeability to produce an action potential. (The mechanism for cold reception is unclear.) The hairs on the body serve as touch receptors, even though they themselves are dead (Figure 19–14b), for around the base of each hair is a collar of sensory nerves that register disturbances in its position. Pressure on the hair is transmitted to the neuron, and from there signals go to the brain. The most highly innervated hairs are found on the face and around the anus and the genitalia.

The most specialized of the skin receptors is the **Pacinian corpuscle,** which is a pressure receptor. The Pacinian corpuscle looks like an onion, with a central nerve ending surrounded by concentric layers of connective tissue, or lamellae. The corpuscles are found deep in the dermis, especially on the hands and feet and near joints. They are also numerous in the sheetlike connective-tissue mesenteries that hold the internal organs in place. The lamellae of the corpuscle are tightly wrapped around the ending of the nerve and enclose a small fluid-filled space. When pressure is put on this stack of membranes, a number of ion channels are opened, thus permitting ion flow across the membrane, which sets up the generator potential. The greater the pressure (that is, with an increase in stimulus strength), the greater the number of open channels and the more ions flow. Current produced, if sufficient, triggers an action potential. In effect, the Pacinian corpuscle is a biological transducer; it converts pressure stimuli into the electrical energy of a nerve impulse. There is experimental evidence that the determination of pressure change by these corpuscles serves not only for touch sensation but also for the perception of movement.

## SUMMARY

**1.** Sense organs act as transducers, collecting information about the outside world (eyes, ears, nose, touch, and taste receptors) and the internal environment (internal sensory receptors) and converting it into nerve impulses. The cerebral cortex integrates, interprets, stores, and acts on these signals, sending messages to effector organs (muscles and glands).

**2.** The olfactory organs, high in the nose, detect odors. Volatile, soluble substances trigger action potentials that pass along the olfactory nerve to the olfactory bulb and then to the cerebral cortex. Odor discrimination probably depends on molecular architecture. The olfactory receptors are subject to fatigue.

**3.** Taste receptors on the tongue have microvilli at their tips. They are stimulated by specific soluble substances, and messages are sent to the cortex. The tip of the tongue senses sweet substances, the sides sense salty and sour, and the back senses bitter flavors.

**4.** Superimposition of the images from each eye allows for stereoscopic vision. The outer sclera of the eye is transparent in front, forming the cornea. The choroid coat, with blood vessels and pigment, underlies the sclera and is visible through the cornea as the iris.

**5.** The amount of light entering the eye via the pupil is controlled by iris muscles. The lens, suspended by the ciliary body, filters out ultraviolet rays and focuses light onto photoreceptor cells (rods and cones) in the retina at the back of the eye. The fovea is the region of keenest vision.

**6.** The anterior eye chamber is filled with the watery aqueous humor, the posterior chamber with the jellylike vitreous humor.

**7.** The eyelids, eyelashes, eyebrows, and transparent epidermal conjunctiva protect the eye in front. Tears from the lacrimal glands moisten the eye and drain away via the lacrimal duct.

**8.** Dim-light-sensitive rods containing visual purple are abundant at the edges; bright-light-sensitive cones containing three different pigments and responsible for color vision are more abundant at the center. Color perceived depends on the number and kind of cones stimulated.

**9.** Nerve impulses are generated by light energy that alters the form of the pigments in the rods and cones; ionic changes in the cellular fluid produce an action potential that travels to the visual cortex via the optic nerve. Dietary deficiency of vitamin A causes night blindness.

**10.** The optic nerve leaves the eye at the blind spot, which lacks photoreceptors. The nerves from each eye partially cross at the optic chiasma before entering the brain.

**11.** The retinal image is inverted, and reinverted by the visual cortex.

**12.** The cornea focuses light onto the retina; the lens makes fine adjustments (accommodation). Nearsightedness, farsightedness, and astigmatism are caused by faulty accommodation, abnormal eye shape, or irregular corneal curvature, and all can be corrected with eyeglasses.

**13.** Sound energy, traveling as waves of disturbed air molecules, is perceived by the ear, which can discriminate volume (as a function of sound wave amplitude), tone quality (as a function of secondary air vibrations), and pitch (as a function of sound wave frequency).

**14.** The external ear (auricle) collects sound waves. The tympanum between the external and middle ear amplifies the vibrations and in turn sets the malleus, incus, and stapes of the middle ear vibrating. The stapes transmits the vibrations to the cochlear fluid in the inner ear (labyrinth).

**15.** In the inner ear, hair cells of the organ of Corti in the cochlea rub against the tectorial membrane and action potentials are transmitted to the cortex via the auditory nerve. Hair cells of the cochlea are sequentially arranged according to frequency (pitch) perception. Amplitude is reflected by oscillations of cochlear fluid, intensity of hair cell stimulation, and transmission of more or fewer impulses to the brain per unit time. Variation in the pattern of hair cell stimulation reflects tone quality.

**16.** Loud sounds produce great pressure in the ear and can cause irreversible damage to the hair cells in the organ of Corti or rupture an eardrum.

**17.** The Eustachian tube connects the middle ear with the pharynx and equalizes air pressure between middle and outer ear.

**18.** The semicircular canals and vestibule of the inner ear are responsible for maintaining balance and equilibrium. When the head is moved, otoliths stimulate sensory hairs in the vestibule of the inner ear and the fluid inertia in the semicircular canals stimulates sensory hairs in a basal chamber.

**19.** The skin, composed of epidermis and dermis, contains an array of variously distributed touch, pressure, and temperature receptors.

## KEY WORDS

| | | | |
|---|---|---|---|
| | aqueous humor | optic chiasma | stirrup (stapes) |
| | posterior chamber | accommodation | oval window |
| transducers | vitreous humor | nearsighted | round window |
| olfactory organs | conjunctiva | farsighted | cochlea |
| taste buds | eyelids | astigmatism | organ of Corti |
| sclera | eyelashes | sound energy | tectorial membrane |
| cornea | eyebrows | frequency | Eustachian tube |
| choroid coat | tears | pitch | threshold of hearing |
| pupil | lacrimal glands | volume | bel |
| iris | lacrimal duct | amplitude | decibel |
| albinism | inverted retina | tone quality | semicircular canals |
| lens | night blindness | external ear (auricle) | vestibule |
| ciliary body | fovea | middle ear | otoliths |
| retina | peripheral vision | inner ear (labyrinth) | skin |
| rods | tunnel vision | tympanum (ear drum) | epidermis |
| cones | optic disc or blindspot | hammer (malleus) | dermis |
| anterior chamber | optic nerve | anvil (incus) | Pacinian corpuscle |

## TOPICS FOR REVIEW AND DISCUSSION

1. Discuss the statement, The sensory receptor itself does not determine sensation.
2. Describe the structure and function of the human eye.
3. How do we hear? Discuss the relationship of noise pollution to deafness.
4. How are the senses of taste and smell related?
5. What is the fovea?
6. How do rods and cones function in vision?
7. Describe some disorders of the eye and how they may be corrected.
8. What is the relationship of vitamin A to vision?
9. Why are sense organs called biological transducers?
10. Are there only five senses? If not, why not?

## C.I.A. Data Show 14-Year Project on Controlling Human Behavior

The Central Intelligence Agency conducted a 14-year program to find ways to "control human behavior" through the use of chemical, biological and radiological material, according to agency documents made public by John Marks, a freelance journalist. "Drugs were part of it," he said, and "so were such other techniques as electric shock, radiation, ultrasonics, psychosurgery, psychology and incapacitating agents, all of which were referred to in documents I have received."

According to Mr. Marks's documents and an earlier Senate investigation, the C.I.A. conducted secret medical experiments from 1949 through 1963 under the code names Bluebird, Artichoke, MK Ultra and MK Delta. The C.I.A. inspector general report in 1963 described the program as the "research and development of chemical, biological and radiological materials capable of employment in clandestine operations to control human behavior."

Does the above excerpt from *The New York Times* reflect public paranoia about the covert actions of the CIA, or does it have basis in fact? Is it possible to modify human behavior by means of drugs, psychosurgery, and the like?

The answer must be a qualified yes. As long ago as the early 1960s, researchers such as Jose Delgado reported using electrical stimulation to change the brain waves of a chimpanzee, to stop a charging bull, to make a female monkey reject her children, and to perform other similar feats. Delgado said that his experimental results seemed to "support the distasteful conclusion that motion, emotion, and behavior can be directed by electrical forces and that humans can be controlled like robots by pushbuttons." By combining classic concepts about the brain with computer technology and sophisticated engineering principles, scientists are in fact discovering new ways of modifying behavior. To what use are these techniques being put?

In epilepsy, seizure control has traditionally depended on anticonvulsant drugs, but for a small number of so-called intractable epileptics, these drugs are ineffective. For these patients, tiny surgically implanted electrodes act as brain-wave circuit breakers, cutting back on the number of impulses that provoke epileptic seizure. The standard treatment of shaking palsy (Parkinson's disease) involves taking large doses of L-dopa, a chemical that can produce multiple side effects that limit and preclude its use. Experiments with a cannula technique, by which tiny channels can be made in the brain itself, can get around this problem. Through the cannula small amounts of the key treatment chemical, dopamine, can be delivered to the precise spot in the brain where the deficiency lies.

A researcher in California is attempting to restore motion to the arms and legs of monkeys experimentally paralyzed by strokes by using electrodes implanted in their lower brain stems. Cingulotomy, boring holes in the skull and cauterizing bundles of nerve cells that connect various parts of the limbic region of the brain, has produced improvements in alcoholic and schizophrenic patients. Removal of part of the amygdala reduced the tendency toward violent, even homicidal rage in patients. With the help of systems engineering, limited visual and auditory perception may become available to the blind and the deaf. Hyperkinetic children by the thousands are being treated and apparently calmed with drugs such as Ritalin.

It should be emphasized that all of this work is aimed at finding new techniques to help those stricken with brain-associated disorders and not at creating a brain-controlled population.

# 20

# Animal and Human Behavior

## 20–1 WHY BEHAVE?

It has been so long since you've seen one another. Where has the time gone? How many years ago was it that you went to school together, spent the summer at the beach, and talked over the problems that you'd had the night before? Now the time for reunion is here at last. With great anticipation you approach the house. Nervously you finger the doorbell, almost taken aback by the measured sound of its chimes. Thoughts of the past race through your mind, causing a smile to cross your lips. What fun it will be to relive those days that you shared together! Suddenly, the door opens wide: your uplifted spirits vanish and your facial expression changes from delightful pleasure to stark terror. Lunging forward toward you is a large, ferociously barking dog; its sharp, white teeth gnash and powerful jaws grip your arm. Fear! Your movements become defensive—you raise your arm to protect your face, you move backward attempting to get the dog away from you, and your heartbeat quickens. You are frightened, and have good reason to be so.

The response of the dog to your presence, and your reaction to it, are examples of behavior. Succinctly, **behavior** is externally directed activity, often involving the response of an organism to an environmental situation. Responses may include motion or cessation of motion in part or all of the body, or secretion from glands. Responses may be initiated by signals from the environment, such as an attacking dog, the presence of food, or a prospective mate, or they may be initiated by internal signals, such as hunger, thirst, or hormonal changes (Box 20A).

In its many forms, behavior is generally adaptive, that is, an animal responds to appropriate stimuli in order to survive and reproduce itself. Your reaction to an attacking dog was a directed and purposeful action designed to promote your survival. The dog also acted appropriately to promote *its* survival. Accommodations to environmental circumstances such as these tend to promote the well-being of the individual. Other examples of behavioral adjustments could benefit the individual in providing food and shelter and in activities related to perpetuation of the species: mate selection, care and rearing of the young, and the establishment of a social order.

By and large the machinery that mediates behavioral responses in an animal is the nervous system.[1] The receipt of stimuli by sense organs is usually the first event in behavior, the input to the system. Reaction of an effector such as a muscle or gland is the last event in behavior, the output. Between the two lies a connecting link, the communication or coordinating channels of the nervous system. For example, when the sight and sound of a hostile dog were received by your senses, messages were transmitted via nerves to the appropriate effectors, and action was taken in accordance with these messages.

Since the nervous system and behavior are so intimately related to one another, it is to be expected that what an animal does will vary according to the capacities of its nervous system. Thus, if animal nervous systems are thought of as arrangements of neuronal "wires," then a simple wiring diagram composed of a few neurons would limit the kinds of behaviors that could be displayed by its possessor. Conversely, a wiring arrangement containing many neurons with the possibility for an almost infinite array of complicated nerve-to-nerve hookups would be matched by complex and exceedingly intricate behavior patterns. This is exactly what we see in animal behavior. However, circuitry is only one facet of behavioral activity. Behavior is also influenced by the state of development of the nervous system during an animal's lifetime. For example, an undeveloped or immature nervous system is capable of much simpler activities than a mature system, as witnessed by the behavioral changes that take place during the development of an infant into a young child. In addition, nervous function (and thus behavior) is affected by repeated performance and by the environmental changes that have been impressed on it. This component of behavior involves learning, in which an individual's behavior may vary from time to time because previous experiences can modify the response to a particular stimulus. For example, a second

---

[1] Plants lack both nervous and muscular systems; therefore they do not exhibit the motor activities that are generally referred to as behavior. Plant movements, often called **tropisms**, involve long-term activity performed over a long period of time. Most of these activities are under the control of hormone-influenced growth patterns.

visit to your long-lost friend might produce some trepidation on your part, rather than your previous pleasant anticipation. Now you know that there might be a ferocious dog on the other side of the door, and perhaps you will take precautions to avoid a repeat performance of your first visit. You have learned by experience.

Animals with simple or immature nervous systems tend to exhibit fairly fixed, or stereotyped, behavioral responses, although these may be reversible; animals with more complex or highly developed nervous systems have an increased range of responses and are generally capable of learning; they can respond to their environment with much greater plasticity. In humans, the fixed, or stereotyped, components of behavior play a minor role.

What we call behavior, therefore, is produced by the sum total of all the visible and invisible influences of the past and the present that traverse the neuronal wires, together with the reactions of effectors. Through behavioral adaptations, individuals as well as species can survive the continuing changes that take place in the environment. In addition, through learning and experience animals need not be endowed with fixed programs of genetic instructions designed to meet every situation or contingency; rather, they can adjust to particular events at certain points in time with great plasticity, or great specificity.

## 20–2 TOWARD UNDERSTANDING BEHAVIOR

The intricate patterns of behavior observed in many animals would not be possible without a muscular system of considerable complexity. Indeed, it is probably true that until a fairly complex muscular system evolved, intricate patterns of behavior were impossible even though the nervous system may have contained the potential for such behavior. Thus, the behaviors displayed by animals depend on a close interplay of the nervous and muscular systems.

When animal behavior is studied on a comparative basis, the animals with simpler nervous systems, tend to show relatively fixed, or stereotyped, responses to a stimulus or set of stimuli. These responses, called taxes, reflexes, or instincts, are in essence inherited properties of the nervous system. Their occurrence and relative importance in the animal kingdom is illustrated in Figure 20–1. In animals, such as birds and mammals (including ourselves), stereotyped patterns make up a smaller part of the behavioral repertoire: taxes are almost nonexistent; simple reflexes, though important, make up a small portion of the total; and variable modes of behavior, such as learning and reasoning, become more prominent. In these animals, patterns of behavior develop or are refined and altered during the lifetime of the individual, and considerable plasticity in behavioral activity is displayed.

Those who study behavior attempt to understand patterns of activity by looking at their subject in a variety of ways. Most begin by simply observing and then describing behavioral patterns. The dog wags its tail as its owner approaches, or the male dog lifts its leg and urinates on a tree. Then they go on to ask, How does this activity promote survival of the animal? Of what *use* is it in the life of the animal? For example, does the behavior avoid conflict? Is it used to mark a territory? Does it enable mating to take place? And finally, through experimentation, behavioral scientists seek to find answers to the question, What makes the behavior happen? In other words, what causes, or promotes it? As is the case with so many areas of human inquiry, opinions differ not so much with respect to observation and description of behavioral phenomena, but in interpretation of their usefulness in the life of the animal and their causative factors.

During the twentieth century, two schools of thought emerged in the field of animal behavior. One group, the **behaviorists,** were primarily experimental psychologists who

© Walt Disney Productions

© Walt Disney Productions

**BOX 20A Purpose is in the mind of the beholder**

People have watched and wondered about animal activities since they first were capable of wonder; however, as a distinct field of study, animal behavior is a newcomer to the scientific scene. The reasons for this are simple enough: behavior is a complex subject that involves the synthesis of several disciplines—neurophysiology endocrinology, evolutionary biology, ecology, and mathematics. Gaps in our knowledge in these areas limit advances in our understanding of why animals behave the way they do. Furthermore, some observers tend to regard much of animal behavior as purposeful, the result of animal consciousness or awareness, and to assume that human desires and a capacity for reason are shared by other animal species. "The animal does this or that because it *wants* . . ." is a common way of describing so-called animal will. This sounds absurd, yet we say a wasp "gets angry," that so-and-so is "clever as a fox," and that birds "love" their babies. Why do we use such phrases? Part of the reason lies in the nature of our language. Human language contains a built-in bias for implying human attitudes, purposes, and motives to animal activities, and this tends to limit the kinds of words we use to describe behavior. The attribution of human conscious attitudes and emotions to animals is called **anthropomorphism,** literally, "human form." Suffice it to say that anthropomorphism is intellectually dangerous and scientifically misleading. Thus, the creations of Walt Disney—Mickey Mouse and Donald Duck to name but two—demonstrate the gamut of human emotions—fear, love, anger, bashfulness—and they delight because they are so human, but in the real world the attribution of such human characteristics to ducks, mice, or other species is totally unwarranted. There is no evidence that conscious awareness—a product of the human brain—is experienced by other organisms. Thus, we should not say that a writhing lobster placed in boiling water feels pain, since the nervous system of the lobster is so very different from the human nervous system that such an extrapolation cannot easily be made. Until evidence to the contrary is presented, it is safer not to apply descriptions of pain, fear, love, desire, and so on to animals other than human beings.

Anthropomorphism has impeded the development of the science of behavior, and it has an ally in teleology. **Teleology** assumes that an animal has an acknowledged goal for its activity. Thus, to say that wings were developed by birds *in order to fly,* or that the heart beats faster *in order to* obtain more oxygenated blood is entirely incorrect. Rather, birds are able to fly *because* they have wings, and the heart obtains more oxygenated blood as a *result* of beating faster.

Both teleology and anthropomorphism are scientifically unproductive and should be avoided.

The British biologist C. Lloyd Morgan (1852–1936) rebelled against the use of anthropomorphism and applied an old principle of logic called Ockham's razor to behavior. (Ockham's razor was named after the fourteenth-century scholar William of Ockham; the allusion to the razor indicates the cutting out of superfluousness.) **Ockham's razor** states that, given a choice of possible explanations for a given phenomenon, the simplest is to be considered the most probable. **Morgan's canon** is a restatement of Ockham's razor, to wit: the actions of an animal should be interpreted in terms of the simplest mechanisms that explain such behavior and permit predictions of future behavior under similar circumstances. (Thus, the writhing of a boiled lobster may be interpreted in the following manner. The sense organs of the lobster receive temperature stimuli that travel along reflex pathways and result in muscle movements; in the natural environment of a lobster, such movements would be clearly adaptive, contributing to the survival of the individual by enabling it to avoid high water temperatures. No conscious awareness, such as pain, need be invoked to describe the lobster's response. Note, however, that the description does not rule out such a possibility.)

Morgan's canon eliminated consciousness in the description of animal behavior and did much to eliminate anthropomorphic interpretations of animal activity.

FIGURE 20–1 A schematic portrayal of the changes that occur in the modes of adaptive behavior in the various kinds of animals. (From V. G. Dethier and E. Stellar, *Animal Behavior, 3rd ed.,* Englewood Cliffs, New Jersey, Prentice-Hall, 1970.)

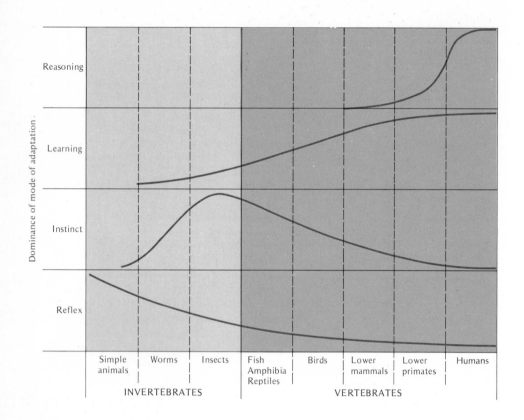

learning. On the other hand, the behaviorists were chastised by the ethologists because they restricted their studies to inbred laboratory subjects and highly artificial environments, and because of their perhaps unjustified extrapolations to human behavior. Further, the ethologists said that the behaviorists tended to ignore the genetic basis for behavior. In essence the two schools of thought boil down to this: is behavior learned or is it innate (hereditary)? Furthermore, which is more important in explaining observed behavior—nature (genes or unlearned behavior) or nurture (experience or learned behavior)? Unfortunately, the nature versus nurture conflict assumes that there are only two distinct and mutually exclusive kinds of behavior, and that each is governed by very different laws. Closer examination of behavioral activity shows that the simple classification of behavior into instinctive (unlearned) versus learned is of limited value. More important is how the behavior develops and how it is adaptive in the life of an animal. Most animals show an interaction of both kinds of behavior; frequently, one may depend upon the other, as we shall see.

## 20–3 SIMPLER TYPES OF BEHAVIOR

### Taxes

The oriented body movements made by animals toward or away from specific stimuli are called **taxes** (singular: **taxis**). Responses toward or away from light, for example, are called **phototaxes;** responses to gravity are called **geotaxes.** If you open a drawer containing a cockroach, the animal responds to the light by moving away from it (a **negative phototaxis**). A newborn rat, its eyes still unopened, moves upward when placed on an inclined plane resting on the surface of a table, indicating that it has a negative response to gravity (a **negative geotaxis**). Behavioral responses may be the result of interplay between two or more taxes. For example, a goldfish in a bowl of water

based their work on the work of an American, J. B. Watson. The behaviorists tried to understand how learning takes place, and they did so by conducting laboratory experiments. They sought to modify behavior in the laboratory by training animals with reinforcement, that is, a positive reward of food or a negative one of electric shock. The Skinner box and the maze were the standard tools of the behaviorists (Box 20B). The white rat became their favorite test animal. The other school of behavior arose in Europe in the early 1900s and consisted of individuals trained in zoology rather than psychology. They called their scientific study of behavior ethology. The **ethologists** studied a variety of animal species both in the laboratory and in the animals' natural environment. They focused most of their attention on birds, fishes, and insects—ani-

mals with relatively fixed, stereotyped behavior patterns. Generally speaking, ethologists do not seek to modify behavior experimentally by training, mazes, and the like, but they examine the role of behavior in an animal's natural environment.

The differing attitudes between ethologists and behaviorists, the varied experimental schemes, and the different kinds of experimental subjects promoted strongly divergent opinions about the mechanisms involved in animal behavior. Clashes between the ethologists and behaviorists were a part of the scientific scene more than 40 years ago, and to a degree the conflict continues to this very day. The ethologists, claimed the behaviorists, tended to explain behavior primarily on the basis of genetically programmed instinct and drive and essentially neglected the importance of orients with the belly side down, responding to both light and gravity. If one destroys the inner ear of the goldfish, where the gravity receptors are located, the fish literally stands on its tail, unable to receive gravitational stimuli, and responds only to the light.

Although these examples of taxes tend to be rather fixed in their response patterns, they are not so rigidly determined that they are without variation. Other factors may modify the basic response. For example, a cockroach in a container that has both a dark and a light side will seek the dark side, but if given an electric shock on the dark side only, it will reverse its normally negative phototaxis. In the simplest sense, the animal has learned. The negative geotaxis of a newborn rat changes when its eyes open and it can respond visually to the edges of the inclined plane. Instead of moving directly toward the upper end of the plane, it may turn around and come down onto the table surface on which the inclined plane rests. Clearly animals respond to more than a single environmental stimulus at one time.

Although some animals in their immature stages will respond to external stimuli in rather simple and fixed ways that we call taxes, the movements need not be "forced," or incapable of modification; rather, they are best described as *relatively* fixed. In addition, taxes may be components in more complex behavioral activity.

## Reflexes

Taxes involve responses of the entire body to a stimulus. **Reflexes** involve responses of a part of the body to a stimulus. Both responses tend to be stereotyped and are derived from the wiring pattern of the nervous system. Thus, when you raise your arm to protect your face from an attacking dog, you respond with reflex actions (See also Chapter 18, page 382). Although the difference between a taxis and a reflex is often determined by the amount of the body

involved in the response, this is not absolute. The knee jerk is a reflex involving only the lower limb, but if goldfishes or cats are turned on their backs, they right themselves by means of a reflex involving almost all parts of the body. Indeed, the taxes of the cockroaches, newborn mice, and the goldfishes involve a series of reflexes. In this sense, the reflex is a fundamental unit of behavior; to a degree, some of the most complex patterns of behavior may be described as the sum total of an array of reflexes. As a consequence, some students of behavior suggest that even the complex behavior of humans can be reduced to combinations of stereotyped (innate or inborn) reflexes and acquired (learned) or conditioned reflexes. The description of complex behavior in higher organisms by reflexes alone cannot be universally applied, however; consequently more complex behavioral activities are designated by other terms.

## 20–4 MORE COMPLEX TYPES OF BEHAVIOR

### Instinct

The term **instinct** as applied to animals refers to fairly complex, stereotyped behavior patterns that are commonly found among members of a particular species. The animal performs the behavior in a functional way the first time it encounters an appropriate cue provided that the animal is of a certain age and motivational state. Generally, instincts are adaptive. Thus, a canary builds a nest just like other canaries even though it is raised in a laboratory and has never seen another canary building a nest. More striking is the fact that the canary builds the nest at the right time of the year so that it is ready to receive the eggs the bird will soon lay. How does the canary "know" how to construct a nest from the proper materials and at such a time that the nest will be ready for the eggs? The answer is instinct.

Human beings, we are often told, are

nothing more than animals among animals, naked apes dominated by their killer instincts. Indeed, the novelist Robert Ardrey wrote, "Man is a predator whose natural instinct is to kill with a weapon." The ethologist and Nobel laureate Konrad Lorenz supports this view by observing that most animal-killing carnivores have instincts inhibiting them from indiscriminately killing their own kind, with two exceptions: rats and humans. Is there in fact a human killer instinct? Can it be identified?

Before attempting an answer (Box 20C), let us consider some examples of instinctive behavior so that we may better see how these relate to notions of human instincts.

### Instinctive behavior patterns

Reproductive behavior in the three-spined stickleback, a brightly colored fresh-water fish, consists of a series of complex behavioral acts: migration, territoriality, aggression, nesting, mating, and parental care (Figure 20–2a). In nature, under the influence of increasing amounts of daylight during the spring, there is an increase in gonadal hormones. The male sticklebacks move out of the school in which they ordinarily live, and, directed by temperature, they migrate to warm, shallow water, where they establish a territory, build a nest, and defend the territory against other male intruders. A male attracts a female by a zigzag courtship dance, leads the female to the nest, fertilizes the eggs, cares for the developing eggs by fanning them, and, once the eggs are hatched, protects the young. Such behavior tempts an anthropomorphic interpretation: it almost looks as if the stickleback "knows" exactly what must be done. Careful experimentation, however, has shown that the animal follows a preprogrammed, fixed action pattern, which remains blocked until an appropriate stimulus (called a **releaser**) activates the behavior. Releasers are sign stimuli that trigger instinctive behavior patterns because the animal possesses an acute neural sensitivity

## BOX 20B Skinner's utopia: panacea or path to hell?

*"Boy, have I got this guy conditioned! Every time I press the bar down, he drops in a piece of food."*

I've had only one idea in my life—a true *idée fixe*. To put it as bluntly as possible—the idea of having my own way. Control expresses it. The control of human behavior. In my early experimental days it was a frenzied, selfish desire to dominate. I remember the rage I used to feel when a prediction went awry. I could have shouted at the subjects of my experiments. "Behave, damn you! Behave as you ought!"

B. F. Skinner *Walden Two*, 1948.

The speaker is T. E. Frazier, a character in *Walden Two* and the fictional founder of the utopian community described in that novel. He is also an alter ego of the author, Burrhus Frederic Skinner, who is both a psychology professor and an institution at Harvard. As leader of the "behavioristic" psychologists, who liken man to a machine, Skinner is vigorously opposed by humanists and by Freudian psychoanalysts.

Skinner's reasoning is that freedom and free will are no more than illusions; like it or not, man is already controlled by external influences. Some are haphazard; some are arranged by careless or evil men whose goals are selfish instead of humanitarian. The problem, then, is to design a culture that can, theoretically, survive; to decide how men must behave in order to ensure its survival in reality; and to plan environmental influences that will guarantee the desired behavior. Thus, in the Skinnerian world, man will refrain from polluting, from overpopulating, from rioting, and from making war, not because he knows that the results will be disastrous, but because he has been conditioned to want what serves group interests.

Is such a world really possible? Skinner believes that it is; he is certain that human behavior can be predicted and shaped exactly as if it were a chemical reaction. The way to do it, he thinks, is through "behavioral technology," a developing science of control that aims to change the environment rather than people, that seeks to alter actions rather than feelings, and that shifts the customary psychological emphasis on the world inside men to the world outside them. Central to Skinner's approach is a method of conditioning that has been used with uniform success on laboratory animals: giving rewards to mold the subject to the experimenter's will. According to Skinner and his followers, the same technique can be made to work equally well with human beings.

Underlying the method is the Skinnerian conviction that behavior is determined not from within but from without. Skinner insists that actions are determined by the environment; behavior is shaped and maintained by its consequences." As Skinner sees it, environments are defective when they fail to make desirable behavior pay off and when they resort to punishment as a means of stopping undesirable behavior. In short, it is punishment or reward that determines whether a particular kind of behavior becomes habitual. But Skinner believes that punishment is generally an ineffective means of control. "A person who has been punished," he writes, "is not less inclined to behave in a given way; at best, he learns how to avoid punishment."

Rats and pigeons were the center of laboratory experiments in which Skinner controlled behavior by setting up "contingencies of reinforcement"—circumstances under which a particular bit of desired behavior is "reinforced" or rewarded to make sure it will be repeated. The behavior Skinner demanded of his pigeons was bizarre—for pigeons. He made them walk figure eights, for example, by reinforcing them with food at crucial moments. By a similar process, Skinner has conditioned pigeons to dance with each other, and even to play ping pong.

All of these conditioning feats were accomplished with the now famous Skinner box. It is a soundproof enclosure with a food dispenser that a rat can operate by pressing a lever, and a pigeon by pecking a key. The dispenser does not work unless the animal has first performed according to a specially designed "schedule of reinforcement."

Skinner himself admits that "pigeons aren't people," but points out that his ideas have already been put to practical use in schools, mental hospitals, penal institutions, and business firms. Skinner-inspired teaching machines have begun to produce what amounts to an educational revolution. Machines now in use in scores of cities across the country present pupils

FIGURE 20–2 The courtship sequence of the three-spined stickleback. (a) A female with a swollen belly (top right) enters the territory of the male. The male begins a zigzag dance, courts, and leads her to the nest. When she enters the nest (bottom), the trembling movements of the male elicit spawning. Later, the male will enter the nest and fertilize the eggs. (b) Schematic drawing showing the courtship sequence. Each action serves as a releaser for the following action. (From N. Tinbergen, *The Study of Instinct,* New York, Oxford University Press, 1951.)

with a succession of easy learning steps. At each one, a correct answer to a question brings instant reinforcement, not with the grain of corn that rewarded the pigeon, but with a printed statement—supposedly just as satisfying—that the answer is right.

Skinner is skeptical about democracy. Observing that society is already using such ineffective means of behavioral control as persuasion and conventional education, he insists that men of good will must adopt more effective techniques, using them for "good" purposes to keep despots from using them for "bad" ones. In his planned society, he says, control would be balanced by countercontrol, "probably by making the controller a member of the group he controls." This would help to ensure that punishment would never be inflicted, Skinner maintains, adding that it was the use of "aversive control" (punishment) that doomed Hitler.

The ultimate logical dilemma in Skinner's thinking is this: What are the sources of the standards of good and evil in his ideal society? Indeed, who decides even what constitutes pleasure or pain, reward or punishment, when man and his environment can be limitlessly manipulated? To one writer, Skinner's "utopian projection is less likely to be a blueprint for the Golden Age than for the theory and practice of hell."

(a)

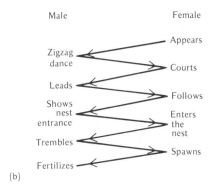

(b)

to these stimuli. For example, a male stickleback courts a female stickleback only if she has a swollen abdomen. However, a male will also display courtship activity if presented with a wooden model that has a swollen belly or if there are females of other species that are gravid. Thus, the specific releaser for male courtship is the swollen abdomen. The male's aggressive defense of the territory also depends on releasers: the red underbelly of a male or a model of wood that is painted red triggers aggressive displays. Indeed, the ethologist Niko Tinbergen reported that a male stickleback showed an aggressive display when a red mailtruck passed by the window on which an aquarium was placed. Leading the female to the nest requires the appropriate female response to the male's courtship dance, and the prodding of the female by the male induces her to spawn. If the experimenter prods a female with a glass rod, she also spawns. The presence of eggs in the nest releases parental behavior, but if the eggs are removed the male shows only courtship displays. In other words, the programmed behavior of the male will not continue unless and until the appropriate releaser is present (Figure 20–2b). This elaborate behavior in sticklebacks is adaptive in that it assists in bringing together and synchronizing the male and female mating act and tends to prohibit errors in the choice of a mating partner.

What governs the instinctive behavior of an animal such as the stickleback? How is it that out of a wide variety of environmental stimuli presented to an individual, only one specific stimulus triggers an appropriate response? It is believed that the response to a stimulus is related to the internal condition of the animal; this internally initiated condition or degree of readiness is called **drive.** Drives are usually directed toward specific goals, and once the goal has been attained the drive energy is reduced, a condition known as **satiation.** Thus, one may speak of an animal's drive for food (hunger

FIGURE 20–3 Herring-gull models and a knitting needle were used to determine the character of the stimulus that elicits response from young gulls. The length of the bar on the right indicates the relative number of responses obtained from each model.

Note that the highest number of responses was obtained from the knitting needle. (From N. Tinbergen, *The Study of Instinct,* New York, Oxford University Press, 1951.)

drive), a mate (sex drive), water (thirst drive), and so on.

In considering drives and releasers as well as the quick execution and rapid termination of instinctive behavior patterns, Konrad Lorenz proposed that drive energy builds up within an animal. An animal in this state would tend to appear restless. Ordinarily the release, or discharge, of activity would be prevented until a specific releaser stimulus was received by a special center in the nervous system, called the **innate releasing mechanism (IRM).** Upon presentation of the releaser, drive energy is released, and a specific instinctive response is produced.

Lorenz' proposal suggests an explanation for some kinds of behavioral events that occur in the life of an animal. For example, when caught in a conflict situation between two opposing drives, some animals will respond with apparently irrelevant behavior called **displacement activity.** A nesting bird, when threatened by a predator, is torn between two conflicting drives: to incubate the eggs and to escape the predator. Rather than either of these, it may begin to inappropriately nibble at its feathers. Displacement activity occurs at the point where the two opposing drives are of equal intensity. This was rather beautifully shown by W. C. Dilger in investigating the territorial behavior of male thrushes. Like many male birds, thrushes warn other males away from their territories by loud singing. Dilger placed a stuffed thrush near a loudspeaker and played a recording of a singing male thrush. The bird in whose territory the speaker was located responded as though his territory was being attacked. If the recording was played softly, aggressive behavior was released and the defending bird attacked the stuffed bird. If the volume was high, escape behavior was released and the defending bird retreated. By alternately raising and lowering the volume, Dilger could make the bird move toward or away from the speaker, even to the extent of teetering on one leg when its conflicting attack and escape drives were perfectly balanced. At

this point, however, some birds began to scratch their heads, preen their wings, peck at the ground, or even go to sleep. The thrush, it seems, had to do something with its behavioral energy: if it could not do something relevant to the situation, it did something irrelevant.

Some authors believe that the thwarting of a single drive may also produce displacement behavior. For example, a thirsty dove prevented from drinking by a sheet of glass in front of its water bowl will peck at the ground nearby. Thwarting or conflict in human behavior is also often resolved by displacement activity; when an individual becomes angered, but for cultural or other reasons is prevented from expression of this rage in a direct way, the individual may resort to pacing, head scratching, yawning, eating, or stretching. On other occasions, the correct behavioral activity may be released but directed at another, more neutral object; this is called **redirected activity.**

The male stickleback defends the small territory in which he builds his nest. At the

territory boundaries, when another male is confronted, the stickleback's tendency to escape or fight are equally strong. As a consequence, during a boundary encounter the male carries out "nest building" activities, but no true nest is built. A bird that is threatened by an aggressive intruder may attack a branch rather than the intruder. An executive angry about something at work may come home and shout at the children.

What is the adaptive significance of such conflict behavior? It has been suggested that displacement, or redirection, allows the resolution of conflict (that is, the dissipation of built-up drive energy, according to Lorenz') rather than "freezing" the animal in a state of paralyzing indecision.

### How an instinct is learned

The feeding behavior of seagull chicks is thought to be instinctive. When the parent gull lowers its head and points its beak at a week-old chick, the chick shows a complex but highly coordinated pecking behavior. It grasps the parent's beak and pulls it until the parent regurgitates food for the chick. Analysis of the chick pecking behavior showed that a parent gull was not required; a wooden gull head produced the same pecking behavior in the chick, and the strength of that pecking response was dependent on the presence of a spot on the adult beak (Figure 20–3). In an experiment using cardboard cutouts resembling gull heads with different arrangements of painted spots, it was discovered that the specific releaser for chick pecking was not the parent but the shape of the bill and the presence of a spot. Indeed, the greatest pecking response was elicited by a knitting needle with three white bands at the tip! A classical instinct, or so it seemed: a behavior that was unlearned, and preprogrammed. Recently, however, this instinctive pattern was reinvestigated with a number of different questions in mind. Does the chick require practice to perfect its aim? Why doesn't the chick peck at the parent's red legs or other objects? Using painted pictures of parent gulls, it could be shown that as the chicks matured, their pecking accuracy increased. This increased targeting was directly related to visual experience acquired by the chicks after hatching—in other words, learned behavior. By using vertical rods of different dimensions and by varying the speed of movement of these rods, it was possible to determine the "beak" that would stimulate the greatest response in gulls of various ages. An 8-cm rod was preferred no matter what the rate of movement. (This is about the mean beak length seen by the chick.) However, it became apparent that older chicks were much more discriminating— they preferred a live gull parent to a model of a gull. Preliminary experiments also suggested that young chicks could be conditioned in their response by the reward of food—in other words, their innate response could be modified. From this study it was concluded that a newly hatched chick is clumsily coordinated and has a poorly aimed but instinctive peck that is elicited by a simple stimulus—the shape and movement of the beak. As a result of reward, in the form of food, the chick learns the characteristics of the parent, and by practicing pecking, it improves its aim. All this strongly suggests that during the normal development of a so-called instinctive behavior, such as pecking, and perhaps of other stereotyped patterns, there is often a learning component. Behavior is thus a combination of innate and learned responses, not simply the one or the other.

Do we humans have instincts? Yes. Without any previous experience, a newborn infant will instinctively suckle the breast and grasp a rod with its hands so firmly that it can support its own weight. Although these patterns tend to fit the term "instinct," that is, they do not seem to depend on learning, they are not refined without experience. The suckling of the infant at the breast becomes more precise and better coordinated with practice. Similarly, the grasping reactions of the infant tend to improve with

increasing experience. Again, in the normal development of instinctive behavior patterns, there is a learning component. Thus behavior cannot be clearly separated into two distinct entities that can be labeled learned or unlearned: the development of a behavior pattern is a complex mosaic produced by the continual interaction of the developing individual with its enviroment. From this, we should be able to conclude that if human beings have aggressive instincts, they may yet be able to learn to control them (Box 20C).

## Learning

"Your mind," said William James, "is the sum of your experience." Indeed, it is as if we begin our lives with minds like clean slates, devoid of any characters, and without any ideas; in the course of time, however, those slates record all we experience. Consider all that you have experienced since birth, and how your mind has changed as you've matured. You learned to walk, to speak, to read and write, to love, and to behave in thousands of other ways. Where would we be without the capacity to learn? Where and how does learning take place?

The experiences of an organism are somehow indelibly recorded in the tangled web of nerve cells. Enduring changes in nervous function that are based on experience permit an organism to alter its future behavior, a condition called learning. When we speak of enduring changes in nervous function and behavior, what do we mean? How long is "enduring"? The nature of the neural changes that take place during the learning process are still incompletely understood. Moreover, as we all know, some of what we learn does not endure—it is forgotten. Is forgetting the permanent loss of what was learned, or is it merely a condition in which the retrieval of information is impossible? Is it a lost or merely a misplaced volume in our library of information? What is the neurological basis for the storage of information? Without memory, learning is

impossible. Once we can definitively characterize memory, then the basis of permanence or transience of learning will become clearer. That time is not yet here. For the present, let us hedge by saying that **learning** is a more or less permanent alteration in behavior that occurs as a result of experience.

**Habituation.** Perhaps the simplest kind of learning is habituation. **Habituation** occurs when a repeated specific stimulus, presented without reward or punishment, results in a decreased response until it may disappear completely. In a sense, habituation is learning *not* to respond to a particular stimulus. It plays an important role in the lives of animals: through habituation, animals avoid wasting time and energy by dropping out responses that are of little significance in their lives. For example, young birds learn not to take flight at the sight of fluttering leaves; crows in a cornfield eventually ignore a scarecrow; when we hear an unexpected sound our attention is aroused, but if the noise recurs repeatedly, we cease to pay attention and eventually may become unaware of it. The "cocktail-party effect" allows us to pay decreasing attention to the group noise around us to the point where we virtually ignore it. Habituation is one of the basic mechanisms involved in training wild animals: if you carefully handle a freshly caught snake, after some hours it may lie completely still in your hands and will no longer strike because it has become habituated to you.

Habituation can be distinguished from the similar phenomena of fatigue and sensory adaptation because it persists even when a stimulus is withheld for some time. A fatigued muscle will fail to respond after repeated stimulation, but this is reversed after a rest period. The sense of smell quickly adapts to odors until they go unnoticed, but again this adaptation is reversed after a period of rest. If you have ever shopped for perfume, you know that after sampling several smells, you can no longer distinguish between them. In sen-

### BOX 20C Are human beings instinctive killers?

Is there, as some have claimed, a human killer instinct? Do humans have an innate, unlearned tendency to kill other humans? How is, or was, this adaptive in the life of the human species? Some writers have observed that humans have "natural" tendencies that include the acquisition and protection of property—an instinct for territorial aggression. Taken to its ultimate limits, the implication has been that humans instinctively kill their own kind. However, the enormous development of the human cerebral cortex and the associated capacity for learning and reasoning have liberated us from behavior based on simple, stimulus-bound responses. In the face of learning, conscious reasoning, and our cultural inheritance, would humans be compelled to respond to a killer instinct if indeed it were present? If conscious override of instincts is possible in humans, how are we to determine if we now possess, or indeed ever possessed, such a killer instinct?

One way of understanding and tracing the development of human behavior is by comparing ourselves with our closest relatives, the primates. Investigations of monkeys isolated from birth, with no opportunity for learning from other monkeys, show that aggression seems to be innate. (This is not the same as a killer instinct, however.) At the period during their lives when aggressive behavior would usually develop, the monkeys showed aggressive tendencies. The same maturational sequences of affection, fear, and aggression observed in primates occur in humans: aggressive tendencies appear in the first 4 to 5 years of life.

Studies of primates in the wild, however, reveal that these animals tend not to be belligerent unless provoked, and they ordinarily do not kill their own kind. Although they have sharp canine teeth and use tools, they do not use them for tearing at the flesh of their fellow primates since they are primarily vegetarians. By extrapolation, this suggests that humans as primates do not have an evolutionary history based on killing.

To some writers, humans as tool makers are equivalent to humans as weapon users. Is such a conclusion justified? Tools may be used as weapons, but most would agree that the primary use of hammers, scrapers, choppers, and knives was and is as tools rather than as weapons and is learned behavior.

Obviously, aggressive behavior is adaptive. Without some aggressive tendencies, organisms would be at the mercy of the nearest predator and carnivores would never hunt for food; but this is interspecific aggression (between members of different species). Intraspecific aggression (between members of the same species) plays a role in the establishment of social order, mating, territoriality, and other relationships. But for most animals, there are built-in inhibitions against carrying aggressive behavior to the point of killing their own kind. (These are known as appeasement gestures—see page 426.)

If aggression *is* innate in humans, as it appears to be in some primates, it poses interesting questions. What are the stimuli that release human aggressive instincts, for example? What are the behavioral mechanisms that normally turn it off? Is aggression being learned, the instinct for it refined, or is it merely released by watching violent scenes on TV? We have seen in herring gulls and human infants that instinctive behavior patterns can be refined by repetition, practice, and learning. Any system that admits that aggression is nonadaptive in current human society, and perhaps seeks to control it, must take these possibilities into account.

The theory of a killer instinct in humans is not new; it is merely original sin revisited. If war is indeed in our genes, a result of instincts that may not be denied, then presumably we can do little to prevent it if the appropriate releasers are provided. An unfortunate side effect of this theory is that it removes from us all responsibility for war, murder, and the like. Such a pessimistic and misleading view of human behavior does little to aid investigations of the causes of human aggression, which are probably complex and primarily a result of learned behavior.

sory adaptation, sensitivity to stimuli within a given sensory modality is temporarily decreased. Following habituation, however, a response can still be elicited by stimuli other than the specific one to which an animal has habituated, even within the same modality. At a noisy cocktail party, you can focus on and respond to a single speaker while disregarding the general noise around you. Habituated to the noise of cars on a highway, you still respond to the screech of brakes.

**Classical (Pavlovian) conditioning.** Perhaps the most familiar of all dogs is not Lassie, but an unnamed dog that lived in the laboratory of the Russian physiologist Ivan Pavlov (1849–1946). Lassie entertains us, but Pavlov's dog instructs us in the mechanisms by which we learn. What Pavlov did was to take an innate reflex, one already programmed into the nervous system, and transfer its response from one stimulus to another; such behavioral modification is called **classical conditioning.** The experimental design was quite simple. When food was presented to a dog, a copious flow of saliva was produced in the dog's mouth by reflex action. However, if a bell was rung regularly at the same time as food was offered to the dog, the ringing of the bell alone would eventually elicit salivation, even when no food was presented. The bell itself is not a specific stimulus since the dog could be conditioned to salivate on a light signal or the clicking of a metronome, for example. The stimulus of food that normally initiates salivation had been replaced by a **neutral stimulus** (bell, light, clicks, etc.) which prior to the conditioning experience would not produce the response (salivation).

Let us consider another example of classical conditioning involving the reflexive act of limb withdrawal. If we were to administer a mild electric shock to your hand, you would rapidly withdraw your arm. If, however, this shock was regularly preceded by some other stimulus, such as a ringing bell, in time just ringing the bell would cause you to pull away your hand. You have been

conditioned! Both examples illustrate how a neutral stimulus can be made to elicit a response which it would not have prior to training.

How does the reflex activity in classical conditioning differ from the innate reflex itself? Innate reflexes persist for life, and, given the appropriate stimulus, the response will always occur. However, in classical conditioning the reflex activity will not be produced unless certain factors necessary for its continuance are satisfied. Four factors are a necessary part of classical conditioning: contiguity, repetition, reinforcement, and interference.

1. **Contiguity.** There must be a close association of the neutral stimulus (e.g., a ringing bell) and the unconditioned, or **natural, stimulus** (e.g., presented food) so that the events occur within a limited period of time, and the order of presentation is specified. For example, the time interval between the neutral stimulus and the natural one cannot be too great, and the natural stimulus (food) cannot be given first. What dog would salivate if you rang a bell after feeding?
2. **Repetition.** The greater the number of pairings made between neutral and natural stimuli, the greater is the response to the neutral stimulus alone.
3. **Reinforcement.** The strengthening of the conditioned response depends on the pairing of a reward (e.g., presented food) with the neutral stimulus (e.g., a ringing bell).
4. **Interference.** If the neutral stimulus is repeatedly presented alone, then the response that it elicits decreases steadily until it is zero. This is called **extinction.** Pavlov believed extinction was due to new learning that interfered with or inhibited the conditioned response. Thus, the repeated ringing of a bell without any food eventually causes the animal to learn that the bell which once meant "food" no longer does; this results in decreased salivary secretion over a period of time, and ultimately the conditioned response no longer occurs.

The following case has been used to support the view of Pavlov that interference is involved in extinction. If during the early period of training an animal is distracted by a loud noise when the bell is rung, there is a reduction in the response, presumably due to external inhibition. However, if the same distracting stimulus is presented during the period when extinction is occurring, then the strength of the conditioned response is increased, presumably because this removes the interference of the new learning; this phenomenon is called **disinhibition.**

The Pavlovian concepts of extinction and interference may apply to memory and forgetting. There is the story (probably apocryphal) of a well-known biologist who specialized in the classification of fishes and who later in his career became the president of a large western university. One of his first goals was to learn the names of all the students he met on campus; however, when he discovered that for every student's name he learned he forgot the name of a fish, he gave up the task of trying to learn student names!

Similar situations occur in our own lives. When we learn something and then there is a long interval before we are tested on the material, we tend to forget it. Indeed, the more similar the material learned in the interval between the initial learning experience and the time of testing, the greater is the degree of forgetting. If the material is dissimilar, there is less loss during the interval, and if sleep occurs between learning and testing, then forgetting is diminished to even a lesser degree. This is why lessons learned just before going to sleep at night are retained with great clarity in the morning.

**Operant (instrumental) conditioning.** A laboratory rat is enclosed in a soundproof chamber with a food dispenser. The rat is rewarded by a pellet of food whenever it inadvertently presses the lever. Eventually the rat learns to press the lever to obtain a pellet of food (Box 20B). How does such instrumental, or operant, conditioning differ from classical conditioning?

In classical conditioning the learning involved is rather simple and passive. The response elicited by the neutral stimulus is programmed into the nervous system, and there is little variability in the response. The animal hears a bell ring and it salivates. Furthermore, the animal cannot control the stimulus; that is the role of the experimenter. **Operant conditioning** involves a more complex kind of learning, in which the animal exerts some operational control over the stimuli received and over its own response; in addition, the behavioral activity that results has some modifying influence on the environment. Consider the caged rat that presses on the lever to obtain a food pellet. Initially, the animal probably jumped around and quite accidentally struck the lever, but after a number of trials it learned to make the proper response. Now it presses the lever as frequently as it requires food; it has modified its feeding situation by its behavior pattern. This situation is quite different from the bell-food-salivation pattern found in classical conditioning, where the animal's behavior does not modify its environment (food received, in this case).

The learning involved in operant conditioning is not restricted to rats; humans do it, too. Las Vegas gamblers, thousands of them standing like robots in front of the slot machines, pour coin after coin into the slot and pull the levers mechanically for hours on end. What makes them behave so when they are fully aware that the odds are against them, that most often they will lose and not win? Why does a gambler continue to pull the lever of a "one-armed bandit" when the rewards seem so remote? The reason is the same as for the rat. The gambler has learned through experience that occasionally there is a jackpot hit, and thus there is a reward for lever pulling (and money invested, too).

These cases of operant conditioning reveal that an important element involved in this kind of learning (as in classical conditioning) is reinforcement. Reinforcements are of two kinds: (1) rewards that result in a repetition of the behavior pattern and (2) punishments that tend to suppress a particular behavioral response (Box 20B). Without reinforcement—that is, in the absence of reward or punishment—operant conditioning does not take place. Reinforcement procedures are involved in training dogs to "shake hands," "sit up," "fetch," and so on. They are also used in training young children to be social beings. Behavior which pleases the parent is rewarded, that which displeases may be punished, as when a child is praised for voiding in the toilet and perhaps even spanked for wetting the bed. The child is being conditioned to deposit body wastes in the same place as the adult members of the family, making life more pleasant for all concerned.

Reinforcement (as well as contiguity, repetition, and interference) applies to both classical and operant conditioning. However, it is important to recognize that although the factors involved are the same, the responses do differ. In classical conditioning the response is a fixed pattern of behavior (a reflex), but in operant conditioning the animal starts out by expressing a variety of responses that are a part of its behavior repertoire, and later one or more of them are reinforced through training while other, unrewarded responses are either extinguished or subject to habituation. There is another difference: in operant conditioning rewards can be given either after each response or intermittently without reducing the strength of the response (witness the intermittence of gambling rewards!).

What is the adaptive significance of operant conditioning in the life of an animal? The learning developed through such conditioning enables an organism to gain some control over its environment, and as such it promotes its welfare. Some researchers believe most, if not all, learning involves conditioning with reinforcement and is of overriding importance in human behavior (Box 20B).

**Trial-and-error learning and reasoning.** Two dishes are set before you: one is green and the other red. You touch each and rapidly withdraw your hand from the green one because it is hot. Quickly you learn that a green dish means hot. Similarly, a rat placed in a simple T maze learns by **trial and error** that one corridor contains food whereas the other does not. In a short time the food-containing corridor is always selected. In these situations a correct response is rewarded (by food) and an incorrect response is discouraged either by punishment (burning) or by an absence of reward (no food). Obviously, operant conditioning and reinforcement are involved in trial-and-error learning. When you consider your own experiences, you can readily appreciate how much of your learning has been and continues to be based on trial and error. Tastes in food, the ability to play games such as tennis and golf, all involve trial-and-error behavior with reinforcement. In a sense this is a very simple type of problem solving.

Let us now consider a more complex kind of learning situation. You are in a basement room containing two boxes, each 2½ ft in height, and you want to open a window that is 10 ft above the ground. How do you do it? Simply by placing the boxes one on top of the other and climbing on the uppermost one. The problem was solved not by trial and error, but by **reasoning,** or **insight learning.** Reasoning is the ability of an animal to solve a problem or respond correctly to a situation not previously encountered. Reasoning permits organisms such as yourself to apply prior learning to a novel situation and to solve the problem without resorting to trial-and-error behavior. Reasoning is most prevalent in the higher primates and humans.

**Imprinting.** One of the most striking things about a mother duck and her ducklings is how closely they follow her. On land they

FIGURE 20–4 Imprinting can go awry, as seen in these goslings following the famous ethologist Konrad Lorenz. (Thomas McAvoy. *Life Magazine* © 1955 by Time Inc.)

FIGURE 20–5 The parts of the human brain. Many of the major structures of the human brain can be seen on its medial surface. The lines on the cerebral hemisphere represent folds in the cerebral cortex. Note that most of the structures pictured here would be cut in order to prepare a view like this one. The corpus callosum, for example, is made up of fibers running into and out of the plane of the page and connecting the two hemispheres. (From D. Krech, R. S. Crutchfield, and N. Livson, *Elements of Psychology,* 2nd ed., New York, Alfred A. Knopf, 1969.)

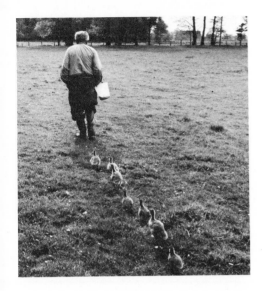

FIGURE 20–4 Imprinting can go awry, as seen in these goslings following the famous ethologist Konrad Lorenz. (Thomas McAvoy. *Life Magazine* © 1955 by Time Inc.)

march in single file, and in the water they swim in linear array, as if tied to an invisible line. What is behind this kind of behavior?

When Konrad Lorenz examined the strong attachment of young birds for their mother, he believed it to result from a special kind of learning in which response to objects presented at a critical period in early life, usually quite restricted in time, were "stamped" into the animal's behavior. The special kind of learning involved came to be called **imprinting.** Such attachment does not have to be directed at a natural object, for newly hatched ducklings will form a more or less irreversible bond to the first large moving object they see after hatching, be it a ball or even the experimenter, and will specifically relate to this object from then on. Figure 20–4 shows a clutch of goslings following Lorenz, on whom they had imprinted. Here, the natural and adaptive value of imprinting has been lost through experimental interference, and instead of staying close to their mother, the animals follow another object. Imprinting in the wild is likely to be adaptive, however, be-

cause the mother is usually the first large moving object seen after hatching. The newborn animal gets a quick behavioral "fix" on its natural parent and is bound to her during its early days when its very survival may depend on the attachment.

Imprinting is a form of learning that profoundly affects social life and mating, and it is particularly strong in certain species of large terrestrial and water birds, such as ducks, where early attachment to the mother

has great survival value. The early experience, presented at a critical developmental period, produces a lasting and almost irreversible effect. Although it is learning, it is apparent that imprinting must be related to special conditions of the nervous system during a restricted period of development, for if the animal is not at this time exposed to the experience, it cannot subsequently be imprinted.

## 20–5 WHERE AND HOW DOES LEARNING OCCUR?

Almost intuitively one feels that learning must occur within the central nervous system, especially in "the great ravelled knot," the brain. We show we believe this when we say, "He hasn't got a thing in his head" in reference to a person of slow learning capacity. How can we determine where learning takes place? Two procedures have been used: neurosurgery, involving removal of a portion of the brain, and electrical stimulation of various loci of the brain. To date, of the large number of studies performed on the brain with an eye toward finding the seat of learning, none have identified a specific site. However, many workers suspect that, in humans at least, the center of greatest importance in many kinds of learning, especially reasoning and the development of language, depends chiefly on one area: the layer of gray matter over the cerebral hemispheres, the cerebral cortex (Figure 20–5). It first appears in reptiles, but shows its greatest development in mammals, especially humans, in whom the cortex is about as large as all the rest of the brain together.

The early anatomists who mapped the brain's cortex found distinct regions that were either sensory or motor in function. There was, however, a vast expanse of the cortex that could not be assigned to either of these categories, and this came to be known as the **association area,** providing a link between sensory and motor activity.

**419**

The neurophysiologists seized upon the association area as the locus of conscious thinking and learning, but later experiments yielded nothing concrete. It is true that destruction of the temporal, frontal, and parietal lobes (Figure 20–5) does produce effects on behavior and on learning, but how do we know that such lesions do not disrupt the normal organization of the brain so that all learning is impaired? No one lesion produces permanent amnesia or inability to learn, but the disruptions do vary in degree. It is as if an animal deprived of a certain region of the brain can compensate and learn with other regions, but at a slower pace. Electrical stimulation of the brain, for example, of the temporal lobes, does produce memory-related experiences, but this does not occur all the time. In addition, how do we know that the electrically stimulated site is the only region activated? It becomes apparent that learning probably occurs at a variety of loci in the brain and there is no single spot responsible for all learning.

By what mechanisms does learning take place? Are the neurons themselves actually changed? A number of possible leads have been suggested recently, but there is no agreement among scientists that any one of them is the sole—or even partial—mechanism involved.

1. **Facilitation.** It has been shown that if a neuron excites other neurons repeatedly through a particular synaptic connection, the passage of stimuli through this pathway is considerably facilitated. Impulses from the same kind of stimulus are not only channeled through the same pathway in the nerve network of the brain but pass through the synaptic gate with greater ease. This principle has been extended to suggest that if use of a neural pathway facilitates transmission, disuse weakens it. Learning thus could involve the well-worn routes of neural transmission.
2. **Growth of nerve pathways.** Although there is little division of neuronal cells after birth, it is entirely possible that learning involves the development of recurrent nerve circuits in which neurons are activated in sequence so that a closed "memory" loop is formed. As a consequence of such sequential activity, neurons could fire continuously and facilitate synapses that impinge on the loop.
3. **Neuronal size.** This theory suggests that frequent use of certain neurons causes them to enlarge, thus engaging in many more synaptic connections. Conversely, disuse or damage results in decreased neuronal size and impaired levels of function.
4. **Proliferation of cells.** Although the number of neurons in the central nervous system is generally fixed shortly after birth, the supportive elements, or glial cells, are continually formed during the course of a lifetime. It has been suggested that greater neuronal activity involves greater numbers of glial cells surrounding the neuron and thus that learning involves glial cells plus neurons. Supporting this is the finding that in dehydrated rats there is an increase in the division rate of glial cells in the "thirst center" of the hypothalamus.
5. **Dendrite spines.** Electron microscope studies of dendrites of neurons have shown that the surface is not smooth, but covered with thousands of tiny spines. Recent evidence suggests that the number of dendritic spines decreases with reduced sensory input and increases with enhanced activity.

At present there is no evidence to exclude any of the above-mentioned suggestions, and it is possible that learning involves a combination of some or all of these.

## 20–6 MEMORY

A creature without memory cannot discover the past; one without expectation cannot conceive a future.
GEORGE SANTAYANA

In the back-to-front world that Alice discovered behind the Looking Glass, the White Queen actually lived in reverse. "There's one great advantage in it," she said, "that one's memory works both ways." Alice remarked, "I'm sure mine only works one way. I can't remember things *before* they happen." To which the White Queen replied, "It's a poor sort of memory that only works backwards."

Although our memories don't work forward as well as backward like that of the White Queen, they do allow us to make certain predictions about the future. **Memory** is the information storage and retrieval process that allows us to bring past experience to bear on present activities and thought. Without memory, learning is impossible.

When you look up a telephone number, study a textbook, or hear a conversation, the energy of sound and light is transformed into electrochemical impulses that are carried along the pathways of the nervous system. This pattern of energy transformation, called **transduction,** is the beginning of learning and memory. Once the stimuli are received in the central nervous system, the coded impulses are attended to immediately, that is, there is a conscious awareness of the incoming information. At the same time, two other events may occur: one in which there is a brief storage, what is commonly called **short-term memory (STM);** the other involves more permanent storage, or **long-term memory (LTM).** STM is comparable to instant replay on TV. The capacity for holding information is of brief duration (seconds to minutes) and is usually restricted to about seven items. STM is involved, for example, in remembering a telephone number and in the situation where you are asked a question and you reply, "What did you say?" but before the question is repeated, you remember what it was. Retrieval of STM is simple and direct, requiring little conscious effort; it stores raw, relatively unprocessed sensory inputs. Unless some further processing occurs, the information held in STM is lost, and the decay is hastened by external interference. Interruption during the time you are looking up a phone number often causes a mistake in dialing and a return to the phone book for another try.

After a fragment of information is held in STM, it is either forgotten or transferred to LTM for more or less permanent storage.

Our understanding of STM is limited indeed. However, it is clear that putting information into the banks of LTM and retrieving it are far more difficult and complicated than is the case with STM. Since associations play an important role in LTM it seems likely that information is stored in an organized fashion. Although the neurological basis for filing information is not clear, there probably does exist some sort of system comparable to the card catalog in a library. This helps to explain why we can best remember material that we have previously organized systematically, but we have no idea whether remembering is due to methods of storage or ease of retrieval. "Cram" sessions do not promote LTM; rather, it is best to space learning at intervals because this seems to facilitate information storage.

The final stage in the processing of information stored in the memory bank is retrieval. How do we pick one piece of information from among the billions held in LTM? We really do not know. Retrieval must involve some kind of search through the files, which may or may not be successful. It is easier to recognize material (for example, information presented in a multiple choice or true-false examination) than to recall it without any cues (for example, an essay exam). Perhaps this is true because the former involves a less comprehensive search, since the category has already been given, whereas in the latter case the entire store of LTM must be surveyed for the item of interest. By analogy it is easier to find the weather report in a newspaper if you are given the section where it will be found rather than randomly searching each page of the paper.

What are the mechanisms involved in memory? The early Greeks believed that the fingers of experience wrote upon a blank slate and in this way a mind was filled with information during a lifetime. Strange and even mystical as this concept may seem, there is some support for it as a result of recent experiments. In 1890, William James suggested that every experience leaves a tiny "scar" on the nerve cells and fibers, registering and storing it for the future. This scar of memory has been called the **engram,** and the search for it in molecular and electrochemical terms continues. It has been found that the electrochemical activity of the brain, the EEG patterns, do change as a result of experience. Indeed, the electrical responses of a single neuron can be modified by experience. Although such findings suggest that functional changes occur in the neurons themselves, it is not yet clear whether these are the essential components that produce learning or whether they are merely correlated events in memory-retrieval processes.

In recent years psychologists and neurophysiologists have speculated and found some evidence of a chemical basis for memory. Experiments have shown that training causes an increase in RNA synthesis in the brain which persists for about 1 hour. It is clear that this is not LTM, but it could be an indication of some of the processes involved in memory storage; on the other hand it could merely be the restoration process of stimulated neurons. Others have suggested that protein synthesis is involved in memory storage; by administration of drugs that inhibit protein synthesis, learning and memory have been impaired. These experiments and others suggest that molecules are synthesized during learning and memory, but it would be presumptuous at this point to conclude that we understand how they function in memory.

The identification of chemical changes in the brain following training has suggested to some that it may be possible to transfer memory from one animal to another. Thus, there has been talk of "memory pills" and the like which will make us "brainier" without recourse to the usual regimens involved in learning. Although there is evidence that injections of RNA and sometimes whole extracts of brains produce learning in animals such as planarian worms and rats, there are an equal number of instances in which the experiments fail. Moreover, it is never quite clear in the seemingly successful trials of memory transfer whether the results are due to a real information transfer or to facilitation of learning. In any case, these experiments provide a fertile ground for exploring the nature of memory. Should information transfer by injection turn out to be feasible, it may be possible to have memory transplants as well as organ transplants. To date, however, no memory molecules are available.

Let us return now to the question of forgetting. Recall that earlier we suggested, in accordance with Pavlov's view, that **forgetting** could be due to interference as a consequence of new learning. It has been suggested that LTM involves both a labile and a stable stage. For information to be stored permanently, it must be consolidated and made stable. If this does not occur, the information is forgotten. For example, if rats are given electroconvulsive shocks each day immediately after training, they are unable to learn a simple task. In humans, a cerebral concussion produces retrograde amnesia, that is, the inability to remember not only the injury itself but events immediately preceding the injury. Memory consolidation in LTM thus seems to depend both on timing and on electrical activity of the nervous system. It is entirely possible that new learning competes with the consolidation process, and thus we forget. As another cause of forgetting, some have suggested that the early (and perhaps later) neurobiological processes that occur during memory have a fixed lifetime and in the course of time they decay or change. As a consequence, memories fade with time.

Forgetting may in fact be highly adaptive. If we were to retain everything impinging on our consciousness, we should soon drown in a flood of information. Selection of the most relevant and useful information is important not only for survival, but to preserve our sanity. In this respect, habituation is a form of learned forgetting.

With the advent of computers, tape machines, and other advances of modern technology that allow us to record and preserve information with enormous ease, we are accumulating a flood of material, often with little regard for its worth or relevance. The written word has allowed us to record, accumulate, and pass on the events of our culture, often overriding the genetic components of our behavior, but the recording of culture today has no built-in mechanism for selection, or for forgetting. Faced with such a wealth of information, we may soon be unable to decide what is important and what is not. We shall be unable to see the wood for the trees, so to speak. Civilization may end not with a bang but in the chaos and confusion derived from the clutter of our recorded cultural inheritance.

## 20–7 SOCIAL BEHAVIOR

Human beings have been described as aggressive, status-oriented, materialistic, territorial animals whose behavior is largely determined by their animal heritage. There is considerable appeal in such a description since there are an endless series of examples of people being unpleasant to one another. Hardly a day passes that we are not told of crime in the cities, wars of aggression, class struggles, and similar events. Are these products of our social organization? What are the strengths and weaknesses of human society?

**Groups and society.** It is a fact: no animal is totally solitary. Although individuals may use the mechanisms of instinct, learning, and reasoning to obtain shelter, to find food, and to protect themselves from enemies, survival frequently depends on social behavior. What do we mean by social behavior? When animals are grouped together as a result of their response to environmental factors, we call this **aggregation,** but when the members of a particular species stay together and cooperate because of their responses to one another, we describe this as **social behavior.** For example, if moths circle about a light bulb or houseflies congregate about an open garbage pail, they are behaving as an aggregate, or group, but they are not exhibiting social behavior; in these cases, the individuals are behaving exactly as they would if each were alone. Despite the fact that there are many of them, they do not interact with each other to any great extent. Social behavior involves the mutual interactions of two or more individuals so that their behaviors are modified. Such an interaction always involves some communication between the individuals—symbolic signs, auditory signals, chemical agents of language (Box 20D). Mating usually involves a special kind of social interaction, wherein a male and female come together for one purpose. Some authors do not regard this as social behavior, since even solitary species must come together for mating and possibly for rearing of the young. However, the behavioral mechanisms that operate within animal societies are often extensions of those that bring organisms together for mating and operate within a family group. Indeed, insect societies, often considered the pinnacle of social organization, are in fact family groups.

What advantages are there to being social? The formation of social groups—societies, if you will—enables a species to go beyond the capacities of its members. In an established society it is possible for individuals to be specialized and to perform different functions so that by virtue of the integration of their special skills that group may display increased complexity and efficiency. Insect societies are an extreme example of this kind of organization (Box 20D). In a sense, by integrating the individual members of a society into a highly organized structure, the whole becomes more efficient and successful than the sum of its individual parts.

The advantages of social life may be many. When a good food source is found by one member, all the others in the group may be attracted to it and share in it (Box 20D). Animals that live in groups tend to be less subject to predation than animals left on their own. For example, when one individual spots an approaching predator it may warn the entire group, or by concerted group action the predator may be driven off. Flocks of birds and schools of fish are so effective in protecting their individual members that predators attempt to isolate an individual before attacking. Further, social behavior may be of critical importance during reproductive periods when territories are established for breeding, for feeding, and for raising of the young.

**Territoriality. Territoriality** is the exclusive occupancy of a place by an animal or group of animals through aggressive defense or display. Dragonflies patrol the ponds in which their eggs are laid, crickets will vigorously fight off male trespassers, a lizard will threaten and engage in combat with a male intruder, and salmon and trout occupy territories during the breeding season. Some of our closest relatives, certain primates, and even we ourselves are territorial animals.

What is the function of territoriality? Territoriality does different things for different species, and some animal species show no territorial behavior. However, in many animals, territoriality plays a role in attracting a mate, in propagating and raising the young, and in ensuring a supply of food. Paradoxically, it may also function in reducing aggression between members of a social group. To maintain a territory a number of behavior patterns are critical. First, the owner of the territory must have the ability to distinguish between those individuals who are intruders, those who are passing through, and those to be attracted to the territory. During the spring the male stickleback fish develops a red belly and establishes a territory. If a strange male enters the territory, the owner assumes a threatening posture, displays its red underside, and warns trespassers off by its threats. The red belly releases male aggressive behavior, for if a female (who lacks a red belly) enters the territory, she does not elicit aggression. Instead the male begins a zigzag courtship dance. Territorial behavior in the stickleback ensures reproduction and also increases efficiency in defense of the territory. The red belly warns off other males and advertises that the territory is occupied. Birds achieve the same thing with song. Their repeated calls are advertisements by the males that the territory is already occupied. If notification and threat do not work to repel an intruder, then physical combat may ensue. Generally, the owner of the territory has the advantage and is virtually undefeatable. Often, territoriality in birds minimizes disruption in large social groups. Many marine birds, such as gulls, form nesting colonies almost on top of each other, but there is little fighting between pairs and each raises its own family within its own small territory.

Territoriality, generally speaking, increases the efficiency of reproduction and in this way benefits the individual. Territoriality may also benefit the species. For example, if a pair of lizards are placed in a large cage they will use the entire territory for feeding and reproducing. If more and more pairs of lizards are introduced into the cage the territories will become smaller and smaller, but the territory is not indefinitely compressible. Ultimately some individuals will not find an area for their needs.

Those individuals that do not gain possession of territory do not breed.

**Social dominance.** Many species of animals have established ways of organizing their populations by means other than territories. One of these is by the establishment of ranked order within a group. In some ways, ranked order is the equivalent of territoriality, but instead of the environment being partitioned into defended areas, the animals in the hierarchy partition themselves while occupying a single territory.

For example, chickens are commonly fed by scattering corn or providing an ample supply of food in a series of feeding troughs. If we were to observe a group of 10 hens that had been living together for some time under such feeding arrangement, we would see little evidence of aggressive behavior. If, however, we modify the feeding situation so that there is a single small trough of grain and the animals are forced to compete with each other for food, then the behavioral pattern changes. One of the hens becomes dominant. It feeds actively, but the others make no effort to share in the food. The dominant hen may scatter some of the grain in its feeding, and others in the group may peck at this, but it is clear that these animals cannot feed directly from the trough. If one of the hens attempts to do so, the intruder is pecked at by the dominant individual, and the intruder shows fear and retires quickly. The dominant individual takes precedence in feeding, and the others can feed only when that individual—the alpha—permits. Usually there is a "second-in-command," a beta-level animal that takes precedence at the trough over all but the alpha animal; there may also be a third and fourth level of dominance and so on down the line to the lowest in the order, a hen that gets pecked by everyone and usually is distinguishable by its bedraggled appearance. A **social hierarchy,** or **peck order,** has been established within the group—so-called because many early studies on this type of social organization involved chickens. In a

peck order, one animal acquiesces to another because of an aggressive relationship. Of course, status within the group may be established not only by pecking but by wing flapping, spur gouging, and other behaviors. The phenomenon of social dominance is quite widespread, and it is most clearly seen in those group-living animals that exhibit a high level of individual aggression. Thus, social wasps, bumblebees, hermit crabs, fishes, lizards, chickens, wolves, baboons, and macaque monkeys often show strong dominance hierarchies.

In stable chicken groups, the order of dominance is clear cut and linear. That is, the alpha individual dominates all the others, whereas the beta individual dominates all but the alpha, and so on. In other cases, there is a two-level arrangement in which a single individual is in complete charge and the other members of the group are all of equivalent subordinate rank.

In all of these situations the dominant individual controls the food, water, roosting place, choice of a mate, and other competitive features. The individuals that rank high in the peck order are easily recognized at sight by their sleek appearance, their confident walk, the way the head is held; in short, by their "high and mighty" display. The hierarchies are formed after encounters among individuals of a group and may involve threats and combat, but once the issue has been settled it is generally semipermanent and mutually accepted. Individuals know their rank and stay in place, and visible fighting is a rare event in the life of the group. Some dominants may posture to "advertise" their alpha status, and in this way through prestige they maintain their dominance. Sometimes it is impossible for an observer to determine a social hierarchy until a crisis situation occurs, when the ranking is displayed very clearly.

While some animals show strong dominance hierarchies, others do not. Thus, in a grazing herd of herbivores the expressions of dominance are very mild because of the even distribution of food on a grassy plain. Not only that, dominance behavior need not be expressed throughout the life of an animal; it may apply only to competitive situations, especially those involving sexual activities.

Social rank is also well recognized among humans, but here the ranks may depend on the kind of activity involved. Thus, an individual could be an alpha tennis player, but an omega in sales. Often, possessions such as houses, clothing, jewels, and cars are used to advertise the position the owner has, or perhaps would like to have, in the social hierarchy.

What are the advantages of a social hierarchy? The establishment of a social order makes a group a closed society. As a consequence each animal knows every other one, knows its status, and is prepared to exclude strangers. If a strange individual attempts to enter such a group, it is usually driven off, or in rare instances, if entry occurs, the individual assumes a subordinate position, thus maintaining the stability of the group. The social hierarchy, once established, is usually highly stable, and this effectively reduces the amount of fighting within the group. As with territoriality, social hierarchies also function to reduce aggression between animals of the same species. For example, when two groups of chickens were studied and one group was permitted to establish a stable hierarchy but the other, by frequent introduction of new indiviuals, was not, the stable group pecked less, ate more, gained more weight, and laid more eggs.

In a peck order it pays to be on top: dominants are able to get more food, and they remain healthier, live longer, and tend to reproduce more frequently. Why then should animals subordinate themselves? Under conditions of stress, that is, when animals have a restricted food supply, dominants get more food and thus gain more weight while the subordinates starve. As a result dominance leads to survival of some individuals. Further, some studies of animal

---

## BOX 20D  The life of the honeybee

Sed inter omniaea principatus apibus, et jure praecipua admiratio.
PLINY. Lib. 11. C5.
(But among all of these species, the chief place belongs to the bees, and rightly are they admired.)

Division of labor in social animals has reached its most complex form in the social insects: the beehive seems to some to provide a model for cooperation in an ideal society. How does it work?

The founder of the hive is the queen bee, an extremely fertile individual who lays two kinds of eggs in cells of the comb: fertilized eggs and unfertilized eggs. The unfertilized eggs develop into haploid males, and the fertilized eggs into diploid females. The males, or drones, have no role in the hive other than to fertilize a future queen; they perform no community tasks—hence the phrase "lazy as a drone." The females, or workers, tend the queen, rear the young, and defend the hive. As a worker matures, she performs a succession of tasks. Newly hatched workers prepare cells to receive eggs and food. After a day or two their brood-food glands develop and they feed larvae. Following this, they re-move nectar from the field workers, pack pollen loads into cells, and keep the hive clean. At about 2 weeks of age, the wax glands develop and the bees build new cells of the comb. At the end of this stage, some become guards at the entrance to the hive. Lastly, in the third week of life, the bees become foragers outside the hive. Their brood-food and wax glands decline, and they collect nectar, pollen, and water.

The hives are extremely efficient family communities. The bees of a given hive recognize each other by a common odor, and their status and needs are communicated among the members by **trophallaxis,** a passing of food substances from one to the other. Thus, a shortage of nectar, pollen, or water is almost immediately communicated to the foragers. A drop in the number of building bees is communicated by a lack of wax in the passed food, and nurse bees will develop wax glands and become builders. Similarly, a dearth of nurse bees produces a redevelopment of nurse glands among the builders, stimulated by a drop in brood-food substance passed among the community. Alarmed bees secrete a substance that excites the others and makes them aggressive. The queen, too, produces a substance that is passed around among the workers by the constant mutual feeding and grooming. When this substance is in short supply, the failure of the old queen is communicated, and a new queen is raised. Queens are raised from fertilized eggs laid in special large comb cells. A future queen gets fed more often with higher quality food (called royal jelly) than a future worker, grows larger, and is, of course, not sterile.

Foraging bees are also able to communicate the location of a food source outside the hive to foragers within by means of special dances up and down the hive combs. The dances are very specific; they communicate distance and direction of the food source.

The division of labor among the three castes in the beehive is extreme. The workers wear themselves out in the service of the community, which benefits at their expense. No matter what, the hive goes on.

Since the genes of the workers die with the workers, the question of how selection operates to maintain these sterile animals has been raised. The answer is that although the workers die, all the female larvae in the hive (offspring of the same queen share a high proportion of the same genes). In this sense, an individual worker's genes are not dying at all. Just as an individual organism's somatic cells die with the organism, and this organism depends on its reproductive organs to keep the line going, so a worker depends on the reproductive organs of the hive—the queen and drone(s)—to reproduce its genes.

In spite of the fact that hives behave (genetically anyway) much as a single organism, we can compare insect societies with vertebrate and even human societies, at least in terms of the way they function. Both occupy territories and communicate hunger, alarm, hostility, caste, and reproductive status by signals other than language. Members can distinguish each other from nonmembers, and **kinship**, or degree of relatedness, is important in maintaining group structure and cohesion. In both insect and vertebrate societies, members share the advantages of division of labor. From a human perspective, however, the similarities are perhaps less important than the differences! To date, attempts to order human societies so that every member knows its place and contributes equally without argument have always produced internal dissent. Chained as we are to the cycle of individual reproduction, individual freedom is prized over social efficiency, and variety remains the spice of human life.

hierarchies show that it is better to be a member of a group, albeit a subordinate, than to be no member at all. Thus, in the European rabbit the dominant individuals enjoy longer lives and produce more offspring than do subordinate members, but the subordinates fare better than the rabbits that are excluded altogether, since these rabbits are much more susceptible to predation and starvation. For the subordinate social animal, it might be said that half a loaf is better than none.

**Courtship, appeasement, and ritual.** Some of the most interesting behavior patterns observed in animals are those associated with mating. If they occur immediately prior to mating, they may fall into the category of **courtship behavior.** We have already described the elaborate mating behavior of the stickleback (page 413). Courtship behavior such as this serves to establish contact between animals and ensure that mating occurs between the right sexes of the right species at the right time.

The sexual partner is often first attracted by special behavior patterns and signals. Birds and insects such as locusts and grasshoppers use courtship songs to attract partners, and many insects use odorous substances. A single female moth can attract males from several miles away. Birds often posture and display, and this is undoubtedly behind the evolution of the magnificent male plumage of many species, such as peacocks and birds of paradise. Some of the most interesting courting behavior has been evolved by the Australian bower birds; to attract a mate, the males build large and elaborate courtship bowers and decorate them with twigs, lichens, fruit, flowers, shells, beetles, and even bones.

Often, a flower or a piece of fruit is presented to the prospective mate. Many animals, including humans, offer gifts to their prospective mates. Terns offer fish to courted females, and some species of predatory flies will offer the females food before mating. Sometimes, infantile behavior inhibits aggression; females of a species rarely

FIGURE 20–6 Behavioral patterns in the black-headed gull. (a) Upright threat posture. (b) Pair-formation sequence. (From N. Tinbergen, *The Study of Instinct,* New York, Oxford University Press, 1951.)

attack the young. Courting male hamsters call like nestling young, and a courting man may speak to his beloved in childlike diminutives. For similar reasons, many animals appease during courtship by covering or hiding signals that normally release aggression. For example, direct gazing at one another is often an aggressive threat gesture, and during courtship many birds turn their heads away from each other. The black-headed gull presents the back of the head to the prospective mate, hiding the black face, which normally releases aggression (Figure 20–6). Coy behavior by human females can be interpreted similarly, and kissing has been regarded by some authorities as a form of appeasement.

**Appeasement gestures** of various kinds may be used to turn off aggression in other situations, as when a member low in a peck order wishes to turn aside an attack by a dominant individual. Low-order wolves roll on their backs in a defenseless posture; a dominant wolf will not attack another in this position. Is aggression in humans inhibited by similar gestures? In human societies, greeting ceremonies such as bowing, raising the hat, or a smile of ''hello'' are thought to be appeasement gestures, which turn aside possible hostility and maintain bonds between individuals. Similarly, attacks on children are normally considered outrageous. Familiarization may act as an inhibitor, for under normal circumstances people are less suspicious of and less likely to attack those they know. The social implications of this are far-reaching. If aggression or even attack is normally inhibited by signals from the attacked, it is not difficult to see how our technology has brought us past the point when such signals can operate effectively. The long-range killing of people unseen by the person with a finger on the button or the trigger removes any possibility for effective appeasement gestures by the victims. Currently, almost the only inhibitor of aggressive behavior on the part of nations is the threat of retaliation. More than 90%

of murders in the United States are performed with guns of some sort, a quick and effective method. Perhaps if the murderers had to do away with their victims slowly, by hand rather than gun, inhibiting appeasement gestures would have a chance to operate.

Often, social behavior patterns take the form of ritual. In courtship and mating, ritual is very common and appeasement gestures have often become ritualized in this connection. **Ritualization** of a behavior pattern indicates that the signals by which animals communicate are distinct and repeated in a predictable way. Further, the ritualized signals are usually symbolic, in that they may have no obvious connection with the behavior released.

For example, some species of birds show ritual feeding prior to mating, and the premating appeasement feeding of predatory flies also qualifies as ritual behavior (page 425). Ritual preening and grooming prior to mating in many birds and mammals fill the same behavioral function of appeasement. Often, ritual sequences of behavior have become extremely exaggerated and repetitive, as in the elaborate mating dances of many bird species. Courting albatrosses perform a repetitive sequence of behavior, including ritual food begging, appeasement gestures, showing of the nest, and preening behavior. The end result is almost a dance: keeping time with each other, the birds wobble from side to side, fence with their bills, make clapping noises by opening and closing their bills sharply, and call to each other. At the end of each courting sequence, the birds bow to each other, point their bills to the ground, sit down, and preen each other. The sequence may be repeated several times before mating actually occurs. These social signals contribute to the mating process, ensuring reproduction.

In other contexts, ritual behavior contributes to the stabilization of animal societies. Ritual fighting may avoid actual combat. Rattlesnakes, for example, never bite each other but push each other from side to side with raised heads: when one is pinned to the ground, it retreats. In most horned mammals, intraspecific fighting is highly ritualized: antelope spar only with the very tips of their sharp horns. Human societies are full of ritual. We have already mentioned the appeasement role of ritual greeting. Organized religion in most of its forms produces cohesion and group efficiency by means of ritual. The pomp and circumstance surrounding kings and queens and parliaments in countries that have them serves to reinforce the top echelons of the dominance hierarchy. Confusion in social interactions—in courting, for example—is prevented by ritual.

## 20–8 PROSPECTS FOR THE FUTURE

The behavior of many people today is extremely disturbed; until we understand the causes, we cannot hope to find a cure. It has been argued that until we know which specific part of the nervous system is responsible for each behavioral pattern, we cannot truly understand or even compare behavioral activities in animals. One author has said that our understanding of behavior and its physiological basis is the widest gap between disciplines in science. This may be true. In order to cope with our social problems, however, we must work with what we have.

Some ethologists, believe that much of our behavior is innate; the implication has been that we are saddled with an inevitable inheritance, an approach that tempts a take-it-or-leave-it attitude to society. Other workers hold the opposite view, that behavior is determined by the environment: what is inherited is a set of capacities, which can be infinitely molded and shaped by the interactions of their possessor with the surrounding world. The truth is probably somewhere in between: we have seen, for example, that inborn behavior patterns, instincts, can be refined by the environment but not completely altered. In coping with the future, an eminent ethologist, Irenaus Eibl-Eibesfeldt, cautions us to remember that "man is not easily molded in every direction by the environment. He resists modification in certain areas more than in others."

Our knowledge of how the brain functions is in fact increasing rapidly. The day when thought, memory, learning, reasoning, insight, and the capacity to symbolize can be explained in physicochemical terms is probably closer than we think. Understanding brings the capacity for manipulation (see chapter introduction). The future of the human species may depend more upon the way in which we use this knowledge than on the possible manufacture of a virulent microbe or the threat of a nuclear holocaust.

## SUMMARY

1. Behavior is externally directed activity, often involving the adaptive response of an organism to its environment.

2. Behavior varies according to the capacity and development of the nervous system and effector organs (muscles) and may vary as a result of experience (learning).

3. Anthropomorphism and teleology should be avoided in discussions of animal behavior. Morgan's canon should be applied in interpreting animal behavior.

4. Behaviorists concentrate on learned behavior and its modification in the laboratory. Ethologists focus on the natural behavior of animals, often in the wild. Some behaviorists, led by B. F. Skinner, believe human behavior is mostly learned and can be modified by conditioning.

5. Simple oriented body movements toward or away from specific stimuli are taxes. Reflexes involve responses of part of the body to a stimulus. Some workers have attempted to explain all behavior in terms of innate and acquired reflexes.

6. Instinctive behavior patterns are stereotyped, inherited, and unlearned. Although they can be modified, refined, or even overridden, the potential to perform them cannot be eliminated.

7. Activation of instinctive behaviors often depends on specific releasers. The internal degree of readiness to respond is known as drive. Release of behavioral activity is prevented until the innate releasing mechanism (IRM) is triggered by a specific releaser stimulus. Once the behavior goal has been reached, the drive is reduced and satiation is achieved.

8. Displacement activity is apparently irrelevant behavior which may be exhibited by animals caught between two conflicting drives, or when thwarted. Released behavior directed at the wrong object is redirected activity.

9. Humans probably have innate aggressive tendencies, but such tendencies can be modified. The influence of learned behavior and culture is of overriding importance, and humans do not have a definable killer instinct.

10. Learning is an alteration of behavior that occurs as a result of experience. Habituation is one of its simplest forms and involves learning not to respond to nonsignificant stimuli.

11. Classical conditioning involves the modification of behavior patterns by the transferring of a response from one releasing stimulus (the natural stimulus) to another (the neutral stimulus). It involves contiguity of both stimuli, repetition, and reinforcement with a reward. It is weakened by interference of other stimuli during the conditioning process. Extinction of classical conditioning occurs in the absence of the neutral stimulus but is subject to disinhibition by the presence of previously interfering stimuli.

12. In operant conditioning, the conditioned animal exerts some operational control over stimuli received and thus exerts controls over its environment. Reward and punishment reinforce operant conditioning and contiguity, repetition, and interference are also important.

13. Operant conditioning and reinforcement are involved in trial-and-error learning. Reasoning, or insight learning, is the ability to respond correctly to a novel situation by the application and integration of prior learning.

14. Imprinting is the stereotyped response of animals to objects presented at a critical period early in life.

15. The cerebral cortex is probably the seat of learning and associative abilities and is highly developed in humans. The nervous mechanisms responsible for learning may involve facilitation, growth of nerve pathways, neuronal enlargement and increased

numbers of synapses, proliferation of glial cells, or increase in dendritic spines.

16. Memory is the information storage and retrieval process that allows us to profit from experience and to learn. Short-term memory (STM) is brief and quickly lost. Long-term memory (LTM) involves transduction of nerve impulses and storage of learned information and seems to depend on timing and electrical activity of the nervous system. The mechanisms of transduction, storage, and retrieval are not well understood, and the search for the engram in chemical and physical terms continues.

Forgetting involves loss or decay of the engram. Some forgetting, such as that involved in habituation, is adaptive.

17. Social behavior involves communication and cooperation between animals, usually with behavior modification. As such, social groups are distinct from aggregations. Social behavior is important in mating and in rearing of the young; it also enables members of a group to operate more efficiently than they would if they were solitary. Insect societies such as bees and termites are the zenith of social organization, and the members of the group often exhibit

structural and physiological as well as behavioral adaptations to group living.

18. Behavior patterns found in social animals include territoriality, social dominance hierarchies, elaborate courtship behavior, appeasement gestures, and ritualization. All of these help to avoid confusion in social interactions, for example, ensuring reproduction, securing a supply of food, raising the young, limiting aggression, and ensuring the efficient workings and continuation of the community— and hence the species.

---

**KEY WORDS**

| | | | |
|---|---|---|---|
| | negative geotaxis | natural stimulus | long-term memory (LTM) |
| | reflexes | repetition | engram |
| behavior | instinct | reinforcement | forgetting |
| tropisms | releaser | interference | aggregation |
| anthropomorphism | drive | extinction | social behavior |
| teleology | satiation | disinhibition | territoriality |
| Ockham's razor | innate releasing mechanism (IRM) | operant conditioning | social hierarchy or peck order |
| Morgan's canon | displacement activity | trial and error | trophallaxis |
| behaviorists | redirected activity | reasoning or insight learning | kinship |
| ethologists | learning | imprinting | courtship behavior |
| taxis (taxes) | habituation | association area | appeasement gestures |
| phototaxes | classical conditioning | memory | ritualization |
| geotaxes | neutral stimulus | transduction | |
| negative phototaxis | contiguity | short-term memory (STM) | |

## TOPICS FOR REVIEW AND DISCUSSION

1. What is behavior? Of what biological significance is behavior in the life of an animal?

2. Why are anthropomorphism and teleology not useful in studies of behavior? What is Morgan's canon?

3. In general, how does behavior in higher organisms differ from that in lower organisms? How is this reflected in the structure of the organism?

4. List the differences between behaviorists and ethologists.

5. Discuss the importance of nurture versus nature in animal behavior.

6. What is sociobiology? How does it seek to explain altruistic behavior in animal species?

7. What are taxes? How do they differ from reflexes?

8. Distinguish between instinctive and learned behavior.

9. Discuss the role of innate releasing mechanisms in instinctive behavior. How do the concepts of drives and releasers explain displacement activity?

10. Give examples of how instincts are "learned" by human beings or by herring gulls.

11. Do you believe humans are innately aggressive? Defend your position.

12. How is habituation adaptive?

13. Distinguish between classical and operant conditioning.

14. Of what importance is conditioning in B. F. Skinner's view of the world?

15. What is imprinting? Why is it so important in water birds?

16. Discuss the physical basis of learning in vertebrates.

17. How is STM related to LTM? What is the engram, and how does it relate to memory?

18. Discuss the adaptive value of forgetting to human life.

19. Describe social behavior in honeybees.

20. What is the role of territoriality in social animals? How is it related to the concept of social dominance? Of what major importance are appeasement and ritualization in social animals?

# 21

# Movement: Skeleton and Muscle

## 21–1 THE SKELETON: TOWER OF SUPPORT AND PROTECTION

The Eiffel Tower, built by Gustave Eiffel for the Paris Exhibition of 1889, was designed to show the potential of steel as a structural material. Today, this symbol of Paris remains an outstanding example of the strength, flexibility, and endurance of steel and a monument to nineteenth-century engineering skills. The most enduring monument to our own existence—itself a remarkable engineering feat—is the skeleton, for long after the body is dead and the soft tissues are destroyed, this bony tower of strength remains (Figure 21–1). The skeleton consists of 206 individual bones (Table 21–1), some hinged and others fused to one another, and it provides the soft, weak flesh with protection. Together with the muscles that are attached to it, it enables us to stand erect, move, jump, and run. The bony skeleton functions in other ways that often go unnoticed: the bone marrow is the site of formation of blood cells, and the matrix of the bone itself acts as a storage depot for mineral salts, such as calcium and phosphorus.

The main axis of the human body is perpendicular to the ground, and the support for this erect position consists of a jointed, flexible column of bones, the **backbone,** or spine. The individual bones are called **vertebrae** (sing. *vertebra*—joint; L.). This is, of course, the reason why animals with backbones are referred to as **vertebrates.** From the vertebrae of the thorax arise a series of bony struts, the **ribs;** they curve around to the front of the body in barrel-stave fashion and join at the sternum,

or breastbone. The rib cage is designed much like a packing crate and shields the heart, lungs, liver, and spleen against damage. Perched atop the backbone is a large bony helmet, the **skull,** with jaws, a prominent chin, and a variety of teeth. The skull and vertebrae enclose and protect the vulnerable brain and spinal cord and together with the ribs are known as the **axial skeleton.**

When a human stands upright, almost the entire weight is carried by the bones of the **pelvis;** the basketlike pelvis acts as an anchor point for the legs, supports the soft internal organs of the body, and marks the lower limit of the body's trunk, or central area. The pelvis is attached to the lower end of the spine, the **shoulder (pectoral) girdle** to the opposite end below the skull. The shoulder girdle marks the upper limit of the body's trunk, and from it stem the bones of the arms. The bones of the arms and legs, together with the bony pelvic and pectoral girdles that attach them to the axial skeleton, are known as the **appendicular skeleton.**

### Bone and cartilage: living reinforced concrete

Bone often appears rather passive in character because of its low metabolic rate and great mineral content, and because the bones we are used to seeing (such as those from a rib roast of beef, the carcass of a chicken, fossils or skeletons in a museum) are dead, dry bones. However, anyone who has witnessed the growth of a child or seen how a broken bone mends itself recognizes the dynamic character of this tissue.

Bone is an organic cement produced by

specialized living cells (Figure 21–2), **osteocytes** (*osteon*—bone; Gk.). It consists of organic materials (35%) and mineral salts (65%). The organic portion consists chiefly of a protein called **bone collagen,** a fibrous substance closely resembling the collagen of other connective tissues; this material yields gelatin when bones are boiled. Between these collagenous fibers is a gelatinous substance composed primarily of the mucopolysaccharide chondroitin sulfate. The organic materials of bone give it a certain flexibility. The inorganic portion of bone, the material that contributes to its hardness and permanency after death, is a complex crystalline array of calcium salts, calcium phosphate and calcium carbonate. In its organization bone is like steel-reinforced concrete. The protein fibers are analogous to the flexible steel rods, and the calcium salts are like the concrete itself. The flexible elements resist breakage when tension is applied, and the rigid mineral matrix resists crushing when pressure is applied.

To appreciate the organization of bone, it is necessary to look at it under the microscope. A thin slice of compact bone[1] (such as that of the upper arm) magnified a few hundred times shows a series of concentric layers of intercellular material (**matrix**) and

---

[1] Bone seen with the unaided eye is often described as being either spongy or compact. The spongy type consists of bony crossbars of various thickness and shape (Figure 21–3); such an arrangement gives rigidity and strength. Compact bone appears to consist of a continuous hard mass, and spaces can be seen in it only with the aid of a microscope. Spongy and compact bone are merely different arrangements of the same elements and do not differ chemically.

**TABLE 21–1 The bones of the human skeleton**

|  | No. of bones |
|---|---|
| **Axial skeleton** | 80 |
| Skull | 29 |
|   Cranium | 8 |
|   Face | 14 |
|   Hyoid | 1 |
|   Ossicles (ear bones) | 6 |
|     Malleus | 2 |
|     Incus | 2 |
|     Stapes | 2 |
| Vertebral column | 26 |
|   Cervical vertebrae | 7 |
|   Thoracic vertebrae | 12 |
|   Lumbar vertebrae | 5 |
|   Sacrum | 1 (5 fused) |
|   Coccyx | 1 (3–5 fused) |
| Thorax | 25 |
|   Sternum | 1 |
|   Ribs | 24 |
| **Appendicular skeleton** | 126 |
| Shoulder girdle | 4 |
|   Clavicle | 2 |
|   Scapula | 2 |
| Upper extremity | 60 |
|   Humerus | 2 |
|   Ulna | 2 |
|   Radius | 2 |
|   Carpals | 16 |
|   Metacarpals | 10 |
|   Phalanges | 28 |
| Pelvic girdle | 2 |
|   Os coxae | 2 |
| Lower extremity | 60 |
|   Femur | 2 |
|   Fibula | 2 |
|   Tibia | 2 |
|   Patella | 2 |
|   Tarsus | 14 |
|   Metatarsus | 10 |
|   Phalanges | 28 |
| Total | 206 |

like osteocytes separated from each other by a matrix of collagen and calcium salts (the "outer space" of the bone). The osteocytes are connected by tiny canals that permit substances to pass from one cell to another and to and from the blood vessels that lie in the center of the system. In this manner the living osteocytes are nourished and their waste products are removed. Bones are usually covered with a fibrous connective-tissue sheath called the **periosteum.**

Cartilage, or gristle, is the more flexible structural material of the skeleton, and it usually contains no mineral salts (Figure 21–4). It is a secretion of specialized cells called **chondrocytes** (*chondros*—cartilage; Gk.). Since cartilage lacks blood vessels, the living cells are nourished by diffusion of materials from the surroundings. Cartilage consists primarily of protein and chondroitin sulfate. Chondroitin sulfate itself is gelatinous, but depending on the nature of its contained fibers, it can be more or less rigid. When chondroitin sulfate is combined with fibers of collagen, it is called fibrocartilage; this kind of cartilage forms the cushions of the discs between the vertebrae and resists breakage. When combined with elastin, the cartilage is flexible like that found in the outer ear. When there is little fiber content, the cartilage is clear and glassy in appearance; this **hyaline cartilage** is found in the windpipe, the ends of long bones, and the embryonic skeleton and is highly resilient. The cartilaginous surfaces are enclosed by a sheath of connective tissue called the **perichondrium,** the source of all new cartilage cells.

### Bone growth: chronometer of the skeleton

"The skeleton punches a time clock from birth to death," W. M. Krogman has said. The sex, approximate age (Figure 21–5), race, and medical history of a deceased individual are accurately recorded in the bones and can be determined from them. For example, it is not unusual for a crimi-

bone cells (Figure 21–3). These are arranged like thousands of miniature solar systems (called **Haversian canal systems**). The hub, or center, of each system contains blood vessels and nerves, and the "planets" encircling the hub consist of layers of spider-

Skull — Sutures

Breastbone — Radius and ulna

Clavicle (collarbone) —

Scapula (shoulder blade) —

Humerus —

Ribs —

Vertebrae (bones of spinal column) —

Pelvis (hipbone) —

Femur (thigh bone) —

Knee cap

Tibia and fibula —

FIGURE 21–2 An osteocyte, as revealed by the electron microscope. (Courtesy of K. R. Porter.)

Nucleus

Uncalcified bone

Calcified bone

Cytoplasm

Plasma membrane

Uncalcified bone

Collagen fibers

nologist, in Holmesian fashion, to determine the sex of a decomposed murder victim from the size of the ridges above the eyes or the shape of the pelvic bones. Indeed, bone is so durable and its developmental patterns so well defined that it provides some of the major clues in unraveling human prehistory. From the structure of fossilized long bones, the size of the skull, and the extent of fusion of the sutures of the brain case, physical anthropologists can often deduce not only the form of members of ancient races, but the kind of work they did, the physical ailments they endured, and the age at which death occurred.

The skeleton of the young embryo initially consists of protein fibers of collagen secreted by the primitive cells called **fibroblasts** (literally "fiber makers"). Later, depending on the location in the body, cartilage is deposited between these fibers so that much of the embryo's skeleton consists of fibrous membranes and hyaline (clear) cartilage. By the eighth week, bone deposition, called **ossification,** has begun.

When we examine the growth of bones, we find that bones generally begin to ossify in the center (Figure 21–6); the process can be most clearly seen in the long bones of the limbs. The bone grows in length in a region just below the tip of the bone and above the shaft itself, called the **growth zone.** The addition of bony material at this region causes the bone to lengthen, and in effect the tip of the bone grows farther and farther away from the middle of the shaft. This is a practical method of growth because it does not interfere with the articulation of the head of the bone with the bone next to it. Gradually, the cartilagenous shaft of the bone is replaced by a bony matrix. Increase in girth occurs by additional layering of bone on the outer surface of the shaft. As the bone increases in thickness, bony material is lost from the central part of the shaft, forming an internal cavity (the **marrow cavity**) that gets larger as the bone diameter increases (Figure 21–6b). The removal of

FIGURE 21-3 The structure of bone. (a) Entire bone. (b) Three-dimensional reconstruction of a slice of bone viewed with the light microscope.

FIGURE 21-4 (top) The structure of cartilage of the glassy type.

FIGURE 21-5 (bottom) The age of bone deposition.

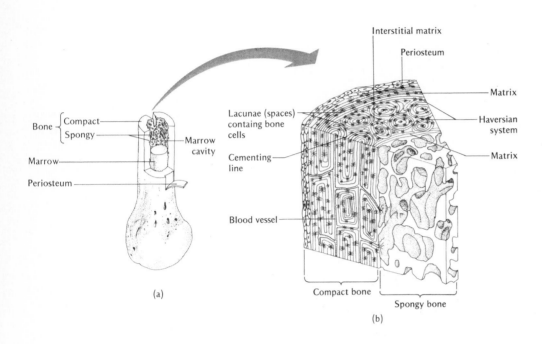

(a)

(b)

Bone { Compact / Spongy }
Marrow cavity
Marrow
Periosteum

Interstitial matrix
Periosteum
Matrix
Lacunae (spaces) containg bone cells
Haversian system
Cementing line
Matrix
Blood vessel
Compact bone
Spongy bone

Cartilage capsule
Chondrocytes
Matrix
Perichondrium

material in the marrow cavity results from the activity of special cells, called **osteoclasts**. Osteoclasts are giant cells containing many nuclei; they resorb bone by secreting enzymes that digest the protein matrix and split the bone salts so that they are easily absorbed by the surrounding fluid. The marrow cavity, once occupied by bone and then by osteoclasts, becomes filled with cells that give rise to red and white cells of the blood. Their hollow structure admirably suits the long bones of the limbs to their function. Built on sound engineering principles, they are extremely strong for the amount of material involved in their form. If they were solid, they would break more easily and would be extremely heavy. The hollow units used to scaffold a building under repair or construction employ the

5 weeks
1.5-2 months
1.5-2 months
1.5-3 months
1.5-3 months
1.5-4 months

Fetus

15-25 years
13-21 years
13-20 years
15-25 years
15-22 years
15-24 years
17-25 years
16-25 years
14-24 years
15-25 years

Adult

FIGURE 21–6 The growth of bones. (a) Growth of a long bone from embryo to adult. (b) Diagram showing the surfaces on which bone is deposited and resorbed during growth to account for the remodeling of the ends of long bones with flared extremities. (Modified from A. W. Ham, *Histology*, Philadelphia, Lippincott, 1969.)

Zone of growth    Cartilage    Bone

Embryo

Fetus

Birth

Juvenile

Adolescent

Adult

(a)

Elongation by growth of cartilage and replacement by bone

(1) Resorbed here

(4) Bone added inside tunnels here

(2) Growing shaft is remodeled by bone being added here

And (3) resorbed here

Shaft elongates because cartilage grows here

And is replaced by bone here

(b)

same principles—lightness and economy of material combined with great strength.

Just prior to maturity, a long bone consists of two strips of tissue, the growth zones, between the tips of the bone and the shaft. When the growth zones become ossified at about 25 years of age, the bone's length is complete. No further increase in length can occur, but new bone growth can be instituted if there is a break in a bone. When such injury occurs, bone cells in the region of the break become active, proliferate, and secrete large quantities of new bone within a few weeks. Bone healing occurs most efficiently in young people and is optimal when the fractured ends are immobilized, brought in close contact, and properly aligned by a splint or cast or by an inserted bone pin.

The initial shape of a bone during its formation is determined genetically, but mechanical stresses, environmental factors (dietary calcium, "vitamin" D), and muscle tension also influence its form. In large part the architecture of a bone reflects the mechanical stress and strain put upon it, and there are struts, buttresses, crossbars, and so on that act to prevent the structure from collapsing. The marvelous engineering involved in bone structure is a product of and regulated by the strains it receives, since the greater the stress put on the bone the greater the activity of the bone cells. Why this is so is not understood. However, this is the reason why bones that are subjected to continuous and excessive loads ordinarily grow thick and strong, whereas bones not used for prolonged periods (such as those

in a plaster cast or those of a person damaged by poliomyelitis) waste away.

## 21–2 MOTION: MUSCLE

Poke your dog or cat; touch a frog, fish, lizard, or bird; swat a fly; nudge a grasshopper or an earthworm. They all respond (most of the time) in the same way: they move. Do the same things to a grapefruit, a pinecone, a rose petal, or a kernel of corn, and they remain as they were before. Animals, ourselves included, move in a purposeful fashion, and basic to such activity is the contraction of muscle.

Muscles (or flesh) are a conspicuous part of the human body, as they are in almost all animals, for approximately one half of our body weight is represented by muscle tissue. Muscles move us from place to place (locomotion), but they are also involved in the less obvious movements of the organs of the body. In the human body there are over 600 different muscles, and when we walk, talk, stand erect, lie down, write, eat, run, dance, creep, crawl, play the piano, and perform a variety of other physical activities, we set these muscles into operation. In addition to playing a role in motion, muscles give the body its characteristic form. The scaffolding of the skeleton is a prime factor in determining body shape, but the muscles that drape the skeleton produce the contours we regard as graceful and beautiful (Figure 21–7).

### The kinds of muscle

Muscles are usually described as **skeletal,** **smooth,** or **cardiac,** depending upon how they look under the ordinary light microscope (Figure 21–8).

**Skeletal muscle.** Skeletal muscle appears to have cross banding, or alternating light and dark stripes, running at right angles to the length of the muscle and is sometimes referred to as **striped** or **striated muscle** (Figure 21–8a). It is called skeletal muscle because it is the kind that is commonly attached to the bones of the skeleton. Skeletal muscle consists of bundles of muscle cells; each cell is multinucleate, and sometimes such a cell is called a **syncytium** (*syn*—together, *kytos*—hollow vessel; Gk.). Skeletal muscles make up most of the fleshy parts of the body. They are supplied with nerves that are under voluntary control, and so contraction of various parts of the body can be consciously willed. Skeletal muscles, which move the limbs, usually act quickly, fatigue more easily, and generally cannot remain contracted for very long periods of time. A wink, an utterance, the movements of the limbs in walking, dancing, and breathing are all produced by the action of skeletal muscles.

As flesh eaters we recognize two kinds

VNDECIMA
MVSCVLO.
RVM TA.
BVLA

FIGURE 21–8 The three kinds of muscle of the human body. (a) Skeletal muscle. (b) Smooth muscle. (c) Cardiac muscle.

(a)

Nucleus
Striation
Myofibrils

Skeletal muscle

(b)

Muscle cells bound together
Nucleus
Smooth muscle cell
Cells separated from each other

Smooth muscle

(c)

Nucleus
Disc
Striation
Myofibrils

Cardiac muscle

of skeletal muscle; these are the types we commonly call dark meat and light meat, or **red muscle** and **white muscle.** They differ in their color because of the presence of the red pigment **myoglobin,** which is richer in red muscle; it becomes brown upon heating, producing dark meat. Myoglobin is a protein similar to hemoglobin and can reversibly bind molecular oxygen. When oxygen is plentiful, the muscle binds and stores it until there is a demand for it.

**Smooth (visceral) muscle.** The muscles of the internal organs (viscera), such as those of the gut, uterus, and blood vessels, are distinct from skeletal muscle in that they have no striations. Such muscles are called smooth muscles, and each is made up of groups or sheets of well-defined uninucleate cells (Figure 21–8b). Smooth muscles are not attached to bones; they usually act slowly, do not fatigue easily, may remain contracted for long periods of time, and are not under conscious control. Smooth muscles are also called **visceral** or **involuntary muscles.** When food is moved along the length of the gut, when the uterus contracts to expel the fetus during delivery, or when blood vessels constrict to reduce the flow of blood or elevate the blood pressure, smooth muscles are in operation.

**Cardiac muscle.** Heart, or cardiac, muscle (*kardia*—heart; Gk.) is located only in the heart. In some respects it embodies the characteristics of both smooth and striated muscles. Cardiac muscle is striated, but it is not under voluntary control (Figure 21–8c). It is not structurally a syncytium (although it functions as one), but it does contract rapidly and is virtually indefatigable—well-adapted for its lifetime job of pumping the blood to every part of the body. Cardiac muscle has an inherent rhythm of approximately 72 beats a minute, and nervous inputs act to modify this, speeding it up or slowing it down (Chapter 18). The metabolism of cardiac muscle is similar to that of red skeletal muscle, but endurance supersedes strength and speed. Cardiac muscle is highly aerobic, and if deprived of oxygen for as little as 30 seconds, it ceases to function.

## Characteristics of muscle

All muscle—smooth, skeletal, and cardiac—has the inherent property of **contractility,** a unique characteristic distinguishing it from any other body tissue. Muscles are so organized that when they contract they reduce the distance between the parts they connect or the space they surround. For example, contraction of the muscles that connect two bones brings the attachment points closer together, causing the bone to move. When cardiac muscle contracts, it reduces the space in the chambers of the heart, and this push on the incompressible fluid contained within causes blood to move from the heart into the blood vessels. Smooth muscles are wrapped around the arteries and the intestines like a cuff, so that contraction causes the diameter of these tubes to narrow. Muscles have two properties in addition to contractility: **extensibility** (ability to be stretched) and **elasticity** (ability to return to original length after having been stretched); together, the triad of contractility, extensibility, and elasticity produces a mechanical device capable of movement. The three kinds of muscles may appear dissimilar, but in the manner by which they work, they are alike.

## Putting muscles to work

In order for a muscle to produce movement of an object such as an arm or a leg, the muscle must be capable of exerting its force on a movable object; that is, it must have something to pull against. In backboned animals like ourselves muscles are attached to the bones of the skeleton by strong bands of connective tissue called tendons. The bones, in turn, are connected to each other by joints, and each muscle is attached so that it bridges a joint; when a muscle contracts, the skeletal components move. The

skeleton thus forms a series of jointed bars and levers with muscles attached—the basic machinery for the movements of limbs, torso, head, and so on.

It is important to realize that muscles are capable of pulling but not of pushing. Reversal of the direction in which a joint is bent must be accomplished by moving a different set of muscles. For this reason, the muscles that move the parts of our body are almost invariably arranged in pairs—one to produce movement in one direction, the other to produce movement in the opposite direction. These paired muscles cooperate to produce body movement, since when one is contracted the other must relax to some extent; since they have opposite actions, they are called **antagonists.** By virtue of the ways in which they are arranged, the muscles of the body can move the body parts in innumerable ways and with great precision. For example, the muscles of the upper arm are arranged in antagonistic pairs (Figure 21–9a). One end of the muscle on the front part of the upper arm (biceps) is fixed to the shoulder bone and upper arm bone; these bones do not move when this muscle contracts (Figure 21–9b). The other end of the biceps muscle is attached to one of the bones in the forearm, and it is this bone that moves when the muscle contracts. The muscle on the back part of the upper arm (triceps) is also attached in the shoulder and forearm region. Bend your elbow and with your other hand feel the contraction of the belly (enlarged region) of your biceps muscle; at the same time run your hand around to the triceps and feel its relaxed condition. (There may be some tenseness, but it certainly does not show a contractile force equal to that of the biceps.) Now extend your forearm, and feel the reversal of contraction and relaxation; the biceps relaxes and the triceps contracts. Now bend your arm halfway and contract both biceps and triceps. The arm becomes rigid, because both sets of muscles contract at the same time.

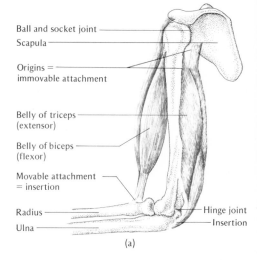

Ball and socket joint

Scapula

Origins = immovable attachment

Belly of triceps (extensor)

Belly of biceps (flexor)

Movable attachment = insertion

Radius

Ulna

Hinge joint

Insertion

(a)

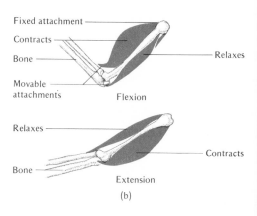

Fixed attachment

Contracts

Bone

Movable attachments

Relaxes

Flexion

Relaxes

Bone

Contracts

Extension

(b)

The biceps is a **flexor** and the triceps an **extensor** muscle because the biceps flexes the elbow and the triceps extends it. Similar groups of antagonistic flexors and extensors are found at the wrist, ankle, knee, and other joints. Other antagonistic muscles are **adductors** and **abductors,** which move parts of the body toward or away from the center line of the body; **levators** and **depressors,** which raise and lower body parts (for example, raising and lowering the lower jaw

FIGURE 21–10 Types of joints. (a) Immovable or slightly movable joints. (b) Ball-and-socket joint of the hip, which allows free movement. (c) Hinge joint of the knee, allowing moderate freedom of movement. (d) Pivot joint in the ankle.

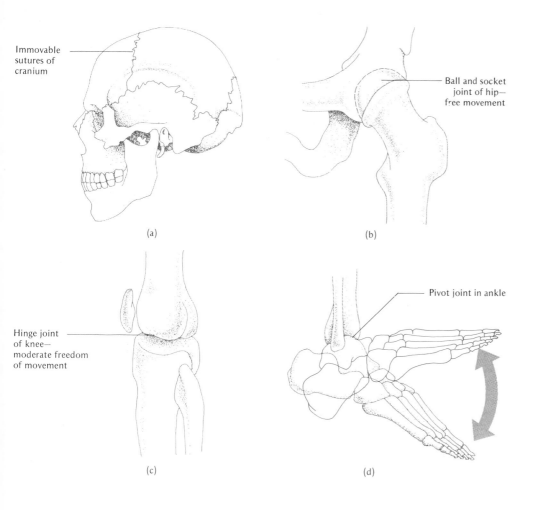

Immovable sutures of cranium

Ball and socket joint of hip— free movement

(a)

(b)

Hinge joint of knee— moderate freedom of movement

Pivot joint in ankle

(c)

(d)

Whenever two movable bones meet at a joint, their ends do not come directly into contact with one another; they are covered with a smooth, slippery cap of cartilage (recall the smooth, shiny ends of a drumstick), and the joint (articular) surfaces are encased in a capsule, (Figure 21–11), made of ligaments and filled with a liquid called **synovial fluid.** The synovial fluid is secreted continuously by the membrane lining the cavity (it is a kind of weeping bearing), and its coefficient of friction (a measure of its frictional resistance) decreases with increased movement, a highly advantageous property for a material at a joint surface. As we age, the synovial fluid is not secreted as quickly as needed, the cartilaginous surfaces of the bone ends tend to become ossified, and as a result there is increased stiffness of joints and difficulty in movement. Where tendons pass over bony protuberances they are subjected to wear. Fluid-filled sacs, placed between the tendon and the bone, called **bursae,** act to cushion the tendon. Chronic inflammation of the joints is called **bursitis, arthritis,** or **rheumatism** (Figure 21–11).

**Tendons**—tough, flexible, and fibrous—are the long cables of connective tissue that anchor muscle to bone. Tendons permit a muscle to act at some distance from the bone it moves. For example, some of the muscles that move the fingers are located in the forearm, but these muscles are attached by long strands of tendons to the finger bones (Figure 21–12a). This can easily be verified by moving your fingers vigorously and noting the rippling of muscles in the upper part of the forearm; you can also feel the muscles operating with the fingers of your other hand. This is the reason why the muscles in the forearm fatigue and ache when you exercise your fingers for long periods of time, as in typing, writing, or playing the piano. The anatomical arrangement of tendons and muscles in the fingers and forearm permits the fingers to perform delicate and precise movements. If the fin-

in eating or speaking); **sphincters** and **dilators,** which decrease or enlarge openings such as the anus and the mouth; **pronators** and **supinators,** which rotate downward-backward and upward-forward, respectively (for example, in turning the palm down or up).

**Joints** are the points of junction between bones (Figure 21–10). Some, such as those between the bony plates of the skull, are immovable (Figure 21–10a) because they

have become fused. The joints concerned with body movements are flexible pivot points and vary in form according to their function: a ball-and-socket joint (Figure 21–10b), allowing free movement in several directions, is found in the hip and shoulder; a hinge joint, permitting movement in a single plane, exists in the elbow and knee (Figure 21–10c); and a pivot joint, showing an intermediate range of movement, is found in the wrist and ankle (Figure 21–10d).

ger muscles were directly fixed to the finger bones, the hand would be clumsy, indelicate, and muscle-bound (Figure 21–12b).

## The molecular machinery of muscle contraction

When you see an animal move, you are impressed with its agility and grace. Perhaps you also wonder, How do its muscles work to produce such activity? If you have ever pondered such a question, you are not alone, for one of the most perplexing questions concerning muscle has been, How does a muscle convert the chemical energy of fuel into mechanical work? Alternatively, the question could be phrased, What are the mechanisms by which muscles contract? The molecular machinery involved in muscle contraction is probably similar in all types of muscles. What follows here pertains particularly to striated muscles only because, up to the present time, these have been the best studied.

The structure of a skeletal muscle is familiar to all of us, for this is the meat we eat. Let us consider a common example, the thigh (drumstick) of a chicken or a turkey. When the bone is stripped from the drumstick, the bulk of the leg, the fleshy part, consists almost entirely of muscle (Figure 21–13a). The muscles are grouped into bundles, and each is surrounded by a sheath, or wrapper, of connective tissue (Figure 21–13b and c). The connective-tissue sheaths permit the individual muscle bundles to function as discrete units. The sheaths of connective tissue join each other, and near the ends of the bone they taper and are gathered to form the tendon. If meat is tough, it is usually due to a high proportion of connective tissue relative to the amount of muscle. With advancing age the amount of connective tissue increases, and this is probably the reason for the decreased tenderness of meat from an older animal. No doubt this is also a factor in decreased muscular strength with advancing age (Figure 21–14).

**FIGURE 21–11** (a) Detailed side view of a joint (the knee). (b) Osteoarthritis. In the early stages of the disease the cartilage at the bone surface begins to degenerate. In time, the missing cartilage is replaced by a hardened bony outgrowth that tends to stiffen the joint, resulting in considerable pain and difficulty in movement.

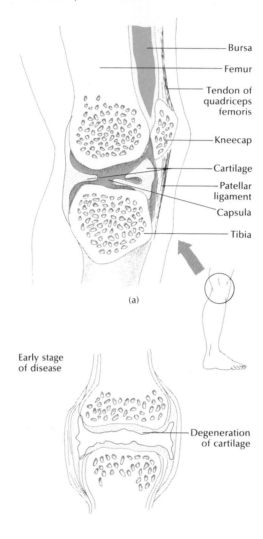

(a)

Bursa
Femur
Tendon of quadriceps femoris
Kneecap
Cartilage
Patellar ligament
Capsula
Tibia

Early stage of disease

Degeneration of cartilage

Late stage

Hardened bone

Bony outgrowth

Cartilage particles

Loss of cartilage

(b)

**FIGURE 21–12** (a) Tendons in the hand permit delicacy in the fingers because only some of the muscles that move the fingers are located in the forearm. (b) The hand would be extremely bulky if the muscles were directly attached to the bones in the fingers. (Modified from G. Hardin, *Biology, Its Principles and Implications,* 2nd ed., San Francisco, Freeman, 1966.)

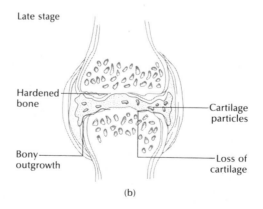

FIGURE 21–13 Skeletal muscle. (a) A drumstick (whole). (b) Cross section through the drumstick at the level shown by the plane in (a). (c) Stereodiagram showing the arrangement of muscle bundles, muscle cells, myofibrils, and connective tissue.

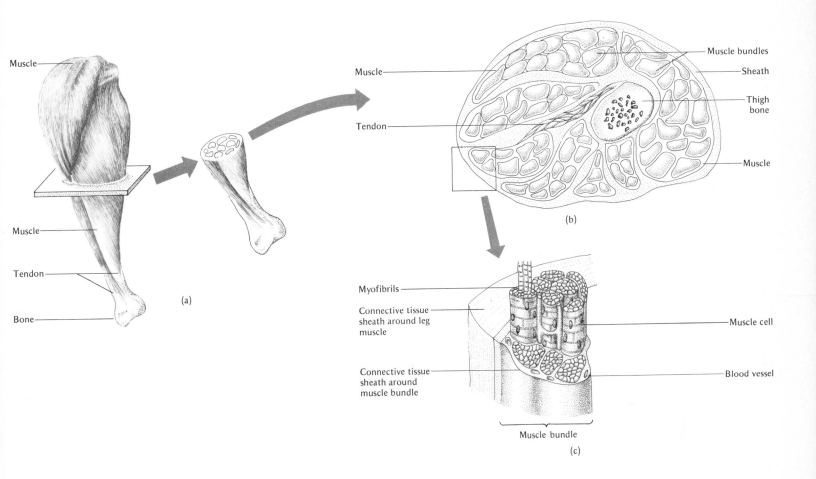

Microscopic examination shows a muscle bundle to consist of muscle cells that run parallel to each other (Figure 21–13c). Each muscle cell is an elongated, multinucleated cylinder of varying length surrounded by a thin, transparent plasma membrane called the **sarcolemma** (*sarkos*—flesh, *lemma*—rind; Gk.) and containing a fluid protoplasm, the **sarcoplasm**.[2] The sarcoplasm contains numerous **myofibrils** (*myo*—muscle; L.), which run the length of the cell and lie parallel to

each other. Each myofibril shows alternating light and dark cross bands. Because each myofibril is aligned in register, that is, precisely side-by-side, the muscle cell appears to be striated or cross-striped. Thus, the components that make up the structure of a skeletal muscle can be written as follows:

Myofibrils ⟶ muscle cells ⟶
muscle bundles ⟶ muscle

If a fresh striated muscle is ground up and extracted, the dry chemical components derived are almost entirely protein. (In fresh muscle, 20% is protein and 80% is water.) Approximately 90% of the muscle

protein is represented by two specific kinds of proteins: **actin** and **myosin.** When actin and myosin are placed in solution in water, they spontaneously combine to form a complex called **actomyosin.** If this actomyosin solution is taken up in a medicine dropper and squirted into a salt solution, it will yield jellylike threads of actomyosin (Figure 21–15a). Such artificial threads contract when ATP is added (Figure 21–15b), but neither myosin nor actin alone will contract in the presence of ATP. It appears that a solution of actin, myosin, and ATP contains all the essential components of the contractile system of muscle, and the actomyosin itself

---

[2] Sarco- is the prefix used in words describing organelles of the muscle cell, because flesh is essentially all muscle.

FIGURE 21–14 Changes in the proportion of muscle and connective tissue in human muscle at various ages. (Modified from G. Hardin, *Biology, Its Principles and Implications,* 2nd ed., San Francisco, Freeman, 1966.)

FIGURE 21–15 (a) Formation of actomyosin thread when a solution of actin and myosin is added to a salt solution. (b) When ATP is added, the thread contracts. (Modified from A. C. Giese, *Cell Physiology,* Philadelphia, Saunders, 1962.)

can liberate energy from ATP to provide the driving force for its own contractions.

If the contraction of muscle involves only the interaction of myosin and actin, how is the system regulated so that the muscles are not always contracted? Recent studies have shown that the actin filaments contain two other kinds of proteins, **tropomyosin** and **troponin.** Both of these proteins lie in the grooves of the helical strands of the actin filament (Figure 21–16). Actin filaments without troponin and tropomyosin strongly bind to myosin in the presence of ATP and magnesium ions, but if troponin-tropomyosin is added to the actin filaments, then the actin-myosin binding does not occur. It is believed that the sites on the actin molecule which normally bind to the myosin are blocked until calcium ions are present. When calcium ions are present, the troponin, which has a very high affinity for calcium, binds the calcium ions and in so doing undergoes a shape change that shifts the tropomyosin, thus exposing the actin binding site. In this way muscle contraction is initiated. When calcium ions are removed, troponin-tropomyosin prevents actin from combining with myosin; this occurs in a resting muscle.

Careful studies with the electron microscope coupled with the technique of x-ray diffraction suggest that the banding pattern of the myofibril is due to the arrangement of actin and myosin within it. The myofibrils show a pattern of light regions (**I bands)** and dark regions (**A bands)** (Figure 21–17). In the middle of the dark A band is a light stripe called the **H zone,** and in the middle of the light I band is a thin, dark line, the **Z line.** When the myofibril contracts, the I bands and the H zones become narrower and a dense zone appears in the A band, but the A band remains the same width; in effect, the A bands are brought closer together.

To explain such observations H. E. Huxley and J. Hanson proposed a sliding-filament model of the contraction of muscle. According to them, the two types of filaments, thick myosin and thin actin, are interdigi-

24 years

51 years

Muscle ——                          —— Connective tissue

73 years

81 years

0.01 *M* KCl

(a)

0.01 *M* KCl + ATP

(b)

tated (Figure 21–18). Each dark A band represents the length of one region of thick myosin filaments; it is darkest at its borders, where the myosin and the actin filaments overlap, and lighter in the middle (H zone), where only the myosin filaments are present. The light I band represents a region of actin filaments, and the Z line is a membranous structure that orients the actin filaments. Movement occurs in the following way. The myosin filaments have fingerlike projections at regular intervals along their length, and these form cross bridges with the actin filaments. The cross bridge is movable, oscillating forward and backward, and the fingerlike myosin projections fit into specialized receptor sites on the actin filament. Attached to the myosin filament is ATP, and when calcium ions appear in the fluids of the muscle fiber (owing to muscle stimulation), the myosin projections form activated myosin, which acts as an enzyme (**ATPase**) and splits the ATP. This provides energy so that the actin filament slides along the myosin filament by a ratchetlike mechanism; the actin filament locks first with one projection, then with one farther along, then with the next, and so on (Figure 21–19). According to Huxley, each ratchetlike movement of the muscle filaments—that is, the formation of each new

FIGURE 21–16 (top) The molecular structure of muscle. (a) Thin filament containing actin, troponin, and tropomyosin. (b) Relationship of thin filament (actin) to thick filament (myosin).

FIGURE 21–17 (bottom) Electron micrograph of striated muscle. (Courtesy of K. R. Porter.)

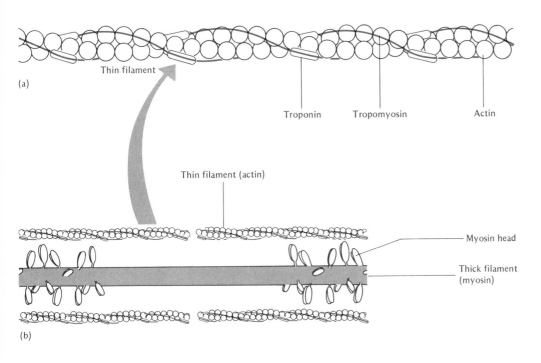

FIGURE 21–18 The Huxley-Hanson model of muscle contraction. The muscle is uncontracted in (a) and fully contracted in (d).

bridge between myosin and actin—requires the energy of one molecule of ATP. When the muscle relaxes, it is presumed that there is no longer a splitting of ATP (calcium ions are removed and ATPase activity is diminished), the myosin bridges no longer combine with the actin filaments, and the muscle spontaneously returns to its original, uncontracted state. (The pull of the surrounding elastic connective tissue may also play a role in relaxation.)

The sliding-filament theory of Huxley and Hanson clearly explains the changes that occur in the banding pattern as the muscle contracts and relaxes. The rigid condition of muscles after death, rigor mortis, is due to the formation of permanent links between actin and myosin in the absence of ATP. In rigor mortis the muscle cell no longer has a supply of ATP, its energy stores are depleted, and the actin-myosin bridges remain permanently fixed as if they had been deprived of their source of lubrication.

### Characteristics of muscle contractions

The events taking place during contraction are similar in all muscle cells. Whether you

FIGURE 21–19 A simplified diagram to show the
function of actin and myosin in the Huxley-Hanson
theory of muscle contraction. (1) The hook moves
downward. (2) The hook attached to actin. (3) The
hook contracts, moving the actin filament inward.

FIGURE 21–20 The motor end plate. (a) Detail of
the motor end plate. (b) Transmission across the
end plate. (c) Movement of an action potential
across the muscle.

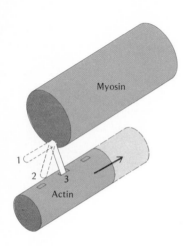

use the muscles in your arm to turn the
page of a book or to lift a weight of 35 lb,
the molecular mechanisms are identical.
However, the force exerted by our arm
muscles is not the same in each case: the
degree of contractile force is directly related
to the amount of work to be performed.
Were this not so, muscular contraction would
be inefficient and lack precision. How does
a muscle regulate its contractile force?

Muscles are supplied with nerves, and
each terminal branch of a nerve cell (axon)
ends in a special rootlike structure called
the **motor end plate** (Figure 21–20a). The
highly branched ends of the nerve cell lie
in a series of gutters, or troughs, formed
by folds in the plasma membrane of the
muscle cell (the sarcolemma). The gap between the ends of the nerve cell and the
muscle membrane is a special kind of synapse. As in the case of neuron-neuron
interactions, each of the tips of the nerve
cell contains small synaptic vesicles containing a chemical transmitter substance
(acetylcholine [ACh] is one of the most
important). When the nerve cell is appropriately stimulated, the synaptic vesicles
discharge their contents into the end-plate
gutter, and transmitter substance diffuses
across the space between nerve cell and
muscle membrane (Figure 21–20b). The

transmitter substance acts on the sarcolemma of the adjacent muscle cell and alters
its permeability to positively charged ions
(particularly sodium ions) present in the
surrounding fluid. As the positive ions rush
into the muscle cell, the polarity of the
sarcolemma becomes first neutral and then
reversed; this change in the electrical potential of the membrane at the motor end
plate is called the **motor-end-plate potential.**
If the magnitude of the motor-end-plate
potential reaches a threshold level, the inrushing positive ions cause a brief decrease
in the muscle's membrane (sarcolemma)
potential, it becomes depolarized, and the
inside of the muscle cell becomes slightly

positive relative to the outside. The depolarization of the sarcolemma is propagated
as a wave over the entire muscle, and this
potential (an action potential) moves outward similar to the way in which waves
move outward to the water's edge when a
pebble is dropped into a pool (Figure 21–
20c). The polarity of the sarcolemma is
restored to its original condition just behind
the wave of depolarization by the extrusion
of positively charged ions (in this case potassium) from inside the muscle cell. As the
action potential traverses the length of the
muscle cell, it promotes the release of
calcium ions from the **sarcoplasmic reticulum**
(a modified endoplasmic reticulum that sur-

### BOX 21A Myasthenia gravis

Myasthenia gravis is a rare human disease that results in paralysis. The cause of the disease is an altered neuromuscular junction: the end plate gutter is widened by about 50%, and the number of clefts on the muscle membrane is significantly reduced* (Figure 21–21). Why should these changes in the neuromuscular junction

FIGURE 21–21 The motor and plate in a normal individual and one with myasthenia gravis.

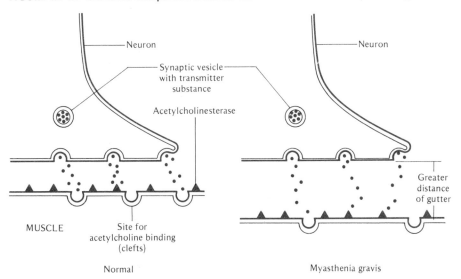

cause muscle paralysis? In victims of the disease, the action of acetylcholine (the neurotransmitter substance) is ineffective because the lengthened amount of time it takes for it to traverse the widened gutter allows acetylcholinesterase to destroy most of that which has been released by the neuron; and with the reduced number of clefts on the muscle membrane, there is less surface on which the neurotransmitter can act. As a consequence an action potential cannot occur, and the muscle is paralyzed. Individuals suffering from myasthenia gravis can have some of their symptoms relieved by the administration of a drug called neostigmine. Neostigmine inactivates acetylcholinesterase, and allows sufficient acetylcholine to accumulate in the gutter so that an end-plate potential can be triggered in the muscle membrane.

---

* The reduced number of acetylcholine receptors results from an autoimmune phenomenon such that in individuals with myasthenia gravis antibodies are formed against the muscle membrane receptors and cause their destruction

---

rounds the packets of myofibrils like a bracelet; Figures 21–17 and 21–22). The calcium ions trigger activation of myosin so that it acts as an ATPase, ATP is split, and the muscle cell contracts as the myofibrils shorten. When the calcium ions are resorbed (presumably they return to the confines of the sarcoplasmic reticulum) or are bound, there is no longer any activation of ATPase, ATP is no longer split, and the muscle lengthens as the myofibrils relax.

Two points of importance are (1) the motor-end-plate potential and the release of calcium from the sarcoplasmic reticulum are graded responses that depend on the strength of the stimulus and (2) the action potential is an all-or-none phenomenon—it either is or is not produced—and it does not vary in amplitude with the strength of the stimulus.

The functional unit of the muscle is a nerve cell and the muscle cells that it innervates, together known as a **motor unit** (Figure 21–20). Usually the muscle cells of a particular motor unit do not lie next to one another, but are spread out over the entire belly of the muscle. In this way stimulation of a motor unit will cause a weak contraction over a broad area of the muscle rather than a single strong contraction at one spot. The number of nerve cells stimulated and the frequency of the action potentials generated in these nerve cells depend on the amount of stimulation received—for example, the amount of pressure on nerve receptors in the skin. The greater the number of nerve cells carrying action potentials, the more muscle cells there will be contracting. The graded response of a muscle depends also upon how many muscle cells are involved in a particular motor unit as well as the threshold of that motor unit (some will be low, others will be high, and still others will be intermediate). Fine or delicate movements involve only a few muscle cells, and although such a system lacks power it is very precise. The eye muscles are an example of this, where a single nerve runs to only five or

FIGURE 21–22 Diagrammatic reconstruction from electron micrographs of a portion of a muscle cell. The section shows the sarcoplasmic reticulum and its relation to the muscle cell and packets of myofibrils.

FIGURE 21–23 Production of tetanus and fatigue by repetitive threshold stimuli.

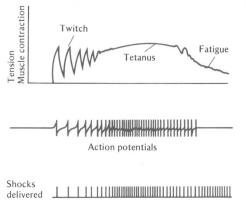

and energy from the breakdown of ATP is utilized. ATP, the driving force of muscle, is formed by the oxidation of fuel materials, such as glycogen and glucose, that are present in the muscle, with pyruvic acid as the initial end product (Chapter 4). If, however, the intensity of exercise rises to an extent that blood cannot deliver oxygen in adequate amounts for the complete oxidation of glucose, the muscle contractions occur anaerobically and lactic acid is formed from pyruvic acid. The lactic acid leaks out of the muscle and passes into the blood. If heavy exercise is continued, the lactic acid content of the blood rises sharply, and eventually so much is present that it no longer leaves the muscle but accumulates there. Excessive amounts of lactic acid depress metabolic activity in the muscle cells and cause decreased irritability. This interferes with the ability of the muscle cell to contract. Muscle fatigue and soreness (cramps) are primarily a result of the accumulation of lactic acid, and this forces cessation of the exercise.

Although the muscle is capable of working in the absence of an oxygen supply for a limited period of time (the exact time being related to the rapidity of lactic acid accumulation), it must eventually have oxygen for oxidizing lactic acid and resynthes-

six muscle cells. By contrast, the calf muscle has a single nerve cell innervating 1,900 muscle cells, and when these contract at the same time, the contraction is powerful.

The preceding discussions about the chemical and electrical changes that occur in a muscle during contraction would lead one to expect that muscles cannot respond to frequent and repeated stimuli, since there would not be enough time between stimuli for the muscle to return to its original, polarized state. This is indeed the case; muscle cells, like nerve cells, have a short period of time immediately after one stimulus when they cannot generate an action potential if a second stimulus is administered; this is the **resting,** or **refractory, period.** The refractory period in most muscles usually lasts about 0.02 second.

If stimuli are given with great rapidity (30 to 350 times per second) and the muscle is unable to relax between stimuli, the contracted state is sustained (Figure 21–23). This condition is called **tetanus** (not to be confused with the disease tetanus, or lockjaw, which produces muscle spasms; Box 21B). Although tetanic contractions do occur normally in our body, if they are continued over a long period of time, the muscle will begin to fatigue and its strength of contraction will diminish even under continued stimulation (Figure 21–23).

What is the reason for muscle fatigue? Why can we not exercise continuously and feel no effects? When we use our muscles to exercise, to maintain posture, or to do any other motor activity, muscular contractions are performing work, heat is released,

FIGURE 21–24 The oxygen debt and its repayment. Area A represents the amount of oxygen needed above the actual amount consumed (oxygen debt). Area B represents oxygen consumed above that needed after exercise (repayment of oxygen debt).

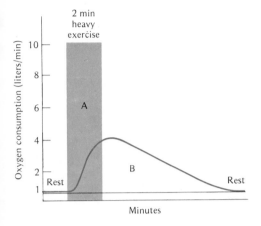

izing glycogen and ATP. The amount of oxygen required for these tasks is called the **oxygen debt,** and it is specified as the quantity of oxygen used in excess of the resting level during physical activity and ending with complete recovery, that is, a return to the resting level (Figure 21–24). Repayment of the oxygen debt is reflected by our heavy breathing after strenuous activity. During this period, some lactic acid is oxidized to provide energy for the conversion of the remainder to glycogen and the restoration of ATP from ADP.

## SUMMARY

**1.** The 206 bones of the skeleton provide for protection, muscle attachment, movement and locomotion, storage of calcium salts, and manufacture of blood cells.

**2.** The skull and vertebral column compose the axial skeleton. The pelvic and pectoral girdle and the bones of the arms and legs form the appendicular skeleton.

**3.** Bone consists of 35% organic collagen and chondroitin sulfate and 65% inorganic calcium salts, arranged in Haversian canal systems in which osteocytes embedded in bone matrix surround a central core of blood vessels and nerves. Bones are surrounded by a periosteum.

---

BOX 21B  Your muscles: use 'em or lose 'em

Muscles become more efficient and capable of performing increased amounts of work as their work load increases, a situation quite unlike that with the machines we create out of "durable" substances such as aluminum and steel, which become worn with use. The more a muscle is used, the larger its size and the greater its strength. The enlargement (hypertrophy) of muscle resulting from growth or exercise is due to an increase in the diameter of the muscle cells rather than an increase in the number of cells or muscle bundles; it is the number of myofibrils per cell that is increased. This change in girth increases the total force of the contractile process.

Muscles that are not continually used **atrophy,** that is, they shrink in size and become weaker. In poliomyelitis the impaired function of the nerve fibers that transmit impulses to the muscle results in diminished stimulation of the muscle, which causes it to waste (atrophy). Muscles deprived of their nerve supply eventually degenerate; in 6 months to 2 years a muscle may be reduced to 25% of its normal size, and the muscle cells are replaced by noncontractile connective tissues. Often the weakening of muscle can be delayed by direct electrical or mechanical stimulation (massage) of the muscle. Muscle atrophy may also occur when there is an enforced period of inactivity, such as immobilization of a limb in a cast after an operation or during an illness that requires extended periods of bed rest; again skeletal-muscle atrophy can be minimized by massage or limited exercise.

We are born with essentially our full complement of skeletal muscle cells and lack the capacity to produce new ones. Accordingly, regeneration of muscle after injury does not occur. However, the surviving cells can increase their size and strength by increasing the synthesis of myofibrils, so that an injured muscle can ultimately perform at its original level with fewer muscle cells. An individual muscle cell may be capable of repair, but any large lesion is replaced by connective tissue, which lacks the contractile properties of the original muscle tissue.

### BOX 21C Paralytic poisons

Deep within the Amazon jungle a Jivaro hunter sits quietly behind a tree, blowgun and quiver of darts hanging at his side. Each dart has a needlelike tip that has been carefully coated with a brownish gum containing the substance curare. As a small wild pig emerges from the dense forest and enters the clearing, the hunter levels his blowgun, places a dart into its barrel, and with a silent puff of air sends the missile toward the prey. The pig jumps as the dart pricks its skin, lurches forward, sways, falls down paralyzed, and in less than 5 minutes has stopped breathing.

A farmer in the southern United States loads a spray truck with an organophosphate pesticide and sets out to spray the crops. As he does so he thinks how the crops will flourish because leaf damage from insects will be minimal. Suddenly, the wind shifts and the farmer is covered with the pesticide. Coming in contact with the pesticide, he reacts as would the insect pest: he becomes paralyzed, breathing movements cease, and death occurs shortly thereafter.

These two anecdotes illustrate the use of paralytic poisons to our benefit and detriment. How do curare and organophosphates work?

Nerves coordinate our body movements by regulating the stimuli that reach our muscles. Since nerves produce transmitter substances that carry messages to the muscles, any substance affecting transmission of these messages at the motor end plate will determine whether a muscle contracts or not. The transmitter substance ACh is released by the synaptic vesicles of certain motor nerves and acts to depolarize the muscle membrane (Figure 21–25a). ACh persists for only a short period of time because it is broken down locally by the enzyme acetylcholinesterase, present in the motor-end-plate region. If ACh were to remain indefinitely, the muscle cells would transmit a continuous series of action potentials, resulting in muscle spasms and ultimately in death.

Certain tribes in South America take advantage of the ACh-cholinesterase system and capture prey or paralyze their enemies by shooting them with darts dipped in the poison curare. When curare enters a wound it is carried to the region of the motor

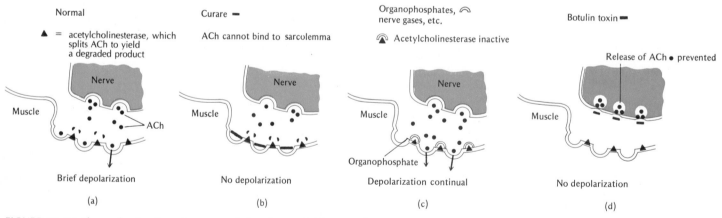

FIGURE 21–25 The mode of action of some paralytic poisons. (a) The normal neuromuscular junction. (b) The end plate affected by curare. (c) The end plate affected by organophosphates or by nerve gases. (d) The end plate affected by botulin toxin.

end plate, and there it binds to the sarcolemma, preventing ACh from reaching the muscle; thus the muscle cannot be stimulated (Figure 21–25b). Continued blockage of impulses across the motor end plate causes paralysis, and death results from asphyxiation since breathing movements are inhibited.

Although curare would seem to have little therapeutic value, its close chemical relative succinylcholine (Anectine) does. During electroshock therapy (EST)*, stimulation of the nerves is frequent and so all-encompassing that muscles may contract forcefully enough to cause bones to break. To counteract these muscle seizures, Anectine is administered to relax muscles so that bone breakage is avoided. The dose administered is low, and its effects disappear in a short time.

Neostigmine, physostigmine (eserine), diisopropyl fluorophosphate, and other organophosphates used as nerve gases and pesticides operate by inhibiting the action of acetylcholinesterase, and thus enhance transmission of messages across the motor end plate (Figure 21–25c). As a result these drugs permit the accumulation of ACh (since it is not degraded), there is spontaneous and continued depolarization-polarization of the sarcolemma, the muscle is continually stimulated, and spastic paralysis results. The antidote for these nerve gases is the drug atropine. Atropine blocks the action of ACh and if used alone would prevent muscle from ever contracting, but since the cause of death from nerve gas is too much ACh, atropine acts as an antidote. (Atropine is also used to dilate the pupils during an eye examination since it relaxes the constrictor muscles of the iris.)

Botulin toxin, a poison produced by the bacterium *Clostridium botulinum*, is the cause of paralytic food poisoning. This toxin blocks the release of ACh (Figure 21–25d) and prevents muscle stimulation; less than 0.001 mg is sufficient to kill a human. By contrast, tetanus toxin, produced by the bacterium *C. tetani*, acts in the spinal cord apparently by suppressing inhibition of muscle antagonists (strychnine acts the same way). As a result

of the lack of inhibition, antagonistic muscles contract simultaneously and the limbs become locked in a state of spastic paralysis (Figure 21–26).

FIGURE 21–26 The nervous control of muscular action. (a) Normal. When stimulus from the brain reaches the biceps and causes contraction, the triceps is stretched. A stretch receptor sends a signal to an interneuron in the spinal cord so that triceps contraction is inhibited. (b) Tetanus. The inhibitory signal is blocked and both muscles contract simultaneously, causing spastic paralysis.

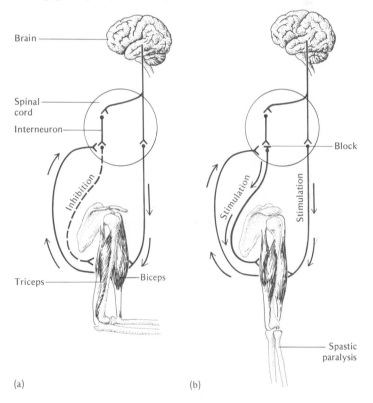

* EST involves the induction of an epileptic-type seizure by electrical stimulation of the brain and is used to treat severe depressive conditions such as catatonic stupor.

**4.** Cartilage, secreted by chondrocytes, contains no mineral salts or blood vessels and is nourished by diffusion. Cartilage may be rigid, flexible, or hyaline. The perichondrium surrounds cartilage and produces chondrocytes.

**5.** The embryonic skeleton is formed of collagen fibers, which are secreted by fibroblasts, and hyaline cartilage. Ossification begins in the center of embryonic bones. The growth zone of long bones is just below the tip. Bone is also added on the outer surface. An internal marrow cavity is formed by osteoclastic resorption. Mechanical stress, diet, and "vitamin" D influence bone formation.

**6.** Skeletal muscles (sometimes called striped muscles or striated muscles), composed of bundles of multinucleate (syncytial) cells, are under voluntary control. Red muscle has more myoglobin than white and binds more oxygen.

**7.** Smooth, or visceral, muscles, composed of groups or sheets of uninucleate cells, are involuntary and not attached to bones.

**8.** Cardiac, or heart, muscle is involuntary striated muscle. A functional syncytium, it has an inherent (myogenic) contraction rate of 72 times a minute, which can be increased or decreased by nervous activity.

**9.** Muscles have properties of contractility, extensibility, and elasticity.

**10.** Skeletal muscles bridge the joints of bones to which they are attached by tendons. Tendons transmit muscular pull and allow muscles to act at a distance from the bones they move. Muscles can pull but not push, and so to produce limb movement in both directions, antagonistic muscles must alternately contract and relax.

**11.** Joints may be fused (as in the skull) or movable. Movable joints may be of a ball-and-socket type (free movement), hinged (movement in one plane), or pivotal (intermediate movement). At movable joints, bones are protected by cartilage lubricated by synovial fluid.

**12.** Skeletal muscle cells are elongate, multinucleate cylinders bounded by a sarcolemma and containing sarcoplasm with myofibrils, which are aligned with their cross bands in register.

**13.** About 90% of skeletal muscle protein is actin and myosin, which forms an actomyosin complex capable of contraction in the presence of ATP.

**14.** In the sliding-filament model of muscle contraction, thick myosin filaments interdigitate with thin actin filaments, producing a banded appearance where they overlap. When muscle is stimulated, $Ca^{2+}$ ions appear, activate the myosin (ATPase), and split ATP, producing energy. The energy causes actin and myosin to form cross bridges and to slide along each other in ratchet fashion. During relaxation, $Ca^{2+}$ is removed, ATP is no longer split, bridges no longer form, and the elasticity of muscle and tissue restore the muscle to its original, uncontracted state. In death, permanent cross bridges are formed in the absence of ATP (rigor mortis).

**15.** A nerve impulse arrives and synapses with a muscle at the motor end plate. Transmitter substance (ACh) diffuses to the muscle sarcolemma, producing a change in membrane permeability. $Na^+$ ions rush in, the sarcolemma is depolarized, a potential is produced, and if it reaches threshold, it is propagated. $Ca^{2+}$ ions are released from the sarcoplasmic reticulum, producing contraction. The sarcolemma is repolarized by the extrusion of $K^+$ ions. The refractory period is 0.02 second. Acetylcholinesterase breaks down the ACh.

**16.** The muscle action potential is all-or-none. The motor-end-plate potential and the release of $Ca^{2+}$ are graded responses.

**17.** The nerve cell and muscle cells it innervates, which may be spread through the body of a muscle, form a motor unit. The number of nerve cells stimulated and the frequency of action potentials generated depend on the amount of stimulation received. The graded response of a muscle to varying stimulation depends on how many muscle cells are involved in a motor unit and on their thresholds.

**18.** Tetanus involves a sustained contracted state when muscles are unable to relax between stimuli.

**19.** Fatigue involves loss of muscle contraction even under continued stimulation. During normal muscle contraction, aerobic respiration produces energy with the formation of pyruvic acid, which ultimately is oxidized to $CO_2$ and $H_2O$. Under intense stimulation lactic acid accumulates, which can cause fatigue with muscle cramps and soreness.

**20.** Muscles hypertrophy with exercise owing to an increase of myofibril numbers and an increase in muscle cell size. Unused muscles atrophy and are replaced by connective tissue.

## KEY WORDS

backbone or spine
vertebrae
vertebrates
ribs
skull
axial skeleton
pelvis
shoulder (pectoral) girdle
appendicular skeleton
osteocytes
bone collagen
matrix
Haversian canal systems
periosteum
chondrocytes
hyaline cartilage
perichondrium
fibroblasts
ossification
growth zone
marrow cavity
osteoclasts
skeletal, striped,
  or striated muscle

smooth, visceral,
  or involuntary muscle
cardiac or heart muscle
syncytium
red muscle
white muscle
myoglobin
contractility
extensibility
elasticity
antagonists
flexor
extensor
adductors
abductors
levators
depressors
sphincters
dilators
pronators
supinators
joints
bursa
synovial fluid
bursitis

arthritis
rheumatism
tendons
sarcolemma
sarcoplasm
myofibrils
actin
myosin
actomyosin
tropomyosin
troponin
I bands
A bands
H zone
Z line
sliding filament model
ATPase
motor end plate
motor-end-plate potential
sarcoplasmic reticulum
motor unit
resting or refractory period
tetanus
oxygen debt
atrophy

## TOPICS FOR REVIEW AND DISCUSSION

1. Describe the molecular machinery of muscle contraction.

2. How may paralytic poisons affect the neuromuscular junction?

3. What is the difference between tetanus (lockjaw) and muscle tetany?

4. During exercise, what is the cause of muscle cramps?

5. Describe the structure of bone.

6. Name the various types of muscles in the human body and give the characteristics of each.

7. Since muscles can only pull, how are various kinds of movement made possible?

8. How can graded muscular activity be achieved when a muscle contracts in an all-or-none fashion?

9. How does the skeleton function in support, protection, and movement?

10. What is the role of the sarcoplasmic reticulum in muscle contraction?

Alice looked round her in great surprise. "Why, I do believe we've been under this tree the whole time! Everything's just as it was!"

"Of course it is," said the Queen. "What would you have it?"

"Well, in *our* country," said Alice, still panting a little, "you'd generally get to somewhere else—if you ran very fast for a long time as we've been doing."

"A slow sort of country!" said the Queen. "Now, *here*, you see, it takes all the running *you* can do, to keep in the same place. If you want to get somewhere else, you must run at least twice as fast as that!"

*Through the Looking-Glass,* Lewis Carroll, 1872. Illustration by John Tenniel.

# 22

# Staying in Place: Homeostatic Controls

## 22–1 KEEPING THINGS IN ORDER, OR, MAINTAINING THE STEADY STATE

The desire to understand how a piece of machinery operates provokes one to dissect it and to ask, How do the parts fit together and work? In our previous discussions of the human organism, we dissected each system, exposed its parts, and analyzed function in some detail. We tried to reveal clearly both the working parts and their operation. Now we must try to put all the pieces together and to look at the body as it actually exists, an integrated whole.

A living organism is an open thermodynamic system; that is, there is a constant flow of energy and matter between it and the environment, a flow that is in dynamic equilibrium, often called the **steady state.** Steady state does not refer to a static, or unchanging, condition. When we speak of normal body temperature, blood pressure, or blood sugar level, we are referring to values that fluctuate slightly about a norm. Maintenance of the norm involves the regulation of input and output so that there is little or no *net* change. To accomplish this, there must be a system of controls that regulates the rates of exchange between the living system and its changing external environment. We can think of ourselves as perched on a continuously moving treadmill. To survive, we must maintain a position of equilibrium on life's treadmill; that is, we must keep pace with its motion so as to appear motionless. Such an appearance of stability—that is, the maintenance of a steady state—is possible only by continuous acquisition of matter and energy. It is achieved

because activity of the treadmill is balanced by activity of the organism; backward motion is balanced by forward motion.

As we have seen, every living cell possesses the capacity for self-regulation. Control of enzyme synthesis, product formation, uptake of matter from the environment, and release of energy are all devices employed by cells to cope with the vagaries of the world around them. The mechanisms used are varied: feedback inhibition, enzyme induction, and so on. In multicellular organisms the environment of the cells is to some degree controlled by the organism. This self-regulated control of the internal environment producing a degree of constancy is called **homeostasis** (*homois*—like or same, *stasis*—standing; Gk.). The more complex an organism is, the more vital the process of homeostasis becomes. When homeostasis fails, the organism first suffers and ultimately may die. Our tissues and organs are functionally integrated by means of homeostatic control systems, each of which is automatic and self-regulating and operates by negative feedback mechanisms.[1] Such a system consists of three components:

1. A receptor mechanism (a sensor, or detector, usually neurons) for monitoring deviations from the regulated state
2. A channel, or transmission mechanism, for transmitting and processing the information received (usually nervous)
3. A response mechanism (an effector,

---

[1] The principles of negative feedback in the thermostat are discussed in Chapter 7.

usually glandular or muscular) for producing a corrective measure so that there is a return to the regulated state

Homeostatic control mechanisms in action have been discussed in previous chapters on reproduction (Chapter 9), the kidney (Chapter 16), the endocrine system (Chapter 17), and the nervous system (Chapter 18). Here we shall examine a single additional example of homeostasis to illustrate how such control enables us to appear motionless in a constantly changing world.

## 22–2 BODY-TEMPERATURE CONTROL

"Ninety-eight point six." This simple phrase has meant "normal" ever since you first had your body temperature taken. Indeed, it is quite true that although the temperature of the surface of the skin, hands, or feet may vary greatly, the **core temperature,** that is, the temperature of the vital organs—heart, liver, intestines, and blood—is relatively fixed, rarely going below 97°F or rising above 104°F. Why, we might ask, is the body temperature so regulated, and how is such regulation achieved?

We have an elaborate system for controlling the body temperature. The temperature of animals such as reptiles, amphibians, and fishes—indeed all animals except birds and mammals—fluctuates with that of their environment (Figure 22–1). These animals are called **poikilotherms** (*poikilos*—varied, *therme*—heat; Gk.) or **ectotherms** (*ecto*—outside; Gk.). There are some disadvantages to ectothermy. For example, a lizard on a cool morning is torpid and slow moving, barely able to drag itself into a

**FIGURE 22–1** A comparison between the body temperatures of an ectotherm and an endotherm. (a) A fish (an ectotherm). (b) A human (an endotherm).

(a)

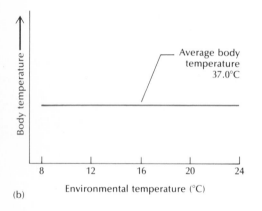

(b)

**FIGURE 22–2** The role of temperature in enzyme activity. (a) Enzyme 1 shows maximum activity at a lower temperature than enzyme 2 and loses activity at a much lower temperature. At the temperature optimum of enzyme 2, enzyme 1 has lost 50% of its activity. (b) If enzyme 1 were inactivated by a temperature rise, substances B, C, and D would not be formed. If enzymes 2 and 3 were equally

(a)

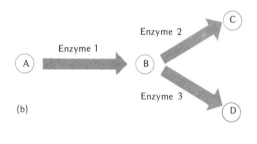

(b)

efficient at the same temperature, C and D would be formed in equal amounts, but if the temperature optima were different the amount of product from B could also be different. If the rates of reactions catalyzed by enzymes 1, 2, and 3 were increased by a temperature rise, the cell could be depleted of A faster than A could be manufactured.

109.4°F or below 77°F. Thus, the maintenance of our body temperature may be a life-or-death affair.

How is constant body temperature of an endotherm achieved? Just as the temperature of a room is regulated by varying the amount of heat produced by the furnace and the rate at which heat leaves the room, so, too, our body balances heat gain and heat loss (Figure 22–3) in order to keep the body temperature at about 98.6°F (37°C). As a result of fuel (food) consumption by our cells, energy is released as heat. A certain amount of energy must be used, and a corresponding amount of heat is produced, just for maintenance. This basal metabolism continues 24 hours a day, asleep or awake. Additional heat may be produced as a result of physical exercise—muscles doing work when we lift something, or run, or shiver. Heat is lost by evaporation, and we may lose or gain heat by radiation and convection, depending on whether the environment is cooler or warmer than the body.

Suppose you exercised vigorously. Would you get warmer or cooler? The answer seems obvious. In exercise heat is produced at a much greater rate than at rest. Heat is not lost from the body as fast as it is gained, and you feel hot. The increase in temperature of blood flowing through the hypothalamus results in physiologic changes. The hypothalamus contains a temperature-control center; when its neurons are stimulated, fewer stimuli are sent to the nerves supplying the muscles of the blood vessels in the skin. Muscles in the walls of the blood vessels relax, the vessels expand (the face becomes ruddy), a large quantity of warm blood flows through the skin, and heat is rapidly lost by radiation. The air close to the skin will also be heated by the blood flowing near the skin surface, the warmed air will tend to move up and away, to be replaced by cooler air, and so on. This movement of unequally heated portions of a gas (or a liquid) is called **convection,** and convection currents increase the rate of heat loss from the body. Finally, impulses from the hypothalamus will be carried by

sunlit spot. All its chemical activities, including the functioning of its muscles, proceed at a slow rate. As the radiant energy of the sunlight warms the lizard, the temperature of the blood rises, its heart beats faster, its metabolic rate speeds up, and soon it can scurry about in search of food or dart away from an attacking enemy. When the body temperature climbs too high, the animal moves to the shade to cool off, and then it can return to the sun or move onto a sun-baked rock to warm up. During the day a lizard can maintain a constant body temperature by moving in and out of the sunshine, but when the sun sets, it must slow down its activity and becomes sluggish. By contrast, our stable body temperature is maintained by the heat of our own metabolism, making us largely independent of the temperature of our environment (Figure

22–1). Humans (and all mammals as well as birds) are **homeotherms,** or **endotherms** (*homois*—same, *endo*—within; Gk.). This environmental independence confers great flexibility on homeothermic animals.

A constant internal temperature has advantages. Each cell of the body is a highly organized system whose chemical reactions are in large part directed by enzymes, and these are often quite sensitive to shifts in temperature. Each enzyme-catalyzed reaction has its own temperature optimum; that is, there is a temperature at which the reaction proceeds most efficiently (Figure 22–2). Too low a temperature will make metabolic reactions proceed slowly and may prevent the formation of materials needed for other vital processes; conversely, too high a temperature can cause changes in the structure of enzymes (denaturation) so that they are rendered nonfunctional. The temperature limits for the human body are very narrow—death usually coming above

FIGURE 22–3 Factors involved in heat gain or loss must be balanced to maintain a constant body temperature. (In a hot environment radiation and convection would result in heat gain.)

sympathetic nerves to the sweat glands in the skin (Figure 22–4). The sweat glands actively secrete a watery fluid; this is deposited on the skin surface. As the sweat evaporates, it has a cooling effect. Why is **evaporation** cooling? To evaporate water, that is, to change it from a liquid to a gas (water vapor), energy is required. Whenever water is evaporated from the body surface, heat energy is lost and the temperature of the body surface drops.

An important factor affecting evaporation is the water-vapor content of the air, its **humidity.** When the days are humid, we tend to feel uncomfortably warm because, although the sweat glands are active, the sweat simply does not evaporate, but remains on the skin or drips off. Most mammals lack sweat glands, and they increase evaporative water loss by panting or by licking their fur. Panting in humans usually occurs while taking a hot bath when sweating cannot cool the body.

The fact that sweat is not pure water (Table 22–1) is of some importance. Sweat contains some salts, principally sodium chloride, so that excessive sweating can deplete body salt, ultimately causing both chemical imbalance and dehydration, heatstroke or sunstroke. This condition can be avoided by increasing the intake of salt as well as water when heavy physical exercise in a hot environment is anticipated.

Let us consider another situation: you enter a walk-in refrigerator set at 32°F (0°C), and you begin to feel cold. During a brief

exposure to the cold, epinephrine is released from the adrenal medulla, and this tends to increase the metabolic rate. (If the exposure to the cold lasts a long time, such as could occur living in an arctic climate, thyroid hormone is secreted in greater

TABLE 22–1 Average composition of sweat and plasma

| Substance | Concentration in sweat (mg/100 ml) | Concentration in plasma (mg/100 ml) |
|---|---|---|
| Sodium | 185 | 325 |
| Potassium | 15 | 15 |
| Calcium | 4 | 10 |
| Magnesium | 1 | 3 |
| Chloride | 310 | 370 |
| Lactate | 35 | 15 |
| Urea nitrogen | 20 | 15 |
| Glucose | 2 | 100 |
| Protein | 0 | 7400 |

Adapted from Y. Kuno, *Human Perspiration*, Springfield, Illinois, Thomas, 1956.

amounts and there is a long-term elevation in the body's metabolic rate.) The hypothalamus sends impulses along the descending tracts of the spinal cord to the body muscles, shivering begins, and more heat is generated. This shivering pathway can be suppressed by input from the cerebral cortex, since a cold person ceases to shiver when engaged in such voluntary activity as stomping the feet or running (which also increases heat production). In addition, there is reflex narrowing of the blood vessels in the skin; as arteriole muscles receive nerve impulses, the amount of blood flowing through the skin is decreased, and heat is conserved by a reduction in the loss from radiation. Hair can help in reducing heat loss from convection: in birds and mammals, when the weather gets cold, feathers and fur puff out to create an insulating blanket of dead air space near the skin surface. The insulation properties of most clothing result from a layer of warm

### BOX 22A Fever: resetting the body's thermostat

During the course of an infection such as a common cold or the flu, it is not uncommon to experience **fever**—an elevation of the body temperature. At the beginning the body reacts as if it were subjected to a cold environment—blood vessels in the skin constrict, the skin pales, there is a reduction in heat loss, and you experience apparent chills and shivering. As a consequence of these heat-conserving mechanisms, the body temperature quickly rises; you become feverish, your face is flushed, and you break out in a sweat. Fever is not a breakdown of the temperature-regulating mechanism, but simply a resetting of the hypothalamic thermostat to a higher point. Thus, at the beginning, although the body temperature is normal, the body acts as if the core temperature were too low and begins to institute measures both for conserving heat and for increasing heat production (Figure 22–5). As a result the body temperature is deviated, and soon it settles at this higher point.

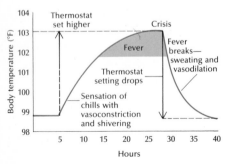

FIGURE 22–5 Fever: a resetting of the body's thermostat.

When the fever breaks (called the crisis), the set point is automatically lowered; now the core temperature is too high, the skin becomes flushed, sweating begins, and mechanisms for increasing heat loss are set into operation. During the early part of such an episode, blankets are put on to combat the feeling of cold, but when the temperature begins to fall, these are thrown off because the skin becomes flushed and sweating begins.

Fever can be harmful. Although the body's tissues can tolerate cooling (temporary body temperatures as low as 85°F do not cause damage), they cannot withstand much heat gain, and chemical reactions may speed up to a dangerous point. Most people suffer convulsions at 106 to 107°F, and 110°F is the absolute limit for life. Indeed, when heat cannot be lost from the body fast enough to prevent a rise in body temperature, a vicious positive feedback cycle ensues: metabolic reactions increase their rate as temperature rises; consequently heat production is increased, the temperature of the body climbs, metabolism goes faster, and so on. Unchecked fever (or exposure to extreme heat) can produce fainting and even death. The best course of action: reduce the body temperature by cooling.

What causes a fever? It is believed that chemical agents called **pyrogens** (*pyr*—flame, *gen*—producer; Gk.) are released by white blood cells during the inflammatory response to a microbial intruder. These pyrogens act (in an unexplained manner) directly on the hypothalamus, causing its set point to be pushed abnormally high. It has been speculated that the high body temperature during a fever helps the body combat the invading microbes.

air trapped in the network of the clothing and not from the material of the fabric itself. Humans have so little body hair that it is ineffective as insulation, but we respond by attempting to raise up our few remaining hairs by contracting the muscles attached to each one (Figure 22–4). All that results is a dimpling of the skin—goose pimples—an ineffectual response to the cold. Sweating ceases in the cold, so that evaporative heat loss is minimized. Additional behavior mechanisms, such as curling into a ball or hunching the shoulders, tend to reduce the surface area of the body exposed to the cold environment, and body heat is conserved.

By a balance of heat loss and heat production, the temperature of the body is regulated; the feedback loops involved are summarized in Figure 22–6. The main center for control of body temperature—our thermostat—is situated in the hypothalamic region of the brain. If the cortex of an endothermic animal's brain is completely removed, such an animal can still regulate its body temperature, but if the hypothalamus is destroyed, this ability is eliminated. The hypothalamus contains a temperature-control center that monitors the temperature of the blood passing through this region of the brain. When the body temperature rises the neurons of the center are activated, sympathetic nerves carry impulses to the sweat glands, blood vessels, and adrenal medulla and there is an increase in heat loss (blood flow is increased, as is sweating). However, when the body is cooled this is sensed by the hypothalamus, the parasympathetic nerves, which run to the sweat glands and blood vessels, produce essentially the opposite effect.

In the home thermostat, you can fool the system by placing a lighted match or an ice-cold rod under the temperature-sensitive element, thus causing the furnace to go on or off without any previous change in the room temperature. The same can be done with the temperature controls of the hypothalamus. If wires implanted in the hy-

FIGURE 22–6 Feedback loops involved in the
maintenance of constant body temperature.

**457**

**STAYING IN PLACE:
HOMEOSTATIC CONTROLS**

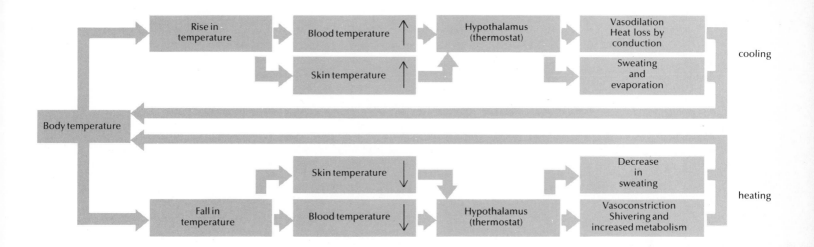

pothalamus are warmed, the animal responds by showing the responses typical of a hot environment —panting, sweating, dilation of skin blood vessels. Conversely, local cooling of the hypothalamus by a chilling of wires implanted in this region of the brain produces responses typical of an animal subjected to the cold.

## SUMMARY

**1.** Living organisms are in dynamic equilibrium with their environments; that is, they maintain a steady state. Although there is input and output, values fluctuate about a norm and there is no net change.

**2.** Maintenance of the norm involves self-regulation, usually by negative feedback mechanisms. The components of a self-regulatory system are receptors, transducing and transmitting mechanisms, and response effectors. Self-regulated maintenance of the internal environment is called homeostasis, and when it fails, death may ensue.

**3.** The body temperature of poikilotherms (ectotherms) fluctuates with their environment, whereas homeotherms (endotherms) have homeostatic mechanisms for maintaining a constant body temperature independent of that of the environ-

ment. These mechanisms are under hypothalamic control and include regulation of the blood supply to the skin, regulation of sweat gland secretion, and evaporative cooling, panting, shivering and erection of hairs.

**4.** Fever involves a resetting of the hypothalamic thermostat to a higher set point under the influence of pyrogens.

### KEY WORDS

steady state
homeostasis
core temperature
poikilotherms or ectotherms
homeotherms or endotherms
radiation
convection
humidity
fever
pyrogens
convection
evaporation

### TOPICS FOR REVIEW AND DISCUSSION

1. Define homeostasis.

2. What is the significance of fever?

3. How is temperature control achieved in the human body?

4. Name some mechanisms that conserve body heat in a cold environment.

5. How do poikilotherms differ from homeotherms?

6. Explain the survival value of homeostasis in vertebrate animals.

7. Compare the human thermostat with the mechanical thermostat.

8. Discuss negative feedback controls.

9. What homeostatic mechanisms come into play at high temperatures?

The past is but the beginning of the beginning, and all that is and has been is but the twilight of the dawn. A day will come when beings who are now latent in our thoughts and hidden in our loins ... shall laugh and reach out their hands amid the stars.

H. G. WELLS

# THE HUMAN POPULATION

We humans have a sense of history. We cope with the present, wonder about our past being and origins, and attempt to forecast the future, hoping that our children will find this planet a habitable place. We are the product of evolution—the ultimate in games of chance. For most creatures—past, present, and future—it is a most unusual game. The participants are unaware that they are playing and know nothing of the game's rules. The prize for winning a round of play is simply the privilege of participating in yet another round of the game; biologically speaking, the winning players perpetuate their kind, and the losers are doomed to extinction. Extinction—leaving the game after losing—is final; there are no second chances. Most of the players will eventually have to pay this penalty. Players entering the next round of the game have a chance of winning that is proportionate to their previous success; that is, the more progeny produced, the greater are the chances that some of these will win, too.

The winner-take-all game of evolution is further complicated by the fact that the rules for selecting the winners can be changed in a rather unpredictable fashion from one round to the next. And in the final analysis, both environmental surroundings and inherited competence of the participants will determine those individuals selected for another round of play. Nature is both adversary and jury in the evolutionary game. In spite of the scarcity of rules, the players' lack of awareness of any rules, and the hidden goals or purposes of the game, evolution proceeds in an orderly fashion. Only the human species, itself a successful player of the game, understands its rules and goals. We are aware of our own participation; we know what constitutes success. But this understanding does not allow us to load the dice in our favor; we are still unable to assure the future success of our own kind.

Evolution is to many the unifying concept of biology. The species, a population of freely interbreeding individuals, stands as the fundamental unit of evolution. The individual organism has importance only as a genetic package within the group. Natural selection acts on the hereditary characteristics of the individual, but its prime target is the total collection of genes in the entire population. Thus, fitness (the chance to play) does not apply to an individual gene or its possessor, but includes all the genes of the breeding group and depends upon the way in which these interact with their surroundings. In the chapters that follow we shall study the transmission of genes from parent to offspring (Chapter 23) and the manner in which genes in the population become scarce or frequent (Chapter 24). Thus, we gain insight into how biological evolution—descent with modification—works (Chapter 25).

An appreciation of population biology enables us to discard the notion of a perfect species. There is and there can be no golden mean for any animal or plant. Genetic diversity within a population provides the biological basis for both our individuality and our freedom; it enables a species to hedge its bets in the game of survival. The more different kinds of individuals there are, the less is the chance that a change in the game's rules will eliminate all the players and thus cause a species to become extinct. Species evolve not by deliberate or conscious efforts of their members to meet a particular environment, but because chance variations in the hereditary characteristics of some individuals enable these to survive and reproduce. Thus, the blind and automatic strategy for living creatures playing the game of evolution is expansion of population size and maintenance of genetic individuality.

Species are genetically continuous in both time and space, since the members share a common pool of genes; the individuals of a species form a reproductive community. Species are also a part of an ecological community, since they interact with both the non-living and the living environment. The world of the next few decades will be determined by an interplay of numbers—numbers of different kinds of people and numbers of environmental resources. We must determine the rules that govern our relationship to our natural surroundings (Chapters 26 and 27). Then, and perhaps only then, can we embark on a collective pattern of play to ensure a decent legacy for our progeny.

FIGURE 23–1 Down syndrome in a 4-year-old girl. (Courtesy of Sanford Schneider.)

FIGURE 23–2 Amniocentesis is accomplished by inserting a hypodermic needle into the amniotic cavity and withdrawing a small amount of fluid and fetal cells. Optimum time for such a procedure is about the sixteenth week of pregnancy.

FIGURE 23–1 Down syndrome in a 4-year-old girl. (Courtesy of Sanford Schneider.)

FIGURE 23–2 Amniocentesis is accomplished by inserting a hypodermic needle into the amniotic cavity and withdrawing a small amount of fluid and fetal cells. Optimum time for such a procedure is about the sixteenth week of pregnancy.

The chromosomal picture of a human male and a female shows that each of the body (somatic) cells contains 46 chromosomes, and these are arranged in 23 pairs (Figure 23–4). Each pair of chromosomes has a slightly different appearance and for the sake of convenience can be assigned a number (Figure 23–4). (The method of preparing chromosomal pictures such as the one shown is described in Box 23A.)

Recall that in your body two types of cell division occur: mitosis and meiosis. Mitosis maintains a constant chromosome number, whereas meiosis halves the number of chromosomes.[2] Meoisis occurs only during the course of germ-cell formation and results in the production of **gametes** (sex cells) containing only one member of each chro-

mosomal pair; thus the chromosomal number of a gamete (egg or sperm) is haploid ($n$). In the human female, mature eggs are produced by meoisis and contain 23 chromosomes; by a similar process the human male produces mature sperm containing 23 chromosomes (Figure 23–5). When a sperm fertilizes an egg, the resultant cell, the **zygote,** contains 46 chromosomes (23 pairs). Thus, every cell of the body contains two sets of genes on two sets of chromosomes, except for the gametes, in which one set of genes occurs on one set of chromosomes.

Compare the chromosomes from the male and female; 22 pairs are similar in form. These are the **autosomes.** One additional pair in the female, designated **XX,** is not similar to the equivalent pair in the male, called **XY.** These are the **sex chromosomes.** Meoisis in the human male produces two kinds of sperm (X-bearing and Y-bearing), but the female produces only X-bearing eggs (Figure 23–5). Since the sex chromo-

somes are responsible for the sex of an individual, the kind of sperm that fertilizes the egg must determine the sex of the offspring. If an X-bearing sperm enters the egg, the genetic constitution is XX, or female; if a Y-bearing sperm fertilizes the egg, the offspring will be a male (XY).

## 23–3 PHENOTYPE AND GENOTYPE

One of the most obvious of all human traits is skin color. Skin color depends principally on the amount of **melanin,** a yellow-black pigment, present in special skin cells called **melanocytes.** If the melanocytes produce a great deal of pigment, the skin is black; if they produce very little, it is white. Melanocytes synthesize melanin from the amino acid tyrosine by a metabolic pathway that can be simply illustrated:

tyrosine $\longrightarrow$ A $\longrightarrow$ B $\longrightarrow$ melanin

Each step in the pathway is catalyzed by a

[2] Mitosis and meoisis are discussed in Chapter 9, and the chromosomal movements are illustrated in Figure 9–1. A review of this material will be helpful to the reader.

## BOX 23A  Preparing chromosomal pictures

The direct observation of human chromosomes was for many years extremely difficult if not impossible. Very few cells could be found in metaphase, when chromosomes are most distinct, and the large number of chromosomes in human cells often caused them to lie on top of each other, making them difficult to count. Indeed, up until 1956 it was believed that humans had 48 chromosomes. In the past 30 years significant technological advances have been made: cells can be grown in glass vessels outside the human body; a chemical agent, colchicine, stops mitosis at metaphase; and cells treated with dilute salt solutions swell and burst, in effect spreading out the chromosomes. Applying these techniques to a drop of blood or to cells removed from the amniotic fluid enables the chromosomes to be analyzed and a **karotype** (chromosome picture) to be prepared (Figure 23–3). By the use of chromosome typing, a number of hereditary defects can be identified, as well as the sex and genetic condition of an unborn child.

FIGURE 23–3 The preparation of a chromosome picture (karotype) for chromsome analysis. Note that the chromosomes shown are actually pairs of chromatids interrupted at metaphase and held together by their centromere. (Modified from H. Curtis, *Invitation to Biology,* New York, Worth, 1972.)

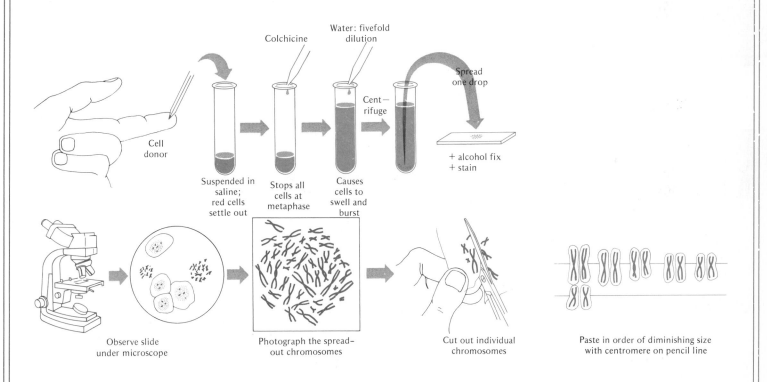

FIGURE 23–4 Human chromosomes. (a) A chromosomal spread from a cell of a human female (top), and (below) the 46 chromosomes arranged in homologous pairs, showing the 22 pairs of autosomes and a pair of sex chromosomes (XX). (b) A similar spread from a cell of a human male (top) and (below) arranged in homologous pairs showing 22 pairs of autosomes and a pair of sex chromosomes (XY). (Courtesy of W. R. Centerwall.)

**FIGURE 23–5** A schematic illustration of meiosis and fertilization.

**465**

GENES IN INDIVIDUALS:
HUMAN INHERITANCE

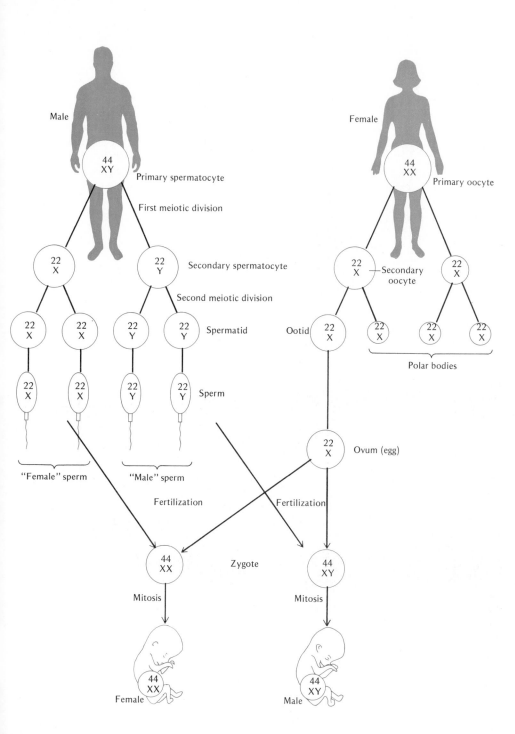

specific enzyme, which in turn is specified by a particular region of the nuclear DNA, a gene:

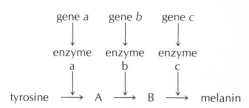

About 1 out of 20,000 humans fails to synthesize melanin because she or he does not produce one of the enzymes in the path from tyrosine to melanin. The skin of such an individual is white or pink (because the red color of the blood cells in the underlying vessels can easily be seen) and the hair is white (Figure 23–6). Such individuals, called **albinos** (*albus*—white; L.), are acutely sensitive to sunlight, are subject to skin cancer, and have poor vision.

Any detectable feature of an organism or a cell, in this case the white-skinned appearance of the albino, is called the **phenotype.** Phenotype (*phainein*—to appear; Gk.) refers to the way in which a trait expresses itself, that is, what can be detected. Blue eyes and brown eyes are different phenotypes; so are red hair, blond hair, brown hair, and black hair. Blood type, nose shape, and many other traits you can think of are also detectable traits—phenotypes—and we use these almost every day to recognize individual persons by their unique array of visible characteristics.

In addition to phenotype, individuals also have a **genotype,** that is, a particular set of genetic instructions inherited from the parents. How is phenotype related to genotype? In each of the body cells there exist pairs of chromosomes that are similar in size, shape, and the kind of genes they carry. Such chromosomes are called **homologous chromosomes.** Each gene may occur in a variety of contrasting forms called **alleles.** Each gene occupies exactly the same position (**locus**) along the length of its chromosome as its partner gene on the homol-

FIGURE 23–6 An albino. (Courtesy of *The Journal of Heredity,* Vol. 39, No. 5, 1948.)

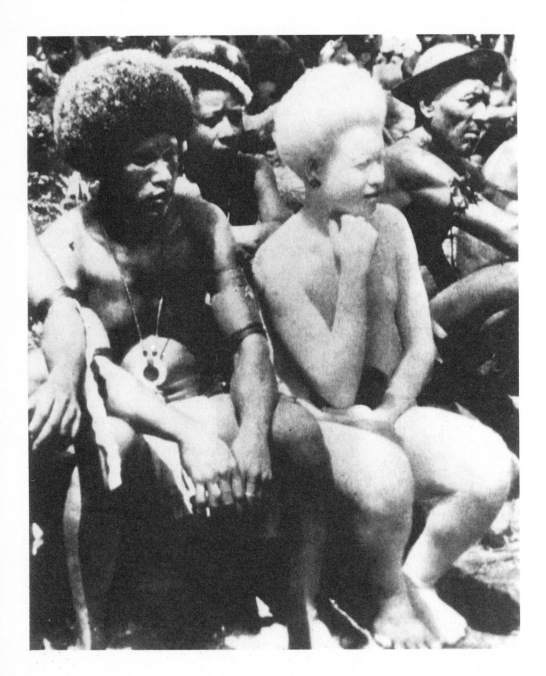

ogous chromosome. Each locus of a single chromosome can carry only one dose of the gene. In terms of the primary products of genes, the alleles produce different forms of the same protein. Albinism is caused by a defective allele coding for a defective enzyme involved in the metabolic pathway of melanin formation from tyrosine. Specifically, the condition arises only when the individual is endowed with two defective alleles. (As long as one allele is normal, the individual will produce the enzyme and be normal in appearance.) Tracing the inheritance of a trait such as albinism from one generation to the next is a basic genetic method. Such a hereditary lineage is called a **family tree** or **pedigree.**

The hypothetical pedigree shown in Figure 23–7 illustrates the genotypes of children resulting from the mating of an albino male with a normal female. All the children are normal. What does this tell us? First, the female parent must carry two normal alleles; second, the male parent must carry two alleles that result in a failure to manufacture melanin. We can conclude from this pedigree that the allele for normal pigmentation is **dominant** over its partner allele, the **recessive,** because the children, who have one normal and one defective allele, have normal skin color.

The dominant allele is customarily symbolized by a capital letter (in this case *A*); the recessive allele, by a corresponding small letter (*a*). The phenotype of the male parent is albino, and his genotype can be written *aa*. The female parent is of normal phenotype, and she must be genotype *AA* (proof of this will become apparent shortly). The children of the mating are all of normal phenotype and have the genotype *Aa*. Persons carrying a pair of similar alleles (both parents in this pedigree) are said to be **homozygous;** those carrying unlike alleles (the offspring in this case) are **heterozygous.**

Let us carry the inheritance of albinism one step further and extend the pedigree of this family for two more generations (Figure 23–7); in the third generation two

FIGURE 23–7 (a) Pedigree for albinism in four generations of a family. By convention, males are symbolized by squares and females by circles. Solid circles or squares represent individuals who show the trait. A horizontal line connecting a circle to a square represents a mating, and a vertical line extending downward from the horizontal one connects to the children produced by the mating. If there are several children from a mating, these are connected by vertical lines to a horizontal one, which in turn links up to the line linking the parents. (b) Matings in generations I and III, showing the genotypes of the parents and possible offspring.

(a)

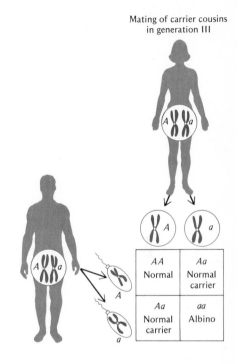

(b)

cousins marry, and some of their offspring in the fourth generation show albinism. Therefore, although the phenotypes of the cousins who marry are normal, these individuals must be heterozygous for albinism, that is, of genotype *Aa*; these parents are designated as **carriers** of the trait.

A number of important points emerge from a study of the family pedigree of albinism. First, genes do not blend, and there is no dilution of a genetic trait from generation to generation. Second, genes are discrete entities that are capable of being expressed in subsequent generations. Third, an offspring receives one and only one member of a pair of alleles from each parent (each gamete contains only one member of a pair of alleles). Fourth, albinism results from a change (**mutation**) in the gene coding for at least one of the enzymes involved in melanin synthesis; the presence of one normal allele, the dominant, is necessary for normal pigmentation. Fifth, a trait determined by a dominant gene will not appear in an offspring unless it also appears in one or both parents.

## 23–4 TRANSMISSION OF GENES

Two principles govern the transmission of genes from parents to offspring: segregation and recombination. Often these principles are called Mendel's first and second laws, after the Austrian monk Gregor Mendel (1822–1884), who worked them out (Box 23B).

The **law of segregation** states the following: (1) each individual starts life as a fertilized egg containing two representatives of each kind of gene; one member of each pair is derived from one parent, and the other member from the other parent; (2) a sexually mature adult (who develops from a fertilized egg) transmits only one member of each pair of genes into each gamete he or she produces. The term "segregation" refers to the fact that although each pair of genes is associated during the lifetime of an individual, when it comes to gamete formation the two genes clearly separate, or segregate. This is related to the behavior of the chromosomes during meiosis (Figure 23–9). The outcomes of nine possible matings involving the recessive trait albinism clearly demonstrate the principle of segregation (Figure 23–10).

The law of independent assortment (also called the **principle of recombination**) states that when an organism matures and produces gametes, the genes may enter into the gametes in a great variety of associations, regardless of their parental origin. Thus, the genes derived from one parent

## BOX 23B  Mendel and his peas

In 1865 Gregor Johann Mendel, an Augustinian monk, described to the Brünn Natural Science Society the inheritance of characters in pea plants after 8 years of painstaking work. The discussion that followed was brief. Sadly, the fundamental importance of Mendel's findings was not understood by anyone in the audience; nevertheless, the society did ask him to publish his lecture in 1866. One copy of the published manuscript was sent to Carl Naegli in Munich, a leading figure in studies of heredity. Letters and views were exchanged between the two men. Naegli, however, did not believe Mendel's explanations and suggested that he work with the hawkweed plant instead of the pea plant. The encounter with Naegli became a disaster for Mendel. After 5 years of intensive effort on the hawkweed, and with his eyesight failing, Mendel wrote to Naegli that the features of inheritance he had discovered with the garden pea did not apply to the hawkweed. (This was in fact not true; the hawkweed rarely reproduces sexually, thus confusing Mendel at the time.)

In 1868 Mendel was elected abbot of the Brünn monastery, an office he thought would allow him ample leisure time to continue his experiments. This was not to be, and by 1871 his productive scientific career came to an end. He died in 1884 at age 62. The mourners who attended the funeral recognized they had lost a dear friend, a dedicated teacher, and a high dignitary, but none at the funeral realized that Mendel had discovered what are at present known as Mendel's laws of heredity. The significance of Mendel's work went unrecognized until 1900, when quite by accident it was rediscovered independently by De Vries in Holland, Tschermak in Austria, and Correns in Germany. Since that time the importance of Mendel's contributions to biology has been clear. Today he is generally acknowledged as the father of genetics.

Here is what Mendel discovered about inheritance. At the beginning he asked a simple question: how is it possible to determine the different kinds of offspring that will result when two pure-breeding varieties are crossed (mated)? Then he went on to select the proper material to answer this question. He chose the garden pea *Pisum* because it showed a constancy of certain characters, he could cross-pollinate plants with ease, and the large garden of the monastery would provide enough space for his plants. By 1856 Mendel had selected 22 varieties and arranged their characters in contrasting traits: round versus wrinkled seeds, tall versus dwarf plants, yellow versus green pods, red versus white flowers, and so on. When two plants differing in only one of these contrasting traits were crossed, the offspring of the first generation, the $F_1$ **(first filial) generation** as it is called, were uniform in appearance and showed only one of the two parental characters; this trait, that was expressed in the presence of a contrasting hereditary factor Mendel called dominant, and the trait that was not expressed in the presence of a contrasting hereditary factor he called recessive. Thus, when he crossed a plant with wrinkled seeds with another having round seeds, the offspring showed only the round-seed character. He found tall was dominant to dwarf, green pods were dominant to yellow pods, and red flower color was dominant to white.

Next, Mendel allowed the $F_1$ plants to self-fertilize, and the progeny of this **second filial generation,** the $F_2$, were found to consist of two types of plants, each resembling one or the other of the original grandparents. No plants were intermediate, and thus there was no blending of the hereditary traits. Unlike his predecessors who had also done plant hybridizations, Mendel counted the numbers of individuals with each of the traits in the $F_2$ generation. He found three fourths of the plants showed the dominant trait and one fourth had the recessive trait. Thus, when he inbred 929 $F_1$ plants showing red flower color, he found the $F_2$ plants to be 705 red-flowered and 224 white-flowered. To explain these results Mendel postulated that each plant contains two hereditary factors—today we call them genes—that affect a particular trait, and during the formation of gametes (pollen and egg) these separate. Each gamete contains only a single member of the pair of parental factors (genes), and by combination of different kinds of gametes a hybrid is produced. Mendel showed that the hereditary factors (genes) segregate, pass undiluted and uncontaminated into the gametes, and do not blend when recombined (at fertilization) to form offspring. This is Mendel's **law of segregation.**

Furthermore, when Mendel took the plants exhibiting the dominant trait from the $F_2$ generation and inbred these to give an $F_3$ generation, about one third of them bred true. In the offspring of the remaining two thirds, grandparental characters once again appeared in a ratio of 3:1. This could occur only if the $F_2$ dominant plants were of two kinds—homozygous and heterozygous (hybrid). All this Mendel symbolized in the following way:

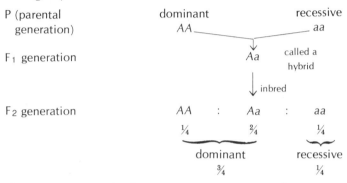

P (parental generation)

dominant          recessive

$AA$ —————————— $aa$

$F_1$ generation                  $Aa$    called a hybrid

inbred

$F_2$ generation      $AA$ : $Aa$ : $aa$

                $\frac{1}{4}$    $\frac{2}{4}$    $\frac{1}{4}$

             dominant      recessive

                 $\frac{3}{4}$         $\frac{1}{4}$

If the $F_2$ $Aa$ were inbred to give an $F_3$ generation, the progeny would again be:

$F_3$ generation      $AA$ : $Aa$ : $aa$

                $\frac{1}{4}$    $\frac{2}{4}$    $\frac{1}{4}$

             dominant      recessive

                 $\frac{3}{4}$         $\frac{1}{4}$

In subsequent experiments Mendel hybridized pea plants that differed not in one but in two or more hereditary characters. For example, he crossed a pea plant with round, yellow seeds with another having green, wrinkled seeds. The offspring ($F_1$) were all uniform, showing round, yellow seeds. However, when these were self-pollinated, the $F_2$ offspring showed all possible combinations of the parental characters in a characteristic ratio: 9/16 round, yellow; 3/16 round, green; 3/16 wrinkled, yellow; and 1/16 wrinkled, green; a ratio of 9:3:3:1 (Figure 23–8). Mendel concluded that when two or more characters were inherited independently of one another, the offspring produced were the results of random assortment of the hereditary factors in the gametes and subsequent recombination of these during fertilization. This is Mendel's **law of independent assortment.\***

\* In present terminology the law of independent assortment may be stated as follows: When two or more pairs of alleles segregate they do so independently of one another. Actually only genes carried on nonhomologous chromosomes are assorted independently, and thus this law is not universal. See page 471.

To us, unlike to Naegli and the people at the Brünn meeting in 1865, Mendel's laws (which apply to peas, flies, mice, humans, and all sexually reproducing organisms) seem obvious, but it should be recalled that all of Mendel's work was done before details of cell division had been worked out and that he was totally unaware of the existence of chromosomes or genes. Thus, the existence of hereditary factors was deduced from only statistical analysis of experimental results and Mendel's brilliant insight; their physical existence was not discovered for many decades.

FIGURE 23–8 Mendel's hybridized peas.

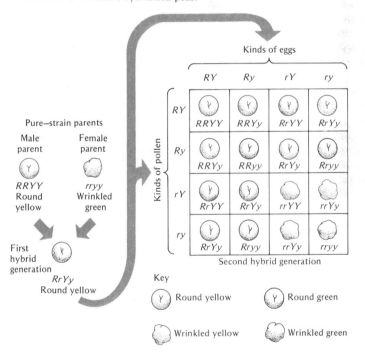

FIGURE 23–9 Meoisis in a heterozygous individual (albinism carrier) illustrates the principle of segregation. Only one pair of chromosomes is shown.

FIGURE 23–10 (below and facing page) Outcome of nine possible crosses (matings) involving the recessive trait albinism. (Modified from E. P. Volpe, *Human Heredity and Birth Defects*, Indianapolis, Bobbs-Merrill, 1971; reprinted by permission.)

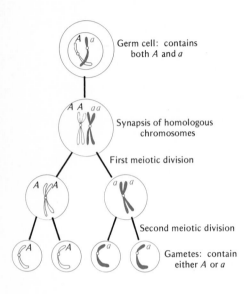

Germ cell: contains both *A* and *a*

Synapsis of homologous chromosomes

First meiotic division

Second meiotic division

Gametes: contain either *A* or *a*

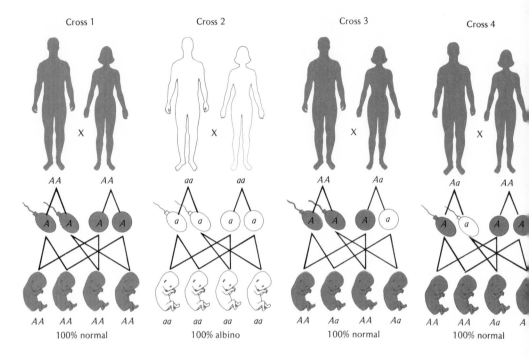

Cross 1     Cross 2     Cross 3     Cross 4

*AA*   *AA*    *aa*   *aa*    *AA*   *Aa*    *Aa*   *AA*

*AA AA AA AA*   *aa aa aa aa*   *AA Aa AA Aa*   *AA AA Aa A*

100% normal    100% albino    100% normal    100% normal

do not necessarily always go together, but they can segregate and form any possible combination; hence the genes are said to recombine (Figure 23–11).

The consequences of the principle of recombination can be examined by following the inheritance of two traits at once. Albinism, as we have already seen, is a recessive trait, and persons of this phenotype have a genotype that can be written *aa*. Persons who are not albinos carry a dominant allele (*A*) and can be either one of two genotypes: *Aa* or *AA* (heterozygous or homozygous). Earlobes of humans may be attached or free (Figure 23–12), and the inheritance of this character is much like that of albinism. Those persons having free earlobes carry a dominant allele (*F*), and such individuals are one of two genotypes: *FF* or *Ff*. Attached earlobes are a recessive trait, and individuals of this phenotype are of a single genotype: *ff*. What kind of offspring would result if an albino man with attached earlobes married a woman heter-

ozygous for both traits, that is, with normal pigmentation and free earlobes? The genotype of the albino with attached earlobes is *aa ff*, and the genotype of his normally pigmented and free-earlobed mate is *Aa Ff*.

Using the principle of segregation, we expect the gametes produced by the albino to be of a single kind: *a*. However, the normally pigmented woman can produce two kinds of gametes: *A* or *a*. Since the albino man has attached earlobes and is homozygous for this trait, only one kind of gamete can be produced: *f*. Thus, the gametes of the albino with attached earlobes are of a single kind: *af*. The normally pigmented woman with free earlobes is heterozygous and can produce two kinds of gametes: *F* or *f*. Since the gene pairs (alleles) for albinism and free earlobes segregate and recombine independently of each other, the normally pigmented mate with free earlobes can produce four different kinds of gametes: *AF*, *Af*, *aF*, and *af*.

The kinds of offspring resulting from such

a mating can be visualized in diagrammatic fashion by making a square (**Punnett square**). In such a Punnett square, the genetic constitution of the gametes is written on the margins and that of the offspring (zygotes) is written within the square:

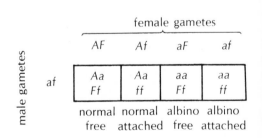

| | female gametes | | |
|---|---|---|---|
| | *AF* | *Af* | *aF* | *af* |
| *af* | *Aa* *Ff* | *Aa* *ff* | *aa* *Ff* | *aa* *ff* |
| | normal free | normal attached | albino free | albino attached |

There result four different kinds of offspring, each with a different genotype and phenotype, and the offspring occur with about equal frequency. If we look at the pattern of meiosis in the normally pigmented, free-earlobed individual, the principle of recombination is easily visualized

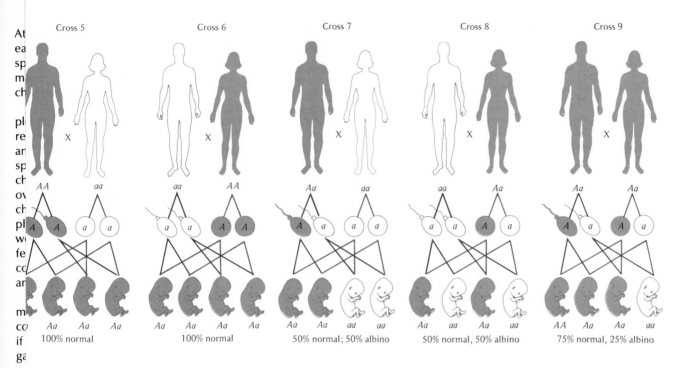

Cross 5 — *AA* × *aa* — *Aa Aa Aa* — 100% normal

Cross 6 — *aa* × *AA* — *Aa Aa Aa Aa* — 100% normal

Cross 7 — *Aa* × *aa* — *Aa Aa aa aa* — 50% normal; 50% albino

Cross 8 — *aa* × *Aa* — *Aa aa Aa aa* — 50% normal, 50% albino

Cross 9 — *Aa* × *Aa* — *AA Aa Aa aa* — 75% normal, 25% albino

(Figure 23–13). What would the offspring look like if both the mother and the father were heterozygous for albinism and free earlobes? (Hint: look at the dihybrid cross made by Mendel shown in Figure 23–8.)

### Linkage: a case of dependent assortment

Genes are not isolated entities that occur independently of one another in the cell; they are carried on chromosomes. It is the chromosomes that segregate independently of each other at meiosis during gamete formation, and these same whole chromosomes recombine during gamete fusion (fertilization). It has been estimated that there are about 100,000 genes in a human being; yet there are only 23 pairs of chromosomes. Thus, many genes occur together on the same chromosome; genes located on the same chromosome cannot separate during meiosis, cannot show independent assortment, and in general must be inher-

ited together as a group. Genes that are on the same chromosome are said to be **linked.** Mendel's law of independent assortment must, therefore, be modified and can apply only to genes that are not linked, that is, to those pairs of genes on different chromosomes.

### Crossing over

About 40 years after Mendel's work on peas, W. R. Bateson and R. C. Punnett of Cambridge University in England discovered linkage. They showed that in pea plants the genes for flower color and pollen-grain shape were located on the same chromosome. When they crossed pea plants with purple flowers and long pollen grains with plants having red flowers and round pollen grains, the offspring had purple flowers and long pollen grains. Thus, purple was dominant to red, and long pollen was dominant to round. The cross can be written:

$$PPLL \text{ purple-long} \quad \times \quad ppll \text{ red-round}$$

$$F_1 \quad PpLl \text{ purple-long}$$

Because the genes for purple-long and red-round are linked, they expected that when they mated their $F_1$ plants with a red-round plant (*ppll*) they would get only two kinds of offspring, purple-long and red-round. They reasoned this to be so because the *PpLl* plant should produce only two kinds of gametes: *PL* and *pl*. However, when they made such a cross there did occur a few plants that were purple-round or red-long. (Contrast this result with the equal frequencies of offspring found when an albino man with attached earlobes was mated with a normally pigmented woman with free earlobes, as described earlier. What would be the frequency of offspring if the genes for normal pigmentation and attached ear-

FIGURE 23–15 (a) A hypothetical pedigree for color blindness in a family. (b) The possible offspring produced from the mating of a color-blind male and a normal female (generation I). (c) The possible offspring produced from the mating of a normal male and a normal female who is a carrier for color blindness. (d) The possible offspring produced from the mating of a color-blind male with a normal female carrier.

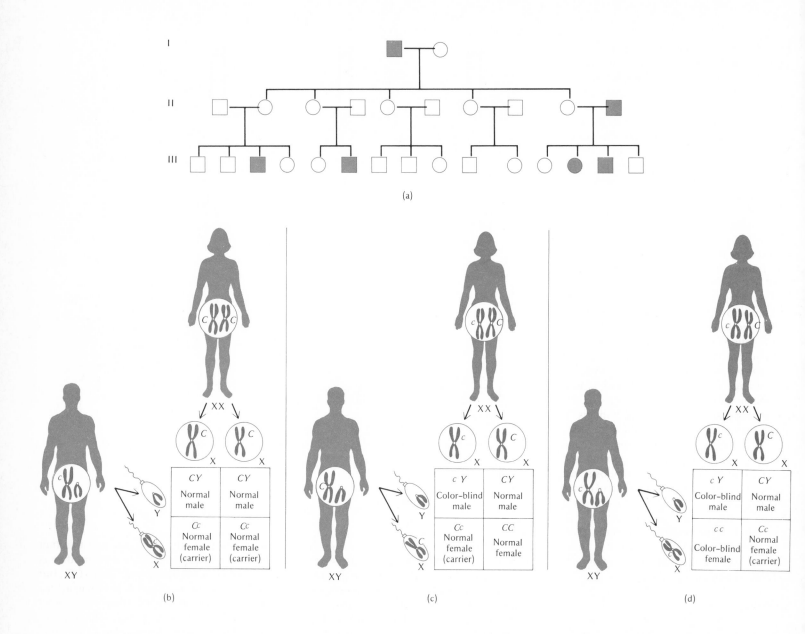

(a)

(b)                     (c)                     (d)

ter, heterozygous for color blindness, has normal red-green vision but is a carrier for the trait. If she marries a man with normal color vision, their sons will be either color blind or normal, and their daughters will be normal or carriers of color blindness (Figure 23–15c). A heterozygous female (Cc) produces two kinds of X-bearing gametes (C and c), whereas a male produces only one. Male offspring receive only a Y chromosome from their father but can receive an X bearing either C or c from their mother; thus the sons can be either one of two genotypes and phenotypes: CY normal or cY color blind. However, daughters receive an X chromosome from each parent and may be either of two genotypes, Cc or CC, but a single pheotype, normal.

Let us consider the pedigree of a family in which the mother is color blind but the father is normal. In such a case the sons are always color blind and the daughters are carriers. A girl will be color blind only if she receives the recessive gene from both

FIGURE 23–16 (a) The nucleus of a cheek cell from a normal male. (b) The nucleus of a cheek cell from a normal female. Arrow indicates the Barr body. (Courtesy of Carolina Biological Supply Company.)

FIGURE 23–17 Diagrammatic representation of the Lyon hypothesis for the formation of the Barr body. (Modified from E. P. Volpe, *Human Heredity and Birth Defects*, Indianapolis, Bobbs-Merrill, 1971; reprinted by permission.)

parents; that is, she must have a color-blind father and her mother must be a carrier or be color blind (Figure 23–15d). If the father is color blind and the mother a carrier, the daughters may be normal or color blind. (See lower right of Figure 23–15a.) Why?

### Is XX twice as good as XY? The Barr body

Since human females have two X chromosomes and males have only one, are women twice as well-off genetically as men? The answer appears to be no; let us see why.

In 1949 Murray Barr was studying the nerve cells of cats to determine if physical changes occurred as a result of fatigue. He found no differences in the cells derived from fatigued or from rested cats, but he did notice that in the nuclei of cells of female cats there was present a dark-staining body. No such body was evident in the nuclei of cells from male cats. Extending these observations to humans, he found exactly the same situation; a dark nuclear body was present only in cells derived from females (Figure 23–16). The dark nuclear body came to be called the **Barr body,** after its discoverer. What is the significance of the Barr body?

The Barr body occurs only in females, and females have two X chromosomes. It appears that the Barr body represents one of the two X chromosomes, tightly coiled and functionless. Thus, in the female only one X chromosome is uncoiled and functional; in any given cell of a female, the genes on only one of the two X chromosomes are expressed.

Once the Barr body was discovered and its role was understood, it became clear why a female does not have twice as many of the enzymes coded for by the genes on the X chromosome as her male counterpart. Theoretically, in the early embryo half the cells have the paternal X as a Barr body and the remainder have the maternal X in this inactive state. In a sense the female is a genetic mosaic because it is purely a matter of chance which X chromosome (the one derived from the mother or the one from

(a)

(b)

the father) will become condensed and inactive. The theory that one of the X chromosomes of the female becomes genetically inactive early in embryonic life and remains in this state throughout adult life was first

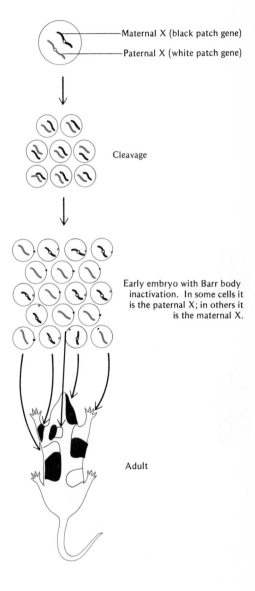

Maternal X (black patch gene)
Paternal X (white patch gene)

Cleavage

Early embryo with Barr body inactivation. In some cells it is the paternal X; in others it is the maternal X.

Adult

proposed by the British geneticist Mary F. Lyon in the early 1960s. In support of her theory (called the **Lyon hypothesis**), she showed that the coats of female mice heterozygous for sex-linked genes affecting coat color showed splotches of dark and light. This patchy distribution of coat color, Lyon explained, is due to the inactivation early in development of one of the X chromosomes (Figure 23–17). A similar condition

## BOX 23C Hemophilia and history

Circumstance often alters the course of history. Disease may be that circumstance. **Hemophilia** (literally "love of blood"; Gk.), a rare disease in which the blood of the afflicted individual clots slowly or not at all, is a case in point. The son of the czar of Russia was a hemophiliac—a bleeder—and because of this the czar and czarina relied heavily on the corrupt and cunning monk Rasputin, who promised a cure. This strange relationship caused a rapid decline in the Russian court. The eldest son of the last king of Spain, Alfonso XIII, died of hemophilia. It could be said that the Russian and the Spanish dynasties both bled to death because they ended with uncrowned successors—the heirs apparent died of hemophilia.

Perhaps the most famous of all hemophiliac families is the royal family of Queen Victoria (Figure 23–18). The family tree illustrates that only the male descendants of the queen were bleeders (Figure 23–19). Why is this so? Hemophilia is a hereditary, sex-linked, recessive trait carried on the X chromosome. Since males have only one X chromosome they will show the trait of hemophilia if they carry the defective allele; however, females, having two chromosomes, would have to have a double dose of the allele for hemophilia to be bleeders. This is an unlikely eventuality since the chance of being homozygous for this rare allele is extremely remote. Furthermore, females showing hemophilia do not survive to maturity; the onset of menstruation is fatal. Hemophilic fathers pass the recessive allele to their daughters, but not to their sons (the male child does not receive an X chromosome from his father), and carrier mothers may pass a defective allele to their sons (their surviving daughters will be carriers). Queen Victoria and two of her daughters, Alice and Beatrice, were carriers, and some of the sons and grandsons of Victoria were hemophiliacs. Since Queen Victoria and Prince Albert were prolific parents and their offspring married into almost all the royal families of Europe, notorious for marrying among themselves, Queen Victoria sowed the seeds that ultimately led to the demise of the European dynasties.

FIGURE 23–18 Victoria and her daughters, shown in a family portrait taken in 1894, illustrate a hereditary dynastic misfortune. Victoria (1) carried the sex-linked mutant allele for hemophilia, as did her daughters Beatrice (2) and Alice (not shown). Alice's daughters, Alexandra (3) and Irene (5), were also carriers. Irene married Prince Henry of Prussia (6), and both their sons were hemophiliacs. Alexandra married Nicholas II of Russia (4), and their son also was a hemophiliac. Also shown are Victoria's sons Edward, the Prince of Wales (7), and Arthur (8) and her daughter Victoria (9), a possible carrier. (Courtesy of The Mansell Collection.)

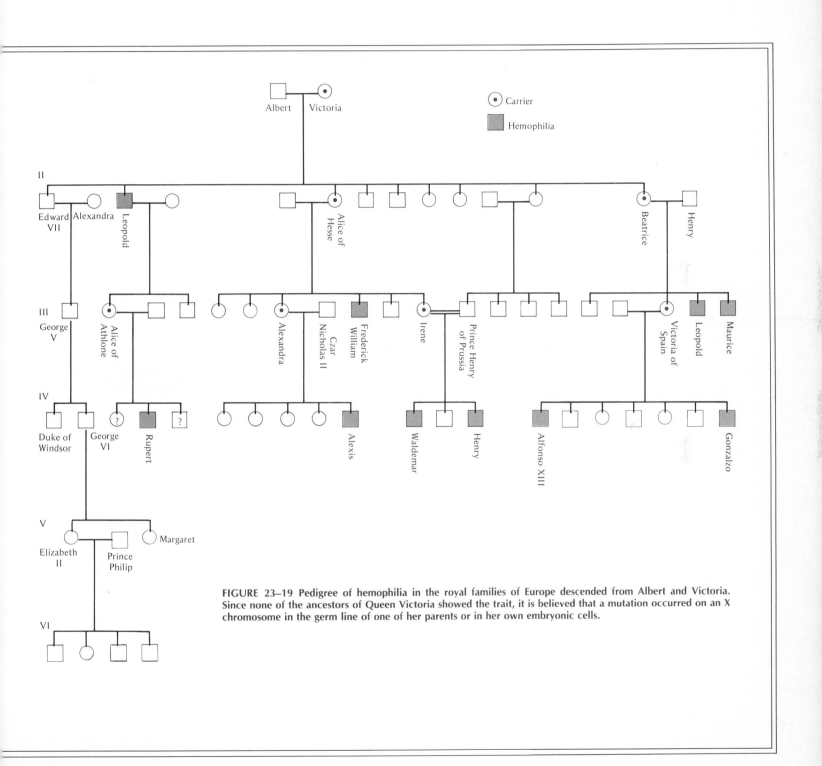

**FIGURE 23–19 Pedigree of hemophilia in the royal families of Europe descended from Albert and Victoria. Since none of the ancestors of Queen Victoria showed the trait, it is believed that a mutation occurred on an X chromosome in the germ line of one of her parents or in her own embryonic cells.**

FIGURE 23–20 Blood typing. Blood from a donor or a potential recipient is typed by placing two drops of blood on a microscope slide. A drop of α-agglutinin is added to one drop and a drop of β-agglutinin to the other. If clumping occurs in both drops, the blood is type AB; if clumping occurs in neither drop, the blood is type O; if clumping occurs in the drop to which α-agglutinin was added, the blood is type A; and if clumping occurs in the drop to which β-agglutinin was added, the blood is type B.

occurs in calico cats, which have blotches of orange and black on their coats. Calico cats are usually female.

The Lyon hypothesis provides a reasonable explanation for the fact that females, with a double dose of the X chromosome, do not produce twice as much gene product as a male with only a single chromosome (carrying the same gene).

## 23–5 BLOOD WILL TELL

### Multiple alleles and blood type

Blood so dominates our thinking about inheritance that even today aristocrats are characterized as "bluebloods," people with behavioral disorders are said to have "bad blood," and those with a passionate disposition are "hot-blooded." Indeed it is not uncommon to denote close family relationships (parent and child, brother and sister) by the term "blood relatives." Prior to the work of Mendel, the belief was common that blood was in fact the inherited material—hence the origin of these terms and their link with ancestry. (In the modern context "blood relative" is used in a general way to imply close genetic ties; a more accurate term would be "DNA relative.") Although the ancient belief that blood is the material of inheritance is incorrect, blood type, or group, is inherited. What is the significance of blood type and how is it inherited?

Transfusion of blood into the body's circulatory system can be life-restoring. The first such miraculous cure via transfusion was made in 1665 by Richard Lower, an English anatomist; he transfused blood from one animal to another, and the recipient animal survived and remained healthy. The achievement caused a flurry of excitement in medical circles, and it was only 2 years later that Jean-Baptiste Denis, physician to Louis XIV of France, attempted a similar blood transfusion in a human. By transfusing 8 oz of lamb's blood into the veins of a young son of an important member of the

| Type of blood from which test serum was derived | Agglutinin | Type of blood being tested (antigen in red blood cells) | | | |
|---|---|---|---|---|---|
| | | A | AB | B | O |
| A | β | | | | |
| B | α | | | | |

royal court, he temporarily restored the dying child. The momentous event, however, ended in tragedy, and public reaction was so strong that it stopped further experiments with blood transfusion. The practice fell into disrepute and was not employed again until the twentieth century, when enough was learned about blood and about the mechanics of transfusion to make the procedure safe.

The most fundamental of all discoveries concerning blood transfusions came from the work of Karl Landsteiner, a Viennese physician. In the 1900s Landsteiner proposed that the blood of one species of animal is not compatible with that of others; in addition, all humans do not possess the same kind of blood. He found that in human plasma there are antibodies (called **isoagglutinins**) that will clump, or agglutinate, red cells that differ from the person's own. If foreign blood cells are transfused into a person, these cells are clumped and destroyed: blood vessels are plugged, hemoglobin is released into the circulation, the kidney tubules become clogged, and the recipient dies of kidney failure in 7 to 10 days.

There are two types of agglutinin antibodies: **alpha** (α) and **beta** (β). The red cells of humans contain specific kinds of antigen, called **A** and **B agglutinogens.** All human blood can be classified into four major

antigenic groups: A, AB, B, and O. The A and B types contain only the A or only the B agglutinogen, respectively; the AB type contains both A and B agglutinogens; and the O type contains neither A nor B. A person with A-type blood has plasma that contains only β-antibody, one with B-type blood has only α-antibody, one with AB-type blood has neither α nor β antibodies, and one with O-type blood has both α and β antibodies.

When blood is taken from an individual (the **donor**) to be transfused into another individual (the **recipient**), both bloods must first be typed to determine if they are compatible (Figure 23–20). The red cells of a donor with A, B, or AB blood have antigenic properties that could be injurious to the recipient. α-antibody and A agglutinogen interact to produce clumping of the red cells; similary β-antibody and B agglutinogen cause red cells to clump. Thus, a person with A- or AB-type blood cannot act as donor to a person with plasma containing α-antibody—that is, a person with O- or B-type blood. In the same way, a person with B- or AB-type blood cannot donate blood to an O or A recipient, since the recipient's β-antibodies would cause the donor's red cells to clump (Table 23–1). We might expect that a person with O blood, having plasma containing both α- and β-antibodies, could donate blood only to another O person,

**TABLE 23–1 Blood types and transfusion**

| Donor's blood type | Recipient's blood type | | | |
|---|---|---|---|---|
| | A | B | AB | O |
| A | − | + | − * | + |
| B | + | − | − * | + |
| AB | + | + | − | + |
| O | − * | − * | − * | − |

+ Incompatible (agglutination occurs).
− Compatible (no agglutination).
* Theoretically, clumping of the recipient's cells should occur here but because the donor plasma (containing isoagglutinins) is diluted out no clumping of cells occurs.

**TABLE 23–2 Genetics of human blood groups**

| Genotype | Phenotype (blood type) | Agglu-tinogen | Isoagglu-tinin (antibody) |
|---|---|---|---|
| $I^A I^A$ or $I^A i$ | A | A | β |
| $I^B I^B$ or $I^B i$ | B | B | α |
| $I^A I^B$ | AB | A and B | None |
| $ii$ | O | None | α and β |

since the donor's plasma antibodies would clump the cells of an A, B, or AB recipient. In practice, however, a pint of O-type blood is so quickly diluted in the body that the donor's α- and β-antibodies have no effect on the red cells of the recipient. Thus, a person with O-type blood can donate to anyone, since such a donor's cells are not capable of clumping when transfused into another person and donor plasma antibodies are diluted and have no effect—such a person is called a **universal donor.** Having no α or β antibodies, an AB person can receive blood from anyone and is called a **universal recipient.**

What is the genetic basis of human blood types? Blood types in human populations are determined by a gene *I* (standing for isoagglutinin) with three different alleles: $I^A$, $I^B$, and *i*. Although there are more than two alleles of a single gene in the popula-tion, no one person has more than two alleles. (Why?) The $I^A$ and $I^B$ alleles are codominant; that is, a person receiving both an $I^A$ and an $I^B$ allele will be of AB blood type. The *i* allele is recessive to the other two, so that $I^A i$ and $I^B i$ genotypes are of A and B blood type, respectively. Persons with a double dose of the recessive allele, that is, genotype *ii*, are blood type O. Table 23–2 shows the relation of genotype to blood type (phenotype).

At the outset of our inquiry into human inheritance we indicated that our main concern would be the simple question, what kinds of offspring can be expected from particular kinds of matings? Blood groups offer a clear system for studies of this kind, and often they play an important role in ascertaining parentage in cases where there is dispute over whether a suspected male is the father of a particular child (Box 23D). There are about 20 different kinds of blood groups, and by using some of these rare groups it is possible to determine with great precision that a particular individual could not possibly be the father of the child in question. It should be emphasized that the genetics of blood typing for determination of paternity can only rule out a suspected father, it cannot provide absolute proof of parentage. (Do you think this is so? Why?)

**The inheritance of Rh factor**

Let us consider the inheritance of another blood group substance, the Rh factor, present on the human red cell. The Rh factor was discovered in 1940 as a result of mixing human red cells with the plasma of a rhesus monkey. If the Rh factor is present, the cells clump in the rhesus monkey plasma. A percentage of the human population has the Rh factor on their red cells; they are Rh positive. The remainder of the population lack it; they are Rh negative. The inheritance of the rhesus factor is that of a simple dominant. Individuals who are homozygous recessive (*rr*) are Rh negative, or Rh⁻, whereas Rh positive, or Rh⁺ persons may be homo-

FIGURE 23–21 Rh incompatibility. (From E. P. Volpe Human Heredity and Birth Defects, Indianapolis, Bobbs-Merrill, 1971; reprinted by permission.)

zygous (*RR*) or heterozygous (*Rr*). (The ABO and Rh alleles show independent assortment). If an Rh⁻ person receives a tranfusion of Rh⁺ blood, she or he builds antibodies against it. (A transfusion of Rh⁻ blood into an Rh⁺ person will not cause antibody production since Rh⁻ cells do not have rhesus factor on their surfaces.) If this person then receives Rh⁺ blood on a subsequent occasion, the Rh⁺ antibodies in the body will clump the tranfused cells. Ordinarily, it is possible to prevent mismatching of tranfused blood, but when incompatibility occurs between a mother and her developing fetus, problems can arise.

About 2% of the infants born to mothers who are Rh⁻ with an Rh⁺ father show an abnormality called erythroblastosis fetalis. Such infants are usually born dead because of severe anemia; those born alive may live only a short time, whereas others suffer from anemia, heart failure, jaundice, or mental retardation. Erythroblastosis fetalis develops because some of the fetal red cells cross the placental barrier and pass into the mother's circulation. If the fetus is Rh⁺, the cells contain *R* antigen. If the mother is Rh⁻, she builds antibodies (agglutinins) to these cells. The agglutinins pass back to the fetus via the placenta and clump and destroy its red cells. To offset these blood losses, the baby's bone marrow and spleen produce red cells rapidly, but the cells poured into the circulation are immature nucleated cells (erythroblasts); thus the reason for the term **erythroblastosis.**

Rarely do fetal cells cross the placenta during pregnancy and so the maternal circulation does not receive much in the way of foreign Rh⁺ cells. However, during delivery, when the placental blood vessels rupture, fetal cell may enter the maternal circulation in abundant quantities, and it is generally believed that greatest sensitization of the mother takes place shortly after delivery of the first Rh⁺ child. Thus, Rh incompatibility between a negative mother and a positive baby seldom occurs with the first pregnancy, but subsequent pregnan-

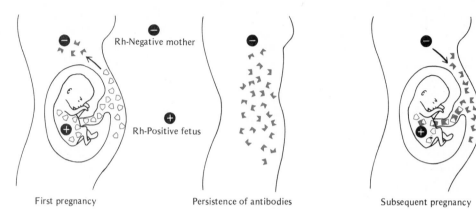

First pregnancy    Persistence of antibodies    Subsequent pregnancy

Antigens ( △ ) stimulate production of antibodies ( ⋈ )    Antibodies destroy antigens ( ▣ )

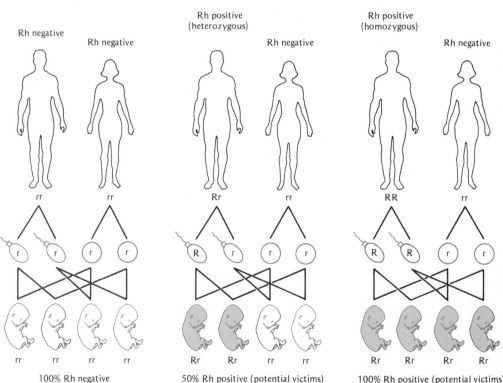

100% Rh negative    50% Rh positive (potential victims)    100% Rh positive (potential victims)

FIGURE 23–22 Distribution of height among adult males living in the United States.

Height of people to nearest inch

cies may prove to be fatal to the newborn. After an initial pregnancy with an Rh⁺ child, the mother's immune system is primed; when challenged with Rh⁺ cells from a second fetus, maternal agglutinins attack the foreign cells, producing severe fetal anemia. (The scheme of inheritance for Rh incompatibility is shown in Figure 23–21).

Two treatments have been used to combat erythroblastosis fetalis. One treatment is to gradually remove the blood of the newborn and transfuse into it Rh⁻ blood. This effectively removes the Rh antibodies in the child's body so that red cell destruction ceases 3 to 5 weeks after birth. Another more recent development is the use of a vaccine on the mother. If an Rh⁻ mother who has not been sensitized previously is given an injection of gamma globulin containing antibodies to Rh⁺ cells no later than 3 days after the birth of her first Rh⁺ child, the cells of the fetus that have passed into the maternal circulation are effectively destroyed; therefore the mother does not build antibodies against the fetal red cells. Unfortunately, the administration of this anti-Rh⁺ gamma globulin is not possible for mothers who have already been sensitized from earlier pregnancies or from transfusion of Rh⁺ blood. The anti-Rh⁺ globulin injection must be repeated for each subsequent Rh⁺ pregnancy to avoid the development or erythroblastosis fetalis in a later child.

## 23–6 POLYGENES AND SKIN COLOR

So far we have discussed the expression of traits in discrete, alternative classes (albino or pigmented skin; attached or free earlobes; A, AB, B, or O blood type). There are, of course, a great many characteristics whose expression appears to be continuous. Some of these are height, weight, body proportions, and skin color. For such characteristics, individuals in a population do not fall into discrete classes, but rather, if arranged in an orderly array, form a continuously graded series (Figure 23–22).

In the early days of genetics it was seri-ously questioned whether such characteristics were controlled by genes at all, since genes (according to the principles of Mendel) are particulate entities that segregate and recombine as individual units. There was a strong tendency on the part of early geneticists to ascribe such characteristics to the simple addition of a series of genes. The logical extension of such thinking is that each individual is merely a collection of unit characters; as we shall see, this concept is erroneous.

Subsequent experiments in genetics have shown that quantitative characteristics are controlled by a large number of genes, called **polygenes,** each producing a small effect. To illustrate polygenic inheritance we shall use a simplified model for the inheritance of human skin color. (There is still incomplete understanding of the inheritance of this characteristic; the information presented is a model for polygenic inheritance and not a presentation of fact.) Let us propose that there are just two loci

with two alleles governing human skin color through all its ranges. Let the genotype *oopp* represent white; then for each capital letter, or pigment-producing allele, substituted in this genotype, there results an increase in skin pigmentation. The darkest or blackest skin color will be represented by the genotype *OOPP*. Table 23–3 shows the phenotypes that correspond to the various combinations of these alleles. This scheme directly represents the dosage of pigment-producing alleles. For the intermediate shades, there is more than one possible genotype; the extremes show only a single genotype. This model for inheritance of skin color involves two loci and five trait classes: there is no dominance in this system, and the phenotype reflects gene dosage. Note that such a system features a tendency to continuous gradation of the character; that is, the expressed trait assumes quantitative proportions.

Now let us examine a model in which three loci determine skin color; in such a

**THE HUMAN POPULATION**

**TABLE 23–3 A model for inheritance of human skin color involving two loci with two alleles**

|  | | OO | | Oo | | oo | |
|---|---|---|---|---|---|---|---|
| PP | | Black | OOPP | Dark | OoPP | Medium | ooPP |
| Pp | | Dark | OOPp | Medium | OoPp | Light | ooPp |
| pp | | Medium | OOpp | Light | Oopp | White | oopp |

| | White | Light | Medium | Dark | Black |
|---|---|---|---|---|---|
| Phenotype: | White | Light | Medium | Dark | Black |
| Color scale: | 0 | 1 | 2 | 3 | 4 |
| Genotype: | oopp | Oopp | OOpp | OOPp | OOPP |
| | | ooPp | OoPp | OoPP | |
| | | | ooPP | | |

**TABLE 23–4 A model for inheritance of skin color in which there are three loci with three alleles**

| Color scale: | 0 | 1 | 2 | 3 | 4 | 5 | 6 |
|---|---|---|---|---|---|---|---|
| Appearance: | | | | | | | |
| Gene dosage: | 0 | 1 | 2 | 3 | 4 | 5 | 6 |
| Genotype: | ooppqq | Ooppqq | OOppqq | OOPpqq | OOPPqq | OOPPQq | OOPPQQ |
| | | ooPpqq | OoPpqq | OOppQq | OOppQQ | OoPPQQ | |
| | | ooppQq | OoppQq | ooPPqq | OoPPQq | OOPpQQ | |
| | | | ooPPqq | ooPpQq | OoPpQQ | | |
| | | | ooPpQq | ooppQQ | ooPPQQ | | |
| | | | ooppQQ | ooPPQq | OOPpQq | | |
| | | | | ooPpQQ | | | |
| | | | | oOpPqQ | | | |

system the color scale and gene dosage would run from 0 → 6 (Table 23–4). The result is simply that the color scale is more finely graded between the extremes. Actually, available evidence indicates that inheritance of human skin color is very much as described, that between three and five genes account for the total variation in pigmentation of human skin, and that there is no dominance. (It is not certain that all the genes have equal effects, however, as we have assumed in the illustrated examples.)

The model of polygenic inheritance shown here makes it easy to understand why the mating of the two extremes (that is, black with black or white with white) breeds true, whereas mating of those of intermediate grades could produce an entire spectrum of skin color in the offspring. In addition, as one moves in shade toward either ex-treme the potential for variation among the progeny is reduced. (Contrary to popular belief, two near-whites cannot have throw-back black offspring, nor can two near-blacks have throwback white offspring.) Although first-generation progeny between the extremes are intermediate, these can in turn produce a variety of shades of skin color.

Note that the pigmentation of human skin, as well as a great many other characteristics (such as height and weight), is strongly modified by environmental factors. The skin of most individuals darkens, upon exposure to ultraviolet light—tanning. Such exposure can often change a lightly pigmented individual into a dark one.[4] This tends to obscure or blur phenotypic bound-

---

[4] The adaptive significance of this is discussed in Chapter 25.

aries, often making the color of the skin vary greatly between the extremes. The tanning effect shows us that phenotypic skin color is not an absolute index of genotype.

Sometimes the expression of a trait depends on the interaction of genes at two different loci. In the discussion of polygenes it was suggested that skin color depends on the dosage of perhaps as many as five pairs of alleles. However, individuals receiving the recessive allelic pair for albinism (aa) will be albino no matter what other gene combination they have for skin pigmentation. The A, a alleles determine whether or not melanin is synthesized, and without the presence of the A allele for melanin production, the genes governing the intensity of pigment formation are not expressed. Such interaction of the gene for albinism with the genes for pigment intensity is called **epistasis** (literally "standing above") because the albino locus determines whether or not the alleles for the loci controlling the degree of pigmentation are expressed and thus it "stands above" them. It is important to distinguish between epistasis and dominance. Epistasis involves interaction between nonallelic genes at two loci, where the phenotypic expression of one gene is masked by an entirely different gene at a different locus. Dominance refers to the interaction between two gene forms or alleles at one locus, where the phenotype is an expression of one allele at the expense of the other.

## 23–7 CHROMOSOMAL ABNORMALITIES

Chromosomal abnormalities can be classified in two categories: alterations in the number of normal chromosomes and structural changes in the chromosome itself.

### Abnormal numbers of chromosomes

Meiosis is not foolproof. On occasion accidents occur that produce an unequal distribution of chromosomes in the gametes.

## BOX 23E Of transplants and genes

On April 26–27, 1986, the Chernobyl Nuclear Power Station, 80 miles from the city of Kiev, suffered a core meltdown in one of its reactors. (Technically, meltdown occurs in reactors containing cooling pools of water, and when this water boils away, the molten fuel core sinks into the earth in a so-called China syndrome, a term popularized by the 1979 movie of the same name, that suggests that the radioactive mass might plunge all the way through the earth.) It was estimated by Soviet authorities that as a result of the meltdown a million curies of radioactivity was released. Some 24,000 people were evacuated from the city, and more than 30 rescue and firefighting personnel lost their lives due to the massive radiation doses and the burns they received. Other workers suffered from soaring fevers and infections because the radiation-ravaged bone marrow could not manufacture enough white blood cells. To assist such individuals with the problems associated with bone marrow depletion a surgical team carried out bone marrow transplants. These transplants were not done, however, until the surgeons were convinced that the transplanted marrow would not be rejected as foreign. This depended on HLA typing of bone marrow donors and recipients. **HLA** stands for **h**uman **l**ympho-cyte-associated **a**ntigen and refers to the presence or absence of specific glycoproteins on the surface of most nucleated cells, but especially on the white blood cells. Antigens of the HLA type are encoded by a group of some 20 different genes, and they may have up to a million alleles. This system provides an astronomical number of different combinations giving an individual's cells a unique antigenic (and genetic) fingerprint. (The high degree of individuality in tissue typing using the HLA system often makes it, rather than ABO and Rh blood typing, the preferred technique for resolving questions of paternity.)

The group of genes that code for such tissue identity antigens is called the **major histocompatability complex** or **MHC** (Figure 23–23).There are two groups of histocompatability antigens, called class 1 and class 2. Class 1 antigens are found on the surface of most nucleated cells as well as helper and suppressor T cells (see p. 284), whereas class 2 antigens are found on the surface of cytotoxic T cells and B cells. The cytotoxic T cell binds most avidly to the surface of those cells that bear a familiar

FIGURE 23–23 The major histocompatibility complex (a) and inheritance of MHC alleles (b). The figure shows a small part of chromosome 6 of two human parents, each of whom is heterozygous at locus A and at locus B of the complex. Their offspring will fall into at least four histocompatibility types, and more, if recombinant chromosomes are formed by crossing over. The child represented on the far right carries a chromosome that is the result of crossing over from one of the parents. The more than 20 known alleles at the A locus and more than 40 known alleles at the B locus can generate nearly 1000 unique chromosome types: A1B1, A1B1, A1B2, . . . , A20B40, . . . . From these, random fertilization can generate nearly a million unique histocompatibility genotypes just considering the A and B loci of chromosome 6. Multiple alleles at other histocompatibility loci generate even greater diversity.

FIGURE 23–24 Nondisjunction during spermato-genesis and the kind of offspring that result when these abnormal sperm fertilize a normal egg.

(self) histocompatability antigen as well as a foreign (nonself) antigen. The cytotoxic T cell receptor binds to both simultaneously. Because transplanted tissue will have some common and some foreign histocompatability an-tigens the cytotoxic T cell will bind to these cells and destroy the transplant, that is, tissue rejection will occur. By closely matching the HLA antigens of donor and recipient it is possible to reduce or delay transplant rejection.

Cytotoxic T cells also kill virally in-fected cells because the T cell binds simultaneously to the normal (self) histocompatability antigen as well as to the virus antigen exposed on the surface of the infected cell. If a cyto-toxic T cell encounters free virus, killing does not take place because there are no histocompatability anti-gens on the virus surface. Because cytotoxic T cells have class 2 antigens and B cells are of class 1, the two cells cannot bind to one another, and lym-phocyte self-destruction does not take place. Because helper and suppressor T cells are of class 2, however, these kinds of T cells can bind to and interact with B cells. The T cell reacts only with antigens on the surface of the cell, not free antigen; therefore, its function is regulated by the fact that it can only bind to cells that have specific antigenic signposts. These signposts are encoded by the histo-compatability genes.

Abnormal sperm

Normal egg

XXY     XXY

Klinefelter syndrome

XXX

Triplo–X female

XYY

XYY syndrome

For example, if the spindle apparatus fails to operate normally, one or more of the chromosome pairs may fail to segregate during cell division, and as a consequence of this (called **nondisjunction**) one of the daughter cells receives extra chromosomes and the other daughter cell is lacking in these chromosomes.

**Abnormal numbers of sex chromosomes.** In 1967 an Olympic gold-medal winner for the women's 100-meter dash was stripped of her records and medals because she failed the "chromosome sex test"; indeed, the International Olympic Committee an-nounced that year that all female athletes would be tested for their sex by chromo-some examination. How can abnormal num-bers of sex chromosomes be produced?

Meiosis in a normal male produces equal numbers of sperm bearing X and Y chro-mosomes (Figure 23–5). However, if non-disjunction occurs during the first or the second meiotic division, the sperm may have abnormal numbers of the sex chro-mosomes (Figure 23–24).[5] If these abnormal sperm fertilize a normal X-bearing egg, the individual suffers from sex-chromosome er-rors.

If an XY-bearing sperm fertilizes an X-

[5] We shall assume that in these cases segregation of autosomes is normal.

FIGURE 23–25 (a) Klinefelter syndrome (*XXY*) in a 24-year-old male. Note the long limbs and horizontal limit of the pubic hair. In some cases there is breast enlargment and a broadening of the pelvis. (b) Karyotype of Klinefelter syndrome. (Courtesy of W. R. Centerwall.)

(a)

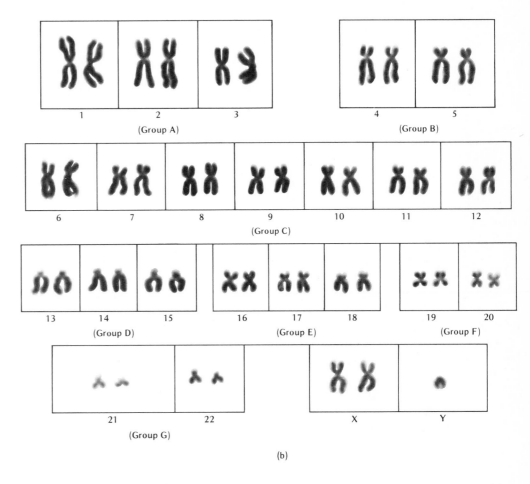

(b)

bearing egg, the individual has one sex chromosome too many and the genotype is *XXY*. This error occurs in males with a frequency of 1 in 500 births, and the condition is called **Klinefelter syndrome,** after the American physician who first described it. Individuals with this syndrome have the external genitalia of a male, but the testes are small and sperm are never produced; the breasts are enlarged and body hair is sparse (Figure 23–25); on occasion the individual is mentally defective. These individuals have a single Barr body. Klinefelter syndrome develops as a result of nondisjunction in the mother (Figure 23–26) and occurs more frequently in males born to older women.

Through nondisjunction in the female, eggs may be produced that have no X chromosome; when such an egg is fertilized by an X-bearing sperm, the offspring is of *XO* genotype (*O* signifying the absence of a sex chromosome). Such eggs fertilized by a Y-bearing sperm are not viable and fail to

FIGURE 23–26 Nondisjunction during oogenesis and the kind of offspring that result when these abnormal eggs are fertilized by normal sperm. (Modified from E. P. Volpe, *Human Heredity and Birth Defects,* Indianapolis, Bobbs-Merrill, 1971; reprinted by permission.)

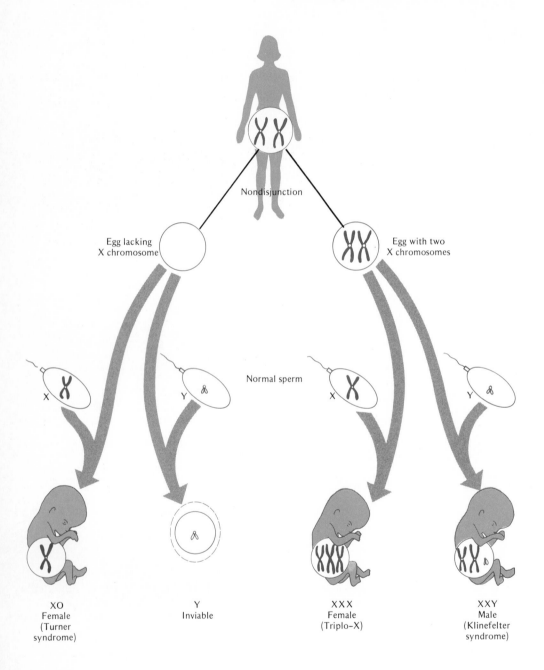

Nondisjunction

Egg lacking X chromosome

Egg with two X chromosomes

Normal sperm

X   Y   X   Y

XO
Female
(Turner syndrome)

Y
Inviable

XXX
Female
(Triplo-X)

XXY
Male
(Klinefelter syndrome)

develop. The *XO* individual suffers from **Turner syndrome** and in external appearance resembles a female (Figure 23–27). However, the breasts are underdeveloped and the ovaries contain only bits of whitish tissue and remain rudimentary. Women with Turner syndrome do not menstruate or ovulate; they have a thick, webbed neck, are short in stature and below normal in IQ, and lack a Barr body. The incidence of Turner syndrome is 1 in 3,500 live female births; only 2% of female embryos carrying the Turner syndrome are born, and 98% are spontaneously aborted.

Thus it can be seen that normal sex determination in the human requires a normal complement of the sex chromosomes, and deficiences or excess numbers of sex chromosomes result in abnormal phenotypes.

**Abnormal numbers of autosomes.** Mary Sinter's younger sister suffers from Down syndrome (see p. 461). Will Mary's unborn child suffer from the same disorder? How does Down syndrome arise?

Down syndrome is usually produced by nondisjunction of chromosome 21 during oogenesis (Figure 23–28), although nondisjunction during spermatogenesis could produce it. If we were to examine the chromosomes of Mary's sister we would find that she has 47 chromosomes instead of 46. The extra chromosome is not a sex chromosome, but an autosome (classified by convention as number 21, one of the smallest chromosomes (Figure 23–29).

In almost all cases of Down syndrome the parents are normal. However, if we examine the relationship between age of the mother and the tendency for offspring to suffer from the syndrome, we find that the older the mother the greater the frequency of such abnormal children (Figure 23–30). Amniocentesis and chromosome analysis will tell Mary Sinter whether her unborn child suffers from Down syndrome. It is highly unlikely that her child will suffer from the disorder, since Mary is young and in good health. However, Mary's own chromosome

(a)

FIGURE 23–27 (a) Turner syndrome (*XO*) in an 11-year-old girl. Note the small stature, shield chest, and broad, webbed neck. The child on the right is her 9-year-old sister. (b) Karyotype of Turner syndrome. (Courtesy of W. R. Centerwall.)

(b)

FIGURE 23–28 The origin of Down syndrome by nondisjunction of chromosome 21 during oogenesis.

FIGURE 23–29 Karyotype of Down syndrome. Note the extra chromosome 21. (Courtesy of W. R. Centerwall.)

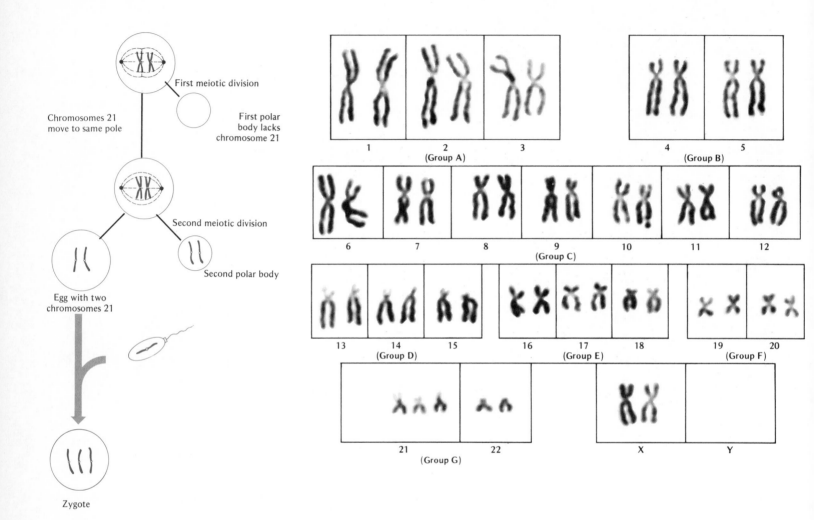

First meiotic division

Chromosomes 21 move to same pole

First polar body lacks chromosome 21

Second meiotic division

Second polar body

Egg with two chromosomes 21

Zygote

1 2 3
(Group A)

4 5
(Group B)

6 7 8 9 10 11 12
(Group C)

13 14 15
(Group D)

16 17 18
(Group E)

19 20
(Group F)

21 22
(Group G)

X Y

constitution should be examined (Box 23A). The reasons for this will become apparent in the next section, when we discuss the genetic cause of a rare kind of Down syndrome.

**Abnormalities in chromosome structure**

We have considered alterations in chromosome numbers and their effects. Let us now consider briefly some of the abnormalities that may occur in the chromosome

itself. Four major alterations in chromosome structure may occur: (1) **deletion,** where a portion of the chromosome is missing; (2) **duplication,** where a portion of the chromosome is repeated (such effects have not been described for humans); (3) **transloca-tion,** where a portion of one chromosome becomes attached to another chromosome; and (4) **inversion,** where the linear array of genes on a chromosome becomes turned around (Figure 23–31).

The consequences of each of these struc-

tural changes are quite variable. If a deletion involves the loss of some important genes, it may affect the phenotype or even the survival of the offspring. In 1963 J. Lejeune described a disorder called **cri-du-chat** (cat-cry) **syndrome** in infants. The affected child has a moonlike face, utters a cry much like that of a mewing cat, and is retarded both physically and mentally (Figure 23–32). The disorder results from a deletion in chromosome 5. It has been suggested that dele-tions are really translocations. To lose a

FIGURE 23–30 The relationship between Down syndrome in the offspring and the mother's age. If the mother is over 40, the child's risk is materially increased.

FIGURE 23–31 Alterations in chromosome structure. (a) Base alteration. (b) Translocation. (c) Inversion. (d) Deletion. (e) Duplication.

(a) Base alteration

(b) Translocation

(c) Inversion

(d) Deletion

(e) Duplication

piece of a chromosome, two breaks must occur on the same chromosome arm and the ends must rejoin. To produce such breaks, a disruptive agent such as x rays would have to score two "hits" very close together on a single chromosome, but this is unlikely. It is more reasonable to expect two hits on two different chromosomes. When this occurs, the broken ends remain "sticky" and tend to join up again. If they join with the broken end of another chromosome, a translocation occurs. At meiosis, the two translocated chromosomes may separate to different gametes. Some will have an abnormally short chromosome and some an extra long chromosome. After fertilization, the fetus may suffer an excess or deficiency of chromosomal material—equivalent to duplication or deletion. Although one would expect an inversion or a translocation to have little or no effect because no genes are lost or duplicated,

this is not so. The order of genes along the length of the chromosome does make a difference, indicating that the position of a gene in relation to other genes affects its function.

We can illustrate the effect of translocation on inheritance by looking once again at Down syndrome. In 5% of persons with Down syndrome the chromosome number is 46. It has been found that in these individuals a portion of chromosome 21 is attached to the end of chromosome 13, 14, 15, 21, or 22 (Figure 23–33). Thus, the child suffering from Down syndrome and having 46 chromosomes actually has the substance of three chromosome 21's: two normal chromosome 21's and one chromosome 21 attached to another chromosome. This is chromosome 15 in the example shown in Figure 23-33. (The only difference evident in the chromosomes as seen under the microscope is that chromosome 15 is lengthened.) A study of the inheritance of this type of Down syndrome shows that one of the parents (called a **Down syndrome carrier**) has 45 chromosomes (the reason being that chromosome 21 is attached, or translocated, to another chromosome). Such a parent may produce four kinds of gametes; when fertilization by a normal gamete occurs, one third of the offspring show Down syndrome (Figure 23–34). Thus, Mary Sinter's karyotype should be determined before the genetic counselor can assure her it is unlikely she will bear a child with Down syndrome. Indeed, if she is a carrier, the chances of her child having Down syndrome will be increased 500 times.

## SUMMARY

**1.** Classical genetics is the study of the mechanisms by which genes are transmitted from one generation to the next.

**2.** The diploid, or 2*n*, chromosome number for humans is 46 (23 homologous pairs). Through amniocentesis and preparation of a karyotype, genetic defects in the unborn can be identified.

**FIGURE 23–32** (a) Karyotype of cri-du-chat syndrome. Note the short arm of one of the number 5 chromosomes. (b) Cri-du-chat syndrome. The child is mentally and physically retarded. (Courtesy of W. R. Centerwall.)

**FIGURE 23–33** In the example illustrated here the translocation of chromosome 21 produces an elongated chromosome 15. Persons with such a constitution are carriers for translocation Down syndrome. (Modified from E. P. Volpe, *Human Heredity and Birth Defects,* Indianapolis, Bobbs-Merrill, 1971; reprinted by permission.)

(a)

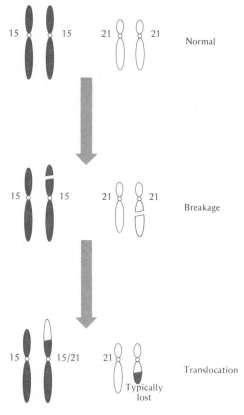

(b)

**3.** Haploid gametes are produced by meiosis. At fertilization, the diploid number is restored in the zygote.

**4.** In humans, there are 22 pairs of autosomes and one pair of sex chromosomes: XX in females, XY in males. Eggs carry an X, sperm may carry an X or a Y; therefore sex of the offspring is determined by the kind of fertilizing sperm.

**5.** A detectable trait is the phenotype. The genetic constitution of the individual is the genotype. Genes that occur at the same locus on homologous chromosomes are alleles.

**6.** An allele that exerts its effect on the phenotype when present in only a single dose is said to be dominant; such gene forms more or less completely mask the

**FIGURE 23–34** Transmission of translocation Down syndrome. There are four possibilities, depending on the manner in which the chromosomes are distributed to the gametes during meiosis. In this example, the translocation is from chromosome 21 to chromosome 15.

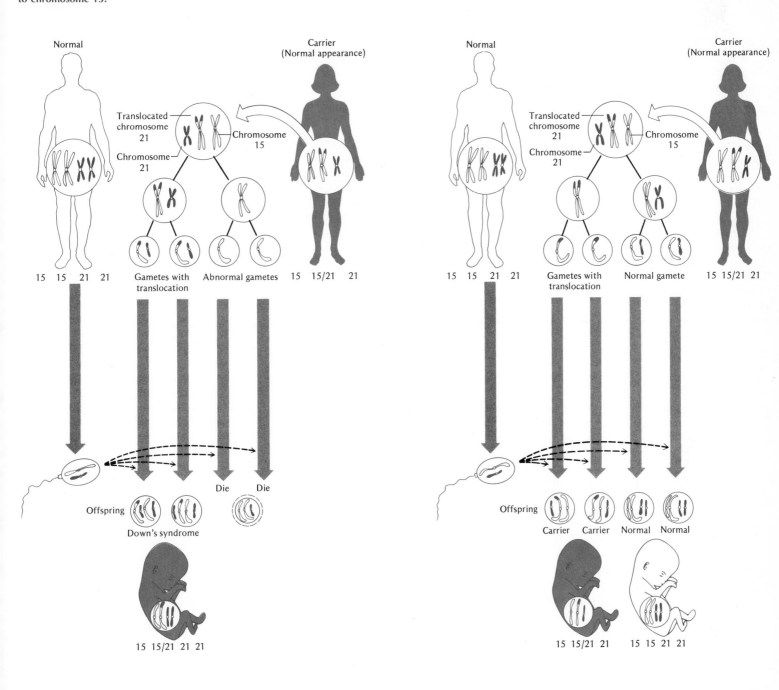

effect of the other allelic form. The latter allelic form is said to be recessive. Recessive alleles have no effect on the phenotype unless present in a double dose. If both members of an allelic pair are the same, the individual is said to be homozygous for that trait, whereas if they are dissimilar, the individual is heterozygous for that trait.

**7.** Gregor Mendel discovered the genetic principles of segregation and independent assortment (recombination) by crossing varieties of peas with contrasting traits. When peas with a dominant trait were crossed with peas with a recessive trait, the $F_1$ generation all showed the dominant trait. When members of the $F_1$ generation were crossed with each other, the ratio of peas showing the dominant trait was 3:1 over those showing the recessive trait. If peas heterozygous for two characters were hybridized, offspring of the $F_2$ generation showed combinations of the parental characteristics in a 9:3:3:1 ratio.

**8.** Mendel's first law, the law of segregation, states that genes do not blend, but behave as independent units and are passed intact from one generation to the next. During gamete formation, members of an allelic pair separate (or segregate) so that the gametes contain only a single member of the allelic pair. Mendel's second law, the law of independent assortment or recombination, applies to the inheritance of two or more traits. It states that the inheritance of any gene pair is independent of the inheritance of all other gene pairs, with each trait being expressed independently of any other.

**9.** In fact, the chromosomes rather than individual genes segregate independently at meiosis, and it is the chromosomes that recombine at fertilization. Genes on the same chromosome are therefore inherited as a group and are said to be linked. Because of this, Mendel's law of independent as-

sortment (recombination) applies to linkage groups of genes on the same chromosome.

**10.** Linkage groups may be broken by crossing over between homologous chromosomes at synapsis during meiotic prophase; in this way variation among offspring is increased.

**11.** Sex-linked genes occur on the sex chromosomes. Since the Y chromosome carries only the genes for maleness and no allelic counterparts for other genes on the X chromosome, males are hemizygous for sex-linked characters. Hence, sex-linked recessive traits such as color blindness and hemophilia occur in males with greater frequency than in females.

**12.** In females, only one X chromosome is functional in any one cell. The other appears as a Barr body. Females are therefore genetic mosaics, depending on whether the maternal or paternal X chromosome is expressed in a particular cell (the Lyon hypothesis). This explains why calico cats are usually female.

**13.** Blood type in humans is determined by a gene with three alleles: $I^A$, $I^B$, and $i$. $I^A$ and $I^B$ are codominant, and $i$ is recessive. $I^A$ and $I^B$ homozygotes will be A and B blood type, respectively, as with $I^A i$ and $I^B i$ heterozygotes, whereas $I^A I^B$ heterozygotes will be AB; $ii$ homozygotes will be blood type O.

**14.** A-type blood contains A agglutinogen but β-antibody. B-type blood has B agglutinogen but α-antibody. AB-type blood has A and B agglutinogen but no antibody, and O blood has no agglutinogen but both types of antibody. A agglutinogen and α-antibody clump red cells, as do B agglutinogen and β-antibody. Therefore, before transfusion of blood from one individual to another, blood types must be matched so that antibody and agglutinogen of the same type do not mix. People with O-type blood are universal donors, however, since the anti-

bodies are quickly diluted by recipient blood and there are no cells with agglutinogen in the donated blood. People with AB-type blood are universal recipients since they have no antibodies to clump transfused cells.

**15.** There are about 20 kinds of blood groups under genetic control, and blood typing has been used to establish paternity in questionable cases.

**16.** Quantitative characteristics are controlled by polygenes. Human skin color is an example in which as many as five alleles may produce a wide range of possible shades of color. Interaction between nonallelic genes may involve epistasis, where the phenotypic expression of one gene or set of genes may be masked by expression of a different gene. The genes for albinism (due to mu-tation of a gene controlling melanin production), for example, show epistasis over all other skin color genes. Since in albinos melanin is not synthesized, the genes determining intensity of melanin deposition have no effect.

**17.** Abnormal chromosome numbers may be produced as a result of nondisjunction during meiosis. Abnormal numbers of sex chromosomes may produce Klinefelter syndrome (*XXY* feminized males) or Turner syndrome (*XO* sterile females). Nondisjunction of autosomes may produce Down syndrome (extra chromosome 21) with characteristic physical symptoms, low IQ, and short life-expectancy; the incidence of Down syndrome increases with the age of the mother.

**18.** Deletion, duplication, translocation, or inversion of various chromosomes may produce cri-du-chat syndrome (deletion in chromosome 5) or Down's syndrome (translocation of extra chromosome 21 to 15). Chromosome abnormalities such as this may be produced by x rays, which can cause chromosome breaks.

## KEY WORDS

Down syndrome
amniocentesis
genetics
physiological or molecular genetics
transmission or classical genetics
chromosomes
diploid number
gametes
zygote
autosomes
sex chromosomes (XX and XY)
karyotype
melanin
melanocytes
albinos
phenotype
genotype
homologous (chromosomes)
allele

locus
family tree or pedigree
dominant
recessive
homozygous
heterozygous
carriers
mutation
$F_1$ (first filial) generation
$F_2$ (second filial) generation
law of segregation
law of independent assortment or principle
  of recombination
Punnett square
linked (genes)
crossing over
sex-linked (genes)
hemizygous
Barr body
Lyon hypothesis
isoagglutinins

$\alpha$-antibody
$\beta$-antibody
A and B agglutinogens
donor
recipient
universal donor
universal recipient
hemophilia
polygenes
epistasis
nondisjunction
Klinefelter syndrome
Turner syndrome
deletion
duplication
translocation
inversion
cri-du-chat syndrome
Down syndrome carrier
HLA (human lymphocyte-associated antigen)
major histocompatability complex (MHC)

## TOPICS FOR REVIEW AND DISCUSSION

1. What is the relationship of phenotype to genotype?

2. What is a karyotype, how is it prepared, and of what value is it in genetic studies?

3. Discuss the molecular basis for albinism, its mode of inheritance, and how it may have arisen.

4. Why is more known about the inheritance of abnormal human traits than of normal ones? Discuss some structural abnormalities of chromosomes.

5. How are Mendel's laws explained by meiosis?

6. Why is Mendel's principle of independent assortment (or recombination) not universally true?

7. What is polygenic inheritance? Give some examples of polygenic traits and their mode of inheritance.

8. What is sex linkage? What is crossing over and what is its biological significance?

9. Discuss multiple alleles and blood group inheritance.

10. Discuss nondisjunction and some of its consequences.

11. What is the relationship of the Barr body to sex-linked inheritance?

12. Discuss the biological significance of sexual reproduction.

13. Discuss the inheritance of Down syndrome.

14. Contrast dominance with epistasis.

## Detecting an Old Killer

Historically, sickle-cell anemia has been an unheralded killer. It does not occur in dramatic epidemics. Its victims in the United States are mostly blacks, whose heritage traces back to populations from West Africa. The malady affects the red blood cells, which normally are spherical. When the anemia victim is under any stress that reduces the oxygen supply in the blood, the red cells elongate into firm gellike crescents, called "sickles," that block narrow capillaries and deprive tissues of vital oxygen. The impaired circulation causes great pain in various parts of the body, enlargement of the heart, and damage to the brain cells. The tendency of the red blood cells to rupture produces severe anemia.

The millions of Americans who carry one defective allele may show mild to severe symptoms of the disease, but the one child in 170 who inherits a sickle-cell allele from each parent has barely an even chance of seeing his or her 20th birthday. Those who do survive into middle age are likely to be crippled.

Sickle-cell anemia cannot be cured, though rapid advances are being made to alleviate the symptoms of the disease. It can be almost completely prevented, provided that partners who both carry the trait avoid having children.

Carriers of the trait can now be identified using a DNA probe, making it possible for the parents to know in advance the probability of their having a child with sickle-cell anemia.

What is the molecular basis of sickle-cell disease? Why is such an obviously debiliating disorder maintained in the population?

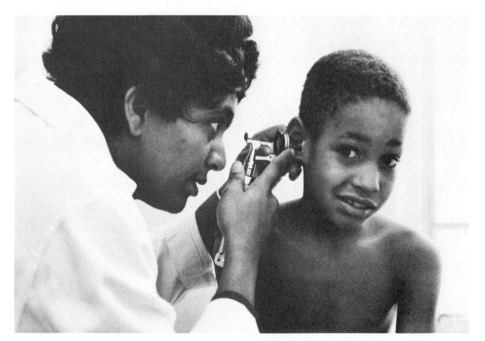

Doctor examining sickle-cell suspect. Incurable, but avoidable. (Photograph by Arnold Hinton. Reprinted by permission, Monkmeyer Press Photo Service.)

The appearance of red blood cells in a person with sickle-cell trait. Notice the crescent-shaped "sickles."

# 24

# Genes in Populations: An Introduction to Evolution

## 24–1 SICKLE CELL: A MOLECULAR DISEASE

Sickle-cell disease was first described in 1910 by J. B. Herrick in a young West Indian student living in Chicago. When air was excluded from a drop of the patient's blood by placing the drop on a microscope slide, ringing it with petroleum jelly, and covering it with a coverglass, the red blood cells showed a dramatic change in shape from round to a sickle form (Figure 24–1). The patient showed other distressing symptoms—clogged blood vessels, pneumonia, rheumatism, heart disease, inflammation of the soft tissues of the hands and feet, and anemia. What is the cause of sickle-cell disease?

In Chapter 23 we considered disorders caused by abnormal chromosome structure or chromosome numbers. Sickle-cell disease and some 1,500 other human diseases are attributed not to visible changes in the chromosomes, but to alterations in the DNA itself. Some of these disorders are very rare, but others are common. Only about 30 of these conditions can be diagnosed in the unborn child by amniocentesis (Figure 23–2), and sickle-cell disease is one of them.

Sickle-cell anemia results when the abnormal recessive gene (Figure 24–2) is inherited in a double dose (*ss*). Heterozygotes, or sickle-cell carriers (*Ss*), typically show no ill effects; however, when oxygen

(a)

(b)

**FIGURE 24–1 Electron micrographs of (a) normal red blood cells and (b) sickled red blood cells. (Courtesy of Philips Electronic Instruments.)**

is limited (for example, at high altitude or on a slide ringed with petroleum jelly), the blood cells of the heterozygote show mild sickling. The heterozygous state is often called **sickle-cell trait.** Individuals who are homozygous for the normal allele (*SS*) do not, of course, show the sickling phenomenon.

The molecular basis of sickle-cell disease is a gene mutation (change) that occurred centuries ago in Africa. In the late 1940s it was found that the hemoglobin molecule present in the red cells of persons having sickle-cell anemia was abnormal. The hemoglobin from persons homozygous for sickle-cell anemia had a different electrical charge from that of normal hemoglobin, and heterozygous persons showed about equal amounts of normal and sickle-cell hemoglobin (Figure 24–3). Closer analysis of the sickle-cell hemoglobin revealed that a change in a single amino acid out of the 287 amino acids in each hemoglobin molecule (substitution of valine for glutamic acid, Figure 24–4) produced profound effects on the structure and function of the hemoglobin. The change in one amino acid altered the electrical charge of the hemoglobin, reduced the ability of the molecule to transport oxygen, changed the shape of the red cells, and created a cascade of disease symptoms. Sickle-cell anemia is an example of **pleiotropy,** a situation in which a single gene affects a great many phenotypic characters (Figure 24–5). It is also a classic example of how a change in a single nucleotide in the DNA molecule can produce a distorted message and an inborn molecular error (the DNA code words for glutamic acid are CTT and CTC, whereas for valine the equivalents are CAT and CAC; Figure 6–8).

## 24–2 OUR CHANGING GENES: MUTATION

What we are and what our children will be depend, in the final analysis, on the nature of the genetic blueprint and how that blueprint is duplicated. Strictly speaking, we did not acquire the genes of our parents, nor will our children receive our genes; rather, parental genes are copied, and the copy is passed on to the progeny. Precision in copying the genetic blueprint and exactness in chromosome duplication ensure that parental traits are passed on intact to the offspring.

A gene is a linear stretch of the DNA molecule that contains the information for producing a protein chain. The kinds of proteins made depend on how accurately the genetic message is read. The transfer of information from parent to progeny depends on the accuracy with which the DNA molecule duplicates itself. Although the copying process involved in the replication of DNA is quite precise, it is not without error. Once in a while a change occurs in the genetic blueprint; this may involve the simple substitution of one base for another in the DNA molecule. (The molecular basis for such changes is discussed in Chapter 6.) The modified gene is reproduced in its altered form. This heritable alteration in the genetic message, called a **gene mutation,** has as its basis a change in the base sequence of the DNA.

Mutations are uncontrollable chance phenomena that cause a change in an organism. Such changes may be relatively minor or they may be severe. Indeed, the vast majority of gene mutations observable today in organisms are changes for the worse and may be lethal[1] (the embryo never survives beyond a few hours or days). When we consider that the organisms that populate the earth today are the products of a long evolutionary history, such changes for the worse produced by mutation are not unexpected. The genes we carry today represent the most favorable mutations, selected and accumulated during the course of time; the chance of a new mutant gene arising that confers an advantage over one

---

[1] Mutations do occur that are not debilitating; the genes for eye color, blood group, and so on mutate without harm. However, in this chapter we are concerned with those diseases that are maintained in the population by mutation.

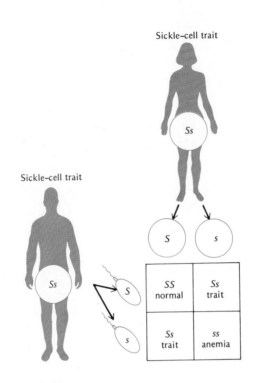

FIGURE 24–2 The mating of two persons with sickle-cell trait can produce normal offspring, offspring with sickle-cell trait, and offspring with sickle-cell anemia.

Sickle–cell trait

Sickle–cell trait

| | |
|---|---|
| SS<br>normal | Ss<br>trait |
| Ss<br>trait | ss<br>anemia |

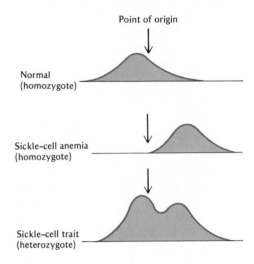

FIGURE 24–3 When a solution of hemoglobin is subjected to an electrical field, its pattern of migration in the field depends on its charge. Note the differing patterns of migration for normal and sickle-cell hemoglobin. Note also that the individual with sickle-cell trait has equal proportions of both kinds of hemoglobin.

Point of origin

Normal (homozygote)

Sickle–cell anemia (homozygote)

Sickle–cell trait (heterozygote)

FIGURE 24–4 A change in a single amino acid in the normal hemoglobin molecule is responsible for sickle-cell hemoglobin's novel properties.

FIGURE 24–5 (bottom) A cascade of consequences connected with sickle-cell anemia.

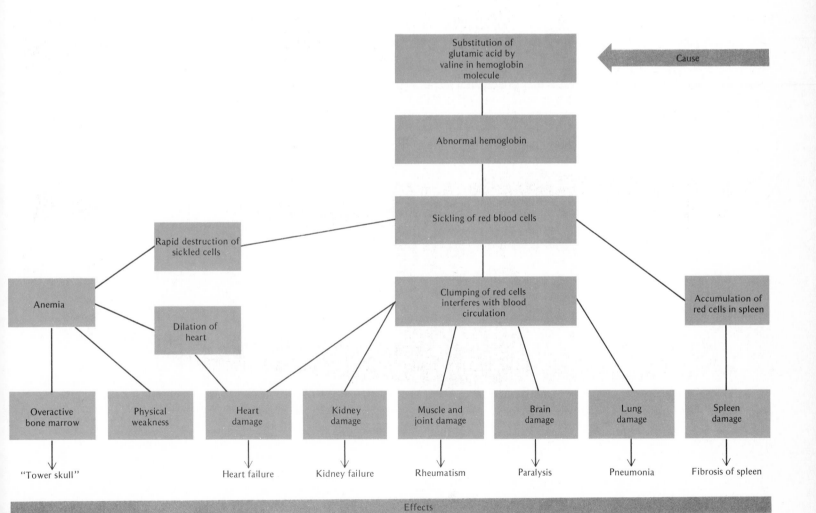

### BOX 24A  Radiation as a mutagen

The Bravo nuclear test on Bikini atoll took place on March 1, 1954. An unexpected wind carried the radioactive products, fallout, more than 80 miles from the target site and showered the Japanese fishing boat *Lucky Dragon* with at least 15 lb of debris. The 23 crewmen received a radiation dose equal to that given off by the entire world supply of radium. One fisherman died, others showed abnormalities in their blood, and most probably suffered genetic damage. On September 13, 1987, two young men entered an abandoned radiotherapy institute in a small suburban village outside of Brasilia, Brazil. They scavenged the site, recovered a stainless steel cylinder from a cancer therapy machine, and sold it to a junkyard. At the junkyard the cylinder was dismantled and the platinum cap was pried open. The junkyard employee who opened the cylinder was fascinated by what he found inside: a glowing blue saltlike substance. He took the luminescent powder home with him, and distributed it to family and friends. One man slept with it under his bed, another carried a lump of it in his pocket, and the children rubbed it on their bodies like carnival glitter. What these unsuspecting people did not know was that the blue powder was radioactive cesium (cesium 137). By the end of October, 244 persons were found to be contaminated, 20 of these had been exposed to sufficiently high levels of radiation (100 to 800 rads) that they had radiation burns on their skin; they themselves were radioactive, and 4 died including the junkyard worker and several members of his family. The eventual toll in terms of cancer and genetic defects cannot yet be accurately determined.

What is radiation, and how does it damage the living cell? Atomic radiation, usually referred to as **ionizing radiation,** includes x rays and gamma rays, which are the shortest and hence the most energetic wavelengths of radiant energy. These energetic waves are capable of knocking out electrons from the atoms of materials through which they pass. The loss of an electron creates a charged atom, an **ion,** and this is highly reactive chemically (Figure 24–6a). Through the chemical activity of ions, the molecules of the living cell may be altered—proteins, especially enzymes, may be inactivated, and bases of the DNA may be substituted, deleted, and rearranged (Figure 24–6b). Loss of a

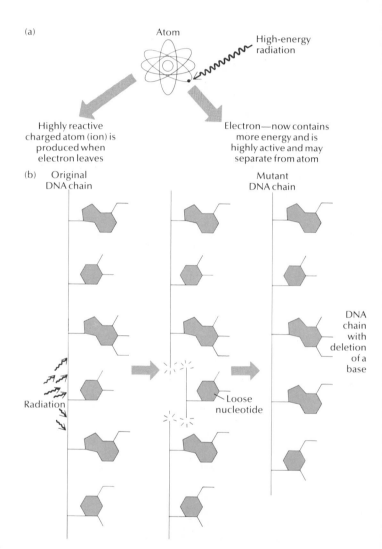

FIGURE 24–6  The effects of radiation on the cell. (a) Ion formation when high-energy radiation strikes an atom. (b) Alteration of DNA base sequence by deletion of a nucleotide (point mutation) when ionizing radiation strikes the DNA chain.

large number of bases in the DNA impairs the cell's ability to synthesize proteins and produces errors in coding. The implications of this are far-reaching, and the effects could even be lethal.

Ionizing radiations are a part of our ecosystem. Radioactive substances occur in soil, water, air, food, and our own bodies; we are continuously being bombarded with cosmic rays from outer space. Together with the other sources of natural radiation, these constitute the **background radiation.** We can do very little about this. Our concern lies with the ever-increasing amounts of radiation that we ourselves have created and that are widely disseminated.

Each of us is exposed to more than twice the radiation received by persons living before the turn of the century. Why is this so? In 1892 Henri Becquerel discovered uranium and the fingerprints of radioactivity—ionization and fogging of photographic plates. Some years later Pierre and Marie Curie isolated the radioactive element radium. These elements (and many others discovered since) are naturally unstable and undergo spontaneous disintegration. As the radioactive atoms decay, energy in the form of gamma rays and particles is emitted, and this is the source of ionizing radiation. Since 1945 we have been able to split the atom and thus create new and totally artificial elements that also decay to emit deadly gamma rays. Detonation of nuclear weapons creates radioactive substances that are let loose into the atmosphere. This material, falling to the earth, is fallout. In 1895 Wilhelm Röntgen discovered that special high-voltage equipment caused disturbances in the electrons of atoms, producing x rays. X rays could then be produced at will. Gamma rays and x rays are quite similar as sources of ionizing radiation; gamma rays are born in the nucleus of an atom, whereas x rays arise in the electron cloud surrounding the atomic nucleus.

X rays opened up a new era of medicine, for they enabled the physician to see inside the body. Splitting the atom created nuclear weapons and nuclear power plants. New sources of radioactivity could be made available for the treatment of cancer, and radioactive elements provided a means of tracing the metabolism of the cell. These are the benefits of living in the age of the atom. What are the hazards?

Ionizing radiation cannot be seen, but its effects, especially those on living matter, are easily detected. Unfortunately this was not immediately realized by the earliest workers. Pierre Curie placed a small fragment of radium on his arm and burned his skin. The pioneers in radiology took few precautions in their exposure to the x-ray beam, and many suffered a life of agony terminated by cancer. The severe injuries caused by the atomic bombs dropped on Hiroshima and Nagasaki are well known. The nuclear reactor successfully employed by Enrico Fermi to produce atomic energy probably contributed to his early death of leukemia at age 54. The signs were all there, but most of the world paid little attention to them. However, in 1927 the subtle genetic effects of ionizing radiation were clearly demonstrated. In that year H. J. Muller bombarded fruit flies *(Drosophila)* with x rays and induced mutations. X rays are **mutagenic** (literally "mutation forming"). Since mutations are random changes in genes, they seldom improve the genetic composition of an organism; most mutations are deleterious, and increasing the mutation rate enhances the probability of disturbing the well-established pattern of inheritance.

Some of the radiation doses we are exposed to are shown in Table 24–1. A dose of 30 rads* is sufficient to double the spontaneous mutation rate. Exposure of a human population of 200 million persons to 10 rads would cause:

| Form of damage | No. of cases in first generation | No. of cases in subsequent generations |
|---|---|---|
| Chondrodystrophic dwarfism | 1,000 | 200 |
| Mental and physical defects | 80,000 | 720,000 |
| Infant mortality | 160,000 | 3,840,000 |
| Embryonic mortality | 400,000 | 7,600,000 |

Such changes occur because the ionizing radiation has interacted with the DNA of the cells undergoing sex-cell formation. The damage to the gametes will show its effect in those yet unborn— a cruel legacy for our children. Exposure to 200 rads causes chromosome abnormalities in the form of rings, fragments, translocations, and two centromeres on the same chromosome.

* A rad is a unit measure of radiation. See Table 24–1.

**TABLE 24–1  The radiation we receive each year**

| Source | Dose (rad)* |
| --- | --- |
| Natural background | 0.1 |
| Fallout | 0.1 |
| Chest x ray | 0.001 |
| Pelvic x ray | 3–6 |
| Upper gastrointestinal tract x ray | 0.2–0.3 |

* A roentgen is the exposure dose and is defined as the amount of radiation that produces $2 \times 10^9$ ion pairs per cubic centimeter of air. (A cubic centimeter of tissue contains 100 billion times this number of atoms.) A rad is a unit of radiation absorption and equals the amount of energy absorbed; 1 rad = 100 erg absorbed per gram of irradiated matter. For our purposes, rad and roentgen are roughly equivalent.

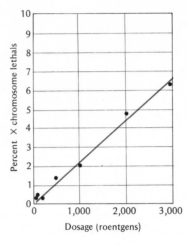

FIGURE 24–7 The relationship of radiation dose to production of mutations in the fruit fly *Drosophila*. It is quite possible that humans are more sensitive to radiation than fruit flies, and therefore lower doses of radiation could produce a similar number of lethal mutations.

Larger doses kill most cells. The exact consequences of exposure to ionizing radiation depend on the individual cell and its metabolic state; the most sensitive cells are those undergoing cell division, especially those of the gonads, stomach, intestines, bone marrow, lymph nodes, and spleen.

As Muller showed more than 60 years ago, the production of mutations in the fruit fly is directly proportional to the total dose of radiation, and the effects are completely independent of the source (Figure 24–7). We have more to fear from the innocent-looking x-ray machine that may be emitting a higher dose than is necessary and is scattering rays throughout the room than from radioactive fallout! Since there is no threshold dose, no x-ray dose is so small as to produce no mutations. Furthermore, doses are additive; the total amount of radiation received is the important factor, not whether the radiation was given in one concentrated dose or in small doses spread out over a long period of time.

Reduction of total-body exposure to radiation lessens the danger of cancer, especially leukemia. (How x rays induce cancer remains uncertain, but it most likely involves somatic mutations.) The best advice: minimize exposure to radiation, especially that received by the ovaries and testes in persons who have not yet passed the childbearing or child-begetting age.

that has an established historical role is quite unlikely. It would be similar to the replacement of a word or two in this paragraph by another word, selected at random, with the retention or improvement of the original meaning. It could happen, but the chances are slim.

If mutation in an organism is often deleterious, what is its significance? Genes arise only from preexisting genes, and mutation is the source of all new genes. Without mutation, evolution could not have progressed beyond the very earliest primitive organisms.

Mutations are chance occurrences. Their appearance has absolutely nothing to do with the needs of an organism or whether the change is advantageous or disadvantageous. On occasion, a mutation may be advantageous and as such may provide the change necessary for the survival of that population of organisms. Let us consider an example. The bacteria called staphylococci cause a variety of human ailments—sore throats, inflamed ears, boils, and so on. Many staphylococcal infections are easily treated by administration of an antibiotic such as penicillin; penicillin kills the bacteria and the infection disappears. On occasion, the staphylococcal infection does not respond to the antibiotic, and the bacteria grow in its presence; we say that such bacteria have lost their sensitivity to penicillin and that they are now penicllin-resistant. Did the penicillin-resistant bacteria arise by an advantageous mutation because the sensitive staphylococci needed a way of combating the antibiotic? No. A chance mutation in the original bacterial population (which was sensitive to penicillin) produced a small number of individuals capable of growing and reproducing themselves in the presence of penicillin. The mutation was not deleterious to these bacteria in the absence of the antibiotic. However, once antibiotic treatment began, the penicillin killed off the sensitive bacterial cells, and only those bacteria that contained the mutant gene could survive in this new anti-

biotic-laden environment. Thus, a mutant gene that previously had little or no effect proved beneficial to the organism under the appropriate environmental conditions. As we shall see, selection of mutant genes is a continuing occurrence and an important part of the evolutionary process in populations of organisms—human as well as bacteria.

What causes mutations? The cause of natural or spontaneous mutations remains uncertain, but it is well known that many external agents can produce mutations. Among these are background radiation (cosmic rays, radioactive elements in the soil and in the food), temperature, and chemicals (mustard gas, peroxides, and so on). Different genes have different mutation rates, but why this is so remains unexplained.

Some mutant genes are decidedly beneficial; that is, an individual carrying such a gene is better able to adapt to the environment. Others are harmful or even lethal to the individual in whom they are expressed. Since the process of evolution involves changes in the quality as well as the quantity of the genes in all members of a species living at that particular time, the consequences of such mutations for the living population as well as for future generations assume some importance. Harmful mutations carried in the germ cells can be regarded as a **genetic burden** (which is also called the **genetic load**) for the whole population.

The entire genetic variability of all members of an interbreeding population is called the **gene pool.** It may be tempting to believe that lethal genes derived from mutation cannot long survive in a population because the individuals carrying such genes are unlikely to reproduce or survive and thus the gene pool will purify itself. This is, of course, true for dominant lethal genes and for individuals homozygous for recessive lethal genes, who will die without reproducing. However, an individual carrying a deleterious gene can function normally if that gene

is compensated for by a normal gene, that is, if the individual is heterozygous for the deleterious gene. Thus, some lethal or deleterious genes persist in the gene pool because the mutant gene is masked by the presence of a normal allele or because the effect of the mutant gene, though not completely masked, is expressed to a lesser degree, and the individual with such a **subvital** (harmful but not lethal) **gene** survives at least long enough to reproduce. (Sickle-cell trait is an example of such a condition.) In this way, deleterious mutations may accumulate in the gene pool of generations yet unborn—a grim legacy for our progeny. This raises the following question: can we reduce the genetic burden we now carry and that of future generations? How can we effect such changes? We shall attempt to answer these questions later in this chapter.

## 24–3 GENES IN POPULATIONS

In our day-to-day encounters with other people, we tend to use individual differences as a sign of recognition. John has red hair, Philip has a jutting jaw, Susan has brown eyes and brown hair, and so on. The most casual assessment of the human population convinces us of one thing: we are not all alike. The variety we see around us depends, at least in its fundamental aspects, on two factors: mutation and sexual reproduction. Mutation, as discussed previously in this chapter, is the source of new genes. But how does sexual reproduction contribute to genetic variation?

An organism that reproduces by asexual means, that is, by mitosis, passes on its chromosomes without genetic change, for in this process chromosomes duplicate themselves with great fidelity. As a consequence, the cellular progeny of mitotic division have a genetic endowment identical to that of the parent cell, unless a mutation has occurred. In addition, since the progeny are derived from a single parent cell, the genes in the offspring are in exactly the same combinations as they were in the parent cell. Mitosis, or asexual reproduction, cannot provide a mechanism for recombining the genes of one individual with those of another.

An organism that reproduces by sexual means has a mechanism for shuffling around genes to produce a staggering array of genetic combinations. Let us consider the situation in ourselves. We began life as a zygote, the result of the fusion of two gametes, an egg from the mother and a sperm from the father. Some of the genes of one parent were combined with those of the other parent in the formation of the zygote. In addition, through meiosis any particular chromosome may be combined with any other chromosome, thus producing new combinations of genes. The number of possible chromosome combinations is given by the formula $2^n$, where $n$ equals the haploid number of chromosomes. Recall that the haploid gamete that results from meiosis has not solely paternal or maternal chromosomes, but a random assortment of these (providing the physical basis of Mendel's principle of recombination [or independent assortment]; see Figure 23–13). To gain some impression of the magnitude of such chromosomal combinations, let us look at our own chromosomal constitution. Each of our cells contains 23 pairs of chromosomes, and in theory the number of chromosomal combinations that could be produced during the formation of the gametes is equal to $2^{23}$, or about 11 million. The number of possible chromosomal combinations that could arise by the fusion of gametes would be equal to $(2^{23})^2$! This number is further increased by crossing over between the chromosomes (page 471 and Figure 23–14). Thus, the number of chromosomal combinations derived from sexual reproduction becomes almost infinite. It is no wonder that each of us is unique in his or her different gene combinations.

Genetic variation, a consequence of mutation and sexual reproduction, is the raw material upon which evolutionary change depends. Evolution involves changes in the genetic makeup of a population through successive generations, that is, with the passage of time. An individual cannot evolve, but a population can. At the moment of fertilization the genetic constitution of an individual is fixed for all time, but the genetic makeup of a population can change with time. In the absence of genetic variation no population of organisms can evolve, and in a changing environment such organisms would soon become extinct. Let us look at the genetic variation in a population of organisms and consider the total number of genes in all the eggs and sperm produced by the parents—the gene pool of that population.

When we study the gene pool of the human population, we are interested in the frequency of occurrence of a particular gene in the entire population. To explain the meaning of **gene frequency,** let us consider a population and a single gene locus on a single pair of chromosomes in that population. The two alleles are $B$ and $b$, and we shall arbitrarily set the frequency of the $B$ allele at 0.5 (that is, 50% of the genes are of this type) and the frequency of $b$ at 0.5. In a more general form we can say that if the frequency of one allele is $p$ and the frequency of the other allele is $q$, then the collective frequency of alleles at the locus for the entire population is:

$$p + q = 1$$

What would happen to the gene frequencies in such a population if there were completely random mating, if mutations did not occur, and if there were no immigration or emigration? In 1908 G. H. Hardy (a mathematician) in England and W. Weinberg (a physician) in Germany provided a mathematical solution to this question. According to the **Hardy-Weinberg law** the frequencies of the genotypes can be described by expanding the binomial expression $(p + q)^2$, that is:

$$p^2 + 2pq + q^2$$

If the gene pool of the population is composed of 0.5 $B$ and 0.5 $b$ genes in the gametes, we would expect the offspring to occur in three distinct genotypes: $BB$, $Bb$, and $bb$. If $p$ is the frequency of $B$ (0.5) and $q$ is the frequency of $b$ (0.5), then on the basis of the Hardy-Weinberg equation, we expect the offspring of such a population to be:

| $p^2$ | + | $2pq$ | + | $q^2$ |
|-------|---|-------|---|-------|
| $BB$ | | $Bb$ | | $bb$ |
| (0.5)(0.5) | | 2(0.5)(0.5) | | (0.5)(0.5) |
| 0.25 | | 0.50 | | 0.25 |

Or, in more familiar terms, 50% of the genotypes in such a population will be either $BB$ (25%) or $bb$ (25%), and 50% of the genotypes will be $Bb$.

Although in most populations the values of $p$ and $q$ are not equal, the calculations remain exactly the same. That is to say, the more-frequent allele in a population will not automatically increase in frequency, nor will the less-frequent allele eventually be lost from the population. Let us see why.

Suppose the frequency of the $B$ gene in the gene pool is 0.9 ($p$) and the frequency of the $b$ gene is 0.1 ($q$). Using the Hardy-Weinberg equation we find:

| $p^2$ | + | $2pq$ | + | $q^2$ |
|-------|---|-------|---|-------|
| (0.9)(0.9) | | 2(0.9)(0.1) | | (0.1)(0.1) |
| 0.81 | | 0.18 | | 0.01 |

That is, 81% of the population is $BB$, 18% is $Bb$, and 1% is $bb$. If we compute the frequencies for the next generation, we find they are the same ones we started with. Similar calculations for subsequent generations turn up the same result: gene frequencies and genotype ratios are unchanged. The Hardy-Weinberg law states that in a sexually reproducing population under certain conditions of stability, the frequency of genes remains constant from generation to generation. Many aspects of the field of population genetics are based on this law.

The Hardy-Weinberg law describes a population that is unchanged from one generation to the next, that is, it describes a situation where evolution is not occuring. In addition, the Hardy-Weinberg law applies only when the following conditions are met:

1. There must be random mating and no selective advantage of one genotype; that is, all the various genotypes have the same survival value.
2. Mutations do not occur.
3. Migration must not occur.

These conditions are rarely found in nature. Once matings are nonrandom, or mutation or migration occurs, or genotypes differ in their mortality and fertility, the Hardy-Weinberg law does not apply and gene frequencies will change from one generation to the next. Since the Hardy-Weinberg law depicts a static evolutionary situation that occurs rarely in a nature, what is its practical value? The value of the principle is twofold:

1. By assuming the Hardy-Weinberg law does apply to a population and then finding out how gene frequencies deviate from this, we can learn something about the various agents involved in evolutionary change.
2. The formula can be used to estimate the frequency of heterozygotes in a population in which heterozygotes appear normal and thus cannot be distinguished readily. Albino heterozygotes and sickle-cell heterozygotes are in this category.

## 24–4 NATURAL SELECTION

We have said that genetic variation is the raw material upon which natural selection works: the term **natural selection** is most frequently associated with the name of Charles Darwin and is the key to his theory of evolution. What exactly is natural selection? Were we really descended from the apes by the forces of natural selection? What is the meaning of a phrase such as "survival of the fittest"? Are economic exploitation and genocide forms of natural selection? Let us begin with two examples: industrial melanism and sickle-cell anemia.

### Industrial melanism

Traits exhibiting more than one phenotype, or morph, are called polymorphisms (literally "several forms"). The British populations of the peppered moth *Biston betularia* are **polymorphic** in that there are two color shades: dark black (or melanic) and light gray (Figure 24–8). Collections of these moths in Great Britain prior to 1800 showed a predominance of the light gray form, and the black forms were so rare that they were prized as collector's items. The Industrial Revolution came in the early 1800s, and a striking change occurred in both the British economy and the peppered moth: the cities became filled with factories, and the dark forms of the peppered moth became more numerous while the lighter forms became rare. In 1848 records from Manchester showed the dark form of the moth to be less than 1% of the population, but by 1898, only 50 years later, the dark form predominated and represented 95% of the population. What is the explanation for the rapid color shift in this moth population?

E. B. Ford and H. B. D. Kettlewell carefully studied these changes in moth coloration, a phenomenon called **industrial melanism.** Their explanation is roughly as follows. Prior to 1800 Britain was agricultural, and the gray color of the moth blended in with the light coloration of the tree trunks on which the moths are often found, protecting the moths from predation by birds. As industrialization proceeded, cities and factories began to dominate the once-rural landscape, and the air was filled with soot and smoke. The replacement of the light-colored moths by the dark moths in regions of heavy industry is attributed to the fact that in these areas the dark forms are protectively colored and more easily escape predation by birds when they alight on the soot-covered trees. Observation of birds feeding on these moths in industrial areas shows that in a single day the birds may reduce the numbers of light-colored moths by 50%, whereas the less conspicuous dark moths remain relatively free from predation. (Attention to environmental pollution in Britain has caused a decrease in smoke and soot in many industrial areas, and in recent years the light-colored moths have reappeared in ever-increasing numbers.)

The dark and light forms of the peppered moth are controlled by a single gene with two alleles; the dark allele is dominant to the light one. Kettlewell believes that the dark form arose by a mutation in the original population of light moths. At first the dominant mutant gene was disadvantageous—birds could easily see the dark moths on the light tree trunk, and so the dark moths were quickly fed upon. However, industrialization tended to produce an environment favorable for the mutant gene. The mutant gene spread rapidly in the population and soon became the more frequent form. This idea, that the genetic constitution of a population changes because some environmental agent favors some individuals more than others and thus promotes evolutionary change, was first clearly stated by Charles Darwin and Alfred Wallace in 1859. They called the process natural selection.

Natural selection is the mainspring of evolution, but in much of the literature, both scientific and popular, it has been misinterpreted. Some have termed it "survival of the fittest," "nature red in tooth and claw," "the law of the jungle," and a "struggle for life." Such notions are essentially without scientific foundation, for in nature selection rarely involves combat. Plants evolve; yet they never fight with one another. Animals of the same species fight infrequently, and when they do so, killing is the exception rather than the rule. As industrial melanism clearly shows, the dark moths did not take over industrial areas by killing the light forms; they merely survived and reproduced their numbers with greater frequency than did the light forms. As a

FIGURE 24–8 Dark and light forms of the peppered moth *Biston betularia* (a) on a dark, soot-blackened tree and (b) on a light, lichen-covered tree. (Courtesy of H. B. D. Kettlewell.)

(a)

(b)

consequence they became the more numerous in the population. Thus, in the modern view natural selection is defined as **differential reproduction,** that is, those organisms best adapted (or fitted) to their environment are the ones that find food and mates more easily; they tend to produce more offspring, which also survive to reproductive age, and these in turn leave more offspring than others in the population. In the case of industrial melanism, the selective agent is clearly the feeding of predatory birds on the peppered moths; however, in most cases it is impossible to identify the factors or agents that enable one genotype to leave more offspring than another.

### Sickle-cell hemoglobin

Natural selection determines whether a gene is rare or common in a population. The process of selection does not create new genes; rather it takes the genes already present in a population and reduces the frequency of a gene that provides less selective advantage. The mechanism whereby this is accomplished is differential reproduction. As a result, and contrary to the belief of some, the most common genes in a population are not always dominant and rare genes are not always recessives. However, sometimes genes with deleterious effects are maintained at a relatively high

frequency in a population. Sickle-cell anemia is an example of such a situation.

Sickle-cell anemia is a severe debilitating disease; the child who is homozygous for this disorder (*ss*) barely has a chance of reaching maturity, and even if he or she does survive the child is likely to be crippled. Since individuals with sickle-cell anemia usually do not survive to reproductive age, we might expect that the abnormal allele would soon be lost from the population. Indeed, the failure of each homozygote to reproduce would deplete the gene pool of two such alleles. Our expectations are not realized. In Africa many populations are polymorphic for the sickle-cell allele.

FIGURE 24–9 (a) Distribution of falciparum malaria. (b) Distribution of sickle-cell anemia.

**505**

**GENES IN POPULATIONS:
AN INTRODUCTION TO EVOLUTION**

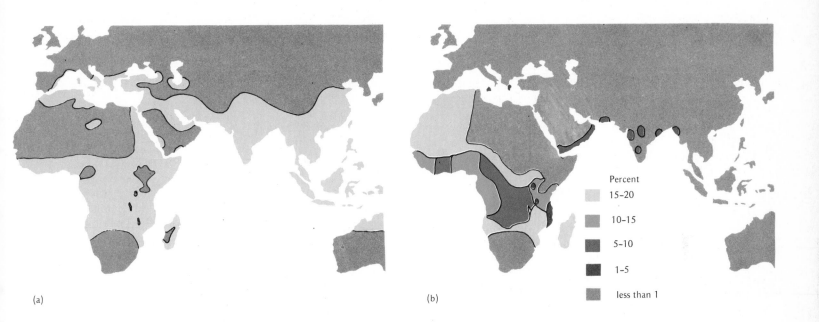

(a)

(b)

Percent

15–20

10–15

5–10

1–5

less than 1

The frequency of sickle-cell trait (*Ss*) exceeds 20% in many areas, and in some local populations the frequency is as high as 40%. What accounts for the high incidence of the sickle-cell allele, which has obvious deleterious effects when it occurs in a double dose?

At first we might suspect that the sickle-cell allele is maintained at a high frequency because there is an exceptionally high mutation rate from $S \longrightarrow s$. However, detailed studies have failed to reveal that the hemoglobin gene is more mutable than others. The geographical distribution of sickle-cell trait shows that it occurs in regions where malignant tertian malaria, produced by the protozoan *Plasmodium falciparum*, is prevalent (Figure 24–9). In 1949 A. C. Allison and his collaborators found that malaria was much less severe in children having sickle-cell trait (*Ss*) than in children with normal hemoglobin. They postulated that the sickle-cell allele in the heterozygous condition provides some degree of protection against malaria. Thus, in those areas where falciparum malaria is prevalent, persons having

sickle-cell trait are more likely to survive to maturity, and these individuals will pass on copies of their genes to the succeeding generation. In malarious areas the heterozygote for sickle-cell hemoglobin is superior in fitness to either of the homozygotes, a condition called **heterosis** or **hybrid vigor.** The *S* and *s* alleles are both maintained in the population because the loss of deleterious alleles by death of the homozygotes (*SS* and *ss*), either from malaria or anemia, is balanced by the gain that results from the enhanced survival and reproduction of the heterozygotes (*Ss*). This phenomenon is known as **balanced polymorphism.**

What happens to the frequency of the sickle-cell allele in areas where malaria has been eradicated? Since the selective advantage of the heterozygote in malaria-free areas would be equal to or less than that of the normal homozygote, we should expect the frequency of the sickle-cell gene to decline. This is exactly what occurs. The frequency of the sickle-cell trait among black Americans living in the United States,

where malaria has been eradicated for more than 50 years, is about 14%.

Again it can be seen that natural selection does not simply eliminate the bad genes and keep the good genes. Rather, selection operates within a population by probing the environment with new gene combinations, and in this way the surviving population increases in fitness; in this view, selection is a positive and creative force enabling a population of organisms to survive in a constantly changing and often hostile environment.

## 24–5 EUGENICS: IMPROVING OUR GENES BY SELECTION

### Negative eugenics

It has been a common practice throughout human history to improve plants and animals by hybridization (controlled mating) and selection. Breeders of livestock have selected for high egg-laying capacity, high meat yield, increased production of milk, high fat content in milk, and so on. The development of high-yield, high-quality strains of wheat, rice, and corn have created "green revolutions" and enhanced food production.

Initially, many such breeding programs were conducted without any genetic knowledge. The general rule applied by the breeder was to cull out the inferior types and retain and inbreed those types carrying the desirable characteristics. The main feature of such a program is to reduce the variability in the population and to remove the undesirable genes.[2]

In the early 1900s when Mendel's principles were rediscovered, the genetic basis for success in hybridization and selection became apparent. Mendelism, coupled with social-class bias in England and Germany and racial bias in the United States, provided the necessary scientific and sociological rationale for fostering programs to "improve" humans by applying the practices of controlled mating and selection. Sir Francis Galton (1822–1911), a cousin of Charles Darwin, publicized the notion of **eugenics** (literally "well born") from 1870 to the time of his death; in 1904 he defined eugenics as a "science dealing with all the influences that improve the inborn qualities of a race." In 1908 Galton and his followers established the Eugenics Society in England, and a few years later a similar group was founded in Germany. Later, eugenics came to be defined as "the study of agencies under social control that may improve or impair the racial (= hereditary) qualities of future generations either physically or mentally." It was almost inevitable that such a program would attract not only altruists, but many persons with strong racial and social-group prejudices. In the United States the beliefs of the eugenicists were reflected by restrictive immigration laws and compulsory sterilization programs for certain undesirable

phenotypes. Between 1907 and 1931, 30 states passed laws requiring or permitting sterilization for more than 24 different classes of defectives; in other cases individuals were institutionalized to prevent them from reproducing. In this way, it was hoped, the numbers of insane, mentally retarded, and epileptic persons would be reduced in society, and future generations would be free of such burdens. In Nazi Germany, Hitler used eugenics to foster a program of "race hygiene" and to justify genocide.

Superficially eugenics sounds both scientifically sound and idealistic. If the program were kept free of cranks, would it work? Once methods for predicting the effectiveness of selection became available and the relationship between the frequency of a gene and the efficacy of selection was understood, the hopes of the eugenics movements were diminished greatly. Eugenics wouldn't work. Let us see why.

If **negative selection** is practiced against a dominant allele (that is, if persons of a certain genotype are prevented from reproducing), in one generation the frequency of the allele will be reduced to the level maintained by mutation. The difficulty about applying negative selection to human disorders is that many disorders are not the result of dominant alleles. However, the condition known as **Huntington's disease**[3] is inherited as a simple dominant, and its incidence could be reduced in the population by a program of education and genetic counseling (Box 24B). But there is a disturbing complication: most persons who carry the dominant allele do not know they carry it because the disease symptoms do not usually develop until middle age, *after* the victim has produced a family and thus passed on the allele for Huntington's disease. Furthermore, persons with Huntington's disease are heterozygous for the defective

---

[2] Inbreeding in humans—that is, consanguineous marriages—creates social and personal burdens. In such cases, the risk is increased that deleterious genes will be expressed in the offspring, as occurs in infantile amaurotic idiocy.

[3] Huntington's disease involves a progressive degeneration of the nervous system: it starts with involuntary twitching of the head, limbs, and body; later, there is a loss of mental and physical powers; and finally death occurs.

---

**BOX 24B  The diabolical disease of Woody Guthrie**

Folksinger and composer Woody Guthrie ("This Land Is Your Land") died in 1967 after suffering from Huntington's disease. Woody had been misdiagnosed, considered an alcoholic, and shunted in and out of mental institutions for many years before an accurate diagnosis of his condition was made. Huntington's disease is a hereditary brain disorder that begins at age 30 or 40 and progresses inexorably to death, usually 10 to 20 years after onset. Each child of an affected parent has a 50% chance of inheriting the disorder. There is no skipping of generations, no way to diagnose the disease early, and no way to distinguish carriers from noncarriers.

Typically the symptoms begin with clumsiness, and then uncontrollable twisting and turning movements develop, followed by forgetfulness, excitability, or total apathy; the final stages are characterized by dementia, loss of memory, and loss of the ability to reason. The disease symptoms are a consequence of the degeneration of neurons in the brain cortex, as well as in the basal ganglia. With such destruction, there are decreased levels of neurotransmitters such as gamma aminobutyric acid and acetylcholine, and alterations in neuron function result.

There is no effective treatment for Huntington's disease, although some tranquilizers do reduce anxiety, depression, and some of the writhing movements. However, there are unpleasant side effects from the high doses of drugs needed to reduce the symptoms. Continued research, it is hoped, will lead to an understanding of the molecular basis of the disease and of how it might be effectively treated.

FIGURE 24–10 The elimination of individuals carrying a recessive allele (homozygous for a particular trait) per generation proceeds at a slower rate as selection pressure decreases. Note that even with complete selection, the percentage never reaches zero.

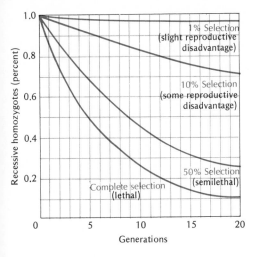

gene, and therefore half the children of a couple wherein only one parent was afflicted would be expected to be normal; prevention of reproduction would disallow both normal and afflicted children. (If the condition could be diagnosed in a fetus by means of amniocentesis, parents with a family history of the disease could elect to abort only those fetuses with the disorder; however, it is not possible at present to diagnose an afflicted fetus by this technique.)

The difficulty of negative selection against a dominant such as the allele responsible for Huntington's disease dims the hopes of a eugenicist; what about negative selection for an allele that is recessive? Again, the problem is recognition. Table 24–2 and Figure 24–10 show that total negative selection against persons homozygous for the recessive allele reduces the frequency of the allele with each succeeding generation. However, recessives remain masked in heterozygotes, and the deleterious recessive allele becomes even more difficult to trace. Selection against the homozygous recessive becomes less and less effective as the gene is reduced in frequency; theoretically, the allele is never eliminated, but by the hundredth generation (in humans that would be 3,000 years) an allele that originally had a frequency of 50% would be reduced to 0.01%. We are drawn, almost inescapably, to the conclusion that negative selection against a recessive gene will not eliminate its presence.

Let us look at a particular case. Persons with sickle-cell anemia (ss) are naturally selected against, that is, the condition is so debilitating and death usually occurs at such an early age that affected individuals are subjected to almost total negative selection. In such a situation, we might ask, how long would it take for the frequency of sickle-

cell anemia to be significantly reduced in the United States[4] from its current level of 6 per 1,000 to a level of 6 per 1,000,000? It has been calculated that to reduce the frequency of sickle-cell anemia 1,000-fold would require 395 generations, or 10,850 years! Thus, active research on sickle-cell hemoglobin and genetic counseling could make sickle-cell anemia a rare disease. If *all* persons with sickle-cell trait (*Ss*) were given genetic counseling and then *all* elected to avoid having children (unlikely possibilities), the frequency of sickle-cell anemia would be reduced to zero in one generation.[5] More important, this is not simply theoretical, since persons with sickle-cell trait (*Ss*) can easily be identified by a blood test. Here parental choice alone can make a critical impact on the gene pool.

Each of us carries, in a concealed condition, about four abnormal alleles which, if they were to become homozygous, would be deleterious. These deleterious alleles constitute our genetic load, or genetic burden. The application of modern medical practice, that is, the prolongation of the life of individuals with apparent genetic defects so that they survive to reproductive age, maintains the pool of defective genes. Can we reduce our genetic load by selecting against heterozygotes? First, can we identify such heterozygotes? Second, if we can identify heterozygotes, can we, in a free and democratic society, prevent the marriage of individuals who potentially could produce all normal children (a heterozygote marrying a normal homozygote) or 75% normal children (if both spouses are heterozygotes)? It is clear, for reasons involving recognition of the heterozygote and imple-

---

TABLE 24–2 Effects of complete selection against a recessive trait

| Generations | Gene frequency | Recessive homozygotes (%) | Heterozygotes (%) | Dominant homozygotes (%) |
|---|---|---|---|---|
| 1 | 0.500 | 25.00 | 50.00 | 25.00 |
| 2 | 0.333 | 1.11 | 44.44 | 44.44 |
| 3 | 0.250 | 6.25 | 37.50 | 56.25 |
| 4 | 0.200 | 4.00 | 32.00 | 64.00 |
| 5 | 0.167 | 2.78 | 27.78 | 69.44 |
| 9 | 0.100 | 1.00 | 18.00 | 81.00 |
| 10 | 0.091 | 0.83 | 16.53 | 82.64 |
| 20 | 0.048 | 0.23 | 9.07 | 90.70 |
| 30 | 0.032 | 0.10 | 6.24 | 93.65 |
| 40 | 0.024 | 0.06 | 4.76 | 95.18 |
| 50 | 0.020 | 0.04 | 3.84 | 96.12 |
| 100 | 0.010 | 0.01 | 1.96 | 98.03 |

From E. W. Sinnott, L. C. Dunn, and T. Dobzhansky, *Principles of Genetics*, 5th ed., New York, McGraw-Hill, 1968.

---

[4] In countries such as the United States, where malaria has been eradicated, the gene in its heterozygous condition confers no selective advantage.

[5] For the purposes of calculation the mutation rate for *S* ⟶ *s* is not considered. Furthermore, mutation would act to delay the reduction of *ss* frequency. The data given are therefore conservative.

mentation of eugenics programs, that total selection against heterozygotes cannot be practiced. Finally, we should note that when genes interact in such a way that the heterozygote is of superior phenotype to one or both homozygotes (for example, the person with sickle-cell trait in malarious areas), then complete elimination is theoretically impossible. As Dobzhansky has said, "A genetic good mixer becomes superior to a genetic rugged individualist."

### Positive eugenics

Suppose instead of negative eugenics we decided to employ **positive eugenics,** that is, to encourage those individuals with desirable phenotypes to produce more offspring. Sir Julian Huxley and Nobel laureate H. J. Muller have advocated the establishment of sperm banks in which semen of men judged to be superior would be deposited. The sperm would be used for artificial insemination, and in this manner the frequency of desirable genes in the gene pool would be increased. It works in cattle; why not humans?

One difficulty encountered in programs of positive eugenics is the definition of "desirable." Can we really agree on those human traits we would want to see in future generations? Suppose we agree that intelligence, adaptability, mental stability, courage, perseverance, energy, and compassion are all desirable traits. How can we test for the genetic basis of these traits? As yet, we do not know of a single human gene that produces any of these desirable phenotypes. In addition, we haven't the vaguest notion how such qualities will fare in a human society a few hundred years from now. A society that cannot decide what is desirable today can hardly forecast the needs of society in the future.

Our best hope for the future lies not in positive or negative eugenics, but in genetic counseling, restriction of family size, adoption of children in consanguineous marriages (first cousins), and maximization of individual choice.

### SUMMARY

**1.** Sickle-cell disease is a genetic abnormality produced by an alteration in the DNA itself. When an individual is homozygous for the recessive allele, sickle-cell anemia results. Such individuals show a sickling of their red blood cells with multiple physical side effects. Heterozygotes are sickle-cell carriers; such individuals show a sickling of their red blood cells when placed under oxygen stress and are said to have sickle-cell trait.

**2.** The molecular basis of sickle-cell disease is a mutation that causes a substitution of valine for glutamic acid in the hemoglobin molecule. When a single allele affects a great many phenotypic characters, it is said to have a pleiotropic effect.

**3.** Mutations are chance phenomena, and most are deleterious or lethal. Selection of occasional beneficial mutations is of overriding importance in evolution.

**4.** Subvital genes may be maintained in a population by heterozygotes. Harmful mutations in the gene pool of a population form its genetic burden, or load.

**5.** Ionizing radiation is mutagenic; there is no threshold and its effects are cumulative.

**6.** Sexual reproduction (as well as mutation) contributes to genetic variation because of independent assortment and crossing over at meiosis. Genetic variation forms the basis of evolution.

**7.** The Hardy-Weinberg law states that in a stable population where there is no migration or mutation, where mating is random, and where all genotypes have the same survival value, gene frequency will remain unchanged ($p^2 + 2pq + q^2$). The law allows prediction of the frequency of heterozygotes with a normal phenotype. Further, measurable deviations in gene frequency indicate agents of evolutionary change are at work.

**8.** Natural selection can be seen to operate in the situation known as industrial melanism. Changes in the coloration of moths in Britain was due to the selective advantage of certain phenotypes; those phenotypes that were favored became the more frequent form—through differential reproduction.

**9.** Evolution involves a change in gene frequency in a population. The alleles involved may be dominant *or* recessive. Recessives, such as that for sickle-cell anemia, may be maintained in a population in higher than expected frequency because of balanced polymorphism. Here, the normally negative effects of the recessive allele are balanced by positive effects of the heterozygote under certain environmental conditions. (Sickle-cell trait shows balanced polymorphism in areas where malaria is endemic; here the heterozygotes [*Ss*] are protected against malaria by the mild sickling of their red cells; they are therefore at an advantage over both homozygote types [*SS* or *ss*] and are said to exhibit hybrid vigor.)

**10.** The genetic basis for success in hybridization and breeding livestock and crops became apparent when Mendel's principles were rediscovered. Eugenicists then sought to apply the same principles to human populations.

**11.** Negative selection against deleterious human alleles is extremely difficult. If the allele in question is recessive, eradication from the gene pool is all but impossible, even if heterozygotes can be easily identified and prevented from breeding. The heterozygote may show heterosis (hybrid vigor), tending to maintain rather than decrease the frequency of the deleterious gene.

**12.** Drawbacks of positive eugenics programs include the difficulty of defining desirable traits and their genetic basis as well as that of predicting their survival value in a changing world. Our best hope lies in our enormous and variable gene pool.

## KEY WORDS

sickle-cell trait
pleiotropy
gene mutation
genetic burden or genetic load
gene pool
subvital gene

gene frequency
Hardy-Weinberg law
ionizing radiation
ion
background radiation
mutagenic
natural selection
polymorphic

industrial melanism
differential reproduction
heterosis or hybrid vigor
balanced polymorphism
eugenics
negative selection
Huntington's disease
positive eugenics

## TOPICS FOR REVIEW AND DISCUSSION

1. What is pleiotropy? Give an example.

2. How do x rays act as mutagens?

3. What assumptions have been made in the derivation of the Hardy-Weinberg law, and why does it represent a static evolutionary situation?

4. What is natural selection?

5. Discuss industrial melanism and its significance to evolutionary thinking.

6. Discuss why and how the sickle-cell allele is maintained in certain populations.

7. Discuss the causes of genetic diversity in populations and the evolutionary significance of such diversity.

8. Why is evolution essentially an irreversible process?

9. Discuss why natural selection and mutation are necessary prerequisites for evolution.

10. Discuss genetic load and its causes.

Hollywood's view of *Australopithecus* as seen in the movie *2001: A Space Odyssey*. (Courtesy of Metro-Goldwyn-Mayer, Inc. © 1968.)

# 25

# Human Evolution

## 25–1 OUR PLACE IN NATURE

In 1836 Charles Darwin (1809–1882), 27 years of age, returned from a worldwide scientific expedition aboard H.M.S. *Beagle* (Figure 25–1). This voyage marked the starting point of his theory of evolution, a theory that began a revolution in biological thinking. On his trip Darwin observed varieties of animals he had never encountered before, and he wondered how such diverse creatures had come into being. Nine years later, thinking on this question, he wrote to a friend, "At last gleams of light have come, I am almost convinced (quite contrary to the opinion I started with) that species are not (it is like confessing a murder) immutable." Among the places visited by Darwin on his trip were the Galapagos Islands. Using patient observation and keen insight (he knew nothing of Mendel or the principles of genetics), Darwin recognized that the organisms isolated for thousands of generations on the various islands of the Galapagos group had gradually evolved in distinctive ways, producing separate species. What is a species?

Life has a common structural and functional basis. There is a unity in biology, and all living creatures are endowed with certain similar properties. However, there is another aspect to life: diversity. Each living organism is distinct and separate from every other one. So impressive is the diversity of life that down through the ages we have been preoccupied with attempts to make some order out of it. To do this we have created systems of classification. Aristotle

(384–322 B.C.), the ancient Greek naturalist, believed that all living things could be arranged into two great classes, or kingdoms: plants and animals. Within each of these two kingdoms further refinements were possible, so that animals and plants could be arranged in a hierarchy. This hierarchy, or ladder, of nature had the simplest creatures on the lowest rungs and the more complex ones at the top. Those animals having a backbone, or spine, were placed on the upper levels; humans, of course, placed themselves at the top, and the lower levels were occupied by spineless creatures. Similar arrangements were made for plants: lower plants were represented by algae and ferns, and the higher plants included those having flowers, seeds, and fruits. The presumption in all this was that the kinds of animals and plants were immutable, or fixed, and each was the product of divine creation. Carl von Linné (1707–1778) (Figure 25–2), believing in original creation and lack of change in organisms, developed an improved system of classification for plants and animals. In 1737 he published *Systema Naturae*, in which he established the convention of using two Latin[1] names for each

organism, the **genus** and the **species** (implying simply "kind"). Thus, according to Linnaeus's system all humans now living are classified as *Homo* (meaning "man") *sapiens* (meaning "wise"). Linnaeus applied the term "species" to plants and animals that were significantly similar to each other, had descended from significantly similar forms that had themselves arisen by special creation, and did not interbreed with other species. Although Linnaeus's view that species remain unchanged through time, a concept called the **fixity of species,** was entirely incorrect (as Darwin clearly recognized), his classification scheme proved so useful in categorizing the various plants and animals that it is used to this day. Thus, the form of the classification system of Linnaeus remains, but the reasoning behind it has changed. Today the classification of organisms represents a summary of physical resemblances as well as evolutionary relatedness. This involves two important ideas: (1) two or more organisms having a large number of significant similarities in function and form are usually closely related and (2) close relationship frequently means common ancestry.

According to the modern view, biological species are defined as "groups of interbreeding natural populations that are reproductively isolated from other such groups."[2] By this definition, members of the same species are potentially capable of

---

[1] The native names for many plants and animals from continents other than Europe were either difficult to pronounce or were ambiguous, and one means of avoiding confusion was to give organisms names that could be understood by most educated Europeans. Latin, the language of scholars, was such a "universal" language. The scholars even Latinized their own names; for example, Carl Von Linné became Carolus Linnaeus.

[2] E. MAYR, *Populations, Species and Evolution,* Cambridge, Mass., Harvard University Press, 1970, p. 12.

**511**

FIGURE 25–1 (a) The voyage of H.M.S. *Beagle*. (b) Portrait of Charles Darwin. (Photograph Derrick Witty. Copyright Gorge Rainbird Ltd. Reprinted by courtesy of The Royal College of Surgeons of England.)

(a)

FIGURE 25–2 Carolus Linnaeus (1707–1778), who devised a classification scheme for plants and animals. (Courtesy of The Bettmann Archive, Inc.)

FIGURE 25–3 (bottom) The hierarchy of classification.

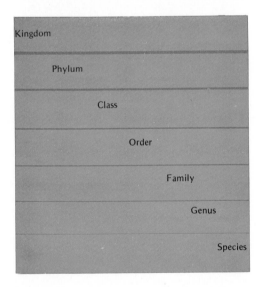

The Linnaean system of classification as used today recognizes both the kingdom and the species; between these levels are five other categories. Thus, species are grouped into **genera** (sing., genus), genera are grouped into **families,** families into **orders,** orders into **classes,** and classes into **phyla** (sing., phylum). The various phyla make up a **kingdom** (Figure 25–3). The levels between genus and kingdom are strictly artificial groupings of organisms having similar qualities; there is no biological definition for these categories.

A biologist who attempts to classify a new plant or animal must observe the structure of the specimen and then determine the proper pigeonhole into which that specimen belongs. In classification, a biologist uses past experience and a number of criteria to narrow the possibilities so that a particular species is placed closest to its relatives. Similarity of **structure, function,** and **development** all enter into the classification of organisms. Structure refers to

body form, or morphology; function, to the manner in which the organ systems operate; and development, to sequences in the life history of the individual organism. Table 25–1 illustrates the classification for the relatives of the domestic cat and of a human. According to this table, the species within a genus are quite similar, but genera differ more markedly in their characteristics. Our cats have more in common with lions and dogs than they do with us; we, on the other hand, are more closely related to apes and monkeys than to our dogs and cats. Indeed, we are the sole living members of the genus *Homo;* there is no species except *H. sapiens.*

Resemblances in structure between one organism and another frequently indicate the degree to which they are related, and this is one basis of classification. Who are our closest living relatives? When our body

**TABLE 25–1 Classification of the domestic cat and of a human**

| Species | Genus | Family | Order | Class | Phylum |
|---|---|---|---|---|---|
| *(F. domestical)* Cat | *(Felis)* Cat | *(Felidae)* Cat | *(Carnivora)* Cat | *(Mammalia)* Cat | *(Chordata)* Cat |
| | | Lynx | Lynx | Lynx | Lynx |
| | | | Lion | Lion | Lion |
| | | | Dog | Dog | Dog |
| | | | | Monkey | Monkey |
| | | | | Horse | Horse |
| | | | | Human | Human |
| | | | | | Bird |
| | | | | | Lizard |
| | | | | | Frog |
| | | | | | Fish |
| *(H. Sapiens)* Human | *(Homo)* Human | *(Hominidae)* Human | *(Primates)* Human | *(Mammalia)* Human | *(Chordata)* Human |
| | | | Monkey | Monkey | Monkey |
| | | | Ape | Lynx | Lynx |
| | | | Lemur | Cat | Cat |
| | | | Tarsier | Dog | Dog |
| | | | | Horse | Horse |
| | | | | | Bird |
| | | | | | Lizard |
| | | | | | Frog |
| | | | | | Fish |

mating and producing fertile offspring, and these in turn can produce fertile progeny. This definition of a species says nothing whatever about how the population looks, and members of the same species—males, females, and young—may differ markedly or slightly in their form (**morphology**).

FIGURE 25–4 A gallery of primates.

**TABLE 25–2 Characteristics shared by humans and other primates**

1. A generalized limb structure.
2. Mobile digits, especially the thumb and the big toe.
3. Flattened nails and sensitive pads on the fingertips, instead of claws.
4. Sharper vision, color vision, and depth perception.
5. A foreshortened snout.
6. Less dependence on the sense of smell.
7. Fewer teeth than ancestral mammals.
8. An expanded and elaborated brain, particularly the cerebral cortex.

structure is compared with that of other organisms, we see that in common with fish, amphibians, reptiles, birds, and a variety of furry creatures humans possess a vertebral column, and so we are classified as vertebrates (subphylum: Vertebrata). Warm-blooded and air-breathing, with a hairy skin and young that are born alive and nursed at the breast (*mamma*—breast; L.), we are entitled to membership in the class of mammals (class: Mammalia). Birds, reptiles (lizards and snakes), amphibians (salamanders, toads, and frogs), and bony fishes neither nurse their young nor have hair, and they belong in different classes: Aves, Reptilia, Amphibia, and Osteichthyes, respectively. Among the mammals, we have features that place us in the order Primates, along with tree shrews, lemurs, tarsiers, monkeys, and apes. What are the characteristics of the primates?

A glance at Table 25–2 and the photographs in Figure 25–4 will show you that humans share many physical features with other modern primates. This suggests that humans and the other primates are closely related and probably descended from a common ancestor. There are, however, additional lines of evidence that, taken together with shared physical characteristics, are very convincing. For example, the chemical composition of the blood of humans, apes, and monkeys is quite similar. A precipitating antiserum prepared against hu-

man blood gives a strong precipitation reaction when mixed with the blood of a gorilla, a somewhat weaker reaction with orangutan blood, and a very weak reaction with baboon blood. When the precipitating antibody to human blood is mixed with ox blood, there is virtually no precipitation. Humans and other primates, particularly the apes, share similarities in blood types, such as ABO, MN, and Rh. We and our primate relatives are subject to the same diseases; syphilis attacks humans and chimpanzees with great intensity, but the disease is less severe in the orangutan and quite mild in the baboon. The chromosomes of humans and apes are also quite similar; chimpanzee and gorilla chromosomes are much more like our own than are those of the orangutan and the gibbon. DNA hybridization shows the chimpanzee and human to be the most closely related, with the gorilla a very close relation. Similar conclusions about relatedness have been drawn from restriction enzyme mapping and gene sequencing data.

The hierarchy of categories for the primate order is shown in Figure 25–5, and the position of man is clearly indicated. Each step in the classification scheme tells us how closely we share characteristics with the other primates. The lower the category in the hierarchy, the more specific are the features of those members of the group, and the more similar they are.

Thus far we have considered humans as primates. But how do humans differ from the other anthropoid primates? What are the unique features that enable us to say, "This specimen before us is a human being and not a gorilla or a chimpanzee"?

A human being is bipedal and walks erect upon the soles of its feet; other primates are four-footed (quadrupedal). A human's legs are long, greatly strengthened, and well-provided with powerful muscles used in walking upright. The adoption of an erect stance frees the hands and arms from a role in locomotion. The human hand is fashioned more effectively into a device for making and using tools. The human cranium

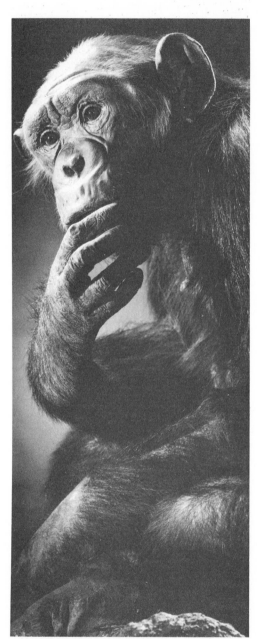

(a) Chimpanzee, a great ape. (Courtesy of the American Museum of Natural History.)

(b) Orangutan, a great ape. (Courtesy of the American Museum of Natural History.)

(c) Gray gibbon, a lesser ape. (San Diego Zoo photograph.)

(d) Gorilla, a great ape. (San Diego Zoo photograph.)

(e) Colobus, an Old World monkey. (Courtesy of the American Museum of Natural History.)

(f) Macaque, an Old World monkey. (San Diego Zoo photograph.)

(g) Langur, an Old World monkey. (San Diego Zoo photograph.)

(h) Lemur, a prosimian. (San Diego Zoo photograph.)

(i) Tarsier, a prosimian. (San Diego Zoo photograph.)

(skull) is dome-shaped and increased in volume over that of our closest primate relatives in order to accommodate our greatly expanded cerebrum. The human brow is steep and high in contrast to the retreating forehead and the ridged brow of the apes. The skull is poised directly above the spinal column, and the pelvis is expanded to form a basket that provides support for the internal organs. Other distinguishing human features include the distinct chin, the female breasts (which are permanently enlarged mammary glands), and, when compared with other primates, the enormous penis. Our closest living relatives, the apes, are born naked, but in time they grow a coat of hair. We are naked apes; we are born so and remain so.

Finally, our ability for thought and language, attributes that shape much of our day-to-day and historic behavior (that is, culture), is developed to a level of complexity that is unique to the human species. No other species within the entire animal kingdom can begin to approach the technology of human civilizations, with all its vast implications. Indeed, it is probably true that most of the significant evolutionary trends for our species will be cultural. The differences between humans and the other primates are presented in Table 25–3 and Figure 25–6.

## 25–3 DARWINISM: FROM FINCHES TO HUMANS

Human beings are the dominant species of vertebrate on this planet. The question of how the species came to be has preoccupied human thought through all of recorded history and, no doubt, even before that period. Each culture has produced its own story of creation, often steeped in mysticism, magic, and symbolism. The Bible describes the creation of the world in 6 days; on the final day God, we are told, made man in His own image and gave him dominion over the fish of the sea, the fowl of the air, the cattle of the earth, and every creeping thing that crawls upon the earth.

FIGURE 25–5 Classification of the primates.

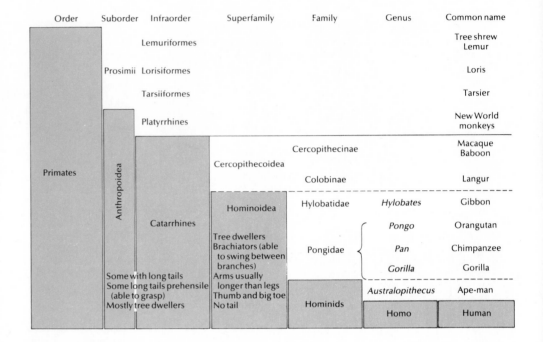

TABLE 25–3 Distinguishing features of anthropoid apes and humans

| Characteristic | Anthropoid apes | Humans |
| --- | --- | --- |
| Locomotion | Brachiating | Bipedal |
| Shoulder | Very mobile | Very mobile |
| Stretching arms | To side | To side |
| Thumb | Small, but used | Large, much used |
| Growth rate | Slow | Slower |
| Sexual maturity | 8 years | 14 years |
| Full growth in males | 12 years | 20 years |
| Infant dependency | 2 years | 6–8 years |
| Female receptivity to sexual intercourse | At ovulation | Continuous |
| Long bones of lower extremities | Shorter than those of upper extremity | Longer than those of upper extremity |
| Tarsal bones | Rather short, toes rather long | Rather long, toes rather short |
| Trunk | Long compared with lower extremities | Short compared with lower extremities |
| Vertebral column | Straight or curved uniformly backward | Alternately curved backward and forward |
| Leg | Curved, knees turned outward | In upright posture, straight in knee and hip joint |
| Joint between skull and vertebral column | At back of skull | Almost in center of base of skull |
| Canines | Large fangs | No larger than premolars |
| Crown of first lower premolar | Has bladelike cutting edge | Unspecialized (bicuspid) |
| Dental arch | Laterally compressed with side rows of teeth almost parallel | Rounded without sharp angles |
| Jaws | Long and large | Short |
| Face | Long, in front of brain, protruding | Short, steep, under brain |
| Brain | Average size one third that of human | Large |

FIGURE 25–6 A comparison of the body structure of three primates. (a) Macaque monkey. (b) Gorilla. (c) Human.

Spine shape

(a) Macaque monkey skeleton

Clavicle

Pelvis

Macaque monkey skeleton

Hand of Macaque monkey

Macaque monkey's arm movements

Neck muscle
Spine shape

(b) Gorilla skeleton

Clavicle

Pelvis

Gorilla

Hand of gorilla

Gorilla's arm movements

Spine shape

(c) Human skeleton

Clavicle

Pelvis

Human

Human hand

Human arm movements

FIGURE 25–7 Charles Darwin at age 73. (Courtesy of the American Museum of Natural History.)

The notion of the special creation of man in a single day was so dominant in current thought that in 1650 Archbishop James Usher of Armagh, Ireland, calculated the date of creation to be 4004 B.C., on October 23, at 9 o'clock in the morning! However, by the late 1700s there appeared reason to doubt the theory that the human species was created in a single dramatic event. At that time ancient human bones and odd-shaped stone tools were found in France, Germany, England, and Belgium—many associated with the bones of extinct animals. Speculation arose that there was a connection between extinct animals, ancient tools, and extinct humans. Critics were quick to point out that such associations could have occurred by chance and that these findings did not constitute proof that all these things existed at the same time.

A turning point in understanding the origins of the human species came not from studies of human bones themselves, but from establishment of the age of the earth. James Hutton (1726–1797), a Scottish physician, and Sir Charles Lyell (1797–1875), a geologist, broke with tradition and suggested that the age of the earth could be determined by studying the successive layers of the rocks (**strata**). The present, they contended, is the key to understanding the past, and only the geological processes that can be observed in action today could have been involved in forming the rock strata. To Hutton and Lyell, the changes in the earth's crust were not the product of repeated catastrophes or some special event, but rather of an orderly process that goes on in nature all the time. Through the passage of long periods of time, the surface of the earth was changing. Strata were produced slowly, taking many thousands of years to form. Hutton and Lyell also contended that the extinction of many species and the formation of new ones must have occurred slowly and continually throughout past time. Support for this contention came from discoveries in the strata of the preserved remains (fossils) of species that do not exist today.

While geologists made progress in estimating the age of the earth, naturalists began to recognize similarities between humans and apes. In 1809, Jean Baptiste de Lamarck (1744–1829) stated that humans were descended from the orangutan; naturally the view met with opposition. The idea of our relation to the other primates was not really accepted until after publication of the writings of Darwin (1871) (Figure 25–7) and especially T. H. Huxley (1863). However, the idea is refuted in some quarters even today.

In 1859 Darwin's work, *On the Origin of Species by Means of Natural Selection, or the Preservation of Favored Races in the Struggle for Life*, appeared. Although he was not the first to propose a theory of evolution, his work was presented in a sober and subdued manner, the intellectual climate was right, and his scholarly ideas were amply documented with supporting evidence; the idea took root. It could be said

that Darwin made evolution respectable. Not only did he provide evidence for the process of evolution and a reasonable explanation for the diversity of organisms, but he proposed a mechanism whereby evolution could work. The mechanism proposed by Darwin was **natural selection.**[3] What was Darwin's evidence for evolution?

Darwin was 22 when he set sail on H.M.S. *Beagle* from Plymouth, England, on December 17, 1831. After the ship reached the Galapagos Islands, he became convinced that evolution must have occurred and that species arose from preexisting species. The Galapagos is a group of 15 or more rocky islands off the coast of Ecuador; it is believed that the islands rose from the ocean floor by volcanic action a million or more years ago (Figure 25–8). The islands were never part of the mainland of South America, nor were they ever connected to one another. In surveying the animal life on the islands, Darwin found very few vertebrates; however, a group of small birds—finches— were quite abundant, and they showed extreme diversity in the form of their beaks as well as in their feeding habits. There were 14 different species of finches; these have been found nowhere else in the world. How, Darwin asked, did these species of finches arise?

Darwin surmised that the ancestors of the present finch populations had been blown to the islands by high winds from the mainland. In time some of these original colonizers spread from one island to the others. Since the finches do not fly readily over large stretches of open water, these populations tended to remain pretty much on their own rocky islands. The original immigrants were split up into separate island populations and came to be geographically isolated. Hence, they could no longer in-

---

[3] The idea of natural selection was independently developed by Alfred Russel Wallace (1823–1913); however, Wallace's work was never as well documented as that of Darwin, and thus his contribution is often minimized. In truth, he should share in some of the credit today, as he did at the time.

FIGURE 25–8 The Galapagos Islands, where Darwin began to formulate his theory of the evolution of animal species. (a) Migration path of the ancestral finch from Ecuador. (b) The exploration pathway of the *Beagle* during its time at the Galapagos Islands.

(a)

(b)

terbreed. In time, chance variations arose among the finches on the separate islands (Figure 25–9a). There was, however, a problem: most of the islands did not contain just a single species of finch, and on some there were up to 10 different species. How did Darwin account for this? He visualized the process as follows. The original population of finches found no predators or other bird competitors on the islands, and so it multiplied its kind. However, in time, food for the finches (primarily ground seeds) came to be a limiting factor. Only those individuals capable of adapting to new environments could survive and reproduce themselves. Darwin believed that the original finch population contained individuals with many differences. If any of these variations permitted individuals to exploit environments not yet occupied by other finches, these individuals would have a greater chance of surviving and leaving offspring (survival of the fittest). Thus, the successful colonization of previously unoccupied habitats would lead to a diversification of species, and each of these species would be better fitted to survive and reproduce under the new conditions than in the ancestral habitat. This spread of a population into a new environment accompanied by divergent adaptive changes from the original one is called **adaptive radiation.**

Adaptive radiation is clearly seen among Darwin's finches. Six of the ground-finch species have heavy, parrotlike beaks for crushing seeds; others have flower-probing beaks for feeding on the flowers of the prickly-pear cactus. One of the tree finches is woodpeckerlike; it has a stout beak for boring into wood, but instead of using its tongue it searches for insect larvae by using a cactus spine. Another finch is warblerlike, with a beak adapted for picking off small insects from the bushes (Figure 25–9b).

According to Darwin, the original population of finches came to be divided into species that were localized in their habitats; offspring of the better adapted forms survived in greater numbers than offspring of less well adapted finches. Aware of the way

FIGURE 25–9 Darwin's finches. (a) How the finches on the Galapagos Islands may have speciated. (b) Adaptive radiation in Darwin's finches.

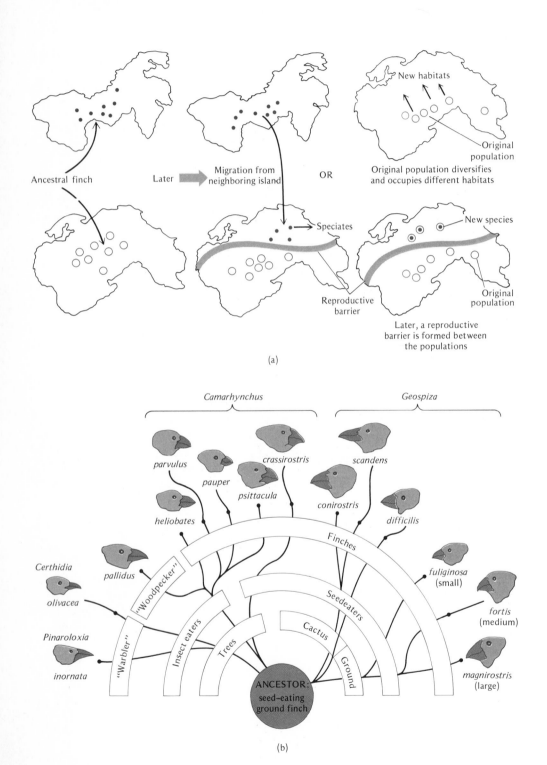

Ancestral finch

Later

Migration from neighboring island

OR

New habitats

Original population

Original population diversifies and occupies different habitats

Speciates

New species

Reproductive barrier

Original population

Later, a reproductive barrier is formed between the populations

(a)

Camarhynchus

Geospiza

parvulus

crassirostris

scandens

pauper

psittacula

conirostris

heliobates

difficilis

Certhidia

pallidus

olivacea

Finches

fuliginosa (small)

Seedeaters

"Woodpecker"

Pinaroloxia

"Warbler"

Insect eaters

Trees

Cactus

Ground

fortis (medium)

inornata

ANCESTOR: seed-eating ground finch

magnirostris (large)

(b)

in which humans could control plant and animal traits by artificial selection, Darwin used the term "natural selection" to indicate that some external agent, rather than conscious choice of the organism, was responsible for favoring certain individual differences and eliminating those that were injurious.

Darwin's theory of evolution and the role of natural selection was based on the premise that there exist natural checks on increases in population size; some of the limiting factors are predators, food availability, competitors, climate, and disease. As a consequence, he reasoned, more individuals of each species will be born than can possibly survive, and thus there ensues a struggle for existence; those individuals within a population having a particular endowment that gives them a better chance at reproductive success will be naturally selected. These selected varieties will in time propagate themselves. Thus, **Darwinian fitness** is reproductive fitness. Natural selection is a blind and opportunistic force that shapes the changes in a population producing new species; it acts as a sieve to cull out the unfit and permits only the fittest to pass through and reproduce their kind; it enables organisms to fit their surroundings, but it cannot anticipate the changes necessary for survival in future environmental situations.

Darwin recognized the importance of variation in a population and its relationship to the evolutionary process. However, he had no knowledge of heredity, and so he ascribed the source of variation to natural forces; to him this was simply an act of faith. Today it is recognized that mutation and sexual recombination are the sources of variation in a population, and these provide the raw materials for evolution. Darwin's mechanism for evolutionary change, natural selection, by itself cannot account for evolution. Another force is necessary for a single species to evolve into two or more species: this force is **reproductive isolation**, which prevents interbreeding be-

FIGURE 25–10 Cartoon lampooning Darwin's suggestion that the human species has an apelike ancestor. (Courtesy of the Granger Collection.)

**523**

HUMAN EVOLUTION

tween species and populations. In the modern view, **evolution** is a change in the gene pool with the passage of successive generations. Evolution of new species involves (1) hereditary variation due to mutation and sexual recombination; (2) natural selection, that is, differential reproduction of certain genotypes; and (3) genetic isolation.

Darwinism came to be a focal point in human thought, and although Darwin never dealt with human evolution in *On the Origin of Species,* it was inevitable that his theory would be applied to humans. Debate on the topic of our origin became lively, and the notion that we were descended from apes was the talk of fashionable salons of the day. In 1871 Darwin himself entered the discussion of human evolution with his publication *The Descent of Man,* in which he presented evidence for his theory of evolution and explained how it shed light on the apelike origins of the human species. For this he was frequently lampooned in the popular press (Figure 25–10). Despite this, in the 130 years since the publication of *On the Origin of Species* his theory has, in a somewhat modified form, survived attacks from various social, religious, scientific, and political groups. Evolution is a biological fact. We are a product of evolution, as is every organism that inhabits the earth.

## 25–4 THE ROAD TO HUMANS

A visit to a zoological garden, a view of monkeys and apes, and we are immediately struck with similarities of appearance, facial expressions, manner of movement, and behavioral patterns between these primates and ourselves. In the face of this sort of circumstantial evidence, it is difficult to believe that only rarely were the similarities between humans and apes recognized. Hindsight is perfect vision, so let us not be too harsh in our judgment of the past. One of the main stumbling blocks in understanding human evolution was a strong belief in

**MR. BERGH TO THE RESCUE.**

THE DEFRAUDED GORILLA. "That *Man* wants to claim my Pedigree. He says he is one of my Descendants."

MR. BERGH. "Now, MR. DARWIN, how could you insult him so?"

the divine creation of animals. Indeed, the Linnaean pattern of classification was considered to be the Creator's plan, and the interrelationships of organisms a part of supernatural design. Then, in 1859, with the publication of *On the Origin of Species,* the idea that humans could have evolved

from a primatelike ancestor began to take hold. At first, it was contended that humans were descended from the apes, but later it was clearly recognized that we could not have evolved from apes like those living today, since they, like us, are recent products of evolution. Rather, modern humans and apes must both be descended from a common ancestral form, now extinct.

In *The Descent of Man* Darwin built his case for human evolution on evidence from living humans and other primates, but he believed that remains of the missing link between apes and humans—the extinct common ancestral form—would be found fossilized in the rocks. Indeed, one means for clarifying the evolution of the human species is to study fossil forms and relate these to the geological time scale. Before we begin the story of our ancestors, we should recognize that the fossil record is far from complete. Yet despite this limitation there is sufficient fossil evidence to suggest the sequence of bodily changes that occurred during the divergence of the hominids from their apelike ancestors. Unhappily, speech and social organization are not fossilized, and thus our reconstructions of these attributes of ancestral humans remain strictly hypothetical.

### The family tree

Who are our nearest relatives? The various primates of today are our closest living relatives, and these are at the ends of divergent lines of evolution. By comparing them with one another biochemically, or by comparing their anatomy with that of fossil forms, we can picture evolutionary relationships in the form of a family tree (Figure 25–11). To provide some idea of how recently modern humans emerged, Figure 25–12 dates the events leading to modern *H. sapiens:* the time scale is shown in terms of millions of years.

**The insectivores.** The primates were derived from **insectivores,** small insect-eating animals whose fossil remains are found in rocks more than 75 million years old. The tree shrews of today are closely related to these fossil animals and are descended from the earliest types of primates. Tree shrews, together with lemurs and tarsiers, which are also derived from the earliest types, are grouped as prosimians (*pro*—before, *simia*—

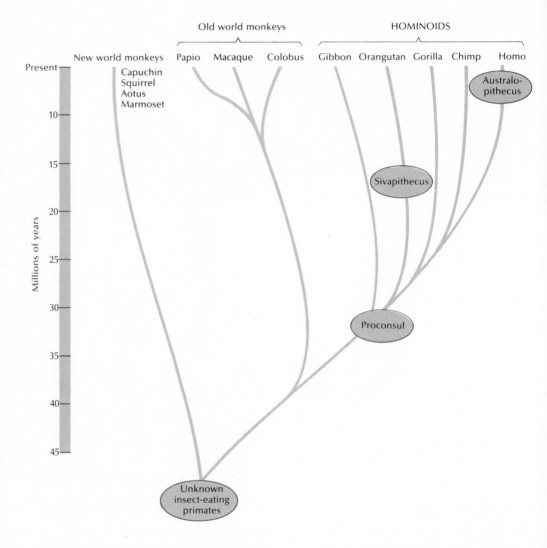

FIGURE 25–11 The human family tree and our primate relatives.

ape; L.). Prosimians were abundant worldwide 65 million years ago; they essentially disappeared from North America 35 million years ago, and today are found only in tropical Asia and Africa, on the island of Madagascar and smaller islands of the Indian Ocean. Prosimians have poorly developed brains, but they do have grasping hands and feet, nonopposable thumbs and big toes, and most have nails instead of claws. Monkeys, apes, and humans (an-

thropoids) probably all arose from a prosimianlike ancestor.

**Proconsul.** The point at which anthropoids diverged from prosimians is uncertain, since the fossil record is quite poor, but in the 1930s L. S. B. Leakey found on an island in Lake Victoria an apelike ancestor, which he called *Proconsul. Proconsul* lived more than 20 million years ago and has the traits of both a monkey (hand, skull, and brain) and an ape (face, jaw, and teeth).

FIGURE 25–12 A possible human family tree.

**525**

**HUMAN EVOLUTION**

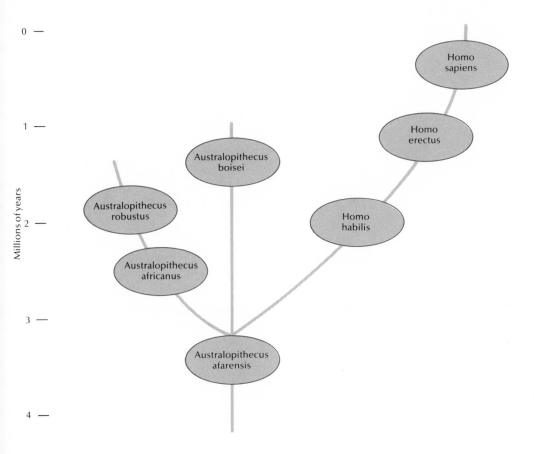

What makes it so certain that *Proconsul* is really anthropoid and not prosimian? The pattern of teeth provides the best proof; prosimians have 34 teeth, but anthropoids have only 32 (Figure 25–14).

**Australopithecus: the earliest hominids.** A remarkable discovery was reported by Raymond Dart of Johannesburg, South Africa, in 1925. Dart, an anatomy professor, was given some fossil bones from a limestone quarry at Tuang. Among these was a skull unlike any seen before. Eventually it turned out to be the skull of a 5- or 6-year-old child, and Dart called the specimen *Australopithecus africanus*. Several years later other skulls and jaws, which were similar to *A. africanus*, were unearthed in South Africa (Figure 25–15). The braincase of these fossils was 450 to 500 ml, about the same size as a modern chimpanzee, and about one third the capacity of a modern day human cranium. The back teeth, the molars and premolars, although large compared with those of present day humans and other members of the genus *Homo*, are typical of hominids, and not hominoids. Fossils of *A. africanus* have been dated to be between 1.5 and 3.0 million years old.

In 1974 Donald Johanson and his colleagues discovered in Ethiopia the fossilized remains of a 20-year-old female *Australopithecus* that was dated to be 3.75 million years old. Unlike most other human fossils that consist of skull fragments and a few teeth, this specimen comprised a good portion of the skeleton (Figure 25–16). The team named the fossil Lucy (after the Beatles' song "Lucy in the Sky with Diamonds"). Lucy was an upright hominid, about 1 meter tall, with a brain capacity of about 500 ml. Based on the kind of teeth, Lucy and her kind, now called *Australopithecus afarensis*, appear to be the common ancestor of both the *Australopithecus* and *Homo* lines (Figure 25–12). Thus, our human ancestry dates back to some time after *A. afarensis*, less than 3.5 million years ago.

Other sites in Africa have yielded hominid fossils that also shed light on the nature of our earliest relatives. Several of the fossil finds had bigger molars and premolars than did *A. africanus*, as well as larger and more robust faces and chewing muscles. These have been called *A. robustus* after their most obvious characteristics. In East Africa, other robustlike fossils have been unearthed, but these have larger teeth and more massive faces and jaws than the *A. robustus* fossils described from South Africa (Figure 25–17). These australopithecines, similar in brain size to *A. robustus*, are 2.5 million years old, and because they appear to be more specialized than *A. robustus*, they have been called *A. boisei*. The few skeletal remains discovered in association with the robust type of fossils suggest that although these hominids were somewhat larger and heavier than *A. africanus*, they were no brainier.

*Australopithecus* lived 3.75 million years ago. These cousins of ours lived in Africa, and came in four varieties (Table 25–4). All stood and ran on their hind legs. The brain was about the size of the brain of a modern ape (Figure 25–18). The jaws were massive and projecting and the molars very large. The incisor teeth were relatively small, and the canines were not of the sharp, projecting kind common to apes but they were larger than ours. (Figure 25–14). One of the factors indicating that *Australopithecus* was a bipedal creature is the position of the foramen magnum, the hole through which

FIGURE 25–13 An artistic reconstruction of human evolution, based on fossil evidence. (a) Pelvic bones. (b) Reconstruction from skeletal remains. (c) Skull.

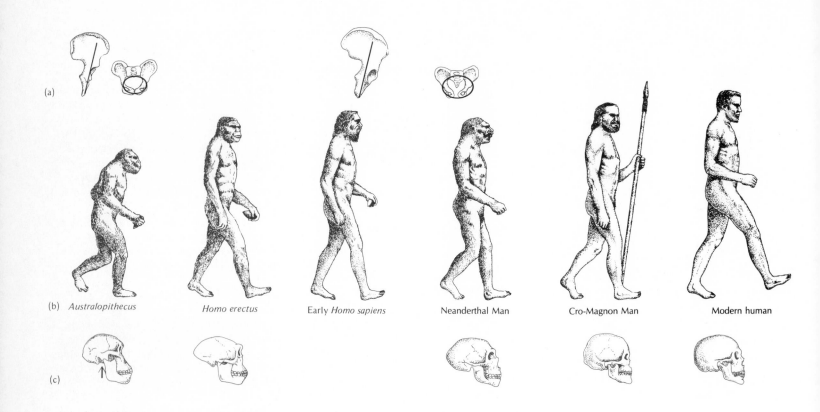

(a)

(b) *Australopithecus*      *Homo erectus*      Early *Homo sapiens*      Neanderthal Man      Cro-Magnon Man      Modern human

(c)

the spinal cord passes through the skull to connect to the brain; it faces almost downward. Thus, this prehuman's head was perched on top of its spine, indicating an erect, upright posture. In quadrupeds (four-footed animals) the spinal cord leaves the cranium from the rear (Figures 25–6 and 25–14). The hipbones provide the most impressive evidence that *Australopithecus* was more humanlike than apelike. In the apes the hipbone is narrow and long, whereas in humans it is flat and broad, with a rear-projecting flange, an adaptation to the human erect posture (Figure 25–13). The flange acts to anchor the large buttock (gluteal) muscles that are used for balancing the trunk on the lower limbs in standing or walking; it forms a kind of basket to cradle

the internal organs and gives attachment to the abdominal muscles that help maintain abdominal tone during standing. The abdominal muscles form a strong barrel that prevents the internal organs from sagging as a result of the pull of gravity. In quadrupeds, the internal organs are suspended from the back (Figure 25–6). Thus, the anatomical evidence indicates that *Australopithecus* stood and walked almost as we do ourselves.

There persist many questions about these prehuman creatures. Some of the most perplexing are, Why did they get up on their hind legs? Why did the canine teeth become reduced in size? The answers are, of course, conjectural, since there is no fossil evidence for behavior. There is, how-

ever, good evidence that during the period in which *Australopithecus* lived there existed considerable expanses of lush savannah with scattered shrubs, trees, and grasses. There were berries and roots in abundance, and because such areas were suitable for grazing, these savannahs were well stocked with game. These areas provided new habitats, abundant in food, and so we surmise the australopithecines came down from the trees in which their own apelike ancestors had lived in order to avail themselves of these new sources of food. Initially, they foraged and returned to the trees, continuing to move from tree limb to tree limb by brachiating movements of their arms, but later they spent more and more time on the ground. Although descent from the

**FIGURE 25–14** (top) Dentition and skull shape in primates.

**FIGURE 25–15** (bottom) Two skulls of *Australopithecus africanus.*

**FIGURE 25–16** *Australopithecus afarensis. A. afarensis* skeleton found at Hadar, Ethiopia, named "Lucy."

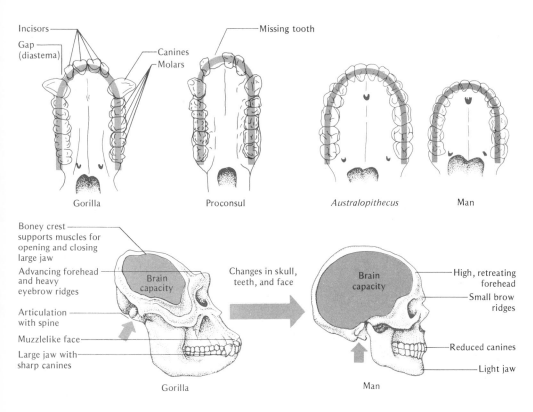

Incisors

Gap (diastema)

Canines
Molars

Missing tooth

Gorilla

Proconsul

*Australopithecus*

Man

Boney crest supports muscles for opening and closing large jaw

Advancing forehead and heavy eyebrow ridges

Brain capacity

Articulation with spine

Muzzlelike face

Large jaw with sharp canines

Gorilla

Changes in skull, teeth, and face

Brain capacity

High, retreating forehead

Small brow ridges

Reduced canines

Light jaw

Man

527

FIGURE 25–17 The robust-type of australopithecines. (left) *A. boisei* and (right) *A. robustus.*

trees does not always result in evolution of upright posture in primates (witness the gorilla), through a lucky combination of anatomy and habits, these ape-humans became bipedal. Being bipedal meant that the hands were freed from locomotor function and could be employed in manipulative skills such as carrying and dragging objects and fashioning tools and weapons (Figure 25–19). Although some biologists suggest that upright posture preceded the use of the hand in fashioning and in using tools, there are compelling arguments that the reverse is true—that toolmaking ability preceded the evolution of upright posture. Apes and monkeys, although tree dwellers, do use their hands and are tool users. They throw stones, they poke with sticks, and they produce sticks by stripping the leaves from vine stems. Tool users get along best by walking on their hind limbs and having their hands free for holding objects; thus, where tool using is important for survival, selective pressure would be toward an upright posture. With the advent of toolmaking, hunting for big game became a possibility, and the brain and the hand were now subject to the molding force of natural selection. Those individuals with better manipulative skills and learning ability would be better adapted and more likely to survive in the new habitat. The destruction of food outside the mouth by the use of hands in ripping and tearing and the ability to fashion tools as weapons of offense and defense

TABLE 25–4 The australopithecines

| |  A. afarensis |  Robust group |  A. africanus | Homo group |
|---|---|---|---|---|
| Brain size | 400–500 ml | 500–550 ml | 450–500 ml | 650–775 ml |
| Dentition | Back teeth generally smaller than *A. africanus*, larger canines, unequal cusps on first premolars. | Very large back teeth; relatively small front teeth | Large front and back teeth | Variable; generally smaller than robust and gracile forms |
| Species | *Australopithecus afarensis* | *Australopithecus robustus* | *Australopithecus africanus* | *Homo habilis* |
| Age (years before present) | 2.9–3.7 million | 1.5–2.5 million | 1.5–3.0 million | 1.5–2.0 million |

FIGURE 25–18 The estimated brain size of anthropoid apes, man-apes, and humans.

FIGURE 25–19 The evolution of tool use.

meant that the teeth (the canines especially) were no longer of such importance for survival, and selective forces began to modify the structure of the skull. In time, the use of tools as weapons of offense and defense became the dominant habit, and with this sort of expertise *Australopithecus* could wander farther away from the trees.

Australopithecus was quick-footed, and became a creature of the open ground. By means of natural selection the offspring of *A. africanus* became better adapted for a predatory life on the ground. Once hunting game became a part of the life of *Australopithecus*, there was selective pressure toward the establishment of base camps and hunting groups, the divison of labor, the accumulation of information, and the fabrication of improved weapons. All these required an increase in brain size as well as complexity, and some form of communication. In this way, stored information could be passed on and used to advantage. The best evidence we have for this is the progressive development of pebble tools (Fig-

ure 25–19). Thus, speech and language became decisive events in the process of hominization. Not only is language an old adaptive pattern in humans, but it is apparently unique to the species. Though many animals make sounds that are signals transmitting information, these constitute a closed system of calls that are all-or-none. As far as we know, only human language can convey many bits of information at the same time.

Once early hominids moved out of the forest they were faced with new dangers of predation; banding together to hunt and acquiring some kind of aggressive behavior pattern would have enhanced the chances for survival. In addition, the earliest humans must have established close-knit social groups for breeding. Much instinctive behavior came to be replaced by learning during a prolonged childhood. Complex learned behavior, based on acquired information, was passed from generation to generation and roughly can be called culture. Behavior became the strongest of all selec-

529

FIGURE 25–20 Java Man, skull and reconstruction. (Courtesy of the American Museum of Natural History.)

tive pressures for human evolution. Thus, we are drawn to the conclusion that human evolution, and especially the foundations of human intelligence, had their roots in a mosaic of adaptive features: bipedalism, hand and tool use, brain development, speech, and breeding pattern. These changes did not occur all at the same time or proceed at the same rate. The trends in hominid evolution including changes in physical appearance and behavior occurred over millions of years. All evidence seems to suggest that *Australopithecus* was the earliest human.

**Homo erectus and Homo habilis.** The next stage of human evolution shows a phenomenal increase in brain size and stretches backward to a time slightly over 1 million years ago. The discovery of the fossil remains of these "true humans" (*Homo*) came in 1887. In that year, E. Dubois, a Dutch anthropologist, discovered in Central Java a skull cap, a lower-jaw fragment, and several thighbones that aroused considerable excitement among students of human evolution. The skull was obviously apelike (Figure 25–20), but the legbones resembled those of a human. This anthropoid ancestor of ours, apelike in skull and human in upright posture, Dubois called *Pithecanthropus* (*pithekos*—ape, *anthropos*—man; Gk.) *erectus*. It is more commonly known as Java Man. For nearly 50 years there was skepticism about Dubois's find because the skull and thighbones seemed so dissimilar in character, but in the late 1930s other fossils of Java Man were discovered. During the latter part of the twentieth century, the status of Java Man was reconsidered, and as a result of these studies he is now termed *Homo erectus* (erect man). The skull of Java Man is unlike that of *Australopithecus*. Its capacity is intermediate between the average skull capacity of the largest living apes and the skull capacity of a modern human, but it is twice that of *Australopithecus* (Figure 25–18). Java Man has a flat, receding forehead; the eyebrow prominences are enormous; the foramen magnum is far for-

ward under the skull, much as it is in ourselves; and the thighbones in shape and proportion are like those of a modern human. All this indicates that although *H. erectus* did not exhibit great intellect and possessed an apelike face, they were too brainy to be classified as apes. They walked upright and had heavy neck and jowl musculature to support a powerful chewing jaw (Figure 25–20).

Finds related to Java Man were made in the late 1920s by a scientific expedition in the village of Choukoutien, about 40 miles southwest of Peking, China. There, in a vast cavern, were unearthed the remains of 40 or more individuals. The diggings also disclosed ample evidence of the use of fire and a plentiful supply of stone tools. This fossil, first called *Sinanthropus pekinensis* (Chinese man of Peking), had a larger cranial capacity than Java Man. However, the jaws were massive and projected forward beyond the nose and the rest of the face. Because of his similarities to Java Man, Peking Man is now also classified as *H. erectus*. In 1975

at Lake Turkana in Kenya there was discovered a skull of *H. erectus* with a brain size of 900 cc. The age of the fossil was 1.5 million years.

At Olduvai Gorge in Tanzania some of the most remarkable fossil finds have been made. One fossil type discovered there has characteristics that bridge those of *Australopithecus* and *Homo erectus*, and these have been classified as *Homo habilis* (literally, handy man). In 1986, Tim White and Donald Johanson discovered a specimen of *H. habilis* that was dated to be 1.8 million years old. This meant that *H. habilis*, the robust australopithecines, and *A. africanus*, lived in Africa at approximately the same time. *H. habilis* was quite small (about 1 meter tall) and had arms that dangled to the knees. *H. habilis* was the first human to make stone tools. But, 1.6 million years ago *H. habilis* was replaced by the taller *H. erectus* whose knuckles no longer hung near the knees. Clearly, a remarkable burst of change in human evolution took place in a 200,000-year period, the time between

*H. habilis* and *H. erectus,* and the time hominids left the trees to walk on the ground. We do not know what provoked such a dramatic and relatively rapid change in human behavior and anatomy, but the clues certainly lie somewhere in Africa.

It is obvious from the fossil record that upright posture and other bodily changes came in advance of cranial development, and we are led to the conclusion that evolution of the postcranial (below the skull) human skeleton was completed over 3.75 million years ago.

Let us try to recreate a picture of the life of *H. erectus.* They were expert hunters of game and dined mostly on meat. They used fire and made quartz tools and a cradle type of hand ax (Figure 25–19). They were cannibalistic and occupied cave sites for about 200,000 to 300,000 years. The earliest signs of fire date back 400,000 years. *Homo erectus* was probably a fire stealer rather than a fire maker; no fire-producing implements have been retrieved from any of the investigated sites. Use of fire enabled the cooking of food and made caves habitable even in the colder seasons. Bones of *H. erectus* have been found in Africa, Java, and China, and present thinking is that the species originated in Africa. How they spread through the continents is unknown, but it is obvious that such migration took place over the centuries and over many generations. Whether *H. erectus* wore clothes or built permanent habitations in addition to caves, we have no idea. We picture them as hunters in small bands, but we know nothing of their social structure, religion, art, or any other cultural practices. The characteristics of such a culture have left no fossil remains. We do not know with any certainty what became of *H. erectus,* but perhaps it is not too far from the truth to surmise that they changed with time to eventually become as we ourselves.

***Homo sapiens:* modern humans.** About 500,000 years ago human mental development had expanded to such a point that the fossils can be considered representatives of *H. sapiens* (Figure 25–18). The earliest find of this period was a skull unearthed in a cave on Gibraltar in 1848; it caused little stir. Then in 1856 near Düsseldorf, Germany, in a valley called Neander, a skull cap and some bones were dug out of a limestone cave. The skull cap was thick, there were massive eyebrow ridges, and the retreating forehead was much flatter on top and bulging in the back than the skull of any present-day human (Figure 25–21). The remarkable discovery, coming just 3 years before the publication of Darwin's *On the Origin of Species,* caused much controversy. T. H. Huxley recognized some very peculiar things about this creature, who came to be called Neanderthal Man. The brain case marked it as the most apelike of all human skulls. Later diggings in Belgium produced skeletons similar to that of Neanderthal Man, and these occurred with the remains of a mammoth, a wooly rhinoceros, and other extinct animals. Neanderthal remains have also been found in Italy, France, Palestine, Siberia, southern Russia, and North Africa. Neanderthal obviously roamed Europe about 100,000 years ago, but was quite unlike those who unearthed his ancient bones. The classic Neanderthal type disappeared about 30,000 years ago. Neanderthal has become the classic concept of the caveman. His name has been synonymous with brutishness: a short thick body with limbs of ungainly proportions, a lumbering gait, and a stooped posture. Was Neanderthal a distinctive and specialized form of *H. sapiens,* a sideline in human evolution? Recent examinations of skeletons suggest that his stooped appearance may have been the result of disease rather than low evolutionary status. One theory is that he suffered from a deficiency of calciferol, aggravated by the diminished sunlight during the Ice Age, and developed severe rickets. New archeological finds in Iraq indicate that he was a skilled hunter and toolmaker, practiced crude surgery, and buried the dead with formal rites. The coarse features of Neanderthal Man are undeniable, but his cultural behavior patterns indicate he was not as apeish as early writings suggest. Even today, the exact status of Neanderthal Man remains controversial.

In 1933 a fossil skull and face were discovered near Steinheim, a town not far from Stuttgart, Germany, and their owner was given the name Steinheim Man. The age of the fossil is about 300,000 years old. The forehead is only moderately recessive, the brow ridges are pronounced, and the nose is broad, but the facial and dental configurations are those of man (Figure 25–22). The cranial capacity is at the lower end of that of a modern human (Figure 25–18). Other fossils of the Steinheim type have been unearthed at Swanscombe, England, and included with the human bones were hand axes. The cranium of the Swanscombe find housed a brain just about the size of a modern human female's brain.

It is apparent that although populations of *H. erectus* still existed during the Lower Pleistocene Era (700,000 to 1,000,000 years ago), individuals of the *H. sapiens* type were also present. Gradually, as the selective advantages of the *H. sapiens* traits began to take effect, there would be a greater proportion of *H. sapiens* in the population.

The final phase in the story of our emergence came about 20,000 years ago, when the Neanderthal inhabitants of Europe were abruptly displaced by a people of a completely modern European type. The remains of these people were found at Cro-Magnon in southern France, and the fossils have therefore been called Cro-Magnon Man. In reality Cro-Magnon Man is just one manifestation of *H. sapiens*. This group of humans was tall and muscular, with a large cranial capacity and fine facial features—in all respects indistinguishable from modern humans. Cro-Magnon Man was the last of the Old Stone Age peoples. He lived in rock shelters and was an accomplished artist; his paintings and sculptures are some of the finest examples of human creativity.

It is unlikely that humans originated in a restricted geographical locality. The Garden of Eden exists only as a metaphor. The

progenitors of the hominoids and the earliest representatives of the human family were probably distributed as widespread breeding communities in India, Europe, Asia, and Africa. The separation of modern peoples into geographical races probably took place as long as 500,000 years ago. The Asian forms migrated to Polynesia and Australia. Some 20,000 years ago Asians crossed the Bering Strait and reached the American continent (Figure 25–23.)

## 25–5 THE RACES OF MAN

### The biology of race

All men have been created equal; most certainly they are not all alike. The idea of equality derives from ethics; similarity and dissimilarity are observable facts. Human equality is not predicated on biological identity, not even on identical ability. People need not be identical twins to be equal before the law, or to be entitled to an equality of opportunity.

And yet, equality is often confused with identity, and diversity with inequality. They are confused so chronically, persistently and obstinately that one cannot help suspecting that people have deep seated wishes to confuse them.

The race problem as described by Dobzhansky is a real one; there is no doubt that the linked concepts of race and prejudice are deeply rooted in man's inhumanity to man. A clear understanding of the biology of race should demonstrate the fallacious reasoning behind racial prejudice.

Humans, you and I, make up a single species. By this we mean we are a group composed of interbreeding populations that are reproductively isolated from other such groups. However, our being of a single species does not reveal anything about the appearance of the members of that species. Indeed, at the species level, it is reproductive compatibility and not appearance that is of importance. Thus, although black bears and grizzly bears occupy the same territory, they do not interbreed, and the same is true for the other species that share our territory; a species remains as a distinct biological entity because its gene pool is isolated from other gene pools.

Species are made up of populations of individuals, and within these populations there exists two kinds of variations: individual and geographical. Individuals in a particular locality, be they bears or humans, show differences in their sex, age, physique, coloration, and so on. This individual variation within a population—**intrapopulation diversity**—depends on genetic variability in a single trait or many traits and is called **polymorphism** (*poly*—many, *morphe*—form; Gk.). It is polymorphism that enables you to tell Jack from Jim and Ellen from Mary. Polymorphic traits may be continuous (weight, height, age) or discontinuous (sex, blood type, eye color) in the population.

Now let us imagine that we expand our examination of a particular species and survey populations in different geographical localities. If we were to study the local populations of humans in Canada, Sweden, China, Ghana, and India, we would find them to be polymorphic. However, if we compared one geographical population with another we would soon see that the polymorphisms of one population were not identical with the polymorphisms of another; this is **geographical variation,** and

FIGURE 25–23 The spread of humans across the face of the earth.

*Dryopithecus* and *Pliopithecus*
Apes
8–18 million years ago

*Australopithecus*
Human-apes
2–5 million years ago

*Homo erectus*
Early humans
400,000–700,000 years ago

To the
Americas
20,000 +
years
ago

*Homo sapiens*
Modern humans
300,000 years ago

their gene frequencies, are termed **subspecies, or races.** Many species of plants and animals, including *Homo sapiens*, are polytypic and consist of races, or subspecies; under the appropriate conditions, that is, genetic or reproductive isolation, subspecies may eventually develop into full species.

The human species is polymorphic and polytypic. Why is there polymorphism? Because of gene mutation and sexual recombination. Why are there races? There are two principal reasons: (1) populations that make up a race, or subspecies, are or have been partially isolated geographically from other populations of the same species; if such isolation is continued, gene flow from one population to the next is restricted and the gene pool takes on a distinctive character; (2) geographically separate populations are subject to different selective pressures, and as a consequence the populations tend to differentiate from one another. Although in most cases it is impossible to identify what is being selected for, it is well established that isolation and selection promote race formation. In this respect it is easy to see that a race is an incipient species—a species in the making.

The term "race," as defined biologically, is equivalent to a subspecies and involves populations within a species that are characterized by differences in gene frequency. There is no agreement on the classification of the races of the human species. W. C. Boyd recognizes 6 races, Carleton Coon describes 30 races, and S. M. Garn classifies human population into 9 categories and 34 local races. (Tables 25–5 and 25–6). Although it is easy to describe differences among human populations in various geographical localities in terms of physique, skin color, hair shape, and so on, many of the traits used in describing human races have only a partial genetic basis and are strongly influenced by environmental factors, such as exposure to the sun and the adequacy of nutrition. Such traits are difficult to measure, and at present there is virtually no

because of it, it is sometimes simple to identify individuals coming from one area or another. It is interesting to note that the closer the populations are geographically, the more similar they are, and the farther apart they are geographically, the more different they appear. Sometimes the variations from one locale to the next are not

sharply defined, but in other cases the distinctions are quite clear. A species showing geographical variation, that is, **interpopulation diversity,** is called **polytypic,** and each population within that species can be shown to differ in the incidence of certain genes. Such differentiated populations occurring within a species, and differing in

**TABLE 25–5 Boyd's classification of the races by blood-group frequencies**

**European (caucasoid)**

High frequencies of Rh, cde, and CDe; moderate frequencies of the other blood-group genes; M usually slightly above and N below 50%

**African (negroid)**

Very high frequency of Rh, cDe; moderate frequencies of the other blood-group genes

**Asiatic (mongoloid)**

High frequency of B; little if any cde

**American Indian**

Most homozygous O, but sometimes high frequencies of A; absence of B; little if any cde; high M

**Australoid**

Moderate to high A; little or no B or cde; high N

**Early European**

High frequency of Rh, cde; no B (Basques are survivors of this group)

Modified from William C. Boyd Science, **140**, 1057–1064, 1963.

**TABLE 25–6 Garn's classification of the races**

**European**
1. Northwest European: population of Scandinavia, northern France and Germany, the Low Countries, the United Kingdom, and Ireland
2. Northeast European: population of Eastern Baltic, Russia, and modern Siberia
3. Alpine: population of central France, southern Germany, Switzerland, and northern Italy, to the Black Sea
4. Mediterranean: population surrounding the Mediterranean, eastward through Asia Minor

**Indian**
1. Indic: population of India, Pakistan, and Ceylon (Note: Garn calls this race Hindu, but inasmuch as Hindu properly identifies a religion, we feel that Indic is more appropriate.)
2. Dravidian: aboriginal population of southern India

**Asian**
1. Classic Mongoloid: population of Siberia, Mongolia, Korea, and Japan
2. North Chinese: population of northern China and Manchuria
3. Turkic: population of western China and Turkestan
4. Tibetan: population of Tibet
5. Southeast Asian: population of South China through Thailand, Burma, Malaya, the Philippines, and Indonesia
6. Ainu: aboriginal population of Japan
7. Eskimo: population of northern maritime fringe of North America and ice-free fringes of Greenland
8. Lapp: population of arctic Scandinavia and Finland

**Melanesian**
1. Papuan: population of mountain highlands of New Guinea
2. Melanesian: population of coastal area of New Guinea and most of the other islands in the Melanesian archipelago

**Polynesian**
1. Polynesian: aboriginal population

2. Neo-Hawaiian: nineteenth- to twentieth-century blend of Polynesian, European, and Asiatic

**Micronesian** (no local races distinguished)

**American**
1. North American (Indian): aboriginal population of Canada and the continental United States
2. Central American (Indian): population of the southwestern United States, Mexico, and Central America to Brazil
3. South American (Indian): population of all South America, except Tierra del Fuego
4. Fuegian: population around the Straits of Magellan
5. Ladino: new Latin-American population resulting from blending of Mediterranean, Central and South American (Indians), Forest Negroes, and Bantu
6. North American: Colored eighteenth- to twentieth-century population blended of Northwest European and Africans

**African**
1. East African: population of the East African Horn, Ethiopia, and Nilotic Sudan
2. Sudanese: population of the Sudan, except for Nilotics
3. Forest Negro: population of West Africa and most of the Congo
4. Bantu: population of South Africa and adjacent parts of East Africa
5. Bushman-Hottentot: surviving post-Pleistocene population in South Africa
6. Pygmy: small-statured population living in the equatorial rain forest
7. South African Colored: population of South Africa produced by a blend of Northwest European and Bantu, plus some Bushman-Hottentot

**Australian**
1. Murrayian: aboriginal population of southeastern Australia
2. Carpentarian: aboriginal population of central and northern Australia

information on their genetic basis. So far no clear-cut racial difference can be shown to exist for these traits. Furthermore, physique and skin color, the two characters most commonly used in race designations, are not critical characteristics of *H. sapiens* from an evolutionary point of view. As far as survival and selection go, it is difficult to pinpoint advantageous or disadvantageous characteristics in an age where humans create their own environment. It could well be argued that the important features of our species are intelligence, compassion, imagination, courage, perseverance, adaptability, and so on. Biologically, the racial differences described by anthropologists remain quite minor and of a secondary quality. The biological unity of modern humans—that is, our being a single species—is much more significant. Human gene pools exhibit a genetic and biological continuity in both time and space. Furthermore, no genetic isolating mechanisms exist for sep-

arating the human races, and even social barriers are inefficient for separating them.

### The significance of race and its origins

"She is a pure-blooded Indian." "The Aryan race was one of superior intellectual and

physical capabilities." "The Jewish race...." "Anglo-Saxons belong to the white race." Are these statements correct? Of course not. Pure races do not exist; races consist of populations showing genetic variability from one another, and therefore a race is defined statistically, not individually. No

FIGURE 25–24 Distribution of skin pigmentation in the world.

**535**

**HUMAN EVOLUTION**

individual can be "typical" of a race. A few misguided individuals have applied a typological definition of race to the human species and have classified us according to artificial criteria based primarily on skin color. This is contrary to the biological concept of race. Racism takes as its basis the erroneous belief in a type specimen for each species or race. Inherent in such thinking is belief in the special creation of each species that remains unchanged throughout the course of time and belief that each kind of creature can be described in an ideal form. Such notions are without scientific foundation. Race, defined in biological terms, is not equivalent to religious groups, language groups, cultural groups, or social status. The classification of human races is quite arbitrary, and often it is used for rather trivial scientific reasons.

Recognizing the arbitrary nature of race designation in humans, let us consider two of the traits that have been used traditionally—skin color and physique—and ask the questions, What is the adaptive significance of race? and, What are its origins?

**Skin color.** If we survey the distribution of skin pigmentation throughout the world before European exploration and colonization blurred population characteristics, we find that dark pigmentation occurred principally among people living around the equator (Figure 25–24). Lighter skin pigmentation occurred in populations living farther away from the equator. What is the adaptive significance of this? There seems little doubt that degree of skin pigmentation is related to environmental conditions. W. F. Loomis suggests that the degree of pigmentation regulates the amount of calciferol (vitamin D) synthesized by the action of ultraviolet light on the skin. Calciferol regulates calcium metabolism, and too little results in inadequate deposition of calcium in the bones; such a deficiency disease, called rickets, produces twisted legs and spine (Chapter 17, Box 17B). In a dark-skinned individual living in the tropics, where the ultraviolet radiation is abundant, many

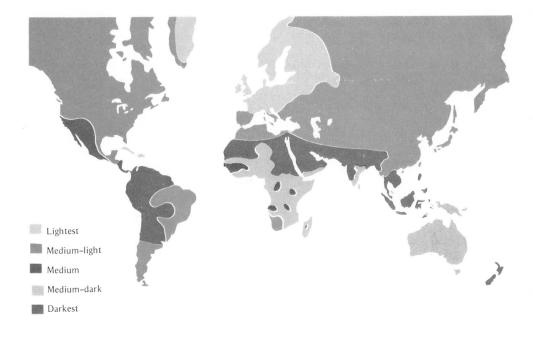

Lightest

Medium–light

Medium

Medium–dark

Darkest

of these rays would be screened out. However, as people moved out of the tropics they received less untraviolet light; they would be faced with a deficiency of calciferol if dark skin prevailed. Those mutations that resulted in a reduction in skin pigmentation would be favored in the temperate zones, since light skin would promote the reception of adequate amounts of ultraviolet light by the skin and permit the synthesis of calciferol in normal quantities. Loomis's hypothesis is attractive, but it requires further documentation.

**Physique.** Body form may be related to cold and heat adaptation. A thin, lean individual has a high surface-to-volume ratio and is well adapted to radiating heat: in warm climates this could offer some selective advantage. Features such as a flat nose, narrow eyelids, padding of the eyelids, and a stocky body with short limbs may all be adaptive for survival in cold climates, since body heat is conserved. Selection for these

alternate physiques doubtless entered into the evolution of the Watusi on the one hand and the Eskimo on the other; these are examples of extreme types, however, and this selective pressure has had little effect on other geographically isolated groups.

## 25–6 WHAT IS OUR EVOLUTIONARY FUTURE?

It is difficult for most of us to conceive of how long we were in becoming what we are today. The development of *H. sapiens* from *Australopithecus* covers a span of over 1 million years—equivalent to 15,000 human life-spans, or about 40,000 generations. A single lifetime is but a fleeting moment in evolutionary time, and it seems to each of us that the evolution of our species stands still. However, change is part of the nature of things. Since change will continue as long as the universe exists, what does the future hold for our species? The prophets of our future speak with assurance and certainty; we shall satisfy ourselves with speculation.

Will humans speciate in the future? Probably not. *Homo sapiens,* the species to which we belong, has failed to speciate and will probably continue in this way for two reasons: (1) humans show great ecological diversity, that is, they occupy a wide variety of habitats, and thus a burst of adaptive radiation into new habitats (such as occurred with Darwin's finches on the Galapagos Islands) is unlikely; (2) reproductive isolating mechanisms develop slowly and never have persisted long enough in humans to prevent gene flow between the races. Indeed, the greater mobility of human beings and their relative independence of the natural environment make geographical isolation and species formation near impossibilities.

Mutation, sexual recombination, and natural selection led to the emergence of *H. sapiens.* We are the first, and at present the only, species that can control its environment to any large extent and plot its evolutionary course. Owing to advances in the medical sciences, many countries have largely succeeded in controlling early death from disease. Many individuals with genetic disorders, who in previous years would not have survived to produce offspring, are now surviving and producing families. Will maintenance of such deleterious genetic factors impair our future? Provided medical care facilities are available, our future will probably be affected to an insignificant degree.

Increased intelligence has been of adaptive value to our survival in a changing world, but since the time of Neanderthal Man there has not been much change in the size of the brain. Will the human brain increase in size? There is no genetic reason why this could not happen if natural selection favored the survival of such a trend. However, it is possible that brain size has reached a plateau, since enlarged size of the brain of a baby would be perilous during childbirth unless there were (1) alterations

in the size of the female pelvis or (2) reduction in the duration of pregnancy; greater brain growth after birth than *in utero* would be another alternative. Such changes have not been selected for, and it has been suggested that increase in the size of the brain ceased not because of selection against increase in size but because larger brain size did not carry selective advantages.

Are we free of natural selection today? When we consider infant mortality and differential fertility in those countries where medical facilities and food are in short supply, it is obvious that natural selection still operates in human populations. However there has been a reduction in selective pressure for adaptations to the environment, such as the ability to resist cold and heat, natural resistance to various diseases, and so on. Our future will depend not solely on our ability to adapt to new habitats, but on our ability to devise a mode of life (culture) that is compatible with the lives of members of our own species and of all other creatures on this planet.

## SUMMARY

**1.** Species are groups of interbreeding natural populations that are reproductively isolated from other such groups.

**2.** The Linnaean system of binomial nomenclature, in which living organisms are known by both genus and species name, is used today. The Linnaean concept of the fixity of species has been superseded by the Darwinian view that organisms of similar structure, function, and development are closely related and have a common ancestry.

**3.** Species are classified into a hierarchy of genera, families, orders, classes, phyla, and kingdoms, reflecting both their similarities and differences.

**4.** Humans belong to the animal kingdom, the subphylum Vertebrata, class Mammalia, order Primates, family Hominidae, genus *Homo,* and species *sapiens.* Humans

are the only living species in the genus *Homo.*

**5.** Humans share many features with other primates. Distinctly human features include bipedalism; structure of the hand, cranium, brow, and pelvis; distinct chin; female breasts; enlarged penis; reduced body hair; enlarged brain; capacity for thought and language; and highly developed culture and technology.

**6.** Establishment of the geological age of the earth eroded theories of the special creation of living organisms. With the publication of Charles Darwin's *On the Origin of Species* and its evidence for natural selection, the theory of evolution began to be accepted.

**7.** Adaptive radiation and speciation among finches of the Galapagos Islands were one of Darwin's case studies in evolution.

**8.** Mutation and sexual recombination are the sources of genetic variation in a population, providing the raw materials on which natural selection can work. Reproductive isolation prevents interbreeding between populations and frequently produces changes in the gene pool. Evolution thus involves hereditary variation, natural selection of the best-adapted (fittest) organisms, differential reproduction (survival of the fittest), and genetic isolation.

**9.** Evolutionary theory also applies to humans, whose closest living relatives are the other primates. Today's primates were descended from an ancient insectivore prosimian stock, whose modern representatives are tree shrews, lemurs, and tarsiers.

**10.** Fossil ancestors of the human species include *Australopithecus,* a bipedal erect hominid with toolmaking ability, a savannahlike habitat, and a brain about half the size of that of modern humans; *Homo erectus (Pithecanthropus,* or Java Man, and *Sinanthropus)* and *Homo habilis* were the first true humans.

**11.** The change from tree-dwelling habitat to life on the plains was probably important in the selection of upright bipedalism. Increased brain size and mental capacity followed since selective pressure favored social development, cooperation, and communication abilities.

**12.** *Homo sapiens* probably appeared about 500,000 years ago.

**13.** Modern humans probably became separated into geographical races about 500,000 years ago. Geographic isolation is responsible for the production of polytypic species, with different gene frequencies forming incipient species (subspecies, or races).

**14.** Isolation of geographic groups restricts gene flow, and such isolated groups are subject to different selection pressures. Thus, isolation and selection promote race formation. Races are subspecies characterized by differences in gene frequency.

**15.** Modern humans are a single species with no true subspecies. Genetic differences among various races are insignificant from an evolutionary viewpoint.

**16.** Differences in human skin pigmentation probably arose as a result of selection for less pigment in areas of less sunlight, since pigmentation regulates calciferol production in the presence of ultraviolet light. Differences in body form may be related to cold and heat adaptation.

**17.** *Homo sapiens* is unlikely to speciate in the near future. Given modern mobility, it is unlikely that reproductive or geographical isolation or adaptive radiation into new habitats will occur. Cultural adaptation to a changing world will probably be of more importance than selection and genetic adaptation.

---

**KEY WORDS**

| | | |
|---|---|---|
| | kingdom | *Proconsul* |
| | structure | *Australopithecus* |
| genus | function | *Homo erectus* |
| species | development | *Homo habilis* |
| fixity of species | strata | *Homo sapiens* |
| morphology | natural selection | intrapopulation diversity |
| genera | adaptive radiation | polymorphism |
| families | Darwinian fitness | geographical variation |
| orders | reproductive isolation | interpopulation diversity |
| classes | evolution | polytypic (species) |
| phyla | insectivores | subspecies or races |

**TOPICS FOR REVIEW AND DISCUSSION**

1. Why can't natural selection alone account for speciation?

2. List the similarities and differences between humans and other primates.

3. Discuss the statement, *Australopithecus* was not an ape.

4. How can evolution be a blind force and yet lead to species that are better adapted than their predecessors?

5. Define a biological species. What are the weaknesses of such a definition? Strengths?

6. What is the significance of Darwin's finches to our thinking about evolution?

7. Discuss the biological basis for race formation and why discussions of human racial superiority are without biological meaning.

8. Describe the significant stages in human evolution and the fossil evidence for each stage.

9. Distinguish between polytypic and polymorphic.

10. John D. Rockefeller Sr. once told a Sunday School class, "The growth of a large business is merely survival of the fittest. . . . The American Beauty Rose can be produced in the splendor and fragrance which bring cheer to its beholder only by sacrificing the early buds which grow around it. This is not an evil tendency in business. It is merely the working out of a law of nature and a law of God." Discuss the biological error implicit in such thinking.

# 26

# Humans and the Environment

## 26–1 WHAT'S ECOLOGY?

You are, for the moment, an astronaut about to leave for a mission to the moon. To provide you with the necessities of life, the small spacecraft is well stocked with food, water, and oxygen; receptacles will be provided to store your liquid and solid wastes, and the carbon dioxide you produce by respiration will be trapped chemically. Prior to lift-off, all the life-support systems as well as the rocket hardware must be in "go" condition or your mission will surely end in disaster.

Stocking a spacecraft with the necessities for life is an obvious prerequisite for space flight. Life-support checklists are routinely employed for a space vehicle not much larger than an automobile, but for another kind of spaceship, the planet Earth, environmental checklists and a balanced environment are often ignored. Months, perhaps years, of planning go into a week-long voyage to the moon, but a trip in space lasting 70 years receives little thoughtful consideration. Indeed, as we shall soon see, Spaceship Earth, carrying billions of human inhabitants and a variety of other living creatures, is as fragile a craft as any ever made. Our survival depends upon maintenance of our life-support systems and an understanding of ecology.

What is ecology and what relationship does it bear to Spaceship Earth?

**Ecology** is taken from the Greek words *oikos*, which means home or house, and *logos*, which means study of. It is the field of biology that involves the study of the relationship between organisms and their biological and physical environments. Perhaps another way of understanding ecology is to look at biology in terms of its levels of organization (Figure 26–1). The molecules of life are organized in specific ways to form cells, cells are grouped into tissues, and tissues are arranged to produce functional organs. The body organs are integrated to produce organ systems, and the entire array of these systems constitutes an organism. Organisms exist not just as single individuals, but in groups called **populations.** The various populations of organisms that interact with one another form a **community;** a living community interacting with its local nonliving factors constitutes an **ecosystem.** Finally, all the ecosystems of the planet are combined to produce a level of organization known as the biosphere (Figure 26–2). The **biosphere**—that film of air, water, and soil extending to a depth of no more than 10 miles—is the relatively thin rind surrounding the surface of the earth where we and all other living creatures exist. Ecology concerns itself with the levels of organization beyond that of the individual organism—population, community, ecosystem, and biosphere.

The biosphere consists of a variety of ecosystems—pond, lake, forest, field, ocean, and so on. However, no ecosystem is an island unto itself. A pond or a lake may be surrounded by a field or a forest, and these in turn may be enclosed by rivers, oceans, and mountains. The existence of such continuity means there are no discrete boundaries between ecosystems, and each eco-

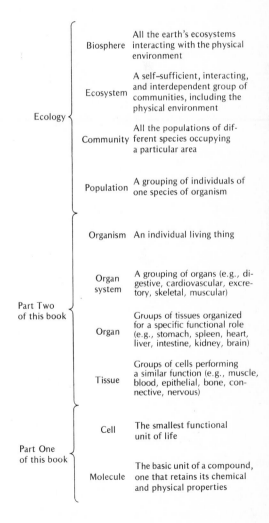

FIGURE 26–1 The hierarchy, or levels of organization, in biology.

| | | |
|---|---|---|
| Biosphere | All the earth's ecosystems interacting with the physical environment | |
| Ecosystem | A self–sufficient, interacting, and interdependent group of communities, including the physical environment | |
| Community | All the populations of different species occupying a particular area | |
| Population | A grouping of individuals of one species of organism | |
| Organism | An individual living thing | |
| Organ system | A grouping of organs (e.g., digestive, cardiovascular, excretory, skeletal, muscular) | |
| Organ | Groups of tissues organized for a specific functional role (e.g., stomach, spleen, heart, liver, intestine, kidney, brain) | |
| Tissue | Groups of cells performing a similar function (e.g., muscle, blood, epithelial, bone, connective, nervous) | |
| Cell | The smallest functional unit of life | |
| Molecule | The basic unit of a compound, one that retains its chemical and physical properties | |

Ecology brackets: Biosphere, Ecosystem, Community, Population.
Part Two of this book brackets: Organism, Organ system, Organ, Tissue.
Part One of this book brackets: Cell, Molecule.

**539**

FIGURE 26–2 The thin film of life—the biosphere.

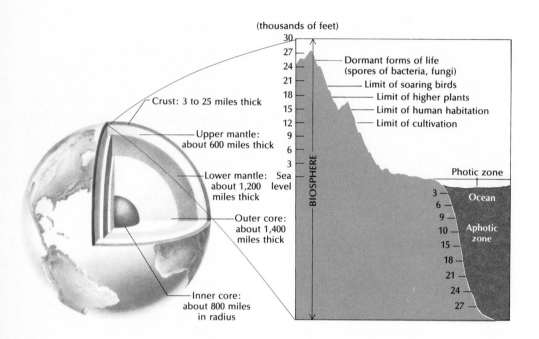

(thousands of feet)

Crust: 3 to 25 miles thick

Upper mantle: about 600 miles thick

Lower mantle: about 1,200 miles thick

Outer core: about 1,400 miles thick

Inner core: about 800 miles in radius

Dormant forms of life (spores of bacteria, fungi)
Limit of soaring birds
Limit of higher plants
Limit of human habitation
Limit of cultivation

BIOSPHERE

Photic zone

Ocean

Aphotic zone

system is partially dependent on what is happening in other systems. Therefore, when a study is made of a particular ecosystem, factors outside the system must be considered as well as those within. As a consequence of this, ecological studies are often complex. (Some of these external factors can be eliminated in the laboratory or in special field experiments when specific ecological principles are studied and tested.)

All living things, from men to the smallest microbe, live in association with other living things . . . an equilibrium is established which permits the different components of biological systems to live at peace together, indeed often to help one another. Whenever the equilibrium is disturbed by any means whatever, either internal or external, one of the components of the system is favored at the expense of the other.[1]

[1] R. Dubos, *The Germ Theory Revisited.* Quoted in S. Wolf and H. Goodell (eds.), *H. G. Wolff's Stress and Disease*, 2nd ed., Springfield, Illinois, Thomas, 1968.

If an ecosystem becomes imbalanced, changes occur that tend to restore the equilibrium, but on occasion the changes are so overwhelming that the compensatory processes could exclude many forms of life. As we shall soon see, this concept is at the core of our current environmental problems.

### 26–2 ENERGY FLOW

All actively metabolizing organisms consist of a complex organization of organic molecules dispersed in a watery medium. For an organism to maintain its organization and reproduce itself there must be available a continuing supply of energy.

As the earth travels through space, it exchanges little in the way of matter with the rest of the universe. Indeed, it may be said that life started on this planet with a fixed supply of raw materials, and these are continuously being recycled. By contrast, the earth is continuously receiving energy

from the sun. Sunlight is the power of life. This is true whether the living form is an enormous blue whale or a tiny hummingbird, a small child on a tricycle or a bulky football player; sunlight powers the pen that writes these words and provides the energy for you to comprehend their meaning. Although all of life depends on the sun, only photosynthesizing creatures are capable of trapping light energy directly and, by using simple raw materials, synthesizing organic compounds; these organisms are called **producers.** In discussions of energy, the term "producer" may sometimes be misleading. Producers do not, indeed they cannot, generate energy out of nothing; rather, they convert light energy into chemical energy. Producers are, in fact, converters or transducers of energy, taking the radiant energy of the sun and chemical elements from the earth and transforming these into useful, energy-rich organic molecules. Because photosynthesizing organisms synthesize their own food (organic molecules), these producers are also called **autotrophs** ("self-feeders").

Since photosynthesizing organisms capture light, they are obviously confined to that portion of the biosphere that receives solar radiation during the day. This region, where fixation of light energy occurs, is restricted to the clearest waters of the oceans to a depth of 300 ft (Figure 26–2). In turbid lakes, rivers, and streams the light may penetrate only 1 in., and thus the availability of light energy for photosynthesizing plants occupying this habitat may reduce their activity to a narrow zone just below the surface of the water. On land, photosynthesis is restricted to an altitude below 18,000 ft, not by the availability of light but by low temperature and lack of oxygen.

The energy flow from the sun to the photosynthesizing autotroph is not the end of our ecological story; it is merely the beginning. Some organisms meet their nutritional needs by feeding on other organisms rather than by manufacturing their own food; these are called **heterotrophs**

FIGURE 26–3 The average solar radiation received by the earth.

**541**

**HUMANS AND THE ENVIRONMENT**

("other feeders"). The heterotroph is a consumer; heterotrophs that feed directly on plants are called **herbivores** or **primary consumers.** Not all animals feed on plants; some feed on other animals. These are also heterotrophs, but they are **secondary consumers,** or **carnivores.** A secondary consumer derives its energy indirectly from the producer (the autotrophic plant) by way of the primary consumer (the herbivore). The hamburger you ate for lunch makes you a secondary consumer. The steer that supplied the hamburger meat was the primary consumer, and the grass upon which that steer fed to provide the meat was the producer.

It is important to recognize that the flow of energy through an ecosystem is unidirectional, not cyclic. The chemical constituents of life—nitrogen, carbon, oxygen, water, and other elements required for life—circulate in the biosphere, but energy does not. This means that the flow of energy is always:

producer ⟶ herbivore ⟶ carnivore
autotroph ⟶ heterotroph

Let us consider the consequences of this unidirectional flow of energy through an ecosystem. The total amount of solar energy fixed on the earth sets an upper limit on the total amount of life the biosphere can support. Another limit is set by the pattern of energy flow through the biosphere. For example, the total supply of solar energy reaching the earth amounts to $13 \times 10^{23}$ gram-calories per year, or 2.5 billion horsepower. This amounts to about 25% of the total incoming solar radiation, the remainder being absorbed by clouds, dust, water, and atmospheric gases. The absorbed radiation serves during its temporary stay on the earth to melt ice, to evaporate water, to generate winds and wave currents, and to warm the waters and land masses of the planet. Much of this absorbed radiation is subsequently lost into space: 10% by direct reflection, 22% by evaporation, and 10% by convection (Figure 26–3). The actual amount

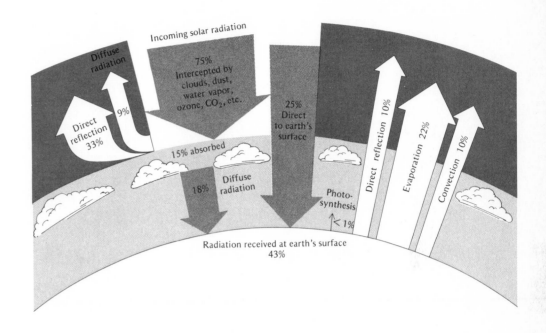

of available solar energy trapped by photosynthesizing organisms is quite small—less than 1% of the total incoming solar radiation. As small as this value is, it provides sufficient energy to synthesize more than 200 billion tons per year of dry organic matter for the world, including our own food.

When an animal feeds on a plant, it succeeds in extracting only 50% of the calories stored in the plant's organic molecules;[2] the remainder of the calories is dissipated in the form of heat. Of the extracted calories, the animal uses 70 to 80% for powering the living system and only 20 to 30% is actually built into organic substance. Thus, the efficiency of conversion

of plant matter into animal matter is 10% or less. A secondary consumer, one that feeds on animal tissue, does a little better (because animal matter has less indigestible material than a plant), but still the efficiency of conversion never exceeds 20% and typically is much less.

The unidirectional flow and efficiency of energy utilization account for the need for a continuous source of energy to prevent the collapse of an ecosystem. Indeed, no ecosystem can maintain itself for an extended period if it is deprived of an energy supply.

## 26–3 FOOD CHAINS AND ECOLOGICAL PYRAMIDS

The transfer of food energy from plants to animals and then to other animals by successive stages of feeding is called a **food chain.** In some cases, the relationships between the organisms involved are so complex that the chain is in the form of a highly

---

[2] The conversion of energy from one form to another is not 100% efficient—a situation described by the Second Law of Thermodynamics. This law states that when a process involving energy transformation occurs, a fraction of the available energy is dispersed in the form of heat and is unavailable for work. (See Chapter 4.)

FIGURE 26–4 Two food chains. (a) Land-based. (b) Water-based (aquatic).

complicated and branching network called a **food web.**

Two food chains, one land-based and the other aquatic, are illustrated in Figure 26–4. A more complicated food web is illus-

trated in Figure 26–5. It should be noted that there are four primary levels in these food chains: plants, herbivores, carnivores, and decay organisms. The products of decay are returned to the plant in the form of

utilizable nutrients, and thus the matter in a food chain may be continuously recycled.

If a food chain is arranged in levels, the first level is occupied by the producers: in a land-based ecosystem these may be grasses and trees; in an aquatic ecosystem, algae, seaweed, and the microscopic phytoplankton. The second level is occupied by the herbivores: on land hoofed animals, rodents, birds, worms, insects, and fungi are herbivores, or primary consumers; in water-based ecosystems molluscs, worms, herbivorous fishes, and microscopic zooplankton occupy this level. The third level is occupied by the carnivores, or secondary consumers: on land these are mountain lions, hawks, foxes, and so on; in the water the carnivores are fishes, seals, and birds. On the fourth level are the carnivores that themselves feed on other carnivores: otters that eat trout, trout that eat insects, and foxes that eat owls. Each level is called a trophic level, after Greek word *trophos* meaning to nurse or feed. Many organisms, including humans, eat both plants and animals and are called **omnivores.** Thus, we and they enter the food chain at a number of trophic levels.

In an ecosystem such as a pond or a forest the energy base is provided by the green plants (producers), the next level above this is occupied by primary consumers (herbivores), and succeeding levels above this are made up of secondary, tertiary, and quaternary consumers (carnivores). If we represent this situation graphically by taking the total amount of dry weight of the organisms in each of these levels, a pyramid of **biomass** is obtained (Figure 26–6).(Biomass is the weight of living organisms in an area.) Another way of looking at the composition of an ecosystem is to represent the energy content at the various levels. The lower levels have a greater energy content than do the higher levels (Figure 26–7). Pyramids of biomass and energy for an ecosystem are a consequence of the Second Law of Thermodynamics.

The biological upper limit of biomass is set by the primary producers, the photosynthesizing organisms responsible for trapping the energy of sunlight. The biomass at each succeeding level is in part determined by the biomass (or energy) available at the level upon which it rests.

**FIGURE 26–6 The pyramid of biomass in a land-based food chain.**

**FIGURE 26–7 The energy pyramid in a land-based food chain.**

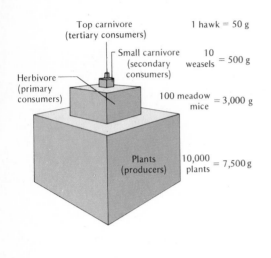

Top carnivore (tertiary consumers) — 1 hawk = 50 g

Small carnivore (secondary consumers) — 10 weasels = 500 g

Herbivore (primary consumers) — 100 meadow mice = 3,000 g

Plants (producers) — 10,000 plants = 7,500 g

Secondary carnivores (tertiary consumers) — $3 \times 10^{19}$ — Lost — Heat and respiration

Carnivores (secondary consumers) — $1 \times 10^{20}$ — Lost — Heat and respiration

Herbivores (primary consumers) — $5 \times 10^{20}$ — Lost — Heat and respiration

Plants (producers) — $1 \times 10^{21}$ — Lost — Heat and respiration

Sun — $1.3 \times 10^{23}$ — Lost — Unabsorbed light

Calories per year

This has great practical significance: the shorter the food chain, the greater will be the available food energy. The less developed nations of the world take advantage of this in their utilization of vegetables and grain foods rather than meat, since energy losses are kept to a minimum when human beings act as herbivores. In countries where meat is a part of the diet and the economy is impoverished, animals used as the source of meat are scavengers, consuming plant wastes not utilizable by humans. The pig is a prime example; it eats the garbage humans do not or cannot eat. The more affluent countries of the world use grain, itself useful as human food, for feeding cattle, since cattle are energetically expensive to produce. Of particular importance in supporting an ever-increasing human population may be attempts to shorten the length of food chains. Thus, more people could be supported on a diet of soyburger than on hamburger or on trout (Figure 26–8). If the world population grows and begins to outstrip the capacity of the earth for meat

production, we may indeed be forced to a grazing diet.

## 26–4 THE DANGER OF ACCUMULATED CHEMICALS

We have considered the flow of energy in a food chain and seen that less than 10% of the energy obtained at one level is stored in the living tissues and available for transfer to the next level; typically more than 90% of the energy is lost as heat to the environment at each step and is therefore not usable by the organism. Another facet of food transfer is the use to which the food itself is put. Usually less than 20% of the food obtained by an animal is used for the construction of the animal's tissues; the remainder is used for work or eliminated by excretion. Small though this amount is, it provides a mechanism for concentrating materials: a substance that is not eliminated is retained, and when passed from one feeding level to the next, it may be concentrated in the tissues two or more times.

Some substances, such as mercury, lead, cadmium, and asbestos, are neither used nor eliminated but are stored in the body, where they may exert a cumulative and damaging effect on a variety of physiological processes. Organic pesticides of the chlorinated hydrocarbon variety (DDT, for example) are another class of long-lasting cumulative poisons stored in living tissues. Other substances may be used by the body even though they are damaging. For example, radioactive elements such as strontium 90, cesium 137, and iodine 131 may be concentrated by transfer from one feeding level to the next; cells receiving high doses of ionizing radiations from such elements can be severely damaged and gross abnormalities induced. Persistent pollutants such as these pose a serious environmental hazard to the "top dogs" in an ecological pyramid, because by the time they reach the top level they have been concentrated many times over. In the more affluent developed nations of the world the food chains are longer, and so the concentration of

FIGURE 26–8 The relationship between length of the food chain and energy efficiency in feeding. Eating farther down on the food chain conserves a larger proportion of energy harvested.

'Tomorrow, the world!'

pollutants may be severe in the members of such societies. Let us look at some of these pollutants that endanger us.

## Mercury

Mental derangement afflicted the Mad Hatter in Lewis Carroll's *Alice in Wonderland.* Minamata disease—characterized by numbed muscles in the arms and legs, impaired speech, and blurred vision—appeared in 1953 in Japanese fishermen who ate seafood from Minamata Bay; of the 134 victims, 47 died. The cause? Mercury poisoning.

Organic mercurials, such as ethyl mercury and methyl mercury, can be deadly. In large amounts methyl mercury can cause brain damage, induce chromosome breaks, and intoxicate an unborn fetus so that it develops cerebral palsy. The chemical basis of such effects seems to be the strong affinity of the organic mercury compounds for the SH (sulfhydryl) groups in proteins, especially those in cellular membranes, causing changes in electrical potential, ion distri-

bution, and movement of fluid. Methyl mercury and ethyl mercury are resistant to degradation and persist in the environment for weeks or months; thus their effects are most damaging and essentially irreversible.

Mercury poisoning can occur by occupational exposure or environmental accumulation. The Mad Hatter's mental derangement was probably caused by chronic exposure to mercury fumes from the mercuric chloride commonly used in processing beaver pelts into men's hats. The fishermen of Minamata Bay developed symptoms of mercury poisoning as a result of accidental ingestion of methyl mercury. The Chisso Chemical Corporation, a plastics manufacturer, used mercuric chloride as a catalyst in the production of urethane and vinyl chloride. After use the mercuric chloride was dumped into Minamata Bay. Once this had settled to the muddy bottom, it was converted by bacterial action into methyl mercury. The mud's methyl mercury content was concentrated to 50 parts per million (ppm) in the fish, and since the fishermen and their families lived almost exclusively on bay fish the concentration in the humans reached over 100 ppm.

In the United States, evidence of abnormal amounts of mercury in water, fish, and game birds has turned up in at least 33 states. The concentrations of mercury in unpolluted waters is about 1 part per billion (ppb), but in the waters around plants producing caustic soda the concentration was found to be 1,800 ppm. Symptoms of methyl mercury poisoning have been associated with blood concentrations of 0.2 ppm, but to maintain this level a 154-lb man would have to ingest 9 lb of fish containing 0.5 ppm each week. The U.S. Food and Drug Administration (FDA) has established a concentration of 0.5 ppm as the allowable limit in fish used for human food.

The principal sources of mercury are fungicides, lumber and paper mills, paint factories, and plants that manufacture chlorine and caustic soda, where mercury is used as a catalyst and is washed away in the residual brine. The mercury deposited in fresh water may remain for centuries after mercury dumping has been stopped. Although there is a natural background of mercury, this is no reason to discount the danger. Mercury is a cumulative poison, and the more mercury released into the environment the greater are the chances that the tolerable level will be exceeded. By restricting entry of mercury into the environment from in-

dustrial sources, by controlling its use as a fungicide, and by reducing the ingestion of heavily contaminated foods, we may avoid future tragedies from mercury poisoning.

## DDT and other chlorinated hydrocarbons

About 100 years ago an obscure German chemist, Othmar Zeidler, synthesized **d**ich-**l**oro-**d**iphenyl-**t**richoroethane, or **DDT.** It lay on the shelf until 1930, when a Swiss entomologist, Paul Muller, tested it for its killing properties on insects and found it most effective. In 1942 DDT came to the United States, where its usefulness as a potent insecticide was quickly recognized. In many countries around the world spraying DDT eliminated the diseases typhus, malaria, yellow fever, and plague—all of which are transmitted by insects. Since World War II the use of DDT has saved many millions of lives and prevented untold human suffering. So widespread was the use of DDT in controlling pest-borne diseases that now the compound is everywhere—the land, the sea, the fatty tissues of animals and humans, and even breast milk. Nobody, no thing is free of DDT. Why does DDT, one of the best and cheapest of the pesticides, now contaminate our environment, not only killing pests but destroying helpful birds and insects and sickening farmers?

DDT, a chlorinated hydrocarbon, is an exceedingly stable material; it breaks down in the environment very slowly (its half-life is 15 years).[3] When DDT is sprayed, it is carried into the air, and depending on the weather conditions, it is rapidly and widely spread from ecosystem to ecosystem. Since it is not very soluble in water (1 ppb), it tends to remain in the environment. Although the amount in the water may be

---

[3] Half-life is the time required for half of a substance to be degraded. Thus, if the half-life of a substance is 100 years, only half of the starting material would present after that period; in 200 years, only 25%; in 300 years, only 12.5%; and so on. (See also p. 18.)

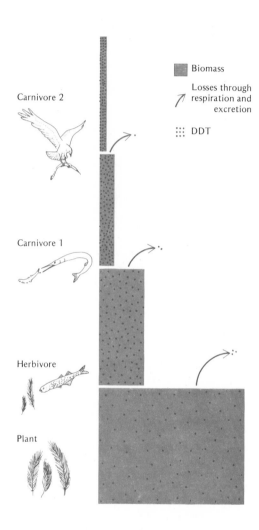

infinitely small, aquatic organisms tend to accumulate DDT because it is fat-soluble. As a consequence, long after the spraying, organisms are continuously exposed to DDT, which they absorb and retain in their fatty tissues. If the organism is a plant, little DDT is lost by respiration; when the plant is eaten, the DDT is transferred virtually intact and concentrated in the fatty tissues of the herbivore. At each feeding transfer, the concentration of DDT in the flesh of the predator is increased (Figure 26–9). Thus, in a Long Island marsh sprayed with DDT, the plankton (microscopic plants and animals) contained 0.04 ppm; the fish (minnows), 1 ppm; and the birds that fed on the minnows, 75 ppm. Similar high concentrations of DDT are found in carnivorous birds and mammals. Human fat on the average contains 122 ppm, and in human breast milk the concentration may be as high as 5 ppm. According to the FDA, the permissible level of DDT in food is 0.05 ppm; thus, if human breast milk were sold with the same restrictions as cow's milk, a nursing mother's milk would be declared unfit for human consumption.

DDT is a poison, and it kills not only insects but myriad other creatures. Unfortunately, we have no clear understanding of the exact mechanism whereby it exerts its killing effect, but it appears likely that its site of action is in the nervous system, since DDT poisoning involves tremors and convulsions.

The widespread use of DDT not only almost eliminated many insect-borne diseases, but by protecting crops from insect damage and destruction, it increased yields by 30 to 40% in underdeveloped nations and by 10% in developed countries. DDT was soon hailed as a miracle insecticide, a cure-all for insect-borne plagues, and a powerful tool in the war against starvation. Then these hopes were dashed: by 1948, resistance to DDT had been developed by 12 species of insects; in 1954, there were 25 resistant species; by 1960, the number had increased to 137 species; and by 1965, there were 165 insect species resistant to DDT. The more we sprayed, the greater were the numbers of resistant species. This is because resistance is a genetic trait; some individuals in an insect population survived exposure to DDT, and their progeny were able to thrive, mate, and lay eggs with complete immunity to DDT. Consequently, the numbers of resistant individuals in that species increased dramatically in only a few generations.

Yet, not all the dangers of DDT stem from resistance, biological magnification, and persistence. A few parts per billion of DDT in the water may depress the photosynthetic activity of algae, and thus the primary productivity of a lake is diminished and ecological disruption begins. Sometimes the spraying of an insecticide destroys the wrong organism at the wrong time and promotes ecological imbalance. For example, the red-spider mite is a destructive pest of spruce trees, but normally it is kept in check by a predatory mite. When spruce forests were sprayed to control the spruce beetle (another insect that damages the spruce needles), the predatory mites and the spruce beetles were both destroyed, but the red-spider mites living on the undersides of the needles survived. The year following the spraying saw a wave of red-spider mite damage in excess of that ever done by the combined efforts of spruce beetles and red-spider mites.

On December 31, 1972, some 10 years after Rachel Carson wrote *Silent Spring* and warned of the threat posed by indiscriminate and widespread use of pesticides, the Environmental Protection Agency banned almost all domestic use of DDT. The growers of cotton, peanuts, and soybeans—three crops that accounted for almost all of the DDT used—must now use methyl parathion, a toxic but highly degradable pesticide. In spite of the ban DDT will still be exported for use in malaria control.

The limited ban on DDT in specific areas seems to be in the public interest, and it will force us to think of insect-control measures less hazardous than the indiscriminate aerial spraying of pesticides. Integrated pest management, that is, the rational use of ecological factors and the moderate use of chemicals, seems to provide a reasonable alternative to DDT and other toxic and persistent pesticides. The future of pest control appears to lie not in the development of more-potent chemical insecticides but in the combined use of safe and specific predators and parasites for eliminating crop pests, the trapping of pests by sex attrac-

tants, the release of sterile males, and the avoidance of single-crop planting.

### Atomic wastes

On the morning of July 16, 1945, at a desert site near Alamogordo, New Mexico, the first atomic bomb was exploded. Since that day we have lived with the atom bomb and its pollutants. Each atom bomb, by a chain reaction, converts a small amount of radioactive matter into blast (50%), heat (35%), and radioactivity (15%). The radioactive materials produced in an atomic blast and let loose into the atmosphere ultimately settle to the earth by gravity and are called **fallout.**

The most important fact about the radioactive materials (**radioisotopes**) in fallout is that for all practical purposes they have the same chemical properties as the nonradioactive forms. Thus, radioactive iodine ($^{131}I$) can be incorporated into thyroxine, the thyroid hormone, as easily as nonradioactive iodine ($^{127}I$). When radioactive isotopes decay, they emit ionizing radiations, and these can damage living tissue or induce mutations (Chapter 24). The exact effects of these radiations depend on the intensity of the radiations, the rate of decay of the isotope, and the place in the body where it is absorbed and stored.

Strontium 90 is a fission product released as a result of nuclear-bomb tests. It is easily spread in the air and can make a complete circuit of the earth in 16 to 25 days—the exact amount and distribution depending on climatic conditions. Strontium 90 is particularly damaging to the blood-forming centers in the bone marrow, since it is chemically very similar to calcium and thus tends to be accumulated in the bones and other tissues rich in calcium. Strontium 90 is relatively long-lived, with a half-life of 27 years, so that its ionizing radiations remain hazardous for a person's entire lifetime.

The route of entry of strontium 90 into human tissues is quite direct. The fallout containing the isotope enters plant tissues from the soil or the air; these plants are

FIGURE 26-12 The nitrogen cycle.

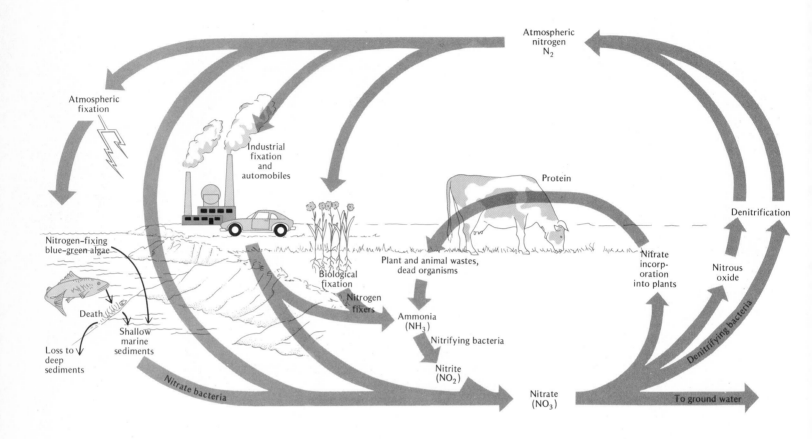

be accumulated in the bodies of organisms, it cycles through the biosphere slowly, and it is ecologically significant because of its limited availability. In some instances, it is the amount of phosphorus alone that determines ecosystem productivity.

The principal reservoirs of phosphorus for the **phosphorus cycle** are phosphate rocks, guano (seabird excreta), and fossilized animals. Through leaching and erosion, mining, and application of fertilizers, phosphorus is released to become available as phosphate to plants. In both plants and animals the phosphate becomes dispersed into a variety of organic constituents; these ultimately return to the soil by decomposition. Soil continuously loses phosphate by leaching, and this ends up in the ocean. There it may be used in the marine ecosys-

tem or it may be lost for long periods of time in deep ocean deposits. The phosphorus cycle is shown in Figure 26–13.

### The water cycle

Most of the stuff of life is water. Without water life cannot exist. Mars and Venus have virtually no water, and our explorations of the moon indicate that it is devoid of water. Mars, Venus, and the moon are all lifeless celestial bodies. By contrast, about 70% of the surface of the earth is covered by water. Water is a renewable resource that is recycled again and again in a complex fashion.

The principal water reservoirs are the oceans. Through evaporation, precipitation, runoff, and groundwater seepage, water

is constantly circulating, and generally the total **water cycle** remains in balance (Figure 26–14). However, it is important to recognize that the relative as well as the absolute amounts of water in an area determine the nature of the ecosystem. The pattern of water distribution on the land via precipitation varies greatly and depends on atmospheric circulation as well as on the topography of the land masses (Figure 26–15). Consequently, some regions of the world are dense forests, while other areas are barren deserts.

It takes vast quantities of water to produce food (recall that in photosynthesis six molecules of water are used in the formation of one molecule of sugar). In more concrete terms, it takes 60 gal of water to produce 1 lb of dry wheat, 200 to 250 gal of water to

FIGURE 26–13 (top) The phosphorus cycle.　　FIGURE 26–14 (bottom) The water cycle.

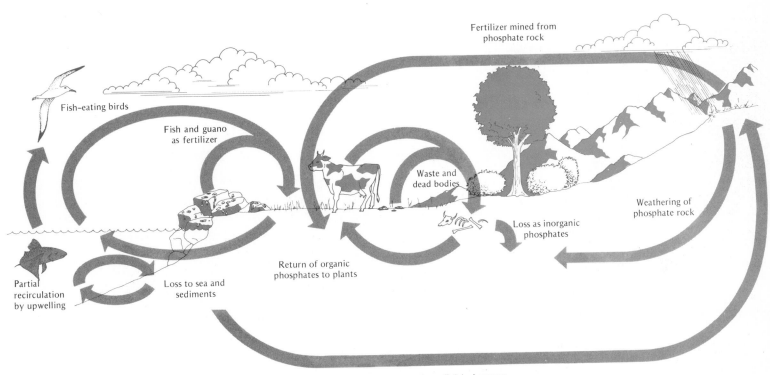

Fertilizer mined from
phosphate rock

Fish-eating birds

Fish and guano
as fertilizer

Waste and
dead bodies

Weathering of
phosphate rock

Partial
recirculation
by upwelling

Loss to sea and
sediments

Return of organic
phosphates to plants

Loss as inorganic
phosphates

Original source:
uplift by geologic processes

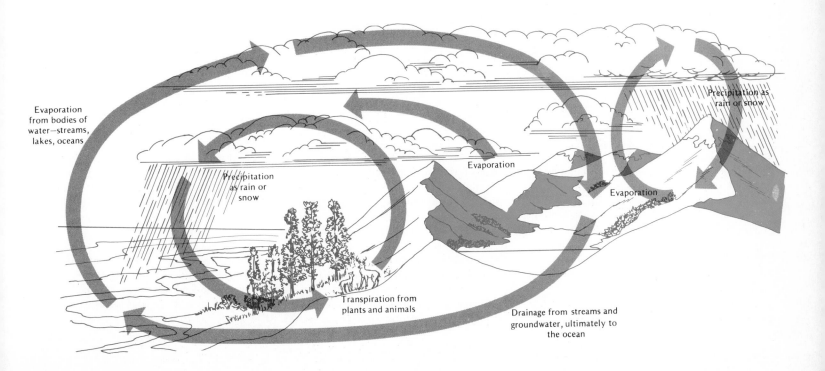

Evaporation
from bodies of
water—streams,
lakes, oceans

Precipitation as
rain or snow

Precipitation
as rain or
snow

Evaporation

Evaporation

Transpiration from
plants and animals

Drainage from streams and
groundwater, ultimately to
the ocean

FIGURE 26–15 The pattern of annual precipitation in the world.

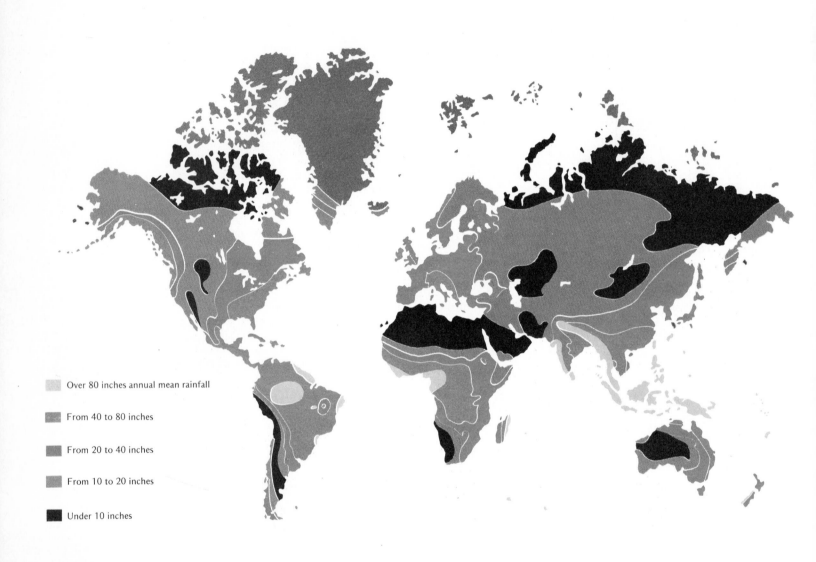

Over 80 inches annual mean rainfall

From 40 to 80 inches

From 20 to 40 inches

From 10 to 20 inches

Under 10 inches

produce 1 lb of rice, 2,500 to 6,000 gal to produce 1 lb of meat, and 1,000 gal to produce 1 qt of milk. Industrial processes utilize staggering amounts of water: it is estimated that 100,000 gal of water are used in the production of a single automobile, and the manufacture of a single copy of a Sunday newspaper uses 150 gal! The amounts of water we waste are phenomenal: shaving, washing, and brushing teeth uses 5 gal; a quick shower or a load of wash takes 30 gal; and flushing the toilet a single time

may use as much as 7 gal. A typical Los Angeles home uses 111 gallons of water per person daily. Of that, 78 gallons is used indoors, the remainder being used for watering lawns and gardens. That is enough water each year to cover more than 146 square miles of land to a depth of 1 foot.

About 97% of the earth's water is salty, and the remainder is mostly in the form of ice in Antartica and Greenland. Only a minute fraction of the earth's water is available for use by living organisms. If we

remove more fresh water from the land masses than is replaced via the water cycle, we put ourselves and all other living things in jeopardy. Witness the water shortages that frequently occur during the summer months in areas of the United States. Groundwater reserves act as "water capital," but these are being reduced by withdrawals at an alarming rate; once withdrawals exceed capital reserve, the water bank will fail (see Box 26B). One authority on the subject contends that Europeans extract

## BOX 26B Ebbing of the Ogallala

There are two documentary images of the Great Plains. The first is a black-and-white photograph of the '30s Dust Bowl, with windblown homesteaders treading the cracked earth. The second: a glossy color shot of the same land 40 years later, showing the lush checkerboard farms of America's breadbasket. Now, as if through a strange reversal in time, the second image threatens to fade into the first. For in another 40 years, the territory could backslide into dust and despair. The Ogallala Aquifer, the vast underground reservoir of water that transformed much of the Great Plains into one of the richest agricultural areas in the world, is being sucked dry.

The aquifer is a California-size deposit of water-laden sand, silt and gravel. It ranges in thickness from 1,000 ft in Nebraska, where two-thirds of its waters lie, to a few inches in parts of Texas. Although it was first tapped in the 1930s, it has been extensively exploited only since the development of high-capacity pumps after World War II. The Ogallala's estimated quadrillion gallons of water, the equivalent of Lake Huron, have irrigated farms in South Dakota, Nebraska, Wyoming, Kansas, Colorado, Oklahoma, Texas and New Mexico, changing a region of subsistence farming into a $15 billion-a-year agricultural center.

For the past three decades, farmers have pumped water out of the Ogallala as if it were inexhaustible. Nowadays they dispense it prodigally through huge center-pivot irrigation sprinklers, which moisten circular swaths a quarter-mile in diameter. The annual overdraft (the amount of water not replenished) is nearly equal to the yearly flow of the Colorado River. Like all aquifers, the Ogallala depends on rain water for recharging, and only a trickle of the annual local rainfall ever reaches it. Gradually built up over millions of years, the aquifer is being drained in a fraction of that time. The question is no longer if the Ogallala will run dry, but when.

On the High Plains of eastern Colorado, the water level has dropped as much as 40 ft since the 1960s. In parts of Oklahoma, it has dipped that much in 4 years. Texas, the thirstiest of the eight states, has consumed 23% of its Ogallala reserves since World War II.

According to a major study, 5.1 million acres of irrigated land (an area the size of Massachusetts) in six Great Plains states will dry up by the year 2020. If current trends continue, Kansas will lose 1.6 million irrigated acres, Texas 1.2 million, Colorado 260,000, New Mexico 224,000, Oklahoma 330,000.

Although the cause of the trouble is obvious, the cure is not. Indeed, there may be no fundamental solution to the ebbing of

Thickness of water layer

0—100 ft.

400—1,200 ft

Projected percent of water supply remaining by the year 2020

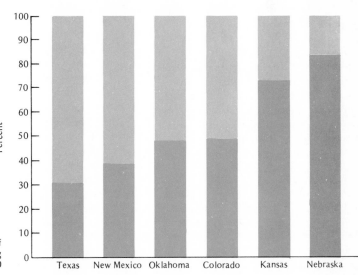

Percent

the Ogallala. "We can prolong the supply," concludes John Weeks, a U.S. Geological Survey engineer who heads a five-year U.S.G.S. study of the situation, "but we are mining a limited resource, like gold, and we can't solve the ultimate depletion problem."

Conservation may forestall the end. Farmers can simply use less water. They are already converting from profitable but water-thirsty corn to water-thrifty crops such as wheat, sorghum, and cotton. Sophisticated laser-guided land graders can now almost perfectly flatten the terrain so that water is not wasted in runoff. Electrodes planted in the fields can measure soil wetness and determine exactly when water is needed. Today, these techniques are rarities, but they may soon be routine. "Water misers" will last longer. But even the stingiest will go under if neighbors are wasteful and the whole aquifer dries up.

The dimensions of the problem have been recognized, but no one is sure whether the shrinking aquifer is a federal, state, or local issue, and no one wants the responsibility of deciding. Several states, including Oklahoma and Colorado, already have established policies limiting water use, but many say such efforts are too little too late. The afflicted states cannot even agree with one another, and unless they all march together, they will all parch separately.

By Richard Stengel. Reported by Sam Allis/ Lubbock and Richard Woodbury/Denver. Copyright 1982 Time Inc. All rights reserved. Reprinted by permission from TIME.

three times more water than the cycle returns for human use, and Americans take out twice the amount returned. Clearly the trend cannot continue unabated. If we are to avoid running out of water, we shall have to be more efficient in our use of it. Once water is in short supply, agriculture will fail, food supplies will diminish, and mass starvation will result. Then it will truly be as Coleridge's Ancient Mariner complained: "Water, water everywhere/nor any drop to drink."

## 26–6 HOMEOSTASIS, CARBON DIOXIDE, AND OZONE

### Homeostasis

An organism maintains its internal environment in a rather constant state by a series of negative feedback loops, a condition known as **homeostasis.** When an organism is out of balance, function becomes abnormal, and disease or death may be the consequence of such an unhealthy situation. The same principle applies to the natural ecosystem. An unbalanced ecosystem leads to instability, survival of the occupants is jeopardized, and if balance is not restored within a short time, the system may undergo irreversible damage.

What is a balanced ecosystem, and how does it come about? Balance in any system implies an equality of opposing forces: a seesaw is balanced when the weights of the persons on each end are equal. In an ecosystem, such as a grassland, a forest, or a desert, there are many opposing forces: organisms are born while others die, water is lost from the soil by evaporation and returned via precipitation, nutrients are leached out of the soil and utilized by producers. All these events tend to balance each other out.

### Carbon dioxide and climate

Ecosystem homeostasis can be seen in the cycling of matter. The regulation of

carbon dioxide levels in the atmosphere provides an example of this. Carbon dioxide is quite soluble in water, and the oceans constitute a vast reservoir of this material. The greater the amount of carbon dioxide in the atmosphere, the warmer the earth becomes because of the **greenhouse effect.** The greenhouse effect occurs because carbon dioxide in the atmosphere acts as do the glass walls of a greenhouse. The glass walls transmit sunlight into the greenhouse, where it is absorbed and reradiated as heat that does not readily exit through the glass; as a consequence the temperature inside the greenhouse becomes higher than that outside. (A similar situation occurs with an automobile that is closed and sitting out in the sun.) There is evidence that shows the concentration of carbon dioxide is rising (Figure 26–16). Human activities have increased the amount by 15 to 25% over the past century. What is not certain, however, is the precise amount of warming and the climatic changes that can be expected from further increases of carbon dioxide. Scientists have attempted to develop models that may serve to predict the possible climatic impacts of increased levels of carbon dioxide. In one model, a doubling or quadrupling of the levels would produce a summer **dry zone** in the North American grain belt, but concomitantly the soil moisture in the monsoon belts would increase. As a result, a new equilibrium was established after several decades of simulated time. The social and economic impacts of the rise in temperature before the time of equilibrium and before humans have adapted is difficult to predict precisely, but they are expected to be significant. It is important to note that the Earth is already 0.5°C warmer than it was a century ago, and in the West Antarctic ice shelves are calving off huge icebergs into the sea. This iceberg melt could result in a rise in sea level of 1.5 mm per year, and were the temperature of the Earth to increase, the rate of calving would also increase. One scenario suggests that were this to occur the sea would rise 3 cm per

FIGURE 26–16 Rising concentration of carbon dioxide in the atmosphere at Mauna Loa in Hawaii. The seasonal variation (color) arises because carbon dioxide is removed from the air by the photosynthetic activity of plants during the growing season and is returned later by the oxidation of plant tissues. Smoother curve (black) shows average change. (Carbon dioxide and world climate Roger Revelle. Scientific American August 1982.)

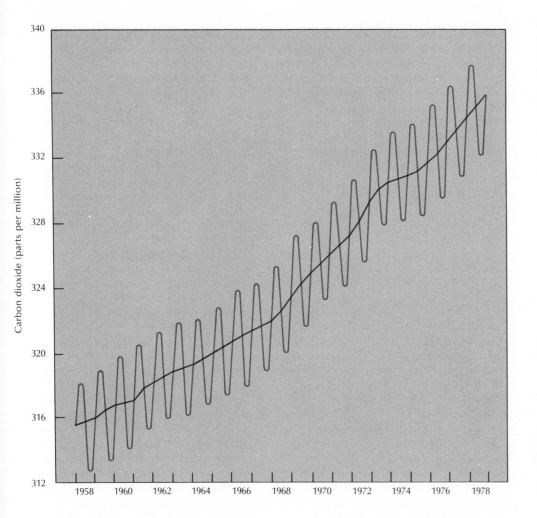

trapped by plants in photosynthesis, and this would cause a rise in the carbon dioxide level in the atmosphere. As South America became industrialized, burning of fossil fuel would increase, and excessive amounts of carbon dioxide would be liberated into the air, perhaps overtaxing the buffering capacity of the oceans. As the carbon dioxide level continued to rise, the greenhouse effect would result in elevated temperatures, and the polar ice caps would melt. A temperature rise of only a few degrees could raise the sea level 30 ft, and most of the coastal land areas (where most of the human population lives) would be flooded.

## The ozone hole and its consequences

An Antarctic survey, published in 1985, indicated that in this region of the world the springtime amounts of ozone in the atmosphere had decreased by more than 40% between 1977 and 1984. The region of depletion was larger than the Antarctic itself and ranged from 12 to 24 km in altitude. The zone containing lower levels of ozone was called the **ozone hole.**

The atmosphere, the ocean of gases that blankets the earth, can be divided into two regions, the troposphere and the stratosphere. The troposphere is where all global weather occurs and it extends from the earth's surface to a height of 10 km. Above this is the stratosphere, which extends to about 50 km.

Ozone ($O_3$) is the form of oxygen that rarely occurs naturally in the troposphere, but it is formed in the stratosphere as a result of ultraviolet bombardment of oxygen. Ozone efficiently screens out ultraviolet light and in so doing it protects the oxygen at lower altitudes from being broken down. Ozone molecules are constantly being made and destroyed, and for millennia the process has been in equilibrium. In 1928 a group of chemists invented a nontoxic, inert gas called chlorofluorocarbons (CFC). The CFCs were used as coolants in refrigerators and as propellants in aerosol sprays.

year or 3 meters per century, and such a rise in sea level would have serious consequences for coastal areas.

Responsible scientists believe that the changes that will come about as a result of increased levels of carbon dioxide will be slow, pervasive environmental shifts. Most will go unnoticed from year to year; however, it might be of considerable benefit to future generations if we began now to think of ways of avoiding the unfavorable effects and the means for taking advantage of the favorable ones.

Consider if you will this somewhat fanciful prediction. As the world population continues to rise, it will be necessary to provide technological benefits to many underdeveloped nations. It has been suggested that damming the Amazon River would provide an economic resource that could be of considerable value to the entire continent of South America. However, the destruction of the Amazonian forests by flooding behind the dam could have disastrous consequences. Flooding the Amazonian jungle would reduce the amount of carbon dioxide

In the troposphere, CFCs are not destroyed but in the stratosphere they are degraded by ultraviolet light. The resulting free chlorine atoms attack the ozone forming chlorine monoxide and oxygen. The chlorine monoxide combines with free oxygen atoms to form oxygen and a chlorine atom that is then capable of destroying more ozone. For every chlorine atom released, 100,000 molecules of ozone are removed from the atmosphere.

Even if CFC use were to stop immediately, the chemicals would persist in the atmosphere for up to 100 years. Concerned that CFCs were depleting the atmosphere of ozone, the United States banned their use in spray cans in 1978. The decline in ozone, however, has continued. Some believe that this decline is the result of spray can use elsewhere in the world as well as continued use of CFCs for purposes other than as an aerosol. In September 1987, 23 nations signed an agreement that would reduce CFC usage to the 1986 level by mid-1990, and to half this amount by 1999.

Although is is generally agreed that CFCs may be the primary cause of the ozone hole, it is conceded that natural processes in the atmosphere may also play a role.

But why, might you ask, should those of us living on the surface of the Earth be concerned about an ozone hole in the stratosphere? Without ozone to screen out the ultraviolet radiation, there will be increased amounts arriving at the surface of the earth. A rough estimate is that a 5% decrease in ozone produces a 10% increase in ultraviolet radiation. It is estimated that a 1% reduction in ozone levels could cause 10,000 more cases of skin cancer a year in the United States alone. A 5% reduction would produce 20,000 to 60,000 additional skin cancers of which about 1,000 to 3,000 would be fatal.

Increased levels of ultraviolet radiation could also impair the growth of some crop plants, as well as phytoplankton, primary producers at the base of the food web. And,

nonbiological damage to paints, fabrics, and plastics would also likely occur. The exact consequences of the ozone hole could be vast, but presently defy detailed prediction.

The complexity of the homeostatic devices in the ecosystem, about which we have incomplete knowledge, leads us to conclude that we should be cautious in our attempts to modify the balance of nature.

## 26–7 THE FORCES THAT SHAPE A COMMUNITY

### Niche and habitat

When we use the phrase: Each of us must find his own niche, we, in an approximate way, speak as some ecologists do. Ecologists, however, are somewhat more definitive. They describe **niche** (or ecological niche) as a species' total functional role in an ecosystem, that is, its unique position in a food web, or the unique set of resources necessary for a species to survive. Ecological niche is not an organism's habitat; it is not the organism's address. No, an ecological niche is an organism's profession or lifestyle. Looked at this way, a niche is a set of ecological conditions under which a species can effectively exploit the available resources so that it can reproduce and colonize similar environments. Niche includes all the abiotic and biotic factors the species needs to survive and reproduce. Describing an animal species' niche requires that we know what it feeds on, what feeds on it, where it lives, the ranges of environmental features that it can tolerate, and the effect it has on other species.

Niche sets the upper limit to population size; in a species' population there cannot be more individuals than opportunities to practice its niche. And, no two species in the same ecosystem can indefinitely occupy exactly the same ecological niche. A corollary of this is: when different species coexist in the same habitat, they have different

ecological niches. The more similar the niches of two species, the greater will be the competition for the same resources. Thus, when two species try to occupy the same niche, one species must change its "profession" or become extinct.

Knowing the ecological niche of a species should enable us to predict the outcome of adding a new factor or removing a factor from an ecosystem; however, because determining the niche of an organism is complex, we frequently find that our descriptions are incomplete, and consequently, our predictions may not be fulfilled.

### Number and distribution limits

Ecologists usually ask two questions: What are the limiting factors for a population of organisms, and what determines the distribution of a species?

There are two prevailing approaches to answering these ecological questions, and both are valid. One approach, called the concept of limiting factors, suggests that any condition or set of conditions that approaches or exceeds the tolerance of an organism or a group of organisms may serve as a limiting factor. Thus, a species or population of organisms would exist only where it can mount an optimum response. Ecologists use the limiting factor approach to identify critical environmental limits, thereby providing an explanation as to why a species is present or absent. Such ecologists are inclined to measure temperature, humidity, or salinity first. The other approach used by ecologists is based on niche theory. Niche theory contends that organisms are fashioned by natural selection to win resources and reproduce. As a consequence, organisms are equipped to hunt, escape, and withstand competitors. Food and enemies are primary to the existence of a species and physical stresses are secondary. An ecologist who follows niche theory precepts usually measures food availability and competitors first to deter-

FIGURE 26–17 The fit of a logistic equation to data on the population size of *Paramecium aurelia* in a laboratory culture.

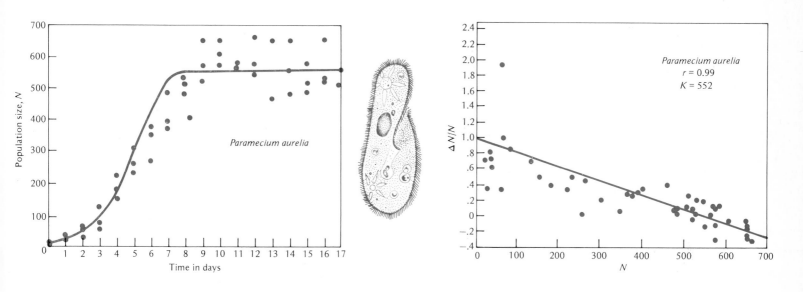

mine their role in species distribution and population size.

Now let us consider some examples that illustrate the checks imposed on the numbers and kinds of species.

In the laboratory, if we place a few individuals of one species of *Paramecium* in a fixed amount of growth medium and then measure the population size over time, we would find that at first the animals would reproduce rapidly, their numbers would increase, and then at a certain time the population would no longer increase in size (Figure 26–17). The curve obtained is called a **sigmoid curve** because of its **S-shape.**

Similar results have been obtained with laboratory cultures of bacteria, yeast, fruit flies, and flour beetles. It is not always possible, however, even in the laboratory, to produce similar sigmoid curves for other animals. For example, mice allowed to feed and reproduce in a finite space do not show a sigmoid growth curve.

One explanation for the sigmoid growth curve is that there is an increasing intensity of competition as animals become more and more crowded. Then, survival rates

drop, death rates rise, and the population levels off when births balance deaths. A mathematical description (called the **logistic equation**) of this phenomenon can be written:

$$R = rN (1 - N/K)$$

$R$ = population growth rate
$r$ = rate of increase
$N$ = number of animals at a particular time
$K$ = number of animals at population equilibrium

$K$ is frequently referred to as the **carrying capacity** of the environment, that is, the maximum number of individuals that can exist under a specified set of conditions.

The value of the mathematical description of sigmoid growth is that it allows one to calculate values for $r$ and $K$ (Figure 26–17), and enables the determination whether a stable population size is present.

Thus far we have examined the growth of one species. What happens with two species? If populations of two species of *Paramecium* are placed in a container, we might expect two possible outcomes: both

species reach a similar maximum population density or the density of one species exceeds the other. Laboratory data confirm that when this experiment is done with two closely related species, one persists whereas the other dies out (Figure 26–18). The principle derived from this experiment is: One species, one niche. This is called the **competitive exclusion principle.**

One implication of these population studies, and similar kinds of laboratory experiments, is that species remain distinct by competition. A second implication is that population size is controlled by competition, a density-dependent factor.

Outside the laboratory, that is, in the field, do density-dependent factors, such as competition or predation, limit population size so that equilibrium is reached? The answer is: Sometimes.

In California, parasitic wasps were introduced to help control red scale, an insect pest of orange trees. One Mediterranean wasp *Aphytis chrysomphali* was (accidentally) introduced in 1900 and became widely distributed. In 1948, another species *A. lignanensis* from China was introduced, and

FIGURE 26–18 (top) Growth of *P. aurelia* and *P. caudatum* populations separately and together. (After Gause, 1934.)

FIGURE 26–19 (bottom) Growth function for reindeer on two similar islands. (From C. J. Krebs: *Ecology*. New York, Harper & Row Publishers, 1972.)

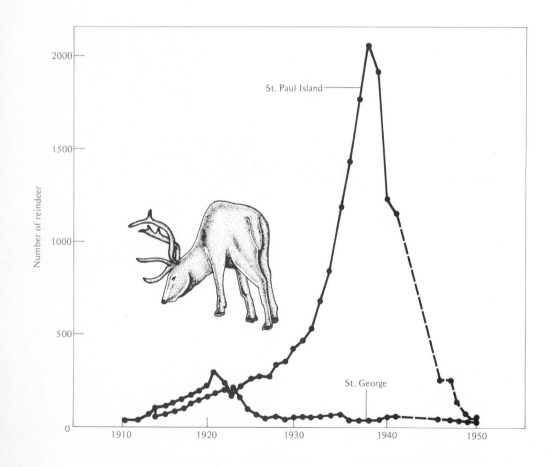

in 10 years it almost completely displaced *A. chrysomphali* from the orchards. In 1956, *A. melinus* was imported from India as a biological control agent, and it displaced *A. lignanensis* from the hotter regions of California, but not the coastal ones. This is an example of competitive exclusion in the field. Because displacement took place without food limitations and without interference from two other parasites that also attack the red scale insect, the mechanism whereby competitive displacement occurred is not clear.

As early as 1891, reindeer were introduced into Alaska to replace the dwindling numbers of caribou, which were the stable economic resource for the Eskimo. In 1911, a dozen reindeer were introduce into two of the Pribiloff islands in the Bering Sea. The islands were completely undisturbed habitats, as at that time there was no hunting and no predators. By 1922, the herd on one island reached a maximum of 222 reindeer, and then declined to a small herd of about 50 animals (Figure 26–19). On the other island, the herd grew larger and by 1938 there were 2,000 animals; then due to overgrazing there was an abrupt crash in the numbers of reindeer so that by 1950 there were only eight animals (Figure 26–19). We do not understand why there were such marked differences between the two islands as they were so similar ecologically, but clearly sigmoid growth did not occur.

Another kind of competition among species can be seen with predators. In 1900 the island of Newfoundland had 40,000 caribou. Twenty-five years later the caribou numbered 200 and were almost extinct. The decline in caribou appeared not to be the result of the natural predator of the caribou, the timber wolf, because it was already extinct in 1911. The explanation is more complex and involves a switching of prey by the predator. In 1864, the snowshoe hare was introduced into Newfoundland. The new introduction resulted in a population explosion, and by 1890 the numbers of hares were so high that trappers could catch 1,000

FIGURE 26–20 Changes in the population of lynx, hare, and caribou in Newfoundland between 1880 and 1980. (After Krebs.)

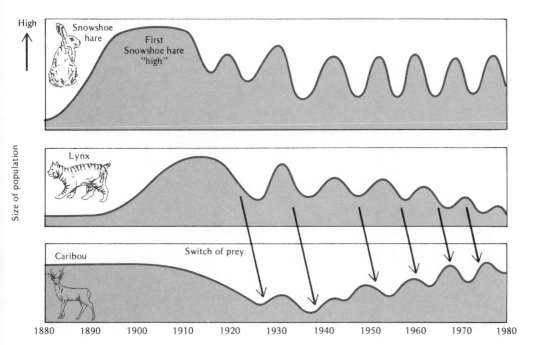

that act on population growth? The answer is: Yes.

In some insect species, population size does not appear to be related to the density of the population. Many populations, such as grasshoppers and thrips, peak in summer and crash later with the arrival of bad weather in the fall and winter. During the winter months, the population exists at equilibrium. Thus, weather conditions, especially temperature and humidity, can and do define population growth as well as affect niche occupancy.

Recognition of this might be of help in predicting whether a new factor when added to a given ecosystem, for example, heated water from a nuclear power plant or a pesticide, will affect size and distribution of a species.

## Resource utilization and community formation

Two species that compete for a resource in short supply can coexist by evolving differences that reduce the competition and make more remote the possibility of extinction. The evolution of competitive abilities that enable organisms to survive under limiting resources is called the species strategy. Among these are foraging, dispersal, and predator avoidance strategies. In addition, there are *r* and *K* strategies. The *r* and *K* designation refers to the two parameters of the sigmoid curve, namely, the rate of increase, *r*, and the saturation density, *K* (see p. 559).

Species that employ the **r-strategy** are opportunists; they have the ability to reproduce rapidly during short favorable seasons, and are able to survive during hostile intervals. Species that use the *r*-strategy usually live in marginal habitats where dispersal and rapid colonization are critical to survival. Such species seldom suffer from interspecific competition and evolve no strong competitive abilities; there is a high chance of death, and consequently a con-

in a single season. The peak in the hare population lasted from 1896 to 1915 (Figure 26–20); after this, there was a rapid decline. The lynx, native to the area, is the chief predator of the hare, and as the hare population increased so did that of the lynx. When the hare population crashed, however, the abundant lynxes sought other prey (Figure 26–20). One alternative was to capture and kill caribou calves. During the years 1911 and 1925, the number of caribou were severely reduced by lynx predation as well as hunting. The decline in the numbers of caribou provoked the lynx to switch to another prey, snowshoe hares.

In 1925, an oscillating cycle of population highs and lows in hares began. The reason for the increase and decline in numbers of hares is that the population increases until limited by food supply; then with a diminished reproduction rate, the population declines. The lynx, as a predator of the hare, shows a similar oscillating cycle with their

increase lagging behind that of the hares. (As the population declines, the lynx reproduce less rapidly and their numbers dwindle; when the hares increase in number, the lynx numbers subsequently rise.) At the highs in the snowshoe hare cycle, the lynx prey on them, and the caribou are spared predation. As a consequence, the caribou herd increased to about 6,000 in 1961.

The predator–prey relationship involving the hare–lynx–caribou tells us that there is considerable difficulty in predicting the effect of introducing a new species into an ecosystem. Who could have imagined that by introducing snowshoe hares in 1864 could result in a decline in caribou? The message is clear: Humans must tread softly when interfering with fragile ecosystems.

The previous examples have illustrated some density-dependent factors that could limit population size and also account for a species niche. Now we might ask the question: Are there density-independent factors siderable amount of energy is devoted to producing large numbers of offspring that can be scattered widely. Weeds and insects are examples of *r*-strategists.

Terrestrial vertebrates, and other species that live at the equilibrium level, are **K-strategists.** These species show a strong interspecific and intraspecific competition, and there is a tendency for more efficient resource utilization. Adaptations for persistence, for life in a crowded habitat, and for having few, large, and well-cared for offspring are often characteristic of *K*-strategists. Most organisms are neither *r* nor *K*, but are a compromise between these two extremes.

Each species niche is filled by individuals that maintain themselves by employing a strategy for surviving and breeding. It is the packing together of niches that results in a community.

## Succession

Communities change with time. If you have ever started a small vegetable garden and then left it unattended for weeks or months, you have been witness to the changes in a mini-ecosystem that occur with the passage of time: crops of vegetables are succeeded by crop after crop of weeds. In the same way, plant and animal populations undergo a series of progressive changes. The sequence of alterations through which an ecosystem passes as time progresses is called **ecological succession.** For any particular environment these changes follow a rather predictable pattern, with particular communities of organisms paving the way for others that will come, until a final stage, or **climax,** is reached. A climax is final or unchanging only in a relative sense, because through the passage of time even a climax ecosystem undergoes changes, with alterations in temperature, altitude, precipitation, sunlight, and so on.

One of the clearest examples of ecological succession is seen at Glacier Bay in Alaska. In the past 200 years, there has been a steady retreat of the glaciers. When a glacier retreats, it leaves a moraine consisting of silt, sand, small rocks, and large boulders. The pattern of succession on this newly exposed land is: First, there appear mosses, fireweed, willows, and cottonwood. Then the area is invaded by alder, and over a 50-year period a dense thicket of bushes up to 9 meters high is produced.

After another 120 years, the alders are invaded by spruce, which then grow into a dense conifer forest. Hemlock invade the

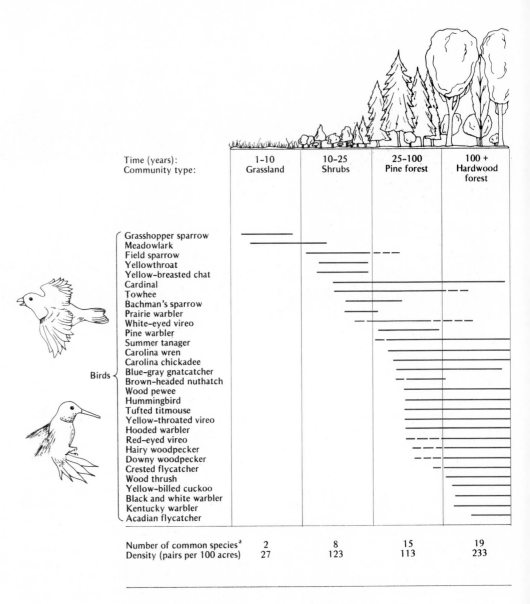

FIGURE 26–21 Succession in an abandoned farmland in Georgia. (Modified from E. P. Odum, *Fundamentals of Ecology,* 2nd edn., Philadelphia, Saunders, 1959.

[a]A common species is arbitrarily designated as one with a density of 5 pairs per 100 acres or greater in one or more of the four community types.

FIGURE 26–22 Succession in a shallow lake with conversion into a dry marsh.

**563**

**HUMANS AND THE ENVIRONMENT**

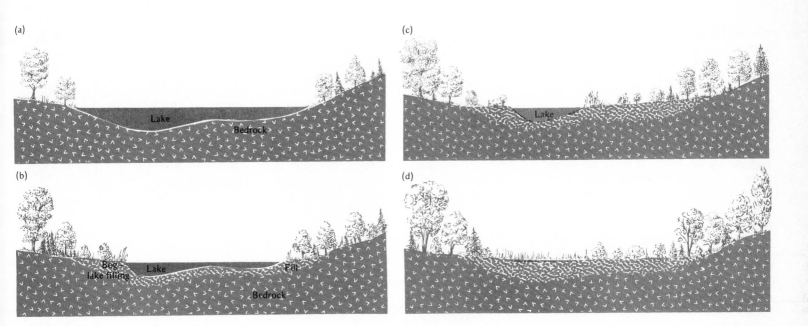

(a)

(b)

(c)

(d)

spruce, and after another 80 years, the situation stabilizes with a climax spruce–hemlock forest. Such a forest remains only in regions where there is good drainage. In areas of poor drainage, the forest floor is invaded by mosses that retain large amounts of water and acidify the soil. The water-logged soil is too deficient in oxygen for root growth, the trees die out, and a bog develops. Thus, in poorly drained areas, the climax vegetation is mosses, whereas in the well-drained areas it is hemlock–spruce.

Closer to home we can follow ecological succession in an abandoned farmland that changes into a forest, or a shallow lake that becomes a marsh and then a forest (Figures 26–21 and 26–22).

The characteristics of succession are: (1) the change in species composition from the early, or pioneering, community to the climax community usually involves increasing plant and animal diversity; (2) biomass increases with time; (3) food chains become more elaborate with succeeding stages; and (4) the climax community is relatively stable under prevailing climatic conditions and tends to be dominated by longer-lived plants.

The nature of the climax community in a given area is determined largely by its climate; the plants and animals of which it is composed share common environmental problems.

Why does succession occur? Could a climax community not be established immediately if soil, climate, rainfall, and seeds of the right plants were present? Probably not. Let us see why. As we follow succession in communities in a given location, we observe that it takes place in a regular and predictable fashion. The pioneering invaders are the grasses that exploit habitats newly opened up by catastrophe—fire, flood, and manmade clearings. Grasses grow fast on bare ground when they receive adequate sunlight and rainfall and relatively small amounts of nutrients. Shrubs and tree seedlings, the next group of immigrants into the area, develop more slowly and cannot at first compete with grasses. However, most grasses are annuals and must reseed themselves and start all over again each year; thus, they come to be at a competitive disadvantage with the perennials—shrubs and young trees—and in time the pioneering grasses give way to these intermediate species. Shrubs build sizable above-ground (stems and branches) and underground (roots and stems) storage structures; their roots use soil nutrients and water more efficiently than grasses, and their branches begin to exclude sunlight from the grasses beneath them. Perennial shrubs do not die back each year, and the shrub-held habitat slowly becomes less suitable for the yearly invasion of grass seeds. Thus the shrubs begin to take over. Shrubs provide a conducive environment both for themselves and for young tree seedlings—shade and a favorably altered soil. The final invaders are equilibrium species[4] (usually, though not exclusively, trees), which produce massive structures and storage organs; because such organisms have adequate reserves of en-

---

[4] Equilibrium species have relatively stable population sizes and are adapted to living in more or less predictable environments.

ergy, they can often withstand long stretches of environmental bad times. Trees provide leaf litter, and this rich source of organic material, when acted upon by decomposers, yields humus. Humus alters the soil itself, promoting water retention and aeration; consequently nutrient cycling becomes more efficient. The increasing shade provided by the canopy of trees tends to exclude the grasses, and these disappear. Shade-loving plants (ground cover or underbrush) move in. The flowers and fruits of these and of the trees act as sources of nourishment for a variety of animals—species diversity increases.

The significant features of succession now become clearer. Pioneering species or *r*-strategists put most of their energy budget into seed production—indeed, that is how they are dispersed from one habitat to another (Figure 26–23). Intermediate species have restricted capacities for dispersal, but they tend to occupy a habitat longer and more tenaciously by building woody structures that can resist environmental changes and by storing nutrients underground. Equilibrium species, the *K*-strategists, build woody roots, trunks, and branches and are adapted to living in a predictable environment; in addition they themselves modify environmental fluctuations by acting as windbreaks, resisting flooding, and retarding soil erosion. Because the climax community is dominated by equilibrium species that have massive woody structures, it has an increased biomass. In time, the opportunistic pioneers must be displaced by the more stable equilibrium species; in effect each community in the successional continuum sows the seeds of its own demise (Figure 26–23).

Is there a grand design to succession so that communities must inexorably proceed to the climax—that "single perfect community" for a given geographical area? No. Succession occurs because of the forces of natural selection:

In the . . . Darwinian view of ecology there is no organizing deterministic principle behind succes-

FIGURE 26–23 Model of succession as a function of rate of invasion. Opportunist species invade early and rapidly (left) but their extinction by competition is also early and rapid (right). The final number of species at climax will depend on the rate of continued invasion (which may proceed for thousands of years) and the rate of local extinction, which eventually should be very slow.

sion. . . . Complex ecosystems are the product of crowding many species into restricted spaces and forcing them to live together and to adapt to each other's presence.[5]

Communities characterized by distinctiveness in important climax species are called **biomes.** There are several ways of classifying biomes but most ecologists agree on eight major terrestrial types: tundra, coniferous forest (taiga), temperate (deciduous and rain) forest, tropical rain forest, tropical savannah, temperate grassland, desert, and chaparral (Figure 26–24).

## 26–8 AGRICULTURE AND UNBALANCED ECOSYSTEMS

The most fundamental principle of ecology is that everything is connected to everything else. In the words of the English poet Francis Thompson: ". . . thou canst not stir a flower, without troubling of a star." All of us resident on Spaceship Earth depend on chemical recycling, and any break in the cycle or alteration in the rate of cycling by removal of too much or too little chemical matter may spell ecological disaster. Agriculture may be the agent to disturb the natural cycling processes.

[5] P. COLINVAUX, *Introduction to Ecology,* New York, Wiley, 1973.

Agriculture is the source of unprecedented supplies of human food and has contributed significantly to our population growth, urbanization, and industrialization. That's the good news; now for the bad. Agriculture by its very nature is an artificial and unbalanced ecosystem. Farmers plant opportunistic pioneering plants because these grow quickly on bare soil and yield edible reproductive structures such as cereal grains and storage stems (sugar beets and potatoes) instead of inedible woody branches and roots. By agricultural practices the trend of succession is reversed and ecological changes are artificially kept in check. For example, when forests become crop fields, equilibrium species are displaced and often become locally extinct; massive inputs of nutrients via fertilizers are required because mineral cycling is low. Crop fields are maintained perennially "young" by the constant attention of human labor. It is necessary to prevent insect pests, fungal parasites, and drought from destroying the precious harvest; to buffer against weather extremes; and to restrict the spread of disease agents or predators. Ecological simplicity and uniformity replace complexity and diversity. Consequently, any society dependent on a single crop is threatened more by drought or plague than another society working on a diversified ecosystem.

FIGURE 26–24 The biomes of North America. The large major types of ecosystems are called biomes. Each has a distinct group of plants and animals.

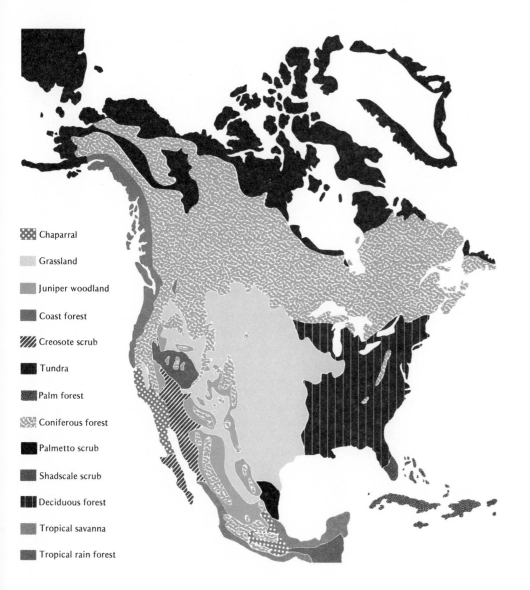

- ▨ Chaparral
- ▢ Grassland
- ▨ Juniper woodland
- ▨ Coast forest
- ▨ Creosote scrub
- ▨ Tundra
- ▨ Palm forest
- ▨ Coniferous forest
- ▨ Palmetto scrub
- ▨ Shadscale scrub
- ▨ Deciduous forest
- ▨ Tropical savanna
- ▨ Tropical rain forest

As the agricultural revolution increased food production, the population grew and people moved from the farms to the cities. The growing demand for food by the ever-increasing population created a drain on the ecosystem; with a greater drain and a slower return, the ecosystem came to be disrupted. Once-fertile lands became barren. The farmer's choice was clear: refertilize or move on to another region where the soil fertility is high. In some cases, by proper management, the soil has been enriched; but in other cases it has been destroyed.

In 1924 a cloud of dust appeared over New York City and blew into the Atlantic Ocean. It was an ecologically important dust cloud, since it was a significant part of the once-rich Oklahoma topsoil. What caused this? In 1889 Oklahoma was opened to homesteaders. The population rose from 60,000 to 390,000 in a single year, and the settlers lived by working the land. The flat, rockless expanses of rich topsoil easily yielded to the plow, and at first the harvests were good. To make way for crops and cattle, the settlers killed off the natural herbivore, the bison, and permitted domestic cattle to overgraze, thus preventing the grasslands from reseeding themselves. The land soon became susceptible to erosion by heavy rains, and as rainwater ran off instead of percolating downward, the water table came to be lower and lower. Depletion of water meant death for perennial plants and the prairie grasses. Soil destruction was further accelerated as the hooves of the vast numbers of cattle compacted the soil and prevented the natural seepage of air and water through the soil. The digging and turning over of the Oklahoma prairie soil rendered it vulnerable to the weather, since there were no longer prairie grasses capable of holding the soil in place during periods of drought. The common agricultural practice of pulling weeds between the rows of crops left the soil susceptible to erosion when heavy rains came. The practice of dust mulching—chopping the top few inches of soil into a fine dust—to bring water to the surface by capillary action during short droughts tended to decrease the concentration of organic matter in the soil (it is brought to the surface and quickly oxidized). Gradually the soil lost its fertility. In less than 35 years the soil was severely depleted of its nutrients, refertilization was incomplete, and the winds and water eroded away the once-rich topsoil. Finally, in 1924 a severe drought struck, the deficient and unprotected soil simply blew away in the winds that swept across the landscape. Rich prairie became a dustbowl because of agricultural mismanagement. Ironically, the prairies that were not managed easily survived the prolonged drought and remain fertile to this day. Some say it will take several thousand years to restore the dustbowl to its full fertility—fertility lost in a single generation by poor agricultural planning.

The lesson of the Oklahoma dust bowl is clear: if technology is to save us from agricultural disruptions, it must recognize that in ecology there is no such thing as independence.

## SUMMARY

**1.** Ecology is the field of biology that concerns itself with studies of populations, communities, and ecosystems as they interact in the biosphere.

**2.** Energy is not recycled through the ecosystem; its flow is unidirectional, from producers (autotrophs) to herbivores, carnivores, and omnivores (heterotrophs).

**3.** According to the Second Law of Thermodynamics, energy conversion is always less than 100% efficient; therefore a continuous supply of energy is needed to maintain an ecosystem.

**4.** The transfer of food energy between the plants and animals of successive feeding stages is called a food chain or food web. Food webs usually involve plants, herbivores, carnivores, and decay organisms that recycle the matter in a food chain or web.

**5.** Because of the Second Law of Thermodynamics, ecosystems can be arranged in pyramids representing biomass and energy. At the base are the producers (plants), followed in ascending levels by herbivores (primary consumers) and carnivores (secondary consumers). Omnivores may enter the pyramid at a number of levels.

**6.** The biomass (or energy) at each successive feeding or trophic level of an energy pyramid is determined by the biomass (or energy) available at the level on which it rests. Approximately 10 to 20% of the energy at one level is available to the next level.

**7.** Autotrophs are at the base of all food chains. By shortening the food chain, the number of energy conversions is reduced and available food energy is increased.

**8.** When materials that are not used or eliminated are passed from one food level to the next, they may be concentrated two or more times over in the tissues of the consumer. The top feeders of a food chain therefore can be the most endangered by environmental pollutants. Examples of such cumulative and damaging substances are mercury, DDT (and other chlorinated hydrocarbons), and radioactive elements.

**9.** Matter, including substances that contain carbon, nitrogen, and phosphorus, is recycled through ecosystems by decay organisms, chiefly bacteria and fungi. Thus, producers, consumers, and decay organisms continuously recycle the matter of the biosphere.

**10.** Ecosystem homeostasis depends on factors such as the recycling of matter and predator-prey relations. Upsetting the homeostatic balance can destroy an ecosystem.

**11.** Ecological succession is the sequence of alterations through which an ecosystem passes with time, from an early pioneering community until a relatively stable climax community, or biome, is reached. During succession, the forces of natural selection lead to increasing organism diversity and biomass and food-chain complexity.

**12.** Biomes are climax communities whose nature is largely determined by climate.

**13.** Agricultural practices produce unnatural and unbalanced ecosystems. Although it is the source of unprecedented food supplies, agriculture reverses normal succession: soil must be artifically enriched to maintain a perpetually "young" community.

## KEY WORDS

populations
community
ecosystem
biosphere
ecology
producers
autotrophs
heterotrophs
herbivores or primary consumers
carnivores or secondary consumers
food chain
food web
omnivores
biomass
fallout
isotopes
decomposers or decay organisms

carbon cycle
nitrogen cycle
nitrogen fixation
nitrogen fixers
denitrifying bacteria
phosphorus cycle
water cycle
homeostasis
greenhouse effect
ecological succession
climax
biome
ozone hole
niche
sigmoid curve
logistic equation
carrying capacity
competitive exclusion principle
*r* and *K* strategists

## TOPICS FOR REVIEW AND DISCUSSION

1. Discuss the meaning of the term "ecology."
2. Why does succession take place in an ecosystem?
3. Discuss the effects of DDT on an ecosystem.
4. How do agricultural practices serve to disrupt ecosystems?
5. Discuss the statement, Energy does not cycle in the biosphere.
6. What are food chains and food webs?
7. How is matter recycled in the biosphere?
8. What are some of the dangers of atomic wastes?
9. What role do decomposers play in the recycling of matter in the biosphere?
10. What is the relationship of the Second Law of Thermodynamics to ecological pyramids?
11. Why is a pound of meat more expensive than an equivalent weight of carbohydrates?
12. Why is it essential to direct urban growth away from prime land?
13. Discuss the mechanisms by which chemicals accumulate in the environment.
14. Discuss homeostasis in the ecosystem.

"Listen to this. A writer way back in 1966 predicted that our generation would have one person to every square foot."

# 27

# Aboard Spaceship Earth

## 27–1 THE INHABITANTS OF SPACESHIP EARTH AND HOW THEY GREW

In April 1970, the world watched in helpless awe as the three astronauts aboard the Apollo 13 spacecraft radioed back to the earth that several systems were malfunctioning and there was little chance they could return to earth. As the people on earth followed the perilous journey of Apollo 13 and its occupants on radio, on TV, and in the press, another dangerous situation received little or no publicity. During the same 4 days that Apollo 13 was in space, aboard the earth 116,000 human beings died of starvation or malnutrition, and half of these were children under 5 years old. Luckily, a corrective solution was found for Apollo 13, and the astronauts did return safely home. No universally acceptable solution has yet been found to save the diseased and dying occupants of Spaceship Earth.

The "spacecraft" we now inhabit, one of finite size and resources, seems to be coming apart at its seams. Material wealth increases, and yet the environment grows poorer; leisure time is more abundant, but there is less space and beauty to enjoy; technological improvements create environmental hazards. Air and water in many places exhibit signs of complete overload, and our overcrowded cities impose intolerable psychological stress. What has gone wrong? The human population is on the increase. Every minute on board our fragile craft more than 250 babies are born. The 85 million new passengers that arrive on earth each year must be fed, clothed, and housed. Each inhabitant makes demands on the finite resources available on the earth, and in turn each contributes to global pollution. There are more hungry and malnourished people on earth today than there were human inhabitants in 1850. Poverty, starvation, destruction, depletion of natural resources, and pollution all ride the coattails of unchecked population growth. Simply stated: our well-being is threatened because there are too many of us.

### Around the bend

Examination of the growth curve describing the increase in human population during the millennia shows that not only has the total population increased markedly over the past 500,000 years, but the rate of increase has also steadily risen (Figure 27–1). The simplest way of appreciating the rate of increase is to look at the **doubling time,** that is, the time it takes for the population to double its size. When the human population went from 5 million in 8000 B.C. to 100 million in A.D. 1, the population increased itself 20-fold; to achieve this required about four doublings: $5 \longrightarrow 10 \longrightarrow 20 \longrightarrow 40 \longrightarrow 80$. This took place over a period of 8,000 years, so that the calculated doubling time was 2,000 years (8,000/4). From A.D. 1 to A.D. 1650 the population swelled from 100 million to 500 million, a fivefold increase requiring 2.5 doublings, or a doubling time of about 600 years (1,600/2.5). The next doubling—from 500 million to 1,000 million—took only 200 years (1650 to 1850), and the human population doubled again in 80 years (1850 to 1930). By 1975, only 45 years from our last calculation, the world population doubled again. At the present rate of increase, by 2025, a time some of us may live to see (and perhaps regret), the world population will be about 8 billion!

Why does the growth rate (or doubling time) change? A population of humans, or any other organism for that matter, tends to increase because the birth rate and the death rate do not keep pace—additions (births) are greater than subtractions (deaths). Reproduction is clearly a positive feedback system, and an unchecked population increases faster and faster, approaching infinity. To understand the nature of this growth phenomenon, let us compare **geometric** (also called **exponential**) and **arithmetic growth.** In

"THEIR BREEDING RATE IS INCREDIBLE."

569

FIGURE 27–1 (top) Growth of the human population for the last 500,000 years. If the Old Stone Age were in scale, it would reach 18 ft to the left. (After *Population Bulletin;* 18, 1.)

FIGURE 27–2 (bottom) A comparison between arithmetic and exponential growth.

arithmetic or linear growth, each increase is constant in amount. Thus, if we begin our calculation with $x$ individuals and the incremental amount is given as $a$ (where $a$ is greater than 1), then in the $n$th generation, there will be $x + na$ individuals. If a population consists of two individuals ($x$) and this is increased by 2 in each succeeding generation ($a$), we would have $2 + 2n$ after $n$ generations (Figure 27–2). In exponential growth, with $x$ individuals at the start, and the increment set at $a$, then there would be $ax$ individuals in the first generation, and $a(ax)$ or $a^2x$ in the second, and $a^nx$ in the $n$th generation. Starting with a population of 2, and with $a$ equal to 2 in each succeeding generation, the population doubles.

Exponential growth is seen in a rapidly dividing population of mitotic organisms, and if plotted on a graph forms a J-shaped curve. Exponential growth is deceptive as initial increases are slow, but then as the bend in the J-shaped curve is rounded, there is a steep, almost vertical, rise.

Recognition of the nature of population growth and its application to humans is not new. In 1755 Benjamin Franklin wrote:

There is, in short, no bound to the prolific nature of plants and animals. . . . Thus, there are supposed to be now upwards of one million English souls in North America (though it is thought scarcely 80,000 had been brought over sea) and yet there is not one the fewer in Britain, but rather more . . .

### The population bomb

**Growth rates.** Two people meet on a corner:

*First person:* We are all indebted to the male alligator for our very lives.
*Second person:* The male alligator? Why?
*First person:* During a single year the female alligator lays over a hundred eggs, but the male alligator eats 98 of these, allowing only a few to survive. So you see, if it were not for the male alligator, we would be up to here (pointing to his nose) in alligators!

This old joke has real meaning in human

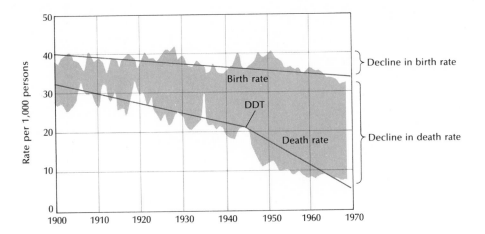

and in the less developed countries it would be about 2.7. The total fertility rate in the United States between 1917 and the year 2000 shows distinct oscillations. Peak baby booms took place after World War I and World War II. Since 1962 the fertility has been dropping, and today it is considerably below the replacement level.

Thus, although it would appear that ZPG has been arrived at in the United States, this is, in fact, not true. The population of the United States and 12 other nations (Great Britain, Norway, Belgium, Switzerland, Italy, Austria, Sweden, East Germany, West Germany, Denmark, Luxembourg, and Hungary) who are close to replacement in fertility rates would see a rise in population. In the United States, it will probably take 50 years to reach ZPG were the present fertility rate maintained. At that point, the U.S. population will exceed 300 million.

It is obvious that a rational approach toward zero population growth (ZPG) requires a lowering of the birth rate and long-range planning for at least 50 years. Do we have that much time? As the astronauts on Apollo 13 were stranded in space, we are stranded on our planet—we do not have the option of leaving Spaceship Earth and beginning anew. All we can do at this point on the bend in the exponential growth curve is try to diminish the steepness of the upward climb.

Perhaps more disturbing, and not revealed by world growth rate figures, is the country-by-country variation in growth rate. At present the growth rate in the United States is 0.7%, and at this rate our population will double in 102 years (Table 27–1). Africa and Latin America have current growth rates of 2.8 and 2.2%, respectively, and their population will double in 25 to 30 years; Asia currently has a rate of 2.1% with a doubling time of 32 years. Within each of these continents the growth rate and per capita income also varies (Table 27–2). What the political, social, and economic results of such diverging patterns in growth and affluence will be is highly speculative; one

terms. During the last 60 years, and especially since the end of World War II, the death rate has been declining because of improved sanitation and medical care (Figure 27–3). Consider the case of Sri Lanka: from 1871 to about 1946 the annual growth rate[1] was 1.7%, but in 1946 DDT was introduced to eliminate the malaria-carrying mosquitoes; the birth rate remained relatively constant, but the death rate declined. Consider the differences in birth and death rates in Sweden, the United States, and Mexico (Figure 27–4). In Sweden and the United States the death rate has declined gradually, much more so than in Mexico. Although during the same time the birth rate in Sweden and the United States also

declined, that in Mexico remained relatively stable. As a consequence, the population of Sweden and the United States has remained relatively stable, whereas that of Mexico increased.

Since 1650 the human population has not had a negative growth rate. Between 1650 and 1750 the world growth rate was 0.3% per year, between 1750 and 1850 it was 0.5%, and between 1850 and 1950 it was 0.8%. By the 1980s the growth rate was close to 1.8%.

To understand this, and to see how demographers project population size, it is necessary to calculate the total fertility rate. The **total fertility rate** is the average of live births born to each woman were she to live through her childbearing years, that is from 15 to 44 years of age. In 1987, the world total fertility rate was 3.6 children per woman, in the less developed countries it was 4.2, and in the more developed countries it was 2.0.

Simple logic would suggest that to maintain a stable population, that is **zero population growth** (ZPG), would require two live births to replace two parents. However, considering mortality of children and the differing sex ratios, replacement in a developed country is 2.1 children per woman,

[1] To calculate the growth rate of a population, we simply subtract the death rate from the birth rate (disregarding immigration and emigration): thus, population growth equals birth rate minus death rate. Let us assume that in 1 year the birth rate for the world was 34 per 1,000 persons in the population, and the death rate was 14 per 1,000. The population growth is therefore 20, and the yearly rate of growth is 2% (20/1,000). Using prepared tables it is possible to calculate the doubling time of a population for a given growth rate (Table 27-1). For example, if the growth rate is 2% per year, the population (irrespective of its original size) will double itself in 35 years.

possibility is that the have-nots will be increasingly agitated to partake of the holdings of the haves.

Health and nutrition must, of necessity, decline in those countries that do not roll back their population growth rate or increase the capacity of their environments to support their population. If malnutrition, starvation, and disease exist, the death rate will exceed the birth rate, the growth rate will become negative, and the population will tend to decline or level off. Pestilence, war, and famine, three of the Four Horsemen of the Apocalypse, provide natural checks on the growth of a population. Decline in the human population from such causes is not unknown. Unfortunately, such catastrophes do not occur by human design, and they strike unexpectedly in supposedly safe areas. In 1348–1350 the Plague probably killed about 25% of the European population. In this century, famine has contributed to between 5 and 10 million deaths in Russia (1918–1922, 1932–1934), 4 million deaths in China (1920–1921), and 2 to 4 million deaths in Bengal (1943).

Natural measures must ultimately check unbridled population growth. However, this is not a very pleasant way to achieve stability. The question presently facing us is whether we can forestall these catastrophes by instituting voluntary measures today that will stem the tide of population growth. Can we do it in time?

**Population structure** The size of a population and whether it will grow or decline depend on the difference between the birth and death rates, which in turn depend on the age and sex ratios of that population. In particular, the number of women of

FIGURE 27–4 Historic trends in birth and death rates in: Sweden (a) and the United States (c), developed countries and Mexico (b), a developing country. Note that the high population growth in Mexico is due to the fact that death rates have declined faster than birth rates. Rapid oscillations in the curves have been caused by wars, epidemics, and periodic "baby booms."

**TABLE 27–1 Doubling times for various rates of annual increase**

| Percentage rate of increase | Doubling time (yr) |
| --- | --- |
| 0.6 | 116 |
| 0.8 | 84 |
| 1.0 | 70 |
| 1.5 | 47 |
| 2.0 | 35 |
| 2.5 | 28 |
| 2.8 | 25 |
| 3.0 | 23 |
| 3.5 | 20 |
| 4.0 | 18 |

**TABLE 27–2 Population growth rate, doubling time, per capita income, and population size for selected countries of the world**

| | Per capita GNP ($) (1985) | Annual growth rate | Number of years to double population | 1987 population (millions) | 2020 population estimate (millions) |
| --- | --- | --- | --- | --- | --- |
| Mexico | 2080 | 2.5 | 28 | 81.9 | 137.8 |
| Honduras | 730 | 3.1 | 22 | 4.7 | 12.0 |
| El Salvador | 710 | 2.6 | 27 | 5.3 | 10.3 |
| Ecuador | 1160 | 2.8 | 25 | 10.0 | 19.7 |
| Algeria | 2530 | 3.2 | 22 | 23.5 | 49.4 |
| Morocco | 610 | 2.5 | 27 | 24.4 | 48.5 |
| Iraq | — | 3.3 | 21 | 17.0 | 43.8 |
| Guatamala | 1240 | 3.2 | 22 | 8.4 | 19.7 |
| Peru | 960 | 2.5 | 28 | 20.7 | 28.0 |
| Pakistan | 380 | 2.9 | 24 | 104.6 | 242 |
| Iran | — | 3.2 | 21 | 50.4 | 130.6 |
| Liberia | 470 | 3.2 | 21 | 2.4 | 6.7 |
| Brazil | 1650 | 2.1 | 33 | 141.5 | 233.8 |
| Malaysia | 2050 | 2.5 | 28 | 16 | 26.3 |
| Bolivia | 470 | 2.6 | 27 | 6.5 | 13.2 |
| Ethiopia | 110 | 2.3 | 30 | 46 | 111.2 |
| Tanzania | 270 | 3.5 | 20 | 23.5 | 68.6 |
| Burma | 190 | 2.1 | 33 | 38.8 | 67.5 |
| Thailand | 830 | 2.1 | 33 | 53.6 | 81.6 |
| India | 250 | 2.1 | 33 | 800 | 1310 |
| Haiti | 350 | 2.3 | 30 | 6.2 | 10.1 |
| World | 2880 | 1.7 | 40 | 5,026 | 7,992 |
| Puerto Rico | 4850 | 1.3 | 54 | 3.3 | 4.1 |
| China, People's Rep. | 310 | 1.3 | 53 | 1062 | 1361 |
| Chile | 1440 | 1.6 | 44 | 12.4 | 14.8 |
| Argentina | 2130 | 1.6 | 43 | 31.5 | 37.2 |
| Japan | 11330 | 0.6 | 124 | 122.2 | 122.9 |
| Spain | 4360 | 0.5 | 147 | 39.8 | 41 |
| Australia | 10840 | 0.8 | 86 | 16.2 | 20 |
| U.S.S.R. | 7400 | 0.9 | 79 | 284 | 355 |
| Canada | 13670 | 0.8 | 91 | 25.9 | 29.3 |
| United States | 16400 | 0.7 | 102 | 243.8 | 268.4 |
| France | 9550 | 0.4 | 178 | 55.6 | 58.4 |
| Denmark | 11240 | −0.1 | — | 5.1 | 4.7 |
| Sweden | 11890 | 0.1 | 636 | 8.4 | 8.0 |
| United Kingdom | 8390 | 0.2 | 462 | 56.8 | 56.5 |
| West Germany | 10940 | −0.2 | — | 61.1 | 50.5 |

From *Population Reference Bureau 1987 World Population Data Sheet*. Washington, D.C., Population Reference Bureau, 1987.

childbearing age in a population is crucial in evaluating its growth rate. Our present world population is young; the young of reproductive age constitute the gunpowder of the population explosion. These young people are already on board Spaceship Earth, and when such a combustible fuel is ignited it can only have disastrous consequences. Compare the age structure of the United States with that of Sweden and Mexico (Figure 27–5). Since the graphs show ages on a percentage basis, the three countries can be directly compared even though the total population sizes differ. It is obvious that Mexico had more young people than the United States and Sweden; this is the condition found in countries showing rapid population growth.

What does the preadolescent bulge in the population of Mexico mean? First, birth rates are high and infant mortality is low. Second, a society so constituted is burdened with a relatively large number of nonproductive individuals. Although in these societies large families are considered an economic advantage—children work on the land and provide security for the parents in their old age—this is a myth. Children in vast numbers put an extreme burden on the educational system, they lead to shortages of teachers and teaching time, and in general, they tend to leave school early. In the economy of such a country, children

surviving into adulthood strain the funds available for medical care and housing. It is the young who are punished for parental sexual indulgence and the desire for economic security. A preadolescent population bulge not only strains the present economy but has a continuing negative effect. As the

children of the bulge reach reproductive age, an astronomical rise in population size will occur if the birth rate remains the same, and this, in turn, will once more inflate the preadolescent group. Thus, the population bulge tends to be self-perpetuating.

Although we have observed that death

FIGURE 27–5 Population age structure diagrams for countries with rapid (Mexico), slow (United States), and zero (Sweden) population growth rates. Dark portions represent prereproductive periods (0 to 14), shaded portions represent reproductive years (15 to 44), and clear portions are postproductive years (45 to 85 +). (Source: Population Reference Bureau.)

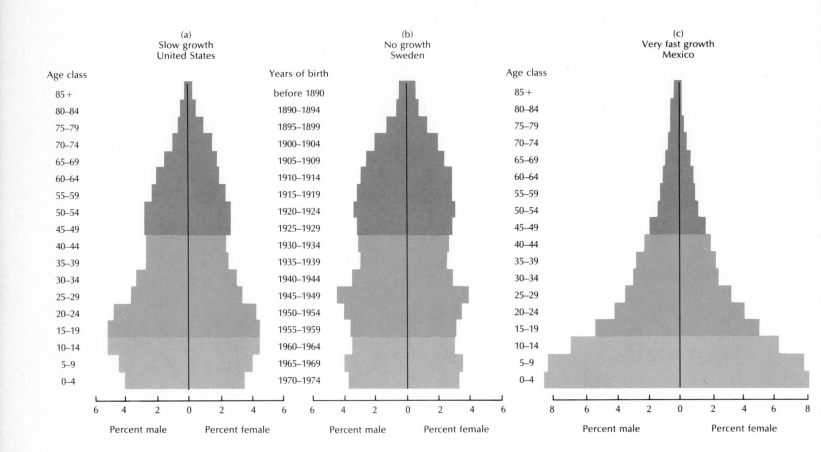

rates may have a marked effect on the growth of a population, it must be recognized that the age at which death occurs is a critical factor. If the victims are in the postreproductive period, the future growth of the population will not be changed at all. In many less developed countries the death rate is high for infants and those of postreproductive age. In these same societies the average age of marriage is very young and there is a tendency to have a great many children during the reproductive period (perhaps to compensate for the high degree of infant mortality), so that the population continues to soar.

Prognostication of population size is a complicated affair. Predicting population changes must take into account the proportion of women of reproductive age, the size of the reproductive group, and fertility (likelihood of producing a child) patterns. These, of course, are influenced by biological, sociological, religious, and political attitudes, many of which cannot be adequately accounted for in statistical evaluations of a population. Social factors and religious and political attitudes may encourage or discourage births; so may the changing role of women in society and the changing attitude toward the child as a supporter of aged parents. Immigration or emigration may affect population structure. War and military service also modify the reproductive potential of a nation, but since these are rather unusual situations, they tend to confound the predictions. To illustrate this, consider the distribution of the female population in Sweden in 1910, 1930, and 1960 (Figure 27–6). This shift from a rapidly expanding population to a relatively stabilized population was influenced by the social and economic effects of World War I and World War II. No study of the characteristics of human populations with regard to size, density, death rate, birth rate, migration, sex ratio, and so on could forecast such a dramatic shift. Predicting where the human population will be in the next few years requires knowledge from many fields and involves great uncertainty.

In a developed country, such as the United States, the number of dependent young is lower than in a less developed country, the work force is proportionately larger, and economic productvity is often greater (Figure 27–5). One cannot completely understand the economics and politics of the

FIGURE 27–6 (top) Population age distribution of females in Sweden in 1910, 1930, and 1960.

FIGURE 27–7 (bottom) Population structure of the United States, 1960 (a), 1975 (b), and 1990 (c).

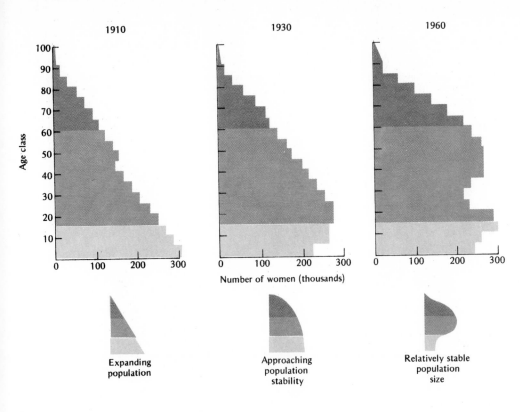

Number of women (thousands)

Expanding population

Approaching population stability

Relatively stable population size

United States today without fully appreciating the impact of reproductive bursts, so-called baby booms. Consider the age structure of the United States in 1960, 1975, and 1990 (Figure 27–7). The baby boom of 1955 to 1965 causes a bulge that moves through the prime reproductive ages of 20 to 30 years between 1980 and 1990. As these baby boomers pass through succeeding age groups, there is need for schools, teachers, housing, employment, medical services, and eventually social welfare programs. In the 1990s the baby boomers will be middle aged, and would represent a significant part of the workforce. And, assuming no increase in death rate, the percentage of people over 64 in the year 2000 will be 13%, and by 2025 there will be 60 million elderly and retired persons. The burden of supporting those of the baby boom will fall on the smaller number of babies born after 1965 who will

(a)

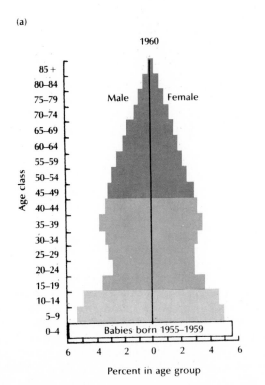

Percent in age group

(b)

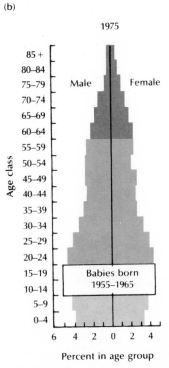

Percent in age group

(c)

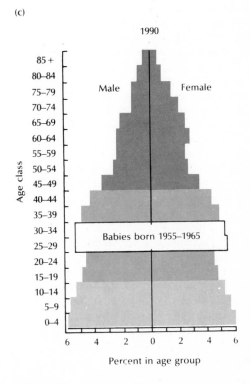

Percent in age group

FIGURE 27–8 (top) Birth rate in the United States, 1910–1975. (After Population Reference Bureau, 1975.)

FIGURE 27–9 (bottom) Total fertility rate for the United States between 1917 and 1984 and projected rate (dashed line) to 2000. The shaded area shows the peak years of the baby boom. (Source: Population Reference Bureau, 1982. *U.S. Population: Where We Are; Where We're Going,* and 1982 U.S. Bureau of Census medium population projections)

make up the workforce. Will such an increase in the numbers of retired persons strain the social welfare system? How will taxes and the federal budget be affected? What will the effect be on jobs, education, availability of labor, immigration, national defense, immigration laws, and political alliances? These are challenging questions, the answers for some of which can be provided by careful planning based on projected age distributions.

In the United States and other more developed countries, infant mortality is low and so is the death rate of the elderly. As noted earlier despite the fact that the birth rate and the fertility rate in the United States has been dropping to the level necessary for ZPG (Figures 27–8 and 27–9), the United States will not attain ZPG in this century. It cannot be stated with any certainty what path we as a nation will follow, but if we want to maintain a nongrowing population of 300 million, now is the time to plan for it. If we are to maintain legal immigration at its present level, 2.1 should be the average number of children per woman so that a stable population size can be achieved before the middle of the twenty-first century.

**Distribution of human populations.** The most significant features of the current population problem are the finite size of the earth, human reproductive potential, and time. *Homo sapiens* appeared on this planet about several million years ago. During the Stone Age (1 million years ago), the human population, numbering in the vicinity of 100,000, was restricted to the continent of Africa (Figure 27–10). Stone-Age people were nomadic hunters, and population was limited by the availability and abundance of prey as well as by what could be captured. In those days, 2 miles of good hunting territory supported one person. About 8000 B.C. the agricultural revolution took place; people learned how to raise crops and domesticate animals. Once they ceased to hunt and began to till the soil, wandering stopped. They settled on the land, formed agricultural communities, and improved methods for producing food.

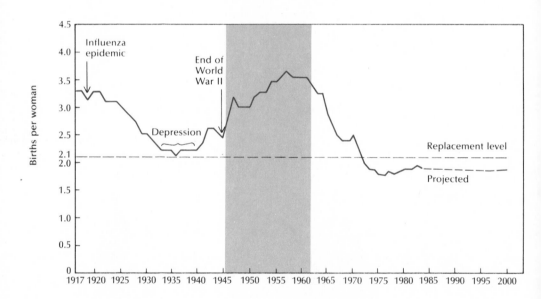

Since there was increased availability of food plus virtually limitless land (more than 20 million square miles of good land is present on the earth's surface), the population increased; humans spread across the continents of Africa, Europe, and Asia, and their density was 0.06 person per square mile. At the time of the birth of Christ, village and urban farming was commonplace, methods of storing and transporting food were improved, and since a farmer could produce more than enough food for his own family, people were freed from the land and could pursue other occupations. Villages contained larger and larger numbers of people, many engaged in a variety of occupations indirectly connected with agriculture, and soon these centers came

FIGURE 27–10 Increase in population density through the ages.

| Date | Area populated | Assumed density per square mile | Total population (millions) |
|---|---|---|---|
| 600,000 B.C. | | 0.006 | 0.125 |
| 200,000 B.C. | | 0.02 | 1 |
| 20,000 B.C. | | 0.06 | 3.34 |
| 8,000 B.C. | | 0.06 | 5.32 |
| 4000 B.C. | | 1.0 | 86.5 |
| A.D. 1 | | 2 | 133 |
| 1650 | | 5 | 545 |
| 1750 | | 7 | 728 |
| 1800 | | 10 | 906 |
| 1900 | | 15 | 1,610 |
| 1950 | | 20 | 2,400 |
| 2000 | | 60 | 6,500 |

Agricultural revolution → (between 8,000 B.C. and 4000 B.C.)

Americas opened up and industrial revolution → (between A.D. 1 and 1650)

to be large enough to qualify as cities. It has been estimated that by about A.D. 1 the human population density was two persons per square mile. By 1650, the development of science, technology, and industrialization brought about new changes in the environment and in human populations. New land, the Americas, opened up, and the human population grew; the density was then five persons per square mile. Two hundred years later (1850), the population reached a density of 12 persons per square mile, and by 1950 it had reached a density of 20 persons per square mile. It has been estimated that by the year 2000, when the human population reaches over 6 billion, there will be 60 persons per square mile; given the present rate of growth, by 2600 there could be one person per square foot of the earth.

Cities first arose in Mesopotamia only 5,000 to 6,000 years ago, but at the present rate of emigration and growth, more than half the world's population will soon live in cities. Not only that, by 2020 half of the human beings in the world will live in a city having 1 million persons, and by 2044 everyone will live in a city of that size. By 2044 we shall exist in wall-to-wall megacities, with the largest containing 1.4 billion people (the projected world population being 15 billion). It is a perplexing and strange situation to us, the inhabitants of cities, to consider that in 1776 not a single city of 1 million existed.

The trend toward city dwelling, or urbanization, in the United States reflects a worldwide change. Accelerated movement from the agricultural regions toward the cities began in 1800. At that time 6% of the U.S. population was urban; by 1850 the proportion living in cities was 15%, by 1900 it was 40%, and today more than 70% of our fellow beings in this country live in the cities or the suburbs. Underdeveloped countries show a similar trend: in South America more than 55% of the population lives in cities; Nairobi, the capital of Kenya, grows larger in population by 7% each year; Lagos, the capital of Nigeria, grows at a rate of 14%,

FIGURE 27–11 The geography of hunger. (Data from *FAO Production Yearbook.*)

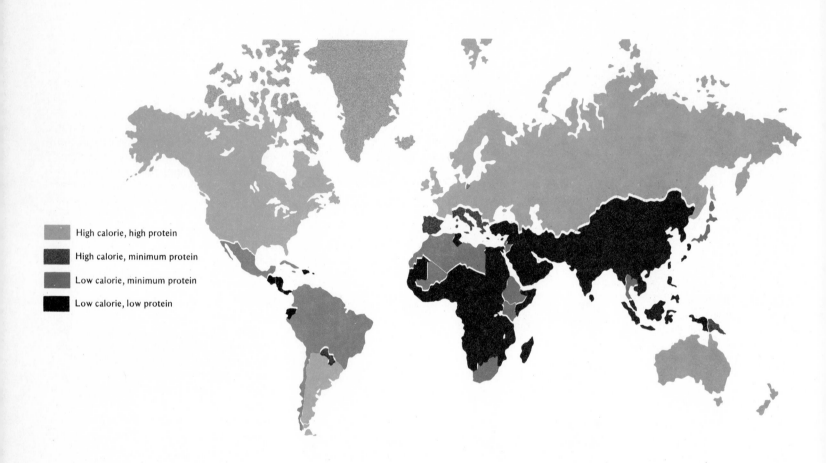

High calorie, high protein

High calorie, minimum protein

Low calorie, minimum protein

Low calorie, low protein

while Los Angeles grows at an annual rate of less than 3%.

Cities have good museums, libraries, theaters, universities, shopping centers, symphony orchestras, and transportation. They also produce many problems that rural areas do not: overcrowding, loss of identity, alienation, anonymity, slums, pollution, and economic dislocations. One continually wonders: are the advantages of urban life balanced by the disadvantages?

### 27–2 IMPLICATIONS OF POPULATION GROWTH

The human population of the earth is increasing exponentially, but planetary resources are not. Obviously, at some point,

as the songwriter said, "Somethin's gotta give." Put another way, if you have a normal pulse beat, it will not quite keep up with the growth in world population. Every time your pulse throbs, the human population of the world will have increased by more than one. Let us look at some of the implications of unlimited population growth.

### Our hungry planet

It has been estimated that more than 20% of the people in the world are not receiving enough calories per day; that is, they are undernourished. Deprived of calories, the individual cannot meet the body's energy demands, tissue reserves are drawn upon, and there is a gradual wasting away, with

death as the final consequence. In addition, 60% of the world's population is malnourished; that is, they lack essential food materials, mostly proteins and vitamins (Figure 27–11). According to the World Bank at least 800 million people in the world have a diet so limited that they do not have enough energy to carry out normal physical activity. Tonight when you go to sleep, remember that more than half the children of the world will go to bed hungry.

In the underdeveloped nations malnutrition takes two primary forms: marasmus and kwashiorkor. **Marasmus** develops when both calories and protein are in short supply; most victims are children less than 1 year old who have been weaned too early or have been given a poor substitute for

FIGURE 27–12 (a) Marasmus. (Photo by Terence Spencer, Courtesy of Time-Life Picture Agency, copyright Time, Inc.) (b) Kwashiorkor. (Courtesy of Sanford Schneider.)

(a)

(b)

mother's milk. The child with marasmus is emaciated and has wrinkled skin and large and sunken eyes (Figure 27–12a). **Kwashiorkor** in African means "the rejected one" and is derived from the fact that children with such symptoms often are displaced from the mother's breast by the arrival of a new baby. The oldest child, about 1 year old, still requires protein, but since the mother can suckle only one child, the displaced child is fed a carbohydrate diet and develops a protein-deficiency disease. The hair and skin are discolored, the belly is bloated due to fluid imbalance and edema, physical growth is impaired, appetite is poor, and in general the child is lethargic (Figure 27–12b). Over half of infant deaths (age 1 to 4 years) in underdeveloped countries result from kwashiorkor. Those children who survive are damaged in other ways: brain development is retarded (the IQ of such children is about 13 points lower

than the IQ of those raised on adequate protein diets), and the body is dwarfed. Protein deficiency during infancy is essentially irreversible, and provision of a normal diet later does not compensate for the early slowing of growth. This is probably because during the first 3 years the brain grows to 80% of its adult size (with more than 50% of its dry weight being protein) and the entire body grows to 20% of its size at maturity.

We, the affluent, drink half of the world's milk and eat three quarters of the world's meat. The dogs in this country eat enough protein to satisfy the requirements of 4 million human beings! Because it is more economical, people living in underdeveloped countries—and even the poor within our own nation—depend on a diet of grain rather than meat. In Asia, 97% of the diet is grain, mainly rice, but among well-fed North Americans only 75% of the diet is in

the form of grains such as rice, corn, and wheat. The disparity between the nutritionally well-off developed countries and the hungry underdeveloped countries is illustrated by the use of grain in the United States: 20 million tons of plant protein are used for feeding livestock, and from this only 2 million tons of meat protein are obtained. The lost protein—18 million tons—could provide much needed protein for the world's population!

The way to feed the hungry, some say, is to cultivate more land, to develop new high-yield strains of grain plants, and to farm the sea. On the surface some of these suggestions have merit, but closer examination shows their deficiencies in solving the hunger problem.

The **carrying capacity** of an ecosystem—the amount of biomass that an ecosystem can support or carry on a sustained basis—depends on the primary productivity of its

FIGURE 27–13 Primary production in grams of dry matter per square meter per day, in the major ecosystems. (Modified from E. P. Odum, *Fundamentals of Ecology*, 2nd edn., Philadelphia, Saunders, 1959.)

photosynthesizing plants. This varies from ecosystem to ecosystem (Figure 27–13). Maximum plant productivity is achieved in efficient agricultural operations, such as those found in the developed countries of the world, and the ideal maximum production capacity based on photosynthetic efficiency and nutrient availability is about 20 g per square meter per day. In the United States there used to be about 9 in. of topsoil that could support good harvests. However, in the last 300 years about one third of that has been destroyed. Farm lands are now converted to suburbs, highways, garbage dumps, and factories at a fantastic rate: 2 acres per minute, or 1 million acres per year. Every day in California agricultural land is lost to urban sprawl, and this state currently produces 29% of the nation's food (Box 27A).

Some have suggested that by utilizing land that could be farmed but at present is not, we could support a larger population. Theoretically, it is possible to increase productivity in arid (dry) and semiarid regions by irrigation (witness southern California and Israel), but to do so requires massive irrigation and vast nutrient additions to improve the soil's fertility. For example, growing crops requires great quantities of water—200 gal to produce the 2,500 Calories required by one person each day—yet 97% of the earth's water is salty. Desalting ocean water for irrigation is costly. Today desalination could supply < 3% of our water needs, and by 2010 it is estimated that 270,000 desalination plants would be required to meet the need for water. What would we do with the salt that is left after desalination? What kinds of pipelines would be needed to transport the fresh water inland? The expense and environmental dislocation produced by mass desalination could be too costly to make the procedure practical.

Enhanced food yields can be obtained by using new strains of wheat and rice—called the **green revolution.** Employing such strains Mexico has increased its wheat yield sixfold

in 20 years. However, the new high-yield varieties require large amounts of water, fertilizer, and pesticides. The ecological consequences of heavy fertilizer and pesticide use are not completely understood and could be dangerous. And, in certain parts of the world the soil is so poor and the climatic interactions so severe that even the addition of fertilizer, water, and agricultural know-how cannot produce crop diversification or increase yields. Paul and Anne Ehrlich and John Holdren have said:

In many ways the problem of revolutionizing LDC (less developed country) agriculture is inextricably tied up with the general problem of LDC "development." Shortages of capital, resources, and trained technicians exist along with lack of effective planning, the absence of adequate storage, transport, and marketing systems, and ineffective demand due to poor income distributions. When these are combined with high rates of population growth, malnutrition, and disease, they make any kind of development extremely difficult, and thus retard agricultural development in particular. It is a vicious cycle—one that will take much more than a new food-production technology to break.[2]

If not the land, how about the sea? Why are the oceans less productive than the land

---

[2] P. EHRLICH, A. EHRLICH, and J. HOLDREN, *Ecoscience Population, Resources, Environment*, San Francisco, Freeman, 1977.

(Figure 27–13)? Large bodies of water, such as open oceans and large lakes, are at a production disadvantage because a large portion of the light energy is absorbed by the water before it reaches the site of maximal mineral supply. In addition, the oceans and larger lakes tend to lack adequate amounts of nutrients. The myth of a food-rich sea is just that—an unsubstantiated illusion. According to J. H. Ryther of the Woods Hole Oceanographic Institution, the maximum fish yield of the oceans is about 100 million tons, and that is only 1.5 times the record fish harvest of 1968. To increase yields it might be possible to harvest lower down the food chain, but this does not seem profitable or practical at present or in the near future. More human calories would be spent on harvesting a thin surface film of plankton than would be gained in consuming the catch!

What about farming the sea by culturing fish and other marine organisms? Could this not be achieved by fertilizing and harvesting the oceans as we do the land? Upwellings of nutrient-laden waters occur naturally in the coastal zones, and such areas have a significantly higher productivity than the open ocean (Figure 27–13). For example, off the coast of Peru, nutrient upwellings permit large blooms of phytoplankton, fishes and fish-eating birds are abundant, the seabirds produce guano in large quantities,

## BOX 27A  Last chance to keep off the grass?

Drawing by Richter;
© 1976 The New Yorker Magazine, Inc.

The admonition to "Go west, young man!" was taken literally by thousands of Americans during the 1950s and 1960s. The slowdown in migration during the early 1970s shows signs of reversing itself as winter-weary Easterners seek to escape to the Sunshine State. What effect is this having on California?

California, the nation's number one agricultural state, contributes almost 10% of the total value of agricultural products in the United States, with 36 million acres of farmed land generating $45 billion worth of agricultural industry receipts in 1986. Without question, agriculture is an extremely important industry in California, and the quality and quantity of the three basic natural resources that are required to support agriculture (soil, air, and water) need to be maintained. Urban development has been diminishing California's commercial agricultural lands by about 44,000 acres annually over the past two decades. However, 50,000 acres of previously nonirrigated lands are said to have been coming into production annually for the first time, resulting in a net annual increase of acres in agriculture production in California each year.

The major drawback to this equation is that it takes far more energy to convert raw land to producing land than it takes to farm the best soil. Poor soils require more heavy equipment, more fertilizer, and hence more energy in order to start producing than do good soils (Table 27–3). One way to conserve our resources is therefore to use our best soils for farming and poorer soils for urban use.

We are not doing this. Since 1965, 23% of California's prime agricultural land and 14% of lesser quality land has become urbanized. Furthermore, since the best land is more intensively cultivated than land of poorer quality, the current pattern of urban expansion will have a more dramatic impact on agricultural production than if the impact were more evenly distributed. If urban projections made for the period between 1965 and 1980 prove to be forerunners of urban expansion, approximately 900,000 acres that were cropland in 1980 will be urban by the year 2000 and none will be left for agriculture by the year 2200, in the absence of four factors. These factors are (1) a decline in population growth, (2) technological advancements increasing agricultural yield on low-quality lands, (3) widespread introduction of a totally new concept of food and fiber production, and (4) external controls that direct urban expansion to less productive land.

Since the first three factors seem at present unlikely to occur, what if anything can be done about redirecting urban expansion?

Currently, state and federal government agencies are examining the problem, but at the local level the pressures for urban development are often enormous. These can reach the dimensions of polarized conflicts, with builders lining up on one side and environmentalists on the other. Some cities in California have put an upper limit on the number of building permits that can be issued annually; others have attempted to plan and direct growth by rating the merits of proposed developments, by imposing agricultural zoning in prime areas, or by attempting to establish agricultural preserves in threatened locations. However, some have questioned the right of government to limit the rights of property owners and the freedom of Americans to move about and live where they please. Legislation at the state and federal levels will probably be required. In the meantime, the future of California's agriculture industry hangs in the balance.

**TABLE 27–3  The agricultural demand for energy**

| Source | % |
|---|---|
| Natural gas (used in the production of fertilizer) | 53 |
| Electric power | 16 |
| Diesel fuels | 17.5 |
| Gasoline | 10 |
| Liquid propane gas | 2.25 |
| Aviation fuel | 0.75 |
| Total | 100 |

and this can be harvested for the production of fertilizer. However, enrichment of the oceans by inducing artificial upwellings would be expensive in terms of energy input. Furthermore, in the offshore areas where such a project might be feasible water pollution poses a serious threat.

Finally, even if we could grow seaweed and algae at reasonable cost, how easy would it be to get people to eat them? How tasty and nutritious will seaweed- or algae-burgers be? We are drawn, almost inescapably, to the conclusion that the seas are essentially biological deserts and likely to remain so.

In spite of the gains made by the green revolution there are more hungry people today than ever before. The more people we feed, the more there are to reproduce. As we feed more people, the population rises; pollution becomes more severe, species composition is adversely affected, and consequently food productivity declines. The land bank is bankrupt. We cannot farm the sea, we cannot produce sufficient quantities of synthetic food cheaply and we cannot reduce our caloric requirements significantly. Even if we could grow enough food to feed our present population, this would only buy time; it would not curtail population growth. Feeding the world's population treats a symptom, but not the disease. To survive, we must control the disease itself, and this means curbing population growth.

## Depletion of resources

Every person on the earth depletes its resources. Paradoxically, it is the developed and affluent countries, whose growth rate is decidedly less than that of the underdeveloped nations, that constitute the most serious threat to our environment. The United States, with 5% of the world's population, uses 35% of the world's resources of fossil fuels, metals, radioactive substances, and the like. The Western nations together, including the United States, Rus-sia, and Japan, account for 25% of the world's population but use 80% of the earth's natural resources. As the consumption of these resources increases, it is automatic that pollution will also increase.

The resources available to us are classified as renewable or nonrenewable. Renewable resources can, with proper management, replace themselves in time; plants and animals are renewable resources. If these are mismanaged, as in the despoilation of forests or the excessive killing of predators or prey, the ecosystem becomes severely imbalanced and renewal is virtually impossible. Nonrenewable resources cannot be replaced; although these materials are not actually lost, they are changed into forms that can no longer be used. Thus, fossil fuels are burned to carbon dioxide and water, radioactive elements decay, and the fertility of the soil may be lost. The mineral resources of our planet have been here since the earth was formed. They are being depleted at an ever-increasing rate because there are more of us using them and our present technology consumes enormous quantities of these substances.

How long will the nonrenewable resources last? Estimates vary with the particular resource. For example, aluminum supplies may last for 570 years, coal and oil for 300 years, but tin, copper, lead, uranium, and zinc may be depleted in one generation (30 years). The rate of depletion is staggering when we consider that it took 1 billion years to produce the earth's coal deposits that we are using up in only a few hundred years. In the last 50 years we have used up more fuel and minerals than in the entire history of the human species. Most of these materials end up in the sea, too diluted for reclamation.

The consequences of depletion of non-renewable resources are obvious: substitute materials must be developed and costs must rise for those substances that become less abundant. Increasingly metals will have to be replaced by plastics, but the substitution is of limited value since plastics are derived from fossil fuels. By switching to new sources of structural materials, we shall deplete other resources.

We are also using up our energy resources at a prodigious rate. Early humans used 2,000 Calories per day, but Amercians now use 200,000 Calories each day. The developed countries use 77% of the world's coal, 81% of its oil, 95% of its natural gas, and 80% of the nuclear energy. Nuclear fission, it is estimated, can supply about half our energy needs by the year 2000, but supplies of uranium (on which the process depends) are expected to last only 30 years more. Discovery of new radioactive fuels and the development of controlled nuclear-fusion reactors could enable future energy demands to be met, but the problems of thermal water pollution and accumulation of radioactive wastes would remain. Nuclear power plants require cooling water in massive amounts, and raising the temperature of the water would soon disrupt the aquatic ecosystem (Box 27B).

## The decline and fall of clean air

People were crawling about, people were whimpering, people were screaming, gasping for breath, touching each other, vanishing in the dark, and ever and anon being pushed off the platform on to the live rail.[3]

These words tell of the collapse of a totally automated society; a society completely subterranean, globally uniform, in which people were fed on synthetic foods and breathed fetid air. The people, if they could be called that, became used to the fetid air and the tasteless food and the dimming illumination until the power source decayed. Fiction or our future? Will the world end from a nuclear holocaust or with a cough, a wheeze, and a gasp from emphysema-scarred lungs?

**The blight of light.** Brown air and gray air are two types of **air pollution.** Brown air

---

[3] E. M. FORSTER, *The Machine Stops.*

BOX 27B Thermal pollution: we can't break even

According to Webster's dictionary, **pollute** means to make or render unclean or impure. Heat energy—waste heat—discharged into the environment is called **thermal pollution.** It is a consequence of the Second Law of Thermodynamics: every energy conversion must add heat to the environment. Thus, the ultimate and inevitable pollutant is heat.

As our demands for energy increase along with population growth more heat will be generated. It is estimated that by the year 2000 the total energy used in the world will have increased by 500%, and in the United States it will rise by 800%. Our power needs double every 10 years. (Think of all the electrical appliances in use right now!) If the insatiable demand for energy were to continue unrestricted, by 2175 all the available land in the United States could be occupied by power plants. Since all our fossil fuels and uranium will be gone long before that time, nuclear fission in breeder reactors (ones that regenerate nuclear fuel) will assume prime importance in supplying our energy needs. Although the fuel in such power plants can be recycled, the heat energy cannot, and it must flow downhill (from warm to cool) into the environment.

Although some of this heat can be used for raising the temperature of greenhouses, heating buildings, and so on, the cost of piping warm water is high, and utilization methods are imperfect. The irony of thermal pollution is this: the warm water that results from cooling of power plants is at too low a temperature for use as an energy reservoir, but is warm enough to threaten aquatic ecosystems. Most aquatic animals cannot exist at temperatures greater than 35°C. As the temperature rises, the solubility of gases decreases; thus oxygen levels in the water will decline and organisms with a high oxygen demand will be damaged or killed. By contrast, higher water temperatures plus increased nutrient load will promote excessive growth of algae—eutrophication—and the ecosystem will be further disrupted. Thermal pollution can make many of our rivers and streams uninhabitable for fishes by the year 2000. Furthermore, as the temperature of the seas increases, the polar ice caps will begin to melt and the level of the oceans will rise. Cities such as London, Los Angeles, and New York will disappear beneath the waters along with a large part of the earth's land mass.

The "energy crunch" of 1973–1974 and 1978–1979 gave people in industrialized countries a foretaste of life in a world where energy is permanently in short supply. The fact that the world's sources of energy are dwindling rapidly was brought home to many of us in the form of lowered thermostats, long lines at gasoline stations, and shortages of many commodities. This confirmed some sufferers in their opinion that more energy is needed. But did they consider the results of increased energy use? Are we caught in a thermodynamic race we cannot win? Will this race destroy all earthly order? If we do nothing, yes! However, by restricting population growth, reducing energy consumption, and, above all, using what we have more wisely, we may yet postpone (almost indefinitely) such a thermodynamic destiny. Ideally, we should ration energy consumption, reduce electrical demands, and raise the cost of power to discourage its reckless use. We can do it if we want to: there is still time left.

covers Los Angeles; it is a pollutant of young cities, and its prime source is the automobile's internal-combustion engine (Figure 27–14). When air containing nitrogen and oxygen is heated to 3000°F, as it is in the automobile engine, nitric oxide (NO) is produced; this reacts with ozone ($O_3$) in the atmosphere and yields highly toxic yellow-brown nitrogen dioxide ($NO_2$). Nitrogen dioxide is harmful to the delicate lining of the lungs, contributing to the development of bronchitis, cancer, emphysema, and cardiovascular damage.

The unburned hydrocarbons of gasoline released into the atmosphere in the presence of nitric oxide and sunlight, undergo chemical reaction to produce peroxy-acetylnitrate (PAN), formaldehyde, and other oxidants that cause the eyes to burn and tear, damage lungs, kill vegetation, and rot rubber and nylon. The abundant sunshine in southern California contributes to the production of ozone by the reaction $NO_2 \rightarrow NO + O$; the oxygen reacts with unburned hydrocarbons and atmospheric oxygen to yield ozone. Automobiles, sunlight, and ozone are a self-perpetuating and dangerous combination that produces photochemical air pollution. Ozone at 1 ppm disrupts photosynthesis (Figure 27–15) and at 0.1 ppm adversely affects the lungs. On a clear day the ozone content is about 0.02 ppm, but on summer air-polluted days in Los Angeles and environs it may be as high as 0.5 ppm!

Incomplete combustion of coal, oil, and gasoline results in carbon monoxide formation. Carbon monoxide inactivates hemoglobin and cytochromes—respiratory pigments. Living for 8 hours in an atmosphere polluted with 80 ppm of carbon monoxide is equivalent to the loss of 1 pint of blood through hemorrhage. In Tokyo the carbon monoxide content of the air often reaches 40 to 50 ppm. On an automobile-jammed highway a motorist may be exposed to 400 ppm! The symptoms of mild carbon monoxide poisoning are headache, nausea, dizziness, blurred vision, and muscle pain.

High levels of carbon monoxide cause convulsions, unconsciousness, and death.

Climate also contributes to air pollution. During a thermal, or temperature, inversion, a layer of warm air sits over a mass of cool air and prevents vertical mixing of the air. The air stagnates and pollutants accumulate (Figure 27–16). Life in such a city becomes nightmarish. High levels of photochemical air pollution have been recorded at one time or another in Sydney, Tokyo, Boston, New York, and Atlanta. However, in the Los Angeles basin air pollutants are a way of life.

**The breath of death.** In medieval times the odor of sulfur dioxide meant the Devil was close by. This idea was not far wrong, for the gray air of older industrialized cities (New York, Chicago, London, Manchester) bedevils the inhabitants with this same gas. Gray air (smog) is encountered in cities where fossil fuels are burned; in addition to sulfur dioxide, it contains soot and dust (particulates) plus toxic metals such as lead and beryllium. Automobiles emit little sulfur dioxide because when gasoline is refined from fuel oil the sulfur is removed. However, coal and heavy oils do contain sulfur, and when these are burned, the sulfur combines with oxygen to form sulfur dioxide. Exposure to 0.2 ppm of sulfur dioxide for 24 hours constitutes a serious health hazard. Sulfur dioxide reacts with water vapor to produce droplets of sulfuric acid. The Parthenon and other monuments of human civilization are disintegrating because of exposure to sulfuric acid. Smog may destroy more than just our monuments. In 1901 over 1,000 deaths in Glasgow and Edinburgh were related to smog, and in December 1952 the London smog caused up to 4,000 deaths.

### Acid rain

Over the last 200 years, the acidity of rain and snow has changed from a solution that was nearly neutral in pH to its present day condition, a dilute solution of dilute sulfuric and nitric acids. In 1974 a storm over Scotland had rain with a pH of 2.4, equivalent to vinegar. **Acid rain** is caused largely by sulfur dioxides and nitrogen oxides emitted by power plants, smelters, factories, and automobiles. These pollutants react with sunlight and moisture to produce an acid soup that descends on us as acid rain, acid fog, and acid particles that literally corrode our environment.

Watersheds over much of the Eastern United States and Canada are especially sensitive to the effects of acid rain because they are underlain by granite and granitoid rocks that are highly resistant to weathering, and the acid rain cannot be neutralized by the soil. Lakes in the Colorado and Wyoming Rockies, the Cascades in Washington, and California's Sierra Nevadas are especially vulnerable.

The clearest effects of acid deposition have been on fish populations. In many thousands of lakes in Norway and Sweden, fish populations have declined or been eliminated once the pH has fallen below 5. In New York's Adirondack Mountains, 212 of the 2,200 lakes and ponds are acidic, dead, and fishless. Canada may suffer the most. It has been projected that if nothing is done to curb acid rain by the end of the century, some 48,000 Canadian lakes will be unable to support fish.

The effects on terrestrial ecosystems are more complex and difficult to predict. In spite of the absence of specifics, however, it is certain that acid rain has the potential to change nutrient cycling. To safeguard freshwater ecosystems, it will be necessary to take immediate steps to reduce the emissions of sulfur dioxide and nitrogen dioxide.

### What can be done about air pollution?

1. Spend more local and federal money to clean the air.
2. Reduce the sulfur content of fossil fuels before burning.
3. Decrease hydrocarbon and nitric oxide emissions from automobiles by installing smog devices on the exhaust.

FIGURE 27–14 Photochemical air pollution. The disappearing landscape during a smoggy day in California. (Courtesy of Air Pollution Research Center.)

4. Use cleaner energy sources (solar, methanol, and hydroelectric) instead of fossil fuels.
5. Improve mass transit in cities, reducing the automobile load.
6. Employ electrostatic precipitators to remove soot and other particulates from the air.
7. Curb sources of pollution—automobile and industrial. (Each day in Los Angeles 4 million cars burn 8 million gal of gasoline producing 3 million tons of carbon monoxide, 200,000 lb of nitrogen dioxide, 400,000 lb of hydrocarbons, and other noxious substances.)

In 1542 Juan Rodriques Cabrillo, the Portuguese explorer, reached Los Angeles. He saw the region blanketed by smoke from Indian fires. He called the basin *La Bahia de los Fumos*—Bay of Smoke—and sailed away convinced nobody could live there. Cabrillo may be proved right if air pollution is not checked.

#### "Water, water everywhere Nor any drop to drink"

As human populations increase in size, waste output also rises. There are two major categories of waste: liquid and solid. **Liquid waste** includes materials that, treated or untreated, are eventually flushed into the waters of the earth—the rivers, lakes, and oceans. Here they are diluted, and agents of decomposition, such as bacteria, break them down and recycle their materials. Until quite recently it had been assumed that the capacity of our natural waters to accept, to dilute, and eventually to purify our liquid wastes was virtually limitless. However, the volume of waste has reached such proportions that dilution no longer suffices and the decomposers cannot work fast enough and may be overcome. The natural process of self-purification is not enough. This has serious implications because these same rivers and lakes serve as our sources of drinking water. Sometimes the wastes themselves are discharged into a river and

FIGURE 27–15 Electron micrographs of the leaves of an 8-day-old bean plant exposed to ozone at a concentration of 1 ppm for 30 minutes, a level comparable to that found in the Los Angeles basin. (Courtesy of W. W. Thomson.) (a) Normal chloroplast. (b) Beginning of smog damage; granulation appears between stacks of membranes (X). At this stage (3 hours after gassing) the plant would appear normal to the unaided eye. (c) Chloroplast damage with extensive granulation and disruption of membranes 24 hours after exposure. The leaves of this plant would have a reduced photosynthetic efficiency.

(a)

(b)
(c)

FIGURE 27–16 Thermal inversion. (a) Normally pollutants are carried away from the ground level because warm air rises. (b) During a thermal inversion, a layer of warm air at higher altitudes traps cooler air beneath, and this tends to accumulate pollutants close to the ground level. (c) Aerial view of an inversion. (Courtesy of Air Pollution Research Center.)

(a)

(b)

(c)

inadvertently recycled before they are broken down—carried downstream to a neighboring town and added to the water supply. As Tom Lehrer tells us, "The things we throw into the [San Franciso] Bay they eat for lunch in San Jose." If measures are not taken to improve treatment of sewage, the pathological bacterial and viral content of our water could provide a source of widespread disease. In a recent survey, 144 out of 155 U.S. cities with populations over 250,000 had measurable traces of sewage in their drinking water.

Agriculture uses water and pollutes it. An orange grove covering 1 acre requires 800,000 gal of water. Spraying of herbicides and pesticides and intensive cultivation to increase crop yields also contaminate our waters. Farm animals produce 10 times the amount of sewage humans do! All this ends up in the water. Additionally, industrial plants contribute over 500,000 different chemicals to our waterways.

'My! How I envy your dazzling white wash!'

BOX 27C  Deep concern: ground water

At the very top of the environmental scientists' list of concerns about pollution damage is something that most Americans probably believe to be safely beyond the reach of contamination: ground water. This is water that lies buried from a few feet to a half mile or more beneath the land's surface in stretches of permeable rock, sand and gravel known as aquifers. In the U.S. there is five times as much water in such subterranean reservoirs as flows through all its surface lakes, streams and rivers in a year. While most ground water is believed to remain pure, concern is rising because it is one of nature's greatest nonrenewable resources. Unlike surface water or the air, ground water is all but impossible to purify once it has become chemically polluted.

Ground water is not exposed to the natural purification systems that recycle and cleanse surface water; there is no sunlight, for example, to evaporate it and thereby remove salts and other minerals and chemicals. Nor can ground water be counted upon to clean itself as it moves through the earth, for it scarcely "flows" at all. Indeed, once ground water becomes polluted, the contamination may last for decades."

In the past, ground water was kept pure because the soil at the earth's surface could be counted on to act as a filtration system, a kind of geological "kidney" that would scrub out bacteria and other insoluble contaminants placed on or in the ground before they could seep down to the water table, the ground water's upper limit. But this filtration system does not reliably screen out the waste chemicals that now leach into the soil from a variety of sources, including cropland that has been sprayed with pesticides, and industrial dumps like the pools into which liquid chemicals are placed so that the water they contain will evaporate.

The EPA has located 181,000 such "lagoons" at industrial and municipal waste disposal sites around the country. In a study of 8,200 of them, the agency found that 72% were just holes in the ground, not lined with concrete or other materials to prevent the chemicals from leaching into the soil; 700 of these unlined lagoons were within a mile of wells tapping ground water.

Bacterial wastes, such as the effluent from residential septic tanks and cesspools, can be filtered fairly simply out of drinking water. But chemical contaminants are another matter. Says EPA Administrator Douglas Costle: "We are not even sure if, not to mention how, chemical contaminants can be removed. Since it

Contaminants    Water-bearing rocks, sand and gravel

takes sophisticated testing just to determine the presence of chemicals.

EPA officials have stated "We cannot even begin to say how much of our drinking water, actual or potential, may have been contaminated. We are going to be doing a lot of detective work."

In 1986 California voters approved by a 2:1 margin Proposition 65, the Safe Drinking Water and Toxic Enforcement Act. This Act requires businesses to warn people before exposing them to chemicals known to cause cancer or birth defects. Businesses that do not comply face penalties of up to $2,500 per day for each exposure. There is a bounty hunter provision. There is also an 800 number hot line so that consumers can learn which products contain potentially dangerous chemicals. The Environmental Defense Fund, the principal author of Proposition 65, says it was designed to persuade businesses that it is cheaper to eliminate toxic chemicals than to endanger the public health. No longer will the government or the individual have to demonstrate that a chemical or product is hazardous but now businesses will have to prove that the chemicals used are safe. Further, the victims will not have to show that they have suffered injury. It is clear Proposition 65 will result in a spate of lawsuits, and many changes in the way agriculture and other industries do business. California's legislation to protect the water we drink may be the forerunner of future regulations elsewhere in the nation.

© *Time* September 22, 1980.

FIGURE 27–17 The growth of a bacterial culture.

What can be done?
1. Recycle sewage water (Table 27–4).
2. Restrict the introduction of agricultural and industrial wastes to the water supply.
3. Conserve water, using only the minimum necessary.
4. Curb population growth.

## The problem of solid wastes

We live in a throwaway age. Hundreds of products are disposable, and many items are packaged in no-deposit, no-return containers. In truth, however, matter—whether it be called disposable or throwaway—cannot be gotten rid of. We can move it, dump it, bury it, burn it, and transform it, but it can never be totally eliminated. Thus, much of our **solid waste**—rubbish, refuse, garbage—remains to litter the landscape.

As a human community grows, so does its waste output. Today's urban dweller discards 4 to 5 lb of solid waste daily—twice the amount discarded 20 years ago. Currently, California produces nearly 39 million tons of garbage a year, and in New York City more than 5 million tons of garbage are collected annually. The bill for collection and disposal is billions of dollars each year, and it is easy to see why when we learn it costs more to dispose of the Sunday *New York Times* than to buy it.

The age-old attitudes toward disposal of solid wastes are proving unsatisfactory. Dumping garbage provides a breeding ground for disease-carrying rats, flies, and mosquitoes and a source of contamination of the water supply. Land for garbage dumping is limited, and because the dump sites are far removed from the urban source, transportation costs are often quite high. Burying wastes requires large tracts of land and locations that are not directly leached into the waterways. Sanitary landfills—compacting garbage and covering this with gravel, soil, or clay—eliminate pollution and unsightliness, but it is estimated that by the year 2000 we shall have run out of landfill sites and the oceans will be too polluted to receive additional garbage. Only combustible garbage can be burned, and this leads to air pollution.

What can be done to improve the disposal of the mountains of solid waste we produce? Recycle it. The aluminum cans that now clutter the environment from sea to shining sea can be remelted, and the 6 million cars junked yearly can be "mined" and melted down. By providing something equivalent to a mining-depletion allowance to car manufacturers, salvage could be made as economical as refining the earth's metallic ores. Glass bottles can be used again and again; a large monetary deposit might supply an incentive for returning these to the store.

We recycle only 20% of the 60 million tons of paper products used annually—why not more? The recycling of a ton of paper would not only cut down on litter but could avoid chopping down 17 trees. As Lamont Cole has pointed out:

Why can't a product be kept off the market until a satisfactory method for its disposal is discovered? And shouldn't the price of a product reflect the cost to society and its ultimate disposal?

Self-destruct cartons and bottles or Mount Trashmores (a ski and toboggan run south of Chicago made from a mountain of trash) scattered across the country hardly seem the perfect remedy for disposal of solid wastes. A more reasonable approach is to make the recycling of wastes profitable, thus balancing economic and ecologic forces.

## 27–3 LIMITS ON POPULATION GROWTH: STRATEGY FOR SURVIVAL

Two hundred years ago Thomas Malthus, an English clergyman, wrote *An Essay on the Principle of Population* (1798), in which he stated that a population that is unchecked increases in a geometric fashion, but the food supply for such a population

TABLE 27–4 Treatment of sewage to recycle water

| Sewage treatment | What is done | Relative Cost (cents/ 1,000 gal) | What is left |
|---|---|---|---|
| Primary | Screening and grinding remove particles | x | Bacteria, pesticides, phosphates, metals |
| Secondary | Activated sludge or trickling filters containing bacteria and protozoa remove nutrients | 2.5x | Pesticides, metals |
| Tertiary | Chlorination and flocculation remove organic matter and soften water; activated charcoal removes odors | 4–10x | Fresh, drinkable water |

FIGURE 27–18 A log-log plot of the human population over the last million years.

**591**

**ABOARD SPACESHIP EARTH**

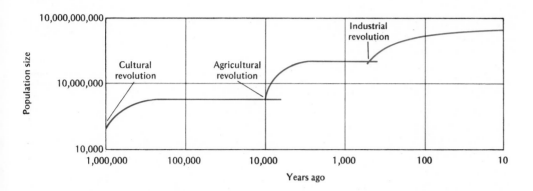

increases only arithmetically. The consequences of overpopulation were, to use Malthus's words, "misery and vice" (starvation, disease, and war). These, he believed, would act as natural checks on population growth and would tend to restore the population to its optimal density. According to the Malthusian theory, a natural population has an optimal density and this density remains relatively constant for a long time.

Under ideal conditions the growth rate of a population is exponential, and the organisms reproduce themselves without impedance. Opposing this growth rate (**biotic potential**) and keeping the population in check is the **environmental resistance,** the sum total of all the environmental factors that act to limit the population (Figure 27–17). Some of the limiting factors are space, temperature, food availability, and oxygen supply. Stabilization of the size of a population probably occurs because of the depletion of food and oxygen, the accumulation of wastes, and other environmental changes that tend to bring the population into a state of dynamic equilibrium—when the death rate equals the birth rate. This equilibrium level is the carrying capacity of the environment, and it represents the maximum population size that can be supported by that particular environment. Although this part of the growth curve is shown as a smooth line, the population actually tends

alternately to overshoot and undershoot this level. These fluctuations reflect changes in environmental resistance as well as differences in the responses of the organisms. If the environment changes (for example, by removal of toxic wastes or availability of new sources of food or new places to live), the carrying capacity will also be shifted.

We can visualize the Malthusian theory in terms of a feedback control system: each population has its own set point around which there may be size fluctuations. To maintain the set point there are a number of feedback controls—when environmental resistance increases, it curbs overpopulation; when it decreases, the population increases in size.

### Is there self-regulation in the growth of the human population?

Malthus concluded that the population of Britain was about optimum in 1800; that is, it was in dynamic equilibrium and if it were to grow (he assumed a doubling time of 25 years), there would be widespread misery in Britain. Malthus was severely criticized for his theory, and Dickens and Hazlitt excoriated him publicly. Indeed, during the 36 years that Malthus lived after publication of *An Essay on the Principle of Population*, both population and prosperity increased in Britain. As a matter of fact, population growth and affluence have been most evident for the last 150 years in the developed

countries of the world. The human population has grown exponentially since the dawn of the species, and there is no evidence of a deceleration in growth rate. Does the Malthusian theory apply to some organisms, but not to us?

If the data on the growth of the human population (Figure 27–18) are plotted on a logarithmic scale, it is possible to indicate both time and population size in some detail and to smooth out year-to-year fluctuations. The population growth curve shows not a single surge, but three surges and two set points: exponential growth occurred 600,000 years ago, corresponding to the cultural revolution; another surge took place 8,000 years ago, marking the onset of the agricultural revolution; and the last one began 200 years ago, establishing the beginning of the industrial revolution. Between the cultural and agricultural revolutions and between the agricultural and industrial revolutions, the human population remained relatively stable and fluctuated around an equilibrium level. The reasons for the abrupt exponential growth of the human population during these revolutions were enhanced food production, opening up of new territories and continents, mechanization, and urbanization. Thus, with each improvement in our ability to obtain food and space, there was established a new carrying capacity, and equilibrium occurred around a new set point. Note that no set point has been reached following the last surge—the curve is still rising. It should be noted also that the carrying capacity can rarely be predicted in advance, but is determined empirically by the present time and conditions.

Thus, although for some time Malthus was considered to be wrong and his critics right, in fact the reverse is true. The reason for the paradox was circumstance: Malthus lived during the time when the industrial revolution was in progress and a new equilibrium level was being established. It is in the long view of human existence that Malthus's theory may prove correct.

## What is the equilibrium level for the human population and how can it be achieved?

What is the carrying capacity of our planet? No one is certain whether it is 5 billion or 100 billion; what is certain is that there is a limit. The limiting factor could be air, water, energy, food, heat buildup, space, or the accumulation of pollutants. J. A. Campbell has estimated the world population that could be supported on existing resources provided consumption remains at the level in effect at present in the United States (Table 27–5); these estimates assume that we shall employ new and more efficient methods for locating and using resources and that the usage will not disturb the balance in the biosphere. These are big assumptions indeed. For example, according to one estimate, the largest world population that could be supported in a fashion similar to that of the average U.S. citizen today is around 1 billion, and that is less than one fifth of the earth's present population. Today most humans, including more than 20 million Americans, live in impoverished and unhealthy conditions. There is yet another defect in these optimistic estimates: if all the world's people were to consume nonrenewable resources at the level of present-day Americans, the metal ore in the earth would be depleted in 24 hours!

We must establish spaceship rules for life on this planet. No longer can we live by what economist Kenneth Boulding calls cowboy or frontier rules, where everything is available in abundance and life is free and easy. One of the first of these spaceship rules must be a decision to establish a set point for our population, and then to curb population growth by governmental, religious, and individual action. Acceptable solutions for limiting population size will vary from person to person and country to country, but the goal for all must be the same: ZPG. We must lower the birth rate, for in this finite world a system involving positive feedback (such as reproduction)

**TABLE 27–5 Maximum world population potentially capable of being supported at present U.S. levels of consumption of existing resources**

| Resource | Population (billions) |
|---|---|
| Maintaining or increasing the overall quality of life | 0.5–2 |
| Preserving the quality of our life support system | 1–5 |
| Heat buildup | 10 |
| Food | 30 |
| Oxygen | 100 |
| Space* | 100 |
| Energy* | 100 |
| Water* | 100 |

*See J. A. Campbell, *Chemical Systems,* San Francisco, Freeman, 1970.

cannot be endured for long. Ultimately, negative feedback controls will emerge to achieve a measure of stability. The natural checks on the human population when it begins to exceed the carrying capacity of the planet will be widespread disease, starvation, warfare, social disorganization, and depletion of the life-support systems.

What can be done to achieve ZPG and maintain a high quality of life as soon as possible?[4] The following recommendations can be made:

1. Reduce the number of spaceship passengers by
   a. Having birth control methods freely applied and readily available
   b. Providing tax incentives to encourage smaller families
   c. Developing educational programs on family planning
   d. Making child adoption easier
   e. Encouraging late marriages
2. Reduce the level of consumption and recycle materials by
   a. Cutting down on use of power and nonrenewable resources
   b. Providing tax incentives for recycling and reducing pollution

[4] Another plan is propounded by P. R. Ehrlich and R. L. Harriman, *How To Be a Survivor,* New York, Ballantine Books, 1971.

c. Improving quality and durability of products

The only question with relation to the future of world population is whether the inevitable decline in rate of growth will come about through a tremendous upsurge in the death rate or through a drastic fall in the birth rate. Over the long haul these two solutions represent our only choice. The former will mean unprecedented human misery: the latter, unprecedented human wisdom.[5]

As the theologian H. Cox has said, "Not to decide, is to decide."

## SUMMARY

**1.** The human world population today is growing annually by 85 million. Because population is increasing geometrically, doubling time is currently only about 40 years.

**2.** Because of improvements in medical care and living standards, the death rate continues to decline drastically, but the birth rate remains constant. Only a decline in the birth rate or an increase in the death rate can produce zero population growth (ZPG).

**3.** In predicting growth rates, population structure is critical. Size and sexual composition of the reproductive age group, average age of marriage, age at which death occurs, fertility patterns, and sociological, political, and religious attitudes are all important.

**4.** With improved agricultural technology and the opening up of industrial job markets, trends in population distribution have been toward concentration in urban centers and away from rural agriculture regions. Advantages of urban life may by offset by the problems of overcrowding, however.

**5.** People in overcrowded, less developed nations generally suffer from marasmus (caloric and protein deficiency) and

[5] From *Man . . . An Endangered Species,* U.S. Department of the Interior, Conservation Yearbook No. 4, Washington, D.C., GPO, 1968.

from kwashiorkor (protein deficiency), both of which hit hardest at the young.

**6.** Carrying capacity of an ecosystem depends on its primary productivity. Productivity of the earth can be increased by enhancing agricultural efficiency through the use of fertilizer, advanced technology, and the development of high-yield plant strains (the so-called green revolution). However, the degree of increase has limits. Suggestions for farming arid lands, irrigation through desalination, and farming the oceans all have major drawbacks. Furthermore, the more people we feed, the more there are to reproduce. The best solution to overpopulation is to curb population growth.

**7.** As resources are depleted, pollution increases. Air pollution from automobile exhaust and industrial discharge is a major problem in many areas of the world. Liquid waste, especially sewage, is increasingly difficult to treat and dispose of as its volume increases with the population. Some solid waste can be recycled, but more needs to be done in this area.

**8.** Thomas Malthus in 1798 pointed out that while food supply increases arithmetically, population increases geometrically. The sigmoid growth curve applied to the human population shows that there have been three phases of exponential growth corresponding to the cultural, agricultural, and industiral revolutions. In each case, new carrying capacities were established as food, water, and other environmental factors ceased to be limiting. We are still in the log phase of the last growth period, and a new carrying capacity for the earth is yet to be established.

**9.** Once the Malthusian population limit is reached, natural checks on population growth are likely to include uncontrollable disease, starvation, warfare, social disruption, and depletion of life-support systems. If this is to be avoided, we must implement measures to control population growth, to reduce levels of consumption, and to recycle materials.

## KEY WORDS

| | |
|---|---|
| | green revolution |
| | air pollution |
| doubling time | liquid waste |
| geometric or exponential growth | pollute |
| arithmetic growth | acid rain |
| total fertility rate | thermal pollution |
| zero population growth (ZPG) | solid waste |
| marasmus | biotic potential |
| kwashiorkor | environmental resistance |
| carrying capacity | |

## TOPICS FOR REVIEW AND DISCUSSION

1. What are the ecological consequences of a declining death rate and a rising birth rate?

2. Discuss why malnutrition is so prevalent in the world today.

3. How are pollution and population size related to one another?

4. Describe some methods for curbing population growth.

5. Why is farming the sea considered to be a myth?

6. What is the Malthusian theory of population growth?

7. What is smog and what are its causes?

8. What is carrying capacity and how does it influence the size of a population? Relate your answer to the human population.

9. What are the difficulties inherent in predicting the population size of a particular country 20 years hence?

10. How can we prevent the depletion of the earth's natural resources?

11. Why is the green revolution a stopgap measure in controlling worldwide hunger?

12. Why do the developed countries of the world have a greater impact on the world's natural resources than do the underdeveloped countries?

13. Why is thermal pollution the ultimate pollutant?

# Epilogue

When we first started down this path (and it has been somewhat long and circuitous), we were looking for an answer to the question, What is life? We have not answered this seemingly simple question altogether satisfactorily because the question is not simple at all. In attempting to find an adequate response to this query, we have explored much of what is known and have defined areas that remain for future investigation and discovery. The three sections of this book form a hierarchy of human biology. First we took an excursion into the microscopic world of the cell—its structure, function, and regulatory controls. Then we moved on to the larger world of the human organism—in health and sometimes in disease. Next we traveled to the broader realms of inheritance, population genetics, and human evolution. Finally, we looked at the ecology of our earth, glanced at some of the dismal consequences of overpopulation, and took an overview of the effects of environmental tampering by human hands.

And now the path ends. What is the message of all these pages? What have we learned from these explorations into the meaning of life?

Clearly, there are solutions to many of our contemporary problems. Humans are possessed of energy, imagination, reason, determination, and compassion: with these we can solve our most pressing difficulties, and our future can be bright. There is no reason why generations yet unborn cannot reap the rich rewards of a productive and meaningful life here on earth.

We travel together, passengers on a little spaceship, dependent on its vulnerable supplies of air and soil . . . preserved from annihilation only by the care, the work, and I will say the love, we give our fragile craft.

ADLAI E. STEVENSON

# APPENDIX A

# Simple Chemistry for Biology

## ELEMENTS AND ATOMS

1. The universe consists of matter and energy.
2. **Matter** has mass and occupies space; that is, it has weight, volume, and density. **Energy** neither occupies space nor has weight; energy is measured by its capacity to do work.
3. Matter is composed of basic substances called **elements,** which cannot be decomposed into simpler constituents by chemical means.
4. At present 105 elements are known (new ones are continually being discovered), and each is designated by a chemical symbol of one or two letters. Thus, hydrogen is represented by H, oxygen by O, carbon by C, nitrogen by N, chlorine by Cl, and so on.
5. The smallest unit of an element, one that retains the chemical characteristics of the particular element, is called an **atom.**
6. An atom, the basic structure of matter, consists of a positive charged center, or **nucleus,** surrounded by a swirling cloud of negative charged particles called **electrons:**

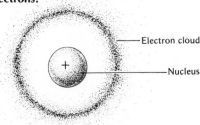

7. The nucleus of an atom contains **protons,** which carry a charge of +1, and **neutrons,** which have no electrical charge.[1] Both protons and neutrons have a mass of 1 (based on an arbitrary unit of atomic mass.)
8. The **atomic number** of a chemical element represents the number of protons in the atomic nucleus; the **mass number** of an element is the sum of the masses of the protons and neutrons. Thus, the nucleus of a carbon atom and an oxygen atom would look as follows:

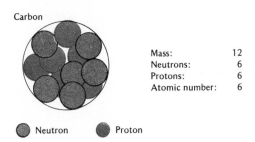

Carbon

| Mass: | 12 |
| Neutrons: | 6 |
| Protons: | 6 |
| Atomic number: | 6 |

○ Neutron  ● Proton

Oxygen

| Mass: | 16 |
| Neutrons: | 8 |
| Protons: | 8 |
| Atomic number: | 8 |

---

[1] Hydrogen, the lightest element, has no neutrons.

9. **Isotopes** are atoms of the same element having the same chemical properties and the same atomic number, but differing in atomic mass. The difference in mass is due to varying numbers of neutrons in the nucleus, the number of protons remaining the same for all isotopes of a given element. Thus, carbon, with an atomic number of 6, has three isotopes with masses of 12, 13, and 14:

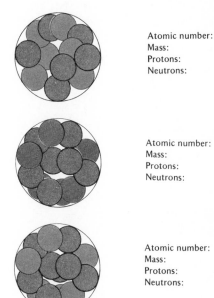

| Atomic number: | 6 |
| Mass: | 12 |
| Protons: | 6 |
| Neutrons: | 6 |

| Atomic number: | 6 |
| Mass: | 13 |
| Protons: | 6 |
| Neutrons: | 7 |

| Atomic number: | 6 |
| Mass: | 14 |
| Protons: | 6 |
| Neutrons: | 8 |

Oxygen, atomic number 8, has three isotopes with masses of 16, 17, and 20. Some isotopes (those designated as **radioactive**) are unstable and undergo nuclear breakdown, liberating radiations and smaller particles. The radioactive isotope of carbon, named carbon 14, is frequently used to follow the chemical reactions of carbon-containing substances in an organism; this and similar radioactive elements are called **tracers.**

10. The electrons surrounding the atomic nucleus have a charge of −1 and have virtually no mass (1/1,850 the mass of a proton). Since the electron cloud has a negligible mass, it is the protons and the neutrons in the nucleus that give an atom almost all its weight. The electrons surrounding the positively charged nucleus occur in discrete shells, or levels, called **orbitals** some distance removed from the nucleus. It is impossible to determine the exact location of a particular electron in its orbital; however, for convenience the electrons of an atom can be shown schematically as a planetary system with discrete orbits for the electrons. For example, an atom of hydrogen can be represented as:

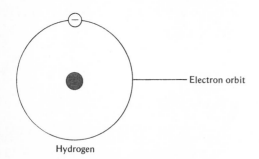

Hydrogen

Carbon can be represented as:

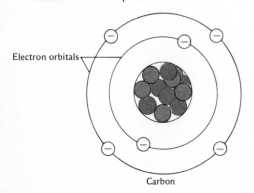

Carbon

11. In a neutral atom the number of negatively charged electrons that orbit the nucleus is balanced exactly by the same number of positive charged protons within the nucleus. A neutral atom has no net charge.

12. The chemical properties of an atom are generally determined by the number of electrons in the outermost orbital(s).

## COMPOUNDS, CHEMICAL BONDS, AND pH

13. The maximum number of electrons each orbital can contain at any one time is two for the orbit closest to the nucleus and eight for the second closest. (Although some atoms contain other orbitals that can hold more than eight electrons, these atoms behave as if they were stable when the outermost orbital contains eight electrons.)

14. An atom having the full complement of electrons in its outermost orbital is chemically unreactive or inert.

15. An atom having fewer than eight electrons in the outermost orbital tends to gain or to lose electrons so that when this orbital becomes filled or emptied the atom attains a stable configuration. (The hydrogen atom, with only a single orbital, requires one additional electron to achieve stability.)

16. When the atoms of two or more elements combine chemically, the resulting product is called a **compound.** Thus, atoms of oxygen and hydrogen may react chemically to form the compound water. Note that the chemical properties of a compound are different from those of its constituent atoms.

17. The basic unit of a compound, one that retains the chemical and physical properties of that compound, is called a **molecule.** For example, two atoms of the element hydrogen and one atom of the element oxygen are chemically bonded together to form a molecule of the compound called water, and the combination of two atoms of oxygen forms molecular oxygen, a gas.

18. The attractive force between two or more atoms in a molecule is called a **chemical bond.** Each bond represents a certain amount of potential chemical energy.

19. An atom that gains an electron becomes negatively charged, whereas an atom that has more protons than electrons is positively charged. Such electrically charged atoms are called **ions.** Ionization may occur when an atom of one element donates one of its electrons to an atom of another element.

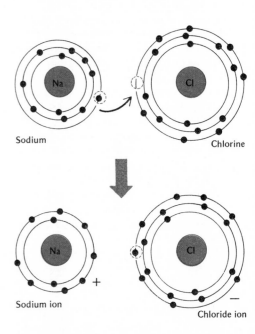

Sodium

Chlorine

Sodium ion

Chloride ion

20. If two ions have opposite electrical charges, they are electrostatically attracted to one another, and the resultant compound is held together by a chemical bond called an **ionic bond.** For example, the attraction of a positive sodium ion to a negative chloride ion produces sodium chloride, or table salt, by ionic bonding. Cystalline sodium chloride is an ionic compound since its constituents are ionized.

21. The ions of ionic compounds have a tendency to break their ionic bonds **(dissociate)** when placed in solution (usually water). This is because the water tends to keep the ions apart. Thus, when table salt, sodium chloride (NaCl), is dissolved in water, free sodium ($Na^+$) and chloride ($Cl^-$) ions are formed.

22. Solutions containing ions can conduct an electrical current. Because of this property, ionic compounds are often called **electrolytes.** By contrast, substances such as table sugar (sucrose), which do not dissociate into ions when placed in water, are **nonelectrolytes.**

23. Acids and bases are important ionic compounds. An **acid** is a substance that dissociates to yield hydrogen ions ($H^+$), also called **protons** because they are hydrogens with only a bare proton and no electrons. A **base** is a substance that dissociates to yield hydroxyl ions ($OH^-$) or that can accept $H^+$ ions.

24. The acidic or base (alkaline) nature of a solution can be measured and described on a scale called **pH.** The pH scale runs from 0 to 14. The midpoint, or neutral value, in the scale is 7, the pH of pure water. At pH 7 the number of $H^+$ and $OH^-$ ions is equal. pH values greater than 7 are found in basic solutions; values less than 7 refer to acid solutions.

```
      acidic              basic
<———————————————————————————————————>
  0 1 2 3 4 5 6  7  8 9 10 11 12 13 14
       ↑            ↑         ↑
 orange juice     blood    soap solution
```

25. pH is defined as the negative logarithm of the molar concentration of $H^+$ ions. A liter of pure water has a hydrogen ion concentration that is $1 \times 10^{-7}$ molar (or 1/10,000,000), and when written as a negative logarithm gives a pH value of 7. A 0.1 molar solution of hydrochloric acid (about 3.6 g of HCl per liter) would dissociate to give a $H^+$ ion concentration of $1 \times 10^{-1}$ molar, and its pH would be 1 (highly acidic). This is a millionfold increase over the hydrogen ion concentration of pure water (pH 7). Since the pH scale is logarithmic, a change of 1 pH unit involves a 10-fold change in $H^+$ concentration.

26. Ionic bonds involve a complete transfer of electrons from one atom to another. However, in some cases chemical bonding involves electron sharing rather than transfer. This is called a **covalent bond.**

27. Carbon combines with the atoms of many other elements by forming covalent bonds; water is made up of two atoms of hydrogen covalently bonded to one oxygen atom. Hydrogen gas is an example of a molecule held together by a covalent bond:

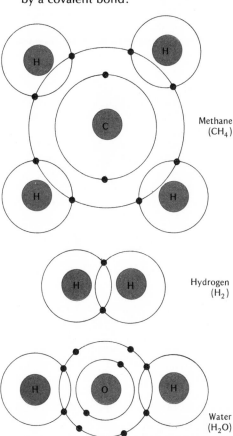

Methane (CH₄)

Hydrogen (H₂)

Water (H₂O)

28. In addition to covalent and ionic bonds, there is another chemical bond, the **hydrogen bond.** Hydrogen bonding, which is much weaker than ionic or covalent bonding, occurs where hydrogen atoms in molecules are electrically attracted to unbonded electrons of nitrogen and oxygen of other molecules— the hydrogen atom acts as a bridge between two other atoms. Water molecules are bonded together by hydrogen bonding, and the three-dimensional structure of proteins and nucleic acids is maintained by hydrogen bonding.

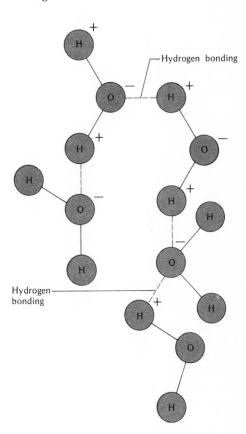

Hydrogen bonding

Hydrogen bonding

## WATER

29. Life as we know it is impossible without water. All cells contain water, and it is only in a watery environment that cells can function. A water molecule is com-

posed of two hydrogen atoms covalently bonded to one oxygen atom. The water molecule is polarized, that is, the molecule has a positively charged end and a negatively charged end. The polarity is a consequence of the nucleus of the oxygen atom attracting more electrons than do the hydrogens, and thus the oxygen end tends to be more electronegative. Also, the geometric configuration of the molecule is such that both hydrogens are placed at one end, creating two positively charged regions and a single negatively charged region:

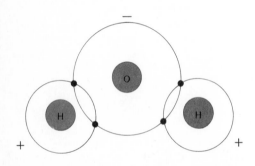

30. Water is a universal solvent, dissolving many substances and thus permitting chemical reactions to take place.
31. Water has a tendency to favor ionization of substances in solution.
32. Water plays an active role in certain chemical reactions, for example, hydrolysis.
33. Water maintains temperature constancy, permitting an organism to resist sudden changes in temperature. This is accomplished because water has a high heat capacity, that is, it can lose and gain large amounts of heat with little change in its own temperature.
34. Water is more dense at 4°C than at 0°C; for this reason, ice floats. This also means that a body of water, such as a lake, freezes from the top down and not from the bottom up, allowing organisms to be protected in deeper waters.

**B.C.** **by Johnny Hart**

© Field Enterprises Inc. 1972. Reprinted by permission.

## CARBON

35. Although water is important in living systems, the chemistry of life is centered on the chemical properties of the carbon atom.
36. Carbon, atomic number 6, has six protons, six neutrons, and six electrons. Since the outermost orbital of carbon contains four electrons, it must borrow, donate, or share four more electrons to become energetically stable.
37. The four electrons in the outer orbital of the carbon atom which can engage in chemical bonding can be represented:

$$-\overset{|}{\underset{|}{C}}-$$

38. Carbon atoms can share electrons with hydrogen, nitrogen, oxygen, and other carbon atoms to form stable compounds. The bonding in such compounds is covalent:

  or  $-\overset{|}{C}-\overset{|}{C}-$

39. The covalent sharing of a pair of electrons between two carbon atoms—the most common kind of bonding in organic compounds—is called a **single bond.** However, carbon atoms may also share

two or three pairs of electrons to form **double** or **triple bonds.** For example, a molecule of ethane has a carbon-carbon single bond, ethylene has a carbon-carbon double bond, and acetylene has a triple bond between carbons:

Oxygen, with six electrons in its outer shell, needs only two more electrons to become energetically stable. If two atoms of oxygen share two pairs of electrons with a single carbon atom, a stable gas, carbon dioxide, results; it contains two carbon-oxygen double bonds:

$$\overset{..}{\underset{..}{O}}::C::\overset{..}{\underset{..}{O}} \qquad \text{or} \qquad O=C=O$$
$$\text{double bonds}$$

40. Carbon-carbon bonding can produce molecules that may be long or short, branched or unbranched, straight or circular. The variety of carbon compounds is virtually endless.

## CHEMICAL REACTIONS

41. In principle, all chemical reactions are reversible, that is:

$$A + B \rightleftharpoons C + D$$

42. All chemical reactions involve changes in energy content.

43. Atoms or molecules interact during a chemical reaction in such a way that electron sharing or exchange takes place.

44. The probability of a chemical reaction occurring is increased when the likelihood of electron-electron interactions is increased.

45. Three ways of increasing the likelihood of two subtances interacting and thus enhancing the rate of a chemical reaction are:
a. Increase the concentration of the reactants (A + B) or decrease the concentration of the products (C + D)
b. Increase the temperature or pressure

c. Arrange the molecules or atoms so that collisions are likely to occur; that is, subdivide or dissolve the substances or provide a large surface area

46. Chemical reactions in which the products contain less energy than the reacting materials release energy (usually in the form of heat) and are called **exergonic reactions.** Exergonic reactions are "downhill" reactions:

$$A + B \longrightarrow C + D + \text{energy}$$

47. Reactions in which the products contain more energy than the reacting materials absorb energy and are called **endergonic reactions.** Endergonic reactions are uphill reactions:

$$\text{energy} + A + B \longrightarrow C + D$$
$$\text{or}$$
$$A + B \longleftarrow C + D + \text{energy}$$

48. In a living system endergonic and exergonic reactions are coupled to one another in such a way that the energy released from an exergonic reaction is used to drive the endergonic one.

49. If the chemical reaction of substances A + B to give products C + D is left to itself, chemical equilibrium will result; that is:

$$A + B \rightleftharpoons C + D$$

At equilibrium the concentrations need not be the same for reactants and products, but the rates of forward and reverse reactions must be the same.

50. A living system cannot exist in a state of chemical equilibrium. In the chemistry of the cell there must be a directionality to the flow of carbon compounds and/or energy. In the reaction of substances A + B to yield the products C + D, the direction will be A + B → C + D and not the reverse if:
a. The concentration of products (C + D) is less than that of the equilibrium concentrations
b. The products (C + D) are removed or used in subsequent reactions
c. Energy is released, thus giving C + D less energy content than A or B

51. Whether a reaction will occur (even if it is exergonic, or "downhill") depends on whether the reactants receive the proper amount of activation energy. The activation energy is the "push" necessary to start the downhill reaction, and its magnitude varies for different reactants.

52. A driving force for chemical reactions can be provided only by a transition from a highly organized state of matter to one that is less organized (unless energy is supplied).

53. Since living organisms obey the same chemical and physical laws as nonliving systems, understanding the mechanisms of chemical reactions enables us to comprehend the way in which living systems—we—work.

# APPENDIX B

# What Ever Happened to Metric?

Austrians have officially given up the *becher* and the *pfiff* as units of volume. The Soviets likewise no longer use the *zolotnik* and the *funt* for weight. So why do Americans cling to such archaic units of measurement as the pound, bushel and inch? Our system of units, a modification of the so-called British imperial system, which even Britain has largely abandoned, is complicated. Converting from inches to feet requires dividing by twelve, (quick how many feet is 97 inches?); going from pounds to ounces calls for multiplying by 16. By comparison, the metric system is a breeze: just move the decimal point, and, presto! five meters equals 500 centimeters equals .005 kilometers.

Besides Burma, the United States is the only nation in the world that has not formally begun converting to metric. There was a time, while Britain was the U.S.'s major trading partner, when it would have been economic suicide to consider switching to metric. In fact, it was precisely such arguments that torpedoed Secretary of State Thomas Jefferson's proposal that the U.S. adopt a decimal-based system in 1790. A study 31 years later by his successor, John Quincy Adams, was similarly unpersuasive. But in 1866, Congress, charged by the Constitution with establishing the nation's weights and measures, declared the metric system valid for "contracts, dealings or court proceedings," and in 1893 officially defined the foot, pound and inch in metric equivalents.

Finally, by the 1960s, most of the rest of the world had gone or was going metric.

**603**

Congress responded with legislation, and in 1975, after years of debate, the Metric Conversion Act became law. The U.S. finally appeared ready for a decisive entry into a new metric era.

Sure enough, signs in both miles and kilometers started to spring up on highways, along with posters exhorting drivers to THINK METRIC. Service stations started pumping gas by the liter. And consumers began to get queasy. "You didn't know how much you wanted, you didn't know how much you got, and you didn't know how much you paid for it," sympathizes G.T. Underwood, director of the Commerce Department's Office of Metric Programs. "But you knew you felt pretty bad about the metric system."

These days, conversion to metric is just a vaguely unpleasant memory for most consumers. The highway signs are largely gone, and the pumps dole out gas mostly by the gallon again. The few visible monuments to metric conversion include liter bottles of soda and liquor, time-and-temperature signs that still flash degrees in Celsius, and gram equivalents on food containers.

The metric system is alive and well, on the other hand, in many areas where it makes sense such as the sciences. An estimated 25% of U.S. manufacturers are metric; more than 60% of FORTUNE 500 companies produce at least some metric products, in contrast to between 10% and 20% in the early 1970s. The automobile industry, for example, is almost entirely metric.

The changeover to the metric system, need not be an all-or-nothing proposition— a remarkably sensible perspective. After all, the reasons for conversion are economic: it is important for U.S. industry to compete in international markets, but there is no particular value in changing the weather report on the nightly news. For most Americans, it seems, an ounce of prevention was worth a kilogram of cure.

© *Time* July 6, 1987

## LENGTH

### SI[1] to English

| | |
|---|---|
| 1 km (kilometer) | = 0.62 mi (mile) |
| 1 m (meter) | = 3.28 ft (feet) |
| 1 cm (centimeter) | = 0.394 in. (inch) |
| 1 μm (micrometer) | = 1/25,400 in. |

### English to SI

| | | |
|---|---|---|
| 1 mi | = 1.609 km | |
| 1 yd (yard) | = 0.9144 m | |
| 1 ft | = 30.48 cm | |
| 1 in. | = 2.54 cm | = 25.4 mm (millimeters) |

### SI

| | |
|---|---|
| 1,000 meters | = 1 kilometer |
| 0.01 meter | = 1 centimeter |
| 0.001 meter | = 1 millimeter |
| 0.000001 meter | = 1 micrometer |
| 0.000000001 meter | = 1 nanometer (nm) |
| 0.0000000001 meter | = 1 Angstrom (Å) |

## WEIGHT

### SI to English

| | |
|---|---|
| 1 kg (kilogram) | = 2.2 lb (pounds) |
| 1 g (gram) | = 0.035 oz (ounce) |

[1] The official name for the new system is International System of Units. This is usually abbreviated "SI" because French is the official language of the General Conference overseeing worldwide conversion and thus "Système Internationale" becomes "SI." Since the international system is essentially, but not totally, the same as the metric system, the term "metric" is sometimes used to describe the new system. However, "SI units" is the official terminology and the one used more and more today.

### English to SI

| | |
|---|---|
| 1 oz | = 28.35 g |
| 1 lb | = 0.4536 kg |

### SI

| | |
|---|---|
| 1000 g | = 1 kilogram |
| 0.001 g | = 1 milligram (mg) |
| 0.000001 g | = 1 microgram (μg) |

## VOLUME

### SI to English

| | |
|---|---|
| 1 liter | = 0.2643 gal (gallon) |
| 1 ml (milliliter) | = 0.03 fl oz |

### English to SI

| | | |
|---|---|---|
| 1 gal | = 3.7854 liters | |
| 1 qt (quart) | = 0.946 liter | = 946 ml |
| 1 pt (pint) | = 0.473 liter | = 473 ml |
| 1 fl oz | = 0.029 liter | = 29 ml |

### SI

| | |
|---|---|
| 1 liter | = 1,000 ml |
| 0.001 liter | = 1 ml |
| 0.000001 liter | = 1 μl (microliter) |

## TEMPERATURE

### SI to English

Degrees Fahrenheit (°F) = (°C × 9/5) + 32
  Note: 9/5 = 1.8

### English to SI

Degrees Celsius (°C) = (°F − 32) × 5/9
  Note: 5/9 = 0.5556

# Index

Page numbers in boldface type refer to definitions of words; these words are also in **boldface** type on that page of the book. Page numbers in *italic* type refer to pages where a figure and/or table appears.

A band, **442**
Abductor muscle, **438**
Abiotic synthesis, **21**
Abortion, 214
   dilation and curettage (D and C), **214**
   saline, **214**
   spontaneous, 214
   suction, **214**
Abcess, dental, 247
Absorption, intestinal, **235, 237**
Acclimation, **316**
Accommodation, **397**
*Acetabularia*, 45, *47*
Acetone, 349
Acetyl coenzyme A, **89,** 92
Acetyl group, **89**
Acetylcholine. *See* ACh
Acetylcholinesterase, 375
Acetylene, 600
ACh, 374, 444
Acid, **599**
Acid rain, **584**
Acidity. *See* pH
Acidosis, 349
Acne, 229
Acquired immunity, **282,** 288
   active, **288**
   passive, **288**
Acromegaly, **343**
ACTH, **341,** 352, 353, 358
Actin, **441,** *444*
Action potential, **367, 369,** 371, 377
   initiation of, 377
   of membrane, 369, 370
   of muscle, 444, 445
Activation energy, **72,** *74*

Activation energy barrier, 74
Activator molecule, 147
Active acquired immunity, 288
Active transport, 32, 34, 35, 59
   in digestion, 238
   in kidney, *328*
Actomyosin, **441,** *442*
Adaptive behavior, 410, 418
Adaptive radiation, 521
Addison's disease, 351
Adductor muscle, **438**
Adenine, 13, **109**
Adenohypophysis, 338. *See also* Anterior
   pituitary
Adenosine diphosphate, 84
Adenosine triphosphate, *See* ATP
Adenyl cyclase, 359
ADH, **329, 341.** *See also* Vasopressin
Adipose tissue, **240**
Adiposogenital dystrophy, 355–356
Adolescent, 173
ADP, **84,** *279*
Adrenal cortex, **350, 351,** 381
Adrenal corticosteroids, 352
Adrenal glands, **350,** *351,* 356, *361,* 455
Adrenal medulla, **350,** 381, 455
Adrenal tumor, 354
Adrenaline. *See* Epinephrine
Adrenocorticosteroids, 352
Adrenocorticotropic hormone. *See* ACTH
Adsorption, 13
Adsorption site, 75
Adult onset diabetes, 241
Aerobes, **85**
Aerobic cells, cyanide, 87
Aerobic respiration, **85,** 89, 91–92
Afterbirth, 196, 199, 203, 207, 208, 209
Age, of earth, 520
Age structure
   Mexico, 574
   Sweden, 574
   U.S., 574

Agglutinins, 293, 478
Agglutinogens, **293, 478**
Aggregation, **422**
Aggression
   and alcohol, 388
   and infantile behavior, 426
   and instinctive behavior, 413
   in primates, 416
   reduction, 426
Agranulocytes, **278**
Agricultural revolution, 576, 591
Agriculture
   in California, 580, 581
   and ecology, 564
   and energy, *581*
AIDS (Acquired immune deficiency syndrome),
   **185,** *190–191,* 290
   affected populations, 190–191
   carriers, *190*
   causes and prevention, 190–191
   death rates, *190*
   distribution, *190*
   history, *290*
   and IV drug use, *190*
   mechanics, *290*
   myths about, *191*
   projected spread, *190*
   and protective behavior, *190*
   and T4 cells, *287*
Air, 301
   gases in, 301
   kinetic energy of, 398
Air pollution, **582,** 584, *585*
Albinism, **226, 394**
   inheritance of, *470–471*
   pedigree in, 466
Albino, **465,** *466,* 467
Albumin, **275,** 276
Alcohol, 63, 237, 241–245, 385–386
Alcoholism, treatment, 247
Aldosterone, 330
*Alice in Wonderland, 32*

Alimentary canal, 233. *See also* Digestive system
Allantoic arteries, **206**
Allele(s), **465,** 466
  blood type, 478
  recessive, *505*
Allergens, **298**
Allergic response, 298
Allergy, 261
Allison, A. C., 504
All-or-none law, **372**
Alpha antibodies, 478
Alpha globulins, **275**
Alpha helix, 69
Alpha waves, **372**
Altitude
  and barometric pressure, *316*
  and oxygen deprivation, 316, *317*
"Alton Giant," 342
Alveolar capillary, 304
Alveolus (alveoli), **303,** 304–309
Amazon rain forest, 557
Amazon River, 557
Ameba(e), 254. *See also* Amoeba
  movement, 28
  nuclear transplant, 45, 46
Amenorrhea, **189**
American Cancer Society, 154, 157
Ames, Bruce, 156
Ames test, 156
Amino acids, **13,** *14,* 30, **68,** 118
  activated, 117
  dietary, 112, 235, 241
  essential, **112**
  laboratory synthesis, 12
  in seminal fluid, 173
  sequence, 121
  stereoisomers of, 62
  world deficiency of, 241
Aminopterin, 76
Ammonia, *322,* 550
Amnesia, 420
Amniocentesis, 202, **461,** *462*
Amnion, **206**
Amniotic fluid, 204
Amniotic sac, 206, 209
Amoeba, *46, 254*
AMP, 17, 375
Amphetamines, 384
Amphibia, 301, 514
Amplitude, sound, **398**
Amylase, 74
Amytal, 386
Anaerobes, **85**

Anaerobic muscle contractions, 446
Anaerobic respiration, **85,** 86, *87*
Anafranil, 384
Anal sphincters, **240**
Analog, 7
Anaphase, **132,** *170*
Anaphylactic shock, **298**
Androgens, **352,** 354
Androstenedione, **352**
Anectine, 384
Anemia, 247, 281
  and heart failure, 281
  sickle cell, *494, 495, 496*
Anger, flight-or-fight responses, 381
Animal, 53
  adaptive behavior, *410*
  cell, *26,* 136
  kingdom, 511
  nervous system, 408
Animalia, 53
Annual growth rate, Sri Lanka, *571*
Annual radiation, 500
ANS, 381
Antagonists, muscle, **438**
Antelope, and ritual fighting, **426**
Anterior chamber, eye, **394**
Anterior pituitary, **338,** *340, 341, 357*
Anthropoids, and humans, *518*
Anthropologists, 433
Anthropomorphism, 409
Antibody, **158, 282**
  alpha, 69, **478**
  and antigen, *288, 292*
  beta, **478**
  blood, 282, 289
  circulating, 293
  colostrum, 288
  fetal, 206
  formation, *289*
  generators, **284**
  and heavy chains, *292*
  and light chains, *292*
  IgE, 298
  lysins, **293**
  monoclonal, 295
  neutralizing, 292
  proteins, 289
  receptor, 284
  recognition site, 289
  response, 288
Antibody-mediated immunity, **285**
Anticodon, **117**
Antidiuretic hormone. *See* ADH

Antigen(s), **284**
  and antibody, *288, 292*
  booster shots, 288
  "not-self," 284
  in tissue transplant, 297
Antigen-antibody reaction, 295
Antigenic determinant, **289**
Antihistimines, **298**
Antimetabolite, **74**
Antithrombin, **281**
Antitoxin, **293**
Antivenin, **293**
Aorta, **254**
Aortic valve, **257**
Ape, characteristics, 514, 515
Apelike ancestor, 523, *529*
Apnea, **314**
Apollo, 569
Appeasement behavior, **425**
Appendicitis, **250**
Appendicular skeleton, 431
Appendix, **250**
Appendix A (Chemistry for Biology) 597–601
Appendix B (Metric System), 603–604
Aqueous humor, 47
Ardrey, Robert, 411
Areola, 209, 211
Aristotle, 511
Arithmetic growth, population, 570
Arms, fetal, 213
Arsenic, and cancer, 153
Arterioles, **254**
Artery, **254**
  atherosclerotic, *66*
  blockage, *66,* 264
  normal, *66*
Arthritis, **439**
Artificial heart, 260
  risks, 260–261
Artificial heart valve, 258
Artificial insemination, 176
Artificial kidney, 320, 330–331
Artificial pacemaker, 268
Artificial valves, 257
Asexual reproduction, 501
Asimov, Isaac, 274
Asphyxia, 305, 314
Association area, **419**
Asters, 131
Asthma, 298, 306
Astigmatism, **397**
Astral rays, **131**
Atabrine excretion, 328

Atherosclerosis, 66, 67, *263,* **264**
  prevention, 266
  in women, 356
Atmosphere, 11, 12, **301**
  carbon dioxide, 21, *557*
  composition, 311
  early earth, 11, 12, 21
  and greenhouse effect, 556
  oxidizing, 12
  pressure, 12
  reducing, 11, 12, 17, 21
Atom, **597**
  electron, **597**
  neutron, **597**
  nucleus, **597**
  proton, **597**
Atomic bomb, 547
Atomic number, **597**
Atomic wastes, 547–549
ATP, 17, 43, *84,* 358, 550
  in aerobic respiration, 85, 92
  in chemical bonds, 93
  formation, 85, 94
  and kidney, 93
  molecule, 85
  and muscle contraction, 441, 443, 445
  and neuron, 375
  and sodium pump, 93, 371
  and transport, 93, 94
  uses, *93*
  yield, 92
ATPase and muscle contraction, **442,** 445, 446
Atrioventricular node (AV), **258**
Atrium, **256**
  contraction, 256
  fibrillation, 259
Atrophy, **447**
Atropine, 384
Auditory nerves, 401
Augmentation, **328**
Auricle, **398**
Australian bower birds, 425
Australopithecus, **525,** *527, 528,* 530
Autoimmune disorder, **284**
Autonomic nervous system. *See* ANS
Autonomous growth, 160
Autosomes, **462**
Autotrophs, 21, 22, **117, 540**
AV bundle, **258**
AV node, 258
Avery, O. T., 108
Axial skeleton, **431**
Axons, 367, 394, 401, 444

Axoplasmic flow, **357**
Azathioprine, 297
Azotobacter, 550
AZT, *290*
Aztecs, 290

B12, 280
B cells, 271, *283,* **284**
B lymphocytes, **284**
Baboons, and social dominance, 423
Backbone, **431**
Background radiation, **499**
Bacteria, 9, 143
  chromosomes, 143–144
  classification, 53
  decomposers, 549
  nitrogen fixing, 550
  phagocytosis of, **35,** 40, **108**
Bacterial culture, growth, *590*
Bacteriophage, **155** *See also* Virus
  life cycle, 54
Balance, 401–403
Balanced diet, 241, *242–246*
Balanced ecosystem, 540
Balanced polymorphism, **505**
Baldness
  cosmetic surgery, *228*
  male, 227
  in women, 227
Ball-and-socket joint, 439
Balsa wood, 49
Barbiturates, 313
  addiction, 385
  tolerance, 385
Barnard, Christian, 297
Barnum, P. T., 343
Barometric pressure, and altitude, 316
Barr body, **475,** 485
Bartholin's glands, 182
Basal body, 42
Basal metabolic rate (BMR), 240
Base, 113, **599**
Base pairing, 111, 116
Base sequence, 113
Base-pair substitution, 161
Basophil, *278*
Bateson, W. R., 472
Battery, *84*
Beadle, G. W., 113
Beatson, G., 159
Beaumont, William, 238
Becquerel, Henri, 499

Bee
  dances, 425
  diploid females, 424
  drone, 424
  eggs, 424
  food glands, 424
  haploid males, 424
  kinship, **425**
  language, 425
  male, 424
  nectar, 424
  queen, 424
  trophallaxis, **424**
  workers (females), 424
Beer, 63, 88
  diuretic effect, **407,** 427
Behavior
  adaptive, *410*
  animal, *410*
  anthropomorphism, *409*
  appeasement, 425, 426
  black-headed gull, *426*
  C.I.A. data, *406*
  complexity, 411, 426
  and conditioning, 417–418
  conflict, 414
  and consciousness, 409
  control, 406
  development, 407
  division of labor, 424
  dominance, 425
  and drive, 410
  duckling, 419
  environment, 410
  experience, 407
  feeding, 414
  and future of man, 427
  gambling, 418
  genetic basis, 410
  innate, 427
  instinctive, 408, 411–415
  learned, 407
  and mating, 422
  monkey, 416
  and nervous system, 407, 408
  pigeon, 412
  plant, 407
  primate, 416
  and punishment, 412
  rat, 418
  and reinforcement, 417
  reproductive, 411
  and rewards, 412

Behavior (*continued*)
  social, **422**–426
  and social implications, 426
  stereotyped, 408
  survival, 407
  and taxis, 410–411
  and temperature control, 456
  territorial, 422–423
Behavioral control, 366
Behaviorists, **408,** 410
Bel, 400
Bel scale of loudness, 400
Bell, Alexander Graham, *400*
Belladonna, 384
Bends (decompression sickness), 317
Benzadrine, 384
3:4 benzpyrene, 153, 154
Berger, Hans, 372
Beriberi, 76
Beta agglutinins, 478
Beta antibodies, **275**
Beta blockers, 266
Beta globulins, 276
Beta waves, **372**
β-galactosidase, 142
Bicarbonate, 309
Biceps, *438*
Bicuspid valve, **257**
Bikini Atoll, *498*
Bile, 249
Bile pigment, 250
Bilirubin, **249**
Biliverdin, **249–250**
Biological world, energy cascade, **85,** *86,* 97–98,
    *99, 100*
Biology hierarchy, *539*
Biomass, **543**
  pyramid, *544*
Biome, **564**
  North American, **565**
Bioplasts, 38
Biosphere, **539,** *540*
Biotic potential, **591**
Bipolar cells, 394
Bipedalism, 525, 530
Birds
  courtship behavior, 425
  habituation in, 425
Bird-of Paradise, 425
  courtship of, 425
Birth, **209**
  breaking of the waters, 209
  canal, 209

date calculation, 189
  uterine contractions, 209
  vaginal show, 209
Birth defects, 213, 217
  causes, 213, 215
  and chromosomes, 215
  clubfoot, 213
  congenital aberrations, **215**
  and disease, 216
  genetic, 215
  harelip, 213
  heart, 215, 216
  hydrocephalic, 213
  influenza, 216
  measles, 216
  mental retardation, 215
  mumps, 216
  rubella, 216
  scarlet fever, 216
  smallpox, 216
  spina bifida, **215**
  split spines, 215
  syphilis, 216
  teratogens, **215**
  and Thalidomide, 213, 215–216
  tuberculosis, 216
  and x-rays, 217
Birth rate, *571–572*
  Sri Lanka, *571–572*
  United States, *576*
*Biston betularia,* 503, *504*
Black-headed gull, behavior, *426*
Bladder, 332, *333*
Blastocyst, *197*
Blastula, 197
Blind spot, **395**
Blocked coronary artery, *264*
Blocked methionine, 121
Blood, **275–299**
  analysis, 280
  pH, 276
  calcium levels, 346
  cells, 275. *See also* Red blood cell(s); White
    blood cell(s)
  centrifugation, *276*
  clot, 279
  color, 276
  count, 280–281
  dialysis, **331**
  donor, **478**
  eosinophil count, 281
  formed elements, 275
  forming tissue, 52

function, 275
  glucose, 60, 329
  glucose level, 61, 329
  group, 479
  immune cells, *288*
  nutrients, *267–275*
  plasma, 275, 277
  plasma cell, *286–287*
  platelet breakdown, 281
  platelets, 279
  quantity, 275
  recipient, **478**
  Rh factor, 479–481
  safety mechanisms, 281
  salts, 275
  scabs, 278
  and seawater, 275
  sugars, 275
  supply, 275
  transfusion, 478, *479*
  types, 478–481, *514*
  typing, *478*
  viscosity, 276
  weight, 275
Blood pressure, **262**
  diastolic, 262
  flow rates, *265*
  measurement, *264*
  and osmotic pressure, 266–270
  and shock, 265, 270
  systolic, **262**
Blood vessels, *256*
  artery, **254**
  of bone, 432
  capillary, 266–269
  constriction of, 263–264
  fetal, 203
  innervation of, 381
  structure of, *256*
  vein, *256*
Bloody nose, *306*
Bloom's, syndrome, 162
"Blue Baby," 208
Body composition, 9
  fat, 65, 66
  fluid, *322*
Body reflexes, **378**
Body temperature, 453–456, *457*
  fetal, 206
"Bokanofsky's Process," 169
Bolus, and digestion, **233**
Bomb calorimeter, **89**
Bonaparte, Napoleon, 354

Bond energy, **83**
Bonding covalent, 141, **599**
Bone, 431–435
  collagen, **431**
  compact, 431
  fetal, 204
  fossil, 433
  growth, 431–*435*
  growth zone, 433
  healing, 431, 435
  marrow, 276, 277, 431, 434, 483
  organization, 431
  resorption, 434
  salts, 431
  of skeleton, *432*
  spongy, 431
  strength, 435
  structure of, *434*
Burkitt's lymphoma, 165
Borlaug, Norman E., 103
Botulin toxin, 448–449
Boulding, Kenneth, 592
Bowels, **240**
Bowman's capsule, **324**
Boyd, W. C., 533, *534*
*Boys From Brazil*, 128
Brain, **378,** 380, *419. See also specific region in
    question*
  association area, 420
  cerebellum, **378,** *380*
  cerebum, **378,** *380*
  corpus collosum, 380
  damage, 372
  development, 530
  electrically manipulated, 365
  embryonic, 199
  endorphins, 383
  fetal, 205
  gray matter, 378
  hypothalmus, *380*
  integrated response, 382
  and learning, 419
  limbic system, *380*
  medulla, **378**
  motor neurons, 380
  and nerves, 365, 377
  pons, 380
  reticular formation, 380
  size, 378, *529*
  stimulation, 365
  structure, 378
  thalamus, 380
  tumor, 372

  ventricles, 377
  waves, **372**
  white matter, 378
Bravo nuclear test, *498*
Bread baking, 88
Breaking of the waters, 209
Breast(s), **209**
  anatomy of, *211*
  development, 68, 209, *212*
  in pregnancy, 211
Breastbone, 431
Breathing, 85, **301**
  capacity, 311
  control, 312
  cycle frequency, 313
  diaphragmatic, 309, 311
  fetal, 209
  inhibition, 316
  movements, 309, *311*
  rate, 313
  reflex system, 311
  reflexes, 216, 312
  triggering mechanisms, 314
  under water, 314–315
Breeder reactors, 583
Breeding pattern, 529
Broad ligament, **177**
Bronchi, **303**
Bronchiolar constriction, 298
Bronchiole, **303**
Bronchitis, 304, 306
  and air pollution, 308
Brow, human, 514
Brown, Robert, 43
Buerger's disease, 155
Bulbourethral glands (Cowper's glands), 173
Bumblebees, and social dominance, 424–425
Bursa, **439**
Bursitis, **439**
"Butter yellow", 153
Bypass surgery, 266

Cabrillo, Juan Rodriguez, 586
Cadmium, 544
Caesar, Julius, 372
Caffeine, 384
Caisson disease (decompression
    sickness), **317**
Calciferol, 309, 348
  in Neanderthal Man, 531
Calcitonin, **344, 346**
Calcium
  in blood, *348*

  in bones, 348
Calcium carbonate, 431
Calcium ions
  level of, 346
  metabolism, *346*
  and muscle contraction, 442, 445
  oxalate, 332
  phosphate, 332, 431
  regulation, *548*
  salts, 431
Calf muscle, 446
Calico cats, 478
Calluses, 223
Caloric values, *242*
  intake, 243
Calories, 89, **183,** 240, 578
  deprivation, 241
  and nutrition, 240
Calving, 556
cAMP, **358**
Campbell, J. A., 592
Cancer, **151,** *152*
  and aging, *160*
  and air pollution, **154**
  autonomy, 151
  benign, *153*
  bladder, 153, 155
  breast, 153, 158, 159
  causes, 153–164
  cells, *160*
  death, 151, 157
  invasive, *153*
  lung, 155
  lymphoma, 162
  metastatic, 152, *153,* 164
  mutations, **161**
  occupational, 153
  prostate, 161
  and radiation, 156–157
  screen, 156
  scrotal, 153
  skin, 151
  and smoking, *154,* 155
  stomach, 161
  and sunburn, *157*
  uterine, 154
  and viruses, 157–160
Cancer hypotheses, 160–164
  mutations, 160
  oncogenes, 162
  transposons, 161
*Cannabis sativa*, **385**
Capillary, **255**

Capillary (*continued*)
  alveolar, 269
  cross section, *267*
  diffusion, *267*
  endothelial cells, 266
  fluid exchange, 267
  hydrostatic pressure, 269
  and tissue space, 267, 269, 270
  wall, 266–267
Carbohydrate diet, 241
Carbohydrate(s), 28, **59**
  fixation, *18*, 102. *See also* Photosynthesis
  production in photosynthesis, 38
  storage, 59
Carbon, **600**
  cycle, **550**, *551*
Carbon dioxide, 305, 550
  in atmosphere, 557
  atmospheric regulation of, 17, 556
  as cellular poison, 301
  exchange, 304
  formation, 99–102
  greenhouse effect, 556
  in plasma, 305
  and respiratory rate, 310–311
Carbon monoxide, 584
Carbonic acid, 309
Carboxyl group, 68
Carboxylase, **88**
Carcinogens, **33**
  Ames test for, *156*
  chemical, 153
  dietary, **153**
  environmental, 153–154, 161
  hormonal, **153**
  hydrocarbons, 153
  smoking, 154
  sunburn, 155
  transposons, 162
Carcinoma, 151
Cardiac arrhythmia, 384
Cardiac constrictor muscle, 248
Cardiac cycle, 269
Cardiac impulse, 258
Cardiac muscle, 258, 436
  metabolism, 258
  rhythm of, 259
Cardiovascular damage, and air pollution, 584
Cardiovascular disease, 263–264
Caries, **247**
Carnivores, **541**, 542
Carotenoids, 39, 98
Carotid arteries, 314

Carrier, **467**
  molecules, 34
  proteins, **326**
Carrying capacity, **559**
Carson, Rachel, 546
Cartilage, 47, 431
  flexible, 432
  hyaline, 433
  rigid, 432
  structure of, *434*
Castration, **352**
Catalyst(s), 17, **72**
  function, 75
  properties, 72
Catecholamines, **375**
Catheter, 333
Cathode ray tube, *33*
Caton, Richard, 372
CAT (Computerized axial tomography, 373
Caudatum population growth, *560*
Cavities, 247
Cell(s), **25**. *See also specific cell type in question*
  alteration, 144
  anaphase, 134, 136–137, *170*
  animal, **28**, *254*
  architecture of, *26, 27*
  B, 284
  blood. *See* Red blood cell(s), White Blood cell(s)
  boundary, 25, 28
  cancer, *77, 160*
  cheek, *475*
  cleavage, **132, 195**
  compartmentalization, 94
  cycle, 137
  cytotoxic T, 484
  daughter, 135
  differentiation, 134
  diploid, 170
  DNA, 38
  drinking, *35*
  eating, *35*
  "engine," 59, 60
  epithelial, 307
  equator, 131
  excitable, **369**
  Fallopian tubes, 42
  fixation, 33
  germ, **171**
  glial, **366, 377**
  green plant, 97
  growth patterns, *160*

haploid, **171**
interphase, **130**, *136*
interstitial, 352
intestinal, 129
lymph-node, 278
mast, 298
mechanical systems, **140**
metaphase, **131**, *133*, 136, 137, 170
mineral requirements of, *246*
muscle, 49, 436, 445, *446*
neoplastic, 162
nerve, 341
normal growth, *160*
olfactory, 391
pathways, *38*
phagocytic, 39
plant, *27*
plasma, 277, 285
primary wall, **49**
prokaryotic, 53
prophase, 136, 137, 170
radiation effect, *498*
respiration, 38, 53, **301**
resting, **130**
sap, **41**
Schwann, 368
secondary wall, **49**
Sertoli, 172
sickled red-blood, 69, 496
skin, 49, *133*, 462
somatic, **171**
specialization, 49
stained, **33**
structure, 25–36
syncytium, **436**
T, **284**, 287
telophase, *135, 136, 170*
tracheal, 42
transformation, 162
types, 25
typical, 25, *26, 27*
unstained, 33
vitamins required, *244, 245*
wall, 27, 48
Cell division, 48, 129, **129, 132**. *See also* Meiosis; Mitosis
  bacteria, 133
  and cancer, 151–152
  dedifferentiation, 134
  implications of, 134
  mechanics, 129–133
  skin, 132
  timing, 133

Cell-mediated immunity, **285**
Cellophane, 49
Cellular bathing solution, 323
Cellular location, photosynthesis, 98–99
Cellular respiration, **301**
Cellulose, **48, 63,** 64
Central nervous system (CNS), 313
  elements, 379
  organization, *379*
  tissue, *52*
Centrifugation of blood, *276*
Centriole, **142,** 43, **130**
Centromere, 131
Cephalin, 67
Cerebellum, *312,* **378**
Cerebral concussion, 313
Cerebral cortex, 313, **378**
Cerebral hemisphere, **378**
Cerebral palsy, 545
Cerebrospinal fluid, **378**
Cerebrum, 312, **378**
Cervix, **182**
  dilation, 209
  in labor, 209
Cesarian section, **214**
CFC's (chlorofluorocarbons), 557
Chain terminator codons, **118**
Chaplin, Charlie, 479
Chargaff, Erwin, 10
Chemical(s)
  body, 59
  bonds, 301, **598**
  and breathing, 301
  and environmental accumulation, 544–549
  food, 59, 301
  and memory, 421
  structure, 107
  and work, 81
Chemical reactions, 72, **601**
Chemical receptors, and respiration, *314*
Chemistry for Biology (Appendix A), *597–601*
Chernobyl Power Plant, *483,* 549
Chest cavity, *34*
Chickenpox, and birth defects, 216
Chickens, and social dominance, 423
Childhood diseases, 288
Children, training of, 418
Chimney sweeps, cancer in, 153
Chimpanzee, 515
Chloasma, **189**
Chloride ions, 327, 369
Chlorinated hydrocarbons, 544
Chlorine, 10

Chlorofluorocarbons (CFCs), 557, 558
p-Chlorophenyl dimethyl urea, 102. *See also*
  CMU
Chlorophyll, **38, 198**
  a and b, 98
  light phase, 98
  molecular structure, 98, *100*
Chloroplast, **38,** 39, *40,* 98
  development, 38
  energy fixation, 38–39
  in eukaryotes, **53**
  grana, **39**
  lamellae, **39**
  stroma, **39,** 102
  structure, *40*
Chlorpromazine, 385
Cholesterol, **67,** *352*
  structure, 57
Choline, in seminal fluid, 173
Cholinergic nerve, **382**
Chondrocytes, **432**
Chondroitin sulfate, **46,** 47, 432
Chorion, **206**
Chorion frondosum, **206**
Chorionic blood vessels, 206
Chorionic gonadotrophin, **189**
Chorionic villi, **206**
Chorionic villi, sampling (CVS), *202*
Choroid coat, **393**
Chromates, and cancer, 153
Chromatid(s), **131,** *132,* 473
  packaging of DNA, 134–135
Chromatin, **130,** *132*
  and hormone-receptor complex, 359–360
  nucleosome, **136**
Chromosome(s), 43, 53, **130,** 132, 134, 169, **461,**
    *464*
  abnormal arrangement, 134
  abnormal structure, 164, **488,** *489*
  abnormalities, 164, 482–489
  analysis, 463, 487
  anaphase, 132, *170*
  ape, 514
  bacterial, 143–144
  base alteration, 489
  coiling, 131
  combinations, 502
  daughter, **132**
  deletion, **488,** *489*
  diploid number, **461**
  distribution, 482
  duplication, 140, **488,** *489*
  female, *133*

giant, **138**
homologous, **170, 465,** 472
human, 514
inversion, **488,** *489*
karotype, *463*
nondisjuncion, **484**
puffs, 139, 140
rearrangements, 162
segregation, 471
sex, **462**
sex test, 484
structure, *132,* 134, 137
synapsis, **170**
synthetic activity, 131
translocation, 164, **488,** *489*
Chromosome 5, 445, 488
Chromosome 15, 416, *490, 491*
Chromosome 21, 444, *488, 489, 490*
Cigarettes and cancer, 154, 155
Cilia, 42, 43, *44,* 180, 303
Ciliary body, **394**
Ciliary muscles, 397
Ciliated epithelial cells, *307*
Cingulotomy, 406
Circulating antibody, 275, 293
Circulation, fetal, 206
Circulatory system, **253, 255**
  artery, 254
  blood vessels, 253
  fetal, 206
  function, 253, 255
  heart, **255–261**
  human, 253
  and respiration, 301
  size, 253
  vein, 255
Cirrhosis, **247,** 276, 387
Cisternae, Golgi, 37
Citric acid, *369*
Citric acid, in seminal fluid, 173
Citric acid cycle, **89,** *90*
City, development of, 581
Clams, *302*
Class, **513**
Classical conditioning, **417,** 418
Classical genetics, **461**
Classification
  cat, *513*
  development, **513**
  function, **513**
  hierarchy, 511, 512
  human, *513*
  of organisms, 173, 571

Classification (*continued*)
  primates, *518*
  structure, *513*
Cleavage, **132, 195,** *196*
Climatic changes, 556
Climax (see also orgasm), **562**
  ecosystem, 563
Clitoris, **182**
Clogged pulmonary artery, 281
Clone, **284**
Cloning, *128*
*Clostridium,* 550
Clot formation, *279*
Clotting factors, **279**
Clyman, Martin, 192
CMU, 102
CNS, 377, 380. *See also* Central nervous system
Coacervate(s), **15,** 17, *20*
  droplets, 15, 16
  formation, 15
Coal depletion, 582
Cobalt, in diet, *77*
Cocaine, 385
Cochlea, **399,** *401*
Cockroach, and negative photaxis, 410
"Cocktail-party effect," 415
Cod-liver oil, 349
Codon, **116**
Coenzyme(s), **76**
Coenzyme A, **89**
Coitus, *175,* **183**
Coitus interruptus, **185**
Colchicine, 131
Cole, Lamont, 590
Collagen, **47,** *48,* 68, 223
Collecting duct, 326–327
Colloidal droplets, 15
Colloidal osmotic pressure, 270
Colloids, 15, **28,** *29*
*Colobus,* 515
Colon, 240
Color, and vision, 394, 395
Color blindness, and pedigree, *474*
Colostrum, **211,** 288
Columnar epithelium, *50*
Coma, 349
Common wart, 151
Communication, 422
Communication, evolution of, 529
Community, 458, **539**
Community, ecological, 558
Compact bone, 431
Compazine, 386

Competitive exclusion, 560
Competitive exclusion principle, **559**
Complement, **295**
Complementary base pairings, **111**
Complementary DNA, 111
Complete proteins, 241
Complex reflex arc, *382*
Compounds, **598**
Concentration of urine, in kidney, 328
Conception, 168. *See also* Test-tube babies
Condensation reaction, **63,** 65
Conditioned reflex, 417
Conditioning, classical (Pavlovian), and gulls, 415, 418
Conditioning, operant, 417–418
Condom, **185**
Cones, retinal, **394**
Confinement, date, 189
Conflict behavior, 414
Congenital aberrations, 215
Conjugated protein, **70,** 304
Conjunctiva, 394
Connective tissue, *51*
  and muscle of, *442*
Conservation, 556
Constipation, **250**
Constitutive enzyme, **143**
Consumer, and recycling matter, 549
Contact dermatitis, 285
Contiguity, and classical conditioning, 417
Contraception, **185**
Contraceptive pill, **186**
Contractility, muscle, **438**
Contraction ventricle, 262
Control system
  feedback, **141**
  fixed, **141**
Controlled mating, 505
Convection, and heat loss, 454–455
Convoluted tubule, kidney, 327
Coon, Carleton, 535
Copper, 77
  depletion, 582
Copulation, *See* Coitus
Cord cells, 173
Core temperature, vital organs, 453
Cornea, **393**
Corona radiata, **179**
Coronary arteries, **264**
Coronary sinus, **264**
Corpora cavernosa, 177
Corpus albicans, **181**
Corpus collosum, *380*

Corpus luteum, **181**
Corpus spongiosum, **177**
Cortex, **350,** *380*
  kidney, **324**
Cortez, 290
Corticosteroids, **352**
Corticosterone, 352
Cortisol, 353
Cortisone, 40, 353
Cosmologists, 10
Costle, 589
Cotton, 48
Coughing, *306*
Courtship, **425,** 426
  albatross, 426
  behavior, **425**
  bird, 425
  bird of paradise, 425
  fly, 426
  gifts, 426
  grasshopper, 425
  and grooming, 426
  hamster, 426
  human, 183
  insect, 426
  and kissing, 426
  locust, 426
  preening, 426
  and releasers, 413
  ritual, **425**
  stickleback, *413*
  tern, 426
Courtship dance, 411
Couzinet, Beatrice, 186
Covalent bond, 141, **599**
Cowper's glands, **173**
Cowpox, 290, 293
Cox, H., 592
Cramps, muscle, 446
Cranial flexure, 199
Cranial nerves, 378, *381*
Cranium, **378.** *See also* Skull
Cretin, **345,** *346*
Crick, Francis, 110, 118
Cri-du-chat syndrome, **488,** *490*
Crisis, temperature, 456
Cristae, **38,** 94
Cro-Magnon Man, *531,* 532
Cross immunity, **291**
Crossing over, **472**
Crows, habituation, 415
Cryptorchidism, **175, 354**
Crystal(s), 5, 6

Cuboidal epithelium, *50*
Cultural revolution, 591
Culture, 536
  evolution of, 529
  human, 514
Cumulus, oophorus, **179**
Curare, 384
Curie, Marie, and Pierre, 499
Curling hair, **73**
Current, **369**
Cyanide, 34, *92*, 371
Cyclamates, and cancer, 153
Cyclic AMP, **358**
Cystitis, **333**
Cytochrome(s), **91,** 99
Cytokinesis, **132**
Cytoplasm, 25, **28,** 29, 121, 359
  cleavage, **132**
  division of, 132
  furrowing, **132**
  streaming, 38, 42
Cytoplasmic enzymes, 86
Cytosine, **109**
Cytoskeleton, **30**
Cytotoxic T-cell, 284, 285, 484

D and C, **214**
Dart, Raymond, 525
Darwin, Charles, 503, 506, 511, *512, 520, 523*
Darwinian fitness, **522**
Darwinism, 518–523
Darwin's finches, 520–*522, 523*
Date of birth, 189
Date of confinement, calculation, 189
Daughter cell, 134
Daughter chromosomes, **132**
Daughter elements, *19*
"David" and immune deficiency, *283*
DCMU, 102
DDT, 546–547
  in food chain, 544, *546*
  half-life, 546
  level permitted by FDA, 547
  and photosynthetic activity, 547
  poisoning, 547
  resistance, 547
Deafness, 400
Deamination, **332**
Death rate, *571, 572*
  Sri Lanka, *571*
  U.S., 572
DeBakey, Michael, 261

Decay, 9, 13
  organisms, **549**
Decibel, **400**
Decidua, **206**
Decomposers, **549**
Decomposition cycle, 550
Decompression sickness, **317**
Dedifferentiation, 134
Deep-sea diving, 317
Deer population regulation, 560
Defecation, **240**
Defecation reflex, 240
Defective genes, birth defects, 215
Degenerate code, **113**
deGraaf, Regnier, 179
Dehydration, 329
Dehydrocholesterol, 348
Dehydrogenations, **83,** 91
Delayed hypersensitivity reaction, **285**
Deleterious genes, 507
Delgado, Jose, 406
Delirium tremens (DTs), 388
Delivery of placenta, 208, 210, *211*
Demerol, 386
Democracy, 412
Dendrites, **366,** *367*
  axon, **367,** 374
  and learning, 420
Denis, Jean Baptiste, 478
Denitrifying bacteria, **550**
Density-dependent factors, 561
Dental abcess, 247
Dentition, primate, 527
Deoxycorticosterone, 352
Deoxyribonucleic acid. *See* DNA
Deoxyribonucleotides, **109**
Deoxyribose, **109**
Depletion
  energy, 582
  mineral resources, 582
Depolarization, 374
  membrane, **369**
  muscle cell, 444
Depressants, 313
Depressor muscle, **438**
Dermis, **223, 403.** *See also* Skin
  collagen, 223
  composition, 223
  elastin, 223
  hair follicles, 223
Desalination, 580
*Descent of Man*, 523
Desensitization, 298

Development
  city, 581
  human, 194–209
Deviated septum, 306
Devries, William, 260
Dexedrine, 384
Dextrose, 31, **60,** *61. See also* Glucose
DHC, 348, 349
Diabetes, **329**
  adult onset, 241
  and atherosclerosis, 349
  causes, 349
  and genetic engineering, 123
  and heart disease, 349
  insipidus, **329**
  juvenile onset, 349, 359
  mellitus, **329**
Dialysis, **331**
Diamox, 332
Diaphragm, **309,** *311*
  contraceptive, **186**
  embryonic, 200
Diarrhea, **250**
Diastole, **259**
Diastolic pressure, **262**
Dichlorophenyl dimethyl urea (DCMU), 102
Dickens, Charles, 591
Diet
  balanced, *241, 243,* 291
  carbohydrate, 241
  dieting, 243
Dietary calcium, 435
Diethylstilbestrol, 153
Differential reproduction, **504**
Differentiation, 147
Diffraction pattern, **110**
Diffusion, **31,** 267, 301
  water, 33
Digestion, 233–234, 235–251
  active transport in, 238
  caloric requirements, *242*
  complete proteins, 241
  and hydrolysis, **235**
  minerals in, 246
  mitosis in, 238
  vitamins in, *241*
  water in, 235
  and work, 238
Digestive enzymes, 37, 236
  aminopeptidase, 236
  amylase, 236
  and bile, 236
  carboxypeptidase, 236

Digestive enzymes (*continued*)
  chymotrypsin, 236
  deoxyribonuclease, 236
  enterokinase, 236
  lactase, 236
  lipase, 236
  maltase, 236
  pepsin, 236
  ptyalin, 236
  rennin, 236
  ribonuclease, 236
  sucrose, 236
  trypsin, 236
Digestive system, **233**
  appendix, 234
  cardiac constrictor, 234
  cecum, 234
  colon and large intestine, 234
  duodenum, 237, *239*
  esophagus, 234
  fetal, 204
  fistula, **238**
  functional organization of, *234*
  ileocolonic sphincter, *234*
  liver and gallbladder, 234
  mitochondria in, 238
  mouth, 234
  pancreas, 234
  pharynx, 234
  pyloric sphincter, 234
  rectum, 234
  small intestine, 234, *237*
  soluble materials, 233
  stomach, 234
Digestive tract, **233**, *235*
  and bolus, 233
  fetal, 204
  ileum, 237
  jejunum, 237
  length, 233
  and mucosa, 233
  muscle tonus, 233
  and peristalsis, *235*
  and submucosa, 233
Dihybrid cross, *469*, 471
Diisopropyl fluorophosphate, 449
Dilatin (diphenylhydantion), 373
Dilation and curettage (D and C), **214**
Dilator muscle, 438
Dilger, W. C., 414
N-dimethylaminobenzene, 153
Dimethylnitrosamine, 154
Diphtheria, 288, 291

Diploid, **170**
Diploid number, **461**
Disaccharides, **61,** 62
  formation, 63
Discharge, urine, 332–333
Disease(s). *See also specific disease in question*
  AIDS, **185,** 190–191, 290
  bacterial, 48
  and birth defects, 216
  Buerger's, 155
  cardiovascular, 264
  Myasthemia gravis, *445*
  protein-deficiency, 578
  viral, 185
Disinhibition, **417**
Displacement activity, **414**
Displacement behavior, 414
Dissociation, **599**
Distal convoluted tubule, 326, 328
Disulfide bridges, **73**
Diuresis, **330**
Diuretics, **330**
Diver paralysis, 317
DNA, 38, 43, **108,** 360, 461, 514, 550
  code, **113,** *114*
  distinction from RNA, 115
  duplication, 109, 111, 141
  helix, 69
  hereditary information, 134
  human, 137
  information content, 141
  ligase, 124
  nitrogenous bases, *109*
  nucleosomes, *139*
  nucleotide, **109,** 116
  organization, **109,** 110
  packaging, 129
  periodicities, **109**
  polymerase, **111**
  promoter region, **144**
  and protein, 113
  reading of code, 118
  recombinant, **123**
  redundant, 137
  replication, **111,** 116
  specific pairing, 110
  stop signal, 121
  strand, 38, *110*
  structure, *138*
  synthesis, 113, 116
  transcription, 121
  Watson-Crick model, *110*
  x-ray diffraction pattern, 110

Dobzhansky, T., 508, 532
Dog
  hemoglobin, 114
  training, 417, 418
Dominance, social, **423**
Dominance hierarchies, 424
Dominant gene, **466**
Donor blood, **478**
Dopamine, 383, 385
Dope, **383**
Dostoevski, 372
Double bonds, **600**
Double helix, *110*, 111
Double sugars, 63
Doubling time and population, 569, 572
Down, J. Langdon, 461
"Downers," 385. *See also* Barbiturates
Down syndrome, 134, **489**
  carrier, **461**
  characteristics, 461
  and chromosomes, 486, 489, 490
  karyotype, *488*
  and mother's age, 486, *489*
  and nondisjunction, 486, *488*
  translocation, 489, *490, 491*
  transmission of, *489, 491*
Drinking center. *See* Hypothalmus
Drinking and thirst, 332
Drinking water, 586
Drive, **413,** 414
Droplets, coacervate, 15, 16
Dropsy, **332**
*Drosophila*, 137, *140*, 472
Drugs, **383**. *See also specific drugs in question*
  addiction, 385
  anesthetics, 386
  and behavior, 385
  and depression, 384
  dilatin, 373
  diuretic, 330
  hallucinogens, *386*
  immunosuppressive, 297
  L-dopa, 383
  and lysosomes, 40
  and memory, 384–385
  narcotics, *386*
  and nervous system, 383
  and neurotransmitter substances, 384
  opiates, 383–384
  and pinocytosis, 34
  placebos, 384
  and pregnancy, 215
  psychological dependency, 383–384

receptor antagonists, 383
and respiratory center, 387
sedatives, 385
stimulants, *386*
and thinking, 384
tranquilizers, 386
withdrawal, 384–385, *386*
Drumstick muscle, *441*
Dry cell, *84*
Dry zone, **556**
Dubois, E., 530
Dugesia, *254*
Duodenal ulcers, **249**
Duodenocolic reflex, **240**
Duodenum, 237, *239*
Duplication, genetic, 489
Dustbowl, 565
Dwarf, pituitary, **342**
Dysentery bacteria, 250

Ear, 398–399
anvil, 399
auricle, 398
and balance, 401
cochlea, 399
eardrum, 398
equilibrium, 401
external, 398
hammer, 399
inner, 398
labyrinth, 398
Organ of Corti, 399
otoliths, 401
oval window, 399
semicircular canals, 401
stirrup, 399
tectorial membrane, 399
tympanum, 398
vestibule, 401
Eardrum, **398,** 399
rupture, 401
Earlobes, 472
Earth
age of, 11, *18–19*
history of, 9–12, *9,* 13, *20, 21,* 22
population, **539**
primitive, 12
spaceship, **569**
Eccrine sweat glands, 230
ECG, 259, 261
abnormal, *261*
Eclipse period, **55**
*E. coli. See Eschericia coli*

Ecological niche, 558
Ecological pyramids, 541
Ecological succession, **562,** *563, 564*
in abandoned farm, *562*
and equilibrium of species, 563
and natural selection, **503,** 505, 520
rate of invasion, *564*
in shallow lake, *563*
Ecology, **539**
and recycling, 540, 549–556
and "Spaceship Earth", 539
Ecosystems, **539,** *565*
and agriculture, 564–566
balance, 540
biomes, **543**
carrying capacity, 559
chemicals in, 544–549
competitive exclusion principle, 560
density dependent factors, 561
energy flow, 540, 541
and homeostasis, 556
and population size, 559
and primary production, *580*
succession in, 562–564
unbalanced, 547, 564
Ectotherm, **453**
and body temperature, *454*
Eddy, Bernice E., 158
Edema, **270, 330**
in pregnancy, 189
EEG, 177, **178,** 372–373
Egg(s)
abnormal, 485
fertilization, **184**–185
formation, 177
human, 170, 171
nucleus, 179
oocyte, **178**
production, 177–178. *See also* Oogenesis
Ehrlich, Anne and Paul, 580
Eibl-Eibesfeldt, Irenaus, 427
Eiffel, Gustave, 431
Ejaculation, *177*
Elasser, W., *6*
Elasticity, muscle, **438**
Elastin, **47,** 223
Elavil, 384
Electric cautery, *192*
Electrical excitation, 365
Electrically manipulated brain, 365
Electricity, principles of, 366, *367*
Electrocardiogram (ECG), *261*
abnormal, *262*

Electrochemical activity and memory, 421
Electrochemical messages, 366
Electrode implant, 365
Electroencephalogram (EEG), **372,** 373
Electrolytes, **599**
Electron(s), **597**
flow, 99
orbitals, **598**
in oxidation, 83–84
in reduction, 83–84
Electron acceptors, 98
Electron microscope, 30, 33
Electron transfer, 102
Electroshock therapy (EST), *449*
Elements, **597**
abundance in universe, 10
in human body, *10*
Elephantiasis, *271*
Embolism, 264, 281
cerebral, 188
pulmonary, 188
Embolus, **188, 281**
Embryo, **195**
abnormal, 202
development, **217**
human, *198*
skeleton of, 199
at 2.5 weeks, *198*
at 3 weeks, *198*
at 4 weeks, *198*
at 5 weeks, *199*
at 6 weeks, 200
at 7 weeks, 201
Embryogenesis, 195
Emergency response, **350**
Emission, **184**
Emotions, and diuretic effect, 332
Emphysema, 154, 306
and air pollution, 308
Emulsion, **29**
Endergonic reactions, **601**
Endocardium, **258**
Endocrine gland(s), **337,** *338,* 360–361, 358. *See also specific gland in question*
hypersecretion, **337**
hyposecretion, **337**
malfunction, 337
and nervous system, 365
organs, **356**
Endocrine system, 365
Endoderm, embryonic, 198
Endometrium, **182,** 206
Endoplasmic reticulum, **36,** 132

Endoplasmic reticulum (*continued*)
  in muscle, 444
  and nuclear membrane, 37
  in prokaryotes, **53**
  protein synthesis, 37
  rough, 36
  smooth, 36
Endorphins, **383**
Endotherm, **454**
  and body temperature, *455*
Energy, 5, **81**, *86*, 97–98, *99, 100*
  agricultural demand, *581*
  daily requirement, 80
  demands, 583
  depletion of sources, 582
  electrical, 81
  of fats, 64
  flow, **540**, 541
  and food, 82
  and food chain, *545*
  in glucose, 83
  and heat, 454
  in kidney, 326
  kinetic, **81**
  Law of Conservation of, 82
  and nutrition, 240
  photosynthetic yield, 97
  potential, **81**
  on primitive earth, 12, 18
  pyramid, *544*
  reservoir, 98
  solar, 540, 541
  sources of, 12, 540–541
Engram, **421**
Enkephalin, **383**
Entelechy, 6
Entropy, **82**
Environment, 539–566
  carrying capacity, 591
  internal, 321, 380
Environmental pollution, radioactive, 549
Environmental Protection Agency, 547
Environmental resistance, **541**
  shifts, 557
Enzyme(s), 5, **17**, 72, **74**. *See also* Catalyst(s)
  active site, 74
  activity, 358, *454*
  constitutive, **143**
  and cyclic AMP, 358
  cytochrome, 77
  digestive, *236*
  of glycolysis, 88
  helpers, 75–77

induction, **142–143**, *144–145*
inhibition, **74**, 76
Krebs-cycle, **89**, *90*
lysosomal, 39
poisoning, **74**, *76*
precursors, 295
protein kinase, 164
in seminal fluid, 173
specificity, 74
substrate-interaction, 74
synthesis, 113, 143
and temperature, 454
tyrosinase, 226
Eosinophils, 278
Epicanthic fold, 461
Epicardium, **258**
Epidermis, **223**, 403
  basal layer, 223
  stratum corneum, **223**
Epididymis, **173**, 184
Epiglottis, 303, 311
Epilepsy, 365, **372**
Epileptic seizure, 365, 372
Epilogue, 595
Epinephrine, **350**, 381, 384
  release of, 381
  and temperature regulation, 455
Epistasis, **482**
Epithelial cells, 307
Epithelial tissues, 50
EPSP, 375, *377*
Equilibrium, 401–403
  environmental, 590–591
Equilibrium species, 563
Ergosterol, 349
Erythroblastosis, **480**, 481
Erythroblasts, **277**
Erythrocytes, **276**. *See also* Red blood cell(s)
*Escherichia coli*, *106, 124*, 137
Eserine, 449
ESPS, 376–377
Essential amino acids, **112**
EST. *See* Electroshock therapy
Ester linkage, **65**
Estradiol, 188
Estrogens, **354**
  at birth, 207
  and breast enlargement, 207
  and cancer, 153
  in ovulation, 181
  structure, *66*
Ethane, 600
Ether, 313

Ethologists, **410**
Ethyl alcohol, 86, 237
Ethyl mercury, 545
Eugenics, 107, 505, **506,** 508
  negative, 505–508
  positive, 508
Eukaryotes, **53**, 122, **148**
Eunuch, **337**
Eustachian tube, 201, **401**
Eutrophication, 583
Evaporation
  and body temperature, 454, **455**
  of early ocean, 13
  and radiation, 541
Evolution, 511, **523**
  of behavior, 408
  brain size, 530
  of communication, 529
  Darwinian, 520–523
  and the gene pool, 501, 523
  human, 502, 523–532, *526*
  of language, 529
  of life, 5
  of man, *526*
  natural selection, 503
  skeleton, 531
  of tool use, *529*
Exchange of materials, 254
Excitable cells, **369**
Excitatory postsynaptic potential (ESPS), **374**
Excretion, 321
Exercise, 446
  and respiratory rate, 314
Exergonic reactions, **601**
Exhalation, 309, 310
Exocrine glands. *50, 337,* 338. *See also specific*
  *gland in question*
Exophthalmos, **345**, *346*
Experiment, 7, **8,** 9
Expiration, **310**. *See also* Exhalation
Expiratory neurons, 312
Exponential growth rate, 570
Extensibility, muscle, **438**
Extensor muscle, **438**
External anal sphincter, **240**
External ear, **398**
Extinction, of behavior, **417**
Extracellular substances, **46**
Extrinsic feedback loop, *313*
Eye
  and accommodation, 397
  astigmatism, 397
  and the camera, *393*

embryonic development, 200
fetus, 203–204
lens, *397*
muscles, 445
and myopia, 397
pigment, 395
pupil, 394
structure, 393–394
tears, 282
Eyebrows, **394**
Eyelashes, **394**
Eyelids, **394**

$F_1$ generation, **468**
$F_2$ generation, **468**
Face
embryo, 200
fetus, 203
Facial hair, 226–227
Facilitation
learning, **420**
neural, 377
FAD, 90
Falciparum malaria, *505*
Fallopian tube, **177**, *192*
cells, 42
and tubal ligation, 192
Fallopius, Gabriel, 177
Fallout radioactive, **548**
Family, **513**
Family tree, **466**. *See also* Pedigree
human, *524–525*
primate, *524*
Famine, 572
Farming the sea, 580
Farsightedness, **397**
Fat(s), 59, **64**
hydrolysis of, 66
percentage of body weight, 54, 65
saturated, **66**
in skin, 223
unsaturated, **66**
Fatigue, sensory, 342, 415
Fatty acids, 31, **65**
Fatty liver disease, **245**
FDA and mercury limits, 546
Feces, **235**, 240
Feedback
control, **141**, *147*
loops, *348, 457*
models, *142–143*
negative, **141**, *143. See also* Negative
feedback

positive, **141**. *See also* Positive feedback
runaway, **141**
Feedback control system, **141**
Female hormones, **354**. *See also* specific
hormone in question
Female reproductive system, **78**, *179, 183*
Fermentation, **88**, 244
Fermi, Enrico, 499
Fern test, **187**
Ferritin, 277
Fertility
patterns, 573
rate, U.S., 576
Fertilization, **169**, 184–185
egg, 184
moment of, *196*
sperm, 184
Fertilizer, 580
Fetal activity, 205
Fetal circulation, *208*
Fetal membranes, 205
Fetus, **203**, *194*
characteristics, 203
development, **217**
growth, 203
and maternal disease, *216*
weight, 205
at 8 weeks, *203*
at 12 weeks, *194*
at 3 months, *204*
at 4–5 months, 205
at 6–7 months, 203
at 8–9 months, 205
Fever, **456**
Fibrillation, **259**
atrial, 259
ventricular, 259
Fibrin, 68, **279**
Fibrinogen, **275**
and menstruation, 182
source of, 276
Fibroblasts, **433**
Fibrous connective tissue, *51*
Fight-or-flight reaction, **350**
Filaria, 270
Filtration, blood, 267
Finch, evolution, 520–521
Finger
embryo, 203
fetus, 206
muscles of, 439
Fingernails
embryo, 229

fetus, 206
growth and function, 229
structure, 229
Fingerprints, 221–222
fetus, 221
Fire, use of, 531
First filial generation, **468**
First Law of Thermodynamics, 82
Fish
and acid rain, 584
body temperature, *454*
gills, *302*
harvest of, 580
and social dominance, 423
Fistula, **238**
Fitness, **522**
Fixed action pattern, 411
Fixed control system, **141**
Fixing of tissues, **33**
Fixity of species, **511**
Flagella, **42**, 43, *44*
Flagellum, *26*
Flavin adenine dinucleotide. *See* FAD
Flavin mononucleotide. *See* FMN
Flax, 48
Fluid balance in body, 321, *322, 329*
FMN, **91**
Focus, *397*
Folic acid, 76
deficiency, 281
Follicle-stimulating hormone. *See* FSH
Food(s)
caloric values, *242*
chemicals in, 59, 85
consumers, 98
daily requirements, *241*
degradation, **235**
digestion of, 233
and energy, 301
oxidation of, 85, 301
producers, 96, 103
pyramid, *98*
requirements, 103
solubility, 233
uptake, 235
Food chain(s), 98, **541**, *544, 545*
biomass, *544*
and DDT, 546
and ecological succession, 541, 544
and energy, 235, *544, 554*
land based, *542*
and producers, 103, 542
Food web, **541**, *543*

Foramen ovale, **208**
Ford, E. B., 503
Forebrain, **378**
Foreplay, 183
Foreskin, **177**
Forgetting, **421,** 422
  and conditioning, 417
Fossil(s), **18,** 520
  dating of, *18*
  forms, 524
  fuels, depletion, 582
  man, 524–532
Fovea, **395**
Fox, Sidney W., *14*
Fractionation of liver cell, 94
Freckles, 224
Frequency, sound, **398**
Friction (in blood pressure), 265
Friedman, Eli, *320*
Fructose, **60,** *61*
  in seminal fluid, 173
Fruit fly
  chromosomes, 132, *138*
  DNA, 132, *138*
FSH, **173,** 179, 182, 341, 352, 354
FSH-releasing factor, 179, 358
Function, in classification, **513**
Fungi, 53
  as decomposers, 549
Furrowing, **132**

Galactose, **60,** *61*
β-Galactosidase, 142
Galapagos Islands, 511, *521*
Gallbladder, 250
  fetal, 204
Gallstones, **250**
Galton, Sir Francis, 500
Gamblers, 418
Gametes, **169, 462,** 467
  chromosomal number of, 169
  formation, *170–171,* 462
Gamma aminobutyric acid (GABA), **376**
Gamma globulin, 68, **275**
Gamma interferon, 286
Gamma rays, 499
Ganglia, sympathetic, 380
Garn, S. M., 533, *534*
Gas, composition in air, 311
Gas exchange, 301, *See also* Respiration
Gastric glands, 337
Gastric juice, and indigestion, 248
Gastric ulcers, **249**

Gastrocolic reflex, **240**
Gastrointestinal (GI) tract, **233**
Gelatin, 31
Gene(s), **113,** 114–115, 117, **169,** 461–489
  action, 139
  activation, 141
  activity, 140
  crossing over, 471, 472, 473
  deleterious, 507
  dominant, 468
  eukaryotes, 122, 147
  expression, 123
  frequency, **502**
  and higher organisms, 146–148
  and histocompatibility, **297**
  lethal, 501
  linked, **471**
  mutation, **496**
  and natural selection, 504
  nonfunctional, 118
  numbers of, 137
  oncogenes, **163**
  operator, **143**
  organization, 138
  polyoma virus, **158**
  recessive, 468
  regulation of, 146–148
  regulator, **143,** 146
  repressor, **143**
  sex-linked, **473**
  structural, **143**
  subvital, **501**
  transfer, 123
  transmission of, 122
  transplantation, *106, 124*
  viral, 158, 164
Gene pool, *483,* **501**
Genera, 513. *See also* Genus
Genetic burden, **501**
Genetic code, 111
  degeneracy of, 113
  and DNA, 116
  implications, 122
  reading, 114
  and RNA, *116*
  transcription, **116**
  translation, *116,* 117–118
  triplet codes, **113,** 118
  "typographical error," 122
Genetic control, 140
Genetic counseling, 461
Genetic engineering, *124*
Genetic farming, *106*

Genetic load, 501
Genetic manipulation, 107, 123, *124,* 125
Genetic mosaic, 475
Genetic recombination, 470, 473
Genetic switching, 140
Genetic transpositions, 161–162
Genetic variation, 502
Genetics, **107,** 461
  and behavior, 410
  and blood types, 478
  classical, **461**
  Law of recombination, **467**
  Law of segregation, **467**
  Mendelian, **468,** 469
  molecular, **461**
  pea, 468, 469
  physiological, **461**
  population, 495, 509
  transmission, **461**
Genitalia
  female, *183*
  male, *172*
Genotype, 465, 470
Genus, **511,** 513
Geographic isolation, 533, 536
Geographic variation, 532, *533*
Geological processes, 520
Geometric growth, 570
Geotaxes, **410**
Germ cells, **171**
"Ghosts," *28*
Giant chromosomes, **138**
Giantism, **343**
Gill clefts, embryonic, *200*
Gills, **302**
  fish, 302, 314–315
  function, 314–315
  mollusc, *302*
Gingivitis, 248
Glands(s) **337.** *See also specific gland in*
      *question*
  endocrine, **337**
  exocrine, 50
  parathyroid, **346**
  pituitary, **338**
  thyroid, **344**
Glans (penis), **177**
Glial cells, **366,** 367
  Schwann cells, 367
Globin, **70,** 307
Globulin, **275**
Glomerular capillaries, 325
Glomerular filtrate, *325*

hyperosmotic, **326**
isosmotic, **326**
Glomerulus, **323,** 324–325
Glottis, **303**
Glucagon, 350
Glucocorticoids, **352**
Glucose, 30, 31, **60**
  active transport of, 347
  aerobic degradation of, 85, 86
  anaerobic respiration of, *85, 87,* 89
  blood level, 61
  degradation of, 74, 89
  metabolism of, 61, 83, 89
  in muscle contraction, 446
  phosphorylation, **86**
  polymers, 59
  transport of, 88
  uptake of, 359
Glutamic acid, 496
Glycerol, **65,** *88*
Glycogen, **63**
  and glucose, 359
  in muscle contraction, 447
  and release of glucose, 59, 349
Glycolipid, 41
Glycolysis, **88**
Glycoprotein, 275
Goiter, **344,** *345*
Goldberger, Dr. Joseph, 76
Golgi, Camillo, 36
Golgi apparatus, **36,** *37*
Gonad, **171**
Gonadotropic hormones, 173, 179, **341,** 352,
  *354,* 358
Gonadotropin, 173
Gonorrhea, 174, 185
Goose pimples, 227
Gorilla, *515*
Graafian follicle, **179**
Graft rejection, 285, 292
Grana, 39
Grand mal seizure, *373*
Granules, 38
Granulocyte, **278**
Grasses, 563
Grave's disease, **345**
Gray matter, 379
  brain, 378
  spinal cord, 278
Green revolution, 580
Greenhouse effect, **556**
Griffith, F., **108**
Gripping reflexes, fetal, *205*

Grooming and courtship, 426
Groups, and society, **422**
Growth, 5
  bone, 431–435
  fetal, 203
  plant, *560*
Growth curve, 569
Growth hormone, **341,** *342,* 356
Growth rate, **570**
Growth zone, **433**
GTP, 118
Guanine, **109**
Guano, 502
Gulls, 414–415
Gum disease, 247–248
Gut, **223.** *See also* Digestive system
Guthrie, Woody, **506**

H ions, 328
Habitat, 558
Habituation, **415**
Hair, **226**
  androgenic hormones, 227
  baldness, 227, *228*
  curling, 68
  and erogenous zones, 227
  and human evolution, 226
  fetal, 204, 227
  follicles, 223
  graying, 227
  human, 220, 226–229
  as ornamentation, 226
  pigmentation, 113
  as protection, 226
  sensory, 401
Hallucinations, 373
Hammer (malleus), **399**
Hamsters, courtship, 426
Hand
  fetal, 203
  human, 440
Hanson, J., 442
Haploid, 171, 462
Hardy, G. H., 502
Hardy-Weinberg law, **502**
Haversian canal systems, 432
Hay fever, 285
Hazlitt, 591
Hearing, 398–401
Hearing loss, 400
Heart, 253–271, **254,** *256, 257*
  artificial valves, 258
  attack, *263, 264*

disease, 154, 263, 264
electrical activity, 258–259
embryonic, 199
fetal, 208
fibrillation, 259
human, 81
innervation, 381
ligaments, 256
Lincoln, Abraham, 252
murmurs, **259**
muscle, 436
parasympathetic nerve, 259
size, 255
sympathetic nerve, 259
transplants, 297
tricuspid valve, **257**
valves, 256–257
wall, 258
Heartbeat, 259
  control of, *259*
  fetal, 202
  regulation of, 259
  refractory period, 259
Heartburn, **248**
''Heartstrings,'' 256
Heat, 81
  balance, *455*
  engine, 81
  metabolic, 83
  pollution, 583
Heatstroke, 455
Heavy chains (immunoglobulin), 292
Height, *481*
Heimlich maneuver, *306*
Helium, in primitive atmosphere, 11
Helper cells, *290*
Heme, **70,** 77, **307,** *309*
Hemizygosity, **473**
Hemocytometer, **280**
Hemodialysis, **331**
Hemoglobin, 68, **276**
  oxygen carrying capacity, 307, **309–310**
  sickle cell, 69
  structure, *71, 72*
Hemophilia, 123, **279, 476**
  and genetic engineering, 123
  inheritance of, *477*
Hemorrhage, **278**
Hemorrhoids, **250**
Hemp, 48
Heparin, **281**
Hepatic portal system, *239*
Hepatitis, **245**

Herbicides, 102
Herbivores, **541,** 542
Hermit crabs, and social dominance, 423
Heroin, 386
Herpes simplex virus, 123
Herrick, J. B., 495
Herring-gull models, *414*
   response to stimulus, *414*
Heterosis, **505**
Heterotrophs, **17,** 20, 22, **540**
Heterozygotes
   frequency of, 505
   selective advantage of, 505
   in sickle cell, 505
Heterozygous, **466**
Hexosaminidase, 41
Hexose, 60
Hiccups, 311
Hierarchy, 424
   in biology, *599*
   social, **423**
High-energy bond, **84,** *85*
High frequency sound, 401
High pressure, 265
Hindbrain, **378**
Hinge joint, *439*
Hippocampus, *380*
Hippocrates, 347
Hiroshima, 157, 499
Histamine, 295, **298**
Histidine, 156
Histocompatibility, complex, *483*
Histocompatibility genes, **297**
Histone, **134,** *139*
Hitler, 128
Hives, 298
HLA, **483**
*H.M.S. Beagle,* 511, *512, 520, 521*
Hodgkin's disease, 158
Holdren, John, 580
Homeostasis, 275, **556**
Homeotherms, **454**
Hominid line, 526
*Homo erectus,* **530**
*Homo sapiens,* 531
   characteristics, 531
Homologous chromosomes, **465**
Homozygote, **446**
Honeybee, life, of, *424*
Hookworm, 281
Hormone(s) 337–361, 365
   anterior pituitary, 338
   calciferol, 348

calcitonin, 346
female, 179
male, **352**
molecular activity of, 358–360
pituitary, 338
and sex differences, 359
triiodothyronine, 344
thyroxine, 344
tropic, **338, 341**
Hormonal system, 337–360
   and nervous system, **337**
HTLV-III. *See* AIDS
Human(s)
   aggression, 415, 416, 426, 529
   and apes, *518*
   behavior, 407–427
   body, 59
   cell type, *137*
   characteristics, *514–518*
   chromosomes, *464*
   circulatory system, *526*
   conception, 168
   environment, 539
   evolution, 502, 523–532, *526*
   female chromosomes, *133*
   gene pool, 501
   growth rate, *570*
   inheritance, 461–493
   instincts, 411, 415, 416
   language, 529
   as primates, 514
   races, **533**
   reasoning, 418
   skeletal evolution, 431–435
   social rank, 424
Human immunodeficiency virus (HIV). *See* AIDS
Human population, 570–582
   growth, 570, *571, 572, 573*
   log-log plot, *591*
Human tissues, morphology, *50, 51, 52*
Humidity, **454**
Humoral immunity, **285**
Hunger, world distribution, *578*
Hunger drive, 413
Huntington's disease, **506**
Hutton, James, 520
Huxley, Aldous, 169
Huxley, Sir Julian, 508
Huxley, T. H., 520
Huxley-Hanson model, *443, 444*
Hyaline cartilage, **432**
Hyaline membrane disease, **310**

Hyaluronidase, 47, 184
Hybrid, vigor, **505**
Hybridization, 505
Hybridoma, *295*
*Hydra,* 253, *254*
Hydration, 329
Hydrazine, 154
Hydrocarbons, and cancer, 153–154
Hydrocortisone, 253
Hydrogen, 11, 599
   bond, **599**
   in early atmosphere, 11
   peroxide, 72
Hydrogenation, **66**
Hydrolysis, **63**
   and digestion, **235**
   of fats, *65, 66*
   of maltose, 63
Hydrostatic pressure, 41, 269
25-Hydroxycalciferol, 348
Hydroxyl ions, 599
Hymen, **182**
Hyperactive immune system, 298
Hypergonadism, **354**
Hyperkinetic children, *406*
Hyperosmotic medium, **32**
Hypersecretion endocrine, **337**
Hypersensitivity, 285
Hyperthyroidism, *346*
Hypertrophy, 447
Hyperventilation, **314**
Hypogonadism, **352**
Hypoosmotic medium, 32
Hypophysis, **338.** *See also* Pituitary, gland
Hyposecretion, endocrine, **337**
Hypothalmic region, 357–358, 456
Hypothalmus, **332,** 341, 354, *355,* **357,** 359, **378,** *380*
   and anterior pituitary, *356*
   releasing factors, 173, 353, 357, 358
Hypothesis, **8**
Hysterectomy, 214
H-zone, **442**

I bands, **442**
Idiocy and PKU, 112
Ileocolonic valve, 240
Image formation, *96,* **396**
Immediate hypersensitivity, **285**
Immovable joints, 439
Immune deficiency, *283*
Immune response, **158, 288**
Immune system, 288, 289

Immunity, **281–295**
  acquired, **282**
  active, 288
  antibody-mediated, **285**
  cell-mediated, **285**
  fetal, 206, 288
  immunoglobulin, 293
  and "memory," 288
  natural, 282
  passive acquired, 288
  and graft rejection, 285
  secondary response, 287
Immunization, 288
Immunoglobulin classes, *293*
Immunological cooperation, **286**
Immunological memory, 287
Immunosuppression, 297
Immunosuppressive drugs, 297
Imprinting, **418,** *419*
In vitro fertilization, *168*
Inbreeding, 505
Incipient species, 533
Incontinence, **233**
Incus, **399**
Indigestion, **249**
Inducer T-cells, 284
Induction, enzyme, 142–143, 144, 145
Industrial melanism, **503**
Industrial revolution, 349, 591
Infant, **195–217**
  birth defects, 217
  grasping reactions, 206
  mortality, 573
  passive immunity, 288
Infection, 288. *See also* Disease(s)
Infectious hepatitis, 288
Infectious mononucleosis, 281
Infertility, 181
Inflammation, **282**
Influenza, 293
  and birth defects, 216
  vaccine, 291
  virus, 293
Inguinal canal, **173,** 175
Inguinal hernia, **175**
Inhalation, model of, 309, 310
Inheritance, 461, 493
  of albinism, *467, 470*
  of attached earlobes, 472
  of blood type, 478–479
  chemical, 107
  of color blindness, *474*
  of Down syndrome, 489

of hemophilia, 476–477
  human, 461–493
  of Klinefelter syndrome, 485
  of Rh factor, 480
  of Turner syndrome, 486
  polygenic, 481
  of skin color, 482
Inhibitory postsynaptic potential (IPSP), **376**
Inhibitory transmitter substance, 374
Innate releasing mechanism (IRM), **414**
Innate responses, 417
Inner ear (labyrinth), **398**
Innervation, body parts, *381*
Insect(s)
  courtship behavior, 426
  societies, *424–425,* 426
Insecticide, 103
Insectivores, **524**
Inspiration, **310**
Inspiratory neurons, 312
Instinct, **411**
  killer, 416
  and learning, 414–415
  pecking, 423
Instinctive behavior, 411–414
Insulin, 68, 329, **347,** *350*
  and glucose, 68, 329, 349
  receptors, 359
Interference
  classical conditioning, 417
  forgetting, 417
Interleukin-I (IL-1), 286, 298
Internal environment, 321
Internal respiration, **301**
International System of Units, 603
Interneurons, **377**
Interphase, 131
  $G_1$, 134
  $G_2$, 134
  S, 134
Interpopulation diversity, **533**
Interspecific aggression, 416
Interstitial cell(s), 352
Interstitial fluid, **265,** 321
Intervillous space, **207**
Intestine, 237–240
  embryonic, *200*
  fetal, 204
  innervation, *381*
Intrapopulation diversity, **532**
Intraspecific aggression, 416
Intrauterine device. *See* IUD
Introns, **122, 148**

Invasive tumor, *150*
Inversion, chromosomal, **488**
  thermal, 588
Inverted retina, 396
Investing membranes, 378
Involuntary movement, 365
Involuntary muscles, **437**
Ion(s), **267, 369, 498, 598.** *See also specific ion in question*
Ionic bond, **598**
Ionization, 598
Ionizing radiation, **498,** 499
IPSP, 376–377
Iris, **394**
Iron, 31
  in blood, 31, 276, 280
  dietary, 77
  filings, 72
Irrigation, 580
Islets of Langerhans, **347,** 350
Isoagglutinins, **478**
Isolation, geographic, 533
Isoleucine, 145
Isosmotic kidney filtrate, **326**
Isosmotic medium, **32,** 328
Isotopes, **597**
IUD, 186
  insertion, *188*
  risks, 187

"Jack-of-all-trades" organ, 221
Jackson, Laird, *202*
Jacob, F., 143
Jacob-Monod model, 143
James, William, 415, 421
"Jarvik-7" artificial heart, 260
Jaundice, 247, **250**
Java man, *530*
Jaw
  embryonic, 200
  fetal, 203
Jellyfish, 252
Jenner, Edward, 290–291
Johnston, Bennet, 548
Joint, **439**
  inflammation, 439
  knee, *440*
  stiffness, 439
  surfaces of, 439
  types, *439*
Jugular vein, 240

$K^+$ ions, 328

Karyotype
  cri-du-chat syndrome, *490*
  Down syndrome, *488*
  Klinefelter syndrome, *485*
Kennaway, 153
Kennedy, John F., 353
Keratin, 58, 68, 73, 223
Ketone bodies, 349
Kettleweill, H. B. D., 503
Kidney, 49, **321,** *322, 324*
  and active transport, 326
  artificial, *330–333*
  ATP, 326
  blood flow, 325
  capillary blood pressure, 325
  cortex, **324**
  dialysis, 320
  epithelial cells, 324
  excretion, 321
  filtration, *326*
  and fluid composition, 321
  function, 323–328
  innervation, 381
  medulla, **324**
  osmosis, 326
  pelvis, 332
  proximal tubule, *327*
  resorption, 326
  salt balance, 323
  secretion, 326
  stones, **332**
  structure, 332, 323–328
  transplants, 297
  tubule, 324–326
  urine concentrations, *328*
  weight, 321, 323
Kidney machine, 330–331
Kidney stones, **332**
Killer instinct, 416
Kinetic energy, **81**
Kingdom, **513**
Kinship, **425**
Klinefelter syndrome, 354, **485**
Knee-jerk reflex, 369
Knee joint, *439, 440*
Koch's postulates, **158**
Kreb cycle, **89,** *90*
Krogman, W. M., 432
K-strategists, **562**
Kwashiorkor, 578, *579*

Labia majora, **182**
Labia minora, **182**

Labor, **209.** *See also* Parturition
  first stage, *209*
  pains, **209**
  second stage, *210*
Labyrinth (inner ear), **398**
Lacrimal duct, **394**
Lacrimal glands, *394*
Lactation, **211,** 212
  and acquired immunity, 288
  as birth control, 212
  fetal, 206
Lacteal, **239,** 240
Lactic acid, 86
  in muscle, 88
Lactiferous duct, **209**
Lactiferous sinuses, **209**
Lactose, **62,** 143
Lacunae, **206**
Lakes, and acid rain, 584
Lakes, succession in, *563*
Lamarck, Jean Baptiste de, 520
Lamellae, chloroplast, 39
Langerhans, Paul, 347
Language
  evolution of, 529
  human, 514
Landsteiner, Karl, 478
Langur, *516*
Lanugo, **205**
Laparoscope, 192
Large intestine, 240
Larynx, **303**
Lavoisier, Antoine Laurent, 240
Law of Conservation of Energy, 82
Law of independent assortment, **467, 469.** *See
    also* Principle of recombination
Law of segregation, **467, 468**
L-dopa, 406
Lead
  depletion, 582
  and environment, 544
Leakey, L. S. B., 524
Learned behavior, 408, 414–420
  and instinct, 414
Learned responses, 415
Learning, **415–422**
  and aggression, 416
  behavior, 410–415
  and the brain, 419
  and classical conditioning, 418
  and habituation, 415
  and imprinting, 419
  and instinct, 414–415

mechanisms, 420
  and memory, 420
  rat, 412
  reasoning, 418
  reinforcement, 379, 418
  trial and error, *418*
Leeuwenhoek, Anton van, *7*
Legallois, Cesar, 312
Leg(s), 514
  fetal, 203
Leg buds, embryonic, *199*
Lehrer, Tom, 588
Lejeune, J., 488
Lemur, *517*
Length, 604
Lenin, 272
Lens, **394,** 396, 397
Letdown reflex, **212**
Lethal genes, 501
Leucoplasts, **39**
Leukemia, 76, 151, 281
  and blood count, 281
  and radiation, 157, 499
Leukocytes, **276.** *See also* White blood cell(s)
Levator muscle, **438**
Lewis, W. H., 34
LH, **173,** 179, 352, 353, 358
Li, C. H., 348
Librium, 386
Life, **5,** 9
  characteristics, 5
  on Mars, 4
  oldest forms, *19*
  origin of, 5, 9, **18**
  produced in laboratory, **14**
Light
  energy, 98, 99
  reception, 393–397
Light chains (immunoglobulin), 292
Lignin, **49**
Limbic system, **378**
Lincoln, Abraham, 252
Lind, 75
Link, Edwin A., 300
Linked genes, **471**
Linnaeus, Carolus, 511, 513
Linne, Carl von. *See* Linnaeus, Carolus
Lipids, 28, **64**
Lipoproteins, 72, 175
Liquid, diffusion in, 33, 267, 301
Liquid waste, 321
Liver, 245, 276
  and albumin, 276

and alpha globulins, 276
and beta globulins, 276
cirrhosis, 245
disease, 245
fetal, 204
and fibrinogen, 276
fractionation, *94*
and glycogen, 63
Living systems, 5, 59, 82, 128
Lizards and social dominance, 423
Locus, **465**
Locust, courtship of, 426
Logistic equation, 559
Long-term memory (LTM), **420**
Loomis, W. F., 535
Loop of Henle, **324**
  ascending, 327
  descending, 327
Lorenz, Konrad, 411, 414, 419
Los Angeles, air pollution, 584
Loudness, 399–401
Louis XIV, 478
Low frequency sound wave, 398, 401
Low pressure, 265, 316
Lower, Richard, 478
LSD, **385**
LTM, 420
Lucy (*Australopithecus*), 525, 527
Lumber, 48
Lung(s), **302,** 303
  area, 303
  asymmetry, 303
  cancer of, 154–157
  capacity, *312*
  circulation, *307*
  dead space, 311
  elastin, 310
  fetal, 204
  function, 303, 309
  innervation, 312
  model, *310*
  passive action of, 303
  weight, 303
Luteinizing hormone (LH), **173,** 179, 341
Lyell, Charles, 520
Lymph, **270,** 275
Lymph nodes, **271**
  and cancer, 271
Lymph vessels, 240
  valves, 270
Lymphatic pump, **270**
Lymphatic system, *270*

Lymphatics, **270**
  mechanism, 270
Lymphocyte(s), **271,** 278, **284.** *See also* B cells, T cells
Lymphoid tissues, 278
Lymphokines, **286,** 285
Lyon, Mary F., 475
Lyon hypothesis, **475**
  and Barr Body, *475*
Lyse, **55**
Lysergic acid diethylamide (LSD), 385
Lysins, **293**
Lysosome(s), 26, **39,** 40, *41*
  and drug action, 40
  enzymes, 37
  and Tay-sachs disease, 41
Lysozyme, 282

Macaque monkeys, and social dominance, 423
McCarty, M., 108
Machu Picchu, 316
MacLoud, C. M., 108
Macrophages, **284**
Magnesium, 77
  dietary, 77
Magnification, **33**
Major histocompatibility complex, **483**
Malaria, 505
Malathion, 375, 384
Male
  climacteric, **354**
  climax, 173–174
  genitalia, 172–174
  hormones, 171, **352**
  menopause, 354
  puberty, 171
  reproductive system, *172*
  sterility, 354
  sterilization, **192**
Malleus, **399**
Malnutrition, 578
Malthus, Thomas, 590
Malting, 244
Maltose, **63**
Mammalia, 514
Mammary glands, 209. *See also* Breast(s)
Man. *See also Homo sapiens*
  body structure, 514
  classification of, *513, 514*
  evolution, 524–532
  special creation, 518
Manganese, 77
Marasmus, **578,** *579*

Marfan syndrome, 252
Marijuana, **385**
Marrow cavity, 277, **433,** 434
Mars, life on, 4
Masculinization, 354
Mass number, **597**
Mast cells, 298
Materials, exchange of, *254*
Maternal diseases and fetus, *216*
Mating, 425–426
  controlled, 505
Mating behavior, 425
Matter, **81, 597**
  three states of, 31
Measles, 286
  acquired immunity to, 289
  and birth defects, 216
  vaccine, 288, 291
Measurement, international system, 603–604
Mechanical systems, **140**
Meconium, **204**
Medici, Marie de, 344
Medulla, 312, **378**
  brain, **378**
  kidney, **324**
Megakaryocyte, **279**
Megavitamin therapy, 243
Meiosis, **170,** *171,* 465, 470, 502
  abnormal, 482, 484, 485
  and crossing over, 473
  and fertilization, *465*
  and gonads, 171
Meiotic nuclear division, *185*
Melanin, **223, 462,** 465, 466
  formation, 224, 462
  and tanning, 225
  synthesis, 462, 465
Melanism, industrial, **503**
Melanocyte, *224*
  and tanning, 224
Melanocyte-stimulating hormone, 225, 353
Melanoma, 151
Melatonin, **356**
Membrane(s)
  depolarization, 369
  features, 49
  plasma. *See* Plasma membrane
  polarization, 369
  potential, 369, 376
  refractory state, 371
  repolarization, 370
  resting potential, **369,** 370

Membrane(s) (*continued*)
  semipermeable, 30–**31**
  transport, 359
  voltage, 369
Membranous structures, **49**
Memory, **420**–422
  chemical basis, 420–421
  and conditioning, 417
  decay, 421
  and drugs, 421
  and learning, 420
  long-term, **420,** 421
  and protein synthesis, 421
  retrieval, 421
  and RNA synthesis, 421
  short-term, **420,** 421
  storage, 421
  transfer, 421
Memory T cells, 286–287
Menarche, **178**
Mendel, Gregor Johann, 467
Mendel's Laws of Heredity, *468,* 506
  and peas, *469*
Meninges, **378**
Menopause, **178,** 354
Menstrual blood, 182
Menstrual cycle, **182**
  and lactation, 212
  ovulation, 182
  proliferation, 182
  secretion, 182
Menstruation, 178, 182, 354
Mental capacity and PKU, 112
Mercury, **545**–546
  effects of, 545
  and environment, 545
  limit in fish, 546
  poisoning, 545
  and skin, 223
Meringue, *71*
Mesoderm, embryonic, 199
Messenger RNA, **115,** 148
Metabolic heat, 254
Metabolic poison, 371
Metabolic rate, **240**
  and temperature control, 454, 455
Metabolism, 4, **5**
  cardiac muscle, 438
  in protoorganism *17*
Metaphase, **131,** *170*
  arrest, 131
  chromosomes, 131–132, *170*
Metastatic cancer, 152

Metastatic tumor, 152
Methadone, 386
Methane, 11, 12, 548
Methedrine, 384, 386
Methyl mercury, 545
Methyl parathion, 547
Metric system, 603–604
MHC, **483**
Microfilaments, 30, **42**
Microscope, *33*
Microtubules, 30, **41,** *42*
Microvilli, **238,** *239*
Micturition, **333**
Midbrain, **378**
Middle ear, **398,** 401
Middle lamella, 48
Migration, *533*
Milk, 213
  composition, *213*
  cow's, 213
  human, 213
  production, *213*
  protein in, 213
  secretion, 209–212
  and vitamin D, 348–349
Milky Way, 11
Miller, Stanley L., 12, *13*
Minamata disease, 545
Mineral resources, depletion, 582
Mineralocorticoids, **352**
Minerals, **77**
  dangers of excess, 243
  in diet, 245
  and digestion, 77, 242
Mitochondria, **37,** 38, *39,* 94, 132
  in digestion, 238
  in kidney function, 326
Mitosis, 130, **132,** *136,* 169, *170,* 501, 502
Mittelschmerz, **187**
Mohammed, 372
Mole, 89
Molecular action
  of hormones, 358–360
Molecular genetics, **461**
Molecular weight, 68
Molecule(s), *29,* **598**
  carrier, 34
  promoters, 144
  in solution, 29
  storage, *60*
Monera, **53**
Mongolism, 461. *See also* Down syndrome
Monkey, *515–517*

Monoclonal antibody, **295**
Monocytes, 278, 284
Monod, J., 143
Monosaccharides, *60,* 61, 235
  fusion, 63
Mons veneris, **182**
Month-after pill, 186
Mora, P., 6
Morgan, C. Lloyd, 409
Morgan, T. H., 472
Morgan's Canon, **409**
Morphine, 313, 386
Morphology, of human tissues, 50–52
Morula formation, *197*
Motility, 49
Motion, 6
  muscle, 438–440
Motion sickness, 403
Motor neurons, **377,** 380
Motor root, 380
Motor unit, **445**
Motor-end-plate, **444,** *445*
  potential, **444**
Mountain sickness, 316
Mouth, 236
  fetal, 203
Movement, 6
  fetal, 205
  perception of, 401–403
mRNA, **115,** 116, 148. *See also* Messenger RNA
MSH, 353
Mucopolysaccharide, chondroitin sulfate, 431
Mucoprotein, 275
Mucosa, **233**
Mucous secretions, 47, 302, 303
Mucus, in seminal fluid, 173
Muller, H. J., 499–508
Muller, Paul, 546
Multicellular organisms, 25, 366
Multiple alleles, 478–481
Multiple sclerosis (MS), **367**
Mumps
  acquired immunity to, 289
  and birth defects, 216
  and male sterility, 174
Murmurs, heart, **259**
Muscle, 435–447, 438, *441*
  abductors, **438**
  action potential, 444, 445, 446
  adductors, **438**
  aging, 440
  antagonists, **438**
  arm, *438*

and ATP, 445, 446
atrophy, 447
body, *436*
bundles, 440, 441
calf, 446
cardiac, **436**, *437*
cell, *446*
characteristics, 438
connective tissue, *442*
contractility of, **438**
contraction, 438, 440, *443, 444*, 445
depressors, **438**
dialtors, **439**
elasticity, **438**
endoplasmic reticulum, 444
extensibility of, **438**
extensor, **438**
eye, 445
fatigue, 437, 439, 446
flexor, **438**
graded response, 445
involuntary, **437**
kinds, 436–440
levators, **438**
molecular contraction, *443*
motion, 438–440
paralysis, 341, 380, 445
pronators, **439**
red, **437**
skeletal, **436**, *437*
smooth, **436**, *437*
sphincter, **439**
striated, **436**, 437, 440, 441, *443*
supinators, **439**
tension and bone growth, 435
tonus, **233**
visceral, **437**
white, **437**
Muscle tissue, *52*
Muscular system and behavior, 408
Mutagenic, 499
Mutagens, *156*
  environmental, 161
Mutation, **5, 122,** 141, 143, **466,** 547
  and evolution, 501
  frameshift, 161
  lethal, 122, 501
  and x-rays, **499**
  and radiation, 122, *498*
Myasthenia gravis, **445**
Myelin sheath, **367,** *368*
Myocardium, **258**
Myofibrils, **441**

Myogenic heartbeat, **258**
Myoglobin, **437**
Myosin, **441,** *444*
Myxedema, **345,** *346*

NAD, **86,** 88, 99
NADH$_2$, 88, 92
NADP, 99
NADPH$_2$, 99, 100
Naegli, Carl, 468
Nagasaki, 157, 499
*Naked Apes,* 226
Naloxine, 384
β-Naphthylamine, 153
Nasal cavity, 303, 305
Nasal epithelium, 391
Nash, Ogden, 298
Natural immunity, **282**
Natural selection, **16**
  as differential reproduction, 17
Neanderthal man, 531
Nearsightedness, **397**
Negative feedback, **141,** *142,* 357
  and blood content, 275
Negative geotaxis, **410**
Negative phototaxis, **410**
Negative selection, **506,** 507
Nelms, Sara, 290
Nembutal, 386
Neoplastic, **151**
Neostigmine, 449
Nephron, **323, 324**
Nerve(s), **366**
  of bone, 432
  cells, 365, 370. *See also* Neuron(s)
  cholinergic, **382**
  conduction, 368
  cranial, 378
  functions, 380
  impulses, **366,** 369, 371. *See also* Action potential
  memory, 383
  parasympathetic, **381**
  pathways, 420
  roots, 380
  spinal, 378
  stimulation, 357, *372*
  stimuli, 371
  sympathetic, **381**
  transmission, 374
  transmission velocity, 374
  vagus, 312, 381
Nerve gas, 384

Nerve impulse, 371–374
Nervous system, 365–389, **377**
  and behavior, 407, 408
  and birth defects, 217
  and brain, 377
  circuitry, *378*
  design of, 378
  and electricity, 368
  and endocrine system, 365
  fetal, 205
  function, 365, 368
  immature, 408
  ionic flow, 370
  mature, 408
  parasympathetic, 381
  peripheral, 380
  and spinal cord, *378*
Nervous tissue, *52*
Nesting, and behavior, 411
Neural tube, *198*
Neuron(s), **366**–369
  adrenergic, 381
  "all-or-none law," 372
  code, 374
  and dendrites, 366
  design, *377*
  excitation, 365
  expiratory, 312
  frequency, *374*
  and glial or Schwann cells, *368*
  inspiratory, 313
  interneurons, **377**
  ions, 369
  membrane potential, 369
  membrane voltage, 369
  and memory, 421
  motor, **377**
  and myelin sheath, *368*
  neuronal "wires," 407–408
  nodes, 374
  nucleus, 36
  operation of, 366
  organelles, 366
  plasma membrane, 366
  polarization, 369
  postsynaptic, *377*
  potassium gates, 370
  refractory period, 371
  at rest, 369
  sensory, **377**
  separation of charges, 369
  sodium gates, 370
  stimulus intensity, 374

Neuron(s) (*continued*)
  threshold stimulus, 371
  types, 367
  work, 369
Neuronal size and learning, **420**
Neurophypophyseal hormones. *See also* Posterior pituitary hormones
Neurosurgery, 419
Neurotransmitter substances, 375
Neurotransmitters, *384*
Neutral atom, 598
Neutral fat, 67
  formation, *65*
Neutral stimulus, **417**
Neutrons, **597**
Neutrophil, **282**, 295
Newborn
  breathing, 314
  regurgitation, 248
Niacin, deficiency, 86
Niche, **558**
Nickel, 153
  and cancer, 153
  and skin, 223
Nicotinamide adenine dinucleotide (NAD), **99**
Nicotinamide adenine dinucleotide phosphate (NADP), 99
Nicotine, 384
Niemann-Pick disease, *202*
Night blindness, **395**
Nine-plus-two arrangement, 42
Nipple erection, 183
Nitrates, 550
Nitric oxide, 584
Nitrites, 550
Nitrogen, 317, 550
  bubbles, 317
  cycle, **550**, *552*
  dioxide, 589
  fixation, **550**
  fixers, **550**
Nitrogenous base, *109*, 113
Nitrogenous waste, 328
Node, **374**
Node of Ranvier, **367**
Noise pollution, *400*
Noncylic photophosphorylation, **99**
Nondisjunction, **484**
  and Down syndrome, *488*
  during oogenesis, *484*
  during spermatogenesis, *484*
Nonelectrolytes, **599**
Noradrenalin, 350

Noradrenergic nerve, **382**
Norepinephrine, 381
  release of, 351
"Normal," 213
North American biomes, 565
Nose, *392*
Nostrils, 302
"Not-self" antigens, 284
Nuclear envelope, 44
Nuclear membrane, 131
  and cell division, 131
Nuclear pores, *45*, 46
Nuclear power plants, 582
Nuclear waste, *548*, 549
Nucleic acids, **13**, 53, **78**
  parasitic integration of, 17
  synthesis, 131
Nucleolar organizer, **44, 132**
Nucleolus, **43**
Nucleoplasm, **43**
Nucleoproteins, 70
Nucleosomes, *138*
Nucleotide(s), **109**
  deletion, 498–499
  DNA, **109**
  pairs, 135
  sequence, **111,** *113,* 118
  structure, *109,* 110
  substitutions, 122
  transcription, 122
Nucleus, **43,** 44, *45*
  atom, **597**
  egg, 185
  function, 44
  interphase, 130
  pores, 46
  prokaryotic, 53
  sperm, 184–185
  transplants, 45
Nurse bees, *424*
Nutrient
  cycling, 584
  movement, *267*
  upwellings, 580
Nutrition, *241*
  and calories, *242,* 578
  and energy, 578
  and metabolism, 240–245
  mineral requirements, *246*
  and vitamins, *244–245*

Obesity, **241**
  and adult-onset diabetes, 241

  causes, 242–243
  and heart disease, 241
  and high blood pressure, 241
Ocean, fish harvest, 580
Ockham's razor, **409**
Odor, 392
Oil depletion, 582
Oil glands. *See* Sebaceous glands
Oils. *See* Fat(s)
Oklahoma dust bowl, 565
Oleoresins, 223
Olfactory bulb, 391
Olfactory nerve, 391
Olfactory organs, **391**
Omnivores, **543**
Oncogenes, **163**
One-gene-one-enzyme hypothesis, **113**
Oocyte, **178,** *196*
  development, 178
Oogenesis, **177,** *185*
  nondisjunction in, *486*
Oparin, A. I., 12, 15
Operant conditioning, **417,** **418**
Operon, **143,** 144, *146*
Ophthalmoscope, 395
Opiates, 343, 386
Opsins, 394, 395
Opsonins, **292**
Opsonization, 295
Optic chiasma, **396**
Optic disc, **395,** *396*
Optic nerve, **396**
Optic neurons, 394
Oral contraceptive pill, 187
  risks of, 188
Orangutan, *515*
Orbitals, of electrons, **598**
Order, **513**
Organ, **49,** 134
  transplant, 297
Organ of Corti, **399**
Organ system, **49**
  embryonic, 199
Organelles, **35**
Organic compound, **11,** 13
Organic molecule, 22, **59**
Organic nutrient, **17**
Organic pesticides, 544
Organic soup. *See* Primitive soup
Organism, 16, 255
  development, 255
  function, 255

primitive, 16, 255
structure, 255
Organophosphate insecticides, 375
Organophosphates, 375
Orgasm, **183**
female, **183–184**
Origin of life, 12
*Origin of Species*, 520, 523
Orwell, George, 366
Os penis, 177
Osmoreceptors, 329
Osmosis, **31,** *32,* 327
in kidney, 327
Osmotic pressure, **31,** 32, 275
blood, 275
hydrostatic, 269
kidney, 329–330
Ossification, 433
Osteoarthritis, 440
Osteoclast, **434**
Osteocyte, **431,** 432, *433*
Otolith, **401**
Ova, 177. *See also* Egg(s)
Oval window, **399**
Ovarian cycle, **178,** *180, 181*
and temperature, 187
Ovary, **177,** *180, 181*
Overweight, 241–243
Ovulation, 179
detection of, 182
failure, 181
Oxidation, **64, 83,** 84
of foodstuffs, 38, 84, 240
glucose, 84–85
Oxidation-reduction reaction, 92
Oxidative combustion, 301
Oxidizing atmosphere, 12
Oxygen, 9, 301, 305
deficiency, 316
diffusion, 307
exchange, 301
need, 305
poisoning, 317
production, 39
transport, 301
Oxygen-carrying capacity, 307
Oxygen debt, **447**
Oxyhemoglobin, **276, 307**
Oxytocin, 68, 209, **341,** 357
in lactation, 212
Ozone, and plants, **586**
Ozone hole, **557,** 558
and skin cancer, 558

*P* wave, **259**
PABA, 77
Pacemaker, **258**
Pacinian corpuscle, **403**
P-aminobenzoic acid (PABA), *77*
P-aminohippuric acid, 228
PAN, 584
Pancreas, **347,** *350, 361*
Panting, 457
Papillae, 393
Parachlorophenylalanine, 384
Paralysis, flaccid, 380
Paralytic poisons, *448–449*
Paramecium, 559
Paraplegics, 380
Parasympathetic nerves, 457
Parasympathetic nervous system, **259, 381**
Parathion, 375, 384
Parathormone, 346–347
Parathyroid glands, **346,** 347, *360*
Parental care, and instinct, 411
Parkinson's disease, *383*
Parturition, **209.** *See also* Birth
Passive immunity, 288
Pasteur, Louis, *9*
Paternity, and blood type, *479*
Pattern baldness, 227
Pavlov, Ivan, 417
Pavlovian conditioning, **417**
Peck order, **423**
Pectin, **48**
Pectoral girdle, **431**
Pedigree, **466**
and albinism, *467*
and color blindness, *474*
Peking Man, 530
Pellagra, 76
Pelvic floor, 183
Pelvis, **431**
Penicillin, 328
evaluation of, 501
excretion of, 328
sensitivity to, 285, 298
Penicillin-resistant bacteria, 501
Penis, 172, **177**
detumescence, 184
ejaculation, 177
erection, 177
Pentoses, 60
Pepsin, 74
Peptic ulcers, **249**
Peptide bond, **68,** *69,* 118
formation, *119*

Peptide chain, 68
Peptide hormones, 357
Perception of movement, 401–403
Pergament, Eugene, 202
Pericardium, **255**
Perichondrium, **432**
Period, menstrual, 182
Periodontal tissue, **244**
Periosteum, **432**
Peripheral blood, 281
Peripheral nervous system (PNS), 380, 381
Peripheral nervous tissue, *52*
Peripheral vision, **395**
Peristalsis, **233**
Peristaltic contractions, *235*
Peristaltic movement, *235*
Peritonitis, **249**
Permanent wave, 73
Permease, 143
Pernicious anemia, 250
Peroxyl-acetyl-nitrate (PAN), 584
Pest management, 546–547
Pesticides, 580
Peter the Great, 312
Petit mal seizure, *373*
PETS (positron emission tomography), 373
PGA, 100
PGAL (phosphoglyceraldehyde), 100
pH, 32, **599**
Phagocytic cells, 277, 282. *See also* White blood cell(s)
Phagocytosis, **35,** 40
Pharyngeal opening, 401
Pharynx, **303**
Phase-contrast microscope, **33**
Phenotype, **465,** 470
Phenylalanine, 112
Phenylketonuria (PKU), **112**
Phenylpyruvic acid, 112
Phipps, James, 291
Phosphate rocks, 552
Phosphoglyceraldehyde, **100**
Phosphoglyceric acid (PGA), 100
Phospholipids, **67**
Phosphorus, 77
in diet, 77, 243
Phosphorus cycle, 550, **552,** *553*
Phosphorylation, **86**
Photochemical air pollution, *585*
Photon, 98
Photophosphorylation, 99
Photoreceptor cells, 394, 395
Photosynthesis, *19,* **21,** 22, **38, 97,** 540, 552

Photosynthesis (*continued*)
  carbohydrate production, 100–102
  cellular location, 98–99
  and chloroplasts, 38, 53, 98
  dark phase, 100, 101
  and earth population, 97–99
  efficiency, 97, 102–103
  light phase, 98
  location, 38, 102
  origin, 19
  and population growth, 103
  reactions, 100–102
  schematic, *102*, 103
  systems I and II, **99,** *101*
Phototaxes, **410**
Phycobilins, 98
Phyla, **513**
Physiograph apparatus, 372
Physiological genetics, **461**
Physique, 123, **535**
Physostigmine, 489
Pigeons, behavior, 412
Pigment, 462
  cells, 41, 113
  photosynthetic, 39, 98
  visual, 394
Pill, contraceptive, **187,** 189
Pineal gland, **356,** *360*
Pineal tumor, 356
Pinocytosis, **35,** 267
Pioneering community, 563
Pioneering plants, 563–609
Pitch, **398,** 401
*Pithecanthropus* (Homo) *erectus*, 530
Pituitary, *181, 360*
  and ADH, 329
  anterior, **338,** *340*
  dwarf, **342,** *343*
  gland, 173, **338,** *339*, 343, 357
  and hypothalmus, 341, 353, 358
  posterior, **341**
  tumor, 396
Pivot joint, 439
PKU
  and genetic engineering, **112**
  and mental retardation, *112*
Placebo, 384
Placenta, **203**
  delivery of, 208, *211*
  and fetal growth, 203
  and material exchange, 207
  regression, 206
  semipermeable membranes, 209

Plague, 572
Planets, 11
  formation, *10*
Plants(s), **53**
  kingdom, 511
  and ozone, 586
  respiration, 102
Plant cell, 27, **48,** *49, 97. See also* Photosynthesis
  mitosis, 132
  vacuoles, 41
  wall, **48**
Plantae, 53
Plaque, 264
Plasma, *27,* **295**
  cell, *286–287*
  components of, *277*
  composition of, *230, 275*
  function, 275
  pH, 276
  proteins, 270
  transport, 321
Plasma cells, 277, 285
Plasma membrane, **25,** *27,* 28, 32, 233, 253
  function, 28
  structure, 67
Plasmablast, **285**
Plasmids, 123, **124**
  chimeras, **124**
Plastics, 49
Plastids, **39**
Plastoquinone, 99
Platelets, **279**
Pleiotropy, **496**
Pleural membrane, **303,** 309
Pleurisy, *306*
Plutonium plants, 549
Pneumonia, 107–108
Pneumococcus, 108
PNS, **377**
Poikilotherms, 453
Poison ivy, 223
Polar body, 179
Poliomyelitis, 289, 380
Poliovirus, 293
Pollution
  air, **154,** 582
  environmental, 544, 589
  heat, 583
  noise, 400
  thermal, **583**
  water, *589*
Polygenes, **481**

Polygenic inheritance, 481, 482
Polygenic traits, **123**
Polygraph, 372
Polymerization, **13, 59,** *60*
Polymorphism, **503, 552**
Polyoma virus, **158**
Polypeptide chain, **68,** *120*
  formation, 120
  ribosome assembly site, *120*
  translation, 121
Polypeptide hormone, 358
Polyribosome, **36,** 118
Polysaccharides, **63**
  chaining, *64*
Polysome, **118,** 120
Polytypic, **533**
Polyunsaturates, 66
Pons, **378,** *380*
Population, 97, 104, 511, **539**
  age structure, *574*
  arithmetic growth, **570**
  bomb, 570
  bulge, 573
  carrying capacity, 579, 591
  changes in animal, *561*
  competitive exclusion principle, 560
  and resource consumption, *592*
  control, 590
  distribution, *575, 576*
  distribution limits, 558
  doubling time, 571, 572
  equilibrium level, 592
  explosion, 571
  exponential growth, **570,** 571
  family size, 574
  fluctuation, 591
  growth, 569, 570, 571, *572*
  in human history, 526–527, 578
  increase in density, *577*
  limits, 590, 591
  log-log plot, *591*
  Malthus and natural selection, 522
  negative feedback, 592
  positive feedback, 592
  regulation, 591
  replacement level, 571
  set point, 592
  structure, **572,** *575*
  world, *593*
  ZPG, 571, 576
Portal veins, 254
Porter, Keith, 36
Positive eugenics, **508**

Positive feedback, **141**
Posterior chamber of eye, **394**
Posterior pituitary hormones, **341**
Postsynaptic neuron, 374
Potassium, 10
    ions, 369
    and neurons, 369
Potential energy, **81**
Pott, Percival, 153
Precipitation, world pattern, *554*
Precipitins, **293**
Precursor cells, 284
Preening, 426
Pregnancy, 189
    and drugs, *215*
    and Rh factor, 480–481
    risk, 215–217
    symptoms, *189*
    test, 189
Pregnenolone, 352
Prepubertal castration, 354
Prepuce, **177**
Pressure, eardrum, 401
Pressure receptor, 403
Pressure stimulus, 391
Presynaptic knob, **374**
Primary cell wall, **48**
Primary consumers, **541**
Primary immune response, **284**
Primary oocyte, 178
Primary productivity, *580*
Primate
    behavior, 416
    body structure, *519*
    characteristics, *514*
    classification, *518*
    dentition, 527
    family tree, *524*
    skull shape, *527*
Primitive earth, 12
    atmosphere, **11**, 12, 17
Primitive organisms, **13**, 14–17
Primitive soup, **12**, *13*, 16, 22
Primitive streak, 198
Primordial Cloud Theory, *10*, 11
Principle of recombination, **467**
Principle of segregation, *470*
Principles of electricity, 368–369
Problem solving, 418
Processed nutrients, 240
*Proconsul,* **524**
Producer, **540**
Progesterone, **354**

at birth, 209
    and breast enlargement, 209
Progestins, 188
Prokaryotes, **53**, 147, 148
    nucleus in, 53
Prolactin, 212, **341**
Promoter region, 144
Pronators, **439**
Prophase, **130,** *170*
Propylthiouracil, 345
Prosimians, 524
Prostaglandins, 179, **356**
    and abortion, 356
    and arterial pressure, 356
    and asthma, 356
    and contraception, 356
    in labor, delivery, 356
    in ovulation, 179
    and peptic ulcers, 356
    and plasma membrane, 356
    in seminal fluid, 173, 356
Prostate gland, **173**
Prosthetic group, 77
Protista, **53**
Protein(s), 28, **68**
    chain, 121
    coagulation, **69**
    conjugated, **70**
    deficiency, 579
    denaturation, **69, 70**
    disposal, 29
    formation, 44
    histone, **134**
    molecules, 71
    primary structure, **69,** *70, 138*
    prosthetic groups, **70**
    secondary structure, **69**
    synthesis, 78, 121
    tertiary structure, **69,** *70*
    translation, **118,** 146
Protein sparing, **241**
Proteinoid, **13,** *14,* 17
Protoearth, 11
Protons, **579–599**
Protooncogenes, 163
Protoorganisms, 16, **17.** *See also* Primitive orga-
    nisms
Protoplasm, 25, 26, **28**
Protozoa, 9
Proximal convoluted tubule, 326
Psychic dependence, 383
Psychology, behaviorists, 408
Ptyalin, 74

Puberty, 179
    and breast development, 179
    female, 179
    male, 351
    and sex hormones, 179, 353–355
Pulmonary artery, 304
Pulmonary circulation, 307
Pulmonary edema, *306*
    and air pollution, 308
Pulmonary osteoarthropathy,
    **308**
Pulmonary pump, **257**
Pulmonary valve, **257**
Pulmonary vein, 305
Pulse, fetal, 199
Punishment, 412
Punnett, R. C., 472
Punnett square, **470**
Pupil, **394**
Purines, 13, **109**
Purkinje fibers, **259**
Purposive behavior, 409
Pus, **282**
Pyorrhea, **248**
Pyrimidines, **109**
Pyrogens, **456**
Pyruvic acid, **86,** *88, 89*

QRC wave, **259**
Quanta, 98
Queen bee, 424–425
Queen Victoria, *476*

R group, **68**
r strategy, **561**
Rabies vaccine, 291
Race, 532–536
    classification, *534*
    differences, 123, 534
    formation, 533
    isolation, 533
    selection, 533
Racism, 532, 535
Radiation, 498–500
    annual amounts, *500*
    and Chernobyl, *483*
    hazards, and causes, 498–500
    and heat, 455
    mutagenic, *498·*
    and mutations, *500*
Radioactive clock, *18*
Radioactive debris, 548–549

Radioactive debris (*continued*)
    fallout, 547
    iodine, 547
Radioactive decay, *18*
Radioactive half-life, *18*
Radioactive iodine, *346*
Radioactivity, **597**
Radiologists, and cancer, 157
Rank order, 423
Rats
    behavior, 412
    learning, 417
    negative geotaxis, **410**
Rates of reversal, sterilization, **192**
Rattlesnake, 426
Rayon, 49
Reaction barrier, 72
Reasoning, insight learning, **418**
Receptor(s), **284,** 365, 391, 392
    agonists, **383**
    antagonists, **383**
    and oxygen, 314
    proteins, 359
    sound, 399
    taste, 393
Recessive allele, and selection, *507*
Recessive gene, **466**
    elimination, 507
    in sickle cell, 495
Recognition site, **289**
Recombinant DNA, **123**
Recombination
    genetic, 470, *472*
    and meiosis, *472*
Rectum, **240**
Recycling
    matter, 549, 550, 556
    solid waste, 590
    water, 552
Red blood cell(s), *28, 34,* 44–45, **276**
    and carbon dioxide, 276
    count, 280
    design, 276
    function, 277
    "ghosts" of, *28*
    osmosis, 277
Red muscle, **437**
Redi, Francesco, *7*
Redirected activity, **414**
Reducing atmosphere, 11, **12,** 17, 93
Reduction, **83**
Reflex arc, **382**
Reflexes, **378,** *382,* **411**

and behavior, 408–418
    conditioned, 417
    fetal, 203
    knee jerk, *302,* 369
    stereotyped, 369
Refractory period of heart, **259**
Refractory period, male, 184
Refractory state, nerves, **371**
Regulation of fluid, 328, 333
Regulator gene, in cancer, 158
Reindeer population growth, *560*
Reinforcement, **417**
Rejection, and immunity, 285
Releaser, **411,** 413, 415
Releasing factors, 357, 413, 415
Releasing hormone, 358
Renal artery, **323**
Renal vein, **323**
Repetition, **417**
Replicase, *16*
Repolarization, membrane, **369**
Repressor protein, 143, 144, 146
Reproduction, **5**
    differential, **504**
Reproductive system, 171–183
    female, 177–183
    male, 171–177
Reserpine, 385
Resolution, 33
Resolving power, 33
Resorption (reabsorption), 326, 329
    kidney, 326
    of sodium, 330
    in tadpole, 40
    of water, 326
Resource depletion, 582
Resources
    nonrenewable, 582
    renewable, 582
Respiration, 38, **301–317,** *302*
    aerobic, 92–93
    cellular, 38, 81–83
    control, 312–317
    diffusion of gases, 301
    evolution of, 93–94
    and exercise, 313
    fetal, 208
    filtration of air, 303
    flatworm, 302
    internal, 302
    kinds of, 301
    location of, 38–39
    prokaryote, 53

    nervous control, 313
    reptile, 301
Respiratory center, **312,** 313, 314
Respiratory chain, **91**
Respiratory exchange surface, 301
Respiratory malfunctions, 306
Respiratory muscles, 309, 311
Respiratory rate, 313
Respiratory rhythm, 313
Respiratory surface, 303
Respiratory system, *303*
    insect, *303*
    mouse, *303*
Respiratory tree, **303,** *304*
Response(s)
    innate, 414–415
    learned, 414–415
Response mechanism, 453
Responsiveness, **5,** 6
Resting cell, **130**
Resting nerve cell, **370**
Resting (refractory) period, muscle, **446**
Restriction enzyme, 514
Rete testis, **173**
Reticulin, *47*
Reticuloendothelial system, **282**
Retina, **394,** *395*
    inverted, *396*
Retinaldehyde, 394
Retroviruses, 163
Reward, 412
Rh incompatability, 479, *480,* 481
Rheumatism, **439**
Rhodopsin, 394
Rhythm, cardiac muscle, 437
Rhythm method, **185**
Rib muscles, 309
Ribonucleic acid, 115. *See also* RNA
Ribonucleotide, **115**
Ribose, **115**
Ribosomal, RNA (rRNA), **117**
Ribosome, *26,* **117**
    binding site, *120,* **121**
    precursors, 44
    in translation, **118**
Ribs, *310,* **431**
Ribulose bisphosphate, **100**
Ribulose phosphate, **100**
Rickets, 348, 349
    and early man, 531
Rickettsiae classification, 53
Right lymphatic duct, **270**
Right-handed (and left-handed) molecules, *62*

Rigid cartilage, 432
Rigor mortis, 443
Ripening fruit, 39, 48
Ritalin, 384, 406
Ritual, **425**
Ritual feeding, 426
Ritual fighting, 426
Ritualization, **426**
RNA, 16, 44, **115.** *See also* Ribonucleic acid
   of cell, *118*
   code words, *114,* 118
   distinctions from DNA, 115
   location, 115
   messenger (mRNA), **115**
   nucleotides, 115
   polymerase, **115,** *120,* 121
   ribosomal (rRNA), 117
   synthesis, 421
   virus, 109
Robertson, J. D., 29
Rods, **394**
Round window, ear, **399**
Rous, Peyton, 157
Rous sarcoma virus, *163*
Royal jelly, 425
rRNA, **117**
*RU-486, 186*
Rubella and birth defects, 216
RuBP, 100
Runaway feedback, **141**
RuP, 100
Ryther, J. H.

SA node, **258**
Saccharin, and cancer, 153
Saccule, 40
Sacroplasmic reticulum, 445, *446*
St. Martin, Alexis, 238
St. Martin's fistula, *238*
Saline abortion, 214
Saliva, 74, 332
Salivary glands, 337
*Salmonella typhimurium,* 157
Salt(s), 28, 31, 323, 328
   balance, 323–328
   concentration gradient, 327
   in seawater, 275
   in sweat, 230
Salt domes, 548
Sarcolemma, **441,** 444
Sarcoma, 151
Sarcoplasm, **441**
Sarcoplasmic reticulum, **444**

Satiation, **413**
Saturated fats, **66**
Saturation curve, oxygen, 310
Scanning electron microscope, 277
Scarlet fever, and birth defects, 216
Schaison, Gilbert, 186
Schick test, 285
Schizophrenic patients, 406
Schwann cell, 368
Scientific method, 8
Sclera, **393**
Scrotum, 172
Scurvy, 75, 175
Sea anemones, 253
Sea farming, 580
Seagull chicks, feeding, 414–415
Sebaceous glands, 211, **221,** 229
Sebum, **229**
Seconal, 386
Second filial generation, **468**
Second genesis, 107
Second Law of Thermodynamics, 82, 86
Secondary cell wall, **48**
Secondary consumers, **541**
Secondary immune response, **287**
Secondary oocyte, 178
Secondary sex characteristics, 177
   Napoleon, 354–355
Sedatives, **384**
Sedimentary rocks, *19*
Selection
   negative, **506**
   and race, 533
   and recessive traits, 507
"Self" antigens, 285
Self-regulation, 453
Self-stimulation, 365
Self-tolerance, **285**
Semen, **173,** 174
   and sperm banks, *176*
   volume of, 174
Semicircular canals, 401
Semilunar valve, **257**
Seminal fluid, **173**
Seminal vesicles, **173**
Seminiferous tubules, **172,** 352, 354
Semipermeability, **31**
Sense organs, 391
Sensory adaptation, 415
Sensory hair, ear, 401
Sensory nerves, 380
Sensory neurons, **377**
Sensory receptors, 365

Serotonin, 385
Sertoli cells, **172**
Serum, **279**
Serum sickness, 288
Sewage treatment, 588, *590*
Sex
   chromosomes, **462**
   determination, 462
   drive, 413
   hormones, **352,** *354–356*
   linkage, **473**
Sex cells, 169–192. *See also* Gametes
Sex characteristics, secondary, 177
Sexual differences, fetal, 205
Sexual intercourse, **183**
   diagrammed, *175*
Sexual organs, fetal, 204
Sexual reproduction, 501, 502
Sexuality and meoisis, 169
Shivering, 456
Shock, **270**
   and allergic response, 298
   and blood pressure, 265
Shope papilloma virus, 157
Short-term memory (STM),
   **420**
Shoulder girdle (pectoral), **431**
Siamese twins, 213
Sickle-cell
   anemia, 494, 495
   characteristics, 495
   consequences, *497*
   distribution, *505*
   frequency, 507
   hemoglobin, **122,** *496, 497*
   inheritance of, *495, 496*
   and malaria, 462, 505
   and negative selection, 504
   trait, **496**
Siegler, Alvin, 192
Sight, 393–397
Sigmoid curve, **559**
*Silent Spring,* 547
Simple reflex arc, 382
Single bond, **600**
Single cell organism, 53
Single sugars, **60**
Sinoatrial node, **258**
Sinuses, **303,** *305*
Sinusoids, **282**
Skeletal muscle, **436**
Skeleton
   fetal, 203

Skeleton (*continued*)
 human, 431–435
 "Lucy," *527*
Skin, **221–230, 403.** *See also* Dermis
 and acne, 229
 apocrine sweat glands, 230
 area, 223
 basal cells, 223
 blood supply, 223
 cancer of, 155, **156,** 465
 cells, 152, 402
 color. *See* Skin color
 dermis, 403
 eccrine sweat glands, 230
 elasticity, **221**
 epidermis, **223, 403**
 fat, 223
 glands of, 229, *361*
 graft, 284
 growth, 152
 pacinian corpuscles, **403**
 penetrating substances, 223
 receptors, 403
 senses, 403
 Stratum corneum, **223**
 Stratum germinativum, **223**
 structure, *222*
 and sunburn, *225*
 sympathetic nerves, 230
 and temperature, 403
 temperature receptors, 403
 thickness, 224
 versatility, 221
 weight, 223
Skin color, **223**
 albinism, 226
 and multiple alleles, 482
 carotene, 223
 and environment, 535
 and epistasis, **482**
 and hemoglobin, 224
 melanin, **223,** 465, 466
 pigment, 223–226, 462, *535*
 and race, 223–224
 senses, *403*
 skin structure, *455*
 and tanning, 155, 224, 482
 and thickness, 224
Skinner, B. F., *412*
Skinner box, 410
Skull, **431,** 439
 primate, *527*
Sliding-filament model, 442

Small intestine, *234, 236, 237*
 area, 238
Smallpox, 290, 291
 and birth defects, 216
 vaccine, 290–291
Smell, 391, *392*
Smith, Homer, 321
Smog, **308**
 damage to chloroplasts, 584
Smoking, 154
 and cancer, 154–157
 Surgeon General's warning, 154
Smooth muscles, **436**
Snake bite, 288
Sneezing, 313
Social behavior, **422–426**
Social dominance, **423–425**
Social hierarchy, **423–424**
Social insects, 424
Social life, advantages, 422
Social order, 423
Society, and groups, **422**
Sodium, 10
 balance, 327
 conservation, 328–330
 excess, 243
 ions, 327, 369
 pump, **34,** 330
 regulation, 328
 resorption, 330
Sodium chloride, 243–244, 327
Sodium-potassium pump, 369
Solar energy, 98
Solar radiation, 11
Solar system
 age of, 11
 origin of, *10*
Sol-gel transformation, **29**
Solid, diffusion in, 29
Solid waste, 590
Solids, in primitive ocean, 13
Solution, 29
Somatic cells, **170,** 460
Somatic nervous system, 381
Somatostatin, 123, 358
Somatotropic hormone, **341**
Somites, 199, 200
Soot, 153
Sound, 398
 energy, **398**
 level readings, *400*
 receptors, 398
 volume, 400

 waves, 398
Spaceship Earth, 564, 569–593
Spallanzani, Lazzaro, *7*
Spare-part surgery, 297
Spark discharge apparatus, *13*
Spastic paralysis, 384
Species, **511,** 532
 classification, 511
 competetive exclusion, 559, 560
 density factors, 561
 diversity, equilibrium, 563, 564
 evolution, 511
 extinction, 520
 fixity of, **511**
 niche, 558, 562
 strategy, 561
Species-specificity, **68,** 114
Spectacles, 397
Speech, 529
Sperm, **172, 173,** *175,* 176
 activation, 184
 banks, *176*
 capacitation, 184
 and fertilization, 173
 infertility, *173*
 maturation, 173
 motility, 174
 nucleus, 184–185
 tails, 42, *174*
Spermatocytes, 173
Spermatogenesis, *173, 174*
 nondisjunction, *484*
Spermatogonia, **172,** 173
Spermatozoa. *See* Sperm
Spermicidal solutions, **186**
Spermiogenesis, **171**
Sphincter muscle, **438**
 urethra, 333
Sphygmomanometer, **261**
Spiegelman Monster, *16*
Spina bifida, **215**
Spinal cord, **378**
Spinal fluid, **378**
Spinal ganglion, **378**
Spinal nerves, **378**
Spinal reflex, 380
Spindle, **131**
Spine, 378–379, **431**
Spinnbarkheit, **187**
Spleen
 fetal, 193
 and immunity, 278
Spongy bone, 391

Spontaneous abortion, 214
Spontaneous generation, **7, 9**
  modern instances, *20*
Spontaneous mutations, 496
Squamous epithelium, *50*
Sri Lanka, *571*
S-shaped growth curve, **559**
Starch, **63**
  and glucose, 59, 63
  hydrolysis, 63
Starr-Edwards heart valve, *258*
Starvation, 103, 241
Steady state, **142, 453**
Steinheim skull, *532*
Stelazine, 386
Stereoisomers, **61,** 62
Stereotyped behavior, 407
Sterility
  female, 181
  male, 173
Sterilization, **192**
  as birth control, 192
  rates of reversal, **192**
  tubal ligation, 192
  vasectomy, 192
Sternum, **431**
Steroids, **67,** 147
  and cancer, 154
  hormones, 147, *351, 359*
  ring, *66,* **351**
  structure, 66
Stethoscope, *264*
Stickleback, 413
  courtship behavior, 411, 413
  territory, 414
Stimulants, **384**
Stimulus
  herring-gull models, *414*
  natural, **417**
  neutral, **417**
Stirrup, **399**
Stomach, 235, 236
  acidity, 236
Stone Age people, 532
Strata, **520**
Stratton, Charlie, 342
*Streptococcus pneumoniae,* 107
Stress, 350
  and subordinance, 424
Stretch receptors, bladder, 333
Striae, abdominal, **189**
Striated muscle, **436**
Striped muscles. *See* Striated muscle

Stroke, 281, 406
Stroma, chloroplast, 39
Strontium, 547
Structure, and classification, **513**
Structural genes, **143**
Structural isomers, **60**
Strychnine, 384
Submucosa, **233**
Subspecies, **533.** *See also* Race
Substance
  breakdown, 36
  synthesis, 36
Substrate, **74**
Subthreshold stimulus, 377
Subvital gene, **501**
Succession, ecological. *See* Ecological succession
Succinylcholine, 449
Sucking reflex, 213
  fetal, 204
  and milk letdown, 212
Sucrase, 74
Sucrose, 31, **61**
Sudden infant death syndrome, 316
Sugar(s), 17, 20, 60
  and digestion, 239
  double. See Disaccharides
  fermentation, 63
  glucose, **60**
  malt. *See* Maltose
  many. *See Polysaccharides*
  *milk. See* Lactose
  phosphorylated, 99
  in plants, 97
  stereoisomer of, 61
  synthesized, 13
  table, 61
  in tooth decay, 247
  in urine, 329
Sugar diabetes (Diabetes Mellitus), 329
Sulfanilamide, 77
Sulfur dioxide, 584
Sulfuric acid, 589
Sulfur-sulfur linkages, 289
Summation, 377
Sun, formation, 11
Sunburn, 155, *225*
Sunstroke, 455
Supinators, **439**
Supporting connective tissue, *51*
Suprathreshold stimulus, 371
Surgeon General's warning, 154
"Survival of the fittest" 502

Suspensions, **29**
Swallowing
  and eustachian tube, 401
  fetal, 204
  and thirst, 332
Sweat, composition of, *230*
  glands, 229–**230**
Sweden, population structure, 573
Sympathetic ganglia, 350
Sympathetic nerve, **259**
Sympathetic nervous system, **259, 381**
Synapse, **374**
  and drugs, 386–387
  fatigue, 373
  structure, *376*
  transmission, *376*
Synapsis, **170**
Synaptic cleft, **374**
Synaptic knob, **367,** *375, 376*
Synaptic vessicles, 444
Syncytium, **436,** 437
Syngamy, 169, 185. *See also*
  Fertilization
Synovial fluid, **439**
Synthesis cycle, *550*
Syphilis, 185, 216, 295, 380
System I, **99,** 101
System II, **99,** 101
*Systema Naturae,* 511
Systemic pump, **257**
Systole, **259**
Systolic pressure, **262**

T cells, **271, 284,** *290*
T lymphocytes, 284
T maze, 418
T wave, **259**
Table sugar, 61
Target organ, **338**
Tarsier, 517
Taste, *392–393*
Taste bud, **393**
Tatum, E. L., 113
Taxes (taxis), 408, **410**
Tay-sachs disease, 41, 204
Tears, 282, **394**
Tectorial membrane, **399**
Teeth, 247
Teleology, 247
Telophase, **132,** *170*
Temperature, 453–457, 604
  atmosphere, 556
  control, 453

Temperature (*continued*)
  and enzyme activity, *454*
  receptor, 403
Temporal lobe, *379*
Tendons, **439**, *440*
Teratogens, **215**
  and birth defects, 215
Terns, courtship, 426
Territorality, **422**, 423
  and aggression, 423
  and behavior, 411, 422–423
  bird, 411, 423
  control, 423
  and reproduction, 423
Tetrahydrocannabinol (THC), 385
Testes, 172
  descent, 175
  hormones, 172. *See also* Androgens
  interstitial cells, 352
  rete, **173**
  retraction, 175
  undescended, 175–176
Testosterone, 172, **173**, *352*
Test-tube babies, *168*
Tetanus, 288, **446**
  and vaccine, 288
Tetany, 347
Tetroses, 60
Thalmus, **378**, *386*, 396
Thalidomide, **215**, 216
  victims, *213*
THC, 385
Theory, 8
Thermal inversion, *588*
Thermal pollution, **583**
Thermodynamics
  laws of, **82**
  model of, *82*
Thermostat, *142*, 456, 457
Thiamine pyrophosphate (TPP), *88*
Thirst, 332
  reflex, 332
Thompson, Francis, 564
Thoracic cavity, 303
Thought, 518
Threshold of hearing, **400**
Threshold stimulus, **371**
Thrombin, *279*
Thrombocytes, 277
Thrombophlebitis, **188**
Thrombus, 264, 281
Thrush, 413
  and behavior, 413

Thurber, James, 24
Thymine, **109**
  dimers, 141
Thymus gland, *284*
Thyroid gland, **344**, 345–346, *360*
  cells in, *33*
  deficiency, 395, *346*
  hormones, *346*, 455
  scan, 346
Thyroidectomy, 345
Thyroid-stimulating hormone (THS), **345**
Thyrotropic hormone, **341**
Thyroxine, **344**
Tin, depletion, 582
Tinbergen, Niko, 413
Tissue(s), **49**, 134
  classification, *50–52*
  connective, *51*
  human types, *50–52*
  "not self," 284
  self, 248
  spaces, 275
  transplanted, 297
  typing, 297
Tissue-transplant antigens, 292
Toenails, fetal, *204*
Toes
  embryonic, *201*
  fetal, 205
"Tom Thumb", 342
Tone quality, **398**
Tongue, 393
Tonsilitis, *306*
Tonsils and immunity, 278
Tool makers, 416
Tool use, *529*
Toolmaking, 528, 529
Tooth decay, 247
Toothache, 247
Total fertility rate, **571**
Touch, 403
Toxins, **293**
  and birth defects, 215
  immunity, 282
Toxoid, **293**
TPP, **88**
Tracers, radioactive, **598**
Trachea, **303**, *305*, 310
Tracheal tube, 305
Training, 418
Tranquilizers, **384**
Transcription, **116**, 117, 146–148
Transducer, **391**

Transduction, and memory, **420**
Transfer RNA. *See* tRNA
Transformation experiments, *108*
Transforming principle, **198**
Transfusion, blood, 478, 480
Translocated chromosomes, 489
Transmission
  of genes, 461–491
  genetics, **461**
Transmitter substance, *377*, 401
Transplants, 297
  bone marrow, 483
  and genes, *483*
  organ, 29
Transport, glucose, 347
Transposons, **162**
Trench mouth, 248
Trial-and-error learning, **418**
Triceps, 438
Trichinosis, 281
Tricuspid valve, **256**
Triglycerides, **239**
Triiodothyronine, **344**
Trioses, 60
Triple bond, 600
Triplet code, 113, 118–119
tRNA, **117**
Trophollaxis, **424**
Tropic hormones, **338**
Trophoblast, *197*, 206
Tropisms, **407**
Tropomyosin, **442**
Troponin, **442**
Tryosine, 462, 466
Trypsin, 74
TSH, 345, 353, 358, 359. *See also* Thyroid-stimu-
  lating hormone
Tubal ligation, **186**, 192
Tuberculin test, 285
Tuberculosis (TB), 216, 285
Tubular fluid, 327
Tumor, **151**
  adrenal, 353
  benign, **151**
  invasive, **151**
  malignant, **151**
  mammary, *159*
  metastatic, **152**, 164
  pituitary, 154
  stages of development, 164
  uterine, 154
Tunnel vision, **395**
Turgor, in plants, 41

Turner syndrome, **486,** *487*
Twins, 123
Tympanum (eardrum), **398**
Typhus, and sterility, 174
"Typical" cell, 23
Tyrosinase, 225
Tyrosine, 375

Ubiquinone, 91
Ulcer, 248
  and diet, 248–249
  duodenal, **249**
  formation, 248
  gastric, 249
  peptic, 249
  and stress, 248–249
  treatment, *249*
Ulcerative colitis, **250**
Ultraviolet light, 141
  and carcinogens, **155**
  and sunburn, *225, 226*
Ultraviolet radiation, 21
Umbilical arteries, 206
Umbilical cord, **206**
  and fetus, 207
Umbilical vein, *211*
Unbalanced ecosystems, 547, 564
Unburned hydrocarbons, 584
Underdeveloped countries, 570–578
Unicellularity, 25
Unit membrane, **28**
United Kingdom, population, 571
United States
  birth rate, 571
  fertility rate, 571
  population structure, 572
Universal donor, **478**
Universal recipient, **478**
Universe, chemical composition, 10
Unsaturated fats, **66**
"Uppers." *See* Amphetamines
Uracil, **115**
Uranium
  and cancer, 153
  depletion, 582
Urban development, 584
Urbanization, 581
Urea, *322*
  cycle, *322*
Ureter, **323, 332**
  ejaculation, 177
Urey, Harold C., 12–13
Uric acid, 332

Urinary calculi, **332**
Urinary sphincters, 333
Urination, 332–333
  control, 333
Urine, **327**
  acidity, 282
  antimicrobial function, 282
  collecting duct, **324**
  composition, *325*
  concentration, *328*
  discharge, 332–333
  formation rate, 329
  and glucose, 327
  output, *329*
  production, 328–329
  regulation of output, *329*
Usher, Archbishop James, 520
Uterine contractions, 209
Uterine cycle, **182**
Uterine lining, 182
Uterine milk, 206
Uterine tubes, **177**
Uterine tumor, 154
Uterus, **182.** *See also* Cervix
  fetal, *207*
  7-week embryonic, *206*
Utricule, 407

Vaccination, 287, *291*
  by graded doses, 288
Vaccine, smallpox, 291
Vaccinia virus, **291**
Vacuole, **41**
Vagina, **182**
  fetal, 204
Vaginal douche, **186**
Vaginal show, 209
Vagus nerve, 312, 381
Valine, 496
Valium, 386
Valve
  aortic, 257
  artificial, 257
  ball-and-ring, 257
  bicuspid, 257
  lymph, *270*
  pulmonary, 257
  semilunar, 257
  venous, 255, 265–266
Variation and evolution, 522
Varicose veins, 189
Variola, **291**
Vas deferens, 172

Vasectomy, **186,** 192
Vasopressin, 68, **329**
Vein(s), **254**
  hepatic portal, *239*
  jugular, 240
  subclavian, 240
  valves, 255, 265–266
Venom
  bee sting, 285
  toxin, 293
Venous pump, **265,** *266*
Ventilation, **301.** *See also* Breathing
Ventricle, **256**
  contraction, 258
  electrical activity, 258
  fibrillation, 259
Venules, **255**
Vermiform appendix, **250**
Vernix caseosa, **204,** 205
Vertebrae, **431**
Vertebral column, 377, 574
Vertebrate structure, 514
Vertebrates, **431,** 513
Vesalius, *367*
Vestibular system, *402, 403*
Vestibule, **401**
  ear, 401
  genital, **182**
Viking lander, 5
Villus (villi), **237**
Vinyl chloride, 154
Viral nucleic acid, *16*
Virus, **18,** *54–55. See also* Bacteriophage
  acquired immune deficiency syndrome. *See*
    AIDS
  and cancer, 55, 158
  and cold sores, 55
  common cold, 55
  eclipse period, 55
  encephalitis, 55
  fever blisters, 55
  infectious hepatitis, 55
  influenza, 55
  life cycle, *54, 55*
  measles, 55
  mumps, 55
  pneumonia, 55
  polio, 55
  polyoma, **158**
  potato, 55
  protein, 68
  rabies, 55
  retrovirus, 163

Virus (*continued*)
    Rous sarcoma, 163
    shingles, 55
    Shope papilloma, 157
    smallpox, 55
    yellow fever, 55
Visceral muscle, **437**
Vision, color, 395
Visual cortex, 396
Visual pigments, 395
Visual purple, 395
Visual reflexes, 396
Vital principle, 9
Vitalism, *6*
Vitalistic force, 9
Vitalists, **6**
Vitamin(s), **76,** 77
    dangers in excess, 243
    and digestion, 243–245
Vitamin A, 243, *245*
    intoxication, 40, 243
    vision, 395
Vitamin B1, 88
Vitamin D, 243, 348
Vitamin K, 244, 297
Vitamin requirements, *244–245*
Vitreous humor, 47, **394**
Vocal cords, **303**
Voltage, 369
    action potential, 369
Volume, **398**
Volumetric measures, 604
Vulva, **182**

Wadlow, Robert, *343*
Wallace, Alfred, 503, 520
Warren, Lavinia, *343*

Wart, 151
Washkansky, Louis, 297
Wasps, and social dominance, 423
Waste
    bacterial, 588, 589
    blood diffusion, *267*
    liquid, **586**
    solid, **590**
Water, **599–600**
    conservation in kidney, 330
    consumption, 553–559
    cycle, **552,** *553, 554–556*
    intake, 328–329
    Ogallala reservoir, *555*
    and plants, 554
    and pollution, 588, 589
    recycling, *590*
    resorption in kidney, 330
    shortage, 554
    treatment of sewage, 588, *590*
Watson, J. B., 410
Watson, James, 110
Watson-Crick model, 110, 134
Wax glands, *424*
Waxes. *See* Fat(s)
Weed killers, 102
Weeks, John, 556
Weights and measures, English/Metric, **603, 604**
    English to metric, **603–604**
Weinberg, W., 502
Wharton's jelly, **207**
Wheelis, Clifford, 192
White blood cell(s), **276,** 277, 278
    count, 280–281
    movement, 278
    and phagocytosis, 40, 282
    types, *278*

White matter, 378, *380*
White muscle, **437**
Whole blood separation, *276*
Whooping cough vaccine, 291
Willke, John, 186
Wilkins, M. H. F., 110
Windpipe. *See* Trachea
Womb. *See* Uterus
Work, **81**
World hunger distribution, *578*
World population
    growth rate, *573*
    maximum, *592*
Wounds and healing, *152*

X-rays, 499, 500
    and birth defects, 217
    and cancer. 156
XX (chromosomes), 462
XY (chromosomes), 462

Yeast, 9
    and fermentation, 88
Yellow fever vaccine, 291
Yolk sac, 199

Z line, **442**
Zeidler, Othmar, 546
Zero population growth. *See* ZPG
Zigzag courtship dance, 423
Zinc, 77
    depletion, 582
Zona pellucida, **179**
ZPG, *571*
Zygote, **169,** 185, 195, **462,** 502
    subdivision, 195

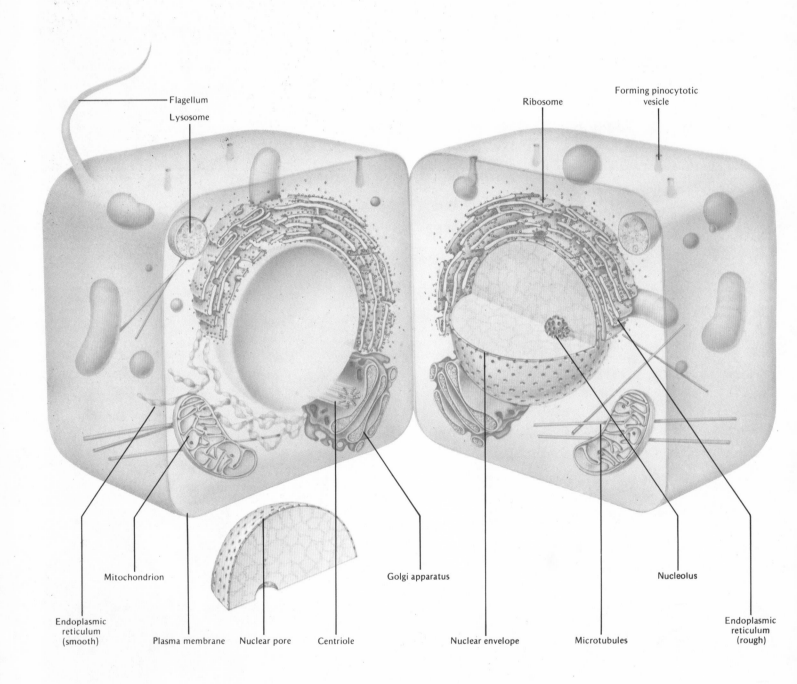

Flagellum

Lysosome

Ribosome

Forming pinocytotic vesicle

Endoplasmic reticulum (smooth)

Mitochondrion

Plasma membrane

Nuclear pore

Centriole

Golgi apparatus

Nuclear envelope

Microtubules

Nucleolus

Endoplasmic reticulum (rough)